ALL ■ IN ■ ONE

CCSP™: Cisco® Certified Security Professional Certification

EXAM GUIDE

Robert E. Larson

Lance Cockcroft

McGraw-Hill/Osborne

New York • Chicago • San Francisco • Lisbon
London • Madrid • Mexico City • Milan • New Delhi
San Juan • Seoul • Singapore • Sydney • Toronto

The McGraw-Hill Companies

McGraw-Hill/Osborne
2100 Powell Street, 10th Floor
Emeryville, California 94608
U.S.A.

To arrange bulk purchase discounts for sales promotions, premiums, or fund-raisers, please contact McGraw-Hill/Osborne at the above address. For information on translations or book distributors outside the U.S.A., please see the International Contact Information page immediately following the index of this book.

CCSP™: Cisco® Certified Security Professional Certification All-in-One Exam Guide (Exams 642-501 SECUR, 642-521 CSPFA, 642-511 CSVPN, 642-531 CSIDS, and 642-541 CSI)

1234567890 DOC DOC 019876543

Book p/n 0-07-222692-7 and CD p/n 0-07-222693-5
parts of
ISBN 0-07-222691-9

Publisher
Brandon A. Nordin

Vice President & Associate Publisher
Scott Rogers

Acquisitions Editor
Nancy Maragioglio

Project Editor
Lisa Wolters-Broder

Acquisitions Coordinator
Jessica Wilson

Technical Editors
Joe Phago
Ole Drews Jensen

Copy Editor
Marcia Baker

Proofreaders
Brian Galloway
Linda Medoff

Indexer
Rebecca Plunkett

Compositors
Apollo Publishing Services
George Toma Charbak

Illustrators
Lyssa Wald
Melinda Moore Lytle
Michael Mueller

Series Design
Peter F. Hancik

This book was composed with Corel VENTURA™ Publisher.

This book is dedicated to my parents, Lou and Elmer Larson,
who provided resources and direction when I was young,
plus freedom, inspiration, and support as I got older.
—Bob

About the Authors

Robert E. Larson lives in the Seattle, Washington area with his wife Jerri and four adult children. Bob has worked full-time as a computer trainer and course developer since 1985, including network training since 1995. Bob got involved with the Cisco Networking Academy program in 1998. He is currently the Cisco Regional Academy contact at Bates Technical College in Tacoma, plus teaches evening and weekend CCNP, Security, and CCIE prep classes at Green River Community College. Bob is currently a member of the Cisco Networking Academy Advisory Council. This is Bob's third Cisco certification book, having also written a CCNA and CCNP book. Bob taught the first Academy CCNA series in Africa in 1999 in Cape Town, South Africa. He has also taught CCNP-level courses in Birmingham, England; Dillingen, Germany; and Vienna, Austria.

Lance Cockcroft, Net+, CCA, MCSE, MCT, CCNP, CCDP, has been a Senior Engineer for many ISP and telecommunications companies, including Bellsouth, Atlanta Broadband, and Southeastern Networks. Lance is currently the Cisco Product Manager for Self Test Software, Cisco's only authorized test prep vendor. Lance writes and oversees the production of all Cisco practice tests for Self Test Software. Lance attended and continues to teach for Kennesaw State University and Southern Polytechnic University located in his hometown of Marietta, Georgia.

About the Technical Reviewers

Ole Drews Jensen began working with computers 21 years ago, and five years later made it his profession. He started out as a programmer in a wide variety of languages, but soon got involved with administering servers and networks. Today Ole is the Systems Network Manager for an enterprise company with several subsidiaries in the recruiting industry, where one of the largest is Carlton Staffing. Ole holds the following certifications: CCNP, MCSE, and MCP+I, and is currently pursuing the new CCSP.

Setotolwane Johannes "Joe" Phago, CCIE # 7105, CCNP, Cisco Firewall Specialist, Cisco VPN Specialist, B.Sc. Computer Science (University of the North, S.A.). He was the first Black South African CCIE and is a graduate of the first Cisco Networking Academy in Africa. Joe is currently Senior Network Analyst at Standard Bank of South Africa, a leading banking and financial services company in S.A. and Africa with a presence on virtually all continents.

CONTENTS

INTRODUCTION

Before You Get Started

Welcome to the *CCSP™: Cisco® Certified Security Professional Certification All-in-One Exam Guide*. This book is here to help you prepare to take–and pass–the following Cisco security certification exams. Even more importantly, it is here to share a pool of knowledge that should help you become more employable in the field. If you strive for knowledge and experience, the certification will come. The CCSP exams are:

- Securing Cisco IOS Networks
- Cisco Secure PIX Firewall Exam
- Cisco Secure Virtual Private Networks
- Cisco Secure Intrusion Detection Systems Exam
- Cisco SAFE Implementation Exam

In this section, we discuss skill building and exam preparation alternatives, the certification exam situation itself, the Cisco certification programs in general, and how this book can help you prepare for Cisco certification exams. We will look at the following:

- Things to do to prepare
- CCNA exam insights
- Cisco Certification Information

CCSP Certification Program

The Cisco Certified Security Professional is a brand-new CCNP-level certification track being driven by the rapidly changing and growing world concern about security. For that reason there have been and will continue to be a great number of changes and additions to the program. There have been three major changes in the program in its first year. At the same time, some of the security products have gone through major upgrades, adding many new and useful features.

What this means to you is that it is very important to keep on top of the current exam numbers and exam objectives. Use the Cisco web site at www.cisco.com and the Learning and Events link to get to the latest certification information. The direct link is: http://www.cisco.com/en/US/learning/le3/learning_career_certifications_and_learning_paths_home.html.

In developing this book, we tried to include the information that is required to pass the various certification exams while at the same time anticipating any new topics that might become exam objectives in the near future.

Because the book covers all five exams, much of the security overview information that appears at the beginning of every book has been consolidated into Chapter 1. Other exam sections may use topics covered in the SECUR exam as foundation. The following table shows the relationships between the exams and chapters. The X indicates the material should be included, while an R is recommended.

CCSP All-In-One Chapter	**SECUR**	**CSVPN**	**CSPFA**	**CSIDS**	**CSI**
Introduction to Network Security					
1. Understanding Network Security Threats	X				X
2. Securing the Network	X				X
Securing the Network Perimeter					
3. Cisco AAA Security Technology	X				X
4. CiscoSecure ACS and TACACS+ Technologies	X				X
5. Securing Cisco Perimeter Routers	X				X
6. IOS Firewall Feature Set - CBAC	X		R		X
7. IOS Firewall Feature Set - Intrusion Detection System	X			R	X
8. IOS Firewall Feature Set - Proxy Authentication	X				X
Virtual Private Networks (VPNs)					
9. Cisco IOS IPSec Introduction	X	X	R		X
10. Cisco IOS IPSec for Pre-Shared Keys	X	R	R		X
11. Cisco IOS IPSec Certificate Authority Support	X	R	R		X
12. Cisco IOS Remote Access Using Cisco Easy VPN	X	X			X
13. Cisco VPN Hardware Overview		X			X
14. Cisco VPN 3000 Remote Access Networks		X			X
15. Configuring Cisco VPN 3002 Remote Clients		X			X
16. Cisco VPN 3000 LAN-to-LAN Networks		X			X
PIX Firewalls					
17. Cisco PIX Firewall Technology and Features			X		X

CCSP All-In-One	SECUR	CSVPN	CSPFA	CSIDS	CSI
PIX Firewalls					
18. Getting Started with the Cisco PIX Firewall			X		X
19. Access Through the PIX Firewall			X		X
20. Advanced PIX Firewall Features			X		X
21. Firewalls and VPN Features			X		X
22. Managing and Maintaining the PIX Firewall			X		X
Intrusion Detection Systems (IDS)					
23. IDS Overview and CSIDS Installation				X	X
24. Alarms and Signatures				X	X
25. CIDS Installation and Configuration				X	X
26. Signature and Alarm Management				X	X
Cisco SAFE Strategy					
27. Cisco SAFE Strategy					X
Appendix A - Access Control Lists	R		R		

How to Protect Yourself Against Exam Changes

Become very familiar with the Cisco web site and how to perform searches for documents. Use the site to stay current on any exam changes. Be sure to look at both the exam description and the *Recommended Training* descriptions. Both will have objectives and topics covered usually as bulleted lists. Consider printing these out and using them as check-off guides to monitor your learning progress. It will also help you to spot new technologies or features introduced in later descriptions.

Release Notes

As you are preparing for a particular topic, perform searches for release notes on that topic, for example *VPN 3000 Concentrator release notes*. Look over the results looking for the latest version; they are not always sorted with the latest at the top. Look particularly at the System Requirements, Upgrading, and New Features sections. Pay particular attention to and feature that was recently added to either the exam or course description on the certifications pages.

Technical Documentation

On the Cisco site, go to the products section for the technology that you are studying and use the links on the left side to find *Technical Documentation* section where you will often find User Guides, Command Reference, Configuration Guides, etc. Each of these documents is available in HTML format and many are available as PDFs.

Find the User Guide or Configuration Guide for the technology (PIX, VPN Concentrator, etc.) and look up the features that are new to you. This is also an excellent way to get a different perspective than the one presented in this or any other book. If you do not have access to some of the technologies (some are very expensive to acquire just for study purposes) look for the Getting Started Guide. Spend some time studying the parts of these documents that are new or unclear for you.

Finally, search for any configuration examples. These documents are often listed under the *Technical Documentation* heading of the product information, or use the search feature. These are typically very specific and usually include diagrams, instructions, configuration output, and useful links. For technologies with web-based interfaces, many include step-by-step instructions with web captures of the entire process.

NOTE Many documents do not require a CCO account, but if asked to login you will be given an opportunity to apply for a CCO account. The process will only require answering some questions. Even the most limited level may make additional documents available to you.

Remember Your Goal

You are, after all, attempting to become recognized as an expert in these technologies. Don't sell yourself short. Look over the most recent (latest version) documents so that you are not surprised by look-and-feel changes or the addition of a key feature on a menu or screen.

Things to Do to Prepare

I cannot emphasize enough how important it is to get some hands-on experience with Cisco devices whenever possible. The exams ask many questions involving the command syntax or web interface page feature options. Experience configuring devices is the best way to become comfortable with any Cisco technology. I have tried to include enough screen captures to assist you if hands-on experience is not possible. The last section covered using Cisco documentation to checkout new features, but it is equally as valuable for building familiarity with devices you do not have access to. In this section we will look at some other options.

Unlike some other certification, memorizing a long list of facts is not necessarily the best approach for Cisco exams. You must be able to apply the information and see it from other perspectives. The following list of resources that can help you study and prepare:

This Book and Related Materials

Preparing for any Cisco certification exam (including the CCSP) requires you to obtain and study materials designed to provide comprehensive information about the subject matter that will appear on your specific exam. This book contains the framework to prepare to pass the exam. The task now is to apply and absorb that information and become comfortable with it. This will present different levels of challenge based on your experience with networking. Obviously, someone who has been working in the field for a period of time will and possibly has another advanced certification, such as CCNP, will have a solid base of knowledge and skills that they can build on. I think this book can be a good tool for that person.

The other type of CCSP student I find is the recent CCNA who is interested in getting into the IT field but has little or no real networking experience. I have tried to write this book for that person, as well. The latter student may need some background material, and may need to look at things from two or more perspectives; the Cisco web site and online articles can help with this.

Labs and Exercises

On the CD-ROM you will find labs and exercises for most of the technologies covered. Even if you do not have access to the required equipment, look over the labs. They have a methodology that will be useful as well as many screen captures or sample output to augment the materials in the related chapter.

SAFE and AVVID Documents

The fifth and final exam for CCSP is the *Cisco SAFE Implementation Exam (CSI 642-541 CSI)*. While based on the series of SAFE documents, such as the *SAFE Blueprint for Small, Midsize, and Remote-User Networks*, every technology, topic, or configuration process covered on the other four exams is fair game. Do yourself a favor and start by downloading the SAFE documents in PDF form. Read them at least the *SAFE Blueprint for Small, Midsize, and Remote-User Networks* before getting too far into the book. Then as you learn about each technology review how it fits into the SAFE strategy. Make sure that you can configure the main connections, such as router VPN to PIX VPN. The SAFE documents have additional configuration examples that should help broaden your knowledge.

Classroom Training

Whether you use this book or not, classroom training for many people is the preferred way to learn complex technologies. In this field that classroom training should be combined with hands-on experience with real routers and switches. There are several possible courses to follow:

Cisco Networking Academies

I believe in this program for the average person. Since 1987, Cisco Systems has set up Networking Academies in more than 10,500 locations around the world. Many are in high schools and the rest are in community colleges, technical colleges, trade schools, universities, and at some service organizations. This highly developed multimedia curriculum, combined with abundant hands-on experience offered part-time, can create a solid foundation. The academies offer CCNA, CCNP, and Fundamentals of Security (SECUR and CSPFA) training and are now branching out to include non-Cisco technologies like UNIX and web design. To learn more about the Academy Program or to locate one in your area, check the following web site: http://www.cisco.com/warp/public/779/edu/academy/.

Cisco Training Partners

In larger cities, for the working administrator with solid foundation skills who truly meets the course prerequisites, these short, often five-day courses can be a quick way to fill in the gaps, gain limited hands-on experience, and move on to certification. I really like these programs for working professionals with a lot of experience. For them, this type of training can be an excellent value. On the other hand, if a person really doesn't fit the target audience and can't keep up with the class, this can be a very expensive reality check. For more information, go to http://www.cisco.com/ and click on the Learning link.

Buying Equipment

Many students do purchase equipment, particularly if their long-term goal is CCNP, CCSP, or CCIE. Cisco vendors like Blackbox and www.cdw.com offer catalogs and knowledgeable support people. I have always had very good luck with eBay (www.ebay.com). Do a search on "Cisco" at the eBay site and there will be thousands of items. The key is that you can't be in a hurry. Watch for the deal that you want, and be ready to walk away. If you are worried about fraud, deal only with sellers who have made many transactions (a number after their ID) and have an easily viewable performance record.

There are two ways to use eBay. First, look at the people offering items. Many have web sites linked to their auctions. See what kind of businesses they are and what other "deals" they have going. Second, if I'm buying a bigger item, I only buy from an auction that will take a credit card. I then use a card that guarantees my purchases. I've bought hundreds of items and I don't feel that I've ever been hurt. I've never had an item fail to be delivered pretty much as advertised.

Virtual Labs and Simulators

While I think simulators do not replace hands-on experience, they are significantly better than nothing at all. It is my understanding that www.boson.com is working on a simulator for these exams.

Practice Exams

I really hate the thought of a person taking a test repeatedly until they know enough of the questions to pass. This leads to what the industry refers to as "paper certifications" or worse "vapor certifications." It's bad for the industry and can't be all that great for the individual. What value is the certification if you get fired from the job because you can't do the work?

Having said that; I do believe in taking practice tests once you have trained and prepared yourself. This serves two purposes. First, it may point out gaps or weaknesses in your training plan. Second, and more importantly, it helps to prepare you for the exam itself. If you have taken the CCNA or CCNP exams, you already know that Cisco exams are like none you've taken before. While they are fair and valid, they are not designed to pass a lot of students. They are designed to see if you know the exam material forwards and backwards. My students have found that the exams at www.boson.com are both challenging and helpful.

Cram Sessions and Brain Dumps

There are web sites called brain dumps, where test-takers try to list as many test questions as they can remember. First, my personal opinion is that these are a waste of time and energy. Second, they violate the non-disclosure agreement that every test-taker agrees to when they take the exam. In the end, you compromise your integrity for a bit of short-term-memory fodder.

What time I've spent at the sites that I'm aware of, I've found a mix of good and bad questions, questions from old exams, questions from the wrong exams, and a small amount of mischief. There are better ways.

One site I like is http://studyguides.cramsession.com/. They have a series of study guides, usually 12-20 pages, for many exams that I recommend to all of my students. While they do not give you questions, they give you lists of things to know. I really do not believe they replace studying. The practice that I follow, and recommend to my students, is that each night for the week before a scheduled exam, read the Cramsession just before bed. Typically, it will lead me to question some points, and after researching I put the results on the margins of the study guide. Their study guide is the only thing that I ever take to a test site. I try to review it once before going into the test site.

Do you need all of the things covered in this section? Probably not. But I've tried to offer a mix to helpful tools and suggestions.

CCSP Exam Insights

Once you have prepared for your exam, you need to register with a testing center. Each computer-based CCSP exam costs $125 (North America), and if you don't pass, you may retest for an additional $125 for each try. In the United States and Canada, tests are administered by Prometric Testing Centers.

You can sign up for a test through Prometric's web site at http://www.2test.com, or you can register by phone at 800-204-EXAM (within the United States or Canada). The web site will not allow you to schedule exams within 48 hours, so use the phone registration for shorter scheduling intervals. It is possible in some markets to take tests on the same day. Be prepared to wait through voice messages.

To sign up for a test, you will need a valid credit card.

To schedule an exam, call the toll-free number or visit the web page at least one day in advance. Before booking the exam make sure that you understand the cancellation process and deadlines, currently before 7 P.M. Central Standard Time the day before the scheduled test time (or you will be charged, even if you don't appear to take the test).

When you want to schedule a test, have the following information ready:

- Exam number and title
- Your name–Exactly the way that you want it to appear on your certificate.
- Your social security, social insurance, or Prometric number (SP)
- A method of payment–Credit card
- Contact telephone numbers–In case of a problem so they can reach you.
- Mailing address–Where you want your certificate mailed.
- Email address–For contact purposes. You will get a confirmation via e-mail.

Once you sign up for a test, you will be informed as to when and where the test is scheduled. Try to arrive at least 15 minutes early–personally, due to traffic congestion, I tell students to show up an hour early. You can always relax and review your notes. I've sat in exams next to students who have showed up late for whatever reason. They seem miserable and I suspect the stress and tension will be reflected in their score.

Photo ID

You will need to bring two forms of identification to the testing site. One form *must* be a photo ID such as a driver's license or a valid passport. The other must have a signature. The test cannot be taken without the proper identification.

Gum, Candy, and Cough Drops

Do yourself a favor and bring something with you. It can always just sit there ignored. But the last thing you want is a dry throat or coughing to disrupt your testing and the silence for your peers.

The Exam Process

When you show up at the testing center, you will need to sign in with an exam coordinator. He or she will ask you to show the two forms of signature identification. After you have signed in and your time slot arrives, you will be asked to deposit any items with you such as books, bags, pagers, or calculators. Make sure that you know where the restrooms and drinking fountain are located. You don't want to plan to need them, but even worse is to have to search for them. You will be escorted into a closed room.

All exams are closed book. You will be furnished with one or two blank sheets of paper and a pen or, in some cases, an erasable plastic sheet and an erasable pen. Before the exam–take a few minutes and write out any important material on the blank sheet. This is particularly important for any formulas or detailed data that you might forget under the stress of the exam. You can refer to this piece of paper any time you like during the test, but you will have to turn it in when you leave.

You will have some time to compose yourself, to record this information, and to take a sample orientation exam before you begin the real test. You will also be required to complete a computer-based survey to track demographics of the test candidates. Typically, if an exam has a 75-minute time limit, you will have 90 minutes to take the sample exam, complete the survey, and take the actual exam. Once you start the actual exam you now have only the exam time limit.

Typically, the room will have up to a dozen computers. Each workstation will be separated from the others by dividers designed to keep you from seeing your neighbor's computer. Keep in mind that the people next to you could be taking a certification exam from an industry totally unrelated to yours, so don't be concerned if someone starts after you or finishes before you. Most test rooms use closed circuit cameras. This permits the exam coordinator to monitor the room.

The exam coordinator will have preloaded the appropriate Cisco certification exam. If there is a problem with the exam, such as version number, screen doesn't display all data, the screen or desk area is dirty, etc., let the coordinator know right away. Do not put yourself at a disadvantage. You can start as soon as you are seated in front of the computer. I suggest that you sit back for a minute and relax. Take a deep breath. If the chair is adjustable, adjust it. Move your arms and legs to release any tension. You are going to be sitting there almost 90 minutes.

All Cisco certification exams allow a certain maximum amount of time in which to complete the work (this time is indicated on the exam by an on-screen counter/clock, so you can check the time remaining whenever you like). All Cisco certification exams are computer generated and most use a multiple-choice format, often with six to eight choices. It is possible, if not likely, that several questions will refer to an exhibit containing dozens of commands from which you will be expected to select one as the answer to a specific question.

Most Cisco exams use some form of simulator in a few questions to test your configuration skills. Typically these are fundamental activities not obscure activities, so make sure that you know how to configure the basics.

While this may sound quite simple, the questions not only are constructed to check your mastery of basic facts and skills about the subject material, but they also require you to evaluate one or more sets of circumstances or requirements. Often, you are asked to give more than one answer to a question, although you will always be told how many to choose. *You get only one pass through the questions*—you cannot mark a question and return to it later.

When you complete a Cisco certification exam, the exam will tell you whether you have passed or failed. All test objectives are broken into several topic areas and each area is scored on a basis of 100 percent. Particularly if you do not pass the exam, select the option on the screen that asks if you want to print the report. The test administrator will print it for you. You can use this report to help you prepare for a second effort, if needed. Once you see your score, you have the option of printing additional copies of the score report. It is a good idea to print it twice.

Remember, if you need to retake an exam, you will have to schedule a new test with Prometric and pay another $125.

Exam Design

All Cisco tests use one of following basic question types:

- Multiple-choice with a single answer
- Multiple-choice with two or more answers (the question will indicate how many answers)
- Multipart with one or more answers (the question will indicate how many answers)
- CLI-based questions (many times, an exhibit will present a sample IOS configuration in which you are asked to choose the correct command or interpret the configuration's output, per the question's directions)
- Drag and drop where steps need to be arranged in order, technologies need to be labeled, or you need to fill in the blanks. Expect a couple of these.
- Simulations to test configuration skills. This will typically be a step in an overall device configuration, such as configuring an interface. Expect no more than a couple of these.

Take the time to read a question at least twice before selecting an answer, and pay special attention to words such as "not" that can radically change the question. If a question seems very simple, great—but read it over once more to make sure that you aren't missing something.

Always look for an Exhibit button as you examine each question. The Exhibit button brings up graphics used to help explain a question, provide additional data, or illustrate network design or program behavior. My perception is that there are fewer exhibits than in the past, with drawings and images included on the screen with the question.

Cisco exams do not allow you to return to questions, so you must make sure to answer the question as best you can before proceeding to the next one. The exam will clearly state before you start whether you can mark answers and return.

Cisco's Testing Format

All Cisco exams are fixed-length with a fixed number of questions. Each candidate will get the same number of questions; the order of the questions can vary, as can the specific questions. If you retake an exam assume there will be different questions. From time to time, questions are replaced and others may not be scored.

Cisco provides a counter in the upper-right corner (near the remaining time) showing the number of questions completed and the number outstanding. Monitor your time to make sure that you have completed at least one-quarter of the questions one-quarter of the way through the exam period and three-quarters of the questions three-quarters of the way through. Have the calculations done in advance, such as 16 questions by 18 minutes.

If you are not finished with 10 minutes remaining, try to pick up the pace. At five minutes remaining, use the remaining time to guess your way through any remaining questions. Guessing is better than not answering because blank answers are always wrong, but a guess may turn out to be right. The important thing is to answer every question.

Some Basic Question-Handling Strategies

For those questions that take only a single answer, usually two or three of the answers will be obviously incorrect, and a couple of the answers will be plausible. Of course, only one can be correct. Unless the answer leaps out at you, begin the process of eliminating those answers that are most obviously wrong.

Many questions assume that the default behavior of a particular command or option is in effect. If you know the defaults and understand what they mean, this will help you with your choice.

Cisco exams are generally pretty straightforward and not intended to beat you out of your certification, but then again they are not designed to be easy. Pay attention, particularly with syntax. Knowing the difference between *access-list 1 deny any* and *access list 1 deny any* should be assumed (note the hyphen).

If the answer seems immediately obvious, reread the question to look for a trap; sometimes those are the ones you are most likely to get wrong.

Typically, at least one answer out of the possible choices for a question can be eliminated immediately because the answer does not apply to the situation or the answer describes a nonexistent issue or option.

If faced with guessing among two or more potentially correct answers, reread the question. Try to picture how each of the possible remaining answers would alter the situation. Be especially sensitive to terminology; sometimes the choice of words (e.g., "remove" instead of "disable") can make the difference between a right answer and a wrong one.

Cisco Certification Program

The Cisco Certification Program currently includes the following separate certificates with various specialty tracks. You should become familiar with and visit regularly Cisco's website at www.cisco.com/go/certifications/.

Cisco reserves the right to change the number of questions and time limits for the exams as it sees fit. Cisco tries to keep this information confidential, although you can check either figure when you register for an exam. The http://studyguides.cramsession.com/ site usually has pretty reliable information about number of questions and time limits.

Receiving Your Certificate

After passing the necessary certification exam(s) and agreeing to Cisco's nondisclosure terms, you will be certified. Official certification normally takes from four to six weeks. The package includes a welcome kit that contains a number of elements:

- Official certificate (suitable for framing)
- A laminated wallet card

- A graduation letter
- A license to use the Cisco certification logo, in advertisements, promotions, documents, resumes, letterhead, business cards, and so on.
- Access to the online Tracking System

Tracking Cisco Certification Status

As soon as you pass any Cisco exam, you must complete a certification agreement. To do this, go to Cisco's Web site www.cisco.com/go/certifications/ and select the Tracking System link. You can also mail a hard copy of the agreement to Cisco's certification authority. You will not be certified until you complete a certification agreement and Cisco receives it in one of these forms.

The Certification Tracking Web site also allows you to view your certification information. Cisco will contact you via email and explain your certification and its use.

Recertification

Cisco requires three-year recertification for the non-CCIE programs. The best place to keep tabs on the Cisco Career Certifications program and its related requirements is on the Web. The URL for the program is www.cisco.com/go/certifications/.

PART I

Introduction to Network Security

CHAPTER

Understanding Network Security Threats

In this chapter, you will learn to:

- Identify the need for network security
- Recognize the causes of network security problems
- Distinguish the four primary types of threats
- Know the four primary types of network attack
- Discover Cisco AVVID and SAFE, and how they relate to network security
- Learn about the Cisco Security Wheel
- Understand network security policy
- Improve network security

To understand, in part, why we are where we are today, you only have to remember that PC is the acronym for personal computer. The PC was born and, for many years, evolved as the tool of the individual. In fact, much of the early interest and growth came as a rebellion to what appeared as exclusionary attitudes and many restrictions of early data-processing departments. Admittedly, many PCs were tethered to company networks, but even then there was often considerable flexibility in software selection, settings preferences, and even sharing of resources such as folders and printers.

As a result, a huge industry of producers developed and sold devices, software, and services targeted at meeting user interests and needs, often with little or no thought about security. Prior to the Internet, a person could keep their computer resources safe simply by being careful about shared floppy disks.

Today, even the PCs of most individuals routinely connect to the largest network in the world (the Internet) to expand the user's reach and abilities. As the computing world grew, and skills and technology proliferated, people with less than honorable intentions discovered new and more powerful ways to apply their craft. Just as a gun makes a robber a greater threat, computers give the scam artist, terrorist, thief, or pervert the opportunity to reach out and hurt others in greater numbers and from longer distances.

This book provides a variety of techniques and technologies to protect computing resources from unauthorized access and loss. This chapter lays the foundation by looking at the need for network security. What are the threats? Who are these people who

Author's Bias

One of the reasons hacking and other forms of network intrusions occur so often is because too many people inside and outside the industry think something is special about computer crime. A mystique surrounds some activities. Some even go so far as to create colorful terms, such as "ethical hackers" or "white hat hackers." The bottom line is this: the person who gains *unauthorized access to another's computer* is no less a criminal than the burglar who gains access to your home. Web site hackers are no more honorable or deserving of special treatment than any other vandal, regardless of their cause or motivation. Once you own, or work for, a company that's had to waste the equivalent of many annual salaries to defend against attacks, fight off an attack, or restore damaged resources, the "victimless" rational of computer crime goes up in smoke.

threaten the data, and what are some of the methods they use? In addition, you'll find many references to outside resources for additional information.

While this book addresses the requirements of the various certification exams, recognizing that the diversity of security threats is far too large for any single book is important. Furthermore, the nature and source of many threats changes on a daily basis, making it important to start building a set of resources, such as web sites, news groups, trade associations, vendor distribution lists, and so forth that can help you try to stay abreast of the changes. Each technology, such as wireless, voice, web pages, and e-mail systems, has its own set of threats that a person must remain aware of.

Identify the Need for Network Security

Pointing at the Internet and indicating that as the point in time when security had to become a part of everyone's computing strategy is easy. Business and individuals alike were faced with protecting their computing resources from the many possible dangers that lurked in the Net. The Internet opened a large door onto a busy street filled with seemingly unlimited commercial and intellectual opportunities. Unfortunately, within that busy street reside the same opportunists we fear in our noncyber lives.

Another way the Internet impacts security is its worldwide reach as a reference library for security experts and, unfortunately, the hacker community as well. In a few minutes, a search for hack, crack, phreak, or spam yields many sites, some with many links to other links.

But blaming the Internet is somewhat unfair. The Internet simply happened to be the first attractive new service with strong mass appeal that brought with it significant security risks. Others that followed include wireless communications and connectivity, instant messaging, and enhanced e-mail services, and undoubtedly more will follow. Increased security awareness and implementation is, by necessity, one of the prices that must be paid for new services that connect people.

Unfortunately, all organizations aren't alike and, therefore, a one-plan-fits-all approach to security won't work. Many factors—from internal company policies to topologies and services supported—impact the decisions about the proper security strategy. Even within an organization, the security requirements can require many different solutions. A single LAN branch location has different security issues than a WAN link or a campus VLAN environment.

Even after the organization assesses its security risks and starts to develop a plan, problems often exist in knowing whether various multivendor tools will work together and be supportable in the long term. One common problem with any multivendor environment (not only networking) is the inevitable finger-pointing when things go wrong. So often, a decision about single vendor or multivendor solutions must be made. Cisco is a big believer in single-vendor, end-to-end solutions—the company was built through acquisitions and R&D to that end, but it's also a solid supporter of standards-based technologies. Standards-based solutions can at least reduce some of the interoperability issues involved in a multivendor solution.

Cisco network and security products are developed under Cisco's AVVID and SAFE strategies to ensure solid standards-based implementations. Both strategies are covered later in this chapter in the "Cisco AVVID and SAFE Strategies" section.

NOTE Multivendor implementations require more than just knowing that the technologies will work together. There can also be a significant support commitment and cost in maintaining resident experts on multiple vendor products. In addition to having to know how to install and provide production support, someone must be a security expert on each vendor line to keep on top of security announcements, vulnerabilities, patches, upgrades, and so forth. The future can change the balance completely. While products from two vendors might "play well together" initially, what happens in the future when a new technology develops and one vendor chooses a standards-based approach while the other chooses a proprietary solution, or maybe not to play at all?

Identify the Causes of Network Security Problems

While many causes exist for security problems, at least three types of fundamental weaknesses open the door to security problems.

- Technology weakness
- Policy weakness
- Configuration weakness

Obviously, we could probably add human weakness and some others, but our purpose is to concentrate on those issues that, once recognized, can be managed, monitored, and improved within a security strategy.

Technology Weakness

Every technology has some known or unknown inherent weaknesses, or vulnerabilities that can be exploited by a sufficiently motivated troublemaker. Some weaknesses are publicized widely in the media because they're associated with a well-known product. Don't fall into the faulty logic that because you don't hear about the other products, they must be secure. Just because no one cares enough to hack a product, doesn't mean it's necessarily secure.

TCP/IP Wasn't Designed for Security

Starting right at the top, TCP/IP wasn't designed with security as a high priority. One of the drawbacks to being the first at anything is the inability to see how others might manipulate and transform a technology into something else. The designers were looking for a reliable vehicle to allow research organizations to share information. The many early protocols and tools that make up the TCP/IP suite were developed in an environment of trust and openness.

Today, various Request for Comments (RFCs), security best practices, security services, and an array of products from many vendors work together to reduce the risks inherent in the environment.

Computer and Network Operating Systems

Regardless of the manufacturer or whether it's an open standard or proprietary product, every operating system (OS) has vulnerabilities that need to be addressed through patches, upgrades, and best practices. Every time a major upgrade comes out, the possibility for new or even revived vulnerabilities can, and does, appear.

While a company tries to produce and deliver a secure final product, the addition of new features, implementation of new standards, and even hardware changes can lead to potential problems that don't get caught in prerelease testing.

Given the number of lines of code in most modern OSs, it isn't wholly unreasonable that some problems will slip through. While our focus is security, the OS developers and product testers are looking at usability, accessibility, features, performance, stability, backward compatibility, and many other characteristics, plus security. Right or wrong, it's also important to remember that security hasn't always been the highest priority of developers, product managers, customers, product reviewers, financial analysts, writers, and so forth.

Network Device Weaknesses

Whether IOS based or embedded in the circuitry, such as application-specific integrated circuit (ASIC), network devices can have vulnerabilities, often called "holes," that can be exploited. Some might lay dormant for years until someone stumbles across one, and either exploits it or documents it. Often the process of documenting and notifying the user base of a problem lays out a roadmap to troublemakers.

When possible patches, IOS upgrades, and best practices should be applied to eliminate or mitigate known problems. In some cases, it might be determined that the device should be abandoned or moved to a part of the network that would be impacted less by the problem.

To find security advisories and related information without a CCO ID, go to http://www.cisco.com and do a search on security.

Policy Weakness

Policy weakness is a catchall phrase for company policies, or a lack of policies, that inadvertently lead to security threats to the network system. Chapter 2 covers in detail the importance and implementation of a written security policy, which is the essential foundation of a good security implementation.

The following examples are some of the policy issues that can negatively impact a businesses computer system:

- **No written security policy** Lack of a documented and adopted plan means the security efforts evolve and are enforced, if at all, in a best-effort manner.
- **Lack of disaster recover plan** Without a plan, the efforts to fight a network attack—or even a physical emergency such as fire, flood, or earthquake—are left to the judgment and knowledge of the staff on hand. Even the best-trained and most experienced staff can make foolish decisions when faced with an unexpected catastrophic event.
- **No policy for software and hardware additions or changes** Whether motivated by increasing productivity or recreation, any addition or upgrade to software or hardware can introduce unexpected security vulnerabilities. Adding an unauthorized wireless access point to a network can throw open a virtual garage door to the network and the company resources. Similarly, an unauthorized screensaver might also be harvesting passwords, user IDs, and other information for someone else.
- **Lack of security monitoring** Even if a secure network is developed, failure to monitor logs and processes or weak auditing allows new vulnerabilities and unauthorized use to evolve and proliferate. The worst case would be not recognizing that a serious loss had occurred or was continuing.
- **Employment policies** Frequent staff turnover, lower than typical compensation, and lack of training opportunities can all impact network security by bringing new untested and underskilled employees into positions of authority and responsibility.
- **Internal policies** Lax business attitudes and practices often create temptations and a relatively safe environment for the opportunist within to ply their craft. This is the "we are all like family here" syndrome. Unfortunately, even some of the best families have a thief in their midst. Similarly, infighting, backbiting, power struggles, or turf struggles can lead to security issues or divert attention, allowing problems to go undetected.

Configuration Weakness

Many network devices have default settings that emphasize performance or ease of installation without regard for security issues. Installation without adequate attention to correcting these settings could create serious potential problems. Some common configuration issues include the following:

- Ineffective access control lists failing to block intended traffic
- Default, missing, or old passwords
- Unneeded ports or services left active
- User IDs and passwords exchanged in clear text
- Weak or unprotected remote access through the Internet or dial-up services

Monitoring vendor announcements and advisories, combined with industry news services, can identify the most common, best-known vulnerabilities and often include the appropriate mitigation solution.

STUDY TIP Know the three causes of security problems.

The Four Primary Types of Network Threats

In an attempt to categorize threats both to understand them better and to help in planning ways to resist them, the following four categories are typically used.

- Unstructured threats
- Structured threats
- Internal threats
- External threats

Unstructured Threats

Unstructured threats often involve unfocused assaults on one or more network systems, often by individuals with limited or developing skills. The systems being attacked and infected are probably unknown to the perpetrator. These attacks are often the result of people with limited integrity and too much time on their hands. Malicious intent might or might not exist, but there is always indifference to the resulting damage caused to others.

The Internet has many sites where the curious can select program codes, such as a virus, worm, or Trojan horse, often with instructions that can be modified or redistributed as is. In all cases, these items are small programs written by a human being. They aren't alive and they can't evolve spontaneously from nothing. Some common terms to be aware of include the following:

Virus	A program capable of replicating with little or no user intervention, and the replicated programs also replicate.
Worm	A form of virus that spreads by creating duplicates of itself on other drives, systems, or networks. A worm working with an e-mail system can mail copies of itself to every address in the e-mail system address book. Code Red and Nimda are examples of high-profile worms that have caused significant damage in recent years.
Trojan horse	An apparently useful or amusing program, possibly a game or screensaver, but in the background it could be performing other tasks, such as deleting or changing data, or capturing passwords or keystrokes. A true Trojan horse isn't technically a virus because it doesn't replicate itself.

The person launching an unstructured attack is often referred to as a *script kiddy* because that person often lacks the skills to develop the threat themselves, but can pass it on anonymously (they think) and gain some perverse sense of satisfaction from the result. E-mail delivery methods have replaced "shared" game disks as the vehicle of choice for distributing this type of attack.

NOTE The term "script kiddy" is a common derogatory term and should be used with caution, if at all. Script kiddy is included here so you know what it means. Remember, the difference between an unstructured attack and a series of all-out denial-of-service attacks might be that the latter attacker is offended or angry.

Unstructured attacks involving code that reproduces itself and mails a copy to everyone in the person's e-mail address book can easily circle the globe in a few hours, causing problems for networks and individuals all over the world. While the original intent might have been more thoughtless than malicious, the result can be a loss of user access while systems are being protected, a loss of reputation if the news that a company's site has been attacked, or a loss of user freedoms as more-restrictive policies and practices are implemented to defend against additional attacks.

In some organizations, if the network is down, entire groups of people can't do their jobs, so they're either sent home or they sit and wait without pay because their income is tied to sales. So even if the hacker "thought" no one would be hurt, the result is often that they just beat some single parent or new hire out of a day's pay.

Each of these results can be quantified in currency and often result in large numbers if and when the perpetrator is prosecuted.

Structured Threats

Structured threats are more focused by one or more individuals with higher-level skills actively working to compromise a system. The targeted system could have been detected through some random search process, or it might have been selected specifically. The attackers are typically knowledgeable about network designs, security, access procedures, and hacking tools, and they have the ability to create scripts or applications to further their objectives.

Structured attacks are more likely to be motivated by something other than curiosity or showing off to one's peers. Greed, politics, racism (or any intolerance), or law enforcement (ironic) could all be motives behind the efforts. Crimes of all types where the payoff isn't directly tied to the attack, such as identity theft or credit card information theft, are also motivations.

International terrorism and government-sponsored attacks on another country's computer infrastructure are becoming well documented. Systems of interest might include utilities, public safety, transportation systems, financial systems, or defense systems, which are all managed by large data systems, each with vulnerabilities.

Internal Threats

Internal threats originate from individuals who have or have had authorized access to the network. This could be a disgruntled employee, an opportunistic employee, or an unhappy past employee whose access is still active. In the case of a past network employee, even if their account is gone, they could be using a compromised account or one they set up before leaving for just this purpose.

Many surveys and studies show that internal attacks can be significant in both the number and the size of any losses. If dishonest employees steal inventory or petty cash, or set up elaborate paper-invoicing schemes, why wouldn't they learn to use the computer systems to further their ambitions? With access to the right systems, a trusted employee can devastate an unsuspecting organization.

All too often, employers fail to prosecute this type of activity. The reasons range from fear of the activity becoming public knowledge to knowing that, quite often, record-keeping systems haven't been developed either to provide adequate evidence or to prove that the transactions, no matter how ludicrous, weren't authorized.

NOTE I was helping a dentist reconstruct a substantial loss by an office manager when we were all served with papers threatening all sorts of repercussions if we spoke to anyone, including the police, about the matter. Because less than three days had passed since the loss was inadvertently exposed, I was shocked at the coolness and speed of the reaction. After a little research, I found this was at least the third dentist in seven years who had been scammed by the same person. The bottom line is that the bonding company and the dentist came to terms, and I never heard another word about it.

External Threats

External threats are threats from individuals outside the organization, often using the Internet or dial-up access. These attackers don't have authorized access to the systems.

In trying to categorize a specific threat, the result could possibly be a combination of two or more threats. The attack might be structured from an external source, but a serious crime might have one or more compromised employees on the inside actively furthering the endeavor.

STUDY TIP Be sure to know the four primary types of threats. They could appear on all four exams.

The Four Primary Types of Network Attack

While there are many variations and often different names, the four most common types of network attacks are

- Reconnaissance attacks
- Access attacks
- Denial-of-service attacks
- Data manipulation attacks

STUDY TIP Some texts and certification exams might consider only the first three as specific types of network attacks, with data manipulation being a variety of access attack.

Reconnaissance Attacks

A *reconnaissance attack*, as the name implies, is the efforts of an unauthorized user to gain as much information about the network as possible before launching other more serious types of attacks. Quite often, the reconnaissance attack is implemented by using readily available information.

Public Information

Employee names and e-mail addresses provide a good start in guessing the user name for an employee's account. Common practice is to use an employee's first initial and last name as the user name for their network computer account. E-mail addresses are also a common user name for computer accounts. Large companies usually have their phone numbers assigned in blocks from the local telephone company, and many large corporations have their own dialing prefix. By using this information, the intruder can begin war dialing all the company phone numbers looking for a dial-up server. Once a dial-up server is found, the intruder can begin guessing account user names based on an employee's first initial and last name or their e-mail addresses. Brute force password crackers are freely available on the Internet. Once a user name has been guessed, it's only a matter of time before a weak password can be cracked.

A *war dialer* is a program used to dial blocks of phone numbers until it finds a computer on the other end of the line. Once a computer is found, the war dialer application records the number dialed for later use by the intruder.

To use a user account on a server or a network, you must first have the user name and password. Discovering the user names is a fairly straightforward process described in the preceding paragraph. Attackers use *password crackers* to crack the passwords to user accounts. Some password crackers find the encrypted password files on the server and decrypt them. When a hacker is unable to retrieve the password files, then brute force password crackers are used. *Brute force password crackers* attempt to log in to a computer account over and over, using multiple password combinations. Some cracking software uses dictionary files, while others attempt every combination of each key on the keyboard—a time-consuming ordeal.

The following are commonly used password crackers:

Microsoft Windows	UNIX
L0phtCrack 4	Qcrack by the Crypt Keeper
PWLVIEW	CrackerJack by Jackal
Pwlhack 4.10	John the Ripper by Solar Designer
PWL-Key	Crack by Alec Muffet
ntPassword	

Internet Protocol (IP) address information is publicly available via the ARIN and many other Internet registering authorities. From www.arin.net, anyone can begin a search using a single known IP address. The search will yield the complete block of IP addresses belonging to the company. Domain Naming Systems (DNS) is another publicly available system that can provide a wealth of information regarding the IP addressing and naming strategies of virtually any company connected to the Internet.

For a company to host its own e-mail, web, ftp, or any other service on the Internet, it must first have each of these servers listed within the DNS infrastructure. These DNS servers list the names of the servers, along with the IP addresses that can be used to access these services. To mitigate these risks, security conscious companies could choose to host these servers and services outside their private networks with a hosting company. This added security is usually rendered obsolete, however, by adding backend connections from the hosting facilities back to their private networks.

Electronic Reconnaissance

The attacker must perform electronic reconnaissance to find what systems and resources are on the network. Unless the attacker has prior knowledge of the target network, he or she must find where the company resources are logically located. Once the company IP addresses are known (see the preceding section, "Public Information"), the attacker can begin to probe and scan the network. The intruder can scan the network looking for vulnerable hosts, applications, or infrastructure equipment.

Scanning the network is typically done using a *ping sweep* utility that pings a range of IP addresses. The purpose of this scanning is to find what hosts are currently live on the network. The ping sweep identifies viable targets on the network. Once the IP address of viable hosts is known, the attacker can then begin to probe those hosts to gather additional information, such as the OS or applications running on those hosts.

Probing is attempting to discover information about the hosts that are on the network. Probing is accomplished by looking for open ports on the available host computers. *Ports* are like virtual doorways to the computer. For a computer to offer or use services on the network, it must first have an open port. Web servers typically use port 80, while FTP servers use port 21. An attacker can find out what services are running on a computer by discovering what ports that computer has opened.

TCP/IP uses port addresses to locate services running on host computers. The port numbers used by an application are that application's address on that host. The address for a web application located on host 10.0.0.1 would be 10.0.0.1:80. This address specifies the host address 10.0.0.1 and the application address of 80. Most common applications use well-defined port numbers. A list of well-known port numbers managed by the Internet Assigned Number Authority (IANA) can be viewed at http://www.iana.org/assignments/port-numbers.

The more ports that are open, the more potential for someone to exploit the services running on the host computer. Once the attacker knows which ports are open, he/or she can use this information further to discover the OS and the application servicing the port.

The purpose of this scanning and probing is to find weaknesses on the network. Intruders know the vulnerabilities of certain OSs and the applications they run. The intruder increases his or her chance of succeeding by finding the weakest point on the network and later attacking that vulnerability. The attacker continues to discover information about the network until they have a complete map of the hosts, servers, and weaknesses to exploit in the future.

Reconnaissance Tools

The most common and widely used hacking tools are *reconnaissance tools*. Many of these tools have been developed by hackers to aid them in their illicit activities. Other tools used by hackers are the same tools commonly used by network engineers to view problems on the network.

As security and intrusion detection have gotten more sophisticated, so has the software used by hackers. Intrusion-detection software looks for people looking at the network. Hackers know that scanning and probing a network is likely to create suspicion and might generate alarms. Because of this, hackers have begun to develop new software that attempts to hide the true purpose of its activity. Reconnaissance tools in common use today include the following:

NMAP	WHOIS
SATAN	Ping
Portscanner	Nslookup
Strobe	Trace

Access Attacks

Access attack is a catch-all phrase to encompass a variety of forms of unauthorized access of computer resources. An access attack could be an outside individual, or a group that uses various methods to gain entry to a network and, from there, steals confidential information or engages in destruction of resources. An access attack could also be an inside (trusted) user getting into areas they aren't authorized to use. Their intentions could be curiosity or the same as the outside hackers.

Gaining Initial Access

In many cases, the first objective is to gain initial access, so additional reconnaissance can be conducted. This reconnaissance could include scouting out resources, IP addresses, and possibly running a network discovery (mapping) program or even a sniffer-type packet-capturing utility, hoping to capture administrative-level passwords.

War dialers can be used to dial a large number of phone numbers looking for modems. A new variation involves sitting in a parking lot or in a building across the street with a laptop and a wireless NIC, looking for unsecured or poorly secured access points.

Again, don't overlook the person on the inside who already has access through an authorized user name and password. Whether connecting from outside or from an inside host, they have the first hurdles resolved.

Social Engineering

The term *social engineering* relative to security came from early hacking efforts on telephone systems and long-distance services. Social engineering is based on the concept of why risk breaking into a system by brute force or tools when you can get some friendly employee to help you do it? Social engineering is generally a hacker's clever manipulation of an employee's natural human tendencies to trust and want to be helpful.

More than one company with elaborate authentication processes, firewalls, virtual private networks (VPNs), and network monitoring software has been left wide open to an attack by an employee unwittingly giving away key information in an e-mail or by answering questions over the phone with someone they don't know. This is one area where the would-be hacker can benefit from a friendly demeanor, a good smile, and knowledge of looking and acting like they belong.

Don't make the mistake of thinking only lower-level employees are prone to this. The fear of appearing not to cooperate with an obviously important activity has led to the comprise of many a manager.

Password-Based Attacks

To use a user account on a server or network, you must first have the user name and password. Discovering the user names is a fairly straightforward process described in the preceding section. Attackers use password crackers to crack the passwords to user accounts. Some password crackers find the encrypted password files on the server and decrypt them. When a hacker is unable to retrieve the password files, then brute force password crackers are used. Brute force password crackers attempt to log in to a computer account over and over using multiple password combinations. Some cracking software uses dictionary files, while others attempt every combination of each key on the keyboard, a time-consuming ordeal.

Commonly used password crackers include the following:

Microsoft Windows	UNIX
L0phtCrack 4	Qcrack by the Crypt Keeper
PWLVIEW	CrackerJack by Jackal
Pwlhack 4.10	John the Ripper by Solar Designer
PWL-Key	Crack by Alec Muffet
ntPassword	

A good password system locks the account after a limited number of tries to thwart this type of attack. The successful hacker has the same access to resources as the users whose accounts they compromised to gain access to those resources.

General password security lapses can put a password in the hands of an intruder. This can be something as simple as passwords written on a desk pad, an appointment calendar, or an address book, to gaining access to a person's home or laptop computer where the logon password is being remembered by the OS. More than one company's security has been compromised by a child accessing the system from home or a friend's house using a password appropriated from a parent.

One-time passwords (OTP) systems and/or cryptographic authentication can almost eliminate the threat of password attacks. OTPs involve using "something you have," such as password-token generator software on your computer, plus something "you know," such as a PIN number. The token software uses the PIN to generate what appears as a unique password. Once the token is used, it won't work again, thwarting the intruder with a sniffer product.

If standard passwords must be used, strong passwords—those that would be difficult to guess—can help. Strong passwords should be at least eight characters long and contain both uppercase and lowercase letters, numbers, and special characters (such as 23!!pandA). While randomly generated passwords might be the best, they're hard to remember and often lead users to write them down.

Gaining Trusted or Privileged Access

Once initial access has been accomplished, the hacker will attempt to exploit any privileges associated with that access, including the ability to get into shared resources. If the initial account has limited access permissions, the hacker will try to gain administrator privileges (root inUNIX). With the higher privileges, the hacker can expand their influence by creating additional accounts they have access to, clean up any logs or history of their activities, and install additional tools for reconnaissance.

Denial of Service (DoS) Attacks

Denial of service (DoS) attacks in their many forms are by far the most infamous, and possibly the most threatening to organizations who conduct any business over the Internet. The primary purpose of any DoS attack is to deny access to a device—or better, an entire network—by bombarding it with useless traffic. This attack has two ways to bury the target. First, the packets themselves can consume 100 percent of a device's resources, thereby preventing it from doing its regular work. Because a firewall or intrusion detection system could often easily defeat this type of attack, the second threat is far greater. The second threat is that the organization's connection(s) to the Internet is filled to capacity with this useless traffic, thereby preventing in or out communications. For this reason, a DoS attack typically can only be defeated by the efforts of the organization's ISP.

Because the ISP's upstream connection, called a *fat pipe,* is typically many times larger than the connection to each customer, the ISP might be completely oblivious to the attack. If the ISP's staff and service policies are less than optimal, the organization under attack might seem doomed. Figure 1-1 shows the relative capacity of the ISP's link to the Internet versus the much smaller links to their customers.

The true DoS attack launched by a single host generally isn't used, except by the least-experienced hackers. Figure 1-2 shows a traditional DoS attack. The two most devastating variations are the distributed denial of service (DDoS) and the distributed deflection denial of service (DRDoS). Both of these attacks enlist the assistance of others, often hundreds, of unsuspecting hosts to assist in the attack, thereby significantly increasing the size of the attack, further shielding the source, and making it harder to defend against.

DDos

DDoS attacks start by the attacker(s) placing Zombie (technically, "bot," short for "robot") programs in a series of compromised computers hooked by relatively high-bandwidth connections to the Internet. These Zombies are programmed to monitor specific Internet Relay Chat (IRC) chat rooms to receive further instructions. The

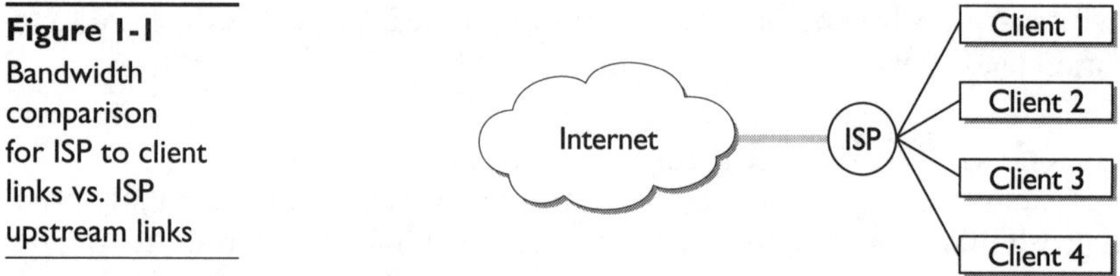

Figure 1-1 Bandwidth comparison for ISP to client links vs. ISP upstream links

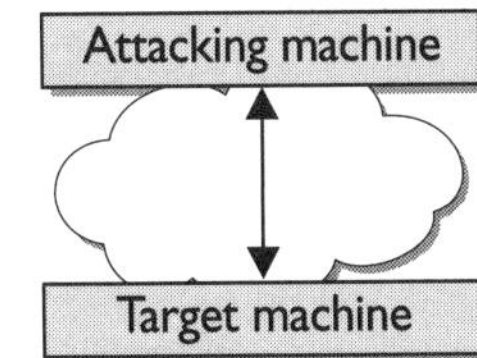

Figure 1-2 DoS attack with a single attacker and a single target

Zombie attack is directed and coordinated by a Zombie Master, who sends instructions to the individual Zombie, who then begins generating a flood of malicious traffic aimed at the target. Figure 1-3 shows a DDoS attack.

Early DoS attacks on some famous web sites involved many computers on university campuses and even some from security agencies. These computers had unprotected security holes, were online around the clock, and provided large connections to the Internet. Today, DSL and cable modem connections make many home and small business computers more attractive as Zombie sites because they often lack the security features and staff to defend against the intrusion.

Some Zombies, once in place, download and install additional applications that can map the local network, capture passwords or keystrokes, and report findings to the instigators of the attacks.

DRDoS

The latest variation on the DoS, the *DRDoS*, involves one or more hosts sending a series of TCP SYN requests or ICMP ping requests to many unsuspecting, even thoroughly secure, hosts using the "spoofed" source address of the target. When these hosts respond to what appears to be a legitimate, nonthreatening request, they collectively create an unsupportable flood of packets aimed at the target. Figure 1-4 shows a DRDoS attack. Again, even if the target device(s) can determine what's happening, only a cooperative ISP can block the traffic before it buries the target's Internet connection.

If the originating source continues to vary the type of packets sent to the reflectors, the filters at the ISP have only temporary or limited usefulness before they need to be changed.

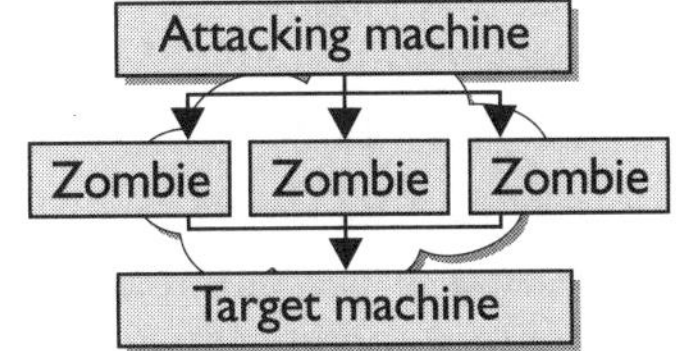

Figure 1-3 DDoS attack involving Zombie remote hosts

Figure 1-4 DRDoS attack showing the interim hosts

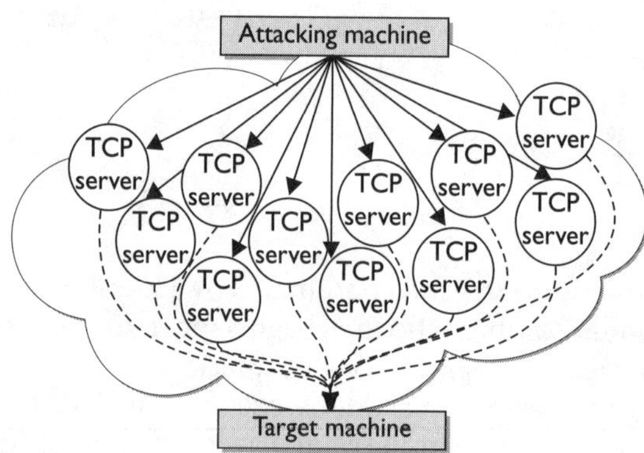

Well-Known DoS Attacks

Knowing about common, well-known attacks can be useful and interesting, and when someone indicates an attack is a variation of the Ping of Death, you will know what that means. Well-known attacks include the following:

- **TCP SYN Flood** Uses the TCP establishment handshake to conduct attacks by creating TCP "half-open" connections, tricking the target or reflector into thinking a session is being established.
- **Ping of Death** Sends one or more oversized ping packets to crash or disable servers and other computer systems. Sending illegal IP datagrams (larger than 65,536 bytes) is possible because of packet fragmentation during transmission. When the fragments are reassembled at the target, it can overflow the buffer and cause a reboot, crash, or hang.
- **Trinoo** A distributed tool (bot) used to launch coordinated UDP flood DoS attacks from many sources. A *Trinoo* network consists of a small number of masters and a large number of bots.
- **Tribe Flood Network (TFN) and Tribe Flood Network 2000 (TFN2K)** Like Trinoo, variations of TFN use a distributed tool to launch coordinated DoS attacks from many sources against the target(s), often using spoofed source IP addresses. TFN bots can generate UDP flood attacks, TCP SYN flood, ICMP echo request flood, and ICMP directed broadcast (for example, smurf) DoS attacks.
- **Stacheldraht** (German for "barbed wire") Combines features of the Trinoo DDoS tool with those of the original TFN, and adds encrypted communications between the attacker and stacheldraht masters and automated agent updates.
- **Trinity** Preys on Linux servers and uses IRC channels to unleash IP packet floods on targeted host machines

Terrorism, Act of War, and Legal Implications

Variations of the DoS attack are likely to be a major component of global terrorism and even a part of government-sponsored acts of aggression against its perceived enemies. The possible devastating that effect a massive distributed attack could have on a country's command and control systems, financial systems, utility grids (power, telephone, transportation, and soon), and other services is something to remember.

While we hope most of us will never be in a position to directly defend against such an attack, it's critical that the resources under our control do not become unwitting hosts to any kind of DDoS attack.

Many lawyers became quite computer savvy and versed in the areas of financial responsibility in preparation for the feeding frenzy they expected from the Year 2000 "bugs." While that threat never materialized, many lawyers are now advising victims of DDoS attacks that the unwitting hosts of the attack bots might have financial liability because of not detecting and eliminating the devices. Security practices that allow these unauthorized residents to do their dirty deeds could carry a hefty price tag.

While the original hacker is careful to conceal their identity and address, they have a whole lot less interest in protecting the bot hosts. If, in fact, lawsuits against remote sites become common, it's not inconceivable that the bot site might be the ultimate target of an attack.

Motivation and Good Sense

While many reasons or rationalizations exist that an individual or group of individuals might choose to launch a form of DoS attack on a network, one thing common to many attacks is anger. Real or imagined, the attacker blames the site, the owners of the site, or the users of the site for some slight, injustice, or wrong doing. Add to this the apparent anonymity the attacker enjoys, and it's generally a no-win situation to provoke or even incur the interest of these individuals needlessly. The size and scope of the Internet means your site can literally fall prey to a "sniper" 12,000 miles way.

Attackers typically have the time, and the cost to them is close to zero. The target is in the opposite position: once the attacks begin, time is virtually nonexistent. The costs, direct and in lost business or reputation, start to soar. Be well aware that no Internet Police Department or anyone else is going to handle this for you.

Don't make yourself a target. Practice good security measures and involve law enforcement in all criminal acts, but be forewarned that personal attacks and even belittling statements like script kiddies might precipitate a career of fighting these attacks. Sometimes, even protective security measures as a result of an attack within your network might escalate the attack.

Time isn't as universal as many of us think. When a network is under attack and the administrator has brought in all the high-priced talent, added new technologies, and possibly even lined up law enforcement, it's common to want the attack to continue long enough to identify and catch the attacker. Remember, other than anger or adrenalin, the hacker has nothing invested and could recognize they can even cause greater losses by being unpredictable. In most cases, the worst that can happen is that the hacker gets locked out.

Techniques to Counteract DoS Attacks

While the threat of DoS attacks can't be eliminated, it can be reduced through the following three methods:

- **Anti-DoS features** Proper implementation and configuration of anti-DoS features available on routers and firewalls can help limit the effectiveness of an attack. These features could include limiting the number of half-open connections allowed at any given time or limiting the number of certain types that can originate from a source address.
- **Antispoofing features** Proper implementation and configuration of antispoofing features on routers and firewalls can help limit a hacker's ability to mask their identity. RFC 2827 filtering should be configured at a minimum (see the upcoming section "IP Spoofing").
- **ISP traffic rate limiting** The ISP agrees to filtering limits on the amount of nonessential traffic that can cross link(s) to the company at one time. The filtering might limit the volume of ICMP traffic, a common source of distributed denial of service (DDoS) attacks, into a network because it's used only for diagnostic purposes.

Data Manipulation Attacks

Data manipulation, or impersonation, is made possible by vulnerabilities in IP protocols and related applications. *Data manipulation attacks* are often called "man-in-the-middle" attacks because the attacks typically involve an individual located between TCP/IP-exploited IP vulnerabilities. Common forms of these attacks include IP spoofing, session replay, session hijacking, rerouting, repudiation, and vandalizing web pages.

IP Spoofing

An *IP spoofing attack* involves an external or internal hacker who pretends to be using a trusted computer by using the address of that computer. The hacker either uses an IP address within the range of trusted internal addresses for the network or an authorized external address that's both trusted and allowed access specified network resources. IP spoofing is often a tool used as part of other attacks, such as any variation of DoS attack, to hide the hacker's identity.

IP spoofing is often limited to the introduction of malicious data or commands into an existing data stream in a peer-to-peer network session. Spoofing a source address might enable data to be sent through a router interface with filtering based on the source address.

The threat of IP spoofing can be reduced, but not eliminated, through the following measures:

- **RFC 2827 filtering** Basically, *RFC 2827 filtering* means filtering out any IP addresses from coming into a network segment that should already be on that segment. If the entire 195.17.1.0 network is attached to a router interface, then no legitimate packets with source addresses in that network should be coming in through the router. This should be applied to edge routers for sure, but it can also be used on internal routers to prevent spoofing within the network. Similarly, limiting any outbound packets leaving the network to ones that have source addresses assigned to that network can prevent a network's hosts from spoofing other networks. This could be the result of an attacker on the inside or a DoS bot on a local host participating in an attack on an outside host. If the company can get its ISP to perform RFC 2827 filtering on packets coming into the network, it would preserve the bandwidth of the link and kill some hack attempts.

NOTE Spoofing could be virtually eliminated if all ISPs filtered client traffic to allow only source addresses assigned to that client. If hackers can't spoof it, this makes going undetected harder.

- **RFC 1918 filtering** *RFC 1918 filtering* means filtering out RFC-defined "private" addresses from entering or exiting the network segment. Because they have no business on the Internet, they shouldn't be there. If private addresses are used in the network, RFC 2827 filtering will include them.
- **Non-IP address authentication** IP spoofing is worthwhile when devices use IP address–based authentication. If you use additional authentication methods, IP spoofing attacks lose much of their value. *Cryptographic authentication* is the strongest form of additional authentication, but if this isn't possible, use strong, two-factor authentication, such as OTP.

Session Replay and Hijacking

Session replay is a form of a man-in-the-middle attack, where the intruder captures a packet sequence and modifies part of the data before forwarding it on normally. This type of attack relies on an inherent weakness in data traffic authentication.

Session hijacking is a form of a man-in-the-middle attack where the attacker takes over an IP session that's underway by spoofing source and/or destination addressing and altering TCP sequence numbering. Typically, a packet sniffer is used to set up the hijacking by allowing the user to see the existing traffic.

Rerouting

Rerouting involves either gaining access to a router to change the route table entries, or spoofing the identity of routers or hosts so traffic is directed to a compromised device. Spoofing ARP replies is even possible. It causes a host to forward packets intended for a specific host or the default gateway to be forwarded instead to another local host. The new destination host can perform its assigned task and then forward the packet on to the correct destination.

Repudiation

Repudiation is the denial of having been a part of a data exchange. This repudiation might be to avoid responsibility for an action. *Nonrepudiation* is a security feature that helps ensure that data has been sent and received by the parties claiming to have sent and received it. Nonrepudiation guarantees that the sender of a message can't later deny (repudiate) having sent the message. Similarly, the recipient can't deny having received the message.

Methods for implementing nonrepudiation include the following:

- **Digital signatures** Unique identifier for an individual, much like a written signature
- **Confirmation services** The message transfer agent creates digital receipts indicating messages were sent and/or received
- **Timestamps** The date and time a document was composed, proving a document existed at a certain time

Cisco AVVID and SAFE Strategies

Cisco Architecture for Voice, Video, and Integrated Data (AVVID) and SAFE are Cisco-comprehensive strategies that help organizations successfully and securely develop and implement end-to-end network designs.

AVVID

The approaching convergence of the telephone services, videoconferencing, IP data networks, software-based services, and a never-ending supply of new technologies introduces many opportunities for both disaster and success. AVVID provides a standards-based network architecture and a comprehensive set of best practices, which allows businesses to develop business and technology strategies that scale to meet the changing demands of e-business. AVVID provides end-to-end networking solutions that help organizations plan rapid deployment of emerging technologies and new Internet-based solutions.

The AVVID end-to-end networking solution includes network client devices, network infrastructure from network platforms to intelligent network services, Internet middleware tools, systems integrator responsibilities, and Internet business solutions. The AVVID strategy addresses the three primary concerns of network deployment: performance, scalability, and availability.

These documents and related links are available free, without a CCO ID from the Cisco web site. To find the current list of documents, either go to the following web site or go to http://www.cisco.com and do a search on AVVID: http://www.cisco.com/warp/public/779/largeent/avvid/cisco_avvid.html.

TIP For the exams and for your own development in the industry, go to the site and at least download the white paper on the AVVID architecture and become familiar with it. This white paper provides a detailed overview that you can use to supplement all the chapters in this book.

SAFE

Cisco's strategy for secure networks (SAFE) started with the original "SAFE: A Security Blueprint for Enterprise Networks," a 66-page plan to provide best-practice information to those involved in designing and implementing secure networks. SAFE represents a defense-in-depth approach to network security design, focusing on the expected threats and the best ways to mitigate those threats, rather than a single set of rules to follow. The result is a "layered approach" to security design and implementation, intended to prevent a failure of one security system from compromising the organization network resources.

Since its introduction, the SAFE program has expanded to include many other blueprints, including "SAFE Extending the Security Blueprint to Small, Midsize, and Remote-User Networks," and a growing number of SAFE documents on topics such as wireless, IP telephony, IPSec VPN, Nimda attack mitigation, and Code-Red attack mitigation. These white papers are available free, without a CCO ID from the Cisco web site. To find the current list of documents, either go to following web site or go to http://www.cisco.com and do a search on SAFE: http://www.cisco.com/warp/public/779/largeent/issues/security/safe.html.

TIP For the exams and for your own development in the industry, go to the site and download at least the original "SAFE: A Security Blueprint for Enterprise Networks" and become familiar with it. This provides a detailed overview you can use to supplement all the chapters in this book. At a minimum, review the foundation material in Appendix B.

Cisco Security Wheel

Cisco developed a process they call the Security Posture Assessment (SPA) to describe a company's network security efforts as a living, evolving entity. The SPA is represented graphically in Figure 1-5. As the graphic shows, developing a network security program is an iterative process that must be continually managed to reduce the risk of loss, while efficiently using company resources.

STUDY TIP You should assume this graphic and the process it represents can be part of all four security exams. As you learn about a new technology, make sure you know where that technology fits in the Security Wheel. For example, intrusion detection systems (IDS) would be a part of the monitoring process.

Even if a company had the capital resources and attempted to develop the "perfect" network security solution, it would still be only the beginning of an on-going process. Like a perfect wave for a surfer or a perfect breeze for a sailor, the perfect security system is at best a moment in time, if not an illusion. The factors that led the company to put in the security system have been busily evolving and changing at the same time. The nearly constant changes occurring in technologies used in the network, types and sources of threats, even changes in data flows within the organization continually introduce new

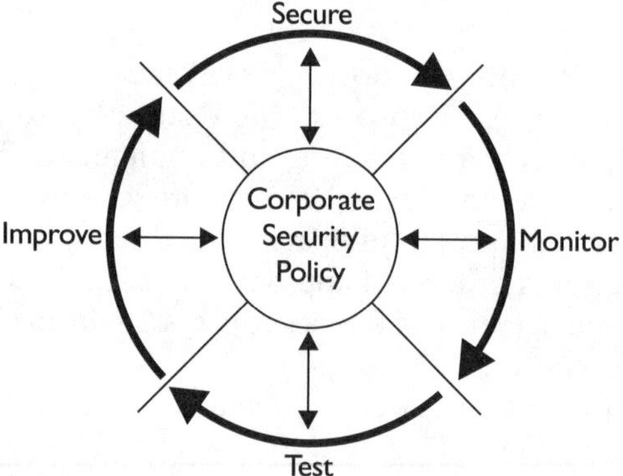

Figure 1-5 Cisco Security Wheel depicting the evolution of a security system

risks that must be anticipated and mitigated. The wheel identifies the four stages of developing a secure system.

- **Secure** After carefully studying the security policy, it's time to secure the network by implementing the processes and technologies required to protect the organization's data and intellectual resources. These could include technologies like VPNs for telecommuters and branch locations, or the addition of firewall devices in the network.
- **Monitor** The security processes and technologies need to be monitored to make sure they provide the security expected. This could involve a variety of activities, ranging from scanning log files to using network management software to detect intrusions, failed attempts, and internal misuse of resources.
- **Test** The test stage can include testing new processes to make sure they meet expectations, testing established processes to see if internal or external changes might have made them less than secure, and periodic audits to see that all processes and policies are being implemented as designed and whether security problems are being dealt with properly.
- **Improve** The improve stage involves developing new plans to adjust the security program for changes in both the internal and the external environment. From implementing "staged" improvements that were built into the original plan to reacting to the latest security threat that could be stalking the network, improvements in both technology and processes are a must.

At the center of the wheel is the network security policy, sometimes referred to as the *corporate* or *enterprise network security policy*. This component, if properly implemented, is the blueprint for the four evolutionary processes of the wheel to follow. The next section looks at the security policy in greater detail.

Network Security Policy

The organization security policy, like the vacation policy or the family leave policy, is an official company document that lays out the expectations of the organization, the processes to be implemented, and the sanctions for those that fail to comply. Without a well-defined and accepted security policy, security becomes an ad hoc process governed by the person in charge at the moment and can (at best) lack any effective usefulness to the organization or (at worse) could lead to significant losses of resources and/or opportunities.

Security policies are covered in detail in the "Site Security Handbook" (RFC 2196). The handbook document defines a security policy as "A formal statement of the rules by which people who are given access to an organization's technology and information assets must abide." It goes on to say that "the main purpose of a security policy is to inform users, staff, and managers of their obligatory requirements for protecting technology and information assets. The policy should specify the mechanisms through which these requirements can be met. Another purpose is to provide a baseline from which to acquire, configure, and audit computer systems and networks for compliance with the policy. Therefore, an attempt to use a set of security tools in the absence of at least an implied security policy is meaningless."

Why Create a Network Security Policy

Any set of policies requires time and effort to produce a useful and effective tool that can be implemented and administered. Some of the benefits and purposes for taking the time to develop a well-structured policy include the following:

- Provides a blueprint for security purchases and implementations
- Defines technologies that can and cannot be added to the network
- Provides the procedures to follow in case of a security incident
- Defines which practices and behaviors are acceptable and which are not
- Defines the sanctions for violations of the policies
- Provides a process and targets to audit existing security
- Defines responsibility throughout all levels of the organization for implementation, monitoring/auditing, sanctioning, funding, and supporting the policies
- Creates a basis for an enforceable legal action
- Provides the baseline for the next step in the evolution of the network security

The Balancing Act

An organization security policy determines how secure or insecure the network and intellectual resources are, what features or functionality is included in the network, and how easy the network resources are to access. A good security policy can only evolve after the organization clearly understands and defines its security goals. Only at that time can intelligent decisions be made about which tools to use, which technologies to allow and/or support, and what restrictions need to be defined and communicated.

Recognizing that the goals of other organizations might not be the same as yours is important. Even competitors within the same industry might have different security needs based on their perceptions, organizational structure, and even whether they are industry leaders or followers. Furthermore, the goals of an organization's vendors—or would-be vendors—might not necessarily be the best to follow. Many network devices include default settings that allow "wide open" operation to maximize throughput and to facilitate adding new devices with little thought for overall network security. For example, notice how many vendors use the top throughput ratings for wireless systems, knowing full well that when security is incorporated, the numbers drop substantially.

A security policy is always the result of compromises and balancing between the following key tradeoffs:

- Security versus ease-of-use
- Security versus services provided
- Security cost versus risk of loss

In the next sections, you will see each of these compromises and the impact each one has on the resulting security.

Security vs. Ease of Use

On the one extreme, a system with no passwords, unlimited access from anywhere, and few restrictions on user behaviors provides the easiest environment for users to work and create within. This also creates an environment where company resources and intellectual property could be easily damaged, lost, or stolen. On the other extreme, frequently changing passwords, restrictive "need to know" access, and draconian penalties for any mistakes can secure the resources at the expense of users being unable to or unwilling to do their jobs to the fullest.

A natural conflict will always exist between the users and the security requirements of an organization. Users often see any restrictions placed on them as interfering with the company's capability to compete and be efficient. Security personnel often see users as security risks, instead of the tools of production that ultimately pay the bills. Figure 1-6 represents the balance between ease of use and network security. The same representation could also be applied to balancing services and cost versus security.

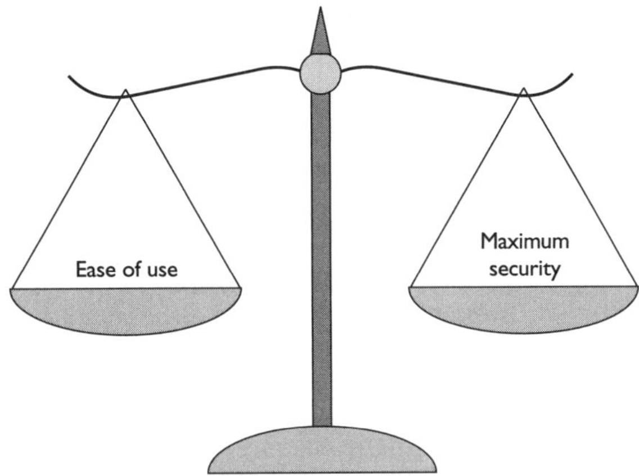

Figure 1-6 Balancing security needs with user ease of use

Security vs. Services Provided

Every service and technology provided to users carries some level of security risks. Some services, such as wireless technologies, involve risks that could be somewhat obvious. Others might involve hidden risks that go unexploited for an extended period of time. In some cases, the decision might be made that the risks outweigh the potential benefits and the service should be eliminated rather than efforts made to secure it.

Security Cost vs. Risk of Loss

This might be the most difficult comparison to make. Implementing a form of security seldom involves just the cost of acquisition, such as the purchase price of a firewall or an authentication server like TACACS+. There can be network performance implications if the new technology increases latency through a device. The new technology or policy could reduce user access or increase user effort in using the technology.

Just as identifying costs associated with implementing some security changes might be difficult, many types and levels of risk can also accrue if the service or policy isn't implemented. The loss could include the following:

- *Loss of company data or intellectual property,* such as the accidental or intentional corruption or deletion of files
- *Loss of service,* such as the loss of a server from a DoS attack, the loss of data storage space because of the replication of nonbusiness files, or the loss of a web site defaced by a hacker
- *Loss of privacy,* such as the copying and/or viewing of company or personnel information by unauthorized users
- *Loss of reputation,* such as the company embarrassment and possible loss of business associated with the disclosure that customer files or credit card information has been accessed by outsiders

NOTE I once had a client who got a call from a police department several states away informing him that his web site was hosting a porn exchange site. The officer provided the exact address and told the client to "take care of it." The officer went on to explain that the call was a courtesy because he was convinced this was an unauthorized use of the server, but that they could just as easily have showed up with warrants and turned the whole place upside down. The site was removed. The company developed a security program, but the client was fearful for a long time that the word might somehow get out and damage his reputation within his client community.

Ultimately, each organization must evaluate its network and intellectual resources to determine the appropriate level of security needed to safeguard those resources, while still enabling the organization to meet its primary mission. This evaluation process often takes time to reach equilibrium and can be altered significantly by events such as a network intrusion or loss of a valuable resource. The lucky groups are those that can learn vicariously from the experiences of others and possibly avoid significant losses of their own.

Network Security vs. Network Operations

Many organizations separate their network security and network operations departments because their missions and pressures are somewhat different. While operations strives to make network resources available in as quick and efficient a method as possible, they might not have the time, resources, or training to analyze the security implications of all situations. Security personnel should have the resources and training to evaluate the organization's needs, without the direct pressures of maintaining a production network. Note, I'm not saying that security personnel can ignore the pressures of running an efficient and reliable production network, only that their main objective is different.

In a perfect world, balance would be struck by having a security staff with previous production experience to better understand their peers in operations, and the operations personnel would have sufficient training and management support for security to perform their jobs effectively, while complying with the security policy.

A Security Policy Is to Be Shared

A *security policy* must be a formal written statement of company policy that has the full support of management and owners. A security policy must be easily disseminated to and scrutinized by users at all levels, operations staff, and managers as a set of security rules that covers all types of information technology, as well as the information stored and manipulated by that technology. To be effective, a security policy must be communicated to users in a clearly understandable form and acknowledged by them through a signed statement, indicating they have read, understand, and will abide by the policy.

Acceptable Use Policy (AUP)

An acceptable use policy (AUP) might logically be included as part of the final security policy. Because of the convergence of technologies, it's common for AUPs to include telephone, copier, personal digital assistant (PDA), and pager, as well as fax activities. The AUP should spell out specifically what users can and cannot do on the various components that make up the network, including the type of activities and traffic allowed on the networks. The AUP should be as explicit as possible to avoid ambiguity or misunderstanding, particularly if sanctions are imposed for failure to comply. For example, an AUP might list prohibited activities like "browsing and engaging in transactions on web auction sites." The AUP could be explained at all employee orientation sessions and signed by each user. This agreement and training should be updated periodically as a refresher and definitely any, time a significant change is made.

Unfortunately, it's not uncommon for new employees to learn about new limitations on access to resources, such as Internet access for personal use only, to find the same information hasn't been distributed to the existing employees. It's particularly dysfunctional when the sanctions involved with a policy are implemented against employees who had no way of knowing they were violating a policy. Handled poorly, this can lead to mistrust, lack of support, and even refusal to use certain resources.

Network Operations and Network Security Training

Networking employees at all levels will require additional training and sign-offs on those portions of the security policy that impact their jobs, but that aren't covered in the AUP. Again, this should be handled proactively with enough detail that each employee understands their responsibilities and the limits of their authority. No one wants to learn that the configuration file they sent to Cisco TAC for help with a problem might cost them their job as a breach of the company security policy.

Who Should Help Create the Security Policy?

For a security policy to be effective, it must have the acceptance and support of all levels of users within the organization. Especially important is that corporate management and ownership (board of directors) fully support the security policy process; otherwise, little chance exists that it will be successful. Also critical is that the resulting policy will eventually fit within the organization and its culture. In particular, a first security policy or a radical change in policy might require some transition time for people to learn and assimilate the new rules. The following people are representative of those who should typically be involved in the creation and review of security policy for a larger organization:

- Company security administrator
- Security incident response team representatives
- IT technical staff representatives (network operations)
- Administrators of organization business units
- Representatives of the user groups
- Responsible upper management
- Corporate legal counsel (in some countries)

The wide variety and sizes of businesses make it impossible to define a single list. The nature of the business and the level of and types of employee contracts and bargaining units might dictate some other attendees. Just because a security policy is necessary and reasonable doesn't set aside a company's requirements to negotiate changes in work rules. More than one organization has been required to rehire with back pay an employee terminated under a security policy rule because it conflicted with a bargaining agreement.

Another group that should be represented is any internal auditors required by industry standards or governmental regulations. Because some policies dictate production of logs, backups, and documentation, it's critical that those policies comply with any relevant laws, regulations, industry standards, or court orders.

If the resulting policy statements are to reach the broadest possible acceptance, the group must be an appropriate mix of involved representatives (stakeholders) that can formulate a set of rules that balance the security requirements with the technical expertise available or obtainable. These policies must have an acceptable impact on the company business model, particularly in any areas perceived to create a competitive advantage. Finally, the budget and policy authority must be present to make sure these policies are supported throughout the organization and funded adequately during both good times and bad. If done properly, the policy should yield the highest level of appropriate security in the most cost-effective manner.

Assets and Threats

Developing a security policy, as in any risk analysis, involves determining what needs to be protected, what it needs to be protected from, and how best to protect it. So the first things to do in the process are

- Identify the assets
- Identify the threats

The process then involves examining all possible risks, ranking those risks by level of severity, and, finally, making cost-effective decisions on what you want to protect and to what extent. It makes no sense to spend more to protect something than its actual worth.

Identifying the Assets

When identifying the assets that need to be protected, some might be obvious, like valuable proprietary information such as product blueprints or designs, intellectual property, and the many hardware components that make up the network. Others might not be so obvious, though, and are often overlooked, such as the people using the systems. While the company doesn't own the people, it could have invested in their skills and development over the years. Similarly, the company might rely heavily on those skills to meet its business objectives. Some users might have no readily identifiable replacements within the current workforce.

The point is to list everything that could be impacted in any way by a security problem:

- **Hardware** Servers, workstations, laptops, printers, scanners, FAX units, routers, switches, firewalls, intrusion detection devices, wireless access points, IP telephones, palm-sized devices, pagers, projection systems, electronic white boards, and communication lines. Don't forget devices that might be at telecommuters' homes, such as DSL routers, printers, and so forth. The move to combine resources like printers and copiers should be acknowledged, even if not yet implemented.
- **Software** User software licenses, custom and off-the-shelf enterprise applications, virus protection software, network and workstation OSs, network device OS, network management applications, utilities of all types, diagnostic programs, and communication/FAX programs.
- **Data** Financial records, business plans and strategies, customer and employee information, sales records (including credit card information), product designs and parts lists, inventories, production schedules, and customer and vendor contracts. Many of these could be parts of one or more databases, while others might be many individual documents in the system. Each type must be identified by its location during execution, where they're stored online, where they're archived offline, any backups, audit logs, and whether they're ever transmitted over communication links. It isn't uncommon to discover entire classes of strategic documents stored only on local hard drives.
- **People** Users, administrators of all types, help desk people, and hardware maintenance.
- **Documentation and licenses** For OSs, applications, hardware, systems, and administrative procedures. Don't forget service agreements and warranties.
- **Supplies** Paper, toner and ink cartridges, and batteries.
- **WAN and Internet services** Contracts and service agreements for communications links, web hosting services, and related contracted services of any kind. Because these services could be in negotiation for some time, be sure to include any works in progress.

While not technically a network component and not appropriate for all companies, as previously mentioned, any company doing business over the Internet ought to consider its reputation and the trust relationships it's developed as an asset. Any attack that damages this reputation could have serious implications for the future well being of that company and its stakeholders.

Identifying the Threats

Once the assets to be protected are identified, it's necessary to identify and assess the threats to those assets. As you saw earlier in this chapter, different names and levels of detail can be applied to these security threats, but, generally, they break down to the following:

- Reconnaissance
- Unauthorized access
- Data manipulation
- Denial of service

The basic goal of security for each asset is to ensure availability, confidentiality, and integrity. Each threat should be examined to assess how it could impact the company assets. Each company can have different perceptions and assessments of the threats, which should be identified and addressed.

STUDY TIP Data manipulation is often included in unauthorized access threats, so keep that in mind if you are asked to identify only three threats.

Evaluating a Network Security Policy

Just as the preceding section showed that different organizations can have different perceptions of threats and place different values on assets, the security policy reflects those differences. Most security studies agree that some of the key characteristics of a security policy should include the following:

- It must be implementable through network administration technologies, by publishing rules and acceptable use policies, or other appropriate methods.
- It must be enforceable with security tools, where appropriate, and with sanctions, where actual prevention isn't technically or financially feasible.
- It must clearly define the areas of responsibility for the users, administrators, and management. Maybe as important, it should clearly identify the limits of authority for each group under predictable circumstances.

Any policy that has serious deficiencies in any of these characteristics stands a better-than-good chance of failing to meet the company objectives.

What Belongs in a Network Security Policy

Each organization will develop a policy based on a variety of factors. Even after exhaustive study and development, the policies need to be updated as new technologies develop or become financially feasible. Some common components of a good security policy include the following:

- **Statement of authority and scope** Who sponsors and authorizes the policy, as well as who it impacts.
- **Access policy** Defines all access privileges and responsibilities to network assets by specifying acceptable use rules for users, network operations staff, and management. These policies should cover adding devices to a network, adding software to systems, modifying software and OS settings, and how and by whom external connections to the network are to be made. The policies should specify any required connect warning messages about "authorized usage and monitoring." Parts of the access policy might become part of acceptable use policy (next).
- **Acceptable use policy** Which user practices and behaviors are acceptable and which are not. This policy often includes technologies, including telephones, cell phones, pagers, copiers, fax machines, computers, access to the Internet, and so forth.
- **Privacy policy** Defines what are reasonable privacy expectations regarding monitoring of e-mail and access to users' files.
- **Remote access policy** Defines how remote users and telecommuters will access the organization networks. This policy might be further broken down to cover specific technologies, such as ISDN access policy, DSL access policy, and cable modem access policy.
- **Wireless access policy** Defines if and under what circumstances a wireless devices or devices can be used with the company network.
- **Antivirus policy** Defines which tools will be used and how they'll be implemented.
- **Password policy** Defines what passwords will look like and how often they must be changed, and it should authorize audits of password files to ensure compliance.
- **Authentication policy** A more comprehensive form of the password policy that defines a local access password policy and establishes guidelines for remote authentication processes, which might include OTPs and the devices that generate them.
- **Router and switch security policy** Defines minimal security configuration for all routers and switches connecting to a production network.
- **Availability statement** Defines what users can expect for resource availability. Known risks, redundancy, and recovery issues should be stated. Hours for routine maintenance downtime should be specified, as well as any notification process used before the system is taken down. Contact information for reporting system and network failures should be included.

- **Accountability policy** Defines the responsibilities of users, network operations staff, and management. This should cover guidelines for routine monitoring, scheduled and unscheduled audits, and guidelines for incident handling (what to do, what not to do, and who to contact in case an intrusion is suspected).
- **IT system and network maintenance policy** Defines how internal and external maintenance people are allowed to handle and access company technology. This should address if, and under what conditions, remote maintenance is allowed and how such access is controlled. If outsourcing is allowed, how it should be managed and the processes that need to be followed should be defined.
- **Violations reporting policy** Defines the types of violations that must be reported and to whom the reports are made. Remember, a low-key atmosphere and even anonymous reporting can result in a greater likelihood that a suspected violation will be reported.The policy should include specific contact information for users, staff, and management for each type of policy violation. Guidelines should include how to handle outside queries about a security incident, detailing who should be responding, and defining the procedures depending on where the contact is from. There may be a different policy or contact person when working with an interested third party, law enforcement, or the media. Defines the procedures if the security incident involves information that might be considered confidential or proprietary. If appropriate, any cross-references to security procedures company policies and/or applicable laws and regulations.

Here's an example. Recently in our area, a policeman was ordered reinstated with about a year's full pay and benefits, plus overtime that would have been earned. While the court agreed that viewing pornography on a department laptop in a public place was a violation of the AUP in place, it disagreed with the penalty for a first violation, determining that termination was too severe. The $86,000 is probably less damaging than the harm done to the department's reputation and credibility.

Make Time for Training and Signing Off

Once the security policy is established, reviewed as needed, and approved by the highest levels in the company, it should be clearly communicated to all users, network staff, and management. Remember, this training of the employees is the only opportunity to express the importance of the effort, the seriousness of the company commitment, and the need for their active participation. Each person should be able to retain for future reference any appropriate sections, including at least the AUP.

Having all personnel sign a statement that indicates they've read, understood, and agreed to abide by the policy is common practice and logical. Note, this signing is of questionable value in protecting the company resources if the policies aren't explained or treated with respect by management. The last security policy I signed was a modified distribution list attached to a stack of papers passed around a conference table. I remember thinking that because virtually nobody read the attached document, it probably wasn't going to modify much existing behavior.

Keep It Flexible

For a security policy to be viable over the long term, it must be as flexible as possible, allowing for growth and changes within the architecture. As much as possible, the policy should be independent from specific hardware and software because these items can be moved or removed on short notice.

The processes for updating the policies should be defined in detail to include the steps to do, the people to include, and who must sign-off on the resulting changes.

Finally, the policies must be reviewed on a regular basis to make sure they're successfully meeting the company security needs. The policies should also be reviewed if any new major technology is added to the network to make sure the technology is covered from day one.

Example of a Network Security Policy

A security policy can take many forms and styles, but one that's easy to get started with is a series of templates produced by the SANS Institute called "The SANS Security Policy Project," available from their web site at http://www.sans.org/newlook/resources/policies/policies.htm.

The System Administration, Networking, and Security (SANS) Institute was established in 1989 as a cooperative research and education organization to provide a forum for security professionals, auditors, system administrators, and network administrators to share the lessons they have learned and find solutions to the challenges they face. Many SANS resources, such as news digests, research summaries, security alerts, and white papers, are free. For more information, their web site is http://www.sans.org.

One of many useful sites SANS hosts is the "SANS/FBI Top Twenty List" (http://www.sans.org/top20.htm), which summarizes the "Twenty Most Critical Internet Security Vulnerabilities." This web site also includes step-by-step instructions and pointers to additional information useful for correcting the flaws.

The writers at SANS have produced about two dozen templates for each of the major policies to be included in a security policy. Each policy is a separate document that allows for easy addition and editing, and each follows the same style shown in the example in the upcoming sidebar.

Securing the Network

Once the security policy is approved, it's time to make sure that any security measures specified or appropriate to the policy are properly installed and configured. The rest of this book focuses on many of those technologies. In the next chapter, beginning in the section on "Improving Network Security," you start looking at those basic configurations that should be a part of every device configuration.

Wireless Communication Policy

1.0 Purpose

This policy (provided here with permission from SANS) prohibits access to <Company Name> networks via unsecured wireless communication mechanisms. Only wireless systems that meet the criteria of this policy or have been granted an exclusive waiver by InfoSec are approved for connectivity to <Company Name>'s networks.

2.0 Scope

This policy covers all wireless data communication devices (that is, personal computers, cellular phones, PDAs, and so forth) connected to any of <Company Name>'s internal networks. This includes any form of wireless communication device capable of transmitting packet data. Wireless devices and/or networks without any connectivity to <Company Name>'s networks don't fall under the purview of this policy.

3.0 Policy

To comply with this policy, wireless implementations must do the following: maintain point-to-point hardware encryption of at least 56 bits; maintain a hardware address that can be registered and tracked, that is, a MAC address; and support strong user authentication that checks against an external database, such as TACACS+, RADIUS, or something similar.

EXCEPTION A limited-duration waiver to this policy for Aironet products has been approved, if specific implementation instructions are followed for corporate and home installations.

4.0 Enforcement

Any employee found to have violated this policy could be subject to disciplinary action, up to and including, termination of employment.

5.0 Definitions

- **Terms** (add terms here)
- **Definitions** (add definitions here)
- **User Authentication** A method by which the user of a wireless system can be verified as a legitimate user independent of the computer or OS being used.

6.0 Revision History

The references to <Company Name> would be replaced by the company or client name and references to **InfoSec** would be replaced by the name of the company department responsible for network security. The reference to Aironet refers to a pioneer wireless manufacturer, since acquired by Cisco. The design with standardized sections and titles makes it easy to add a policy unique to the organization that would fit right in.

Monitoring Network Security

The security policy should specify the methods to be implemented in the routine monitoring of the network. The purpose of security monitoring is not only to observe a network attack, but also to point out potential weaknesses that could be exploited. The one thing monitoring should verify is whether the security policy is being followed.

Monitoring could be as simple as an orderly collection and review of the various log files that network devices generate as a normal part of operation. Simply viewing failed login authentications for a server can indicate attempts to break into the system or maybe just some individuals that need additional training. At the other end of the spectrum are sophisticated devices like IDS that can monitor traffic looking for patterns or signatures that would indicate something is amiss. If a potential problem is discovered, the IDS sensor can notify the IDS director management console, which can then start a process to block (shun) the attack. It could involve creating an access control list in a router or firewall specifically to block further contact from that source. IDS technology is covered in Chapter 7, and then again in Chapters 23 to 26.

Auditing Network Security

Whereas monitoring is a routine general process of watching the network for potential problems with the network security, auditing is a more specific test or series of tests on the network to determine the effectiveness of the security measures, as well as compliance with the policy and any relative regulations. Auditing, like monitoring, should be specifically defined, and allowed within the formal security policy.

The random nature of audits as compared to routine monitoring makes them useful in detecting unauthorized internal activity within the system. For this reason, audits shouldn't become routine or scheduled. Much of their usefulness is diminished if your troublemakers can predict when an audit will occur.

Shareware tools are available on the Internet and even many operator-triggered system tests can be automated by the use of scripts. Checklists of features to audit for many technologies are available on the various security web sites. Some auditing is low tech. It can be as simple as periodically reviewing the tape backups to confirm the backup was run when scheduled, that it covered everything specified, and that the tape has a usable file. Other reasons for audits might include the following:

- Any addition to or change to systems in the network. Has the new system or the change (upgrade) possibly brought with it some unknown problem? This shouldn't be an optional audit.
- Spot checks of policy compliance.
- Regularly checking password files for compliance with the password policy.
- Router and switch configuration compliance to make sure all appropriate security requirements are included.

Commercial auditing tools or even network intrusion tools like Cisco Secure Scanner can perform ongoing auditing, including looking for potential security holes. Some of these tools come from a variety of vendors, but might only run on certain management stations. This is one area where UNIX seems to have a clear edge.

Improving Network Security

Just as the image of the security wheel implies, network security is a constantly evolving and growing process. This process is driven by the changing and growing nature of the business on one side leading to more and more resources and possibly links to more outside sources. Pressing from another side is the bad guys outside of your network who are constantly gathering better tools, often the same ones you'll be learning about. They also don't have a security policy preventing them from trying the latest and greatest hack posted on the Internet. They could also have "cracked" copies of licensed tools and software the company can't afford. If potential attacks from two growing fronts weren't bad enough, internal users are becoming savvier about the workings of the network. Economic turmoil can often bring out a side of people that even they might not have known existed under other circumstances.

So what is the company to do? Start by recognizing that what you have today in the form of network security becomes the baseline from which the future is built. There's no going back to last year, so today becomes the beginning of time. Planning and development must always look at the next level of safety the network security can be moved to. Meanwhile, caution and good practices would suggest the following:

- Monitor the security alerts from all network device vendors and install the recommended patches and upgrades.
- Stay current on the latest threats, vulnerabilities, and tools by monitoring security web sites and newsgroups, such as www.sans.org, www.cert.org and www.cisecurity.org.
- Implement and follow the existing network security policies, including incident investigation and reporting. Lax implementation and enforcement leads to potential vulnerabilities and can undermine commitment to security.

- Update the security policy on a regularly scheduled basis, plus any time a new technology is added to the network or an existing technology is removed.
- Ongoing security training and awareness should be a priority at all levels within the company.
- Encourage a sense of trust and friendliness to encourage employees to "ask first" when in doubt and to encourage reporting of potential security incidents.

Chapter Review

Technologies like the Internet, wireless connectivity, instant messaging, and others have introduced new levels of concern for network security. In addition to providing additional access points to the network, the Internet is also a reference resource for hackers and security experts. Unfortunately, no rules or limitations exist on the information that can be posted, so it's easy for harmful information to be widely distributed.

The secure network design example is to lay a basic design foundation for discussions throughout the book. Basically, three types of networks are separated by a firewall device, which can be a router running firewall features, a server running firewall features, or a dedicated firewall device. The three types of networks are the following:

- **Inside** Those trusted hosts and networks that make up the area to be protected.
- **Outside** Those hosts and networks that pose a threat to the inside network. In many cases, the outside includes a perimeter router, the ISP, the Internet, and any networks attached to it.
- **DMZ** A network of shared servers, or bastion hosts, that provide resources to both the outside network and the inside network users.

The firewall configuration allows relatively free access from the outside to the DMZ; access from the DMZ to the inside is limited to sessions originating inside; and access from the outside to the inside is generally blocked, except in rare well-protected exceptions.

The three most common weaknesses or vulnerabilities that cause network security problems include technology weaknesses, such as IP or OS holes; policy weaknesses, such as missing or weak security policies; and configuration weaknesses, such as insecure default settings.

The four primary threat designations are unstructured, structured, inside, and outside. These designations can be used in combinations like outside—unstructured to better define the type of attack.

The four most common attack types include reconnaissance attacks, access attacks, denial of service attacks, and data manipulation attacks. Many references, including the PIX Firewall exam, consider data manipulation attacks to be variations of access attacks.

Cisco Architecture for Voice, Video, and Integrated Data (AVVID) and SAFE are Cisco-comprehensive strategies that help organizations to successfully and securely develop and implement end-to-end network designs.

Questions

1 Which of the following is *not* a common cause of network security problems?

A. Technology weakness

B. Configuration weakness

C. Planning weakness

D. Policy weakness

2. Which four of the following are primary types of network threats?

A. Planned threats

B. Unstructured threats

C. External threats

D. Structured threats

E. Internal threats

3. A virus is an example of which of the types of network threats?

A. Planned threats

B. Unstructured threats

C. External threats

D. Structured threats

E. Internal threats

4. Which of the following is *not* one of the four primary types of network attack?

A. Access attacks

B. Data manipulation attacks

C. Reconnaissance attacks

D. Programmed attacks

E. Denial of service attacks

5. In a reconnaissance attack, which one of the following is *not* a part of target discovery?

A. Ping sweeps

B. Ping of Death

C. Port scans

D. DNS queries

6. Which one of the following is an example of social engineering relative to security?

A. Guessing a password based on a person's vanity license plate

B. All users in a department using the same user name and password

C. Giving your password to the home office technician, so they can test your account

D. Using a password of eight characters, uppercase and lowercase, plus numbers

7. A standard DoS attack typically includes which one of the following?

A. An attacker, a series of Zombies, and the target

B. An attacker, a war dialer, and the target

C. An attacker, a series of Zombies, and the target

D. An attacker and the target

8. Which of the following is *not* a well-known DoS attack?

A. Ping of Death

B. Tribe Flood Network

C. Trinoo

D. TCP SYN Flood

E. Script kiddy

9. IP spoofing is an example of which of the following?

A. DoS attack

B. Reconnaissance attacks

C. Data manipulation attacks

D. Brute force attack

10. RFC 2827 filtering refers to which of the following?

A. Filtering private IP addresses

B. Filtering based on trusted external addresses

C. Filtering based on source addresses that belong on a network segment

D. Filtering based on destination addresses that belong on a network segment

11. Which of the following involves denying responsibility for a transaction?

A. Session replay

B. Rerouting

C. Repudiation

D. Session hijacking

12. Which of the following provides a standards-based network architecture and comprehensive set of best practices that allow businesses to develop business and technology strategies, which scale to meet the changing demands of e-business?

A. SAFE

B. DrDos

C. AVVID

D. Digital signatures

13. RFC 1918 filtering refers to which of the following?

A. Filtering private IP addresses

B. Filtering based on trusted external addresses

C. Filtering based on source addresses that belong on a network segment

D. Filtering based on destination addresses that belong on a network segment

14. Which of the following best describes a good security plan for an organization?

A. Set it and forget it

B. Ad hoc

C. Evolutionary

D. Rigid

15. Which one of the following is *not* a part of the Cisco Security Wheel?

A. Monitor

B. Administer

C. Test

D. Secure

16. What is at the center of the Cisco Security Wheel?

A. Strong network support staff

B. Improvement

C. Network security policy

D. Flexibility

17. According to the "Site Security Handbook" (RFC 2196) a security policy is

A. An informal set of suggestions by which people who are given access to an organization's technology and information assets should abide.

B. A formal statement of the rules by which people who are given access to an organization's technology and information assets must abide.

C. A formal statement of the rules by which network administrators can control access to an organization's technology and information assets.

D. RFC 2196 doesn't deal with this issue.

18. Which of the following is *not* a reason to create a network security policy?

A. It provides a blueprint for security purchases and implementations.

B. It defines technologies that can and cannot be added to the network.

C. It provides the procedures to follow in case of a security incident.

D. It frees up network security personnel to work on other projects.

E. It provides a process and targets to audit existing security.

19. Developing a security policy is often described as a balancing act. Which three of the following are common compromises that need to be made?

A. Security cost versus risk of loss

B. Security cost versus local or federal regulations

C. Security versus ease of use

D. Security versus services provided

E. Local or federal regulations versus ease of use

20. When evaluating risk associated with a security breach, which three of the following might result from someone accessing the companies sales order entry system?

A. Loss of reputation

B. Loss of company data or intellectual property

C. Loss of temper

D. Loss of service

E. Loss of privacy

21. Which of the following might be included in an acceptable use policy (AUP)?

A. Acceptable and unacceptable Internet activities

B. Penalties or sanctions for violating the policy

C. Acceptable and unacceptable e-mail activities

D. Acceptable and unacceptable telephone use

E. Acceptable and unacceptable copier or fax use

F. All of the above

22. Which of the following is likely to result in a security policy that will meet the needs of an organization?

A. The network security staff develops the policy.

B. The network security staff and network operations staff develop the policy.

C. Representatives of all major groups that use and manage the networks, plus representatives of management develop the policy.

D. The network security staff and company management develop the policy.

23. In developing a security policy, as in any risk analysis, the first two things you must identify are the

A. Opportunities

B. Assets

C. Hardships

D. Threats

24. According to the RFC, which of the following is *not* a characteristic required of a good security policy?

 A. It must be implementable through network administration technologies, by publishing rules and acceptable use policies, or other appropriate methods.

 B. It must clearly define the areas of responsibility for the users, administrators, and management. Maybe as important, it should clearly identify the limits of authority for each group under predictable circumstances.

 C. It must be state of the art, implementing all the latest, most advanced technologies and procedures to protect the company resources.

 D. It must be enforceable with security tools, where appropriate, and with sanctions, where actual prevention isn't technically or financially feasible.

25. When a group of sales reps plug a wireless access point into a network jack so they can use wireless NICs on their laptop, they

 A. Greatly increase their mobility and freedom

 B. Increase the number of usable connections to the network

 C. Probably violate the wireless access policy of the security policy

 D. Add a hub that will reduce the bandwidth to each user

26. Which of the following statements best describes monitoring and auditing?

 A. They are two terms for the same process.

 B. Auditing is routine scheduled reviewing of security, while monitoring is random and unpredictable reviewing of security.

 C. Monitoring catches bad guys outside the network, while auditing catches bad guys inside the network.

 D. Monitoring is routine scheduled reviewing of security, while auditing is a random and unpredictable reviewing of security.

Answers

1. C. Planning weakness
2. B. Unstructured threats; C. External threats; D. Structured threats; and E. Internal threats
3. B. Unstructured threats
4. D. Programmed attacks
5. B. Ping of Death

6. C. Giving your password to the home office technician so they can test your account. There is never a reason to give someone your password, or for a legitimate tech to ask for it.
7. D. An attacker and the target
8. E. Script kiddy
9. C. Data manipulation attacks
10. C. Filtering based on source addresses that belong on a network segment
11. C. Repudiation
12. C. AVVID
13. A. Filtering private IP addresses
14. C. Evolutionary
15. B. Administer
16. C. Network security policy
17. B. A formal statement of the rules by which people who are given access to an organization's technology and information assets must abide
18. D. It frees up network security personnel to work on other projects.
19. A. Security cost versus risk of loss; C. Security versus ease of use; and D. Security versus services provided
20. A. Loss of reputation B. Loss of company data or intellectual property; and E. Loss of privacy; (While loss of temper might occur, this isn't one of the risk criteria.)
21. F. All of the above
22. C. Representatives of all major groups that use and manage the networks, plus representatives of management develop the policy.
23. B. Assets and D. Threats
24. C. It must be state of the art implementing all of the latest and most advanced technologies and procedures to protect the company resources. (While a good idea, this might be far from cost-effective for many organizations.)
25. C. Probably violate the wireless access policy of the security policy (While all the statements are true, within the context of this course, this is *the* important issue.)
26. D. Monitoring is routine scheduled reviewing of security, while auditing is a random and unpredictable reviewing of security.

CHAPTER 2

Securing the Network

In this chapter, you will learn how to:

- Secure network design example
- Improve network security
- Secure network devices
- Use access control lists (ACLs) to secure the network

As you saw in the preceding chapter, the network has many threats. Developing a comprehensive security program to combat those threats requires planning in the initial stages, and a lot of tweaking and revising as time goes on. Just as the organization attempts to move the network to a more secure state, the threats are also evolving, changing and often growing stronger. Network security will never be a "set it and forget it" world.

This book looks at many technologies and methods to secure access to and operation of the computer networks. While many variations exist, some of the most important ones include the following concepts.

Physical security	Once stated, this seems so obvious, but it's often overlooked. Network devices must be physically secured from unauthorized access or even theft. Password recovery techniques make it quite easy for anyone to access and reconfigure a device if they can have physical access to it.
Vulnerability patching	Network devices from workstations to routers have or develop vulnerabilities that can usually be mitigated by applying software patches, performing upgrades, and disabling any unnecessary services.
Encryption	If making the data path absolutely secure isn't possible, then encrypt the data. Encryption, such as IPSec, means anyone capturing the data will find useless gibberish.
Firewalls	Firewalls filter traffic based on predefined permit-and-deny rules. Ideally, a firewall devotes 100 percent of its resources to protecting the network.

Intrusion detection	Intrusion detection systems (IDS) detect certain patterns of data that match known "signatures" of improper activities. The IDS system can then notify network management or even implement measures to block the activity.
Authorization systems	Secure authorization systems, such as one-time passwords (OTP), limit the usefulness of a password that's been compromised or captured through sniffing activity.

In this chapter, you learn some other simple techniques to improve network security. Some of these techniques should be familiar from other certifications, but each one provides a small piece of the strategy necessary to secure the network.

Secure Network Design Example

To lay a foundation for discussion of secure networks, this section looks at some basic terms and concepts used throughout the book. In security terms, you have three types of networks to consider: inside, outside, and an optional network called the demilitarized zone (DMZ). A *firewall* is the device that separates or joins these areas. The firewall can be a router running a firewall feature set or a specialty server, or it can be a specialty device such as the Cisco PIX that does nothing but provide firewall services. Figure 2-1 shows a simplified view of the three areas and the firewall.

Figure 2-1 A firewall separating the three security areas

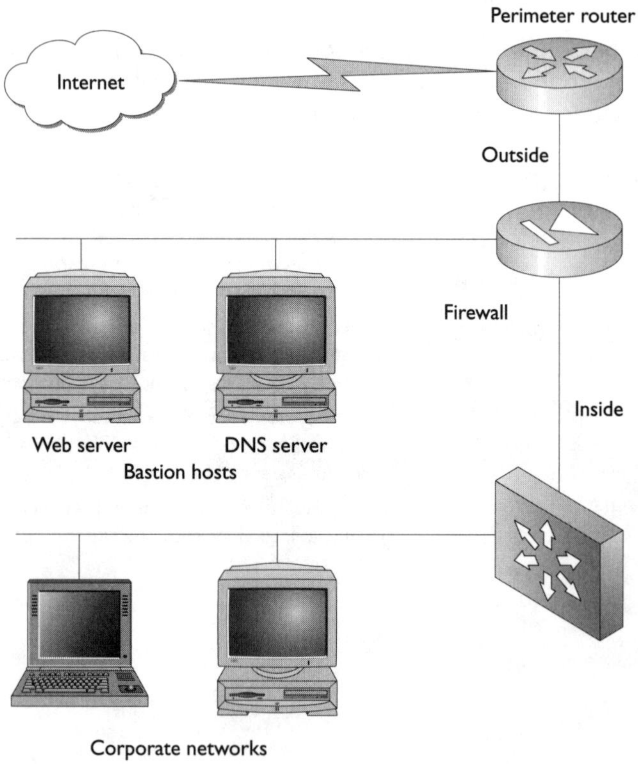

The typical firewall device has three or more LAN interfaces: one each for the inside and outside networks, and one for each DMZ network. Some early firewalls and those used in small implementations like branch locations or telecommuter residences might only have two interfaces for separating the inside network from the outside world. Today the LAN interfaces are typically Fast Ethernet or Gigabit Ethernet, but there's no reason they couldn't be Ethernet, Token Ring, or Fiber Distributed Data Interface (FDDI).

Inside Network

Inside networks are also referred to as the *internal* or *private networks*. The inside area is made up of the network(s) of the organization, including all workstations and servers not shared with the outside world. These devices are considered *trusted* and in need of protection from the outside world. The inside area is typically under one administrative authority and operates under a common security plan.

A firewall is normally used to separate the inside network from the outside world, but a firewall can also be used to separate internal departments if additional security is required. For example, a school might choose to place a firewall between the student network and the faculty network.

Outside Network

Outside networks are also referred to as the *external* or *public networks*. The outside area, or *untrusted area*, is considered to be all devices and networks beyond the direct control of the organization's administration and security policies. The outside area would typically include the perimeter router, the ISP, the Internet, and all networks attached to it.

While not necessarily the greatest actual threat to many networks, the international scope of the Internet means an organization can face threats from anywhere in the world for reasons that could seem ludicrous at home.

Demilitarized Zone (DMZ)

The demilitarized zone (DMZ) is made up of one or more isolated LAN networks that contain shared server resources, such as web, DNS, and e-mail servers. These servers are available to the outside world. These shared servers are often called *bastion hosts, bastion servers,* or even *sacrificial hosts*. Bastion hosts must be secured and receive highest priority security maintenance because of their vulnerability to the outside world and increased likelihood of attacks. A bastion server typically runs only those specific services being shared, and all other services will be stopped or turned off.

The firewall must be configured to allow quite loose, but regulated, access to the DMZ from the outside network while at the same time protecting the inside network. Inside network users need access to the server resources in the DMZ and are typically allowed limited access, possibly restricting access to only those sessions originating within the inside network.

Generally, the firewall will be configured to prevent access from the outside to the inside, possibly limiting access to those sessions originating from the inside network. Other, unsolicited, access from the outside would be blocked in most cases. One common exception might be the e-mail server(s) if it resides in the inside network instead of the DMZ. Securing this type of connection is covered in the firewall chapters.

Securing Network Devices

The rest of the chapters in this book cover technologies and processes to secure the corporate network. Some are pretty simple, while others are more elaborate. The remainder of this chapter covers some basic techniques that should be a part of any basic router or switch configuration, regardless of its role or placement within the network. Many of these might be familiar to you from your earlier certifications. While this list of tasks is by no means exhaustive, it does represent the types of details that must be covered to make sure our networks are secure.

Physically Secure the Devices

All network devices need to be in a physically secure environment, whether in a locked data closet, a locked cabinet, or both. In most cases, if routers and switches can be physically accessed, they can be compromised. With Cisco devices, the only things required to compromise the system are a console cable kit and a terminal system, which today can include many palm-sized devices. Password recovery techniques are well known and easy to implement.

While password recovery lets a person with less than CCNA skills take control of the device, an equal fear should be the person with a screwdriver who decides to take the device(s) and worry about accessing them later. Cisco devices are typically hot items on web auction sites, often with several thousand listings on any given day. While corporate data centers typically have secure facilities, many small businesses and small branch offices might rely on Telco closets for router placement. Before agreeing to place devices in a Telco closet, consider that, in many cases, every building tenant has direct or indirect access to that closet.

Other reasons for centralizing network devices into a single room include facilitating environmental features like climate control (heating and cooling), stable power with Uninterruptible Power Supply (UPS) backups, secure access including locks and protection from over the wall or under the floor access, and possibly increased human presence to provide a deterrent. If the data room is busy with many people having access, it might make good sense to put key devices into locked cabinets.

Securing Administrative Access

One of the fundamental requirements in protecting the network is to secure the administrative access to any network device. With Cisco devices, administrative access to the device could allow someone to reconfigure features or even possibly use that device to launch attempts on other devices. Some of the basic techniques for securing administrative access would include the following:

- Setting User mode passwords
- Setting Privilege mode passwords
- Encrypting passwords in the configuration files
- Setting an MOTD banner to advise about the security restrictions
- Setting access privilege levels
- Restricting Telnet access to the device
- Restricting web browser access to the device
- Restricting SNMP access to the device

The first five techniques are covered in this chapter, while the last three are covered in Chapter 3, which deals with access control lists.

User Mode Passwords

This section reviews and expands on the techniques for assigning passwords to the three potential access points to the *User* mode, the entry level into a Cisco device. In Chapter 3, you learn how to use authentication servers, such as TACACS+ and RADIUS, with AAA authentication services for securing access to Cisco devices.

The User level on a Cisco router often has three potential access points. They include the following:

- **Console (con) port** Access for the console cable. Figure 2-2 shows a typical console port on a router.
- **Auxiliary (AUX) port** A console-like access that can be attached to an external modem for a dial-up connection.
- **Virtual terminal (vty) ports** The access points for Telnet sessions.

The default configuration for each of these interfaces, shown in the following code listing, doesn't include a password. Since the release of version 12.0 of the IOS, the virtual terminals and AUX ports require that a password is set. If none is set, the user will be rejected with the message "password required, but none set." The console port doesn't

Figure 2-2 Console port on an 800 model telecommuter router

have this requirement, so it's a good idea always to set a password to prevent anyone with a laptop and a console cable from accessing the device.

```
interface FastEthernet0/0
 ip address 192.168.0.1 255.255.255.0
!
line con 0          <-Console connection
 login
line aux 0          <-AUX connection
 login
line vty 0 4        <-Virtual terminal connections
 login
end
```

The basic password configuration for each is the same. The password is defined with the **password** command and the **login** command. Passwords can be 1 to 25 character, and can include uppercase and lowercase letters, as well as numbers, to comply with complex password requirements in the password policy. The result might look like the following listing:

```
!
line con 0
 password cisco1
 login
line aux 0
 password cisco2
 login
line vty 0 4
 password cisco3
 login
end
```

The passwords used should comply with the password policy portion of the network security policy. You could use the same password for all three, but this isn't a secure solution. Someone attempting to access the device through one of these three methods will be prompted only for a password, at which time they need to supply the appropriate one.

User Name/Password with Login Local You can require both a user name and a password, as well as have the opportunity to create different combinations for different users. The first step is to develop a local database of acceptable user name and password combinations in the Global Configuration mode. Like all passwords, these are case- ensitive, can include text and numerals, and should comply with the password policy. The user names aren't case sensitive. Two examples might include the following:

```
Rtr1(config)#username remote password acC3ss
Rtr1(config)#username scott password woLfe7
```

To finish the configuration, change the login command to **login local** for the interface(s) that you want to use this feature. In the following example, only the virtual terminal lines are being changed.

```
username remote password access
username scott password wolfe
```

```
!
line con 0
 password cisco1
 login
line aux 0
 password cisco2
 login
line vty 0 4
 login local
end
```

After making the changes, the next Telnet session login might look like the following:

```
User Access Verification

Username: remote                <-Used the remote / acC3ss combination
Password:
Rtr1>exit                       <-Successful attempt

User Access Verification

Username: scott                 <-Used scott / WOLFE7 combination - note case
Password:
% Login invalid                 <-Wrong case on the password)

Username: ScOtT                 <-Used ScOtT / woLfe7 combination - note case)
Password:
Rtr1>                           <-Used the correct case on the password)
```

The important things to remember are that the user name isn't case sensitive, while the password is. Furthermore, if more than one entry is in the local database, then any valid combination is acceptable.

Privilege Mode Passwords

Access security for the Privilege mode involves being prompted for a password only if an **enable password** or **enable secret** password has been previously defined in Global Configuration mode. If neither is set, no security allowing any user to view and/or change the device configuration exists for the Privilege mode. Someone could even set a password and lock out other users.

The older **enable password** command followed by the desired password creates a cleartext entry in the running configuration that could be viewed by anyone seeing the configuration. The more secure **enable secret** command followed by the desired password creates an encrypted entry in the running configuration that can't be understood by anyone just seeing the configuration. If both **enable password** and **enable secret** are configured, only the **enable secret** is used. The **enable password** is ignored.

The following entries demonstrate both commands, and then use a **show run** command to display the configuration. All passwords are case sensitive and should comply with the password policy.

```
Rtr1#conf t
Rtr1(config)#enable password test
Rtr1(config)#enable secret cisco
Rtr1(config)#^z
Rtr1(config)#show run
```

```
!
enable secret 5 $1$4F6c$D5iYCm31ri1cA9WwvAU220
enable password test
```

Notice the enable secret password can't be recognized, but the enable password is easily recognized. If only the enable password had been set, anyone seeing the configuration could get the password that would let them reconfigure the router.

Password Encryption

If you look over the previous examples, you'll notice all passwords are in cleartext, except for the enable secret password. This means prying eyes might gather a password. You can secure the passwords in Global Configuration mode by typing the **service password-encryption** command. This permanently encrypts all passwords, so make sure you know what they are. The following abbreviated output demonstrates the command and the results:

```
Rtr1#conf t
Rtr1(config)#service password-encryption              <-command
Rtr1(config)#^Z
Rtr1#sho run
version 12.0
service timestamps debug uptime
service timestamps log uptime
service password-encryption                           <-command
!
hostname Rtr1
!
enable secret 5 $1$4F6c$D5iYCm31ri1cA9WwvAU220
enable password 7 15060E1F10                         <-enable password
!
username remote password 7 070E224F4B1A0A            <-local database
username scott password 7 02110B570D03               <-local database
!
line con 0
 password 7 121A0C041104                             <-line con password
 login
line aux 0
 password 7 121A0C041104                             <-line aux password
 login
line vty 0 4
 login local
!
end
```

Note, typing **no service password-encryption** won't cause the passwords to revert to cleartext. The system will no longer encrypt new passwords, but the existing ones remain encrypted. Make sure you know a password before you encrypt it.

Message of the Day Banner (MOTD)

It's possible and prudent to create a message that will appear to everyone logging in to the User mode. This message should be a polite warning of company security policies for unauthorized access. Some courts have held that if this isn't explicitly stated—telling people to stay out, then it's an implicit invitation to come in and raise havoc.

To configure this message, use the **banner motd** command in the Global Configuration mode. The syntax is a little unusual in that you type the command, followed by a character you don't plan to include in the message. This character becomes a delimiter, in that everything you type after it until the character appears again will be part of the message. An example would be **banner motd *No Unauthorized Access*** where the asterisks indicate the beginning and the end of the message. The asterisks won't appear in the message.

You can make multiple-line messages by using SHIFT-ENTER at the end of the line and ignoring the warning message that appears the first time you try it. The following lines demonstrate this technique. Typing a new MOTD replaces any existing one.

```
Rtr1#conf t
Rtr1(config)#banner motd * Unauthorized Access Could Result In Termination
Enter TEXT message.  End with the character '*'.          <-Ignore this

If you have any trouble with this device, call:
Mark Smith in IT Tech Support
Phone: (555) 555-1111 ext 1234*
Rtr1(config)#^Z
Rtr1#
```

The next login attempt would look like the following:

```
Unauthorized Access Could Result In Termination

If you have any trouble with this device, call:
Mark Smith in IT Tech Support
Phone: (555) 555-1111 ext 1234
User Access Verification
Password:
```

Three other options can be used with the **banner {exec | incoming | login | motd}** command that allow for variations on when the banner can be used. The MOTD option has been included because it causes the warning to appear at login for all users and is the most frequently used. You can use the help feature to see the other options.

Privilege Levels

Cisco devices numbered 0 through 15 have 16 privilege levels. By default, any user who can furnish the user-level password or user name/password combination can gain User exec mode access to the device, which is privilege level 1. From there, if the user knows the enable secret password, they can access the Privilege exec mode, or privilege level 15. The three predefined privilege levels on Cisco devices include the following:

- **1** User exec mode only (prompt is router>), the default level for login
- **15** Privileged exec mode (prompt is router#), the Enable mode
- **0** Seldom used, but includes five commands: disable, enable, exit, help, and logout

To determine or confirm the current privilege level, type the **show privilege** command. It would look like this in Privilege mode:

```
Rtr1#show privilege
Current privilege level is 15
Rtr1#
```

Privilege levels 2 through 14 can be defined by the admin to provide limited features to some users by assigning specific commands to the level using the **privilege** command. The syntax is

privilege *mode* {level *level command* | reset *command*}, where

mode	Indicates the configuration level being assigned. This includes all router configuration modes, including exec, configure, and interface.
level	Indicates the level being defined.
command	Indicates the command to be included. If you specify exec mode, then the command must be an **exec mode** command.
reset	Resets the privilege level of the command to the default privilege level.

A possible application of this feature might look like the following lines, which are creating a new Privilege mode for a part-time administrator.

```
Rtr1(config)#privilege exec level 7 ping
Rtr1(config)#privilege exec level 7 show startup-config
Rtr1(config)#privilege exec level 7 show ip route
Rtr1(config)#privilege exec level 7 show ip int brief
Rtr1(config)#enable secret level 7 tESt7
```

The following lines show how the new privilege level would be accessed and a confirmation of the new level:

```
Rtr1>enable 7
Password:
Rtr1#show privilege
Current privilege level is 7
Rtr1#
```

Any attempt to run a command other than those specifically defined for this privilege level returns the same error message as any attempt to run a command from the wrong mode. As you will see in Chapter 4, AAA authentication provides some additional options for this feature.

Note that the privilege feature only limits user access if the user only knows the enable secret password for the defined level. If the user knows any other level password, then they can go there as well.

Using Access Control Lists to Secure the Network

Access control lists (ACLs) are powerful tools that are often at the heart of many other processes, including security processes. ACLs can be a good starting point for adding security and traffic management to a network, but they can't protect the network by themselves. Devices like firewalls and proxy servers, as well as good security practices—password management, physical security, and solid administrative policies—should be used to augment them.

STUDY TIP While ACLs aren't a specific exam objective, they're fundamental in many security implementations and processes. Newer operating system (OS) versions for devices like PIX firewall boxes and Catalyst switches use Cisco IOS–like features and commands and, therefore, incorporate access list capabilities. Make sure you're comfortable with how access lists are constructed and how they work. If you need a refresher on ACLs, go to Appendix A.

Standard ACLs

This section includes examples of standard IP ACLs with various wildcard Mask options to perform the following security-related tasks.

- Traffic filtering
- Limiting access to Telnet sessions
- Limiting access to HTTP sessions
- Filtering routing updates
- Limiting the **debug ip packet** analysis and, therefore, CPU use

Before looking at these examples, let's look at a technique that can be used in test labs to make a limited pool of devices look more diverse. In some of the next exercises, having more than one LAN interface on the routers would be useful, but this isn't required. The next section looks at using loopback interfaces as a simple work-around in the lab.

Using Loopback Interfaces on Lab Routers

What do you do if your router has only a single Ethernet interface? Or worse, what if one of your lab routers has only a Token Ring LAN interface and you don't have a Multistation Access Unit (MAU) unit to plug it in to, so the interface won't come up? Short of getting another device, the only solution is to create loopback interface(s). What are loopback interfaces?

- They are logical interfaces, in that they don't connect to any cables and, therefore, they have no hosts. Loopback interfaces are logical interface only.

- They are "up" by default and remain up unless administratively shut down with the **shutdown** command.
- They can be configured as a host, a subnet, a network, or a supernet, like any other interface.
- They can be included in the routing updates like any other interface.
- They can be used as a ping, a Telnet destination, or a source.
- Some routing protocols, such as OSPF and BGP, use loopbacks as router IDs.

Configuring a loopback interface is similar to creating a subinterface. The syntax is

router(config)#interface loopback *num*
router(config-if)#ip address *ip-address subnet-mask*

The *num* is any whole number between 0 and 2147483647. It won't accept module-type notation, like 0/1.

Note, the **no shutdown** command isn't required and would only be used with loopback interfaces following a **shutdown** command.

Here is an example:

```
router(config)#interface loopback 0
router(config-if)#ip address 192.168.3.1 255.255.255.255
```

The Layer 3 addresses can be either an IP or an IPX interface configuration (AppleTalk isn't supported on all router platforms). The example is a 32-bit mask, called a *host mask,* because it specifies a single host, not a network or a subnetwork. Some routing protocols, such as Open Shortest Path First (OSPF), use loopback interfaces as router IDs and prefer the host mask to avoid problems. With protocols such as RIP, IGRP, and EIGRP, you can use any mask that serves your purpose.

Traffic Filtering

Traffic filtering is a common use for standard access lists used when the plan is to block all packets from a specific source host or group of hosts from reaching a portion of the network. Figure 2-3 shows a simple two-router network that might represent two branch locations of a smaller business.

The following code represents two access lists created on the Rtr1 router. ACL 10 allows only a single host (192.168.2.20) from the Rtr2 LAN and all hosts from the Rtr1 LAN to go out to the Internet. By not adding a permit any statement, all other hosts are denied.

```
Rtr1(config)#access-list 10 permit host 192.168.1.20.0.0.0.255
Rtr1(config)#access-list 10 permit 192.168.1.20 0.0.0.255
Rtr1(config)#access-list 20 permit host 192.168.2.20
Rtr1(config)#access-list 20 deny 192.168.2.0 0.0.0.31
Rtr1(config)#access-list 20 permit any
Rtr1(config)#int s0
Rtr1(config-if)#ip access-group 10 out
Rtr1(config-if)#int e1
Rtr1(config-if)#ip access-group 20 out
```

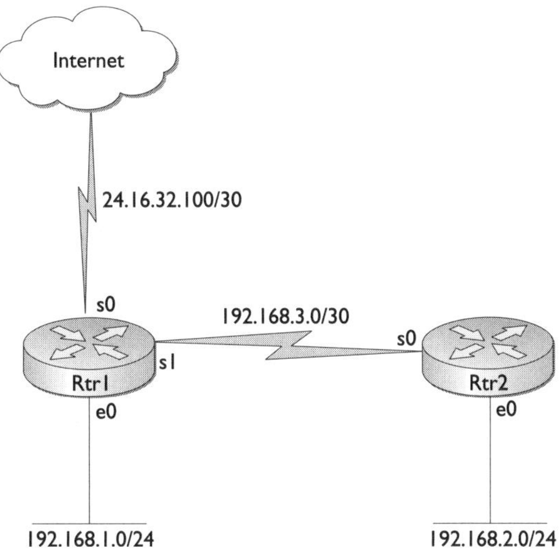

Figure 2-3 Two-router network with two ACLs

The first line of ACL 20 permits host (192.168.2.20) from the Rtr2 LAN to access the LAN on Rtr1. The second line blocks the rest of 192.168.2.0 subnet mask 255.255.255.224, or addresses 192.168.2.0 to 192.168.2.31 from the Rtr1 LAN. The final line allows the rest of Rtr2 LAN and anything coming in over the Internet.

Placement of Standard ACLs Most administrators deduce quickly that if packets can be discarded as early as possible, this will reduce bandwidth requirements on links and router CPU cycles used to process packets that are going to be dumped anyway. Unfortunately, with standard ACLs, the only criterion for making the determination to permit or deny is the source address—the destination is unknown. Standard access lists are generally placed as close to the destination network segment as possible to exercise the most control. For example, in Figure 2-3 in the preceding section, a standard ACL blocking a certain Internet address from entering the Rtr2 LAN would need to be placed on the Rtr2 e0 interface outbound. While s0 on Rtr1 would save more router resources, it would also block access to the Rtr1 LAN. Similarly, applying it to s0 on Rtr2 would work for now, but what if additional interfaces are used later? They would also be blocked.

Looking at Figure 2-3, if ACL 20 had been placed inbound on the Serial 1 interface of Rtr1 or outbound on s0 of Rtr2, this would have saved resources, but this would also have blocked access to the Internet for hosts 192.168.2.1 to 192.168.2.19 and 192.168.2.21 to 192.168.2.30.

Log Option Since v11.3 of the IOS, the Log option at the end of an ACL statement results in logging packets that meet the ACL criterion. How and where the logging is stored is controlled with the **logging console** command. The simplest form of the Log option causes a message to be printed to the console screen the first time the ACL is activated, and then every five minutes while the ACL is still being used. The first report indicates only the first packet, while the subsequent reports summarize the number of occurrences.

The following output lines show the result of adding the Log option to an ACL that blocks the access of host 192.168.1.10 to a LAN.

```
Rtr1(config)#access-list 50 deny   192.168.1.10 log
Rtr1config)#access-list 50 permit any
Rtr1(config)#int e0
Rtr1(config-if)#ip access-group 50 out
Rtr1(config-if)#^Z
Rtr1 #
11:29:37: %SEC-6-IPACCESSLOGS: list 50 denied 192.168.1.10 1 packet
Rtr1 #
11:34:53: %SEC-6-IPACCESSLOGS: list 50 denied 192.168.1.10 27 packets
Rtr1#
```

In the example, the last two lines indicate the workstation attempted to ping a LAN host (192.168.5.1) seven times from the Command window. The first packet was recorded in the first log entry. The other 27 packets, 4 per ping, were reported five minutes later.

The **logging console** command in Global Configuration mode can be used to modify the Log options, which includes specifying a host address running Syslog server software to forward all log entries for permanent storage. Chapter 5 has a section demonstrating the various logging options.

Limiting Access to Telnet Sessions

Using Figure 2-4, assume the company wants to limit Telnet access to Rtr1 to users on the Rtr2 LAN and a single outside address 42.17.17.45, which is the router administrator's home computer. Just as it's possible to filter the physical interfaces, such as Ethernet 0 and serial 1, standard access lists can be used to filter the virtual ports, thereby limiting telnet access to the routers.

Five virtual ports, or vty lines, typically are designated as vty 0 4, allowing up to five telnet sessions to be established. Similar to setting Telnet passwords, you can set identical restrictions on all vty lines at one time.

Figure 2-4 Two-router network for two branch locations

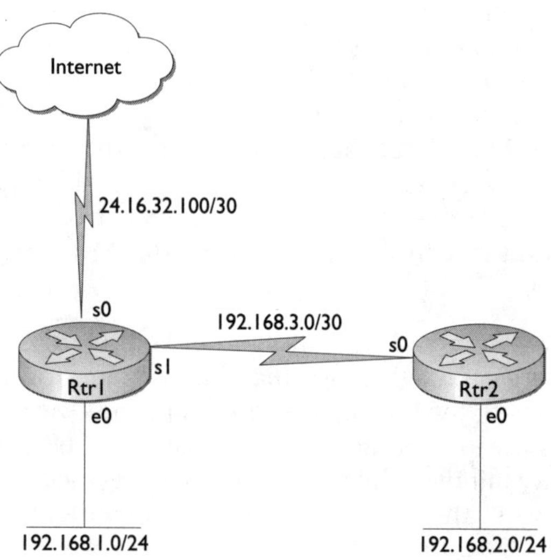

In the following output, inbound access list 15 limits access to the router to users specified by the company. The lack of a permit any statement limits the access to those hosts defined in lines one and two. ACL 16 prevents any user who successfully Telnetted into the router to Telnet to another device. They can only exit out after doing their assigned tasks.

```
Rtr1(config)#access-list 15 permit 192.168.2.0 0.0.0.255
Rtr1(config)#access-list 15 permit 42.17.17.45
Rtr1(config)access-list 16 deny any
Rtr1(config)#line vty 0 4
Rtr1(config-line)#access-class 15 in
Rtr1(config-line)#access-class 16 out
Rtr1(config-line)#password cisco
Rtr1(config-line)#login
```

The important keyword here is "access-class," which is used in place of access-group when you're applying an ACL to a virtual interface.

The following code shows the result when another router, or a host on any other subnet/ network, tries to Telnet into Rtr1. It's important to realize that this implementation of the access-class applies to the entire router, not only to one direction on an interface.

```
Rtr2>telnet 192.168.3.1          <-could have used 192.168.1.1
Trying 192.168.3.1...
% Connection refused by remote host
```

The following lines show the result of a permitted user (who cleared access-list 15 and supplied the password) trying to telnet onto another router. The output assumes an IP HOST table was set up with both IP addresses associated with the name Rtr2 (Rtr1(config)#ip host rtr2 192.168.3.2 192.168.2.1). Telnet attempts both interfaces, but is denied at each attempt.

```
Rtr1>telnet Rtr2
Trying Rtr2 (192.168.3.2)...
% Connections to that host not permitted from this terminal
Trying Rtr2 (192.168.2.1)...
% Connections to that host not permitted from this terminal
Rtr1>
```

Show Line VTY Command The **show line vty 0 4** command lists the virtual terminals and shows that the access lists are applied. The **AccO** (ACL outbound) and **AccI** (ACL inbound) display the ACL numbers. Running the command to verify that your access lists are, in fact, applied to all virtual terminals is always a good idea.

```
Lab-X#show line vty 0 4
 Tty Typ   Tx/Rx  A Modem  Roty AccO AccI   Uses   Noise  Overruns   Int
   2 VTY          -   -     -   16   15      0       0      0/0       -
   3 VTY          -   -     -   16   15      0       0      0/0       -
   4 VTY          -   -     -   16   15      0       0      0/0       -
   5 VTY          -   -     -   16   15      0       0      0/0       -
   6 VTY          -   -     -   16   15      0       0      0/0       -
```

Limiting Access to HTTP Sessions

Many Cisco devices allow access to the User and Privilege modes via a web browser. Figure 2-5 shows an example of the opening screen for a 2500 model router. While not as extensive or friendly as some manufacturer's web interfaces, it does enable the user to view the interfaces, view the diagnostic log, ping the device, execute commands, and open a telnet session.

For this feature to work, the **ip http server** command must be issued in Global Configuration mode because the default is for the service to be off. The command allows the device to act as an HTTP server. Many company security policies require the feature to be turned off by issuing a **no ip http server** command to reduce the exposure to unauthorized access.

Another alternative is to use a standard ACL to limit which host(s) can access the device from a web interface. The basic steps include the **ip http server** command, any

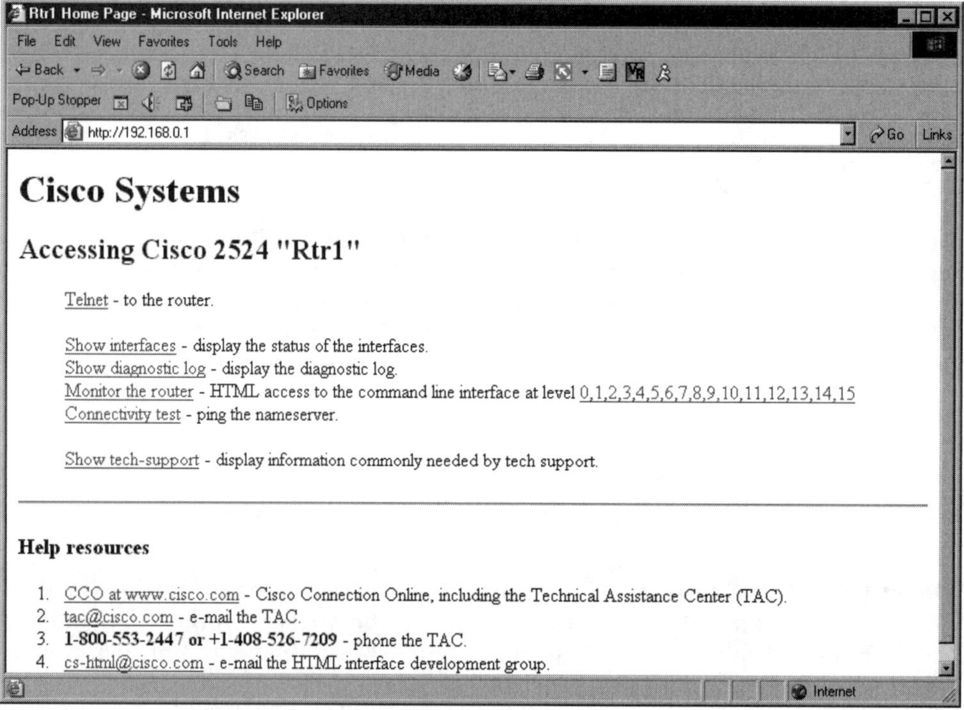

Figure 2-5 Web browser access to a 2500 router

ACL statement(s) required to define the authorized host, and the **ip http access-class** {*acl-num* | *acl-name*} command. The following lines show an example of the commands:

```
Rtr1#conf t
Rtr1(config)#ip http server
Rtr1(config)#access-list 90 permit 192.168.0.10
Rtr1(config)#access-list 90 permit 192.168.5.0 0.0.0.31
Rtr1(config)#access-list 90 permit 192.168.45.0 0.0.0.255
Rtr1(config)#ip http access-class 90
Rtr1(config)#^Z
Rtr1#
```

The lack of a permit any statement limits access to those specifically defined in the permit statement(s). Any time the device is accessed with a web browser, a login screen appears asking for a user name and password. With the previous configuration, the device host name (Rtr1) would be the user name and the enable secret password would be the password.

Controlling the access further is possible with the **ip http authentication** command, which supports several methods of establishing the user name/password combinations. The syntax would be:

ip http authentication {aaa | enable | local | tacacs}

AAA	The AAA authentication feature covered in Chapter 4
Enable	Uses the enable password for authentication (the default HTTP)
Local	Uses the local user database (user name/password) defined in Global mode
Tacacs	The TACACS or XTACACS server authentication covered in Chapter 5

Limiting the debug ip packet Analysis and, Therefore, CPU Use

The **debug ip packet** command displays in real-time all IP packet activity passing through a router. This is, unfortunately, extremely hard on CPU resources. In fact, a router running at 50 percent capacity can be buried by the command dominating the CPU use. Many organizations ban all use of the command for this reason. A second problem with the command is the screen is often overwhelmed by output, making it difficult to see the expected information.

Fortunately, the command syntax, **debug ip packet** [*acl-num*], allows an ACL to be created to filter the specific traffic of interest. In the following example, the output is limited to any traffic originating in the 192.168.0.0 network. Any valid host address, subnet, or network address can be used.

```
Rtr1#conf t
Rtr1(config)#access-list 20 permit 192.168.0.0 0.0.0.255
Rtr1(config)#^Z
Rtr1#debug ip packet ?                        <-shows the options
  <1-199>       Access list
  <1300-2699>   Access list (expanded range)
  detail        Print more debugging detail
  <cr>
```

```
Rtr1#debug ip packet 20
IP packet debugging is on for access list 20
Rtr1#
00:05:28: IP: s=192.168.0.1 (local), d=224.0.0.10 (Ethernet0),
    len 60, sending broad/multicast
00:05:28: IP: s=192.168.0.10 (Ethernet0), d=192.168.0.1 (Ethernet0),
    len 56, rcvd 3
```

The options shown in the **debug ip packet ?** indicate extended ACLs could be used to filter, based on destination address, protocol, or port numbers.

Extended Access Lists

Extended access lists provide a higher level of traffic control by being able to filter packets based on the protocol, source and/or destination IP address, and source and/or destination port number. For example, an extended access list can block an address (or group of addresses) in a particular network from accessing the FTP services on a specific server, while still allowing other services.

Restrict Application Traffic

Implicit in using TCP and UDP access list statements is that it becomes possible to support or suppress certain higher level applications. Because port numbers are associated with applications, allowing or denying access to a specific port number determines if that application can be used and which devices can access it. Setting up network segments to carry only one or two types of traffic—say, NNTP news or SMTP mail—becomes possible. Access lists can be established to prevent any other traffic from entering that particular segment. These ACLs not only focus on the source and destination of the packets, but also on the service offered. The following table shows some common port numbers and the related services (applications).

ftp	File Transfer Protocol	20, 21
Telnet	Telnet, Remote Terminal	23
smtp	Electronic Mail (servers)	25
pop3	POP Mail (users)	110
nntp	Network News	119

More examples are included in the sections dealing specifically with TCP and UDP filtering.

TCP's Established Option The Established option is a TCP-only feature that can use the connection-oriented attributes of the TCP to limit traffic coming into a network or network segment to those sessions that originated from within that network. The established condition is only true if the ACK (acknowledge) or RST (reset) bits are set to one in the TCP header, indicating an already established connection. A packet with no ACK or RST bit set, but a SYN (synchronize) bit set to one, is used to establish a new connection and can then be denied. Figure 2-6 demonstrates the three-step "handshake" that TCP uses to establish a connection.

PART I

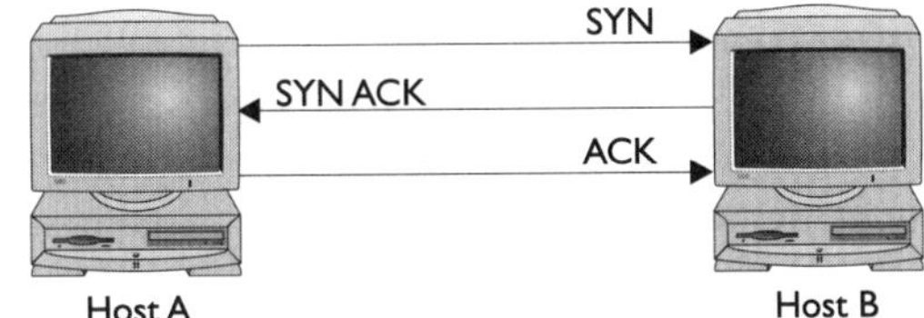

Figure 2-6 TCP three-way handshake to establish a session

The following output demonstrates allowing any host to respond to web and Telnet requests that originated within the 192.168.1.0 network, but blocks all other TCP packets.

```
access-list 101 permit tcp any 192.168.1.0 0.0.0.255 established
access-list 101 permit tcp any 192.168.1.0 0.0.0.255 any eq telnet
access-list 101 deny   tcp any any
access-list 101 permit ip  any any
```

The Established option can help reduce the risk of a common type of hacker attack that buries a host in SYN requests, preventing it from handling normal business. Because a sophisticated hacker can manipulate the TCP header bits, this tool needs support from other tools to protect against that threat.

Look over the following ACL statement using the Established option. This is a common first effort when trying to limit web activity to those sessions originating within the network. So what's wrong with the statement?

```
access-list 101 permit tcp any 192.168.1.0 0.0.0.255 eq www established
```

Remember, www is an "alias" for port 80. A web session originating inside would use port 80 as the destination, but would designate a port above 1024, such as 1065, as the source port. This means the returning packet would have port 80 as the source and port 1065 as the destination. The ACL is looking for port 80 as the destination. The following output might work better:

```
access-list 101 permit tcp any eq www 192.168.1.0 0.0.0.255 established
```

When working with the Established feature, it's important to make sure you understand what the mnemonic and any port numbers stand for, if you use the port numbers. Another approach is represented in the following code lines, which allow any established sessions, but block all other TCP traffic.

```
access-list 101 permit tcp any 192.168.1.0 0.0.0.255 established
access-list 101 deny   tcp any any
```

NOTE *Source-port filtering*, the process of filtering data on the source port of a packet, isn't secure because a skilled hacker could easily change a source port on a packet, which could then pass through the filter.

Named Access Lists

Since Cisco IOS Release 11.2, it's possible to use a text name for access lists in many cases. Some new features were added to named ACLs that make them more than just text names. The benefits of using named access lists are described in the following paragraph:

Time-Based Access Lists

Until recently, an access list was either implemented or not. An administrator would have to change the configuration to include a feature, such as blocking Internet access, and then would have to physically remove either the ACL or the access-group statement to allow access. This wasn't convenient if the goal was to block employee access during work hours, but to allow access at other times of the day.

Since version 12.0 of the IOS, it's possible to create access lists that can incorporate date- and time-sensitive features. This allows filtering to occur only during certain hours of the day or on certain days of the week. IP and IPX extended access lists are currently the only functions that can use time ranges. *Time ranges* enable the network administrator to specify when the permit or deny statements in the access list are in effect. Both named or numbered access lists can use the time range feature.

Two separate tasks are required to implement time ranges:

- Define a time range.
- Reference the time range.

Define a Time Range

Three basic commands are used to implement the time-based features in extended ACLs:

- time-range
- periodic
- absolute

The **time-range** command is used to create (name) a time range, while the absolute and periodic commands are used to define the days and times included in the named range. While multiple periodic entries are allowed per time-range command, only one absolute entry is allowed.

If a **time-range** command has both absolute and periodic values specified, then the periodic items are evaluated only after the absolute start time is reached, and aren't evaluated any further after the absolute end time is reached.

The time-range Command

The **time-range** command is used to enable Time-Range Configuration mode and name time ranges for functions, such as extended access lists. The command is issued in Global Configuration mode. The syntax is:

```
Router(config)#time-range time-range-name
```

time-range-name	User-specified name of the time range

The following output demonstrates defining a time range named NoDayAccess. Remember, the name *is* case sensitive.

```
Router(config)#time-range NoDayAccess
```

The periodic Command

The **periodic** command is used to specify a recurring range of days and times to be included in the time-range created in the previous command. Using this command allows a feature to be implemented on only certain days of the week and within certain hours. The command is issued in the Time-Range Configuration mode, which is activated by the **time-range** command. The syntax is

Router(config-time-range)#periodic *days-of-the-week hh:mm* to [*days-of-the-week*] *hh:mm*

days-of-the-week	Used to define the days included in the time-range
hh:mm	Defines the beginning or ending time of the time range. *hh* is the 24-hour time and *mm* is the minute.

The first occurrence of the *hh:mm* argument is the starting hours:minutes that the time range is in effect. The second occurrence is the ending hours:minutes the statement is in effect. Times are expressed using the 24-hour clock; therefore, 8:00 P.M. would be typed as **20:00**. The keyword **to** is required to complete the range, as in ***start-time** to **end-time***.

NOTE Remember, all time specifications are interpreted as local time. To ensure the time range entries take effect at the desired times, the software clock should be synchronized using the Network Time Protocol (NTP) or some other authoritative time source.

The *days-of-the-week* argument can seem complicated until you become used to it. Used properly, this can be used to represent a single day or combination of days using the following keywords:

Monday, **Tuesday**, **Wednesday**, **Thursday**, **Friday**, **Saturday**, **Sunday**—day names

daily Monday through Sunday

weekdays Monday through Friday

weekend Saturday and Sunday

The following examples should help you understand the process. The following lines create a time range for a single day named MondayDays, and then define the day and hours (8:00 A.M. to 5:30 P.M.).

```
Router(config)#time-range MondayDays
Router(config-time-range)#periodic monday 8:00 to 17:30
```

When multiple days can be defined by the keywords daily, weekday, and weekend, the keyword is used. The next lines creates a time range named WeekdayEves, and then define hours (5:00 P.M. to 10:00 P.M.). In this example, the feature is to be implemented Monday through Friday.

```
Router(config)#time-range WeekdayEves
Router(config-time-range)#periodic weekdays 17:00 to 22:00
```

When multiple days other than those defined by the keywords daily, weekday, and weekend are required, the days are listed separated by spaces. The next lines create a time range named TuThuEves and then defines the days and hours (5:00 P.M. to 10:00 P.M.).

```
Router(config)#time-range TuThuEves
Router(config-time-range)#periodic tuesday thursday 17:00 to 22:00
```

With a recurring time range on consecutive days, other than those defined by the keywords, the days are also listed separated by spaces. The next lines create a time range named SunMonTue and then define the hours (5:00 P.M. to 10:00 P.M.) included each day.

```
Router(config)#time-range SunMonTue
Router(config-time-range)#periodic sunday monday tuesday thursday 6:00 to 9:00
```

With a time range that "spans" consecutive days, the optional *days-of-the-week* after the **to** is used. The next lines create a time range named MonToWed, and then define the start and ending time as 8:00 A.M. Monday to Wednesday at 5:00 P.M.

```
Router(config)#time-range MonToWed
Router(config-time-range)#periodic Monday 8:00 to Wednesday 17:00
```

Multiple periodic entries are allowed per **time-range** command.

The absolute Command

Use the **absolute time-range** command to specify a time range to be in effect each day. The command is issued in the Time-Range Configuration mode, which is activated by the **time-range** command. The syntax is

Router(config-time-range)#absolute [start *time date*] [end *time date*]

The start and end times use the 24-hour clock. The dates are in a text form, such as June 1, 2003.

The following sample defines a time range from 8:00 December 18, 2003, until 8:00 January 3, 2004:

```
Router(config)#time-range holidays-closed
Router(config-time-range)#absolute 8:00 18 december 2003 8:00 3 january 2004
```

Only one absolute entry is allowed per **time-range** command. If a **time-range** command has both absolute and periodic values specified, then the periodic items are evaluated only after the absolute start time is reached, and aren't evaluated any further after the absolute end time is reached.

Reference the Time Range

An extended access control list can be either a numbered or a named ACL. In each case, the Time-Range option is added to provide an additional qualifier for the permit|deny statement. The basic syntax for a named ACL would be

> Router(config)#ip access-list extended *name*
> Router(config-ext-nacl)# {permit | deny} {*protocol* | *protocol-keyword*}{*source wildcard* | any} [*operator source-port*] {*destination wildcard* | any} [*operator destination-port*] [precedence *precedence*] [tos *tos*] [log | log-input] [options] **[time-range *time-range-name*]**

The basic syntax for a numbered ACL would be

> Router(config)#access-list *acl#* {permit | deny} {*protocol* | *protocol-keyword*}{*source wildcard* | any} [*operator source-port*] {*destination wildcard* | any} [*operator destination-port*] [precedence *precedence*] [tos *tos*] [log | log-input] [options] **[time-range *time-range-name*]**

The following time range example with a periodic statement denies web traffic to employees on the Ethernet LAN for Monday through Friday during business hours (8:00 A.M. to 6:00 P.M.).

```
time-range no-web
  periodic weekdays 8:00 to 18:00
!
ip access-list extended block-web
  deny tcp any any eq www time-range no-web
  permit ip any any
!
interface ethernet 0
  ip access-group block-web in
!
```

The following example uses a time-based access list to allow a LAN to begin accessing the network beginning at 8:00 A.M. on January 1, 2003. The access will continue until stopped. The access list and time range together permit traffic on Ethernet interface 0 starting.

```
time-range new-lan
  absolute start 8:00 1 January 2003
!
ip access-list extended start-service
  permit ip 192.168.15.0 0.0.0.255 any time-range new-lan
!
interface ethernet 0
  ip access-group start-service in
```

The following example uses a time-based access list to block a LAN from accessing the network beginning at midnight on December 31, 2003.

```
time-range stop-lan
  absolute end 23:59 31 December 2003
!
ip access-list extended stop-service
  permit ip 192.168.15.0 0.0.0.255 any time-range stop-lan
!
interface ethernet 0
  ip access-group stop-service in
```

The following example uses a time-based access list to permit weekend employees to browse the Internet for a two month test period from 8:00 A.M. on June 1, 2003, to 6:00 P.M.on July 31, 2003.

```
time-range web-test
absolute start 8:00 1 June 2003 end 18:00 31 July 2003
periodic weekends 00:00 to 23:59
!
ip access-list extended lan-web
  permit tcp 192.168.15.0 0.0.0.255 any eq www time-range web-test
!
interface ethernet 0
  ip access-group lan-web in
```

The show time-range Command

The **show time-range** command can be used to display the current status of the time ranges and list the periodic and absolute attributes.

```
Rtr1#show time-range
time-range entry: WeekdayEves (inactive)
   absolute start 08:00 01 December 2004 end 08:00 03 January 2005
   periodic weekdays 17:00 to 22:00
time-range entry: weekdayeves (active)
   used in: IP ACL entry
time-range entry: worktime (active)
   absolute start 08:00 01 December 2004 end 08:00 03 January 2005
   periodic weekdays 8:00 to 18:00
   used in: IP ACL entry
Rtr1#conf t
```

The output shows two defined time ranges **WeekdayEves** and **worktime**, but it also shows another undefined time range, **weekdayeves**. The output shows it was used in an ACL, indicating someone tried to use **WeekdayEves** and forgot that the names are case sensitive. The result in this case will be that since no times are defined, the ACL statement will be active all of the time.

Chapter Review

Many simple device configuration techniques can add to the security of the network. To a great extent, these often fall into the category of commonsense practices, such as using administrative access passwords on all device access points.

As Cisco moves more and more devices to IOS-based command structures, access lists remain a need-to-know technology. While not a complete security solution, access lists are an integral part of any security program.

Standard access lists filter based on source address alone, creating a simple, yet powerful, tool for blocking all traffic or access to a host, subnet, or network. Standard ACLs can be used for traffic filtering, limiting access to Telnet sessions, limiting access to Web browsers trying to access a Cisco router or switch, filtering routing updates, and focusing commands like **debug ip packet** to conserve router resources.

Extended access lists can be used to filter on protocol, source address, destination address, source and destination port identifiers for TCP and UDP traffic, and various powerful options. The TCP Established option can be used to limit TCP traffic only to what originated within the network.

Named access lists are a variation on the numbered ACLS supporting for standard and extended versions. Named ACLs are easier to create than numbered lists, and allow limited editing and deletion of specific statements that can't be done with numbered lists. They can be descriptive of their purpose and, therefore, easier for follow-up support to work with. Some IOS features and all IOS versions prior to 11.2 don't support named ACLs, requiring some thought in mixed environments. Some newer features like reflexive ACLs only work with named lists, so it's probably safe to say they're going to be a bigger, rather than smaller, part of the future.

Questions

1. Which of the following interface types is least likely to be on a firewall appliance?
   - A. Fast Ethernet
   - B. Serial
   - C. Ethernet
   - D. Token Ring
2. Which of the following would not be considered a basic security step in a router configuration?
   - A. Setting access privilege levels
   - B. Setting an MOTD banner to welcome the user to the device
   - C. Encrypting passwords in the configuration files
   - D. Setting all passwords
3. Which of the following is *not* true about numbered access lists?
   - A. An ACL is made up of one or more permit or deny statements.
   - B. If an ACL doesn't have at least one permit statement, it will deny everything.
   - C. All ACL statements with the same number are part of the same ACL.
   - D. New statements are always added to the top of the list statements.
   - E. ACL statements must be entered sequentially to be processed properly.
   - F. An ACL can be added to (appended), but not edited. Any attempt to edit an item will delete the entire ACL.
4. Which one of the following will deny access to a class C network?
   - A. Rtr1(config)#access-list 15 deny 192.168.1.0 255.255.255.0
   - B. Rtr1(config)#access-list 15 deny 192.168.1.0 0.0.0.255

C. Rtr1(config-acl)#access-list 15 deny 192.168.1.0 255.255.255.0

D. Rtr1(config-acl)#access-list 15 deny 192.168.1.0 0.0.0.255

5. What is the ACL line to deny the subnet 192.168.1.16 subnet mask 255.255.255.240?

   A. access-list 15 deny 192.168.1.16 0.0.0.255

   B. access-list 15 deny 192.168.1.0 0.0.0.16

   C. access-list 15 deny 192.168.1.16 0.0.0.15

   D. access-list 15 deny 192.168.1.16 0.0.0.31

6. With the Log option for ACLs, a message appears when the first match occurs, and then at what interval as long as matches continue?

   A. One minute

   B. Five minutes

   C. Ten minutes

   D. Thirty minutes

7. When limiting access to Telnet sessions, which command would work?

   A. access-group 15 in

   B. access-group 15 out

   C. access-class 15 in

   D. access-class 15 out

   E. access-session 15 in

8. Which two commands could be used to secure the web browser access to a device?

   A. ip http server

   B. no ip http server

   C. ip http access-class 90

   D. ip http access-group 90

9. Which of the following protocols uses the established option?

   A. UDP

   B. ICMP

   C. TCP

   D. IGRP

10. Numbered extended ACLs are created in which mode?

   A. Privilege mode

   B. Global Configuration mode

C. Local Configuration mode

D. Access Configuration mode

11. Which statement is *not* true about named access lists?

A. Named access lists aren't compatible with older IOS releases (pre-11.2).

B. A standard access list and an extended access list can't have the same name.

C. Names must begin with an alphanumeric character and are case sensitive.

D. All processes that use access lists can use a named ACLs

12. Which statement will create a named extended ACL?

A. Rtr1(config)#ip extended access-list tcp-control

B. Rtr1(config)#ip access-list named extended tcp-control

C. Rtr1(config)#ip access-list extended tcp-control

D. Rtr1(config-ext-nacl)#ip access-list extended tcp-control

13. The time-based ACL statements are relative to which one of the following?

A. The computer clock

B. The world clock

C. The router clock

D. The day, month, and year

14. Which command will define a periodic time range?

A. Router(config-time-range)#periodic tuesday thursday 17:00 to 22:00

B. Router(config-time)#periodic tuesday thursday 17:00 to 22:00

C. Router(config-time-range)#periodic tuesday, thursday 17:00 to 22:00

D. Router(config-time)#periodic tuesday, thursday 17:00 to 22:00

15. Which statement is true about defining a time range?

A. A time range can have either periodic or absolute times.

B. A time range can have one periodic and multiple absolute times.

C. A time range can have multiple periodic and one absolute time.

D. A time range can have one periodic and one absolute time.

16. Which one of the following is true about the Established option in a TCP access list?

A. Outbound traffic is limited to established customers.

B. Outbound traffic is limited to sessions originating outside the network.

C. Inbound traffic is limited to sessions originating outside the network.

D. Inbound traffic is limited to sessions originating inside the network.

17. In the following ACL, what is the impact of the third statement?

```
access-list 101 deny tcp 192.168.3.0 0.0.0.255 192.168.1.0 0.0.0.255
access-list 101 deny tcp 192.168.3.0 0.0.0.255 any eq ftp
access-list 101 permit tcp 192.168.3.0 0.0.0.255 192.168.1.0 0.0.0.255 eq www
access-list 101 deny tcp any 192.168.1.0 0.0.0.255 any eq telnet
access-list 101 permit ip any any
```

A. It allows network 192.168.3.0 to access 192.168.1.0 for web access.

B. It allows network 192.168.1.0 to access 192.168.2.0 for web access.

C. It allows network 192.168.3.0 to access any network for web access.

D. The line does nothing at all.

Answers

1. B. Serial. Firewall device, such as the PIX box, use LAN interfaces
2. B. Setting a MOTD banner to welcome the user to the device
3. D. New statements are always added to the top of the list statements (They're actually appended to the bottom of the list.)
4. B. Rtr1(config)#access-list 15 deny 192.168.1.0 0.0.0.255
5. C. access-list 15 deny 192.168.1.16 0.0.0.15
6. B. Five minutes
7. C. access-class 15 in
8. B. no ip http server; c. ip http access-class 90
9. C. TCP
10. B. Global Configuration mode
11. D. All processes that use access lists can use a named ACL.
12. C. Rtr1(config)#ip access-list extended tcp-control
13. C. The router clock. If the router clock is wrong, the statements will be implemented wrong.
14. A. Router(config-time-range)#periodic tuesday thursday 17:00 to 22:00
15. C. A time range can have multiple periodic and one absolute time
16. D. Inbound traffic is limited to sessions originating inside the network.
17. D. The line does nothing at all. All TCP traffic from 192.168.3.0 to 192.168.1.0 was denied in the first statement

PART II

Securing the Network Perimeter

- **Chapter 3** Cisco AAA Security Technology
- **Chapter 4** CiscoSecure ACS and TACAS+/Radius Technologies
- **Chapter 5** Securing Cisco Perimeter Routers
- **Chapter 6** IOS Firewall Feature Set—CBAC
- **Chapter 7** IOS Firewall—Intrusion Detection System
- **Chapter 8** IOS Firewall—Authentication Proxy

CHAPTER

Cisco AAA Security Technology

In this chapter, you will learn how to:

- Describe the Cisco AAA model
- Describe and configure the AAA system and each of its three components
- Test the NAS AAA configuration using applicable **debug** and **show** commands

Cisco IOS software provides features for simple access control, such as local user name authentication, line password authentication, and enable password authentication. These methods, represented in the following output, are commonly used when you first learn to work with the Cisco IOS.

```
no service password-encryption
enable secret 5 $1$s3/7$C4ngFihNBDwqlmdj1
!
username xyzdotcom password cisco
!
line con 0
 password cisco
 login
line aux 0
 password cisco
 login
line vty 0 4
 login local
end
```

These features don't provide the same degree of access control that's possible by using AAA, however. In this chapter, you look at the methods used by Cisco's AAA security technology to control remote access to the network. While AAA is supported on many devices and can be expected on each of the certification exams, this chapter introduces AAA within the context of securing the Network Access Server (NAS). This traditionally has been called "securing the dial-up connection," using NAS routers to handle the incoming modem and ISDN sessions. As you see in the chapters that cover PIX and PIX IOS, AAA uses the same methods to control remote access from the Internet.

The Cisco AAA Model

Cisco's AAA network security services provide the principal structure to manage who has access to the network, what services they're permitted to use, and a record of what they did while logged on. The three components of AAA include the following:

Authentication	Identifies and verifies the remote user. This process can take the form of a simple password or user name/password combination verified locally by the NAS, or it could use one or more authentication servers and technologies, such as one-time passwords (OTPs) or tokens.
Authorization	Determines what devices, features, or services a specific remote user is authorized to access in the network, such as network resources or services. This concept is much like that of user permissions in the Windows server model.
Accounting	Allows the network administrator to define a process for tracking the services remote users are accessing. The data collected can be used for client billing, auditing, or network planning.

NAS Servers

NAS servers, sometimes simply called *access servers*, are routers with interfaces designed to service the remote users of the company. A simple example would be the older 2501s with two serial interfaces connected to two modems, or the 2503 with two serial and an ISDN interface to provide access service to a small number of dial-in users, such as employees dialing in from their motel rooms.

Other combinations include the 2509–2512 series that have one or two special 68-pin interfaces that can each support up to eight modem connections with an octal cable. As modem service is being replaced by DSL and cable connections, these units are dropping in price and are becoming popular today as terminal servers. As a terminal server, a single console connection to an access server can be used to provide up to 16 console connections to other devices.

NOTE While this isn't a CCSP exam requirement, a lab (Terminal Server.pdf) on this book's CD-ROM demonstrates configuring and using a terminal server to save time in the lab or production network.

Most of the common modular routers have, or have had, interfaces with multiple serial and/or multiple ISDN interfaces to provide modem and ISDN access service to larger organizations and early ISPs. Figure 3-1 shows a four-port serial interface for a 4000 series router that could connect to four modems or four ISDN devices. The 4000s also offered similar modules with four or eight ISDN interfaces.

Figure 3-2 shows an NM-16A module for a 2600 or 3600 series router with two of the 68-pin serial interfaces mentioned earlier. With octal cables, these two connectors support 16 connections. Four of the interfaces on the NM-32A allow 32 connections.

Figure 3-1 Four-port serial module for a 4000 series router

At the top end, the AS5x00 series routers can support dozens to thousands of outside connections in a variety of combinations. The AS5400 and AS5800 routers provide the capability to terminate ISDN, 56K analog modem, fax, and VoIP calls on the same interface. The AS5400 can support over 600 connections, while the AS5800 can support 2,000.

For more information, go to http://www.cisco.com on the Web and choose the link for Products. Access Servers are listed under product categories. No CCO account is needed for much of the information.

Why Authenticate?

Not too long ago, PCs didn't require a user to type in their user name and/or a password. The computer powered up, and whoever was sitting at the keyboard had full access to

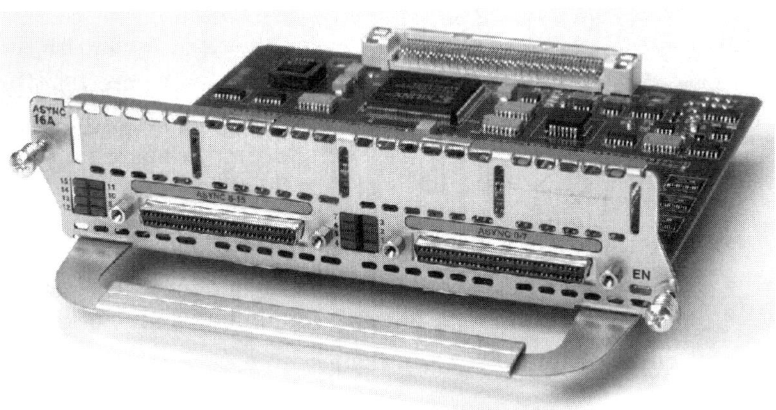

Figure 3-2 NM-16A module for 2600/3600 routers

anything stored on the machine. Even many networked computers were configured without a login requirement because, after all, "everybody was just like family." This would be the ultimate "open" system.

It didn't take long to determine that possibly everyone in the family doesn't need to see the checkbook program or read each other's e-mails, but, to protect those resources, it was necessary to know who was sitting at the keyboard. Some applications experimented with using passwords, and people learned to use password protection on shared resources like folders or printers. Once a password was created, it had to be shared with anyone who needed access. If more than one shared resource existed, one of two problems arose. Either unique passwords were necessary for each resource, requiring some users to keep track of multiple passwords and the resource they were associated with, or the same password was used, which meant any user who had legitimate access to one protected resource now had the password for all protected resources.

If someone left under less-than-favorable circumstances, all passwords known to that person had to be changed, and then the other users had to be told about the changes. These early efforts showed right away that leaving security up to the individual users wasn't reliable and wouldn't scale well as the network group.

Many organizations have this same problem with the user names/and or passwords used to access their network devices, such as routers and switches, by storing the access user name and/or password locally on the device. The following output demonstrates access requiring only a password (line con 0 and line aux 0) and access using the local database (line vty 0 4).

```
!
username xyzdotcom password cisco
!
line con 0
 password cisco
 login
line aux 0
 password cisco
 login
line vty 0 4
 login local
end
```

The preceding techniques were covered in Chapter 2. While both methods work, they have the same shortfalls and security issues as the early networking administrators faced with user data and applications. The example could be made more secure by using techniques covered in Chapter 2, including the following:

- Using a different password for each access point
- Using complex passwords containing eight or more characters, incorporating uppercase and lowercase letters, plus numbers and symbols
- Requiring routine password changes
- Using the **service password-encryption** command to hide the passwords from wandering eyes that could see the configuration

The encryption also reduces the chances of someone being able to capture the passwords if the configuration is included in a Telnet session. Telnet transmits all communications in cleartext.

Centralized Authentication

The lack of scalability and reliability limitations associated with locally stored authentication can only be overcome by using some form(s) of centralized authentication server. Network operating systems (OSs) typically have this feature at their core. In addition to allowing access to the network, this system usually is linked to a mechanism for matching login IDs with permissions to use protected resources. While all authenticated users might have permission to use any of the network printers, only members of the "accounting" group might be granted "permission" to access to the Accounting Department servers. And maybe only those accounting group members who are also part of the "payroll" group might be granted access to the payroll software and data.

If a payroll accountant leaves the company under any circumstances, it's only necessary to delete their user account, which also removes them from the accounting and payroll groups, maintaining security for those assets.

AAA is a technology that can work independently or with the network security system to provide centralized authentication, authorization, and accounting security for network devices and remote user access. Figure 3-3 demonstrates a simple example of AAA and a NAS server providing secure access to a company network. With only authentication features, the remote user could have access to both the server (web server possibly)

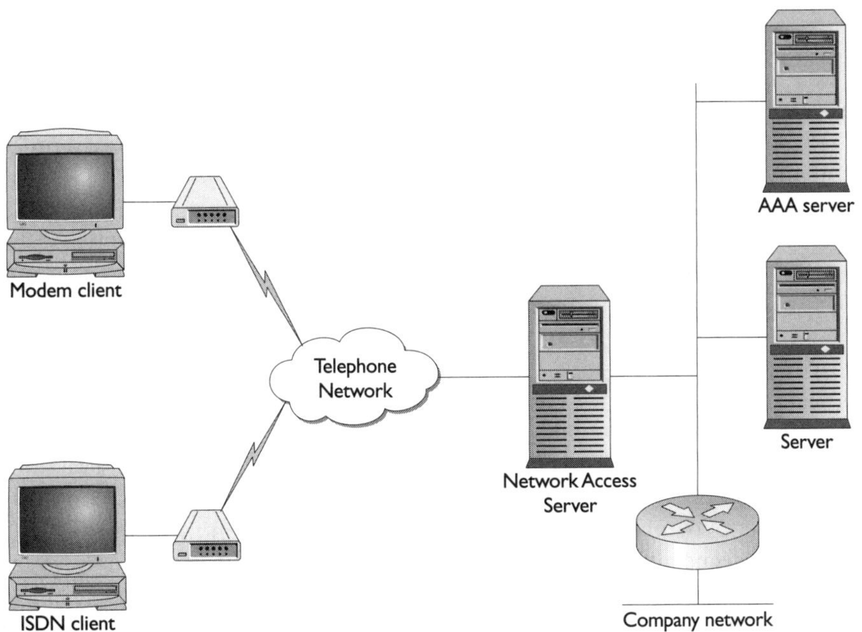

Figure 3-3 AAA and NAS server providing secure remote access to a network

and the company network. With authorization implemented, it would be possible to allow the modem user access to both, while limiting the ISDN user to one or the other.

AAA Benefits

Cisco's AAA technology centralized network access security provides many benefits to the organization and network administrator, including the following:

- Increased flexibility
- Increased security
- Scalability
- Standard authentication methods
- Multiple backup systems

Increased Flexibility

AAA's support of authorization, in addition to authentication, means access can be maintained on a "need to have" basis, without having to maintain multiple passwords. The accounting support means that user auditing and cost-allocation policies can be implemented, as well as providing a trail that might be useful in troubleshooting network problems.

Increased Security

Multiple devices with the *same* locally administered user name/password offer a low level of security. Everyone having access to everything, without regard for need, also unnecessarily increases risk. Multiple locally administered passwords would appear to increase security, but might lead to employees writing down passwords if too many exist to remember. This situation would be exacerbated if complex passwords were implemented.

AAA, with its centralized security database and authorization features, allows a single secure user name/password combination for each employee and yet allows restricting access to a "need to have" basis. At the same time, AAA allows for rapid resolution of compromised passwords or terminated employees.

Scalability

AAA is a template approach to security management that remains reliable and flexible as the network grows larger and more complex. By centralizing the security databases and supporting authorization, AAA avoids the nightmare of managing many user name/password combinations in a growing environment or the alternative "weak" security of using a small number of combinations. Locally stored authentication means any time there's a potential of a compromised user name/password or termination of an employee, each device "should" be reconfigured. The more devices that exist, the greater the amount of effort. AAA avoids this in much the same way that server security is maintained under the same circumstances.

Standard Authentication Methods

AAA supports RADIUS, TACACS+, and Kerberos security protocols for securing dial-in sessions. These protocols provide secure authentication, including encrypted communications and interaction with network server security systems. The next section compares these three systems.

Multiple Backup Systems

AAA supports multiple security servers, such as TACACS+, on the same network to provide redundancy in case of device failure or link congestion. In addition, AAA allows for multiple authentication methods to be specified so, if the first one is unavailable, then a second or third option could be used. For example, if the specified TACACS+ server is offline, the locally stored user name/password database could possibly be used or maybe even the enable password. These alternatives must be defined in advance or access could be blocked until the specified service is restored.

TACACS+, RADIUS, and Kerberos Support

AAA supports all three of these security protocols to control dial-up access into networks. You look, in turn, at each, but note that Cisco supports Kerberos as a legacy security protocol for those networks already committed to it. Cisco Secure Access Control Server (ACS), covered in the next chapter, only implements TACACS+ and RADIUS databases.

At the most obvious level, each of these three protocols does the same thing. Each provides a secure authentication process that allows remote users to access an organization's network resources. At the nuts and bolts level, these are quite different systems, requiring several chapters to detail. The good news is this: that detailed information exists in many places, including Cisco's web site, which is where it's going to stay. This chapter covers those features and differences that might be on the certification exams and would allow a person to choose among them for implementation, or at least to move ahead with intelligent research.

Kerberos is covered first, and then TACACS+ and RADIUS are compared to help determine which should be implemented as part of Cisco Secure ACS.

NOTE It's important to make sure that TACACS+, RADIUS, or Kerberos server services are properly configured before adding the client features to the NAS. Otherwise, you could lock yourself out and require a password recovery.

Kerberos

Kerberos derives its name from the three-headed dog that guards the gates of Hades in Greek mythology. *Kerberos,* the security protocol, is an authentication system developed at the Massachusetts Institute of Technology (MIT), which uses the Data Encryption Standard (DES) cryptographic algorithm for encryption and authentication. Kerberos is based on the assumption that internal users are no more inherently trustworthy than external users and, therefore, applies security and encrypted communications for services like Telnet for all users.

Kerberos is designed to enable two parties to exchange private information across an otherwise open network like the Internet by assigning a unique key, called a *ticket,* to each user that logs on to the network. The ticket is then embedded in messages to identify the sender of the message. Kerberos is based on the concept of a trusted third party, called the *key distribution center (KDC),* a Kerberos authentication server (AS), performing secure verification of all users and services on the network. This verification involves exchanging encrypted authentication messages without transmitting the user password.

The "lite" explanation of using Kerberos to gain network access might help.

1. A remote user opens a PPP connection to an organization's NAS router.
2. The router prompts the user for a user name and a password.
3. The router then uses only the user name to request a ticket or credential verifying the user identity (TGT) from the key distribution center (KDC).
4. Assuming the user name is known to the KDC, an encrypted TGT is sent back to the router, which includes (among other things) the user's identity. The ticket has a limit life of eight hours to reduce the exposure to an unauthorized capture and replay attempt.
5. The router uses the password from Step 2 to decrypt the TGT. If the decryption is successful, the remote user is authenticated to the router and granted access to the network.

When a remote user successfully authenticates at a boundary router, the user and the user's machine become part of the network. Another TGT from the KDC is necessary to access network services because the original TGT is stored on the router and isn't used for additional authentication, unless the user physically logs on to that router.

Securing a network service involves a double encryption. When a user requests access to a network service, such as a printer or Telnet access to a host, the KDC creates a service credential. This service credential contains the client's identity, the desired network service's identity, and a time limit. The service credential is encrypted first using a password shared by the KDC and the service. The result is encrypted again using the user's TGT as the key.

The target service uses the TGT supplied by the user to perform the first decryption. If the result can be successfully decrypted using the password shared by the KDC and the service, then the service is available.

Since Cisco IOS 11.2, organizations already using Kerberos 5 security can use their existing authentication servers to authenticate their routers and switches. The IOS software Kerberos authentication capabilities support the following network services:

- Telnet
- rlogin
- rsh
- rcp

The previous applications are said to be *Kerberized,* applications and services that have been modified to support the Kerberos credential infrastructure and encrypted communications.

Driver's License Analogy An analogy commonly used for Kerberos is a state driver's license, wherein the state is the KDC that issues a TGT, the license. The license contains information that can authenticate the user: the picture and description items. In addition, the permissions, such as motorcycle endorsement, and restrictions, such as glasses required, associated with the license are also included. Like a TGT, the license also has an expiration time after which it's no longer valid.

Some states include an authentication code made up of portions of the key supplied data, such as name and birth date. Any crude attempt to alter part of the key data makes the authentication code not match.

To complete the analogy, a third party accepts the TGT, license, and, after confirming the picture and description, trusts that the state did a reasonable job in confirming the identity before issuing the license, and thereby accepts it as proof of identity, age, or the right to drive.

For more information, go to http://www.cisco.com on the Web and perform a search for Kerberos. If you'll be working in a Kerberos environment, add a search for Configuring Kerberos to get assistance on using the Kerberos commands. No CCO account is needed for much of the information.

RADIUS

Remote Authentication Dial-In User Service (RADIUS) is an access server authentication, authorization, and accounting protocol developed by Livingston Enterprises, Inc., now a division of Lucent Technologies. RADIUS is a system of distributed security that secures remote access to networks and network services against unauthorized access.

RADIUS is a fully open protocol, distributed in source code format that can be modified to work with any security system currently available on the market. Numerous implementations of RADIUS server code are commercially and freely available. Cisco's servers include CiscoSecure ACS for Windows, CiscoSecure UNIX, and Cisco Access Registrar. Several IETF RFCs define the RADIUS protocol, but currently it's still a proposed standard.

A RADIUS implementation is made of the three following components:

- Protocol using UDP/IP communication.
- RADIUS server—a service running on a central Windows or UNIX server, typically at the customer's site.
- RADIUS client—a service residing in the dial-up access servers that can be distributed throughout the network. Cisco added RADIUS client support beginning with IOS v11.1.

Client/Server Model A NAS router running the RADIUS client service passes user information to defined RADIUS server(s), and then acts, based on the response received. The RADIUS server responds to all user connection requests, authenticating the user, and then forwarding all configuration information needed for the client to provide the service to the user. RADIUS servers can act as proxy clients for other types of authentication servers. The RADIUS server, after reviewing the credentials, replies to the client with one of the following responses:

- **Accept** The user is authenticated.
- **Reject** The user is not authenticated and access is denied. The user will be prompted to reenter the user name/password.
- **Challenge** A request for more information from the user to confirm identity.
- **Change Password** The user must change their password.

Network Security Technology RADIUS clients and servers use a shared secret technology for all authentications transactions. The shared secret is never sent over the network. To eliminate the possibility of someone successfully snooping a user's password on an unsecured network, any transmitted user passwords are sent encrypted between the client and RADIUS server.

Flexiblity RADIUS server supports a variety of methods to authenticate a user, including PPP PAP or CHAP, MS-CHAP, UNIX login, and others.

Interoperability The other side of any open standard is that it doesn't always guarantee interoperability with other vendors' implementations'. RADIUS's implementations between different vendors can vary because the RADIUS standard specifically allows vendors to offer custom features or attributes in what are called *AV pairs.* If a vendor device doesn't recognize the AV pair, it ignores it. To demonstrate the variations, the IETF implementation supports attributes, while Ascend supports 254. Cisco currently supports 58 attributes on Cisco Secure ACS, access servers, Ethernet switches, PIX firewalls, and VPN 3000 concentrators.

TACACS+

Terminal Access Controller Access Control System Plus (TACACS+) is an authentication protocol that allows an NAS to communicate with an authentication server to determine if a user has access to the network.

TACACS+, a new protocol developed by Cisco, replaces two earlier industry standards: TACACS and XTACACS (Extended Terminal Access Controller Access Control System). TACACS+ isn't compatible with the two older protocols. Cisco has submitted TACACS+ protocol specification in a draft RFC to the IETF for development of a standard and for those customers interested in developing their own TACACS+ software.

TACACS+ server services are maintained in a database on a TACACS+ daemon running on a Windows 2000/NT or UNIX host. Cisco's servers supporting TACACS+ include CiscoSecure ACS for Windows, CiscoSecure UNIX, and Cisco Access Registrar. Cisco Access Servers (Cisco Secure ACS) can implement both TACACS+ and RADIUS. The underlying architecture of TACACS+ protocol complements the AAA architecture.

TACACS+ and RADIUS Compared

This section compares several key features of TACACS+ and RADIUS to help understand the strengths and weaknesses of each. While counterpointing many of these comparisons is possible and the information is useful, remember, in the long run, it's Cisco's certification and their comparison.

Authentication and Authorization RADIUS combines the authentication and authorization services. The access-accept packets sent by the RADIUS server in cleartext to the client contain authorization information. Accounting is a separate service on the RADIUS server.

TACACS+ fully supports the AAA architecture by separating the authentication, authorization, and accounting. This allows the flexibility of using another service, such as Kerberos, for authentication, while still using TACACS+ for authorization and/or accounting.

UDP vs. TCP TACACS+ uses TCP for connection-oriented transport between clients and servers. TCP port 49 is reserved for TACACS+. RADIUS uses UDP for best-effort delivery, requiring additional variables to be defined, such as retransmit attempts and time-outs to compensate.

The acknowledgements (TCP ACK) provide indications that a request has been received within (approximately) a network round-trip time (RTT). This same TCP process uses RST (reset) packets to provide immediate indication of a failed (or offline) authentication server. UDP can't tell the difference between a failed server, a slow server, and a nonexistent server.

TCP keepalive packets can be used to watch for failed servers and to facilitate rapid failover between multiple connected authentication servers.

TCP scales better and adapts better to growing and/or congested networks.

Challenge/Response RADIUS supports only unidirectional challenge/response from the RADIUS server to the RADIUS client. TACACS+ supports bidirectional challenge/response like CHAP between the two NASs.

Multiprotocol Support Both TACACS+ and RADIUS support SLIP and PPP encapsulation protocols, but RADIUS doesn't support the following TACACS+ supported protocols:

- Novell Asynchronous Services Interface (NASI)
- X.25 PAD connection
- Net BIOS Frame Protocol Control protocol
- AppleTalk Remote Access protocol (ARAP)

Packet Encryption RADIUS encrypts only the password in the access-request packet from the client to the server, using MD5 hashing for security. The remainder of the packet is in cleartext exposing information such as user name, authorized services, and accounting to be captured by snooping.

TACACS+ encrypts the entire data payload of the packet leaving only the standard TACACS+ header in cleartext. While leaving the body of the packets unencrypted is possible for debugging purposes, normal operation fully encrypts the body for more secure communications. A field in the header indicates whether the body is encrypted.

Router Management RADIUS doesn't support limiting the user access to specific router commands as a tool for router management or terminal services.

TACACS+ supports two methods for controlling the authorization of router commands on either a per-user or a per-group basis.

- Assign commands to privilege levels and have the router use TACACS+ to verify that the user is authorized at the specified privilege level.
- Explicitly define the commands allowed on a per-user or a per-group basis on the TACACS+ server.

AAA System Components

Access control is the way to manage who is allowed access to the NAS and what services they're allowed to use once they have access. Authentication, Authorization, and Accounting (AAA) network security services provide the primary framework through which to set up access control on the router or access server. AAA is comprised of three independent security functions included in the name:

- Authentication
- Authorization
- Accounting

AAA as Facilitator

AAA is designed for flexibility by enabling the administrator to configure the type of authentication and authorization on a per-line (per-user) or per-service basis. During configuration, the types of authentication and authorization to be allowed are defined by creating method lists, and then applying those method lists to specific services or interfaces. The method lists are used to authenticate dial-in users. These lists create an ordered list of security protocols to be used for authentication, thus creating a backup system for authentication in case the initial method fails. For example, the preferred authentication method might be TACACS+, but if the TACACS server isn't available, then use the local user name/password database. Finally, if the user name/password entries have been removed, then use the enable password.

AAA uses protocols, such as RADIUS, TACACS+, and Kerberos, to administer its security functions. If a router or access server is acting as an NAS, then AAA is the means through which the NAS communicates with the RADIUS, TACACS+, or Kerberos security server.

Steps to Configure AAA

Configuring AAA is relatively simple once the basic process is understood. The basic steps to configure AAA security on a Cisco router or access server are the following:

1. Enable AAA by using the **aaa new-model** global configuration command.
2. If you decide to use a separate security server, such as RADIUS, TACACS+, or Kerberos, configure security protocol parameters to use the appropriate server(s).
3. Define the method lists for authentication by using an **aaa authentication** command.
4. Apply the method lists to a particular interface or line, if required.
5. (Optional) Configure authorization using the **aaa authorization** command.
6. (Optional) Configure accounting using the **aaa accounting** command.

You will look at Steps 3 through 6 in the next sections. For now, you will concentrate on starting AAA and telling it how to find the authentication server, assuming one will be used.

NOTE The exam and this book only use the TACACS+ and RADIUS features. For more information on configuring Kerberos, go to http://www.cisco.com/ on the Web and perform a search for configuring Kerberos. No CCO account is needed for much of the information.

Enable AAA

To enable the AAA access control model on the router or NAS, in global configuration mode, type the **aaa new-model** command. Use the no form of the command to disable the AAA. The syntax is

```
Rtr1(config)#aaa new-model
Rtr1(config)#no aaa new-model
```

There are no variables. The words simply turn the feature on and off. Once entered, the CON, VTY, AUX, and TTY lines require a user name and a password for access. Any previous password configuration for those lines is automatically removed.

Define the Security Server—TACACS+

If a TACACS server host is used for authentication, use the **tacacs-server host** global configuration command. Use the no form of this command to delete the specified name or address. The syntax is

```
Rtr1(config)#tacacs-server host {hostname | ip address} [single-connection] [port port#]
    [timeout seconds] [key string]
Rtr1(config)#no tacacs-server host hostname
```

hostname	Name of the TACACS+ server.
ip-addresss	IP address of the TACACS+ server.
single-connection	(Optional) Specify that the router maintain a single open connection for confirmation from the AAA/TACACS+ server. This command contains no autodetect feature and fails if the host isn't running a CiscoSecure daemon.
port	(Optional) Overrides the default, which is port 49.
port#	(Optional) Port number of the server (range 1 to 65535).
timeout	(Optional) Overrides the global timeout value set with the global **tacacs-server timeout** command for this server only.
seconds	(Optional) New timeout interval in seconds.
key	(Optional) Specify an authentication and encryption key. This must match the key used by the TACACS+ daemon. Specifying this key overrides the key set by the global command **tacacs-server key** for this server only.
string	(Optional) Character string to use as the authentication and encryption key.

Multiple **tacacs-server host** commands can be used to specify additional host servers. The Cisco IOS software searches for hosts in the order in which they're specified. Use the single-connection, port, timeout, and key options only when running AAA/TACACS+ server.

Because some of the parameters of the **tacacs-server host** command override global settings made by the **tacacs-server timeout** and **tacacs-server key** commands, this command can be used to enhance security on a network by uniquely configuring individual TACACS+ connections.

The following example specifies a TACACS host named tac-serv1:

```
Rtr1(config)#aaa new-model
Rtr1(config)#tacacs-server host tac-serv1
```

The next AAA example specifies that the router first try the CiscoSecure TACACS+ host 192.168.1.4. If 192.168.1.4 is unavailable, then use tac-serv1:

```
Rtr1(config)#aaa new-model
Rtr1(config)#tacacs-server host 192.168.1.4
Rtr1(config)#tacacs-server host tac-serv1
```

The next AAA example specifies that the router consult the CiscoSecure TACACS+ host named 192.168.1.4 on port number 51. The timeout value for requests on this connection is three seconds. The encryption key is a_secret.

```
Rtr1(config)#aaa new-model
Rtr1(config)#tacacs-server host 192.168.1.4 single-connection port 51
     timeout 3 key a_secret
```

Define TACACS+ Server Key Option After enabling AAA with the **aaa new-model** command, the authentication and encryption key must be set using the **tacacs-**

server key global configuration command. Use the no form of this command to disable the key.

Rtr1(config)#tacacs-server key *key*
Rtr1(config)#no tacacs-server key [*key*]

key	A character entry, this key must match the key used on the TACACS+ daemon. Any leading spaces are ignored, *but spaces within and at the end of the key aren't ignored*. Don't enclose the key in quotation marks unless they're part of the key.

The following example shows an AAA TACACS+ implementation with the authentication and encryption key set to seattle19:

```
Rtr1(config)#aaa new-model
Rtr1(config)#tacacs-server host 192.168.1.4
Rtr1(config)#tacacs-server key seattle19
```

Define the Security Server—RADIUS

To specify a RADIUS server host, use the **radius-server host global** configuration command. Use the no form of this command to delete the specified RADIUS host. The syntax is

Rtr1(config)#radius-server host {*hostname* | *ip-address*} [auth-port *port-number*] [acct-port *port-number*] [timeout *seconds*] [retransmit *retries*] [key *string*] [alias{*hostname* | *ip-address*}]
Rtr1(config)#no radius-server host {*hostname* | *ip-address*} [auth-port *port-number*] [acct-port *port-number*] [timeout *seconds*] [retransmit *retries*] [key *string*]

hostname	DNS name of the RADIUS server.
ip-address	IP address of the RADIUS server.
auth-port	(Optional) To specify a UDP destination port for authentication requests.
port-number	(Optional) Port number for authentication requests. The host isn't used for authentication if it's set to 0.
acct-port	(Optional) To specify a UDP destination port for accounting requests.
port-number	(Optional) Port number for accounting requests. The host isn't used for accounting if it's set to 0.

Use multiple radius-server host commands to specify multiple hosts. The software searches for hosts in the order in which they're specified.

The following example specifies host1 as the RADIUS server and uses default ports for both accounting and authentication.

```
Rtr1(config)#aaa new-model
Rtr1(config)#radius-server host host1.domain.com
```

The next example defines port 12 as the destination port for authentication requests and port 16 as the destination port for accounting requests on a RADIUS host named 192.168.1.4. Because entering a line resets all the port numbers, you must specify a host and configure both the accounting and authentication ports on a single line.

```
Rtr1(config)#aaa new-model
Rtr1(config)#radius-server host 192.168.1.4 auth-port 12 acct-port 16
```

To use separate servers for accounting and authentication, use the zero port value, as appropriate. The following example specifies that RADIUS server192.168.1.4 be used for accounting, but not for authentication, and that RADIUS server host1 be used for authentication, but not for accounting:

```
Rtr1(config)#aaa new-model
Rtr1(config)#radius-server host 192.168.1.4 auth-port 0
Rtr1(config)#radius-server host host1.domain.com acct-port 0
```

Define RADIUS Server Key Option After enabling AAA with the **aaa new-model** command, the authentication and encryption key must be set using the **radius-server key** global configuration command. Use the no form of this command to disable the key:

Rtr1(config)#radius-server key *key*
Rtr1(config)#no radius-server key [*key*]

key	A character entry, this key must match the key used on the RADIUS daemon. Any leading spaces are ignored, *but spaces within, and at the end of the key, aren't ignored.* Don't enclose the key in quotation marks unless they're part of the key.

The following example shows an AAA RADIUS implementation the authentication and encryption key set to seattle19:

```
Rtr1(config)#aaa new-model
Rtr1(config)#radius-server host 192.168.1.4
Rtr1(config)#radius-server key seattle19
```

Authentication

Authentication is the way a user is identified prior to being allowed access to the network and network services. The authentication process can include a login and password dialog box, challenge and response, messaging support, and any encryption used.

You configure AAA authentication by defining a named list of authentication methods, and then applying that list to various interfaces. The method list defines the types of authentication to be performed and the sequence in which they'll be performed. The method list must be applied to a specific interface before any of the defined authentication methods will be performed. The only exception is the default method list (which, by coincidence, is named "default"). The default method list is automatically applied to all interfaces if no other method list is defined. A defined method list overrides the default method list.

Steps to Configure AAA

Configuring AAA is relatively simple once the basic process is understood. The basic steps to configure AAA security on a Cisco router or access server are as follows:

1. Enable AAA by using the **aaa new-model** global configuration command.
2. If you decide to use a separate security server, such as RADIUS, TACACS+, or Kerberos, configure security protocol parameters to use the appropriate server(s).
3. Define the method lists for authentication by using an **aaa authentication** command.
4. Apply the method lists to a particular interface or line, if required.
5. (Optional) Configure authorization using the **aaa authorization** command.
6. (Optional) Configure accounting using the **aaa accounting** command.

You will look at Steps 3 and 4 in this section.

Define the Method Lists

After identifying the authentication server and defining an associated encryption key, now it's time to define method lists for authentication. Use the **aaa authentication** command to name the list and define the authentication method in the order they're to be tried.

The **aaa authentication** ***purpose*** command has several options, including the following implementations:

- **aaa authentication login**   Authentication at login
- **aaa authentication ppp**   Authentication methods for interfaces running PPP
- **aaa authentication nasi**   Authentication for Netware Asynchronous Services Interface
- **aaa authentication arap**   Authentication method for AppleTalk Remote Access protocol

The book and the exams will concentrate on the login and PPP options. The configuration is similar except for the method choices, which can be overcome by using the **?** to display the options while configuring.

Define the Method Lists—Login

To set AAA authentication at login, use the **aaa authentication login** global configuration command. Use the no form of this command to disable AAA authentication. The syntax is

Rtr1(config)#aaa authentication login {default | *list-name*} *method1* [*method2...*]
Rtr1(config)#no aaa authentication login {default | *list-name*} *method1* [*method2...*]

default	Uses the listed authentication methods as the default list to be used when a user logs in
list-name	A character string used to name the list of authentication methods that can be specified to be used when a user logs in
method	At least one of the keywords described in the next table

The *method* argument identifies the list of methods the authentication algorithm tries, in the stated sequence. Method keywords are described in the following table.

Keyword	Description
group tacacs+	Use the list of all TACACS+ servers to authenticate services.
group radius	Use the list of all RADIUS servers to authenticate services.
group *group-name*	Use a subset of RADIUS or TACACS+ servers for authentication, as defined by the server group *group-name*.
local	Use the local user name database for authentication.
local-case	Use the case-sensitive local user name database for authentication.
Enable	Use enable password for authentication.
Line	Use the line password for authentication.
krb5	Use Kerberos 5 for authentication.
krb5-telnet	Use Kerberos 5 Telnet authentication protocol when using Telnet to connect to the router.
none	Use no authentication—no security.

The additional methods of authentication are used only if the preceding method returns an error, not if it fails. To ensure that the authentication succeeds, even if all methods return an error, specify none as the final method in the command line.

Implementing Authentication Method Lists

The authentication method lists are implemented on interfaces with the **login authentication** {**default** | *list-name*} command. If no list is implemented on an interface with the **login authentication** command, a default list to be used can be specified with the default keyword, followed by the methods.

If authentication isn't specifically set for a line, the default is to deny access and no authentication is performed. Use the **show running-config** command to display currently configured lists of authentication methods.

The following example creates an AAA authentication list called *XYZ-access*. This authentication first tries to contact a TACACS+ server. If no server is found, TACACS+ returns an error and AAA tries to use the enable password. If this attempt also returns an error (because no enable password is configured on the server), the user is allowed access with no authentication.

```
Rtr1(config)#aaa new-model
Rtr1(config)#tacacs-server host 192.168.1.4
Rtr1(config)#tacacs-server key seattle19
```

```
Rtr1(config)#aaa authentication login XYZ-access group tacacs+ enable none
Rtr1(config)#line vty 0 4
Rtr1(config-line)#login authentication XYZ-access
```

The following example creates the same list, but sets it as the default list that's used for all login authentications if no other list is specified. It adds the local user name/password database as the second choice.

```
Rtr1(config)#username last password hope
Rtr1(config)#aaa new-model
Rtr1(config)#tacacs-server host 192.168.1.4
Rtr1(config)#tacacs-server key seattle19
Rtr1(config)#aaa authentication login default group tacacs+ local enable none
```


Define the Authentication Method Lists—PPP

To set AAA authentication at login, use the **aaa authentication ppp** global configuration command. Use the no form of this command to disable AAA authentication. The syntax is

Rtr1(config)#aaa authentication ppp {default | *list-name*} *method1* [*method2*...]
Rtr1(config)#no aaa authentication ppp {default | *list-name*} *method1* [*method2*...]

default	Uses the listed authentication methods as the default list to be used when a user logs in
list-name	Character string used to name the list of authentication methods that can be specified to be used when a user logs in
method	At least one of the keywords described in the next table

The *method* argument identifies the list of methods the authentication algorithm tries, in the stated sequence. Method keywords are described in the following table.

Keyword	Description
group tacacs+	Use the list of all TACACS+ servers to authenticate services.
group radius	Use the list of all RADIUS servers to authenticate services.
group *group-name*	Use a subset of RADIUS or TACACS+ servers for authentication, as defined by the server group *group-name*.
local	Use the local user name database for authentication.
local-case	Use the case-sensitive local user name database for authentication.
Enable	Use enable password for authentication.
Line	Use the line password for authentication.
krb5	Use Kerberos 5 for authentication.
if-needed	Does not authenticate if the user has already been authenticated on a TTY line.
none	Use no authentication—no security.

The additional methods of authentication are used only if the preceding method returns an error, not if it fails. To ensure the authentication succeeds even if all methods return an error, specify none as the final method in the command line.

Implementing Authentication Method Lists

The PPP authentication method lists are implemented on interfaces with the **ppp authentication** {**default** | *list-name*} command. *These lists contain up to four authentication methods that are used when a user tries to log in to the serial interface.* If no list is implemented on an interface with the **ppp authentication** command, a default list to be used can be specified with the default keyword followed by the methods.

If authentication isn't specifically set for a line, the default is to deny access and no authentication is performed. Use the **show running-config** command to display currently configured lists of authentication methods.

The following example uses the previous named list example and adds a PPP authentication list named PPP-access. This authentication first tries to contact a TACACS+ server. If no TACACS+ server is found, the user is allowed access with no authentication.

```
Rtr1(config)#aaa new-model
Rtr1(config)#tacacs-server host 192.168.1.4
Rtr1(config)#tacacs-server key seattle19
Rtr1(config)#aaa authentication login XYZ-access group tacacs+ enable none
Rtr1(config)#aaa authentication ppp PPP-access group tacacs+ none
Rtr1(config)#interface serial 0/1
Rtr1(config-if)#encapsulation ppp
Rtr1(config-if)#ppp authentication ppp-access
```

The following example creates the same list, but sets it as the default list used for all login authentications if no other list is specified, and adds the if-needed method.

```
Rtr1(config)#username last password hope
Rtr1(config)#aaa new-model
Rtr1(config)#tacacs-server host 192.168.1.4
Rtr1(config)#tacacs-server key seattle19
Rtr1(config)#aaa authentication login default group tacacs+ local enable none
Rtr1(config)#aaa authentication ppp default if-needed group tacacs+ none
```

Authorization

AAA authorization works by assembling a set of attributes that describe what the user is authorized to perform or access. These attributes are compared to the information contained in a database for a given user, and the result is returned to AAA to determine the user's actual capabilities and restrictions. The database can be located locally on the access server or the router, or it can be stored remotely on a RADIUS or TACACS+ security server. Remote security servers, such as RADIUS and TACACS+, authorize users for specific rights by associating attribute-value (AV) pairs, which define those rights, with the appropriate user. All authorization methods must be defined through AAA.

As with authentication, you configure AAA authorization by defining a named list of authorization methods, and then applying that list to various interfaces.

Steps to Configure AAA

Configuring AAA is relatively simple once the basic process is understood. The basic steps to configure AAA security on a Cisco router or access server are

1. Enable AAA by using the **aaa new-model** global configuration command.
2. If you decide to use a separate security server, such as RADIUS, TACACS+, or Kerberos, configure security protocol parameters to use the appropriate server(s).
3. Define the method lists for authentication by using an **aaa authentication** command.
4. Apply the method lists to a particular interface or line, if required.
5. (Optional) Configure authorization using the **aaa authorization** command.
6. (Optional) Configure accounting using the **aaa accounting** command.

You will look at Step 5 in this section.

Define the Authorization Method Lists

Use the **aaa authorization** command to enable authorization and to create named methods lists, defining authorization methods that can be used when a user accesses the specified function. Method lists for authorization define the ways authorization will be performed and the sequence in which these methods will be performed.

A *method list,* as in authentication, is simply a named list describing the authorization methods to be queried (such as RADIUS or TACACS+), in sequence. Method lists enable one or more security protocols for authorization to be designated, thus ensuring a backup system in case the initial method fails. Cisco IOS software uses the first method listed to authorize users for specific network services. If that method fails to respond, the Cisco IOS software selects the next method listed in the method list. This process continues until successful communication occurs with a listed authorization method or all methods defined are exhausted.

NOTE The Cisco IOS software attempts authorization with the next listed method only when no response occurs from the previous method. If authorization fails at any point in this cycle (meaning the security server or local user name database responds by denying the user services), the authorization process stops and no other authorization methods are attempted.

Use the **aaa authorization** global configuration command to set parameters that restrict a user's network access. Use the no form of this command to disable authorization for a function. The basic syntax is

Rtr1(config)#aaa authorization {*authorization-type*} {default | *list-name*} *method1* [*method2*...]Rtr1(config)#no aaa authorization {*authorization-type*}

The first step is to choose which of the eight authorization types AAA supports is to be validated. The actual syntax and choices include

Rtr1(config)#aaa authorization {**network** | **exec** | **commands** ***level***| **reverse-access** | **configuration** | **config-commands** | **auth-proxy** | **ipmobile**}
{default | *list-name*} *method1* [*method2…*]

network	All network-related service requests, including SLIP, PPP, PPP NCPs, and ARAP.
exec	Is the user allowed to run an EXEC shell?
commands *level*	Specific command level to be authorized (0 through 15).
reverse-access	Reverse access connections, such as reverse Telnet.
configuration	Downloads the configuration from the AAA server.
config-commands	Configuration mode commands.
auth-proxy	Authentication Proxy Services.
Ipmobile	Mobile IP services.

Once the authorization type is selected, the rest is just like the authentication process.

default	Uses the listed authorization methods that follow this argument as the default list of methods for authorization
list-name	Character string used to name the list of authorization methods
method1 [*method2…*]	One of the keywords listed in the following table

The actual method lists are specific to the type of authorization being requested. The six methods Cisco IOS software supports for authorization are described in the following table.

Method	**Description**
group tacacs+	Uses the list of all TACACS+ servers to provide authorization services. TACACS+ authorization defines specific rights for users by associating attribute-value (AV) pairs, which are stored in a database on the TACACS+ security server, with the appropriate user.
group radius	Uses the list of all RADIUS servers to provide authorization service. RADIUS authorization defines specific rights for users by associating attributes, which are stored in a database on the RADIUS server.
if-authenticated	Allows the user to access the requested function if the user is authenticated.
local	Uses the local database for authorization, as defined by the user name command, to authorize specific rights for users. Only a limited set of functions can be controlled by the local database.
krb5-instance	Uses the instance defined by the **Kerberos Instance Map** command.
none	The NAS doesn't request authorization information. Authorization isn't performed over this line/interface.

When creating a named method list, a particular list of authorization methods for the indicated authorization type is defined. Once defined, method lists must be applied to specific lines or interfaces, as with authentication, before any of the defined methods will be performed. The **authorization** command causes a request packet, containing a series of AV pairs, to be sent to the RADIUS or TACACS+ daemon as part of the authorization process. The daemon can do one of the following:

- Accept the request as is.
- Make changes to the request.
- Refuse the request and refuse authorization.

Implementing Authorization Method Lists

To configure AAA authorization using named method lists, perform the following tasks beginning in Global Configuration mode:

Task	Command
Create an authorization method list for an authorization type and enable authorization.	aaa authorization {*authorization-type*} *list-name* [*method1* [*method2*...]]
Enter Line Configuration mode on which you want to apply the authorization method list. or Enter the Interface Configuration mode for the interfaces to which you want to apply the authorization method list.	line [aux | console | tty | vty] *line-number* [*ending-line-number*] or interface *interface-type interface-number*
Apply the authorization list to the line(s). or Apply the authorization list to the interface.	authorization {*authorization-type*} *list-name* or ppp authorization *list-name*

The following example defines the network authorization method list named XYZ-auth, which specifies TACACS+ authorization will be used on serial lines using PPP. If the TACACS+ server fails to respond, the local network authorization will be performed.

```
Rtr1(config)#aaa new-model
Rtr1(config)#tacacs-server host 192.168.1.4
Rtr1(config)#tacacs-server key seattle19
Rtr1(config)#aaa authentication login XYZ-access group tacacs+ enable none
Rtr1(config)#aaa authentication ppp PPP-access group tacacs+ none
Rtr1(config)#aaa authorization network xyz-auth group tacacs+ local
Rtr1(config)#interface serial 0/1
Rtr1(config-if)#encapsulation ppp
Rtr1(config-if)#ppp authentication ppp-access
Rtr1(config-if)#ppp authorization xyz-auth
```

Accounting

Accounting enables you to track the services users are accessing, as well as the amount of network resources they're consuming. When AAA accounting is activated, the NAS reports user activity to the TACACS+ or RADIUS security server (depending on which security method you have implemented) in the form of accounting records. Each accounting record is comprised of accounting AV pairs and is stored on the access control server. This data can then be analyzed for network management, client billing, and/or auditing. All accounting methods must be defined through AAA. As with authentication and authorization, you can configure AAA accounting by defining a named list of accounting methods, and then applying that list to various interfaces.

Steps to Configure AAA

Configuring AAA is relatively simple once the basic process is understood. The basic steps to configure AAA security on a Cisco router or access server are the following:

1. Enable AAA by using the **aaa new-model** global configuration command.
2. If you decide to use a separate security server, such as RADIUS, TACACS+, or Kerberos, configure security protocol parameters to use the appropriate server(s).
3. Define the method lists for authentication by using an **aaa authentication** command.
4. Apply the method lists to a particular interface or line, if required.
5. (Optional) Configure authorization using the **aaa authorization** command.
6. (Optional) Configure accounting using the **aaa accounting** command.

You will look at Step 6 in this section.

Define the Accounting Method Lists

When **aaa accounting** is activated, the NAS monitors either RADIUS accounting attributes or TACACS+ AV pairs pertinent to the connection, depending on the security method you implemented. The NAS reports these attributes as accounting records, which are then stored in an accounting log on the security server. The **aaa accounting** command enables accounting and enables you to create named method lists defining specific accounting methods on a per-line or per-interface basis. Use the no form of this command to disable accounting. The basic syntax is

Rtr1(config)#aaa accounting {***accounting-type***} {default | *list-name*} {***accounting-method***}
method1 [*method2...*]

Rtr1(config)#no aaa accounting {***accounting-type***}

The first step is to choose which of the eight authorization types that AAA supports should be validated. The syntax and choices include

Rtr1(config)# aaa accounting {**system** | **network** | **exec** | **connection** | **commands** ***level*** | **nested** | **update**} {default | *list-name*} {***accounting-method***} *method1* [*method2...*]

system	All system-level events not associated with users, such as reloads. Don't use named accounting lists, only use the default list for system accounting.
network	All network-related service requests, including SLIP, PPP, PPP NCPs, and ARAP.
exec	Creates accounting records about user EXEC terminal sessions on the NAS, including user name, date, start, and stop times.
connection	All outbound connections from the NAS, such as Telnet, local-area transport (LAT), TN3270, packet assembler/disassembler (PAD), and rlogin.
commands *level*	Specific command level to track for accounting (0 through 15).
nested	Provides accounting when starting PPP from EXEC, generate NETWORK records before EXEC-STOP record.
update	Enables periodic interim accounting records to be sent to the accounting server.

Once the accounting type is selected, you must specify the accounting method to be used in recording the results. The syntax and choices include

Rtr1(config)#aaa accounting {*accounting-type*} {default | *list-name*} {**start-stop** | **wait-start** | **stop-only** | **none**} *method1* [*method2...*]

start-stop	Sends a *start accounting notice* at the beginning of a process and a ***stop accounting notice*** at the end of a process. The *start accounting record* is sent in the background. The requested user process begins, regardless of whether the start accounting notice was received by the accounting server.
wait-start	Sends both a start and a stop accounting notice to the accounting server. But, if the *wait-start* keyword is used, the requested user service does *not* begin until the start accounting notice is acknowledged.
stop-only	Sends a *stop accounting notice* at the end of the requested user process.
None	Disables accounting services on this line or interface.

For minimal accounting, use the stop-only keyword. For more detailed accounting, include the start-stop keyword. For even more accounting control, include the wait-start keyword, which ensures the start notice is received by the RADIUS or TACACS+ server before granting the user's process request.

When **aaa accounting** is activated, the network access server monitors either RADIUS accounting attributes or TACACS+ AV pairs pertinent to the connection, depending on the security method implemented. The network access server reports these attributes as accounting records, which are then stored in an accounting log on the security server. The default | *list-name* and *method* options are just like in the authentication and authorization process. Individual named accounting method lists are specific to the indicated accounting type. *System accounting* doesn't use named accounting lists. Only the default list for system accounting can be defined.

default	Uses the listed accounting methods that follow this argument as the default list of methods for accounting
list-name	Character string used to name the list of accounting methods
method1 [*method2*...]	One of the keywords listed in the following table

Accounting method keywords are described in the following table.

Keyword	Description
group tacacs+	Uses the list of all TACACS+ servers to provide authorization services. The NAS reports user activity to the TACACS+ security server in the form of accounting records. Each accounting record contains accounting attribute-value (AV) pairs and is stored on the security server.
group radius	Uses the list of all RADIUS servers to provide authorization service. The NAS reports user activity to the RADIUS security server in the form of accounting records. Each accounting record contains accounting attribute-value (AV) pairs and is stored on the security server.
group | *group-name*	Uses a subset of RADIUS or TACACS+ servers for accounting, as defined by the server group *group-name*.

Method lists for accounting define the way accounting will be performed. Named accounting method lists enable the option to designate a particular security protocol to be used on specific lines or interfaces for particular types of accounting services.

Implementing Accounting Method Lists

AAA accounting is disabled by default. If the **aaa accounting** command for a particular accounting type is issued without a named method list specified, the default method list is automatically applied to all interfaces or lines (where this accounting type applies), except those with a named method list explicitly defined. (A defined method list always overrides the default method list.) If no default method list is defined, then no accounting takes place.

To configure AAA accounting using named method lists, perform the following tasks beginning in Global Configuration mode:

Task	Command
Create an accounting method list and enable accounting.	aaa accounting {*accounting-type*} *list-name* {*accounting-method*} *method1* [*method2*...]
Enter Line Configuration mode on which you want to apply the accounting method list. or Enter the Interface Configuration mode for the interfaces to which you want to apply the accounting method list.	line [aux | console | tty | vty] *line-number* [*ending-line-number*] or interface *interface-type interface-number*

Task	Command
Apply the accounting list to the line(s). or Apply the accounting list to the interface.	aaa accounting {*accounting-type*} *list-name* or ppp accounting *list-name*

The following example defines the network accounting method list named XYZ-acct, where command accounting services are provided by a TACACS+ security server with a stop-only restriction.

```
Rtr1(config)#aaa new-model
Rtr1(config)#tacacs-server host 192.168.1.4
Rtr1(config)#tacacs-server key seattle19
Rtr1(config)#aaa authentication login XYZ-access group tacacs+ enable none
Rtr1(config)#aaa authentication ppp PPP-access group tacacs+ none
Rtr1(config)#aaa authorization network xyz-auth group tacacs+ local
Rtr1(config)#aaa accounting network xyz-acct group start-stop tacacs+
Rtr1(config)#interface serial 0/1
Rtr1(config-if)#encapsulation ppp
Rtr1(config-if)#ppp authentication ppp-access
Rtr1(config-if)#ppp authorization xyz-auth
Rtr1(config-if)#ppp accounting xyz-acct
```

Testing AAA Configuration

Troubleshooting AAA can be rather comple—because it's used so often with other features, such as PPP—so remembering to use the troubleshooting commands associated with any protocols or technologies working with AAA is important. This section looks at some common commands for confirming AAA configuration and activity.

When working with AAA in a specific environment, such as dial-up modems, ISDN, or PPP, don't overlook Cisco's web site for more information. Go to http://www.cisco.com on the Web and perform a search for AAA or ISDN AAA. No CCO account is needed for much of the information.

The show Commands

Two **show** commands useful in debugging AAA are

show running-config	To verify that local AAA is configured correctly
show tacacs	To verify network connectivity between NAS and AAA server

The debug Commands

Cisco **IOS debug** command output provides a valuable source of information and feedback concerning state transitions and functions within the AAA environment. In addition to **debug** command output gathered directly from devices running Cisco IOS, the

Cisco AAA server can be configured to collect operational diagnostics. Use the following debug commands to capture AAA-related transitions and functions:

debug condition user *username*	Sets conditional debugging for a specific user and generates output debugs related to the user
debug aaa authentication	Displays authentication information with TACACS+ and RADIUS client/server interaction
debug aaa authorization	Displays authorization information with TACACS+ and RADIUS client/server interaction
debug aaa accounting	Displays accounting information with TACACS+ and RADIUS client/server interaction
debug tacacs	Displays TACACS+ interaction between the IOS client and the AAA server
debug radius	Displays RADIUS interaction between the IOS client and the AAA server
debug ppp negotiation	Shows if a client is passing PPP negotiation
debug ppp authentication	Shows if a client is passing PPP authentication
debug ppp error	Displays protocol errors and error statistics associated with PPP connection negotiation and operation

Chapter Review

Remote dial-up connections to the corporate network are made up of several dial-in technologies, including modem and ISDN connections, as well as virtual connections via the Internet. Access control is the process of controlling who can access the network and what resources they're allowed to use. Cisco's Authentication, Authorization, and Accounting (AAA) network security services configured on a router or network server implement this access control.

The three security components of AAA are designed to let you define and configure the type of authentication, authorization, and accounting in a detailed and consistent manner through the use of method lists, and then apply those method lists to specific services or interfaces according to your security plan. Method lists define a sequence of implementation processes that allow backup methods in case the initial method fails.

Authentication is the process of identifying users through user name and password verification methods that allow only approved individuals to access the network.

Authorization is the process of matching authenticated users with the permissions or privileges to use network resources

Accounting is the process of tracking or logging the different types of resources or services the remote users are accessing. This data can then be analyzed for auditing, troubleshooting, network management, and network planning client billing. The AAA databases can be remotely stored on one or more TACACS+ or RADIUS servers. Authentication and authorization databases can be stored locally on the access server.

AAA benefits include

- Scalability
- Flexibility and granularity
- Multiple implementation methods, which provide redundancy
- Support of standard authentication methods, such as RADIUS, TACACS+, and Kerberos

Questions

1. Which of the following is *not* one of the three components of AAA?

   A. Accounting

   B. Acknowledgement

   C. Authorization

   D. Authentication

2. Which one of the following is the process of determining what devices, features, or services a specific remote user has permission to access in the network, such as network resources or services?

   A. Accounting

   B. Acknowledgement

   C. Authorization

   D. Authentication

3. Which of the following is a term for the router with interfaces designed to service the remote users of the company?

   A. Remote server

   B. NAS

   C. Access point

   D. Authentication server

4. Which one of the following is *not* one of the three security protocols to control dial-up access into networks supported by AAA?

   A. TACACS+

   B. Kerberos

   C. RADIUS

   D. ASICS

5. Which of the following security protocols is considered legacy and is supported for those organizations already implementing it?
   A. TACACS+
   B. Kerberos
   C. RADIUS
   D. ASICS
6. Which of the following is a security protocol developed by Livingston Enterprises, Inc., now a division of Lucent Technologies?
   A. TACACS+
   B. Kerberos
   C. RADIUS
   D. ASICS
7. Which of the following is a security protocol developed by MIT?
   A. TACACS+
   B. Kerberos
   C. RADIUS
   D. ASICS
8. Which of the following is a security protocol developed by Cisco and submitted to IETF as a proposed standard?
   A. TACACS+
   B. Kerberos
   C. RADIUS
   D. ASICS
9. Which of the following is *not* an advantage of TACACS+ over RADIUS?
   A. Uses TCP for connections
   B. Supports multiple protocols, including ARAP, NASI, and X.25 PAD
   C. Fully supports the AAA architecture by separating the components
   D. Supports server-based security databases
10. Which command enables the AAA access control model on the router?
    A. tacacs-server host
    B. radius-server host
    C. aaa new-model
    D. tacacs-server key *key*

11. Which command identifies the TACACS+ server host to be used for authentication?
    A. Rtr1(config)#tacacs-server key seattle19
    B. Rtr1(config-if)#tacacs-server key seattle19
    C. Rtr1(config)#tacacs-server host Seattle
    D. Rtr1(config-if)#tacacs-server host Seattle
12. In the following command, what is the first authentication method?
    aaa authentication login XYZ-access group tacacs+ enable none
    A. Group servers
    B. TACACS+
    C. enable password
    D. None
13. Which of the following combines the authentication and authorization into a single database?
    A. TACACS+
    B. Kerberos
    C. RADIUS
    D. None of the above
14. Which command verifies network connectivity between the NAS and the AAA server?
    A. show running-config
    B. show tacacs
    C. debug tacacs
    D. debug aaa authentication
15. Which of the following is *not* an AAA benefit?
    A. Scalability.
    B. Automatic installation and configuration.
    C. Flexibility and granularity.
    D. Multiple implementation methods provide redundancy.

Answers

1. B. Acknowledgement
2. C. Authorization
3. B. NAS

4. D. ASICS
5. B. Kerberos
6. C. RADIUS
7. B. Kerberos
8. A. TACACS+
9. D. Supports server-based security databases (They both support this feature.)
10. C. **aaa new-model**
11. C. **Rtr1(config)#tacacs-server host Seattle**
12. B. TACACS+
13. C. RADIUS
14. B. **show tacacs**
15. B. Automatic installation and configuration.

CHAPTER 4

Cisco Secure ACS and TACACS+/RADIUS Technologies

In this chapter, you will learn how to:

- Describe Cisco Secure ACS
- Use the features and architecture of CiscoSecure ACS for Windows
- Understand the features of CiscoSecure ACS for UNIX
- Install CiscoSecure ACS 3.0 for Windows NT or Windows 2000
- Administer and troubleshoot CiscoSecure ACS for Windows
- Make use of TACACS+ overview and configuration
- Configure Cisco Secure ACS and TACACS+
- Verify TACACS+

This chapter looks at the features and architecture of the Cisco Secure Access Control Server (ACS) application. The chapter also covers the general process of preparing to install and configure the current versions of ACS support for Windows 2000/NT and UNIX (Solaris). Before starting installation, it's important for you to have the correct instructions for Cisco Secure ACS, for the appropriate network OS and OS version.

For the most recent information, go to http://www.cisco.com on the Web and choose the link for Products | Security Components under the Product Categories heading. Access servers are listed under product categories. Or, perform a search on Cisco Secure ACS. This search should also reveal any recent security announcements and mitigation techniques. No CCO account is needed for much of the information. Be aware that some Windows references refer to NT or ACS NT, but also include Windows 2000.

NOTE Special Cisco Secure ACS upgrade and reinstallation requirements and steps must be followed to make sure everything goes smoothly. The process varies, depending on whether the original configuration settings are to be incorporated in the new installation. Always get the latest upgrade instructions.

Describe Cisco Secure ACS

The *Cisco Secure ACS* is a server-based application offering a centralized user-access control strategy for the various access gateways to your network, as shown in Figure 4-1. Cisco Secure ACS supports the user Authentication, Authorization, and Accounting (AAA) features covered in the preceding chapter and is covered in several chapters pertaining to PIX firewalls.

ACS allows the administrator to manage user access for Cisco IOS routers, firewalls, Cisco Catalyst switches, and virtual private networks (VPNs), as well as newer technologies, such as dial-up and broadband DSL, cable access solutions, voice over IP (VoIP), Cisco wireless implementations, and third-party vendor Terminal Access Controller Access Control System Plus (TACACS+) offerings.

ACS is a strategic product at Cisco, incorporating new, advanced features as they become available to increase the diversity and granularity of implementations. Current support includes user and administrative access reporting, database synchronization and user importation tools, Lightweight Directory Access Protocol (LDAP) user authentication support, dynamic quota generation, restrictions such as time of day and day of week, and user and device group profiles.

CiscoSecure ACS for Windows and UNIX

There's no exam or practical purpose for this chapter to include detailed steps for installing, reinstalling, and upgrading Cisco Secure ACS. The network OS, ACS version, and new install versus upgrade/reinstall variables make using the most recent instructions downloaded from Cisco's site the only prudent solution.

Experience with installing server applications, careful reading of the correct installation instructions, and cautious progress can save you the hassle of having to start all over.

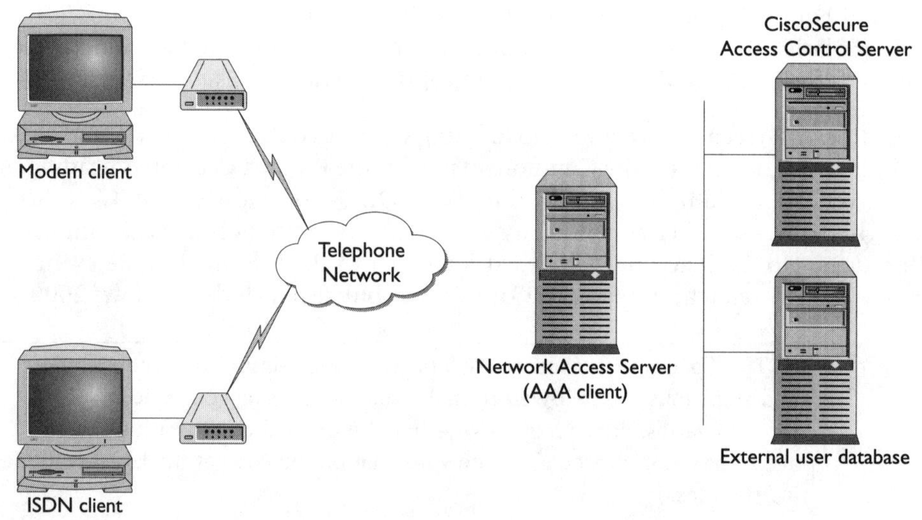

Figure 4-1 Cisco Secure ACS with an NAS AAA client

This section concentrates on system requirements and preparation that would be beneficial when you choose to install Cisco Secure ACS.

Features and Architecture of Cisco Secure ACS for Windows

The latest Windows version is Cisco Secure ACS version 3.0 for Windows 2000 and NT, supporting both RADIUS and TACACS+ server systems. New features included in Cisco Secure ACS version 3.0 allow network administrators to scale and deploy secure network services with centralized control, access management, and accounting within the Cisco Secure ACS framework. Using Cisco Secure ACS, network administrators can control

- Which users can access the network from either wired or wireless connections
- What privileges each user will have while in the network
- What accounting information is kept for capacity planning, account billing, or security audits
- What access and command controls are enabled for each configuration administrator

Features and Benefits

Specific features included in Cisco Secure ACS version 3.0 are the following.

IEEE 802.1x—Access Control for Switched LAN Users

The IEEE 802.1*x* standard brings new security services to the local area network (LAN) by letting network administrators control which users can access their switched LAN environment. The 802.1*x* standard manages port-level access control by using the Cisco Secure ACS Extensible Authentication Protocol (EAP), which is carried on RADIUS.

EAP Message Digest 5 (EAP-MD5) and EAP Transport LAN Services (EAP-TLS)

EAP is an IETF RFC standard for various authentication methods carried over any Point-to-Point Protocol (PPP) connection. *EAP-MD5* is a user name/password method incorporating MD5 hashing for security. *EAP-TLS* uses X.509 digital certificate technology to provide both Cisco Secure ACS server and client authentication. EAP-TLS also supports dynamic session key negotiation.

Microsoft Challenge Authentication Protocol (MSCHAP) Support

Cisco Secure ACS now supports MSCHAP version 2.0 exchanges and MSCHAP password change service for Microsoft Dial-Up Networking clients, Cisco VPN clients, and any other desktop client supporting MSCHAP version 2.0 password change service. A user whose password has expired now is automatically prompted to change their password after their next login.

Multiple LDAP Support

Cisco Secure ACS supports user authentication using records kept in a directory server through the LDAP, including Novell and Netscape, using a generic LDAP interface. New in Cisco Secure ACS version 3.0 is the capability to define multiple, different LDAP sources for user lookups. This lets you define a different LDAP repository to search for users. Another new feature is the capability to define secondary, backup LDAP servers, for times when a primary LDAP server is unavailable.

Device Command Sets (DCS)

Device Command Sets (DCS) is a new TACACS+ administration tool that uses a central Cisco Secure ACS graphical user interface (GUI) mechanism to control the authorization of each command on each device via per-user, per-group, or per-network device group mapping. DCS provides a method to group and name command profiles, which can then be paired with users, groups of users, or device groups. The new features and tools provide greater granularity, scalability, and manageability in setting authorization restrictions for network administrators.

Per-User Access Control Lists (ACL)

Per-user Access Control Lists (ACL) is a Cisco PIX Firewall Solution service that allows administrators to define access control lists (ACL) of any length, for users or groups of users using the Cisco Secure ACS GUI.

New NAS Wildcard, Multi-NAS, and Named Access Filters Features

NAS wildcard support for device, device group entry, and NAS filtering enables easier device entry and management in the Cisco Secure ACS system.

Multi-NAS allows the administrator to create shared NAS profile templates that define a group of network devices with the same attributes: shared key, authentication method, or login/accounting parameters. Multi-NAS also enables administrators to provide multiple IP addresses or ranges of IP addresses.

Named access filters simplify and facilitate assigning the same access filter to multiple devices or device groups.

User-Extensible Vendor-Specific Attributes (VSAs)

The Cisco Secure ACS now supports user-defined outbound Vendor-Specific Attributes (VSAs) using the web GUI, including support for Broadband Service Manager (BBSM) implementations.

Cisco Secure ACS Benefits

Cisco Secure ACS is a powerful access control system with many high-performance, flexibility, and scalability features for the growing WAN or LAN. Some of the benefits of the Windows 3.0 version include the following.

Ease of use	A web-based user interface simplifies and distributes configuration for user profiles, group profiles, and ACS configuration.
Product flexibility	AAA support is integrated in the Cisco IOS Software, allowing Cisco Secure ACS to be implemented across virtually any Cisco NAS.
Scalability	Built to support large networks with support for redundant servers, remote databases, and backup user database services.
Extensibility	LDAP authentication forwarding supports user authentication using profiles stored in directories or databases from leading vendors, such as Microsoft, Netscape, and Novell.
Administration	The capability to assign different access levels to each Cisco Secure administrator, plus the option to group network devices, facilitates easier control, flexibility, and granularity in defining, changing, and enforcing security policy administration.
Management	Shares Windows user name/password management by using Windows 2000 Active Directory and NT database support, as well as using the Windows Performance Monitor for real-time statistics viewing.
Protocol flexibility	Simultaneous TACACS+ and RADIUS support allows flexible implementation of VPN or dial support at both ends of Internet Protocol Security (IPSec) and Point-to-Point Tunneling Protocol (PPTP) tunnels.
Token server support	Token server support for RSA SecurID, Passgo, Secure Computing, ActiveCard, Vasco, and CryptoCard.
Control	Supports dynamic quotas for time-of-day, network usage, number of logged sessions, and day-of-week access restrictions.

PART II

Cisco Secure ACS for Windows Internal Architecture

Cisco Secure ACS for Windows NT/2000 version 3.0 servers is designed to be modular and flexible to scale from simple to complex networks. Cisco Secure ACS includes the following service modules:

CSAdmin

CSAdmin is the service for the Cisco Secure ACS internal web server that eliminates the need for a third-party web server. Once installed, Cisco Secure ACS must be configured from its HTML interface, which requires that CSAdmin be running. CSAdmin is a multithreaded application allowing multiple administrators to access it at the same time. CSAdmin is best for distributed, multiprocessor, and clustered environments.

While starting and stopping the other services from within the Cisco Secure ACS HTML interface is possible, this doesn't include starting or stopping CSAdmin. If CSAdmin stops abnormally through an external action, Cisco Secure ACS is only accessible from the Windows NT/2000 server on which it's running. CSAdmin can be started or stopped from the Windows NT/2000 Service menu.

CSAuth

CSAuth is the authentication and authorization service used to permit or deny access to users. CSAuth is the database manager that determines whether access should be granted and defines the privileges for a particular user. Cisco Secure ACS can access several different databases for authentication purposes. When a request for authentication arrives, Cisco Secure ACS checks the database configured for that user. If the user is unknown, Cisco Secure ACS checks the database(s) configured for unknown users. The database options include the following:

- **Cisco Secure ACS user database** The fastest option involves locating the user name and checking the password against the internal Cisco Secure ACS user database, as depicted in Figure 4-2. This avoids any delay while Cisco Secure ACS waits for a response from an external user database.
- **Windows NT/2000 user database** CSAuth passes the user name and password to Windows NT/2000 for authentication using its user database. Windows NT/2000 then provides a response approving or denying validation. Figure 4-3 represents Cisco Secure ACS using the network OS security database to authenticate users.
- **Novell NDS option** Uses the Novell NDS service to authenticate users. Cisco Secure ACS supports one tree, but the tree can have multiple Containers and Contexts. The Novell requester must be installed on the same Windows server as Cisco Secure ACS.

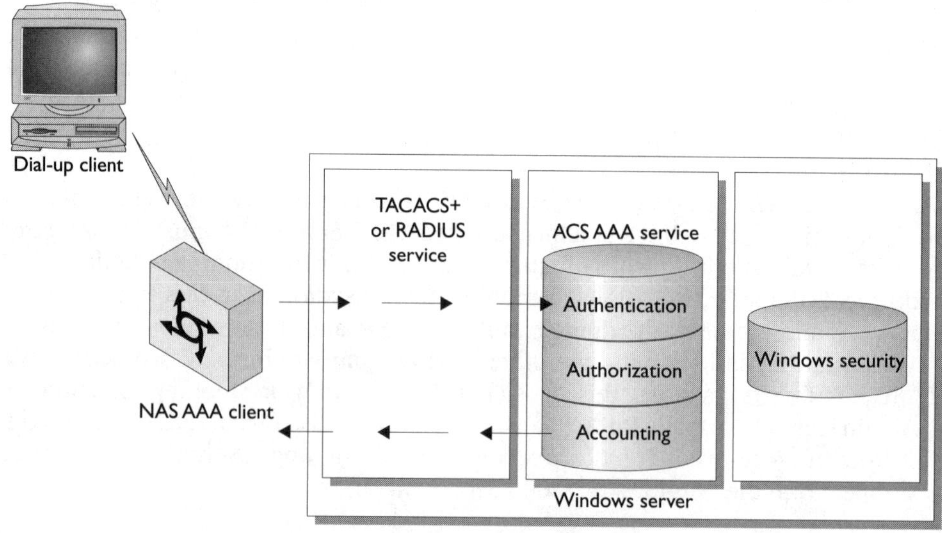

Figure 4-2 Cisco Secure ACS using its own database to authenticate users

- **ODBC** Open Database Connectivity (ODBC)–compliant SQL databases use the ODBC standardized API developed by Microsoft and are now used by most major database vendors. A benefit of ODBC in a web-based environment is easy access to data storage programs, such as Microsoft Access and SQL Server.
- **UNIX passwords** Cisco Secure ACS includes a password import utility to import passwords from a UNIX database.
- **Generic LDAP** Cisco Secure ACS supports authentication of users against records kept in a directory server through the LDAP. Both PAP and CHAP passwords can be used when authenticating against the LDAP database.
- **Token Card servers** Cisco Secure ACS supports token servers, such as RSA SecurID, and SafeWord AXENT, and any hexadecimal X.909 Token Card, such as CRYPTOCard. Cisco Secure ACS either acts as a client to the token server or, in other cases, uses the token server's RADIUS interface for authentication requests. Figure 4-4 shows the Token Card server interacting with Cisco Secure ACS.

When the user authenticates using one of the defined methods, Cisco Secure ACS obtains a set of authorizations from the user profile and any groups the user belongs to. This information is stored with the user name in the Cisco Secure ACS user database. Some authorizations are the services the user is entitled to, such as IP over PPP, IP pools from which to draw an IP address, access lists, and password aging information. The authorizations, with the authentication approval, are then passed to the CSTacacs or CSRadius modules to be sent to the requesting device.

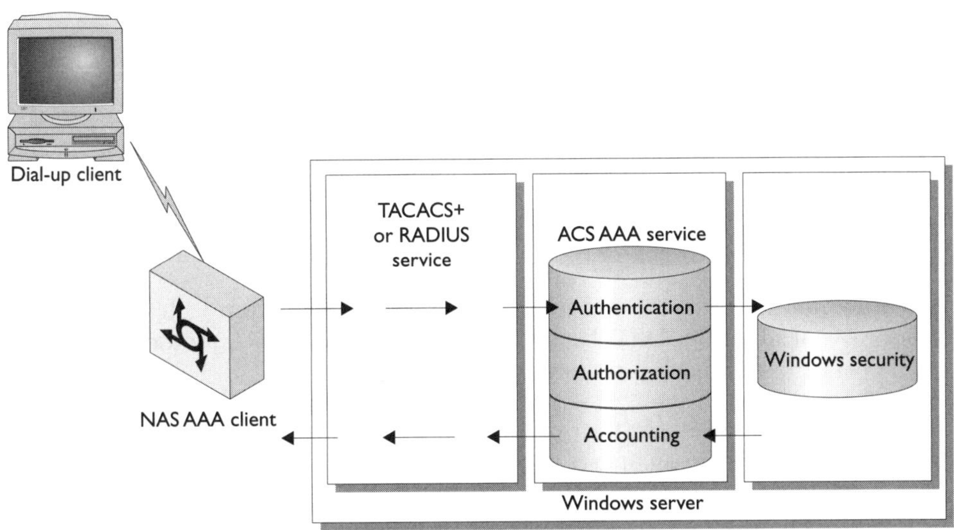

Figure 4-3 Cisco Secure ACS using Windows security database for authentication

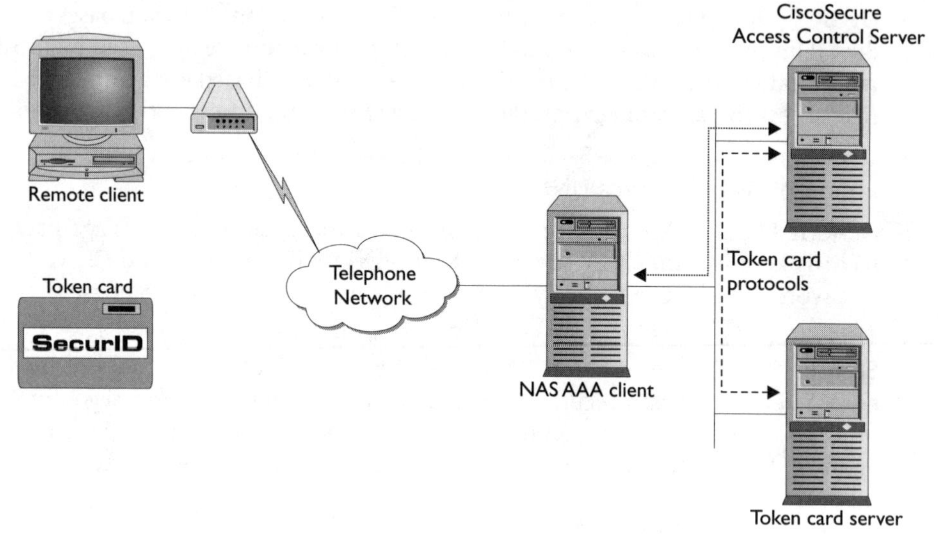

Figure 4-4 Remote user authentication using Token Card

CSDBSync

CSDBSync is an alternative to using the ODBC dynamic link library (DLL) to synchronize the Cisco Secure ACS database with third-party RDBMS systems. Because version 2.4, CSDBSync synchronizes AAA client, AAA server, network device groups (NDGs), and proxy table information.

CSLog

CSLog is the service that captures and places logging information. CSLog gathers data from the TACACS+ or RADIUS packet and CSAuth, and formats the data into the comma-separated value (CSV) files that can be imported into spreadsheets supporting the format.

CSMon

CSMon minimizes downtime in a remote access network environment. CSMon works for both TACACS+ and RADIUS by automatically detecting which protocols are in use. CSMon performs four basic activities:

- **Monitoring** Monitors the overall status of Cisco Secure ACS and the host system it's running on. It uses the Windows Event Log and Performance Monitor to monitor overall system health, including disk, CPU, and memory utilization.
- **Recording** Records and reports all exceptions to a special log file that can be used to diagnose problems.

- **Notification** Alerts the administrator to potential problems and real events regarding Cisco Secure ACS, and records all such problems. The default notification method is Simple Mail Transfer Protocol (SMTP) e-mail, but scripts can be written to enable other methods, such as pager notification.
- **Response** Can be configured to attempt to fix detected problems automatically and intelligently, such as running scripts to restart stopped services.

CSTacacs and CSRadius

The *CSTacacs* and *CSRadius* services communicate between the CSAuth module and the access device requesting authentication and authorization services. CSTacacs is used to communicate with TACACS+ devices, and CSRadius is used to communicate with RADIUS devices. Both services can run at the same time. CSTacacs and CSRadius services must be configured from CSAdmin.

Each module can be started and stopped individually from within the Microsoft Service Control Panel; or, with the exception of CSAdmin, each can be stopped from within the Cisco Secure ACS HTML interface.

System Performance

Cisco Secure ACS's performance capabilities, like most server services, are largely dependent on the resources of the Windows server it's installed on. Other factors include network topology, network management, and the selection of user authentication databases. Common sense would rightly indicate that a faster processor, increased memory, and high-speed connectivity will increase both the speed and volume of authentications per second.

The following items are general indicators of system performance, but the actual Cisco Secure ACS performance on a particular network could vary based on the environment and AAA configuration.

- **Maximum users supported** Technically, no limit exists to the number of users the Cisco Secure ACS user database can support if disk space is available. Cisco has successfully tested Cisco Secure ACS with databases greater than 100,000 users. While a single Cisco Secure ACS server using multiple databases might be able to support 300,000 to 500,000 users, using replicated multiple Cisco Secure ACS servers would increase that number substantially.
- **Transaction processing** A single minimal ACS server with a 10,000 user database might be able to process 80 RADIUS logins, plus approximately 40 TACACS+ logins per second. Increasing memory and/or the number and size of the processors would increase these numbers, while increasing the size of the database will reduce performance.
- **Maximum number of AAA client devices** Approximately 2,000 network devices running any AAA client.

Features of CiscoSecure ACS for UNIX

The most recent UNIX version is *CiscoSecure Access Control Server v2.3 for UNIX (Solaris)* to control the authentication, authorization, and accounting of users accessing the corporate network, Internet, or intranet. Using Cisco Secure ACS, network administrators can control the following:

- Which users can access the network from either wired or wireless connections
- What privileges each user can have while in the network
- What accounting information is kept for capacity planning, account billing, or security audits

Features and Benefits

CiscoSecure ACS v2.3 for UNIX provides the following features that allow network administrators to scale and deploy secure network services with centralized control, access management, and accounting within the Cisco Secure ACS framework:

- Simultaneous TACACS+ and RADIUS support for flexibility in implementation.
- HTML/JAVA GUI simplifies and speeds configuration for user and group profiles. SSL is also supported for secure server configuration.
- Administration of users using groups for maximum flexibility and to facilitate enforcement and changes of security policies.
- Token caching of passwords.
- Local and remote domain declaration.
- Virtual private dial-up network (VPDN) allows dial-up users to connect securely to a corporate network through a third-party ISP. VPDN can use AAA servers such as RADIUS and TACACS+ and services for better scalability of VPDN.
- Import mechanism to rapidly import a large number of users.
- Relational database support using Oracle, Sybase, or the included SQL Anywhere.
- Password support that includes Cleartext, DES encrypted, Bellcore S/Key, UNIX /etc/passwd file, Challenge Handshake Authentication Protocol (CHAP), Password Authentication Protocol (PAP), and AppleTalk Remote Access (ARA).
- Token server support for CryptoCard, Secure Computing, and Security Dynamics.
- Time-of-day and day-of-week access restrictions.
- User restrictions based on NAS name, port name, or remote address, including calling line ID (CLID.)
- Disabling of an account on a specific date.
- Disabling of an account after *n* failed attempts to thwart brute force attacks.
- Accounting information stored in the relational database.

Preparing to Install UNIX ACS

Cisco Secure ACS operates on UNIX Server as a service. Remembering the performance issues covered earlier, the UNIX server computer must meet the following minimum hardware and software requirements.

Hardware Requirements

The server must meet the following minimum hardware requirements:

- Sun SPARCstation 20
- CD-ROM drive
- 128MB of RAM
- 256MB of disk swap space
- 500MB of disk space

Software Requirements

The server must meet the following software requirement:

- Solaris V2.51 or V2.6, V7, V8

Third-Party Software Requirements

The server must have a compatible web browser installed. Both Java and JavaScript must be enabled for any web browsers to be used to administer Cisco Secure ACS. Cisco Secure ACS has been tested with the following browsers:

- Microsoft Internet Explorer versions 5.0 and 5.5
- Netscape Communicator version 4.76

External Databases

- Oracle v7.33
- Sybase v11.1

NAS Minimum IOS Requirements

- Cisco IOS v11.1 (TACACS+)
- Cisco IOS v11.2 (RADIUS)

Installing Cisco Secure ACS 3.0 for Windows

Cisco Secure ACS operates on Windows 2000 Server or NT 4.0 Server as a service. Cisco Secure ACS can operate on Windows 2000 Advanced Server and Windows 2000 Datacenter Server implementations *if Microsoft Clustering Services are not installed*. Cisco Secure ACS can run on a domain controller or a member server.

Hardware Requirements

Remembering the performance issues just covered, the Windows server computer must meet the following minimum hardware, operating system (OS), and third-party software requirements.

- Intel class Pentium 550 MHz PC or compatible
- 256MB of RAM
- 250MB of free disk space or more if you're running your database on the same machine
- Minimum resolution of 256 colors at 800 × 600 or lines

Operating System Requirements

The server must be running a functioning English-language version of one of the following Microsoft Windows OSs:

- Windows 2000 Server with Service Pack 1 or Service Pack 2 installed
- Windows 2000 Advanced Server with Service Pack 1 or Service Pack 2 installed (Microsoft Clustering Services must *not* be installed)
- Windows 2000 Datacenter Server with Service Pack 1 or Service Pack 2 installed (Microsoft Clustering Services must *not* be installed)
- Windows NT Server 4.0 with Service Pack 6a installed

While, technically, Windows service packs can be applied either before or after installing Cisco Secure ACS, if the service packs are installed before the Cisco Secure ACS software, the process will go more smoothly. If not, the Cisco Secure ACS installation program displays warnings that the required service pack isn't present. If a service pack message is displayed, continue the installation, and then install the required service pack *before* starting user authentication with Cisco Secure ACS.

Third-Party Software Requirements

The server must have a compatible web browser installed. Both Java and JavaScript must be enabled for any web browsers to be used to administer Cisco Secure ACS. Cisco Secure ACS has been tested with the following browsers:

- Microsoft Internet Explorer versions 5.0 and 5.5
- Netscape Communicator version 4.76

NAS Minimum IOS Requirements

- Cisco IOS v11.1 (TACACS+)
- Cisco IOS v11.2 (RADIUS)

Network Requirements

The following network requirements should be in place before you begin to install Cisco Secure ACS:

- A web browser meeting the previous third-party software requirements must be properly installed on any Windows server to be used to administer Cisco Secure ACS.
- For full TACACS+ and RADIUS support on any Cisco IOS devices, make sure the AAA clients are running Cisco IOS Release 11.2 or later.
- Make sure any non-Cisco IOS AAA clients can be configured with TACACS+ or RADIUS support, or both.
- Make sure the Windows server can ping the AAA clients.
- For Cisco Secure ACS to use the Grant Dial-In Permission To User feature when authorizing Windows network users, this option must be selected in the Windows NT User Manager or Windows 2000 Active Directory Users And Computers for the applicable user accounts.
- Make sure all network cards in the server that will host the Cisco Secure ACS software are enabled. Disabled NICs will slow installation because of delays caused by Microsoft CryptoAPI.
- Make sure any dial-in, VPN, or wireless clients can successfully connect to the applicable AAA clients.

Back Up Server Data

As with any major change to a server, backing up the Windows server installation, including the Windows Registry, makes sense. When upgrading or reinstalling Cisco Secure ACS, note the following issues:

- Back up the Cisco Secure ACS configuration and database, and then copy the backup file to a drive other than one that's local to the Cisco Secure ACS server.
- When upgrading Cisco Secure ACS, the backup created can't be used after a successful upgrade. This backup only provides a recovery option for the previous Cisco Secure ACS installation.
- The ACS Backup feature temporarily stops any Cisco Secure ACS services during the backup.

Gathering Information Required During Installation

During new Cisco ACS installations or any upgrades and reinstallations that don't preserve the existing configuration, specific information about your Windows server and an AAA client on your network need to be entered. Collect the applicable information before beginning the installation procedure. Upgrades or Cisco Secure ACS reinstallations intended to preserve the existing configuration and database don't require this information.

To collect information required during the installation of Cisco Secure ACS, follow these steps:

1. For the first AAA client to be configured to use Cisco Secure ACS's AAA services, determine which AAA protocols and vendor-specific attributes you want to implement.
   - TACACS+ (Cisco IOS)
   - RADIUS (Cisco Aironet)
   - RADIUS (Cisco BBSM)
   - RADIUS (Cisco IOS/PIX)
   - RADIUS (Cisco VPN 3000)
   - RADIUS (Cisco VPN 5000)
   - RADIUS (IETF)
   - RADIUS (Ascend)
   - RADIUS (Juniper)
   - RADIUS (Nortel)
2. Record the name of the AAA client.
3. Record the IP address of the AAA client.
4. Record the Windows 2000/NT server IP address.
5. Record the TACACS+ or RADIUS key (shared secret).

Administering and Troubleshooting Cisco Secure ACS for Windows

Once installed, Cisco Secure ACS is configured and administered using a web browser through the HTML interface, enabling easy configuration from any host on the LAN or WAN. The Cisco Secure ACS HTML interface uses HTML and some Java functions for ease of use. This program design keeps the interface straightforward and responsive. Figure 4-5 shows the Cisco Secure ACS HTML interface.

From the HTML interface, you can easily view and edit user and group information, stop and restart services, add or change remote administrators, modify AAA client information, back up the system, view reports, and more. Reports track connection activities,

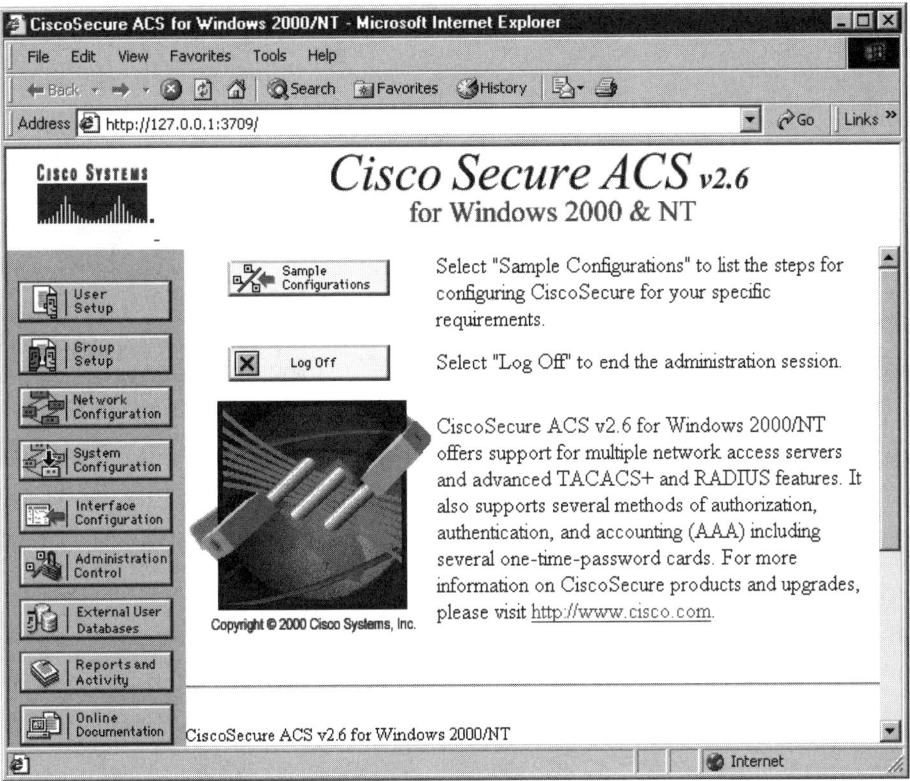

Figure 4-5 Cisco Secure ACS HTML interface

show users who are logged in, list any failed authentication and authorization attempts, and show a history of the recent tasks of administrators.

The HTML interface has three vertical frames that perform the following functions:

- Navigation bar
- Configuration area
- Display area

Figure 4-6 shows the three frames of the ACS HTML configuration screen.

Navigation Bar

The *navigation bar,* the gray frame on the left of the browser window, contains the task buttons. Each button changes the configuration area (second panel) to a section of the

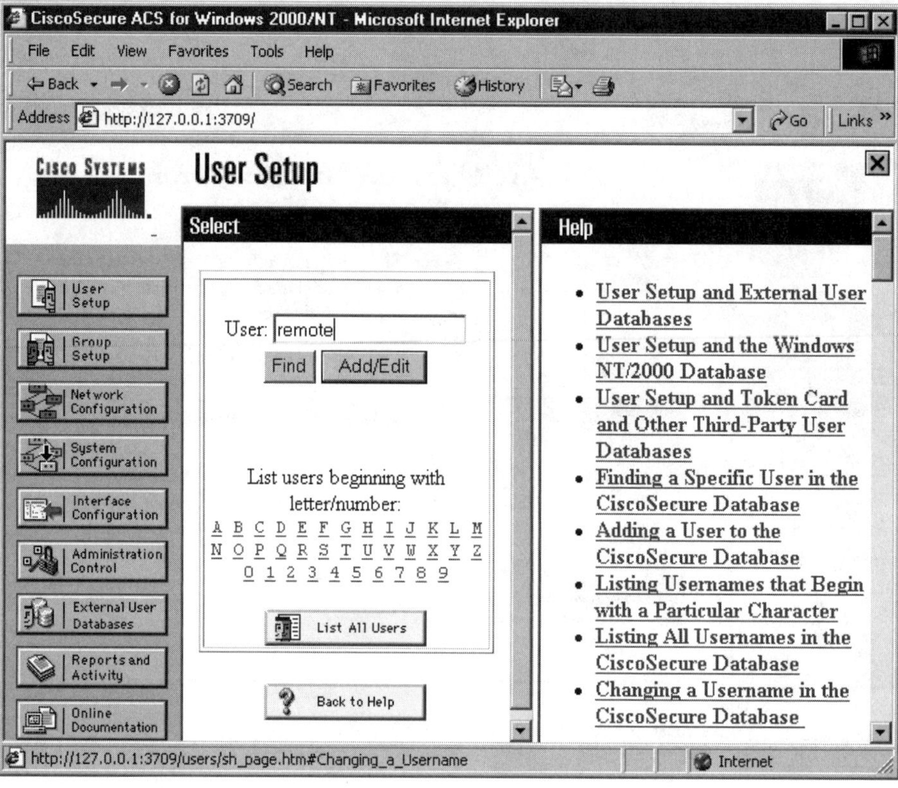

Figure 4-6 ACS configuration screen

Cisco Secure ACS application. This frame doesn't change; it always contains the following buttons:

User Setup	Add and edit user profiles.
Group Setup	Configure network services and protocols for user groups.
Network Configuration	Add and edit network access devices.
System Configuration	Configure database information and accounting.
Interface Configuration	Display or hide product features and options.
Administration Control	Define and configure access policies.
External User Databases	Configure external databases for authentication.
Reports And Activity	Display various accounting and logging summaries.
Online Documentation	View the Cisco Secure ACS User Guide.

PART II

Configuration Area

The *Configuration Area*, middle frame, displays web pages that belong to one of the sections represented by the buttons in the navigation bar. The configuration area is where you add, edit, or delete program setup information. For example, in Figure 4-6, it's possible to find a particular user and change their user information.

Most configuration pages have an appropriate Submit button at the bottom that's used to confirm your changes. Figure 4-7 shows the Submit button options. The Submit + Restart button is used for those configuration changes that require stopping and restarting the services. If you don't click the Submit button or click the Cancel button, the changes won't be saved.

Display Area

The Display Area, right-side frame, shows one of the following options, depending on the button selected in the navigation bar.

Online Help	Basic help about the page currently shown in the Configuration Area. This help isn't intended to be in-depth information but, instead, basic information about the topic in the middle frame. For more detailed information, click Section Information at the bottom of the page to go to the applicable part of Online Documentation.
Reports Or Lists	Displays available lists or reports, including accounting summary reports. Most listings are hyperlinks to the specific configuration views, so clicking the link enables you to edit that item.
System Messages	Displays system and error messages after you submit your changes, indicating the nature of the problem. Any incorrect information remains in the Configuration Area for easy review and correction.

Accessing the HTML Interface

The HTML interface can be reached by using a web browser from anywhere on the network at either of the following URLs. The first two lines show the syntax, while the last two are examples.

```
http://windows-server-IP-address:2002
http://windows-server-host-name:2002
http://192.168.1.3:2002
http://wilson:2002
```

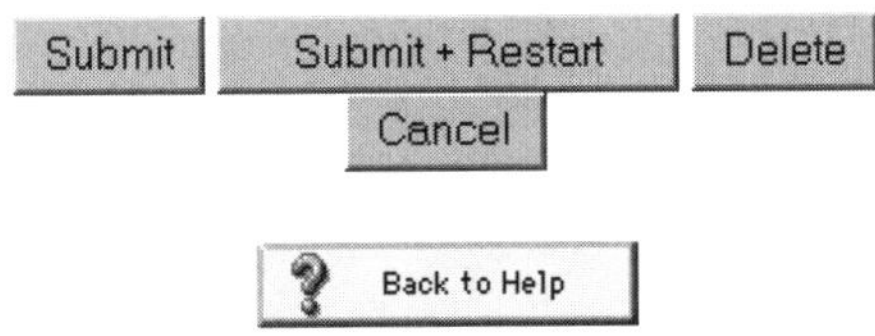

Figure 4-7 Configuration Area Submit and Cancel buttons

If Cisco Secure ACS is installed on the local server you're accessing with a web browser, it's possible to use either of the following two URLs. These commands take advantage of default naming and addressing standards.

```
http://localhost:2002
http://127.0.0.1:2002
```

Remote administrative sessions always require a login using a valid administrator name and password, as configured in the Administration Control section.

To access the Cisco Secure ACS configuration HTML interface, follow these steps:

1. Open a web browser.
2. In the Address or Location bar in the web browser, type the applicable URL.
3. If the Cisco Secure ACS for Windows 2000/NT Login page appears, follow these steps:
    a. Type a valid Cisco Secure ACS administrator name in the User name box.
    b. Type a valid administrator password in the Password box.
    c. Click the Login button.

The Cisco Secure ACS for Windows 2000/NT initial page appears, as shown earlier in Figure 4-5.

Logging Off the HTML Interface

Click the Logoff button to end the ACS session. Failure to do so might allow unauthorized access by someone using the web browser after you, or even unauthorized access through the HTTP port left open to support the administrative session. Cisco Secure ACS can timeout unused administrative sessions.

Remote Administrative Session Issues

Many organization security policies wouldn't allow remote access to resources like the Cisco Secure ACS server. For this reason, various technologies are designed to keep outsiders safely outside the network. The nature of these technologies is often inconsistent with the ACS architecture.

While this isn't always practical, the recommendation is that remote administration sessions not have any of the following technologies between the administration browser and the Cisco Secure ACS server.

- HTTP proxy server
- NAT gateway
- Firewall devices

Each of these technologies can interfere with or prevent connection between the browser and the ACS server. Because these are common technologies, particularly when accessing the ACS server from outside the network, the following explanations and suggestions might be useful.

HTTP Proxy Servers Because of the way proxy servers work between clients and servers, a web browser configured to use a proxy server for a remote administrative session will appear to Cisco Secure ACS server as originating from the IP address of the proxy server, not the address of the remote workstation. ACS remote administrative session tracking requires that each browser resides on a workstation with a unique IP address. ACS administrative sessions using a proxy-enabled web browser is neither tested nor supported.

Suggestion: If the web browser is configured to use a proxy server, disable HTTP proxying before attempting the remote Cisco Secure ACS administrative session.

NAT Gateway If a remote session uses a web browser on a workstation behind a NAT gateway, the gateway substitutes a global "public" address for the workstation's real local IP address. When ACS receives the HTTP requests, the NAT device's public IP address conflicts with the workstation's private IP address *included in the content of the HTTP requests.* Cisco Secure ACS won't allow this.

If the Cisco Secure ACS server is behind a NAT gateway, you could try to configure the NAT gateway to forward all connections to port 2002 to the Cisco Secure ACS server, retaining the port 2002. In addition, all the ports allowed using the HTTP port allocation feature must be similarly mapped. Cisco hasn't tested this and it doesn't support this implementation.

Firewall Devices Firewalls implementing NAT would fall into the last section. For firewalls not performing NAT, remote ACS administrative sessions conducted across the firewall will require additional configuration of both the ACS software and the firewall. This is necessary because ACS assigns a random HTTP port at the beginning of a remote administrative session.

The firewall must be configured to allow HTTP traffic across the range of ports ACS is configured to use. This can be configured using the HTTP port allocation feature to configure the range of TCP ports to be used by Cisco Secure ACS for remote administrative HTTP sessions. The firewall must also be configured to permit HTTP traffic through port 2002 because this is the port a remote web browser must access to initiate an administrative session.

To reduce the risk of malicious discovery of an active administrative port by an unauthorized user, keep the HTTP port range as narrow as possible. Any unauthorized user would have to impersonate, or "spoof," the IP address of the legitimate remote host to use the active administrative session HTTP port.

Suggested Configuration Sequence

No single set of steps, or even order of steps, exists for configuring ACS. The size and topology of the network, the types of network access supported, and even the technological skills of the administrative staff will all be factors. The CCO latest documentation, and security alerts, as well as the ACS documentation feature, should always be consulted before and during the final implementation begins. The following sequence is keyed to the functions represented in the navigation toolbar.

Configure Administrators

Configure at least one administrator (Administration Control button), or there's no remote administrative access and all configuration activity must be done from the server. The administrative policy and security policy should dictate the number and details of administrator accounts.

Configure the ACS Web Interface

You can configure ACS HTML interface (Interface Configuration button) to show only those features and controls you plan to use. This streamlines ACS, making it less difficult to use, less intimidating, and easier to train new administrators to use. The downside, of course, is that features and controls aren't available and are possibly unknown to the staff because they aren't present.

Aspects of the web interface that can be configured in this section include the following:

- **User Data Configuration Options** You can add (or edit) up to five fields for recording information on each user.
- **Advanced Options** Over 20 options ranging from User-Level Network Access Restrictions to Voice-over-IP (VoIP) Accounting options.
- **Protocol Configuration Options for TACACS+** Settings enable the display or hiding of TACACS+ administrative and accounting options.
- **Protocol Configuration Options for RADIUS** Settings enable the display or hiding of RADIUS administrative and accounting options.

Figure 4-8 shows some of the configuration options available in setting up TACACS+.

Configure System

Figure 4-9 shows some of the dozen or more features that can be configured within the System Configuration section (System Configuration button). This is where the Logging options are made that can be used later to produce reports. ACS comprises several Windows NT/2000 services. The Service Control page provides basic status information about the services, and enables you to configure the service log files, and to stop or restart the services.

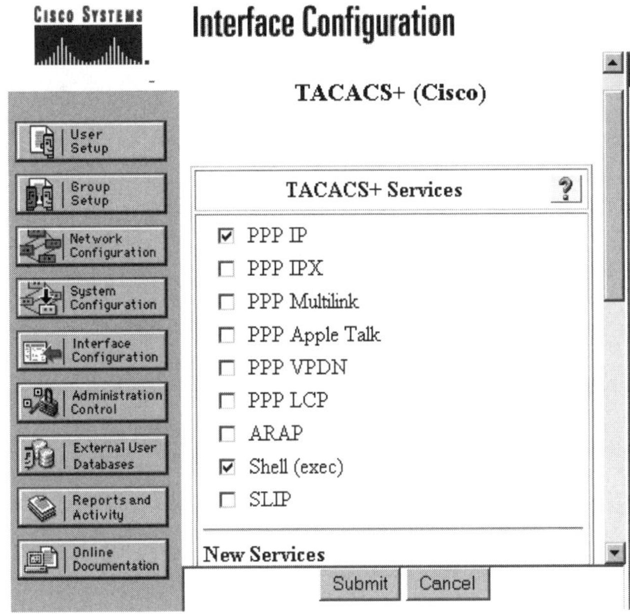

Figure 4-8 Interface configuration setting TACACS+ features

Configure Network

Figure 4-10 shows the network configuration (Network Configuration button) used to control distributed and proxied AAA functions. This section is used to establish the identity, location, and grouping of AAA clients and servers, and to determine what authentication protocols each is to employ.

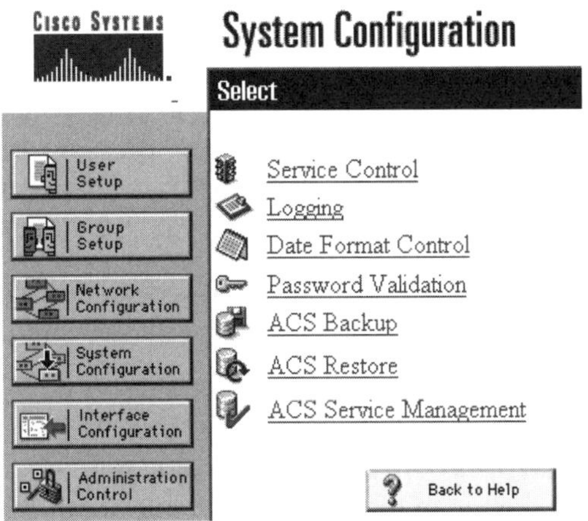

Figure 4-9 ACS System Configuration options

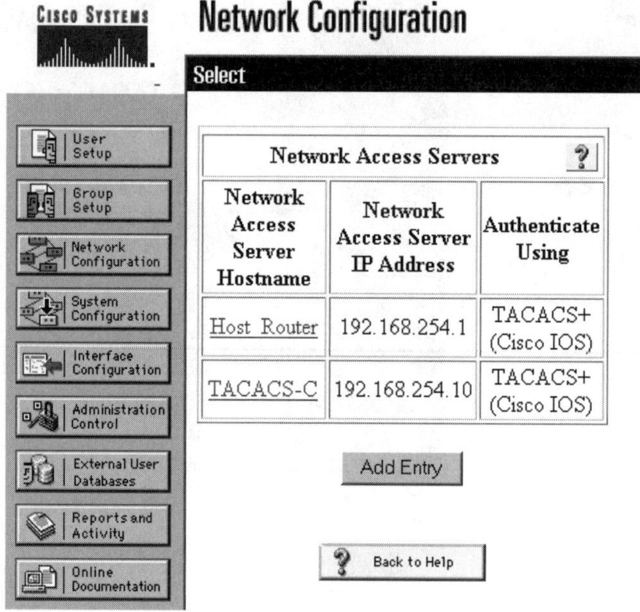

Figure 4-8 Network configuration showing the NAS router and the AAA server

Configure External User Database

The External User Databases button is used to implement an external database to establish and maintain user authentication accounts. This configuration usually is based on the existing network administration mechanisms. In addition to implementing an external user database (or databases), this section is used to define requirements for ACS database replication, backup, and synchronization.

Configure Shared Profile Components

The Shared Profile Components section enables administrators to develop and name reusable, shared sets of authorization components, which might be applied to one or more users, or groups of users, and referenced by the assigned name within their profiles. These include network access restrictions (NARs), command authorization sets, and downloadable PIX ACLs.

- NARs enable the administrator to define additional authorization conditions that must be met before a user can gain access to the network.
- Command authorization sets provide a central mechanism to control the authorization of each command on each network device.
- Downloadable PIX ACLs enable the creation of an ACL once, in Cisco Secure ACS, and then load that ACL to any number of PIX firewalls that authenticate using the Cisco IOS/PIX protocol.

These shared profile components enhance the scalability of the selective authorization feature. Shared profile components, once configured, can be applied to many users or groups, and they eliminate having to configure the authorization explicitly for each user group for each possible command on each possible device.

Configure Groups

Figure 4-11 shows some of the features that can be assigned to groups (Group Setup button), much the same way group permissions are used in the Windows authentication model. It's always easier to deal with group privileges, permissions, or features, and then make sure the appropriate users are in the correct groups. This not only facilitates setting up a new user, it also facilitates removing all of a user's permissions and features when they leave the organization.

Configure Users

Figure 4-12 shows defining a User account (User Setup button). Once the groups are defined, it's time to create the user accounts. Note, unlike the Windows groups methods, a user can belong to only one user group and user level settings always override group level settings.

Configure Reports

The Reports And Activity section (Reports or Lists button) is used to specify the nature and scope of logging that ACS performs, which, ultimately, determine the reports that can be generated.

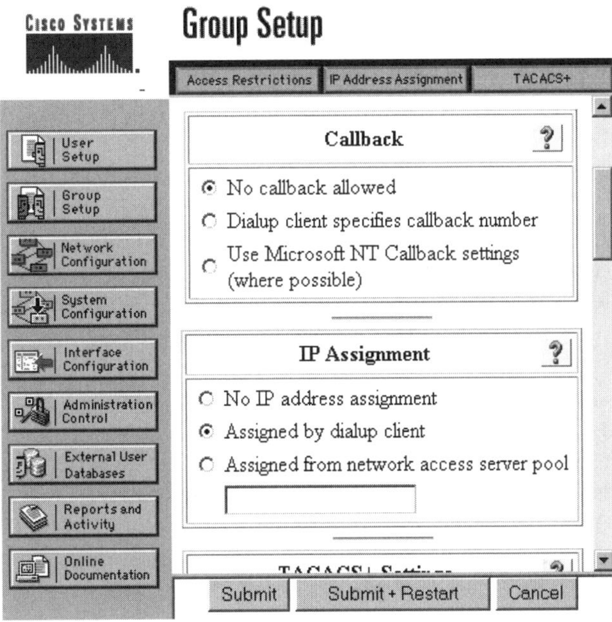

Figure 4-9 Example of group setup options

Figure 4-10 User account entry screen

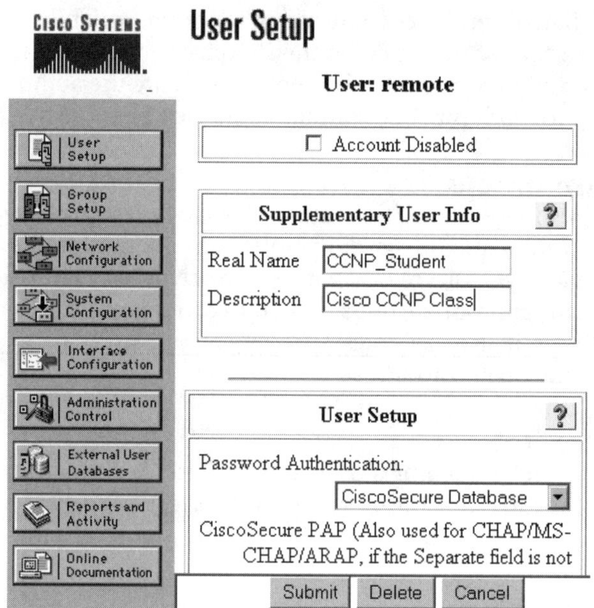

TACACS+ Overview

TACACS+ is an authentication protocol that allows a network access server to communicate with an authentication server to determine if a user has access to the network.

TACACS+ is a new protocol developed by Cisco that replaces two earlier industry standards—TACACS and XTACACS (Extended). TACACS+ is *not* compatible with the two older protocols. Cisco has submitted TACACS+ protocol specification in a draft RFC to the IETF for development of a standard and for those customers interested in developing their own TACACS+ software.

TACACS+ server services are maintained in a database on a TACACS+ daemon running on a Windows 2000/NT or UNIX host. Cisco's servers supporting TACACS+ include CiscoSecure ACS for Windows, CiscoSecure UNIX, and Cisco Access Registrar. Cisco Access Servers (Cisco Secure ACS) can implement both TACACS+ and RADIUS. The underlying architecture of TACACS+ protocol complements the AAA architecture.

TACACS+ fully supports the AAA architecture by separating the authentication, authorization, and accounting. This allows the flexibility of using another service, such as Kerberos, for authentication, while still using TACACS+ for authorization and/or accounting.

TACACS+ uses TCP for connection-oriented transport between clients and servers. TCP port 49 is reserved for TACACS+. The acknowledgments (TCP ACK) provide indications that a request has been received. This same TCP process uses RST packets to provide immediate indication of a failed (or offline) authentication server. TCP keepalives can be used to watch for failed servers and to facilitate rapid failover between multiple connected authentication servers. TCP scales better and adapts better to growing and/or congested networks.

TACACS+ supports bidirectional challenge/response, like CHAP, between the two network access servers.

In addition to supporting SLIP and PPP encapsulation protocols, TACACS+ supports the following protocols:

- Novell Asynchronous Services Interface (NASI)
- X.25 PAD connection
- Net BIOS Frame Protocol Control protocol
- AppleTalk Remote Access protocol (ARAP)

Packet Encryption TACACS+ encrypts the entire data payload of the packet, leaving only the standard TACACS+ header in cleartext. While it's possible for debugging purposes to leave the body of the packets unencrypted, normal operation will fully encrypt the body for more secure communications. A field in the header indicates whether the body is encrypted.

- TACACS+ supports two methods for controlling the authorization of router commands on either a per-user or per-group basis.
- Assign commands to privilege levels and have the router use TACACS+ to verify that the user is authorized at the specified privilege level.

Explicitly define on the TACACS+ server the commands allowed on a per-user or per-group basis.

Configuring Cisco Secure ACS and TACACS+

Basic Cisco Secure ACS configuration for TACACS+ support is performed using the Interface Configuration button on the ACS HTML interface. The interface settings enable you to display or hide TACACS+ administrative and accounting options. You can simplify the HTML interface by hiding the features you don't use. Figure 4-13 shows configuring TACACS+ options and features.

The TACACS+ section includes three areas:

TACACS+ Services Settings	This section lists the most commonly used TACACS+ services and protocols. Select each TACACS+ service to appear as a configurable option on either the User Setup page or the Group Setup page.
New Services	Specify any services or protocols unique to your network configuration.
Advanced Configuration Options	Advanced TACACS+ features.

PART II

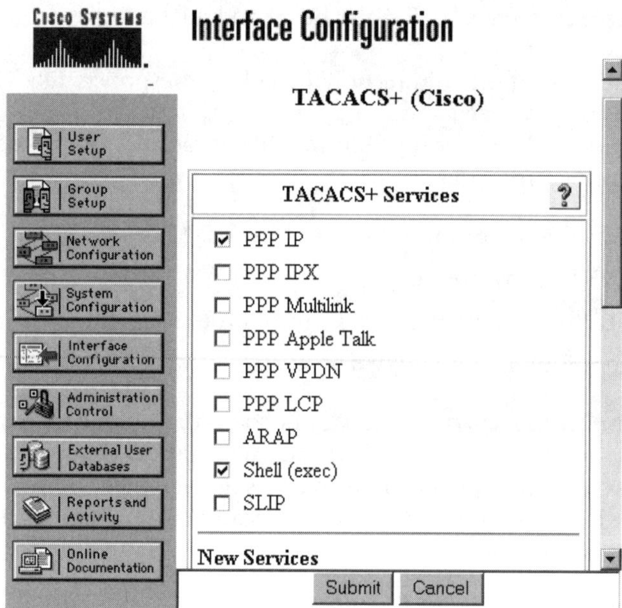

Figure 4-11 Configuring TACACS+ features

To configure the user interface for TACACS+ options, follow these steps:

1. Click the Interface Configuration button.
2. Click TACACS+. The TACACS+ Interface Configuration section appears.
3. In the TACACS+ Services table, select the check box for each TACACS+ service you want displayed on the applicable setup page.
4. To add new services and protocols, follow these steps:
   a. In the New Services section of the TACACS+ Services table, type in the Service and Protocol to add.
   b. Use the appropriate check box to select those to be displayed for configuration either under User Setup or Group Setup, or both.
5. In the Advanced Configurations Options section, select the check boxes of the display options you want to enable.
6. When you finish setting TACACS+ interface display options, click Submit. The selections made in this procedure determine what TACACS+ options Cisco Secure ACS displays in other sections of the HTML interface.

Configure NAS to TACACS+ Server Communication

Chapter 3 looked at the various commands to implement AAA features on the NAS. This chapter reviews the basic commands to allow the AAA client running on a NAS to locate and communicate with a Cisco Secure ACS TACACS+ server.

To define one or more TACACS servers, use the **tacacs-server host** global configuration command. Use the no form of this command to delete the specified server. The syntax is

Rtr1(config)#tacacs-server host {*hostname* | *ip address*} [single-connection] [port *port#*]
    [timeout *seconds*] [key *string*]
Rtr1(config)#no tacacs-server host *hostname*

hostname	Name of the TACACS+ server.
ip-addresss	IP address of the TACACS+ server.
single-connection	(Optional) Specify that the router maintain a single open connection for confirmation from the AAA/TACACS+ server. This command contains the no autodetect feature and fails if the host isn't running a CiscoSecure daemon.
port	(Optional) Overrides the default, which is port 49.
port#	(Optional) Port number of the server (range 1 to 65535).
timeout	(Optional) Overrides the global timeout value set with the global **tacacs-server timeout** command for this server only.
seconds	(Optional) New timeout interval in seconds.
key	(Optional) Specify an authentication and encryption key. This must match the key used by the TACACS+ daemon. This key overrides the key set by the global command **tacacs-server key** for this server only.
string	(Optional) Character string to use as the authentication and encryption key.

Multiple **tacacs-server host** commands can be used to specify additional host servers. The Cisco IOS software searches for hosts in the order in which they're specified. Use the single-connection, port, timeout, and key options only when running an AAA/TACACS+ server.

Because some of the parameters of the **tacacs-server host** command override global settings made by the **tacacs-server timeout** and **tacacs-server key** commands, this command can be used to enhance security on a network by uniquely configuring individual TACACS+ connections.

The following AAA example specifies that the router first try the CiscoSecure TACACS+ host 192.168.1.4. If 192.168.1.4 is unavailable, then use tac-serv1.

```
Rtr1(config)#aaa new-model
Rtr1(config)#tacacs-server host 192.168.1.4
Rtr1(config)#tacacs-server host tac-serv1
```

The next AAA example specifies that the router consult the CiscoSecure TACACS+ host named 192.168.1.4 on port number 51. The timeout value for requests on this connection is three seconds. The encryption key is a_secret.

```
Rtr1(config)#aaa new-model
Rtr1(config)#tacacs-server host 192.168.1.4 single-connection port 51
     timeout 3 key a_secret
```

Define TACACS+ Server Key Option

The authentication and encryption key must be set using the **tacacs-server key** global configuration command. Use the no form of this command to disable the key.

Rtr1(config)#tacacs-server key *key*
Rtr1(config)#no tacacs-server key [*key*]

key	A character entry, this key must match the key used on the TACACS+ daemon. Any leading spaces are ignored, *but spaces within and at the end of the key are not ignored.* Don't enclose the key in quotation marks unless those quotation marks are part of the key.

The following example shows an AAA TACACS+ implementation with the authentication and encryption key set to seattle19:

```
Rtr1(config)#aaa new-model
Rtr1(config)#tacacs-server host 192.168.1.4
Rtr1(config)#tacacs-server key seattle19
```

Verifying TACACS+

Troubleshooting and verifying TACACS+ can be rather complex because it's used so often with other features, such as PPP. Remember to use the troubleshooting commands associated with any protocols or technologies working with TACACS+.

The show Commands

Two show commands that are useful in debugging AAA are the following:

show running-config	To verify local TACACS+ is configured correctly, enter
show tacacs	To verify network connectivity between NAS and AAA server

The debug Commands

Cisco IOS debug command output provides a valuable source of information and feedback concerning state transitions and functions within the AAA environment. In addition to debug command output gathered directly from devices running Cisco IOS, the Cisco AAA server can be configured to collect operational diagnostics. Use the following debug commands to capture AAA-related transitions and functions.

debug condition user *username*	Sets conditional debugging for a specific user and generates output debugs related to the user
debug aaa authentication	Displays authentication information with TACACS+ client/server interaction
debug aaa authorization	Displays authorization information with TACACS+ client/server interaction

debug aaa accounting	Displays accounting information with TACACS+ client/server interaction
debug tacacs	Displays TACACS+ interaction between the IOS client and the AAA server
debug ppp negotiation	Sees if a client is passing PPP negotiation
debug ppp authentication	Sees if a client is passing authentication
debug ppp error	Displays protocol errors and error statistics associated with PPP connection negotiation and operation

Configure NAS to RADIUS Server Communication

Chapter 4 looked at the various commands to implement AAA features on the NAS. This chapter reviews the basic commands to allow the AAA client running on a NAS to locate and communicate with Cisco Secure ACS RADIUS+ server.

To define one or more RADIUS servers, use the **radius-server host global** configuration command. Use the no form of this command to delete the specified RADIUS host. The syntax is

Rtr1(config)#radius-server host {*hostname* | *ip-address*} [auth-port *port-number*] [acct-port *port-number*] [timeout *seconds*] [retransmit *retries*] [key *string*] [alias{*hostname* | *ip-address*}]
Rtr1(config)#no radius-server host {*hostname* | *ip-address*} [auth-port *port-number*] [acct-port *port-number*] [timeout *seconds*] [retransmit *retries*] [key *string*]

hostname	DNS name of the RADIUS server.
ip-address	IP address of the RADIUS server.
auth-port	(Optional) To specify a UDP destination port for authentication requests.
port-number	(Optional) Port number for authentication requests. The host isn't used for authentication if set to 0.
acct-port	(Optional) To specify a UDP destination port for accounting requests.
port-number	(Optional) Port number for accounting requests. The host isn't used for accounting if set to 0.

Use multiple **radius-server host** commands to specify multiple hosts. The software searches for hosts in the order they're specified.

The following example specifies host1 as the RADIUS server and uses default ports for both accounting and authentication.

```
Rtr1(config)#aaa new-model
Rtr1(config)#radius-server host host1.domain.com
```

The next example defines port 12 as the destination port for authentication requests and port 16 as the destination port for accounting requests on a RADIUS host named

192.168.1.4. Because entering a line resets all the port numbers, you must specify a host and configure both the accounting and authentication ports on a single line.

```
Rtr1(config)#aaa new-model
Rtr1(config)#radius-server host 192.168.1.4 auth-port 12 acct-port 16
```

To use separate servers for accounting and authentication, use the zero port value as appropriate. The following example specifies that RADIUS server 192.168.1.4 be used for accounting, but not for authentication, and RADIUS server host1 be used for authentication, but not for accounting:

```
Rtr1(config)#aaa new-model
Rtr1(config)#radius-server host 192.168.1.4 auth-port 0
Rtr1(config)#radius-server host host1.domain.com acct-port 0
```

Define RADIUS Server Key Option

The authentication and encryption key must be set using the **radius-server key** global configuration command. Use the no form of this command to disable the key.

Rtr1(config)#radius-server key *key*
Rtr1(config)#no radius-server key [*key*]

key	A character entry, this key must match the key used on the RADIUS daemon. Any leading spaces are ignored, *but spaces within and at the end of the key are not.* Don't enclose the key in quotation marks unless they're part of the key.

The following example shows an AAA RADIUS implementation with the authentication and encryption key set to seattle19:

```
Rtr1(config)#aaa new-model
Rtr1(config)#radius-server host 192.168.1.4
Rtr1(config)#radius-server key seattle19
```

Chapter Review

The CiscoSecure Access Control Server (ACS) is a server-based application offering centralized user access control support for the various network devices. CiscoSecure ACS can be installed on either Windows or UNIX servers that meet minimum resource requirements.

ACS allows the administrator to manage user access for Cisco IOS routers, firewalls, Cisco Catalyst switches, and virtual private networks (VPNs), as well as newer technologies like dial-up and broadband DSL, cable access solutions, voice over IP (VoIP), Cisco wireless implementations, and third-party vendor TACACS+ offerings.

ACS is a strategic product at Cisco, incorporating new advanced features as they become available to increase the diversity and granularity of implementations. Current support includes the use of network OS security databases and management tools, user and administrative access reporting, database synchronization and user importation tools, Lightweight Directory Access Protocol (LDAP) user authentication support, dynamic quota generation, and restrictions such as time of day and day of week, as well as user and device group profiles.

Questions

1. Which two of the following are server platforms supported by Cisco Secure ACS?
   A. Novell NetWare
   B. Microsoft Windows
   C. UNIX (Sun Solaris)
   D. Linux
2. Which one of the following isn't controllable by a network administrator using Cisco Secure ACS for Windows?
   A. What accounting information is kept for capacity planning, account billing, or security audits
   B. What privileges each user will have while in the network
   C. What encryption method will be used for interdevice communications
   D. Which users can access the network from either wired or wireless connections
   E. What access and command controls are enabled for each configuration administrator
3. Which IEEE standard is being introduced to support CiscoSecure ACS in the LAN?
   A. 802.1q
   B. 802.11b
   C. 802.1*x*
   D. 802.3au
4. True or False. Cisco Secure ACS for Windows does *not* support MSCHAP version 2.
   A. True
   B. False
5. True or False. Cisco Secure ACS for Windows supports per-user access control lists.
   A. True
   B. False
6. True or False. Cisco Secure ACS for Windows requires a choice between TACACS+ and RADIUS support.
   A. True
   B. False

PART II

7. Cisco Secure ACS supports Token Card authentication on which platform?
   A. Windows only
   B. UNIX only
   C. Both UNIX and Windows
   D. Neither one
8. Which Cisco Secure ACS for Windows service is the internal web server?
   A. CSAuth
   B. CSMon
   C. CSLog
   D. CSAdmin
9. Which Cisco Secure ACS-supported database would provide fastest authentication?
   A. Windows NT/2000 user database
   B. Novell NDS
   C. Token Card servers
   D. CiscoSecure user database
10. Which of the following does *not* impact Cisco Secure ACS server performance?
    A. Number and size of the CPUs
    B. Amount of server memory
    C. Number of users in the database
    D. Remote users connection speed
11. Which of the following won't work as a Cisco Secure ACS platform?
    A. Windows 2000 Server
    B. Windows 2000 Advanced Server
    C. Windows 2000 Datacenter Server
    D. Windows 2000 Professional
    E. Windows NT Server 4.0
12. True or False. Cisco Secure ACS for Windows and UNIX are identical, and they provide the same features and service.
    A. True
    B. False
13. True or False. One limitation of Cisco Secure ACS for UNIX is its lack of support for TACACS+.
    A. True
    B. False

14. Once installed, Cisco Secure ACS is configured and administered using what?
    A. CLI only
    B. Web browser only
    C. CLI and/or web browser
    D. Windows Management Interface
15. Which two of the following will only access the ACS HTML interface using a web browser from the server on which Cisco Secure ACS is installed?
    A. http://*Windows-server-IP-address*:2002
    B. http://localhost:2002
    C. http://*Windows-server-host-name*:2002
    D. http://127.0.0.1:2002

Answers

1. **B. and C.** Microsoft Windows and UNIX (Sun Solaris)
2. **C.** What encryption method will be used for interdevice communications
3. **C.** 802.1*x*
4. **B.** False. With ACS for Windows v3.0, it now supports MSCHAP.
5. **A.** True
6. **B.** False. It will support both simultaneously.
7. **C.** Both UNIX and Windows
8. **B.** CSMon
9. **D.** CiscoSecure user database because it's internal to ACS
10. **D.** The remote users connection speed
11. **D.** Windows 2000 Professional. It must be a version of the server.
12. **B.** False
13. **B.** False. Cisco Secure ACS for UNIX supports both.
14. **B.** Web browser only
15. **B.** http://localhost:2002 and d. http://127.0.0.1:2002

CHAPTER 5

Securing Cisco Perimeter Routers

In this chapter, you will learn about:

- Eavesdropping
- Limiting unnecessary services
- Denial of service attacks
- Unauthorized access
- Lack of legal IP addresses
- Rerouting attacks
- Lack of information about an attack

This chapter looks at those IOS features that can be used on the borders of the network to ward off unwanted and malicious traffic. Chapters 6 and 7 pick up with those additional features included in the Cisco IOS Firewall feature set. In many ways, this chapter pulls together information covered in the first three chapters. In Chapter 1, you learned that the four most common types of network attacks are reconnaissance attacks, access attacks, denial of service (DoS) attacks, and data manipulation attacks.

The *perimeter router* is the first line of defense against each of these threats. While the perimeter router can often thwart reconnaissance, access, and data manipulation attacks, it typically requires the assistance of the company's ISP to deal with DoS attacks.

Perimeter Router Terms and Concepts

A *network*, like a city or village, has an area where the network meets the outside world. Unlike a city, this interface is limited to those devices—hopefully routers—that have connections both to the inside of the network and with the outside world. Typically, an ISP is at the other end of that connection, and then the Internet.

In the preceding two chapters, you looked at network access servers (NAS), which also constitute a part of the network boundary. These NAS connections are a little different, in that security technologies like AAA can be set up to limit access to only those remote dial-in users with preestablished login authority. On the other hand, the network boundary, or perimeter, routers often must allow access to persons unknown to the corporate shared resources, such as web and FTP servers. Furthermore, perimeter router connections also provide access for the Internet, which then exposes the network to other risks.

Simple Secure Network Design

In Chapter 1, you saw a simplified example of a secure network design. Figure 5-1 expands on that view. The perimeter router represents the border crossing or the demarcation point between the outside world and the internal network.

In a small branch office or in a telecommuter's home, a single perimeter router might be the only barrier between the inside and outside network. The features and configuration of that lone device would be the only line of defense. Many larger networks use a design similar to that shown in Figure 5-1, called screened subnet architecture. In *screened subnet architecture,* two devices work together with a router as the perimeter device and the firewall as the second line of defense. The result is three types of networks: inside, outside, and an area called the demilitarized zone (DMZ).

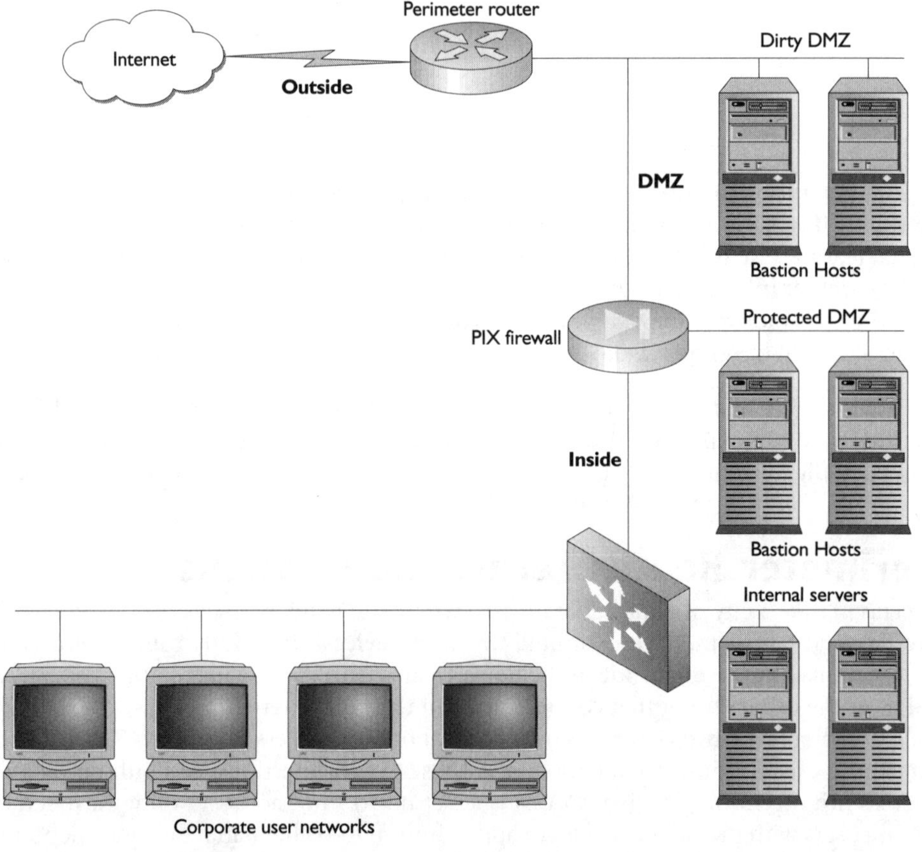

Figure 5-1 Network design with perimeter security

Inside Network

Inside networks are also referred to as the internal or private networks. The *inside area* is made up of the corporate network(s), including all workstations and, typically, any servers not shared with the outside world. These devices are considered trusted and can be accessed freely by other inside hosts. These *trusted* devices need to be protected from the outside world and even from attackers that might have compromised the DMZ area(s). The inside area is under one administrative authority and operates under a common security plan.

The inside area is often connected to one of the firewall interfaces, the *inside interface.* Additional firewalls might be used within the inside area to offer secure separation between two or more subnets. The company security policy might specify a firewall between the accounting/finance departments and the other operating units.

Outside Network

The *outside network* is also referred to as the external or public network. The outside area, or *untrusted area,* is considered to be all devices and networks beyond the direct control of the organization's administration and security policies. The outside area typically includes everything beyond the external interface of the perimeter router, the ISP, and the Internet and all networks attached to it.

The outside network wouldn't normally be attached directly to a firewall device because of media and data framing issues. A firewall device like the Cisco PIX devices have LAN interfaces only requiring another device between the firewall and the serial WAN connection. The perimeter router, possibly a lower-end model, provides the media conversion, framing transition, and any first-line security services.

Demilitarized Zone (DMZ)

The DMZ can be two or more areas inside the network perimeter, but not on the *inside* of the firewall device. The first type of DMZ, often called the *dirty DMZ* or *dirty net,* is the LAN segment between the perimeter router and the firewall. This area has only the protection of the perimeter router and the individual security features of any devices placed there. The second type of DMZ is made up of one or more additional LAN interfaces on the firewall. These areas are often called *protected DMZs* because they have the additional protection offered by the firewall device.

Not uncommonly, some firewall devices offer six or more interfaces, allowing for multiple protected DMZs with different security requirements. Special thought would have to be given to whether any performance benefits from the dirty DMZ only being "filtered" once is offset by the increased risk to whatever is placed out there.

DMZs contain shared server resources, such as web, DNS, and e-mail servers. These servers are available to the outside world. These shared servers are often called bastion hosts, bastion servers, or even sacrificial hosts. *Bastion hosts* must be hardened, and they receive the highest priority security maintenance because of their vulnerability to the outside world and increased likelihood of attacks. A *bastion server* typically runs only those specific services being shared, and all other services will be stopped or turned off.

The dirty DMZ is bordered by the outside interface of the firewall device and the internal interface of the perimeter router. The firewall must be configured to allow loose, but regulated, access to the protected DMZ from the outside network, while at the same time protecting the inside network. Inside network users need access to the server resources in the DMZ and are typically allowed limited access, possibly restricting access to only those sessions originating within the inside network.

Firewall

A *firewall* is a device that separates or joins the inside network to the dirty DMZ and any optional protected DMZs. The firewall can be a router-running firewall feature set, a specialty server with two or more NICs in different networks, or a specialty device like the Cisco PIX that does nothing but provide firewall services. While suitable applications exist for each type of firewall, generally best is to use a dedicated device performing only security features, and leave routing and serving to other devices.

In a network like the example in Figure 5-1, the firewall would typically be configured to prevent access from the outside to the inside, possibly limiting access to those sessions originating from the inside network. The firewall configuration might allow inside users access to DMZ resources, while providing some defense for the inside from attackers who compromise a bastion host.

Unsolicited access from the outside directed to the inside would typically be blocked. Certain well-thought-out exceptions and configurations could be created, so e-mail server(s) residing on the inside network, instead of the DMZ, could still exchange e-mails. Securing this type of connection is covered in the firewall chapters.

The typical firewall device has two or more LAN interfaces: one each for the inside and outside networks. Optionally, an additional LAN interface can exist for each protected DMZ network. Today, the LAN interfaces are typically Fast Ethernet or Gigabit Ethernet, but there's no reason they couldn't be Ethernet, Token Ring, or FDDI.

Some small firewalls used in implementations like branch locations or telecommuter residences could only have two interfaces for separating the inside network from the outside world. In those small implementations, the inside interface could connect to a user machine via a crossover cable, or to a small hub or switch. The external interface would often connect to the DSL, cable modem, or ISDN device. The Cisco 806 router, shown in Figure 5-2, with an Ethernet interface, four-port hub, Cisco IOS, and supporting the firewall feature set, is an example.

While a firewall is normally used to separate the inside network from the outside world, also possible is to use a firewall to separate internal departments where additional

Figure 5-2 Cisco 806 router for telecommuter or small office firewalls

security is required. For example, a school might choose to place a firewall between the student network and the faculty network. In this case, the firewall might have only two interfaces, with the *inside* interface connected to the protected network and the *outside* interface connected to the network perceived as the potential threat.

Perimeter Router

The *perimeter router* is typically a standard router providing a serial connection to the outside world and a LAN connection to the internal network. The perimeter router should provide any filtering of outside traffic to implement basic security for the dirty DMZ and preliminary filtering for the inside network. This device could be running the firewall feature set for additional security options.

Because the perimeter router is often connected to a slower WAN interface on one side and it doesn't normally provide routing functions for internal networks, the LAN interface speed isn't as critical as making sure adequate memory and features exist to handle the outside connection. Even if the inside network is 100MB and all protected DMZ interfaces are full-duplex 100MB, if the Internet connection is a T1 (1.54MB), then a 10MB LAN interface on the perimeter router shouldn't impede traffic. Even most DSL or cable connections would be well below 10MB.

While bandwidth issues are important, feature sets are important on perimeter routers. Routers clear down to the 800 series support access list, firewall features, and so forth, making low-end devices attractive in some perimeter implementations. If intrusion detection features are needed, though, you should know that the firewall feature sets for devices below the 2600 devices don't include them. So, while a 1700 or 2500 device might handle the traffic, it won't provide intrusion detection services.

The next chapter looks at the Cisco IOS firewall feature set and the additional features it can add to the perimeter router.

Eavesdropping

Eavesdropping, using packet-sniffing tools, allows attackers to read transmitted information, including logon information and database contents. Eavesdropping can yield information, such as credit card information, which can be used in later transactions, damaging both the customer and the business that allowed the breach.

A related problem involves eavesdropping and session replay in which the attacker retransmits the captured data, such as a session logon sequence to gain access to network resources.

Router Solutions

If you're using a dynamic routing protocol that supports authentication, a good idea is to enable that authentication. This prevents some malicious attacks on the routing infrastructure and it can also help to prevent damage caused by misconfigured "rogue" network devices.

Configuring Authentication Example

Many routing protocols support authentication and the commands vary somewhat, but the following example demonstrates the feature using RIP version 2.

RIP version 1 doesn't support authentication, but RIP version 2 allows RIP authentication on a per-interface basis. RIP supports two modes of authentication: plaintext authentication and MD5 authentication. The default is plaintext authentication. Don't use plaintext authentication for security purposes because the unencrypted authentication key is sent in every RIP version 2 packet. Interfaces on both sides of the link must be configured for MD5 authentication using the same key number and key string.

The key chain determines the set of keys that can be used on the interface. If a key chain isn't configured, no authentication is performed on that interface, not even the default authentication.

The following commands configure RIP authentication. The first three are configured in Global Configuration mode and the last two are in Interface Configuration mode.

Command	Purpose
key chain *name*	Names a key chain. Could contain more than one key for added security.
key *number*	Defines the first key in the key chain.
key-string *string*	Defines the key value—must be identical on both ends of the link.
ip rip authentication key-chain *name*	Enables RIP authentication.
ip rip authentication mode {text | md5}	Uses MD5 digest authentication (or defaults to plain text authentication).

```
Rtr1:
key chain seattle
key 1
key-string 9631
!
interface Ethernet 0
  ip address 192.168.1.1 255.255.255.0
!
interface Serial 0
  ip address 192.168.2.1 255.255.255.252
  ip rip authentication mode md5
  ip rip authentication key-chain seattle
!
router rip
  version 2
  network 192.168.1.0
  network 192.168.2.0

Rtr2:
key chain seattle
key 1
key-string 9631
!
interface Ethernet 0
```

```
  ip address 192.168.3.1 255.255.255.0
!
interface Serial0
 ip address 192.168.2.2 255.255.255.252
 ip rip authentication mode md5
 ip rip authentication key-chain seattle
 clockrate 64000
!
router rip
 version 2
 network 192.168.3.0
 network 192.168.2.0
```


Verifying MD5 Authentication

By configuring the Rtr1 and Rtr2 as shown, all routing update exchanges are authenticated before being accepted. Verify this by observing the output obtained from the **debug ip rip** command:

```
Rtr1#debug ip rip
RIP: received packet with MD5 authentication
RIP: received v2 update from 192.168.2.2 on Serial0
     192.168.3.1/24 via 0.0.0.0 in 1 hops
```

MD5 authentication uses the one-way, MD5 hash algorithm in which the routing update doesn't carry the actual password (key) for the purpose of authentication. A128-bit message, generated by running the MD5 algorithm on the password, and the message are sent along for authentication. The recipient device runs the same hash using the key information configured and, assuming it generates the same 128-bit message, the update will be accepted. MD5 hashing is covered in greater detail in Chapter 8.

Encryption and Tunneling

Data separation using tunneling technologies, such as generic routing encapsulation (GRE) or Layer 2 Tunneling Protocol (L2TP), provides effective data privacy. When privacy requirements call for the use of digital encryption technology, protocols such as IPSec provide the added protection when implementing VPNs. The IPSec and VPN chapters, 9 through 16 and 21, cover these features in detail.

Hub and Switch Issues

While less-common than a few years ago, the shared media technology of hubs made them susceptible to sniffing attacks. All an intruder needed was access to any port in the collision domain and they could monitor all traffic. Just changing to switches reduced the threat because the only traffic visible on the port is traffic directed to the attached host or broadcasts.

Many switches support *port monitoring* or *port spanning,* which allows traffic from ports designated for capture to the port designated as the monitor port. The sniffer is attached to this port. Care should be taken to prevent port monitoring.

Limit Unneeded TCP/IP and Other Services

As a general rule, any unnecessary service should be disabled on perimeter routers. The following services are often useful, but should be disabled if they aren't being used.

TCP and UDP "Small Services"

By default, Cisco devices offer the small services: echo, chargen, and discard. These services, especially their UDP versions, are infrequently used for legitimate purposes, but can be used to launch DoS and other attacks, which would otherwise be prevented by packet filtering.

The small services are disabled by default in Cisco IOS 12.0 and later software. In earlier software, they can be disabled using the **no service tcp-small-servers** and **no service udp-small-servers** commands.

Finger

Cisco routers support the "finger" service used to identify which users are logged into a network device. This information can be useful to an attacker. The "finger" service can be disabled with the **no service finger** command.

NTP

The Network Time Protocol (NTP) isn't a particularly dangerous feature. If NTP is being used, be sure to configure a trusted time source and use proper authentication. Corrupting the time on network devices can subvert certain security protocols and cause some processes to fail to synchronize or function. If NTP isn't being used on a particular router interface, it can be disabled with the interface command **no ntp enable**.

CDP

Cisco Discovery Protocol (CDP) is a fairly useful feature, but on the network perimeter, it can be dangerous because it announces the following to any system on a directly connected segment: that the router is a Cisco device, the model number, and the Cisco IOS version being run. This information could be used to exploit vulnerabilities in the router. The CDP protocol can be disabled with the global configuration command **no cdp running**. CDP can be disabled on a particular interface with the **no cdp enable** command.

Denial of Service Attacks

The following Cisco features can be used to increase the basic security measures related to the way in which the router forwards IP packets.

Controlling Directed Broadcasts

An *IP directed broadcast* is a datagram sent to the subnet broadcast address. The directed broadcast is routed through the network as a unicast packet until it arrives at the target subnet, where it's converted into a link-layer broadcast. Only the last router, the one directly connected to the target subnet, can positively identify a directed broadcast.

IP directed broadcasts are used in *smurf* DoS attacks, in which the attacker sends ICMP echo requests from a falsified source address to a directed broadcast address. This causes all the hosts on the target subnet to send replies to the falsified source. By sending a continuous stream of these requests, the attacker can create a much larger stream of replies, burying the smurfed host and their link to their ISP.

The **no ip directed-broadcast** command on an interface causes discards directed broadcasts, such as 192.168.12.255, that would otherwise "explode" into link-layer broadcasts at that interface. The **no ip directed-broadcast** command is the default in Cisco IOS software version 12.0 and later.

Flood Management

As you saw in Chapter 1, many DoS attacks rely on floods of useless packets that congest network links, slow hosts, and overloaded routers. Being aware of where performance bottlenecks lie is important in flood management. If a DoS flood is burying a T1 line, then filtering the flood at the source end router can help, while filtering at the destination end will have little or no effect.

If an "underpowered" router is the bottleneck, then adding additional filtering will probably make things worse. In this case, increasing memory or replacing the device might have to be part of the solution.

Transit Floods

In some cases, Cisco's quality of service (QoS) features can be used against some kinds of floods on serial links. Using weighted fair queuing (WFQ), the default for low-speed serial lines in recent versions of Cisco IOS software, has proven effective against ping floods, but less effective against SYN floods. A *ping flood* appears to WFQ as a single traffic flow, whereas each packet in a SYN flood generally appears as a separate flow. A smurf reply stream falls somewhere between the two. Cisco QoS features are covered extensively on Cisco's web site.

TCP Intercept

The *TCP Intercept* feature is designed specifically to reduce the impact of SYN flooding attacks on hosts. TCP Intercept is available in some IOS versions for many routers with model numbers of 4000 or greater. A device supporting TCP Intercept can literally step in as a proxy and handle TCP session requests for a server that is under attack or heavy load. The device attempts to complete the TCP 3-way handshakes, forwarding successful attempts to the server and discarding the rest.

Antispoofing with RPF Checks

Cisco IOS versions that support Cisco Express Forwarding (CEF) can have the router check the source address of any packet against the interface through which the packet entered the router. If, according to the routing table, the input interface isn't a feasible path to the source address, the packet is then dropped. The feature is known as a *reverse path forwarding (RPF)* check and is enabled with the command **ip verify unicast rpf**.

Unauthorized Access

The perimeter router is the first line of defense against external threats. Features like using access lists to perform traffic filtering, covered in Chapter 2 and Appendix A, can help in the battle. In this section, you learn about the Dynamic and Reflexive access lists.

Address Filtering

RFC 2827 filtering involves filtering out any IP addresses from coming into a network segment, which should already be on that segment. If the entire 195.17.1.0 network is attached to a router interface, then no legitimate packets with source addresses in that network should be coming in through the router. This should be applied to perimeter routers for sure, but it can be used on internal routers to prevent spoofing within the network. Similarly, limiting any outbound packets, leaving the network to ones that have source addresses assigned to that network, can prevent a network's hosts from spoofing other networks. This could be the result of an attacker on the inside or a DoS bot on a local host participating in an attack on an outside host. If the company can get its ISP to perform RFC 2827 filtering on packets coming into the network, it would preserve the bandwidth of the link and kill some hack attempts.

RFC 1918 filtering involves filtering out RFC-defined private addresses from entering or exiting the network segment. Because they have no business on the Internet anyway, they shouldn't be there. If private addresses are used in the network, RFC 2827 filtering will include them. The following is a standard ACL approach, although an extended or named list would also work.

```
interface serial 0
ip access-group 10 in
access-list 10 deny 10.0.0.0 0.255.255.255
access-list 10 deny 172.16.0.0 0.15.255.255
access-list 10 deny 192.168.0.0 0.0.255.255
access-list 10 permit any
```

Dynamic (Lock-and-Key) Access Lists

Assume the network is secured with ACLs regulating traffic in, out, and through the network. Decisions were made to be conservative in allowing traffic to access the resources. So everything that can be blocked is being dealt with. What if you need some flexibility to deal with some necessary exceptions? *Dynamic access lists,* often called *lock-and-key access lists,* can literally create temporary openings to your network for specific IP traffic.

Figure 5-3 shows an example of a company network that might have limited TCP access to the internal networks to those sessions that originated from within the LAN. To accomplish this, they might have used the TCP ACL established option. The organization still wants to allow the network administrators access from the outside to reduce the number of evening and weekend callouts, particularly for forgotten passwords, locked accounts, and so forth.

The point of lock-and-key is to grant temporary IP access to specific hosts that would normally be blocked. The process works like this:

1. A user Telnets to the router configured with the dynamic ACL. The router can be a perimeter router protecting the entire network or an internal router protecting certain segments.
2. The router challenges the user to authenticate. The authentication method used is whatever security has been applied to Telnet sessions (*line vty* settings) in the router configuration. Options include using standard passwords, local user name/password entries, or AAA.
3. Once successfully authenticated, the Telnet session is terminated and the router creates a temporary ACL that allows traffic between the specific host(s) and resources defined in the ACL statements.
4. The user(s) can then have temporary access through the router.
5. When the time limit defined in the ACL is reached, the temporary ACL list is removed and a new authentication is required to continue.

Properly configured, dynamic access lists provide the same benefits as standard and static extended access lists with the additional security benefit of authenticating users, thereby reducing the opportunity for network break-ins by hackers.

Creating a Lock-and-Key System

Creating a dynamic ACL is a two-step process that includes building or modifying an ACL that will be applied to a router interface, and then configuring the virtual terminal access to support the feature.

Figure 5-3
Simple example of lock-and-key access

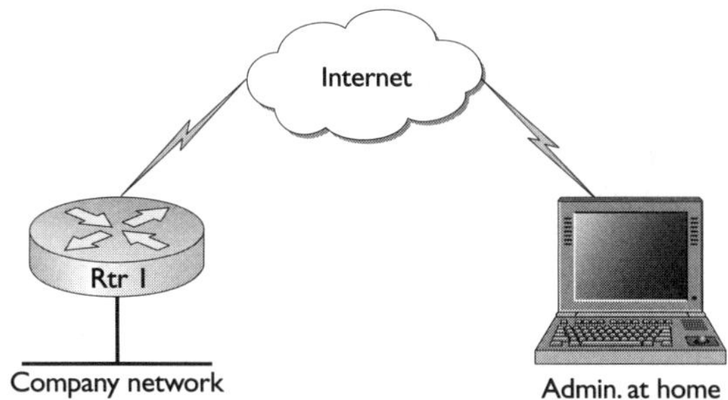

The Dynamic ACL Statements The dynamic access list feature is an option for both numbered and named extended access lists for TCP, UDP, ICMP, and IGMP traffic. The [dynamic *dynamic-name* [timeout *minutes*]] options precedes the {permit | deny} choice.

The basic syntax for a numbered ACL would be the following:

Router(config)#access-list *acl#* **[dynamic *dynamic-name* [timeout *minutes*]]** {permit | deny} *protocol* | *protocol-keyword*} {*source wildcard* | any} [*operator source-port*] {*destination wildcard* | any} [*operator destination-port*] [precedence *precedence*] [tos *tos*] [log | log-input] [options]

The basic syntax for a named ACL would be as follows:

Router(config)#ip access-list extended *name*
Router(config-ext-nacl)#**[dynamic *dynamic-name* [timeout *minutes*]]** {permit | deny} {*protocol* | *protocol-keyword*} {*source wildcard* | any} [*operator source-port*] {*destination wildcard* | any} [*operator destination-port*] [precedence *precedence*] [tos *tos*] [log | log-input] [options]

dynamic	Identifies this access list as a dynamic access list, meaning it can create a temporary ACL.
dynamic-name	The name of the temporary ACL to be created.
timeout *minutes*	Specifies the absolute length of time (in minutes) a temporary ACL can exist. **Warning:** The default is infinite, which allows an entry to remain permanently until an administrator deletes it. Always set a timeout to close this "hole" in your security.

The following simple example creates a named access list with a dynamic access list statement. Line two allows any host to telnet to the router (IP address 201.5.45.87). Line three enables a dynamic list entry called **allow-in**. The statement allows router access to any IP traffic from the authenticated host or the host network. It also limits the temporary access to 60 minutes, regardless of activity.

```
Rtr1(config)#ip access-list extended filter-in
Rtr1(config-ext-nacl)#permit tcp any host 201.5.45.87 eq telnet
Rtr1(config-ext-nacl)#dynamic allow-in timeout 60 permit ip any any
```

Because the dynamic ACL will be applied to an interface and because only be one ACL can exist in each direction per protocol, the dynamic statements are typically going to be added to an existing ACL that's already regulating traffic through that interface.

The Virtual Terminal Statements The [dynamic *dynamic-name* [timeout *minutes*]] options precede the permit | deny choice.

Router(config-line)#autocommand access-enable [host] [timeout *minutes*]

autocommand	Executes the **access-enable** command when a user authenticates through a Telnet session into the router.
access-enable	Enables the lock-and-key access feature by enabling the router to create a temporary access list entry in a dynamic access list.
host	Limits access to the host that originated the Telnet. If not included, the temporary ACL allows access by all hosts on the network defined by the ACL **dynamic** statement network mask.
timeout	Specifies an **idle timer** (in minutes) for the temporary ACL entry. If the temporary ACL statement isn't accessed within this time period, the statement is deleted and requires the user to authenticate again. The default is for the entries to remain permanently.

The following example creates a single password—cisco—and then enables the dynamic ACL to create a temporary ACL limited to the host that authenticated. If five minutes pass between exchanges, the temporary entry is deleted.

This example could be one solution to the problem in Figure 5-3 to allow an administrator to access the network from home.

```
Rtr1(config)#username itadmin password cisco
Rtr1(config)#ip access-list extended filter-in
Rtr1(config-ext-nacl)#permit tcp any host 199.45.5.7 eq telnet
Rtr1(config-ext-nacl)#permit tcp any any established
Rtr1(config-ext-nacl)#permit icmp any any
Rtr1(config-ext-nacl)#dynamic allow-in timeout 60 permit ip any any log
Rtr1(config-ext-nacl)#int s0/0
Rtr1(config-if)#ip address 199.45.5.7 255.255.255.0
Rtr1(config-if)#ip access-group filter-in in
Rtr1(config-if)#line vty 0 4
Rtr1(config-line)#login local
Rtr1(config-line)#autocommand access-enable host timeout 5
Rtr1(config-line)#^Z
Rtr1#
```

Line 1 defines an acceptable user name/password combination.

Line 11 stipulates that the local database of user names and passwords will be used to authenticate. If multiple user name/password combinations had been configured, any set would be accepted.

Line 3, permit tcp any host 199.45.5.7 eq telnet, allows anyone to access the lock-and-key router. The "any" could be replaced by a host address, permit tcp host 24.12.117.91 host 199.45.5.7 eq telnet, if the admin has a permanent IP address. This reduces the opportunities for outsiders to access the network. Even if it can't be reduced to a single IP address, a network address and wildcard mask could limit exposure.

Line 6, dynamic allow-in timeout 60 permit ip any any, specifies the temporary ACL will be called allow-in, limits the temporary ACL statements to 60 minutes, and specifies the temporary ACL statements will allow any host access to any network for IP traffic. If the host option is left off line 12, the temporary ACL will be open to any host in the world. By replacing the first "any" with a network address and a wildcard mask, the exposure could be limited. Replacing the last "any" with a host address or a network address and a wildcard mask, all authenticated access would be limited to the defined address(es). An example of changes to line six could be the following: dynamic allow-in timeout 60 permit ip 24.12.117.0 0.0.0.255 192.168.0.0 0.0.0.255.

Line 12 limits access to only the host address that authenticated and sets the idle timer to five minutes.

Line 10, line vty 0 4, specifies that all five virtual terminal sessions will be configured for lock-and-key. But, what if you have to Telnet into that router for administration purposes? The router is going to authenticate us, and then close the Telnet session just like everyone else. The following lines show an alternative that configures virtual lines 0 through 3 (4 total) to lock-and-key while saving the final session, line vty 4, for separate configuration.

```
!
line vty 0 3
  login local
  autocommand access-enable host timeout 10
line vty 4
  password cisco
  login
  rotary 1
```

The rotary Command Because normal virtual sessions are assigned in round-robin fashion, knowing which session is being accessed is impossible. The **rotary 1** command, shown in the example, makes it possible to specify a port number (3001) when setting up the Telnet session, and thereby specify the virtual session. The numbers in the 3000 range are reserved for this purpose, so adding 3000 to a rotary value used will access the correct line. The Telnet 199.45.5.7 3001 command would access the vty session 4. If the rotary statement had been rotary 17, the Telnet command would have used 3017.

Display Dynamic Access Lists

Displaying a temporary access list is much like any other access list using the **show access-list [acl# | acl-name]** or **show ip access-list [acl# | acl-name]** commands from Privilege Exec mode. The trick is this: the temporary access-list lines are only present when they're in use. After the absolute or idle timeout parameter has activated, the temporary entries are cleared. The number of matches displayed indicates the level of activity for that statement since the last time the counters were cleared.

```
Rtr1#sho access-lists
Extended IP access list filter-in
    permit tcp any host 199.45.5.7 eq telnet (66 matches)
    permit tcp any any established (232 matches)
    permit udp any any eq rip (44 matches)
    Dynamic allow-in permit ip any any log
      permit ip host 192.168.0.14 any log (21 matches) (time left 253)
Rtr1#
00:36:10: %SEC-6-IPACCESSLOGP: list filter-in permitted tcp 192.168.0.14(1107) -
> 192.168.2.1(2001), 2 packets
Rtr1#
```

Line seven identifies the host that authenticated and specifies that 21 packets were permitted. The time left is 253 seconds. Each time another match is made, the idle timer is reset to 300, the five minutes specified in the **autocommand access-enable host timeout** 5 command.

Reflexive Access Lists

As you learned in Chapter 3, the TCP Established option could be useful in limiting access to the local networks to those sessions that originated from inside the network. Any packets originating from the outside that are trying to establish a connection would be rebuffed. But what about other protocols like UDP and ICMP that aren't connection oriented? In fact, a similar problem occurs with TCP applications that send on one port and receive on another. Either way, the established feature doesn't always work in these cases.

A feature of IP-named extended access lists, called *reflexive access lists,* provides what is referred to as *reflective filtering.* Any IP packet going out of a filtered port will create a temporary access list statement inbound, which is a mirror image of the outgoing packet source and destination information. This temporary opening remains active until a TCP FIN packet is received or the idle timer expires. The idle timer timeout feature is critical for protocols that don't have a session-ending message, such as UDP and ICMP.

If host 192.168.0.10 wants to use TCP port 1045 to establish a telnet session with 192.168.1.2 in another network through its TCP 23 (telnet) port, the access list statement to allow this—if one had to be created—would look like the following:

```
permit tcp host 195.168.0.10 eq 1045 host 192.168.1.2 eq 23
```

What gets created is a temporary reflected inbound statement, which looks like the following:

```
permit tcp host 192.168.1.2 eq 23 host 195.168.0.10 eq 1045
```

Reflexive access lists can filter network traffic based on IP upper-layer protocol information by using port numbers. They create temporary ACL statements that permit returning IP traffic for sessions originating from within the network, but prevent other IP traffic from outside. They use reflexive filtering that can only be defined in *named extended IP access lists.*

Reflexive access lists can be an important part of securing your network against spoofing and certain DoS attacks. They can be a major component in a router firewall defense strategy. Reflexive access lists are relatively simple to use and provide greater control over which packets enter your network than do basic access lists.

Selecting the Interface to Use

Reflexive access lists are generally applied to a perimeter router. You can apply reflexive ACLs to either the external or the internal interface. Whenever possible, the reflexive ACL should be configured on the outside interface to block unwanted IP traffic.

Figure 5-4 shows two topologies that might be found on the perimeter of the company network. The topology on the left is a basic perimeter router. In this case, the reflexive ACL can be applied to the external interface (serial) and keep all blocked traffic out of the router.

The topology on the right shows a single-device firewall design for supporting shared servers in a DMZ network. In this case, putting the reflexive ACL on the external interface would undoubtedly interfere with legitimate traffic going to the DMZ area. Placing

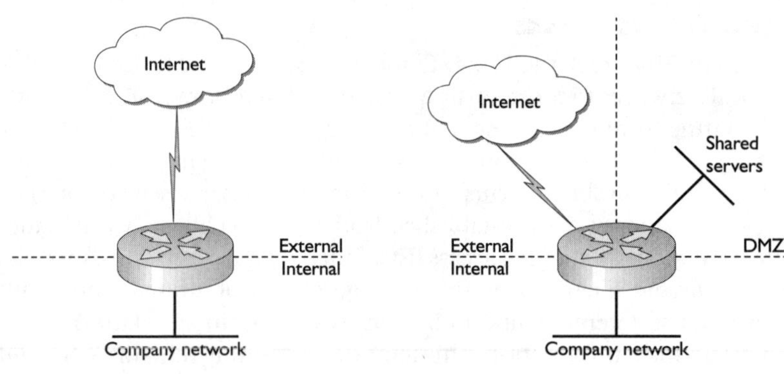

Figure 5-4 Topology impacts on interface selection

the ACL on the internal interface can protect the local network, while not interfering with traffic to and from the shared resources in the DMZ.

Configure Reflexive Access Lists

Reflexive access lists aren't applied directly to an interface but, instead, are nested into an extended-named IP access list that's applied to an interface. Because of the concept of nesting, reflexive access lists don't have the usual implicit deny-all at the end of the list.

Two primary commands need to be configured in building reflexive access lists: the **reflect** command and the **evaluate** command. In addition, the **ip reflexive-list timeout** command is for setting the idle timer.

The reflect Statement The keyword **reflect** in a **permit** statement is the key to creating the return entries in the temporary access list. The **reflect** statement in an outbound ACL creates the entries in the inbound ACL when packets matching the condition(s) are recognized.

The ACL that contains the **reflect** statement can also contain regular **permit** and **deny** statements, either before or after the **reflect** statement. If a match occurs, the packet will be processed but won't trigger a temporary entry in the reflexive access list.

The basic syntax is

Rtr(config)#ip access-list extended *name*
Rtr(config-ext-nacl)#permit *protocol source destination* reflect *name* [timeout *seconds*]

protocol	Any TCP/IP protocol that can use named extended ACLs
source and destination	Same as any ACL source and destination, including keywords **host** and **any**, wildcard masks, and port numbers
name	Name of temporary reflexive ACL to be created
timeout	Optional idle timer for this line only that overrides the absolute timeout set by the **ip reflexive-list timeout** global configuration command (default is 300 seconds)

Examples follow the discussion of the evaluate statement in the next section.

The evaluate Statement The **evaluate** statement is the final configuration entry in another named extended IP access list that partners with the **permit/reflect** statements previously discussed. The syntax is as follows:

Router(config-ext-nacl)#evaluate *name*

name	Name of temporary reflexive ACL specified in the **permit/reflect** statements

The following is a simple example where outgoing TFTP and HTTP traffic is allowed and generates return openings in a temporary ACL called newlist. The Telnet entries in both ACLs are only an example of normal ACL statements that don't generate entries in newlist.

```
Internet serial 0
  ip access-group ok-out out
  ip access-group ok-in in
!
ip access-list extended ok-out
  permit tcp any any eq telnet
  permit udp any any eq tftp reflect newlist
  permit tcp any any eq www  reflect newlist
!
ip access-lst extended ok-in
  permit tcp any any eq telnet
  evaluate newlist
```

Two named access lists, ok-out and ok-in, are applied to the external serial interface.

ok-out contains two **reflect permit** statements, plus a normal Telnet statement. Outbound TFTP and HTTP packets will create entries in a temporary access list named newlist, which reverses the source and destination designations of the outbound packets.

The ok-in evaluate newlist statement incorporates the newlist statements.

The ip Reflexive-list timeout (Seconds) Command The global mode command **ip reflexive-list timeout** ***seconds*** specifies the length of time reflexive access list statements remain in the ACL if no packets in that session are detected. Each new matching packet rests the timeout timer. If no timeout statement is specified, the default timeout value is 300 seconds. The next example shows changing the idle timeout to two minutes.

External Interface Example The following is a simple example of a reflexive ACL applied to an external interface allowing the LAN (192.168.0.0) users access to the Internet and the DNS servers.

```
ip reflexive-list timeout 120
!
Interface serial 0
  ip access-group lan-out out
  ip access-group lan-in in
!
ip access-list extended lan-out
```

```
  deny icmp any any
  permit tcp any any eq dns reflect ok-packets timeout 240
  permit tcp any any eq www reflect ok-packets
!
ip access-list extended lan-in
  deny icmp any any
  evaluate ok-packets
```

The first line changes the global timeout value to two minutes for all reflexive access lists entries on this router that don't specify their own timeout value. Line nine sets a four-minute idle timer for the DNS packets only.

Internal Interface The following is a simple example of a reflexive ACL applied to an internal interface allowing the LAN (192.168.0.0) users access to the Internet and the DNS servers. Typically, this implementation would be used if there's another network (DMZ) of shared servers. Placing the ACL on the external interface would interfere with the outside access to the servers.

```
Interface ethernet 1
  ip access-group lan-in in
  ip access-group lan-out out
!
ip access-list extended lan-in
  deny icmp any any
  permit tcp any any eq dns reflect ok-packets timeout 120
  permit tcp any any eq www reflect ok-packets timeout 180
!
ip access-list extended lan-out
  deny icmp any any
  evaluate ok-packets
```

The two **permit/reflect** entries set their own timeout, two and three minutes, respectively. Without these timeout settings, they would be governed by the global default (300 seconds).

Viewing Reflexive Access Lists

Reflexive access lists can be displayed using the **show access-list** command. No reflexive access list entries will appear if no outbound traffic has triggered the reflexive access list. After a HTTP session is initiated from within the network, the **show access-list** command could display the following:

```
Extended IP access list lan-in
  permit icmp any 195.168.1.0 0.0.0.255 echo-response
  permit tcp any host 195.168.1.20 eq 80 (7 matches)
  permit bgp any any (4 matches)
  evaluate ok-packets
Extended IP access list lan-out
  permit tcp 195.168.1.0 0.0.0.255 any eq 80 reflect ok-packets timeout 180
  permit tcp 195.168.1.0 0.0.0.255 any eq 53 reflect ok-packets
Reflexive IP access list ok-packets
  permit tcp host 201.37.14.127 eq www host 195.168.52 eq 80 (5 matches)
    (time left 140 seconds)
```

Reflexive Access Lists Caveats Some applications, like FTP, allow port numbers to be changed during a session, meaning the port numbers of returning packets aren't the same as the originating packet. Reflexive access lists can't resolve this and the return packet will be denied—even if it's part of the same session. Passive FTP is an option that will work with reflexive access lists if the FTP site supports it.

Reflexive access lists can't examine data in the packet beyond the Layer 4 (OSI model) information, such as TCP and UDP port numbers and the related IP addresses. They can't follow the application as you just saw with the FTP discussion in the preceding paragraph.

Lack of Legal IP Addresses

Organizations are facing two related challenges. First, the depletion of registered IP addresses means that getting blocks of "real" addresses larger than class C is virtually impossible. Second, trying to scale larger organizations with a hodge-podge of class C addresses will reduce routing efficiency. The following private address pools (RFC 1918) provide the only logical solution, but they can't go out on the Internet.

10.0.0.0–10.255.255.255	1 class A	16.6+ million hosts
172.16.0.0–172.31.255.255	16 class Bs	1+ million hosts
192.168.0.0–192.168.255.255	256 class Cs	65,000+ hosts

Network Address Translation (NAT) is a mechanism that allows private addresses to be translated to real addresses, so they can travel through the Internet. NAT allows an organization with unregistered "private" addresses to connect to the Internet by translating those addresses into globally registered IP addresses. Incoming traffic is translated back for delivery within the inside network.

NAT can save an organization the hassle of readdressing its network when it changes ISPs. The real addresses leased from the original ISP can continue to be used, but must be translated at the perimeter to addresses that will summarize to the new ISP. This can be a real sanity saver when an ISP fails without notice to clients.

NAT can also provide a limited level of network privacy by hiding internal IP addresses from external networks. The external hosts will see the assigned "real" address and respond to that address.

NOTE Important to know is that some applications, such as some e-mail programs, capture the internal address and store it in the data portion of the IP packet, which means that under some circumstances the internal address can be seen by the outside world. Programs like McAfee SpamKiller display the entire path back to the source, including the internal local addresses.

This chapter covers Cisco IOS NAT and how to configure it, typically on a perimeter router. You must understand NAT technology and concepts because these are revisited in the Firewall chapters (6–8 and 17–20) and IPSec chapters (9–16 and 21) and can be on any of the exams. In some form, NAT is available on personal routers (cable and DSL connections), firewall devices like the PIX devices, and proxy servers working as firewalls. This section covers basic NAT operations and the following NAT implementations:

- Static NAT
- Dynamic NAT
- Dynamic NAT with overloading (PAT)

NAT Technology and Terminology

NAT is the process of altering the IP header of a packet, so the source local address of the internal host is replaced in the header by real global addresses. In some cases, the destination address might also be modified. This swapping process is performed by a NAT device, usually on the network perimeter. The NAT server then maintains a table of the translations that allows returning packets to be addressed with the correct internal address. Figure 5-5 is a simple example of NAT where the local hosts (10.0.0.0 private network) are translated by the NAT device to global addresses in the 192.168.1.0 network.

When an outside host sends a response to 192.168.1.97 or 192.168.1.98, the NAT router checks the current table of network address translations, and then replaces the destination address with the original inside source address.

NOTE Obviously, 192.168.1.0 isn't a globally routable "real" network, but we'll use only private addresses in all examples for two reasons. The public addresses belong to someone, and the current or future owners might not agree with their use. Second, inevitably, someone will build a "practice" lab like the ones in the book and a slim possibility would exist for impacting the real owners of the address.

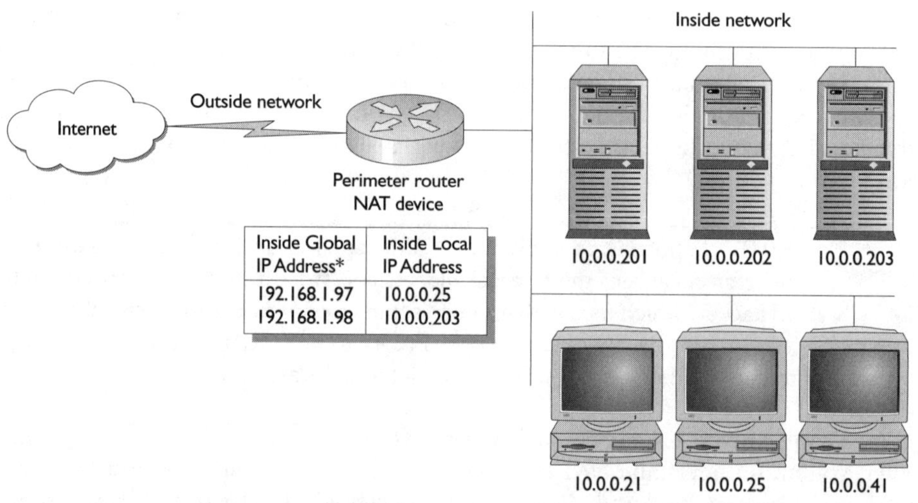

Figure 5-5 NAT translation for inside network 10.0.0.0

Cisco IOS Software uses the following terms when working with NAT. While other implementations might change the terms, the concepts remain the same:

- **Inside local address** The configured IP address assigned to a host on the inside network. Quite often, these addresses are drawn from the RFC 1918 private address pools. They could also be real addresses officially assigned to some other organization.
- **Inside global address** The inside global address is the translated address. This is the IP address the outside world sees for an inside host. Typically, these addresses are allocated from a pool of real IP addresses provided by the ISP.
- **Outside local address** The IP address of an outside host as it appears to the inside network. Because these addresses are only used on the inside network, they might not necessarily be real public addresses. They can be assigned from the RFC 1918 private address pools.
- **Outside global address** The configured IP address assigned to a host in the outside network. This address is a real address assigned from the globally routable pool.

NAT translations can occur dynamically or statically, and can be used for a variety of purposes, as described in the following sections.

Device Interfaces

A key concept in all NAT translations is identifying the internal (inside) interface(s) and the external (outside) interface(s). NAT needs to know which interfaces are connected to inside networks and which are connected to outside networks. Only packets moving between inside and outside interfaces can be translated. At least one inside interface and one outside interface for each border router must be defined. The following configuration additions would be typical for a perimeter router with a single serial connection to the Internet and a single LAN:

```
interface Serial0/0
  ip nat outside
!
interface FastEthernet0/0
  ip nat inside
```

Outside interfaces should never be included in internal route tables and must remain unknown to internal hosts. Similarly, internal addresses should never be advertised or shared with the outside world. The internal interface typically is either the default gateway for hosts that share that network or the next-hop address for default routes set on other internal routers.

Static NAT

Static translation involves permanently mapping an inside local address to an inside global address. For most organizations, this would be reserved for those network servers shared with the outside world that, therefore, need to keep the same address. This is particularly true for servers, such as web or e-mail servers, that will have domain name translations in DNS servers. Any change in their global address results in missed traffic until the DNS server system is fully resolved to the change. This might take the form of those dreaded 404 Page Not Found Errors when searching the Web.

Except in the smallest of networks, or those with few users authorized to go out into the Internet, static NAT isn't a suitable implementation for users because it requires a one-for-one ratio of real addresses to inside addresses.

Configuring Static NAT

To enable static NAT of an inside source address; use the **ip nat inside source** command in global configuration to create a single static translation. To remove the static translation, use the no form of this command. The syntax is

Rtr1(config)#ip nat inside source static *local-ip global-ip*
Rtr1(config)#no ip nat inside source static *local-ip global-ip*

local-ip	Local IP address assigned to an inside host—often taken from RFC 1918 pool
global-ip	Globally unique IP address of an inside host as it appears to the outside world

Creating three static translations for servers in the example at the beginning of this section might look like the following:

```
Rtr1(config)#ip nat inside source static 10.0.0.201 192.168.1.105
Rtr1(config)#ip nat inside source static 10.0.0.202 192.168.1.106
Rtr1(config)#ip nat inside source static 10.0.0.203 192.168.1.106
```

Confirming NAT Translations

To see the NAT translations, use the **show ip nat translations** command. The results would look something like the following output. The translations appear immediately because they're permanent. An outside user could access these servers by using the 192.168.1.105–107 addresses, assuming no access lists prevent it.

```
Rtr1#show ip nat translations
Pro Inside global    Inside local     Outside local    Outside global
---  192.168.1.105    10.0.0.201       ---              ---
---  192.168.1.106    10.0.0.202       ---              ---
---  192.168.1.107    10.0.0.203       ---              ---
Rtr1#
```

To see any NAT activity, use the **show ip nat statistics** command. The results would look something like the following output. The Total active translations summarizes the current status, while hits and misses indicates no traffic has been attempted. If an outside host were to ping one of the servers, the hits would show the number of packets—four or five.

```
Rtr1#show ip nat statistics
Total active translations: 3 (3 static, 0 dynamic; 0 extended)
```

```
Outside interfaces:
  Serial0/0
Inside interfaces:
  FastEthernet0/0
Hits: 0  Misses: 0
Expired translations: 0
Dynamic mappings:
Rtr1#
```


Dynamic NAT

You can configure dynamic NAT in the following three steps:

- Define a pool of global IP addresses to be allocated.
- Use a standard ACL to define the local addresses eligible for translation.
- Link the pool of global addresses with the eligible local addresses.

Define a Pool of Global IP Addresses to Be Allocated

To define a pool of global IP addresses for NAT, use the **ip nat pool global** configuration command. To remove one or more addresses from the pool, use the no form of this command. The command defines a pool of addresses using start address, end address, and either netmask or prefix length. The **pool** command can define either an inside global pool or an outside local pool. The syntax is

Rtr1(config)#ip nat pool *name start-ip end-ip* {netmask *netmask* | prefix-length *prefix-len*}
Rtr1(config)#no ip nat pool *name*

name	Name of the pool
start-ip	Starting IP address that defines the range of addresses in the address pool
end-ip	Ending IP address that defines the range of addresses in the address pool
netmask *netmask*	Network mask that defines address bits identifying the network ID
prefix-length *prefix-len*	CIDR notation indicating how many bits make up the netmask

Examples:

```
Rtr1(config)#ip nat pool 2net-out 172.16.2.10 172.16.2.20 netmask 255.255.255.0
Rtr1(config)#ip nat pool 3net-out 172.16.3.10 172.16.3.99 prefix-length 24
```

Use a Standard ACL to Define the Local Addresses Eligible for Translation

A standard access list is used to define the internal addresses that can and can't be translated. In Global Configuration mode on SanJose1, make the following entries:

Examples:

```
Rtr1(config)#access-list 1 permit 192.168.1.0 0.0.0.255
Rtr1(config)#access-list 1 deny 192.168.2.5
Rtr1(config)#access-list 1 permit 192.168.2.0 0.0.0.255
```

Link the Pool of Global Addresses with the Eligible Local Addresses

To enable dynamic NAT of the inside source addresses, use the second form of the **ip nat inside source** command. To remove the static translation or remove the dynamic association to a pool, use the no form of this command. The syntax is

Rtr1(config)#ip nat inside source list {acl# | acl-name} {pool *name* | interface *dialer-name*}
Rtr1(config)#no ip nat inside source list {acl# | acl-name}{pool *name* | interface *dialer-name*}

list *acl#* | *acl-name*	Standard IP ACL number or name (packets permitted by the ACL are allowed to translate)
pool *name*	Name of the address pool from which global IP addresses are dynamically allocated
interface *dialer-name*	Name of the dialer interface on which the PPP/IPCP address negotiation takes place

Examples:

```
Rtr1(config)#ip nat pool 3net-out 172.16.3.10 172.16.3.99 netmask 255.255.255.0
Rtr1(config)#ip nat inside source list 1 pool 3net-out
Rtr1(config)#access-list 1 permit 192.168.2.0 0.0.0.255
```

Clearing the NAT Translation Table

Some dynamic translations stay in the translation table for 24 hours. Clearing dynamic NAT translations from the translation table before they timeout is possible by using the **clear ip nat translation** * command. This is particularly useful when testing NAT configuration.

Static NAT entries are immediately reestablished in the table.

Additional options exist for clearing only part of the table. Use the **clear ip nat translation ?** feature, if necessary.

Changing the NAT Default Inactivity Timeout Timers

TCP translations inactivity timeout defaults to 24 hours, unless an RST or FIN bit packet is seen on the stream, in which case they timeout in one minute. To change the amount of time after which NAT translations timeout, use the global configuration **ip nat translation** command. To disable the timeout, use the no form of this command.

Rtr1(config)#ip nat translation timeout *seconds*
Rtr1(config)#no ip nat translation timeout

timeout	Applies to dynamic translations, except for overload (PAT) translations. Default is 86,400 seconds (24 hours).
seconds	Seconds after which the specified port translation times out.

Examples:

The following example demonstrates changing the NAT default timeout value to 120 seconds on Rtr1.

```
Rtr1(confif)#ip nat translation timeout 120
```

Additional timer options are covered in the overload (PAT) section.

Dynamic NAT with Overloading (PAT)

Unless an organization has a large pool of global IP addresses, it seems the basic dynamic NAT translations could prove too limiting and cumbersome. Furthermore, having to maintain a large pool of global addresses somewhat defeats the address preservation aspects of private addresses.

The alternative is to have the NAT router create a unique identifier for every session by using a single global IP address and appending a port number, such as 1.1.1.1:1540. While over 65,000 port numbers exist, the effective limit is about 4,000. This means an organization could use and pay for only one real IP address and allow up to 4,000 hosts out onto the Internet. Even if NAT has a pool of two or more IP addresses to work with, the IOS version of NAT chooses to continue using the first IP address in the pool for subsequent translations.

This process is referred to as *dynamic overloading* or as Port Address Translation (PAT). To implement the feature requires adding only the one word **overload** to the **ip nat inside source list** command. An example would be as follows:

```
Rtr1(config)#ip nat pool 3net-out 172.16.3.10 172.16.3.99 netmask
     255.255.255.0
Rtr1(config)#ip nat inside source list 1 pool 3net-out overload
Rtr1(config)#access-list 1 permit 192.168.2.0 0.0.0.255
```

When the router receives the packet from an inside computer, it saves the computer's local IP address and port number to a NAT table. The router replaces the local IP address with a global IP address and adds the same port number. The translation table now has a mapping of the computer's nonroutable IP address and port number along with the router's IP address. The **show ip nat translation** command displays the result.

```
Rtr1#show ip nat translation
Pro Inside global      Inside local        Outside local    Outside global
icmp 172.16.2.5:1536   192.168.0.21:1536   10.0.0.5:1536    10.0.0.5:1536
tcp  172.16.2.5:1095   192.168.0.21:1095   10.0.0.19:21     10.0.0.19:21
tcp  172.16.2.5:1094   192.168.0.21:1094   10.0.0.45:23     10.0.0.45:23
Rtr1#
```

The first column (Pro), which has been blank before, now shows the protocol used.

When a packet comes from the destination computer, the router checks the destination port on the packet. The router then looks in the address translation table to see which computer on the stub domain the packet belongs to. It changes the destination address and the destination port to the one saved in the address translation table and sends it to that computer. The NAT router continues to use that same port number for the duration of the connection. The timer is reset each time the router accesses an entry in the table. If the entry isn't accessed again before the timer expires, the entry is removed from the table.

Changing the PAT Default Inactivity Timeout Timers

When port translation (PAT) is configured, a finer control exists over specific translation entries because each entry contains more context about the traffic using it. A separate entry is made for each timer. The syntax is

Rtr1(config)#ip nat translation {udp-timeout | dns-timeout | tcp-timeout | finrst-timeout} *seconds*

Rtr1(config)#no ip nat translation {udp-timeout | dns-timeout | tcp-timeout | finrst-timeout}

udp-timeout	Applies to the UDP port. Default is 300 seconds (five minutes).
dns-timeout	Applies to DNS connections. Default is 60 seconds.
tcp-timeout	Applies to the TCP port. Default is 86,400 seconds (24 hours).
finrst-timeout	To set the timeout value after a Finish or Reset TCP packet before terminating a connection. Default is 60 seconds.
seconds	Seconds after which the specified port translation times out.

Examples:

```
Rtr1(confif)#ip nat translation udp-timeout 120
Rtr1(confif)#ip nat translation dns-timeout 30
Rtr1(confif)#ip nat translation tcp-timeout 600
```

Dynamic NAT sessions can only be initiated by an internal host. Initiating a NAT translation from outside the network is impossible. To some extent, this adds a level of security to the internal network. This might also help explain why the dynamic timeout timer for overload (PAT) sessions is so short. The window of opportunity stays open just long enough to make sure legitimate replies like web pages, FTP and TFTP copies, and ICMP messages can get in.

Debugging IP NAT

To see the actual translation process and troubleshoot NAT problems, use the **debug ip nat** command and related options. As with all **debug** commands, this can have serious impacts on production routers and should be used judiciously. The **debug ip nat** output looks like this:

```
Rtr1# debug ip nat
IP NAT debugging is on
06:37:40: NAT:  s=192.168.0.10->172.16.2.5, d=172.16.1.97 [63]
06:37:40: NAT*: s=172.16.1.97, d=172.16.2.5->192.168.0.10 [63]
06:37:41: NAT*: s=192.168.0.10->172.16.2.5, d=172.16.1.97 [64]
06:37:41: NAT*: s=172.16.1.97, d=172.16.2.5->192.168.0.10 [64]
06:37:42: NAT*: s=192.168.0.10->172.16.2.5, d=172.16.1.97 [65]
06:37:42: NAT*: s=172.16.1.97, d=172.16.2.5->192.168.0.10 [65]
06:37:43: NAT*: s=192.168.0.10->172.16.2.5, d=172.16.1.97 [66]
06:37:43: NAT*: s=172.16.1.97, d=172.16.2.5->192.168.0.10 [66]
Rtr1#
06:38:43: NAT: expiring 172.16.2.5 (192.168.0.10) icmp 1536 (1536)
Rtr1#undebug all
All possible debugging has been turned off
```

The previous output shows the results of a ping from workstation to Rtr2.

You can see both translations as the pings pass both ways through the NAT router. The number at the end of the row is the same for both translations of each ping. The *s*= indicates the source, *d*= indicates the destination, and -> shows the translation.

The previous 06:38:43 entry shows the expiration of a NAT translation.

Using the **debug ip nat ?** command indicates you can refer to an access list number to define specific traffic to debug. The detailed option provides the port numbers, as well as the IP address translations. The following output shows the results of a ping from workstation to Rtr2. The second and third NAT output lines show the actual verification of IP address and port number assignment.


```
Rtr1#debug ip nat ?
  <1-99>    Access list
  detailed  NAT detailed events
  <cr>

Rtr1#debug ip nat detailed
IP NAT detailed debugging is on
07:03:50: NAT:  i: icmp (192.168.0.10, 1536) -> (172.16.1.97, 1536) [101]
07:03:50: NAT:  address not stolen for 192.168.0.10, proto 1 port 1536
07:03:50: NAT:  ipnat_allocate_port: wanted 1536 got 1536
07:03:50: NAT*: o: icmp (172.16.1.97, 1536) -> (172.16.2.5, 1536) [101]
07:03:51: NAT*: i: icmp (192.168.0.10, 1536) -> (172.16.1.97, 1536) [102]
07:03:51: NAT*: o: icmp (172.16.1.97, 1536) -> (172.16.2.5, 1536) [102]
07:03:52: NAT*: i: icmp (192.168.0.10, 1536) -> (172.16.1.97, 1536) [103]
07:03:52: NAT*: o: icmp (172.16.1.97, 1536) -> (172.16.2.5, 1536) [103]
07:03:53: NAT*: i: icmp (192.168.0.10, 1536) -> (172.16.1.97, 1536) [104]
07:03:53: NAT*: o: icmp (172.16.1.97, 1536) -> (172.16.2.5, 1536) [104]
Rtr1#
```

Rerouting Attacks

A router ICMP redirect message directs a host to use another router as its path to a particular destination because it has a better route. The rules say a router will send redirects only to hosts on its own local subnets. No user host will ever send a redirect and no redirect will travel more than one network hop. Unfortunately, attackers don't play by the rules. Some attacks are based on this.

Figure 5-6 shows a situation where using the host default gateway wouldn't reach the target destination in network 10.1.1.0. The following debug message shows Rtr1 sending a debug message to host 192.168.1.10 to use router Rtr2 (192.168.1.200) as the gateway to reach the destination 10.1.1.10.

```
Rtr1#debug ip icmp
ICMP packet debugging is on
ICMP: redirect sent to 192.168.1.10 for dest 10.1.1.10, use gw 192.168.1.200
Rtr1#
```

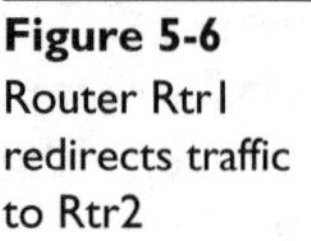

Figure 5-6 Router Rtr1 redirects traffic to Rtr2

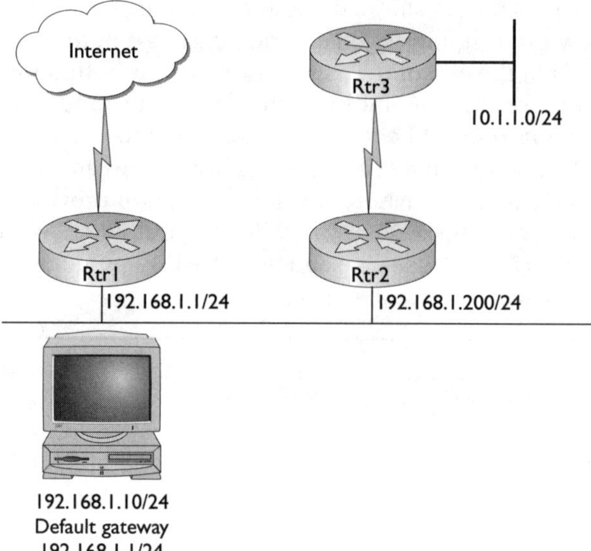

By default, Cisco routers send ICMP redirects. You can use the interface subcommand **no ip redirects** to disable ICMP redirects. Another solution is to use an ACL to filter out any incoming ICMP redirects. The following code contains examples of each:

```
Rtr1(config)#interface ethernet 0
Rtr1(config-if)#no ip redirects
Rtr1(config-if)#^Z
Rtr1#
Rtr1#conf t
Rtr1(config)#access-list 125 deny   icmp any any redirect
Rtr1(config)#access-list 125 permit ip any any
Rtr1(config)#interface serial 0
Rtr1(config-if)#ip access-group 125 in
Rtr1(config-if)#^Z
Rtr1#
```

This filtering prevents only redirect attacks by remote attackers, but does nothing against an attacker that has internal access to the same segment as a host that's under attack.

Event Logging on Perimeter Routers

Perimeter router logs can be invaluable in troubleshooting, capacity planning, and dealing with security incidents. For security purposes, the events to log are interface status changes, changes to the system configuration, access list matches, events detected by the firewall, and intrusion detection features. System logging events might be reported to a variety of destinations, including the following:

- The system console port (**logging console** command). Because many console ports are unattended or are connected to terminals with no historical storage, this information might be unavailable to reconstruct a major event.
- Servers running the syslog daemon can send logging information to a server with the **logging** ***server-ip-address*** command, and you can control the urgency threshold for logging to the server with the **logging trap** ***urgency*** command. Even if you have a syslog server, you should probably still enable local logging. If you don't have access to a syslog server, go to Kiwi Enterprises at http://www.kiwisyslog.com /index.htm and download its free Kiwi Syslog Daemon.
- Remote sessions on VTYs and local sessions on TTYs (**logging monitor** and **terminal monitor** commands).
- Most routers can save system logging information to a local RAM buffer. This buffer is a fixed size and retains only the most recent information, and the contents are lost whenever the router is reloaded. Use the **show memory** command to make sure your router has enough free memory to support a logging buffer. Create the buffer using the **logging buffered** ***buffer-size*** configuration command.

If the router has a real-time clock or is running NTP, time-stamp log entries by adding the **service timestamps log datetime msecs** command to the configuration.

Access List Violation Logs

With traffic filtering and access control ACLs, you should consider logging packets that violate the filtering criteria. Older Cisco IOS software versions use the **log** keyword option, which captures the IP addresses and port numbers of packets matching an access list entry. Newer IOS versions use the **log-input** keyword, which adds receiving interface information and the MAC address of the host that sent it.

To manage file size and minimize performance impacts, configure logging for those critical access list entries. Don't log entries that will match a large number of packets and generate little useful information, such as the **permit any** statement.

Chapter Review

This chapter focused on the IOS features that could be used on the perimeter router as a first line of defense against security threats. The perimeter configuration of the network often includes both a perimeter router and a firewall as the second line of defense. The firewall separates the inside network from the DMZs. The dirty DMZ is protected only by the perimeter router, while the protected DMZ has the firewall and perimeter router between it and the outside.

Network security can be enhanced by disabling unused services, such as CDP, finger, and TCP and UDP small services.

Cisco IOS offers a rich selection of routing and route security tools, such as controlling directed broadcasts, blocking ICMP redirects, routing protocol authentication, and flooding control.

Controlling network access and traffic using address filtering, dynamic access lists, and reflexive access lists can all contribute to increased security.

Questions

1. True or False. In the screened subnet architecture network model, the inside network is everything from the perimeter router in to the corporate network.

   A. True

   B. False

2. Which one of the following is considered the trusted network?

   A. Inside

   B. Outside

   C. Dirty DMZ

   D. Protected DMZ

3. Which of the following would *not* be a function of a perimeter router in a screened subnet architecture network?

   A. Providing a serial connection to the outside world

   B. Providing any filtering of outside traffic

   C. Providing LAN routing

   D. Implementing basic security for the dirty DMZ

4. True or False. CDP facilitates a secure environment on a perimeter router.

   A. True

   B. False

5. Which one is *not* true about IP directed broadcast?

   A. It's a datagram sent to the subnet broadcast address.

   B. It's routed through the network as a unicast packet.

   C. Only the router directly connected to the target subnet can positively identify it.

   D. It can be blocked by a smurf defense.

6. True or False. Filtering incoming ICMP redirects on a perimeter router should never cause any problems.

   A. True

   B. False

7. Which two of the following reduces spoofing attacks?
   A. RFC 2827 filtering
   B. Weighted fair queuing
   C. RFC 1918 filtering
   D. Routing protocol authentication
8. Which of the following is most like the TCP established option?
   A. Dynamic ACL
   B. Lock and key
   C. Reflexive ACL
   D. Finger ACL
9. In NAT terminology, what's the IP address of a network member computer?
   A. Inside local
   B. Outside local
   C. Inside global
   D. Outside global
10. Which statement is *not* true about Network Address Translation (NAT)?
    A. It's a mechanism that allows private addresses to be translated to use the Internet.
    B. It can be configured both static and dynamic on the same router.
    C. It provides good security by hiding internal IP addresses.
    D. It reduces the cost of IP addresses.
11. True or False. Static NAT entries appear in the translation table the first time they're used.
    A. True
    B. False
12. Which command shows the NAT table?
    A. show ip nat statistics
    B. show run
    C. show ip nat translations
    D. show ip nat table
13. What one word changes dynamic NAT to PAT?
    A. PAT
    B. Overflow

C. Overload

D. Rotary

14. Which command sets the idle timeout for a dynamic (lock-and-key) access list?

A. access-list 101 dynamic temp-in timeout 30 permit ip any any

B. ip dynamic-list timeout 30

C. autocommand access-enable host timeout 30

D. ip reflexive-list timeout 30

15. Which statement is true about reflexive access lists?

A. They create temporary holes into the network security, based on a successful Telnet authentication.

B. They only work with TCP traffic.

C. They create temporary holes in the network security–based specific outbound traffic.

D. They rely on named standard access lists.

Answers

1. **B.** False. It's everything in from the inside interface of the firewall.
2. **A.** Inside
3. **C.** Providing LAN routing
4. **B.** False. It announces to any system on a directly connected segment that the router is a Cisco device, the model number, and the Cisco IOS version being run.
5. **D.** It can be blocked by a smurf defense.
6. **A.** True. They shouldn't come from outside the segment.
7. **A.** RFC 2827 filtering and **C.** RFC 1918 filtering
8. **C.** Reflexive ACL
9. **A.** Inside local
10. **C.** It provides good security by hiding internal IP addresses. It provides limited privacy.
11. **B.** False. They appear when created.
12. **C.** show ip nat translations
13. **C.** Overload
14. **C.** autocommand access-enable host timeout 30
15. **C.** They create temporary holes in the network security–based specific outbound traffic.

CHAPTER

IOS Firewall Feature Set—CBAC

In this chapter, you will learn how to:

- Recognize Cisco IOS Firewall security problems and solutions
- Use Context-Based Access Control (CBAC)
- Configure the Cisco IOS Firewall
- Use the two methods of IOS Firewall Administration

With the growing awareness of, and commitment to, network security as the way to secure business transactions both internally and over the Internet, more and more businesses are recognizing that security concepts and features must be integrated into the network design and infrastructure.

According to Cisco advertising, 80 percent of the Internet backbone routers run Cisco IOS software, making it the most fundamental component of today's network infrastructure. The Cisco IOS software-based security features, combined with the wide range of products supported, make it a logical solution for any organization's end-to-end Internet, intranet, and remote access network security requirements.

This chapter looks at the key components of the IOS Firewall features, and compares the functionality and limitations to the PIX Firewall devices. PIX Firewall devices are introduced in the next chapter, and then expanded on later in the advanced PIX chapters.

STUDY TIP The material in this chapter is part of the exam objectives for both the Managing Cisco Network Security (MCNS) and Cisco Secure PIX Firewall Advanced (CSPFA) exams.

Introduction to Cisco IOS Firewall

The *Cisco IOS Firewall* is a feature set option for Cisco IOS software, that is available for a wide range of Cisco routers and switches. It provides advanced firewall capabilities, as well as other security technologies such as intrusion detection and authentication.

The Cisco IOS Firewall is only one part of the growing Cisco Secure product family. It joins and integrates with other Cisco Secure products, such as Cisco Secure Access Control

Server (ACS), Cisco Secure PIX Firewall devices, Cisco Secure Intrusion Detection System (IDS), Cisco Secure Scanner, and Cisco Secure Policy Manager (CSPM), plus a variety of consulting and training services options. As key components of Cisco AVVID strategy, Cisco Secure network security solutions improve the network's capability to support mission-critical Internet applications.

Cisco IOS software firewall feature set provides an extensive array of security tools, enabling the administrator to configure a firewall providing the appropriate level of functionality to meet security policy requirements. Whether as a stand-alone unit or working in tandem with a dedicated firewall device, the IOS firewall features provide flexible and reliable options to extend the security protection throughout the network.

Router-Based Firewall Functionality

Cisco IOS Firewall is available on the Cisco 800, uBR900, 1400, 1600, 1700, 2500, 2600, 3600, 7100, 7200, and 7500, as well as RSM series routers. By supporting such a wide variety of router platforms, the firewall features will scale to meet any network's bandwidth, performance, and security requirements. The firewall features are also available on the Catalyst 5000 switch.

No absolute rules exist for choosing the right Cisco router for implementing the firewall and security features. While an organization's size and security requirements must be factored in, the following general guidelines can be used as a starting point.

- Small office/home offices (SOHO): Cisco 800, uBR900 series, 1600, and 1720 series
- Branch and extranet implementations: Cisco 2500, 2600, and 3600 series
- Central office or high-volume locations: Cisco 7100, 7200, 7500, and RSM series

Integration with Cisco IOS Software

The *Cisco IOS Firewall feature set* is an optional security solution integrated into the network through selecting the correct Cisco IOS software. The integration of the firewall features into the IOS means the organization security policy can be implemented and enforced throughout the network. Whether securing the links between departments or partner networks, or between the organization and the Internet, the IOS implementation allows for an end-to-end security solution that can grow and change with the organization.

The Cisco IOS Firewall is also completely interoperable with, and often enhances, other features, such as AAA, NAT, Cisco encryption technology (CET), and system logging, as well as standard and extended access control list features, such as Time-Based and Lock n Key.

VPN, IPSec Encryption, and QoS Support

When combined with Cisco IPSec technology, the Cisco IOS Firewall features provide integrated and enhanced virtual private network (VPN) functionality. VPNs are rapidly evolving as the standard for providing secure data communications over public networks like the Internet.

The firewall features work with the IOS encryption, tunneling, and quality of service (QoS) features to ensure timely and reliable delivery of data and provide robust perimeter security, while providing advanced bandwidth management, intrusion detection, and service-level validation. The Firewall Authentication Proxy feature can provide user authentication and authorization for Cisco VPN client software.

Several chapters are dedicated to IPSec and to VPN implementation and features, but it's important to recognize that both the firewall and the IPSec features are separate IOS options that might be selected to match the objectives of the security policy. Figure 6-1 shows a sample of the Cisco IOS Upgrade Planner from the Cisco web site. Notice that the firewall features, identified as FW, and the IPSec features, IPSEC 56, are available in various combinations on different platforms. You can have either, both, or neither. Often memory and flash requirements will increase for each, as might the cost.

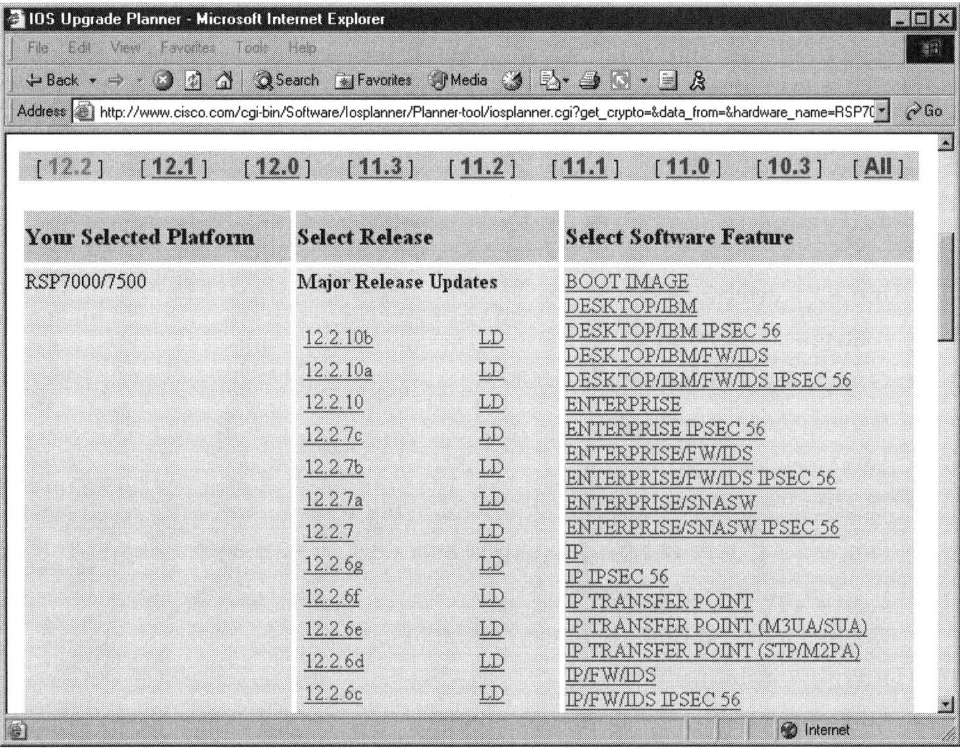

Figure 6-1 Cisco CCO IOS Upgrade Planner showing feature sets

Does the IOS Image Support Firewall and IPSec Features?

How do you tell if the IOS on a router supports the firewall or the IPSec features? Cisco and vendors who use Cisco IOS on their devices follow a naming convention for software images. The device IOS convention identifies the platform, the features of the image, and the area of memory used by the image at runtime. For the image c2600-jos56i-mz.120-4 .T.bin, the name is the portion up to the first period and everything else is version/release information. The three components of the name are separated by dashes. In the example,

- The platform is a Cisco 2600 series router.
- The *o* feature code indicates firewall features. The 56i indicates 56-bit IPSec encryption. The *s* indicates a group of features, such as NAT, ISL IBM, MMP, VPDN/L2F, VOIP, and ATM. The *j* indicates enterprise features.
- The *m* indicates that the software runs from RAM, and the *z* indicates the image is zipped.

For more information on naming convention and version numbers, go to http://www.cisco.com/warp/public/620/4.html. Naming is in Section 2.2. No CCO account is required to view this document.

Feature Summary

The Cisco IOS Firewall feature set adds the following security features to a broad selection of Cisco routers:

- Intrusion detection
- Authentication proxy
- Context-Based Access Control (CBAC)
- Dynamic port mapping
- Java blocking
- Denial of service (DoS) detection and prevention
- Simple Mail Transfer Protocol (SMTP) attack detection and prevention
- IP fragmentation attack prevention
- Configurable real-time alerts and audit trail
- Failover capabilities
- Microsoft NetShow application support

The 800, UBR904, 1600, and 2500 series of routers support all the previous firewall features, except authentication proxy and intrusion detection. There's no firewall feature set support for the 4000 series routers, but there is VPN support.

Context-Based Access Control (CBAC)

Context-Based Access Control (CBAC) is a per-application control mechanism that adds advanced traffic filtering functionality to firewalls that isn't limited, as are access lists, to examining packets at the network or transport layer. While CBAC examines both of these layers, it also examines the application-layer protocol data to monitor the state of a given TCP or UDP session. This means, as multiple channels are created or used by applications such as SQL*Net, FTP, and RPC, CBAC can respond by creating temporary openings in the firewall access lists to allow return traffic and additional data connections for specified sessions that originated from within the protected network. This application-layer awareness and capability to evolve with the traffic is beyond the capabilities of access list technologies.

Quick Access List Review

Before continuing with CBAC, it's important to be clear about how standard and extended ACLs work. By definition, standard ACLs filter only on source network addresses and are, therefore, limited to Layer 3 capabilities. Extended ACLs are able to filter on port numbers extending their reach into Layer 4. In both cases, any ACL allowing traffic to enter a network is, in fact, a hole in the firewall or perimeter security that can possibly be exploited by others.

The preceding chapter introduced reflexive ACLs as an alternative to creating permanent holes through the network security. Temporary ACL statements can be created for inbound traffic based on outbound traffic reducing risk of exploitation. Unfortunately, reflexive ACLs are limited to Layer 4 filters, like any other extended ACL. Furthermore, reflexive ACLs can't deal with changes in port designations by the outside host, such as FTP. The outbound address/port combinations for the source and destination are "mirrored" to create the inbound openings. Another limitation of reflexive ACLs is that they're limited to single channel applications.

CBAC Advantages

Understanding CBAC might be made easier if you think of it as reflexive ACLs without the limitations. CBAC adds inspection intelligence to ACL capabilities by reading the entire packet for application status information, which is stored in the state table. Like reflexive ACLS, CBAC watches outbound traffic to determine what packets to let in; but unlike reflexive ACLs, CBAC can make decisions based on how the application behaves, not only the addresses and port number it uses.

CBAC can open any additional inbound channels required for returning data that were negotiated by the outgoing data for a particular application.

When a session times out or ends, the state table and ACL entries are deleted, and the opening closes to additional traffic.

CBAC can be configured to inspect and filter the following IP sessions and application-layer protocols:

- All TCP sessions, regardless of the application-layer protocol (sometimes called *single-channel* or *generic TCP inspection*).
- All UDP sessions, regardless of the application-layer protocol (sometimes called *single-channel* or *generic UDP inspection*).
- CU-SeeMe (White Pine version only), an Internet videoconferencing program developed as freeware by Cornell University. WhitePine, Inc., sells an enhanced commercial version.
- FTP doesn't support third-party connections (three-way FTP transfer). Allows data channels with the destination ports 1024 to 65535. CBAC won't open a data channel if the FTP client-server authentication fails.
- HTTP (Java blocking).
- Microsoft NetShow.
- UNIX R-commands, such as rlogin, rexec, and rsh.
- RealAudio.
- H.323, such as NetMeeting and ProShare
- Real-Time Streaming Protocol (RTSP): CBAC supports the following RTSP data transport modes.
  - Standard Real-Time Transport Protocol (RTP)   IETF standard (RFC 1889) for real-time audio and video applications, such as Cisco IP/TV and Apple QuickTime 4 software. RTP uses the RTP Control Protocol (RTCP) to manage the multimedia data stream.
  - RealNetworks Real Data Transport (RDT)   Proprietary protocol developed by RealNetworks used for RealServer G2. Uses RTSP for communication control and RDT for the data connection and retransmission of lost packets.
  - Interleaved (Tunnel Mode)   Uses the control channel to tunnel RTP or RDT traffic.
  - Synchronized Multimedia Integration Language (SMIL)   Layout language that allows the creation of multimedia presentations made up of music, voice, image, text, video, and graphics elements. Uses multiple RTSP control and data streams between the player and the servers. Currently available only for RTSP and RDT, but SMIL is a proposed specification of the World Wide Web Consortium (W3C). RealNetworks RealServer and RealServer G2 support SMIL, while Cisco IP/TV and Apple QuickTime 4 don't.
  - RPC   Sun RPC, but not DCE RPC.
  - Simple Mail Transport Protocol (SMTP)   CBAC can inspect SMTP, but not Extended Simple Mail Transport Protocol (ESMTP).

- SQL*Net
- StreamWorks
- TFTP
- VDOLive

CBAC Limitations

As with all things that seem too good to be true, some limitations must be recognized and worked around:

- Only IP TCP and UDP traffic is inspected by CBAC, so ICMP traffic and any other Layer 3 protocols need to be filtered using extended ACLs.
- Any traffic where the router is the source or destination won't be inspected. CBAC will filter traffic passing through, but not traffic originating or terminating on that device.
- Because CBAC only detects and protects against attacks that travel through the firewall, it doesn't normally protect against attacks originating from within the protected network. Deploying CBAC on an intranet-based router is possible.
- CBAC can't inspect in-transit IPSec traffic. Because the IPSec traffic is encrypted, CBAC can't interpret it and, therefore, drops it. CBAC and IPSec can *only* work together at tunnel endpoint by applying IPSec to the external interface and CBAC on the internal interface.

Memory and Performance Issues

You need to consider two issues when determining which model of router to use for CBAC and how much memory to install.

- CBAC uses about 600 bytes of memory per connection established.
- A slight amount of additional CPU processing is used to inspect packets. While evaluating long access lists can negatively impact performance, CBAC mitigates this by hashing ACLs, and then evaluates the hash.

CBAC Process

The following steps describe the sequence of events for CBAC configured on an external interface connected to the Internet. The example starts with an outbound packet, which is the first of a new TCP session configured for CBAC inspection.

1. The outbound packet reaches the firewall's external interface.
2. The packet is checked against the interface's existing outbound ACL, and the packet is permitted. A denied packet would be discarded at this point and couldn't be evaluated by CBAC to allow inbound traffic. With no outbound traffic, there shouldn't be returning traffic.

3. If the packet's application is configured for CBAC inspection, CBAC inspects the packet to determine and record the state information of the connection. As a new session, a new state table entry is created for the new connection. If the application isn't configured for CBAC inspection, it would go directly to Step 5.
4. Using the state information, CBAC creates a temporary entry inserted at the beginning interface's inbound extended ACL. This temporary entry is designed to allow inbound packets that are part of the same session.
5. The outbound packet is forwarded out the interface.
6. When an inbound packet from the just-established session reaches the interface, it's evaluated against the inbound ACL and permitted by the temporary entry created in Step 4.
7. The packet permitted in Step 6 is then inspected by CBAC, and the connection's state table entry is updated as necessary. Based on this updated state information, the inbound extended ACL temporary entries can be modified to permit only packets that are valid for the current state of the connection.
8. Additional inbound and outbound packets from the connection are inspected to update the state table and the temporary inbound ACL entries as needed. The packets are forwarded through the interface.
9. When the connection terminates or times out, the related entries in the state table and the inbound ACL are deleted.

Configuring CBAC

To configure CBAC, perform the following tasks. Each task is described in the following sections.

- Set Audit Trails and Alerts
- Set Global Timeouts and Thresholds
- Define Port-to-Application Mapping (PAM)
- Define Inspection Rules
- Apply Inspection Rules and ACLs to an interface
- Test and Verify

Set Audit Trails and Alerts

Real-time alerts send syslog error messages to central management consoles upon detecting suspicious activity, allowing network managers to respond immediately to intrusions. Enhanced audit-trail features use syslog to track all transactions, recording time stamps, source host, destination host, ports used, session duration, and the total number of transmitted bytes for advanced, session-based reporting.

Cisco IOS Firewall alerts and audit-trail features are now configurable, enabling more flexible reporting and error tracking. The configurable audit-trail features support modular tracking of specific CBAC-supported applications and Java blocking. Both the real-time alerts and the audit-trail features are supported by a variety of third-party reporting tools.

Use the Global Configuration Mode command **ip inspect audit-trail** to turn on CBAC audit-trail messages. The messages are displayed on the console after each CBAC session closes. Use the no form of the command to turn off the feature. The syntax is

```
Rtr1(config)#ip inspect audit-trail
Rtr1(config)#no ip inspect audit-trail
```


This command has no arguments or keywords. By default, the audit-trail messages aren't displayed. This command was introduced in IOS 11.2 P.

The following messages are two examples of audit-trail messages. To determine which protocol was inspected, refer to the responder's port number following the responder's IP address.

```
%FW-6-SESS_AUDIT_TRAIL: tcp session initiator (192.168.1.13:33192)
     sent 22 bytes -- responder (192.168.129.11:25) sent 208 bytes
%FW-6-SESS_AUDIT_TRAIL: ftp session initiator 192.168.1.13:33194)
     sent 336 bytes -- responder (192.168.129.11:21) sent 325 bytes
```

CBAC alert messages are displayed on the console by default. Use the Global Configuration Mode command **ip inspect alert-off** to disable these messages. To reenable CBAC alert messages, use the no form of the command. The syntax is

```
Rtr1(config)#ip inspect alert-off
Rtr1(config)#no ip inspect alert-off
```

This command has no arguments or keywords. This command was introduced in IOS 12.0(5)T.

Logging While it isn't a CBAC feature, make sure logging is enabled and a syslog server is specified, so any incidents are properly logged for future reference.

```
Rtr1(config)#service timestamps log datetime
Rtr1(config)#logging host
Rtr1(config)#logging facility facility-type
Rtr1(config)#logging trap level
```

The commands,—in order,—do the following:

1. Adds the date and time to syslog and audit-trail messages.
2. Defines the host name or IP address of the host to send syslog messages to.
3. Configures the syslog facility in which error messages are sent.
4. (Optional) Limits messages logged to the syslog servers based on severity. The default is level 7 (informational).

Set Global Timeouts and Thresholds

This section looks at configuring the following global timeouts and thresholds used by CBAC.

- TCP SYN and FIN wait times
- TCP, UDP, and DNS idle timers
- TCP flooding thresholds (DoS indicators)

These are global default settings used by CBAC to determine how long to maintain state table entries and as indicators of possible DoS attacks. Each command has a default value and, therefore, needs to be set only to change the default to implement a security policy better.

TCP Session Establishment Timer Use the Global Configuration Mode command **ip inspect tcp synwait-time** to define the number of seconds the software will wait for a TCP session to reach the established state before dropping the session. The session is considered to have reached the established state after the session's first SYN bit is detected. Use the no form of this command to reset the timeout to the default of 30 seconds. The syntax is

```
Rtr1(config)#ip inspect tcp synwait-time seconds
Rtr1(config)#no ip inspect tcp synwait-time
```

This command was introduced in IOS 11.2 P. The default is 30 seconds.

The value specified for this timeout applies to all TCP sessions inspected by CBAC.

TCP Session Termination Timer Use the Global Configuration Mode command **ip inspect tcp finwait-time** to define how many seconds a TCP session will still be managed after the firewall detects a FIN-exchange. The *FIN-exchange* occurs when the TCP session is ready to close. Use the no form of the command to reset the timeout to the default of five seconds. The syntax is

```
Rtr1(config)#ip inspect tcp finwait-time seconds
Rtr1(config)#no ip inspect tcp finwait-time
```

This command was introduced in IOS 11.2 P. The default is five seconds.

The timeout set with this command is referred to as the *finwait timeout.* It applies to all CBAC-inspected TCP sessions.

TCP Session Inactivity Timer Use the Global Configuration Mode command **ip inspect tcp idle-time** to specify the TCP idle timeout—the number of seconds a TCP session will still be managed after no activity. Use the no form of the command to reset the timeout to the default of 3,600 seconds (one hour). The syntax is

```
Rtr1(config)#ip inspect tcp idle-time seconds
Rtr1(config)#no ip inspect tcp idle-time
```

This command was introduced in IOS 11.2 P. The default is 3,600 seconds (one hour).

When CBAC detects a valid TCP packet that's the first in a session for a protocol CBAC is inspecting, the software creates a new state table entry with the information. If no TCP packets for a particular session are detected for the time defined by the TCP idle timeout, the software drops that session entry from the state table and ACL.

This global value can be overridden for specific interfaces by defining a set of inspection rules with the Global Configuration Mode command **ip inspect name**. This command only applies the new timeout to any new or existing inspection rules *that don't have an explicitly defined timeout.*

UDP Session Inactivity Timer Use the Global Configuration Mode command **ip inspect udp idle-time** to specify the UDP idle timeout, the number of seconds a UDP "session" will still be managed after no activity. Use the no form of the command to reset the timeout to the default of 30 seconds. The syntax is

```
Rtr1(config)#ip inspect udp idle-time seconds
Rtr1(config)#no ip inspect udp idle-time
```

This command was introduced in IOS 11.2 P. The default is 30 seconds.

When CBAC detects a valid UDP packet that's the first in a session for a protocol CBAC is inspecting, the software creates a new state table entry with the information. Because UDP is a connectionless service, no actual sessions exist, so the software approximates sessions by examining the information in the packet and determining if the packet is similar to other UDP packets (for example, similar source/destination addresses) and if the packet was detected soon after another similar UDP packet.

Because UDP is a connectionless service, no actual sessions exist as with TCP, so CBAC approximates sessions. It does this by examining the packets and determining if they're similar (source/destination addresses and ports) to other UDP packets. If no UDP packets for a particular session are detected for the time defined by the UDP idle timeout, the software drops those session entries from the state table and ACL.

This global value can be overridden for specific interfaces when you define a set of inspection rules with the Global Configuration Mode command **ip inspect name**. This command only applies the new timeout to any new or existing inspection rules *that don't have an explicitly defined timeout.*

DNS Session Inactivity Timer Use the Global Configuration Mode command **ip inspect dns-timeout** to specify the DNS idle timeout, the length of time a DNS-name lookup session will still be managed after no activity. Use the no form of the command to reset the timeout to the default of five seconds. The syntax is

```
Rtr1(config)#ip inspect dns-timeout seconds
Rtr1(config)#no ip inspect dns-timeout
```

This command was introduced in IOS 11.2 P. The default is five seconds.

When CBAC detects a valid UDP packet for a new DNS-name lookup session for a protocol CBAC is inspecting, the software creates a new state table entry with the information.

If the software detects no packets for the DNS session for a time period defined by the DNS idle timeout, the software then drops that session entry from the state table and ACL.

The DNS idle timeout applies to all DNS-name lookup sessions inspected by CBAC and overrides the global UDP timeout. The DNS idle timeout value also enters Aggressive mode and overrides any timeouts specified for specific interfaces when you define a set of inspection rules with the **ip inspect name** command.

Maximum Incomplete Sessions High/Low Threshold An unusually high number of half-open sessions can indicate a DoS attack is occurring. For TCP, *half-open* means that the session hasn't reached the established state. For UDP, *half-open* means that the firewall has detected traffic from one direction only.

CBAC measures both the total number of existing half-open sessions and the rate of session establishment attempts. Both TCP and UDP half-open sessions are counted in the total number and rate measurements. Measurements are made once a minute.

When the number of existing half-open sessions rises above the threshold set by the **ip inspect max-incomplete high** command, the software then deletes half-open sessions until the number of existing half-open sessions drops below the threshold set by the **ip inspect max-incomplete low** command.

The global value specified for this threshold applies to all TCP and UDP connections inspected by CBAC.

Use the Global Configuration Mode command **ip inspect max-incomplete high** to define the number of existing half-open sessions that will cause the software to start deleting half-open sessions. Use the no form of the command to reset the threshold to the default of 500. The syntax is

```
Rtr1(config)#ip inspect max-incomplete high number
Rtr1(config)#no ip inspect max-incomplete high
```

This command was introduced in IOS 11.2 P. The default is 500 half-open sessions.

Use the Global Configuration Mode command **ip inspect max-incomplete low** to define the number of existing half-open sessions that will cause the software to stop deleting half-open sessions. Use the no form of the command to reset the threshold to the default of 400 half-open sessions. The syntax is

```
Rtr1(config)#ip inspect max-incomplete low number
Rtr1(config)#no ip inspect max-incomplete low
```

This command was introduced in IOS 11.2 P. The default is 400 half-open sessions.

The following example causes the CBAC to start deleting half-open sessions when the number of half-open sessions rises above 800 and to stop when the number drops below 500.

```
Rtr1(config)#ip inspect max-incomplete high 800
Rtr1(config)#ip inspect max-incomplete low 500
```

One Minute Incomplete Sessions High/Low Threshold This is an extension of the preceding threshold, accelerating the process to respond to a rapid increase in incomplete sessions. These rate thresholds are measured as the number of new session connection attempts detected in the last one-minute sample period.

The global value specified for this threshold applies to all TCP and UDP connections inspected by CBAC.

Use the Global Configuration Mode command **ip inspect one-minute high** to define the number of new unestablished sessions that will cause the software to start deleting half-open sessions. Use the no form of the command to reset the threshold to the default of 500. The syntax is

```
Rtr1(config)#ip inspect one-minute high number
Rtr1(config)#no ip inspect one-minute high
```

This command was introduced in IOS 11.2 P. The default is 500 half-open sessions.

Use the Global Configuration Mode command **ip inspect one-minute low** to define the rate of new unestablished TCP sessions that will cause the software to stop deleting half-open sessions. Use the no form of this command to reset the threshold to the default of 400. The syntax is

```
Rtr1(config)#ip inspect one-minute low number
Rtr1(config)#no ip inspect one-minute low
```

This command was introduced in IOS 11.2 P. The default is 400 half-open sessions.

The following example causes the software to start deleting half-open sessions when more than 1,000 session establishment attempts are detected in the last minute and to stop when fewer than 750 sessions are detected in the last minute:

```
Rtr1(config)#ip inspect one-minute high 1000
Rtr1(config)#ip inspect one-minute low 750
```

Maximum Incomplete Sessions Per Destination Host Threshold An unusually high number of half-open sessions with the same destination host address can indicate that a DoS attack is being launched against the host. Use the Global Configuration Mode command **ip inspect tcp max-incomplete host** to specify threshold and blocking time values for TCP host–specific DoS detection and prevention. Use the no form of the command to reset the threshold and blocking time to the default values. The syntax is

```
Rtr1(config)#ip inspect tcp max-incomplete host number block-time seconds
Rtr1(config)#no ip inspect tcp max-incomplete host
```

number	Specifies how many half-open TCP sessions with the same host destination address can exist at a time, before the software starts deleting half-open sessions to the host. Use a number from 1 to 250.
block-time	Specifies blocking of connection initiation to a host.
seconds	Specifies how long the software will continue to delete new connection requests to the host.

This command was introduced in IOS 11.2 P. The default is 50 half-open sessions and 0 minutes.

When the numbers of half-open sessions with the same destination host address rises above this threshold, CBAC will delete half-open sessions choosing a method based on the block-time seconds setting. If the timeout is

0 (the default)	CBAC will delete the oldest half-open session for the host for every new connection request to the host. This ensures the number of half-open sessions to a given host will never exceed the threshold.
Greater than 0	CBAC will delete all existing half-open sessions for the host, and then block all new connection requests to the host until the block-time expires.

The software also sends syslog messages whenever the max-incomplete host number is exceeded and when blocking of connection initiations to a host starts or ends.

The global values specified for the threshold and blocking time apply to all TCP connections inspected by CBAC.

The following example changes the max-incomplete host number to 70 half-open sessions and changes the block-time timeout to 90 seconds.

```
Rtr1(config)#ip inspect tcp max-incomplete host 70 block-time 90
```

Define Port-to-Application Mapping (PAM)

Flexible, per-application port mapping allows CBAC-supported applications to be run on nonstandard TCP and UDP ports. PAM allows network administrators to customize access control for specific applications and services to meet the distinct needs of their networks.

The **ip port-map** command associates TCP or UDP port numbers with applications or services, establishing a table of default port mapping information at the firewall. This information is used to support network environments that run services using ports that are different from the registered or well-known ports associated with a service or application. PAM also supports port mapping for specific host(s) or subnet(s) by using standard ACLs.

The port mapping information in the PAM table is one of three types:

- System defined
- User defined
- Host specific

System-Defined Port Mapping Initially, PAM creates a set of system-defined entries in the mapping table using well-known or registered port mapping information set up during the system startup. The Cisco IOS Firewall CBAC feature requires the system-defined mapping information to function properly. The system-defined mapping information can't be deleted or changed. It isn't possible to assign an application to an existing system-defined mapping, such as attempting to map HTTP services to port 25 (SMTP). The following table shows the well-known or registered port mapping information.

Application Name	Registered Port Number	Protocol Description
Cuseeme	7648	CU-SeeMe Protocol
Exec	512	Remote process execution
ftp	21	File Transfer Protocol (control port)
http	80	Hypertext Transfer Protocol
h323	1720	H.323 Protocol (such as MS NetMeeting and Intel Video Phone)
login	513	Remote login
msrpc	135	Microsoft Remote Procedure Call
netshow	1755	Microsoft NetShow
real-audio-video	7070	RealAudio and RealVideo
smtp	25	Simple Mail Transfer Protocol
sql-net	1521	SQL-NET
streamworks	1558	StreamWorks Protocol
sunrpc	111	SUN Remote Procedure Call
tftp	69	Trivial File Transfer Protocol
vdolive	7000	VDOLive Protocol

User-Defined Port Mapping Network applications that use nonstandard ports require user-defined entries in the mapping table. Use the Global Configuration Mode command **ip port-map** to create user-defined entries ports to application mapping. Use the no form of the command to delete user-defined PAM entries. The command can't be used to change system-defined port mappings. The syntax is

Rtr1(config)#ip port-map *appl-name* port *port-num* [list *acl#*]
Rtr1(config)#no ip port-map *appl-name* port *port-num* [list *acl#*]

appl-name	The name of the application with which to apply the port mapping
port	Indicates a port number maps to the application
port-num	Port number (1 to 65535)
list	The port mapping information applies to a specific host or subnet
acl#	Standard ACL number used to identify the host(s) or subnet(s)

This command was introduced in IOS 12.0(5)T. No default values.

This example shows PAM entries that define a range of nonstandard ports for HTTP services.

```
Rtr1(config)#ip port-map http port 8000
Rtr1(config)#ip port-map http port 8001
Rtr1(config)#ip port-map http port 8002
```

Host-Specific Port Mapping User-defined entries in the mapping table can include host-specific mapping, which establishes port mapping information for specific hosts or subnets. In some situations, it might be necessary to override the default port mapping information for a specific host or subnet, including a system-defined default port mapping information. Use the list option for the **ip port-map** command to specify an ACL for a host or subnet that uses PAM.

In this example, a specific host uses port 8000 for FTP services. ACL 1 identifies the server address (192.168.0.100), while port 8000 is mapped with FTP services:

```
Rtr1(config)#access-list 1 permit 192.168.0.100
Rtr1(config)#ip port-map ftp port 8000 list 1
```

In the next example, the same port number is required by different services running on different hosts. Port 8000 is required for FTP services by host 192.168.0.100, while port 8000 is required for HTTP services by host 192.168.0.175. ACL 10 and ACL 2 identify the specific hosts, while PAM maps the ports with the services for each ACL.

```
Rtr1(config)#access-list 1 permit 192.168.0.100
Rtr1(config)#access-list 2 permit 192.168.0.175
Rtr1(config)#ip port-map ftp port 8000 list 1
Rtr1(config)#ip port-map http port 8000 list 2
```

This example shows a failed attempt to assign the RealAudio application to port 21, which is normally reserved for FTP services. Following that is the correct method to define the host using ACL 1. With this configuration, host(s) in List 1 won't recognize FTP activity on port 21.

```
Rtr1(config)#ip port-map realaudio port 21
Rtr1(config)#Command fail: the port 21 has already been defined for
         ftp by the system.
         No change can be made to the system defined port mappings.
Rtr1(config)#access-list 1 permit 192.168.0.100
Rtr1(config)#ip port-map realaudio port 21 list 1
```

Verify Port to Application Mapping Use the Privileged EXEC Mode command **show ip port-map** to display the Port to Application Mapping (PAM) information. This command displays the port mapping information at the firewall, including the system-defined and user-defined information. Include the application name to display only the entries for that application. Include the port number to display only the entries for that port. The syntax is

Rtr1#show ip port-map [*appl-name* | port *port-num*]

This command was introduced in IOS 12.0(5)T.

The following example shows the port mapping information for FTP services:

```
Rtr1#show ip port-map ftp
Default mapping: ftp             port 21                  system defined
Host specific:   ftp             port 1250   in list 1    user defined
```

Define Inspection Rules

To define a set of inspection rules, use the **ip inspect name** command with the same inspection name for each protocol you want CBAC to inspect. Each set of inspection rules must have a unique inspection name, which shouldn't exceed the 16-character limit. Typically, if inspection is configured for a protocol, return traffic entering the internal network is only permitted if the packets are part of a valid, existing session for which state information is being maintained.

Define either one or two sets of rules per interface. A single set can be used to examine both inbound and outbound traffic, or you can define two sets: one for outbound traffic and one for inbound traffic. To define a single set of inspection rules, configure inspection for all the desired application-layer protocols and for TCP or UDP, as desired. This combination of TCP, UDP, and application-layer protocols join together to form a single set of inspection rules with a unique name.

In general, to configure CBAC inspection for a protocol, packets for that protocol should be permitted to exit the firewall by configuring the appropriate ACL if necessary. Packets for that protocol will only be allowed back in through the firewall if they belong to a valid existing session. Without outbound packets, there can be no existing session. Each protocol packet is inspected to maintain information about the session state.

Use the Global Configuration Mode command **ip inspect name** to define a set of inspection rules. Use the no form of this command to remove the inspection rule for a protocol or to remove the entire set of inspection rules. The syntax is

Rtr1(config)#ip inspect name *inspection-name protocol* [alert {on | off}] [audit-trail {on | off}] [timeout *seconds*]
Rtr1(config)#no ip inspect name *inspection-name protocol* (removes a protocol inspection rule)
Rtr1(config)#no ip inspect name (removes the entire set of inspection rules)

inspection-name	Name of inspection rules set. Up to 16 characters. To add a protocol to an existing set of rules, use the same *inspection-name*.
protocol	Application protocol name is supported by CBAC.
alert {on | off}	(Optional) Each inspected protocol can override the default settings created by the global **ip inspect alert-off** command.
audit-trail {on | off}	(Optional) Each inspected protocol can override the default settings created by the global **ip inspect audit-trail** command.
timeout *seconds*	(Optional) Each inspected protocol can override the default global TCP or UDP idle timeouts, but won't override the global DNS timeout.

This command was introduced in IOS 11.2P. Configurable alert and audit-trail, IP fragmentation checking, and NetShow protocol support were added in 12.0(5)T.

TCP and UDP Inspection Configuring TCP and UDP inspection will permit *any* TCP and UDP packets to enter the internal network through the firewall, even if the application-layer protocol isn't configured to be inspected. TCP and UDP inspection doesn't recognize application-specific commands or processes and might not permit all returning packets for that application. Any returning application packets with port numbers different than the exiting packet will be blocked.

Application-layer protocol inspection takes precedence over the TCP or UDP packet inspection. For example, with FTP inspection, all control channel information will be recorded in the state table, and all FTP traffic is permitted back through the firewall if the control channel information is valid for the state of the FTP session. Any TCP inspection in this case becomes irrelevant.

Generic TCP and UDP inspection is much like reflexive ACLs, in that the packets entering the network must exactly match an existing session. This match is based on having the same source/destination addresses and source/destination port numbers as the existing packet, except reversed. Otherwise, the inbound packets are blocked at the interface.

The following example causes the software to inspect TCP sessions and UDP sessions, and to specifically allow FTP and Real Audio traffic back through the firewall for existing sessions only. UDP traffic has the audit-trail feature on, while the FTP timeout is changed to three minutes.

```
Rtr1(config)#ip inspect name letusin tcp
Rtr1(config)#ip inspect name letusin udp audit-trail on
Rtr1(config)#ip inspect name letusin ftp timeout 180
Rtr1(config)#ip inspect name letusin realaudio-video
```

H.323 Inspection If you want CBAC inspection to work with Microsoft NetMeeting 2.0 traffic, an H.323 application-layer protocol, it's necessary also to configure inspection for TCP because NetMeeting 2.0 uses an additional TCP channel not defined in the H.323 specification. No special configuration options exist for H.323

To add Microsoft NetMeeting 2.0 inspection, it's necessary to add only the following entry because TCP inspection is on in the initial example:

```
Rtr1(config)#ip inspect name letusin h323
```

HTTP Inspection (Java Blocking) With the proliferation of Java applets available on the Internet, protecting networks from malicious applets has become a major concern to network managers. The Java blocking feature can be configured either to filter or to completely deny access to Java applets.

Java inspection enables Java applet filtering at the firewall. *Java applet filtering* distinguishes between trusted and untrusted applets by relying on a list of external sites you designate as "friendly." If an applet is from a friendly site, the firewall allows the applet through. If the applet isn't from a friendly site, the applet is blocked. Alternatively, you could permit applets from all sites, except sites specifically designated as "hostile."

Java blocking uses only numbered standard access lists to define friendly and hostile external sites. ACL "permit" statements define traffic from friendly sites, while ACL "deny statements" define traffic from hostile sites. If Java blocking is defined using an ACL number and no matching ACL exists, all Java applets will be blocked.

NOTE CBAC can't detect or block encapsulated or "zipped" Java applets. Applets in .zip or .jar format aren't blocked at the firewall. CBAC also doesn't detect or block applets loaded via FTP, gopher, or HTTP on a nonstandard port.

Use the no form of the command to remove Java blocking from the inspection set. The syntax is

Rtr1(config)#ip inspect name *inspection-name* [http [java-list *acl#*]] [alert {on | off}] [audit-trail {on | off}] [timeout *seconds*]

Rtr1(config)#no ip inspect name *inspection-name* http

http	Specifies Java applet blocking
java-list *acl#*	A "numbered standard" ACL used to define friendly sites.

The next example would add blocking of all Java applets to the inspection set.

```
Rtr1(config)#ip inspect name letusin http
```

If the next example was used instead, all Java applets would be blocked except those originating from the server 192.168.0.10.

```
Rtr1(config)#access-list 15 permit 192.168.0.10
Rtr1(config)#ip inspect name letusin http java-list 15
```

RPC Inspection *RPC inspection* allows the specification based on program numbers. To define multiple program numbers, create multiple entries for RPC inspection, each with a different program number. If a program number is specified, all traffic for that program number is permitted. Any program number that isn't specified will have all traffic for that program number blocked.

Use the no form of the command to remove RPC inspection from the inspection set. The syntax is

Rtr1(config)#ip inspect name *inspection-name* [rpc program-number *number* [wait-time *minutes*]] [alert {on | off}] [audit-trail {on | off}] [timeout *seconds*]

Rtr1(config)#no ip inspect name *inspection-name* rpc

rpc program-number *number*	The RPC program number to permit.
wait-time *minutes*	(Optional) Number of minutes to keep a small hole in the firewall to allow subsequent RPC connections from the same source address, and to the same destination address and port. Default is zero minutes.

The following example adds two RPC program numbers to the inspection set.

```
Rtr1(config)#ip inspect name letusin rpc program-number 100002
Rtr1(config)#ip inspect name letusin rpc program-number 100010
```

Fragment Inspection (DoS Attacks) CBAC inspection rules can help protect hosts against DoS attacks involving fragmented IP packets. Even if the firewall prevents an attacker from completing a connection to a protected host, the attacker might still be able to disrupt services provided by that host in two ways: by sending a large number of "noninitial" IP fragments or by sending a complete set of fragmented packets through a router that has an ACL that filters out the first fragment of the packet. Either way, the remaining fragments can tie up host resources as it tries in vain to reassemble the incomplete packets.

Using fragmentation inspection, the CBAC maintains an interfragment state for IP traffic. Noninitial fragments are discarded unless the corresponding initial fragment has already been permitted to pass through the firewall. Noninitial fragments received before the corresponding initial fragments are discarded. Because many circumstances exist that can cause out-of-order delivery of legitimate fragments, fragmentation inspection can have a severe performance implications. For this reason, fragment inspection is off by default.

Use the no form of the command to remove fragment inspection from the inspection set. The syntax is

Rtr1(config)#ip inspect name *inspection-name* fragment [max *number* timeout *seconds*]

Rtr1(config)#no ip inspect name *inspection-name* fragment

fragment	Specifies fragment inspection for the named inspection set.
max *number*	This is the maximum number of unassembled packets for which state structure information memory space is allocated by the IOS. Unassembled packets are those arriving before the initial packet for a session. Range is 50 through 10,000 entries, with 256 being the default. Because memory is allocated for these state structures, the larger the number, the more memory is reserved, possibly causing memory resources to be exhausted.
timeout *seconds* (fragmentation)	The number of seconds a packet state structure remains active. When the timeout value expires, the router drops the unassembled packet, freeing that structure for use by another packet. The default timeout value is one second. If timeout is set to more than one second, it's automatically adjusted by the IOS if the number of "free" state structures dips below certain thresholds. If the number of free states is less than 32, the timeout is divided by 2. If the number of free states is less than 16, the timeout is set to one second.

Even if the system is under heavy attack from fragmented packets, legitimate fragmented traffic, if any, will still get some fraction of the firewall's fragment state resources and, more important, regular unfragmented traffic can pass through the firewall unimpeded.

The following example adds fragment checking to that software inspection set. The firewall will allocate 100 state structures, meaning 100 initial fragments for 100 different packets sent through the router can be stored before new ones must be discarded. The timeout value for dropping unassembled packets is set to four seconds.

```
Rtr1(config)#ip inspect name letusin fragment max 100 timeout 4
```

SMTP Inspection SMTP inspection searches SMTP commands for illegal commands. Packets with illegal commands are dropped, and the SMTP session will hang and eventually time out. An illegal command is any command except for the following legal commands: DATA, EXPN, HELO, HELP, MAIL, NOOP, QUIT, RCPT, RSET, SAML, SEND, SOML, and VRFY.

Use the no form of the command to remove fragment inspection from the inspection set. The syntax is

Rtr1(config)#ip inspect name *inspection-name* smtp [alert {on | off}] [audit-trail {on | off}] [timeout *seconds*]
Rtr1(config)#no ip inspect name *inspection-name* smtp

The following example adds SMTP inspection with default audit-trail and alert setting.

```
Rtr1(config)#ip inspect name letusin smtp
```

Apply Inspection Rules and ACLs to an Interface

It's time to apply the inspection set to a router interface. If the interface connects to the external network, apply the inspection rules to outbound traffic. If the interface connects to the internal network, apply the inspection rules to inbound traffic. By applying the rules to outbound traffic, then returning inbound packets will be permitted if they belong to a valid connection with existing state information. This connection state must be initiated with an outbound packet.

Normally, you apply only one inspection rule per interface. The only exception is if you want to enable CBAC in two directions between two departments or partner networks. To configure CBAC in both directions on a single firewall interface, apply two rules, one for each direction.

Use the interface configuration **ip inspect** command to apply a set of inspection rules to an interface. Use the no form of the command to remove the set of rules from the interface. The syntax is

Rtr1(config-if)#ip inspect *inspection-name* {in | out}
Rtr1(config-if)#no ip inspect *inspection-name* {in | out}

in	Applies the inspection rules to inbound traffic (relative to the router)
out	Applies the inspection rules to outbound traffic (relative to the router)

This command was introduced in IOS 11.2.

This example applies a set of inspection rules named letusin to an external interface's outbound traffic. The inspection set is the one created in the example and isn't repeated here. Inbound IP traffic is permitted only if the traffic is part of an existing session created by the letusin inspections. All other inbound traffic will be denied unless it's the specific ICMP traffic allowed by the inbound ACL 101. The outbound ACL 150 specifies the traffic that can leave the network.

```
Rtr1(config)#access-list 101 deny udp any any
Rtr1(config)#access-list 101 deny tcp any any
Rtr1(config)#access-list 101 permit icmp any any echo-reply
Rtr1(config)#access-list 101 permit icmp any any packet-too-big
Rtr1(config)#access-list 101 permit icmp any any time-exceeded
Rtr1(config)#access-list 101 permit icmp any any traceroute
Rtr1(config)#access-list 101 permit icmp any any unreachable
Rtr1(config)#access-list 150 permit tcp any any
Rtr1(config)#access-list 150 permit udp any any
Rtr1(config)#access-list 150 permit icmp any any
Rtr1(config)#interface serial0
Rtr1(config-if)#ip inspect letusin out
Rtr1(config-if)#ip access-group 150 out
Rtr1(config-if)#ip access-group 101 in
```

PART II

Select the Interface

When implementing CBAC, deciding whether to configure CBAC on an internal or an external interface of your firewall is necessary. In firewall terminology, *internal* refers to the interface(s) where sessions must originate for the traffic to be permitted through the firewall. *External* refers to the interface(s) where sessions can't originate. Sessions originating from the external side will be blocked.

Figure 6-2 shows a simple topology common on perimeter routers or networks without a protected DMZ. CBAC would be configured on the external interface—Serial 0—to prevent unwanted traffic from entering the firewall and the internal network.

Figure 6-3 shows a common topology that includes a protected DMZ for shared servers. CBAC is configured for the internal interface—Ethernet 1—allowing external traffic free access to the DMZ. At the same time, external traffic is prevented from entering the internal network, unless it's part of a session initiated from within the internal network.

To provide firewall security between two departments or two partner networks, configure CBAC in two directions. CBAC can be configured in two directions at one or more interfaces. First, configure CBAC in one direction using the appropriate internal and external interface designations. Then, configure CBAC in the other direction with the interface designations swapped.

CBAC on an External Interface Create an outbound standard or extended IP access list and apply it to the external interface. This ACL permits all packets to be allowed to exit the network, including any packets you want inspected by CBAC.

Create an inbound extended IP access list and apply it to the external interface. This ACL denies any traffic to be inspected by CBAC. When an outbound packet triggers CBAC, a temporary opening is created in this inbound ACL to permit only traffic from a valid existing session. If the inbound ACL is configured to permit the desired traffic, then CBAC creates unnecessary openings in the firewall for packets that would be allowed anyway.

CBAC on an Internal Interface Create an inbound standard or extended IP access list and apply it to the internal interface. This ACL permits all packets to be allowed to exit the protected network, including any packets you want inspected by CBAC.

Create an outbound extended IP access list and apply it to the internal interface. This ACL denies any traffic to be inspected by CBAC. When an inbound packet triggers CBAC, a temporary opening is created in this outbound ACL to permit only traffic from a valid existing session.

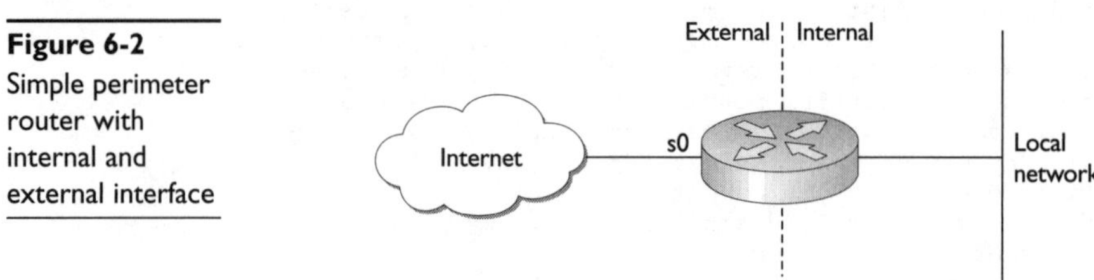

Figure 6-2 Simple perimeter router with internal and external interface

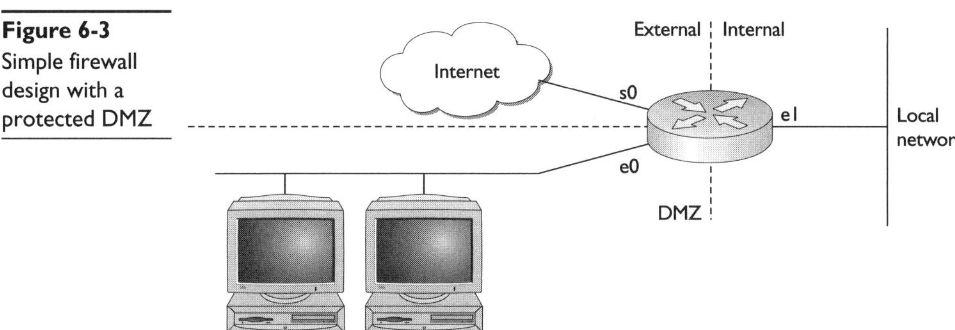

Figure 6-3 Simple firewall design with a protected DMZ

Test and Verify

Use the Privilege EXEC Mode command **show ip inspect** with its various options to view CBAC configuration and session information. The syntax is

Rtr1#show ip inspect {name *inspection-name* | config | interfaces | session [detail] | all}

config	Shows the complete CBAC inspection configuration.
interfaces	Shows interface configuration for applied inspection rules and ACLs.
session [detail]	Shows existing CBAC inspection sessions. (Optional) keyword **detail** displays more information about the sessions.
all	Shows all CBAC configuration and all sessions being tracked and inspected by CBAC.

This command was introduced in IOS 11.2 P.

The following example shows sample output for the **show ip inspect name testinspect** command, where testinspect is the inspection rule set. The output shows the protocols as inspected by CBAC and the idle timeouts for each.

```
Rtr1#show ip inspect name testinspect
Inspection Rule Configuration
 Inspection name testinspect
    tcp timeout 3600
    udp timeout 90
    ftp timeout 2400
```

The following, which is sample output for the **show ip inspect config** command, shows CBAC configuration, including global timeouts, thresholds, and inspection rules:

```
Rtr1#show ip inspect config
Session audit trail is disabled
one-minute (sampling period) thresholds are [500:750] connections
max-incomplete sessions thresholds are [500:750]
max-incomplete tcp connections per host is 50. Block-time 0 minute.
tcp synwait-time is 30 sec -- tcp finwait-time is 5 sec
tcp idle-time is 3600 sec -- udp idle-time is 90 sec
dns-timeout is 5 sec
Inspection Rule Configuration
 Inspection name testinspect
```

```
    tcp timeout 3600
    udp timeout 90
    ftp timeout 2400
```

This output demonstrates the **show ip inspect interfaces** command:

```
Rtr1#show ip inspect interfaces
Interface Configuration
 Interface Ethernet0
  Inbound inspection rule is testinspect
    tcp timeout 3600
    udp timeout 90
    ftp timeout 2400
  Outgoing inspection rule is not set
  Inbound access list is not set
  Outgoing access list is not set
```

This output demonstrates the **show ip inspect sessions** command, indicating an FTP session and showing the source and destination addresses and port numbers (separated by colons):

```
Rtr1#show ip inspect sessions
Established Sessions
 Session 25A3318 (192.168.0.17:20)=>(192.168.1.9:47091) ftp-data SIS_OPEN
 Session 25A6E1C (192.168.1.9:47098)=>(192.168.0.17:21) ftp SIS_OPEN
```

This output demonstrates the **show ip inspect sessions detail** command, including times, number of bytes sent, and which access lists are applied:

```
Rtr1#show ip inspect sessions detail
Established Sessions
 Session 25A335C (192.168.0.17:20)=>(192.168.1.9:47091) ftp-data SIS_OPEN
   Created 00:00:07, Last heard 00:00:00
   Bytes sent (initiator:responder) [0:3416064] acl created 1
   Inbound access-list 100 applied to interface Ethernet0
 Session 25A6E1C (192.168.1.9:47098)=>(192.168.0.17:21) ftp SIS_OPEN
   Created 00:01:34, Last heard 00:00:07
   Bytes sent (initiator:responder) [196:616] acl created 1
   Inbound access-list 100 applied to interface Ethernet0
```

IOS Firewall Management

You can administer the IOS Firewall features in two methods: the traditional command-line interface (CLI) and Cisco ConfigMaker.

Command Line Interface

For users who are familiar with the CLI, its primary advantage is that it can be used across virtually the entire product line. As with any complex skill, the more familiar you become with the CLI, the easier it becomes. Strengths of the CLI include

- Similarity across product lines.
- Functional online help to assist with complex tasks.

- Virtually every feature can be accessed or configured.

On the possible downside, the initial exposure to CLI can be intimidating and confusing. The additions and changes in commands with new releases can be a challenge to keep up with.

NOTE A technician I met early in my career told me the Cisco CLI was the way "to keep the fools that shouldn't be touching routers away." While I've never found that in any Cisco document, I suspect the result might be on the mark, even if the intent is not.

ConfigMaker

Cisco ConfigMaker is an easy-to-use Microsoft Windows–based software tool designed to configure smaller network Cisco routers, switches, hubs, and other network devices. Advanced features include implementing security policies and managing the Cisco IOS Firewall quickly and efficiently with GUI-based management. Cisco ConfigMaker 2.1 and later versions include a Security Wizard for step-by-step guidance for quick configuration

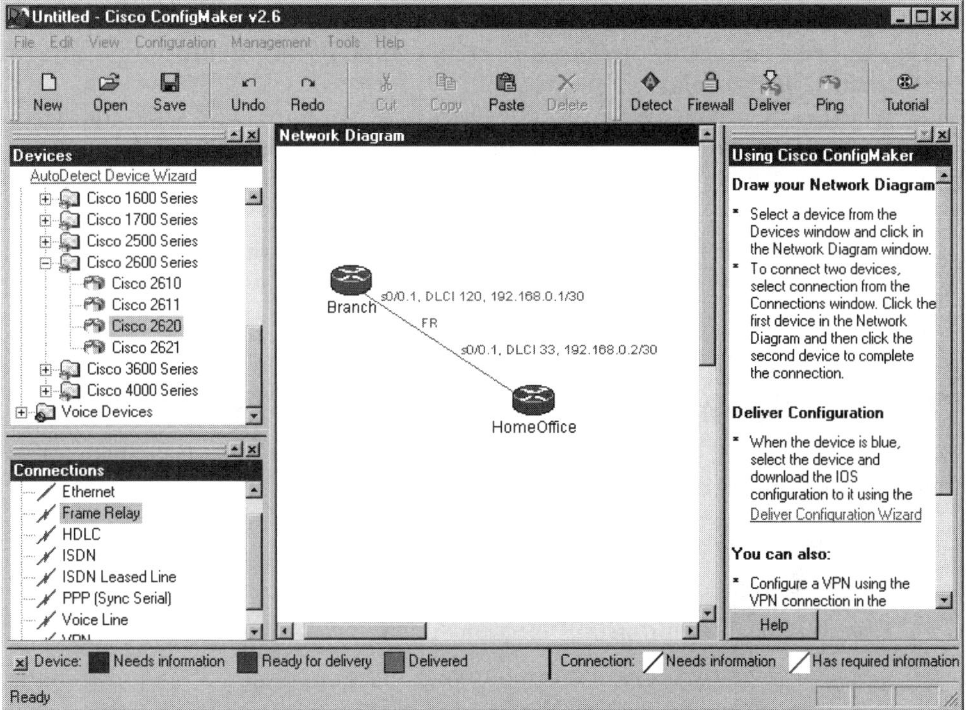

Figure 6-4 Cisco ConfigMaker tool for network design and implementation

of security policy for the Cisco IOS Firewall. They also support NAT and IPSec configuration. Figure 6-4 shows the ConfigMaker interface.

ConfigMaker prompts, wizards, and help screens guide users through the setup process. Online WAN configuration worksheets list important information the network administrator must obtain from the Internet service provider (ISP) or WAN service provider before configuring the devices. The program includes a multimedia movie tutorial.

Configurations can be downloaded or uploaded to the appropriate devices from a standalone PC or over the network.

Configuration wizards include the following:

Task wizards	Prompt user through processes and for key information.
AutoDetect Device Wizard	Can automatically detect and identify the configuration of any supported Cisco device on the network and any WAN or voice interfaces installed in a modular router.
Address Network Wizard	Quick-and-easy completion of complex network addressing procedures by using supplied address ranges and assigning the addresses to selected devices or the entire network.
Security Wizard	Enable policy-based configurations for efficient setup of the Cisco IOS Firewall feature set for Cisco 1600 and 2500 series routers.
Deliver Configuration Wizard	Once the configuration is complete, the wizard can automatically download it through the console port or over the network.

ConfigMaker supports routers up through the 4000 series, but little or no support exists for the Catalyst switches.

To download ConfigMaker, go to the Cisco web site, http://www.cisco.com/warp/public/cc/pd/nemnsw/cm/index.shtml, or do a search for ConfigMaker. No CCO account is required, but you're asked to supply some information before downloading.

STUDY TIP For those of you attempting to certify without access to devices, look at this product, which will at least challenge and assist you in working with many of the technologies covered in the exams.

Chapter Review

The Cisco IOS Firewall feature set, a part of the Cisco Secure system, is made up of the following four interrelated features:

- Cisco IOS Firewall Context-Based Access Control
- Port to Application Mapping
- Cisco IOS Firewall Intrusion Detection System
- Cisco IOS Firewall Authentication Proxy

Context-Based Access Control (CBAC) allows the firewall to take the access list type filter to a much higher level. Whereas ACLs are limited to Layer 3 and Layer 4 information for filtering, the CBAC can incorporate knowledge of the operation of supported application protocols to make decisions. This allows for more flexibility in the number of and port addressing of communications channels through the firewall.

Other CBAC features allow for monitoring and reacting to common DoS attacks and e-mail attacks involving unauthorized SMTP commands.

Port to Application Mapping (PAM) allows the flexibility of incorporating nonstandard TCP and UDP port numbers in the secure openings through the firewall.

Questions

1. True or False. IPSec is a part of the Cisco IOS Firewall feature set.
   A. True
   B. False
2. True or False. The Cisco IOS Firewall feature set is implemented on all Cisco router series.
   A. True
   B. False
3. Which of the following IOS features is *not* part of the Firewall feature set?
   A. Intrusion detection
   B. Context-Based Access Control (CBAC)
   C. AAA
   D. Java blocking
4. True or False. CBAC can incorporate application layer information in its filtering.
   A. True
   B. False
5. In the following command, what does the 30 represent?
   Rtr1(config)#ip inspect tcp idle-time 30
   A. Minutes
   B. Packets
   C. Seconds
   D. Hours
6. True or False. CBAC can filter TCP, UDP, and ICMP traffic.
   A. True
   B. False
7. The memory required for each CBAC connection is what?
   A. 600 bits
   B. 600 bytes

C. 600K

D. Varies with the data

8. Which of the following is *not* a step in configuring CBAC?

A. Set audit trails and alerts.

B. Set global timeouts and thresholds.

C. Define inspection rules.

D. Remove all nonstandard Port-to-Application Mapping.

E. Apply inspection rules and ACLs.

9. Which of the following is a DoS protective measure?

A. RPC inspection

B. Fragment inspection

C. SMTP inspection

D. HTTP inspection

10. Which of the following defines the number of seconds the software will wait for a TCP session to reach the established state before dropping the session?

A. Rtr1(config)#ip inspect tcp synwait-time 20

B. Rtr1(config-if)#ip inspect tcp synwait-time 20

C. Rtr1(config)#ip inspect tcp finwait-time 20

D. Rtr1(config-if)#ip inspect tcp finwait-time 20

11. In the following command, what does the number 800 represent?
Rtr1(config)#ip inspect max-incomplete high 800

A. Seconds

B. Minutes

C. Half-open TCP sessions

D. DNS-name lookup session

12. What does the following command do?
Rtr1(config)#ip port-map realaudio port 21

A. Assigns port 21 to be used by Real Audio.

B. States a preference for port 21 to be used by Real Audio.

C. The command will fail because CBAC doesn't support Real Audio.

D. The command will fail because port 21 is reserved for FTP.

13. True or False. ConfigMaker is an alternative for configuring Firewall features.

A. True

B. False

14. Which two commands might be useful against DoS attacks?
    A. Maximum Incomplete Sessions High/Low Threshold
    B. UDP Session Inactivity Timer
    C. TCP Session Termination Timer
    D. One Minute Incomplete Sessions High/Low Threshold
15. Which statement is *not* true about CBAC?
    A. Only IP TCP and UDP traffic is inspected by CBAC.
    B. CBAC doesn't normally protect against attacks from within the protected network.
    C. CBAC and reflexive ACLs work well together.
    D. CBAC can't inspect in-transit IPSec traffic.

Answers

1. **B.** False. They're used together often, but they're separate feature sets.
2. **B.** False. It is implemented only on the Cisco 800, uBR900, 1400, 1600, 1700, 2500, 2600, 3600, 7100, 7200, and 7500 and RSM series routers.
3. **C.** AAA It is in the regular IOS feature set.
4. **A.** True
5. **C.** Seconds
6. **A.** False. It's limited to TCP and UDP traffic.
7. **B.** 600 bytes
8. **D.** Remove all nonstandard Port-to-Application Mapping.
9. **B.** Fragment inspection
10. **A.** Rtr1(config)#ip inspect tcp synwait-time 20
11. **C.** Half-open TCP session
12. **D.** The command will fail because port 21 is reserved for FTP.
13. **A.** True
14. **A.** Maximum Incomplete Sessions High/Low Threshold and **D**. One Minute Incomplete Sessions High/Low Threshold
15. **C.** CBAC and reflexive ACLs work well together

CHAPTER 7

IOS Firewall—Intrusion Detection System

In this chapter, you will learn how to:

- Use Cisco IOS Firewall IDS
- Initialize the IOS Firewall IDS
- Configure, disable, and exclude signatures
- Create and apply IDS audit rules

With the growing awareness of, and commitment to, network security as the way to secure business transactions—both internally and over the Internet—more and more businesses are recognizing that security concepts and features must be integrated into the network design and infrastructure.

According to Cisco advertising, 80 percent of the Internet backbone routers run Cisco IOS software, which makes it the most fundamental component of today's network infrastructure. The Cisco IOS software-based security features, combined with the wide range of products supported, makes it a logical solution for any organization's end-to-end Internet, intranet, and remote access network security requirements.

This chapter looks at the Cisco IOS intrusion detection system (IDS) features that are now a part of the IOS Firewall feature set on many router platforms. In the last four chapters of this book, you willlearn about the Cisco Secure IDS appliances that make up the first team in Cisco's intrusion detection strategy.

STUDY TIP The material in this chapter is only part of the exam objectives for the Managing Cisco Network Security Exam (MCNS 640-100), but reviewing it when you prepare for the IDS with Policy Manager Exam (IDS 9E0-572) will help you see how the products can be compared and used together.

Intrusion Detection System (IDS)

An intrusion detection system (IDS) device inspects all network activity passing through it and identifies suspicious patterns that might indicate a network or device attack. IDS can be categorized three ways.

Misuse detection vs. anomaly detection	With *misuse detection,* the IDS analyzes the data stream and compares it to databases of known attack signatures. The IDS can only look at previously documented, specific attacks. This is similar to the process many virus-scanning programs use, and, like those programs, the protection is only as good as the database of attack signatures available. In *anomaly detection* (or *profile detection*), the administrator defines the baseline profile of the "normal" network traffic characteristics. The IDS monitors network segments and compares their state to the baseline, looking for deviations or anomalies.
Network-based vs. host-based systems	With network-based systems (NIDS), such the Cisco IDS 4200 Series appliances, the individual packets flowing through a network are analyzed by dedicated devices. As specialty devices, NIDS have been optimized to detect suspicious packets, which, typically, are overlooked by a firewall's filtering rules. A *host-based system* is IDS software configured on key resources such as servers, routers, or switches to examine activity on that device.
Passive system vs. reactive system	When a *passive system* detects a potential security threat, it logs the pertinent information and signals an alert message. A *reactive system* would log the event and send out the alert but, at the same time, the IDS responds to block traffic from the suspected malicious source.

This capability to react to an evolving threat allows IDS implementations to provide protection beyond that of a firewall without IDS features. Furthermore, firewalls tend to be configured to look for bad traffic coming into the network, but remain oblivious to internal traffic. IDS can simultaneously protect the network from internal and external threats.

IOS Firewall Intrusion Detection System

The IOS Firewall IDS feature acts as an inline sensor, watching packets and sessions as they flow through the router, scanning each for pattern matches to any known IDS signatures. When packets in a session match a signature, the IDS system can be configured to do the following:

- Send an alarm to a Syslog server and/or to a Cisco Secure IDS Director centralized management device (formerly the NetRanger system).
- Discard the packet.
- Reset the TCP connection.

While enabling both the firewall and intrusion detection features of the CBAC security engine to support a network security policy is preferable, each of these features can be enabled independently and on different router interfaces.

Devices Supporting the IOS Firewall IDS Features

Cisco IOS software-based intrusion detection is available on the Cisco uBR900, 1720, 2600, 3600, 7100, 7200, and 7500 series routers, and the RSM for Catalyst 5000 switches.

The IDS technology has been included with the firewall feature set since version 12.1 or 12.2 of the IOS, depending on the device platform. More models might be supported later. You must choose a feature set that contains the firewall and IDS features when you order or upgrade the device IOS. For this reason, a router IOS that supports the firewall features doesn't necessarily mean that the IDS technology is included. Figure 7-1 shows a sample of the Cisco IOS Upgrade Planner from the Cisco web site for the model 1720 router. Notice that the firewall features (FW) and the intrusion features (IDS) are available in combination with various protocols and features, such as IPX. The IOS releases with firewall features without IDS are typically capped at version 12.0(4). Memory and flash requirements often increase, as does the cost of the IOS when additional features are added.

The following IOS image names are the latest 1720 release for IP with the firewall features only, while the second listing includes the IDS features. The last two entries are for a 2600 and a 7000 with RSP, respectively, with each having Enterprise and IPSec features. The *o* indicates firewall features, while the o3 indicates firewall and IDS features.

```
c1700-oy-mz.120-5.T1.bin
c1700-o3y-mz.122-12a.bin
c2600-jk8o3s-mz.122-12.bin
rsp-jk8o3sv-mz.122-10b.bin
```

[12.2] [12.1] [12.0] [11.3] [11.2] [11.1] [11.0] [10.3] [All]

Your Selected Platform	Select Release	Select Software Feature
1720	**Major Release Updates** 12.2.12a LD 12.2.12 LD 12.2.10b ED 12.2.10a LD 12.2.10 LD 12.2.7c LD 12.2.7b LD 12.2.7a LD 12.2.7 LD 12.2.6h LD 12.2.6g LD 12.2.6f LD 12.2.6e LD 12.2.6d LD 12.2.6c LD 12.2.6b LD	IP IP PLUS IP PLUS 40 IP PLUS 56 IP PLUS IPSEC 56 IP/ADSL IP/ADSL PLUS IP/ADSL PLUS IPSEC 56 IP/ADSL/FW/IDS PLUS IPSEC 56 IP/ADSL/IPX/AT/IBM PLUS IP/ADSL/IPX/AT/IBM/FW/IDS PLUS IPSEC 56 IP/ADSL/IPX/AT/IBM/VOICE/FW/IDS PLUS IPSEC 56 IP/ADSL/IPX/FW/IDS PLUS IP/ADSL/IPX/VOICE/FW/IDS PLUS IP/ADSL/VOICE PLUS IP/ADSL/VOICE PLUS IPSEC 56 IP/ADSL/VOICE/FW/IDS PLUS IP/ADSL/VOICE/FW/IDS PLUS IPSEC 56 IP/FW IP/FW PLUS IPSEC 56 IP/FW/IDS IP/FW/IDS PLUS IPSEC 56

Figure 7-1 Cisco CCO IOS Upgrade Planner showing IDS feature sets

Cisco IDS Attack Signatures

The most recent Cisco IOS Firewall IDS uses 59 *attack signatures,* representing a broad cross section of intrusion-detection signatures, which identify severe breaches of security and the most common network attacks and information-gathering scans. Unlike virus protection software, IDS signatures aren't updated periodically by the system. Currently, the number of signatures only changes if a version upgrade contains any additions or deletions. The Cisco IOS Firewall IDS signatures are categorized into four types:

- Info Atomic
- Info Compound
- Attack Atomic
- Attack Compound

To understand these categories better, the signature keywords are as follows:

Info	Information-gathering activity, such as a port sweep.
Attack	Attacks attempted into the protected network, such as denial of service (DoS) attempts or the execution of illegal commands during an FTP session.
Atomic	Simple patterns, such as an attempt to access a specific port on a specific host.
Compound	Complex patterns, such as a sequence of operations distributed across multiple hosts over an arbitrary period of time.

The intrusion detection signatures included in the Cisco IOS Firewall were chosen from a broad cross section of intrusion detection signatures as representative of the most common network attacks and information-gathering scans. A small sample of the signatures is included in the following table.

Sig ID	Signature Name	Sig Type	Description
1100	IP Fragment Attack	Attack, Atomic	Triggers when any IP datagram is received with the more fragments flag set to 1 or if an offset is indicated in the offset field.
2003	ICMP Redirect	Info, Atomic	Triggers when an IP datagram is received with the protocol field in the IP header set to 1 (ICMP) and the type field in the ICMP header set to 5 (Redirect).
2154	Ping of Death Attack	Attack, Atomic	Triggers when an IP datagram is received with the protocol field in the IP header set to 1 (ICMP), the Last Fragment bit is set, and (IP offset × 8) + (IP data length) > 65535. In other words, the IP offset plus the rest of the packet is greater than the maximum size for an IP packet.
3050	Half-open SYN Attack/SYN Flood	Attack, Compound	Triggers when multiple TCP sessions were improperly initiated on any of several well-known service ports. Detection of this signature is currently limited to FTP, Telnet, HTTP, and e-mail servers (TCP ports 21, 23, 80, and 25, respectively).

For a complete listing and more information on IDS signatures, go to http://www.cisco.com and do a search for Cisco IOS Firewall IDS Signature List, and then look through the resulting choices for the same phrase in bold.

False Positives

The signatures integrated into the IOS software monitor for severe breaches of security. They are used to watch for those data flows you wouldn't normally expect to see in an operating network. A *false positive* is an erroneous report from an IDS, indicating it detected a potentially malicious pattern. The pattern appears to matches a signature but, in fact, is a valid and acceptable transmission. Any intrusion detection technology can and does report false positives. This can be looked at as erring on the side of security or caution, but it can also block necessary traffic.

The IOS-based intrusion-detection features were developed with flexibility in mind, so individual signatures could be disabled in case of false positives.

Cisco Secure IDS Director Support

The Cisco IOS Firewall intrusion detection capabilities have an enhanced reporting mechanism that permits logging to the Cisco Secure IDS Director console in addition to a Syslog server to provide a consistent view of all intrusion detection sensors throughout a network. Administrators can deploy the IOS Firewall IDS to complement their existing IDS systems. This allows IDS protection to be deployed to areas that might not support a Cisco Secure IDS Sensor. The IOS Firewall IDS signature features can be deployed alongside or independent of other Cisco IOS Firewall features.

The Cisco Secure IDS consists of three components:

- Sensor
- Director
- Post Office

Cisco *Secure IDS Sensors*, dedicated high-speed network appliances, analyze the content and context of individual packets to determine if traffic constitutes a threat. If a data stream appears unauthorized or suspicious, such as a ping sweep or a SATAN attack, the sensors can detect the policy violation in real-time, forward alarms to a Cisco Secure IDS Director management console, and remove the offender from the network.

The *Cisco Secure IDS Director* is a software-based management system that can monitor the activity of multiple Cisco Secure IDS Sensors located on local or remote network segments. Events are sent to the Director by an IDS Sensor or an IDSM that detects a security violation. The *smid daemon* on the Director interprets this event information and passes it to the *nrdirmap daemon,* which is responsible for displaying this information on the Director's maps.

Depending on the severity of an alarm, the alarm icon displays in different colors: red for severe, yellow for moderate, green otherwise. The Cisco Secure IDS Director is an application that runs on either HP or Sun Solaris UNIX workstations. The Director is covered in detail in the final chapter of this book.

The *Cisco Secure IDS Post Office Protocol* is the communication backbone that allows Cisco Secure IDS services and hosts to communicate with each other. All communication is supported by a proprietary, connection-based protocol that can switch between alternative routes to maintain point-to-point connections.

NOTE Version 2.2.2 of the Cisco Secure IDS Director replaces the name "Cisco Secure IDS Post Office Protocol" with "Communication Service." The version 2.2.2 Installation program replaces the nr.postofficed daemon.

Performance Implications

The impact on performance of the IOS intrusion detection features depends on the number of signatures enabled, the router platform, the overall traffic level on the router, and other features enabled on the router—such as encryption, CBAC, and so on. Because the router is working as a security device, no packets are allowed to bypass the security mechanisms. The IDS process in the IOS Firewall router acts as a filter in the packet path, thus searching each packet for signature matches. Because the entire packet is searched in many cases, the state information, and even the application state and awareness, must be maintained by the router.

IOS IDS vs. Cisco Secure IDS

The *Cisco Secure IDS Sensor* is a dedicated appliance that passively monitors the network and reacts to suspicious signatures indicating potential malicious activity. The IDS device can be configured to block this activity. The Cisco IOS-based IDS system is an integral component of the IOS software and, therefore, lies directly in the packet path, rather than being a separate appliance. The IOS IDS technology expands the perimeter protection capabilities offered by the IOS Firewall by being able to take appropriate actions on packets and data flows that appear to be malicious network activity or to violate the organization security policy.

Other differences include the following:

- The Cisco Secure IDS Sensor device processing speed is faster than that of the IOS feature because of the shared resources design of the integrated router-based solution.
- The Cisco Secure IDS Sensor device includes more signatures than the intrusion detection feature on the Cisco IOS Firewall.
- The Cisco Secure IDS Sensor device can reconfigure a Cisco router by dynamically adding an access control list to block intruders, but the IOS version can't do this.
- The Cisco Secure IDS Sensor device can be managed remotely by the Cisco Secure IDS Director. While the IOS version can send output to the IDS Director, it doesn't take instructions from it.

PART II

When to Choose the Cisco IOS Firewall IDS Features

Because the IOS Firewall IDS supports intrusion detection features for a wide range of Cisco router platforms, it can make a powerful addition to any network perimeter. The features can be especially useful in locations where a router is being deployed to provide additional security between network segments, such as between the organization and a partner site.

The Firewall IDS features can provide increased protection between intranet connections, such as branch-office connections to the corporate office or even providing additional security for an internal department like an R&D program. Three examples of IOS Firewall IDS supporting the security goals of all sizes of organizations include:

- Small and medium-sized businesses looking for a cost-effective way to add IDS features to their security policies for their network router(s).
- Enterprise customers looking for a cost-effective way to extend their IDS security protection and policies across all network boundaries, including branch-office, intranet, and extranet perimeters.
- Service providers that want to provide router-based managed firewall and intrusion detection services for their customers.

The IOS IDS support of the Cisco Secure IDS Director security-management system allows many routers and the Catalyst 6500 family of switches to provide additional security and visibility into the network in support of the organization's Cisco Secure IDS appliance implementation. The Cisco Secure IDS appliance features and implementation are covered in detail in the last four chapters of this book.

Cisco IOS Firewall IDS Configuration Task List

Use these four basic steps to configure the IDS features if the network is using the Cisco Secure Director:

- Initialize Cisco IOS Firewall IDS (required)
- Initialize the Post Office (required)
- Configure and apply audit rules (required)
- Verify the configuration (optional)

The second step is only applicable when working with the Director. If the network isn't using the Director, a logging feature within initializing the Post Office steps should still be used to create a history of the IDS activity.

STUDY TIP The MCNS 640-100 exam doesn't assume the Cisco Secure Director is present, and therefore doesn't (at press time) require you to know those commands. The commands are included here to complete the coverage and in anticipation that the exam objectives could change. Assume the commands in the other three steps are required.

Initializing the IOS Firewall IDS

Only two commands initialize Cisco IOS Firewall IDS on a router. This section introduces the purpose, syntax, and examples of each.

The ip audit smtp spam Command

Use the **global configuration mode** command **ip audit smtp spam** to set the threshold beyond which you suspect e-mail messages contain spam. Use the no version of this command to set the number of recipients to the default setting. The syntax is

```
Rtr1(config)#ip audit smtp spam recipients
Rtr1(config)# no ip audit smtp spam
```

recipients	Integer (1–65535) that designates the maximum number of recipients in a mail message before a spam attack is suspected. The default is 250.

This command was introduced in IOS 12.0(5)T. The default is 250.

The following example changes the maximum number of e-mail recipients to 70:

```
Rtr1(config)#ip audit smtp spam 70
```

The ip audit po max-events Command

Use the **global configuration mode** command **ip audit po max-events** to specify the maximum number of event notifications placed in the router's event queue. Additional events are dropped from the queue for sending to the CiscoSecure IDS Director. This command can be used regardless of whether the Cisco Secure IDS Director is used. Use the no version of this command to return the number to the default setting. The syntax is

```
Rtr1(config)#ip audit po max-events number_events
Rtr1(config)#no ip audit po max-events
```

number-of-events	Integer (1–65535) that designates the maximum number of events allowed in the router event queue. Increasing this number could impact memory and performance—each event in the queue requires 32KB of memory.

This command was introduced in IOS 12.0(5)T. The default is 100.

The following example changes the maximum number of events queued to 50.

```
Rtr1(config)#ip audit po max-events 50
```

Initializing the Post Office

Only three commands initialize the Post Office system on a router. This section introduces the purpose, syntax, and examples of each. If the Cisco Secure IDS Director isn't being used, the only command that should be used is the **ip audit notify** command to specify that alarms be sent to a Syslog server to preserve a record of the event.

NOTE Each time a change is made to the Post Office configuration, the router must be reloaded.

The ip audit notify Command

Use the **global configuration mode** command **ip audit notify** to specify the method(s) of event notification. If alarms are to be sent to a Cisco Secure IDS Director, use the **nr-director** keyword in the command syntax. If alarms are to be sent to a Syslog server, use the **log** keyword in the command syntax. The two commands can be used together to log to both devices. Use the no version of this command to return the number to the default setting. The syntax is

```
Rtr1(config)#ip audit notify {nr-director | log}
Rtr1(config)#no ip audit notify {nr-director | log}
```

nr-director	Sends messages in Director format to the Cisco Secure Director or Sensor
log	Sends messages in syslog format

This command was introduced in IOS 12.0(5)T. The default is to send messages in syslog format.

The following example directs logging to both the Cisco Secure IDS Director and a Syslog server.

```
Rtr1(config)#ip audit notify nr-director
Rtr1(config)#no ip audit notify log
```

While they're not a part of IDS, the following commands must also be issued to identify the Syslog server, using the IP address or host name and direct logging input to the server.

```
Rtr1(config)#logging 192.168.1.10
Rtr1(config)#logging on
```

Without these commands, the output would be displayed on the router console and would look like the following output. Notice the output includes the IDS signature detected, plus the source and destination IP addresses.

```
01:04:33: %IDS-4-ICMP_ECHO_SIG: Sig:2004:ICMP Echo Request - from 192.168.1.10 t
o 192.168.2.1
01:04:34: %IDS-4-ICMP_ECHO_REPLY_SIG: Sig:2000:ICMP Echo Reply - from 192.168.2.
1 to 192.168.1.10
```

The previous signatures triggered are

2000 ICMP Echo Reply (Info, Atomic)	Triggers when an IP datagram is received with the IP header protocol field set to 1 (ICMP) and the type field in the ICMP header set to 0 (Echo Reply)
2004 ICMP Echo Request (Info, Atomic)	Triggers when an IP datagram is received with the IP header protocol field set to 1 (ICMP) and the type field in the ICMP header set to 8 (Echo Request)

Figure 7-2 shows what the entries might look like in a Syslog server. The sample uses a free Syslog daemon from Kiwi Enterprises.

If messages are sent to the Cisco Secure IDS Director, then it's necessary also to configure the Cisco Secure Director's Post Office transport parameters for both the router (using the **ip audit po local** command) and the Cisco Secure IDS Director (using the **ip audit po remote** command).

The ip audit po local Command

Use the **global configuration mode** command **ip audit po local** to specify the local Post Office parameters used when sending event notifications to the Cisco Secure IDS Director. Use the no form of this command to set the local Post Office parameters to their default settings. The syntax is as follows:

Rtr1(config)#ip audit po local hostid *host-id* orgid *org-id*
Rtr1(config)#no ip audit po local [hostid *host-id* orgid *org-id*]

host-id	Unique integer (1–65535) that identifies the router
org-id	Unique integer (1–65535) that identifies the organization to which both the router and the Director belong

This command was introduced in IOS 12.0(5)T. The default organization ID is 1. The default host ID is 1.

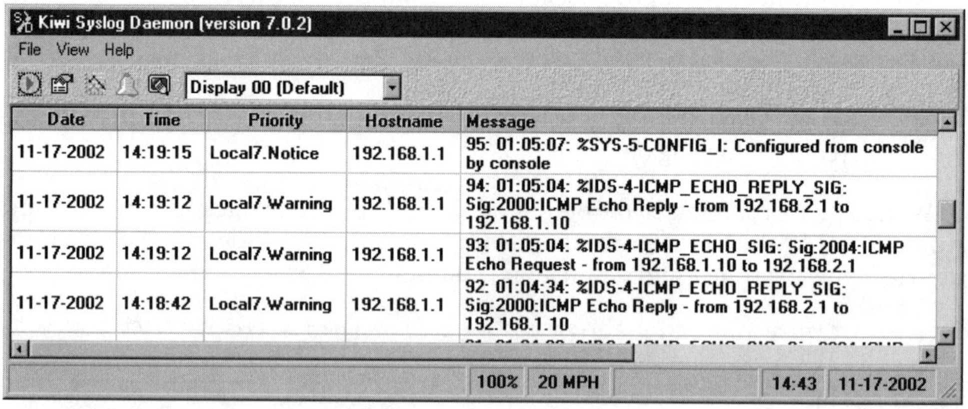

Kiwi Syslog Daemon (version 7.0.2)

File View Help

Display 00 (Default)

Date	Time	Priority	Hostname	Message
11-17-2002	14:19:15	Local7.Notice	192.168.1.1	95: 01:05:07: %SYS-5-CONFIG_I: Configured from console by console
11-17-2002	14:19:12	Local7.Warning	192.168.1.1	94: 01:05:04: %IDS-4-ICMP_ECHO_REPLY_SIG: Sig:2000:ICMP Echo Reply - from 192.168.2.1 to 192.168.1.10
11-17-2002	14:19:12	Local7.Warning	192.168.1.1	93: 01:05:04: %IDS-4-ICMP_ECHO_SIG: Sig:2004:ICMP Echo Request - from 192.168.1.10 to 192.168.2.1
11-17-2002	14:18:42	Local7.Warning	192.168.1.1	92: 01:04:34: %IDS-4-ICMP_ECHO_REPLY_SIG: Sig:2000:ICMP Echo Reply - from 192.168.2.1 to 192.168.1.10

100% 20 MPH 14:43 11-17-2002

Figure 7-2 Sample Syslog output showing IDS activity

In the following example, the local host is assigned a host ID of 777 and an organization ID of 25:

```
Rtr1(config)#ip audit po local hostid 777 orgid 25
```

The ip audit po remote Command

Use the **global configuration mode** command **ip audit po remote** to specify one or more sets of Post Office parameters for Cisco Secure IDS Director(s) receiving event notifications from the router. A router can report to more than one Director by adding an **ip audit po remote** command for each Director. Use the no form of this command to remove a Director's Post Office parameters as defined by host ID, organization ID, and IP address. The syntax is

Rtr1(config)# ip audit po remote hostid *host-id* orgid *org-id* rmtaddress *ip-add* localaddress *ip-add* [port *port-num*] [preference *pref-num*] [timeout *seconds*] [application {director | logger}]

host-id	Unique integer (1–65535) that identifies the router.
org-id	Unique integer (1–65535) that identifies the organization to which both the router and the Director belong.
rmtaddress *ip-add*	The Director's IP address.
localaddress *ip-add*	The router's interface IP address.
port-num	The UDP port the Director listens for alarms (the default is 45000).
pref-num	The relative priority of the route to the Director (1 is the default). If more than one route is used to reach the same Director, then one must be a primary route (preference 1) and, the other, a secondary route (preference 2).
seconds	The integer representing the heartbeat timeout value—in seconds—the Post Office waits before it determines a connection has timed out (the default is 5).
app-type	Either *director* (Cisco Secure IDS Director) or *logger* (the default is director).

This command was introduced in IOS 12.0(5)T. The default organization ID is 1, the default host ID is 1, the default UDP port number is 45000, and the default preference is 1. The default heartbeat timeout is five seconds.

Director vs. Logger Application

Use *logger application* instead of the default *director* when sending Post Office notifications to a sensor. Sending to a logging application means no alarms are sent to a GUI. Instead, the Cisco Secure IDS alarm data is written to a flat file, which can then be processed with scripts or filters, such as perl and awk, or staged to a database. Use logger only in advanced applications where you want the alarms only to be logged and not displayed.

Multiple Routes to the Same Director

More than one route can be established to the same Director by giving each route a preference number that establishes the relative priority of routes. The router always attempts to use the lowest numbered route, switching automatically to the next higher number when a route fails and then switching back when the route begins functioning again.

In this example, two routes for the same dual-homed (residing on two networks) IDS Director are defined.

```
Rtr1(config)#ip audit po remote hostid 777 orgid 25 rmtaddress 192.168.1.3 localaddress 192.168.1.1 preference 1
Rtr1(config)#ip audit po remote hostid 777 orgid 25 rmtaddress 192.168.6.3 localaddress 192.168.6.1 preference 2
```

The router will use the first entry to establish communication with the Director, host ID 777, and organization ID 25. The router will switch to the secondary route if the preferred route fails. When the preferred route returns to service, the router switches back and closes the secondary route.

In this example, the Director is assigned a longer heartbeat timeout value, with a default of five seconds, because of predictable network congestion. This is also designated as a logger application.

```
Rtr1(config)#ip audit po remote hostid 727 orgid 25 rmtaddress 192.168.4.3 localaddress 192.168.4.1 timeout 10
application logger
```

After you configure the router, it's necessary to add the Cisco IOS Firewall IDS router's Post Office information to Cisco Secure IDS Sensors and Directors communicating with the router. This process is covered in the last four chapters of the book.

NOTE Remember, if the Post Office features are added or changed, then it's necessary to save the configuration and reload the router.

Creating and Applying Audit Rules

The Cisco IOS IDS technology works as an inline sensor, monitoring packets as they travel between the router's interfaces. If a packet, or group of packets, in a session matches an active signature, the IOS IDS can perform any or all of the following actions based on the predefined router configuration.

- **Alarm** Sends an alarm to a Syslog server and/or a Cisco Secure IDS Director
- **Drop** Discards the packet
- **Reset** Resets the questionable TCP connection

Two basic steps are necessary to set up the packet auditing process for the Cisco IOS Firewall IDS router.

1. Create an audit rule specifying which signatures are to be applied to packet traffic and the specific action(s) to take when a match is found.
2. Apply the audit rule to a router interface, specifying a traffic direction (in or out).

As packets pass through an interface covered by the audit rule, they're monitored by a series of audit modules in the following order:

- IP module
- TCP, UDP, or ICMP modules (as appropriate)
- Application-level modules

If a pattern matching a known signature is found by any audit module, then the following action(s) occur, based on the instructions included in the router configuration. Any or all of the actions can be configured.

Action	Result
alarm	The module completes its audit. It sends an alarm to the Syslog and/or IDS Director. The packet is forwarded to the next module.
drop	The packet is dropped from the module, discarded, and not sent to the next module.
reset	If this is a TCP session, the reset flag (bit) is set On and sent to both ends of the session. The packets are forwarded to the next module.

NOTE Cisco recommends the drop and reset actions be used together.

If multiple signature matches occur as a packet is processed by a module, only the first match triggers the specified action—the packet is either discarded (drop) or moved immediately to the next audit module (alarm or reset). Additional matches in other modules can trigger additional alarms, but only one per audit module. This separates the IOS IDS implementation from the Cisco Secure IDS Sensor appliance, which identifies all signature matches for each packet.

Creating an Audit Rule

The idea is to define an audit rule, specifying which signatures should be applied to packet traffic and the action(s) to take when a match is found. The signature list can have a single signature, all available signatures, or a partial list of the signatures. The signatures can be informational and attack signatures. Signatures can be disabled in case of false positives or to meet the unique requirements of the network environment.

Using the **ip audit info** and **ip audit attack** commands is necessary to set the default actions for respective signatures. Both types of signatures can take any or all of the following actions: alarm, drop, and reset.

Define Info Audit Actions

Use the **global configuration mode** command **ip audit info** to specify the default action(s) for info-type signatures. Use the no form of this command to set the default action for info signatures. The syntax is

```
Rtr1(config)#ip audit info {action [alarm] [drop] [reset]}
Rtr1(config)#no ip audit info
```

Action	Sets an action for the info signature to take when a match occurs
Alarm	Sends an alarm to the console, IDS Director, or to a Syslog server
Drop	Drops the packet
Reset	Resets the TCP session

This command was introduced in IOS 12.0(5)T. The default action is Alarm.

In the following example, the default action for info signatures is set to all three actions:

```
Rtr1(config)#ip audit info action alarm drop reset
```

Define Attack Audit Actions

Use the global configuration mode command ip audit attack to specify the default action(s) for attack-type signatures. Use the no form of this command to set the default action for info signatures. The syntax is

```
Rtr1(config)#ip audit attack {action [alarm] [drop] [reset]}
Rtr1(config)#no ip audit info
```

action	Sets an action for the info signature to take when a match occurs
alarm	Sends an alarm to the console, IDS Director, or to a Syslog server
drop	Drops the packet
reset	Resets the TCP session

This command was introduced in IOS 12.0(5)T. The default action is alarm.

In this example, the default action for attack signatures is set to all three actions:

```
Rtr1(config)#ip audit attack action alarm drop reset
```

Create Named Audit Rules

Use the **global configuration mode** command **ip audit name** to create audit rules for info and attack signature types. Any signatures disabled with the **ip audit signature** command don't become a part of the audit rule created with the **ip audit name** command. Use the no form of this command to delete an audit rule. The syntax is

```
Rtr1(config)ip audit name audit-name {info | attack} [list standard-acl] [action [alarm] [drop] [reset]]

Rtr1(config)no ip audit name audit-name {info | attack}
```

audit-name	The name for an audit specification.
info	Specifies that the audit rule is for info signatures.
attack	Specifies that the audit rule is for attack signatures.
list	Specifies an ACL to attach to the audit rule.
standard-acl	The integer representing an access control list. Use with the list keyword.
action	Sets an action for the info signature to take when a match occurs.
alarm	Sends an alarm to the console, IDS Director, or a Syslog server.
drop	Drops the packet.
reset	Resets the TCP session.

This command was introduced in IOS 12.0(5)T. The default action is alarm.

In this example, the default action for attack signatures is set to all three actions:

```
Rtr1(config)#ip audit attack action alarm drop reset
```

The following example creates an audit rule named Audit.99 for info signatures that's configured with all three actions:

```
Rtr1(config)#ip audit name Audit.99 info action alarm drop reset
```

This example demonstrates disabling signature 1000 and then creating an info signature audit rule named Audit.33 that doesn't include that signature:

```
Rtr1(config)#ip audit signature 1001 disable
Rtr1(config)#ip audit name Audit.33 info action alarm drop reset
```

Using ACLs with Named Audit Rules

Using a Standard ACL to help define the traffic to be audited by an audit rule is possible. In the following example, an audit rule named Attack.7 is created that uses ACL 25, which is defined later in the configuration. The ACL doesn't behave the way you'd assume, particularly if you're thinking of it as if it were filtering interface traffic. Instead, when used in this context, the deny statements are indicating that the private networks—192.168.0.0 to 192.168.255.0—aren't filtered through the audit process because they're trusted hosts. All other hosts are defined by the permit any statement and are to be processed by the audit rule.

```
Rtr1(config)#ip audit name Attack.7 list 25
Rtr1(config)#access-list 25 deny 192.168.0.0 0.0.255.255
Rtr1(config)#access-list 25 permit any
```

If some individual hosts or subnets should have been included in the audit, the following example shows how this might be addressed.

```
Rtr1(config)#ip audit name Attack.7 list 25
Rtr1(config)#access-list 25 permit host 192.168.1.117
```

```
Rtr1(config)#access-list 25 permit 192.168.100.16 0.0.15
Rtr1(config)#access-list 25 permit 192.168.8.0 0.0.1.255
Rtr1(config)#access-list 25 deny 192.168.0.0 0.0.255.255
Rtr1(config)#access-list 25 permit any
```

Disabling Individual Signatures

Use the **global configuration mode** command **ip audit signature** to attach a policy to a signature. You can implement two policies: disable a signature or qualify the audit of a signature with an access list. This command is generally used to disable the auditing of a signature or to exclude specific hosts or network segments from being audited. Use the no form of this command to remove the policy. If the policy disabled a signature, then the **no** command re-enables the signature. If the policy attached an access list to the signature, the **no** command removes the access list. The syntax is

```
Rtr1(config)#ip audit signature signature-id {disable | list acl-list}
Rtr1(config)#no ip audit signature signature-id
```

signature-id	A unique integer that specifies a signature in the Director Network Security Database
disable	Disables the ACL associated with the signature
list	Specifies an ACL to associate with the signature
acl-list	The ACL configured on the router

This command was introduced in IOS 12.0(5)T. The default is that no policy is attached to a signature.

Using ACLs When Disabling Individual Signatures

You can use the **ip audit signature** command to apply ACLs to individual signatures to help filter out sources of false alarms. When attaching an ACL to a signature, then it's also necessary to create an audit rule with the **ip audit name** command and to apply that named rule to an interface with the **ip audit** command.

In this example, the 1001 signature is disabled and signature 1004 has ACL 10 attached. As in the preceding example, the ACL doesn't behave as you might initially assume. The hosts on the defined network aren't filtered through the signature because they're trusted hosts or, possibly, because they're causing false positives to occur. All other hosts are defined by the permit any statement and are to be processed by the audit rule.

```
Rtr1(config)#ip audit signature 1001 disable
Rtr1(config)#ip audit signature 1004 list 10
Rtr1(config)#access-list 10 deny 192.168.45.0 0.0.0.255
Rtr1(config)#access-list 10 permit any
```

Apply the Audit Rule to the Interface(s)

The *audit rule* is applied to an interface on the router specifying a traffic direction (in or out) in much the same way that ACLs are applied. As with ACLs, in or out is referenced to the center of the router, not to the connected network. An *inbound rule* is auditing traffic coming into the router from the specified interface. In deciding which interfaces to use and whether to apply the audits in or out, consider the following information.

Inbound Audits

When an audit rule is applied to the in direction on an interface, packets are audited before the inbound ACL has a chance to discard them. This order allows the administrator, Syslog server, and/or IDS Director to be alerted if an attack or information-gathering activity is underway, even if the router would normally reject the activity.

Outbound Audits

When an audit rule is applied to the out direction on an interface, an *outbound rule*, packets are audited after they enter the router through another interface. In this case, an inbound ACL on the other interface might discard packets before they're audited, meaning the administrator, Syslog server, and/or IDS Director won't be alerted of an attack or information-gathering activity that's occurring. Even though the attack or information-gathering activity was thwarted, the network is unaware of it, and so, while the attacker is preparing their next assault, the administrator doesn't even know to prepare for it.

Applying the Audit Name

Use the **interface configuration mode** command **ip audit** to apply an audit specification created with the **ip audit name** command to a specific interface and for a specific direction. Use the no version of this command to disable auditing of the interface for the specified direction. The syntax is

```
Rtr1(config-if)#ip audit audit-name {in | out}
Rtr1(config-if)#no ip audit audit-name {in | out}
```

audit-name	Name of an audit specification created with the **ip audit name** command
in	Inbound traffic—toward the router
out	Outbound traffic—away from the router

This command was introduced in IOS 12.0(5)T. The default that no audit specifications are applied to an interface or direction is implied.

In the following example, the default action for attack signatures is set to all three actions, and the audit specification—Attack.7—is applied inbound on the Ethernet interface:

```
Rtr1(confisg)#interface e0
Rtr1(config-if)#ip audit Attack.7 in
```

Define the Protected Networks

After you apply the audit rules to the router interfaces, use the **global configuration mode** command **ip audit protected** to specify whether an address is on a protected network. A single address at a time or a range of addresses can be entered at one time. You can make as many entries to the protected networks list as needed. In case of a detected attack, the corresponding event contains a flag that denotes whether the source and/or destination of the packet belong to a protected network.

Use the no form of this command to remove network addresses from the protected network list. If you specify an IP address for removal, that address is removed from the list. If you don't specify an address, then *all IP addresses* are removed from the list. The syntax is

Rtr1(config)#ip audit protected *ip-addr* [to *ip-addr*]
Rtr1(config)#no ip audit protected [*ip-addr*]

to	Specifies a range of IP addresses
ip-addr	IP address of a network host

This command was introduced in IOS 12.0(5)T. The default is that if no addresses are defined as protected, then all addresses are considered outside the protected network.

The following example shows three individual addresses and two ranges of addresses to be added to the protected network list. The final entry shows an address removed from the protected list.

```
Rtr1(config)#ip audit protected 192.168.5.1
Rtr1(config)#ip audit protected 192.168.5.8
Rtr1(config)#ip audit protected 192.168.5.211
Rtr1(config)#ip audit protected 192.168.4.1 to 192.168.4.254
Rtr1(config)#ip audit protected 192.168.6.1 to 192.168.7.254
Rtr1(config)#no ip audit protected 192.168.4.75
```

Verifying the IDS Configuration

Four **show** commands are used to verify and monitor IDS configuration and performance. These commands include

- **show ip audit statistics**
- **show ip audit configuration**
- **show ip audit interface**
- **show ip audit all**

The show ip audit statistics Command

Use the **show ip audit statistics** EXEC command to display the number of packets audited and the number of alarms sent, among other information. This command shows any signatures used, how many interfaces are configured for audit, and a summary of session information.

```
Rtr1#show ip audit statistics
Signature audit statistics [process switch:fast switch]
  signature 2000 packets audited: [1:569]
```

```
  signature 2004 packets audited: [2:569]
Interfaces configured for audit 2
Session creations since subsystem startup or last reset 3
Current session counts (estab/half-open/terminating) [1:0:0]
Maxever session counts (estab/half-open/terminating) [1:1:0]
Last session created 00:00:10
Last statistic reset never
Rtr1#
```


The clear ip audit statistics Command.

To reset the audit statistics for packets analyzed and alarms sent, use the **clear ip audit statistics EXEC** command. This command could be handy to eliminate historical data when trying to see current activity. If the data is being logged, clearing these counters shouldn't present any downside. The syntax is

```
Rtr1#clear ip audit statistics
```

The show ip audit configuration Command

Use the **show ip audit configuration** EXEC command to display additional configuration information, including default values that might not be displayed using the **show run** command. You can tell this configuration is logging to a Syslog server only and not doing anything more than logging events for info signatures (alarm only). It's performing all three actions on attack signatures:

```
Rtr1#show ip audit configuration
Event notification through syslog is enabled
Event notification through Net Director is disabled
Default action(s) for info signatures is alarm
Default action(s) for attack signatures is alarm
Default threshold of recipients for spam signature is 25
PostOffice:HostID:0 OrgID:0 Msg dropped:0
          :Curr Event Buf Size:0  Configured:100
Post Office is not enabled - No connections are active
Audit Rule Configuration
 Audit name Audit-1
    info actions alarm
    attack actions alarm drop reset
Rtr1#
```

The show ip audit interface Command

Use the **show ip audit interface EXEC** command to display the interface configuration. This command shows the auditing being done on each interface.

```
Rtr1#show ip audit interface
Interface Configuration
 Interface FastEthernet0
  Inbound IDS audit rule is Audit-1
    info actions alarm
    attack actions alarm drop reset
  Outgoing IDS audit rule is not set
```

```
 Interface Serial1
  Inbound IDS audit rule is Audit-1
    info actions alarm
    attack actions alarm drop reset
  Outgoing IDS audit rule is not set
Rtr1#
```

The show ip audit all Command

Use the **catch-all** command—**show ip audit all**—to include the output from the previous commands:

```
Rtr1#show ip audit all
Event notification through syslog is enabled
Event notification through Net Director is disabled
Default action(s) for info signatures is alarm
Default action(s) for attack signatures is alarm
Default threshold of recipients for spam signature is 25
PostOffice:HostID:0 OrgID:0 Msg dropped:0
           :Curr Event Buf Size:0  Configured:100
Post Office is not enabled - No connections are active
Audit Rule Configuration
 Audit name Audit-1
    info actions alarm
    attack actions alarm drop reset
Interface Configuration
 Interface FastEthernet0
  Inbound IDS audit rule is Audit-1
    info actions alarm
    attack actions alarm drop reset
  Outgoing IDS audit rule is not set
 Interface Serial1
  Inbound IDS audit rule is Audit-1
    info actions alarm
    attack actions alarm drop reset
  Outgoing IDS audit rule is not set
Rtr1#
```

Chapter Review

The Cisco IOS Firewall Intrusion Detection System has been a feature of a growing list of Cisco router platforms running the firewall feature set since version 12.0(5). The IDS features are currently available on the Cisco uBR900, 1720, 2600, 3600, 7100, 7200, and 7500 series routers, as well as the RSM for Catalyst 5000 switches.

The IOS-based IDS features extend the Cisco Secure IDS appliance and host-based software features to include the router-based firewalls. The IDS features can be especially useful in locations where a router is being deployed to provide additional security between network segments, such as between the organization and a partner site. The key advantage of an IDS-enabled device is the capability to take preconfigured steps to thwart an attack, rather than simply report it.

The most recent Cisco IOS Firewall IDS uses 59 attack signatures representing a broad cross section of intrusion detection signatures that identify severe breaches of security, as well as the most common network attacks and information-gathering scans.

Four basic steps configure the IDS features if the network is using the Cisco Secure Director (NetRanger). Those steps include initializing Cisco IOS Firewall IDS (required), initializing the Post Office (required), configuring and applying audit rules (required), and verifying the configuration (optional).

The MCNS exam objectives only include the first, third, and fourth steps because the IDS Director is covered in the IDS exam. In the configuring audit rules step, it's possible to disable certain signatures because they're unneeded or create false positive responses. You can also exempt some hosts from the auditing process reflecting their trusted status or to avoid false positive responses.

Questions

1. Which of the following is *not* a method of categorizing IDS systems covered in this chapter?
   A. Misuse detection vs. anomaly detection
   B. Network-based vs. host-based systems
   C. Open vs. proprietary
   D. Passive system vs. reactive system
2. True or False. The Cisco IOS Firewall feature set is implemented on all Cisco router series.
   A. True
   B. False
3. Which of the following IOS features is always found with the IDS features on the new IOS?
   A. VPN features
   B. Firewall feature set
   C. AAA
   D. Java blocking
4. Which of the following is *not* an action the IOS IDS can be configured to do?
   A. Drop
   B. Shut down
   C. Alarm
   D. Reset
5. Cisco IDS is based on matching traffic patterns to which of the following?
   A. Virus profiles
   B. Autographs
   C. Signatures
   D. Traffic baselines

6. Which of the four basic steps to configure the IDS features isn't required?
   A. Initializing the Post Office
   B. Initializing Cisco IOS Firewall IDS
   C. Verifying the configuration
   D. Configuring and applying audit rules
7. Which two of the following are the commands to initialize Cisco IOS IDS on a router?
   A. Rtr1(config)#ip audit notify {nr-director | log}
   B. Rtr1(config)#ip audit smtp spam *recipients*
   C. Rtr1(config)#logging on
   D. Rtr1(config)#ip audit po max-events *number_events*
8. Which of the following signature keywords means "information-gathering activity, such as a port sweep"?
   A. Attack
   B. Atomic
   C. Info
   D. Compound
   E. Apply Inspection Rules and ACLs
9. Which of the following signature keywords means "simple patterns, such as an attempt to access a specific port on a specific host"?
   A. Attack
   B. Atomic
   C. Info
   D. Compound
10. According to the text, how many IDS signatures are supported in the IOS version of IDS?
    A. 39
    B. 59
    C. 79
    D. The number changes with daily updates.
11. With the **ip audit info** and **ip audit attack** commands, how many actions can be applied?
    A. 1
    B. 2

C. 3

D. Depends on where it's applied

12. Which command will disable the IDS signature 1001?

A. Rtr1(config-if)#ip audit signature 1001 disable

B. Rtr1(config)#ip audit signature 1001 disable

C. Rtr1(config-if)#ip audit signature disable 1001

D. Rtr1(config)#ip audit signature disable 1001

13. In the command **Rtr1(config)#ip audit name Attack.7 list 25**, what does the 25 represent?

A. The IDS signature

B. The first 25 matching packets

C. An ACL number

D. The hold-time for attack packets

14. What does the **ip audit *audit-name*** command do?

A. Creates an IDS audit specification

B. Is used to disable an IDS signature

C. Applies an IDS audit specification to an interface

D. No such command

15. Which is *not* a valid IDS **show** command?

A. show ip audit transactions

B. show ip audit statistics

C. show ip audit configuration

D. show ip audit interface

Answers

1. **C.** Open vs. proprietary is *not* a category used.
2. **B.** False. This is implemented only on the Cisco 800, uBR900, 1400, 1600, 1700, 2500, 2600, 3600, 7100, 7200, and 7500, and RSM series routers
3. **B.** Firewall feature set is always with IDS in the IOS.
4. **B.** Shut down
5. **C.** Signatures
6. **C.** Verifying the configuration

7. **B. and D. Rtr1(config)#ip audit smtp spam *recipients*** and **Rtr1(config)#ip audit po max-events *number_events***
8. **C. Info**
9. **B. Atomic**
10. **B.** 59
11. **C.** 3: Alarm, Drop, and Reset
12. **C.** Rtr1(config)#ip audit signature 1001 disable
13. **C.** An ACL number
14. **C.** Applies an IDS audit specification to an interface
15. **A.** show ip audit transactions is *not* a real command

CHAPTER 8

IOS Firewall—Authentication Proxy

In this chapter, you will learn how to:

- Use authentication proxy concepts and processes
- Understand AAA server configuration
- Make use of AAA router configuration
- Apply authentication proxy configuration on the router
- Verify authentication proxy configuration

One of the concerns of every network administrator with a connection to the outside world is how to make sure only approved users can access resources. A secondary need is to make sure those approved users are limited to the resources and services specified in the organization security policy. In this chapter, you will learn about the Cisco IOS Firewall authentication proxy features and the steps necessary to configure them.

STUDY TIP The material in this chapter is part of the new exam objectives for only the Managing Cisco Network Security (MCNS). This was also included in a lighter form in the objectives for the old Cisco Secure PIX Firewall Advanced (CSPFA) exam.

Cisco IOS Firewall Authentication Proxy

The Cisco IOS Firewall authentication proxy feature allows network administrators to implement security policies on a per-user basis through personalized ACLs. Without firewall authentication proxy, user identity and any authorized access was associated with a user's IP address. Any single security policy had to be applied to an entire user group or subnet. Now, users can be identified and authorized on the basis of their per-user policy, and any access privileges can be customized based on their individual access profiles.

With the authentication proxy feature, users can log in to the network or access the Internet via HTTP. Their specific access profiles are automatically retrieved and applied from a Cisco Secure Access Control Server (ACS), or another RADIUS or TACACS+ authentication server. The user profiles are active only while there's active traffic from the authenticated user.

The authentication proxy is supported on the latest IOS versions (12.2) of the SOHO 70, 800, uBR900, 1720, 2600, 3600, 7100, 7200, and 7500 series routers. Earlier versions won't support the feature on the smaller units (SOHO 70 to 1720s). Authentication proxy is compatible with other Cisco IOS security features, such as NAT, CBAC, IPSec encryption, and VPN client software.

How the Authentication Proxy Works

Unlike many Cisco IOS Firewall features that operate transparently to the user, the authentication proxy feature requires some user interaction on the client host. When a user, using a web browser, initiates an HTTP session through a firewall configured to support the authentication proxy, the process is triggered. The first thing the authentication proxy checks is to see if the user has already been authenticated. If so, the connection is completed without further intervention. But, if no valid authentication entry exists, the authentication proxy responds by providing a screen that prompts the user for a user name and a password. Figure 8-1 shows the message that greets the user.

In the sample, the Rtr1 text is the host name defined for the firewall router. The rest of the text might vary slightly with the version of Cisco Secure ACS and the operating system (OS) platform.

The users must successfully authenticate by supplying a valid user name and password combination recognized by the defined authentication server. Figure 8-2 shows a successful attempt response.

If the authentication attempt failed, the authentication proxy would display a message stating Authentication Failed! and then prompt the user for retries. After five failed attempts to authenticate, the user would wait two minutes, and then would have to initiate another HTTP session to trigger authentication proxy.

User Profiles and Dynamic ACL Entries

With a successful authentication, the user's authorization profile stored on the AAA server is downloaded to the firewall to create dynamic access control entries (ACEs). These temporary ACEs are added to the inbound ACL for an input interface and to the

Figure 8-1 Authentication proxy login screen

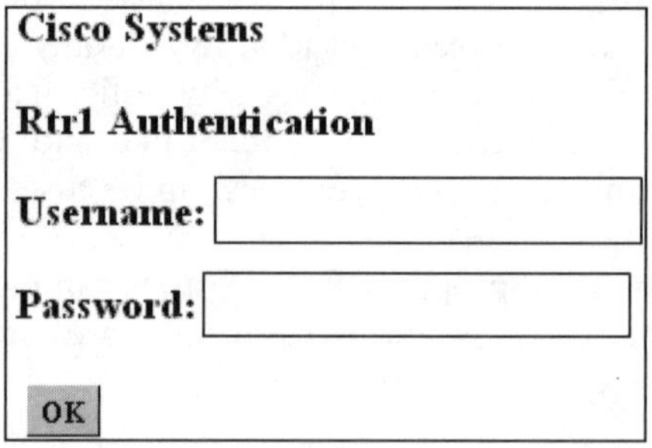

Cisco Systems

Rtr1 Authentication

Username:

Password:

OK

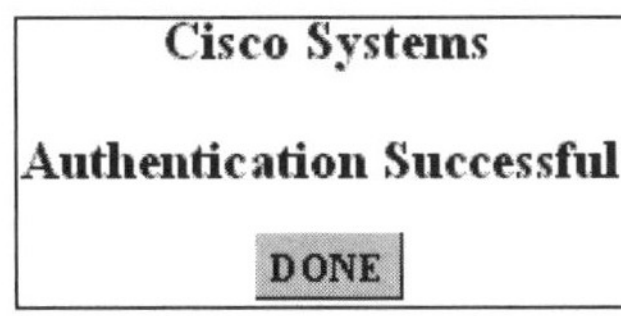

Figure 8-2 Authentication successful attempt response message

outbound ACL of an output interface, if an output ACL exists at the interface. These temporary ACEs configure the firewall to allow only the authenticated users access to the network that was specifically permitted by the authorization profile. For example, the user could only initiate a Telnet session through the firewall if either Telnet or all of TCP is specifically permitted in that user's profile. The following example is a TACACS+ user profile stored on a Windows AAA server.

```
default authorization = permit
key = test
user = newuser1 {
login = cleartext test
service = auth-proxy
{
priv-lvl=15
proxyacl#1="permit tcp any any eq 69"
proxyacl#2="permit icmp any host 192.168.7.2"
proxyacl#3="permit tcp any any eq ftp"
proxyacl#4="permit tcp any any eq ftp-data"
proxyacl#5="permit tcp any any eq telnet"
proxyacl#6="permit tcp any any eq smtp"
}
}
```

The various proxyacl#*n* lines will be downloaded as ACEs in the firewall router to allow the defined protocol or activity. Notice no deny statements exist because all traffic should have already been denied by a standard ACL. These entries are creating the exceptions. All source addresses are set to any because they'll be replaced by the IP address of the authenticating user.

The following output shows input ACL (160) following the user on host 192.168.1.10 successfully authenticating. The first six permit statements represent the downloaded user profile enabling the specified features for the authenticated user. The last four lines are the "real" ACL entries.

```
Rtr1#show ip access-lists
Extended IP access list 160
permit tcp host 192.168.1.10 any eq 69
permit icmp host 192.168.1.10 host 192.168.4.2
permit tcp host 192.168.1.10 any eq telnet
permit tcp host 192.168.1.10 any eq ftp
permit tcp host 192.168.1.10 any eq ftp-data
permit tcp host 192.168.1.10 any eq smtp
deny tcp any any eq telnet
deny udp any any
permit tcp any any (76 matches)
permit ip any any
```

Idle Timer

With a successful authentication, the authentication proxy sets up an inactivity (idle) timer for the created user profile. As long as any authorized user traffic goes through the firewall, the idle timer is continuously reset and the user's host doesn't trigger the authentication proxy. The **ip auth-proxy auth-cache-time** ***minutes*** command is used (covered in the section "Authentication Proxy Configuration on the Router") to set the idle timer. The default is 60 minutes.

If the idle timer expires, the authentication proxy then removes the user's profile information and any related dynamic ACEs in the access lists. Any subsequent traffic from the client host is blocked until they initiate another HTTP session to trigger the authentication proxy.

Secure Authentication

The authentication proxy uses a JavaScript applet to help establish a secure authentication session with the user's web browser. This secure authentication prevents a client from mistakenly submitting a user name/password combination to a network web server other than the authentication proxy router. For this to work, user browsers must allow JavaScripts prior to initiating the HTTP connection. With the JavaScript feature enabled on the browser, secure authentication is done automatically and the user sees the authentication message displayed earlier in Figure 8-2.

NOTE There is a work-around for networks that won't allow the JavaScript feature. While this technique works, it's neither automatic nor particularly reassuring to the user. The Cisco online documentation has the steps to follow if the JavaScript feature can't be enabled.

Applying the Authentication Proxy

Figure 8-3 shows a simple authentication proxy implementation where a single connection exists to the local, protected network and a serial connection exists to the Internet via an Internet service provider (ISP). Access control lists are applied inbound on both interfaces to block all incoming traffic. The lone exception is this: an opening must be created that allows the AAA server to communicate with the firewall router.

One strategy is to apply the authentication proxy in the inbound direction for any router interface for which per-user authentication and authorization is required. By applying the authentication proxy inbound, all user connection requests are intercepted before they're processed by any IOS or firewall features. If the user authentication attempt fails, the connection request is dropped.

The authentication proxy feature supports using a standard access list to specify a particular host or group of hosts whose initial HTTP traffic triggers the proxy. How the authentication proxy will be applied should be driven by the organization security policy.

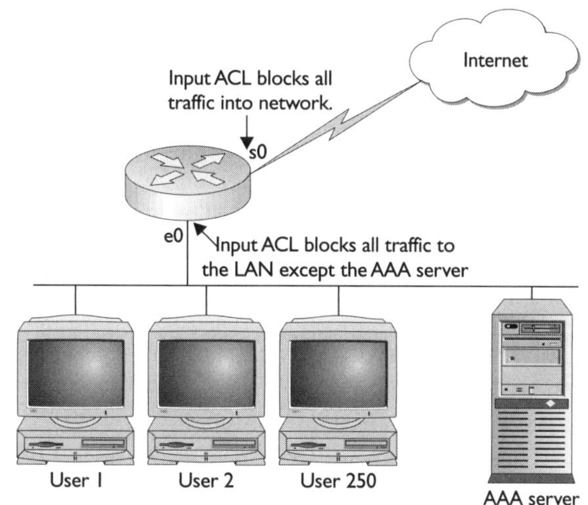

Figure 8-3 Simple network implementation for authentication proxy

Comparison with the Lock-and-Key Feature

Chapter 5 covered another IOS feature—lock-and-key—which seems to provide a similar service to authentication proxy. Lock-and-key also uses authentication and dynamic access lists to provide user access through a firewall. The following table compares the authentication proxy and lock-and-key features.

Authentication Proxy	Lock-and-Key
Triggers on HTTP connection requests.	Triggers on Telnet connection requests.
TACACS+ or RADIUS authentication and authorization.	TACACS+, RADIUS, or local authentication.
Access list entries are created from profile information retrieved from the AAA server only.	Access lists are configured on the router only.
Access privileges are granted on a per-user and host IP address basis.	Access privileges are granted on the basis of the user's host IP address only.
ACLs can have multiple entries defined by the user profiles on the AAA server.	Access lists are limited to one entry for each host IP address.
Allows DHCP-based host IP addresses, meaning users can log in from any host location and obtain authentication and authorization.	Associates a fixed IP address with a specific user. Users must log in from the host with that IP address.

Compatibility with Other Features

The authentication proxy works transparently with the Cisco IOS Firewall intrusion detection system and Cisco IOS IPSec encryption features. This section looks at issues related to authentication proxy and features, such as NAT, CBAC, VPN client software, AAA, and one-time password (OTP) features.

CBAC Compatibility

Authentication proxy *does not create ACEs to support returning data traffic or data channel traffic*, so you must either create static ACLs to allow the return traffic or configure the CBAC inspection rules in the firewall configuration. Remember, static ACLs increase the network vulnerability because they're permanent "holes" in the firewall, whereas a CBAC "hole" only exists as long as it's needed.

Configuring CBAC with any authentication proxy implementation is the most reliable and secure method to ensure return traffic for authorized user connections through the firewall.

Network Address Translation (NAT) Compatibility

Authentication proxy can be successfully implemented on a network using network address translation (NAT) if the CBAC features are configured. Figure 8-4 shows a firewall router performing NAT translation on traffic heading out into the Internet.

With the NAT service, the client local IP address is translated to a "real" global address for any packets traveling out into the Internet. This translation is stored in a NAT translation table on the router, so returning traffic can be retranslated back to the appropriate local address. For example, traffic from host 192.168.1.2 might travel out through the Internet using 172.16.1.1:2070.

But, earlier, when 192.168.1.2 used authentication proxy, a set of temporary ACEs were established using 192.168.1.2 as the authenticated address, not 172.16.1.1. Depending on where those ACEs were applied, our user might not have ACEs to allow the traffic to pass through the router.

Assuming authentication proxy is applied inbound on the LAN interface (e0) only, temporary ACEs are created inbound on that interface to allow that user the use of whatever protocols and features were defined in the downloadable profile. Because NAT will

Figure 8-4 Firewall router performing NAT translations

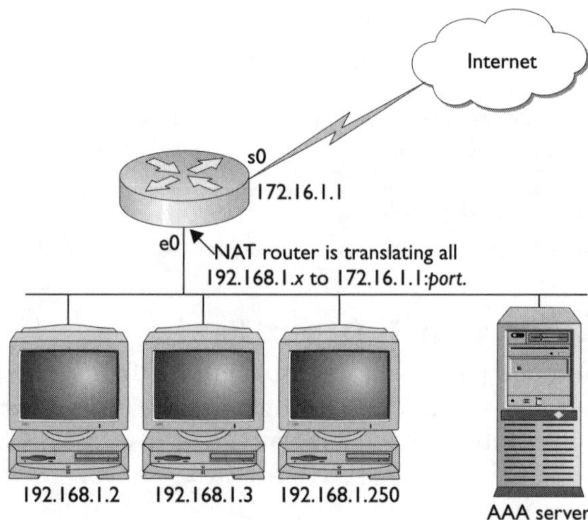

occur outbound after the traffic has passed through the LAN interface, everything should be okay so far. The NAT translations on returning traffic shouldn't be an issue because the returning traffic is unfiltered outbound on the LAN interface. Even if the traffic was filtered, the addresses have been retranslated back to the local addresses before heading out into the LAN.

But, what if the ACEs were applied to the Serial 0 interface? Now the traffic reaching the interface doesn't match the original dynamic ACEs created by the authentication proxy. Configuring CBAC when using authentication proxy with NAT services will take care of the problem by using the translated addresses to create matching ACEs. CBAC makes sure the NAT translated address for the session is associated with the original host address.

When in doubt, use CBAC with NAT and the authentication proxy feature.

VPN Client Compatibility

Authentication proxy can add an extra layer of security and access control for VPN client sessions. A VPN client initiating an HTTP connection through the firewall router is treated like any other user. The authentication proxy checks for a prior client authentication. If a valid authentication is found, authorized traffic is permitted. If not, the HTTP request triggers the authentication proxy and the user is prompted for a user name and password.

Once the VPN user authenticates successfully, the authentication proxy retrieves the user profile from the AAA server. The source address in the user profile entries is then replaced with the IP address of the authenticated VPN client from the decrypted packet.

Compatibility with AAA Accounting Features

Authentication proxy supports the AAA Accounting feature by being able to generate "start" and "stop" accounting records with enough detail to be used successfully for billing and security auditing purposes. This also allows the network administrator to monitor the actions hosts that have used the authentication proxy service.

If the accounting Start option has been enabled, a start record will be generated every time an authentication proxy cache entry and associated dynamic access control list entry are created. Any subsequent traffic from the authenticated host will be recorded when the ACEs created by the authentication proxy receive the packets. The accounting feature saves data about this event in a data structure stored with the data of other users on a defined server.

When the authentication proxy cache expires and is deleted along with the related ACEs, any additional data, such as elapsed time, is added to the accounting information and a stop record is sent to the server.

Operation with One-Time Passwords (OTS)

Authentication proxy supports the use of one-time passwords (OTPs) because AAA supports them. Remember, OTPs typically require an additional authentication server and will require additional configuration of the AAA server. When using an OTP, the user enters the user name and OTP in the HTML login page as usual.

One minor difference is this: the user must enter the correct token password within the first three attempts. If a user has made three consecutive incorrect entries, they must enter two valid token passwords in succession before authentication is granted by the AAA server.

Security Vulnerability Issues

Any time holes are punched through a firewall defense, an increased vulnerability occurs to those who would capitalize on those vulnerabilities. Because authentication proxy should be configured with CBAC, it only makes sense to implement the CBAC attack defenses introduced in Chapter 6.

Denial of Service (DoS) Attacks

Any time a firewall experiences a high level of connection requests requiring authentication, legitimate network users might experience delays in making needed connections or the connection could be rejected and the user would need to try reestablishing the connection. For each request, the authentication proxy prompts the users for login credentials. A high number of open requests could indicate that the router is the subject of a denial of service (DoS) attack.

As a protective mechanism, the authentication proxy monitors incoming HTTP requests, limits the number of open requests, and then drops any additional requests until the number of open requests has fallen below 40.

Source Address Spoofing

Spoofing a source address involves a hacker substituting a known or suspected trusted address for their address both to gain access and conceal their identity. When an HTTP session triggers a successful authentication proxy session, a dynamic opening is created in the firewall by reconfiguring an interface with temporary user-access privileges. As long as this opening exists, it's always technically possible for another user to detect the source IP address information and spoof the address to gain access behind the firewall.

Spoofing is a problem inherent to all access list implementations. Important to realize is that the authentication proxy feature doesn't cause this address spoofing problem, but it does have some level of vulnerability. The authentication proxy doesn't specifically address this problem.

Before Configuring Authentication Proxy

Authentication proxy (auth-proxy) is available only on Cisco IOS Software containing the firewall feature set since version 12.0.5.T.auth-proxy can be used to authenticate inbound or outbound users, or both, by using a web browser to pass through the firewall and authenticate on a TACACS+ or RADIUS server. Traditional access lists are in place to block all traffic. After authentication, the AAA server passes temporary access list entries to the firewall router to allow predefined types of traffic.

Authentication proxy has certain requirements that must be met for effective use of this technology in a network. This section looks briefly at some of the system requirements, as well as the skill sets required of a network administrator tasked with implementing and supporting Cisco secure authentication proxy.

- Client hosts must be running one the following software browsers. These client browsers must have the JavaScript capabilities enabled for secure authentication.
  - Microsoft Internet Explorer 3.0 or later
  - Netscape Navigator 3.0 or later
- Because the authentication proxy activates only on HTTP connections, HTTP services must be running on the standard (well-known) port 80 on the firewall router.
- The authentication proxy feature and related access list entries only apply to traffic passing through the router. Any administrative traffic with the router as the destination is authenticated by the standard authentication methods provided by IOS software.
- Authentication proxy doesn't support concurrent use, meaning it can't be used for multiple users to log in from the same host device at the same time. The authentication and authorization apply only to the first user to submit a valid user name and password. Any others are ignored until the first user ends their session.
- Load balancing between multiple AAA servers isn't supported. Requests only go to any additional AAA server if the first one configured times out.
- Because authentication proxy can use standard access lists, how access lists are used to filter traffic before configuring the authentication proxy is important. For more information on how to configure and use access lists, see Chapter 2 and Appendix A.
- The authentication proxy is a feature of the Cisco Authentication, Authorization, and Accounting (AAA) strategy. It's important to understand how to configure AAA user authentication, authorization, and accounting before you attempt to configure the authentication proxy. For more information on how to configure AAA, see Chapters 3 and 4.
- To create a completely secure and successful implementation of the authentication proxy feature of the Cisco IOS Firewall, you must configure CBAC on the firewall. CBAC features are typically required to allow filtering of protocols permitted by the downloadable user profiles. For more information on configuring and using the CBAC features, see Chapter 6.

Cisco suggests the following tips for implementing the auth-proxy features to reduce the impact on the existing network and the variables involved. This makes it easier to see if the process is being implemented as defined in the security policy.

- Confirm that traffic is flowing properly through the firewall before configuring auth-proxy. Remember, other firewall features exist, such as ACLs and CBAC, that can restrict traffic flow.
- To reduce disruption of the network during testing, modify any existing access list or add an access list to deny access to only one test client.

PART II

- Confirm that only the one test client can't get through the firewall and that all other hosts can pass through.
- Add the **exec-timeout 0 0** command under the console port (line con 0) and/or virtual type terminals (line vty 0 4) to prevent your sessions from timing out while you're busy on other devices or reading online documentation. The first 0 is minutes, the second 0 is seconds: exec-timeout 20 30 would set the idle timer to 20 1/2 minutes. The 0 0 combination turns off the idle timer.

Authentication Proxy Configuration Task List

The authentication proxy feature requires an AAA server running Cisco Secure Access Control Server (ACS) to be present on the network. This is necessary to configure the AAA server to enable the features.

Next, the router running the firewall feature set, typically the perimeter router, must be configured by performing the following tasks:

- Configuring AAA support
- Configuring the HTTP server feature
- Configuring the authentication proxy
- Verifying the authentication proxy

Technically, only the first three tasks and configuring the AAA server are required. Skipping the optional verifying is done only at risk to the resources you're charged to protect. The next section looks first at configuring the AAA server, and then at the firewall router.

AAA Server Configuration

Cisco Secure ACS must be configured on a Windows 2000/NT or UNIX server to support either TACACS+ (Cisco preferred) or RADIUS authentication. The next lines demonstrate installing Cisco Secure ACS v2.6 for Windows 2000/NT, which is the latest version at press time. The example assumes a TACACS+ implementation. This information is included as representative of the process, but it's important to make sure you have the latest instructions matching the platform and version of the Cisco Secure ACS software.

To get the latest instructions, go to the Cisco web site at www.cisco.com and search for IOS auth-proxy, and then scan for a document referring to Implementing Authentication Proxy. While searching for Implementing Authentication Proxy could be more direct, the former also includes Command Reference listings and examples for working with other firewall features you might find useful.

The configuration steps are as follows:

1. Open a web browser.

2. In the address or location bar in the web browser, type the applicable URL, using the IP of a remote server, or either http://localhost:2002 or http://127.0.0.1:2002 if you're working directly on the server.
3. If the Cisco Secure ACS for Windows 2000/NT login page appears, follow these steps:
   - Type a valid Cisco Secure ACS administrator name in the User Name box.
   - Type a valid administrator password in the Password box.
   - Click the Login button.
   - The Cisco Secure ACS for Windows 2000/NT initial page appears (Figure 8-5).
4. Click the Interface Configuration option on the left side of the opening screen. The three-column format of the screen includes links for help on the right-hand side, if necessary.
5. From the Interface Configuration screen, select TACACS+ (Cisco IOS). Note, this is also where you could choose a RADIUS (IETF) implementation. Figure 8-6 shows the Interface Configuration screen.

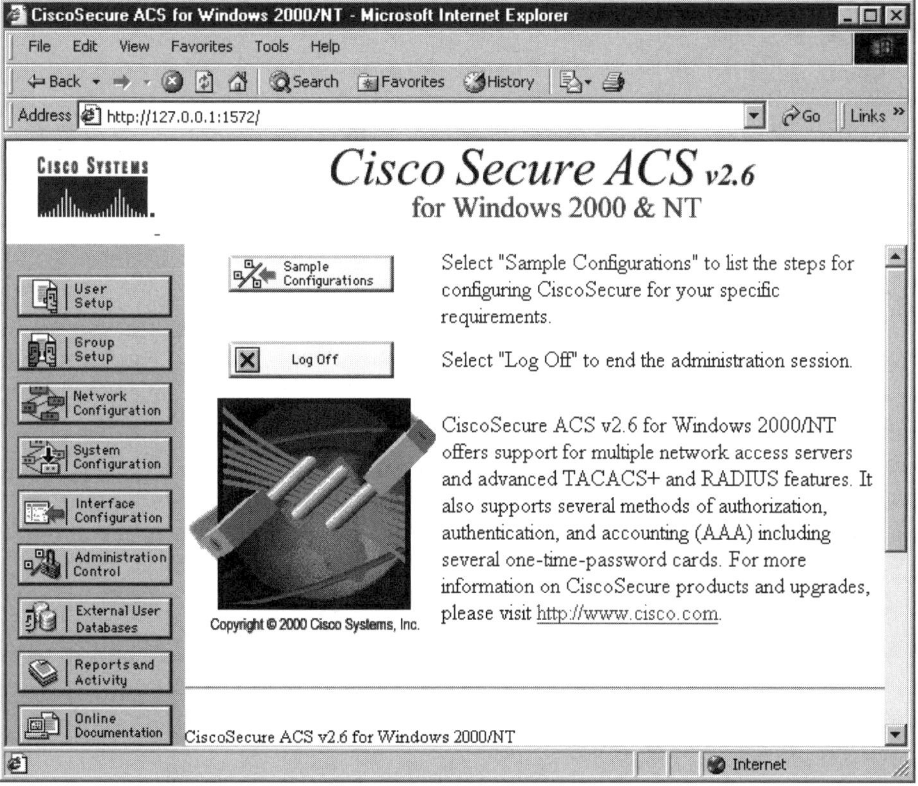

Figure 8-5 Cisco Secure ACS for Windows opening screen

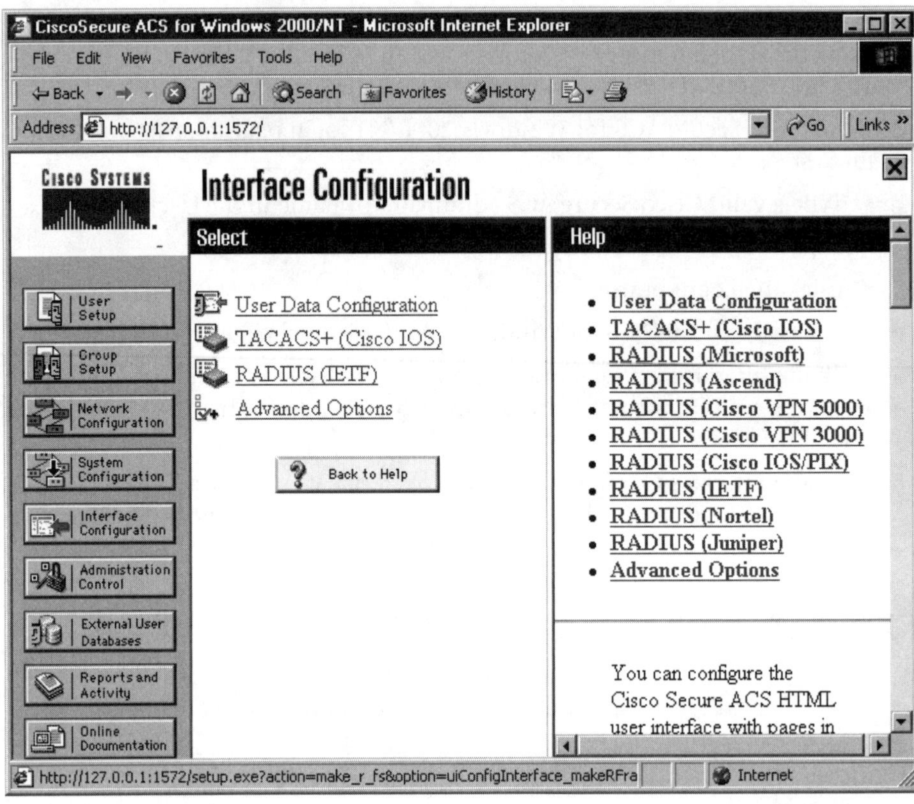

Figure 8-6 Interface Configuration screen showing the TACACS+ and RADIUS options

6. On the resulting screen, scroll down in the center column until you can see the .New Services section (Figure 8-7). Select (check) the Group option for the first blank row, and then type **auth-proxy** in the Service column. Leave the Protocol column blank. Do *not* click the Submit button yet.
7. Further down the same screen, in the Advanced Configuration Options (Figure 8-8), select the Display window for each service selected in which you can enter customized **TACACS+** attributes. Look over the other choices, including the option to create a time-of-day schedule for services. Click the Submit button.
8. Return to the button bar on the left side of the screen and click the Group Settings option. When the next screen appears, choose Edit Settings. You'll be editing the default group settings, but you can use the drop-down list to select a particular group.

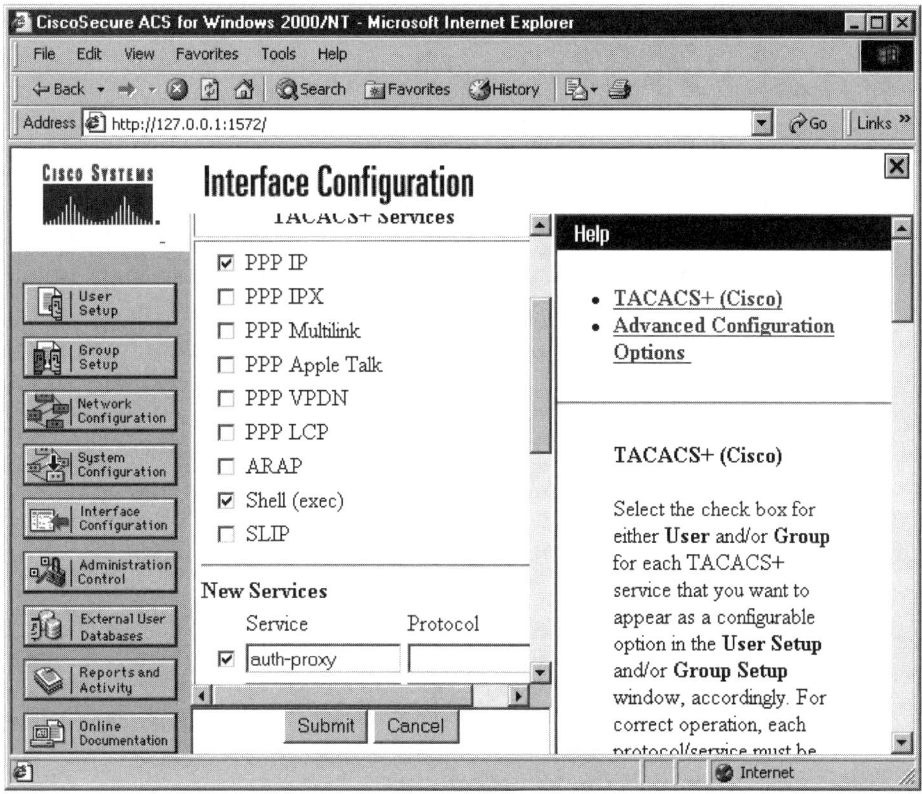

Figure 8-7 TACACS+ configuration page showing the New Services section

9. Find and select the Auth-Proxy option. This is several sections down in the center panel.
10. The authentication proxy features require a per-user downloadable user profile configuration on the AAA server. When the user uses the auth-proxy feature to access the network, the appropriate profile is downloaded and becomes a series of temporary ACL entries on the firewall router. The following is an example of what a user profile looks like on a TACACS server.

```
default authorization = permit
key = test
user = newuser1 {
login = cleartext test
service = auth-proxy
{
priv-lvl=15
proxyacl#1="permit tcp any any eq 69"
```

```
proxyacl#2="permit icmp any host 192.168.7.2"
proxyacl#3="permit tcp any any eq ftp"
proxyacl#4="permit tcp any any eq ftp-data"
proxyacl#5="permit tcp any any eq telnet"
proxyacl#6="permit tcp any any eq smtp"
}
}
```

11. This profile can be created at this point using a type of access control list. Remember the following:
    - Use the **proxyacl#*n*** attribute when configuring the access lists in the profile
    - for both RADIUS and TACACS+ attribute-value (AV) pairs.
    - Note, the **proxyacl#*n*** values are numbered sequentially
    - The privilege level must be set to 15 for all users.
    - Each user profile access list entry can contain only the **permit** keyword.
    - Use the **any** keyword for the source address in each entry. The source address of the host making the authentication proxy request will replace the **any** keyword when the user profile is downloaded to the firewall.

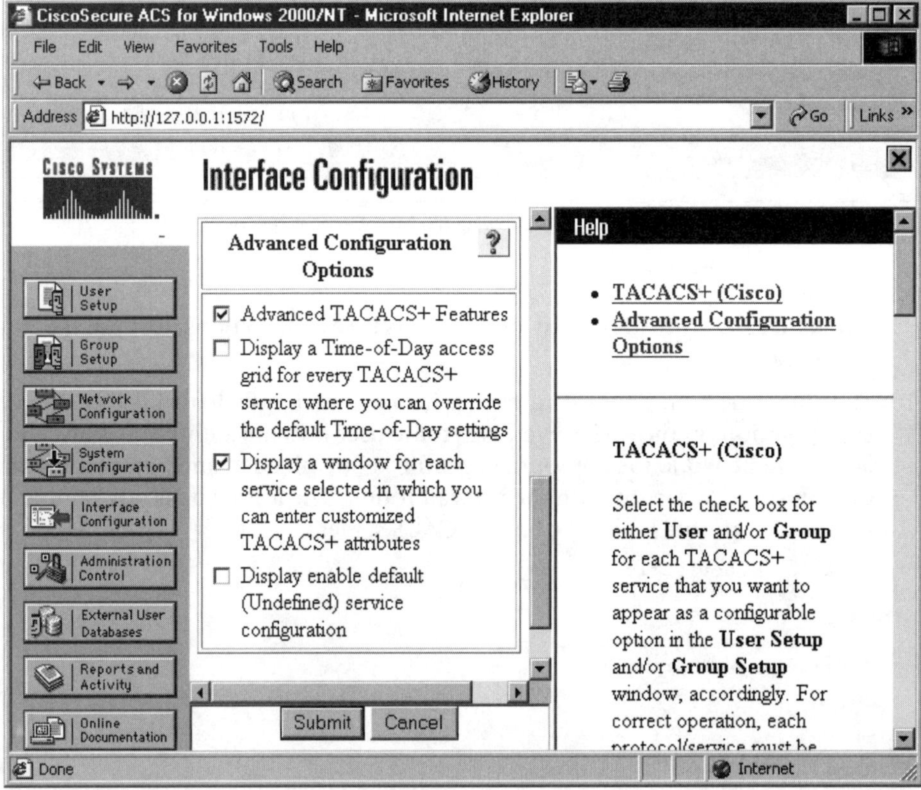

Figure 8-8 Advanced TACACS+ configuration options

In the box following the auth-proxy selection, type the following lines. These lines enable new users to create ICMP, TCP, and UDP sessions.

```
priv-lvl=15
proxyacl#1=permit icmp any any
proxyacl#2=permit tcp any any
proxyacl#3=permit udp any any
```

12. Figure 8-9 shows the completed entries and the various activation buttons. Click the Submit + Restart button when the entry is complete.

NOTE The techniques and exact commands for creating these user downloadable profiles vary with the OS platform and the version of the software. Always check the online documentation before proceeding.

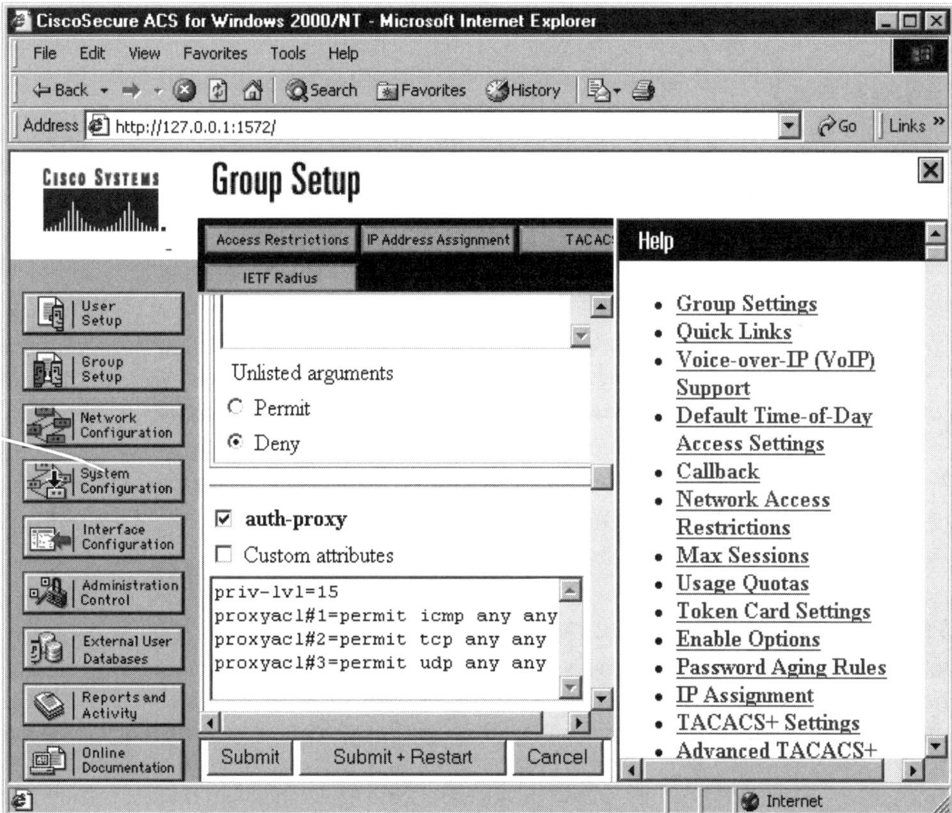

Figure 8-9 Downloadable profile entries and activation buttons

AAA Router Configuration

The following eight tasks are required to enable AAA authentication proxy services. These tasks must be configured in Global Configuration mode before authentication proxy can be configured. Fortunately, the first four tasks should be familiar from Chapter 3.

- Enable AAA.
- Define the security server (TACACS+ or RADIUS).
- Define a server key (TACACS+ or RADIUS).
- Define the list of login authentication methods.
- Enable authentication proxy for AAA.
- Activate authentication proxy accounting.
- Create an ACL entry to allow return traffic from the AAA server to the firewall.
- Enable the HTTP server feature to work with AAA.

Enable AAA

To enable the AAA Access Control model on the router or NAS, in Global Configuration mode, type the **aaa new-model** command. Use the no form of the command to disable the AAA. The syntax is

```
Rtr1(config)#aaa new-model
Rtr1(config)#no aaa new-model
```

No variables exist. The words simply turn the feature on and off. Once entered, the CON, VTY, AUX, and TTY lines require a user name and a password for access. Any previous password configuration for those lines is automatically removed.

NOTE Technically, the **aaa new-model** command not only implements AAA, but also prohibits any of the earlier **TACACS** and **extended TACACS** commands.

Define the Security Server

Defining one or more security servers that provide the authentication services is necessary. The server or servers can be TACACS+, RADIUS, or both. The method lists specified in the **authentication, authorization,** and **accounting** commands determine which type of server should be used for each service and, if both are specified, in which order. If multiple servers of either type are specified, the Cisco IOS software searches for hosts in the order in which they're specified.

Both protocols support Timeout Timer options for defining how long the device will wait for a reply from the specified host before moving on to any remaining server. Both also support Key options, which, if configured on both the server and the firewall router, provide a level of device authentication. The key, if defined, travels in the request packet and is treated as a password or authentication token by the server. If the key doesn't match the one configured on the server, the request is denied.

The ***protocol*-server host** command is used to define the security server. While they're quite similar, the RADIUS version has more options.

Define the Security Server—TACACS+

If a TACACS+ server host is used for authentication, use the **tacacs-server host global configuration** command. Use the no form of this command to delete the specified name or address. The syntax is

```
Rtr1(config)#tacacs-server host {hostname | ip address} [single-connection] [port port#]
    [timeout seconds] [key string]
Rtr1(config)#no tacacs-server host hostname
```

hostname	Name of the TACACS+ server.
ip-addresss	IP address of the TACACS+ server.
single-connection	(Optional) Specify that the router maintain a single open connection for confirmation from the AAA/TACACS+ server. This command contains no autodetect feature and fails if the host isn't running a Cisco Secure daemon.
port *port#*	(Optional) Overrides the default port number (49) with any number from 1 to 65535.
timeout *seconds*	(Optional) Overrides the global timeout value set with the global **tacacs-server timeout** command for this server only.
key *string*	(Optional) Specifies an authentication and encryption key. This must match the key used by the TACACS+ daemon. Overrides the key set by the **global** command **tacacs-server key** for this server only.

Because some of the parameters of the **tacacs-server host** command override global settings made by the **tacacs-server timeout** and **tacacs-server key** commands, this command can be used to enhance security on a network by uniquely configuring individual TACACS+ connections.

Define TACACS+ Server Key Option The global authentication encryption key is set with the **global configuration** command **tacacs-server key.** This key value must match the key value configured on the TACACS+ server, if one is used. Use the no form of this command to disable the key. The syntax is

```
Rtr1(config)#tacacs-server key string
Rtr1(config)#no tacacs-server key [string]
```

string	Any leading spaces are ignored, *but spaces within and at the end of the key are not.* Don't enclose the key in quotation marks unless they're part of the key.

The following example specifies a global timeout of seven seconds, a global key of cisco-key, and then three TACACS+ servers. The first one—tac-serv1—is the one all requests are sent to first. If those requests aren't answered before the timeout timer expires (seven seconds), the next two servers are tried in order. The global timeout and key settings only apply to the first two servers because the third one has overriding options defined.

```
Rtr1(config)#aaa new-model
Rtr1(config)#tacacs-server timeout 7
Rtr1(config)#tacacs-server key cisco-key
Rtr1(config)#tacacs-server host tac-serv1
Rtr1(config)#tacacs-server host 192.168.1.4
Rtr1(config)#tacacs-server host 192.168.6.4 port 1500 timeout 3 key cisco9
```

Define the Security Server—RADIUS

To specify a RADIUS server host, use the **radius-server host global configuration** command. Use the no form of this command to delete the specified RADIUS host. The syntax is

Rtr1(config)#radius-server host {*hostname* | *ip-address*} [auth-port *port-num*] [acct-port *port-num*] [timeout *seconds*] [retransmit *retries*] [key *string*] [alias{*hostname* | *ip-address*}]
Rtr1(config)#no radius-server host {*hostname* | *ip-address*} [auth-port *port-num*] [acct-port *port-num*] [timeout *seconds*] [retransmit *retries*] [key *string*]

hostname	DNS name of the RADIUS server.
ip-address	IP address of the RADIUS server.
auth-port *port-num*	(Optional) To specify a UDP destination port for authentication requests. The host isn't used for authentication if set to 0.
acct-port *port-num*	(Optional) To specify a UDP destination port for accounting requests. The host isn't used for accounting if set to 0.

The following example defines port 12 as the destination port for authentication requests and port 16 as the destination port for accounting requests on a RADIUS host named 192.168.1.4. Because entering a line resets all the port numbers, you must specify a host and configure both the accounting and authentication ports on a single line.

```
Rtr1(config)#aaa new-model
Rtr1(config)#radius-server host 192.168.1.4 auth-port 12 acct-port 16
```

To use separate servers for accounting and authentication, use the zero port value, as appropriate. The following example specifies RADIUS server192.168.1.4 be used for accounting, but not for authentication, and RADIUS server host1 be used for authentication, but not for accounting:

```
Rtr1(config)#aaa new-model
Rtr1(config)#radius-server host 192.168.1.4 auth-port 0
Rtr1(config)#radius-server host host1.domain.com acct-port 0
```

Define RADIUS Server Key Option The global authentication encryption key is set with the **global configuration** command **radius-server key**. This key value must match the key value configured on the RADIUS server, if one is used. Use the no form of this command to disable the key. The syntax is

Rtr1(config)#radius-server key *string*
Rtr1(config)#no radius-server key [*string*]

string	Any leading spaces are ignored; *but spaces within and at the end of the key are not.* Don't enclose the key in quotation marks unless they're part of the key.

The following example specifies a global timeout of seven seconds, a global key of cisco-key, and then three RADIUS servers. The first—rad-serv1—is the one all requests are sent to first. If those requests aren't answered before the timeout timer expires (seven seconds), the next two servers are tried in order. The global timeout and key settings only apply to the first two servers because the third one has overriding options defined.

```
Rtr1(config)#aaa new-model
Rtr1(config)#radius-server timeout 7
Rtr1(config)#radius-server key cisco-key
Rtr1(config)#radius-server host rad-serv1
Rtr1(config)#radius-server host 192.168.1.4
Rtr1(config)#radius-server host 192.168.6.4 timeout 3 key cisco9
```

Define AAA Group Server (Optional)

The **global configuration mode** command **aaa group server** provides a way to group existing defined server hosts. By grouping a set of servers, you can use the group name with other **AAA** commands to select that subset of server hosts to use them for a particular service. A server group is comprised of server hosts of a particular type. Currently, the IOS supports RADIUS and TACACS+ server hosts. The **aaa group server** command lists the IP addresses of the selected server hosts from the global protocol-server host list. To remove a server group from the configuration list, enter the no form of this command. The syntax is

Rtr1(config)#aaa group server {tacacs+ | radius} *group-name*
Rtr1(config)#no aaa group server tacacs+ | radius *group-name*

group-name	Character string used to name the group of servers

The command was introduced in IOS version 12.0(5)T. There are no default values.

The command can only be entered after the **aaa new-model** command turns on the AAA features. The entry is followed by one or more server server-name statements identifying the servers to be included in the group. The next two sample outputs demonstrate this; be sure to note the prompt for the server entries.

The following example uses the three TACACS+ servers created in the earlier example and selects only two them to be included in the server group.

```
Rtr1(config)#aaa new-model
Rtr1(config)#tacacs-server timeout 7
Rtr1(config)#tacacs-server key cisco-key
Rtr1(config)#tacacs-server host tac-serv1
Rtr1(config)#tacacs-server host 192.168.1.4
Rtr1(config)#tacacs-server host 192.168.6.4 port 1500 timeout 3 key cisco9
Rtr1(config)#aaa group server tacacs+ tac-1
Rtr1(config-sg-tacacs+)#server tac-serv1
Rtr1(config-sg-tacacs+)#server 192.168.6.4
```

The following RADIUS example shows the configuration of an AAA group server named rad-1, which includes two of the three defined servers:

```
Rtr1(config)#aaa new-model
Rtr1(config)#radius-server timeout 7
Rtr1(config)#radius-server key cisco-key
Rtr1(config)#radius-server host rad-serv1
Rtr1(config)#radius-server host 192.168.1.4
Rtr1(config)#radius-server host 192.168.6.4 timeout 3 key cisco9
Rtr1(config)#aaa group server radius rad-1
Rtr1(config-sg-radius)#server rad-serv1 auth-port 1800 acct-port 1801
Rtr1(config-sg-radius)#server 192.168.6.4 auth-port 1802 acct-port 1803
```

The server statement allows the auth-port and acct-port to be defined. If not specified, the default value of auth-port is 1645 and the default value of acct-port is 1646. The output for next paragraph demonstrates this.

With either protocol, if you attempt to create the server group without first defining the servers with ***protocol*-server host** commands, you'll get the following error messages because the IOS attempts to verify the server presence. Notice the entry with

```
Rtr1(config)#aaa new-model
Rtr1(config)#aaa group server radius rad-1
Rtr1(config-sg-radius)#server rad-serv1
Translating "rad-serv1"...domain server (255.255.255.255)
                              ^
% Invalid input detected at '^' marker.

Rtr1(config-sg-radius)#server 192.168.6.4
Rtr1(config-sg-radius)#
00:02:11: %RADIUS-4-NOSERV: Warning: Server 192.168.6.4:1645,1646 is
not defined.
Rtr1(config-sg-radius)#^z
Rtr1#show run
Building configuration...
!
hostname Rtr1
!
aaa new-model
aaa group server radius rad-1
 server 192.168.6.4 auth-port 1645 acct-port 1646
!
```

Notice that the entry with a named server—rad-serv1—returned an invalid input error and the command was rejected. The entry that used the server IP address—192.168.6.4—returned a system warning message indicating that the specified address can't be found, but the entry was accepted. The **show run** command in the same output confirms this. The result is identical for TACACS+. So, if you're going to define servers by name, it's critical for your **ip host** table to be created or your **ip name-server** command(s) to be issued before creating your server groups.

Define Login Authentication Methods List

To use AAA authentication for device login, use the **aaa authentication login global configuration** command. Use the no form of this command to disable AAA authentication. The syntax is

Rtr1(config)#aaa authentication login {default | *list-name*} *method1* [*method2. . .]*
Rtr1(config)#no aaa authentication login {*default* | *list-name*} *method1* [*method2. . .*]

default	Uses the listed authentication methods as the default list when a user logs in.
list-name	Character string used to name the list of authentication methods that can be specified to use when a user logs in.
method	At least one of the keywords described in the next table.

The *method#* arguments identify the list of methods the authentication algorithm tries, in the stated sequence. Method keywords are described in the following table.

Keyword	**Description**
group tacacs+	Use the list of all TACACS+ servers to authenticate services.
group radius	Use the list of all RADIUS servers to authenticate services.
group *group-name*	Use a subset of RADIUS or TACACS+ servers for authentication, as defined by the server group *group-name* in the preceding section.
Local	Use the local user name database for authentication.
local-case	Use case-sensitive local user name database for authentication.
Enable	Use the enable password for authentication.
Line	Use the line password for authentication.
krb5	Use Kerberos 5 for authentication.
krb5-telnet	Use Kerberos 5 Telnet authentication protocol when using Telnet to connect to the router.
None	Use no authentication—no security.

The additional methods of authentication are used only if the previous method returns an error, not if it fails. To ensure that the authentication succeeds, even if all methods return an error, specify None as the final method in the command line.

Examples of this command are included in the next section.

Enable Authorization Proxy (auth-proxy) for AAA

To configure AAA authorization to all proxy authentications, use the global configuration mode command **aaa authorization** to enable authorization and to create a method list, defining authorization methods that can be used when a user accesses the specified function.

In Chapter 3, you learned a method list is simply a list describing the authorization methods to be queried (such as RADIUS or TACACS+), in sequence. Method lists enable one or more security protocols to be used for authorization, thus ensuring a backup system if the initial method fails.

Use the auth-proxy option of the **global configuration** command **aaa authorization** to set parameters for proxy authentications. Use the no form of this command to disable AAA authentication proxy. The general syntax of the command is

```
Rtr1(config)#aaa authorization {authorization-type} {default | list-name} method1 [method2. . .]
Rtr1(config)#no aaa authorization {authorization-type}
```

The AAA authorization types include the following:

```
Rtr1(config)#aaa authorization {network | exec | commands level| reverse-access |
    configuration | config-commands | auth-proxy | ipmobile}
    {default | list-name} method1 [method2. . .]
```

The authorization proxy feature uses the **auth-proxy** keyword. Unlike other AAA authorization options, this one requires the keyword **default**, not allowing the creation of a named list. Also, this feature only allows three method options: group tacacs+, group radius, and group *group-name*. The actual syntax and choices include

```
Rtr1(config)#aaa authorization auth-proxy default method1 [method2. . .]
```

The proxy authentication feature only allows three method options: group tacacs+, group radius, and group *group-name*.

group tacacs+	Uses the list of all TACACS+ servers defined with the **tacacs-server host** command to provide authorization services. The servers are tried in sequential order from the top, first entered.
group radius	Uses the list of all RADIUS servers defined with the **radius-server host** command to provide authorization services. The servers are tried in sequential order from the top, first entered.
group *group-name*	Uses the list of specified TACACS+ or RADIUS servers defined with the **aaa group server** command to provide authorization services. The servers are tried in sequential order within the group from the top, first entered.

The following example uses TACACS+ servers for both login authentication and proxy authorization.

```
Rtr1(config)#aaa new-model
Rtr1(config)#tacacs-server timeout 7
Rtr1(config)#tacacs-server key cisco-key
Rtr1(config)#tacacs-server host 192.168.1.4
Rtr1(config)#aaa authentication login default group tacacs+ local secret
Rtr1(config)#aaa authorization auth-proxy default group tacacs+
```

The following example uses RADIUS servers for both login authentication and proxy authorization.

```
Rtr1(config)#aaa new-model
Rtr1(config)#radius-server timeout 7
Rtr1(config)#radius-server key cisco-key
Rtr1(config)#radius-server host 192.168.1.4
Rtr1(config)#aaa authentication login default group radius local secret
Rtr1(config)#aaa authorization auth-proxy default group radius
```

The following example uses the three TACACS+ servers used earlier and selects only two of them to be included in the server group.

```
Rtr1(config)#aaa new-model
Rtr1(config)#tacacs-server timeout 7
Rtr1(config)#tacacs-server key cisco-key
Rtr1(config)#tacacs-server host tac-serv1
Rtr1(config)#tacacs-server host 192.168.1.4
Rtr1(config)#tacacs-server host 192.168.6.4 port 1500 timeout 3 key cisco9
Rtr1(config)#aaa group server tacacs+ tac-1
Rtr1(config-sg-tacacs+)#server tac-serv1
Rtr1(config-sg-tacacs+)#server 192.168.6.4
Rtr1(config)#aaa authentication login default group tac-1 local secret
Rtr1(config)#aaa authorization auth-proxy default group tac-1
```

Activate Authentication Proxy Accounting

The **aaa accounting** command enables accounting and creating named method lists to define specific accounting methods on a per-line or per-interface basis. Use the **global configuration mode** command **aaa accounting auth-proxy** to activate the security server that will monitor the accounting information. The router reports these attributes as accounting records, which are then stored in an accounting log on the security server. Use the no form of this command to disable accounting. The basic syntax is

Rtr1(config)#aaa accounting auth-proxy default {***accounting-method***} *method1* [*method2. . .*]

The accounting methods include the following four choices:

start-stop	Sends a start accounting notice at the beginning of a process and a stop accounting notice at the end of a process. The start accounting record is sent in the background. The requested user process begins regardless of whether the start accounting notice was received by the accounting server.
wait-start	Sends both a start and a stop accounting notice to the accounting server. But, if the **wait-start** keyword is used, the requested user service does *not* begin until the start accounting notice is acknowledged.

stop-only	Sends a stop accounting notice at the end of the requested user process.
None	Disables accounting services on this line or interface.

For minimal accounting, use the **stop-only** keyword. For more detailed accounting, include the **start-stop** keyword. For even more accounting control, include the **wait-start** keyword, which ensures the start notice is received by the RADIUS or TACACS+ server before granting the user's process request.

Unlike other AAA authorization options, this one requires the keyword **default**, not allowing the creation of a named list. Also, this feature only allows three method options: group tacacs+, group radius, and group *group-name*.

group tacacs+	Uses the list of all TACACS+ servers defined with the **tacacs-server host** command to provide authorization services. The servers are tried in sequential order from the top, first entered.
group radius	Uses the list of all RADIUS servers defined with the **radius-server host** command to provide authorization services. The servers are tried in sequential order from the top, first entered.
group *group-name*	Uses the list of specified TACACS+ or RADIUS servers defined with the **aaa group server** command to provide authorization services. The servers are tried in sequential order within the group from the top, first entered.

The following example uses TACACS+ servers for both login authentication and proxy authorization.

```
Rtr1(config)#aaa new-model
Rtr1(config)#tacacs-server timeout 7
Rtr1(config)#tacacs-server key cisco-key
Rtr1(config)#tacacs-server host 192.168.1.4
Rtr1(config)#aaa authentication login default group tacacs+ local secret
Rtr1(config)#aaa authorization auth-proxy default group tacacs+
Rtr1(config)#aaa accounting auth-proxy default start-stop group tacacs+
```

ACL Entry for Return Traffic from the AAA Server

Typically, it's necessary to create an ACL entry to allow the AAA server TACACS+ or RADIUS return traffic to get to the firewall. If CBAC has already been configured, an input ACL should already be implemented on an interface. Because two ACLs can't be on the same interface monitoring traffic that's traveling in one direction, it's necessary to add the appropriate entries to that ACL.

If there's no existing ACL, consider the following

- The *source* address is the IP address of the AAA server.
- The *destination* is the IP address of the router interface nearest to the AAA server.
- Do you want to permit ICMP traffic?
- Block all other traffic.
- Apply the ACL inbound on the interface connected to the AAA server.

The syntax of the specify entry required for the return traffic looks like the following:

```
Rtr1(config)#access-list acl# permit tcp host source eq tacacs host dest
```

In the following example, ACL 105 blocks all inbound traffic on interface Ethernet0/0, except for traffic from the AAA server, assuming that traffic from the AAA server would come in through Ethernet0/0. The permit ip any any statement allows any ICMP traffic through.

```
interface Ethernet0/0
  ip address 192.168.1.1 255.255.255.0
  ip access-group 105 in
!
access-list 105 permit tcp host 192.168.1.20 eq tacacs host 192.168.1.1
access-list 105 deny   tcp any any
access-list 105 deny   udp any any
access-list 105 permit ip any any
```


Configuring the HTTP Server

To use authentication proxy, the HTTP server on the firewall must be configured and the HTTP server authentication method set to use AAA. You can accomplish this in three basic steps. The first two are required, while the third offers some optional capabilities.

1. Enable the HTTP server on the router. The authentication proxy process uses the HTTP server features to communicate with the client for user authentication. The syntax is

   ```
   Rtr1(config)#ip http server
   ```

2. Set the HTTP server authentication method to AAA. The following output shows the authentication options. This isn't a method list, so only one can be chosen. The final line demonstrates the AAA implementation. The syntax is

   ```
   Rtr1(config)#ip http authentication ?
     aaa     Use AAA access control methods
     enable  Use enable passwords
     local   Use local username and passwords
     tacacs  Use tacacs to authorize user
   Rtr(config)#ip http authentication aaa
   ```

3. (Optional) Specify an access list for the HTTP server. This standard access list can identify which IP address(es) can access the HTTP session. If used, the *acl#* is the same as the one applied to the interface in the **ip auth-proxy name *auth-proxy-name* http** command in the next section. The syntax is

   ```
   Rtr1(config)#ip http access-class acl#
   ```

The following example enables the HTTP server on the router using the AAA authentication. The ACL 75 denies all host connections to the HTTP server.

```
Rtr1(config)#ip http server
Rtr1(config)#ip http authentication aaa
Rtr1(config)#ip http access-class 75
Rtr1(config)#access-list 75 deny any
```

Authentication Proxy Configuration on the Router

Configuring authentication proxy on a firewall router involves using three variations of the **ip auth-proxy** command in the Global Configuration mode. Then, the same **ip auth-proxy** command is used in the Interface Configuration mode to apply the rule to the interface. The variations include the following commands:

- **ip auth-proxy auth-cache-time**
- **ip auth-proxy auth-proxy-banner**
- **ip auth-proxy name**
- **ip auth-proxy** (interface configuration)

Remember, the **aaa authorization auth-proxy** command, covered earlier, is used together with the **ip auth-proxy name** command covered in this section. The former enables the AAA auth-proxy feature, while the latter defines the specific rules to apply. Together, these two commands create the authorization policy to be used by the firewall.

The ip auth-proxy auth-cache-time Command

Use the **global configuration ip auth-proxy** command with the auth-cache-time option to set the authentication proxy global idle timeout value. This *cache idle timer* monitors the length of time (in minutes) that an authentication cache entry, along with its associated dynamic user access control list entry, is managed after a period of inactivity. When that period of inactivity expires, the authentication entry and the associated dynamic access list entries are deleted.

If CBAC is also configured on the router, the auth-cache-time timeout value must be set higher than the idle timeout for any context-based access control protocols. If not, when the authentication proxy timer expires and removes the user profile and any associated dynamic user ACLs, idle connections could be monitored by CBAC. Deleting these ACL entries can cause the idle connections to hang.

The reverse isn't a problem when the CBAC idle timeout value is shorter. CBAC always resets the idle connections whenever the CBAC idle timeout expires, which would then be before the authentication proxy removes the user profile. Use the no form of the command to restore the default. The syntax is

```
Rtr1(config)#ip auth-proxy auth-cache-time min
Rtr1(config)#no ip auth-proxy auth-cache-time
```

auth-cache-time *min*	Specifies the minutes of inactivity an authentication cache entry and the associated dynamic user ACL entry will exist before being deleted. Acceptable values: 1 to 2,147,483,647 minutes.

This command was introduced in IOS 12.0(5)T. The default value is 60 minutes.

The following example sets the authorization cache idle timeout to 20 minutes.

```
Rtr1(config)#ip auth-proxy auth-cache-time 20
```

The ip auth-proxy auth-proxy-banner Command

To display a banner, such as the router name, in the authentication proxy login page, use the **ip auth-proxy auth-proxy-banner** command in Global Configuration mode. Use the ***banner-text*** argument to specify a customer banner other than the default. To disable the banner display, use the no form of this command. The syntax is

Rtr1(config)#ip auth-proxy auth-proxy-banner [*banner-text*]
Rtr1(config)#no ip auth-proxy auth-proxy-banner [*banner-text*]

banner-text	(Optional) Specifies a text string to replace the default banner, which is the name of the router. This command is similar to the standard IOS message of the day (MOTD) command. The text string should be written in the following format: *C banner-text C* , where *C* is a delimiting character. This delimiting character can be any character that won't be used in your message.

This command was introduced in IOS 12.0(5)T. By default, the command is disabled. If the command is issued without the banner-text option, the router host name will appear.

The first example adds the router name to the display in the authentication proxy login page. The second example personalizes the message using the # as the delimiter. The show run output shows the result regardless of the delimiter selected.

```
Rtr1(config)#ip auth-proxy auth-proxy-banner
Rtr1(config)#ip auth-proxy auth-proxy-banner # Jerri's Perimeter Router #
Rtr1#show run
!
ip auth-proxy auth-proxy-banner ^C Jerri's Perimeter Router ^C
ip auth-proxy auth-cache-time 20
!
```

The ip auth-proxy name Command

The **ip auth-proxy name** command is used to create a named authentication proxy rule. The command includes several options that increase the administrator's ability to control access. The rule is applied to an interface on a router using the **ip auth-proxy** command. To create an authentication proxy rule, use the **global configuration mode** command **ip auth-proxy name**.

Use the no form of this command with a rule name to remove the specific authentication proxy rules. If no rule name is specified, the no form of this command removes all the authentication rules on the router and disables the proxy on all interfaces. The syntax is

Rtr1(config)#ip auth-proxy name *auth-proxy-name* http [list {*acl#* | *acl-name*}]
[auth-cache-time min]
Rtr1(config)#no ip auth-proxy [name *auth-proxy-name*]

auth-proxy-name	Associates a name, up to 16 alphanumeric characters long, with an authentication proxy rule.
http	The protocol that triggers the authentication proxy—only HTTP is supported.
list {*acl#* | *acl-name*}	(Optional) Uses a standard (1–99), extended (100–199), or named ACL with the authentication proxy rule to control which hosts can use the authentication proxy. Traffic not matching the ACL is blocked. If no list is specified, all HTTP traffic connections arriving at the interface are subject to authentication.
auth-cache-time *min*	(Optional) Overrides the global default authentication proxy cache timer for the named authentication proxy rule. Values can be 1 to 2,147,483,647. The default value is set by the **ip auth-proxy auth-cache-time** command.

This command was introduced in IOS 12.0(5)T. Support for named and extended access lists was added with the IOS 12.2 release. Until then, only standard ACLs could be used.

The first example creates the authentication proxy rule **net_users**. Because no ACL is specified in the command, all connection sessions using HTTP traffic will trigger the authentication window and process.

```
Rtr1(config)#ip auth-proxy name net_users http
```

The next example creates the authentication proxy rule **sales_users**. The **auth-cache-time 15** sets the idle timer for this rule only to 15 minutes. The *"list 77"* reference and related ACL defines the hosts, the 192.168.3.0 network that is allowed to authenticate. All other traffic is blocked.

```
Rtr1(config)#ip auth-proxy name sales_users http auth-cache-time 15 list 77
Rtr1(config)#access-list 77 permit 192.168.1.0 0.0.0.255
```

In this last example, the first command disables only the **sales_users** rule, while the last line disables the authentication proxy on all interfaces and removes any rules from the router configuration, as well as any related ACL entries.

```
Rtr1(config)#no ip auth-proxy name sales_users
Rtr1(config)#no ip auth-proxy
```

The auth-proxy Interface Configuration

Use the **interface configuration** command **ip auth-proxy** to apply the named authentication proxy rule to a firewall interface. Connection-initiating HTTP traffic passing into the interface is intercepted for authentication if no existing authentication cache entry exists.

If no ACL is defined as part of the rule, traffic from all hosts is given the opportunity to authenticate. If an ACL is referenced in the rule, only those IP addresses of hosts that match the ACL is allowed to attempt to authenticate. Traffic from all other addresses is discarded.

Use the no form of this command with a rule name to disable that specific authentication proxy rule on the interface. If a rule isn't specified, the no form of this command disables the authentication proxy on the interface.

Rtr1(config)#ip auth-proxy *auth-proxy-name*
Rtr1(config)#no ip auth-proxy [*auth-proxy-name*]

auth-proxy-name	The name of the authentication proxy rule to apply to the interface. The authentication proxy rule is defined using the **ip auth-proxy name *auth-proxy-name*** command.

This command was introduced in IOS 12.0(5)T. No default behavior or values.

This example applies the authentication proxy rule sales_users to interface Ethernet0.

```
Rtr1(config)#interface e0
Rtr1(config-if)#ip address 192.168.4.2 255.255.255.0
Rtr1(config-if)#ip access-group 100 in
Rtr1(config-if)#ip auth-proxy sales_users
Rtr1(config-if)#ip nat inside
Rtr1(config-if)#no shutdown
```

Verify Authentication Proxy Configuration

To check the current authentication proxy configuration, use the privileged **EXEC mode** command **show ip auth-proxy configuration**.

In this example, the global authentication proxy idle timeout is 20 minutes, the named authentication proxy rule is "sales_users," and the idle timeout value for this rule is 15 minutes. The display shows no host list is specified, meaning all connections initiating HTTP traffic at the interface are subject to the authentication proxy rule.

```
Rtr1#show ip auth-proxy configuration
Authentication global cache time is 20 minutes
Authentication Proxy Rule Configuration
 Auth-proxy name sales_users
    http list 77 auth-cache-time 15 minutes
```

The auth-proxy Cache

When the authentication proxy is in use, dynamic access lists grow and shrink as temporary authentication entries are added and deleted. After users initiate HTTP connections through the router, use the privileged **EXEC mode** command **show ip auth-proxy cache** to display the list of authentication entries.

The authentication proxy cache lists the host IP address, the source port number, the timeout value for the authentication proxy, and the state of the connection. If the authentication proxy state is HTTP_ESTAB, the user authentication was successful.

```
Rtr1#show ip auth-proxy cache
Authentication Proxy Cache
 Client IP 192.168.1.10 Port 31219, timeout 15, state HTTP_ESTAB
```

Clearing the auth-proxy Cache

To clear authentication cache entries manually from the firewall before they time out, use the **clear ip auth-proxy cache** command in privileged EXEC mode. Use the Asterisk option to delete all authentication cache entries. Enter a specific IP address to delete an entry for a single host. The syntax is

Rtr1#clear ip auth-proxy cache {* | *host-ip-address*}

Displaying Dynamic ACL Entries

When the authentication proxy is in use, dynamic access list entries are added and removed as temporary authentication sessions are added and deleted. When no open sessions exist, there won't be any dynamic entries. To display any dynamic access list entries, use the **show ip access-lists** command in privileged EXEC mode. The number of matches displayed in parentheses indicates the number of times the access list entry was used.

Both the idle timeout parameter and the **clear ip auth-proxy cache** command from the last section can cause no dynamic entries to occur in the display. The syntax to display any access lists configured on the firewall, including dynamic ACL entries, is

Rtr1# show ip access-lists

This following shows the ACL entries prior to any authentication proxy sessions.

```
Rtr1#show ip access-lists
Extended IP access list 160
 deny tcp any any eq telnet
 deny udp any any
 permit tcp any any (41 matches)
 permit ip any any
```

This next output shows the same ACL following user authentication. The first six lines represent the downloaded user profile enabling the specified features for the authenticated user. The last four lines are the same lines as in the previous example after more traffic.

```
Rtr1#show ip access-lists
Extended IP access list 160
permit tcp host 192.168.1.10 any eq 69
permit icmp host 192.168.1.10 host 192.168.4.2
permit tcp host 192.168.1.10 any eq telnet
permit tcp host 192.168.1.10 any eq ftp
permit tcp host 192.168.1.10 any eq ftp-data
permit tcp host 192.168.1.10 any eq smtp
deny tcp any any eq telnet
deny udp any any
permit tcp any any (76 matches)
permit ip any any
```


For more information, go to the Cisco web site http://www.cisco.com and search for authentication proxy. No CCO account is required.

The debug Commands

While they aren't specifically exam objectives, the following **debug** commands can be useful in troubleshooting or simply watching authentication proxy processes. As with all **debug** commands, remember, debug can have a detrimental effect on production routers.

Rtr1#debug ip auth-proxy {function-trace}	Displays the authentication proxy functions
Rtr1#debug ip auth-proxy {http}	Displays auth-proxy–related HTTP events

The following **debug** commands are AAA tools but, because authentication proxy relies on AAA, they can be useful in troubleshooting.

Rtr1#debug {tacacs | radius}	Displays TACACS+ or RADIUS information.
Rtr1#debug aaa authentication	Displays information on AAA/TACACS+ authentication. Shows the methods of authentication and the results.
Rtr1#debug aaa authorization	Displays information on AAA/TACACS+ authorization. Hows the methods of authorization and the results.

CBAC Configuration

As you learned earlier in this chapter, authentication proxy *does not create ACEs to support returning data traffic or data channel traffic.* So, it's necessary either to create static ACLs to allow the return traffic or to configure the CBAC inspection rules in the firewall configuration. Because static ACLs increase the network vulnerability (they're permanent "holes" in the firewall) and the CBAC "hole" only exists as long as needed, the solution is quite simple.

Configuring CBAC with any authentication proxy implementation is the most reliable and secure method to ensure return traffic for authorized user connections through the firewall. Chapter 6 covered CBAC in detail. The following exercise shows an example of adding CBAC to the configuration after the authentication proxy is defined.

Chapter Review

The authentication proxy is user authentication and authorization technology, which is a part of Cisco IOS Firewall feature set. The feature is supported on a growing list of platforms using the latest IOS versions (12.2), including the SOHO 70, 800, uBR900, 1720, 2600, 3600, 7100, 7200, and 7500 series routers. Earlier versions won't support the feature on the smaller units (SOHO 70 to 1720s). Authentication proxy is compatible with other Cisco IOS security features, such as NAT, CBAC, IPSec encryption, and VPN client software.

The Cisco IOS Firewall authentication proxy feature allows network administrators to implement security policies on a per-user basis through personalized ACLs. Without firewall authentication proxy, user identity and any authorized access was associated with a user's IP address. Any single security policy had to be applied to an entire user group or subnet. Now, users can be identified and authorized on the basis of their per-user policy, and any access privileges can be customized, based on their individual access profiles.

With the authentication proxy feature, users can log in to the network or access the Internet via HTTP, and their specific access profiles are automatically retrieved and applied from a Cisco Secure ACS, or other RADIUS or TACACS+ authentication server. The user profiles and the resulting temporary ACL entries are active only while active traffic exists from the authenticated user. By default, the temporary openings close after 60 minutes of inactivity.

The authentication proxy feature requires that an AAA server running Cisco Secure Access Control Server (ACS) be present on the network. Configuring the AAA server to enable the features is necessary.

Next, the router running the firewall feature set, typically the perimeter router, must be configured by performing the following tasks:

- Configuring AAA support (required)
- Configuring the HTTP server feature (required)
- Configuring the Authentication Proxy (required)
- Verifying the Authentication Proxy (optional, but valuable)

Skipping the optional verifying is done only at risk to the resources you're charged to protect.

Questions

1. What protocol does the authentication proxy use to trigger an authentication session?

   A. Telnet

   B. HTTPS

   C. TFTP

   D. HTTP

2. Which two protocol authentication servers can be used with authentication proxy?
   - A. TACACS
   - B. Kerberos
   - C. RADIUS
   - D. TACACS+
3. Authentication proxy allows how many attempts to enter a valid user name and password?
   - A. 1
   - B. 3
   - C. 5
   - D. unlimited
4. True or False. User profile entries stored on the AAA server are made up of **permit** and **deny** statements used to create temporary ACL entries on the firewall router.
   - A. True
   - B. False
5. In the temporary ACL entry **permit icmp host 192.168.1.10 host 192.168.4.2**, which address probably represents the authenticated user?
   - A. 192.168.1.10
   - B. 192.168.4.2
   - C. It can be either one.
   - D. There's no way to know.
6. True or False. Authentication proxy is supported on all router platforms since v12.2.
   - A. True
   - B. False
7. In the **ip auth-proxy auth-cache-time *units*** command, what are the idle timer units?
   - A. Bits
   - B. Seconds
   - C. Minutes
   - D. Hours
8. Which technology does authentication proxy use to provide secure authentication?
   - A. HTTPS
   - B. DirectX

C. JavaScript

D. All of the above

9. According to the text, which of the following is the reason to configure CBAC with authentication proxy?

   A. CBAC's attack prevention features.

   B. CBAC is so easy to configure.

   C. Authentication proxy doesn't create ACEs to support returning data traffic.

   D. CBAC has its own authentication functions.

10. The IOS Firewall authentication proxy feature works with which technology?

    A. Dial-in connection

    B. Console connections

    C. HTTP sessions

    D. Telnet sessions

11. What additional IOS feature allows the authentication proxy to work with NAT services?

    A. AAA Accounting

    B. CBAC

    C. VPN client

    D. One-time passwords

12. Which command is *not* a step in setting up an IOS Firewall authentication proxy?

    A. Configuring the HTTP server

    B. Configuring the authentication proxy

    C. Configuring AAA

    D. Configuring CBAC

13. How many open sessions does authentication proxy support before refusing additional sessions?

    A. 24

    B. 40

    C. 100

    D. 500

14. When creating the inbound ACL on the firewall for authentication proxy, all traffic is typically blocked except which one of the following that's absolutely required?

    A. Outbound traffic to the AAA server

    B. Local user Telnet traffic

C. Return traffic from the AAA server

D. Local user HTTP traffic

15. When configuring the authentication proxy features, all commands are variations of which of the following?

A. Rtr1#ip auth-proxy auth

B. Rtr1(config)#ip auth-proxy auth

C. Rtr1(config-if)#ip auth-proxy auth

D. Rtr1(config-ap)#ip auth-proxy auth

Answers

1. **D.** HTTP
2. **C. and D.** RADIUS and TACACS+
3. **C.** Five tries
4. **B.** False. User profiles contain only **permit** statements.
5. **A.** 192.168.1.10
6. **A.** False. IOS versions (12.2) support authentication proxy on the SOHO 70, 800, uBR900, 1720, 2600, 3600, 7100, 7200, and 7500 series routers.
7. **C.** Minutes (default 60)
8. **C.** JavaScript
9. **C.** Authentication proxy does *not* create ACEs to support returning data traffic.
10. **C.** HTTP sessions
11. **B.** CBAC
12. **D.** Configuring CBAC
13. **B.** 40
14. **C.** Return traffic from the AAA server
15. **B.** Rtr1(config)#ip auth-proxy auth

PART III

Virtual Private Networks (VPNs)

CHAPTER 9

Cisco IOS IPSec Introduction

In this chapter, you will learn to:

- Recognize Virtual Private Networks
- Apply tunneling protocols
- Work with IPSec
- Use Cisco IOS IPSec technologies
- Learn about Cisco IOS Cryptosystem components
- Understand security associations
- Know the five steps for IPSec
- Make use of IPSec support in Cisco Systems products

As businesses grow and create branch locations or encourage employees to work at least part-time from home, the need to maintain remote connectivity to the organization's information systems becomes a bigger concern. At the same time, many businesses are incorporating "just in time" scheduling into many of their processes, which requires vendors, suppliers, and even customers to have immediate access to production or purchasing information.

At one time, network security could be managed quite well simply by not allowing any outside access to the company resources. If information was needed, employees either reported to their desk to retrieve the information or telephoned someone at the office to get the needed data. Both of these solutions would be considered unacceptably slow today for many firms.

Earliest remote connections were often made with dedicated (leased) lines that provided quite secure connections for a price. Typically, that price went up according to distance. A branch office across town might require only a few hundred dollars per month for connectivity, whereas the same size branch across the country could cost many times as much. The two factors that most directly impacted the cost were bandwidth required and distance covered.

WAN technologies like analog modem, ISDN, T1/E1, T3/E3, frame relay, and cell relay (ATM) all offer reliable, secure connectivity with varying degrees of performance. The problem is they can be expensive. Lack of universal access to some of these technologies in many parts of the country or world means companies often have to install and support multiple technologies. Even for companies that routinely use dedicated lines, the problem still exists of what to do with branch locations, vendors, suppliers, or traveling employees located halfway around the world.

The advent of the Internet naturally caught the imagination of many organizations—large and small—as a possible way to extend their networks for a relatively small cost. All they had to do was give up was security and often performance. The goal became to develop a way of providing a secure connection within an inherently non-secure environment, a virtual private network. Many attempts have been made to create these VPNs and many proprietary solutions are competing for this growing business. In Chapters 10 through 16, the focus is on Cisco's implementation of IPSec, an industry standard for providing private connections over public networks. Figure 9-1 shows some of the many types of connections that an organization might try to incorporate into its VPN strategy.

Virtual Private Networks

A virtual private network (VPN) is a secure connection within a public (non-secure) network. This security is typically implemented by some form of user and/or device authentication and encryption of the data stream creating a secure, private tunnel between

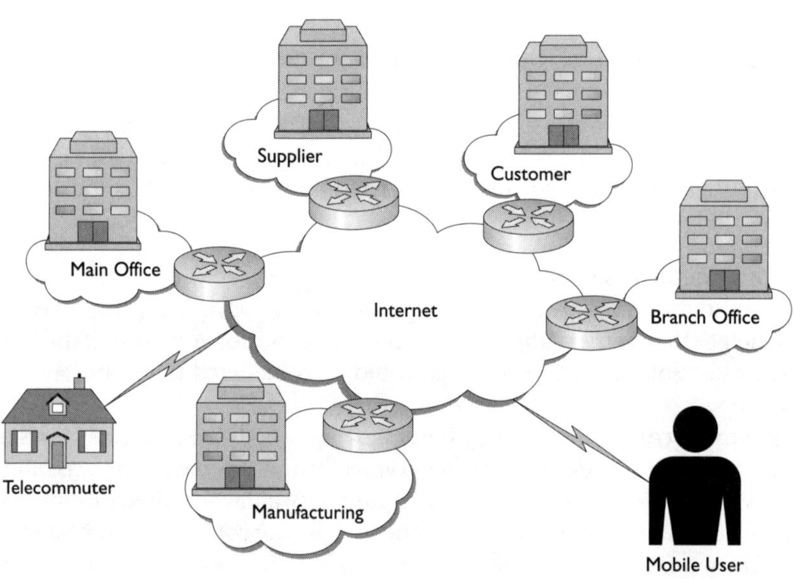

Figure 9-1 VPN opportunities to extend the corporate LAN services

a remote endpoint and a gateway. The sensitive nature of some communications requires the help of VPNs to provide the following three services:

Confidentiality	Ensures that only the intended recipient can read the transmitted data while, at the same time, thwarting efforts by other parties that might intercept it. Confidentiality is provided by encryption algorithms, such as DES or 3DES.
Authentication	Verification of the identity of a person or process that sent the data. Authentication is provided by mechanisms, such as exchanging digital certificates.
Integrity	Ensures the data received is exactly what was transmitted from the source without alterations or additions. Integrity is provided by hashing algorithms, such as MD5 or SHA.

While many VPN strategies and technologies exist, let's start by defining some basic terminology that can help describe VPNs. VPNs come in two basic types:

- Remote access
- Site-to-site

Each of these two VPN types can be further broken down into either of the following categories:

- Intranet access
- Extranet access

Remote-Access

Remote access involves connecting individual users to a LAN to provide secure, encrypted network access for telecommuters, traveling employees, and one-person offices of consultants, contractors, brokers, vendors, and so forth.

Early remote-access VPN often involved contracting (outsourcing) with enterprise service providers (ESPs), such as CompuServe. The ESP provided the network infrastructure and client software for the user computers. Many of these systems used dial-up (modem) services called virtual private dial-up networks (VPDN). ESPs were often too expensive for small to medium-sized organizations or they weren't interested in supporting that size client.

Today, many companies provide their own VPN connections through the Internet, allowing access to remote users running VPN client software through their Internet service providers (ISPs). The rapid expansion of cable modems and DSL has made it possible for telecommuters and other fixed location users to replace slower modem and ISDN services with fast connections, at a fraction of the cost of dedicated lines. Fast Internet connections offered in many hotels and the new wireless access facilities in many public places, such as airports and convention centers, means traveling employees can also use fast secure remote VPN connections. Examples in Figure 9-2 show two common types of remote-access VPN.

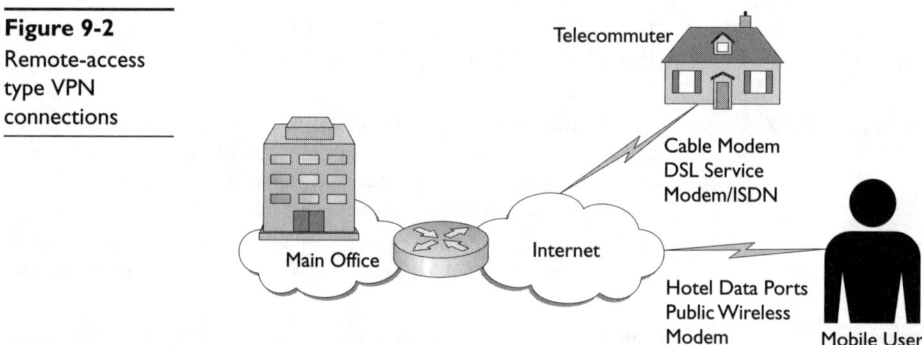

Figure 9-2 Remote-access type VPN connections

The three basic types of VPN connections include

- Access VPN
- Intranet VPN
- Extranet VPN

Access VPN

Access VPNs allow the organization's remote users to access company intranet or extranet over a shared infrastructure. Access VPNs provide secure connectivity for mobile users, telecommuters, and small branch offices using analog modems, ISDN, DSL, cable modems, and wireless IP.

Intranet and extranet VPNs are covered in the next paragraphs.

Site-to-Site

Site-to-site, or LAN-to-LAN, VPNs involve a secure connection between two end devices such as routers, firewalls, or VPN hardware devices. The hosts on each LAN connected to those end devices can access the other LAN via the secure connection based on the organization security policy and the placement of shared resources. Common examples of site-to-site VPN implementation could include connecting branch offices, vendor sites, dealer sites, or customer offices to the corporate network. Figure 9-3 shows the types of connections that might be VPN candidates.

Intranet VPN

Intranet VPN would involve allowing the remote user or connected site to have access to the company internal network and resources. A typical example might be a branch office connecting to the corporate network allowing all branch employees access to e-mail and other corporate resources. Individual telecommuters and traveling employees would be candidates to use a VPN to connect to the company intranet.

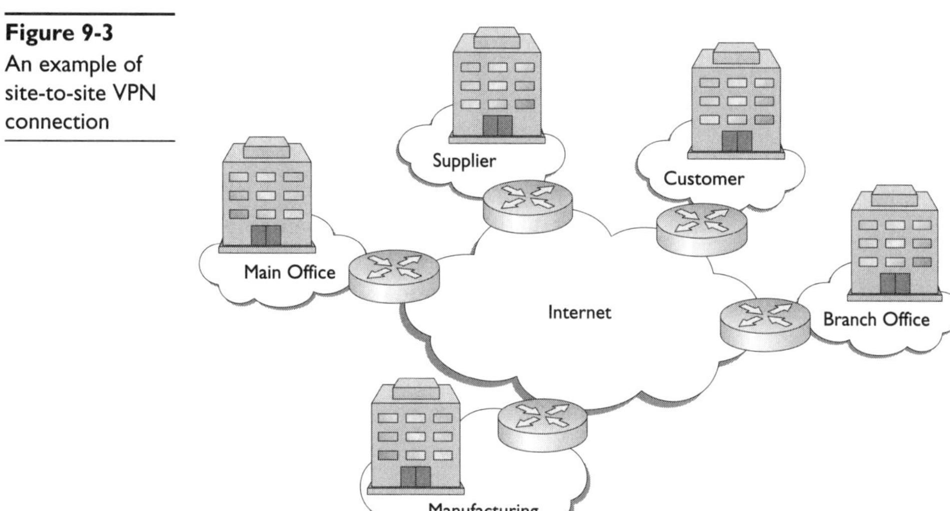

Figure 9-3 An example of site-to-site VPN connection

Extranet VPN

Extranet VPN might be one or more special networks established to share resources with vendors, suppliers, customers, consultants, business partners, and other nonemployee groups. The extranet creates a shared environment for collaborative efforts. An example might be a company web server network that allows dealers to check inventory, place orders, and track deliveries. This limits access and exposure to only those resources needed by the shared, while protecting the others.

Extranet access could be either site-to-site or a remote-access connection to a nonemployee, such as a consultant or a broker.

The extranet could be a DMZ on the network that requires some level of authentication to access and is, therefore, unavailable to the general public. If anyone could access it, this would be an Internet. Figure 9-4 shows VPN connection types supported by Cisco technologies.

Layer 2 VPNs

In an effort to provide secure connections through the public networks, service providers developed their own proprietary technologies or combinations of technologies. Some of these early VPN implementations were Layer 2 technologies, while others were Layer 3.

Using the broad definition of a VPN as "a private network built upon or within a public network," public X.25, Frame Relay, and ATM networks' use of virtual circuits within their public networks can be considered VPNs. The shared nature of these technologies allowed them to be less expensive than comparable dedicated circuits. These types of VPNs are generically referred to as Layer 2 VPNs. Unfortunately, these services don't address universal access because they are unavailable in many parts of the country and world.

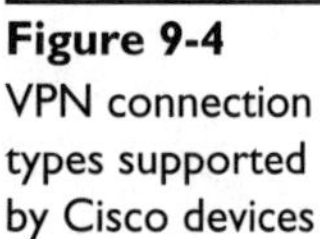

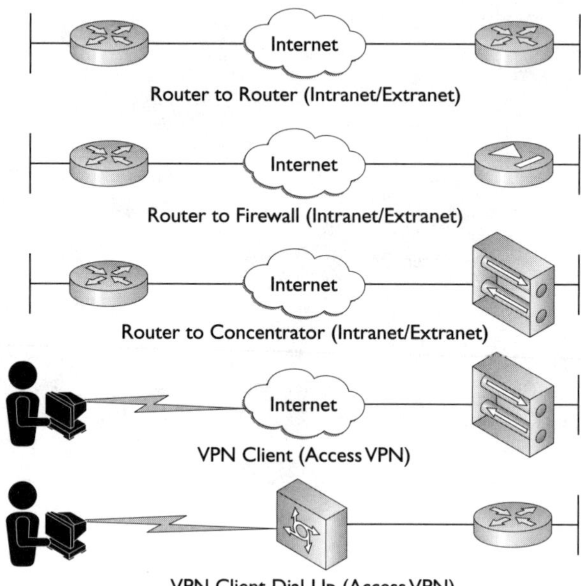

Figure 9-4 VPN connection types supported by Cisco devices

Layer 3 VPNs

The dominant emerging form of VPNs are those networks constructed across shared IP backbones, called *IP VPNs.* Because the Internet is the largest and most widely accessible of the public networks, this is where the greatest research and development is aimed. The early Layer 3 VPN implementations were provided by private companies that developed security implementations on top of the published TCP/IP and Internet standards. Cisco encryption technology (CET) was an early Cisco proprietary Layer 3 VPN technology.

The biggest drawback to these early efforts was the lack of interoperability between different manufacturers. While a strong case can be made for a single vendor end-to-end solution, the reality is this: all-too-common business mergers and acquisitions often mean companies are forced to merge different vendor VPN strategies and technologies.

A second issue is that not all vendors make products for all implementations within the network. For example, a vendor might have a strong VPN line for connecting branch locations and could even have client software for individual remote users, but they might lack a solution for small multiuser connections using cable modems or DSL service.

IPSec as an Emerging Leader

IP Security (IPSec) is a standards-based suite of protocols developed by the Internet Engineering Task Force (IETF) to provide secure exchange of packets at the IP layer (Layer 3). IPSec is rapidly becoming the most widely deployed VPN implementation. Cisco has adopted IPSec for its VPN products.

The single biggest problem with using the Internet—or any TCP/IP network—for private communication is the lack of security. The underlying protocols simply weren't designed with security as a high priority. While it's easy to place blame using hindsight, a fair analysis would recognize that not only was the technology brand new, but also that no one involved could have visualized the masses from every corner of the Earth individually accessing the resulting network.

The evolution of the World Wide Web as a more or less unregulated playground for every interest and activity has lead to a growing number of miscreants bent on causing problems. Add to this the technologically incompetent and those who see the Internet as a tool for political and religious warfare, and you can understand why the neighborhood has become an unfriendly place.

The security concerns in using the Internet for conducting private communications can fall into the following categories:

- Loss of privacy
- Loss of data integrity
- Identity spoofing
- Denial-of-service

The ultimate goal in developing an IPSec standard is to address these threats without the need for expensive host hardware or application modifications and changes.

IPSec and the Future

Remember, IPSec is a new and still-evolving pool of standards and protocols. The IETF working group for IPSec has dozens of draft proposals they're working on to extend the capabilities and interoperability of IPSec with other common network technologies, such as NAT/Firewall traversal and MIB standards.

The mandate is for IPSec to be in IP Version 6 when it's finally implemented. Once this occurs, we'll all be using IPSec in its latest form. For more information on the IPSec working group and its current activities go to the following site: http://www.ietf.cnri.reston.va.us/html.charters/ipsec-charter.html.

NOTE While this book is current at press time, probably no other features warrant constant monitoring of Cisco documentation and releases covering IOS and device upgrades more than IPSec and VPNs. Each new release seems to bring expanded support for technologies like wireless, firewalls, and even basic IPSec protocols supported.

Other VPN Implementations

Data security can be performed at many levels, including having the user applications encrypt the data. This was a feature supported on many user applications, such as Microsoft Excel and Word. In each case, the users supplied a password when they saved a document and, next, the data was scrambled using the password as an encryption key. The recipient then needed to supply exactly the same password to open the document. While somewhat effective, this method relied on the user to implement it, forward the password in a secure fashion to the recipient, and never forget the password for the life of the document. Many corporate disasters occurred when an employee left the company, for whatever reason, and critical data was unavailable.

In an effort to remove user involvement from the process, technologies were developed that operated at the application layer, but remained invisible to the end user. Some of these applications provided only partial solutions to the problem. Secure Sockets Layer (SSL) is an example of application encryption for web browsers that protects the confidentiality of data sent from supported applications, but it doesn't protect data sent from other applications. Each host system on the network and all applications must be SSL installed and configured to work efficiently. While this is better than having the user manage encryption, too many opportunities still exist for the system to fail. SSL typically requires increased administrator involvement when computers or applications are added or changed.

Why Use VPNs?

VPN benefits to the organization can include significant cost savings because the service provider network supplies the brunt of the hardware and support for the WAN connections. The savings can be substantial, especially when comparing the price of bandwidth available from DSL and cable connections to the Internet versus the cost of dedicated or frame relay links.

Particularly in supporting remote users, the Internet provides a low-cost alternative for enabling access to the corporate network, instead of maintaining large modem banks and paying costly phone bills. With just a local phone call to an ISP in many places around the world, a user can have access to the corporate network. In some cases, VPNs enable organizations to save between 30 and 70 percent over competing remote-access solutions.

An organization might see improved geographical coverage, especially in communities or regions where dedicated links or frame relay links are unavailable or prohibitively expensive. The rapid deployment of cable modems, DSL service, and even some public wireless networks can allow the telecommuter opportunities that would be impractical at modem speeds. High-speed data ports in hotels and motels that can be secured through VPN connections mean traveling employees can often do more tasks on the road than simply checking their e-mail. In many cases, VPNs mean simplified WAN operations and increased networking reliability.

VPN Analogy

A network with remote sites can be thought of as a group of islands served by a public ferry system. While this internetwork of ferries allows residents to move from place to place at a reasonable cost, there's no privacy and any scheduling, routing, and rules are up to the ferry provider.

An alternative would be to build bridges among the islands, but the cost would be high and some islands might have too few residents to make the cost worthwhile. These dedicated links, as in WANs, would provide privacy and more freedom of movement. Unfortunately, like WANs, where distance determines the cost of the bridge, it's possible to create situations where connecting a distant small site with even minimal service could cost many times that of servicing a much larger and closer group.

Another alternative could be personal watercraft of some type. These boats could provide private transportation, routing, and scheduling at the direction of their owner. Even if the people on the ferry see a boat, they have no idea what's going on inside, or even its source or destination. Relative to building bridges, adding more boats as needed would be inexpensive.

With all the variety in boat types—from canoes and kayaks to luxury yachts—at least it's possible that some marinas might not support all types, thereby limiting the boat owner's ability to make connections. If a single standard was adopted by all marinas, such as power boats between 15 and 35 feet, then the boat owner would be free to choose from many vendors as long as they met the standard. The marinas, as service providers, could still support other options in addition to the standard.

Tunneling Protocols

Most VPNs use the concept of tunneling to create a private network that extends across the Internet. Conceptually, it's as if a secure tunnel has been built between two end devices (routers, firewall, or VPN device). Data can be directed into one end of the tunnel and it travels securely to the other end. These end devices, or tunnel interfaces, are typically the perimeter router firewalls for the LANs being connected.

Technically, no tunnel exists and the process doesn't resemble a tunnel, but the term "tunneling" somewhat describes the end result of traffic being able to pass through a non-secure environment without concerns about eavesdropping, data hijacking, or data manipulation. *Tunneling* is a process of encapsulating an entire data packet as the payload within a second packet, which is understood by the network and both end points. Depending on the protocols used, the new payload—the original packet—can be encrypted. Figure 9-5 is a common graphical representation of Layer 3 tunneling technology.

The tunneling process requires three different protocols:

- **Carrier protocol** The network protocol used to transport the final encapsulation
- **Encapsulating protocol** The protocol used to provide the new packet around the original data packet. Examples: IPSec, GRE, L2F, L2TP, PPTP
- **Passenger protocol** The original data packet that's been encapsulated. Examples: IP, IPX, NetBEUI

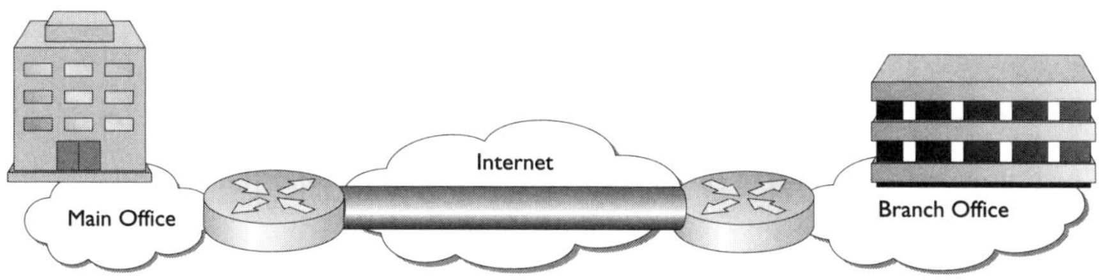

Figure 9-5 Layer 3 VPN tunneling representation

Through tunneling techniques, you can pass non-IP packets or private IP addressed packets through a public IP network. You can even route NetBEUI—the famous non-routable protocol—once it's been encapsulated for tunneling through a VPN. What happens is the new data frame, or packet, is, in fact, a legal packet with proper addressing to travel through the network. Hidden safely within the payload portion of this new frame is the original packet, which needs the assistance and/or protection.

L2F, L2TP, and PPTP are all three Layer 2 tunneling protocols that support Access VPN solutions by tunneling PPP.

Layer Two Forwarding (L2F) Protocol

L2F is a tunneling protocol developed by Cisco Systems, which is similar to PPTP developed by Microsoft. Both protocols enable organizations to set up VPNs that use the Internet backbone for transporting traffic. L2F is supported by other vendors, such as Shiva and Nortel.

Recently, Microsoft and Cisco agreed to merge their respective protocols into a single, standard protocol called Layer Two Tunneling Protocol (L2TP) an IETF and industry-standard Layer 2 tunneling solution. Microsoft supports L2TP in Windows 2000/XP client software for client-initiated VPN tunnels.

Layer 2 Tunneling Protocol (L2TP)

L2TP is an emerging IETF standard and one of the key building blocks for VPNs in the dial access space. L2TP combines the best features of Cisco's Layer 2 Forwarding (L2F) and Microsoft's Point-to-Point Tunneling Protocol (PPTP), enabling mobile workforces to connect to their corporate intranets or extranets wherever and whenever they require.

L2TP is a standard way to build Access VPNs that simulate private networks using a shared infrastructure, such as the Internet. These Access VPNs offer access for mobile users, telecommuters, and small offices through dial, ISDN, xDSL, and cable.

Benefits of L2TP include per-user authentication, dynamic address allocation from an address pool or by using DHCP server, plus RADIUS and AAA support.

Generic Routing Encapsulation (GRE)

GRE is an early Layer 3 tunneling technology that has existed for years. Cisco has supported this tunneling technology since Cisco IOS software version 9.21. IPSec is the new IETF standard for Layer 3 encryption and encrypted tunnels supported by the Cisco IOS software since version 11.3(3)T.

How IPSec Works

IPSec is a complex method of exchanging data that involves many component technologies and numerous encryption-method options. This chapter covers the major protocols and processes that make up IPSec. Configuring these protocols and processes is covered in Chapters 10 through 16. Recognizing that IPSec operation can be broken down into the following five main steps might be useful.

Step 1	Traffic deemed "interesting" initiates an IPSec session. Access lists determine which data traffic will be protected by the IPSec technology. Other traffic will travel through the public network without IPSec protection.
Step 2	Called *IKE Phase One* A secure channel is established between two peers. Each peer determines whether the other peer can be authenticated and whether the two peers can agree on Internet Key Exchange (IKE) security rules for exchanging data.
Step 3	Called *IKE Phase Two* IPSec session is established between the two peers. Stricter IPSec security rules and protocols are established between the peers.
Step 4	Data transfer Data is transferred between IPSec peers using the IPSec-defined security rules and protocols.
Step 5	*IPSec tunnel termination* IPSec session ends through deletion or by timing out.

The complexity of VPNs in general and IPSec in particular can get a little intimidating, but, remember, at the highest level, this is just like many other communications sessions. Some data requires special attention, a session is opened, the data is exchanged, and the session is torn down. Even a simple telephone call to someone special can be an analogy.

- Step 1 Something important occurs that can't wait until the next time you speak to that person.
- Step 2 The telephone call is placed and, through the ringing and answering, you can determine you're talking to the person you expected.
- Step 3 Because the subject matter is private and important, you might ask if the person is alone, so they can speak freely.
- Step 4 Once an acceptable level of privacy is assured, the information can be shared.
- Step 5 When the information has been exchanged, both parties hang up.

These steps are revisited again in the section "IKE SAs versus IPSec SAs."

Cisco IOS IPSec Technologies

IPSec acts at the network layer, protecting and authenticating IP packets between participating IPSec peers, such as VPN software clients, VPN 3002 hardware clients, Cisco routers, PIX Firewalls, and the VPN 3000 Series Concentrators. Cisco IPSec VPNs provide the following network services:

- **Data integrity** The IPSec receiver can authenticate packets sent by an IPSec sender to make sure the data hasn't been modified during transmission.

- **Data origin authentication** The IPSec receiver can authenticate the source of any IPSec packets received. This service is dependent on the data integrity service.
- **Anti-replay** The IPSec receiver can detect and reject replayed packets.
- **Data confidentiality** IPSec can encrypt data packets before transmitting them across a network in a form that can only be unencrypted by the destination target.

IPSec Security Overview

IPSec is a framework of several open standards that provides data confidentiality, data integrity, and data authentication in exchanges between participating VPN peers at Layer 3. IPSec technologies can be used to authenticate and protect data flows between IPSec peers. The two main IPSec security protocols are the following:

- Authentication Header (AH)
- Encapsulating Security Payload (ESP)

In addition, IPSec uses other existing encryption standards to complete the protocol suite. These encryption standards are covered in the section "Other IPSec Encryption Standards."

Authentication Header (AH)

The Authentication Header (AH) security protocol provides only data authentication and integrity for IP packets forwarded between two systems. It does *not* provide encryption services for data confidentiality.

The AH authentication is provided by both ends of the tunnel performing a one-way hash calculation on the packet using a shared key value. The function of a message digest hash is never to be decrypted, but to provide a check value for the receiving party to verify data hasn't been modified. While performing a hash calculation isn't difficult, trying to modify the packet and end up with exactly the same resulting message digest is difficult. The hashing algorithm was designed to be nonpredictable and, therefore, hard to duplicate.

The fact that creating the two one-way hash calculations involves using a shared secret key known to the two systems means authenticity is guaranteed.

AH can also help to implement antireplay protection by requiring the receiving host to set the replay bit in the header to indicate the packet was seen.

AH Authentication and Integrity The AH authentication and integrity function is applied to the entire IP packet, except for those IP header fields that must change in transit; such as the Time To Live (TTL) field, which is decremented by the routers along the path. Figure 9-6 shows the AH process diagrammatically. The AH process works as follows:

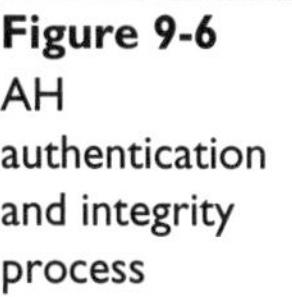

Figure 9-6 AH authentication and integrity process

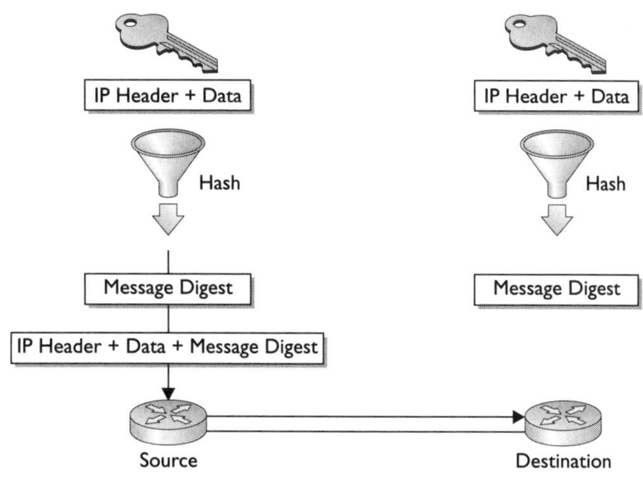

Step 1	The IPSec source device performs a hash function on the IP header and data payload using a key value known also by the destination device.
Step 2	The resulting message digest is appended to the original packet as a part of creating a new packet for transit.
Step 3	The new packet is transmitted to the IPSec peer device.
Step 4	The receiving device separates the original IP header and data payload from the message digest and it performs a hash function on the IP header and data using the key value shared with the source. If the resulting message digest doesn't exactly match the one received from the source, it's rejected by the destination device.

Even a single bit change or substitution in the transmitted packet creates a different hash result and can cause the packet to be discarded. Even if the packet were captured in transit and the IP packet information was in Cleartext, the hacker doesn't know the shared key.

Encapsulating Security Payload (ESP)

The *ESP security protocol* provides confidentiality via encryption, data origin authentication, data integrity, optional antireplay protection, and limited traffic flow confidentiality by defeating traffic flow analysis. Authentication and integrity can be provided via the same algorithms used by AH. Confidentiality can be implemented independent of the other services.

The ESP confidentiality is accomplished by performing encryption at the IP packet layer. ESP supports a variety of symmetric encryption algorithms, but the default for IPSec is 56-bit DES. This particular cipher must be implemented to conform to the IPSec standard and to ensure interoperability with other vendor IPSec products. Cisco products support DES plus 3DES for even stronger encryption.

DES Encryption Algorithm Data Encryption Standard (DES) is a popular symmetric-key encryption method that uses a 56-bit key to ensure secure, high-performance encryption. The first public encryption standard, DES is based on an algorithm developed by IBM. DES is used to encrypt and decrypt packet data turning cleartext into ciphertext via an encryption algorithm. The receiving device uses a decryption algorithm and the same shared key value to restore the cleartext. Figure 9-7 shows the encryption process.

Specialized "DES cracker" machines, while uncommon, can recover a DES key after only a few hours, so Cisco recommends 3DES as the main encryption algorithm for VPN.

Triple DES Algorithm (3DES) Cisco products implementing IPSec can use the Triple DES (3DES) algorithm as a much stronger encryption method. *3DES* is a variation of the 56-bit DES that breaks the data up into 64-bit blocks, and then processes each block three times, each time with an independent 56-bit key. This process effectively doubles encryption strength over 56-bit DES.

Both DES and 3DES offer adequate performance for production network applications. Now that DES/3DES encryption is available in ASIC hardware in products, such as the VPN 3002 Hardware Client Device and VPN 3000 Series Concentrators, you can add encryption to a VPN with little impact on overall system performance.

Advanced Encryption Standard (AES) AES encryption technique was recently approved as a Federal Information Processing Standard (FIPS)-approved cryptographic algorithm (FIPS PUB 197). *AES* is based on the Rijndael (pronounced *Rhine Dahl* or *Rain Doll*) algorithm, which defines how to use 128-, 192-, or 256-bit keys to encrypt 128-, 192-, or 256-bit source blocks (all nine combinations of key length and block length are possible). AES offers greater flexibility than even 3DES because it supports multiple key sizes and multiple encoding passes.

Release 3.6 of Cisco VPN products introduce support for AES (128 and 256 bit), providing a stronger encryption standard option and improved remote access performance for both software and hardware clients. Cisco is working with the IETF IPSec Working Group to push for a new specification outlining how AES will work within the IPSec framework.

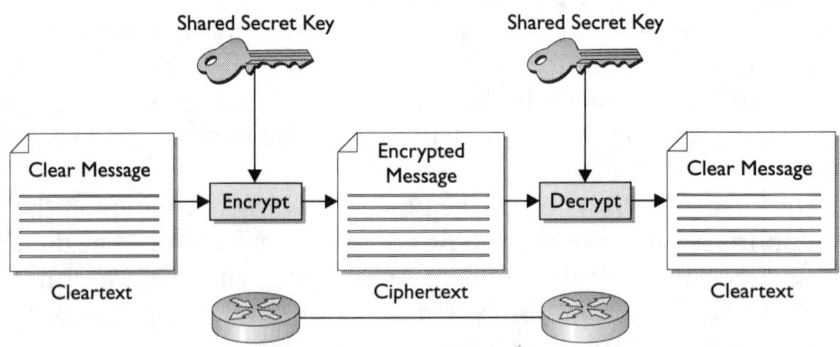

Figure 9-7 DES encryption process

Choosing Between AH and ESP

Deciding to use AH or ESP in a particular situation might seem confusing, but remember these two basics: any time more services are required, you can expect additional resources will be consumed. The same can be expected of throughput so, if a service isn't needed, don't use it. Follow both of these rules:

- If you need to make sure that data from an authenticated source is transferred with integrity, but confidentiality isn't necessary, then use the AH protocol. This saves the additional overhead and bandwidth associated with ESP encryption.
- If data confidentiality (privacy through encryption) is required, then ESP must be used. ESP can provide authentication and integrity for the packets via the same algorithms used by AH.

Other IPSec Encryption Standards

IPSec employs several different technologies to provide a complete system of confidentiality, integrity, and authenticity. These technologies are as follows:

- **Message Digest 5 (MD5)**–A hash algorithm is used to authenticate packet data.
- **Secure Hash Algorithm-1 (SHA-1)**–A hash algorithm is used to authenticate packet data.
- **Diffie-Hellman (DH)**–A key exchange standard allows two parties to establish a shared secret key to be used by encryption algorithms.
- **Rivest, Shamir, and Adelman Signatures (RSA)**–A public-key cryptographic system used for authentication.
- **Internet Key Exchange (IKE)**–A hybrid protocol that provides setup utility services for IPSec, including authentication of the IPSec peers, negotiation of IKE and IPSec security associations (SAs), and establishment of keys for encryption algorithms used by IPSec.
- **Certificate authority (CA)**–Cisco router and PIX Firewall support of CAs allows the IPSec-protected network to scale by providing the equivalent of a digital ID card for each device.

NOTE Internet Security Association Key Management Protocol (ISAKMP) is synonymous with IKE in Cisco router or PIX Firewall configuration commands. The keyword ISAKMP is always used instead of IKE.

Transport and Tunnel Mode

In configuring IPSec, one of the early decisions that must be made is whether the session is a Tunnel or a Transport mode connection. This distinction impacts other configuration decisions that have to be made.

Transport Mode

Transport mode is used between two end-host devices or between a remote host and a gateway device, where the gateway is the actual destination device. An example of a gateway device being the target destination would involve an encrypted Telnet session to configure a router or a PIX Firewall. In either case, this is basically a one-device to one-device connection. Figure 9-8 shows two possible examples of a Transport mode connection. In VPN 1, administrator Nancy must be able to access the perimeter router from home to check the status and make any configuration changes. In VPN 2, Nancy needs to access a server to make user or group account changes. In each case, a host-to-host connection exists.

NOTE Both examples are offered with the warning that these practices might be banned by a security policy. Allowing a VPN to pass through any perimeter router and/or firewall to get directly into the protected LAN is an especially risky proposition.

Transport Mode Encryption In Transport mode, if encryption is performed, only the upper-layer IP protocol fields (IP packet payload) are encrypted, leaving the IP header untouched. The IP header must be left unencrypted, so the packet can be routed through the network. Any device recording a packet in transit would be unable to read the data, but could easily determine the source and destination information.

Tunnel Mode

Tunnel mode is the most common mode involving a VPN connection between two gateway devices or a connection between an end-station and a gateway device. The Tunnel mode connection would be common between a branch office and the main office providing multiple hosts on the branch LAN to multiple shared resources on the main network. An example of the end-host to gateway VPN tunnel would be a traveling employee or telecommuter connecting to the company network to access shared resources, such as e-mail, files, printing, and so forth.

In Figure 9-9, each of the connections to the main office would normally be a Tunnel mode connection between the two routers. The mobile user or telecommuter would typically have a VPN tunnel connection from their workstation to the Main Office router.

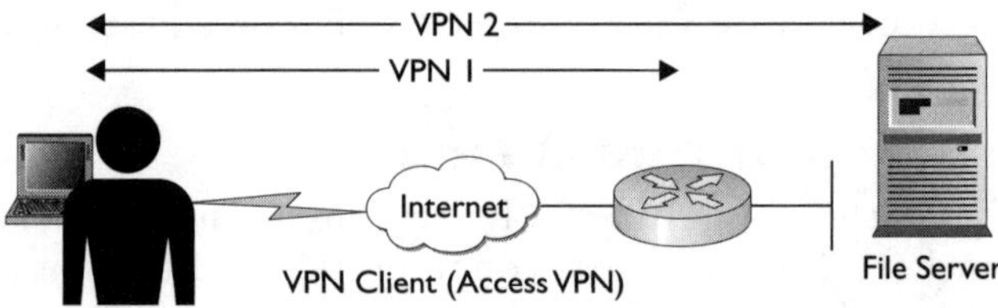

Figure 9-8 VPN Transport mode connections

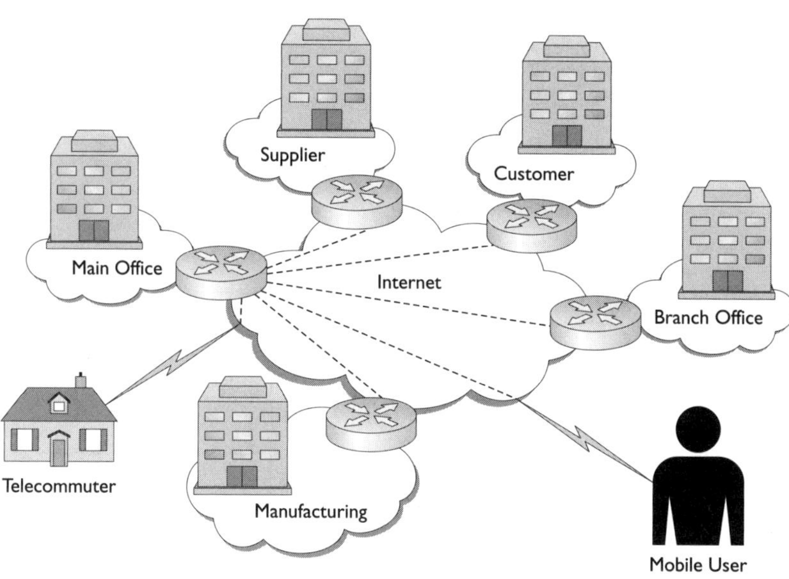

Figure 9-9 Typical Tunnel mode VPN connections

Tunnel Mode Encryption The more secure Tunnel mode encrypts both the IP header and the payload. This is possible because while the packet is in transit through the tunnel, it's fully encapsulated in a packet that uses the tunnel endpoints as the source and destination address. Any device recording a packet in transit would be unable to read any part of the original packet and could only determine the end points of the tunnel.

Tunnel Mode Benefits Tunnel mode allows a router or VPN hardware host device to act as an IPSec proxy, which means the device performs encryption services for the hosts. The Tunnel mode endpoint device is used to protect datagrams that originate from or are destined to non-IPSec host systems, making the process invisible to end users. Another great advantage is the source and the destination addresses are invisible while encrypted.

AH Transport and Tunnel Mode

Figure 9-10 compares AH Transport mode versus AH Tunnel mode. In *AH Transport mode,* AH authentication and integrity services protect the original IP packet by hashing the header fields that don't change in transit through the network, plus the data payload. Fields like TTL aren't included.

The AH header, which is the result of the hashing algorithm, is inserted after the IP header and before the data payload (higher layer fields) in the original packet. Because no encryption is involved, the IP header destination address is readable by any Layer 3 device encountered in transit and any fields, such as TTL, are still available for required changes. One advantage of Transport mode is it only adds a few bytes to each packet.

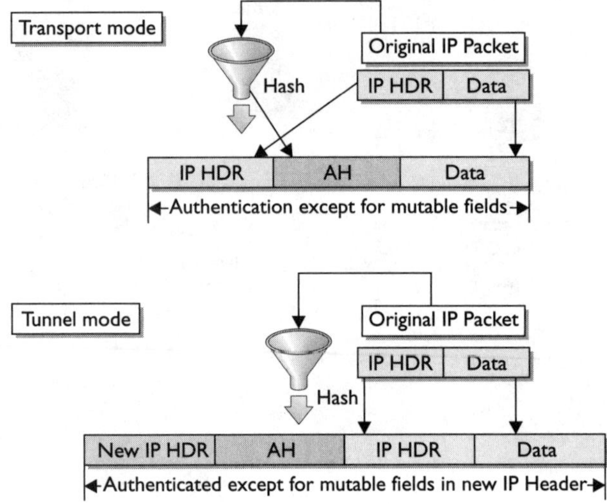

Figure 9-10 AH Transport mode versus AH Tunnel mode

In *AH Tunnel mode,* the entire original IP header and data becomes the "payload" for the new packet: a new IP header reflecting the end points of the VPN tunnel is added and the hash is performed on the resulting packet. The new IP header is protected exactly the same as the IP header in Transport mode. The fields that change in transit are excluded. The hash result again becomes the AH header following the new IP header.

Remember, both AH methods provide sender authentication and integrity verification that nothing in the data has been changed, but neither mode prevents the information from being read by an eavesdropper or a packet capture device.

A second, more serious concern is this: AH is incompatible with NAT. This is an issue if NAT occurs after the AH packet has been built because NAT changes the source IP address. This can cause the hash value stored in the AH header not to match the one generated at the destination peer and cause the packets to be rejected. This would always be a problem with AH Transport mode because the host computer is the source and, therefore, NAT would have to occur in transit. With planning, Tunnel mode would work if NAT were performed before the AH packet was built, for example, if NAT was performed at the firewall and IPSec at the perimeter router. Figure 9-11 shows how AH and NAT can be implemented to work together.

ESP Transport and Tunnel Mode

Figure 9-12 compares ESP Transport mode versus ESP Tunnel mode. In *ESP Transport mode,* the IP payload is encrypted, while the original IP header is left intact. An ESP header is inserted after the IP header and before the upper-layer protocol header (original Layer 3 data), while an ESP trailer is appended after the original data. The inserted ESP header contains a Security parameter index (SPI) value to identify the VPN security association, a sequence number field, and authentication data to verify packet authenticity.

In Transport mode, only the original data and ESP trailer fields are encrypted. The IP header isn't encrypted because some fields will be required by a Layer 3 device encountered in transit. The ESP header field isn't encrypted because it's needed by the destination peer to decipher the payload.

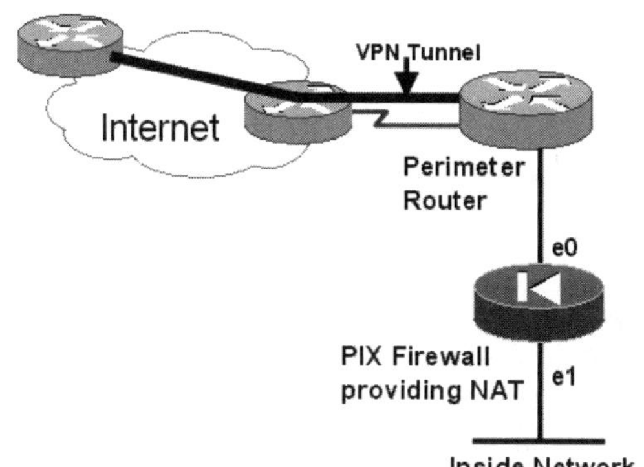

Figure 9-11 AH implementation to work with NAT

If ESP authentication is used, the upper-layer protocols (original data payload) are hashed with the ESP header and trailer, and then appended to the packet as the ESP Authentication field. Cisco IOS software and the PIX Firewall refer to this authentication service as ESP HMAC. ESP Transport mode doesn't authenticate any portion of the IP header itself.

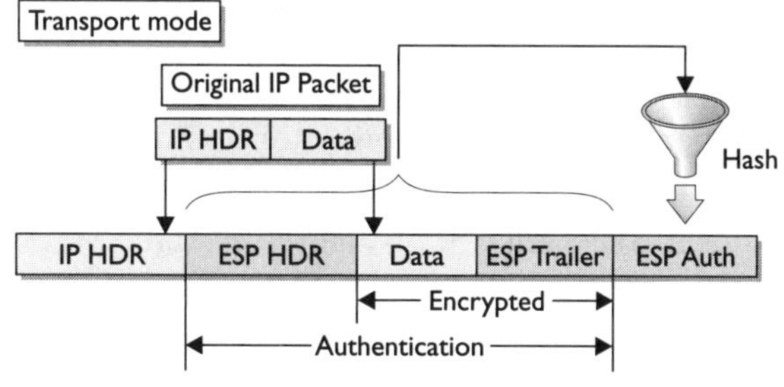

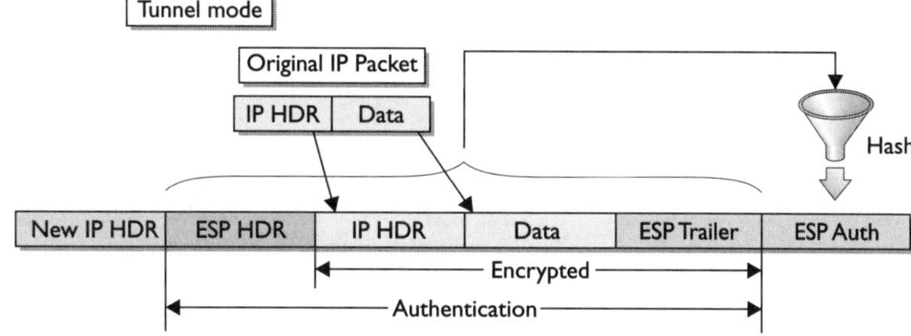

Figure 9-12 ESP Transport mode versus AH Tunnel mode

In ESP Tunnel mode, as in AH, a new IP header reflecting the end points of the VPN tunnel is added. Both encryption and authentication incorporate the entire original IP header.

When both authentication and encryption are selected, encryption is performed before authentication. This order facilitates rapid detection and rejection of replayed or bogus packets by the receiving peer, potentially reducing the impact of denial-of-service (DoS) attacks.

Choosing AH versus ESP

Both AH and ESP support both MD5 and SHA-1 hashing algorithms for authentication. The main difference between ESP and AH authentication is this: ESP doesn't protect any IP header fields in Transport mode. Both ESP and AH authenticate all IP header fields in Tunnel mode.

IPSec Transforms and Transform Sets

One set of decisions that must be made early in the IPSec implementation is whether to use AH or ESP, or MD5 or SHA-1 hashing, combined with Transport or Tunnel mode. These decisions create what are called transforms.

An *IPSec transform* defines a single IPSec security protocol—AH or ESP—with its associated security algorithms and mode. You can see the possible transform choices in Figure 9-13.

Two possible transform choices might include the following:

- AH protocol with HMAC-MD5 authentication algorithm in Transport mode, where authentication and performance are important, but encryption security isn't required.
- ESP protocol, 3DES encryption algorithm, and HMAC-SHA-1 authentication algorithm in Tunnel mode, where both data confidentiality and authentication are critical. Performance will be traded away for improved security.

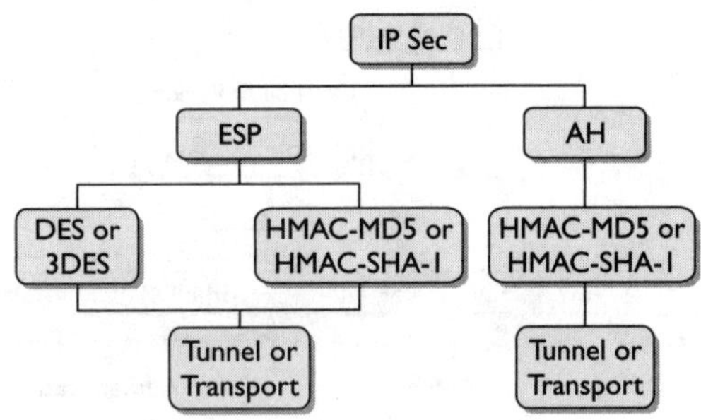

Figure 9-13 IPSec transform options

The actual transforms supported might vary by device type. VPN devices support a slightly different group than the PIX Firewall. The following are transforms supported by the IOS-based devices.

AH Transforms—Choose up to one

Transform	Description
ah-md5-hmac	AH with the MD5 (HMAC variant) authentication algorithm
ah-sha-hmac	AH with the SHA (HMAC variant) authentication algorithm
ah-rfc1828	Older version of the AH protocol (RFC 1828)

ESP Encryption Transforms—Choose up to one

Transform	Description
esp-des	ESP with the 56-bit DES encryption algorithm
esp-3des	ESP with the 168-bit DES (Triple DES) encryption algorithm
esp-rfc1829	Older version of the ESP protocol (RFC 1829). Doesn't support using ESP authentication transform
Esp-null	ESP without cipher. Can be used with esp-md5-hmac or esp-sha-hmac for ESP authentication without encryption. Shouldn't be used in production network because of the lack of security

ESP Authentication Transform—Choose up to one, only if you also selected the esp-des or esp-3des transform (not esp-rfc1829)

Transform	Description
esp-md5-hmac	ESP with the MD5 (HMAC variant) authentication algorithm
esp-sha-hmac	ESP with the SHA (HMAC variant) authentication algorithm

Transform Sets

A *transform set* is a combination of up to three individual IPSec transforms designed to implement a specific security policy for secure data transmission. The transform sets represent the choices available during IPSec security negotiation between two IPSec peers. The peers must agree to use a particular transform set for protecting a particular data flow or the exchange can't occur. Transform sets are limited to no more than one AH transform, plus no more than two ESP transforms: one for encryption and one for authentication.

Some possible examples of acceptable transform combinations include the following:

- ah-md5-hmac   AH protocol with MD5 authentication
- esp-des   ESP protocol with DES encryption

- esp-3des and esp-md5-hmac ESP protocol with DES encryption, plus ESP MD5 authentication
- ah-sha-hmac and esp-des and esp-sha-hmac AH protocol with SHA-1 authentication, ESP DES encryption, plus ESP SHA-1 authentication
- ah-rfc1828 and esp-rfc1829 Legacy AH protocol with ESP encryption

When configuring transform sets, the parser prevents you from entering invalid combinations. Transform sets are discussed in greater detail in Chapters 10 and 11 when configuring IPSec is covered.

Cisco IOS Cryptosystem Components

You should be familiar with two terms used in network security. While these terms are quite closely related, they aren't quite as interchangeable as they might first seem.

Encryption	The process of translating data into a secret code, which can only be read or processed after being decrypted using a secret key or password. Encryption typically involves using a mathematical algorithm for combining the original data, referred to as plaintext or Cleartext, with one or more keys—character strings of numbers and/or text known only to the sender and the recipient. The resulting output is *ciphertext*. Encryption is the most effective way to achieve data security.
Cryptography	The science or study of encryption and decryption techniques. A system for encrypting and decrypting data is called a *cryptosystem*. While it's technically possible for encrypted data to be deciphered using *cryptanalysis*, or code-breaking techniques, most modern cryptography techniques are virtually unbreakable.

The Internet, wireless technologies, and other forms of electronic communication are making electronic security technologies increasingly important. Current cryptography technologies being widely used include SSL for web traffic, Secure Shell (SSH) for Telnet sessions, Pretty Good Privacy (PGP) to protect e-mail messages, and IPSec Layer 3 secure communications.

How Encryption Works

Simply encryption uses a mathematical algorithm to scramble a message to create the cipher text. A *key* is used by the algorithm to determine the scramble pattern. The same key can then be used to unscramble or decipher the message. While this isn't a perfect analogy, a deadbolt on a door is nothing more than a chunk of metal until someone inserts a key that can manipulate the tumblers and advance the bolt. The lock and the door are then secure until the correct key is used to reverse the process. Like the door analogy, more than one person might have the key but, without the correct key, the lock won't budge. Also, somewhat like the door analogy, cipher text might require multiple keys both to lock and unlock. Figure 9-14 shows a common, simplified view of encryption.

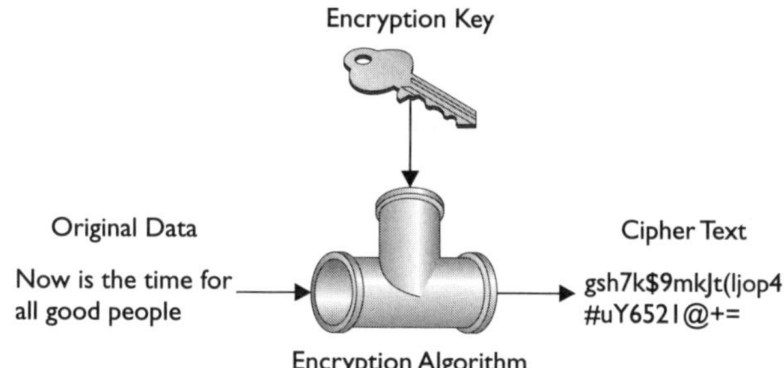

Figure 9-14 Cleartext being processed using a key to produce cipher text

The key terms in the process include data, key, encryption algorithm, and cipher text.

Data

The *data* is the information to be encrypted. This data could be text from an e-mail, text and numbers from a credit card transaction, user name and password combinations, music, graphics, videos, or voice conversations. Data arriving to be encrypted might possibly have already been encrypted one or more times in earlier processes. If cipher text is the result of three encryptions, then it must be deciphered three times in the correct order with the appropriate key(s).

Key

A *key* is a fixed-length digital sequence of characters used to scramble the source data. A longer key typically provides a higher level of security than a shorter key. DES is an industry-standard, symmetric-key encryption method that uses a 56-bit key. Triple-DES (3DES) uses three separate encryptions with unique 56-bit (168-bit) keys for stronger security. Newer AES technology uses 128-, 192-, or 256-bit keys for even greater security.

Government Regulation Recognizing that encryption keys are tightly regulated in many countries is important. Exporting from the United States or Canada technologies using encryption keys longer than 56 bits—even for use by overseas branches of domestic companies—is currently illegal. Similarly, possession of some key technologies could be a serious crime in certain countries. Export controls on strong encryption (greater than 56-bit DES strength) vary according to type, strength, destination territory, end use, and end user. A person would be foolhardy to assume that violations of import or export controls on this type of technology would be overlooked or resolved with an apology. Terrorism, drug trafficking, and racketeering concerns can make even a sloppy transaction to a third party, who then transships the technology illegally, a serious legal problem.

Encryption Algorithm

The mathematical formula used by the encryption process to scramble the data is an *encryption algorithm*, and DES and MD5 are examples. Algorithms are often used in combinations to encryption cryptosystems like IPSec.

Cipher Text

The encrypted result is virtually useless to anyone who lacks the correct key. The length of the key, and the number and types of incorporated encryptions determines the cipher text's capability to withstand unauthorized access. Ultimately, the security of a cryptosystem depends on the secrecy of one or more of the keys, rather than with the secrecy of the encryption algorithm. A strong cryptosystem has a large number of possible keys, making it time- and resource-consuming to try all possible keys (brute force). Brute force attacks, as depicted on television, where a computer generates potential keys, are typically more fantasy than reality.

Cryptography Types

Three basic types of cryptographic functions are used for authentication, integrity, and confidentiality. They include the following:

Symmetric encryption	Often called *secret key encryption*, uses a shared key and the same encryption algorithm to encrypt and decrypt a message.
Asymmetric encryption	Often called *public key encryption*, uses two different, but related, keys for the encryption algorithm. To encrypt a message, both a public key and a private key are used. The sender uses the public key to encrypt the message and the recipient uses the private key to decrypt the encrypted message.
Hash function	A *hash function* is a one-way encryption used to authenticate information. The information is "hashed," and then transmitted with the hash value. The destination peer can perform the same hash, and then compare the result to the transmitted hash value. If they match, the probability is high that the data is complete and unchanged.

Encryption Alternatives

Encryption can occur at various levels within the network to meet the organization's specific objectives. Using the Open Systems Interconnection (OSI) or the Transmission Control Protocol/Internet Protocol (TCP/IP) reference model, the encryption can be placed at the data-link layer, the network layer, or the application layer. Figure 9-15 shows a diagram of encryption at each of the layers.

Data-Link Layer

Data-link layer (L2) encryption can be implemented in devices other than the router on switched links where security is a concern. Because this method encrypts the network layer header, as well as the data, traffic must be decrypted before entering the next router. The concern would be if traffic had to pass through many routers, the decryption and reencryption would need to be repeated each time, leading to latency issues. Another concern involves trust because the data passes through these routers as Cleartext.

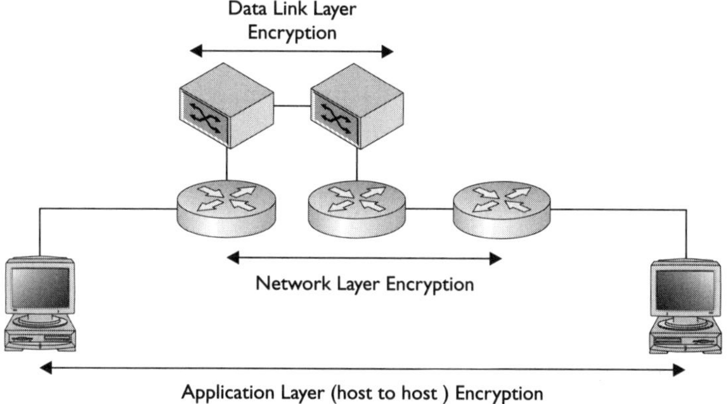

Figure 9-15 Encryption implementation options

Network Layer

Network layer (L3) encryption is done between two layer 3 devices. While Transport mode involves encrypted connections between an end host and a VPN endpoint device, such as routers on the network, the more common implementation is between two VPN endpoints, such as a VPN hardware client device, a router, a firewall, or a VPN concentrator. This means Cleartext data travels between the actual host and the VPN source endpoint where it's encrypted and forwarded on to the VPN destination endpoint, where the transmission is decrypted and forwarded to the destination host as Cleartext. One security concern is that the data is unencrypted during part of the trip, although we hope it would be in the internal secure LAN networks on both ends.

Note, the VPN endpoints might be many routers (hops) away and the interim routers needn't be VPN-aware. Because the packets must be routed through the network, the IP header must remain in Cleartext. While IPSec uses this approach, the layer 3 header information that's vulnerable refers to the VPN tunnel endpoints and not to the source and destination hosts. The original IP header is safely encrypted in the data section of this transport packet.

Layer 3 implementations should use Quality of Service (QoS) features end-to-end to ensure priority delivery through the network, particularly with time-sensitive data.

Application Layer

Application layer (TCP/IP 4 or OSI 7) encryption is implemented on each host using encryption features built in to the user applications. SSL providing secure web transactions or e-mail applications using PGP are both examples of application-layer encryption. While providing the ultimate in end-to-end security, application layer encryption does require all users to share the same encryption tools, even if they work on different hardware and software platforms. And it also relies on each user be somewhat knowledgeable about the encryption tools.

Hashing

As explained earlier, a hash is a one-way encryption method used to authenticate that data received is exactly the same as the data transmitted. The following basics about hashing are important to understand.

- A hash algorithm's function is to provide data integrity verification, not necessarily character-for-character translations of data.
- The hash process typically generates a fixed length number value derived from a variable length string of text.
- The hash output is often substantially smaller than the source text itself.
- The hash algorithm is sufficiently complex to make producing the same hash value with any other text combination extremely unlikely.

Hashed Message Authentication Codes (HMAC)

IPSec supports improved versions of Message Digest 5 (MD5) and Secure Hash Algorithm 1 (SHA-1) hash functions for cryptographically secure authentication. As with everything else in the security arena, hashing algorithms have evolved into HMACs, which build on the proven security of hashing algorithms by implementing additional cryptographic processes.

The HMAC algorithm involves having the original message text encrypted (hashed) using the sender's private key, resulting in a keyed, fixed-length checksum as output. The checksum value is appended to the message as a signature. The destination peer runs the same HMAC on the received message data, using the same private key. The resultant hash is compared with the received hash value, which should match exactly. Figure 9-16 shows this combination of source message and encryption key.

Figure 9-16 HMAC hash process showing the private encryption key

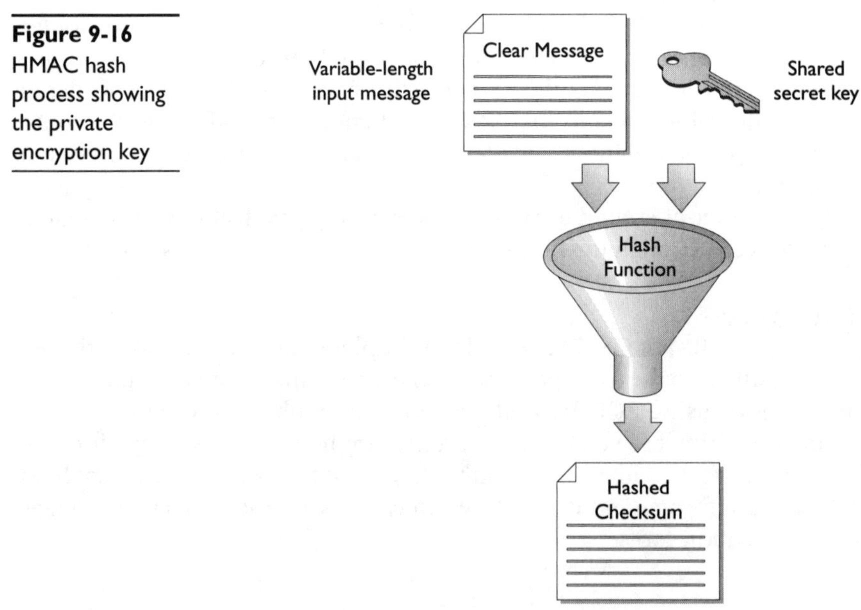

HMAC-MD5-96 Also known as HMAC-MD5 (RFC 1321), this hashing technique is based on MD5 developed by Ronald Rivest of MIT and RSA Data Security Incorporated. HMAC-MD5 uses a 128-bit secret key to produce a 128-bit authenticator value. Once produced, the 128-bit value is truncated to only the first 96 bits and stored in the AH or ESP authenticator field of the new packet. At the destination peer, the 128-bit authenticator value is computed and the first 96 bits are compared to the value stored in the authenticator field.

While the MD5 algorithm used alone was found vulnerable to collision search attacks and other known weaknesses, the vulnerability doesn't impact HMAC-MD5.

HMAC-SHA-1-96 Also known as HMAC-SHA-1 (RFC 2404), this hashing technique is based on SHA-1 specified in FIPS-190-1 combined with HMAC technology. HMAC-SHA-1 uses a 160-bit secret key to produce a 160-bit authenticator value. The 160-bit authenticator value is truncated to the first 96 bits and stored in the AH or ESP authenticator field of the new packet. At the destination peer, the 160-bit authenticator value is computed and the first 96 bits are compared to the value stored in the authenticator field.

Because of the longer key value, HMAC-SHA-1 is cryptographically stronger than HMAC-MD5, but it requires more CPU cycles to compute. Therefore, HMAC-SHA-1 should be the choice if slightly superior security is required. HMAC-MD5 should be the choice if slightly superior performance is required.

Diffie-Hellman Key Agreement (DH)

Diffie-Hellman (DH) is a public key encryption method that provides a mechanism for two IPSec peers to establish a shared secret key that only they know, while communicating over an insecure channel. DH is critical to IPSec operations because the shared secret key is used to encrypt data using the secret key encryption algorithms specified in the IPSec Security Associations, such as DES or MD5. Security Associations are covered later in this section.

DH algorithms and calculations are quite complex, using exponentiation of large numbers, between 768 and 1,536 bytes. Even simple calculations can take up to four seconds on a Cisco 2500. Fortunately, DH boils down to the following relatively simple conceptual steps:

- Each IPSec peer generates a public and private key pair. The public key is a mathematical derivative of the private key, conceptually like a series of unique office door keys might all be derived from a master key that can open every office.
- Each peer keeps its own private key secret and never shares it with anyone.
- Each peer sends its public key over the insecure channel.
- Each peer combines the other peer's public key with its own private key and computes the shared secret number that will be the same on each peer.

- The shared secret number is converted by each peer into a shared secret key. This shared secret key is never exchanged between the peers, which avoids the chance of it being captured in transit on the insecure link.

The end result of the DH process is this: each IPSec peer has the three following keys for each IPSec peer relationship it maintains.

- A *private key*, which is kept secret and never shared. The private key is used to "sign" outgoing messages to the IPSec destination peer.
- A *public key*, which is shared with the IPSec destination peer. The public key is used by the destination peer to verify a "signature" on a transmission.
- A *shared secret key*, which is used to encrypt data using any shared secret encryption algorithm, such as DES, 3DES, MD5, SHA-1, and so forth. This shared secret key is derived from the DH key generation process just described.

Defining a DH Group

The only real configuration in defining the DH process is to assign a DH group level. The groups supported might vary based on the device and the operating system (OS) release. Cisco IOS devices currently support DH Groups 1, 2, and 5. Group 5 provides the greatest security and is the most recently added, in IOS v12.1(3)T. The default group on most devices is Group 1.

DH Group	Description
1	The 768-bit Diffie-Hellman group
2	The 1,024-bit Diffie-Hellman group
5	The 1,536-bit Diffie-Hellman group

Security Association (SA)

The concept of Security Associations (SAs) is fundamental to understanding and configuring IPSec. An *SA* is a relationship between two or more potential VPN endpoints, which describes how those endpoints will use security services (technologies and protocols) to communicate securely. In establishing each secure communication connection, IPSec can provide services for encryption, integrity, and/or authenticity services. Once the services are selected, the two IPSec peers must determine exactly which algorithms to use for each service, such as DES or 3DES for encryption and MD5 or SHA for data integrity.

Once the services are selected and the algorithms chosen to implement those services, the two peers must exchange or implement session keys required by the algorithms. Is this beginning to sound complicated? How can you keep track of all these choices and decisions? The security association is the mechanism IPSec uses to manage these decisions and choices for each IPSec communication session. A basic component of configuring IPSec services on a client, router, firewall, or VPN concentrator is defining SA parameters.

IKE SAs versus IPSec SAs

The next section shows you that two types of SAs are used in configuring IPSec, just as there are two stages in establishing IPSec. *IKE SAs* describe the security parameters between two IKE devices, the first stage in establishing IPSec. *IPSec SAs* pertain to the actual IPSec tunnel, the second stage.

At the IKE level, a single IKE SA is established to handle secure communications both ways between the two peers. The following is an example of the type of information that would be included in an IKE SA.

Description	Example
Authentication method used	MD5
Encryption and hash algorithm	3DES
DH group used	2
Lifetime of the IKE SA in seconds or kilobytes	86,400
Shared secret key values for the encryption algorithms	Preshared

At the IPSec level, SAs are unidirectional—one for each direction. A separate IPSec SA is established for each direction of a communication session. Each IPSec peer is configured with one or more SAs, defining the security policy parameters to use during an IPSec session. To establish an IPSec session, peer 1 sends peer 2 a policy. If peer 2 can accept this policy, it sends the policy back to peer 1. This establishes the two one-way SAs between the peers.

IPSec Security Association (SA)

Each IPSec SA consists of security parameter values, such as a destination address, a unique security parameter index (SPI), the IPSec transforms used, the security keys, and additional attributes, such as IPSec lifetime. The SPI value becomes a unique record identifier (key field) linked to the SA parameters in the Security Parameter Databases in the RAM of peer devices.

Each IPSec SA consists of values such as

Description	Example
Peer (destination) address	10.1.1.23
Security parameter index (SPI)	7C123A9C
IPSec transforms used	AH, HMAC-SHA-1
Security keys	12345CD8765EF432A
Additional attributes (such as IPSec lifetime)	43,200

Five Steps of IPSec Revisited

This section discusses the individual steps required for a successful IPSec data exchange in greater detail. While IPSec incorporates many component technologies and offers multiple encryption options, the basic operation can be broken down into the following five main steps. Figure 9-17 show a graphical representation of the IPSec process.

Step 1	Interesting traffic initiates an IPSec session—Access lists interpret IPSec security policy to determine which traffic will be protected by IPSec.
Step 2	IKE Phase One—IKE authenticates peers and negotiates IKE SAs to determine if a secure channel can be established between the peers.
Step 3	IKE Phase Two—IKE negotiates the stricter IPSec SA parameters between the peers.
Step 4	IPSec data transfer—Qualifying data is transferred between IPSec peers.
Step 5	IPSec tunnel termination—IPSec session terminates through deletion or by timing out.

Step 1—Determine Interesting Traffic

Data communications covers a wide gamut of topics, sensitivity, and security requirements. Just as all rumors you hear aren't worth repeating, often much network traffic isn't worth securing, such as an employee's personal web browsing. Any security measures can come at the expense of network resources and performance, so a method must exist to determine what traffic is protected and what traffic travels normally through the public network.

The *VPN security policy* generally determines which type of traffic is considered "interesting" and, therefore, protected. How the VPN security policy gets implemented depends on the device platform. Cisco routers and the PIX Firewall use access lists to define the traffic to secure. The access lists are then incorporated in a crypto policy, which causes traffic associated with permit statements to be encrypted, while traffic associated with deny statements is sent unencrypted.

Figure 9-17 IPSec session five steps

Host A
Router A
Router B
Host B
1. Host A sends interesting traffic to Host B.
2. Router A and B negotiate an IKE phase one session.
IKE SA
IKE Phase 1
IKE SA
3. Router A and B negotiate an IKE phase two session.
IPSec SA
IKE Phase 2
IPSec SA
4. Information is exchanged via IPSec tunnel.
IPSec Tunnel
5. IPSec tunnel is terminated.

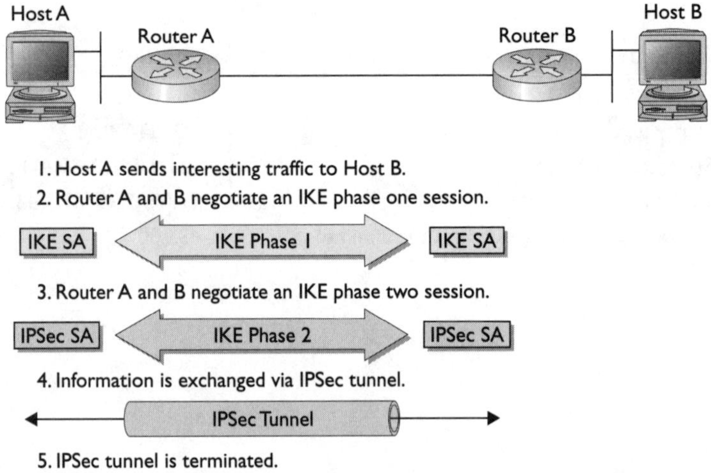

Cisco VPN Client and some VPN management software tools allow the use of menu windows to define connections to be secured by IPSec.

Both methods of identifying interesting traffic are covered in Chapters 10 through 16.

Step 2—IKE Phase One

IKE is a key management protocol standard used in conjunction with IPSec. While IPSec can be configured without IKE, the use of IKE enhances the IPSec with additional features and makes it scalable. IKE authenticates each peer in an IPSec session, automatically negotiates two levels of SAs, and handles the exchange of session keys. This is accomplished in two phases: Phase One and Phase Two.

NOTE IKE was formerly known as the Internet Security Association Key Management Protocol/Oakley (ISAKMP/Oakley) or ISAKMP. In Cisco documents, it's typically referred to as IKE, but configuration commands still use the ISAKMP keyword. Just recognize that the two mean the same thing, but might not be interchangeable.

IKE Phase One's main purpose is to authenticate the IPSec peers and to set up a secure channel between the peers. To accomplish this, IKE Phase One performs the following functions:

- Authenticates while protecting the identities of the IPSec peers
- Negotiates a common IKE SA policy between peers to protect the IKE exchange
- Performs a DH exchange to create shared secret keys
- Sets up a secure tunnel to negotiate IKE Phase Two parameters

IKE Phase One occurs in two modes: Main mode and Aggressive mode.

Main Mode

Main mode has three two-way exchanges between the peers to create the secure connection and develop the common SAs, while protecting the identities of the IPSec peers.

- First exchange   The security algorithms and hash methods to be used to secure the IKE exchanges are agreed on to create the common IKE SA for each peer.
- Second exchange   A DH exchange is performed to generate shared secret keying material to be used by each peer to generate shared secret keys. *Nonces,* pseudorandom numbers, are sent to the other peer, signed, and returned to prove their identity.
- Third exchange   The peer's identity is verified using the peer's IP address or fully qualified domain name (FQDN), such as ian@testco.com, in encrypted form.

The resulting IKE SA in each peer is bidirectional and specifies IKE exchange choices for the authentication method, encryption and hash algorithms, DH group, the lifetime of the IKE SA in seconds or kilobytes, and the shared secret key values for the encryption algorithms.

Aggressive Mode

As the name implies, in the *Aggressive* mode, only a single three-way exchange is performed. In the initial exchange, the sender defines the proposed IKE SA values and adds their DH public key, a nonce to be signed by the other party, and an identity packet to verify their identity via a third party.

The peer sends everything back that's required to complete the exchange, plus their DH public key. The only thing left is for the initiator to confirm the exchange.

While Aggressive mode is faster than Main mode, it exposes the peers to discovery because both sides have exchanged information before you have a secure channel. The possibility exists to sniff the wire and discover who formed the new SA.

Peer Authentication

Would-be IPSec peers must authenticate themselves to each other before IKE can proceed. IKE Phase One has three methods to authenticate IPSec peers in Cisco products. The two peers must negotiate a common authentication protocol from the following choices:

- Preshared keys—A key value entered into each peer manually (out of band) and used to authenticate the peer.
- RSA signatures—Uses a digital certificate authenticated by an RSA signature.
- RSA encrypted nonces—Uses RSA encryption to encrypt a nonce value (a random number generated by the peer) and other values.

A common value used by all authentication methods to help identify the peer is the peer identity (ID). Some ID values include the peer's IP address or their FQDN, such as ian.testco.com.

Preshared Key Authentication With this method, the same preshared key is configured on each IPSec peer. These IKE peers can authenticate each other by generating a hash of their ID, plus the key appended to the ID before transmission. If the receiving peer can create the same hash value using its preshared key, it authenticates the source peer. Figure 9-18 shows the preshared key authentication exchange.

While preshared keys are easier to configure than configuring the IPSec policy values on each IPSec peer, they don't scale well and potential security risks can be associated with getting the key to the peer.

RSA Signature Authentication RSA Signature Authentication is a public-key cryptosystem supported by IPSec for IKE Phase One authentication. This technology was developed in 1977 by Ron Rivest, Adi Shamir, and Leonard Adleman. RSA is the first letter of each developer's last name.

Figure 9-18 Preshared key authentication exchange

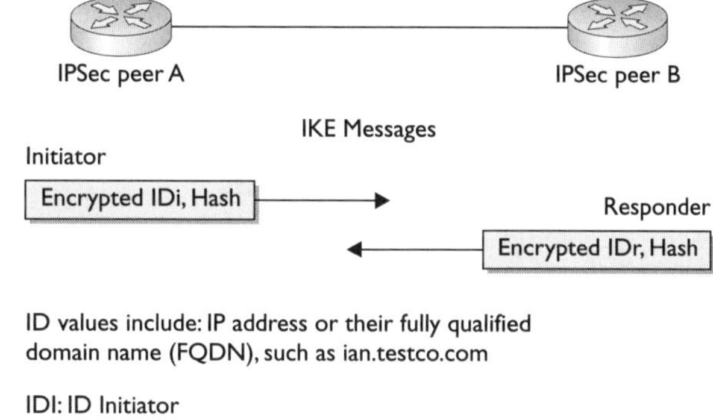

RSA signatures use a CA to generate a unique digital-identity certificate for each peer for authentication. The digital-identity certificate is similar in function to the pre-shared key, but provides stronger security.

To authenticate for an IKE session, the initiator and responder send each other their ID values, identity digital certificates, and an RSA signature value consisting of various IKE values, all encrypted using the negotiated IKE encryption method (DES or 3DES). Figure 9-19 shows an RSA signature authentication exchange.

RSA Encryption Authentication The RSA-encrypted nonces authentication method uses the RSA encryption public key cryptography algorithm. This technology requires that each party generate a pseudorandom number (a nonce) and encrypt it (and possibly other publicly and privately available information), using the other party's RSA public key. Authentication occurs when each party decrypts the other party's nonce with its local private key, and then uses the decrypted nonce to compute a keyed hash.

A drawback to this method is this: either side of the exchange can plausibly deny that it took part in the exchange. Cisco IOS software is the only Cisco product that supports this authentication method. Figure 9-20 shows an RSA encryption authentication exchange.

Figure 9-19 RSA signature authentication exchange

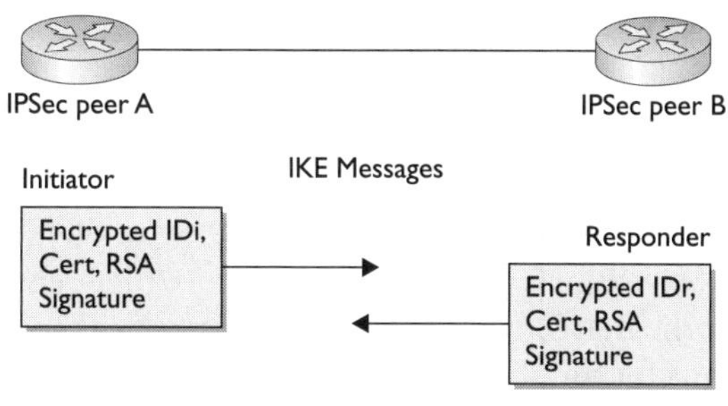

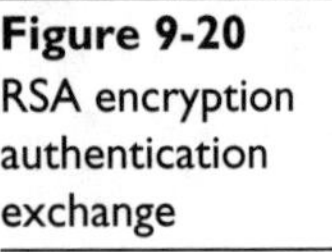

Figure 9-20 RSA encryption authentication exchange

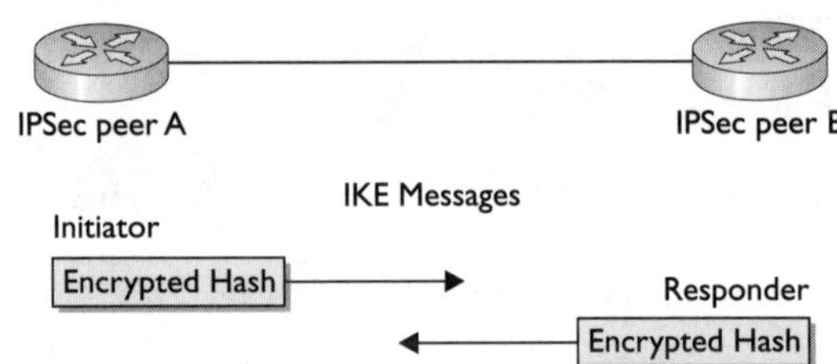

CAs and Digital Certificates CAs and Digital Certificates are covered in greater detail in Chapter 11, but for our purposes here, they represent a digital identification system whereby an independent third party vouches for them. Conceptually, this is similar to most state driver's licenses when used as identification. The merchant accepting the ID accepts that the state has performed adequate verification to be reasonably sure the identity is valid.

The distribution of security keys through an untrusted network, such as the Internet, involves questionable levels of risk.

CAs are trusted third-party organizations, such as Verisign, Entrust, and Netscape, which provide digital certificates. The peers wanting to use digital certificates register with a CA. Once the CA verifies the client's credentials, a digital certificate is issued. The *digital certificate* contains the certificate bearer's identity (name or IP address), the certificate serial number, the certificate expiration date, and a copy of the certificate bearer's public key.

The digital certificate standard format is defined in the X.509 specification. Cisco supports X.509 version 3.

Step 3—IKE Phase Two

IKE Phase Two has only one mode, *Quick mode*, which occurs after IKE has established the secure tunnel in Phase One. In Quick mode, IKE

- Negotiates a shared IPSec policy
- Establishes IPSec SAs
- Derives shared secret keys used for the IPSec security algorithms

To negotiate the IPSec SAs, the sender forwards one or more transformsets, including transform combinations and related settings that represent the sender's security requirements/preferences for the new IPSec session. The receiving peer compares these requirements to its own transform sets (requirements/preferences). If one matches, then the recipient returns that single transform set, indicating a mutually agreed on transform and algorithms for the IPSec session.

Quick mode is also used to renegotiate a new IPSec SA any time the IPSec SA lifetime expires. If PFS (next section) isn't specified, Quick mode refreshes the key generation material used to create the shared secret keys derived from the DH exchange in Phase One.

Perfect Forward Secrecy (PFS)

When Perfect Forward Secrecy (PFS) is specified in the IPSec policy, a new DH exchange is performed for each Quick mode, providing new key material and, thereby, greater resistance to cryptographic attacks. Because each DH exchange requires large exponentiations, this option increases CPU use and can reduce performance.

Nonces

Quick mode exchanges nonces to provide replay protection. These nonces are used to generate new, shared, secret key material and to prevent replay attacks from generating bogus SAs.

Step 4—IPSec Data Transfer

Information is exchanged via the IPSec session based on the method for defining interesting traffic. Packets are encrypted and decrypted at the IPSec peers using any encryption specified in the IPSec SA.

Step 5—Session Termination

The IPSec session can be terminated because the traffic ended and the IPSec SA was deleted or the SA can time -out based on either SA lifetime setting. The SA timeout can be after a specified number of seconds or a specified number of bytes passed through the connection. The keys are discarded when SAs terminate, requiring IKE to perform a new Phase Two and, possibly, a new Phase One negotiation. New SAs can be established before the current ones expire, maintaining uninterrupted data flows.

IPSec Support in Cisco Systems Products

The choice of Cisco VPN technology depends on the type of VPN being developed, remote-access or site-to-site, plus the current and projected size of the resulting network. The Cisco components required to build the VPN might include any or all of the following options:

- Client VPN software, such as Easy VPN Remote, provides secure remote access to central Cisco routers, PIX Firewalls, and VPN Concentrators. The VPN client runs on the Windows OS.
- VPN hardware clients, such as Cisco VPN 3002, provide hardware-based encryption services for each remote user or small branch.
- Cisco VPN 3000 Series Concentrators provide powerful remote access and site-to-site VPN capabilities for the network with many VPN connections. The series supports an easy-to-use management interface.
- Cisco Secure PIX Firewall provides a highly secure VPN gateway alternative to the router or concentrator devices.

- IOS-based VPN-optimized routers for branch and remote user connections. Routers supporting this include the Cisco 800, UBr900 cable access router/modem, 1400 DSL router/modem, the 1700, 2600, 3600, 7100, 7200, and 7500 series routers. The Cisco 7100 Series VPN Router is an integrated VPN router that provides solutions for VPN-centric environments.
- Cisco Secure Intrusion Detection System (CSIDS) and Cisco Secure Scanner can be used to monitor and audit the security of the VPN.
- Cisco Secure Policy Manager and Cisco Works 2000, two Cisco network management software applications, provide VPN-wide system management.

Because VPN technology is so new and no single standard evolved quickly, many companies developed turnkey solutions, which could be implemented and administered easily by the client or consultant services. Cisco developed several VPN solutions built around each of the three following technologies. You learn about each technology in the next eight chapters.

- **VPN 3000 Series Concentrator** Most models use a hardware-based VPN solution with advanced encryption and authentication. *VPN concentrators* are designed and built specifically to provide high availability, high performance, and scalability. The modular design of the 3015 to 3080 models includes Scalable Encryption Processing (SEP) modules that allow the organization to increase capacity and throughput. This scalability supports small businesses, with up to 100 remote-access users, to large organizations, with up to 10,000 simultaneous remote connections.
- **Cisco Secure PIX Firewall** The *PIX Firewall* is a hardware security device that combines features like NAT, proxy server, packet and stateful filtering, and VPN features into a single device. The PIX unit uses a proprietary OS that trades the capability to handle a large variety of protocols and services for extreme robustness and performance by focusing on IP security.
- **VPN-Optimized Router** Cisco routers running an IOS with the VPN feature set provide routing, security, scalability, and QoS for businesses from small office/home office (SOHO) access to central-site VPN aggregation for the large-scale enterprise.

Chapter Review

This chapter looked at how VPNs can be used to extend the corporate networks securely using public networks, such as the Internet. The two basic VPN types are remote access and site-to-site. The three types of VPN connectivity are access VPN, intranet VPN, and extranet VPN. The two VPN modes are transport and tunnel.

While a variety of Layer 2 and Layer 7 VPN implementations exist, IPSec and IETF Layer 3 standards seem to dominate the market today. IPSec technologies include a variety of authentication and encryption methods.

Questions

1. Which is *not* one of the three basic types of VPN connections?
   A. Access VPNs
   B. Intranet VPNs
   C. Internet VPNs
   D. Extranet VPNs
2. Which is *not* one of the concerns in using the Internet for conducting private communications?
   A. Loss of privacy
   B. High cost
   C. Loss of data integrity
   D. Identity spoofing
3. Which one of the following is a Layer 2 tunneling protocol supported by Microsoft and Cisco?
   A. PPTP
   B. L2F
   C. L2TP
   D. GRE
4. With which security protocol is the data *not* encrypted?
   A. AH
   B. EST
   C. ESP
   D. Diffie-Hellman
5. What is the size of the encryption key for DES?
   A. 40 bit
   B. 56 bit
   C. 128 bit
   D. 168 bit
6. Which one of the following is *not* an encryption algorithm?
   A. DES
   B. 3DES
   C. ESP
   D. AES

7. Which is the most secure hashing algorithm?
    A. MD5
    B. SHA-1
    C. HMAC MD5
    D. HMAC SHA-1
8. With which security mode is the original IP header encrypted?
    A. AH Transport
    B. AH Tunnel
    C. ESP Transport
    D. ESP Tunnel
9. Which is *not* a valid transform?
    A. ah-md5-hmac
    B. esp-rfc1829
    C. ah-des
    D. esp-sha-hmac
10. Transform sets can contain how many AH transforms?
    A. 1
    B. 2
    C. 3
    D. None
11. Which cryptography type is also called public key encryption?
    A. Symmetric encryption
    B. Asymmetric encryption
    C. Hash function
    D. Cipher text
12. Which Diffie-Hellman key exchange offers the most security?
    A. 5
    B. 2
    C. 1
    D. 0
13. In an IPSec session, what is the minimum number of SAs that will be created?
    A. 1
    B. 2

C. 3

D. 6

14. At what point are the IPSec peers authenticated?

A. IKE Phase One

B. IKE Phase Two

C. IKE Phase Three

D. Interesting Traffic

15. What is a nonce?

A. A large prime number

B. A random number

C. A pseudorandom number

D. A digital signature

Answers

1. C. Internet VPNs
2. B. High cost
3. C. L2TP
4. A. AH
5. B. 56 bit
6. C. ESP
7. D. HMAC SHA-1
8. D. ESP Tunnel
9. C. ah-des
10. A. 1
11. B. Asymmetric encryption
12. A. 5
13. C. 3—1 IKE and 1 in each direction for IPSec
14. A. IKE Phase One
15. C. pseudorandom number

CHAPTER 

Cisco IOS IPSec for Preshared Keys

In this chapter, you will learn to:

- Configure IPSec encryption tasks
- Configure IPSec manually

Using Internet Key Exchange (IKE) with preshared keys for authentication of IP Security (IPSec) sessions is relatively easy to configure, but it doesn't scale well. The process for configuring IKE preshared keys in Cisco IOS software for Cisco routers consists of four major tasks. This chapter looks at each configuration task in detail.

Configure IPSec Encryption Tasks

The good news is only four tasks are required to configure IPSec for preshared keys. The bad news is each task has multiple tasks that can initially seem overwhelming. The four tasks Cisco uses, which you can expect on the exam, are as follows:

- Task 1 Prepare for IKE and IPSec
- Task 2 Configure IKE
- Task 3 Configure IPSec
- Task 4 Test and verify IPSec

Don't make this more complicated than necessary. Task 1 is nothing more than making sure you've tested the existing network and gathered the information you need for Tasks 2 and 3. Task 2 is configuring for IKE Phase 1, while Task 3 is configuring for IKE Phase 2. Finally, Task 4 is checking your work.

The following task list shows the four tasks broken down into their individual steps. The steps are numbered to include the task number, as well as to help keep them straight. These steps are repeated in the chapter summary with the key commands listed for each step.

Figure 10-1 shows the networks that provide an example scenario used throughout this chapter. The goal is to create a secure VPN tunnel between Rtr1 at the company main office, and Rtr2 at one of almost 100 branch offices in North America, Europe, and Africa.

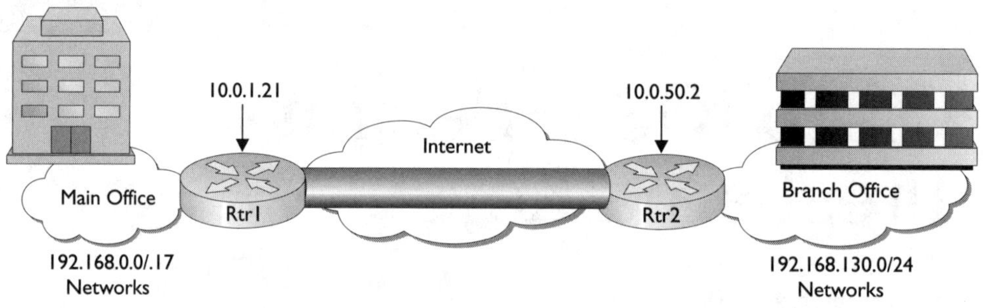

Figure 10-1 Chapter scenario VPN session to be configured

Task 1 Prepare for IKE and IPSec

- Step 1-1 Identify IPSec peers
- Step 1-2 Determine the IKE (IKE Phase 1) policies
- Step 1-3 Determine the IPSec (IKE Phase 2) policies
- Step 1-4 Check the current configuration
- Step 1-5 Ensure the network works without encryption
- Step 1-6 Ensure access control lists are compatible with IPSec

Task 2 Configure IKE

- Step 2-1 Enable or disable IKE
- Step 2-2 Create IKE policies
- Step 2-3 Configure preshared keys
- Step 2-4 Verify the IKE configuration

Task 3 Configure IPSec

- Step 3-1 Configure transform set suites
- Step 3-2 Configure global IPSec security association lifetimes
- Step 3-3 Configure crypto ACLs
- Step 3-4 Configure crypto maps
- Step 3-5 Apply the crypto maps to the interface

Task 4 Test and verify IPSec

- Step 4-1 Display the configured IKE policies
- Step 4-2 Display the configured transform sets
- Step 4-3 Display the current state of the IPSec SAs
- Step 4-4 Display the configured crypto maps
- Step 4-5 Debug IKE events
- Step 4-6 Debug IPSec events

The assumption is this: the main office has reserved networks 192.168.0.0 through 192.168.127.0 for itself and will use one class C for each branch in the remaining 192.168.128.0 to 192.168.255.0 addresses.

The example uses private addresses to avoid using public addresses that might belong to others and to make it easier for those who choose to try to create the configuration in a test lab.

Task 1 Prepare for IKE and IPSec

Successful implementation of an IPSec network requires testing of the existing network and advance planning before any configuration begins. Insufficient testing and planning can lead to troubleshooting problems or configuration errors. Some preparation and planning steps include the following:

- Step 1-1 Identify IPSec peers
- Step 1-2 Determine the IKE (IKE Phase 1) policies
- Step 1-3 Determine the IPSec (IKE Phase 2) policies
- Step 1-4 Check the current configuration
- Step 1-5 Ensure the network works without encryption
- Step 1-6 Ensure Access Control Lists are compatible with IPSec

The actual order of these steps could be varied based on personal preferences and implementation circumstances.

Step 1-1 Identify IPSec Peers

An important part of defining a comprehensive IPSec policy is to identify the IPSec peer pairs that must be configured. In the chapter scenario, expanded in Figure 10-2, each remote site will connect only to the Main Office router and, therefore, requires only simple configuration. The Cisco router at the Main Office must be configured for peer communications with each of the remote sites and telecommuter(s). Each peer must support IPSec. Because many different types of peer devices exist, it's important to identify all potential peers and determine their VPN capabilities. Possible peer devices could include, but aren't limited to, the following:

- Cisco routers
- Cisco Secure PIX Firewalls
- Cisco Secure VPN 3000 Concentrators
- Cisco Secure VPN 3002 Hardware Client device
- Cisco Secure VPN Software Client
- Other vendor IPSec products that conform to IPSec standards
- CA servers

It's important to recognize that IPSec features supported and default settings can vary between Cisco product families, as well as versions of the operating system (OS) being used. This is most important for the Main Office router in the scenario because it must be able to establish common IKE and IPSec policies with each remote device. This also demonstrates why many companies limit the number of devices supported by defining standards for telecommuters or branch offices.

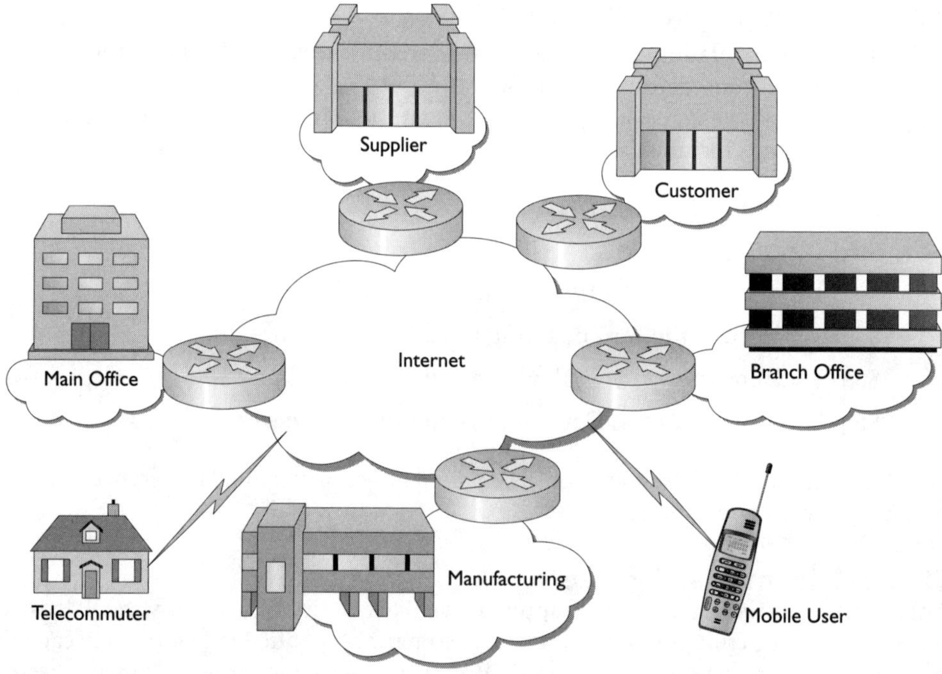

Figure 10-2 Chapter scenario network showing peer connections

The result of this analysis might be a table like the following:

Location	Device	Version (or OS)
Main Office	Cisco 7100 router	12.2(8)T with FW and VPN
Telecommuters (24)	Cisco 900 Cable/DSL router	12.2(8)T with FW and VPN supports 3DES
Mobile users (16)	Cisco VPN Software Client	v3.6-3DES
Branch offices (80) North America	Cisco 2600/3600 routers	12.2(8)T with FW and VPN supports 3DES
Branch offices (20) Europe/Africa	Cisco 2600/3600 routers	12.2(8)T with FW and VPN supports DES only
Manufacturing (1)	Cisco PIX 525 Firewall	OS v6.2-3DES

Step 1-2 Determine the IKE (IKE Phase 1) Policies

IKE is a hybrid protocol that implements the Oakley key exchange and the Skeme key exchange inside the Internet Security Association and Key Management Protocol (ISAKMP) framework. (ISAKMP, Oakley, and Skeme are security protocols implemented by IKE.)

The purpose of IKE Phase 1 is to authenticate the peers and negotiate a secure session between those peers. This creates a stable platform for IKE Phase 2 to negotiate the IPSec tunnel. The word "negotiate" makes this sound like a complex process, which might involve contentious arguments late into the night. In reality, at each phase, the session instigator submits one or more security policies, which will then be compared by the destination peer against its preconfigured security policies. If a match is found, a session is then established. If no match is found, the session is terminated. From a practical standpoint, if a VPN session can't be established between the two peers, then one of the devices must be configured to include a set of policies acceptable to the other.

The objective here is to develop one or more IKE security policies based on the overall company security policy. Each policy will require decisions about five security options: authentication method, encryption algorithm, hashing algorithm, Diffie-Hellman group, and SA lifetime. This can make IKE seem more complicated than it is. To get some perspective, we aren't configuring a connection to an unknown or an untrusted entity. Instead, we're connecting a branch of the company to the main office system. Chances are both are governed by the same security policy so, while some choices must be made, the list of possibilities shouldn't be infinite.

In many cases, the decision could be that 3DES will be the encryption, MD5 will perform hashing functions, preshared keys will be used for authentication, and so forth, and that would be configured on each router. So, why have multiple policies with different option combinations? The answer depends on the router and the number of VPN connections that it needs to support. In our example, if each branch only connects to the main office, then they only need the policy that matches the main office router.

The main office router could need a couple of IKE policy choices because all branch offices might be unable to support the same policy. This might not be a vendor or a product platform issue, but a legal issue. While all the North American branches can be configured with 3DES encryption, export controls could prevent the foreign branches from using anything but DES. So, a second policy needs to be available for those connections.

Research the Parameter Options The following table shows the five security features that must be decided, including the current options, defaults, and which choice provides the greatest security. A good idea is always to confirm these options and defaults as IOS versions change. It only makes sense that the IOS will assimilate new IPSec standards as they're established.

Parameter	Choices	Keyword	Default	Strongest
Message encryption algorithm	DES 3DES	des 3des	des	3des
Message integrity - hash algorithm	SHA-1 (HMAC variant) MD5 (HMAC variant)	sha md5	sha	sha
Peer authentication method	RSA signatures RSA encrypted nonces preshared keys	rsa-sig rsa-encr pre-share	rsa-sig	rsa-sig
Diffie-Hellman group (key exchange)*	768 bit 1,024 bit	1 2	1	2
IKE SA lifetime	60 to 86,400 seconds		86,400	60

*Some VPN devices support D-H group 5 (1,568 bit), but it might be a while before IOS devices support this level of key exchange.

Develop the Parameter Preferences To complete the IKE planning process, what would make sense is to create a table of the preferred combination of security features, plus one or more fallback options for those devices or locations that can't support the preferred package. The resulting table might look like the following:

Parameter	Preferred (stronger)	2nd Choice	3rd Choice
Encryption algorithm	3des	des	des
Hash algorithm	sha	sha	md5
Authentication method	preshare	preshare	preshare
DH key exchange group	2	2	1
IKE SA lifetime	43,200	43,200	86,400

In comparing the two tables, you should see that RSA-SIG would be a preferred authentication method over preshared keys. This chapter deals with using preshared keys, while Chapter 12 covers Certificate Authority (RSA-SIG). RSA encrypted nonces are addressed in the last section of this chapter.

NOTE You can't use SHA together with DES encryption on Cisco's VPN software client version 3.6. Part of the problem with determining a set of preferences is being aware of the different platform limitations.

Using our scenario for this chapter, the Preferred column represents our configuration preferences for all North American branches and would be the only options configured. The 2nd Choice column would be for those overseas branches that can support the Preferred configuration, except for the export restriction on triple DES. Assuming they don't form VPN sessions with anyone else, this would be the only choice configured on those devices. The 3rd Choice column might represent extremely small branches or telecommuters using small personal routers with limited resources and options. This also represents the lowest level of parameter options the main office will accept for a VPN connection. The only device that will have all three choices configured is the main office router.

Because any parameter that isn't defined will use the existing default value, the actual table could look like the following example. Either table can be used in Task 2 to configure the IKE parameters.

Parameter	Preferred (stronger)	2nd Choice	3rd Choice
Encryption algorithm	3des		
Hash algorithm			md5
Authentication method	preshare	preshare	preshare
DH key exchange group	2	2	
IKE SA lifetime	43,200	43,200	

Step 1-3 Determine the IPSec (IKE Phase 2) Policies

Once the choices are made for IKE Phase 1, it's time to turn to those parameters required to complete IKE Phase 1. This is where the IPSec tunnel is negotiated and, ultimately, the IPSec SAs established. As in Phase 1, the goal is to define one or more sets of IPSec security parameters defining the IPSec security policy, based on the overall company security policy.

The information gathered is required in Task 3 when IPSec is configured. To facilitate that process, gather the following information into a table similar to the one developed for Phase 1 for each peer for which sessions will be established.

Transforms (or transform sets)	IPSec transforms or build transform sets, plus the VPN mode to provide the optimal security and performance balance
Peer address	Peer IP address for this session
Peer host name	What is the peer host name for this session?
IP address to protect	Which source hosts are to be protected for this session?
Traffic to protect	What applications should be protected for this session?
SA establishment method	Will SAs be manually established or established via IKE?

Most of the choices to be configured, such as peer address and host name, are straight-forward. The transforms or, if necessary, the transform sets, involve determining the security features required, and then striking a balance between security level and performance implications. Chapter 9 introduced Transforms and Task 3, later in this chapter, looks at configuring them.

The following table might represent the IPSec values for the chapter scenario:

Parameter	Site 1	Site 2
Transform (set)	esp-des, tunnel	esp-des, tunnel
Peer host name	Rtr2	Rtr1
Peer IP address	10.0.50.2	10.0.1.21
Hosts to be encrypted	192.168.0.0/25	192.168.30.0/24
Traffic to be encrypted	TCP	TCP
SA establishment	ipsec-isakmp	ipsec-isakmp

Step 1-4 Check the Current Configuration

It's important to check the current Cisco router configuration to see if any existing IPSec policies are configured that could be useful for, or interfere with, the new IPSec policies. If appropriate, previously configured IKE and IPSec policies can be used to save configuration time. This section looks at three commands useful in discovering existing IKE and IPSec policies.

The show running-config Command The basic **show running-config** command is always a good starting point. In the following partial output, the lines in boldface are the IKE and IPSec configuration statements.

```
Rtr2#show run
!
hostname Rtr2
!
enable secret 5 $1$ojfF$eAp7xa0hU4E678XaibAQa
!
crypto isakmp policy 1
hash md5
authentication pre-share
crypto isakmp key test_key1 address 10.0.1.21
!
crypto ipsec transform-set trans1 esp-3des
crypto ipsec transform-set trans2 ah-md5-hmac esp-des
crypto ipsec transform-set trans3 esp-sha-hmac esp-null
!
crypto map test_map1 1 ipsec-isakmp
set peer 10.0.1.21
set security-association lifetime seconds 43200
set transform-set trans1 trans2 trans3
match address 101
!
interface Ethernet0
 ip address 192.168.130.1 255.255.255.0
 no mop enabled
!
interface Serial0
 ip address 10.0.50.2 255.255.255.252
 no ip mroute-cache
 no fair-queue
 crypto map test_map1
```

```
!
ip classless
ip route 0.0.0.0 0.0.0.0 10.0.50.1
access-list 101 permit tcp 192.168.130.0 0.0.0.255 192.168.0.0 0.0.127.255
dialer-list 1 protocol ip permit
!
```

The show crypto isakmp policy Command The following is an example of the output from the **show crypto isakmp policy** command, which can be used to view all existing IKE policies. Notice the default parameters are displays at the bottom of the output.

```
Rtr1#show crypto isakmp policy
Protection suite of priority 100
        encryption algorithm:   DES - Data Encryption Standard (56 bit keys).
        hash algorithm:         Secure Hash Standard
        authentication method:  Pre-Shared Key
        Diffie-Hellman group:   #2 (1024 bit)
        lifetime:               43200 seconds, no volume limit
Default protection suite
        encryption algorithm:   DES - Data Encryption Standard (56 bit keys).
        hash algorithm:         Secure Hash Standard
        authentication method:  Rivest-Shamir-Adleman Signature
        Diffie-Hellman group:   #1 (768 bit)
        lifetime:               86400 seconds, no volume limit
Rtr1#
```

The show crypto map Command The **show crypto map** command is useful for displaying any previously configured crypto maps. If possible, these can be used to save configuration time, but they can interfere with the new IPSec policy.

```
Rtr1#show crypto map
Crypto Map "testmap" 50 ipsec-isakmp
        Description: VPN Link to branch office in Tacoma, WA
        Peer = 10.0.50.2
        Extended IP access list 125
            access-list 125 permit tcp 192.168.0.0 0.0.127.255 192.168.130.0
  0.0.0.255
        Current peer: 10.0.50.2
        Security association lifetime: 2300000 kilobytes/1800 seconds
        PFS (Y/N): Y
        DH group:  group2
        Transform sets={ CPU-HOG, }
        Interfaces using crypto map testmap:
                    Serial0
Rtr1#
```

The show crypto ipsec transform-set Command The **show crypto ipsec transform-set** command can be used to view previously configured transform sets. Whenever possible, these transforms can, and should, be used to save configuration time.

```
Rtr1# show crypto ipsec transform-set
Transform set MD5-DES: { esp-des esp-md5-hmac  }
   will negotiate = { Tunnel,  },

Transform set DES-ONLY: { esp-des  }
   will negotiate = { Tunnel,  },
```

```
 Transform set CPU-HOG: { ah-md5-hmac  }
   will negotiate = { Tunnel,  },
   { esp-des esp-md5-hmac  }
   will negotiate = { Tunnel,  },

Transform set AH-ONLY: { ah-sha-hmac  }
   will negotiate = { Tunnel,  },
Rtr1#
```

Step 1-5 Ensure the Network Works Without Encryption

All peer-to-peer connectivity must be verified before configuring IPSec encryption. Basic troubleshooting techniques become more difficult, if not impossible, once encryption is in place.

While the router **ping** command can be used to verify basic connectivity between peers, equally important is that all important applications and related data are confirmed to be accessible. This can only be accomplished by testing those applications before beginning IPSec configuration.

Skipping this step can lead to wasted time trying to debug IPSec configuration only to discover eventually that the underlying connectivity was never tested. A simple rule of thumb is this type of mistake is always exposed when it can embarrass you the most.

Step 1-6 Ensure Access Control Lists Are Compatible with IPSec

Make certain any existing access lists on VPN device and perimeter router don't block IPSec traffic. Perimeter routers frequently implement restrictive security policies using ACLs. These policies often deny all inbound traffic that isn't responding to a specific outbound request. This restriction often blocks inbound IPSec traffic necessary to establish a VPN session.

Specific permit statements must be added to the inbound ACL to allow IPSec traffic. The following ports and protocol access should be left open:

- **IKE/ISAKMP** UDP port 500/keyword: isakmp
- **Encapsulating Security Payload (ESP)** IP protocol number 50/keyword: esp
- **Authentication Header (AH)** IP protocol number 51/keyword: ahp

The first step is to use the **show access-lists** command to determine if any ACLs will block IPSec traffic.

Assuming an inbound ACL is causing problems, it must be edited, placing entries at the beginning to permit IPSec traffic. The following shows an example of the lines that should be added to Rtr2's existing ACL 110.

```
Rtr2# show running-config
!
interface Serial 0
 ip address 10.0.50.2 255.255.255.252
 ip access-group 110 in
!
access-list 110 permit ahp host 10.0.1.21 host 10.0.50.2
access-list 110 permit esp host 10.0.1.21 host 10.0.50.2
```

```
access-list 110 permit udp host 10.0.1.21 host 10.0.50.2 eq isakmp
    ---balance of ACL statements---
```

Task 2 Configure IKE

The second major task in configuring the IPSec VPN is to configure the IKE parameters gathered in Task 1, Step 2. Configuring IKE involves the following four steps:

- Step 2-1 Enable or disable IKE
- Step 2-2 Create IKE policies
- Step 2-3 Configure preshared keys
- Step 2-4 Verify the IKE configuration

This section looks at these four steps and the associated commands.

Step 2-1 Enable or Disable IKE

The first step in configuring IKE is to make sure IKE is globally enabled. While IKE is enabled globally by default, the **crypto isakmp enable** command makes sure the feature is on. Use the no form of the command to disable IKE. Because IKE is a global **mode** command, it needn't be enabled or disabled for individual interfaces. Some circumstances might warrant using an ACL entry to block ISAKMP access (UDP port 500) on interfaces not being used for IPSec to reduce the chances of a denial of service (DoS) attack. The command syntax and an example follow.

```
Rtr2(config)# crypto isakmp enable
Rtr2(config)# no crypto isakmp enable
```

Step 2-2 Create IKE Policies

Now, it's time to define a suite of ISAKMP (IKE) policy details gathered during the planning task, Task 1, Step 2 (repeated in the following with defaults in italics). The goal is to create a suite of IKE policies, so you can establish IKE peering between two IPSec endpoints.

Parameter	Preferred (stronger)	2nd Choice	3rd Choice
Encryption algorithm	3des	*des*	*des*
Hash algorithm	*sha*	*sha*	md5
Authentication method	preshare	preshare	preshare
DH key exchange group	2	2	*1*
IKE SA lifetime	43,200	43,200	*86,400*

Using the scenario example, Rtr2 only needing to connect to Rtr1, might be configured with only the preferred (most secure) set of parameters because that set will also be on Rtr1. On the other hand, Rtr1, needing to peer with various devices both domestically and internationally, might need multiple policies to accommodate the different peers. The trick is to configure the policies, so the preferred policy is evaluated by the peer first, and then the second and third choices. This ensures the agreed policy is always the highest mutually agreeable choice.

The crypto isakmp policy Command Use the global **crypto isakmp policy** command to define an IKE policy containing a set of parameters used during IKE negotiation. Use the no form of this command to delete an IKE policy. The command syntax and an example follow.

Rtr1(config)#[no] crypto isakmp policy *priority*
Rtr1(config)#crypto isakmp policy 100
Rtr1(config-isakmp)#

priority	Unique identifier for the IKE policy used to order, or prioritize, the policies. Acceptable range 1 to 10,000 with 1 being the highest possible priority.

This command invokes the ISAKMP policy configuration (config-isakmp) mode, which allows the six IKE parameters to be defined. The no form of each parameter removes that setting. Exit is used to end the session and any undefined parameters use the default values. The actual choices ware based on the table made in Task 1, Step 2. The following shows the syntax for each parameter, followed by the entries for the preferred policy.

```
Rtr1#conf t
Rtr1(config)#crypto isakmp policy 100
Rtr1(config-isakmp)#authentication {pre-share | rsa-encr | rsa-sig}
Rtr1(config-isakmp)#encryption {des | 3des}  (depending on feature set)
Rtr1(config-isakmp)#hash {md5 | sha}
Rtr1(config-isakmp)#group {1 | 2}
Rtr1(config-isakmp)#lifetime <60 to 86400 seconds>

Rtr1(config)#crypto isakmp policy 100
Rtr1(config-isakmp)#authentication pre-share
Rtr1(config-isakmp)#encryption 3des
Rtr1(config-isakmp)#hash sha
Rtr1(config-isakmp)#group 2
Rtr1(config-isakmp)#lifetime 43200
Rtr1(config-isakmp)#exit
```

Because the preferred policy was assigned 100 as a priority, the second and third choices must be progressively larger to control the order in which they're offered to a peer. A possible choice might be 200 and 300, respectively, enabling newer policies to be assigned priorities that would allow them to be prioritized according to changes in the company security policy. Using 1, 2, and 3 might initially be easy to understand, but it could force reconfiguring the devices if a new feature like AES encryption is implemented.

The following shows the steps to configure the second and third preference, taking advantage of default values to save configuration:

```
Rtr1#conf t
Rtr1(config)#crypto isakmp policy 200
Rtr1(config-isakmp)#authentication pre-share
Rtr1(config-isakmp)#group 2
```

```
Rtr1(config-isakmp)#lifetime 43200
Rtr1(config-isakmp)#crypto isakmp policy 300
Rtr1(config-isakmp)#authentication pre-share
Rtr1(config-isakmp)#hash md5
Rtr1(config-isakmp)#exit
```

Branch Office Configuration Implications Assuming the chapter scenario, if each branch will only be connecting VPNs to the main office, configuring only one of the IKE policies for each branch should be necessary. Assuming the domestic branches can all support 3DES, policy 100 would seem appropriate. For any foreign branches that can't use 3DES because of export restrictions, then policy 200 seems the likely candidate. If any branch initiates a session with the main office, both peers would have the same policy. The same is true for a session initiated by the main office to any branch; even the foreign branches could accept the second policy offered.

This whole discussion is based on using a single IKE policy between peers for any encrypted traffic. If the security policy called for 3DES for only certain types of traffic and DES for others, then configuring a second policy on the remote peers would be necessary.

The show crypto isakmp policy Command Use the **show crypto isakmp policy** command to verify the entries, display the default policy, and confirm that the nonconfigured parameters took on the default values.

```
Rtr1#show crypto isakmp policy
Protection suite of priority 100
        encryption algorithm:   3DES - Triple DES (168 bit keys).
        hash algorithm:         Secure Hash Standard
        authentication method:  Pre-Shared Key
        Diffie-Hellman group:   #2 (1024 bit)
        lifetime:               43200 seconds, no volume limit
Protection suite of priority 200
        encryption algorithm:   DES - Data Encryption Standard (56 bit keys).
        hash algorithm:         Secure Hash Standard
        authentication method:  Pre-Shared Key
        Diffie-Hellman group:   #2 (1024 bit)
        lifetime:               43200 seconds, no volume limit
Protection suite of priority 300
        encryption algorithm:   DES - Data Encryption Standard (56 bit keys).
        hash algorithm:         Message Digest 5
        authentication method:  Pre-Shared Key
        Diffie-Hellman group:   #1 (768 bit)
        lifetime:               86400 seconds, no volume limit
Default protection suite
        encryption algorithm:   DES - Data Encryption Standard (56 bit keys).
        hash algorithm:         Secure Hash Standard
        authentication method:  Rivest-Shamir-Adleman Signature
        Diffie-Hellman group:   #1 (768 bit)
        lifetime:               86400 seconds, no volume limit
Rtr1#
```

NOTE Although the output shows "no volume limit" for the lifetimes, currently it is only possible to configure a time IKE lifetime (such as 86,400 seconds); volume limit lifetimes aren't used.

Step 2-3 Configure Preshared Keys

IPSec peers authenticate each other during IKE negotiations using the preshared key and their IKE identity. The *IKE identity* can either be the device IP address or the host name. The router IOS defaults to the IP address and doesn't add a line to the configuration, unless the host name option is used.

To use the host name identity method, use the global **crypto isakmp identity** command. The no form of this command resets the default value (address). The command syntax is as follows:

Rtr1(config)#[no] crypto isakmp identity {address | hostname}
Rtr1(config)#crypto isakmp identity hostname

Using the host name identity method makes the most sense if a DNS server is available on the network to resolve the name. If not, the following example shows using an **IP Host** command entry on the router to handle the name resolution:

```
Rtr1(config)#ip host Rtr2.domain.com 10.0.50.2
```

Use the global **crypto isakmp key** command to configure a preshared authentication key whenever you specify preshared keys in an ISAKMP policy. Use the no form of the command to delete a preshared authentication key. The command syntax for both the address and the host name option is as follows:

Rtr1(config)#[no] crypto isakmp key *keystring* address *peer-address* [*mask*]
Rtr1(config)#[no] crypto isakmp key *keystring* hostname *peer-hostname*

keystring	The preshared key. Any combination of alphanumeric characters up to 128 bytes. Must be identical on both peers.
mask	(Optional) Defines a subnet address for the remote peer. Indicates the remote peer ISAKMP identity will be established using the preshared key only. With the mask, keys are no longer restricted to only two users. Added v12.1(1)T.

A given preshared key is shared between two peer devices. While it's possible for Rtr1 in the scenario to use the same key with all remote peers, the more secure approach is to use different keys with each pair of peers.

The next example shows IKE and preshared key (cisco123) for Rtr1 and Rtr2 using the address identity method. The IKE policies are compatible. Because the hash algorithm SHA-1 is the default value, it needn't be configured.

```
Rtr1(config)#crypto isakmp key cisco123 address 10.0.50.2
Rtr1(config)#crypto isakmp policy 100
Rtr1(config-isakmp)#authentication pre-share
Rtr1(config-isakmp)#encryption 3des
Rtr1(config-isakmp)#group 2
Rtr1(config-isakmp)#lifetime 43200
Rtr1(config-isakmp)#exit
```

```
Rtr2(config)#crypto isakmp key cisco123 address 10.0.1.21
Rtr2(config)#crypto isakmp policy 100
Rtr2(config-isakmp)#authentication pre-share
Rtr2(config-isakmp)#encryption 3des
Rtr2(config-isakmp)#group 2
Rtr2(config-isakmp)#lifetime 43200
Rtr2(config-isakmp)#exit
```

Because both devices are under the administrative policies of a single entity, it makes sense that the policy priority value might be the same on both devices. That isn't a requirement, though, and it would be unlikely when the two peers are from different organizations. The important thing is the parameters are the same.

NOTE One exception to matching parameters is the lifetime can be shorter on the destination peer and that value will be used. The shorter of the two lifetimes is always used. A shorter lifetime, in theory, increases the security.

Step 2-4 Verify the IKE Configuration

Use the **show crypto isakmp policy** command to display configured and default policies. An example of IKE policy for Rtr1 is shown in the Step 2-2 section. The **show running-config** command can also be useful, but the parameters using default values are omitted for brevity.

Task 3 Configure IPSec

The next major task in configuring Cisco IOS IPSec is to configure the IPSec parameters gathered in Task 1, Step 3. The general steps used to configure IPSec encryption on Cisco routers are summarized as follows. This chapter looks at each configuration step in detail.

- Step 3-1 Configure transform set suites
- Step 3-2 Configure global IPSec security association lifetimes
- Step 3-3 Configure crypto ACLs
- Step 3-4 Configure crypto maps
- Step 3-5 Apply the crypto maps to the interface

Step 3-1 Configure Transform Set Suites

In Chapter 9, an IPSec transform was defined as a single IPSec security protocol—AH or ESP—with its associated security algorithms and mode. Technically, a *transform* is the list of operations done on a dataflow to provide data authentication, data confidentiality, and since IOS v12.2(8) data compression. Some of the supported transform choices are shown in Figure 10-3.

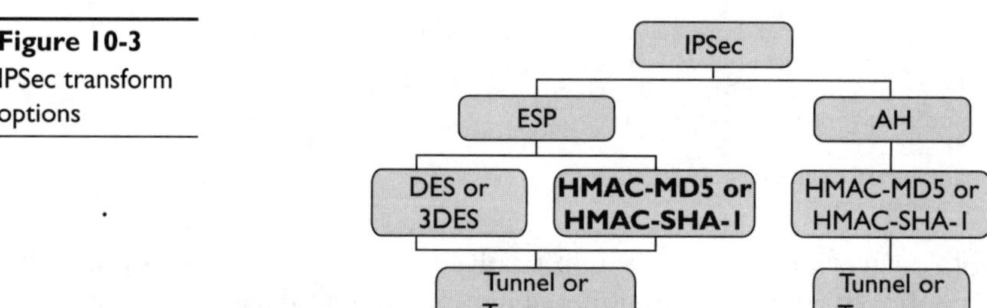

Figure 10-3 IPSec transform options

The actual transforms supported might vary by device type. VPN devices could support a slightly different group than the PIX Firewall. The following are transforms supported by the IOS-based devices:

AH Transforms—Pick up to one:

Transform	Description
ah-md5-hmac	AH with the MD5 (HMAC variant) authentication algorithm
ah-sha-hmac	AH with the SHA-1 (HMAC variant) authentication algorithm

ESP Encryption Transforms—Pick up to one:

Transform	Description
esp-des	ESP with the 56-bit DES encryption algorithm
esp-3des	ESP with the 168-bit DES (Triple DES) encryption algorithm
Esp-null	ESP without cipher. Can be used with esp-md5-hmac or esp-sha-hmac for ESP authentication without encryption. Shouldn't be used in a production network because of the lack of security

ESP Authentication Transform—pick up to one, but only if you also selected the esp-des or esp-3des transform (not esp-rfc1829):

Transform	Description
esp-md5-hmac	ESP with the MD5 (HMAC variant) authentication algorithm
esp-sha-hmac	ESP with the SHA-1 (HMAC variant) authentication algorithm

IP Compression Transform—pick up to one:

Transform	Description
comp-lzs	IP compression with the LZS algorithm. (IOS v12.2((8)) or later)

The compression algorithm used in the *comp-lzs* transform is Lempel-Ziv-Stac (LZS) compression, the most widely accepted lossless compression algorithm at this time. Compression is implemented on Layer 3, like hardware encryption, and can considerably reduce bandwidth requirements to support IP Security (IPSec).

Transform Sets A *transform set* is a combination of up to three individual IPSec transforms designed to implement a specific security policy to protect a particular dataflow. The transform sets represent the security choices available during IPSec SA negotiation between two IPSec peers in IKE Phase 2 quick mode. The following are two examples of transform sets:

- **ah-sha-hmac and esp-des and esp-sha-hmac** AH protocol with SHA-1 authentication, ESP DES encryption, plus ESP SHA-1 authentication.
- **esp-3des and esp-md5-hmac** ESP protocol with DES encryption, plus ESP MD5 authentication.

The IKE Phase 2 quick mode operates much like the Phase 1 negotiation. The initiator sends one or more transform sets to the destination peer. The destination peer compares them in order against its own preferred transform sets. If a match is found, the destination peer returns the transform to the initiator peer to complete the "negotiation." The peers must share a common transform set or the exchange can't occur. If the peers can't agree on a transform set, this means one or the other will need to configure a matching set of policies.

Transform sets are limited to three transforms with no more than one AH transform, plus no more than two ESP transforms. Transform sets combine the following IPSec features:

- Payload authentication, example: AH transform
- Payload encryption, example: ESP transform
- IPSec mode (transport or tunnel)

You can define multiple transform sets, and then specify one or more of these sets using a crypto map entry. Use the global **crypto ipsec transform-set** command to define a transform set. Use the no form of the command to delete a transform set. The command syntax is as follows:

Rtr1(config)#crypto ipsec transform-set *transform-set-name trans1* [*trans2* [*trans3*]]
Rtr1(config)#no crypto ipsec transform-set *transform-set-name*

The command invokes the Crypto-Transform Configuration mode that can be used to define up to four transform sets. Use the **exit** command to end the configuration. Once defined, the transform sets can be specified in a crypto map entry. The following example shows the creation of four transform sets:

```
Rtr1#conf t
Rtr1(config)#crypto ipsec transform-set MD5-DES esp-md5-hmac esp-des
Rtr1(cfg-crypto-trans)#crypto ipsec transform-set DES-ONLY esp-des
Rtr1(cfg-crypto-trans)#crypto ipsec transform-set AH-ONLY ah-sha-hmac
Rtr1(cfg-crypto-trans)#crypto ipsec transform-set CPU-HOG ah-md5-hmac
  esp-md5-hmac esp-des
Rtr1(cfg-crypto-trans)#exit
Rtr1(config)#
```

When IKE isn't being used to establish SAs, a single transform set must be configured and the transform set isn't negotiated.

Step 3-2 Configure Global IPSec Security Association Lifetimes

IPSec security associations that use the shared secret keys time out together, based on the SA lifetime configured. This section looks at configuring a global lifetime value to be used when a particular crypto map entry doesn't have lifetime values configured. When a router receives a negotiation request from a peer, it uses the smaller of the lifetime value proposed by the peer or the locally configured global lifetime value for the new security associations.

Two lifetimes exist—a "timed" lifetime and a "traffic-volume" lifetime that can be configured. The SA and keys expire when the first of these lifetimes expires.

Any changes made to a global lifetime are only applied when the crypto map entry doesn't have a lifetime value specified. The change isn't applied immediately to existing security associations, but will be used in subsequent SA negotiations.

Use the global **crypto ipsec security-association lifetime** command to set the global lifetime. For a timed lifetime, use the *seconds* form of the command. The *kilobytes* form causes the security association to time out after the specified traffic limit (in kilobytes) has been protected. The lifetime values are ignored for manually established security associations installed using an **ipsec-manual crypto map** command entry. To reset a lifetime to the default value, use the no form of the command. The command syntax is as follows:

> Rtr1(config)#crypto ipsec security-association lifetime {seconds *seconds* | kilobytes *kilobytes*}
> Rtr1(config)#no crypto ipsec security-association lifetime {seconds | kilobytes}

The default value for a timed lifetime is 3,600 seconds (one hour) with the range of acceptable values between 120 and 86,400 (one day) seconds. The default value for a traffic volume lifetime is 4,608,000 kilobytes (10 megabytes per second for one hour) with the range of acceptable values between 2,560 and 536,870,912 kilobytes. Using shorter lifetimes can make it harder for an intruder to mount a successful key recovery attack because the attacker has less data encrypted under the same key to work with. The downside is shorter lifetimes require more CPU processing time for establishing new security associations.

The following example shortens the timed lifetime to 1,800 seconds (30 minutes) and the traffic-volume lifetime to 2,300,000 kilobytes. The **show crypto ipsec security-association-lifetime** command confirms the result.

```
Rtr1(config)#crypto ipsec security-association lifetime seconds 1800
Rtr1(config)#crypto ipsec security-association lifetime kilobytes 2300000


Rtr1#show crypto ipsec security-association-lifetime
Security association lifetime: 2300000 kilobytes/1800 seconds
Rtr1#
```

How These Lifetimes Work The SA and associated keys expire when either lifetime expires. To help ensure a new SA is ready when the old one expires, the new SA negotiation starts either 30 seconds or 256 kilobytes before the existing SA lifetime expires. If no traffic has passed through the tunnel during the entire life of the SA, a new one isn't negotiated until IPSec sees another packet that should be protected.

Step 3-3 Configure Crypto ACLs

Access lists, specifically crypto ACLs, play a substantial roll in how IPSec processes data flows. Crypto ACLs perform the following functions:

- Define the data flow to be protected by IPSec (permit statements).
- Define the data flow to pass unprotected by IPSec (deny statements).
- Check outbound traffic to see if it should be protected by IPSec.
- Check inbound traffic to discard traffic that should have been protected by IPSec. The assumption is if it's unprotected, it isn't from the source.
- Determine whether to accept requests for IPSec SAs for requested data flows when processing IKE negotiations.

Only extended IP ACLs can be used to create crypto ACLs. These extended IP ACLs select the IP traffic to encrypt by protocol, IP address, network, subnet, and port. While the basic ACL syntax is unchanged, the result is slightly different for crypto ACLs. Crypto ACLs are only deciding which traffic to protect and which to allow access through unprotected. A *permit statement* means the matching packet must be protected, while a *deny statement* means the matching packet needn't be protected. Any actual packet filtering must be done with another ACL. The crypto ACL determines only *if* the packet is protected. The level and type of protection is determined by the IKE and IPSec SAs.

Allowing one type of data traffic to receive one combination of IPSec protection is possible—such as authentication only—and other traffic to receive a different combination, such as both authentication and encryption. To do this, you must create two different crypto ACLs to define each of the two different types of traffic. The resulting ACLs are then used in different crypto map entries defining the different IPSec policies.

Using the Any Keyword Cisco strongly recommends avoiding the **any** keyword for specifying source or destination addresses whenever possible. A permit any any statement causes all outbound traffic to be protected and discards any unprotected inbound traffic, including packets for routing protocols, NTP, echo, echo response, and so forth.

If using the **any** keyword in a permit statement is unavoidable, be sure to precede the statement with as many deny statements as necessary to identify any traffic to be allowed through unprotected.

Mirrored ACLs The same outbound IPSec ACL that determines which outbound traffic will be protected by IPSec is also used to "catch" noncompliant inbound traffic. For example, if all TCP traffic is to be protected, then any unprotected inbound TCP traffic must have been introduced at some point other than the IPSec source. This is both an elegant and a simple system, but it relies on having ACLs at each end, which are virtually mirror images of each other. This means the source addresses/ports and destination addresses/ports are literally reversed on the peer.

In the following example, using the chapter scenario, each peer will protect outbound TCP traffic, discard any unprotected inbound TCP traffic, and, because of the implicit deny any statement, each will allow all other traffic to pass unprotected and unfiltered.

```
Rtr1(config)#access-list 125 permit tcp 192.168.0.0 0.0.127.255
   192.168.130.0 0.0.0.255

Rtr2(config)#access-list 150 permit tcp 192.168.130.0 0.0.0.255
   192.168.0.0 0.0.127.255
```

Compare that to the next example, where the Rtr1 Admin decided to protect outbound UDP traffic without adding the same ACL statement to Rtr2. Now, as requested, all outbound UDP traffic will be protected. But maybe what isn't expected is the inbound UDP traffic continues to be unprotected and, therefore, mistaken as interlopers and discarded. While this is a somewhat glaring example and would probably be noticed quite quickly, it's an easy and troublesome mistake to make when new protocols or services are added to a network.

```
Rtr1(config)#access-list 125 permit tcp 192.168.0.0 0.0.127.255
   192.168.130.0 0.0.0.255
Rtr1(config)#access-list 125 permit udp 192.168.0.0 0.0.127.255
   192.168.130.0 0.0.0.255

Rtr2(config)#access-list 150 permit tcp 192.168.130.0 0.0.0.255
   192.168.0.0 0.0.127.255
```

In the next step, the crypto ACL is associated to a crypto map assigned to a specific interface.

Step 3-4 Configure Crypto Maps

Crypto map entries must be created for IPSec to set up SAs for traffic flows that must be protected. Crypto map entries created for IPSec set up security association parameters, tying together the various parts configured for IPSec, including

- Which traffic should be protected by IPSec (crypto ACL)
- Which IPSec peers the protected traffic can be forwarded to—the peers with which a security association can be established
- Which transform sets are to be used with the protected traffic
- How keys and security associations should be used or managed (or what the keys are, if IKE isn't used)
- Other parameters that might be necessary to define an IPSec SA

As with applying packet filtering, it's only possible to apply one crypto map set to a particular interface. You can apply the same crypto map to multiple interfaces to apply the same policy to all included interfaces. The crypto map set can include a combination of IPSec using IKE and IPSec with manually configured SA entries.

To create more than one crypto map entry for a particular interface, use a unique sequence number (seq-num) of each map entry. The number assigned to the seq-num shouldn't be arbitrary; it's used to rank multiple crypto map entries within a crypto map set. Within a crypto map set, a crypto map entry with a lower seq-num has a higher priority and is evaluated before a map entry with a higher seq-num. Be sure to space the sequence numbers to allow for future technology to be inserted without having to completely reconfigure.

Use the global **crypto map** command to create a crypto map entry and enter the Crypto Map Configuration mode. Use the no form of the command to delete a crypto map entry or set. Use the **crypto map *map-name seq-num*** command without a keyword to modify an existing crypto map entry. Once a crypto map entry is created, you can't change the global configuration parameters because those parameters determine which **configuration** commands are valid at the crypto map level. For example, once a map entry is created as ipsec-isakmp, it can't be changed to ipsec-manual. It must be deleted and reentered.

The command syntax follows:

Rtr1(config)#crypto map *map-name seq-num* ipsec-manual
Rtr1(config)#crypto map *map-name seq-num* ipsec-isakmp [dynamic *dynamic-map-name*][discover]
Rtr1(config)#no crypto map *map-name* [*seq-num*]

map-name	Identifies the crypto map set. Assigned when the crypto map was created.
seq-num	A sequencing number assigned to a crypto map entry that determines its processing order. A lower number is used before a higher number.
ipsec-manual	Indicates IKE will *not* be used to establish the IPSec SAs for protecting the traffic specified by this crypto map entry.
ipsec-isakmp	Indicates IKE *will* be used to establish the IPSec SAs for protecting the traffic specified by this crypto map entry.
dynamic	(Optional) Specifies this crypto map entry is to reference a preexisting dynamic crypto map. *Dynamic crypto maps* are policy templates used in processing negotiation requests from a peer IPSec device. None of the **crypto map configuration** commands are available with this option.
dynamic-map-name	(Optional) Name of the dynamic crypto map set to use as the policy template.
discover	(Optional) Enables peer discovery. Added in v12.0(5)T to support Tunnel Endpoint Discovery (TED).

By default, no crypto maps exist and peer discovery isn't enabled.

After typing the **crypto map** command, the Crypto Map Configuration mode is invoked, as shown in the following output:

```
Rtr1(config)#crypto map testmap 50 ipsec-isakmp
% NOTE: This new crypto map will remain disabled until a peer
        and a valid access list have been configured.
Rtr1(config-crypto-map)#
```

From here, the **set** command can be used to define the crypto map parameters. You can also add a description, a match statement to link the crypto ACL that defines the traffic, and, finally, exit to end the session. The following example demonstrates pulling choices from the earlier exercises:

```
Rtr1(config)#crypto map testmap 50 ipsec-isakmp
Rtr1(config-crypto-map)#description VPN Link to branch in Tacoma, WA
Rtr1(config-crypto-map)#set peer 10.0.50.2
Rtr1(config-crypto-map)#set security-association lifetime seconds 1800
Rtr1(config-crypto-map)#set pfs group2
Rtr1(config-crypto-map)#set transform-set CPU-HOG
Rtr1(config-crypto-map)#match address 125
Rtr1(config-crypto-map)#exit
Rtr1(config)#
```

This next example demonstrates creating a second crypto map entry for *testmap* that creates a VPN to San Antonio, TX. Because of the larger seq-num (100), this choice is always considered after the original entries.

```
Rtr1(config)#crypto map testmap 100 ipsec-isakmp
Rtr1(config-crypto-map)#description VPN Link to branch in San Antonio, TX
Rtr1(config-crypto-map)#set peer 10.1.195.130
Rtr1(config-crypto-map)#set security-association lifetime seconds 2700
Rtr1(config-crypto-map)#set pfs group2
Rtr1(config-crypto-map)#set transform-set DES-ONLY
Rtr1(config-crypto-map)#match address 150
Rtr1(config-crypto-map)#exit
```

After crypto map entries are defined, the crypto map set is assigned to interfaces using the **crypto map** (interface IPSec) command, covered in the next section.

Step 3-5 Apply the Crypto Maps to the Interface

The last step in configuring IPSec is to apply the crypto map set to an interface with the **crypto map** command while in Interface Configuration mode. Use the no form of the command to remove the crypto map set from the interface. The command syntax is as follows:

Rtr1(config-if)#crypto map *map-name*

The IPSec SAs initialize as soon as the crypto map statement is entered. Because only one crypto map set can be assigned to an interface, crypto maps using the same map-name could have multiple entries designated by a different seq-num. The crypto map entry with the lowest seq-num is considered the highest priority and is evaluated first.

In the following example, crypto map testmap will be applied to the serial interface:

```
Rtr1(config)#interface serial 0
Rtr1(config-if)#crypto map testmap
Rtr1(config-if)#exit
```

Task 4 Test and Verify IPSec

The Cisco IOS software contains several **show, clear,** and **debug** commands that can be useful in testing and verifying IPSec and ISAKMP configuration and operations. The following steps provide a checklist to test and verify the correct configuration and operations of the VPN connection:

- Step 4-1 Display the configured IKE policies
- Step 4-2 Display the configured transform sets
- Step 4-3 Display the current state of the IPSec SAs
- Step 4-4 Display the configured crypto maps
- Step 4-5 Debug IKE events
- Step 4-6 Debug IPSec events

Step 4-1 Display the Configured IKE Policies

Use the **show crypto isakmp policy** command to view the parameters for each IKE policy, as the following example shows. Multiple policies are listed in priority order with the highest priority (first compared) listed first. The IKE default settings are shown at the end.

```
Rtr1#show crypto isakmp policy
Protection suite of priority 100
        encryption algorithm:   3DES - Triple DES (168 bit keys).
        hash algorithm:         Secure Hash Standard
        authentication method:  Pre-Shared Key
        Diffie-Hellman group:   #2 (1024 bit)
        lifetime:               43200 seconds, no volume limit
Protection suite of priority 200
        encryption algorithm:   DES - Data Encryption Standard (56 bit keys).
        hash algorithm:         Secure Hash Standard
        authentication method:  Pre-Shared Key
        Diffie-Hellman group:   #2 (1024 bit)
        lifetime:               43200 seconds, no volume limit
Protection suite of priority 300
        encryption algorithm:   DES - Data Encryption Standard (56 bit keys).
        hash algorithm:         Message Digest 5
        authentication method:  Pre-Shared Key
        Diffie-Hellman group:   #1 (768 bit)
        lifetime:               86400 seconds, no volume limit
Default protection suite
        encryption algorithm:   DES - Data Encryption Standard (56 bit keys).
        hash algorithm:         Secure Hash Standard
        authentication method:  Rivest-Shamir-Adleman Signature
        Diffie-Hellman group:   #1 (768 bit)
        lifetime:               86400 seconds, no volume limit
Rtr1#
```

Step 4-2 Display the Configured Transform Sets

Use the **show crypto ipsec transform-set** command to view the transform sets configured on the device. The command syntax shows an optional parameter that allows limiting the output to only a single transform set.

Rtr1#show crypto ipsec transform-set [tag *transform-set-name*]

Any time the keyword tag is used in **IOS** commands, it can be interpreted as "named" or "labeled" and is followed by a name. If no keyword and name are used, all transform sets configured are displayed as in the following example:

```
Rtr1#show crypto ipsec transform-set
Transform set DES-ONLY: { esp-des  }
   will negotiate = { Tunnel,  },

Transform set MD5-DES: { esp-des esp-md5-hmac  }
   will negotiate = { Tunnel,  },

Transform set CPU-HOG: { ah-md5-hmac  }
   will negotiate = { Tunnel,  },
   { esp-des esp-md5-hmac  }
   will negotiate = { Tunnel,  },

Transform set AH-ONLY: { ah-sha-hmac  }
   will negotiate = { Tunnel,  },
Rtr1#
```

Step 4-3 Display the Current State of the IPSec SAs

Use the **show crypto ipsec sa** command to display the settings of the current security associations. The command supports three parameters to limit the display and an option to generate a more detailed output of the selected choices. The syntax is as follows:

Rtr1#show crypto ipsec sa [map *map-name* | address | identity | interface-id] [detail]

map *map-name*	Limits the display to any existing security associations created for the crypto map set named *map-name*. (Optional)
Address	Lists all existing security associations, sorted by the destination address, and then by protocol (AH or ESP). (Optional)
Identity	Displays only the flow information, not the SA information. (Optional)
Interface-id	Limits the display to a single interface.
Detail	Displays detailed error counters. (Optional)

When no optional keyword is used, all security associations are displayed, sorted by interface, and then by traffic flow. Within a flow, the SAs are listed by protocol (ESP/AH) and direction (inbound/outbound).

```
Rtr1#show crypto ipsec sa

interface: Serial0
```

```
     Crypto map tag: testmap, local addr. 10.0.1.21

   local  ident (addr/mask/prot/port): (192.168.0.0/255.255.128.0/6/0)
   remote ident (addr/mask/prot/port): (192.168.130.0/255.255.255.0/6/0)
   current_peer: 10.0.50.2
     PERMIT, flags={origin_is_acl,}
    #pkts encaps: 60, #pkts encrypt: 60, #pkts digest 60
    #pkts decaps: 60, #pkts decrypt: 60, #pkts verify 60
    #pkts compressed: 0, #pkts decompressed: 0
    #pkts not compressed: 0, #pkts compr. failed: 0, #pkts decompress failed: 0
    #send errors 60, #recv errors 0

     local crypto endpt.: 10.0.1.21, remote crypto endpt.: 10.0.50.2
     path mtu 1500, media mtu 1500
     current outbound spi: 20890A6F

     inbound esp sas:
      spi: 0x36724AA4(913459876)
        transform: ah-md5-hmac esp-md5-hmac esp-des
        in use settings ={Tunnel, }
        slot: 0, conn id: 58, crypto map: testmap
        sa timing: remaining key lifetime (k/sec): (4607461/90)
        IV size: 8 bytes
        replay detection support: Y

     inbound ah sas:

     inbound pcp sas:

     outbound esp sas:
      spi: 0x338E791F(864975135)
        transform: ah-md5-hmac esp-md5-hmac esp-des
        in use settings ={Tunnel, }
        slot: 0, conn id: 59, crypto map: testmap
        sa timing: remaining key lifetime (k/sec): (4607461/90)
        IV size: 8 bytes
        replay detection support: Y

     outbound ah sas:

     outbound pcp sas:

Rtr1#
```

Step 4-4 Display the Configured Crypto Maps

Use the **show crypto map** command to display the crypto map configuration. The two optional parameters allow showing only the crypto map set applied to the specified interface or the crypto map set associated with the specified map-name. The syntax is as follows:

Rtr1#show crypto map [interface *interface* | tag *map-name*]

```
Rtr1#show crypto map
Crypto Map "testmap" 50 ipsec-isakmp
        Description: VPN Link to branch office in Tacoma, WA
        Peer = 10.0.50.2
        Extended IP access list 125
            access-list 125 permit tcp 192.168.0.0 0.0.127.255 192.168.130.0
```

```
    0.0.0.255
         Current peer: 10.0.50.2
         Security association lifetime: 2300000 kilobytes/1800 seconds
         PFS (Y/N): Y
         DH group:  group2
         Transform sets={ CPU-HOG, }
         Interfaces using crypto map testmap:
                  Serial0
Rtr1#
```

Step 4-5 Debug IKE Events

```
Rtr1#debug crypto isakmp
Crypto ISAKMP debugging is on
Rtr1#
```

Step 4-6 Debug IPSec Events

```
Rtr1#debug crypto ipsec
Crypto IPSEC debugging is on
Rtr1#
```

Crypto System Error Messages for ISAKMP

Cisco IOS software can generate many useful system error messages for IKE/IPSec. The IOS sends these error messages to the console and, optionally, to a Syslog server. Understanding that not all system error messages indicate problems with the system is important. Some are purely informational and others could help diagnose problems with communications lines, internal hardware, or the system software.

> %CRYPTO-6-IKMP_AUTH_FAIL: Authentication method failed with host 10.0.50.2

How to Read System Error Messages System error messages begin with a percent sign (%) and are structured as follows:

> %FACILITY-SEVERITY-MNEMONIC: Message-text

FACILITY	Code consisting of two or more uppercase letters that indicate the facility to which the message refers. A facility can be a hardware device, a protocol, or a module of the system software.
SEVERITY	A single-digit code (0 to 7) reflecting severity. The lower the number, the more serious the situation. Logging traps are based on these values.
MNEMONIC	Code that uniquely identifies the error message.
Message-text	Text string describing the condition. Can contain detailed event information, including port numbers, network addresses, or memory addresses. Variable fields change from message to message and are represented here by short strings enclosed in square brackets ([ ]). A decimal number, for example, is represented as [dec].

For a detailed description of the error messages, search on the Cisco site for Cisco IOS System Error Messages.

Pay close attention to these messages during initial configuration and trouble shooting because they can provide the clues to what's going wrong. Once the configuration is up and running, if these messages are being logged to a server, they can help identify and solve problems that arise with data handling. The following is a sample IPSec system error message:

%CRYPTO-6-IKMP_AUTH_FAIL: Authentication method [dec] failed with host [*IP_address*]

Explanation: The IKE process was unable to authenticate its SA with its remote peer.

%CRYPTO-6-IKMP_MODE_FAILURE: Processing of [chars] mode failed with peer at [*IP_address*]

Explanation: Negotiation with the remote peer failed.

%CRYPTO-6-IKMP_NOT_ENCRYPTED: IKE packet from [*IP_address*] was not encrypted and it should've been.

Explanation: A portion of the IKE is unencrypted and a portion is encrypted. This message should have been encrypted, but wasn't. This would occur if the ACLs aren't mirror images of each other on the peers. See Task 3, Step 3 for details.

Configuring IPSec Manually

You can configure the IPSec keys manually. This section provides a brief overview of how this is done and why manual key use isn't generally recommended.

Use the **set session-key** command in Crypto Map Configuration mode to specify the IPSec session keys manually within a crypto map entry. The command is only available for ipsec-manual crypto map entries. They aren't used with ipsec-isakmp entries because the SAs and corresponding keys are automatically established via the IKE negotiation. Use the no form of this command to remove IPSec session keys from a crypto map entry. The command uses the following syntax:

Rtr1(config)#crypto map *map-name seq-num* ipsec-manual
Rtr1(config-crypto-map)#set session-key {inbound | outbound} ah *spi hex-key-string*
Rtr1(config-crypto-map)#set session-key {inbound | outbound} esp *spi* cipher *hex-key-string* [authenticator *hex-key-string*]
Rtr1(config-crypto-map)#no set session-key {inbound | outbound} ah
Rtr1(config-crypto-map)#no set session-key {inbound | outbound} esp

PART III

inbound	Sets the inbound IPSec session key. Both inbound and outbound must be set.
outbound	Sets the outbound IPSec session key. Both inbound and outbound must be set.
ah	Sets the IPSec session key for the AH protocol. Use if the crypto map entry transform set includes an AH transform.
esp	Sets the IPSec session key for the ESP. Use if the crypto map entry transform set includes an ESP transform.
spi	Specifies the security parameter index (SPI), a number used to uniquely identify a security association. *SPI* is an arbitrary value assigned by the admin between 256 and 4,294,967,295 (FFFF FFFF).
hex-key-string	The session key in HEX format. The key is an arbitrary HEX string of 8, 16, or 20 bytes. If the crypto map's transform set includes A DES algorithm—use at least 8 bytes per key An MD5 algorithm—use at least 16 bytes per key An SHA algorithm—use at least 20 bytes per key Keys longer than the previous sizes are truncated.
cipher	Indicates the key string is to be used with the ESP encryption transform.
authenticator	(Optional) Indicates the key string is to be used with the ESP authentication transform. This argument is required only when the crypto map entry's transform set includes an ESP authentication transform.

Use the following rules to determine when to create keys:

- If the crypto map transform set includes an AH protocol, IPSec keys must be defined for AH for both inbound and outbound traffic.
- If the crypto map transform set includes an ESP encryption protocol, IPSec keys must be defined for ESP encryption for both inbound and outbound traffic.
- If the crypto map transform set includes an ESP authentication protocol, IPSec keys must be defined for ESP authentication for inbound and outbound traffic.

The SPI is used to identify the security association used with the crypto map. When defining multiple IPSec session keys within a single crypto map, it's permissible to assign the same SPI number to all keys. Session keys must be the same for both peers. Before assigning a SPI, confirm with the peer's admin that the same SPI isn't used more than once for the same destination address/protocol combination.

If a session key is changed, the SA using the key will be deleted and reinitialized.

```
Rtr1(config)#crypto map testmap2 50 ipsec-manual
Rtr1(config-crypto-map)#set peer 10.0.10.133
Rtr1(config-crypto-map)#match address 100
Rtr1(config-crypto-map)#set transform-set encrypt-des
Rtr1(config-crypto-map)#set session-key inbound esp 300 32a87b445c98701c
Rtr1(config-crypto-map)#set session-key outbound esp 300 32a87b445c98701c
```

Configuring IPSec Manually Is Not Recommended

Cisco recommends using IKE to set up the SAs because it's difficult to ensure the SA values match between peers and D-H is a more secure method for generating secret keys between peers. Other reasons not to configure IPSec manually include the following:

- Manual keying doesn't scale well.
- The result can be insecure because of difficulty in creating secure keying material manually.
- Manually established SAs never expire.
- ACLs used for crypto map entries using ipsec-manual are restricted to a single permit statement. Any other entries are ignored.

Chapter Review

This chapter looked at steps involved in configuring IPSec with preshared keys. The steps and related commands are summarized in the following task list.

Task 1 Prepare for IKE and IPSec

- Step 1-1 Identify IPSec peers
- Step 1-2 Determine the IKE (IKE Phase 1) policies
- Step 1-3 Determine the IPSec (IKE Phase 2) policies
- Step 1-4 Check the current configuration

  show running-config

  show isakmp

  show crypto map
- Step 1-5 Ensure the network works without encryption

  ping
- Step 1-6 Ensure access control lists are compatible with IPSec

  show access-lists

Task 2 Configure IKE

- Step 2-1 Enable or disable IKE

  crypto isakmp enable
- Step 2-2 Create IKE policies

  crypto isakmp policy

  authentication

  encryption

  hash

  lifetime
- Step 2-3 Configure preshared keys

  crypto isakmp key
- Step 2-4 Verify the IKE configuration

  show crypto isakmp policy

PART III

Task 3 Configure IPSec

- Step 3-1 Configure transform set suites
  crypto ipsec transform-set
- Step 3-2 Configure global IPSec security association lifetimes
  crypto ipsec security-association lifetime
- Step 3-3 Configure crypto ACLs
  access-list
- Step 3-4 Configure crypto maps
  crypto map
- Step 3-5 Apply the crypto maps to the interface
  interface
  crypto map

Task 4 Test and verify IPSec

- Step 4-1 Display the configured IKE policies
  show crypto isakmp policy
- Step 4-2 Display the configured transform sets
  show crypto ipsec transform set
- Step 4-3 Display the current state of the IPSec SAs
  show crypto ipsec sa
- Step 4-4 Display the configured crypto maps
  show crypto map
- Step 4-5 Debug IKE events
  debug crypto isakmp
- Step 4-6 Debug IPSec events
  debug crypto ipsec

Questions

1 Which one of the following is *not* one of the tasks required to configure IPSec for Preshared Keys?

A. Configure IPSec

B. Prepare for IKE and IPSec

C. Test and verify IPSec

D. Configure the crypto map

2. Which of the following VPN products would be common for mobile users?

A. Cisco 1700 router

B. Cisco 900 Cable/DSL router

C. Cisco VPN Software Client

D. Cisco VPN Hardware Client

3. Which one of the following is a hybrid protocol that implements the Oakley key exchange?

   A. IPSec

   B. Crypto map

   C. IKE

   D. Hash algorithm

4. Which of the following is a peer authentication method?

   A. 3DES

   B. SHA-1

   C. MD5

   D. Preshared keys

5. Which of the following preparation steps is done using the **ping** command?

   A. Identify IPSec peers

   B. Check the current configuration

   C. Ensure the network works without encryption

   D. Ensure access control lists are compatible with IPSec

6. Which one of the following is *not* an IKE Phase 1 parameter?

   A. Encryption algorithm

   B. Traffic to protect

   C. Authentication method

   D. DH key exchange group

7. To make sure the router ACLs are IPSec-compatible, which is *not* required to be permitted?

   A. Port 500

   B. Port 510

   C. Protocol 51

   D. Protocol 50

8. If the **crypto isakmp policy** command were used to create policies with the following priorities, which would be processed first?

   A. 1000

   B. 500

   C. 12

   D. 25

9. If the crypto isakmp policy lifetime is set to 43,200, to what does the 43,200 refer?
   A. 43,200 bytes of protected throughput
   B. 43,200 hours
   C. half a day
   D. 43,200 lines of protected throughput
10. Which command shows the IKE policies and default values?
    A. show running-config
    B. show isakmp policy
    C. show crypto ike policy
    D. show crypto isakmp policy
11. A transform set can contain up to how many transforms?
    A. 4
    B. 6
    C. 3
    D. 1
12. Which is *not* a function of a crypto ACL?
    A. Define the dataflow to be protected by IPSec
    B. Discard inbound traffic that should have been protected by IPSec
    C. Filter outbound traffic for access to the Internet
    D. Define the data flow to pass unprotected by IPSec
13. Which of the following is *not* true?
    A. The crypto ACL determines the traffic to be protected
    B. The global **crypto map** command ties together the IPSec parameters
    C. The interface **crypto map** command applies the crypto map to an interface
    D. The global **crypto map policy** command sets the implementation priority
14. Which command shows IPSec performance indicators?
    A. show crypto map
    B. show crypto ipsec sa
    C. show crypto ipsec transform-set
    D. show crypto isakmp policy

15. Which statement is *not* true about the ipsec-manual form of the **crypto map** command?
    A. It doesn't scale well
    B. The result can be insecure because of difficulty in manually creating secure keying material
    C. It enhances the flexibility of the crypto ACLs
    D. Manually established SAs never expire

Answers

1. D. Configure the crypto map
2. C. Cisco VPN Software Client
3. C. IKE
4. D. Preshared keys
5. C. Ensure the network works without encryption
6. B. Traffic to protect
7. B. Port 510
8. C. 12
9. C. half a day
10. D. show crypto isakmp policy
11. C. 3
12. C. Filter outbound traffic for access to the Internet
13. D. The global **crypto map policy** command sets the implementation priority
14. B. show crypto ipsec sa
15. C. It enhances the flexibility of the crypto ACLs

CHAPTER 11

Cisco IOS IPSec Certificate Authority Support

In this chapter, you will learn to:

- Learn about CA support overview
- Configure CA support tasks
- Understand RSA encrypted nonces overview

This chapter looks at configuring Cisco IOS IPSec using a certificate authority (CA). After presenting an overview of the configuration process, the chapter covers planning before beginning configuration, and the major tasks and steps required for successful implementation of an IPSec network. These steps involve how to configure CA support, as well as IKE policies and IPSec. Descriptions of all required steps are provided.

CA Support Overview

With public/private key encryption technology, each key is a unique encryption device. If, in fact, no two keys are ever identical, it's possible to use a key to identify its owner. Keys are always created and used in pairs: one is the private key; the other is the public key. You can then encrypt data with the public key, which only the corresponding private key can decrypt.

The public key can be distributed to anyone who needs to share secure information with the owner of the private key. The private key, on the other hand, is never duplicated or distributed to anyone: it remains secure on the owner's computer or server. While not as secure as limiting keys to pairs, the same public key can be duplicated and distributed to multiple users who need to share information with the private key owner. The public key holders would be unable to exchange information using the shared key. The downside is the public key no longer identifies a unique host.

A fundamental problem with public key cryptosystems is this: all users must be careful to make sure they're always encrypting to the correct person's key. In an environment where keys can be physically exchanged in person or configured by a single administrator, this shouldn't be a problem. Unfortunately, neither of these key-exchange methods scales well, particularly over large geographical areas. One common solution for key exchanges is to use public servers, such as e-mail servers. Unfortunately, the threat of man-in-the-middle attacks must be considered a potential threat. Figure 11-1 shows

Figure 11-1 Rtr1 sharing secure data with Rtr10 using a public key

Rtr1 communicating securely with Rtr10, using a public key BCD sent to Rtr10. The attacker can see the traffic, but can't decrypt it.

In the man-in-the middle scenario, the culprit posts a phony public key using the real name and user ID of the legitimate holder of the private key with whom the user expects to share data. Now any data encrypted using the phony public key can only be decrypted by the holder of the matching private key—the attacker. In Figure 11-2, the hacker has posted a new public key using Rtr1's name and ID. Rtr10, not realizing the ruse, implements the new key. The attacker can now decrypt the traffic, but Rtr1 can't.

In a public key environment, it's absolutely critical that the public key used to encrypt data is, in fact, a legitimate public key of the intended recipient and not a forgery. Common sense indicates that requiring an administrator to configure both devices or physically deliver the public keys won't scale well. Even if this is physically possible, the process would present a significant cost burden, even in regional networks. There must be another way. Digital certificates (certs) can simplify the task of sharing public keys, while verifying the public key belongs to the "real" owner.

Digital Certificates

A *digital certificate* is a form of credential much like a driver's license or a passport in the paper-based world. Like its paper counterparts, the digital certificate has information on

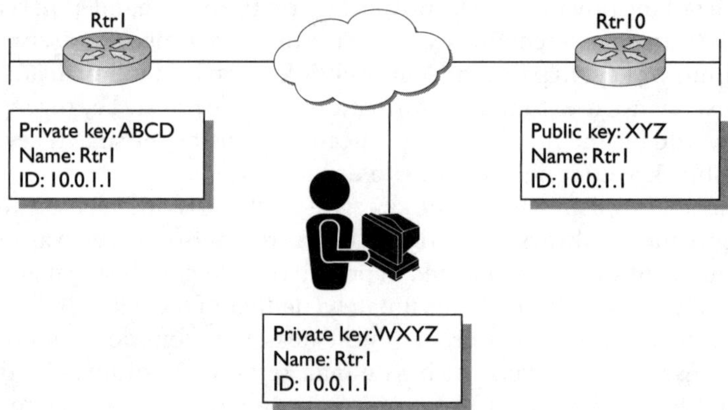

Figure 11-2 The attacker and Rtr10 now share a key, allowing the attacker to decrypt the messages.

it that identifies the holder, plus some uninvolved third-party authorization, which indicates they confirmed the holder's identity.

A digital certificate has additional information included with the holder's public key that helps others to verify the key is genuine. This additional information, like a person's picture on a driver's license or a passport, can thwart attempts to substitute an unauthorized public key.

A digital certificate contains the following three items:

- Public key
- Certificate information—Identifying information about the holder, such as ID, name, and so forth
- One or more digital signatures

The *digital signatures* indicate the certificate information was verified and attested to by a trusted independent third party. Understanding that the digital signature doesn't guarantee the authenticity of the certificate as a whole is important. What it verifies is only that the signed identity information belongs to or is bound to the attached public key. Don't let this get too complicated. In the case of a passport, the government is verifying that the picture and identifying information belong to the passport number. But, the passport can be expired or revoked by a court order. Similarly, digital certificates can expire or be revoked.

Conceptually, a digital certificate is a public key with a tag containing one or more forms of ID, plus a seal of approval by a trusted third party. Figure 11-3 shows a conceptual representation of a digital certificate.

Certificate Distribution

Chapter 10 looked at preshared public keys, but this manual distribution method is only practical to a certain point. After that, having an exchange system that can provide the necessary security, storage, and exchange mechanisms becomes necessary, so coworkers, business partners, and even strangers could establish secure communications, if necessary.

These public key exchange systems can take the form of storage-only repositories called *Certificate Servers*, or they can be much more structured systems providing additional key management features. These latter systems are called *Public Key Infrastructures*.

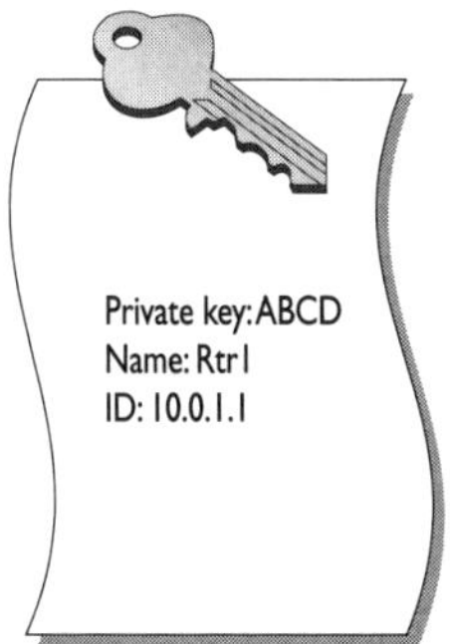

Figure 11-3 Conceptual representation of a digital certificate

Certificate Servers

A certificate server, also called a *cert server* or a *key server*, is a database service running on an existing or dedicated server that allows users to submit and retrieve digital certificates. The cert server typically offers additional administrative features that allow the company to implement and maintain its security policies. For example, the cert server can be configured to allow only certain types of keys to be stored.

Public Key Infrastructures (PKI)

A Public Key Infrastructures (PKI) includes the storage capabilities of a certificate server, but it also provides additional certificate management functions, such as the capability to issue, store, retrieve, revoke, and trust certificates. A powerful feature of a PKI system is the concept of a Certification Authority (CA). CAs are responsible for managing certificate requests and issuing certificates to participating IPSec network peers. These services provide centralized key management for the participating peers. CAs simplify the administration of IPSec network devices (peers) in networks containing multiple IPSec-compliant devices, such as with the Cisco Secure PIX Firewall units and Cisco routers.

The CA creates the digital certificate, and then digitally signs it using its own private key. Any CA client can then use the shared CA public key to authenticate a certificate's digital signature and, thereby, the integrity of the certificate contents, including the certificate holder public key and the identity of the certificate holder.

Conceptually, the CA functions in the digital environment much like the government passport or driver's license office in the nondigital world.

IPSec with CAs

When using IPSec with a CA, configuring keys among all the potential IPSec peers isn't necessary. Instead, each participating device is individually enrolled with the CA, requesting a certificate for the device. Once this is done, each participating device can dynamically authenticate itself to all the other participating peers.

Adding a new IPSec device to an existing network is similarly simplified. In each case, it's only necessary to configure the new device to request a certificate from the CA.

How CA Certs Are Used by IPSec Peers

As you learned in Chapter 9, any time two IPSec peers want to establish an IPSec-protected communication session between them, they must first authenticate each other. This authentication is done with IKE and, without it, IPSec protection can't occur.

Without a CA, the peers authenticate themselves to the remote peer, using either preshared keys (Chapter 10) or RSA-encrypted nonces (see the section "RSA Encrypted Nonces Overview.") Both methods require previously configured keys on both peers. PIX Firewall devices currently don't support RSA-encrypted nonces.

With a CA, each peer authenticates itself by sending a valid digital certificate to the remote peer. The peer's unique certificate was issued and validated by the CA, encapsulates the peer's public key and IDs, and works because all participating peers recognize the CA as an authenticating authority. This process is called *IKE with an RSA signature*.

Each peer can continue sending its own certificate for additional IPSec sessions, as well as to additional IPSec peers, until the certificate expires. When a certificate expires, the peer administrator must request a new one from the CA.

Certificate Revocation List (CRL)

CAs can revoke otherwise valid certificates for peers that will no longer participate in IPSec. These revoked certificates are listed in a certificate revocation list (CRL), which each peer can check before accepting another peer's certificate. Revoked certificates, like expired passports or driver's licenses, aren't recognized as valid by other peers.

Registration Authority (RA)

Some CAs extend their reliability and availability by supporting registration authority (RA) as part of their implementation. An *RA* is a server that acts as a proxy for the CA, so CA functions can continue when the CA is offline or otherwise unavailable.

Cisco IOS CA Standards

Cisco IOS supports the following open CA standards:

- **Internet Key Exchange (IKE)** A hybrid protocol that implements Oakley and Skeme key exchanges inside the ISAKMP framework. IKE is covered in Chapters 9 and 10.
- **Public-Key Cryptography Standard #7 (PKCS #7)** A standard developed by RSA Data Security, Inc. used to encrypt and sign certificate enrollment messages.
- **Public-Key Cryptography Standard #10 (PKCS #10)** A standard syntax developed by RSA Data Security, Inc. for certificate requests.
- **RSA Keys** *RSA* is the public-key cryptographic system developed by RSA Data Security, Inc. RSA keys come in pairs: one public key and one private key.
- **X.509v3 Certificates** An *X.509 certificate* is a collection of a standard set of fields containing information about a user or device and their corresponding public key. The X.509 standard defines what information goes into the certificate and describes how to encode it (the data format). The encoded information is used with the IKE protocol when authentication requires public keys.

Simple Certificate Enrollment Protocol (SCEP)

Developed by a Cisco, Verisign, Entrust, Microsoft, Netscape, and Sun Microsystems initiative, Simple Certificate Enrollment Protocol (SCEP) provides a standard way of managing the certificate lifecycle. This initiative is important for furthering open development for certificate handling protocols that can help ensure interoperability with devices from many vendors.

SCEP provides the following two authentication methods:

- Manual authentication
- Authentication based on a preshared secret

Manual Mode

In the Manual mode, the entity that submits the request is required to wait until the CA operator can verify its identity, using any reliable out-of-band method. An MD5 hash "fingerprint" generated by and included in the PKCS10 must be compared out-of-band between the SCEP clients and CAs (or RAs, if appropriate) to enable verification.

Preshared Secret Mode

With a preshared secret method, the CA server distributes a shared secret to the end entity, which can then be used to associate an enrollment request uniquely with the end entity. To maintain the integrity of the method, the distribution of the shared secret must be private, allowing only the end entity to know the secret.

Challenge Passwords

When an enrollment request is initiated, the end entity is asked to provide a challenge password. With the *preshared secret* method, the end entity must type in the distributed secret as the password. With the *manual authentication* method, the challenge password is also required because the server might challenge an end entity for a password before any certificate can be revoked. Eventually, the challenge password is included as a PKCS#10 attribute and is sent to the CA server as encrypted data. The PKCS#7 envelope protects the privacy of the challenge password using DES encryption.

CA Servers Interoperable with Cisco Routers

CA interoperability permits Cisco IOS devices, PIX Firewalls, Cisco VPN Hardware devices, and CA servers to communicate so the VPN device can obtain and use digital certificates supplied by the CA. While IPSec can be implemented in the network without using a CA, the CA with SCEP provides enhanced manageability and scalability for IPSec.

The list of CAs supported could vary from VPN platform to platform, for example, PIX Firewalls might not support the same options as IOS devices or VPN hardware devices. A good idea is always to check the Cisco online documentation for the particular device and version of the operating system (OS) to confirm support and appropriate version numbers. The following are CA providers that support SCEP to interoperate for enrolling Cisco IOS routers:

- VeriSign
- Entrust Technologies, Inc.
- Baltimore Technologies
- Microsoft Corporation

VeriSign OnSite 4.5

The VeriSign's OnSite 4.5 solution provides a fully integrated enterprise PKI to issue, control, and manage IPSec certificates for PIX Firewalls and Cisco routers. VeriSign administers the CA themselves, providing the certificates as a service. VeriSign OnSite service specifics include the following:

- **Requirements**—No local server requirements. Routers must be running IOS v 12.0.6 or higher and must have a retry count set to greater than 60.
- **Standards supported**—SCEP, x509 certificate format, and PKCS# 7, 10, 11, and 12.

For more information on VeriSign products and features, consult their web site at www.verisign.com.

Entrust Technologies

One major difference between CA servers is where the server is located and who administers it. *Entrust* is a software solution that's installed and administered by the user on a local network server. The Entrust/PKI service is able to issue digital IDs to any device or application supporting the X.509 certificate standard. This implementation offers a secure, flexible, and low-cost solution from one PKI. Entrust/PKI service specifics include the following:

- **Requirements**—Entrust software runs on the Windows servers (for Cisco interoperability), Solaris 2.6, HP-UX 10.20, and AIX 4.3 OSs. Requires RSA usage-keys configured on the routers. Cisco IOS release 11.(3)5T and later.
- **Standards supported**—CA services, RA capabilities, SCEP, and PKCS#10.

For more information on Entrust products and features, consult their web site at www.entrust.com.

Baltimore Technologies

Baltimore Technologies supports SCEP in UniCERT, its CA server, as well as the PKI Plus toolkit, making it easy for customers to implement certificates in their networks. *UniCERT* is a software solution installed and administered by the user on a local network server. Baltimore Technologies service specifics include the following:

- **Requirements**—The current release of the UniCERT CA software module is available for Windows servers. Must use Cisco IOS release 12.0(5)T and later.
- **Standards Supported**—The following standards are supported with this CA server: X509 v3, CRL version 2, PKCS# 1, 7, 10, 11, and 12, and many more protocols.

For more information on Baltimore products and features, consult their web site at www.baltimore.com.

Microsoft Windows 2000 Certificate Services Microsoft has integrated SCEP support into the Windows 2000 CA server via the Security Resource Kit for Windows 2000. This SCEP support allows Microsoft clients to obtain certificates and certificate revocation information from Microsoft Certificate Services for all of Cisco's VPN security solutions.

- **Requirements**—Intel-based PC running Windows 2000 Server. Cisco IOS release 12.0(5)T or later.

- **Standards Supported**—The following standards are supported with this CA server: X.509 version 3, CRL version 2, PKCS #7, #10, and #12, and many more protocols.

For more information on Microsoft products and features, consult their web site at www.microsoft.com.

Enroll a Device with a CA

The basic process for enrolling an IPSec peer with a CA includes the following steps. Most of these steps have been automated using the SCEP protocol supported by many CA server providers. Each CA vender determines how long certificates are valid.

- **Step 1** Configure the router for CA support.
- **Step 2** Generate a public and private key pair on the router.
- **Step 3** The router authenticates the CA server.
- **Step 4** The router sends a certificate request to the CA.
- **Step 5** The CA creates and signs an identity (ID) and root certificate and, optionally, an RA certificate.
- **Step 6** The CA sends the certificates to the router and posts the certificates in its public repository (directory).

The configuration commands are covered under Task 2 "Configure CA support" activities.

Configure CA Support Tasks

Configuring for RSA signatures consists of five major tasks, each requiring multiple steps. This chapter covers the CA configuration tasks and steps in detail, but those tasks and steps identical to those covered in Chapter 10 for preshared keys aren't repeated. Refer to Chapter 10 for a detailed explanation of these steps.

The five major tasks Cisco uses and which you can expect on the exam to configure CA support are as follows. The major difference is the insertion of a new Task 2 specifically for configuring CA support.

- Task 1 Prepare for IKE and IPSec
- Task 2 Configure CA support
- Task 3 Configure IKE
- Task 4 Configure IPSec
- Task 5 Test and verify IPSec

A summary task list showing the five tasks broken down to their individual steps and key commands is included in the Summary. As in Chapter 10, the steps are numbered to include the task number, as well as to help keep them straight.

Figure 11-4 shows the example networks from Chapter 10. These networks provide an example scenario used throughout this chapter. The goal is to create a secure VPN tunnel between Rtr1 company main office and Rtr2 at one of almost 100 branch offices in North America, Europe, and Africa. The assumption is this: the main office has reserved networks192.168.0.0 through 192.168.127.0 for itself and will use one class C for each branch in the remaining 192.168.128.0 to 192.168.255.0 addresses.

Because not all configuration steps are repeated in this chapter, using the same scenario as Chapter 10 means a person performing the configurations along with the text can refer to Chapter 10 for assistance.

Task 1—Prepare for IKE and IPSec

Successful implementation of an IPSec network requires testing of the existing network and advance planning before any configuration begins. Insufficient testing and planning can lead to troubleshooting problems or configuration errors. Some preparation and planning steps include the following:

Step 1–1 and Step 1–2 are covered in detail in this chapter. The other steps are presented for review purposes, but aren't covered in this chapter. Chapter 10 has detailed coverage of Steps 1–3 through 1–6.

- Step 1–1 Plan for CA support
- Step 1–2 Determine the IKE (IKE phase one) policies
- Step 1–3 Determine the IPSec (IKE phase two) policies
- Step 1–4 Check the current configuration

  show running-configuration

  show isakmp [policy]

  show crypto map
- Step 1–5 Ensure the network works without encryption

  ping

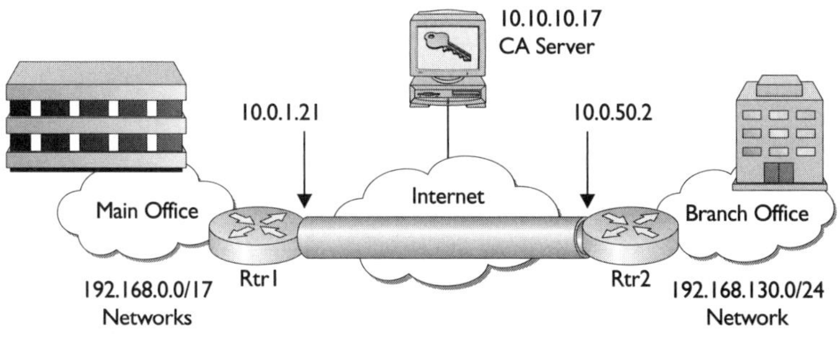

Figure 11-4 Chapter scenario VPN session to be configured

- Step 1–6 Ensure access control lists are compatible with IPSec
  show access-lists

The order of these steps could be varied based on personal preferences and implementation circumstances.

Step 1–1 Plan for CA support

Configuring CA is a complicated process, but having a detailed plan reduces the chances of improper configuration. Some basic information to be decided or collected includes the following items:

- **Determine which CA server is being used.** The organizations providing CA services vary in capabilities, requirements, and the resulting configuration. Once the service provider is selected, the requirements could include the RSA key type required, CRL capabilities, and support for RA mode.
- **Identify the CA server IP address, host name, and URL.** Information to use Lightweight Directory Protocol (LDAP).
- **Identify the CA server administrator contact information.** This arranges for the certificates to be validated if the process isn't automatic.

The actual information required for all CA features varies with the organization providing the CA support and can change over time with a specific organization. A good idea is always to check the CA supplier and Cisco documentation. Figure 11-5 shows the information that would be useful in configuring VeriSign CA support.

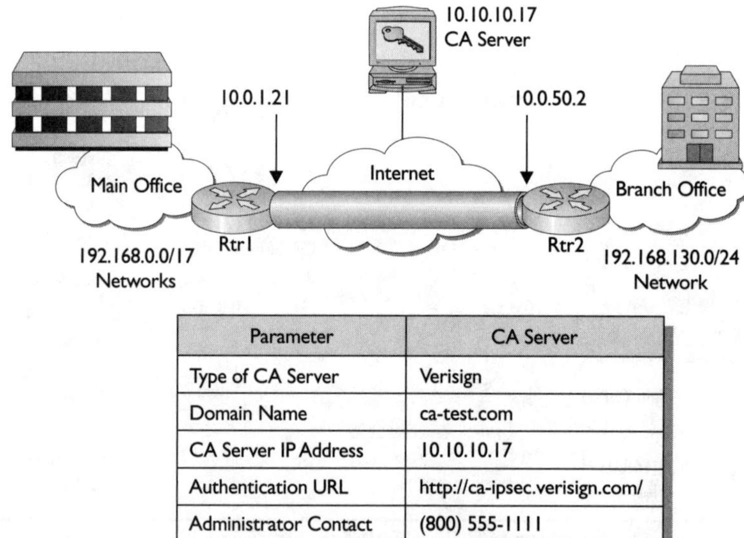

Parameter	CA Server
Type of CA Server	Verisign
Domain Name	ca-test.com
CA Server IP Address	10.10.10.17
Authentication URL	http://ca-ipsec.verisign.com/
Administrator Contact	(800) 555-1111

Figure 11-5 Configuration parameters for VeriSign CA support

Step 1–2 Determine the IKE (IKE phase one) policies

The objective here is to develop one or more IKE security policies, based on the overall company security policy. Each policy is going to require decisions about five security options: authentication method, encryption algorithm, hashing algorithm, Diffie–Hellman group, and SA lifetime.

Defining the IKE phase one policies is basically the same as with preshared keys except the authentication method will use RSA Signatures. Cisco IOS software supports preshared keys, RSA encrypted nonces, or RSA signatures to authenticate IPSec peers.

To complete the IKE planning process, what would make sense is to create a table of the preferred combination of security features, plus one or more fallback options for those devices or locations that can't support the preferred package. The resulting table might look like the following:

Parameter	Preferred (stronger)	2nd Choice	3rd Choice
Encryption algorithm	3des	des	des
Hash algorithm	sha	sha	md5
Authentication method	rsa-sig	rsa-sig	rsa-sig
DH key exchange group	2	2	1
IKE SA lifetime	43,200	43,200	86,400

NOTE You can't use SHA together with DES encryption on Cisco's VPN software client version 3.6. Part of the problem with determining a set of preferences is being aware of the different platform limitations.

Using our scenario for this chapter, the *Preferred* column represents our configuration preferences for all North American branches and would be the only options configured. The *2nd Choice* column would be for those overseas branches that can support the Preferred configuration, except for the export restriction on triple DES. Assuming they don't form VPN sessions with anyone else, this would be the only choice configured on those devices. The *3rd Choice* column might represent small branches using small routers with limited resources and options or telecommuters using Cisco's VPN software. This would also represent the lowest level of parameter options that the main office will accept for a VPN connection. The only device that will have all three choices configured will be the main office router.

Task 2—Configure CA Support

Configuring Cisco IOS CA support can be quite complicated and requires ten steps to complete. The planning steps performed in Task 1 and the first three commands in this section ensure the actual router CA support configuration goes smoothly. The process necessary to configure CA support on Cisco routers includes the following steps:

- Step 2–1 Manage the NVRAM memory usage (optional)
- Step 2–2 Set the router time and date

- Step 2–3 Configure the router host name and domain name
- Step 2–4 Generate an RSA key pair
- Step 2–5 Declare a CA
- Step 2–6 Authenticate the CA
- Step 2–7 Request your own certificate
- Step 2–8 Save the configuration
- Step 2–9 Monitor and maintain CA interoperability (optional)
  Request a CRL. Delete your router's RSA keys.

  Delete both public and private certificates from the configuration.

  Delete peer's public keys.
- Step 2–10 Verify the CA support configuration

Step 2–1 Manage the NVRAM Memory Usage (Optional)

Certificates and CRLs are stored in NVRAM on the router, and each certificate and CRL requires a moderate amount of memory. The types of certificates stored locally on the router include the following:

- The router's own certificate
- The CA's root certificate
- Two RA certificates if the CA supports RAs

If the CA doesn't support an RA, there will be one CRL stored on the router. Otherwise, there will be multiple CRLs.

Depending on the router model, the NVRAM available, and whether the CA supports RAs, storing certificates and CRLs locally shouldn't be a problem. But memory might become an issue with smaller routers, limited NVRAM, and a CA that supports RAs. If the CA supports an RA and a large number of CRLs end up being stored on the router, it can consume a large amount of NVRAM space.

To preserve limited NVRAM, you can specify that certificates and CRLs won't be stored locally, but can be retrieved from the CA as needed. While this method can save NVRAM, it could cause a slight performance reduction and puts additional traffic out on the network.

The crypto ca certificate query Command Use the global configuration mode **crypto ca certificate query** command to specify that certificates and CRLs shouldn't be stored locally but, instead, retrieved from the CA as needed. This command puts the router into Query mode. To cause certificates and CRLs to be stored locally (the default), use the no form of this command. The command syntax is as follows:

```
Rtr1(config)#crypto ca certificate query

Rtr1(config)#no crypto ca certificate query
```

NOTE Remember, this command should only be used if NVRAM resources are inadequate to service the CA support locally.

Step 2-2 Set the Router Time and Date

For CA support to function properly, the router must have an accurate time and date to enroll with a CA server. The clock must be set accurately before generating RSA key pairs and enrolling with the CA server because the keys and certificates are time-sensitive.

Like many time-dependent processes, CA support features use the router software clock. The *software clock* runs from when the system powers up or a **reload** command is used and keeps track of the current date and time. The software clock can be set from a number of sources and, in turn, can be used to distribute the current time through various mechanisms to other systems. If no other system or process initializes the clock, it uses a date in the past as the seed value. (My lab 1720 uses 16:00:00 PST Sun Feb 28 1993).

If a router has a built-in hardware clock, the software clock is initially set at power up or reload, based on the time in the hardware clock. The software clock can then be updated from the following time sources:

- Network Time Protocol (NTP)
- Simple Network Time Protocol (SNTP)—some models
- Manual configuration

Because the software clock can be dynamically updated, it has the potential to be more accurate than the hardware clock. In fact, updating the hardware clock from the software clock after synchronization is common.

The software clock can provide time to the following services:

- CA support features
- Access lists
- Logging and debugging messages
- User show commands
- NTP
- The hardware clock

The software clock stores time internally based on Coordinated Universal Time (UTC), also known as Greenwich Mean Time (GMT). The next sections look at configuring information about the local time zone and summer time (daylight saving time), so the time is always displayed correctly relative to the local time zone.

Network Time Protocol (NTP) NTP is an industry protocol developed to facilitate time synchronization of network devices. NTP Version 3 uses UDP transport and is documented in RFC 1305.

A specified device in a NTP network usually gets its time from an *authoritative time source*, such as a radio clock or an atomic clock attached to a time server. NTP then periodically distributes this time across the network. NTP is an extremely efficient protocol, requiring no more than one packet per minute to synchronize two machines to the accuracy of within a millisecond of one another.

NTP uses the concept of a stratum to describe how many NTP "hops" a device is away from an authoritative time source. A stratum 1 time server typically has an authoritative time source directly attached, a stratum 2 time server receives its time via NTP from a stratum 1 time server, and so on.

Devices in a Cisco network can be configured to be a NTP server, master, or peer. The Cisco implementation of NTP doesn't support stratum 1 service, recommending instead that time service be synchronized with a public NTP server available in the IP Internet. Note, it's important to recognize that not all Cisco devices support NTP fully. PIX firewalls just added NTP support with v6.2 of the PIX OS, while IOS devices added support with IOS 10.0.

NTP devices avoid synchronizing to a device with inaccurate time in two ways. First, NTP will never synchronize to a device that isn't synchronized itself. Second, NTP will compare the time reported by several devices and won't synchronize to a device with a time significantly different than the others, even if its stratum is lower. This strategy effectively builds a self-organizing tree of NTP servers.

NTP devices are usually statically configured to create associations; each device is given the IP address of any devices with which it should form associations. In a LAN environment, configuring NTP to use IP broadcasts is often advantageous. This implementation reduces configuration complexity because each device is configured to send or receive broadcast messages.

Use the global configuration **ntp peer** command to configure the software clock to synchronize a peer or to be synchronized by a peer. To disable the feature, use the no form of this command. The syntax is as follows:

Rtr1(config)#ntp peer ip-address [version *ver-num*] [key *keyid*]
[source *interface*] [prefer]

Rtr1(config)#no ntp peer ip-address

ip-address	IP address of the peer providing, or being provided, the clock synchronization
ver-num	NTP version number (1 to 3)* (Optional)
keyid	Authentication key to use when sending packets to this peer (Optional)
source	Names the interface (Optional)
interface	Name of the interface from which to pick the IP source address (Optional)
prefer	Makes this peer the preferred peer that provides synchronization (Optional)

*If the default version (3) doesn't result in NTP synchronization, try NTP version 2 (NTPv2).

The following example allows a router to synchronize its software clock with the peer at IP address 192.168.1.45 using the default settings over the FastEthernet 0 interface.

```
Rtr1(config)#ntp peer 192.168.1.45 source fastethernet 0
```

Use the interface configuration **ntp broadcast client** command to receive NTP broadcast packets on a specified interface. To disable this capability, use the no form of this command.

Rtr1(config-if)#ntp broadcast client

Rtr1(config-if)no ntp broadcast client

Simple Network Time Protocol (SNTP) SNTP is a simplified, client-only version of NTP supported on smaller Cisco routers, such as the 1000, 1600, and 1700 platforms. SNTP devices can only receive the time from NTP servers. They can't be used to provide time services to other systems.

While SNTP is simple to implement, it's more vulnerable to a misbehaving server than an NTP client and should be used only when strong authentication isn't required for the following reasons:

- Accuracy to within 100 milliseconds versus 2 milliseconds for NTP
- Doesn't provide complex filtering and statistical mechanisms of NTP
- Doesn't authenticate traffic, although extended ACLs can be configured

SNTP clients can be configured to request and accept packets from NTP servers or to accept NTP broadcast packets from any source.

Use the global configuration **sntp broadcast client** command to use the SNTP to accept NTP traffic from any broadcast server. To prevent the router from accepting broadcast traffic, use the no form of this command.

Rtr1(config)#sntp broadcast client

Rtr1(config)#no sntp broadcast client

The following example demonstrates using the **sntp broadcast client** command and the **show sntp** command to display the results.

```
Router(config)#sntp broadcast client
Router(config)#end
Router#show sntp
SNTP server     Stratum   Version   Last Receive
10.0.115.2         4         3        00:00:21   Synced   Bcast
Broadcast client mode is enabled.
```

The clock timezone Command To specify the router time zone, use the configuration mode **clock timezone** command. The command sets the time zone and an offset from UTC, displayed by the router. The command syntax is as follows:

Rtr1(config)#clock timezone *zone hour-offset* [*minute-offset*]

zone	Name of the time zone to be displayed (typically a standard acronym).
hour-offset	Hours offset from UTC.
minute-offset	Minutes offset from UTC. (Optional). This argument is for those cases where a local time zone is a percentage of an hour different from UTC/GMT.

The following example demonstrates setting the time zone to Central Standard Time (CST) in the United States. The -6 indicates CST is 6 hours behind UTC.

```
Rtr1(config)#clock timezone CST -6
```

The *zone* entry isn't a keyword. What you type is what you'll get, including case usage. Spaces aren't allowed. The following example demonstrates creating a custom entry. The **show clock** command displays the current settings. Notice the date and time setting is old, indicating the router hasn't had the software clock set. This is covered in the next section, "The clock set Command."

```
Rtr1(config)#clock timezone Pacific.Standard.Time -8
Rtr1(config)#^Z
Rtr1#show clock
*17:51:09.799 Pacific.Standard.Time Sun Feb 28 1993
Rtr1#
```

For more information on UTC, time zones, and common time zone abbreviations, go to http://www.timeanddate.com/worldclock.

The clock set Command If the system time is synchronized by a valid outside timing mechanism, such as a Network Time Protocol (NTP), or if it can be set using the router hardware clock, it shouldn't be necessary to set the software clock. Use this command if no other time sources are available.

To set the router's time and date manually, use the privileged EXEC **clock set** command. This command isn't available in Configuration mode. The time specified in this command is relative to the configured time zone. The command syntax is either of the following:

Rtr1#clock set *hh:mm:ss day month year*

Rtr1#clock set *hh:mm:ss month day year*

hh:mm:ss	Current time in hours, minutes, and seconds (24-hour format)
day	Current day of the month
month	Current month (by name)
year	Current year (4-digit format)

There are no defaults and all elements are required, even the seconds. The following example sets the time to 6:15 P.M. on December 15, 2004. While the full month can be typed out, it's only necessary to type the first three letters. The output is the same, regardless of whether the entry is abbreviated or the case of the entry.

```
Rtr1#clock set 18:15:00 15 december 2004
Rtr1#show clock
18:15:28.279 PST Wed Dec 15 2004
Rtr1#
```

Setting the Software Clock from the Hardware Clock If the router has a hardware-based clock, it's possible to set the software clock to the new hardware clock setting by using the following **privilege EXEC mode** command. If the router doesn't have a hardware clock, the command is rejected.

```
Rtr1#clock read-calendar
```

Setting the Hardware Clock To update the hardware clock with the current software clock setting, use the following **privilege EXEC mode** command. If the router doesn't have a hardware clock, the command is rejected.

```
Rtr1#clock update-calendar
```

You can periodically update the hardware clock (calendar) from a NTP time source, using the global configuration **ntp update-calendar** command. To disable the periodic updates, use the no form of this command.

```
Rtr1(config)#ntp update-calendar
Rtr1(config)#no ntp update-calendar
```

Configuring Daylight Saving Time To configure daylight saving time (summer time) in areas where it starts and ends on a particular day of the week each year, use the following global configuration **mode** command. To avoid automatically switching to summer time, use the no form of this command.

Rtr1(config)#clock summer-time *zone* recurring [*week day month hh:mm week day month hh:mm* [*offset*]]

zone	Time zone name, such as PDT for Pacific Daylight Time, to be displayed when summer time is in effect
recurring	Summer time starts and ends on the corresponding specified days every year
week	Week of the month, 1 to 5 or last (Optional)
day	Day of the week (Sunday, Monday, and so on) (Optional)
month	Month (January, February, and so on) (Optional)
offset	Number of minutes to add during summer time (default is 60) (Optional)

The first *week day month hh:mm* is when daylight saving time starts, while the last one represents when it ends.

The following example specifies that summer time starts on the first Sunday in April at 2 A.M. and ends on the last Sunday in October at 2 A.M.:

```
Rtr1(config)# clock summer-time PDT recurring 1 Sunday April 2:00 last Sunday
October 2:00
```

For those areas that have a varying daylight saving time, it's possible to configure the exact date and time of the next summer time event by using either of the following global configuration **mode** commands. To avoid automatically switching to summer time, use the no form of this command.

Rtr1(config)#clock summer-time *zone* date *month date year hh:mm month date year hh:mm* [*offset*]

Rtr1(config)#no clock summer-time *zone* date *month date year hh:mm month date year hh:mm* [*offset*]

Rtr1(config)#clock summer-time *zone* date *date month year hh:mm date month year hh:mm* [*offset*]

Rtr1(config)#no clock summer-time *zone* date *date month year hh:mm date month year hh:mm* [*offset*]

date	Summer time starts on the first specific date listed in the command and ends on the second specific date in the command
date	Date of the month (1 to 31)
month	Text month (January, February, and so on) (Optional)
year	Four-digit year (1993 to 2035)
offset	Number of minutes to add during summer time (default is 60) (Optional)

In the following example, daylight saving time (summer time) for Pacific Daylight Time is configured to start on April 26, 1997 at 2 A.M. and end on October 12, 1997at 2 A.M. The **show clock** command with the Detail option displays the current settings:

```
Rtr1(config)#clock summer-time PDT date 26 Apr 2004 2:00 12 Oct 2004 2:00
Rtr1(config)#^Z
Rtr1#show clock detail
18:23:40.399 PST Thu Apr 15 2004
Time source is user configuration
Summer time starts 02:00:00 PST Mon Apr 26 2004
Summer time ends 02:00:00 PDT Tue Oct 12 2004
Rtr1#
```

Monitoring Time and Calendar Services To monitor clock, calendar, and NTP EXEC services, use the following commands in EXEC mode, as needed:

Rtr1#show calendar	Displays the current *hardware* clock time.
Rtr1#show clock [detail]	Displays the current *software* clock time.
Rtr1#show ntp associations [detail]	Displays the status of NTP associations.
Rtr1#show ntp status	Displays the status of NTP.

Step 2–3 Configure the Router Host Name and Domain Name

If the router's host name and domain name haven't been configured, it's necessary to configure them for CA support to work correctly. The host name is used in prompts and default configuration file names. The domain name is used to define a default domain name, which the Cisco IOS software uses to complete unqualified host names.

Use the global configuration **hostname** command to specify or modify the host name for the network server. The command syntax is as follows:

Rtr1(config)#hostname *host-name*

Use the global configuration **ip domain-name** command to define a default domain name that the Cisco IOS software uses to complete unqualified host names (names without a dotted-decimal domain name). To disable the default domain name, use the no form of this command. The command syntax is as follows:

Rtr1(config)#ip domain-name *dom-name*

The following example shows configuring a host name and default domain name:

```
Router(config)#hostname Rtr1
Rtr1(config)#ip domain-name ca-test.com
```

Name Resolution Alternative In a system without a DNS server, using the global configuration **ip host** command to define a static host name-to-address mapping is possible. Each host name can be associated with up to eight IP addresses separated by spaces. To remove the name-to-address mapping, use the no form of the command. The command syntax is as follows:

Rtr1(config)#ip host *name address1* [*address2...address8*]

The following example shows creating an IP Host entry to resolve the CA server name because it can't be resolved using DNS features:

Rtr1(config)#ip host ca-server 192.168.1.100

Step 2–4 Generate a RSA Key Pair

RSA signatures support two mutually exclusive types of RSA key pairs.

- General-purpose keys
- Special-usage keys

When generating RSA key pairs, you can indicate whether to generate general-purpose keys or special-usage keys. If the usage-keys keyword isn't specified in the **crypto key generate rsa** command, the general-purpose keys are generated.

General Purpose Keys With general purpose keys, only one pair of RSA keys is generated. The generated pair is used for any IKE policies specifying either RSA signatures or RSA-encrypted nonces. Therefore, a general purpose key pair might get used more frequently than a special usage-key pair, increasing the chances of compromise.

Special-Usage Keys If the *usage-keys* option is specified, two separate pairs of RSA keys are generated for signing and encryption. One pair is used with any IKE policy that includes RSA signatures as the authentication method. The other pair is used with any IKE policy that specifies RSA encrypted nonces as the authentication method. RSA encrypted nonces are covered in the "RSA Encrypted Nonces Overview" section.

If the security policy specifies to have both types of RSA authentication methods in the IKE policies, it would be best to generate special-usage keys. By using the special-usage keys, each key isn't unnecessarily exposed. Otherwise, the single key is used for both authentication methods, increasing that key's exposure.

Modulus Length The key generation process can be both a lengthy and resource-intensive process, depending on the router platform and the length of the key modulus specified. When generating RSA keys, the system will prompt for the number of bits to use in the modulus key. The default is 512 bits, with a range of choices from 360 to 2,048 bits. A longer modulus provides stronger security, but takes longer to generate and use. A modulus of less than 512 bits is generally considered too vulnerable. Under some circumstances, a short modulus might not function properly with IKE policies. Cisco recommends using a minimum modulus of 1,024 bits.

The following table compares the processing time for generating general-purpose key pairs with various-length modulus values.

Platform	360 bits	512 bits	1,024 bits	2,048 bits
Cisco 2500	11 seconds	20 seconds	4 minutes, 38 seconds	more than 1 hour
Cisco 4700	less than 1 second	1 second	4 seconds	50 seconds

The crypto key generate rsa command The global configuration **crypto key generate rsa** command is used to generate RSA key pairs for a Cisco device, such as a router. If the router already has RSA keys, a warning is displayed, along with a prompt to replace the existing keys with new keys. The command syntax is as follows:

Rtr1(config)#crypto key generate rsa [usage-keys]

usage-keys	Specifies two RSA special-usage key pairs should be generated (that is, one encryption pair and one signature pair), instead of one general-purpose key pair. (Optional)

NOTE If the host name and the IP domain name weren't created in Step 2–3, the **crypto key generate rsa** command will fail.

This command isn't saved in the router configuration. The keys generated are saved in the private configuration in NVRAM, however, which is never displayed to the user or backed up to another device.

The following example shows generating a special-usage key pair followed by the **show crypto key mypubkey rsa** command demonstrating the result:

```
Rtr1(config)#crypto key generate rsa usage-keys
The name for the keys will be: Rtr1.ca-test.com
Choose the size of the key modulus in the range of 360 to 2048 for your
  Signature Keys. Choosing a key modulus greater than 512 may take
  a few minutes.

How many bits in the modulus [512]: 2048
Generating RSA keys ...
[OK]

Rtr1(config)#^Z
```

```
Rtr1#show crypto key mypubkey rsa
% Key pair was generated at: 00:21:00 PST Dec 16 2004
Key name: Rtr1.ca-test.com
 Usage: Signature Key
 Key Data:
  30820122 300D0609 2A864886 F70D0101 01050003 82010F00 3082010A 02820101
  009407CE 65AF10C8 A8D0023F 4CF157FE C359B0BF B21D86C8 9415D8EB B62878AB
  C559AD80 B6B5FD2F F2D4DEAD B6181350 9F937A17 BD23F2C0 CA0759DF 2D51F12C
  B60B2E9F 4F0ECD86 4B3C2B7E 5E30A4E7 D1C47D22 6ADEF189 BB99197E BAA741FF
  6014E0D5 426F37A8 6722A920 93DCB02F 6D5D6670 D3E4DAD1 7ECC6DF2 02D52A45
  53B45062 BF1685BC DF042887 79349774 82BC82E6 CA276477 65645CF6 E78E350E
  0C259D9F 366FD38F B78D16E2 F48839D5 DBA0D138 99CD26C1 3333C03D 1BBBD5B4
  7509E413 38D25619 EB5C4138 4B539EDB B0080E40 5FC179BA B1A5A5EF 0CD1CC2C
  BB6D018A D3BA4CD9 8F502553 7FEFB1D0 070177C5 DBAC2EBE 19D9E1A2 052F2B44
  A5020301 0001
% Key pair was generated at: 00:25:16 PST Dec 16 2004
Key name: Rtr1.ca-test.com
 Usage: Encryption Key
 Key Data:
  30820122 300D0609 2A864886 F70D0101 01050003 82010F00 3082010A 02820101
  00C50963 248DD7E2 E21191E4 1AD6A0D7 2D8EF5E5 8952B071 1FF8C18E C6E5F53B
  37DBB9E2 52A3BD1B 9C02444B EABC0E85 96C9866B 164AE96F CD27F448 C1C93028
  5B8A024D 7939E533 66D0CC37 6F512BF9 1432E6EC 791DC05D 4059A552 17EF7326
  664DB438 847461E4 8ECBBEB0 622E0CA3 1EA97ECA DF9B5C8F 65A0D887 23CADB33
  6F3D3BA4 C1962E66 C7753335 A41D63AE 1DB69086 6A63AF1C F008B7FD 94F41240
  087150CA 1422730E 3D06F070 09F4C630 09F6B3A0 8838E2F7 9CEDC701 DCBB7D6E
  0178D788 5235DBE0 033681C8 23CF2134 2DDC4151 CF86152B 391F456A 74135B61
  EB15D797 CECE8493 FEC16D9C 47BE7410 D0EF2353 61A3C108 08325630 8519D89D
  07020301 0001
% Key pair was generated at: 00:25:22 PST Dec 16 2004
Key name: Rtr1.ca-test.com.server
 Usage: Encryption Key
 Key Data:
  307C300D 06092A86 4886F70D 01010105 00036B00 30680261 00B7ED8C E4C06C08
  C8DE36F5 DDEEEB78 A0F1FA0E 4C8CAC32 2B4AC0A4 B813F56F FEA8B7F7 5C372C66
  55A1189E 0A373898 846B0679 497F9474 29EB1088 E31ED19E 771C10C6 C35A98D0
  226AEDB3 FE42066A A81FD230 4FFCBCD0 0159D879 6F632FFA 1F020301 0001
Rtr1#
```

Step 2–5 Declare a CA

Use the global configuration **crypto ca identity** command to specify what CA the router will use. The CA might require a particular name, such as its domain name. Use the no form of this command to delete all identity information and certificates associated with the CA. The command syntax is as follows:

Rtr1(config)#crypto ca identity *name*

Rtr1(config)#no crypto ca identity *name*

If the CA has been previously declared and updating its characteristics is all that's required, just specify the name previously created. Performing the **crypto ca identity** command initiates the ca-identity Configuration mode, where CA characteristics can be defined, as shown in the following output:

```
Rtr1(config)#crypto ca identity ca-ipsec
Rtr1(ca-identity)#?
```

PART III

```
CA identity configuration commands:
  crl          CRL option
  default      Set a command to its defaults
  enrollment   Enrollment parameters
  exit         Exit from certificate authority identity entry mode
  no           Negate a command or set its defaults
  query        Query parameters

Rtr1(ca-identity)#
```

Some of the more common CA characteristics that can be defined in ca-identity Configuration mode include the following. Use the no form of the commands to remove the feature.

enrollment url	URL of the CA—required
enrollment mode ra	RA mode—required if the CA system supports a registration authority (RA).
query url	URL of the Lightweight Directory Access Protocol (LDAP) server—required if the CA supports an RA and the LDAP protocol.
enrollment retry period	Minutes the router will wait between sending certificate request retries. Range 0 to 60 minutes. Default is one minute. (Optional)
enrollment retry count	Number of certificate request retries the router will send before giving up. Range 1 to 100. Default is 0, which allows an infinite number of retries. (Optional)
crl optional	Specify whether the router can accept other peers' certificates if the certificate revocation list isn't accessible. Without this command, CRL checking is mandatory. (Optional)

The following is an example of the identity options that might be used with Verisign as the CA service provider. The choices and options vary with provider.

```
Rtr1(config)#crypto ca identity ca-ipsec
Rtr1(ca-identity)#enrollment url http://ca-ipsec.verisign.com/
Rtr1(ca-identity)#query url ldap://ca-ipsec.verisign.com/
Rtr1(ca-identity)#crl optional
Rtr1(ca-identity)#enrollment mode ra
Rtr1(ca-identity)#enrollment retry count 10
Rtr1(ca-identity)#enrollment retry period 5
Rtr1(ca-identity)#exit
Rtr1(config)#
```

The crypto ca identity is only significant locally. It needn't match the identity defined on any VPN peer.

Step 2–6 Authenticate the CA

The router needs to authenticate the validity of the CA by obtaining its self-signed certificate containing the CA's public key. Because the CA's certificate is self-signed, its public key should be manually authenticated by contacting the CA administrator.

If the CA support is using RA mode, the **enrollment mode ra** command in Step 2–5, then RA signing and encryption certificates will accompany the CA certificate.

To authenticate the certification authority (and RA, if appropriate), use the global configuration **crypto ca authenticate** command. Use the same name used to declare the CA with the **crypto ca identity** command:

Rtr1(config)#crypto ca authenticate *name*

If the CA doesn't respond within the timeout period defined in the **ca identity** commands, the command will fail. If this happens, you must reenter the command. The following show a representation of a successful CA authentication:

```
Rtr1(config)#crypto ca authenticate ca-ipsec
Certificate has the following attributes:
Fingerprint: 9876 5432 1098 7654 3210
Do you accept this certificate? [yes/no]
```

While the command isn't saved to the router configuration, the public keys embedded in the received CA (and RA) certificates are saved to the configuration as part of the RSA public key record called the "RSA public key chain."

Step 2–7 Request Your Own Certificate

The next step requires the local router to obtain its certificate from the CA using the global configuration **crypto ca enroll** command. Use the same name as when you declared the CA using the **crypto ca identity** command. Use the no form of this command to delete a current enrollment request:

Rtr1(config)#crypto ca enroll *name*

Rtr1(config)#no crypto ca enroll *name*

The router needs a signed certificate from the CA for each of the router's RSA key pairs. With a RSA general purpose key request in Step 2–4, this command will obtain one certificate corresponding to the general purpose RSA key pair. If the RSA key request was for special-usage keys, this command will return two certificates corresponding to each of the special-usage key pairs. This task is also known as *enrolling* with the CA.

If certificates already exist for each key pair, the command will fail and a prompt will appear, advising the existing certificates be removed first. Removing the existing certificates is accomplished with the **no certificate** command.

Responding to Prompts During the enrolling process with the CA, several prompts appear. The actual prompts can vary with the CA provider and over time. The following example is included as representative of what you can expect.

First, you must create and verify a challenge password. This *challenge password* is important because it's required if you ever need to revoke the router's certificate(s). The password can be up to 80 characters in length. This password isn't stored anywhere by the router, so you must remember it or secure it in a safe place. A lost password might not absolutely prevent revocation, but the CA administrator will undoubtedly require additional authentication of the router administrator identity.

Second, a prompt will ask for a subject name in the certificate. In the following example, the fully qualified domain name of the local device was used.

Third, a prompt will ask whether to include the router's serial number in the certificate. This is an internal board serial number rather than the one on the case. While the serial number isn't used by IPSec or the IKE process, it can be used by the CA to authenticate certificates or to associate a certificate with that particular router.

Fourth, a prompt will ask whether to include the router's IP address. This might not be a good idea in some cases because the IP address binds the certificate more tightly to a specific entity. If the router is moved, requiring a new IP address, then requesting a new certificate would also be necessary. If including the IP address is selected, a prompt will ask for the interface of the IP address. The interface should correspond to the interface to which the crypto map is applied.

The following example shows an RSA general-purpose key pair request for a certificate from the CA. Ultimately, the router displays the certificate fingerprint, at which time the local administrator verifies the fingerprint by calling the CA administrator. If the fingerprint is correct, the router administrator accepts the certificate.

A delay might occur between when the certificate request is sent and when the certificate is received by the router. The length of any delay depends on the CA authorization process.

```
Rtr1(config)#crypto ca enroll ca-ipsec
%
% Start certificate enrollment ..
% Create a challenge password. You will need to verbally provide this
password to the CA Administrator in order to revoke your certificate.
For security reasons your password will not be saved in the configuration.
Please make a note of it.
Password: ca-password
Re-enter password: ca-password
% The subject name in the certificate will be: rtr1.ca-test.com
% Include the router serial number in the subject name? [yes/no]: yes
% The serial number in the certificate will be: 01234567
% Include an IP address in the subject name [yes/no]? no
Interface: fastethernet 0
Request certificate from CA [yes/no]? yes
% Certificate request sent to Certificate Authority
% The certificate request fingerprint will be displayed.
% The 'show crypto ca certificate' command will also show the fingerprint.
Rtr1(config)#
```

At a later time, the router receives the certificate from the CA and displays a confirmation message, such as the following:

```
Rtr1(config)#Fingerprint: 1234 9876 5432 1098 7654
%CRYPTO-6-CERTRET: Certificate received from Certificate Authority
Rtr1(config)#
```

If the certificate request can't be granted for any reason, a message like the following is displayed at the router instead:

```
%CRYPTO-6-CERTREJ: Certificate enrollment request was rejected by
  Certificate Authority
```

Step 2–8 Save the Configuration

After completing the router configuration for CA support, the configuration should be saved using the **copy running-config startup-config** command.

Step 2–9 Monitor and Maintain CA Interoperability (Optional)

The following housekeeping measures are optional and will vary, based on the CA server requirements and operational circumstances:

- Request a CRL
- Delete your router's RSA keys
- Delete both public and private certificates from the configuration
- Delete peer's public keys

Request a CRL When the router receives a certificate from a peer, it will download a CRL from either the CA or from a CA-designated CRL distribution point. The router then looks for the certificate on the CRL to make sure it hasn't been revoked. The router won't accept the certificate and it won't authenticate the peer if the certificate appears on the CRL. A CRL can continue to be reused with other certificates until the CRL expires. If the router receives a certificate after the CRL has expired, it will download the latest CRL.

If the CA system supports RAs, multiple CRLs can exist. The certificate in question will indicate which CRL applies and should be downloaded by the router for authentication. If the router doesn't have or is unable to download the appropriate CRL, the certificate will normally be rejected. The exception to this would be if the router configuration contains the **crl optional** feature under the **crypto ca identity** command. With the **crl optional** command, the router will still try to get the required CRL, but failing that, it can accept the peer's certificate anyway. The router will continue to try to get the CRL.

If the CA server requires a local CRL, use the global configuration **crypto ca crl request** command to request an immediate download of the latest CRL. Use the same name used to declare the CA with the **crypto ca identity** command:

Rtr1(config)#crypto ca crl request *name*

An example for the chapter scenario would look like the following:

```
Rtr1(config)#crypto ca crl request ca-ipsec
```

Delete Router's RSA Keys While this could seem like a harsh step, it might be necessary to delete a router's RSA keys if you had reason to believe the RSA keys were compromised. This process can't be undone and all new key exchanges would have to wait until new RSA key requests could be processed.

Use the global configuration **crypto key zeroize rsa** command to delete all the router's RSA keys. The syntax and an example follow:

```
Rtr1(config)#crypto key zeroize rsa
```

Delete Both Public and Private Certificates from the Configuration The **crypto key zeroize rsa** command in the last step deletes all RSA keys generated by the router. In addition to this command, it would be necessary to perform two additional tasks:

- Request the CA administrator revoke the router's certificates at the CA. The challenge password created when the router's certificates were originally enrolled must be supplied.
- The router's certificates must be manually removed from the configuration using the **certificate** command in Certificate Chain Configuration mode. The syntax would be as follows:
  Rtr1(config-cert-chain)#no certificate certificate-serial-number

In the following example, the **show** command is used to determine the serial number(s) of the certificate to be deleted:

```
Rtr1#show crypto ca certificates
Certificate
  Subject Name
    Name: rtr1.ca-test.com
    IP Address: 10.0.1.21
  Status: Available
  Certificate Serial Number: 9876543210ABCDEF9876543210ABCDEF
  Key Usage: General Purpose

CA Certificate
  Status: Available
  Certificate Serial Number: 0192837465A0B1C2D3E4F50192837465A
  Key Usage: Not Set
Rtr1#config t
Rtr1(config)#crypto ca certificate chain ca-ipsec
Rtr1(config-cert-chain)#no certificate 0192837465A0B1C2D3E4F50192837465A
% Are you sure you want to remove the certificate [yes/no]? yes
% Be sure to ask the CA administrator to revoke this certificate.
Rtr1(config-cert-chain)#exit
Rtr1(config)#
```

To delete the CA's certificate, you must remove the entire CA identity, which also removes all certificates associated with the CA—the router's certificate, the CA certificate, and any RA certificates. Use the global configuration **no crypto ca identity** command to remove the CA identity. The syntax is

Rtr1(config)#no crypto ca identity *name*

The following example demonstrates using the **no crypto ca identity** command to remove the CA identity:

```
Rtr1(config)#no crypto ca identity ca-ipsec
% Removing an identity will destroy all certificates received from
```

```
 the related Certificate Authority.

Are you sure you want to do this? [yes/no]: y
% Be sure to ask the CA administrator to revoke your certificates.
Rtr1(config)#
```

Delete Peer's Public Keys If a peer's RSA public keys have been compromised, it could be necessary to delete the peer's public keys. Use the following commands to accomplish this task:

Rtr1(config)#crypto key pubkey-chain rsa

Rtr1(config-pubkey-chain)#no named-key key-name [encryption | signature]

or

Rtr1(config-pubkey-chain)#no addressed-key key-address [encryption | signature]

The global configuration **crypto key pubkey-chain rsa** command enters the Public Key Chain Configuration mode.

The choice of *named-key* or *addressed-key* depends on which keys were created originally. If only general purpose RSA keys were generated, don't use either of the encryption or signature keywords. If the IPSec remote peer generated special-usage keys resulting in two pairs of keys, then you must perform the appropriate command twice and use the encryption and signature keywords in turn. Similarly, using the encryption or signature keywords makes it possible to delete only one type of key.

Step 2–10 Verify the CA Support Configuration

The following commands can be used to verify any configured CA certificates:

- show crypto ca certificates
- show crypto key mypubkey rsa
- show crypto key pubkey-chain rsa

The show crypto ca certificates Command The **show crypto ca certificates** command is used to display the details of any CA certificates. The syntax reveals other interesting options:

Rtr1#show crypto ca [certificates | crls | roots]

```
Rtr1#show crypto ca certificates
Certificate
  Subject Name
    Name: rtr1.ca-test.com
    IP Address: 10.0.1.21
  Status: Available
  Certificate Serial Number: 9876543210ABCDEF9876543210ABCDEF
  Key Usage: General Purpose

CA Certificate
  Status: Available
```

```
  Certificate Serial Number: 0192837465A0B1C2D3E4F50192837465A
  Key Usage: Not Set
Rtr1#
```

The show crypto key mypubkey rsa Command Use the **show crypto key mypubkey rsa** EXEC command to view the RSA public keys associated with this router. The following output from the **show crypto key mypubkey rsa** command shows the results of RSA keys generated, using the **crypto key generate rsa usage-keys** command with a 2,048-bit modulus.

```
Rtr1#show crypto key mypubkey rsa
% Key pair was generated at: 00:21:00 PST Dec 16 2004
Key name: Rtr1.ca-test.com
 Usage: Signature Key
 Key Data:
  30820122 300D0609 2A864886 F70D0101 01050003 82010F00 3082010A 02820101
  009407CE 65AF10C8 A8D0023F 4CF157FE C359B0BF B21D86C8 9415D8EB B62878AB
  C559AD80 B6B5FD2F F2D4DEAD B6181350 9F937A17 BD23F2C0 CA0759DF 2D51F12C
  B60B2E9F 4F0ECD86 4B3C2B7E 5E30A4E7 D1C47D22 6ADEF189 BB99197E BAA741FF
  6014E0D5 426F37A8 6722A920 93DCB02F 6D5D6670 D3E4DAD1 7ECC6DF2 02D52A45
  53B45062 BF1685BC DF042887 79349774 82BC82E6 CA276477 65645CF6 E78E350E
  0C259D9F 366FD38F B78D16E2 F48839D5 DBA0D138 99CD26C1 3333C03D 1BBBD5B4
  7509E413 38D25619 EB5C4138 4B539EDB B0080E40 5FC179BA B1A5A5EF 0CD1CC2C
  BB6D018A D3BA4CD9 8F502553 7FEFB1D0 070177C5 DBAC2EBE 19D9E1A2 052F2B44
  A5020301 0001
% Key pair was generated at: 00:25:16 PST Dec 16 2004
Key name: Rtr1.ca-test.com
 Usage: Encryption Key
 Key Data:
  30820122 300D0609 2A864886 F70D0101 01050003 82010F00 3082010A 02820101
  00C50963 248DD7E2 E21191E4 1AD6A0D7 2D8EF5E5 8952B071 1FF8C18E C6E5F53B
  37DBB9E2 52A3BD1B 9C02444B EABC0E85 96C9866B 164AE96F CD27F448 C1C93028
  5B8A024D 7939E533 66D0CC37 6F512BF9 1432E6EC 791DC05D 4059A552 17EF7326
  664DB438 847461E4 8ECBBEB0 622E0CA3 1EA97ECA DF9B5C8F 65A0D887 23CADB33
  6F3D3BA4 C1962E66 C7753335 A41D63AE 1DB69086 6A63AF1C F008B7FD 94F41240
  087150CA 1422730E 3D06F070 09F4C630 09F6B3A0 8838E2F7 9CEDC701 DCBB7D6E
  0178D788 5235DBE0 033681C8 23CF2134 2DDC4151 CF86152B 391F456A 74135B61
  EB15D797 CECE8493 FEC16D9C 47BE7410 D0EF2353 61A3C108 08325630 8519D89D
  07020301 0001
% Key pair was generated at: 00:25:22 PST Dec 16 2004
Key name: Rtr1.ca-test.com.server
 Usage: Encryption Key
 Key Data:
  307C300D 06092A86 4886F70D 01010105 00036B00 30680261 00B7ED8C E4C06C08
  C8DE36F5 DDEEEB78 A0F1FA0E 4C8CAC32 2B4AC0A4 B813F56F FEA8B7F7 5C372C66
  55A1189E 0A373898 846B0679 497F9474 29EB1088 E31ED19E 771C10C6 C35A98D0
  226AEDB3 FE42066A A81FD230 4FFCBCD0 0159D879 6F632FFA 1F020301 0001
Rtr1#
```

The show crypto key pubkey-chain rsa Command Use the **show crypto key pubkey-chain rsa** EXEC command to view any peer RSA public keys stored on the router:

Rtr1#show crypto key pubkey-chain rsa [name *key-name* | address *key-address*]

name *key-name*	Name of the particular public key to view (Optional)
address *key-address*	Address of the particular public key to view (Optional)

The following is sample output from the **show crypto key pubkey-chain rsa** command:

```
Rtr1#show crypto key pubkey-chain rsa
Codes: M - Manually configured, C - Extracted from certificate
Code   Usage         IP-Address     Name
M      Signature     10.0.1.21      rtr1.ca-test.com
M      Encryption    10.0.1.21      rtr1.ca-test.com
C      Signature     10.0.50.2      rtr2.ca-test.com
C      Encryption    10.0.50.2      rtr2.ca-test.com
```

Task 3—Configure IKE

Task 3 is configuring IKE parameters determined in Task 2. The steps required are identical to configuring preshared keys in Chapter 10, except for setting the authentication method parameter in Step 2. Configuring IKE consists of the following steps and commands:

- Step 3–1 Enable or disable IKE

  crypto isakmp enable
- Step 3–2 Create IKE policies

  crypto isakmp policy

  authentication

  encryption

  hash

  group

  lifetime
- Step 3–3 Set the IKE identity to address or host name

  crypto isakmp identity
- Step 3–4 Verify the IKE configuration

  show crypto isakmp policy

  show crypto isakmp sa

Step 3–2 Create IKE Policies

Now, it's time to define a suite of ISAKMP (IKE) policy details gathered during the planning task, Task 1 Step 2 (repeated in the following with the defaults in italics). The goal is to create a suite of IKE policies, so it's possible to establish IKE peering between two IPSec endpoints.

Parameter	Preferred (stronger)	2nd Choice	3rd Choice
Encryption algorithm	3des	*des*	*des*
Hash algorithm	*sha*	*sha*	md5
Authentication method	*rsa-sig*	*rsa-sig*	*rsa-sig*
DH key exchange group	2	2	*1*
IKE SA lifetime	43,200	43,200	*86,400*

Using the scenario example, Rtr2 only needing to connect to Rtr1, might be configured with only the preferred (most secure) set of parameters because that set will also be on Rtr1. On the other hand, Rtr1, needing to peer with various devices both domestically and internationally, might need multiple policies to accommodate the different peers. The policies are configured using priority numbers, so the preferred policy is evaluated by the peer first, and then by the second and third choices. This ensures the agreed policy will always be the highest mutually agreeable choice.

The crypto isakmp policy Command Use the global **crypto isakmp policy** command to define an IKE policy containing a set of parameters used during IKE negotiation. Use the no form of this command to delete an IKE policy. The command syntax and example are as follows:

Rtr1(config)#[no] crypto isakmp policy *priority*

Rtr1(config)#crypto isakmp policy 100

Rtr1(config-isakmp)#

priority	Unique identifier for the IKE policy used to order, or prioritize, the policies. Acceptable range 1 to 10,000, with 1 being the highest possible priority.

This command invokes the ISAKMP Policy Configuration (config-isakmp) mode, which allows the six IKE parameters to be defined. The no form of each parameter removes that setting. Exit is used to end the session and any undefined parameters will use the default values. The actual choices are based on the table made in Task 1 Step 2. The following shows the syntax for each parameter, followed by the entries for the preferred policy.

```
Rtr1#conf t
Rtr1(config)#crypto isakmp policy 100
Rtr1(config-isakmp)#authentication {pre-share | rsa-encr | rsa-sig}
Rtr1(config-isakmp)#encryption {des | 3des}  (depending on feature set)
Rtr1(config-isakmp)#hash {md5 | sha}
Rtr1(config-isakmp)#group {1 | 2}
Rtr1(config-isakmp)#lifetime <60 to 86400 seconds>

Rtr1(config)#crypto isakmp policy 100
Rtr1(config-isakmp)#authentication rsa-sig
Rtr1(config-isakmp)#encryption 3des
Rtr1(config-isakmp)#hash sha
Rtr1(config-isakmp)#group 2
Rtr1(config-isakmp)#lifetime 43200
Rtr1(config-isakmp)#exit
```

Because the preferred policy was assigned 100 as a priority, the second and third choices must be progressively larger to control the order in which they're offered to a peer. A possible choice might be 200 and 300, respectively, allowing newer policies to be assigned priorities that would allow them to be prioritized according to changes in the company security policy.

The following shows the steps to configuring the second and third preference, taking advantage of default values to save configuration:

```
Rtr1#conf t
Rtr1(config)#crypto isakmp policy 200
Rtr1(config-isakmp)#group 2
Rtr1(config-isakmp)#lifetime 43200
Rtr1(config-isakmp)#crypto isakmp policy 300
Rtr1(config-isakmp)#hash md5
Rtr1(config-isakmp)#exit
```

Step 3–3 Set the IKE Identity to Address or Host Name

Use the global **crypto isakmp identity** command to set the ISAKMP identity of the remote peer to be used during IKE negotiations. The IKE identity can either be the device IP address or the host name. The router IOS defaults to the IP address and doesn't add a line to the configuration, unless the host name option is used.

To use the host name identity method, use the global **crypto isakmp identity** command. The no form of this command resets the default value (address). The command syntax is as follows:

Rtr1(config)#[no] crypto isakmp identity {address | hostname}

Rtr1(config)#crypto isakmp identity hostname

Using the host name identity method makes the most sense if a DNS server is available on the network to resolve the name. If not, the following example shows using an **IP Host** command entry on the router to handle the name resolution:

```
Rtr1(config)#ip host Rtr2.domain.com 10.0.50.2
```

Task 4—Configure IPSec

Task 4 is configuring Cisco IOS IPSec to the IPSec parameters developed in Task 1. The steps are identical to those used to configure preshared keys in Chapter 10. The steps and commands used to configure IPSec encryption on Cisco routers are summarized as follows:

- Step 4–1 Configure transform set suites

  crypto ipsec transform-set
- Step 4–2 Configure global IPSec security association lifetimes

  crypto ipsec security-association lifetime
- Step 4–3 Configure crypto ACLs

  access-list
- Step 4–4 Configure crypto maps

  crypto map
- Step 4–5 Apply the crypto maps to the interface

  interface

  crypto map

Task 5—Test and Verify IPSec

Cisco IOS software contains a number of **show**, **clear**, and **debug** commands useful for testing and verifying IPSec and ISAKMP. While many of these commands are used the same as when configuring preshared keys, Step 5–7 introduces two debug options that are unique to RSA signatures. To test and verify that Cisco IOS IPSec VPN is correctly configured, use the following commands:

- Step 5–1 Display the configured IKE policies
  show crypto isakmp policy
- Step 5–2 Display the configured transform sets
  show crypto ipsec transform set
- Step 5–3 Display the current state of the IPSec SAs
  show crypto ipsec sa
- Step 5–4 Display the configured crypto maps
  show crypto map
- Step 5–5 Debug IKE events
  debug crypto isakmp
- Step 5–6 Debug IPSec events
  debug crypto ipsec
- Step 5–7 Debug CA events
  debug crypto key-exchange
  debug crypto pki commands

RSA Encrypted Nonces Overview

The *RSA-encrypted nonces authentication method* uses the RSA-encryption public key cryptography algorithm. This technology requires each party to generate a pseudorandom number (a nonce) and encrypt it (and possibly other publicly and privately available information), using the other party's RSA public key. Authentication occurs when each party decrypts the other party's nonce with their local private key, and then uses the decrypted nonce to compute a keyed hash.

The major drawback to implementing this technology is it's somewhat difficult to configure and, therefore, more difficult to scale to a large number of VPN peers. RSA-encrypted nonces require peers to possess each other's public keys, but they don't use a CA. Two methods can be used for peers to get each others' public keys:

- Manually configure and exchange RSA keys
- Use the RSA signatures used previously during a successful ISAKMP negotiation with the remote peer

Another potential drawback to this authentication method is this: either side of the exchange can plausibly deny they took part in the exchange. Cisco IOS software is

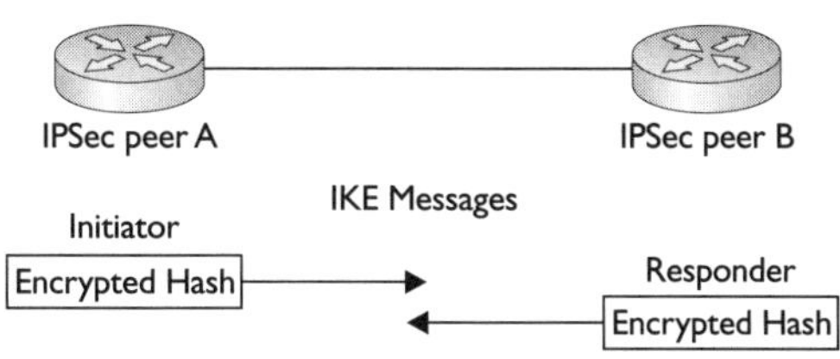

Figure 11-6 RSA-encryption authentication exchange

the only Cisco product that supports this authentication method. Figure 11-6 shows a RSA-encryption authentication exchange.

This section provides a short overview of configuring IPSec using RSA-encrypted nonces. Only those tasks and steps that are unique to RSA-encrypted nonces are presented. Configuring RSA encryption is similar to preshared keys and CA support. It's introduced using the same outline with commands introduced when those technologies were covered in Chapter 10 and earlier in this chapter. The following are the major tasks for configuring RSA-encrypted nonces:

- Task 1 Prepare for IKE and IPSec
- Task 2 Configure RSA keys manually
- Task 3 Configure IKE for IPSec to select RSA encryption
- Task 4 Configure IPSec (typically, the same as preshare keys)
- Task 5 Test and verify IPSec

Task 2—Configure RSA Keys

The steps and commands used in Task 2 are included in the following items. While this display is intended to demonstrate the similarities to technologies already covered, a thorough coverage of the tasks and steps to configure RSA-encrypted nonces can be found in the Cisco IOS Security Configuration Guide online.

Configuring RSA keys involves the following six steps:

- Step 2–1 Plan for RSA keys.
- Step 2–2 Configure the router's host name and domain name.

  hostname

  ip domain-name
- Step 2–3 Generate the RSA keys.

  crypto key generate rsa usage-keys
- Step 2–4 Enter peer RSA public keys.

  crypto key pubkey-chain rsa

  addressed-key *ip-addr*

  named-key *name*

- Step 2–5 Verify the key configuration.

  show crypto key mypubkey rsa

  show crypto key pubkey-chain rsa
- Step 2–6 Manage RSA keys—Remove old keys.

  crypto key zeroize rsa

Chapter Review

This chapter looked at steps involved in configuring IPSec for CA support. The steps and related commands are summarized in the following task list:

Task 1 Prepare for IKE and IPSec

- Step 1–1 Plan for CA support
- Step 1–2 Determine the IKE (IKE phase one) policies
- Step 1–3 Determine the IPSec (IKE phase two) policies
- Step 1–4 Check the current configuration

  show running-configuration

  show isakmp [policy]

  show crypto map
- Step 1–5 Ensure the network works without encryption

  ping
- Step 1–6 Ensure access control lists are compatible with IPSec

  show access-lists

Task 2 Configure CA support

- Step 2–1 Manage the NVRAM memory usage (Optional)

  crypto ca certificate query
- Step 2–2 Set the router's time and date

  ntp broadcast client

  sntp broadcast client

  clock set
- Step 2–3 Configure the router's host name and domain name

  hostname

  ip domain-name

  ip host
- Step 2–4 Generate an RSA key pair

  crypto key generate rsa

- Step 2-5 Declare a CA
  crypto ca identity
  enrollment url
  query url
  crl optional
  enrollment mode ra
  enrollment retry count
  enrollment retry period
- Step 2-6 Authenticate the CA
  crypto ca authenticate
- Step 2-7 Request your own certificate
  crypto ca enroll
- Step 2-8 Save the configuration
  copy running-config startup-config
- Step 2-9 Monitor and maintain CA interoperability (Optional)
  Request a CRL
  crypto ca crl request
  Delete your router's RSA keys:
    crypto key zeroize rsa
  Delete both public and private certificates from the configuration:
    no certificate certificate-serial-number
    no crypto ca identity
  Delete peer's public keys:
    no named-key key-name
    no addressed-key key-address
- Step 2-10 Verify the CA support configuration
  show crypto ca certificates
  show crypto key mypubkey rsa
  show crypto key pubkey-chain rsa

Task 3 Configure IKE

- Step 3-1 Enable or disable IKE
  crypto isakmp enable
- Step 3-2 Create IKE policies
  crypto isakmp policy

PART III

authentication

encryption

hash

group

lifetime

- Step 3–3 Configure preshared keys

  crypto isakmp key

- Step 3–4 Verify the IKE configuration

  show crypto isakmp policy

Task 4 Configure IPSec

- Step 4–1 Configure transform set suites

  crypto ipsec transform-set

- Step 4–2 Configure global IPSec security association lifetimes

  crypto ipsec security-association lifetime

- Step 4–3 Configure crypto ACLs

  access-list

- Step 4–4 Configure crypto maps

  crypto map

- Step 4–5 Apply the crypto maps to the interface

  interface

  crypto map

Task 5 Test and verify IPSec

- Step 5–1 Display the configured IKE policies

  show crypto isakmp policy

- Step 5–2 Display the configured transform sets

  show crypto ipsec transform set

- Step 5–3 Display the current state of the IPSec SAs

  show crypto ipsec sa

- Step 5–4 Display the configured crypto maps

  show crypto map

- Step 5–5 Debug IKE events

  debug crypto isakmp

- Step 5–6 Debug IPSec events

  debug crypto ipsec

Questions

1. A digital certificate is conceptually most like which type of document?
   A. Event admission ticket
   B. Vehicle license plate
   C. Passport
   D. Social Security card
2. Which of the following is *not* a common name for a database service running on an existing or dedicated server that allows users to submit and retrieve digital certificates?
   A. Certificate server
   B. CRL
   C. Cert server
   D. Key server
3. What does the acronym PKI stand for?
   A. PIX Key Interchange
   B. Private Key Interchange
   C. Public Key Infrastructures
   D. PIX Key Interface
4. Digital certificates are generated by which of the following?
   A. Sending peer
   B. Certificate authority
   C. Receiving peer
   D. The government
5. When checking a certificate against a CRL, what happens if a match occurs?
   A. The certificate is accepted
   B. A new CRL is requested
   C. The certificate is rejected
   D. The request is sent to the CA
6. Which of the following is a server that acts as a proxy for the CA, so CA functions can continue when the CA is offline or otherwise unavailable?
   A. CRL
   B. CAR
   C. CA
   D. RA

7. Which of the following is an initiative for furthering open development for certificate-handling protocols that can help ensure interoperability with devices from many vendors?

   A. PKI

   B. CA

   C. LDAP

   D. SCEP

8. Which of the following is *not* a CA provider supported by the Cisco IOS?

   A. Entrust Technologies, Inc.

   B. Symantic

   C. VeriSign

   D. Microsoft

9. Which is the IKE keyword for CA support authentication method?

   A. rsa-sig

   B. pki

   C. rsa-encr

   D. preshare

10. Which command specifies that certificates and CRLs should *not* be stored locally, but should be retrieved from the CA as needed?

    A. **no ntp peer ip-address**

    B. **crypto key generate rsa**

    C. **crypto ca identity**

    D. **crypto ca certificate query**

11. In the following command, what does the word "six" represent?

    ```
    Rtr1(config)#clock timezone CST -6
    ```

    A. The number six is a sequence number

    B. Six hours behind NY standard time

    C. Six hours behind UTC/GMT

    D. Six hours ahead of UTC/GMT

12. Given the following command, how many RSA key pairs will be generated?

    ```
    Rtr1(config)#crypto key generate rsa usage-keys
    ```

    A. 1

    B. 2

    C. 3

    D. 4

13. Which command is used to define the CA?
    A. **crypto ca enroll**
    B. crypto **ca identity**
    C. **crypto ca authenticate**
    D. **crypto key zeroize rsa**
14. Which command removes all certificates associated with the CA—the router's certificate, the CA certificate, and any RA certificates?
    A. **no named-key key-name**
    B. **no crypto ca identity**
    C. **crypto key zeroize rsa**
    D. **no certificate**
15. Which of the following is *not* required for CA support on Cisco IOS devices?
    A. Hostname defined
    B. Special-usage keys ordered
    C. Domain name defined
    D. Software clock set

Answers

1. C. Passport
2. B. CRL
3. C. Public Key Infrastructures
4. B. Certificate authority
5. C. The certificate is rejected—it has been revoked
6. D. RA
7. D. SCEP—Simple Certificate Enrollment Protocol
8. B. Symantic
9. A. rsa-sig
10. D. **crypto ca certificate query**
11. C. Six hours behind UTC/GMT
12. B. 2
13. B. **crypto ca identity**
14. B. **no crypto ca identity**
15. B. Special-usage keys ordered

CHAPTER 12

Cisco IOS Remote Access Using Cisco Easy VPN

In this chapter, you will learn to:

- Understand the Cisco Easy VPN
- Use the Cisco Easy VPN server
- Use the Cisco Easy VPN Remote
- Make use of the Cisco VPN 3.6 Client
- Do easy VPN server configuration tasks
- Preconfigure the Cisco VPN 3.6 client
- Understand the new Management Center for VPN routers
- Use the easy VPN Remote Phase Two
- Know about the Cisco VPN Firewall feature for VPN Client

This chapter looks at the Cisco VPN Client software as part of the Cisco Easy VPN strategy to deliver easy to use, reliable VPN connectivity. Many features require supporting configuration in an IOS router, a PIX Firewall, or a Cisco VPN Concentrator. That specific configuration was addressed in Chapters 10 and 11.

Introduction to Cisco Easy VPN

Cisco Easy VPN is a component of the Cisco Unified Client Framework, in which VPN management is centralized across all Cisco VPN devices. This strategy simplifies VPN deployment for remote offices and telecommuters, reduces deployment complexity, and conserves human resources. The Cisco Easy VPN strategy incorporates all VPN platforms, including VPN software client, VPN 3002 hardware client, Cisco routers, Cisco PIX Firewalls, and Cisco VPN 3000 Concentrators.

The Cisco Easy VPN strategy is comprised of two types of implementations:

- Cisco Easy VPN Server
- Cisco Easy VPN Remote

Cisco Easy VPN Server

The *Cisco Easy VPN Server service* allows a growing number of Cisco IOS routers, PIX Firewalls, and Cisco VPN 3000 Concentrators to act as VPN head-end devices in site-to-site or remote access VPNs. These head-end devices provide the VPN connections, as well as a configuration source for the Cisco Easy VPN Remote sites. The Cisco Easy VPN Server is available on numerous Cisco VPN routers, including Cisco UBR900, 1700, 2600, 3600, 7100, 7200, and 7500 series routers running Cisco IOS Release 12.2(8)T, Cisco PIX Firewalls, and all Cisco VPN 3000 Concentrators. Use the Cisco online documentation to verify any new platforms supported because new supported platforms have been added with each new release.

Basic feature configuration and security policies defined on the head-end device are pushed to the remote VPN site before the connection is established. This insures those connections have current configurations and policies in place. In the case of the VPN 3002 Hardware Device, firmware updates can be maintained using the same feature.

Cisco Easy VPN Server-enabled devices can provide VPN tunnel termination for mobile remote workers running Cisco VPN client software, allowing them to access the headquarters' intranet.

Some of the benefits of the Cisco Easy VPN Server implementation for rolling out remote VPN connections include the following:

- Centrally stored configurations allow dynamic configuration of end-user VPN connections and require less manual configuration by end users and field technicians, reducing errors and additional service calls.
- VPN security policy management can be centralized.
- Supports large-scale, rapid deployments with minimal remote user provisioning.
- When used with a remote VPN device, such as a router, firewall, or VPN hardware client, this eliminates the need for end-user VPN devices or client software.

Client Connection Process

In general terms, an Easy VPN Remote device or a VPN Software Client version 3.x/4.x initiates a connection with a Cisco router configured as a Easy VPN Server. During the connection establishment the exchange includes device authentication via IKE, user authentication via IKE Extended Authentication (Xauth), VPN policies that are pushed down to the client, and then the IPSec SA is established.

The following is a more detailed look at the client/server session establishment.

1. The client initiates IKE Phase One exchange. If a preshared key is to be used for authentication, the exchange is initiated via IKE Aggressive mode. In this case, the group name entered while configuring the client with the web application is used to identify the group profile. If digital certificates are used, the exchange will be via IKE Main mode and the organizational unit field of a distinguished name will be used to identify the appropriate group profile.

2. The client attempts to negotiate an IKE SA with the Easy VPN Server. To reduce client configuration policies weren't defined, so all supported combinations of encryption and hash algorithms for authentication, plus supported Diffie-Hellman (DH) group sizes, are proposed.
   The Easy VPN Server Device accepts the first proposal received that matches its configured policies. Assuming a policy match is achieved, device authentication is completed and user authentication can begin.
3. If the Easy VPN Server is configured for Xauth, the server issues a user name/password challenge to the client. The resulting entries are verified against using AAA supported protocols, such as TACACS+, RADIUS, or one-time password token cards using AAA proxy. This step is particularly important if the peer is a remote client or a remote device is configured as a remote client.
4. The system parameters are pushed from the server to the client. These parameters can be configured to include an IP address (required) and the following optional information: DNS address(es), domain name, WINS address(es), local NAT pool name, access list, split tunnel attributes, and so forth. The access list defines the traffic to be protected through the VPN tunnel.
5. The Easy VPN Server can use reverse route injection (RRI) to create static routes and inject them into any dynamic routing protocols for distribution to surrounding devices. With dynamic crypto maps, a static route is created for each subnet or host protected by the remote peer when the peer establishes its IPSec security association. With *static crypto maps,* a static route is created for each destination using an extended access-list rule.
6. Once all parameters are transferred to the client, IKE Phase Two Quick mode is used to negotiate IPSec SAs to complete the connection.

PART III

Cisco Easy VPN Remote

The Cisco Easy VPN Remote provides a remote VPN client feature, which is currently supported on the following platforms: Cisco 800, 1700, and UBR900 Series Routers, Cisco PIX 501 Firewalls, and Cisco VPN 3002 Hardware Client device. As with all new technologies, the Cisco online documentation includes any new platforms supported.

The Cisco Easy VPN Remote feature eliminates much of the basic VPN configuration by implementing Cisco's Unity Client protocol, which allows most VPN parameters to be defined at a VPN remote access server. These basic configuration and security policies are "pushed" down from the Cisco Easy VPN Server during the initial connection. Configuration changes, software upgrades, and, in some cases, firmware updates can also be pushed down to the remote site. This can reduce local VPN configuration requirements and ongoing VPN support at the remote location.

The Cisco Easy VPN Remote feature allows for "push" configuration and automatic management of the following details:

- Managing security keys for encryption and decryption.
- Negotiating tunnel parameters, including IP addresses, algorithms, lifetime, and so forth.

- Establishing tunnels according to the defined security parameters.
- Enabling and configuring NAT/PAT translation, plus any related access lists.
- User authentication based on user names, group names, and passwords, as well as X.509 digital certificates.
- Authenticating, encrypting, and decrypting data through the tunnel.

The Cisco Easy VPN Remote feature supports the following two modes of operation:

Client	The private hosts protected behind the Easy VPN Remote device are a separate network that remains invisible and nonroutable to the central site. The local hosts are assigned their IP addresses from the Easy VPN Remote device DHCP server feature. The Cisco Easy VPN Remote feature automatically configures the NAT/PAT translation and any required access lists to implement the VPN tunnel. Because all traffic to the central network has the Public interface IP address, PAT both supplies and manages unique port number mappings to use in combination with the IP address.
Network Extension	The Cisco Easy VPN Remote device establishes a secure site-to-site connection with the central site device. PAT isn't used, allowing the client hosts to have direct access to the hosts on the corporate network. The local stations behind the VPN Remote device are fully routable and the local network is visible to the central site. As the name implies, the local network becomes a part of the organization's intranet.

Split Tunneling

Split tunneling is a useful feature that provides the capability to have a secure tunnel to the central site, while simultaneously maintaining a Cleartext connection to the Internet through the Internet service provider (ISP). The Cisco Easy VPN Remote device uses PAT to protect the local workstations during split tunneling to the Internet. Figure 12-1 shows secure a VPN tunnel and split tunneling for web browsing.

If the organization security policy prohibits split tunneling, it can be blocked by creating a policy on the central site device, which is then pushed down to the remote device.

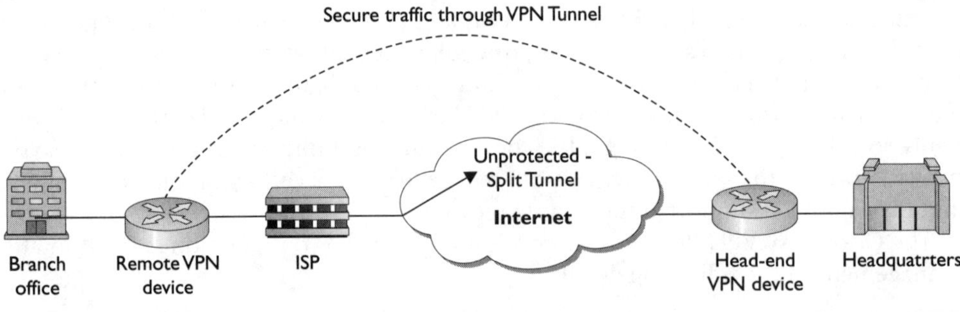

Figure 12-1 A secure VPN tunnel and split tunneling for web browsing

Cisco VPN 3.6 Client

The VPN Client is a thin design software program, which is easy to deploy and operate providing secure, end-to-end encrypted tunnels. The client software is available from the Cisco web site for use with any Cisco central site VPN product and is included free of charge with any Cisco VPN 3000 Series Concentrator.

The client software can be preconfigured for large, rapid deployments that require little end-user intervention. VPN access policies and configurations are downloaded and updated using push technology from the central VPN head-end device when a connection is established. This centralized push technology makes deployment and management quite simple, as well as highly scalable.

The Cisco VPN Client software is available in versions to support most Windows versions, Sun Solaris (UltraSparc 32 and 64 bit) UNIX, Linux (Intel), as well as Mac OS X 10.1 and 10.2 (Jaguar).

The Cisco VPN Client software, regardless of the host operating system (OS), is compatible with the following Cisco products:

- Cisco IOS Software Releases 12.2 T and later
- Cisco PIX Firewall Software Version 6.0 and later
- Cisco VPN 3000 Series Concentrator with Software Version 3.0 and later

How the VPN Client Works

The VPN Client works with a central Cisco VPN device to create a secure tunnel connection between the host computer and the corporate network. VPN Client uses Internet Key Exchange (IKE) and Internet Protocol Security (IPSec) tunneling protocols to make and manage the secure connection. Some of the steps include the following:

- Negotiating tunnel parameters, such as IP addresses, algorithms, lifetime, and so on.
- Establishing tunnels according to the defined parameters.
- Authenticating users based on user names, group names, passwords, and X.509 digital certificates.
- Establishing user access rights, including hours of access, connection time, allowed destinations, allowed protocols, and so forth.
- Managing security keys for encryption and decryption.
- Authenticating, encrypting, and decrypting data through the tunnel.

Connection Technologies

The VPN Client supports each of the following technologies for connecting to the Internet and, thereby, accessing the destination VPN endpoint.

- Plain Old Telephone Service (POTS)

- Integrated Services Digital Network (ISDN)
- Cable/modem
- Digital Subscriber Line (DSL)
- LAN connection

Easy VPN Server Configuration Tasks

The specific commands to configure the Easy VPN Server features vary, depending on the hardware platform. Other command options, such as the Auto Upgrade feature, apply to VPN Hardware Client devices only. Examples of the type of configuration tasks that need to be implemented on the VPN Server to support Easy VPN Clients include the following. The first three are required, while all others are optional.

- Enabling Policy Lookup via AAA (required)
- Defining Group Policy Information for Mode Configuration Push (required)
- Applying Mode Configuration and Xauth (required)
- Enabling Reverse Route Injection for the Client (optional)
- Enabling IKE Dead Peer Detection (optional)
- Configuring RADIUS Server Support (optional)
- Verifying Easy VPN Server (optional)

In addition, the Easy VPN Server feature enables Cisco IOS routers to push new and/or enhanced VPN policy parameters to any remote access Easy VPN client (hardware or software). This feature adds support for the following functions:

- Mode Configuration Version 6 Support—based on an IETF draft submission.
- Xauth Version 6 Support—based on an IETF draft submission.
- IKE Dead Peer Detection (DPD) —a new keepalive scheme.
- Split Tunneling Control—enables clients to have intranet and Internet access at the same time, without requiring Internet access to use the VPN tunnel.
- Initial Contact—to facilitate reestablishing lost connections.
- Group-Based Policy Control—Policy attributes, such as IP addresses, DNS, and split tunnel access can be enabled on a per-group or per-user basis.

Preconfiguring the Cisco VPN 3.6 Client

To use the VPN Client, at least one connection entry must be configured to define the following information:

- The Cisco VPN Remote Server to connect to.

- Preshared keys—The IPSec group to which the system administrator assigned the client. The group determines the level and type of access that will be available once connected. The group membership could define the user authentication method used, the hours the client can access the network, if and how many simultaneous logins are allowed, and even the IKE and IPSec algorithms the VPN Client will use.
- Certificates—The name of the certificate being used for authentication (if used).
- Optional parameters.

You can create multiple connection entries so the VPN Client software can be used to connect to multiple networks, although not at the same time.

Creating a New Connection Entry

Because the order of the following steps is important, we'll view this as if it were a lab exercise. While it isn't difficult, if the end user is going to do the initial configuration, the network administrator should furnish the information in written form with at least minimal instructions.

1. Start the VPN Client by choosing Start | Programs | Cisco Systems VPN Client | VPN Dialer from the Start button menu. Figure 12-2 shows the menu sequence.
2. The VPN Dialer application starts and displays the Cisco Systems VPN Client, as shown in Figure 12-3.

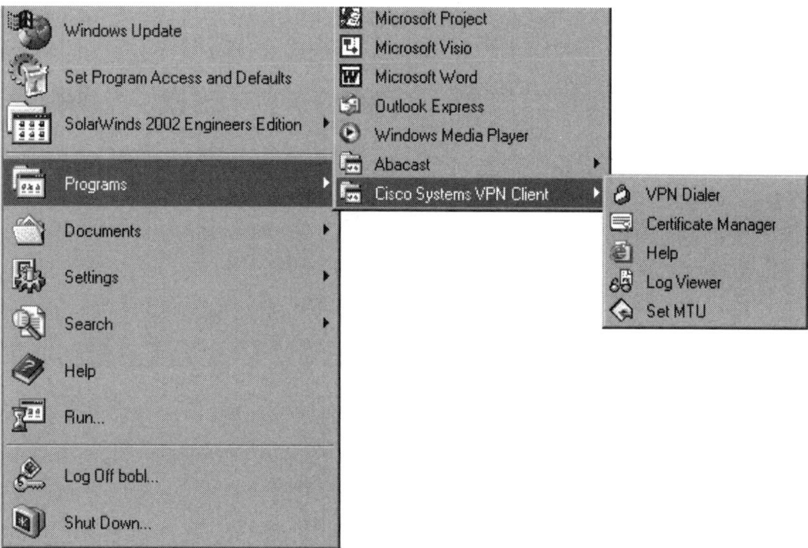

Figure 12-2 Starting the Cisco VPN Client software

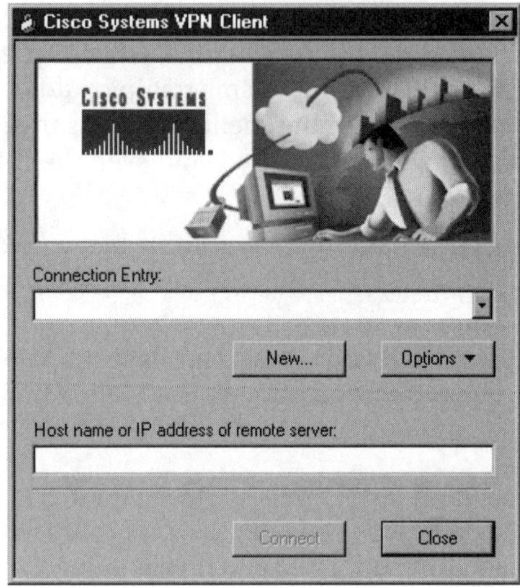

Figure 12-3 Cisco Systems VPN Client opening dialog box

3. On the Cisco Systems VPN Client main dialog box, click the NEW button. The first New Connection Entry Wizard dialog box appears, as shown in Figure 12-4.
4. Each connection on a host machine must have a unique name. The same name can be used for all users in a group who don't share a computer. If the users are configuring this unique name, the name and description might be defined by the network administrator to reduce any possible user doubt.
   Both the name and description can contain spaces and neither is case-sensitive. When the entries are complete, click the NEXT button.

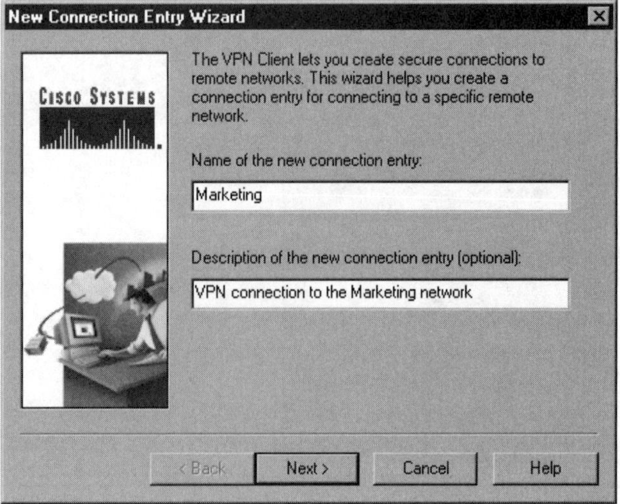

Figure 12-4 Define connection name and description

5. The next dialog box appears asking for host name or IP address of the server. This is the VPN head-end device to which the client will be connecting. Depending on the network, this could be either an IP address or a host name. The network administrator will furnish the proper form. This needs to be typed in exactly. Figure 12-5 shows an example of using an IP address to define a VPN device.
6. After typing the host name or IP address of the remote VPN device, click the NEXT button.
   The third New Connection Entry Wizard dialog box appears, asking for either the group information supplied by the network administrator or the digital certificate to be used to authenticate this client.
   Figure 12-6 shows an example of choosing group authentication. Notice the group name is displayed in Cleartext, but the passwords are masked for security. What isn't so obvious is that all three entries are case-sensitive. When the entries are complete, click the NEXT button.
7. Figure 12-7 shows the fourth and final New Connection Entry Wizard dialog box. The BACK button can be used to change earlier entries or the FINISH button can complete the process.
   When the final dialog box closes, the new connection entry now appears in the Connection Entry drop-down list on the VPN Client's main dialog box.

Trying Out the New Connection

Use the following steps to Start the VPN Dialer:

1. Start the VPN Client just as before.
   The VPN Dialer displays the Cisco Systems VPN Client main dialog box with the connection information from the earlier steps, as shown in Figure 12-8. If multiple connections were created, the Connection Entry: drop-down list would be used to choose the desired connection entry.

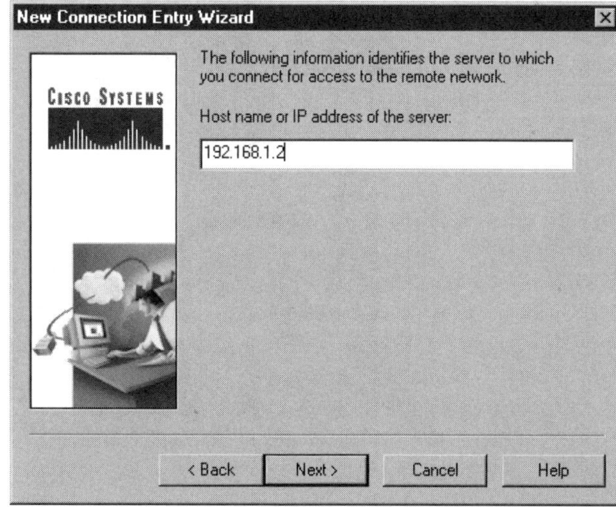

Figure 12-5 Using an IP address to define a VPN head-end device

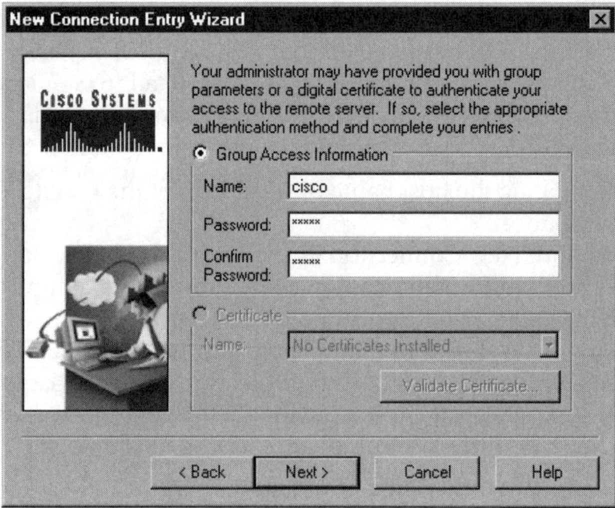

Figure 12-6 Entering the IPSec group and password

2. Clicking the CONNECT button starts the connection.
   Figure 12-9 shows the connection progress dialog box.
3. The remaining screens will vary, depending on the authentication system used to verify the user. Figure 12-10 displays a Windows-type login screen.

Customizing the Connection

Figure 12-11 shows how to customize the connection and the available options. From copying (cloning) the connection settings, to deleting it, to launching third-party

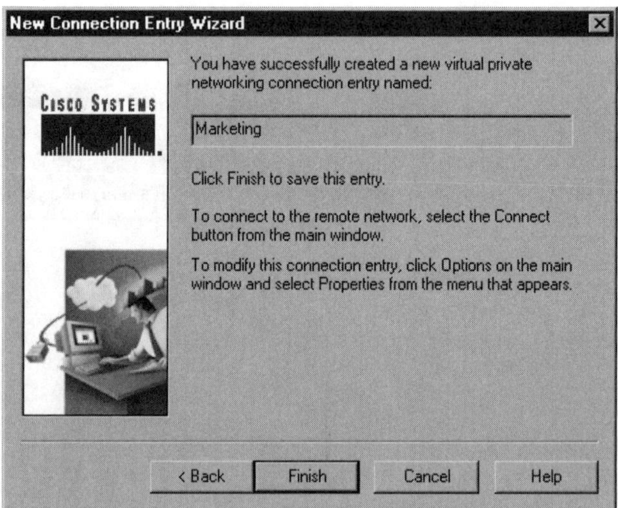

Figure 12-7 Final New Connection Entry Wizard dialog box

Cisco Systems VPN Client
Cisco Systems
Connection Entry:
Marketing
New...
Options
Host name or IP address of remote server:
192.168.1.2
Connect
Close

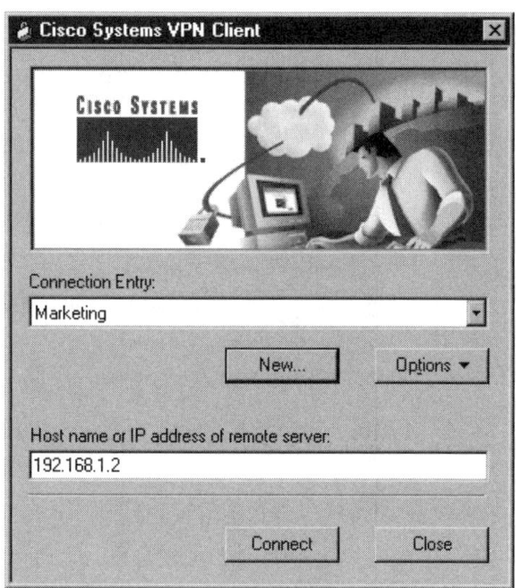

Figure 12-8 The Cisco Systems VPN Client main dialog box is ready to connect.

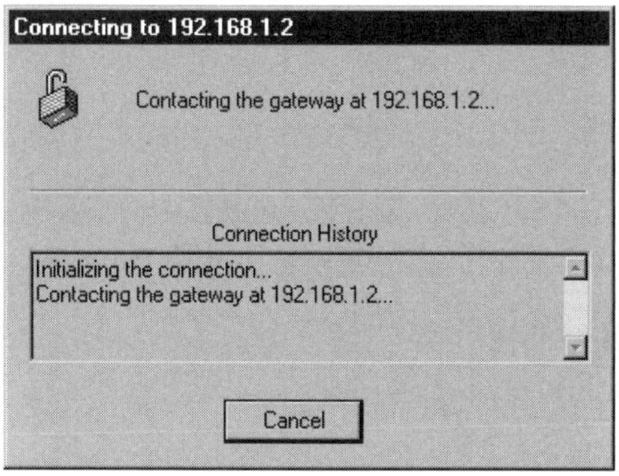

Connecting to 192.168.1.2
Contacting the gateway at 192.168.1.2...
Connection History
Initializing the connection...
Contacting the gateway at 192.168.1.2...
Cancel

Figure 12-9 VPN connection progress dialog box

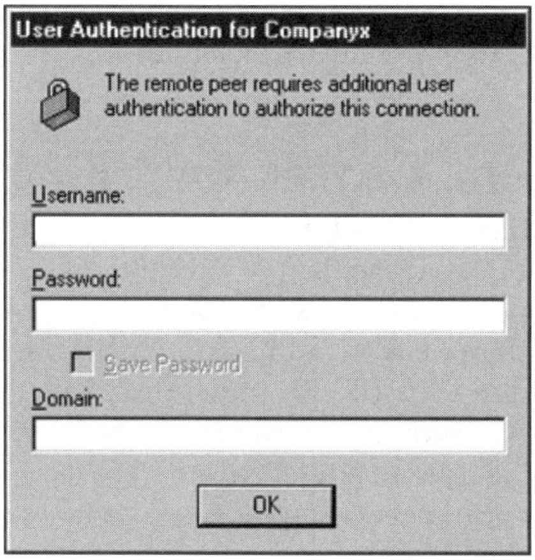

User Authentication for Companyx
The remote peer requires additional user authentication to authorize this connection.
Username:
Password:
Save Password
Domain:
OK

Figure 12-10 Windows user authentication box

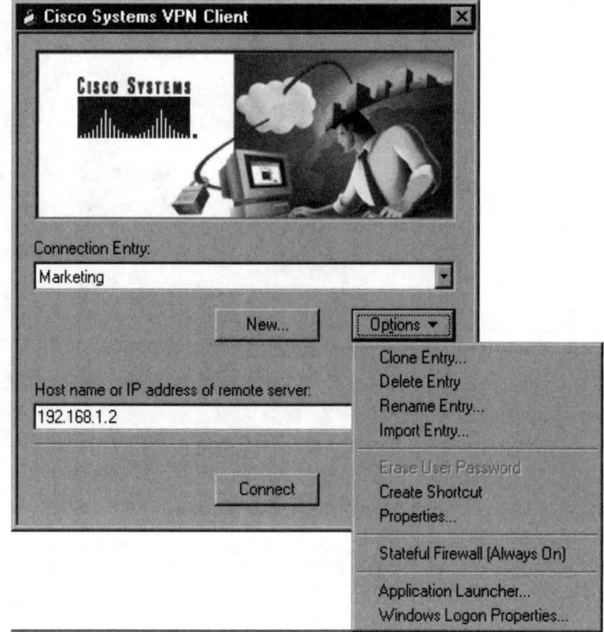

Figure 12-11 VPN Client customization options

applications, this tool offers some useful options. A new feature is support for the following personal firewalls (in addition to PIX support).

- Cisco Integrated Firewall (CIC)
- ZoneAlarmPro 2.6.3.57
- ZoneAlarm 2.6.3.57
- Zone Integrity
- BlackIce Agent and BlackIce Defender 2.5

Management Center for VPN Routers

Management Center for VPN Routers v1.1 (Router MC) is a web-based application designed for large-scale management of VPN and firewall configurations running on Cisco routers. Management Center for VPN Routers is one of the components of Cisco Works.

Router MC enables network administrators to configure and maintain VPN connections between multiple Cisco VPN routers using a hub-and-spoke topology. Router MC features support provisioning all critical connectivity, security, and performance parameters for a large-scale site-to-site VPN.

Router MC supports overlaying a VPN over a Frame Relay network for added security. It can be used to facilitate the migration from leased-line connections to Internet or intranet-based VPN connections.

Router MC-developed firewall and/or VPN configurations can be deployed to individual devices or groups of devices. The hierarchical device grouping and policy inheritance features of Router MC make it possible to configure multiple like devices simultaneously.

Features and Benefits

The Router Management Center offers features, such as smart rules hierarchy, resiliency support via IKE and generic routing encapsulation (GRE), import and deployment to files or devices, wizards-based support for setup of IKE and VPN tunnel policies, reusable building blocks, and more. The main features and benefits of the Router Management Center's are summarized as follows:

- Web browser interface—Makes it easy to define and deploy policies.
- Simplified policy definitions—Wizard-based interface that steps the user through the creation of IKE policies, tunnel policies, and transform sets.
- Support for a large number of devices—Uses device grouping, Smart Rules hierarchy, and reusable policy components to enable VPN configurations that scale to thousands of devices.
- Enhanced resiliency with IKE keepalives or GRE for failover—Supports IKE keepalives or GRE, with EIGRP or OSPF routing protocols, to provide failover options.
- Transparent translation of VPN policies to CLI commands—Web interface allows simplified and quick configuring and managing VPN policies. The application translates the VPN policies into CLI commands to be deployed to devices.
- Flexible deployment to files or devices—Choice of deploying configurations directly to devices as CLI commands or generates files containing CLI commands, which can be written to devices later.
- Configuration rollback—Possible to restore a device's previous configuration if not satisfied with a configuration after deploying VPN policies.
- Frame Relay network support—Deploy hub-and-spoke VPN configurations over a Frame Relay network.

Router MC v1.1 Firewall Features

Router MC v1.1 added support for the following firewall functionality features:

- Support for configuring ordered access rules to be assigned per interface.
- The ability to view a list of access rules per device or device group.
- Context Based Access Control (CBAC) feature support, including availability of the inspect action for access rules, alert and audit settings, fragmentation settings, DNS timeouts, protocol timeouts, and Denial of Service (DoS) prevention by monitoring half-open connections.

PART III

Router MC v1.1 Enhanced VPN Features

Router MC v1.1 added support for the following VPN features:

- Enhanced Certification Authority (CA) enrollment features, including support for trust-point and autoenrollment commands for devices running IOS 12.2(8)T and higher
- Advanced Encryption Standard (AES) encryption algorithm for use in IKE policies and transform sets
- High Availability (HA) groups of hubs, using Hot Standby Routing Protocol (HSRP)
- Multiple failover and routing policies within the Router MC device hierarchy
- Catalyst VPN Services Module support as a hub endpoint
- Network Address Translation (NAT) traversal
- Dialer interfaces

Router MC Server Requirements

Router MC is a component of Cisco's VPN/Security Management Solution (VMS) which integrates CiscoWorks, VPN Monitor, CiscoWorks Common Services, and other individual applications.

Requirement Type	Minimum Requirement
Hardware	Intel-based computer with 1 GHz or faster Pentium processor. Color monitor with video card capable of 16-bit color. CD-ROM drive. 10 Mbps (or faster) network connection.
Memory (RAM)	1GB.
Available disk space	9GB. 2GB virtual memory. NTFS file system (recommended).
Software	ODBC Driver Manager 3.510 or later. One of the following: Windows 2000 Professional. Windows 2000 Server. Service Pack 3.

Router MC Client Requirements

You can access all product features from any PC client meeting or exceeding the following hardware, software, and browser requirements.

Requirement Type	Minimum Requirement
Hardware	Intel-based computer with 300 MHz or faster Pentium processor.
Memory (RAM)	256MB.
Available disk space	400MB virtual memory.
Software	One of the following: Windows 98 Windows NT 4.0 Windows 2000 Server or Professional with Service Pack 2.
Web browser	Internet Explorer 6.0 or 5.5 with Service Pack 2. (Netscape Navigator not supported at this time.)

Router MC User Permissions

Router MC requires all users to log in with a user name and a password, which must be authenticated by the CiscoWorks server (default) or by a Cisco Secure Access Control Server (ACS) v3.1. Once authenticated, Router MC determines the user's defined role within the application. The role determines the set of tasks or operations the user is authorized to perform. Only those menu items, Table of Contents items, and buttons associated with authorized tasks are visible to the user. All others are hidden or disabled.

CiscoWorks Server Roles and Router MC Permissions

CiscoWorks supports the following five role types corresponding to typical functions within an organization:

Help desk	Read-only access for viewing devices, device groups, and the entire scope of a VPN.
Approver	Can review policy changes and can either approve or reject them. Can also approve or reject deployment jobs.
Network operator	Can make policy changes (except device inventory changes), as well as create and deploy jobs. Activities and jobs must be approved by an Approver.
System administrator	Can perform CiscoWorks server tasks and can make changes to the device hierarchy, such as move or delete devices. Can change administrative settings.
Network administrator	Can perform all CiscoWorks server and Router MC tasks. Can add users to the system with CiscoWorks or ACS. Can set user passwords and assign user roles and privileges.

If ACS authentication is used, the roles are different because of the group and task orientation of ACS. Each role is made up of a set of permissions that determine the role's level of access to Router MC tasks. User groups are assigned a role and each user in the group can perform all the Router MC tasks in the role. Use the Cisco online feature to get the most current configuration and implementation information if ACS will be used.

Easy VPN Remote Phase Two

Cisco Easy VPN Remote Phase Two features introduced with Cisco IOS v 12.2(8)YJ provide greater flexibility and feature options to Easy VPN Remote client devices, including Cisco 806, 826, 827, 828, and 1700 series routers, plus the Cisco uBR905 and uBR925 cable access routers. The goal is to provide the greatest flexibility in high-performance connections to the Internet, combined with the security of VPN, while minimizing the client-side configuration and support.

Easy VPN Remote Phase Two features still rely on most VPN parameters being defined at a VPN remote access server, such as a Cisco VPN 3000 concentrator, PIX Firewall, or a Cisco IOS router. When the IPSec client then initiates the VPN tunnel connection, the VPN remote access server pushes the IPSec policies to the IPSec client and creates the corresponding a VPN tunnel connection.

Supported VPN Servers

VPN Remote Phase Two requires that the destination server support the new features. The following device and OS combinations currently meet the requirements.

- Cisco uBR905 and uBR925 cable access routers running Cisco IOS v12.2(8)YJ or later
- Cisco 806, 826, 827, 828, 1700 series, 2600 series, 3600 series, 7100 series, 7200 series, and 7500 series routers running Cisco IOS v12.2(8)YJ or later
- Cisco PIX 500 series running software release 6.2 or later
- Cisco VPN 3000 series devices running software release 3.11 or later

The Cisco 806, 826, 827, 828, 1700 series routers, and uBR905 and uBR925 cable access routers support simultaneous remote client and remote server roles, allowing them to provide easy-to-implement VPN connections from small branch locations to corporate centers. The device is a client to the corporate center and a server to their VPN remote clients.

Phase Two Features

Cisco Easy VPN Remote Phase Two provides automatic management of the following features:

- Manual Tunnel Control
- Multiple Inside Interface Enhancements
- Multiple Outside Interfaces Support
- NAT Interoperability Support
- Local Address Support for Easy VPN Remote
- Cable DHCP Proxy Enhancement

- Peer Hostname Enhancement
- Proxy DNS Server Support
- PIX Interoperability Support
- Cisco IOS Firewall Support
- Simultaneous Easy VPN Client and Server Support
- Cisco Easy VPN Remote Web Manager

Manual Tunnel Control

With the original Cisco Easy VPN Remote, the VPN tunnel connects automatically on configuration. If the tunnel times out or fails, it automatically reconnects or retries indefinitely. Phase Two implements manual control over IPSec VPN tunnels, making it possible to establish and terminate the tunnel on demand. The manual feature is implemented with a new subcommand under the **crypto ipsec client ezvpn** command. The syntax is as follows:

```
Rtr1(config)#crypto ipsec client ezvpn name
Rtr1(config-crypto-ezvpn)#connect [auto | manual]
```

Automatic is the default setting, compatible with Phase One functionality. As such, the subcommand with the autoparameter is only needed to reverse the manual option.

With the manual option, the Easy VPN Client waits for the following command to attempt to establish the connection or to reestablish a timed out or failed session:

```
Rtr1#crypto ipsec client ezvpn connect name
```

Use the following **clear** command to disconnect an established tunnel.

```
Rtr1#clear crypto ipsec client ezvpn [name]
```

Multiple Inside Interface Enhancements

Phase One supports only one inside interface on the remote client router. The **crypto ipsec client ezvpn *name* inside** command option allows designating up to three inside interfaces. Each inside interface supports only one tunnel. The syntax is as follows:

```
Rtr1(config-if)#interface interface-id
Rtr1(config-if)#crypto ipsec client ezvpn name [outside | inside]
```

The following example shows configuring an outside interface using the default designation outside:

```
Rtr1(config)#interface ethernet 0
Rtr1(config-if)#crypto ipsec client ezvpn vpn1 inside
```

PART III

Multiple Outside Interfaces Support

Phase One supports only one outside interface on the remote client router. The **crypto ipsec client ezvpn *name* outside** command option allows designating up to four outside interfaces. The default option is outside. The syntax is as follows:

```
Rtr1(config-if)#interface interface-id
Rtr1(config-if)#crypto ipsec client ezvpn name [outside | inside]
```

This feature is applicable only to platforms, such as the Cisco 1700 series routers, that support multiple outside interfaces.

While each inside or outside interface supports only one tunnel, multiple inside interfaces can be mapped to one outside interface.

The following example shows configuring an outside interface using the designation outside. As the default, the outside didn't need to be included:

```
Rtr1(config)#interface serial 0/0
Rtr1(config-if)#crypto ipsec client ezvpn vpn1 outside
```

NAT Interoperability Support

With the Easy VPN Client, the features automatic NAT and access list configuration replaced any existing NAT and access list configuration. If a tunnel timed out or dropped its connection, the NAT and access configuration were removed automatically, preventing any Internet access even to nontunnel destinations.

Cisco Easy VPN Remote Phase Two supports interoperability with locally configured NAT. When the IPSec VPN tunnel is down, the router automatically restores the previous NAT configuration. Users can continue to access nontunnel Internet connections when the tunnel times out or disconnects.

Local Address Support for Easy VPN Remote

Easy VPN Remote Phase Two provides an interface configuration option, which makes it possible to specify the interface to use in determining the IP address as the source of VPN tunnel traffic. Typically, the loopback interface is the interface used to source tunnel traffic. The syntax is as follows:

```
Rtr1(config)#crypto ipsec client ezvpn name
Rtr1(config-crypto-ezvpn)#local-address interface-id
```

The following example shows the **local-address** subcommand used to specify the loopback0 interface for sourcing tunnel traffic:

```
Rtr1#config t
Rtr1(config)#crypto ipsec client ezvpn telecom-client
Rtr1(config-crypto-ezvpn)#local-address loopback0
Rtr1(config-crypto-ezvpn)#
```

Cable DHCP Proxy Enhancement

With Phase Two, cable providers can use the Cable DHCP Proxy feature to obtain a public IP address, assign it to the loopback interface, and then have the cable modem interface get its IP address from the loopback interface. The Phase Two feature enhancement applies to the existing **cable-modem dhcp-proxy interface** configuration command for the uBR905 and uBR925 cable access routers.

For the router to configure the loopback interface automatically with the public IP address obtained from the DHCP server, the loopback interface must be created before issuing the **cable-modem dhcp-proxy interface** command.

The following example shows a loopback interface created first, and then the loopback interface being specified, so the router automatically assigns it with the public IP address:

```
Rtr1#config t
Rtr1(config)#interface loopback 0
Rtr1(config-if)#interface cable-modem 0
Rtr1(config-if)#cable-modem dhcp-proxy interface loopback0
```

NOTE The **cable-modem dhcp-proxy interface** command is currently only supported for the Cisco uBR905 and uBR925 cable access routers.

Peer Host Name Enhancement

When defining the VPN peer, you can use either an IP address or a host name. When a host name is used, a DNS lookup is performed immediately to resolve the name to an IP address. Because Phase Two supports manual tunnel control, and to support DNS entry changes, the host name text string is stored and the DNS lookup is performed at the time of the tunnel connection. The host name enabling syntax is as follows:

```
Rtr1(config)#crypto ipsec client ezvpn name
Rtr1(config-crypto-ezvpn)#peer [ip-address | hostname]
```

The following shows the crypto entries:

```
Rtr1(config)#crypto ipsec client ezvpn vpn-client
Rtr1(config-crypto-ezvpn)#connect auto
Rtr1(config-crypto-ezvpn)#group vpn-client-grp key vpn-client-password
Rtr1(config-crypto-ezvpn)#local-address Loopback0
Rtr1(config-crypto-ezvpn)#mode client
Rtr1(config-crypto-ezvpn)#peer vpn-server
```

Proxy DNS Server Support

When the VPN connection to the corporate network is up, the enterprise DNS servers should resolve domain names to IP addresses. But when the VPN connection to the enterprise is down, the ISP or cable provider DNS servers should be used to resolve DNS requests.

An Easy VPN Remote Phase Two router can be configured to act as a proxy DNS server. As a proxy DNS server for LAN, the router receives DNS queries from local users on behalf of the enterprise DNS server. The DHCP server sends out the router's LAN address as the DNS server IP address. When the VPN tunnel connection comes up, the router forwards the DNS queries to the enterprise DNS server. Otherwise, they're forwarded to the ISP DNS.

To enable the proxy DNS server functionality with the **ip dns server** command in Global Configuration mode, use the following commands beginning in Global Configuration mode.

PIX Interoperability Support

Cisco Easy VPN Remote Phase Two more fully supports the Cisco PIX Firewall v6.2 features than the original implementation of Easy VPN Remote.

Cisco IOS Firewall Support

Cisco Easy VPN Remote Phase Two more fully supports the Cisco IOS Firewall feature set than the original implementation of Easy VPN Remote.

Simultaneous Easy VPN Client and Server Support

Cisco Easy VPN Remote Phase Two more fully supports configuring simultaneous Easy VPN Client and Cisco Easy VPN Server support on the same Cisco 1700 series routers. You can configure one outside interface as a Cisco Easy VPN Server and another outside interface on the same router as a Cisco Easy VPN Client. Figure 12-12 shows an example of a router (Rtr2) acting as both an Easy VPN Client and a Server.

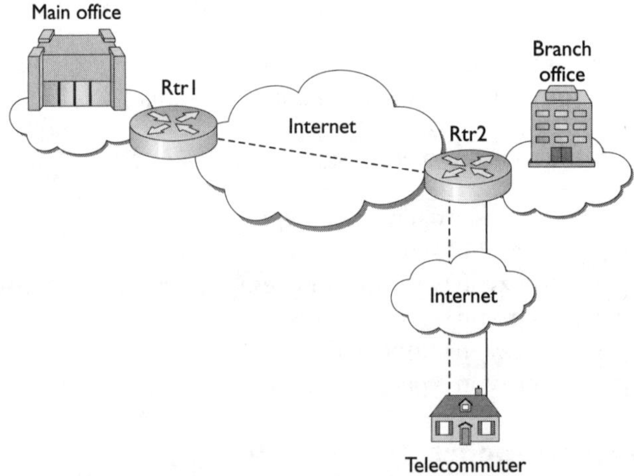

Figure 12-12 Router (Rtr2) acting as both an Easy VPN Client and a Server

The following example shows the configuration for the VPN client and server features on Rtr2. Some lines were eliminated to conserve space:

```
Rtr2#show run
version 12.2
!
hostname Rtr2
!
aaa new-model
aaa authorization network vpn-client-grp local
aaa session-id common
!
ip subnet-zero
no ip domain-lookup
ip ssh time-out 120
ip ssh authentication-retries 3
!
crypto isakmp policy 10
 authentication pre-share
 group 2
crypto isakmp client configuration address-pool local loc-pool
!
crypto isakmp client configuration group vpn-server-grp
 key vpn-grp-key
 dns 192.168.0.13 192.168.0.15
 wins 192.168.0.14 192.168.0.16
 domain vpn-test.com
 pool loc-pool
!
crypto ipsec transform-set trans-set-1 esp-3des esp-md5-hmac
!
crypto ipsec client ezvpn client1
 connect auto
 group vpn-client-grp key vpn-grp-key
 mode client
 peer 1.1.100.17                              (Rtr1)
!
crypto dynamic-map dyn-map 1
 set transform-set trans-set-1
!
crypto map dyn-map isakmp authorization list vpn-server-grp
crypto map dyn-map client configuration address respond
crypto map dyn-map 1 ipsec-isakmp dynamic dyn-map
!
interface FastEthernet0/0
 description Connection to Branch Office - VPN Clients
 ip address 5.0.0.1 255.0.0.0
 crypto ipsec client ezvpn client1 inside
!
interface Serial0/0
 description Connection to Corporate Network - VPN Server
 ip address 1.0.0.1 255.0.0.0
 no fair-queue
 crypto ipsec client ezvpn client1
!
interface Serial0/1
 description Connection to telecommuters - VPN Clients
 ip address 1.2.0.1 255.255.0.0
```

```
 crypto map dyn-map                          (for server functionality)
 crypto ipsec client ezvpn client1 inside    (for client functionality)
!
ip local pool loc-pool 1.2.0.3 1.2.0.31
ip classless
!
line con 0
line aux 0
line vty 0 4
end
Rtr2#
```

Cisco Easy VPN Remote Web Manager

Cisco Easy VPN Remote Phase Two introduced using the Cisco Easy VPN Remote Web Manager to manage the Cisco uBR905 and Cisco uBR925 cable access routers. The Cisco Easy VPN Remote Web Manager is a built-in web-interface application resident on the uBR905 and uBR925 devices. The Web Manager enables the user to avoid the command-line interface (CLI) to perform the following functions:

- See the current status of any Easy VPN Remote Phase Two tunnels
- Connect or disconnect a tunnel configured for manual control
- Reset a tunnel configured for automatic connection
- Be prompted for Xauth information if Xauth information is needed

Cisco VPN Firewall Feature for VPN Client

The VPN Client software now includes an integrated stateful firewall feature set that provides protection to the client. The feature set protects the VPN Client PC from Internet attacks both from split-tunneling implementations and IPSec tunnel connections to a VPN Concentrator. This feature is called Stateful Firewall (Always On).

Overview of Software Client Firewall Feature

The built-in Stateful Firewall (Always On) service provides even tighter security by blocking all new inbound sessions from all networks, regardless of whether a VPN connection is active. The Stateful Firewall filtering applies to both encrypted and nonencrypted traffic. Outbound traffic creates entries in a state table, which allows returning packets to be allowed through. Any sessions originating on the outside interface are blocked by default, though, because no state table entries exist.

Two exceptions exist to this no unsolicited inbound traffic rule. The first involves supporting DHCP services: DHCP client requests to a DHCP server pass out on one port, but the resulting responses return through a different port. The Stateful Firewall feature is programmed to know this and allows that specific inbound traffic. The second exception is edge services processor (ESP) traffic through ESP modules from the secure gateway. The Stateful Firewall software recognizes ESP traffic as packet filters, and not as session-based filters, and allows it through.

To enable the Stateful Firewall, click Stateful Firewall (Always on) on the Options menu, as shown in Figure 12-13. The check in front of the option indicates the Stateful Firewall (Always On) feature is enabled. This feature is disabled by default. The feature can be enabled or disabled by clicking the entry in the VPN Client Options menu.

During a VPN connection, you can view the status of the firewall features by double-clicking the lock icon in the taskbar system tray or right-clicking the same icon and choose Status from the resulting menu. You can also enable or disable the feature from the same menu. The result is a three-tab window, as shown in Figure 12-14, with the firewall features on the third tab. The information displayed on the tab varies according to the configured firewall policy.

Defining a Client Firewall Policy

The VPN Concentrator network administrator can define and manage the firewall policy using the Configuration | User Management | Base Group or Group | Client FW tab. You can choose from three options:

- Are You There
- Centralized Protection Policy
- Client/Server

The Are You There Feature

Since v3.1, the Cisco VPN Client supports the Are You There (AYT) feature. When the AYT feature is enabled, the VPN Client polls the local firewall every 30 seconds to make

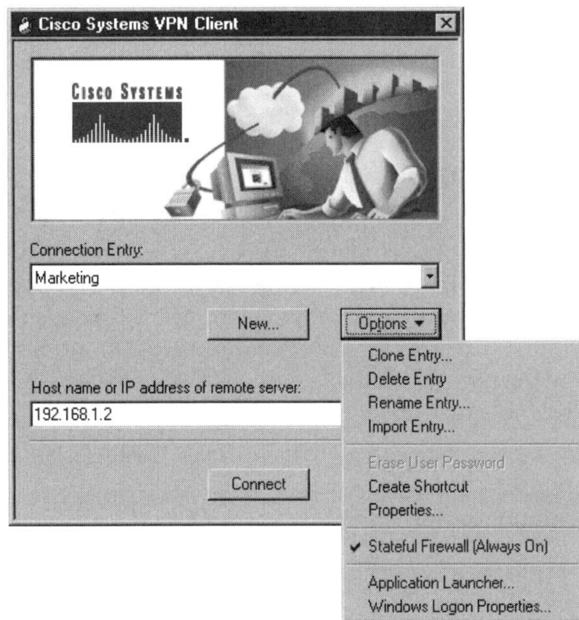

Figure 12-13 Stateful Firewall (Always on) on the Options menu

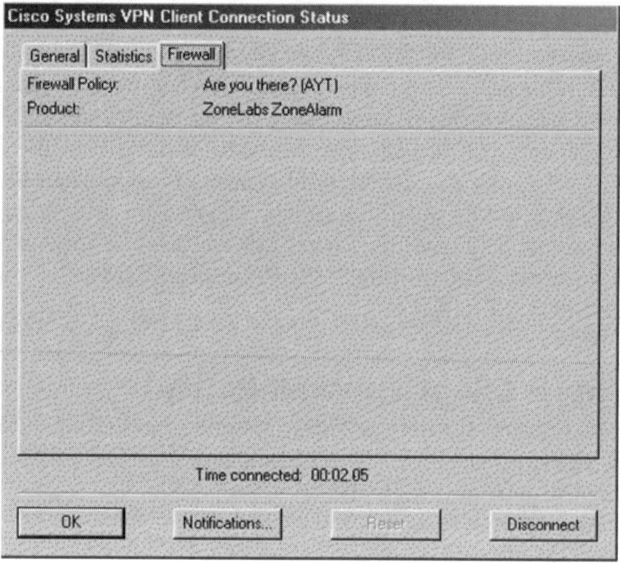

Figure 12-14 Cisco System VPN Client Connection Status information box

sure it's still running. While the VPN Client confirms the firewall is running, it doesn't confirm that a specific policy is enforced.

If the security policy requires that remote users have firewalls running on their PCs, the VPN Concentrator can allow these clients to connect only if they have the designated firewall installed and running. If the designated firewall isn't running, the connection attempts fails. Once the connection is established, the VPN Client uses the AYT feature to monitor the firewall to make sure it's running. If the firewall stops for any reason, the VPN Client immediately drops the connection to the VPN Concentrator.

The Cisco System VPN Client Connection Status information box Firewall tab shows only the firewall policy (AYT) and the name of the firewall product, as shown in Figure 12-14 earlier.

The Central Policy Protection Feature

Central Policy Protection (CPP) is a stateful firewall policy that leverages the Cisco Integrated Client feature by letting the VPN Concentrator manage the client firewall policies. The specific policy rules are defined by the administrator on the VPN Concentrator, and then pushed down to the VPN Client every time a connection is attempted. The VPN Client then enforces these policy rules for all nontunneled (split-tunnel Internet) traffic while the tunnel is active.

Because CPP works only on out-of-tunnel Internet traffic, if the client is operating in a tunnel-everything mode, enabling CPP has no effect.

The Cisco System VPN Client Connection Status information box Firewall tab shows the firewall policy, the firewall in use, and firewall rules, as shown in Figure 12-15.

Firewall Rules

The Firewall Rules section of the Status box shows all the firewall rules currently implemented on the VPN Client. The rules are arranged in order of importance, with the highest importance at the top. All but the last two rules are defined by the VPN administrator to allow inbound and outbound traffic between the VPN Client and the secure gateway, as well as between the VPN Client and the private networks with which it communicates. Because the rules are implemented from the top down, the VPN Client enforces them before trying the two CPP default rules at the bottom. This approach lets the traffic flow to and from private networks.

The bottom two rules define the filter's default actions, which are to drop both inbound and outbound traffic. These rules are implemented only if the traffic doesn't match any of the preceding rules.

To see the full fields of a specific rule, click the first column in the top half of the Firewall Rules: window; the selected rule is displayed in the bottom half of the window.

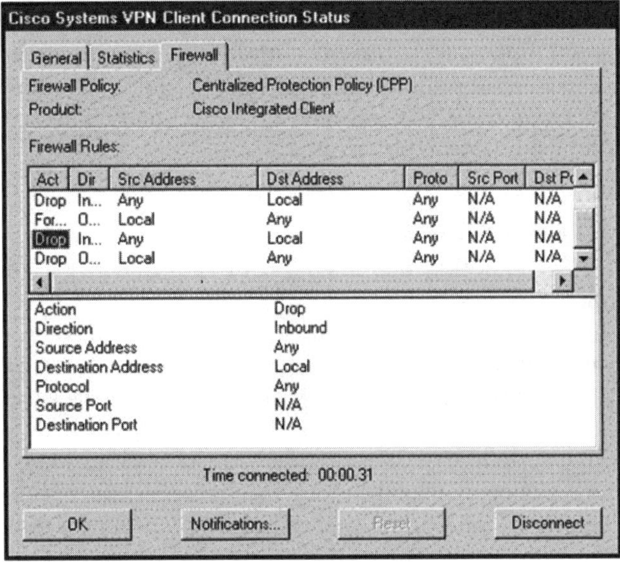

Figure 12-15 Firewall tab for CPP

A firewall rule includes the following fields and options:

Action	Action to be taken if the data traffic matches the rule: **Drop**—Discard the session. **Forward**—Allow the session to go through.
Direction	Direction of traffic to be affected by the rule: **Inbound**—traffic coming in to the local machine. **Outbound**—traffic going out from the local machine.
Source Address	Source address of the traffic this rule affects: **Any**—all traffic, for example, drop any inbound traffic. **IP address and subnet mask**—A specific host address. **Local**—The local machine for outbound traffic.
Destination Address	Destination address this rule affects: **Any**—All traffic. **Local**—Local machine if the direction is inbound.
Protocol	The Internet Assigned Number Authority (IANA) number of the protocol covered by this rule concerns (6 for TCP, 17 for UDP).
Source Port	Source port used by TCP or UDP.
Destination Port	Destination port used by TCP or UDP.

The Stateful Firewall Process

In the stateful Cisco Integrated Client, firewall protocols TCP, UDP, and ICMP automatically allow inbound responses to outbound packets. To allow inbound responses to outbound packets for any other protocols, the network administrator needs to define specific filters on the VPN Concentrator. These are then passed down to the VPN Client the next time a session is established.

Client/Server Feature

The Client/Server policy supports the Zone Labs Integrity solution. *Zone Labs Integrity* is a Client/Server firewall solution in which the Integrity Server acts as the firewall server that pushes firewall policy to the Integrity Agent residing on the VPN Client PC. Because Integrity is a fully functional stateful personal firewall, it can intelligently decide on network traffic based on application layer information, as well as on traditional Layer 3 and 4 fields.

The Cisco System VPN Client Connection Status information box Firewall tab shows the firewall policy as Client/Server, the name of the product as ZoneLabs Integrity Agent, the user ID, session ID, and the addresses and port numbers of the firewall servers, as shown in Figure 12-16.

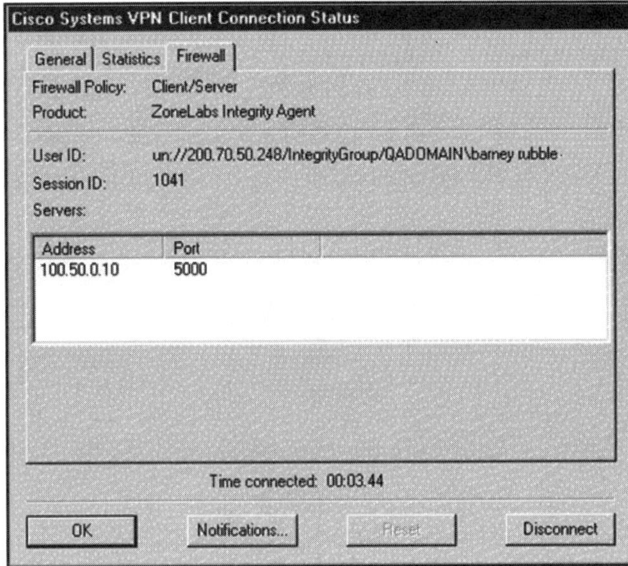

Figure 12-16 Client/Server Firewall tab

Client Firewall Statistics

The Statistics tab on the Cisco System VPN Client Connection Status dialog box shows statistics on the VPN Client data packets processed during the current session or since the statistics were reset. The data collected includes the following information. Figure 12-17 shows the Statistics tab information.

Bytes in	Total data received after the secure packets have been decrypted.
Bytes out	Total amount of encrypted data transmitted through the tunnel.
Packets decrypted	Total number of data packets received on the port.
Packets encrypted	Total number of secured data packets transmitted out the port.
Packets bypassed	Total number of packets not processed by the VPN Client because they didn't need to be encrypted, such as local ARPs and DHCP.
Packets discarded	Total number of packets the VPN Client rejected because they weren't from the VPN peer device.

Clicking the RESET button clears these counters, but doesn't impact the other two tabs. Clearing the counters often makes seeing the current activity easier, particularly if some time has passed since the last reset.

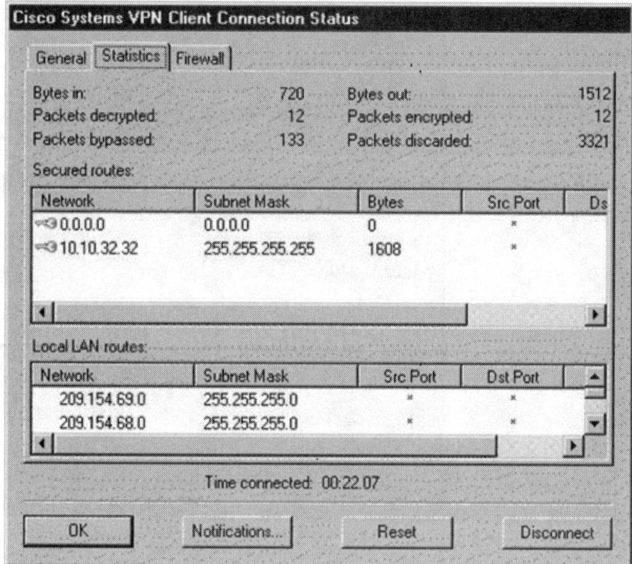

Figure 12-17 VPN Client connection statistics

Chapter Review

Cisco Easy VPN is part of Cisco's Unified Client Framework, in which VPN management is centralized across all Cisco VPN devices. The goal is to simplify VPN implementation, at least at the remote end. The Easy VPN strategy incorporates all VPN platforms, including VPN software client, VPN 3002 hardware client, Cisco routers, Cisco PIX Firewalls, and Cisco VPN 3000 Concentrators.

Cisco Easy VPN strategy incorporates centrally stored and managed configurations with dynamic configuration of end-user VPN devices. This should require less manual configuration by end users and field technicians, reducing errors and additional service calls.

The Cisco Easy VPN strategy has two main components: the Cisco Easy VPN Server and the Cisco Easy VPN Remote. The Easy VPN Server service allows a growing number of Cisco IOS routers, PIX Firewalls, and Cisco VPN 3000 Concentrators to act as VPN head-end devices in site-to-site or remote-access VPNs. In addition to providing VPN connections, these devices would store the client configurations and "push" those settings down to the Easy VPN Remote devices on their next connection.

Cisco VPN client software is available, for many common computer OSs bring those systems directly in contact with the VPN networks. While this isn't a full part of the Easy VPN Remote family, the software client shares similar features and ease of configuration.

Questions

1. Which of the following Cisco products is *not* a Cisco Easy VPN Server?
   A. PIX Firewall
   B. IOS routers
   C. IDS Manager
   D. VPN Series Concentrator
2. Which two of the following are modes of operation of Cisco Easy VPN Remote?
   A. Server
   B. Client
   C. Network extension
   D. Push
3. Split tunneling refers to which one of the following?
   A. Running two simultaneous VPN connections
   B. Allowing two-way simultaneous exchanges
   C. Unsecured Internet connections in addition to secure VPN sessions
   D. Load balancing VPN circuits
4. Which of the following is marketed as both an Easy VPN Client and an Easy VPN Server?
   A. Cisco 800
   B. Cisco 1700
   C. PIX 501
   D. Cisco VPN 3002
5. Which one of the following technologies is *not* typically used by VPN Clients?
   A. DSL
   B. Cable modem
   C. Dial-up modems
   D. T1 dedicated line
6. Which one is *not* a required Easy VPN Server configuration task?
   A. Applying Mode Configuration and Xauth
   B. Enabling Policy Lookup via AAA
   C. Configuring RADIUS Server Support
   D. Defining Group Policy Information for Mode Configuration Push

7. Which of the following is a new VPN keepalive scheme?
   A. Split Tunneling Control
   B. IKE Dead Peer Detection (DPD)
   C. Initial Contact
   D. Group-Based Policy Control
8. In setting up a Cisco VPN client connection to use preshared keys, what information is used to authenticate the connection?
   A. Digital certificates
   B. Local IP address
   C. Server IP address
   D. Group name and password
9. With which one of the following must the user configure their computer to support VPN?
   A. PIX Firewall with VPN service
   B. IOS Router with VPN service
   C. VPN 3002 Hardware client
   D. Cisco VPN Client
10. Which VPN implementation would *not* usually include NAT or PAT?
    A. PIX Firewall with VPN service
    B. IOS Router with VPN service
    C. Cisco VPN Client
    D. VPN 3002 Hardware client
11. Which of the following is *not* true about Management Center for VPN Routers v1.1 (Router MC)?
    A. It's a component of Cisco Works
    B. It uses a web interface
    C. It's a router-based Java application
    D. Developed configurations can be deployed directly to a device
12. Which of the following is *not* a supported feature of Management Center for VPN Routers v1.1 (Router MC)?
    A. Configuration rollback
    B. Transparent translation of VPN policies to CLI commands
    C. Simplified policy definitions
    D. Command-line interface for easy configuration

13. Which of the following Cisco Easy VPN Remote Phase Two features is only supported on the Cisco uBR905 and Cisco uBR925 cable access routers?

    A. Multiple Inside Interface Enhancements

    B. Simultaneous Easy VPN Client and Server Support

    C. Cisco Easy VPN Remote Web Manager

    D. NAT Interoperability Support

14. Which two of the following can be used for the Router Management Center server?

    A. Windows NT server

    B. Windows 2000 Professional

    C. Windows 2000 Server

    D. Sun Solaris 8.0 or above

15. Which of the following Cisco Easy VPN Remote Phase Two features allows a loopback address to be defined as the VPN tunnel source?

    A. Manual Tunnel Control

    B. Peer Host Name Enhancement

    C. Local Address Support

    D. NAT Interoperability Support

Answers

1. C. IDS Manager
2. B. Client and C. Network extension
3. C. Unsecured Internet connections in addition to secure VPN sessions
4. B. Cisco 1700
5. D. T1 dedicated line
6. C. Configuring RADIUS Server Support
7. B. IKE Dead Peer Detection (DPD)
8. D. Group name and password
9. D Cisco VPN Client
10. C. Cisco VPN Client
11. C It is a router-based Java application—it's a Windows 2000 application.
12. D. Command-line interface for easy configuration—Web interface

13. **C.** Cisco Easy VPN Remote Web Manager
14. **B.** Windows 2000 Professional and **C.** Windows 2000 Server
15. **C.** Local Address Support

Cisco VPN Hardware Overview

In this chapter, you will learn to:

- Use Cisco products to enable a secure VPN
- Know about Cisco VPN 3002 Client devices
- Recognize Cisco VPN 3000 Concentrator devices

In this chapter, you learn about VPN hardware technologies supported by Cisco. Specific configuration is covered in the relevant chapters. Router-based VPNs are covered in Chapters 10 and 11. VPN client software is covered in Chapter 12. VPN connections to PIX Firewalls are covered in Chapter 21, and Cisco VPN 3000 Series devices are covered in Chapters 14 and 15.

Cisco Products Enable a Secure VPN

A wide variety of Cisco products actively support VPN connections throughout the network. Cisco's Unified Client Framework strategy enables all adhering VPN client technologies to connect to any Cisco central-site VPN concentrators, including the Cisco 3000 series VPN concentrators, PIX Firewalls, and Cisco IOS-based routers.

The Cisco VPN software client is typically provided at no charge with central site concentrators, so the software client is inexpensive to deploy and scale to large numbers. These VPN clients have specific limited operating system (OS) support and might require some level of support. These software clients could be impractical in those extranet environments where the organization doesn't own or control the remote PC, such as in a franchise or customer location. The organization might not want to absorb the expense associated with maintaining and supporting non-company workstations.

Cisco small router and firewall devices can be an inexpensive way to provide security features like stateful firewall and VPN capabilities to remote sites. Unfortunately, these devices don't scale beyond a few hundred devices. Deployment, monitoring, and ongoing support can be inconvenient, time-consuming, and expensive because of the variety of features and options that must often be manually configured at both ends of the connection.

The Cisco VPN 3000 Series Concentrator, combined with the Cisco VPN 3002 Hardware Client device, scales to support customers with 100 or fewer remote access users to large organizations with up to 10,000 simultaneous connections. The Cisco VPN 3000 Series Concentrator is available in both nonredundant and redundant configurations, providing the customer with multiple options to design and build robust, reliable, and cost-effective networks.

What's New?

The latest Cisco VPN 3000 Series Concentrator OS, release 3.6, is the most recent version at press time. This release includes simplified VPN Software Client—Easy VPN—which allows minimal client configuration and "push" technology to download the configuration from the concentrator. Additional release 3.6 features include AES support, expanded support for Microsoft's Integrated VPN Client in Windows 2000/XP, and security for wireless environments.

The new Cisco VPN 3002 Hardware Client, covered in the next section, combines easy implementation and rollout, plus high scalability, with the performance, reliability, and stability of a hardware device.

The Cisco VPN 3000 Series Concentrator Wireless Client Support for Elliptic Curve Cryptography (ECC) provides faster information processing by personal digital assistants (PDAs) and smart phones.

The Cisco VPN 3000 Series Concentrator, Cisco VPN 3002 Hardware Client, and the Cisco VPN Client work together with the Cisco Internet Mobile Office to provide mobile professionals with secure, high-speed broadband connectivity to their networks in airports, convention centers, hotels, and a growing number of other public spaces.

Cisco VPN 3002 Client Devices

The Cisco *VPN 3002 Hardware Client* was specifically designed for those organizations with many remote users and sites that need to operate as secure clients in a VPN environment. The 3002 combines the ease of configuration and installation, plus the scalability of a software VPN client, with the stability and reliability of a hardware platform.

The VPN 3002 Hardware Client eliminates the need to install and configure VPN client software on the local workstation(s), plus it supports workstations running any OS, including Windows, Sun Solaris UNIX, Mac, and Linux. Each 3002 client appliance can connect one or more devices, including workstations, servers, hubs, cash registers, printers, and IP telephones to a company's central network. Figure 13-1 shows the book- sized (2 × 8.6 × 6.5 inches) 3002 device.

Figure 13-1 Cisco VPN 3002 Client device (front view)

The VPN 3002 is designed with simplicity and reliability of installation. It has few local setup parameters that must be configured. Additional parameters and policy are "pushed" to the device from the central site (head-end) device with the first connection. In Chapter 15, you see how little installation configuration must be done to connect to the corporate network.

The user simply plugs the minimally configured VPN 3002 device into a DSL/cable connection, router, or other wide area network (WAN) access devices at the remote site. The central site VPN concentrator takes over, using push policy features to centrally set policy, manage, and upgrade the device. This central control and management approach minimizes the need to rely on remote users to deploy or maintain the unit. Tunnel setup and policy configuration is automated, so companies needn't dedicate IT staff to configure individual devices manually. Troubleshooting aids and centralized monitoring features are built into the 3002 software to ensure proper operation after the unit is set up.

This ease of installation and because the 3002 can coexist with other types of VPN clients on the network make it an ideal choice for the organization that needs to set up and support dozens, or even thousands, of remote end users who need secure network connections from geographically dispersed branch or home office sites. Some examples that might fit this business model include fast food outlets, grocery store-based banking operations, retail chains, insurance or brokerage offices, employment offices, vehicle dealerships, drugstores, and the like.

In calculating return on investment (ROI), larger enterprises typically find the initial price of the hardware client is more than offset by the savings from reduced or eliminated service calls common with supporting software VPN clients. The same is true when compared to supporting expanding LAN-to-LAN networks with their complex configuration requirements at central and remote sites, particularly if on-site support is limited.

Cisco VPN 3002 Client Models

The *3002 Client,* a small-footprint, book-sized device designed for wall mount or table top operation, currently comes in two models. The *CPVN3002-K9* has two 10/100 Mbps RJ-45 Ethernet autosensing interfaces: one for the outside or public connection and one for the inside or private connection. This makes the device ideal for placement between a DSL or a cable modem, either connected directly to a workstation or to multiple hosts via a separate switch or hub.

The *CVPN3002-K9* sports a single 10/100 Mbps RJ-45 Ethernet autosensing interface for the public connection plus eight 10/100 Mbps Ethernet autosensing interfaces via an integrated switch. This device can provide simplified installation for the small office or home that needs to connect several computers to the network, or the switch can connect to additional switches, providing connections for up to 253 host devices. Figure 13-2 shows the back of the 8E unit.

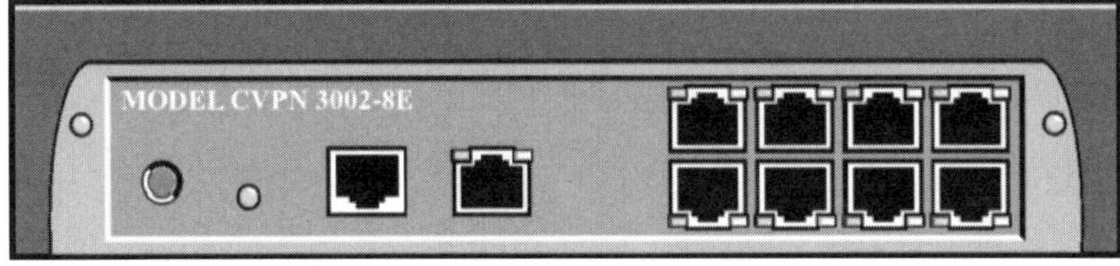

Figure 13-2 Cisco VPN 3002 Client with built-in 8-port switch

Client and Network Extension Modes

The Cisco VPN 3002 supports two modes of operation to offer implementation choices based on flexibility, security, and easy configuration. Those modes are

- Client mode
- Network Extension mode

A large VPN implementation might frequently have both types of operation.

Client Mode

In *Client mode,* the VPN 3002 emulates the VPN client software appearing to the main network like a remote user. The private hosts protected behind the VPN 3002 are a separate network that remains invisible and nonroutable to the central site. The local hosts are assigned their IP addresses from the VPN 3002 Dynamic Host Control Protocol (DHCP) server feature, while the public port can use the VPN 3002 DHCP client feature to acquire its IP address from an ISP. From a cost and address preservation standpoint, it would make sense for the local IP addresses to be private IP addresses.

To help secure the local network and to allow local hosts to travel out of the network in Client mode, the VPN 3002 uses Port Address Translation (PAT). Because all traffic to the central network will have the public interface IP address, PAT supplies and manages unique port number mappings to be used in combination with the IP address.

Split tunneling is a useful feature that provides the capability to have a secure tunnel to the central site, while simultaneously maintaining a clear text tunnel to the Internet through the ISP. The VPN 3002 uses PAT to protect the local workstations during split tunneling to the Internet. If the organization security policy prohibits split tunneling, it can be blocked by creating a policy on the central site device, which is then pushed down to the 3002 Client.

The VPN 3002 Client can only create outbound connections, so no way exists for an outside source to initiate a connection with the VPN 3002 or through it to the stations behind.

Network Extension mode

In *Network Extension* mode, the VPN 3002 establishes a secure site-to-site connection with the central site device. The local stations behind the VPN 3002 are fully routable and the local network is visible to the central site. As the name implies, the local network becomes part of the organization's intranet. VPN and 3002 configuration and security policies are pushed from the central site.

In Network Extension mode, the private addresses are assigned manually and permanently, allowing central site host and applications to reliably reach any local server, printer, POS terminal, IP phone, or other device critical to the business.

PAT provides security for local host traffic heading to the Internet through split tunneling. This outbound PAT on the VPN 3002 provides centralized security control because no configuration parameters exist for local users to adjust, which could possibly cause the central site to be compromised.

Standards Supported

To support fast, easy, and reliable deployment and scalability to thousands of sites, the Cisco VPN 3002 Hardware Client is a full-featured VPN client that incorporates IPSec and other industry standards. The 3002 support for the Cisco VPN Client Release 3.5 software, using the Unified Client Framework, enables it to connect to any Cisco central-site VPN Concentrator, including the Cisco 3000 Series VPN Concentrators, PIX Firewalls, and Cisco IOS–based routers.

The 3002 supports the following standards and protocols. The details of configuring these features are covered in Chapter 15.

- DHCP client and server services are supported. DHCP *client* implementation allows the public interface to be assigned an IP address from the head-end device on first connection. This is both easier and more reliable than end-to-end statically assigned addresses, which are typically required for LAN-to-LAN devices. DHCP *server* support allows the private interface(s) to assign IP addresses to up to 253 stations behind the Cisco VPN 3002.
- Three methods of NAT Transparent IPSEC, including the UDP method implemented in the original product release, IPSec/TCP method, and ratified IPSec/UDP NAT-T specification, which includes autodetection and fragmentation avoidance.
- PAT can be configured on the 3002 to hide the stations behind the Cisco VPN 3002 private interface(s) from external view and attack.
- IPSec encryption protocols, including 56-bit DES or 168-bit Triple DES for securing the data transmissions.
- MD5, SHA-1, HMAC with MD5, and HMAC with SHA-1 authentication algorithms.
- IPSec tunneling protocol with Internet Key Encryption (IKE) key management.
- AAA RADIUS accounting and security from the central site.
- H.323 support allows users to host and access NetMeeting sessions or to access other H.323 applications, such as voice-over IP (VoIP).
- Embedded web management interface accessible via local web browser, Secure Shell (SSH)/Secure Socket Layer (SSL), or conventional console port.
- SNMP MIB-II for monitoring, configuration, and event logging.

Cisco VPN 3002 Hardware Client Features

The following summarizes the features and benefits provided by the Cisco VPN 3002 Hardware Client devices. Those requiring configuration are addressed in Chapter 15, when configuring the client is covered or, because many features are "pushed" down from the central site, they're enabled and configured in Chapter 14.

Auto Upgrade

The client update feature was added in version 3.0 for the VPN 3002 Hardware Client and version 3.1 for the Cisco VPN software client. If the central device supports the feature (v3.0 for VPN Concentrators), the central device can be used to upgrade the software and configuration on the client. In the case of the VPN 3002 Hardware Client, firmware upgrades can also be pushed down to the client.

For VPN 3002 Hardware Clients, the *client update* allows administrators to update software and firmware automatically for the 3002 device. If an upgrade is needed, the unit upgrades automatically from an internal TFTP server specified on the central site VPN Concentrator. The process of maintaining security, managing the system, and upgrading it is transparent to the end user.

For Cisco VPN software clients the process is a little less automatic. This is more of a notification mechanism with an assisted upgrade. The client update for the Cisco VPN software clients allows central location administrators to notify the client users automatically when it's time to update. Then action is required on the part of users to retrieve and install the newer software.

Authentication Features

The VPN 3002 supports the following two levels of client authentication mechanism that supplies a high level of security for both the VPN 3002 and the users behind the VPN 3002:

- Interactive Unit Authentication
- Individual User Authentication

The VPN 3002 *Interactive Unit Authentication* technology uses Saved or One Time Passwords to reauthenticate itself to the head-end device. With Saved passwords, the 3002 client device needn't reauthenticate if the tunnel cycles. With One Time passwords, the device must be reauthenticated each time the tunnel cycles. The VPN 3002 supports preshared secrets, digital certificates, and tokens for this authentication.

The VPN 3002 *Individual User Authentication* feature can be set to require each user behind the VPN device to authenticate before traversing the tunnel. This feature can require the users behind the 3002 to use preshared secrets or tokens to authenticate. The individual authentication can be used by itself or in conjunction with Interactive Unit Authentication to maximize security.

To simplify the process and make it as transparent as possible to the end users, this technology automatically intercepts any user attempting to traverse the VPN tunnel and redirects them to a browser page to authenticate. The user needn't initiate or remember to initiate the security authentication because this is done automatically. If a user is only attempting to access the Internet via split tunneling, that user isn't prompted to authenticate.

Load Balancing and Failover

The VPN 3002 hardware device (release 3.5) and the Cisco VPN software client (v3.0) both support Cisco's VPN 3000 load-balancing strategy. To implement load balancing, multiple concentrators are grouped together logically on the same private LAN-to-LAN network in a virtual cluster. These VPN Concentrators can be configured to direct session traffic transparently to the least-loaded device, thus distributing the load among all devices. In addition to increasing efficient use of system resources, this strategy provides increased performance, high availability, and reliability.

The VPN 3002 supports up to 10 back-up concentrators, in case the primary location is down or otherwise unavailable. The 3002 cycles through each backup concentrator in order until it makes a successful connection, maximizing network availability to the client.

PPPoE Support

Point-to-Point Protocol over Ethernet (PPPoE) is a specification for connecting Ethernet users to the Internet using a common broadband medium, such as a DSL line, a cable modem, or a wireless device. Many ISPs now require PPPoE authentication for DSL or other access to their networks. The VPN 3002 supports PPPoE Client mode to access these networks. Users need only to authenticate to the PPPoE server the first time and VPN 3002 then authenticates for all the user's subsequent attempts.

Cisco VPN 3000 Concentrator Devices

The Cisco VPN 3000 Series Concentrator is a growing family of VPN devices specifically designed and built to provide fast, reliable, and secure remote access to organization network resources. These devices combine with Cisco VPN client software and hardware to incorporate high availability, high performance, and scalability, plus advanced encryption and authentication technologies to allow customers to implement the latest VPN technology, while protecting and persevering in their communications investments.

The VPN 3000 platform offers customer-upgradeable and field-swappable components to increase capacity dramatically, while maintaining the original device, rack space, and power requirements. Scalable Encryption Processing (SEP) modules can be added to the 3015 to 3060 model case to enable users to add capacity and throughput easily.

The Cisco VPN 3000 Concentrator series comes in several models to meet organization capacity requirements and applications. The platform includes models to support customers with 100 or fewer remote access users to large organizations with up to 10,000 simultaneous remote connections. The latest Cisco VPN Software Client is provided at no additional charge with unlimited distribution licensing with all versions of the Cisco VPN 3000 Concentrator.

The Cisco VPN 3000 Concentrator platform offers models that can be implemented in both redundant and nonredundant configurations, offering the organization flexibility in design and budget management. In addition, advanced routing support, such as OSPF, RIP, and NAT, are available.

Cisco VPN 3000 Concentrator Models

The VPN 3000 Concentrators create virtual private networks (VPNs) by creating secure connection across a TCP/IP network, such as the Internet, that allows remote end users to connect to the corporate network. The VPN Concentrator can be used to create single-user-to-LAN connections for connecting traveling employees or telecommuters, plus LAN-to-LAN connections for connecting remote sites. The VPN 3000 family of VPN concentrators currently come in the following five models, offering support for a few secure connections up to 10,000 sessions:

- Cisco VPN 3005
- Cisco VPN 3015
- Cisco VPN 3030
- Cisco VPN 3060
- Cisco VPN 3080

The *3005* is a unique 1U rack-mountable nonupgradeable device. The others share a common 2U rack-mountable chassis that allows choices in number of power supplies and SEP units. These units support after purchase upgrade options that allow the VPN security architecture to grow with the organization.

The following features are common to all Cisco VPN 3000 Concentrator Models:

- 10/100 Ethernet autosensing interfaces:
  - Model 3005: Two interfaces
  - Models 3015-3080: Three interfaces
- Motorola PowerPC CPU
- SDRAM memory for normal operation
- Nonvolatile memory (NVRAM) for critical system parameters
- Flash memory for file management

NOTE While each 3000 series device still specifies a T1/E1 optional interface, a Cisco Systems announcement is of the end of sale of Cisco VPN 3000 WAN Interface products, including all T1 and E1 WAN modules for VPN 3000 Concentrator Series products.

Cisco VPN 3005 Concentrator

The *3005* is a fixed-configuration VPN platform designed for small-to-medium networks with bandwidth requirements up to full-duplex T1/E1 (4 Mbps maximum performance) and up to 100 simultaneous sessions. Figure 13-3 shows the front and rear views of a VPN 3005. The basic configuration and expansion capabilities include the following:

- Software-based encryption
- Single power supply
- Expansion capabilities:
  - Optional WAN interface module with dual T1/E1 ports

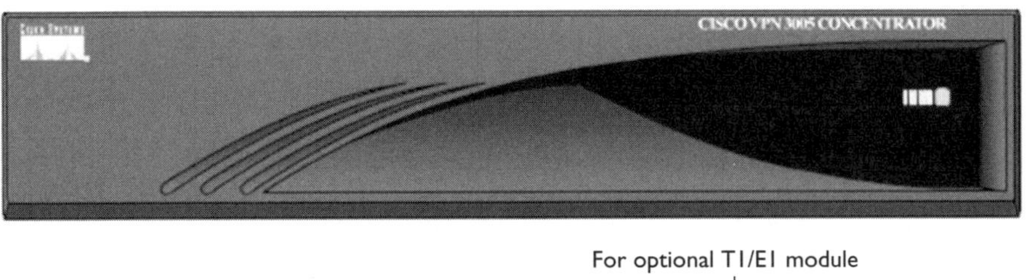

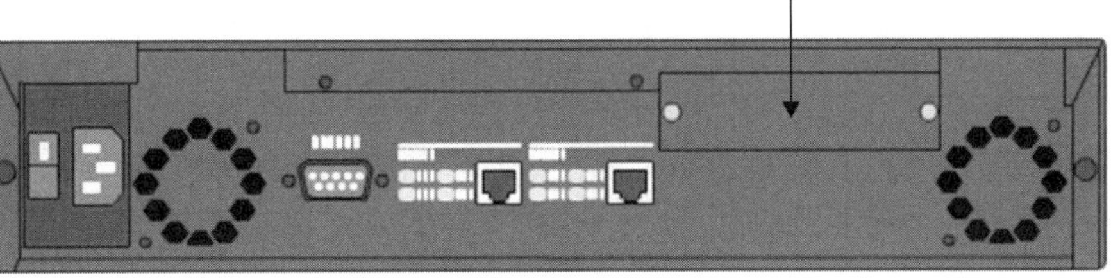

Figure 13-3 VPN 3005 front and rear views

Cisco VPN 3015 Concentrator

Like the Cisco VPN 3005, the *3015* is a VPN platform designed for small-to-medium networks with bandwidth requirements up to full-duplex T1/E1 (4 Mbps maximum performance) and up to 100 simultaneous sessions. Also, like the 3005, the default encryption processing is performed in software. Unlike the 3005, the 3015 is field-upgradeable to the VPN 3030 and 3060 models by adding memory and SEP modules. Figure 13-4 shows the front and rear view of a VPN 3015. The larger units look the same except that SEP modules and the redundant power supply replace the blank covers. The basic configuration and expansion capabilities include the following:

- Software-based encryption
- Single power supply
- Expansion capabilities:
    - Optional WAN interface module with dual T1/E1 ports
    - Up to four Cisco SEP hardware encryption modules
    - Optional redundant power supply

Cisco VPN 3030 Concentrator

The *3030* is a VPN platform designed for medium-to-large networks with bandwidth requirements from full T1/E1 through fractional T3, up to 50 Mbps maximum performance.

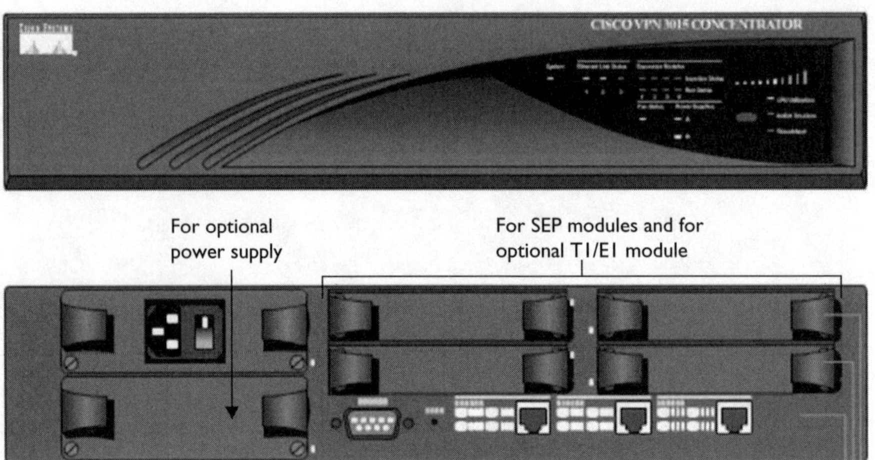

Figure 13-4 VPN 3015 front and rear views

The 3030 can support up to 1,500 simultaneous sessions. The basic configuration and expansion capabilities include the following:

- One SEP module for hardware-based encryption
- Single power supply
- Expansion capabilities:
    - Optional WAN interface module with dual T1/E1 ports
    - Up to three additional SEP hardware-based encryption modules
    - Optional redundant power supply

Cisco VPN 3060 Concentrator

The *3060* is a VPN platform designed for large networks requiring the highest level of performance and reliability, with high-bandwidth requirements from fractional T3 through full T3/E3 or greater connections. The 3060 can support up to 5,000 simultaneous sessions. The basic configuration and expansion capabilities include the following:

- Two SEP modules for hardware-based encryption
- Optional dual redundant power supplies (hot swappable)
- Expansion capabilities:
    - Optional WAN interface module with dual T1/E1 ports
    - Up to two additional SEP hardware-based encryption modules

Cisco VPN 3080 Concentrator

The *3080* is a top-of-the-line platform fully optimized to support large enterprise networks requiring the highest level of performance with support for up to 10,000 simultaneous remote access sessions. The basic configuration and expansion capabilities include the following:

- Four SEP modules for hardware-based encryption
- Dual redundant power supplies (hot swappable)
- Expansion capabilities:
    - Optional WAN interface module with dual T1/E1 ports

Side-by-Side Model Comparison

The following table summarizes the key features of the Cisco VPN 3000 Concentrator series of devices.

	3005	3015	3030	3060	3080
Simultaneous Users	100	100	1,500	5,000	10,000
Encryption Throughput	4 Mbps	4 Mbps	50 Mbps	100 Mbps	100 Mbps
Encryption Method	Software	Software	Hardware	Hardware	Hardware
Encryption (SEP) Module	0	0	1	2	4
Expansion Slots Available	0	4	3	2	0
Redundant SEP	N/A	N/A	Option	Option	Yes
System Memory	32MB fixed	64MB	128MB	256MB	256MB
T1 WAN Module	Fixed Option	Option	Option	Option	Option
Dual Power Supply	Single	Option	Option	Option	Yes
Client License	Unlimited	Unlimited	Unlimited	Unlimited	Unlimited
Hardware	1U, Fixed	2U, Scalable	2U, Scalable	2U, Scalable	2U

Standards Supported

To support fast, easy, and reliable deployment and scalability to thousands of remote users and sites, the Cisco VPN 3000 Concentrators are full-featured VPN devices that incorporate IPSec and other industry standards. The 3000 series support the following standards and protocols. Any details for configuring these features are covered in Chapter 14.

- Tunneling Protocols: IPSec, PPTP, L2TP, and L2TP/IPSec
- Encryption/Authentication: IPSec Encapsulating Security Payload (ESP) using DES/3DES (56/168 bit) or AES (128, 192, 256 bit) with MD5 or SHA, MPPE using 40/128 bit RC4
- Key Management: Internet Key Exchange (IKE) and Diffie–Hellman (DH) Groups 1, 2, 5, 7 (ECDH)

- NAT: NAT Transparent IPSec, IPSec/TCP, Ratified IPSec/UDP (with autodetection and fragmentation avoidance). Ratified IPSec/UDP support for NAT-T provides autodetection behind a NAT/PAT device, such as a small or home office router, and adds multivendor interoperability
- Routing: RIP, RIP2, OSPF, reverse route injection (RRI), static, automatic endpoint discovery, classless interdomain routing (CIDR)
- Release 3.6 includes DHCP relay/proxy for customers using the Cisco VPN 3000 Concentrator as an edge device in wireless configurations because it removes the need for an additional DHCP server
- Dynamic Domain Naming System (DNS) population (DDNS/DHCP) allows administrators to associate a remote access computer with its current IP address
- IPSec fragmentation policy control, including support for Path MTU Discovery (PMTUD)
- PPPoE Automatic Maximum Transmission Unit (MTU) adjustment for the network driver interface specification WAN (NDISWAN) during install improves remote access client operation in PPPoE DSL environments
- MovianVPN (Certicom) Handheld VPN Client with ECC

Cisco VPN 3000 Concentrator Features

The following summarizes the features and benefits provided by the Cisco VPN 3000 Concentrator devices. Chapter 14 addresses those that require configuration.

Modular Design (Models 3015 to 3080)

The Cisco SEP modules provide hardware-based encryption, ensuring consistent performance throughout the rated capacity for models 3030 through 3080. With multiple SEP modules, the devices became distributed-processing architecture, providing enhanced performance and increased reliability through redundancy. This modular design provides investment protection, redundancy, and a simple upgrade path, plus it minimizes the impact on rack space and power supply allocation.

Digital Design

The all-digital design of the VPN 3000 device provides high-degree reliability with solid, long-term performance, while providing 24-hour continuous operation. Incorporated into each unit is a robust instrumentation package for real-time monitoring and alerts.

Windows Compatibility

The VPN 3000 series' close support for Microsoft hosts, including Windows 2000/XP clients, makes large-scale client deployment and seamless integration with related network systems. The VPN 3000 supports the following Microsoft protocols:

- Microsoft PPTP/MPPE/MPPC, MSCHAPv1/v2, and EAP/RADIUS pass-through for EAP/TLS and EAP/GTC support

- Microsoft L2TP/IPsec for Windows 2000/XP (including XP DHCP option for route population)
- Microsoft L2TP/IPsec for Windows 98, Windows Millennium (Me), and Windows NT Workstation 4.0

VPN 3000 Release 3.6 added three improvements to support Microsoft's Integrated VPN Client including

- Microsoft L2TP/IPSec Extensible Authentication Protocol (EAP) pass-through support (TLS and GTX/SDI) for working from behind a PAT/NAT device with the VPN Client
- DHCP—XP route list population (split tunneling)
- IPSec/User Datagram Protocol (UDP) NAT-T compatibility (expected release by Microsoft in 2003)
- Support for Windows Installer (MSI) installation (Windows NT/20000XP only), providing the system administrator with the capability to customize installation packages and track system changes made during client installation

Security

The VPN 3000 Series support for current and emerging security standards, including RADIUS, NT Domain Authentication, RSA SecurID, one-time passwords (OTP), and digital certificates offering large-scale client deployment and seamless integration with external authentication systems, as well as interoperability with third-party products.

VPN 3000 release 3.6 offers two notable enhancements to concentrator encryption and security, including

- Advanced Encryption Standard (AES) addition to the concentrator offers a stronger encryption option and provides performance benefits for both the Cisco VPN 3002 Hardware Client and the Cisco VPN Client.
- RSA SecurID (SDI) Version 5.0 support. Users can now take advantage of the load balancing and resiliency features found in the RSA SecurID Version 5.0.

Advanced packet-filtering capabilities provide additional network security. Filtering options include source and destination IP address (Layer 3), port and protocol type (Layer 4), fragment protection, time and day access control, and FTP session filtering.

User and group-level policy management can be implemented for maximum flexibility and granularity in controlling network and feature access control.

High Availability

The VPN 3000 Series' redundant subsystems and multichassis failover capabilities help to ensure maximum system uptime and remote user connectivity. Redundant SEP and power supply options within individual devices promote reliability in a single or multidevice configuration. Multiple concentrators can be configured for both load-balancing and failover redundancy, providing protection and capacity to high-volume critical systems.

Extensive instrumentation and monitoring capabilities, as well as support for Cisco network management software applications, provide network managers with real-time system status and early-warning alerts.

A new feature in Release 3.6 is improved bandwidth limiting and traffic-shaping capabilities on the Cisco VPN 3000 Concentrators. This allows network administrators to assign minimum and maximum bandwidth parameters on a per-user basis. The administrator can establish limits on users with high-bandwidth use.

Robust Management

The Cisco VPN 3000 Concentrator can be managed using web-based applications from any standard web browser using HTTP or HTTPS. The VPN 3000s also support CLI commands using Telnet, Secure HTTP, SSH, and via a console port.

The VPN concentrator devices support configuration and monitoring capabilities for both the enterprise user and the service provider.

VPN concentrator device access levels can be configured per user and/or per group allowing configuration and maintenance control consistent with the organization security policies.

Monitoring and Logging

The Cisco VPN 3000 Concentrators support the following technologies for providing monitoring and logging services:

- Syslog output
- Configurable SNMP traps
- Event logging and notification via e-mail (SMTP) and, therefore, pager
- Automatic FTP backup of event logs
- SNMP MIB-II support
  General Statistics
  System Status
  Session Data (including Client Assigned IP, Encrypted Type Connection Duration, Client OS, Version, and so forth)

VPN 3000 Concentrator Client Support

Remote access VPN clients use the three following common connectivity techniques to reach the central site:

- VPN client software installed on PCs or workstations
- Hardware VPN routers
- Firewalls and hardware clients

Cisco Easy VPN could be the perfect solution for all three techniques, particularly with large implementations and limited local support.

Cisco Easy VPN

The *Cisco Easy VPN* is a software enhancement for existing Cisco routers and security appliances that can simplify VPN deployment for remote offices and telecommuters. Easy VPN is based on the Cisco Unified Client Framework using a centrally located Easy VPN Server, which is configured with all parameters required of remote device. The remote Easy VPN client can be preconfigured for mass deployments and initial logins require little user intervention. The full client configuration is "pushed" down from the Easy VPN Server when the client connects.

Cisco Easy VPN centralizes VPN configuration and management, thereby reducing the complexity of VPN deployments. The Cisco Easy VPN strategy incorporates all Cisco VPN client implementations into a single deployment, including IOS routers, PIX Firewalls, the VPN 3002 Hardware Client, and software VPN clients. This system offers consistent policy and key management methods, thus simplifying remote side setup and administration.

Using this feature, security policies defined and updated at the head-end are pushed to the remote VPN client, ensuring those connections have current policies in place before any connection is established. In addition, a Cisco Easy VPN Server-enabled device can terminate VPN tunnels initiated by mobile remote workers running Cisco VPN client software on PCs. This flexibility makes it possible for traveling workers or telecommuters to access the corporate intranet for critical data and applications.

The Cisco Easy VPN client on a hardware device supports both the VPN Client and Network Extension modes discussed earlier.

The Cisco Easy VPN client feature currently supports the following hardware platforms. It might be necessary to upgrade the IOS on older devices to have the feature. Be sure to check the Cisco web site to see if other models have been added.

- Cisco 806, Cisco 826, Cisco 827, and Cisco 828 routers
- Cisco uBR905 and Cisco uBR925 cable access routers
- Cisco 1700 series routers
- PIX 500 Series Firewalls
- Cisco VPN 3002 Hardware Client

The Cisco Easy VPN Server feature supports the following hardware platforms. As with the client, it might be necessary to upgrade the IOS have the feature. Be sure to check the Cisco web site to see if other models have been added.

- Cisco VPN 3000 Concentrators
- PIX 500 Series Firewalls
- Most Cisco IOS routers

The Cisco Easy VPN Remote feature provides for automatic management of the following details:

- Negotiating tunnel parameters—Addresses, algorithms, lifetimes, and so on
- Establishing tunnels according to the defined parameters

- Automatically creating the NAT/PAT translation and any associated access lists
- Authenticating users—Making sure users are who they say they are, by way of user names, group names, and passwords
- Managing security keys for encryption and decryption
- Authenticating, encrypting, and decrypting data through the tunnel
- Client software upgrades for the VPN 3002

The Cisco VPN Client provides support for Windows 95, 98, Me, NT 4.0, 2000, XP, Linux (Intel), Solaris (UltraSparc-32bit), and MAC OS X 10.1, including centralized split-tunneling control and data compression. VPN client configuration was covered in Chapter 12.

Cisco VPN 3002 Hardware Client

The Cisco VPN 3002 Hardware Client was designed for organizations with many remote office environments. The *3002* combines the ease of use and scalability of a software client with the reliability and stability of a hardware platform. The 3002 client supports Easy VPN Remote, allowing it to connect to any Easy VPN server site concentrator. The VPN 3002 Hardware Client works invisibly with any OS supporting IP, including Solaris, Mac, and Linux.

The VPN 3002 is available with or without a built-in 8-port switch and allows up to 253 station connections in a single network.

Release 3.6 included two significant feature enhancements for the VPN 3002 Hardware Client device:

- Software-based AES providing an enhanced security option through stronger encryption capabilities. As with the Cisco VPN Client, enhanced remote access performance also exists on the Cisco VPN 3002 Hardware Client.
- H.323 Fixup feature allows remote access users—in Client mode—behind the Cisco VPN 3002 Hardware Client, to use NetMeeting or other H.323 applications. H.323 requires no configuration on either the VPN Concentrator or the VPN 3002.

Wireless Client Support

With release 3.0, all Cisco VPN 3000 Concentrators support ECC. This is a new Diffie–Hellman Group, which allows for much faster processing of keying information by devices with limited processing power, such as PDAs and smart phones. Cisco VPN 3000 Concentrators can now securely terminate tunnels from IP-enabled wireless devices, allowing a whole new class of users to access enterprise information securely, while preserving the investment in VPN termination equipment in the enterprise data center.

Cisco Internet Mobile Office

The Cisco VPN 3000 Series Concentrator, Cisco VPN 3002 Hardware Client, and the Cisco VPN Client work together with the Cisco Internet Mobile Office to provide mobile professionals with secure, high-speed broadband connectivity to their networks in airports, convention centers, hotels, and a growing number of other public spaces.

Chapter Review

This chapter looked at the various hardware implementations for Cisco VPN technologies and focused mainly on the VPN 3002 Hardware Client and the VPN 3000 Series Concentrators. The VPN 3002 is typically implemented at remote sites in larger organizations. They can be augmented by Cisco IOS routers, PIX Firewalls, and VPN client software running directly on the host PC.

The 3002 comes in two models: a two-port unit that can support a single client or pass through to a hub or switch and a model with a built-in 8-port 10/100 switch. Both devices can support up to 253 users on the LAN interface and a maximum of 100 simultaneous secure connections back to the central network.

The Cisco VPN 3002 supports two modes of operation to offer implementation choices based on flexibility, security, and easy configuration: Client mode and Network Extension mode. A large VPN implementation might frequently have both types of operation. In Client mode, the VPN 3002 emulates the VPN client software appearing to the main network like a single remote user. The hosts protected behind the VPN 3002 are a separate network that remains invisible and nonroutable to the central site. In Network Extension mode, the VPN 3002 establishes a secure site-to-site connection with the central site device. The local stations behind the VPN 3002 are fully routable and the local network is visible to the central site.

The VPN 3002 supports a growing range of VPN standards and technologies, plus some implementation features to simplify large VPN implementation and support. These features include Easy VPN Client, which allows a thin installation on the 3002 and the final configuration pushed down to the 3002 on first connection to the VPN Concentrator. The 3002 also supports Auto Upgrade, which allows the VPN Concentrator to push any needed software or firmware upgrades down to the client.

The VPN 3002 supports the following two levels of client authentication mechanism that supplies a high-level of security for both the VPN 3002 and the users behind the VPN 3002: Interactive Unit Authentication authenticates the VPN device during the VPN setup, while Individual User Authentication requires each user behind the 3002 to authenticate before using the VPN tunnel.

The VPN 3002 hardware device (release 3.5) and the Cisco VPN software client (v3.0) both support Cisco's VPN 3000 load-balancing and failover strategies that allow for more efficient use of the Concentrators and provide backup alternatives if a Concentrator fails.

The Cisco VPN 3000 Series Concentrator is a growing family of VPN devices designed and built to provide fast, reliable, and secure remote access to organization network resources. These devices work with the Cisco VPN client software and various Cisco VPN hardware devices to incorporate high availability, high performance, and scalability, plus advanced encryption and authentication technologies to the network.

The VPN 3000 Concentrator platform offers customer-upgradeable and field-swappable components to increase capacity dramatically, while maintaining the original device, rack space, and power requirements. Scalable Encryption Processing (SEP) modules can be added to the 3015 to 3060 model case to enable users to add capacity and throughput easily.

The Cisco VPN 3000 Concentrator series comes in several models to meet organization capacity requirements and applications. The platform includes models to support customers with 100 or fewer remote access users to large organizations with up to 10,000 simultaneous remote connections. The latest Cisco VPN Software Client is provided at no additional charge with unlimited distribution licensing with all versions of the Cisco VPN 3000 Concentrator.

Questions

1. What is the protocol the Cisco VPN 3000 Series Concentrators use to provide Wireless Client Support for personal digital assistants (PDAs) and smart phones?

   A. H.323

   B. Elliptic Curve Cryptography (ECC)

   C. IPSec/UDP NAT-T

   D. PPPoE

2. The VPN 3002 Hardware Client supports how many simultaneous VPN connections?

   A. 10

   B. 50

   C. 100

   D. 253

3. The Cisco VPN 3002 supports which two modes of operation?

   A. Split Tunneling mode

   B. Client mode

   C. DHCP mode

   D. Network Extension mode

4. The VPN 3002 DHCP "client" service is implemented on which interface?

   A. Private

   B. DMZ

   C. Public

   D. It is user configurable on any interface

5. The VPN 3002 DHCP "server" service is implemented on which interface?

   A. Private

   B. DMZ

   C. Public

   D. It is user configurable on any interface

6. Which one of the following is *not* a VPN 3002–supported feature?
   A. Auto Upgrade
   B. Interactive Unit Authentication
   C. PPPoE
   D. Individual User Authentication
   E. Wireless client
7. Which is *not* a model of VPN 3000 Concentrator?
   A. 3005
   B. 3010
   C. 3030
   D. 3060
   E. 3080
8. Which model of VPN 3000 Concentrator supports only two 10/100 interfaces?
   A. 3005
   B. 3010
   C. 3030
   D. 3060
   E. 3080
9. What is the maximum number of simultaneous VPN connections supported by any VPN 3000 Concentrator?
   A. 1,000
   B. 5,000
   C. 10,000
   D. 100,000
   E. No limit
10. What is the maximum number of SEP modules that can be installed in a VPN 3000 Concentrator?
    A. 1
    B. 2
    C. 3
    D. 4
11. Which one is *not* a security protocol supported by the VPN 3000 series devices?
    A. Diffie-Hellman (DH) Groups 1, 2, 5, 7 (ECDH)
    B. RRI (reverse route injection)

C. AES (128, 192, 256 bit)

D. DES/3DES (56/168 bit)

12. Which one is *not* a common remote access VPN client connectivity technique to reach the central site?

    A. VPN switch

    B. Firewalls and hardware clients

    C. Hardware VPN routers

    D. VPN client software installed on PCs or workstations

13. With the Cisco Easy VPN strategy, where is the security policy configured?

    A. Cisco Easy VPN Client

    B. Cisco Easy VPN Server

    C. Cisco VPN Client

    D. NAS

14. The Cisco Internet Mobile Office provides mobile professionals with what service?

    A. VPN connectivity while on airplanes

    B. PDA connectivity within the network

    C. VPN connectivity from home

    D. Secure, high-speed broadband connectivity in public places

15. Which of the following can *not* be a Cisco Easy VPN server?

    A. PIX Firewall

    B. IOS Router

    C. VPN 3000 Concentrator

    D. VPN 3002 hardware device

Answers

1. **B.** Elliptic Curve Cryptography (ECC)
2. **C.** 100
3. **B.** Client mode. and D. Network Extension mode
4. **C.** Public
5. **A.** Private
6. **E.** Wireless client
7. **B.** 3010

8. A. 3005
9. C. 10,000
10. D. 4
11. B. RRI (reverse route injection)
12. A. VPN switch
13. B. Cisco Easy VPN Server
14. D. Secure, high-speed broadband connectivity in public places
15. D. VPN 3002 hardware device

CHAPTER 14

Cisco VPN 3000 Remote Access Networks

In this chapter, you will learn to:

- Describe VPN Concentrator user interfaces and startup
- Discuss VPN Concentrators in IPSec VPN implementations
- Configure VPN remote access with preshared keys
- Configure VPN remote access with digital certificates
- Configure VPN users and groups
- Configure Cisco VPN 3000 client support
- Configure the Cisco VPN client autoinitiation feature
- Monitor and administer Cisco VPN 3000 remote access networks

This chapter introduces working with the Cisco VPN 3000 Concentrators for basic operations, as well as for advanced features and options. The 3000 series devices were introduced and described in Chapter 13. That information won't be repeated here, but the features introduced are explored and the configuration steps defined.

The VPN 3000 devices, the concentrator series, and the remote client device all support the following three main activities:

- Configuration
- Administration
- Monitoring

This chapter looks at all three activities on the 3000 series Concentrators.

Basic VPN concepts, such as preshared keys and using Certificate Authorities to implement digital certificates, were covered in Chapters 9 through 11. While the features are configured in this chapter, the underlying technologies aren't addressed beyond an explanation for the processes being discussed. The menu-driven and web-based interfaces used with the VPN 3000 devices change the implementation steps, but three primary tasks are still used to ensure a successful installation:

1. Prepare for IKE and IPSec
2. Configure the features
3. Verify and monitor configuration

The VPN Concentrator creates a virtual private network (VPN) by creating a secure connection across a public Transmission Control Protocol/Internet Protocol (TCP/IP) network, such as the Internet. It can create single user to local area network (LAN) (remote user) connections and LAN-to-LAN connections.

The VPN Concentrator functions as a bidirectional tunnel endpoint using various standard protocols to perform the following tasks:

- Establish tunnels
- Negotiate tunnel parameters
- Authenticate users
- Assign user addresses
- Encrypt and decrypt data
- Manage security keys
- Manage data transfer across the tunnel

Network configurations and VPN placement can vary widely. Chapter 27 introduces the Cisco SAFE strategy and how VPN devices fit into the secure network design. The *VPN Concentrator* is a flexible and functional device that can satisfy most applications. This chapter discusses configuring the VPN 3000 Series Concentrator to support VPN remote access implications. Chapter 15 reviews the VPN 3002 remote access client device. Chapter 16 covers the VPN Series Concentrator to support VPN LAN-to-LAN networks.

VPN Concentrator User Interfaces and Startup

The VPN 3000 Concentrator and the VPN 3002 Hardware Client support both a specialized command-line interface (CLI) and a web-based interface (Concentrator or Client Manager). You can do exactly the same tasks with either interface. The choice ultimately boils down to personal preference but, in general, the Manager web-based interface might be easier to learn and navigate if you're familiar with the Windows interface and browsers. The Help feature on the Concentrator Manager is much better than the CLI.

To manage the device with something other than the console cable, the CLI must be used to configure at least the private interface to be part of a network accessible by one or more hosts with either a web browser or Telnet capabilities.

Quick Configuration

The Quick Configuration Wizard that appears at initial startup allows configuring the minimal parameters needed to make the VPN Concentrator functional. While optional, this wizard and a console connection provide a relatively quick and easy way to add enough configuration to allow access from a network PC. Quick Configuration can be performed entirely from the CLI or switched to the Concentrator Manager any time after the first two steps. The Quick Configuration options, as shown in the following output, appear only once and can only be used once, unless the device is rebooted with the Reboot with Factory/Default option.

```
Login: admin
Password:                               (doesn't display)

               Welcome to
              Cisco Systems
       VPN 3000 Concentrator Series
          Command Line Interface
Copyright (C) 1998-2003 Cisco Systems, Inc.
-- : Set the time on your device. ...
> Time
Quick -> [ 10:13:37 ]
```


CLI Quick Configuration Steps

The CLI Quick Configuration Wizard prompts guide you through the following configurations steps:

1. Set the system time, date, time zone, and daylight saving time values.
2. Configure the VPN Concentrator private network interface (Ethernet 1) by responding to the following prompts:

```
This table shows current IP addresses.
    Interface              IP Address/Subnet Mask    MAC Address
---------------------------------------------------------------
| Ethernet 1 - Private |    0.0.0.0/0.0.0.0       |
| Ethernet 2 - Public  |    0.0.0.0/0.0.0.0       |
| Ethernet 3 - External |   0.0.0.0/0.0.0.0       |
---------------------------------------------------------------
** An address is required for the private interface. **
> Enter IP Address
Quick Ethernet 1 -> [ 0.0.0.0 ] 192.168.1.1

> Enter Subnet Mask
Quick Ethernet 1 -> [ 255.0.0.0 ] 255.255.255.0

1) Ethernet Speed 10 Mbps
2) Ethernet Speed 100 Mbps
3) Ethernet Speed 10/100 Mbps Auto Detect
Quick -> [ 3 ]

1) Enter Duplex - Half/Full/Auto
2) Enter Duplex - Full Duplex
3) Enter Duplex - Half Duplex
Quick -> [ 1 ]
```

Once these settings are made, the remainder of the Quick Configuration can be completed with the VPN Concentrator Manager (Cisco's recommended method). If the CLI method is used, similar prompts would guide the configuration through the following features:

1. Configure any other interfaces. At a minimum, the Ethernet 2 public interface must be configured. An additional Ethernet 3 interface could be on models 3015-3080 and/or optional WAN interfaces.
2. Define information that identifies your VPN Concentrator on the network, such as the system name, IP address of the DNS, registered Internet domain name, and default gateway to which the VPN will forward unknown packets.
3. Define which tunneling protocols and encryption options are to be used.
4. Define the method(s) for assigning IP addresses to protected clients on the private interface as the defined tunnel is established.
5. Specify one of five types of servers to authenticate users: the concentrator's internal server, the external RADIUS server, the external NT Domain server, external server, or the external SDI (RSA Security Inc. SecurID) server, or Kerberos/Active Directory server.
6. When using the VPN Concentrator internal authentication server, populate the internal user database with at least one user, each with a user name and password, and, if *per-user address assignment* is specified, an IP address and subnet mask.

NOTE The maximum number of entries (groups and users combined) varies by model:
Model 3005/3015–100
Model 3030–500
Model 3060/3080–1,000

7. When using IPSec tunneling protocol, the remote-access client connects to the VPN Concentrator via a group name and password, which needs to be configured.
8. Change the admin password to improve system security.
9. Save the configuration file (menu option) to complete quick configuration.

Concentrator Manager Quick Configuration

The Concentrator Manager Quick Configuration assumes the first two steps of the CLI Quick Configuration were performed, so the private interface can be accessed by a web browser. As with the CLI version, you can only go through the quick configuration steps one time, unless the device is rebooted ignoring the Configuration File option.

The web browser session is opened using the admin/admin case-sensitive user name/password combination. The one-time screen, as shown in Figure 14-1, allows using the Quick Configuration Wizard to add additional settings.

The wizard then leads you through the same configuration options offered earlier in the CLI section. While they aren't identical, the Quick Configuration Wizard is similar to the one used by the VPN 3002 Hardware Client device, covered in detail in Chapter 15.

Main

Welcome to the VPN 3000 Concentrator Series Manager

The **VPN 3000 Concentrator Series** has booted, and you must now supply some configuration parameters to make it operational.

To configure the *minimal* parameters, click here to start Quick Configuration.

To configure *all* features, click here to go to the Main Menu..

Figure 14-1 VPN Concentrator Manager Quick Configuration option screen

The example about preshared keys in the section "Remote Access VPNs with Preshared Keys" assumes the Quick Configuration wasn't done, and it covers the screens and settings at that time.

STUDY TIP VPN, PIX, and IDS technologies, features, and versions are quickly changing and improving. In some cases, three versions were released in the past year. Because the Cisco web site no longer specifies the versions covered, confirming as many processes as possible with the online documentation makes sense. For the latest information on the Quick Configuration Wizards, go to www.cisco.com and search for VPN Quick Configuration. Then look for the most recent version of the Getting Started Guide. This guide has step-by-step instructions with the most current screen features. Similar searches on any technologies that you can't work with hands-on would be good way to avoid being surprised in this rapidly changing environment.

Command-Line Interface (CLI) Basics

The VPN 3000 Concentrator CLI is a built-in, menu-driven configuration, administration, and monitoring system, which can be accessed via the device console port or a Telnet (or Telnet over SSL) session. Both Telnet options are enabled by default on the private network interface once the interface is configured with an IP address in the LAN. The CLI supports the same configuration options as the HTML-based VPN 3000 Concentrator Manager covered in the section "Concentrator Manager (Web Interface)."

NOTE The VPN 3000 concentrators use a straight-through serial connection. A serial cable with 9-pin adapter can be used on the concentrator end, and then whatever connection is required for the serial interface on the PC.

To use a straight-through jumper cable, one of the Cisco 9-pin adapters (gray posts) from a Cisco console configuration kit is required on the concentrator. The VPN 3002 uses a standard Cisco console kit with a roll-over cable that plugs into an RJ-45 interface on the device.

Console port access is similar to the IOS routers using a terminal emulator program, such as HyperTerminal. Pressing ENTER few times might be necessary to get the login prompt to appear. Login user names and passwords for both console and Telnet access are the same. The factory-supplied default is configured and enabled for administrators using admin for both the login and password. Entries are case-sensitive. The following output shows the initial login and the main menu:

```
Login: admin
Password:                              (doesn't display)

                Welcome to
               Cisco Systems
       VPN 3000 Concentrator Series
          Command Line Interface
Copyright (C) 1998-2003 Cisco Systems, Inc.

1) Configuration
2) Administration
3) Monitoring
4) Save changes to Config file
5) Help Information
6) Exit

Main ->
```

Making changes typically involves making one or more menu choices, and then answering any appropriate prompts. The following are some things to remember about the CLI interface:

- Password entries are case-sensitive.
- The interface displays current or default entries in brackets, for example, [192.168.1.1].
- Use the ENTER key on the console keyboard to complete a choice.
- Any configuration changes take effect as soon as they're entered. These changes are part of the active, or running, configuration. To make this the boot configuration used when the device is rebooted, you must save the configuration (Main menu option #4).

Help

The Help menu system is somewhat limited, displaying only the following information when 5 is entered at the Main menu. Context-sensitive Help is unavailable and the familiar question mark (?) doesn't activate help features. The Help feature in the Hardware Client Manager is much better and offers context-sensitive assistance like most Windows applications.

```
Main -> 5
Cisco Systems.  Help information for the Command Line Interface
```

```
From any menu except the Main menu.
-- 'B' or 'b' for Back to previous menu.
-- 'H' or 'h' for Home back to the main menu.

For Data entry
-- Current values are in '[ ]'s. Just hit 'Enter' to accept value.

1) View Help Again
2) Back

Help ->
```

The *B* and *H* options (and especially the *H* option) come in handy when you're navigating the device menus. Pressing *H* returns you to the Main menu.

Saving Configuration File Changes

Configuration and administration changes made using Options 1 and 2 on the Main menu take effect immediately and become a part of the active, or running, configuration. Like the Cisco routers, if the VPN 3000 is rebooted without saving the active configuration, any changes will be lost.

Saving changes to the system configuration (CONFIG) file is a one-step process from the Main menu. At the Main -> prompt, typing the numeral 4 will save changes without additional steps or confirmation.

```
1) Configuration
2) Administration
3) Monitoring
4) Save changes to Config file
5) Help Information
6) Exit

Main -> 4
```

The system writes the current (active) configuration to the CONFIG file and redisplays the main menu.

Configuring the Private Interface

To access the Concentrator using the Manager web interface, you must have the workstation in the same subnet at the private interface. If the Quick Configuration Wizard wasn't used for a new or unconfigured Concentrator, the CLI is used to configure the interface. The following output shows the steps from the Main menu:

```
1) Configuration
2) Administration
3) Monitoring
4) Save changes to Config file
5) Help Information
6) Exit

Main -> 1
```

```
1) Interface Configuration
2) System Management
3) User Management
4) Policy Management
5) Back

Config -> 1                              (shows the current settings)

This table shows current IP addresses.
  Intf         Status       IP Address/Subnet Mask         MAC Address
-------------------------------------------------------------------------
Ether1-Pri|      UP      | 192.168.10.1/255.255.255.0 | 00.03.A0.88.CE.AC
Ether2-Pub|Not Configured|      0.0.0.0/0.0.0.0       |
-------------------------------------------------------------------------
DNS Server(s): DNS Server Not Configured
DNS Domain Name:
Default Gateway: Default Gateway Not Configured

1) Configure Ethernet #1 (Private)
2) Configure Ethernet #2 (Public)
3) Configure Power Supplies
4) Back

Interfaces -> 1                        (to set the Private interface)

1) Interface Setting (Disable, DHCP or Static IP)
2) Set Public Interface
3) Select IP Filter
4) Select Ethernet Speed
5) Select Duplex
6) Set MTU
7) Set Port Routing Config
8) Set Bandwidth Management
9) Set Public Interface IPSec Fragmentation Policy
10) Back

Ethernet Interface 1 -> 1                (to set a Static IP address)

1) Disable
2) Enable using DHCP Client
3) Enable using Static IP Addressing

Ethernet Interface 1 -> [ 3 ] 3

> Enter IP Address                 (current value appears in brackets)
Ethernet Interface 1 -> [ 192.168.10.1 ] 192.168.1.10

> Enter Subnet Mask
Ethernet Interface 1 -> [ 255.255.255.0 ]
Ethernet Interface 1 -> h                          (return to Main menu)
```

Concentrator Manager (Web Interface)

The VPN 3000 Concentrator Manager (Manager) is an HTML-based interface application that makes configuring, administering, monitoring, and managing the VPN 3000 device possible with a web browser on a PC in the private network.

By default, the Manager uses HTTP, which is convenient, but messages are transmitted in Cleartext. If security requires it, the Manager supports secure, encrypted HTTP connection over Secure Sockets Layer (SSL) protocol, known as HTTPS.

Browser Requirements

The Manager application supports either Microsoft Internet Explorer (IE) version 4.0 or higher or Netscape Navigator version 4.5–4.7. For the best results, Cisco recommends Internet Explorer. JavaScript and Cookies need to be enabled in the browser. Another recommendation is to install any updates and patches.

Recommended Display Settings

Cisco recommends the following monitor display settings for the best viewing:

- Screen area—1024 × 768 pixels or greater. (Minimum 800 × 600 pixels)
- Colors—256 colors or higher.

Browser Navigation Toolbar

Earlier implementations of the Manager were the CLI converted simply to a web interface. Each new version includes better Windows function integration. In particular, Help, a Java-based applet, is getting friendlier and more useful.

Cisco doesn't recommend using the browser navigation toolbar buttons Back, Forward, or Refresh/Reload with the Manager, unless you're specifically instructed to do so. To maintain access security, clicking the Refresh/Reload button automatically logs out the Manager session and returns to the login screen. Using the Back or Forward buttons could possibly display old Manager displays with incorrect data or settings. If you're concerned, the IE View | Full screen (F11) feature will eliminate the temptation.

Connecting to the Concentrator Manager

To access the VPN 3000 Concentrator Manager application using HTTP over a web browser, type the VPN 3000 private interface IP address (such as 192.168.1.10) in the browser Address or Location field. The browser automatically supplies the http:// prefix.

The browser displays the login screen shown in Figure 14-2.

Logging in to the Manager application is the same for Cleartext HTTP or secure HTTPS. At this point, a valid user name/password combination can be entered to gain access. Both entries are case-sensitive. Internet Explorer users can use the TAB key to move from field to field. The Clear button can be used to start over.

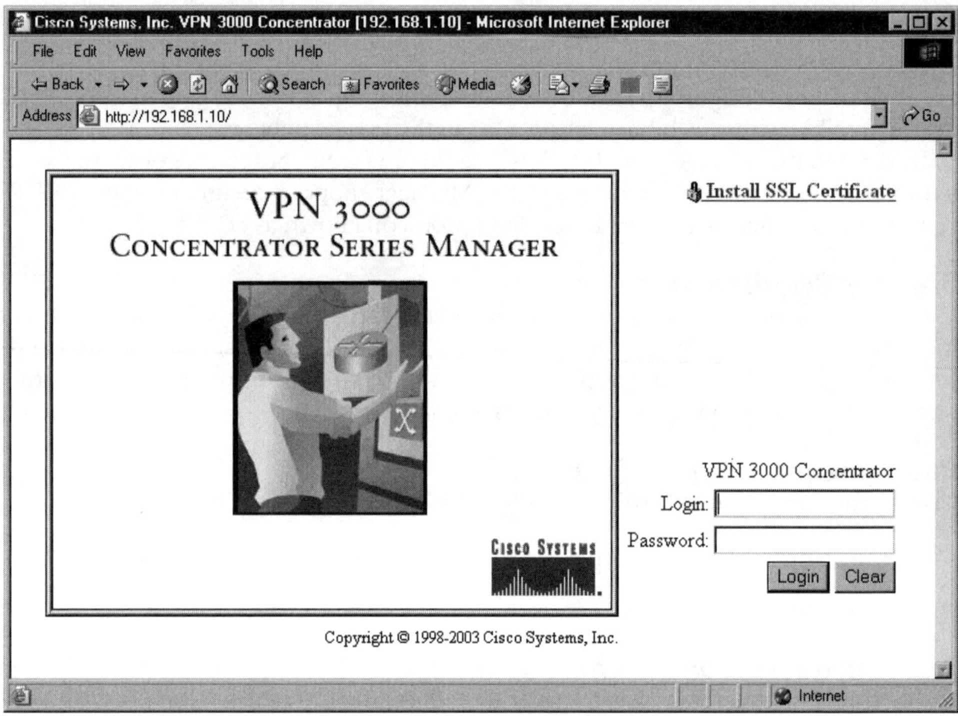

Figure 14-2 VPN 3000 Concentrator Manager login screen

An unconfigured unit will have the default Administrator combination admin/admin for initial entry.

Figure 14-3 shows the opening screen that appears, offering access to the three main application modules: Configuration, Administration, and Monitoring. The application tree on the left-hand side offers explorer-like navigation capabilities to move quickly from feature to feature. The menu tree can be expanded and contracted as needed. The figure shows the Configuration section expanded to show the second-tier choices. The same three choices are displayed in the upper-right corner for times when the left-side panel isn't displayed. The upper-right corner also offers quick access to the Main menu and the Help system, as well as support phone numbers and web pages.

The main body of the window provides a good overview of the various screen components and options of the application, including explanations for service icons that will appear in the upper-right corner.

The VPN 3000 Concentrator Reference, available online or on the documentation CD-ROM that came with the device, covers how to set up the device for installing an SSL Certificate in the browser for HTTPS connectivity.

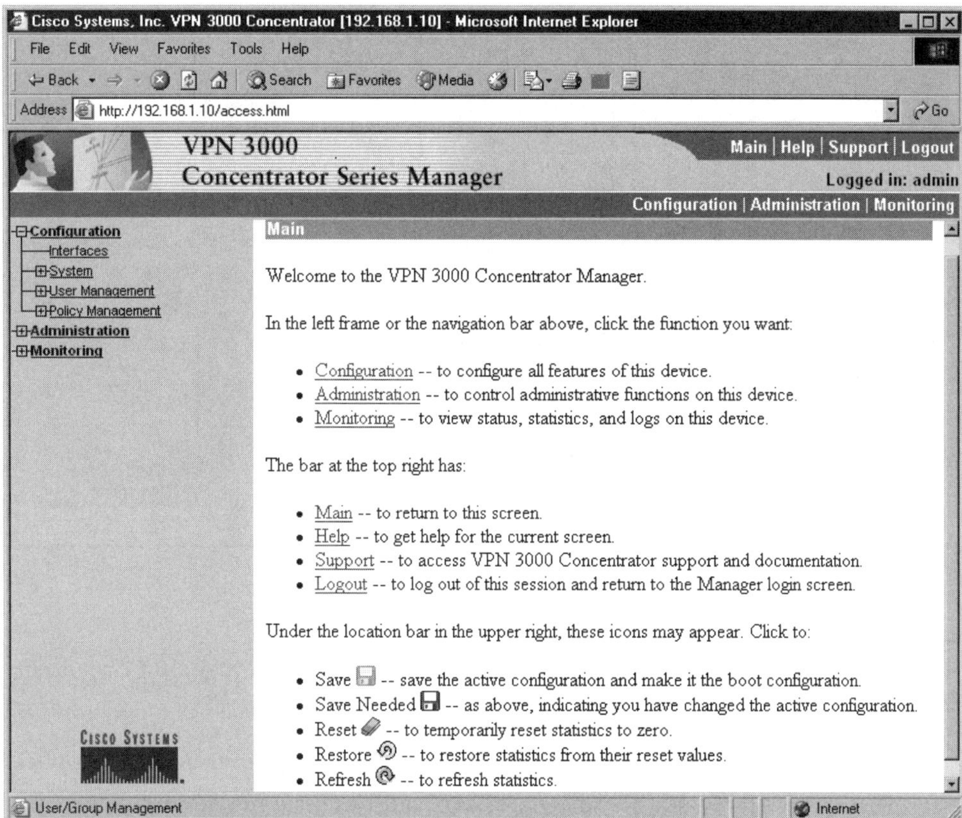

Figure 14-3 Manager opening screen

Manager Organization

The Manager, exactly like the CLI, is made up of three major sections and many second- and third-level subsections:

- Configuration
- Administration
- Monitoring

Configuration The Configuration menu is used to set all parameters that govern the unit's use and functionality as a VPN device. Cisco supplies default parameters that cover typical installations and uses. Figure 14-4 shows the Configuration menu fully expanded. The insert graphic shows the four second-tier options.

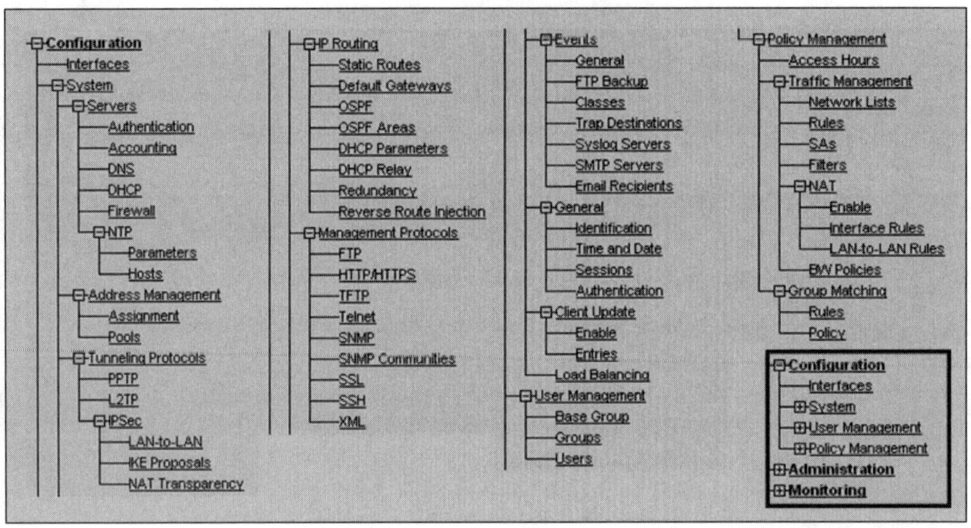

Figure 14-4 Configuration menu fully expanded

The Configuration section provides access to configure all VPN 3000 Concentrator features:

- **Interfaces**—Ethernet interfaces, DNS servers, domain name, and power supplies
- **System**—system-wide parameters: servers, address assignment, tunneling protocols, IP routing, IPSec, management protocols, events, identification, and the Client autoupdate feature
- **User Management**—create and modify groups and users
- **Policy Management**—access hours, network lists, rules, security associations, filters, and NAT and group matching

Administration The Administration menu manages the higher level functions that keep the 3000 unit operational and secure, such as who is allowed to configure the system, what software runs on it, and managing its configuration files and digital certificates. Only the administrator account can use the VPN Concentrator Manager. Figure 14-5 shows the Administration menu fully expanded out.

The Administration section provides access to control VPN 3000 Concentrator administrative functions:

- **Administer Sessions**—statistics and logout capability for all sessions
- **Software Update**—update concentrator and VPN client software
- **System Reboot**—system reboot options, including save and scheduling choices
- **Ping**—use ICMP ping to determine connectivity to an address

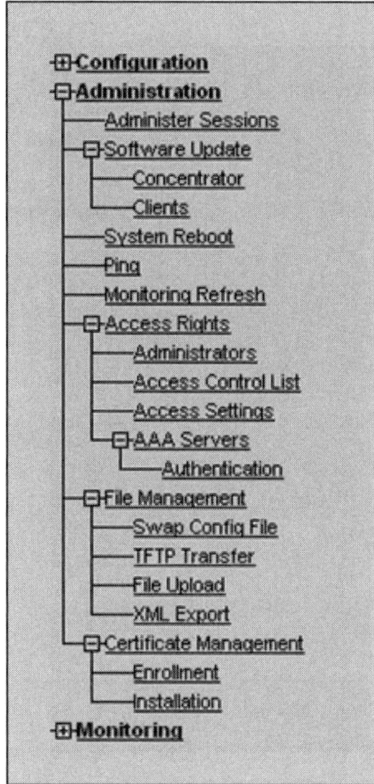

Figure 14-5 Administration menu fully expanded

- **Monitoring Refresh**—enable automatic refresh of Monitoring screens
- **Access Rights**—configure administrator profiles, access, sessions, and AAA
- **File Management**—view, save, delete, swap, and transfer files
- **Certificate Management**—install, enroll, and manage digital certificates

Monitoring The *Monitoring* menu is used to track many statistics and the status of many items essential to system administration and management. You can see the state of any LEDs that show the status of hardware subsystems in the device, as well as statistics stored and available in standard MIB-II data objects. Figure 14-6 shows the Monitoring menu fully expanded. The insert graphic shows the five second-tier options.

The Monitoring section of the Manager displays the VPN Concentrator status, sessions, statistics, and event logs. The Monitoring screens are read-only "snapshots" of data or status at the time the selection was made. These aren't real-time monitors. Most screens offer a Refresh button in the upper-right corner of the screen, which can be used to get a fresh image. The data on the screen can't be modified.

This section of the Manager lets you view VPN 3000 Concentrator status, sessions, statistics, and event logs.

- Routing Table—current valid routes and protocols
- Filterable Event Log—event logging with filtering capabilities

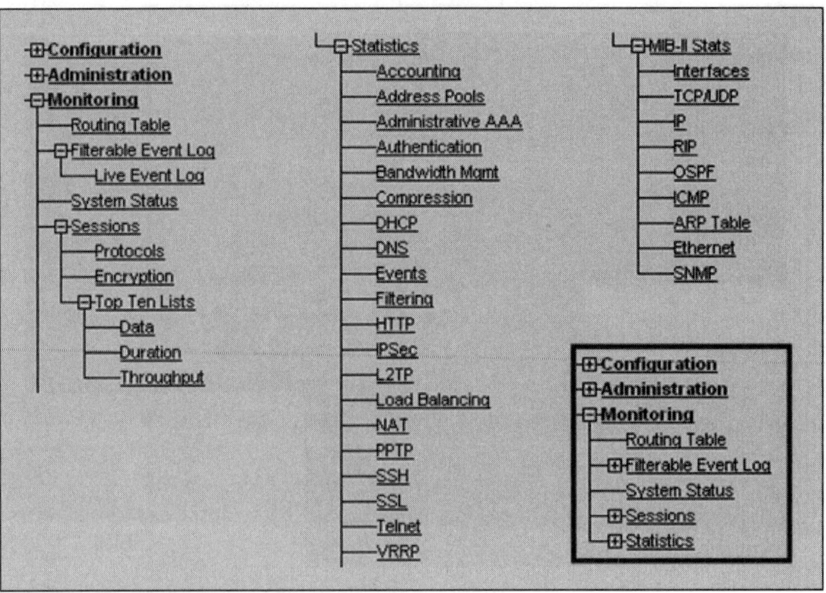

Figure 14-6 Monitoring menu fully expanded

- System Status—current software revisions, uptime, front-panel LEDs, network interfaces, SEP modules, and power supplies
- Sessions—all active sessions and "top ten" sessions, encryption and protocol data
- Statistics—accounting, address pools, administrative AAA, authentication, bandwidth management, compression, DHCP, DNS, events, filtering, HTTP, IPSec, L2TP, load balancing, NAT, PPTP, SSH, SSL, Telnet, and VRRP and MIB-II statistics

Figure 14-7 shows an example of a Monitoring screen using the Monitoring | System Status menu option. This screen shows the current version of the software, device serial number, the time the unit has been up, as well as CPU and Fan statistics. The device images show LED status and optional components, plus interface, modules, and power supplies with embedded links that display component statistics if clicked on.

Help

Figure 14-8 shows the result of selecting Configuration | Interfaces in the left panel, and then clicking the Help button in the upper-right corner. The context-sensitive Help window works like any Windows help document.

NOTE Help is a Java application, so Java must be enabled to see it and you might need to turn off any pop-up window protection software.

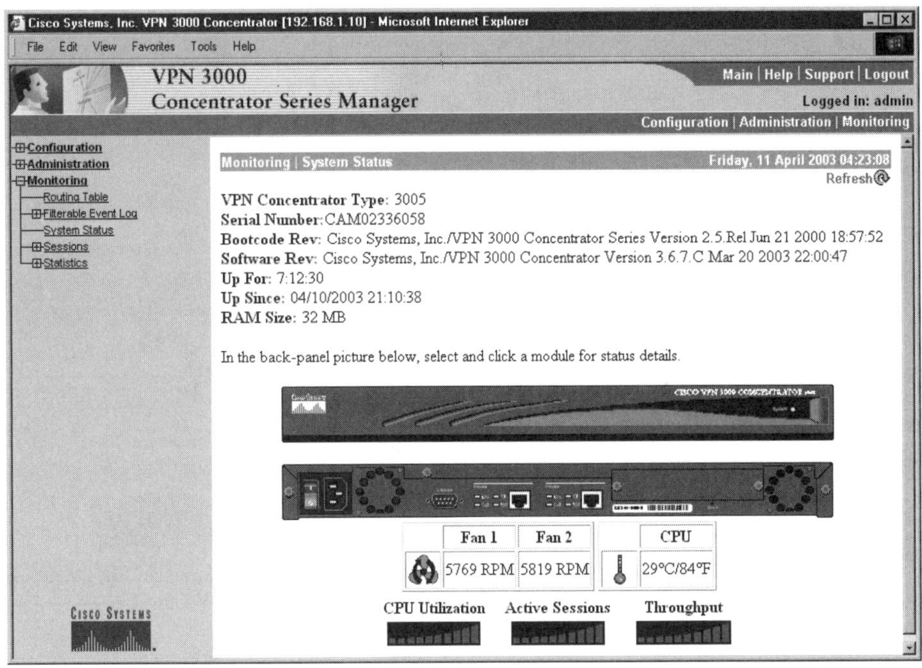

Figure 14-7 System monitoring screen

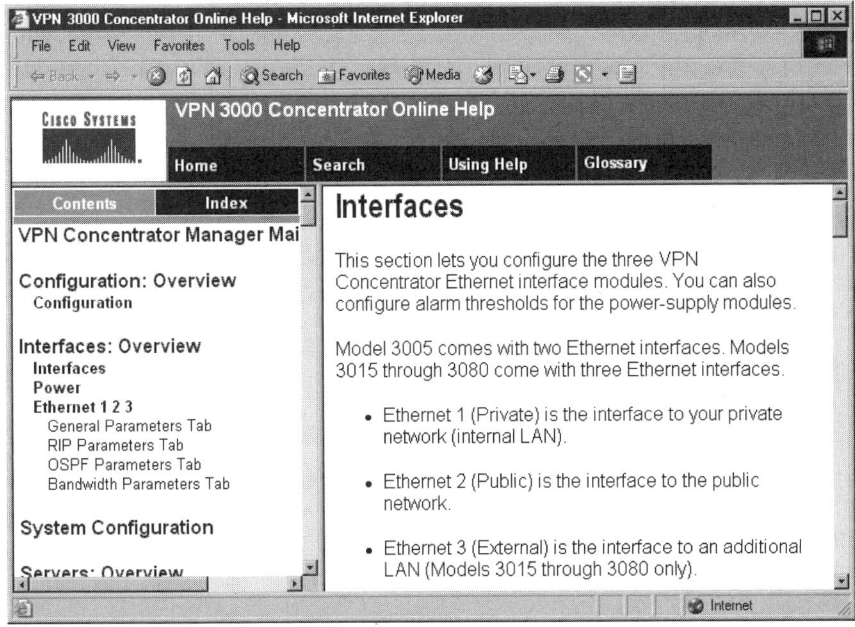

Figure 14-8 VPN 3000 Concentrator Manager Help system

PART III

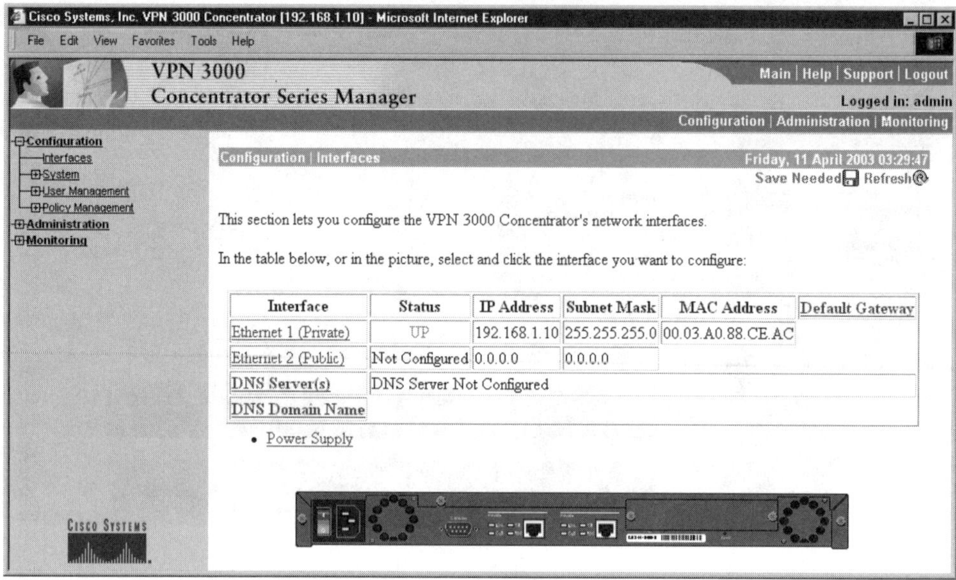

Figure 14-9 Typical Manager screen with reminder icons

Basic Operations

The Manager application takes advantage of the graphical interface to display as much information as feasible. Figure 14-9 shows the result of selecting Configuration | Interfaces from the menu. Notice the application map in the left-side panel shows where the screen is located in the structure. The figure might not show this, but the actual selection is highlighted.

In the upper-right corner, two icons remind you that changes must be saved and the screen needs to be refreshed—the data has timed out and is considered stale. This is a most useful reminder when counters and statistics are displayed. Clicking the icon activates the indicated service.

In the example figure, the back side of the device is displayed. In larger models, this would indicate any options that were added to the device.

VPN Concentrators in IPSec VPN Implementations

The Cisco VPN Concentrator series of devices has two basic VPN implementations:

- Remote access
- LAN-to-LAN

A large VPN implementation might frequently have variations of both types. It wouldn't be uncommon to have several LAN-to-LAN connections for branch office links combined with many remote access connections for traveling executives, sales professionals, and telecommuters.

Remote Access Networks

Remote access involves connecting individual users to a LAN to provide secure, encrypted network access for telecommuters, traveling employees, and one-person offices of consultants, contractors, brokers, vendors, and so forth.

Today, many companies provide their own VPN connections through the Internet, allowing access to remote users running VPN client software over dial-up technologies through their Internet service providers (ISPs). The rapid expansion of cable and DSL markets makes it possible for telecommuters and other fixed location users to replace slower modem and ISDN services with fast connections at a fraction of the cost of dedicated lines.

Fast Internet connections offered in many hotels and the new wireless access facilities in many public places, such as airports, convention centers, and even fast-food restaurants, means traveling employees can also use fast, secure, remote VPN connections. Figure 14-10 shows two common types of remote access VPN examples.

Remote access VPN implementations with VPN Concentrators is covered in the upcoming section "Remote Access VPNs with Preshared Keys." Chapter 15 covers the VPN 3002 client device, which allows a single appliance to provide remote access VPN connectivity and protection to small groups at a single location.

LAN-to-LAN Networks

LAN-to-LAN (site-to-site) VPNs are an alternative WAN infrastructure used to create secure connections between two end devices, such as routers, firewalls, or VPN Concentrators. The hosts on each LAN connect to those end devices and can access the other LAN via the secure connection based on the organization security policy and the placement of shared resources.

Common examples of site-to-site VPN implementation could include connecting branch offices, vendor sites, dealer sites, or customer offices to the corporate network. Figure 14-11 shows the types of connections that might be VPN candidates.

LAN-to-LAN VPN implementations with VPN Concentrators are covered in Chapter 16.

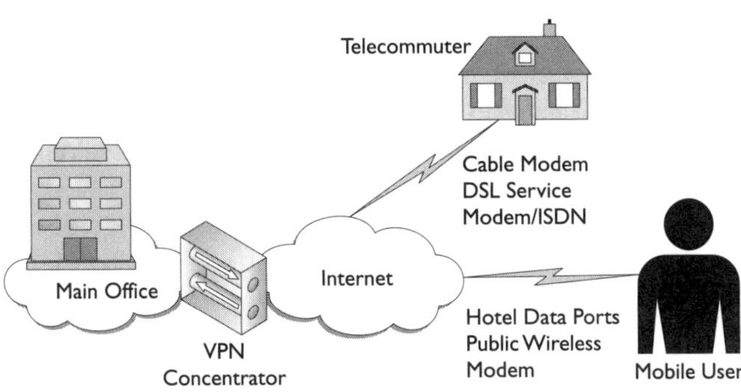

Figure 14-10 Remote access type VPN connections

PART III

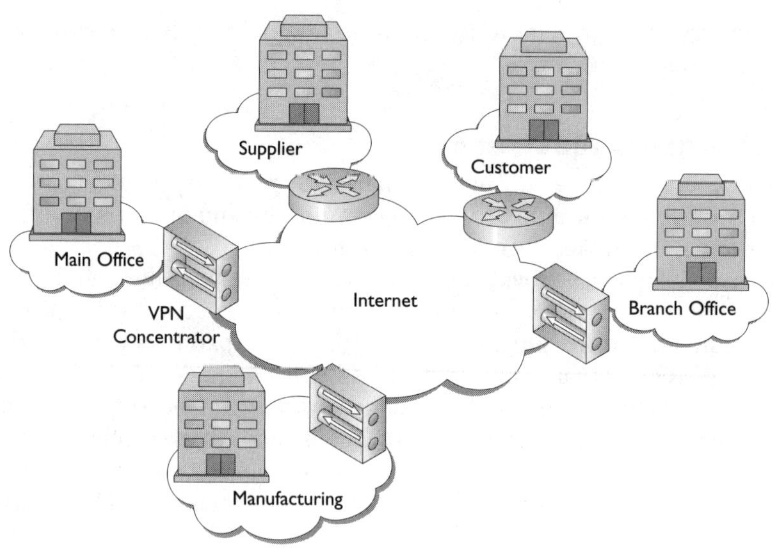

Figure 14-11 LAN-to-LAN VPN connection example

Remote Access VPNs with Preshared Keys

This section discusses configuring VPN 3000 Concentrators to support remote access implementations. Remote access VPN clients can use any of the four following common connectivity technologies:

- VPN client software installed on PCs or workstations
- VPN 3002 Hardware Client
- Router supporting VPN
- Firewall supporting VPN

The proliferation of low-cost small routers and firewall devices is making this an attractive and more secure option for many remote users. Cisco's small routers and firewall all support remote access options. For this example, we assume the remote users are using VPN client software. In any case, two levels of authentication need to occur. First, the device must authenticate itself to the concentrator or peer device, and then the user typically must authenticate on the network to gain access.

Cisco Easy VPN is a software enhancement that enables all three types of remote access clients to connect easily to the central site with minimal end user involvement. This is most important with large implementations and sites with limited local support. Chapter 12 covered the VPN client software, Chapter 15 covers the VPN 3002 Hardware Client, and Chapter 21 covers the PIX VPN connections, including Easy VPN. In this chapter, we focus on the VPN Concentrator that would connect to each of these technologies.

Figure 14-12 shows a scenario to use in the VPN remote-access configuration example. The Internet was simplified, in case someone wants to configure the scenario as a lab

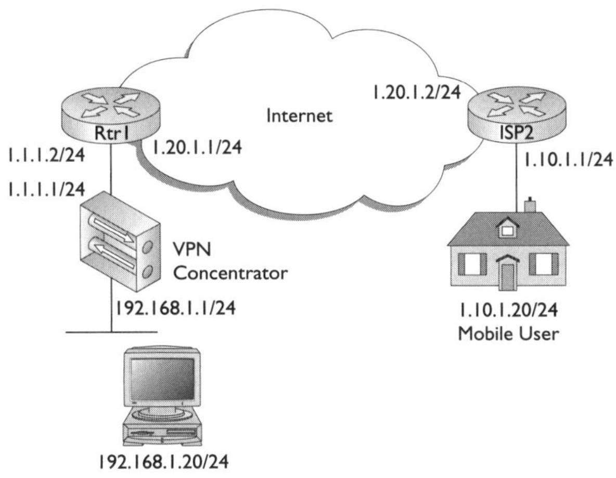

Figure 14-12 VPN Concentrator remote access scenario

exercise. The network behind Rtr1 could be the central site for a large number of remote clients and could contain multiple LANs.

NOTE The Concentrator Manager is used whenever possible in this example, but all steps could be accomplished using the CLI by following the same menu selections.

Preshared Keys

As Chapter 9 explained, VPN peer devices can authenticate each other using preshared keys or with digital certificates and certificate authorities. This section discusses using preshared keys and the section "Digital Certificates" looks at the changes required to use digital certificates. Three types of preshared keys exist.

- **Unique keys**—Each IP address has a unique key associated with it, providing a high level of security, but requiring much greater administrative overhead. While manageable for LAN-to-LAN implementations, it doesn't scale well for remote access networks with many users or a growing pool of users.
- **Group keys**—In this implementation, preshared keys are assigned to one or more groups. Managing new users becomes easier and more scalable by requiring only that the user be made a group member and given the appropriate passwords. This concept of groups has many other benefits, including the capability to separate different types of users based on access method (router vs. software client) for autoupdate features or even based on Security Policy access limitation differences. By default, the VPN Concentrator has one group: the Base Group. Additional groups can be added as needed, using the Base Group setting as defaults that can be modified as necessary.

- **Wildcard keys**—With a wildcard preshared key, it's possible to allow one or more clients to use a shared secret key to authenticate encrypted tunnels to the gateway. To be configured on the Concentrator, all devices must be using preshared keys. This option can be more prone to security problems, such as man-in-the-middle attacks, if a key is compromised. In that case, all keys must be changed.

Initial Configuration

The following example assumes either the Quick Configuration wasn't used or the related features should be changed. At a minimum, the private interface must be configured for the VPN 3000 Concentrator using the CLI. While the CLI can also be used to configure the Public Interface and any default routes, this exercise performs those tasks using the Manager interface. The following lists the correct addresses for the scenario:

VPN Concentrator: 192.168.1.1/24.

```
              Welcome to
             Cisco Systems
       VPN 3000 Concentrator Series
          Command Line Interface
Copyright (C) 1998-2003 Cisco Systems, Inc.

1) Configuration
2) Administration
3) Monitoring
4) Save changes to Config file
5) Help Information
6) Exit

Main ->1

1) Interface Configuration
2) System Management
3) User Management
4) Policy Management
5) Back

Config -> 1                             (shows the current settings)

This table shows current IP addresses.
  Intf         Status       IP Address/Subnet Mask          MAC Address
-----------------------------------------------------------------------
Ether1-Pri|      UP      | 192.168.10.1/255.255.255.0 | 00.03.A0.88.CE.AC
Ether2-Pub|Not Configured|      0.0.0.0/0.0.0.0       |
-----------------------------------------------------------------------
DNS Server(s): DNS Server Not Configured
DNS Domain Name:
Default Gateway: Default Gateway Not Configured

1) Configure Ethernet #1 (Private)
2) Configure Ethernet #2 (Public)
3) Configure Power Supplies
4) Back

Interfaces -> 1                       (to set the Private interface)
```

```
1) Interface Setting (Disable, DHCP or Static IP)
2) Set Public Interface
3) Select IP Filter
4) Select Ethernet Speed
5) Select Duplex
6) Set MTU
7) Set Port Routing Config
8) Set Bandwidth Management
9) Set Public Interface IPSec Fragmentation Policy
10) Back

Ethernet Interface 1 -> 1                  (to set a Static IP address)

1) Disable
2) Enable using DHCP Client
3) Enable using Static IP Addressing

Ethernet Interface 1 -> [ 3 ] 3

> Enter IP Address                  (current value appears in brackets)
Ethernet Interface 1 -> [ 192.168.10.1 ] 192.168.1.1

> Enter Subnet Mask
Ethernet Interface 1 -> [ 255.255.255.0 ]
Ethernet Interface 1 -> h                           (return to Main menu)
```


Basic Browser Configuration

Once the CLI is used to configure the private interface, you can use a browser on a PC on the same network to complete the configuration. The following steps assume the private interface was configured and a successful web session was established using a client on the LAN attached to that interface.

Setting the Public Interface

Use the Configuration | Interfaces | Ethernet 2 menu options to get to the screen, as shown in Figure 14-13. Select Static IP Addressing, and then enter the IP address and the appropriate mask. This same screen allows making choices on interface speed, full- or half-duplex, MTU size, fragmentation preferences, and whether the interface can be a DHCP client.

Check the DHCP Client check box if it's necessary to obtain the IP address, the subnet mask, and the default gateway for this interface via DHCP from an ISP. This would be more common at a branch location or any small client that doesn't require permanent static IP addresses for shared servers. If this check box is selected, don't make entries in the IP address and subnet mask fields that follow.

To make this interface a public interface, check the Public Interface check box designating the interface is part of a public network, such as the Internet. A public interface must be configured before you can configure NAT and IPSec LAN-to-LAN. Designate only one VPN Concentrator interface as a public interface.

Notice the tabs on this screen would allow configuring RIP, OSPF, and Bandwidth Management features. While static routes are common with Concentrators, some LAN-to-LAN features, such as Network Autodiscovery, require or can take advantage of this support.

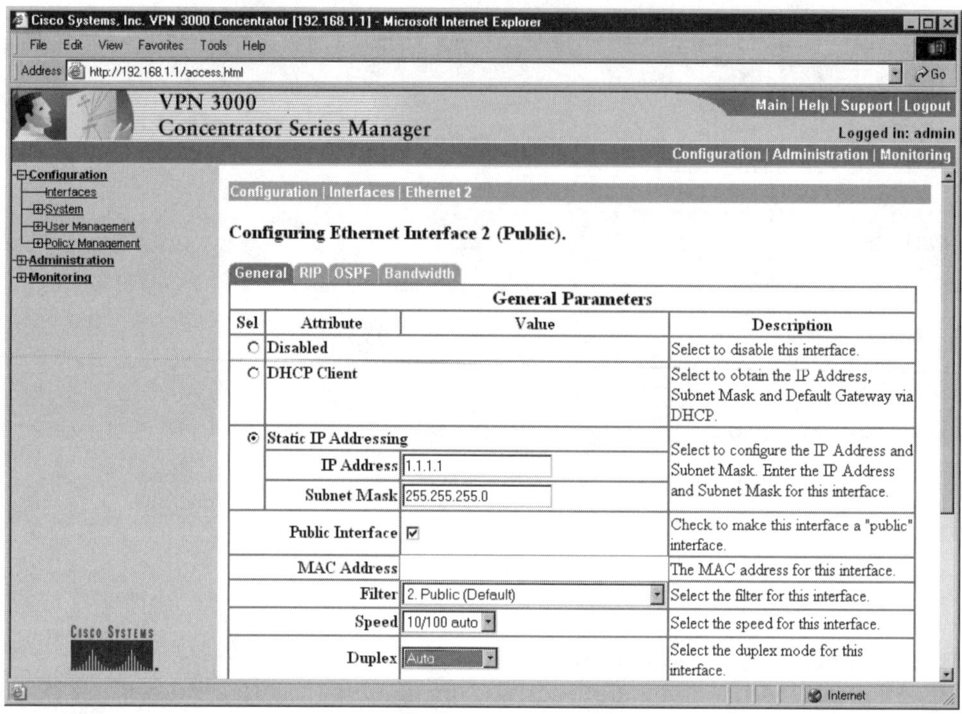

Figure 14-13 Configuring the public interface

Clicking the Apply button applies the choices and returns to the Configuration | Interfaces screen, which confirms the new IP address and mask.

Defining the Default Gateway (Optional)

Default routes or *default gateways* are used to forward packets addressed to unknown networks to avoid having to discard the packet. The not-too-practical alternative is that all routers, firewalls, and VPN devices would have to know all the routes in the world.

The default route for the Concentrator to which you forward all outside bound packets can be defined either by choosing the Default Gateway link on the Configuration | Interfaces screen or by using the Configuration | System | IP Routing | Default Gateways menu to add these special forms of static routes. Figure 14-14 shows the resulting screen with the appropriate entries to use Rtr1 as the default gateway for the network.

In the example scenario, if no additional routers are in the LAN, the PCs in the LAN would use the Concentrator private address for their default gateways.

Verifying Configuration

Returning to the Configuration | Interfaces screen, as shown in Figure 14-15, confirms the default gateway was defined and provides a reminder icon to save the configuration.

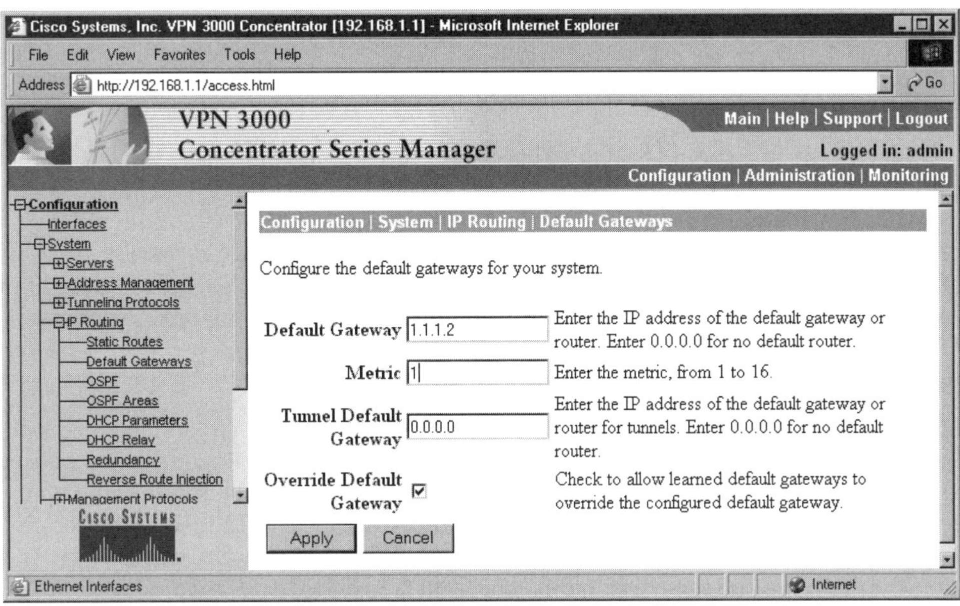

Figure 14-14 Setting the default gateway for the Concentrator

This same screen confirms the interface configurations and whether the two interfaces are up or down. If either interface is down, this could be caused by any of the following:

- You might need to click the Refresh icon.

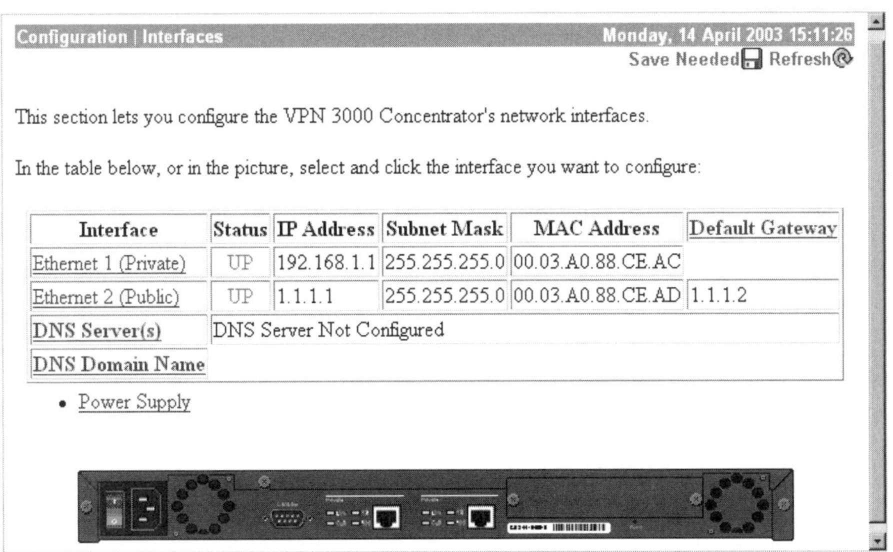

Figure 14-15 Using the Configuration | Interfaces screen to confirm configuration

- You might have used the wrong cable. Use straight through to the hub or the switch; otherwise, use a crossover.
- The device on the other end might be misconfigured or unconfigured.

At this point, you should be able to use the Administration | Ping screen to ping other devices on the network to verify connectivity. As with the IOS Routers and PIX Firewalls, a good idea is always to verify connectivity before configuring encryption and access control measures. While pinging the Concentrator public interface is possible, it won't be possible to ping through to the LAN or the private interface. Also, opening Telnet or browser sessions with the Concentrator from the outside network won't be possible.

Adding the Static Routes

Use the Configuration | System | IP Routing | Static Routes menu to add any necessary static routes. Unless configured earlier using the CLI, the Static Routes box should be empty or show only any configure default gateway. Use the Add button to bring up the screen, shown in Figure 14-16, to add any static routes required. The figure shows configuring a route specifically to the network the remote host is on. Because the default gateway would accomplish the same result, this static rout is included only as an example.

On the static route screen, you can specify the Destination Router Address (next-hop) or the Interface (Concentrator Public). Clicking the Add button returns to the Configuration | System | IP Routing | Static Routes screen. Figure 14-17 shows the Static Routes screen with a default gateway, a static route pointing to a next-hop router and another one pointing at the Concentrator public interface. The last entry shows a possible

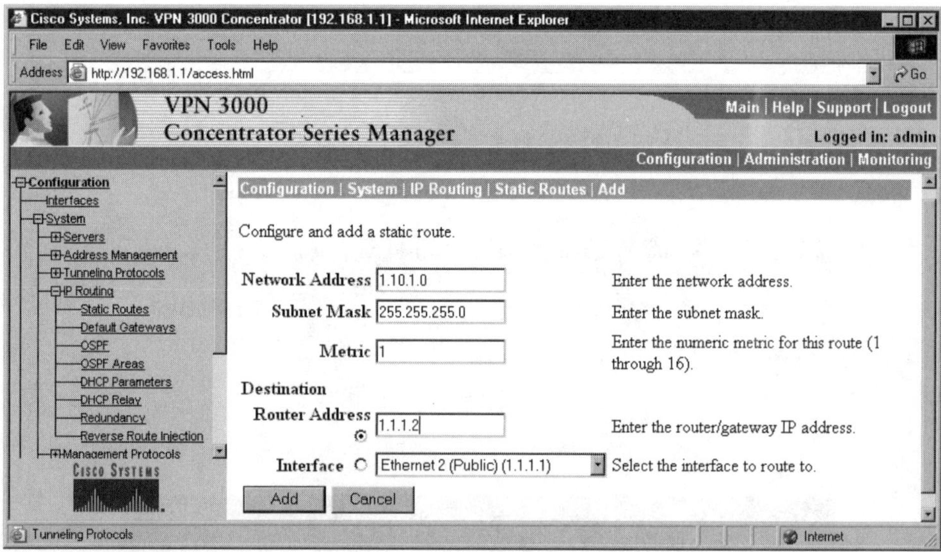

Figure 14-16 Creating a new static route

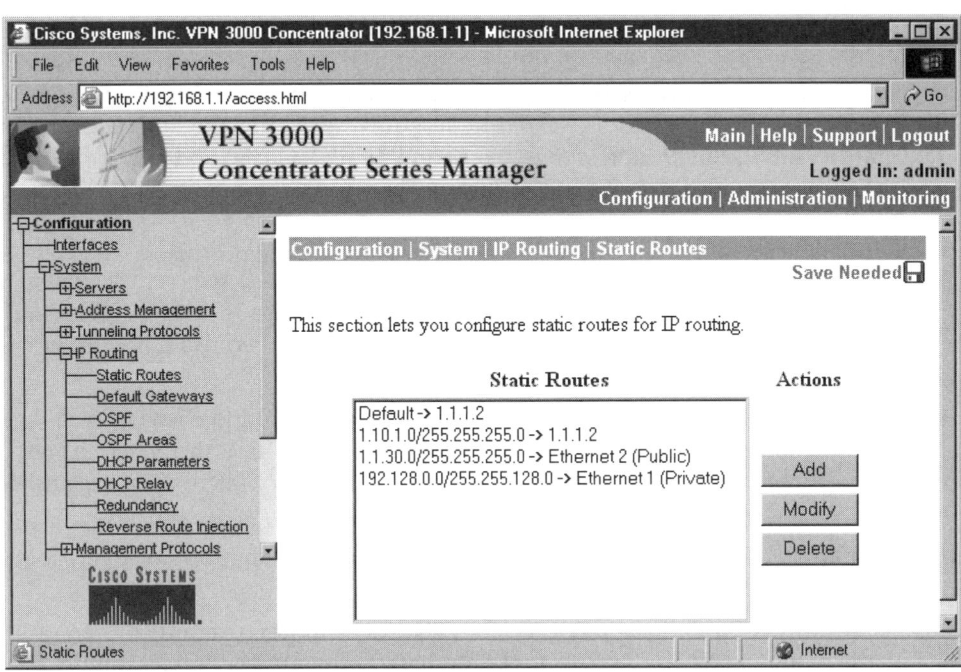

Figure 14-17 Defined default and static routes

configuration if the LAN protected by the Concentrator included the 192.168.0.0 to 192.168.127.0 networks built around additional routers and/or Layer 3 switches.

General System Information

Use the Configuration | System | General menu to add or modify any of the following. The time and date settings are critical to the proper operation of IPSec, especially when working with certificate authorities. Each related screen is self-explanatory.

- **Identification**—system name, contact person, device location
- **Time and Date**—device time and date
- **Sessions**—maximum simultaneous sessions
- **Authentication**—global authentication parameters

Define Inside Address Assignment Method

Remote users have network addresses associated with their local network or, more likely, their ISP network. To function within the private network (LAN), it's necessary to assign suitable "inside" addresses to these users. Conceptually, this is similar to a reverse NAT.

Use the Configuration | System | Address Management | Assignment menu to define how the remote users are assigned addresses within the private network. The screen shown in Figure 14-18 is used to select prioritized methods for assigning IP addresses to clients as a tunnel is established. The Concentrator tries the selected methods in the order listed, until it finds a valid IP address to assign. A minimum of one method must be selected or any combination of choices will be evaluated. There is no default method. The figure shows using an address pool defined on the VPN Concentrator.

Four possible methods exist for assigning addresses to the remote users:

- **Use Client Address**—enables the client to specify its own IP address. This isn't a good security strategy. Don't use this option for IPSec because IPSec doesn't allow client-specified IP addresses.
- **Use Address from Authentication Server**—used to assign IP addresses retrieved from an authentication server (AAA) on a per-user basis. This is the preferred and most secure method, if an authentication server (external or internal) is being used.
- **Use DHCP**—used to obtain IP addresses from a DHCP server. This is the most manageable and the most scalable of the two remaining options available to IPSec networks.
- **Use Address Pools**—used to have the VPN Concentrator assign IP addresses from an internally configured pool. Internally configured address pools are the easiest method of address pool assignment to configure. Use the Configuration | System | Address Management | Pools screens covered in the next section to define and prioritize the address pools.

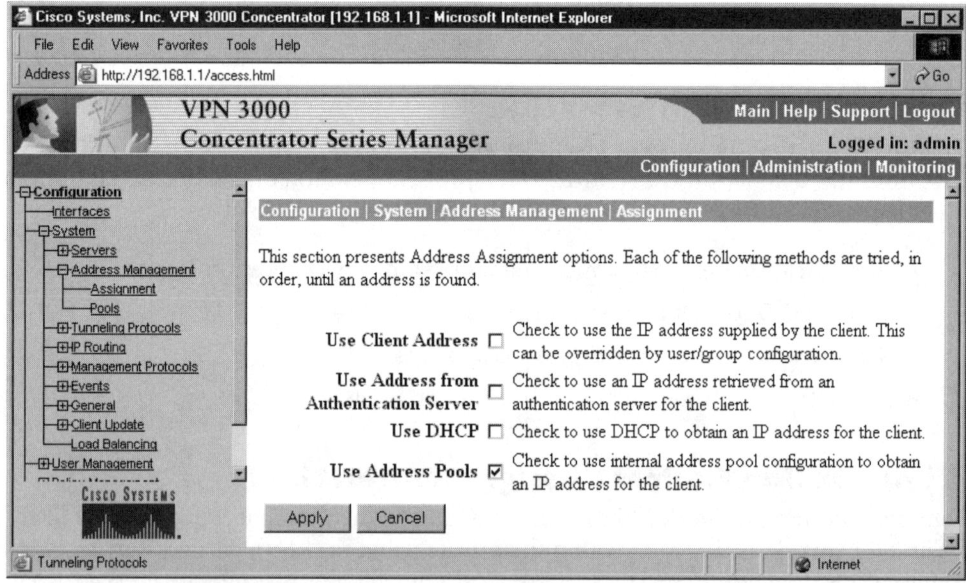

Figure 14-18 Selecting an inside address assignment method for remote users

If the assignment method uses addresses that aren't from the local subnet on the private interface, then it's necessary to add routing for those subnets.

Define Inside Address Pool for Remote Users

Use the Configuration | System | Address Management | Pools menu to add or modify the inside address pool to be used by remote users, making them part of the inside network. Initially, the IP Pool Entry box is empty. Click the Add button to bring up the screen shown in Figure 14-19, which shows it is using the last 54 addresses in the inside network. Note, these addresses shouldn't be assigned to inside hosts or included in any DHCP pools used in the network.

Clicking the Add button implements the pool and returns to the Configuration | System | Address Management | Pools screen, as shown in Figure 14-20, to confirm the pool was added. The Add, Modify, and Delete buttons can be used to create new, to edit existing, or to remove existing pools. The Move Up/Move Down buttons are used to change the priority of the address pools: the higher a pool is in the list, the more likely the addresses are to be used. No Undo option exists yet on any of the configuration options.

Configuring Groups and Users

VPN features and configurations are assigned and "pushed" down to clients on the basis of group and user assignment and configuration. As with basic network-resource sharing, this is always most scalable and easier to administer if features are assigned to defined groups. Individual users are then put in groups to assign features to them. Then, if a person leaves or changes his or her job role, that person only needs to be removed from the group.

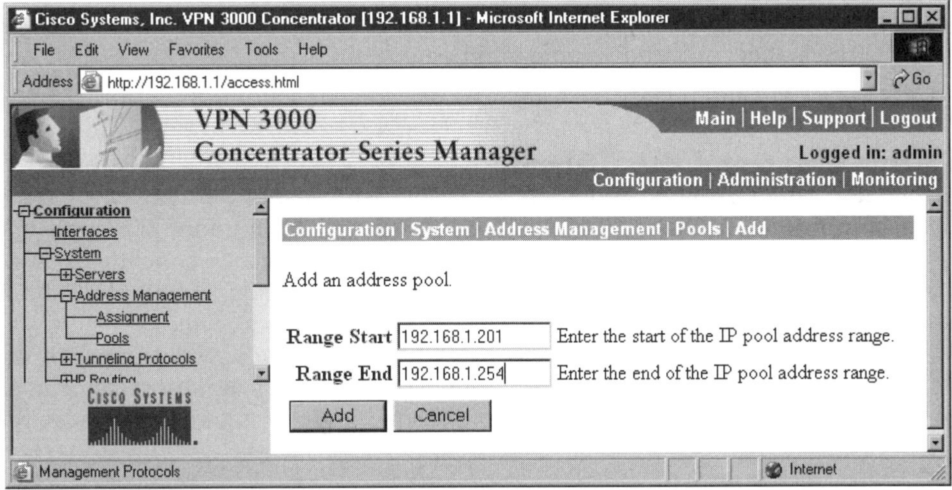

Figure 14-19 Defining a pool of addresses for remote users to use

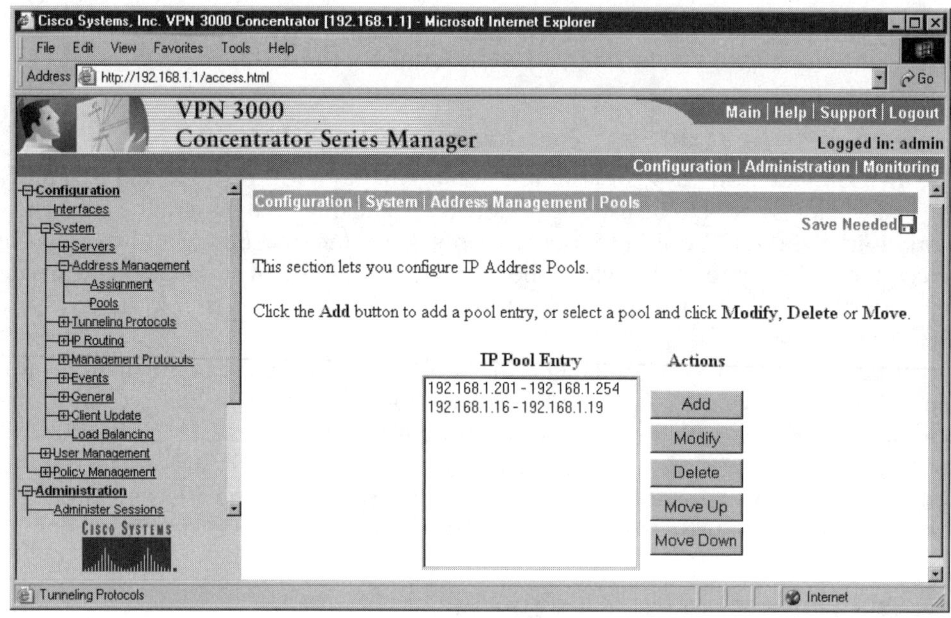

Figure 14-20 Managing IP address pools for remote users

The Configuration | User Management screen is used to configure VPN 3000 Concentrator group and user parameters for IPSec, PPTP, and L2TP. The following are the three configuration options:

- **Base Group**—default group and user parameters
- **Groups**—add and modify groups and group parameters
- **Users**—add and modify users and user parameters

Setting Group and User Defaults

While modifying the Base Group default settings isn't absolutely necessary, Cisco's default setting might not match the network or company security policy. The Configuration | User Management | Base Group screen shows a series of tabs—currently six—that can be used to define default settings for the various users (clients). Figure 14-21 shows the default settings for the General tab, which applies to all groups and users.

Most of the options are self-explanatory and the Help system provides enough information, including default values, in most cases to make intelligent choices. Remember, most of these options might be moot because of specific group and user settings, as well

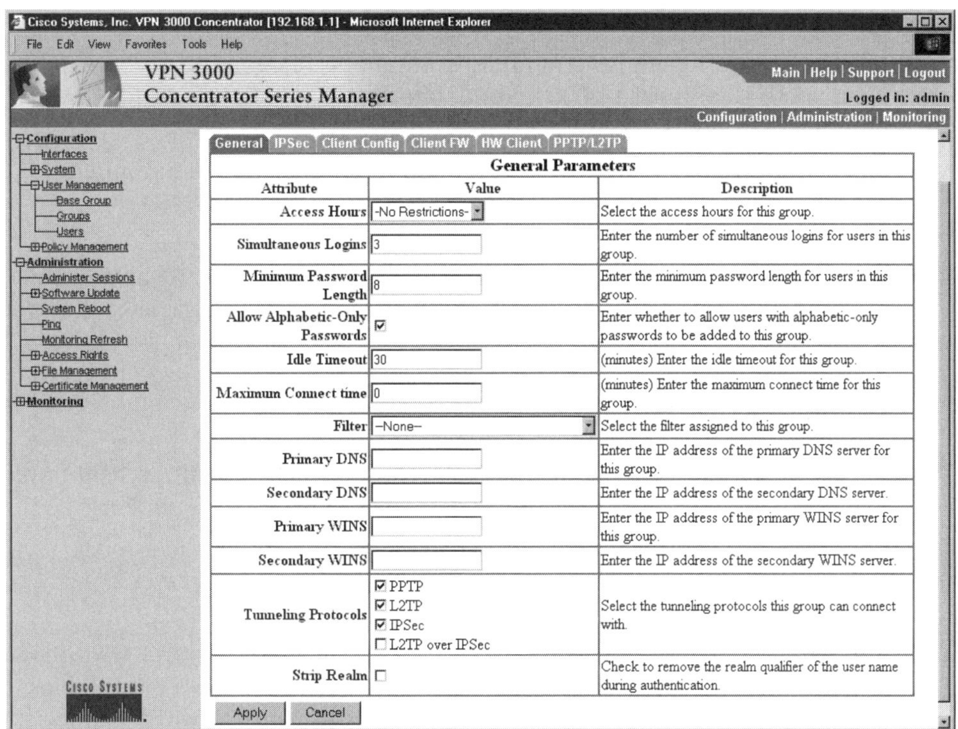

Figure 14-21 General Default Settings tab

as limitations imposed by the local client device. The following options are included as examples or to show interesting features:

- **Access Hours**—Drop-down menu button to select the hours remote access users can access the VPN Concentrator. The default entries are as follows:
  - **No Restrictions**—No restrictions on access hours.
  - **Never**—No access at any time.
  - **Business Hours**—Access 9 A.M. to 5 P.M., Monday through Friday. To configure access hours, use the Configuration | Policy Management | Access Hours screen. Any additional named access hours you create will appear on the list.
- **Simultaneous Logins**—For a single internal user. Default is 3. Minimum is 0, which disables login and prevents user access. No maximum limit.

- **Minimum Password Length**—Default is 8. Minimum is 1. Maximum is 32.
- **Idle Timeout**—Default is 30 minutes. Minimum is one minute. Maximum is 2,147,483,647 minutes (4,000+ years). Use 0 to disable timeout and allow an unlimited idle period.
- **Maximum Connect Time**—Default is 0 minutes, which allows unlimited connection time. Minimum is one minute. Maximum is 2,147,483,647 minutes (4,000+ years).
- **SEP Card Assignment**—The VPN Concentrator models 3015 and above can contain up to four SEP modules to handle encryption. This parameter allows configuring the load on each SEP module.
- **Tunneling Protocols**—Protocols to be supported. Clients can use only the selected protocols. The choices include the following:
    - **PPTP**—Point-to-Point Tunneling Protocol. Checked by default. A client-server protocol popular with Microsoft clients, especially older OS versions.
    - **L2TP**—Layer 2 Tunneling Protocol. Checked by default. A client-server protocol that combines many features from PPTP and L2F (Layer 2 Forwarding).
    - **IPSec**—IP Security Protocol. Checked by default. Used by both LAN-to-LAN (peer-to-peer) connections and client-to-LAN (remote access) connections. Cisco VPN Client is an IPSec client specifically designed to work with the VPN Concentrator.
    - **L2TP over IPSec**—L2TP using IPSec for security. Unchecked by default. A client-server protocol providing interoperability with Windows 2000 VPN clients. L2TP packets are encapsulated within IPSec, thus providing an additional authentication and encryption layer.

Setting IPSec Defaults

The Configuration | User Management | Base Group screen with the IPSec tab selected is used to configure IP Security Protocol parameters that apply to the base group. This section would apply if IPSec or L2TP over IPSec were selected on the General Parameters tab. Figure 14-22 shows the default settings. The options are self-explanatory and the Help system provides enough information, including default values, to make appropriate choices.

The IPSec SA option contains a drop-down menu button to select the default IPSec security association (SA) assigned to IPSec clients during tunnel negotiation. Re mote-access clients must have a default SA defined, while LAN-to-LAN connections ignore this selection and use parameters from the Configuration | System | Tunneling Protocols | IPSec LAN-to-LAN screens.

The Default Preshared Key option (the third option from the bottom) is used to define the preshared secret key. Use a minimum of four options and a maximum of

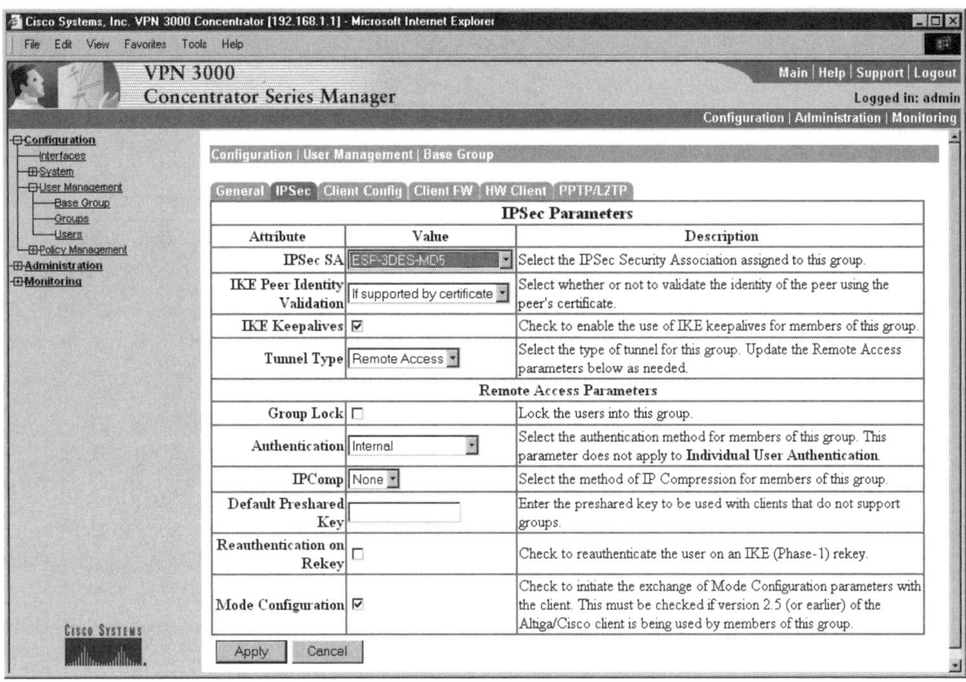

Figure 14-22 Setting IPSec defaults

32 alphanumeric characters. This option allows the following VPN clients to connect to the VPN Concentrator:

- VPN clients that use preshared secrets, but don't support "groups," such as the Microsoft Windows XP L2TP/IPSec client
- VPN router devices that are creating inbound connections from nonfixed IP addresses using preshared secrets

Setting Client Defaults

The remaining four tabs are used to configure client-specific default settings. These are the configuration features that are pushed down to the appropriate client the next time the device connects to the Concentrator. The *Client Config* tab is used to set general client features that might apply to all Cisco VPN Clients. The remaining three tabs are for setting those defaults features unique to that type of client.

Figure 14-23 shows the Cisco Client parameters such as login banners, choosing IPSec over UDP, and defining up to ten IPSec Backup Servers.

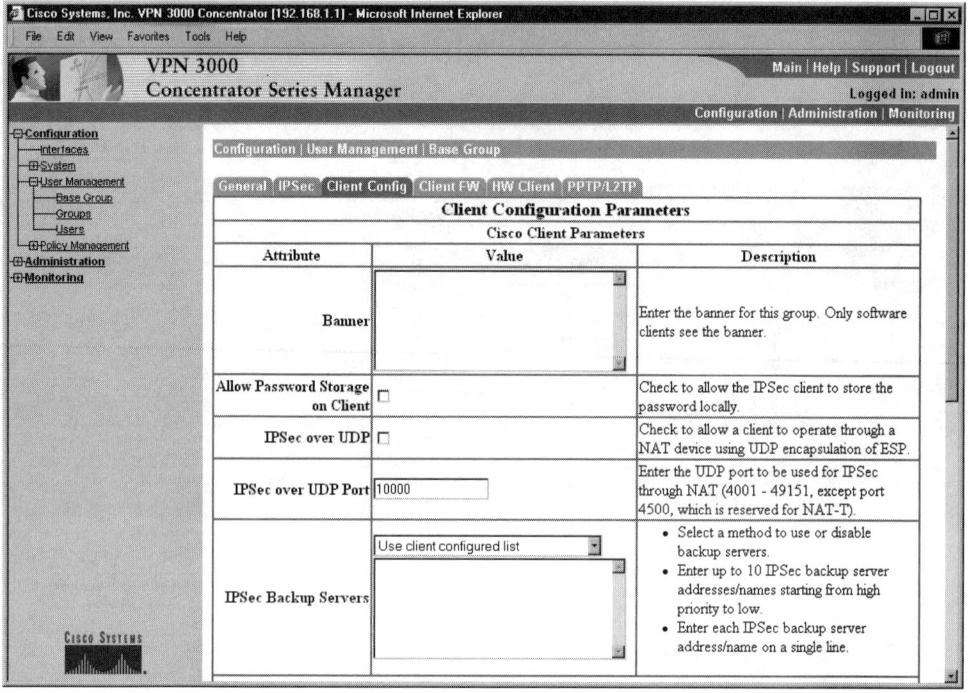

Figure 14-23 Setting Cisco Client default parameters

Figure 14-24 shows the rest of the previous screen, which includes setting two Microsoft Client parameters and three Common Client parameters. This is the screen where split tunneling is allowed by default for VPN Clients.

Split Tunneling Policy

Split tunneling allows the IPSec client to go directly to the Internet in Cleartext form for those destinations that don't require encryption. Split tunneling applies only to remote-access IPSec tunnels, not to LAN-to-LAN connections.

Split tunneling eases the device-processing load, simplifies traffic management, and speeds untunneled traffic. Split tunneling is a traffic management feature, not a security feature. In fact, for optimum security, split tunneling isn't recommended. Because only the VPN Concentrator, not the IPSec client, can enable split tunneling, it's possible to control implementation and minimize security vulnerabilities.

Split tunneling is disabled by default on both the VPN Concentrator and the client. To enable and configure the feature, all entries are made on the VPN Concentrator, and then pushed down to the IPSec client. The default split-tunneling policy is *Tunnel Everything,* which disables split tunneling. No traffic goes in clear text or to any destination

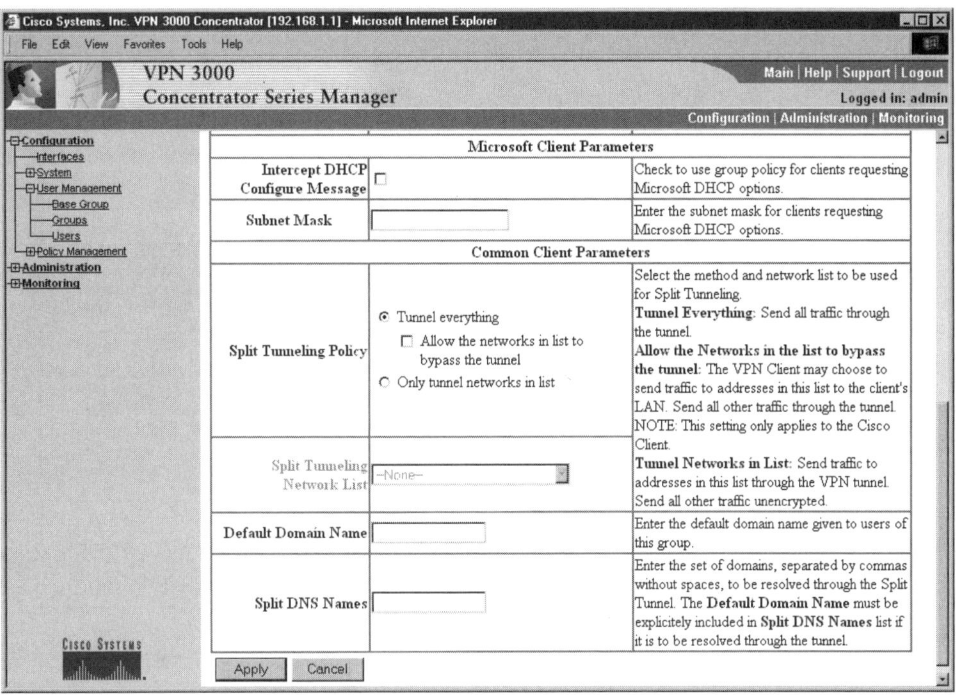

Figure 14-24 Setting Microsoft Client parameters and Common Client parameters

other than the VPN Concentrator. Remote users in this group reach Internet networks through the corporate network and don't have access to local networks.

The *Allow Networks in List to Bypass Tunnel* allows the administrator to define a list of networks to which traffic can go without passing through the tunnel. This allows remote users to access devices on their local networks, such as printers, while still connected to the corporate network through a tunnel.

Only Tunnel Networks in List allows remote users to access Internet networks without tunneling through the corporate network.

Client Firewall Requirements

The *Client FW Parameters* tab, as shown in Figure 14-25, is used to configure firewall parameters for VPN Clients running Microsoft Windows. The features are currently unavailable for hardware clients or other non-Windows software clients. If the Firewall Required option is selected, the client won't be allowed to connect to the protected network without meeting the defined requirements. The firewall feature protects the user PC and, thereby, the corporate network, from intrusions originating from the Internet or the user LAN.

PART III

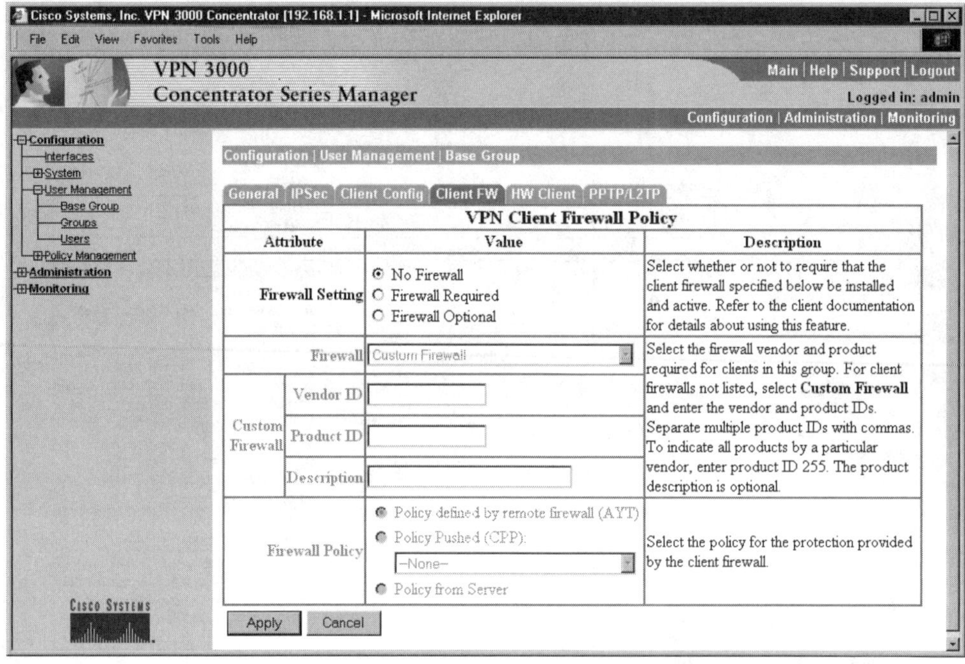

Figure 14-25 Defining client firewall default requirements

VPN 3002 Hardware Client Defaults

The *HW Client Parameters* tab, shown in Figure 14-26, is used to enable and configure interactive hardware client authentication and individual user authentication. These features are covered in the next chapter when the VPN 3002 Hardware Client is covered in greater detail.

Creating or Modifying Other Groups

The Base Group features set in the last sections automatically apply to all users accessing the VPN Concentrator. If the security policy requires defining multiple groups with unique features and/or requirements, the Configuration | User Management | Groups screen, shown in Figure 14-27, can be used to configure access and usage parameters. A *group* is a collection of users treated as a single entity. Groups inherit parameters from the Base Group. The figure includes a group created in the next section.

To create and use groups beyond the Base Group requires using an internal authentication server. The authentication server must be one of the following:

- RADIUS—An external RADIUS server is the default.
- NT Domain—An external Windows NT Domain server.
- SDI—An external RSA Security Inc. SecurID server.

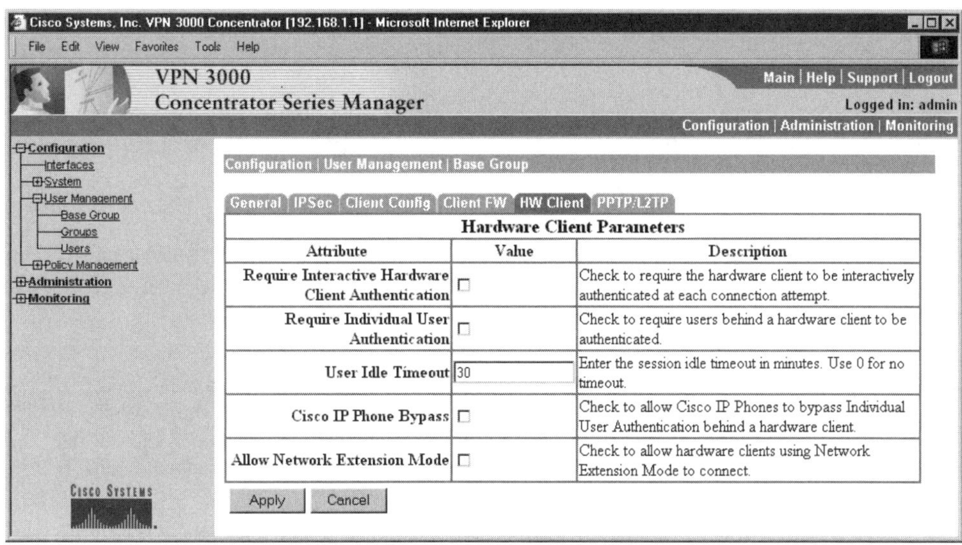

Figure 14-26 Defining VPN 3002 Hardware Client defaults

- Internal Server—The internal VPN Concentrator authentication server. With this server, you can configure a maximum of 100, 500, or 1000 groups and users (combined) in the internal database depending on the model number.

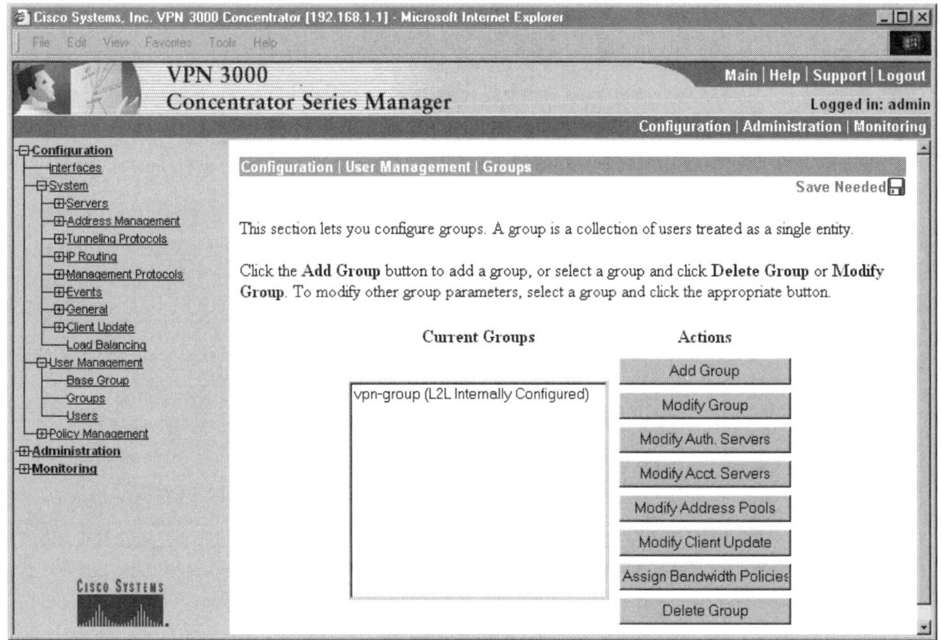

Figure 14-27 Screen to create and manage user groups

- Kerberos/Active Directory – Windows 2000/XP and Linux/Unix authentication server.

If no external server was defined, a link appears on the Groups or Users screen to create an internal server. Creating the internal server is simply a matter of clicking the link and choosing the Internal Server option.

Adding a Group The Configuration | User Management | Groups | Add screen, shown in Figure 14-28, shows the seven tabs used to define the configuration parameters for a new group. The *Identity Parameters* tab is used to configure the name, password, and authentication server type for this group.

Group Name	Unique case-sensitive name for this specific group. Maximum length is 64 characters. Changing a group name automatically updates the group name for all users in the group. For remote access users connecting with digital certificates, this name must match exactly the Organizational Unit (OU) field of the user's identity certificate.
Password	Unique case-sensitive password for this group. Minimum length is four characters. Maximum is 32 characters. The field displays only asterisks.
Verify	Reenter the group password to verify it. The field displays only asterisks.
Type	Use the Type drop-down menu button to select the authentication server type.

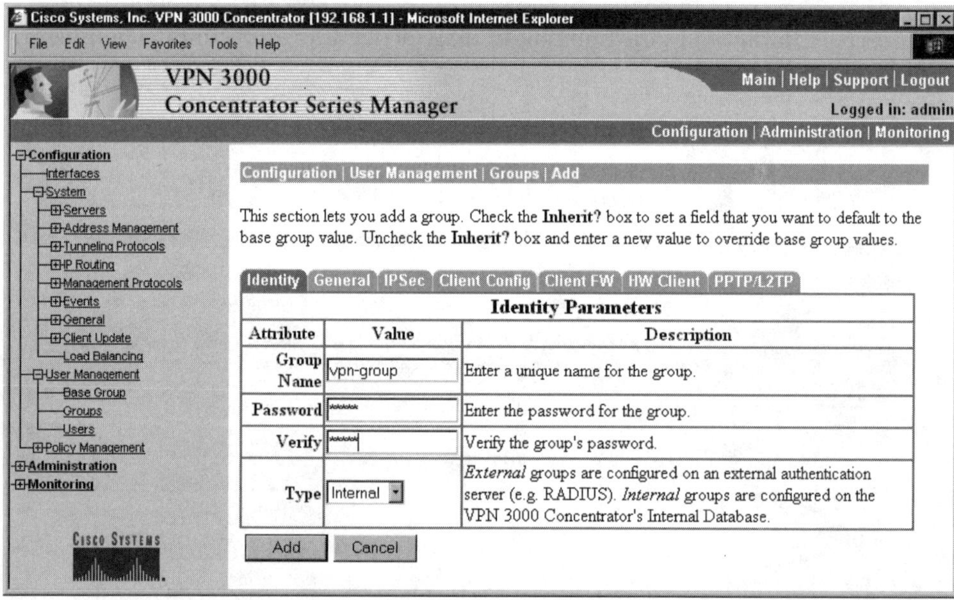

Figure 14-28 Creating a group and defining a password

The six remaining tabs are used to change any options that either weren't defined in the Base Group tabs with the same names or when the Base Group options need to be overridden. Figure 14-29 shows the parameter screens have a column to inherit the feature settings from the Base Group. A check mark in the Inherit? column indicates to inherit the default setting.

Creating or Modifying Users

The Configuration | User Management | Users screen, shown in Figure 14-30, allows configuring access, usage, and authentication parameters for users. Users inherit the feature parameters from the specific group to which they belong. Configuring users in this section requires configuring them in the VPN Concentrator internal authentication server. The authentication server is a properly configured RADIUS, NT Domain, SDI server, Internal Server, or Keberos/Active Directory server.

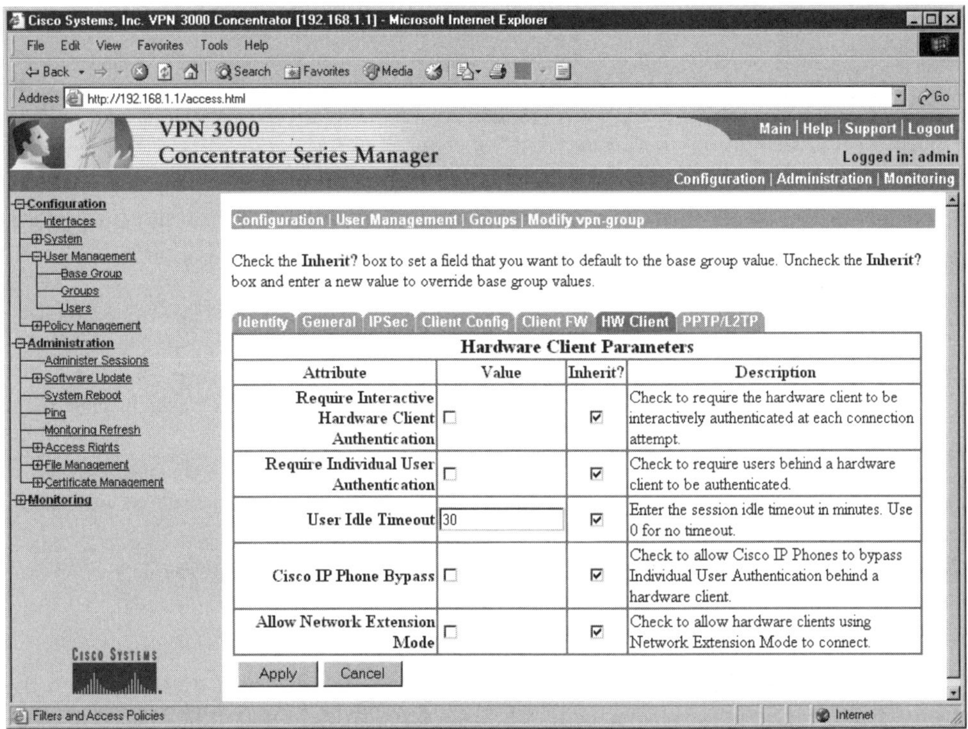

Figure 14-29 Group parameters screen showing the Inherit option

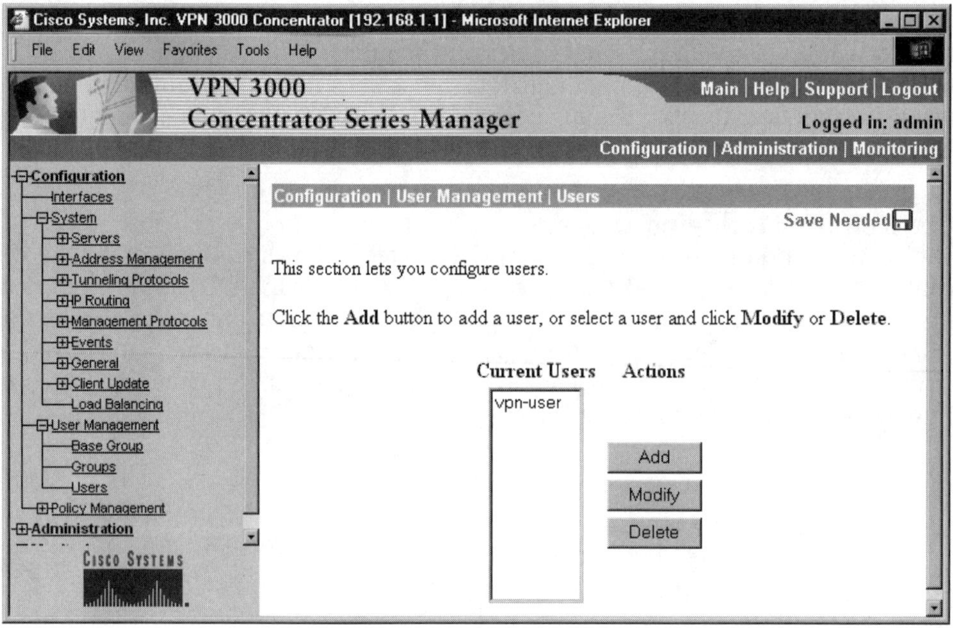

Figure 14-30 User management screen for adding users

Using the Add button brings up the Identity Parameters tab, as shown in Figure 14-31, used to configure the name, password, group, and IP address for this user.

User Name	Unique, case-sensitive name for this user. Maximum length is 64 characters. If the name is changed, this user profile replaces the existing profile.
Password	Unique, case-sensitive password for this user. Minimum length must satisfy the minimum for the group to which the user is assigned. Maximum length is 32 characters. The field displays only asterisks.
Verify	Reenter the user password to verify it. The field displays only asterisks.
Group	Drop-down menu used to select the group to assign this user. The list shows all defined groups plus the Base Group.
IP Address	Only if Use Address from Authentication Server on the Configuration | System | Address Management | Assignment screen. Otherwise, leave this field blank.
Subnet Mask	Same as IP address field.

The other three tabs are used to specify parameters for this user that vary from the group. Each feature has an Inherit check box, selected by default, which is used to override the group feature settings.

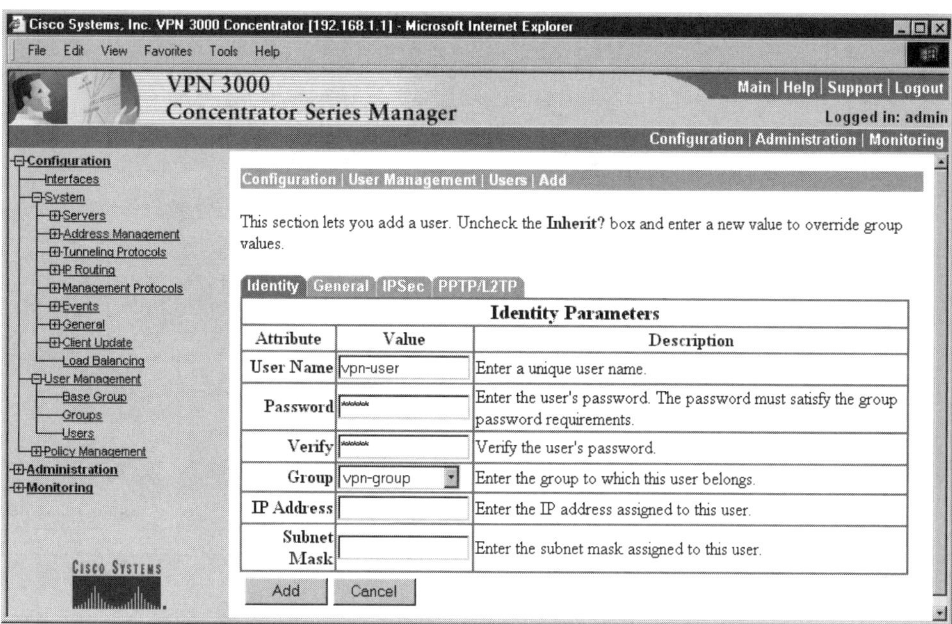

Figure 14-31 Defining a VPN user

Other Configuration Options

This section covers some additional and useful configuration options that are available. Note, other options related to backup servers, load balancing, client update features, and so forth for remote client devices are included at the end of Chapter 15.

These configuration options are accessed from the Configuration menu. Figure 14-32 shows the variety of the configurable settings. The following examples represent the process and the level of granularity attainable.

Configuration | Policy Management | Access Hours

This menu option makes it possible to configure the hours that remote-access groups and users can access the VPN Concentrator. These hours don't apply to LAN-to-LAN connections. Figure 14-33 shows the default screen with the default settings. Never is self-explanatory. Business Hours include Monday through Friday, 9 A.M. to 5 P.M.

Figure 14-34 shows the screen (Configuration | Policy Management | Access Hours | Modify) used either to modify the Business Hours settings or to create another definition based on these settings. To modify existing settings, select the choice on the initial screen

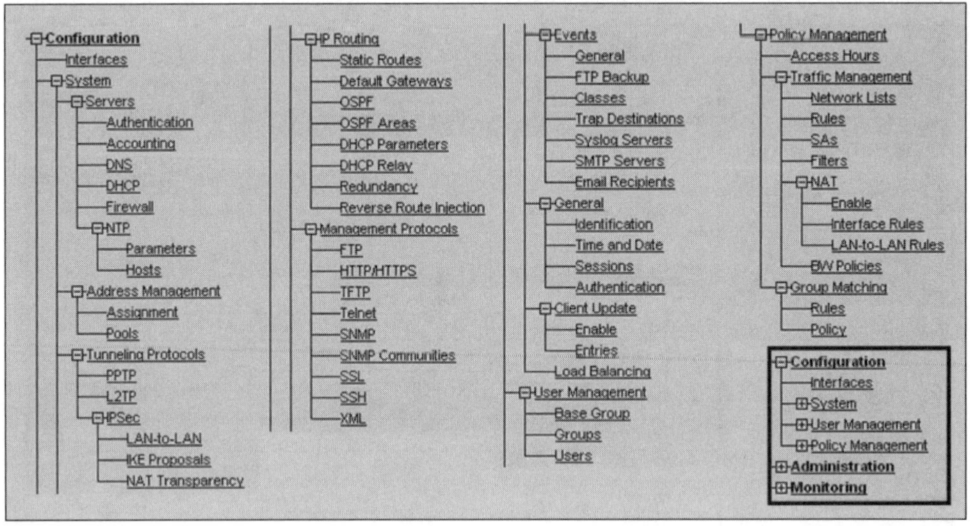

Figure 14-32 Configuration menu options

and click the Modify button. Note, the first column drop-downs allow defining whether to include (during) or exclude the row in the access hours. The Name box at the top could

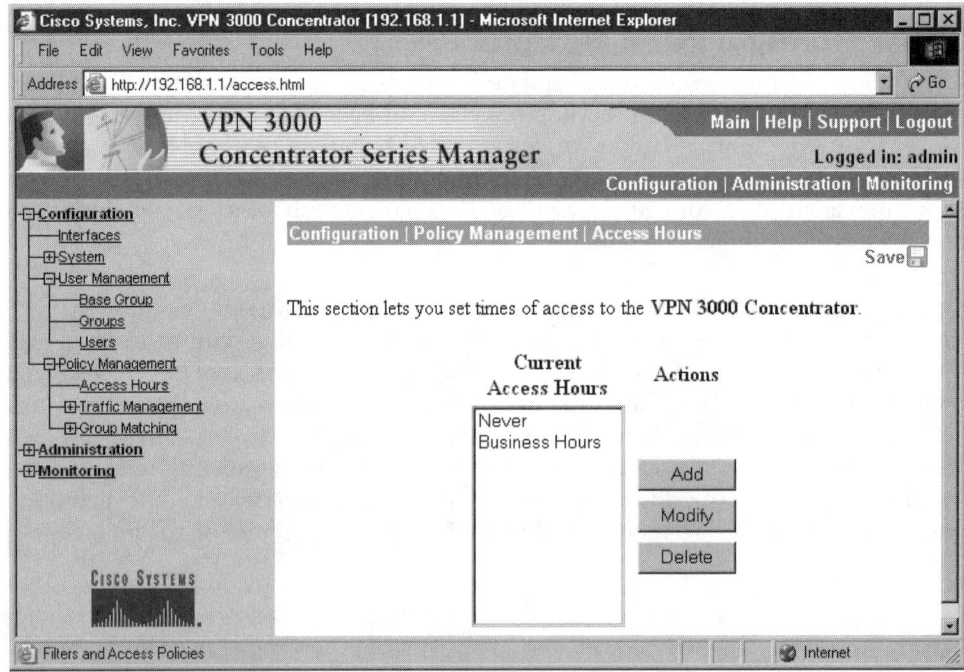

Figure 14-33 Default access definitions

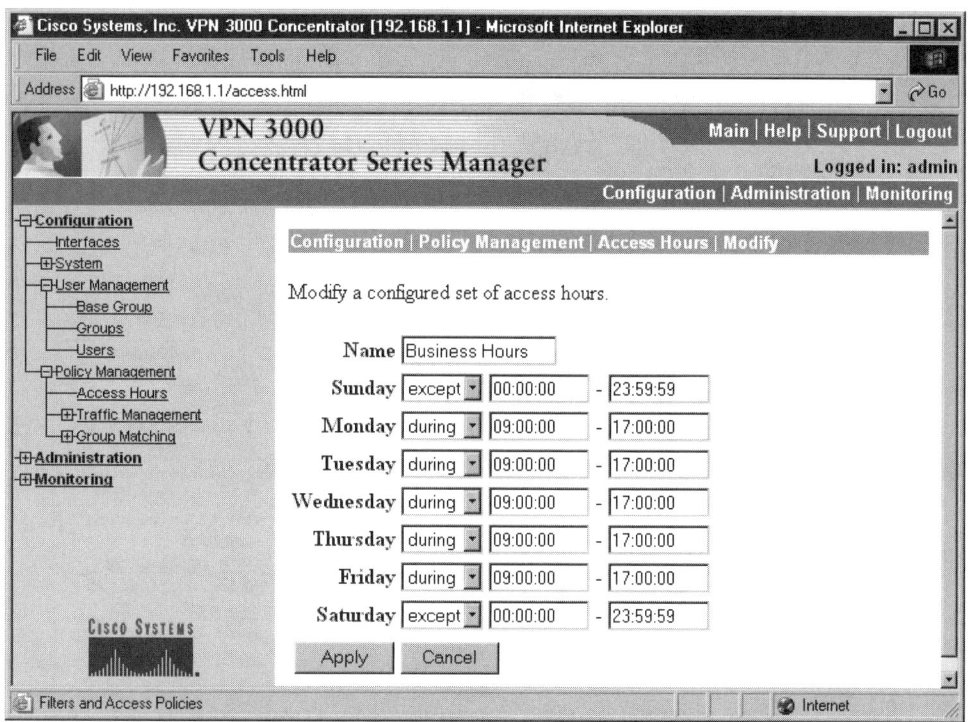

Figure 14-32 Modify or add a new access definition

be used to create a second range East Coast Hours for any groups in another time zone. The Apply button saves the changes, while the Cancel button abandons them.

Figure 14-35 shows the screen (Configuration | User Management | Groups | Modify *grp-name*) used to apply the previous access setting to a specific group. This is a common process in working with group settings where the feature needs to be configured, and then applied to the specific group. The first drop-down allows selecting any defined access time. Note, changing an existing access time definition will impact any groups or users who have that definition assigned to them.

Configuration | System | IP Routing

The VPN Concentrator can be configured to support RIP routing, plus the following routing features to communicate with other routers within the private network and to determine network connectivity, status, and optimum paths for sending data traffic.

- Static Routes—Manually configured route table entries.
- Default Gateways—Routes of last resort for otherwise unroutable traffic.
- OSPF—Open Shortest Path First routing protocol, including Area support.
- DHCP—Define global parameters for DHCP features.

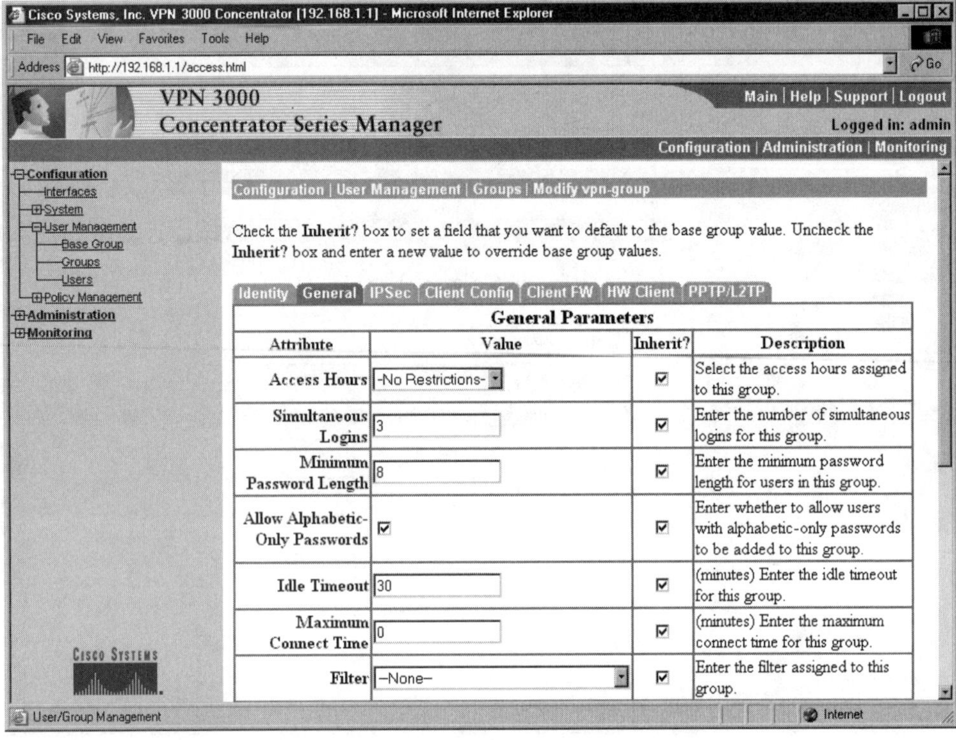

Figure 14-33 Change access hours for a specific group

- Redundancy—Virtual Router Redundancy Protocol parameters.
- Reverse Route Injection (RRI) —VPN Concentrator can add routes to its routing table for remote hardware or software clients.

Configuration | System | Management Protocols

The VPN 3000 Concentrator Series offers the following common built-in servers, supporting a variety of useful protocols used to manage devices and the network:

- FTP—File Transfer Protocol
- HTTP—Hypertext Transfer Protocol
- HTTPS—HTTP over SSL (Secure Sockets Layer) protocol
- SNMP—Simple Network Management Protocol
- SNMP Community Strings—Identifiers for valid SNMP clients
- SSL—Secure Sockets Layer protocol
- SSH—Secure Shell
- Telnet—Terminal emulation protocol and Telnet over SSL

- TFTP—Trivial File Transfer Protocol
- XML—Extensible Markup Language

Digital Certificates

As you learned in Chapters 9 and 11, a *digital certificate* is a form of credential, much like a driver's license or a passport in the paper-based world. Like its paper counterparts, the digital certificate has information on it that identifies the holder, plus the certificate authorities (CA), a trusted third-party that "signs" the certificates to confirm the holder's identity.

A digital certificate has additional information included with the holder's public key, which helps others to verify the key is genuine. This additional information, like a person's picture on a driver's license or a passport, can thwart attempts to substitute an unauthorized public key.

A digital certificate contains the following three items:

- Public key
- Certificate information—Identifying information about the holder, such as IP address, name, serial number, company, department, and so forth
- One or more digital signatures—Supplied by a CA

Certificate Types

CAs issue digital certificates for use in the Public Key Infrastructure (PKI). *PKI* uses public-key/private-key encryption methodology to ensure security. Some terms to remember include the following:

- **CA certificate**—Certificate used to sign (authenticate) other certificates.
- **Root certificate**—CA certificate that's self-signed.
- **Subordinate certificate**—Certificate issued by another CA certificate.
- **Identity certificates**—Certificates for specific systems or hosts.

VPN Concentrator and Certificates

To authenticate using digital certificates, at least one identity certificate and its root certificate must exist on the VPN Concentrator; there could be more. The VPN Concentrator model determines the maximum number of CA and identity certificates allowed.

- **Models 3015–3080**—Maximum of 20 root or subordinate CA certificates and 20 identity certificates.
- **Model 3005**—No more than six root or subordinate CA certificates and two identity certificates.

In both cases, CA certificate maximums include any supporting registration authority (RA) certificates.

PART III

All models of VPN Concentrator can have only one SSL certificate installed.

All digital certificates and private keys are automatically stored in the VPN Concentrator's Flash memory. Saving them is unnecessary. These stored items aren't listed and they can't be displayed using the Administration | File Management menu. All stored private keys are encrypted. Once installed on the VPN Concentrator, the identity certificate appears in the Digital Certificate list for configuring both IPSec LAN-to-LAN connections and IPSec SAs.

Certificate Revocation List (CRL)

The VPN Concentrator can be configured to enable CRL information caching in RAM to speed the process of verifying the revocation status of certificates. When the VPN Concentrator needs to check the revocation status of a certificate, it first checks to see if the CRL exists in cache and that it hasn't expired. If the CRL has expired, a new one is requested, but if it hasn't expired, the Concentrator searches the list of revoked serial numbers for the certificate serial number. If a match exists, the authentication fails.

Time Issues

Digital certificates have an expiration date beyond which they're of no value, much like the driver's license and passport examples in the paper-based world. Note, because of this expiration date, the VPN Concentrator time and date must be correct and synchronized with network time.

A second time issue is this: certificate enrollment and installation process must be completed within one week of generating the request. Otherwise, the request is deleted.

Enrolling and Installing Certificates

To use digital certificates for authentication, you must first enroll with a CA, and obtain and install the CA certificate on the VPN Concentrator. Then, you can enroll and install an identity certificate from the same CA. You can enroll and install digital certificates manually or automatically. The automatic method is a new feature that uses Simple Certificate Enrollment Protocol (SCEP), a secure messaging protocol that requires minimal user intervention to enroll and install certificates using only the VPN Concentrator Manager. SCEP was introduced in Chapter 11. SCEP is quicker than enrolling and installing digital certificates manually, but SCEP is available only if it meets the following two conditions:

- The CA must support SCEP.
- Enrolling must be done via the Internet.

If the CA doesn't support SCEP or if digital certificates are enrolled by other means, such as by e-mail or floppy disk, then they must be processed using the manual method, which requires more steps.

In either case, whichever method is used to install a CA certificate must also be used to request identity or SSL certificates from that CA.

Certificate Task Summary

Regardless of whether SCEP or the manual method is used, the following tasks must be completed to obtain and install certificates:

1. Request and install the required CA certificate(s).
2. Create an enrollment request for one or more identity certificates.
3. Request an identity certificate from the same CA that issued the CA certificate(s).
4. Install the identity certificate on the VPN Concentrator.
5. Enable CRL checking and caching.
6. Enable certificates.

Using SCEP to Manage Certificates

The following steps demonstrate using SCEP to enroll and install digital certificates. To use SCEP to enroll identity or SSL certificates, SCEP must also be used to obtain the associated CA certificate. The Manager doesn't allow enrolling a certificate from a CA unless that CA certificate was installed using SCEP. The certificate obtained using SCEP can issue other SCEP certificates and is, therefore, referred to as *SCEP-enabled.*

Using SCEP to Obtain and Install CA Certificates Automatically

Follow these steps for each CA Certificate you want to obtain:

1. Use the Concentrator Manager navigation system to display the Administration | Certificate Management screen, as shown in Figure 14-36.
2. Click the *Click here to install a CA certificate* option at the top of the screen. The Administration | Certificate Management | Install | CA Certificate screen appears, as shown in Figure 14-37.

   The previous link option is only available on this screen if no CA certificates have been installed on the Concentrator. If the link is missing, click the *Click here to install a certificate* option, the third link in the last figure. The Administration | Certificate Management | Install screen is displayed, from which you can choose Install CA Certificate.
3. Click the SCEP (Simple Certificate Enrollment Protocol) link to display the Administration | Certificate Management | Install | CA Certificate | SCEP screen, shown in Figure 14-38. Enter the following information in the two fields:

   URL—The URL of the CA's SCEP interface.

   CA Descriptor—Some CAs require and provide a descriptor to identify a certificate. If the CA doesn't use a descriptor, enter one of your own. Something must be entered in this field.

   Click Retrieve.

   Once complete, the CA certificate is installed on the Concentrator and appears in the Certificate Authorities box of the Administration | Certificate Management screen (as shown in the previous Figure 14-36).

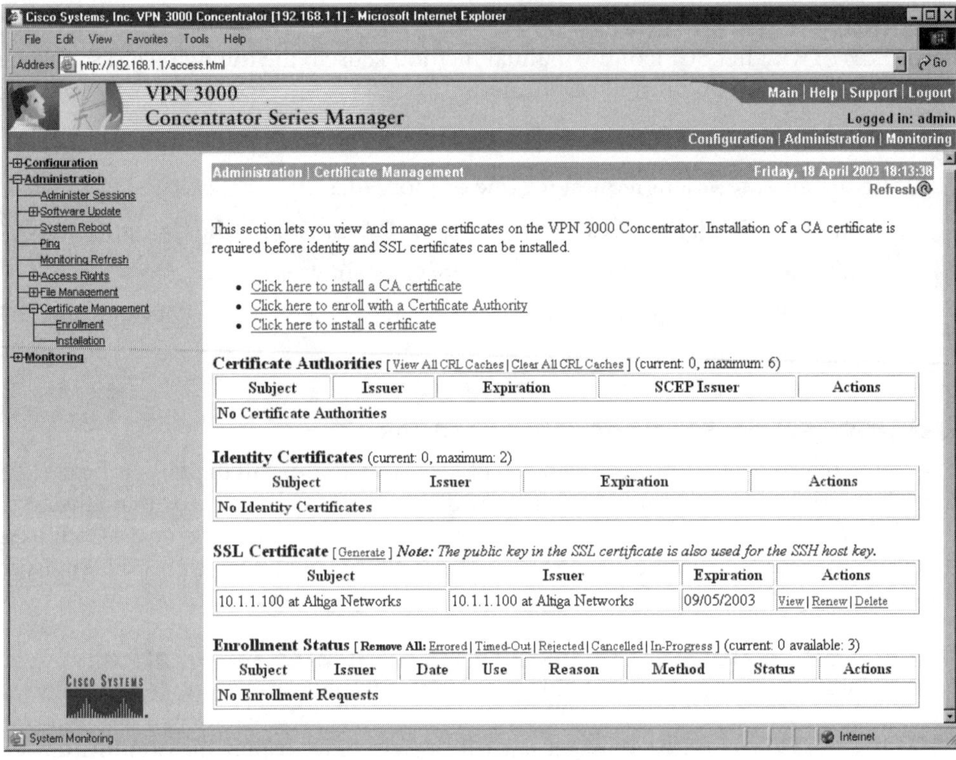

Figure 14-34 Certificate management screen

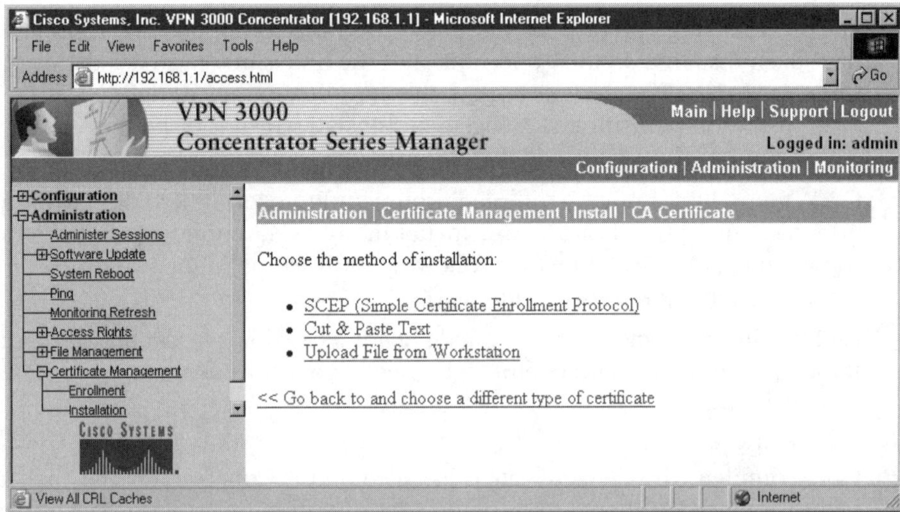

Figure 14-35 Install CA Certificate screen

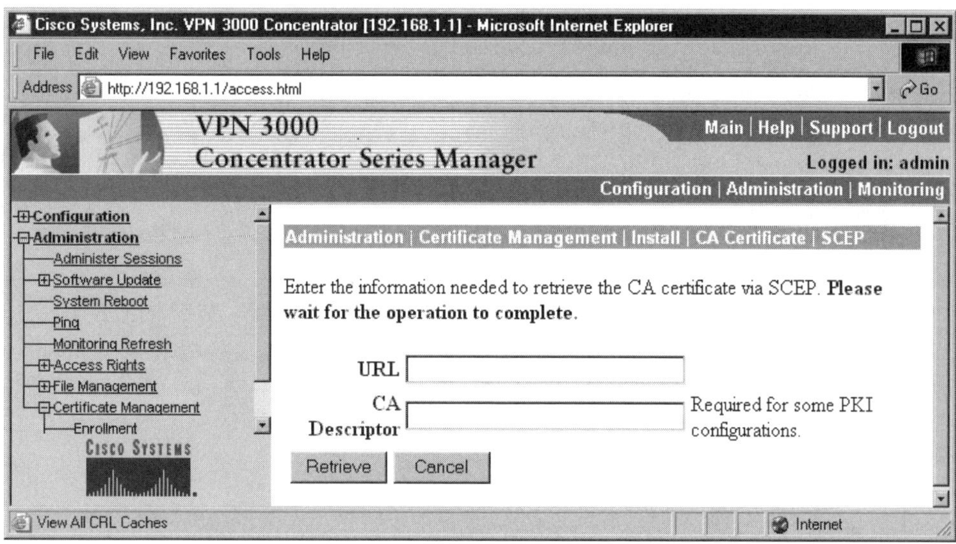

Figure 14-36 CA certificate request information

Using SCEP to Enroll and Install Identity Certificates Automatically

Follow these steps for each identity certificate you want to obtain:

1. Using the Administration | Certificate Management screen from the previous Figure 14-36, Click the *Click here to enroll with a Certificate Authority* link.The Administration | Certificate Management | Enroll screen displays, as shown in Figure 14-39.
2. Click the *Identity Certificate* link to display the Administration | Certificate Management | Enroll | Identity Certificate screen, as shown in Figure 14-40. If SCEP-enabled CA certificates were on the VPN Concentrator, they would be listed as links beneath the Enroll via PKCS10 Request (Manual) shown in the figure.

   The link title includes the name of the CA certificate in the following format: Enroll via SCEP at Certificate Name. So, a CA certificate on the Concentrator named "CA-Test" would look like the following:

   - Enroll via PKCS10 Request (Manual).
   - Enroll via SCEP at CA-Test.
3. Click the link to the SCEP certificate to be enrolled and the Administration | Certificate Management | Enroll | Identity Certificate | SCEP screen display, as shown in Figure 14-41.

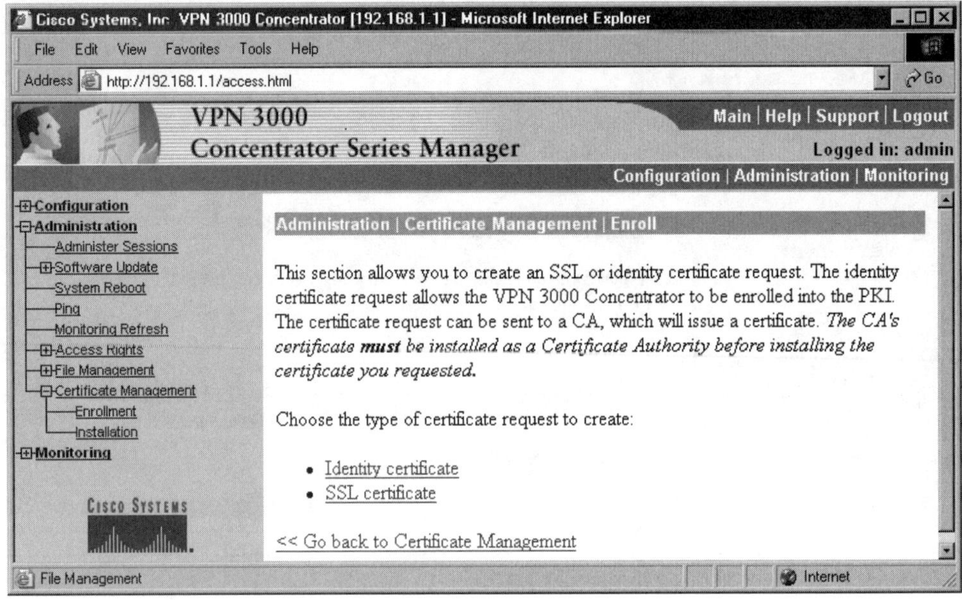

Figure 14-37 Certificate management enrollment screen

4. Complete the fields and click the Enroll button.

   Some CAs require manual verification of credentials and this can take some time—the certificate request could enter Polling mode. In this case, the

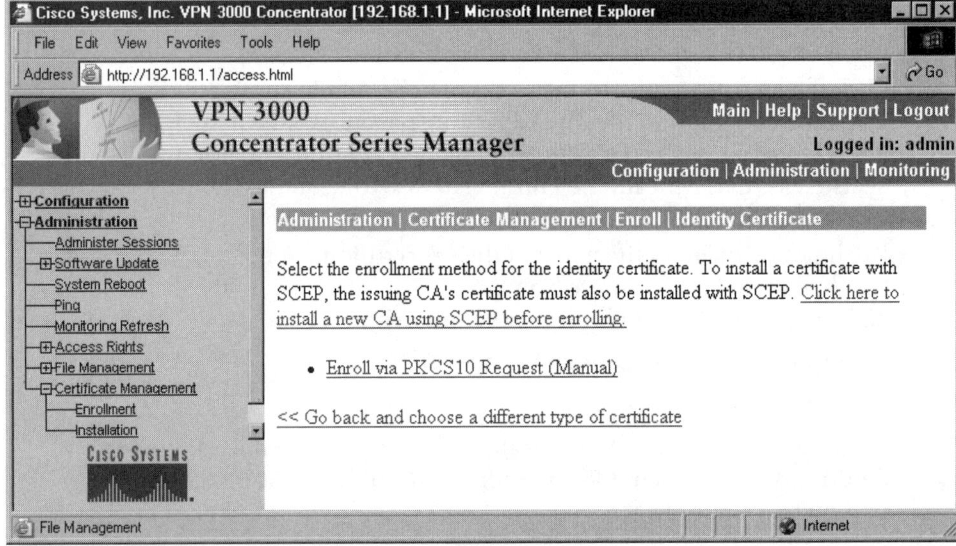

Figure 14-38 Enrollment Identity screen to select a certificate

Administration | Certificate Management | Enroll | Identity Certificate | SCEP

Enter the information to be included in the certificate request. **Please wait for the operation to finish.**

Common Name (CN)	Enter the common name for the VPN 3000 Concentrator to be used in this PKI.
Organizational Unit (OU)	Enter the department.
Organization (O)	Enter the Organization or company.
Locality (L)	Enter the city or town.
State/Province (SP)	Enter the State or Province.
Country (C)	Enter the two-letter country abbreviation (e.g. United States = US).
Subject AlternativeName (FQDN)	Enter the Fully Qualified Domain Name for the VPN 3000 Concentrator to be used in this PKI.
Subject AlternativeName (E-Mail Address)	Enter the E-Mail Address for the VPN 3000 Concentrator to be used in this PKI.
Challenge Password / **Verify Challenge Password**	Enter and verify the challenge password for this certificate request.
Key Size RSA 512 bits	Select the key size for the generated RSA key pair.

Enroll | Cancel

Figure 14-39 Screen to add certificate enrollment information

Concentrator will resend the request to the CA a defined number of times, until either the CA responds or the process times out.

Once the CA responds and issues the certificate, the VPN Concentrator installs it automatically and displays the Administration | Certificate Management | Enrollment | Request Generated screen, as shown in Figure 14-42.

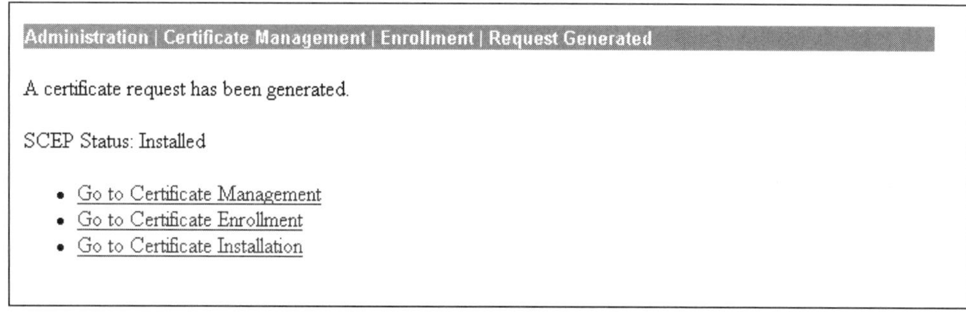

Figure 14-40 SCEP Status: Installed

Using the Certificates

Once the certificate is installed on the VPN concentrator, you must change settings for IKE negotiation. This requires two screen entries, the IKE transform to be used and the IPSec SA information.

IKE Configuration

Use the Manager navigation to locate the Configuration | System | Tunneling Protocols IPSec | IKE Proposals screen, shown in Figure 14-43. This screen displays both the Active and Inactive IKE options available on the Concentrator.

You can change an existing Active proposal from preshared keys to certificates or create a new one. Select an existing proposal, and then click the Modify button or click the Add button. Either way, a screen similar to the one shown in Figure 14-44 appears.

You only have one choice here. Use the Authentication mode drop-down list and select RSA Digital Certificate. Then click the Apply button.

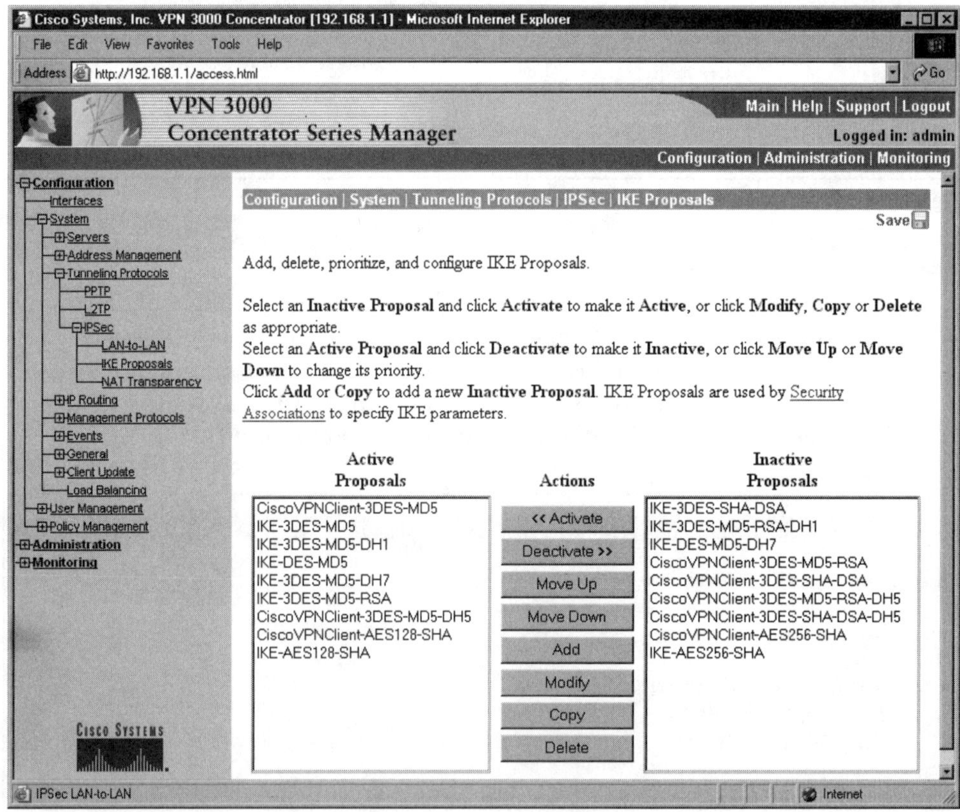

Figure 14-41 IKE Proposal options

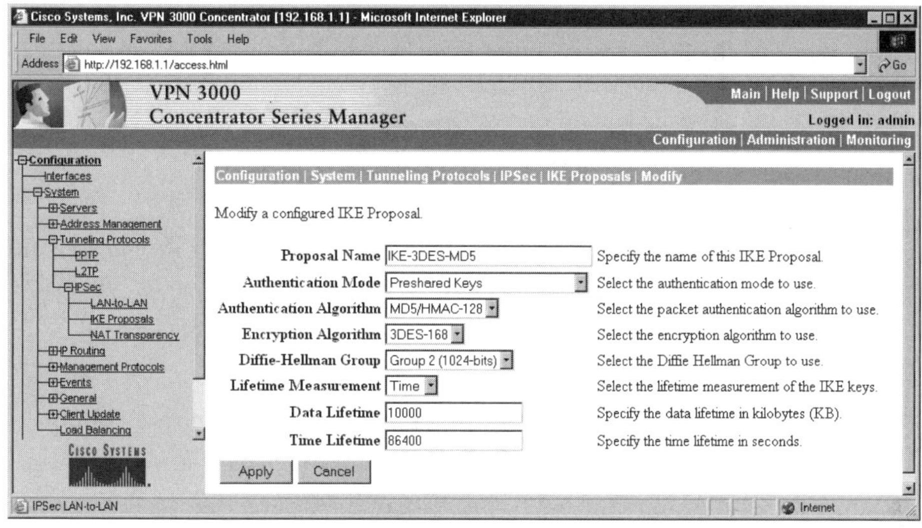

Figure 14-42 IKE Proposal option to be modified

IPSec Configuration

Use the Manager navigation to locate the Configuration | Policy Management | Traffic Management | Security Associations | Modify screen for the appropriate IPSec SA. The resulting screen is large, but the bottom panel, as shown in Figure 14-45, is all that must be changed.

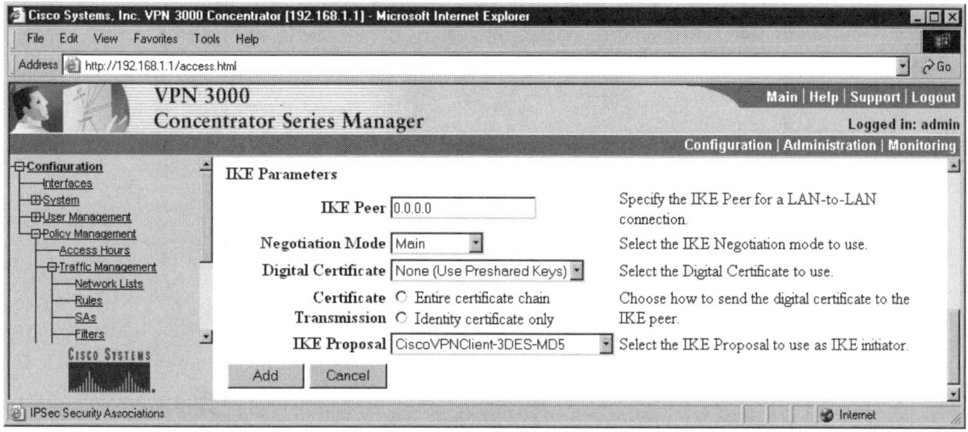

Figure 14-43 Defining the IKE parameters for the IPSec SA

Use the Digital Certificate drop-down list to select the appropriate certificate name.

If necessary, use the IKE Proposal drop-down list to select the IKE proposal defined in the last section, and then click Apply.

Configure Cisco VPN Client Support

Now, it's necessary to configure the Cisco VPN Client. While the full process was covered in Chapter 12, the following steps are used to contact the VPN Concentrator. Bring up the VPN Client on the PC using the Start | Programs | Cisco Systems VPN Client | VPN Dialer.

1. Click the New button.
2. Name the connection, as shown in Figure 14-46, and click the Next button.
3. Enter the Group name just created, and then click the Next button.
4. Enter the IP address of the public interface of the Concentrator.
5. Click the Finish button.
6. Click the Connect button, as shown in Figure 14-47, to establish the connection.
7. When prompted, enter the user name and the password, and then click OK.

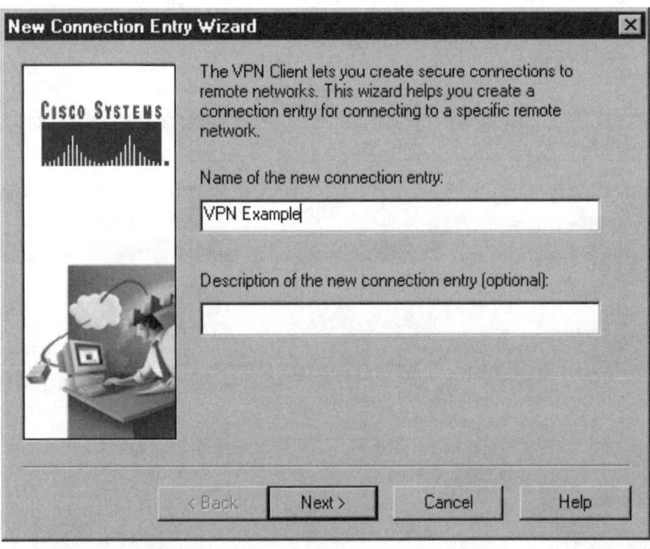

Figure 14-44 New Connection Entry Wizard box

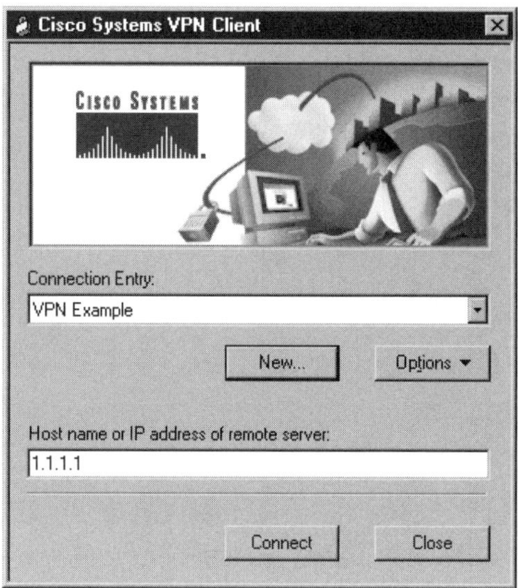

Figure 14-45 Cisco Systems VPN Client box

VPN Client Autoinitiation Feature

VPN Client Autoinitiation (Automatic VPN initiation) is a new feature that provides secure connections to hosts using a wireless LAN (WLAN) environment by connecting through a VPN 3000 Series Concentrator. With autoinitiation configured on the VPN Client, the Client becomes active immediately after the PC boots up, or after exiting Standby or Hibernation mode. The client establishes a VPN tunnel to the Concentrator defined for its network, prompts the user to authenticate, and allows that user network access.

In the WLAN network, the wireless client first associates itself to a wireless Access Point (AP). The installed VPN Client uses the IP address range it receives from the wireless connection to launch a VPN connection request automatically to the corresponding VPN Concentrator on site. The resulting IPSec VPN connection provides secure wireless 802.11*x* traffic for the wireless host. Without a successful VPN connection, the wireless host won't have access to the network resources.

The vpnclient.ini File

Currently, no wizard exists to perform this configuration, so it's necessary to edit the vpnclient.ini file manually for the VPN Client to activate autoinitiation. This file is located in the VPN Client folder, under Program Files in the Windows environment. The file created previously in Chapter 12 looks like the following:

```
[main]
StatefulFirewall=1
EnableLog=1
[LOG.IKE]
LogLevel=1
[LOG.CM]
LogLevel=1
[LOG.PPP]
```

The changes can be made to the [Main] section by double clicking the file name. The file will then open in Notepad. Saving a copy before you begin might be a good idea.

Preparation

As with any configuration, gathering the needed information before you begin makes sense. The following information is needed to configure autoinitiation.

- The network IP addresses for the client network
- The subnet mask for the client network
- The names for all connection entries users are using for their connections

Configuration

To configure autoinitiation, you need to add the following three keywords and appropriate values in the [Main] section of the vpnclient.ini file:

- **AutoInitiationEnable**—enables or disables autoinitiation. 1 = enable, 0 = disable.
- **AutoInitiationRetryInterval**—defines the number of minutes to wait before retrying the autoinitiation connection. Range is one to ten minutes. The default is one minute.
- **AutoInitiationList**—defines a series of section names that follow this entry. Each one contains the network details needed to autoinitiate. Entries include network address, subnet mask, and a connection entry name, specifying a connection entry profile (.pcf file). You can have a maximum of 64 section (network) entries.

Next, you need to define the networks listed that are associated with the section names in the AutoInitiationList section. While the following is a simple example, it shows enabling autoinitiation for two networks. This feature could represent a significant advantage in a corporate environment, where some personnel frequently work in multiple locations.

```
[main]
AutoInitiationEnable=1                  (turns the feature on)
AutoInitiationRetryInterval=3           (sets a 3 minute wait)
AutoInitiationList=TacomaWLAN,
ViennaWLAN                              (identifies 2 WLANs)
[TacomaWLAN]                            (config info for Tacoma)
Network=10.95.254.0
Mask=255.255.255.0
ConnectionEntry=TacProf                 (connection profile named TacProf.pcf)
[ViennaWLAN]                            (config info for Vienna)
Network=192.168.1.0
Mask=255.255.255.0
ConnectionEntry=VieProf                 (connection profile named VieProf.pcf)
StatefulFirewall=1
EnableLog=1
[LOG.IKE]
LogLevel=1
[LOG.CM]
LogLevel=1
[LOG.PPP]
```

VPN 3000 Configuration

The configuration steps for this feature required on the 3000 Concentrator are the same as any other VPN Client group. Defining a new group and confirming that all Security Policy issues are addressed and enabled might be wise. This can also make administering and monitoring these users easier, as well as providing autoupdate configurations, if necessary.

Administer and Monitor Remote Access Networks

This section looks briefly at the Administration and Monitoring features of the Cisco VPN 3000 Concentrator Series.

Administration

The VPN 3000 Concentrator Series provides a rich set of administration tools and features that keep the system operational and secure. Configuring the system sets the parameters that govern its use and functionality as a VPN device, but administration involves higher-level activities, such as who is allowed to configure the system and what software runs on it. Only those logged in as administrators can access and use the Administration tools. Figure 14-48 shows a breakdown of the Administration menu.

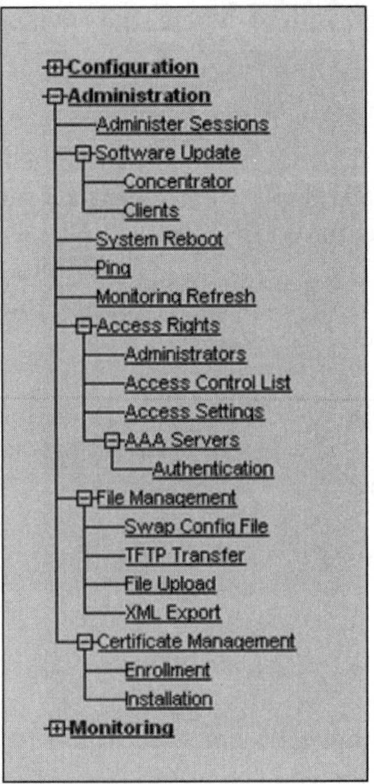

Figure 14-46 VPN 3000 Administration menu

Earlier sections in this chapter looked at some of the Administration features, such as managing Concentrator access hours and digital certificates. This section briefly discusses some other features that might be useful in a remote access environment.

Summarizing VPN Activity

The VPN 3000 Concentrator Series provides a recap of the current sessions currently underway by using two similar screens, the Administration | Administer Sessions screen option and the Monitoring | Sessions screen. Figure 14-49 shows the Administration | Administer Sessions screen.

Both screens have the Group drop-down box that allows looking at only a single group. Both screens have two additional outputs rows, which are not shown in the previous figure. One is a detail view of the current Remote Access sessions and the other is a detail view of the current administrative sessions.

The primary difference between the views is this: the Administration | Administer Sessions screen has links, just below the Group drop-down box, which can be used to log out of all active sessions of a given tunnel type at once. This could be handy if new

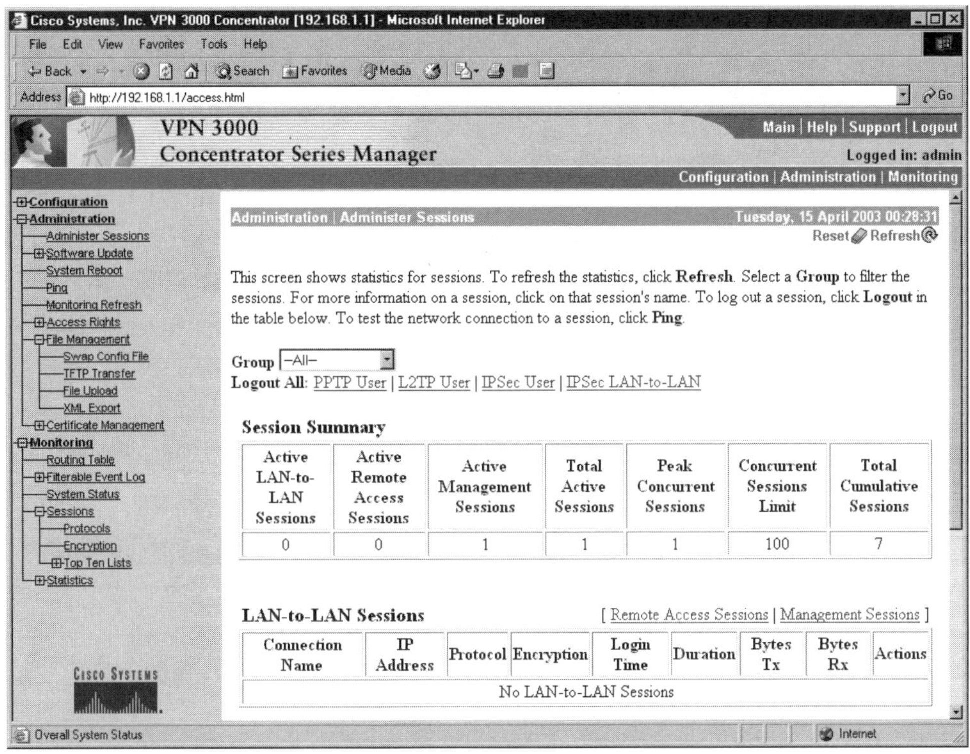

Figure 14-47 The Administration | Administer Sessions screen summarizing VPN activity

security parameters were configured and you decide to force all current sessions to comply, instead of waiting for the next session.

To log out of the sessions, click the appropriate label. The Manager displays a prompt to confirm the action. This action immediately terminates all sessions of the given tunnel type. No user warning or Undo option occurs.

Ping

The Administration | Ping screen, shown in Figure 14-50, lets you use the ICMP ping utility to test network connectivity. This is most useful when working with and troubleshooting remote user connections. The VPN Concentrator sends an ICMP Echo Request message to the defined host. If the host is reachable, the screen displays a simple IP address is alive message, such as *192.168.1.20 is alive.* If the host is unreachable, the Manager displays an Error message. You can also ping hosts from the Administration | Administer Sessions screen.

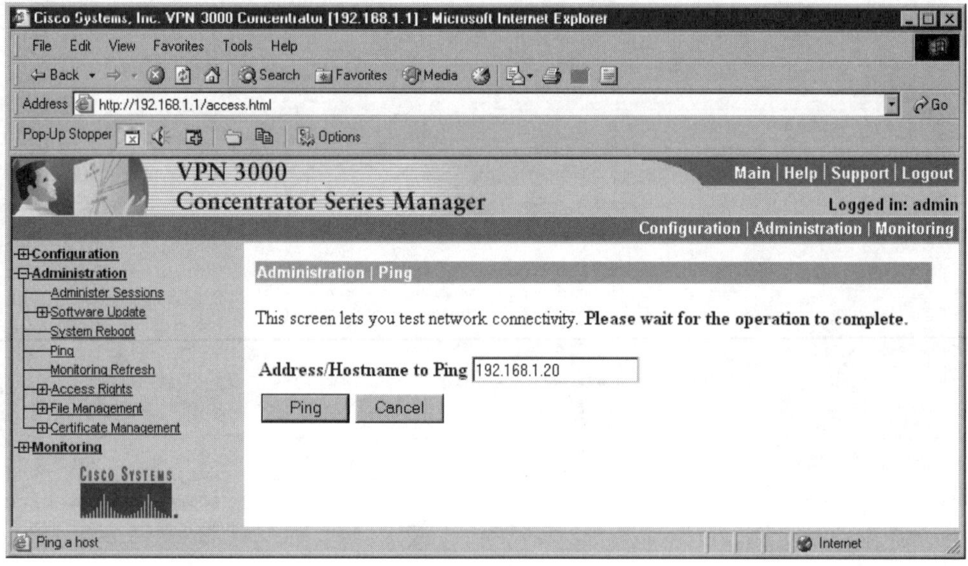

Figure 14-48 Ping screen

System Rebooting

The Administration | System Reboot screen, as shown in Figure 14-51, allows the administrator to reboot or shut down the VPN Concentrator with various options. Rebooting the system automatically logs you out and displays the main login screen. If the browser appears to hang during a reboot, preventing you from logging in, wait a minute for the reboot to finish.

The choices should be self-explanatory.

Software Update

The Administration | Software Update screen has only two links that allow the administrator to update either the VPN Concentrator executable system software or the VPN Client software. The two links are as follows:

- **Concentrator**—Uploads the software image to the VPN Concentrator
- **Client**—Updates the VPN 3002 Hardware Client software

Clicking the Concentrator link brings up the Administration | Software Update | Concentrator screen, as shown in Figure 14-52. The process uploads the executable system software to the VPN Concentrator, which then verifies the integrity of the software image.

To specify the new software file, enter the complete path name of the new image file or click the Browse... button to find and select the file from the workstation or network.

This process can take a few minutes to upload and verify the software. The system will display a simple progress bar.

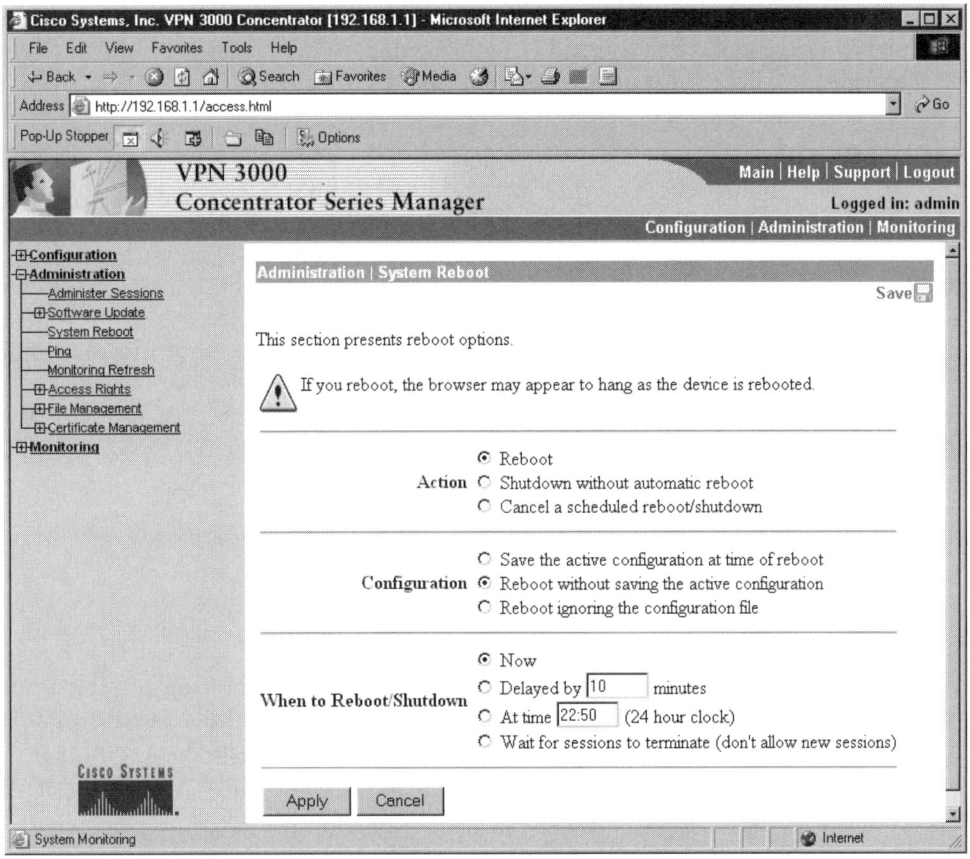

Cisco Systems, Inc. VPN 3000 Concentrator [192.168.1.1] - Microsoft Internet Explorer

Address http://192.168.1.1/access.html

VPN 3000
Concentrator Series Manager

Main | Help | Support | Logout
Logged in: admin
Configuration | Administration | Monitoring

Configuration
Administration
Administer Sessions
Software Update
System Reboot
Ping
Monitoring Refresh
Access Rights
File Management
Certificate Management
Monitoring

Administration | System Reboot

Save

This section presents reboot options.

If you reboot, the browser may appear to hang as the device is rebooted.

Action: Reboot / Shutdown without automatic reboot / Cancel a scheduled reboot/shutdown

Configuration: Save the active configuration at time of reboot / Reboot without saving the active configuration / Reboot ignoring the configuration file

When to Reboot/Shutdown: Now / Delayed by 10 minutes / At time 22:50 (24 hour clock) / Wait for sessions to terminate (don't allow new sessions)

Apply Cancel

System Monitoring

Figure 14-49 System reboot and shutdown options

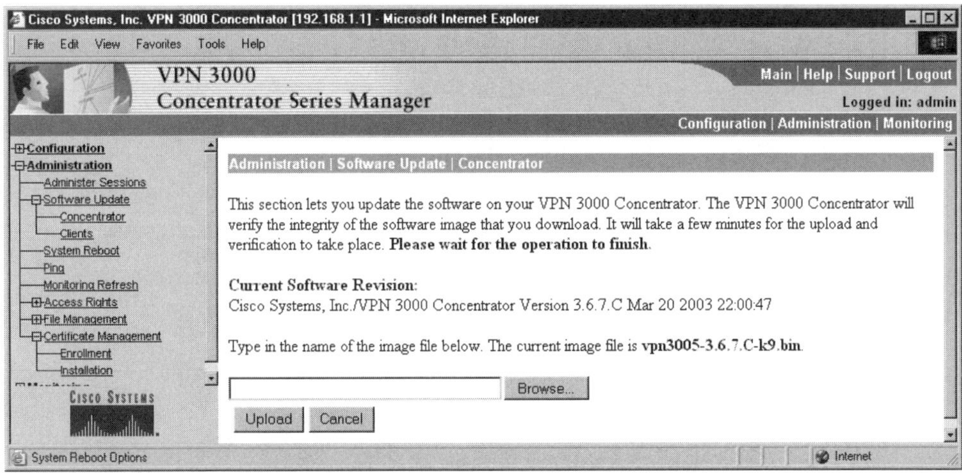

Figure 14-50 VPN Concentrator software upgrade screen

You must reboot the VPN Concentrator to run the new software image. The system prompts you to reboot when the update is finished.

Updating the Client software is covered in Chapter 15.

Monitoring

The VPN 3000 Concentrator compiles many statistics, and it tracks the status of many processes and activities essential to system administration and management. The Monitoring windows can be used to view the status items and statistics. You can see the state of LEDs that show the status of hardware subsystems in the device. Figure 14-53 shows a breakdown of the Monitoring menu.

The Monitor menu option provides opportunities to see snapshot summaries of activity broken down by protocol or encryption type. An option, Monitoring | Sessions | Top Ten Lists, shows statistics for the top ten currently active sessions, sorted by the following:

- Data—total bytes transmitted and received
- Duration—total time connected
- Throughput—average throughput (bytes/sec)

Routing Table

The Monitoring | Routing Table screen displays the current VPN Concentrator routing table. As with the routers, the routing table shows the best valid forwarding paths the system knows about. These routes can be static routes, or learned via routing protocols or interface configurations. Figure 14-54 shows a simple route table with related information.

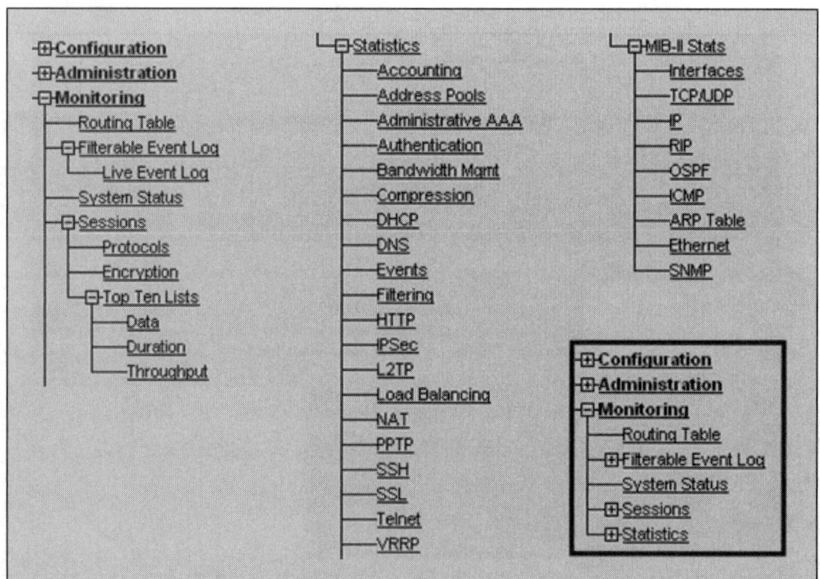

Figure 14-51 Monitoring menu options

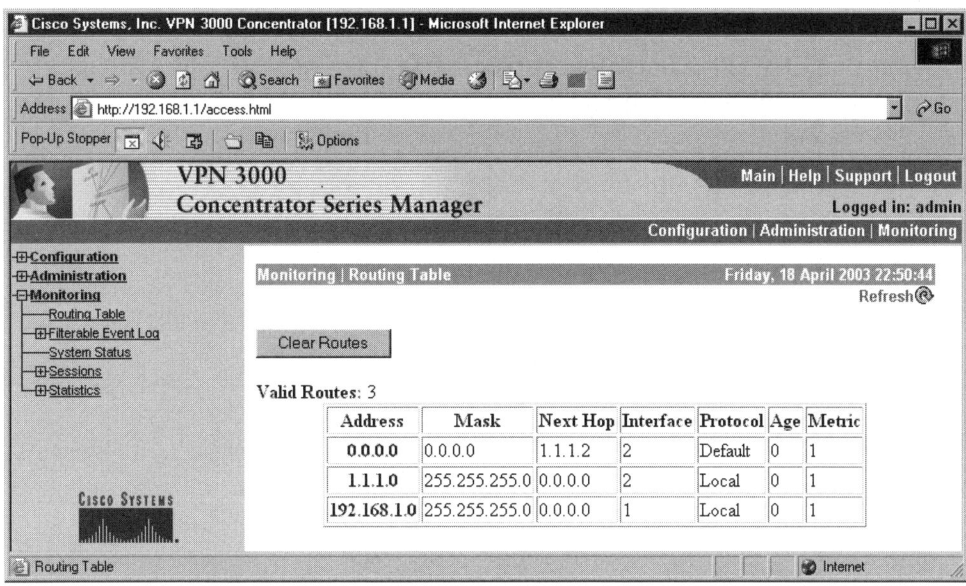

Address	Mask	Next Hop	Interface	Protocol	Age	Metric
0.0.0.0	0.0.0.0	1.1.1.2	2	Default	0	1
1.1.1.0	255.255.255.0	0.0.0.0	2	Local	0	1
192.168.1.0	255.255.255.0	0.0.0.0	1	Local	0	1

Figure 14-52 Routing table entries

Additional monitoring options are included in Chapter 15.

Chapter Review

The Cisco VPN 3000 Concentrator devices are a series of specialty appliances that perform VPN gateway services for organizations of all sizes. The VPN Concentrator can be used in remote access implementations, providing secure connections for mobile users and Small Office/Home Office (SOHO) locations, as well as LAN-to-LAN connections providing VPN access between branch locations. Many networks use the Concentrators for both types of networks.

Concentrator configuration and operations are via a menu-driven architecture, accessed by either a text-based CLI or a web-based interface. Generally, all tasks and functions can be performed using either interface, but the CLI must be used initially to configure an IP address on the private interface to allow web access.

The Concentrator functions and menu options break into three areas: Configuration, Administration, and Monitoring. Configuring the system sets the parameters that govern its use and functionality as a VPN device, but administration involves higher level activities, such as who is allowed to configure the system and what software runs on it. The Monitoring screens can be used to view the status of the many processes and activities essential to system administration and management, as well as the statistics the Concentrator compiles.

Questions

1. To make the VPN Concentrator accessible to a web browser, which interface must be configured by the CLI?

   A. Ethernet 0

   B. Ethernet 1

   C. Ethernet 2

   D. Ethernet 3

2. The VPN 3000 Concentrator CLI console connection uses which of the following?

   A. A standard Cisco console kit with cable

   B. A rollover cable with no adapters required

   C. A straight-through serial connection

   D. A straight-through RJ-45 cable with no adapters required

3. What is the following screen?

   Welcome to
   Cisco Systems
   VPN 3000 Concentrator Series
   Command Line Interface
   Copyright (C) 1998-2003 Cisco Systems, Inc.
   -- : Set the time on your device. ...
   > Time
   Quick -> [10:13:37]

   A. CLI startup menu

   B. Manager startup menu

   C. CLI Quick Configuration

   D. Manager Quick Configuration

4. Which of the following is *not* one of the Quick Configuration steps?

   A. Define which tunneling protocols and encryption options will be used

   B. Change the admin password to improve system security

   C. Define the method(s) for assigning IP addresses to protected clients

   D. Define the IP routing method to be used

5. Which of the following wouldn't a VPN Concentrator normally connect to in a remote access implementation?

   A. VPN 3002 Client

   B. VPN Client software

C. VPN 3000 Concentrator

D. PIX Firewall

6. Which is *not* one of the three types of preshared keys?

A. Unique

B. User

C. Group

D. Wildcard

7. When using the VPN Concentrator internal authentication server, which is *not* an accurate maximum number of entries (groups and users combined)?

A. Model 3005/3015—100

B. Model 3030—500

C. Model 3060—800

D. Model 3080—1,000

8. Which of the following is *not* one of the four possible methods for the VPN Concentrator to assign IP addresses to the remote users?

A. Use Address from Authentication Server

B. Use a DHCP Server

C. Use NAT inside

D. Use Address Pools

E. Use Client Address

9. What does the term split tunneling refer to?

A. The capability to establish multiple simultaneous VPN connections

B. The capability to allow multiple users to share a VPN connection

C. The capability to allow the IPSec client to go directly to the Internet in Cleartext form for those destinations that don't require encryption

D. The capability to create different VPN connections based on security requirements

10. Which statement is true about VPN Concentrator client firewall requirements?

A. Used to require a personal firewall for all VPN clients

B. Used to configure firewall parameters for VPN Clients running on PIX firewalls

C. Used to configure firewall parameters for VPN Clients running on non-Windows PCs

D. Used to configure firewall parameters for VPN Clients running Microsoft Windows

11. Which is *not* a supported type of user authentication server?
    A. RADIUS server
    B. TACACS+ server
    C. Internal server
    D. RSA Security Inc. SecurID (SDI) server
    E. NT Domain server
12. When using the Identity Parameters tab to define a group, which of the following is *not* included?
    A. User name
    B. Group name
    C. Password
    D. Authentication server type
13. Which routing method is *not* supported using Configuration | System | IP Routing?
    A. Static routes
    B. OSPF
    C. Default gateways
    D. EIGRP
14. Which of the following is *not* a digital certificate type?
    A. Subordinate certificate
    B. CA certificate
    C. Secondary certificate
    D. Root certificate
    E. Identity certificate
15. Which is *not* one of the three keywords added to the [Main] section of the vpnclient.ini file for VPN Client Autoinitiation?
    A. AutoInitiationList
    B. AutoInitiationRetryInterval
    C. AutoInitiationNetworks
    D. AutoInitiationEnable

Answers

1. **B.** Ethernet 1
2. **C.** A straight-through serial connection
3. **C.** CLI Quick Configuration
4. **D.** Define the IP routing method to be used
5. **C.** VPN 3000 Concentrator (used for LAN-to-LAN implementations)
6. **B.** User
7. **C.** Model 3060—800 (should be 1,000)
8. **C.** Use NAT inside
9. **C.** Enables the IPSec client to go directly to the Internet in Cleartext form for those destinations that don't require encryption
10. **D.** Used to configure firewall parameters for VPN Clients running Microsoft Windows
11. **B.** TACACS+ server
12. **A.** User name
13. **D.** EIGRP
14. **A.** Secondary certificate
15. **C.** AutoInitiationNetworks

CHAPTER 15

Configuring Cisco VPN 3002 Remote Clients

In this chapter, you will learn to:

- Configure the VPN 3002 using the CLI
- Configure the VPN 3002 device Remote Access
- Configure a variety of VPN 3000 and 3002 features
- Configure for a backup server and for load balancing
- Configure the client auto-update feature

This chapter looks at configuring the Cisco VPN 3002 Remote Hardware Client for basic operations, as well as advanced features and options. The 3002 device was introduced and described in Chapter 13. That information won't be repeated here, but the features introduced will be explored and the configuration steps defined.

The Cisco VPN 3002 Hardware Client communicates with a VPN 3000 Series Concentrator to create a VPN across a TCP/IP network (such as the Internet). The VPN 3002 requires minimal configuration, and allows the VPN administrator to monitor, configure, and upgrade multiple VPN 3002 hardware clients from a central location.

The VPN 3002 Remote Hardware Client is a small, footprint-dedicated device designed for organizations with many remote users and sites that require secure VPN connections. Figure 15-1 shows the book-sized (2 × 8.6 × 6.5 inches) 3002 device.

The VPN 3002 Hardware Client device can be used to connect one or more devices, including workstations, servers, hubs, cash registers, printers, and IP telephones to a company's central network. Each 3002 unit eliminates the need to install and configure VPN client software on the local workstation(s), plus it supports workstations running any TCP/IP supporting operating system (OS), including Windows, Sun Solaris UNIX, Mac, and Linux.

Currently, the 3002 case supports two models: the VPN 3002 has one public and one private 10/100BASE-T Ethernet interface, and the VPN 3002-8E has one public interface and a built-in 8-port 10/100-Mbps auto-sensing Ethernet switch as its private interface. Each 3002 can connect to LAN switches providing connections for up to 253 host devices. Figure 15-2 shows the back of the both models. The upper unit is the 3002-8E that incorporates the integrated switch, which can provide simplified installation for the

Figure 15-1 Cisco VPN 3002 Client device (front view)

small office or home needing to connect several computers to the network. The lower unit is the VPN 3002, which has a single private interface.

Both models share the following features found in many Cisco devices:

- Motorola PowerPC CPU
- Software-based encryption
- SDRAM memory for normal operation
- NVRAM for storing system configuration parameters
- Flash memory for file management and device OS
- Single power supply

The VPN 3002 in the Network

The VPN 3002 Hardware Client fits into the network anytime a relatively small group of users need secure VPN connections to the corporate network. Figure 15-3 shows both an overall view of the small branch connecting to the corporate network via a VPN 3002 and a more detailed view of the possible local connection using cable or DSL services.

Figure 15-2 Cisco VPN 3002 Client models

VPN Modes

The Cisco VPN 3002 supports two modes of operation to offer implementation choices based on flexibility, security, and easy configuration. Those modes are as follows:

- Client mode
- Network Extension mode

A large VPN implementation might frequently have both types of operation.

Client Mode

In *Client* mode (also called *PAT* mode), the VPN 3002 emulates the VPN client software appearing to the main network like a single remote user, isolating all devices on the VPN 3002 private network from the corporate network. The private hosts protected behind the VPN 3002 are a separate network that remains invisible and can't be routed to by the central site hosts. The local hosts are assigned their IP addresses from the VPN 3002 private interface configured as a DHCP server, while the public network port can be configured to use DHCP client feature to acquire its IP address from an Internet service provider (ISP).

The 3002 device uses Port Address Translation (PAT) on the public interface to help secure (hide) the local network and to allow local hosts to travel out of the network in Client mode. Because all traffic to the central network will have the Public interface IP address, PAT supplies and manages unique port number mappings to be used in combination with the IP address.

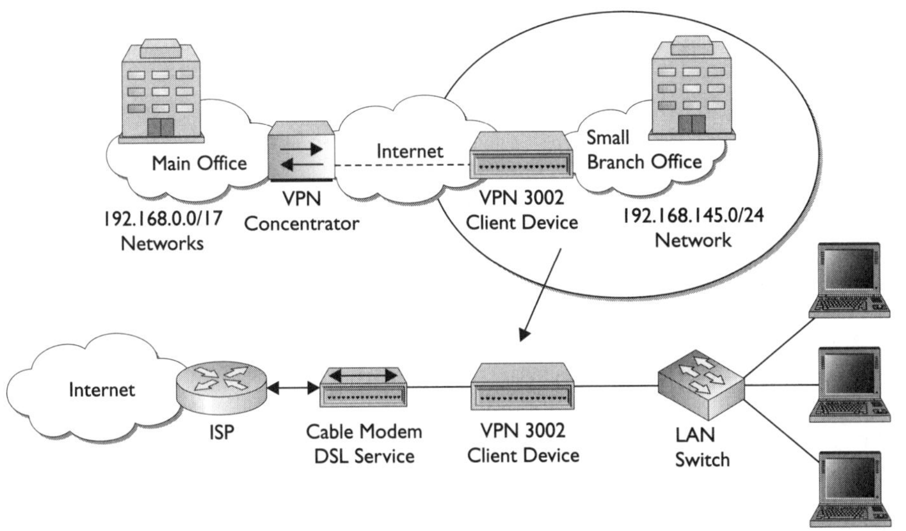

Figure 15-3 VPN 3002 connection overview and detail view

PART III

Because the VPN 3002 configured for Client mode can only create outbound connections, there's no way for an outside source—even from the corporate network—to initiate a connection with the 3002 unit or through it to the workstations behind.

Client Mode and Split Tunneling *Split tunneling* provides the capability to have a secure tunnel to the central site, while simultaneously maintaining an unsecured clear-text tunnel to the Internet through the ISP. PAT is used to protect the local workstations during split tunneling to the Internet. The network and addresses on the private side of the VPN 3002 remain hidden and can't be accessed directly from the Internet. If the organization security policy prohibits split tunneling, it can be blocked by creating a policy on the central site device, which is then pushed down to the 3002 Client.

Network Extension Mode

In *Network Extension* mode, the VPN 3002 establishes a secure, site-to-site connection with the central site device. The local stations behind the VPN 3002 are fully routable and the local network is visible to the central site. As the name implies, the local network becomes part of the organization's intranet. VPN and device configuration and security policies are pushed from the central site. The VPN 3002 must initiate the tunnel to the central site but, after the tunnel is up, either side can initiate data exchange.

In Network Extension mode, the private address can be assigned using the DHCP server. Any shared resources in the protected network that must be accessed by the central area hosts should be assigned manually to allow central site hosts and applications to reliably reach any local server, printer, POS terminal, IP phone, or other device critical to the business.

Network Extension Mode and Split Tunneling PAT provides security for local host traffic heading to the Internet through split tunneling. The network and addresses on the private side of the VPN 3002 are accessible over the tunnel, but are protected from the Internet because they can't be accessed directly. This outbound PAT on the VPN 3002 provides centralized security control because no configuration parameters exist for local users to adjust, which might cause the central site to be compromised.

Network Extension Mode per Group VPN software versions 3.6 and later let a network administrator restrict the use of Network Extension mode. The administrator can now enable/disable Network Extension mode on the VPN Concentrator for VPN 3002 hardware clients on a per-group basis.

Network Extension mode is the default setting on the VPN Concentrator. If the concentrator is configured to disallow Network Extension mode for a group, all VPN 3002s in the group must be configured for Client (PAT) mode.

IPSec VPNs

The VPN 3002 Hardware Client supports IPSec for secure connections to a central-site VPN Concentrator over a VPN tunnel. The VPN 3002 Hardware Client, which supports one tunnel at a time, running software release 3.6 or higher, supports the following IPSec implementations, but only one for each tunnel.

- IPSec over TCP
- IPSec over NAT-T
- IPSec over UDP

IPSec over TCP

IPSec over TCP encapsulates encrypted data traffic within TCP packets. This allows the VPN 3002 to operate in networks where standard ESP (Protocol 50) or IKE (UDP 500) can't function, or they can only function by modifying existing firewall rules. IPSec over TCP enables secure tunneling through NAT and PAT devices, and through firewalls by encapsulating both the IKE and IPSec protocols within TCP packets.

To use IPSec over TCP, both the VPN 3002 and the VPN Concentrator must meet the following requirements:

- Run version 3.5 or later software.
- Enable IPSec over TCP.
- Configure both the VPN 3002 and the VPN Concentrator to use the same port for IPSec over TCP.

NOTE IPSec over TCP doesn't work with proxy-based firewalls.

IPSec over NAT-T

NAT Traversal (NAT-T) allows IPSec peers to establish a connection through a device using NAT. NAT-T accomplishes this by encapsulating IPSec traffic in UDP datagrams (port 4500), thereby providing NAT devices with needed port information. NAT-T technology auto-detects any NAT devices and only encapsulates IPSec traffic when necessary.

The VPN 3002 hardware client uses NAT-T by default and requires no special config uration. The VPN 3002 first attempts NAT-T, and then uses IPSec over UDP if a NAT device isn't autodetected. The UDP packets allow IPSec traffic to pass through firewalls, which would normally reject and discard it.

To use NAT-T, the VPN 3002 must meet the following requirements:

- Run version 3.6 or later software.
- Port 4500 on any firewall between the VPN 3002 and the VPN peer must be open.
- Reconfigure any existing IPSec over UDP using port 4500 to a different port.
- Use the Configuration | Interfaces | Public screen to select the second or third options for the Fragmentation Policy parameter. These options let traffic travel across NAT devices that don't support IP fragmentation, while not impeding NAT devices that do support IP fragmentation.

IPSec over UDP

The VPN 3002 supports UDP NAT/Firewall Transparent IPSec. This technology encapsulates encrypted data traffic within UDP packets to provide secure connections between a VPN 3002 and a VPN Concentrator through a device, such as a firewall performing NAT.

The VPN 3002 uses frequent keepalives to ensure the mappings on the NAT device remain active. The VPN 3002 doesn't require special configuration for this feature, but the following minimum requirements must be met.

- Both the VPN 3002 and the VPN Concentrator must be running Release 3.0.3 or higher.
- IPSec over UDP must be enabled on the VPN Concentrator for the group to which the VPN 3002 belongs.

NOTE Cisco technology doesn't currently support a topology with multiple VPN 3002 Hardware Clients behind a single NAT device.

Configuring the 3002 Device

The VPN 3002 has been designed for simplicity and reliability of installation. It has few local setup parameters that must be configured. Basic configuration parameters, security policy, and even device upgrades are "pushed" to the device from the central site (head-end) device with the next connection. The user simply plugs the minimally configured VPN 3002 device into a DSL/cable connection, router, or other wide area networks (WANs) access device at the remote site.

This central control and management approach minimizes the need for skilled users or dedicated IT staff to deploy or maintain the connection. Troubleshooting aids and centralized monitoring features are built into the 3002 software to ensure proper operation after the unit has been set up.

The 3002 supports both a specialized command-line interface (CLI) and a Hardware Client Manager (web-based interface). In reality, they are similar to each other, much like the built-in web interface for routers like the 2600 series. From a practical standpoint, you can do exactly the same tasks with either interface. The primary difference is shown in Figure 15-4, where you can see the Explorer-like program structure on the left side and links to the three program modules in the upper-right corner. These two features make navigating the web-based interface significantly easier and quicker. The Help feature on the Hardware Client Manager is much better than the CLI.

Command-Line Interface (CLI)

The VPN 3002 Hardware Client CLI is a built-in, menu-based configuration, administration, and monitoring system that can be accessed via the system console port or a Telnet (or Telnet over SSL) session. Both Telnet options are enabled by default on the private network interface. The CLI supports the same configuration options as the HTML-

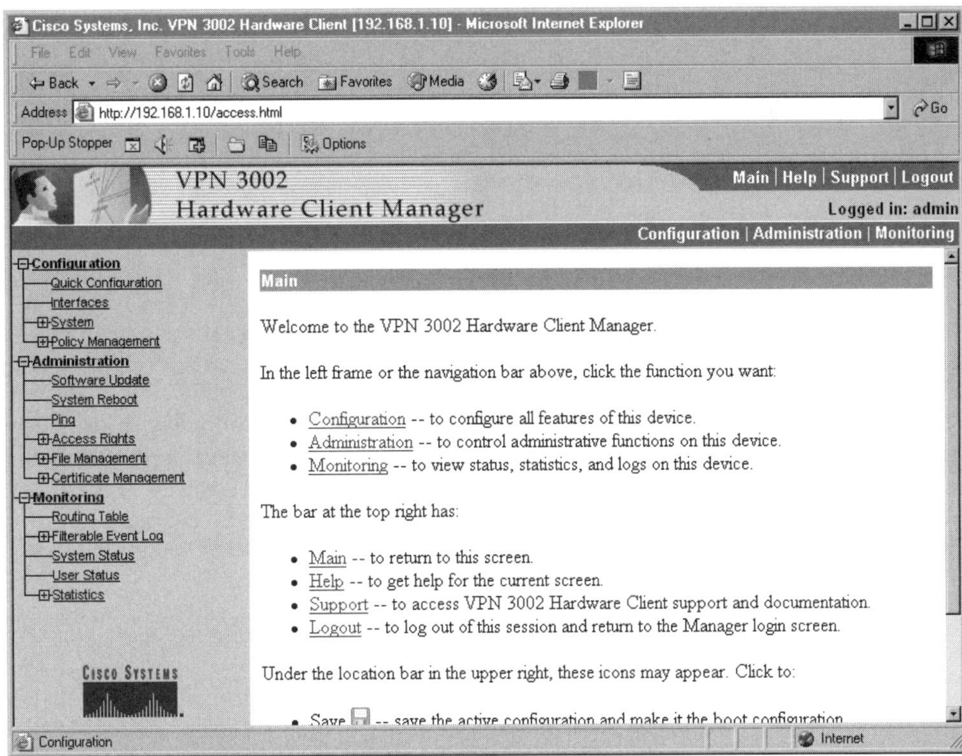

Figure 15-4 VPN 3002 Hardware Client Manager

based VPN 3002 Hardware Client Manager covered in the section "The Hardware Client Manager."

NOTE The VPN 3002 uses a standard Cisco console kit and plugs into a RJ-45 interface on the device. The VPN 3000 concentrators use a straight-through jumper cable and needs one of the RJ-45 to DB-9 converters.

Console port access is similar to the IOS routers using a terminal emulator program, such as HyperTerminal. You might need to press ENTER until the login prompt appears. Login user names and passwords for both console and Telnet access are the same. The factory-supplied default is configured and enabled for administrators using admin for both the login and the password. Entries are case-sensitive. Access and user names/ passwords are set using the Administration | Access Rights | Administrators menus. The following output shows the initial login and main menu:

```
Login: admin
Password:                          (doesn't display)
```

```
                Welcome to
               Cisco Systems
         VPN 3002 Hardware Client
          Command Line Interface
Copyright (C) 1998-2003 Cisco Systems, Inc.

1) Configuration
2) Administration
3) Monitoring
4) Save changes to Config file
5) Help Information
6) Exit

Main ->
```

Help

The *Help* menu system is somewhat limited, displaying only the following information when 5 is entered at the Main menu. Context-sensitive Help isn't available and the familiar question mark (?) doesn't activate Help features. The Help feature in the Hardware Client Manager is much better, offering context-sensitive assistance like most Windows applications.

```
Main -> 5
Cisco Systems.  Help information for the Command Line Interface

From any menu except the Main menu.
-- 'B' or 'b' for Back to previous menu.
-- 'H' or 'h' for Home back to the main menu.

For Data entry
-- Current values are in '[ ]'s. Just hit 'Enter' to accept value.

1) View Help Again
2) Back

Help ->
```

As it turns out, the *B* and *H* options—and particularly the *H* option—will come in handy when you navigate the Device menus. Pressing *H* returns you to the Main menu.

Saving Configuration File Changes

Configuration and administration changes made using menu options 1 and 2 on the Main menu take effect immediately and become a part of the active, or running, configuration. Like the Cisco routers, if the VPN 3002 is rebooted without saving the active configuration, any changes will be lost.

Saving changes to the system configuration (CONFIG) file is a one-step process from the Main menu. At the Main -> prompt, typing 4 will save changes without additional steps or confirmation.

```
1) Configuration
2) Administration
```

```
3) Monitoring
4) Save changes to Config file
5) Help Information
6) Exit

Main -> 4
```

The system writes the current (active) configuration to the CONFIG file and redisplays the main menu.

Second Level Menus

Familiarity with the menu system will come with experimentation and experience, but the following examples expand the menus one level. The following output reflects choosing the Configuration (1) option. Notice the prompt changes to reflect the new menu:

```
1) Configuration
2) Administration
3) Monitoring
4) Save changes to Config file
5) Help Information
6) Exit

Main -> 1

1) Quick Configuration
2) Interface Configuration
3) System Management
4) Policy Management
5) Back

Config ->
```

The following output reflects choosing the Administration (2) option from the Main menu:

```
1) Configuration
2) Administration
3) Monitoring
4) Save changes to Config file
5) Help Information
6) Exit

Main -> 2

1) Software Update
2) System Reboot
3) Ping
4) Access Rights
5) File Management
6) Certificate Management
7) Back

Admin ->
```

The following output reflects choosing the Monitoring (3) option from the Main menu:

```
1) Configuration
2) Administration
3) Monitoring
4) Save changes to Config file
5) Help Information
6) Exit

Main -> 3

1) Routing Table
2) Event Log
3) System Status
4) User Status
5) General Statistics
6) Back

Monitor ->
```

Shortcut Numbers

Once you become familiar with the structure of the CLI, you can quickly access any level by entering a series of numbers, corresponding to menu choices, separated by periods. For example, entering 2.2.2.1.2 at the Main-> prompt saves the configuration and reboots the device immediately. The result looks like the following, beginning at the Main menu:

```
1) Configuration
2) Administration
3) Monitoring
4) Save changes to Config file
5) Help Information
6) Exit

Main -> 2.2.2.1.2

Done

Login:
```

The following are the steps that were fast-forwarded through, beginning at the Main menu:

```
1) Configuration
2) Administration
3) Monitoring
4) Save changes to Config file
5) Help Information
6) Exit

Main -> 2
```

```
1) Software Update
2) System Reboot
3) Ping
4) Access Rights
5) File Management
6) Certificate Management
7) Back

Admin -> 2

1) Cancel Scheduled Reboot/Shutdown
2) Schedule Reboot
3) Schedule Shutdown
4) Back

Admin -> 2

1) Save active Configuration and use it at Reboot
2) Reboot without saving active Configuration file
3) Reboot ignoring the Configuration file
4) Back

Admin -> 1

1) Cancel Scheduled Reboot/Shutdown
2) Reboot Now
3) Reboot in X minutes
4) Reboot at time X
5) Reboot wait for sessions to terminate
6) Back

Admin -> 2

123 03/31/2003 15:41:12.460 SEV=1 REBOOT/1 RPT=1
Reboot scheduled immediately.
Done
```


The Hardware Client Manager (Web Interface)

The VPN 3002 Hardware Client Manager is an HTML-based interface that makes it possible to configure, administer, monitor, and manage the VPN 3002 device with a web browser. The easiest way to use the web interface is to connect to the VPN 3002, using any PC with a web browser on the private network behind the VPN 3002.

By default, the Client Manager uses HTTP, which is convenient, but messages are in clear text. If security requires it, the Client Manager supports a secure, encrypted HTTP connection over Secure Sockets Layer (SSL) protocol, known as HTTPS.

Browser Requirements

The VPN 3002 Hardware Client Manager supports either Microsoft Internet Explorer (IE) version 4.0 or higher or Netscape Navigator version 4.5–4.7. For the best results, Cisco recommends Internet Explorer, and JavaScript and cookies must be enabled in the browser. The other recommendation is that any updates and patches be installed.

Recommended Display Settings

Cisco recommends the following monitor display settings for best viewing:

- Screen area   1,024 × 768 pixels or greater (Minimum 800 × 600 pixels)
- Colors   256 colors or higher

Browser Navigation Toolbar

Earlier implementations of the Client Manager were basically the CLI converted simply to a web interface. Each new version includes much better Windows function integration. *Help*, a Java-based applet, in particular, is getting friendlier and more useful.

Cisco still doesn't recommend using the browser navigation toolbar buttons Back, Forward, or Refresh/Reload with the Client Manager unless specifically instructed to do so. To maintain access security, clicking the Refresh/Reload button automatically logs out the Manager session and returns to the login screen. Using the Back or Forward buttons could possibly display old Manager displays with incorrect data or settings. If you're concerned about this, the IE View | Full screen (F11) feature will eliminate the temptation.

Connecting to the Client Manager

To access the VPN 3002 Client Manager application using HTTP over a web browser, type the VPN 3002 private interface IP address (such as 192.168.1.10) in the browser Address or Location field. The browser will automatically supply the http:// prefix.

The browser displays the VPN 3002 Hardware Client Manager login screen, as shown in Figure 15-5.

Logging in to the Manager application is the same for clear-text HTTP or secure HTTPS. The 3002 supports three types of accounts that can access the device: Administrator, Config, and ISP. Only the Administrator account is enabled by default using admin/admin for the user name/password. Internet Explorer users can use the TAB key to move from field to field. The Clear button can be used to start over.

Figure 15-6 shows the opening screen that appears, offering access to the three main application modules. This screen provides a good overview of the various screen components and options to maneuver through the application. The application tree on the left-hand side offers Explorer-like navigation capabilities to move quickly from feature to feature. This feature alone makes the web interface significantly easier to use than the CLI.

The VPN 3002 Hardware Client Reference, available online or in the CD-ROM documentation that came with the device, covers how to set up the device for installing an SSL Certificate in the browser for HTTPS connectivity.

Client Manager Organization

The Client Manager, exactly like the CLI, is made up of three major sections and many second and third level subsections:

- **Configuration**—Sets all VPN 3002 parameters that govern the unit's use and functionality as a VPN device.

- **Quick Configuration**—A series of steps that supply the minimal parameters needed to make the VPN 3002 operational.
- **Interfaces**—Ethernet parameters for public (outside) and private (inside) interfaces.
- **System**—Sets system-wide function parameters, such as server access, IPSec tunneling protocol, built-in management servers, event handling, IP-routing, and system identification.
- **Policy Management**—Enables PAT and certificate validation.
- **Administration**—Manages the higher-level functions that keep the 3002 unit operational and secure, such as who is allowed to configure the system and what software runs on it, as well as managing its configuration files and digital certificates.
- **Monitoring**—Views routing tables, event logs, system LEDs and status, and statistics and user session data.

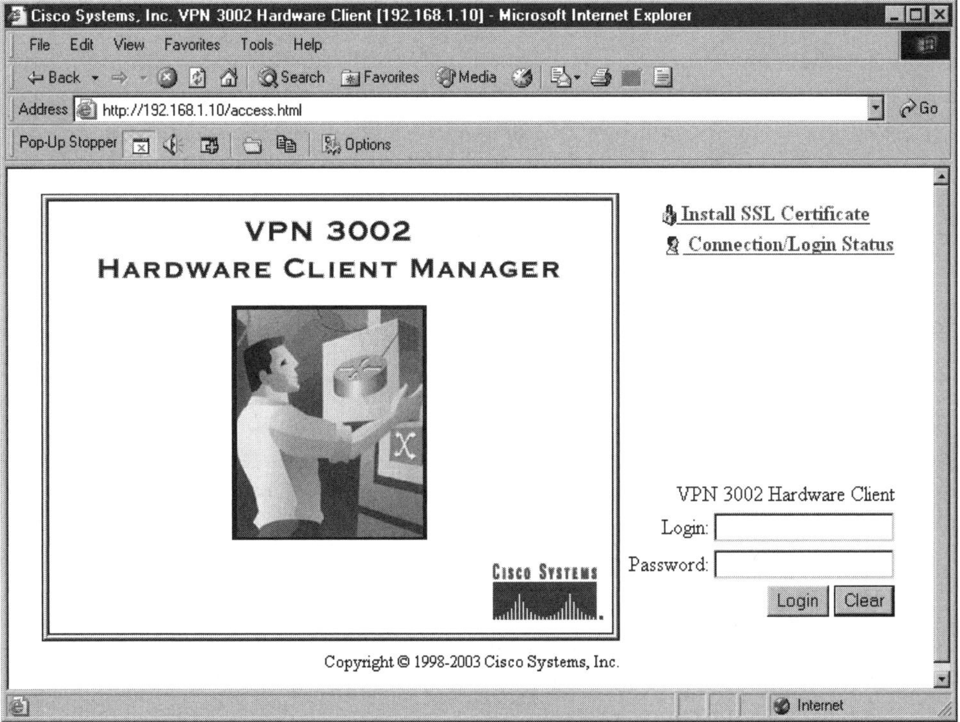

Figure 15-5 VPN 3002 Hardware Client Manager login screen

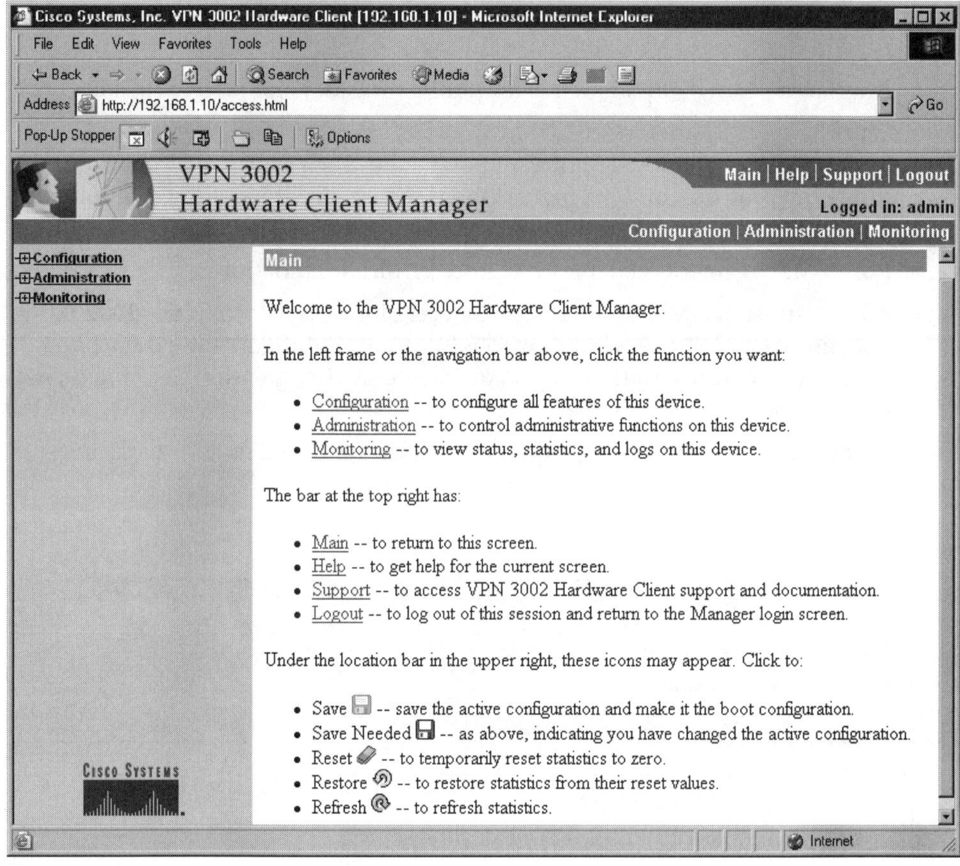

Figure 15-6 Client Manager opening screen

Help

Figure 15-7 shows the result of selecting Administration | Ping in the left panel, and then clicking on the Help button in the upper-right corner. The Help window works much like any Windows help document.

Second-Level Menus

The Client Manager structure tree in the leftmost panel can be expanded using standard Windows techniques. Figure 15-8 shows the three menus expanded and the Configuration menu expanded to three levels.

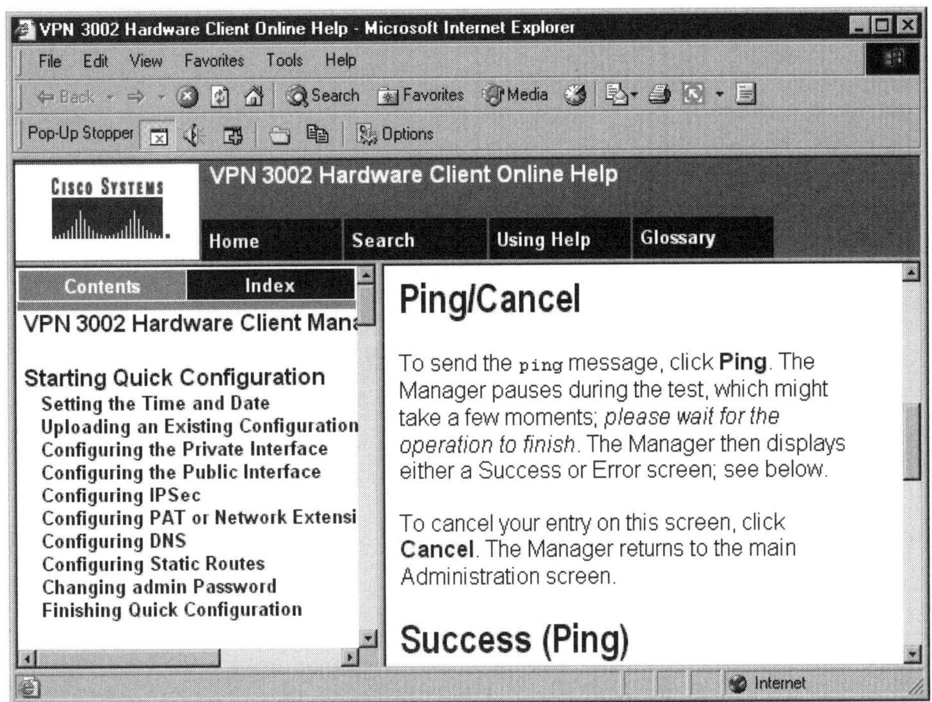

Figure 15-7 VPN 3002 Client Manager help system

Common Configuration Tasks

This section looks briefly at how to use both interfaces to accomplish routine configuration tasks. While conceptually these will be familiar, please remember that neither interface has been aligned with the familiar IOS and this can be a little confusing.

Upgrading the Software

When upgrading with the CLI, you must download the latest OS for the 3002 and store it in the source directory for the TFTP server. Make sure the TFTP server is running. The web interface uses an upload process that only requires the new software is installed on the computer.

The following output shows the upgrade steps to use when working with the CLI, starting at the Main menu:

```
1) Configuration
2) Administration
3) Monitoring
4) Save changes to Config file
5) Help Information
```

PART III

```
6) Exit

Main -> 2                                  (select Administration)

1) Software Update
2) System Reboot
3) Ping
4) Access Rights
5) File Management
6) Certificate Management
7) Back

Admin -> 3                 (select Ping to test connectivity to TFTP)

> Ping host                (prompt is confusing. Enter IP address only)
Admin -> 192.168.1.20
Host 192.168.1.20 (192.168.1.20) is alive. The round trip time is 3.96 ms

> Ping host
Admin ->                   (press ENTER to return to Admin menu)

1) Software Update
2) System Reboot
3) Ping
4) Access Rights
5) File Management
6) Certificate Management
7) Back

Admin -> 1                                    (select Software Update)
```

The first prompt asks for the upgrade file name. The file name for the current OS, or for the OS you tried to get on a previous attempt that failed, is displayed in square brackets. Type the new name and press ENTER. The second prompt is asking for the TFTP server address. Type the address and press ENTER. Finally, a prompt will allow modifying the two initial entries, continuing to file transfer, or exiting from the process.

```
Name of the file for main code upgrade? [old.bin] vpn3002-3.6.7.C-k9.bin
IP address of the host where the file resides? [10.1.0.1] 192.168.1.20

(M)odify any of the above (C)ontinue or (E)xit? [M] c
Erasing flash...This can take several seconds to complete!

Starting the TFTP download...
Loading........................................
Verifying.........................................complete
SUCCESS: New code image will become active on next reboot!

Reboot now? (Y/N) [Y]                          (press ENTER to confirm)
Reboot scheduled immediately...
64 03/29/2003 21:44:38.110 SEV=1 REBOOT/1 RPT=1
Reboot scheduled immediately.

Done

Login: admin
Password:
```

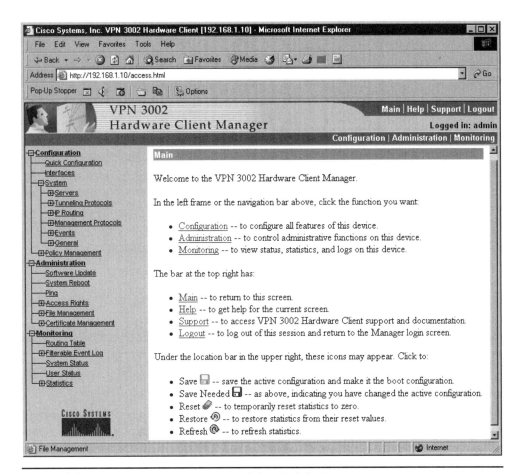

Figure 15-8 Client Manager menu tree expanded on the left side

Figure 15-9 shows the Update process using the Web interface. Expanding Administration in the left-panel tree and choosing Software Update brings up this screen. Note, a Ping option should also be used first to verify connectivity to the TFTP server.

NOTE A Ping option exists that should be used first to verify connectivity to the TFTP server. The screen is straightforward: browse for the OS file on your local computer or a server you have access to, and then click the Upload button.

Quick Configuration

Quick Configuration (Configuration | Quick Configuration) starts a series of screens to provide basic connectivity for the VPN 3002. See the section "VPN Hardware Configuration"

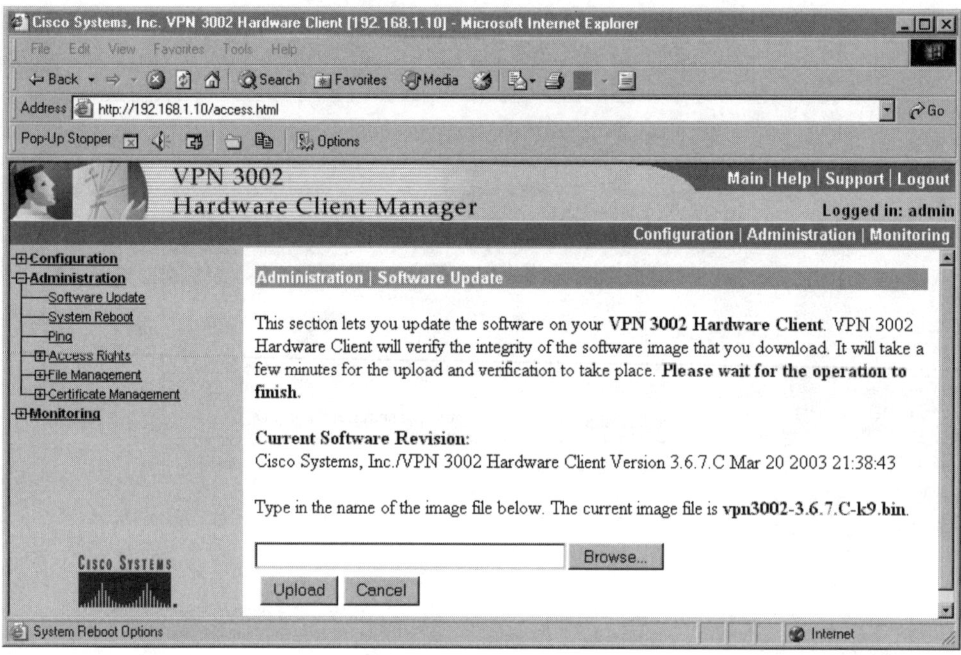

Figure 15-9 VPN 3002 Update process using the web interface

for an example of these features. The Quick Configuration on the web interface consists of the following ten steps (the CLI steps are slightly different). When appropriate, the current settings will appear in square brackets as the default value.

1. Set the system time, date, and time zone.
2. Configure the Private Interface Ethernet interface. To use Network Extension mode, you must configure an IP address other than the default.
3. Optionally upload an already existing configuration file.
4. Configure the Public Interface Ethernet interface to a public network.
5. Specify a method for assigning IP addresses.
6. Configure the IPSec tunneling protocol with group and user names, and passwords and encryption options.
7. Set the VPN 3002 to use either PAT or Network Extension mode.
8. Configure DNS.

9. Configure static routes.
10. Change the admin password for security.

System Status

Use the Monitoring | System Status menu to check the status of several software and hardware variables. The resulting data is a snapshot of the device feature at the time the screen is displayed. From this screen, you can display the status of the IPSec tunnel security associations (SAs) and tunnel duration. On the web interface, the device front and rear panels are displayed with embedded links that display port statistics. Figure 15-10 shows the web-based output for displaying system status.

The following is the CLI output from choosing Monitoring | System Status (3.3) from the menus:

```
System Status
-------------
VPN Concentrator Type: 3002
Serial Number: CAM02223438
Bootcode Rev:
  Cisco Systems, Inc./VPN 3002 Hardware Client Version 3.0.Rel Feb 26
  2001 10:39:17
Software Rev:
  Cisco Systems, Inc./VPN 3002 Hardware Client Version 3.6.7.C Mar 20
  2003 21:38:43
Up For 3:29:12
Up Since 03/30/2003 19:41:58
RAM Size: 16 MB
No Tunnel Established - Public Interface not configured.

1) Refresh System Status
2) Reset System Status
3) Restore System Status
4) Connect Now
5) Disconnect Now
6) View Memory Status
7) Back

Status ->
```

PPPoE Support

Point-to-Point Protocol over Ethernet (PPPoE) incorporates two widely used and understood standards: PPP and Ethernet. The *PPPoE* specification connects hosts on an Ethernet to the Internet through a common broadband medium, such as DSL line, cable modem, or a wireless device. With PPPoE, the principles of Ethernet supporting multiple users in a LAN are combined with the principles of PPP, which uses serial

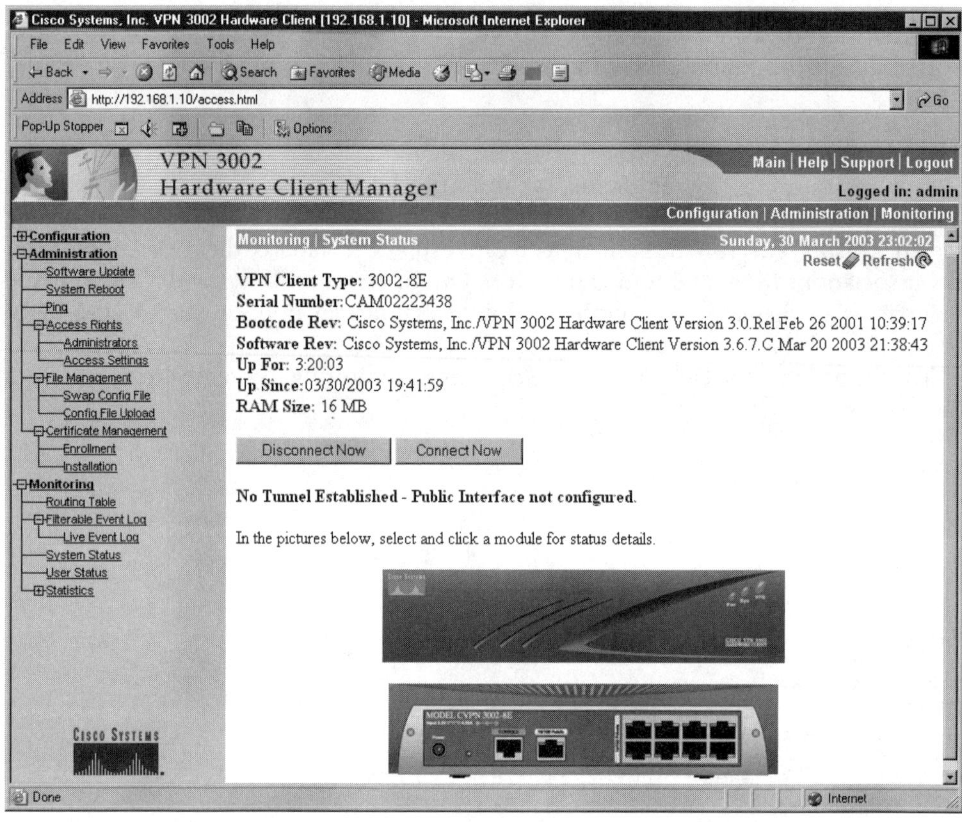

Figure 15-10 Web interface displaying system status

connections. The VPN 3002 supports PPPoE Client mode on the public interface to access these networks. Users need only to authenticate to the PPPoE server the first time and, for all subsequent attempts, VPN 3002 will authenticate for the user.

Figure 15-11 shows the public interface screen (Configuration | Interface | Public). The feature is supported on the CLI by following the same menu options. To configure PPPoE, you must furnish the following information, which is generally provided by the ISP.

- A valid PPPoE user name
- The PPPoE password for the user name entered previously
- The PPPoE password again to verify it

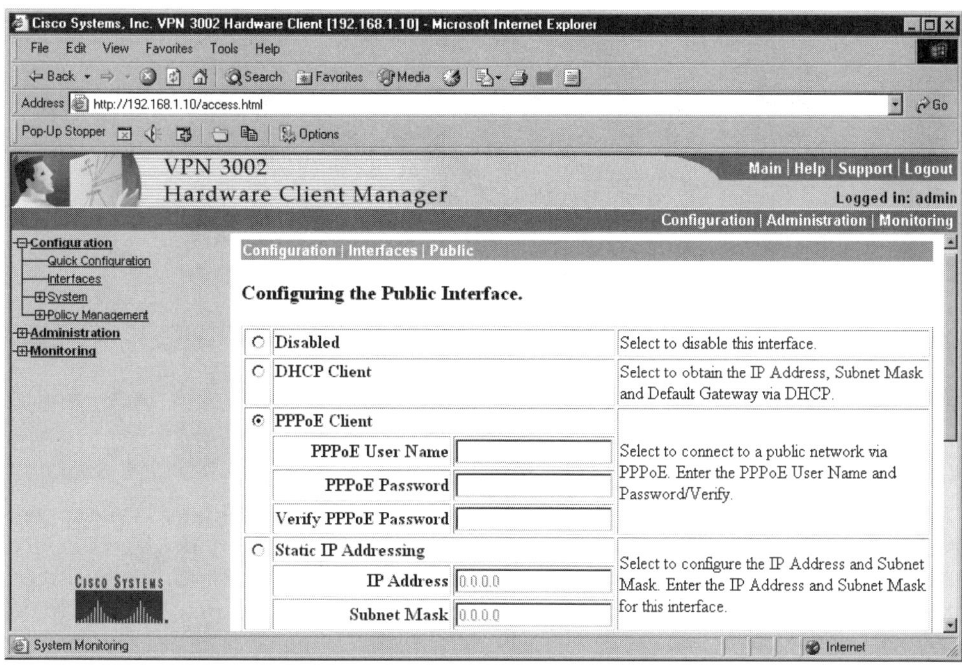

Figure 15-11 PPPoE configuration on the public interface screen

Basic Configuration for the VPN 3002

The Quick configuration ten-step process in either CLI or web-based Client Manager can be used to supply the minimal parameters needed to make the VPN 3002 operational. The Client Manager is used in this section, but it shouldn't be any trick to follow along in the CLI.

The following discussion assumes a successful login and choosing Configuration | Quick Configuration in the left-side panel. The actual configuration is based on Figure 15-12, showing a small branch location connecting through a VPN 3002 client to a VPN Concentrator at the main office.

The scenario assumes the main office has reserved the networks 192.168.0.0 to 192.168.127.0 for its internal use. The other private class C addresses have been assigned as needed to the company's branch locations. The figure shows a small branch location assigned the 192.168.145.0 network.

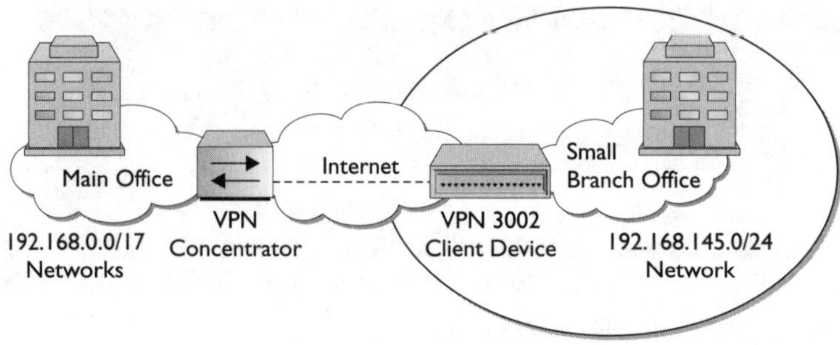

Figure 15-12 VPN 3002 configuration scenario

Set the System Time, Date, and Time Zone

The Client Manager window displays the Configuration | Quick | Time and Date screen.

Figure 15-13 shows the entry screen used to set the time and date on this device. The choices are self-explanatory. Notice all ten steps are listed at the top of the screen, allowing a person to jump to any feature. Click the Continue button to advance to the next screen.

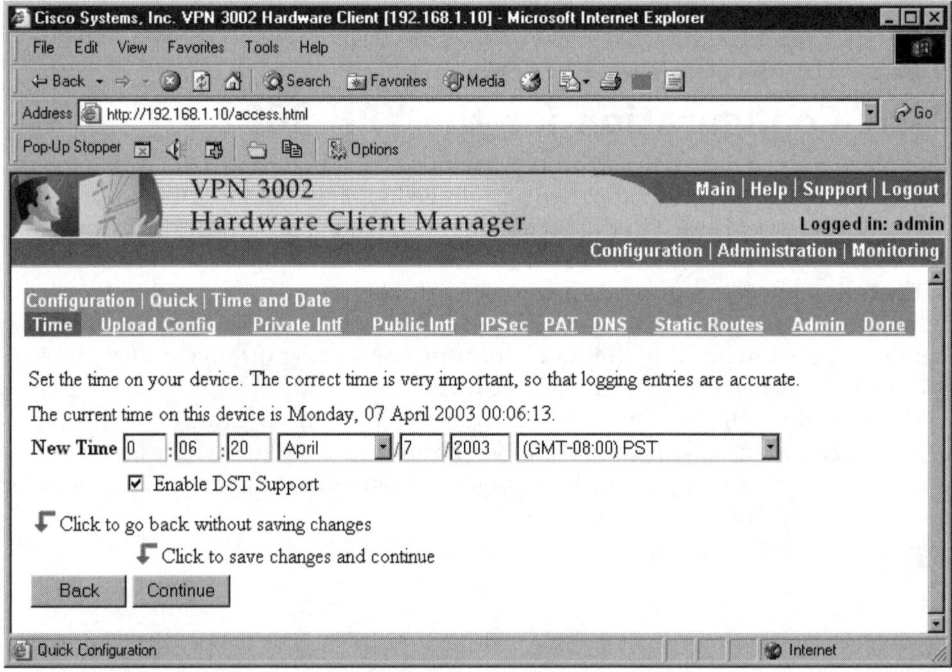

Figure 15-13 Screen to set date, time, and time zone for the device

Optional—Upload an Existing Configuration File

The Client Manager window displays the Configuration | Quick | Upload Config screen.

Figure 15-14 shows the option screen used to use HTTP or HTTPS to transfer (upload) configuration files from a host to the VPN 3002 flash memory. This could be a time-saver if you need to restore a lost or damaged configuration.

Click No to continue to the next section or click Yes to upload an existing configuration file.

Configure the Private Interface

The Client Manager window displays the Configuration | Quick | Private Interface screen.

Figure 15-15 shows the screen used to configure the VPN 3002 private interface. This is the protected LAN interface of the network. The top portion of the screen displays the current configuration settings. The following is a possible example:

IP Address 192.168.1.10/ 255.255.255.0
DHCP Server Enabled (192.168.1.21–192.168.1.254)

The first question determines whether to reconfigure the IP address for the private interface. The Yes/No choices are self-explanatory.

The second question deals with using DHCP to define the address for the private interface. The first choice ultimately brings up a screen to configure the DHCP server

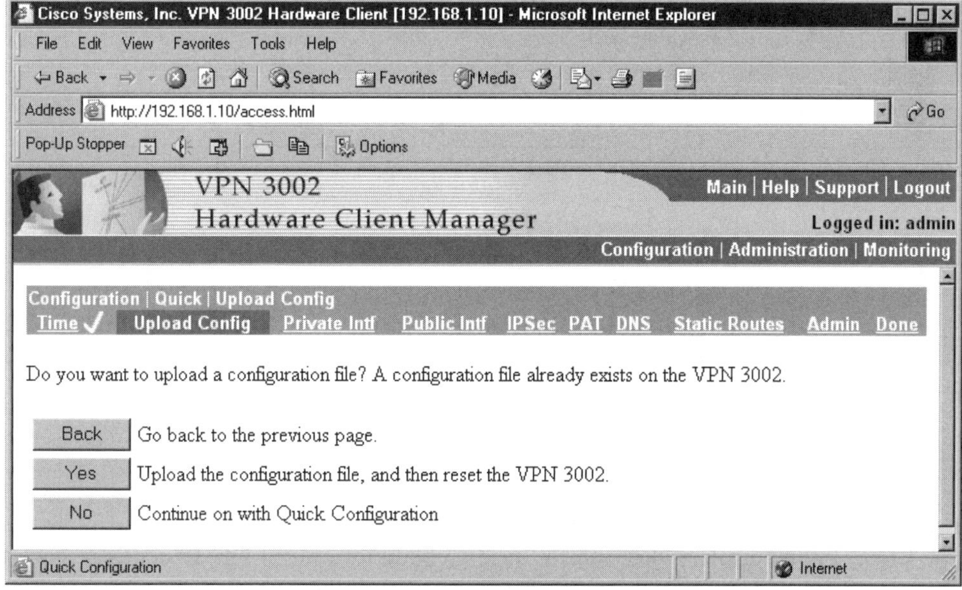

Figure 15-14 Choice to upload an existing configuration file

PART III

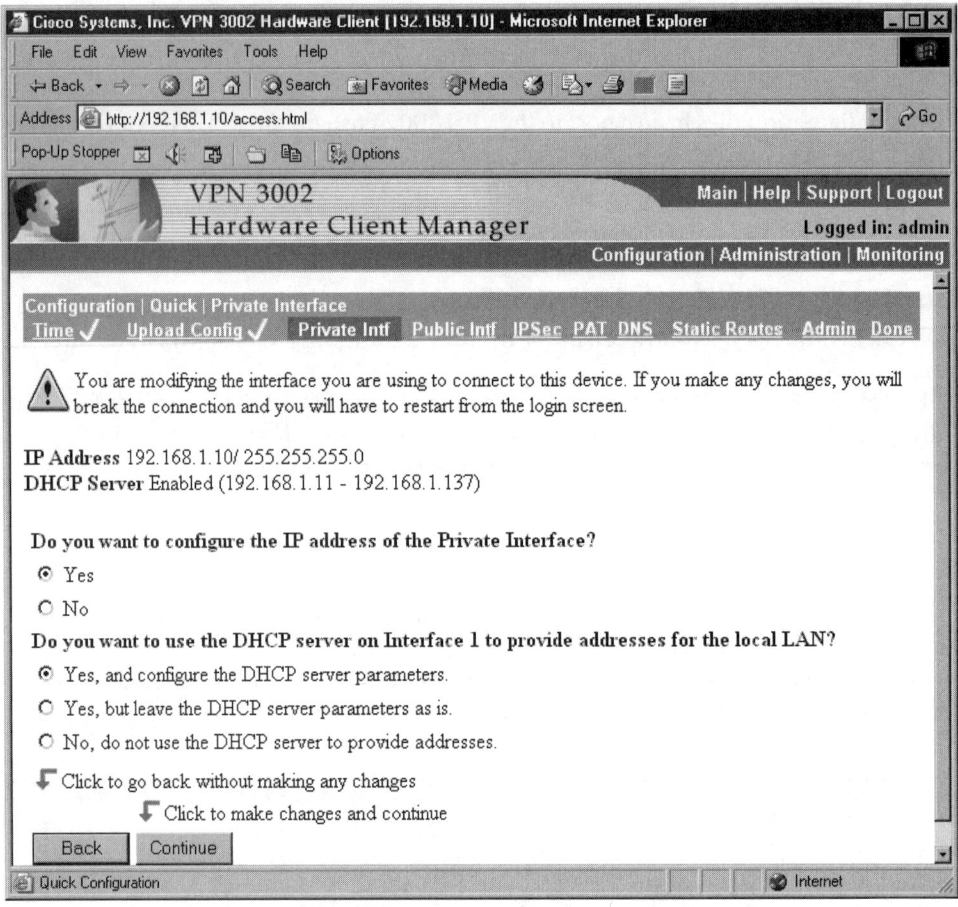

Figure 15-15 Configure the private interface

parameters, as shown in Figure 15-16. The second choice would be used while reviewing the settings. The third choice would be used to configure the interface address manually. Click the Continue button to implement the advance of the choice to the appropriate next screen.

For the VPN 3002 to operate in Network Extension mode, you must change the private interface IP address from the default setting 192.168.10.1.

Configuring the DHCP Server

The Client Manager Configuration | Quick | Private Interface | DHCP Server screen is used to enable and configure the VPN 3002 private interface to serve as a DHCP server for the private network hosts. This allows IP hosts on the LAN to obtain IP addresses automatically from a limited pool of addresses for a fixed length of time or for a lease

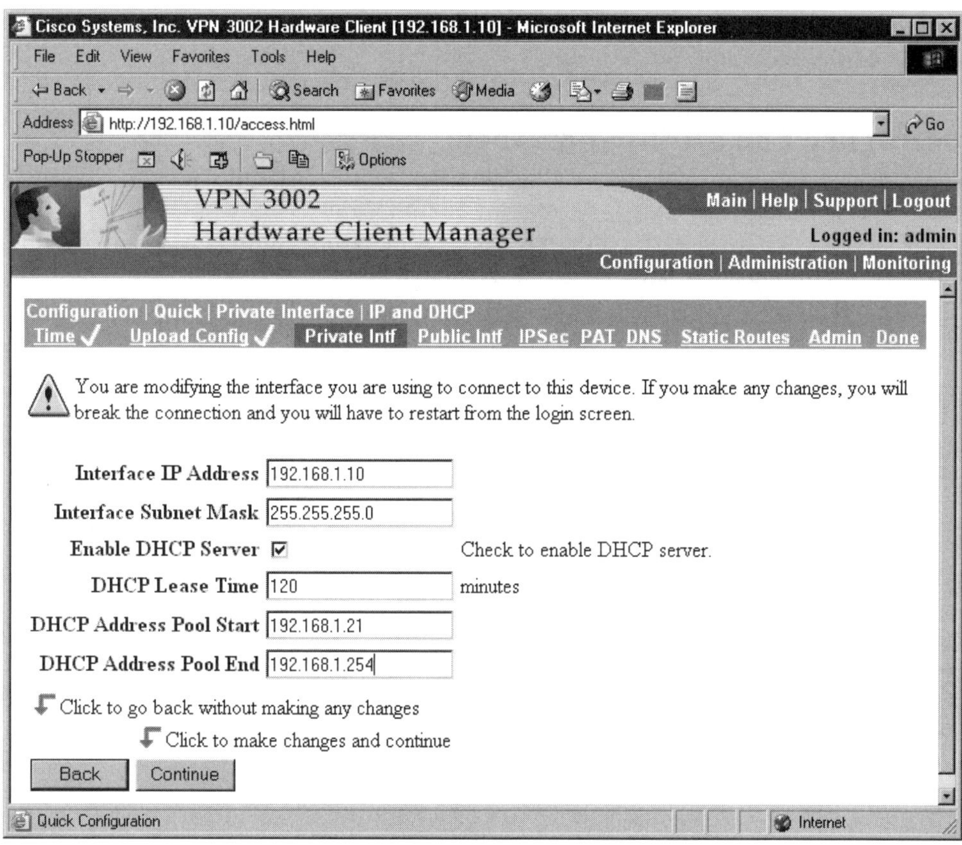

Figure 15-16 Configuring the DHCP server

period. DHCP simplifies host configuration by allowing the network settings to be learned from the DHCP server rather than statically configured.

Check the Enabled box to enable DHCP services for the private interface.

The DHCP Lease Timeout field can be set between 5 and 500,000 minutes. The default is 120 minutes. After the lease time expires, the lease can be renewed or returned to the address pool. This Lease Timeout period applies only when the tunnel to the VPN Concentrator is established. When the tunnel isn't established, the Lease Timeout period is five minutes.

The next two fields are used to define the starting and ending address of the DHCP. The example reflects the first 20 addresses were excluded from the pool, so they might be permanently assigned to shared resources, such as printers and servers. The default pool is 127 IP addresses and the start of the range is the next IP address after that of the current private interface.

If changes were made, the Manager displays the Configuration | Quick |

Private Interface | DHCP server address pool screen used confirms that the DHCP server address pool range was entered.

Configure the Public Interface

The Client Manager, displaying the Configuration | Quick | Public Interface screen, is shown in Figure 15-17.

This is the interface used to connect to an ISP and to the central network. The public interface can obtain an IP address in one of three ways:

- DHCP client
- PPPoE
- Static addressing

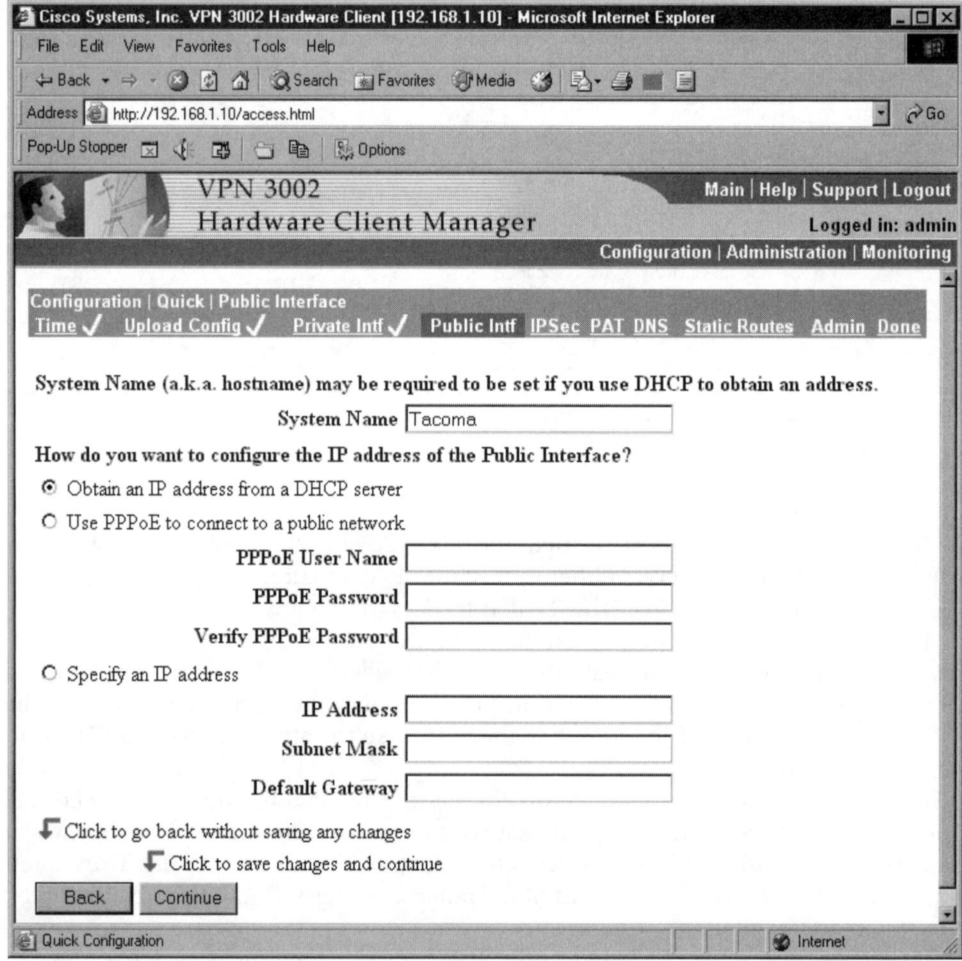

Figure 15-17 Screen to configure the public interface

Once the choice is made, PPPoE and static addressing need some address information. The PPPoE information would generally be provided by the ISP.

The system name, also known as a host name, is optional unless DHCP is chosen to obtain an IP address and the ISP requires a host name. As a DHCP client, the upstream DHCP server assigns the public interface IP address, subnet mask, and default gateway.

Configure the IPSec

The Client Manager displays the Configuration | Quick | IPSec screen.

This screen lets you configure the IPSec parameters, enabling the VPN 3002 to connect to the VPN Concentrator or to other IPSec security gateways, such as the Cisco PIX firewall or Cisco IOS routers. Figure 15-18 shows the IPSec configuration screen.

The Remote Server field is for the IP address or host name of the VPN Concentrator to which this VPN 3002 hardware client connects. If a host name is used, a DNS server must be available to resolve the name.

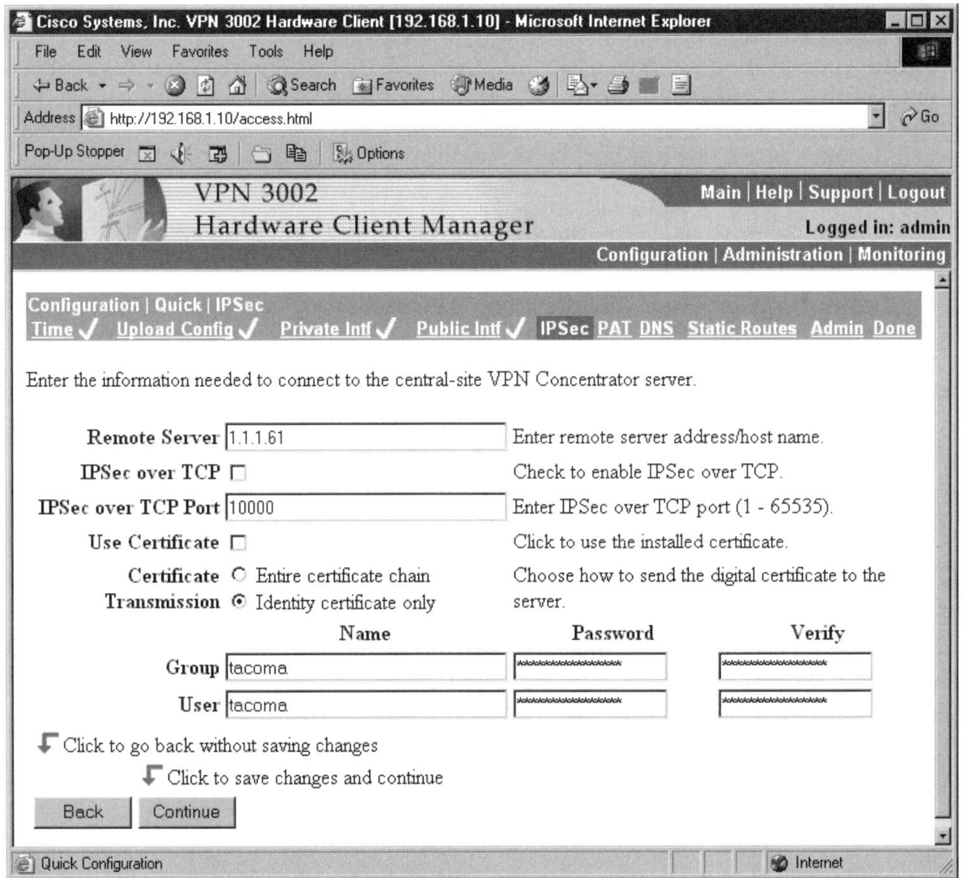

Figure 15-18 IPSec configuration screen

As mentioned previously, NAT-T is the default, but you can check the IPSec over TCP box to use TCP. The TCP feature must also be enabled on the VPN Concentrator to which this VPN 3002 connects.

Specify the IPSec over TCP port number; only one port number can be specified. The VPN 3002 port must also be configured on the VPN Concentrator to which this VPN 3002 connects.

The *Use Certificate* box specifies digital certificates for authentication. With digital certificates, you needn't enter a group name and group password.

Digital Certificates

You have two Select a Certificate Transmission options:

- **Entire certificate chain**—to send the peer the identity certificate and all issuing certificates, including the root certificate and any subordinate CA certificates.
- **Identity certificate only**—to send the peer only the identity certificate.

Preshared Keys

The following information has to be consistent with that configured for this VPN 3002 on the central-site VPN Concentrator.

- Group Name field—unique name for this group (up to 32 characters, case-sensitive).
- Group Password field—unique password for this group (4 to 32 characters, case-sensitive). The field displays only asterisks.
- Group Verify field—reenter the group password.
- User Name field—unique name for this user in the group (up to 32 characters, case-sensitive).
- User Password field—unique password for this user (4 to 32 characters, case-sensitive). The field displays only asterisks.
- User Verify field—reenter the user password.

Choose Client (PAT) Mode or Network Extension Mode

The Client Manager displays the Configuration | Quick | PAT screen.

The next screen is used to specify either Client (PAT) mode or Network Extension mode. The default Yes selects Client mode; No selects Network Extension mode. Figure 15-19 shows the selection screen.

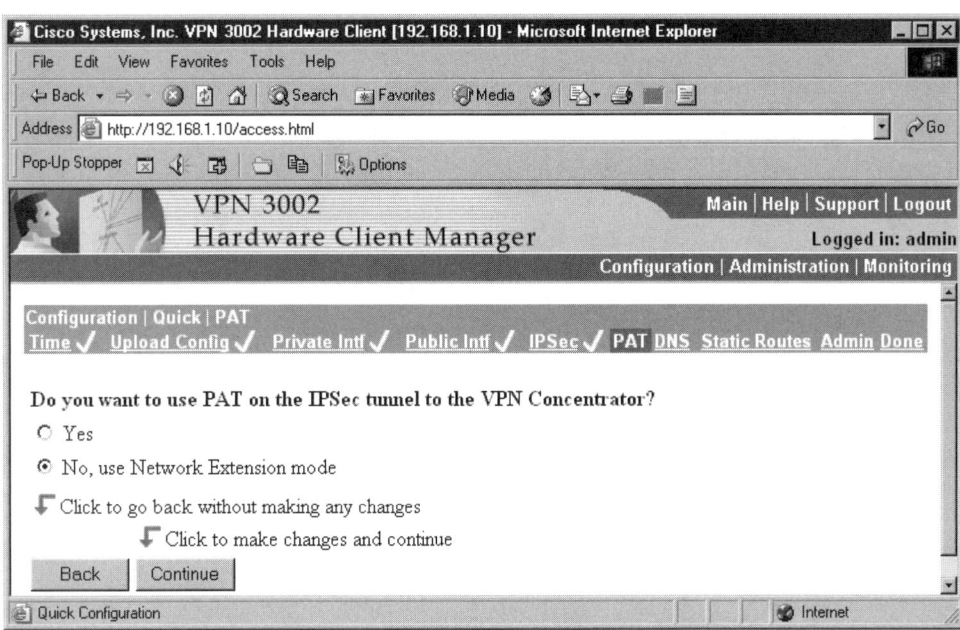

Figure 15-19 Client mode or Network Extension mode choice

Configure DNS

The Client Manager displays the Configuration | Quick | DNS screen.

As shown in Figure 15-20, this screen is used to specify a DNS server for the local ISP, so Internet host names can be used instead of IP addresses for servers when configuring and managing the VPN 3002. While host names are easier to remember, using IP addresses avoids problems that might occur with the DNS server offline or congested.

If a host name was used to identify the central-site VPN Concentrator on the IPSec configuration screen, a DNS server must be configured on the VPN 3002.

If used, the IP address of the local DNS server is entered in the DNS Server field. The local ISP domain name is entered in the Domain field.

Configure Static Routes

The Client Manager displays the Configuration | Quick | Static Routes screen.

The Static Routes list shown in Figure 15-21 displays any existing static IP routes that were configured. The format is destination network address/subnet mask -> outbound destination. Use this screen to add or delete static routes for IP routing.

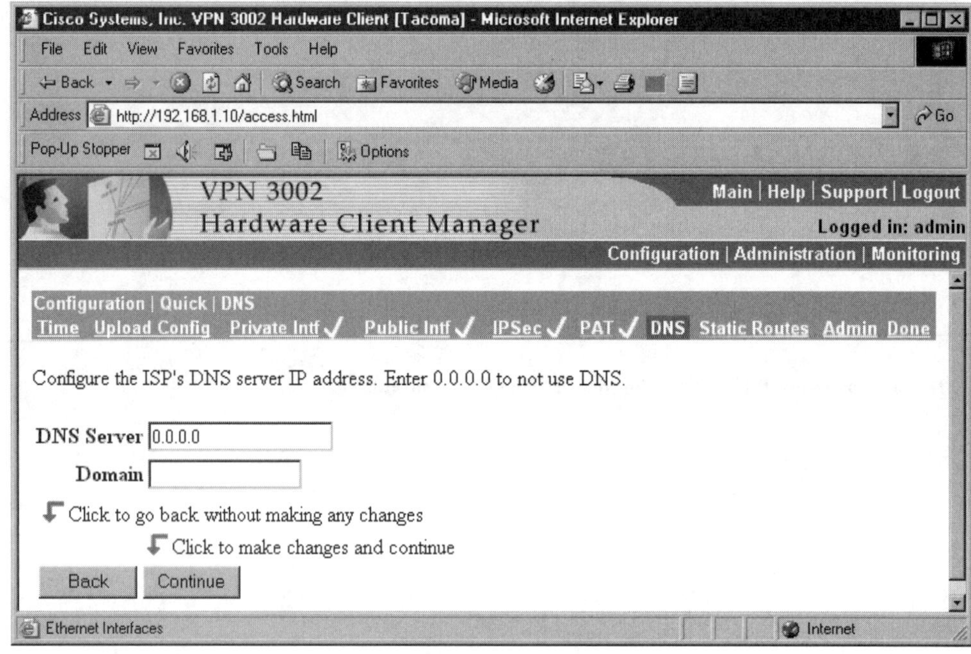

Figure 15-20 Define ISP DNS server and domain name (optional)

Clicking the Add button displays the Configuration | Quick | Static Routes | Add screen, as shown in Figure 15-22. This screen lets you add a new static route to the IP routing table. The options are pretty straightforward. The Subnet Mask automatically defaults to a standard classful subnet mask, but it can be changed as needed.

The Metric field allows assigning a cost for the route. The range is 1 to 16, where 1 is the lowest cost. The device always tries to use the least costly route. This makes creating floating static routes possible, where two routes to the same network can be given different metrics to reflect a preference.

The last choice is between using a next-hop address or the local VPN 3002 interface. For the Interface option, the drop-down menu button can be used to select a configured VPN 3002 interface as the outbound destination.

Change the Admin Password

The Client Manager displays the Configuration | Quick | Admin Password screen.

The screen is used to change the password for the administrator account (admin). The default password is also admin. Obviously, this isn't secure for the most powerful account on the device. Changing this password makes sense to improve device security.

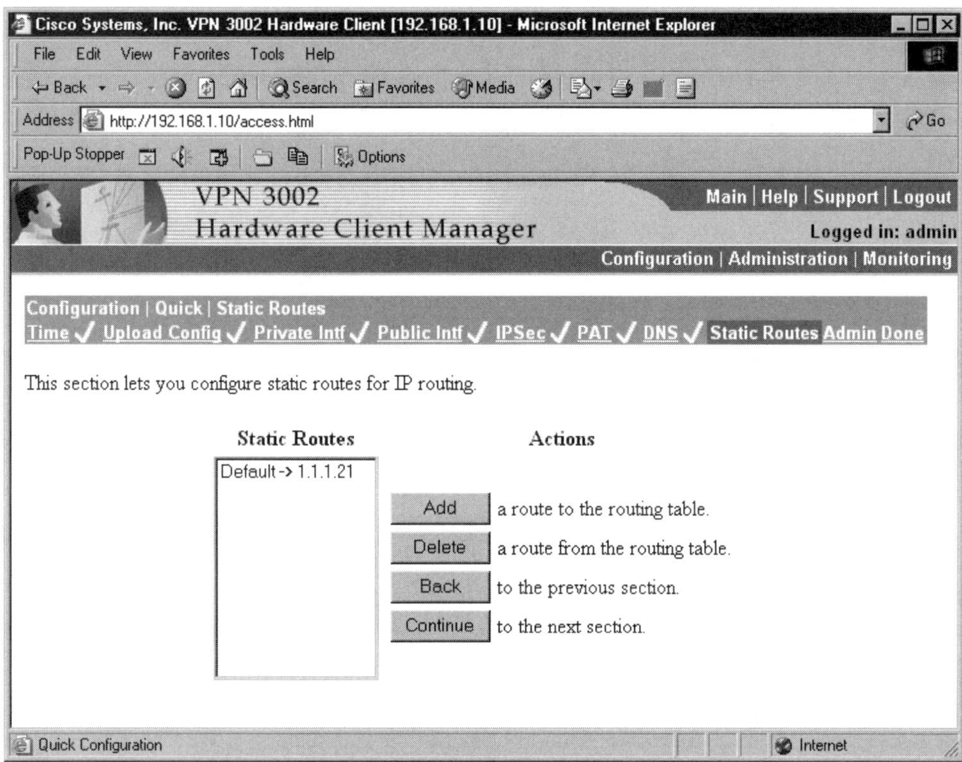

Figure 15-21 Existing static routes

When the password is set, the Quick configuration is done and a message screen much like the opening screen confirms that.

The Quick configuration can be used again to make changes or the Configuration menu can be used to change specific features or add options.

Modifying Options

The Quick configuration is used to configure the minimum requirements for connecting to a VPN Concentrator. Modifying or adding options later to a VPN Concentrator is easy. For example, when the DHCP server was configured on the private interface, only minimal features were defined. Once the initial configuration is in place, use the Configuration menu to set additional features. Figure 15-23 shows the DHCP Options screen and the left-side panel shows how to get there. This is where additional servers could be defined.

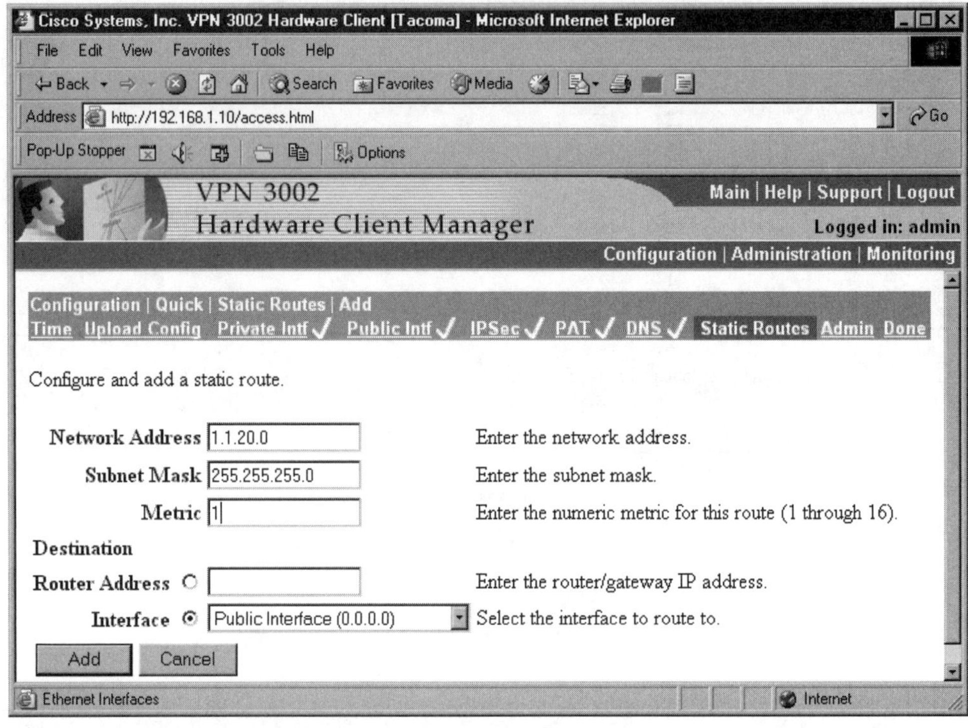

Figure 15-22 Adding a static route to the VPN 3002

Other VPN 3002 Software Features

The VPN 3002 software supports the following features:

Interactive Hardware Client Authentication

Interactive hardware client authentication, sometimes called *interactive unit authentication,* prevents VPN 3002 private LAN users from accessing the central site until the VPN 3002 unit authenticates. In this scenario, the VPN 3002 doesn't use a saved user name and password for authentication. Instead, a valid user name and a password for the 3002 must be manually entered each time.

The VPN 3002 sends the user name and the password to the VPN Concentrator when it initiates a tunnel session. The VPN Concentrator can authenticate the connection using either an internal or an external server. The tunnel is only established if the user name/password combination is valid.

Interactive hardware client authentication is configured on the VPN Concentrator, which then pushes the policy down to the VPN 3002 at the next connection.

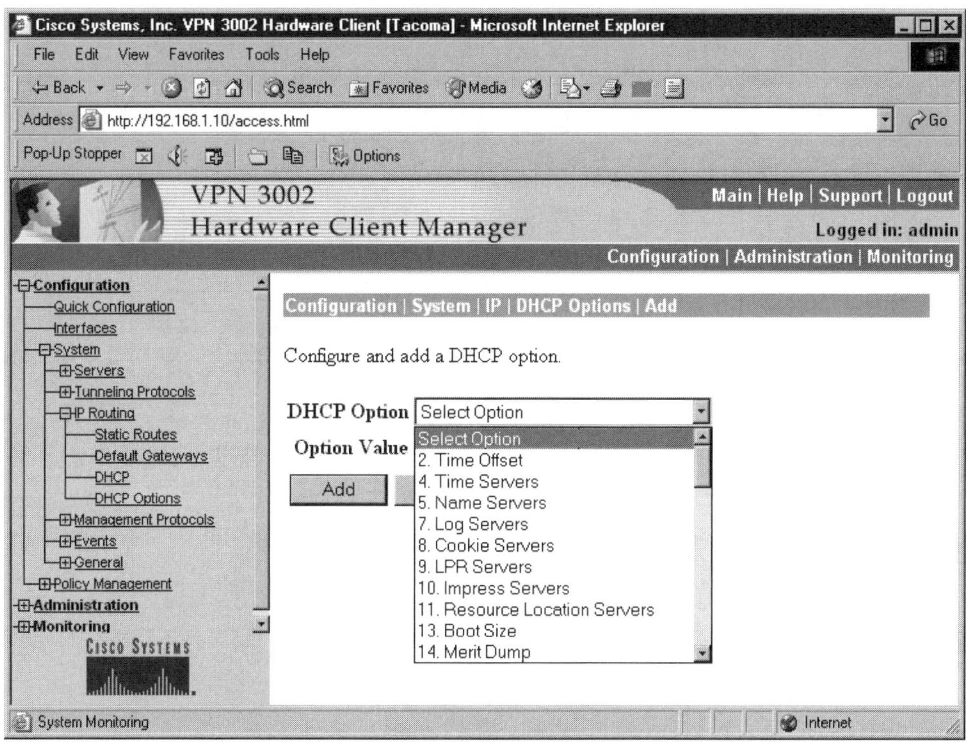

Figure 15-23 DHCP Options configuration screen

Configuring Interactive Unit Authentication

The Hardware Client parameters tab on the VPN 3000 Concentrator Series Manager is used to configure several features for the VPN 3002 and its users in the base group. The feature will be "pushed" down to the client devices the next time the VPN 3002 establishes a session. The menu selection is Configuration | User Management | Base Group, HW Client parameters tab.

Check the Require Interactive Hardware Client Authentication check box, as shown in Figure 15-24.

Individual User Authentication

Individual user authentication protects the central site from access by unauthorized individuals on the VPN 3002 private network. It accomplishes this by requiring each user to open a web-browser session and manually enter a valid user name and password combination to gain access to the network behind the VPN Concentrator, regardless of

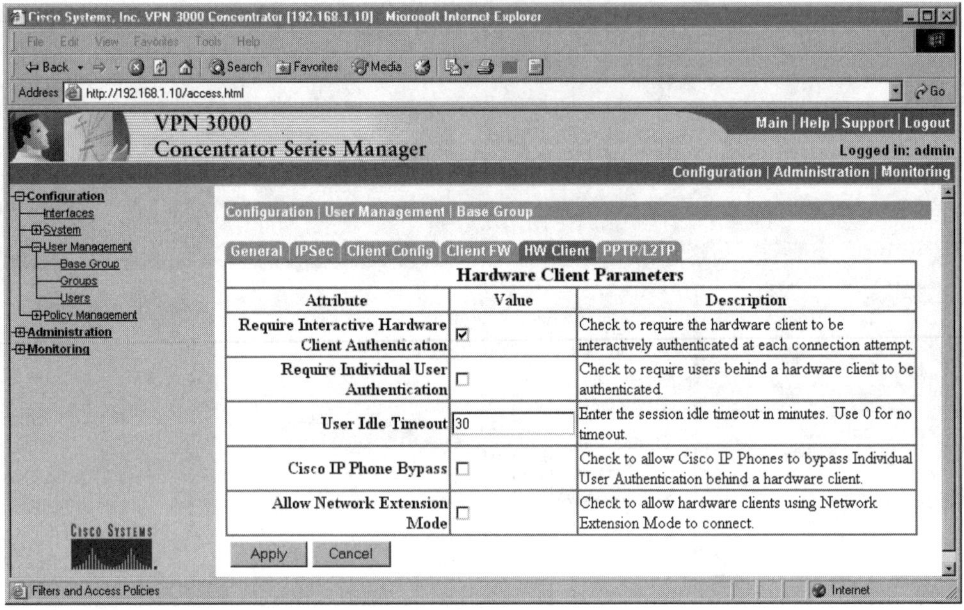

Figure 15-24 Configure Interactive Hardware Client Authentication

whether a VPN tunnel already exists. A successful login results in the browser displaying the appropriate default home page.

This feature can only be used with a browser, not the command-line interface. Attempts to access non-web-based resources, such as e-mail, on the network behind the VPN Concentrator will fail until a successful browser authentication occurs.

To simplify the process and make it as transparent as possible to the end users, this technology automatically intercepts any users attempting to traverse the VPN tunnel and redirects them to a browser page to authenticate. Users needn't initiate or remember to initiate the security authentication because it's done automatically. If users are only attempting to access the Internet via Split Tunneling, they aren't prompted to authenticate. Each user can maintain a maximum of four simultaneous login sessions.

Individual user authentication is configured on the VPN Concentrator, which then pushes the policy down to the VPN 3002 at the next connection.

Configuring Individual User Authentication

This feature is enabled on the same screen as the last feature. The menu selection is Configuration | User Management | Base Group, HW Client parameters tab, as shown in Figure 15-24 in the previous section.

Check the Require Individual User Authentication check box. This feature can be used separately or in conjunction with the Interactive Hardware Client Authentication.

LEAP Bypass

IEEE 802.1X is a standard for authentication on wired and wireless networks providing wireless LANs with strong mutual authentication between clients and authentication servers. 802.1X provides dynamic per-user, per-session wireless encryption privacy (WEP) keys, thereby removing administrative overhead and security concerns related to static WEP keys.

Lightweight Extensible Authentication Protocol (LEAP) is Cisco Systems 802.1X wireless authentication technology that implements mutual authentication between a wireless client and a RADIUS server. The authentication credentials, including a password, are always encrypted before they're transmitted over the wireless medium.

LEAP Bypass allows LEAP packets from devices behind a VPN 3002 to travel across a VPN tunnel before individual user authentication. This allows wireless workstations using access point devices to establish LEAP authentication, and then authenticate again using individual user authentication, if enabled.

Without this technology, LEAP users behind a VPN 3002 are caught in a Catch-22. They can't authenticate on the wireless network because they can't access the VPN tunnel to get to the RADIUS. They can't access the VPN tunnel because they haven't authenticated on the wireless network.

The VPN Concentrator administrator enables LEAP Bypass on a per group basis at the central site, using a check box on the HW Client tab on the Group configuration page. The LEAP packets travel over the tunnel to a RADIUS server via ports 1645 or 1812.

LEAP Bypass functions properly if the following conditions are met.

- Interactive unit authentication must be disabled, otherwise, a non-LEAP (wired) device needs to authenticate the VPN 3002 before LEAP devices can connect using the tunnel.
- Individual user authentication is enabled, otherwise, LEAP Bypass isn't needed.
- The VPN 3002 device can be in either Client mode or Network Extension mode.
- Wireless Access points must be Cisco Aironet Access Points.
- The Cisco Aironet Access Point must be running Cisco Discovery Protocol (CDP).
- The wireless NICs for the PCs can be from other manufacturers.

While the LEAP and LEAP Bypass technologies are sound, some security risk always exists in allowing any unauthenticated traffic to traverse the secure tunnel.

PART III

IPSec Backup Servers

The IPSec backup servers feature provides alternatives for the VPN 3002 hardware client to connect to the central site when its primary VPN Concentrator is unavailable. Backup servers can either be configured individually on the VPN 3002 device or on a per-group basis on the central-site VPN Concentrator. When configured on the central-site VPN Concentrator, the Concentrator pushes the backup server policy to all VPN 3002 hardware clients in the group.

The following characteristics apply to the IPSec backup server feature:

- Each VPN 3002 must connect to the primary VPN Concentrator at least once to download a backup server list. A backup server list can't be downloaded from a backup server.
- If the primary VPN Concentrator is unavailable to download the backup server list and the VPN 3002 has a previously configured backup server list, it can continue to connect to the servers on that list.
- If the VPN 3002 has tried all designated backup servers on the list and can't connect, it doesn't automatically retry. The following trigger a new round of attempts:
    - In Network Extension mode, the VPN 3002 attempts a new connection after four seconds.
    - In Client mode, the VPN 3002 attempts a new connection when the user clicks the Connect Now button on the Monitoring | System Status screen or when data passes from the VPN 3002 to the VPN Concentrator.
- Any changes to the configuration of the backup server's list during an active VPN 3002 session won't take effect until the next time the VPN 3002 connects to its primary VPN Concentrator.
- The VPN Concentrator backup servers needn't be aware of each other.

The group name, user name, and any passwords configured for the VPN 3002 must be identical for the primary VPN Concentrator and all backup servers. Also, if interactive hardware client authentication and/or individual user authentication are configured for the VPN 3002 on the primary VPN Concentrator, they must be configured on backup servers as well.

Configure IPSec Backup Servers—VPN 3002 Client

You can configure the backup server feature from the primary VPN Concentrator or the VPN 3002. Use the Configuration | System | Tunneling Protocols | IPSec screen to configure backup servers directly on the VPN 3002. From this screen, shown in Figure 15-25, you can configure up to ten servers, ranging from the highest priority on the top to the lowest priority on the bottom. The Backup Easy VPN Servers window is only a small text box allowing direct entry and insertions.

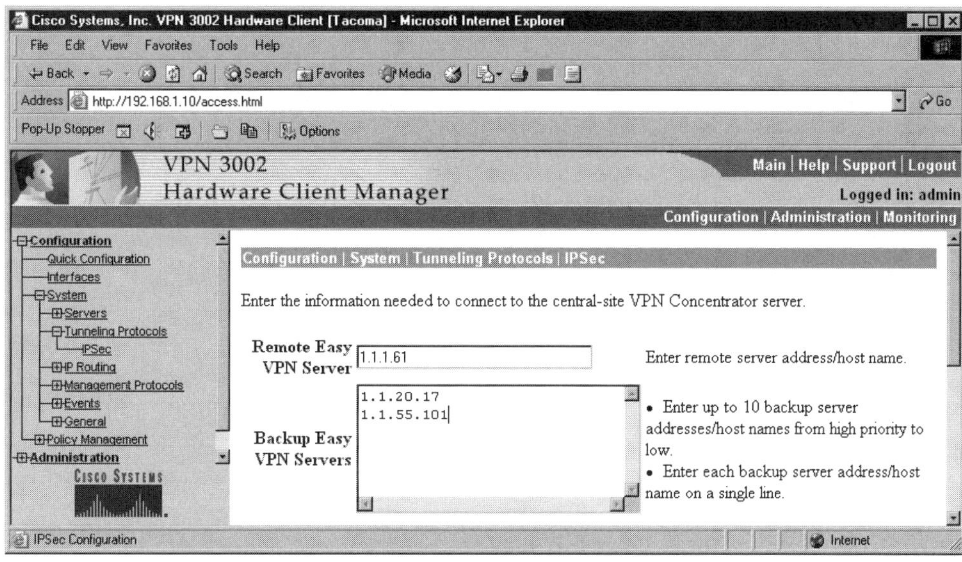

Figure 15-25 Configure backup servers directly on the VPN 3002 Client

Configure IPSec Backup Servers—VPN 3000 Concentrator

To configure backup servers for the VPN 3002 from the VPN Concentrator, use the Configuration | User Management | Base Group, Client Config tab, as shown in Figure 15-26. The backup server's list will apply the next time the 3002 connects to its primary concentrator.

In the IPSec Backup Servers section, use the drop-down list box to select a method to use or disable backup servers. The three choices are as follows:

- Use client configured list
- Disable and clear client configured list
- Use list below

Enter up to ten IPSec backup server addresses/names starting from the highest priority to the lowest. Enter each IPSec backup server address/name on a single line.

IPSec Server Load Balancing

The load balancing feature makes it possible to distribute remote sessions among two or more VPN Concentrators connected on the same network. Load balancing provides efficient use of system resources, while providing increased performance and high availability by directing remote sessions to the least-loaded device.

The load balancing is used only with remote sessions with VPN Concentrators initiated by either the Cisco VPN Client (3.0 or later) or the Cisco VPN 3002 Hardware

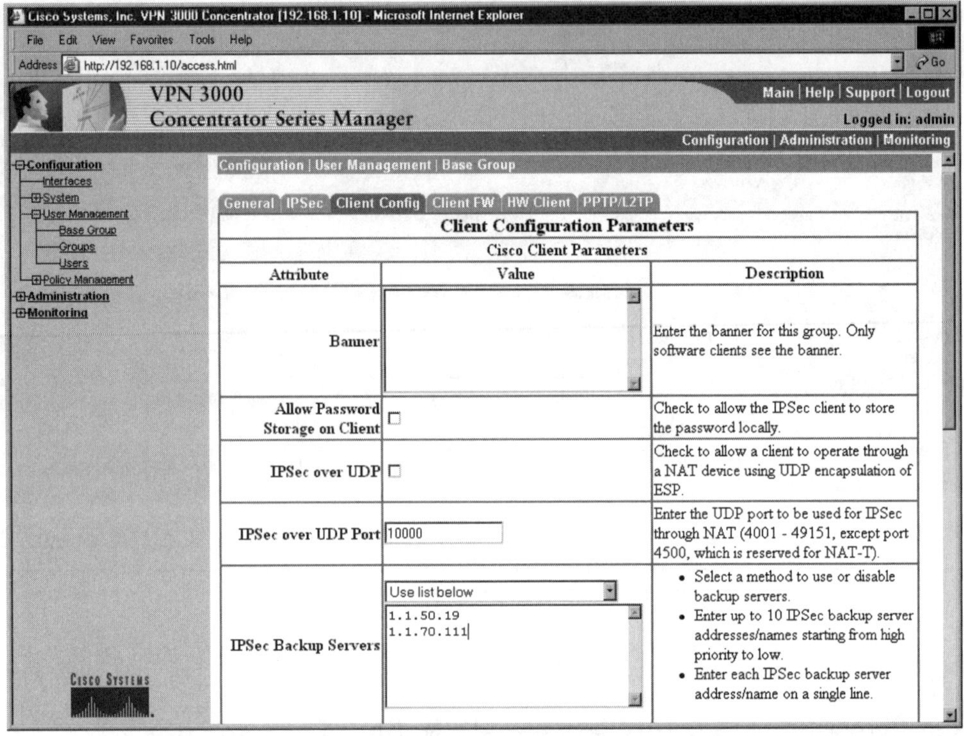

Figure 15-26 Configure backup servers on the VPN Concentrator

Client (3.5 or later). All other VPN clients, including LAN-to-LAN connections, can connect to a VPN Concentrator on which load balancing is enabled, but they can't participate in load balancing.

Load balancing requires no configuration on the VPN Client or VPN 3002.

Configure a Server for Load Balancing

Before configuring load balancing on a VPN Concentrator, you must complete the following two tasks:

- Configure the private and public interfaces.
- Configure the filters for the private and public interfaces to allow the Virtual Cluster Agent (VCA) load balancing protocol.

Configure Interfaces Use the Configuration | Interfaces window to check to see if the public and private interfaces were defined and each has status UP. If either interface is undefined, it must be defined before proceeding.

Virtual Cluster To implement load balancing, you must group together two or more VPN Concentrators logically on the same private LAN-to-LAN network, private subnet, and public subnet into a virtual cluster. The virtual cluster appears to outside clients as a single virtual cluster IP address.

All devices in the virtual cluster are used to distribute session loads. The *virtual cluster master* directs incoming calls to the other devices, referred to as *secondary devices*. By monitoring all devices, the virtual cluster master can distribute the session load based on the activity of each device. The virtual cluster master role isn't assigned to a specific physical device, but can shift among devices, as needed. This flexibility is particularly important if the current virtual cluster master fails. In this case, one of the secondary devices takes over and immediately becomes the new virtual cluster master.

A VPN Client wanting to initiate a session connects to the virtual cluster IP address. The virtual cluster master returns the public IP address of the cluster host with the least load to the client. The process is transparent to the user because the VPN client connects directly to that designated host without any user involvement or messages.

If a cluster machine fails, the terminated sessions reconnect immediately to the virtual cluster IP address where the virtual cluster master repeats the reassignment process. Even if the failed device is the virtual cluster master, one of the secondary cluster devices immediately and automatically takes over as the new virtual session master. Multiple device failures in the cluster should also be resolved, as long as one cluster device remains available.

Configure Filters Use the following VPN Concentrator steps to configure the filters for the private and public interfaces to allow the VCA load balancing protocol.

1. In the Configuration | Interfaces window, select Ethernet1 (Private).
   The Configuration | Interfaces | Ethernet1 window appears.
2. Choose the General tab.
3. Use the drop-down Filter menu button and select Private (Default).
4. Click on Apply.
5. In the Configuration | Interface window, select Ethernet2 (Public).
   The Configuration | Interfaces | Ethernet2 window appears.
6. Choose the General tab.
7. Use the drop-down Filter menu button and select Public (Default).
8. Click Apply.
9. Go to the Configuration | Policy Management | Traffic Management | Filters window.
10. Choose Private (Default) from the Filter list.
11. Select Assign Rules to Filter. The Configuration | Policy Management | Traffic Management | Assign Rules to Filter window appears.

12. Verify that VCA In (forward/in) and VCA Out (forward/out) are in the Current Rules in Filter list. If necessary, add them to the list.
13. Click on Done.
14. In the Configuration | Policy Management | Traffic Management | Filters window, choose Public.
15. Choose Assign Rules to Filter. The Configuration | Policy Management | Traffic Management | Assign Rules to Filter window appears.
16. Verify VCA In (forward/in) and VCA Out (forward/out) are in the Current Rules in Filter list. If necessary, add them to the list.
17. Click Done.
18. Click the Save Needed icon in the upper-right corner to save the changes.

Configure Load Balancing Use the Configuration | System | Load Balancing screen to enable load balancing on the VPN Concentrator, as shown in Figure 15-27. The process takes two steps:

1. Configure the cluster—Define the common virtual cluster IP address, UDP port (if necessary), and IPSec shared secret value for every device in the cluster.
2. Configure the device —Enable load balancing on the device, and then define the device-specific properties. These values can vary, based on device type and option features.

VPN Virtual Cluster IP Address	A single IP address identifying the virtual cluster. This address must be within the address range shared by all VPN Concentrators in the cluster.
VPN Virtual Cluster UDP Port	A UDP destination port number to use for load balancing if another application is already using the default port.
Encryption	Specifies all load-balancing communication between the VPN Concentrators is encrypted.
IPSec Shared Secret	Available only if Encryption is checked. The shared secret is a common password used to authenticate all virtual cluster members. IPSec uses this shared secret as a preshared key to establish secure tunnels between virtual cluster peers.
Priority	Priority (1 to 10) for this VPN Concentrator within the virtual cluster. The higher the value, the more likely this device could become the virtual cluster master either at startup or when an existing master fails.

H.323 Support in PAT Mode

VPN 3002 client software supports H.323, the packet-based multimedia communications standard developed by the International Telecommunication Union (ITU). A variety of multimedia applications use the H.323 standard to implement real-time audio,

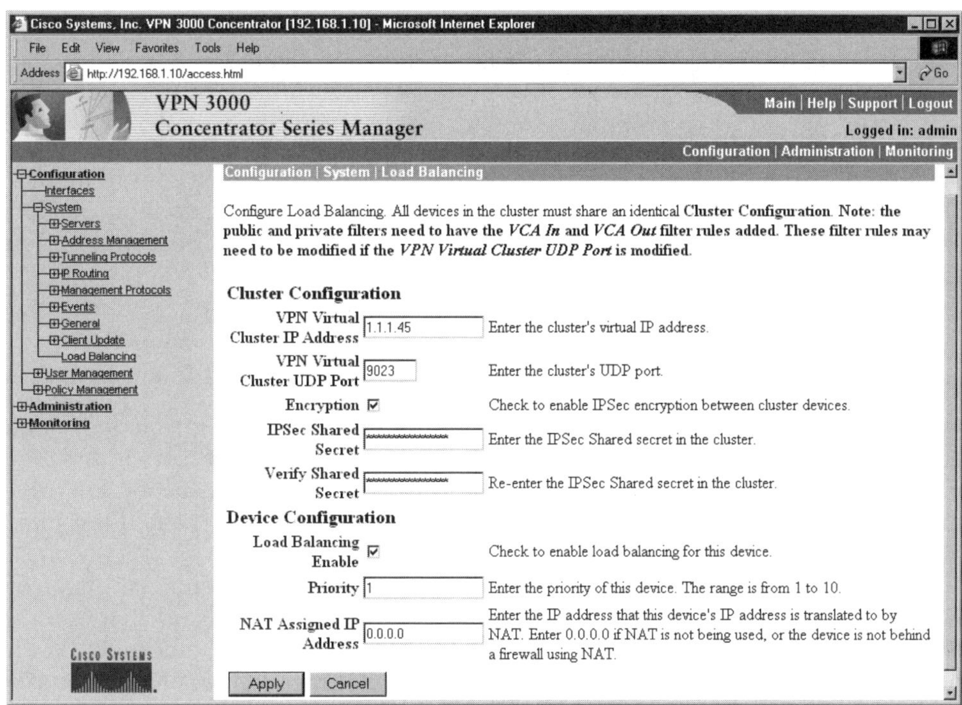

Figure 15-27 Configuring load balancing

video, and data communications. This H.323 support allows the VPN 3002 to support Microsoft NetMeeting. H.323 support requires no configuration on the VPN 3002.

Simple Certificate Enrollment Protocol (SCEP)

You can enroll and install digital certificates on the VPN 3002 manually or automatically. The automatic method is a new feature that uses the Simple Certificate Enrollment Protocol (SCEP) to streamline enrollment and installation. SCEP is a secure messaging protocol that requires minimal user intervention and was introduced in Chapter 11.

This automatic method is quicker than enrolling and installing digital certificates manually, but is available only if the following two conditions are met.

- The CA must support SCEP.
- Enrolling must be done via the Web.

If the CA doesn't support SCEP or if digital certificates are enrolled by other means, such as e-mail or floppy disk, then they must be processed using the manual method.

To allow retrieving the CA certificate via SCEP, use the Administration | Certificate Management | Install | CA Certificate | SCEP, as shown in Figure 15-28.

XML Management

The VPN 3002 now supports an XML-based interface that allows the administrator to use an external management application. These management applications can be Cisco products or third-party tools. XML data can be sent to the VPN Concentrator using HTTPS, SSH, or standard file transfer protocols, such as FTP or TFTP.

This feature is enabled by default and doesn't require configuration.

Reverse Route Injection (RRI)

A VPN Concentrator can be configured to add routes to its routing table for remote hardware or software clients. The VPN Concentrator then advertises these routes to its private network via RIP or OSPF, making the VPN 3002 protected networks known to the main network. This feature is called reverse route injection (RRI) and it was introduced in version 3.5 of the VPN 3000 Concentrator code.

Figure 15-29 shows the VPN scenario used earlier. The scenario assumes the main office has reserved the networks 192.168.0.0 to 192.168.127.0 for its internal use. The other private class C addresses were assigned as needed to branch locations. RRI could be implemented so all main office routers know about the branch office LAN. This assumes the branch office is configured for Network Extension mode.

RRI requires no configuration on the VPN 3002.

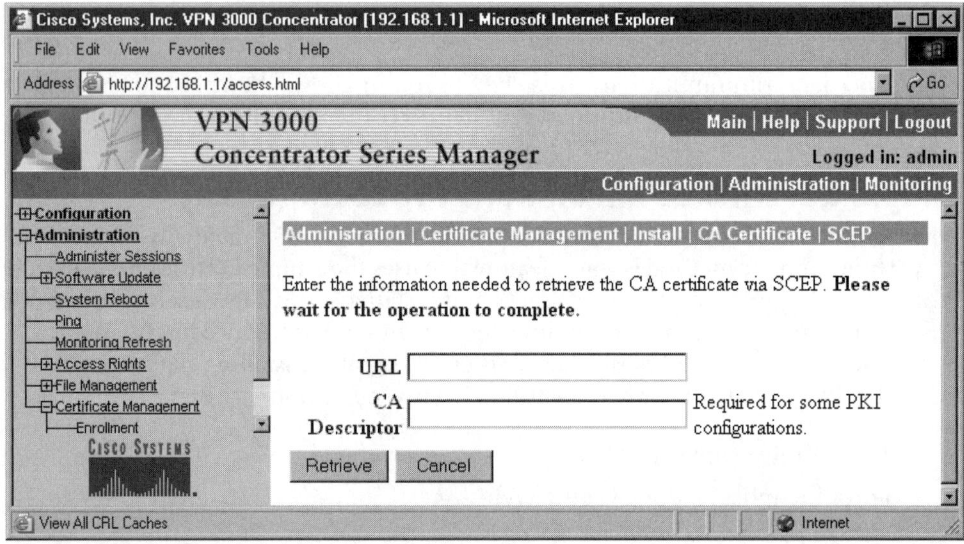

Figure 15-28 Using SCEP to enroll certificates

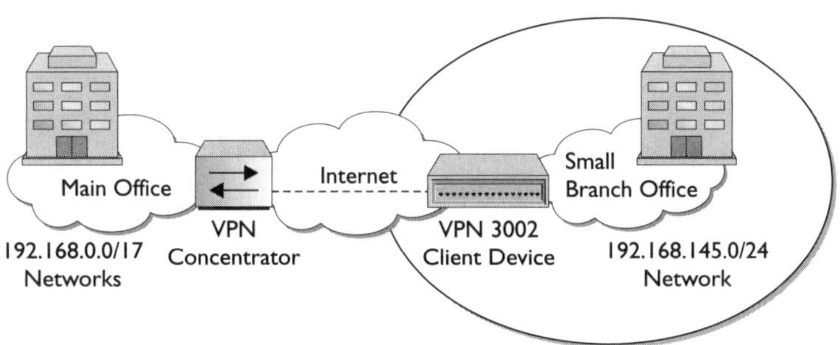

Figure 15-29 VPN scenario network with the main office using RRI

VPN Client Support

Client RRI can be used on all VPN Clients connecting to the VPN Concentrator. This option applies to all remote software clients and VPN 3002 Hardware Clients using Client (PAT) Mode. To configure Client RRI on the VPN Concentrator, go to Configuration | System | IP Routing | Reverse Route Injection, and then select the check box for Client Reverse Route Injection. This selection adds host routes for each remote client to the VPN Concentrator routing table. The VPN Concentrator adds a host route when the client connects and deletes it when the client disconnects. This box is unchecked by default.

Network Extension RRI

This option is for VPN 3002 Client in Network Extension mode (NEM) only. To configure Network Extension RRI on the VPN Concentrator, go to Configuration | System | IP Routing | Reverse Route Injection and select the check box for Network Extension Reverse Route Injection. This selection adds a network route for each network behind a VPN 3002 Hardware Client to the routing table on the VPN Concentrator. The VPN Concentrator adds the route when the VPN 3002 connects and deletes the route when it disconnects. This box is unchecked by default.

Figure 15-30 shows the Configuration | System | IP Routing | Reverse Route Injection screen where both of the RRI features can be configured. The example shows adding the protected LAN from the scenario example.

AES Support and Diffie-Hellman Group 5

VPN software version 3.6 introduced support for Advanced Encryption Standard (AES), which is more secure than DES and more efficient than 3DES. AES supports 128-, 192-, and 256-bit key strengths. 128-bit AES is significantly faster than 168-bit 3DES and little performance difference exists between 256-bit AES and 168-bit 3DES. AES support was also added to the PIX Firewall with v6.3(1).

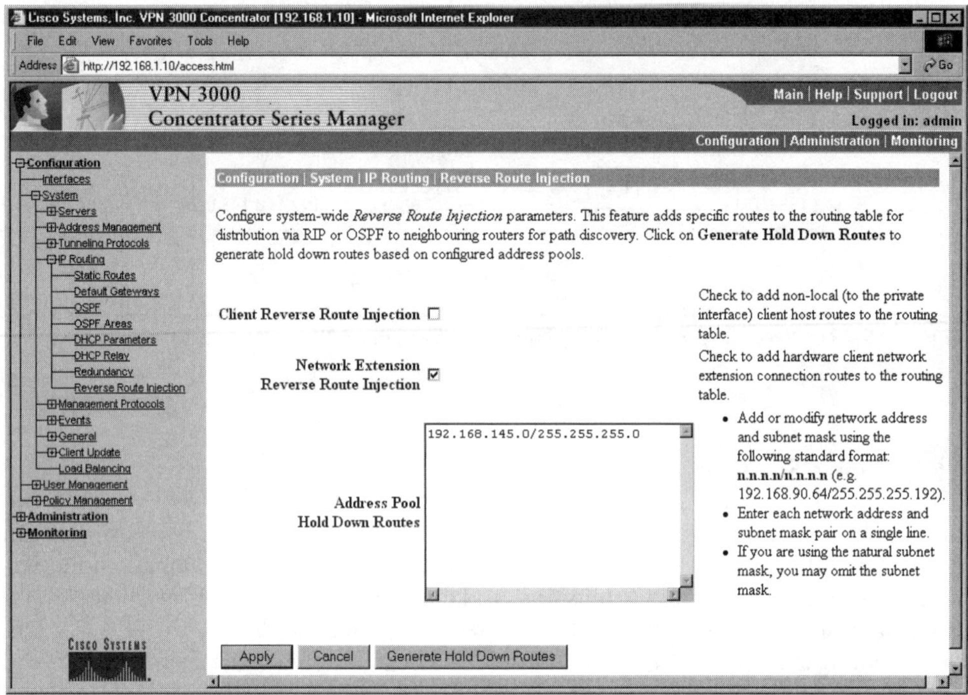

Figure 15-30 Configuring Reverse Route Injection

VPN software version 3.6 also introduced support for Diffie-Hellman Group 5 (1,536-bit key), which provides greater key exchange security. This feature is set as part of IPSec configuration on the VPN Concentrator, as shown in Figure 15-31.

Push Banner to VPN 3002

An administrator can create a banner on the VPN 3000 Concentrator and push it to the VPN 3002. This allows the organization to provide information to users about their network, terms for use, liability, and other issues. The maximum banner length is 510 characters. Any characters, including newline (ENTER key) can be used. Use the Configuration | User Management | Base Group, Client Configuration parameters tab on the VPN Concentrator, as shown in Figure 15-32.

The banner displays only when individual user authentication is enabled.

Delete with Reason

Delete with reason is a part of the system-messaging process that can be used for alerts and troubleshooting. Delete with reason causes the VPN Concentrator to send reasons for VPN Concentrator-initiated disconnects to any impacted software clients or VPN 3002 hardware clients. The client device then decodes the reason and displays it in the event log.

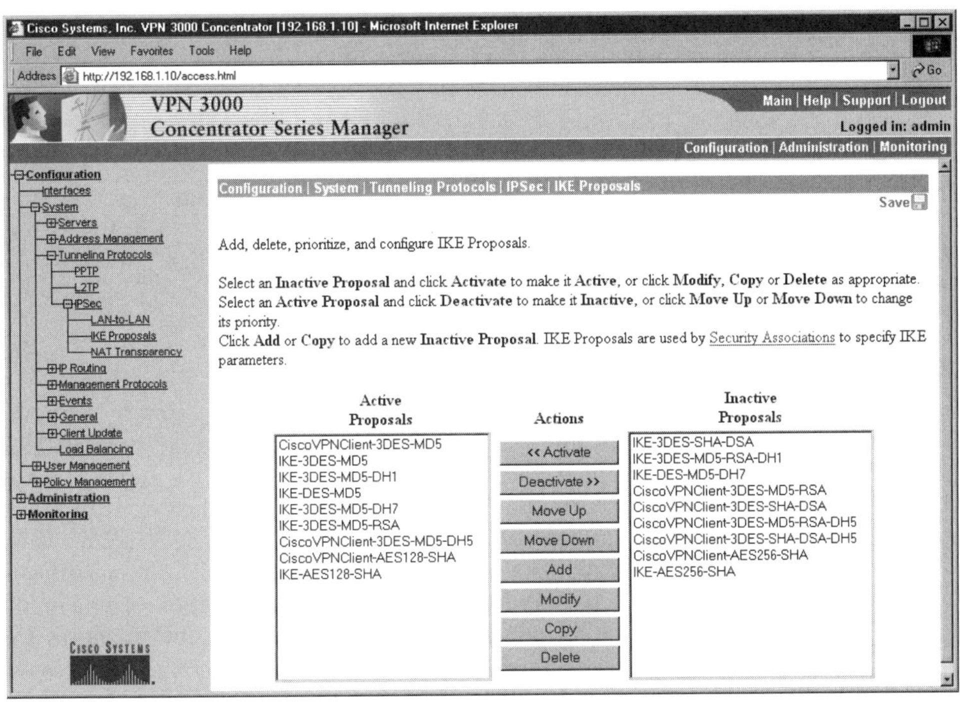

Figure 15-31 Configuring IKE proposals, including AES and DH 1, 5, and 7

Similarly, the VPN 3002 sends reasons for any VPN3002-initiated disconnects to the VPN Concentrator at the central site. The VPN Concentrator decodes the reason and displays it in the event log.

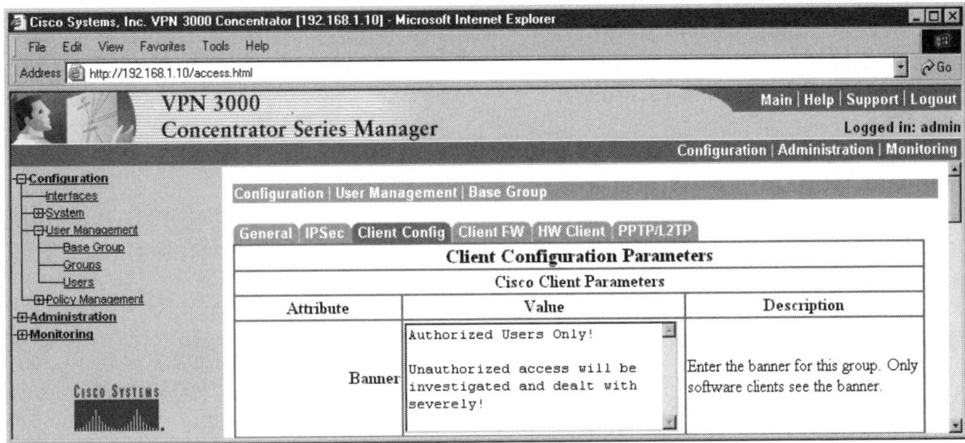

Figure 15-32 Configuring a banner to be pushed to VPN 3002s

The feature isn't currently supported by the Cisco PIX Firewalls.
The feature is active by default, but an administrator can disable it.

Auto-Update Feature

The *client update* feature was added in version 3.0 for the VPN 3002 Hardware Client allowing VPN central devices, such as VPN Concentrators, to upgrade the software and configuration on the client. In the case of the VPN 3002 Hardware Client, firmware upgrades can also be pushed down to the client.

VPN 3002 Hardware Clients

For VPN 3002 Hardware Clients, the client update allows an administrator to update software and firmware automatically for the 3002 device. If an upgrade is needed, the unit upgrades automatically from an internal TFTP server specified on the central site VPN Concentrator. The process of maintaining security, managing the system, and upgrading it is transparent to the end user.

To avoid update failures and reduce downtime, the VPN 3002 stores image files in two locations: the active and the backup location. The *active location* contains the image currently running on the system. Updating the image overwrites the image in the backup location. That new image is tested to validate it and, if successful, the image is identified as the active location for the next reboot. If the update isn't validated, the client doesn't reboot, and the invalid image doesn't become active. If the update process fails to download a valid image, it will retry up to 20 times, waiting three minutes between attempts. Any unsuccessful updates are logged with information indicating the type of failure.

Cisco VPN Software Clients

For Cisco VPN software clients, the process is a little less automatic: it's more of a notification mechanism with an assisted upgrade. The client update for the Cisco VPN software clients allows central location administrators to notify the client users automatically when it's time to update. Then action is required on the part of users to retrieve and install the newer software.

Configuring Auto-Update

Use the Configuration | System | Client Update menu options of the VPN 3000 Concentrator Manager to configure the client update feature. This screen, as shown in Figure 15-33, offers the following two options.

Enable	Enables or disables client update.
Entries	Configures updates by client type, acceptable firmware and software versions, and their locations.

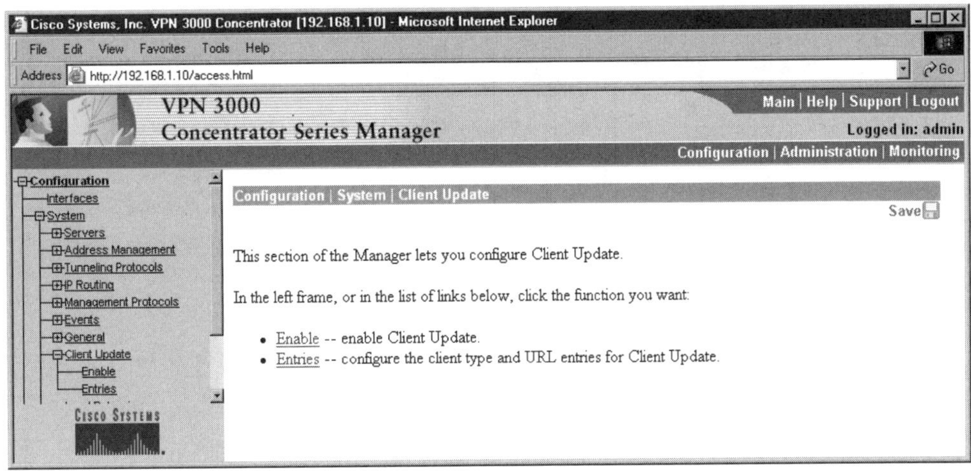

Figure 15-33 Client auto-update screen

1. The Configuration | System | Client Update | Enable screen has only an Enable check box. Select it and click the Apply button to enable or disable the client update feature. The Manager returns to the Configuration | System | Client Update screen.
2. The Configuration | System | Client Update | Entries screen, shown in Figure 15-34, is used to add, modify, or delete client update entries. The update entry list shows the available client updates. If no updates were configured, the list shows "--Empty--".

Use the Add button to configure a new client update entry. The Manager opens the Configuration | System | Client Update | Entries | Add screen, as shown in Figure 15-35.

To modify an existing entry, highlight the update in the Update Entry list and click the Modify button. The Manager opens the Configuration | System | Client Update | Modify screen, which looks like the Add screen.

The Delete button can be used to remove a client update entry.

Chapter Review

This chapter looked at configuring the VPN 3002 client and the VPN 3000 concentrators to support the VPN client features.

The VPN 3002 Hardware Client is a dedicated VPN device that can be used to connect one or more devices, including workstations, servers, hubs, cash registers, printers, and IP telephones to a company's central network. The 3002 unit eliminates the need to install and configure VPN client software on the local workstation(s), plus it supports workstations running any TCP/IP supporting OS.

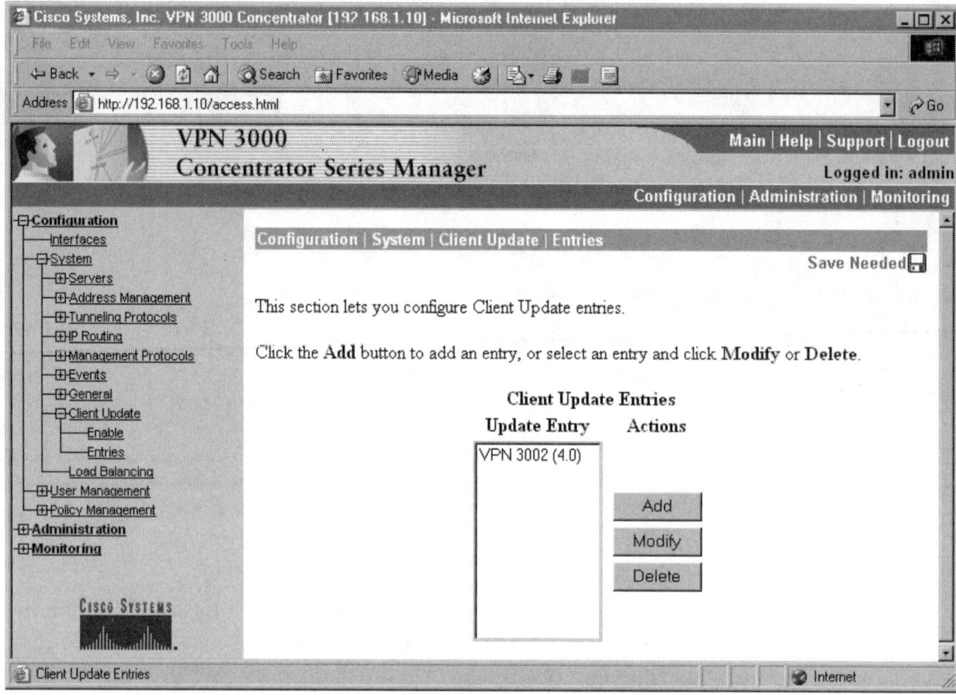

Figure 15-34 Configuration | System | Client Update | Entries screen

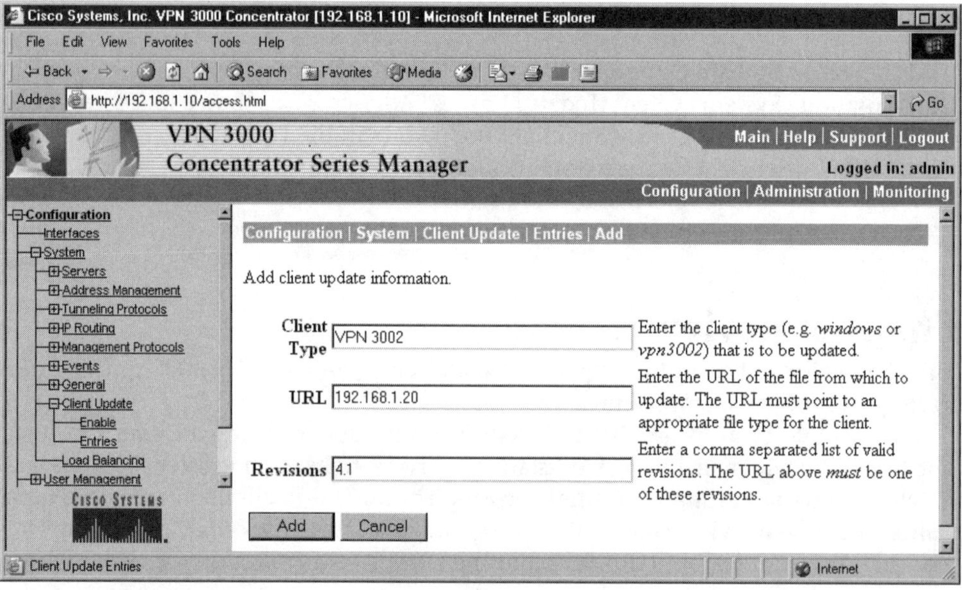

Figure 15-35 Adding or modifying a client update entry

Configuring the VPN 3002 can be accomplished using a menu-driven version of the CLI or the more user-friendly Client Manager web-based application. The two systems have virtually identical steps and menu options making it easier to use both as needed.

The Quick Configuration option is used to provide the basic parameters required for connecting to a VPN Concentrator, which will "push" the basic IPSec configuration and security policy features down to the client. A wide variety of features can be configured on the VPN Concentrator to be pushed out to either VPN 3002 or VPN software clients. An auto-update feature facilitates configuration, software, and firmware upgrades.

Questions

1 What is another name for VPN PAT mode?

A. Network Extension mode

B. Client mode

C. Network Extension Mode per Group

D. Split tunnel mode

2. Which of the following is *not* an IPSec implementation used by the VPN 3002?

A. IPSec over TCP

B. IPSec over UTP

C. IPSec over NAT-T

D. IPSec over PPTP

3. The VPN 3002 CLI is most like which of the following?

A. Cisco IOS routers

B. Cisco Catalyst 5000 and 6000 switches

C. The PIX Firewall

D. None of the above

4. Which one of the following is *not* one of the three main menu sections for the VPN 3002?

A. Monitoring

B. Reporting

C. Configuration

D. Administration

5. What is the command to upgrade the VPN 3002 software?

A. copy tftp flash

B. copy tftp nvram

C. copy tftp backup

D. None of the above

6. Which of the following is a growing protocol for connecting ISPs through broadband connections like DSL/cable systems?
   A. PPP
   B. PPPoE
   C. Ethernet
   D. BGP
7. What is the first feature(s) set with Quick Configuration?
   A. Upload an Existing Configuration file
   B. Configure the Public Interface
   C. Set the System Time, Date, and Time Zone
   D. Configure DNS
8. Where might the DHCP Server feature be configured on the VPN 3002?
   A. Public interface
   B. Private interface
   C. Public or private interfaces
   D. None of the above
9. In which two cases would PAT always be used on outbound traffic?
   A. Network extension mode
   B. Split tunnels
   C. Client mode
   D. PPPoE
10. Which feature can be configured on either the VPN 3002 or the Concentrator?
    A. Interactive Unit Authentication
    B. IPSec Server Load Balancing
    C. Individual User Authentication
    D. IPSec backup servers
11. Which feature requires Virtual Cluster protocol configuration?
    A. Interactive Unit Authentication
    B. IPSec Server load balancing
    C. Individual User Authentication
    D. IPSec backup servers

12. Reverse Route Injection refers to which of the following?
    A. Inserting main network routes in remote network route tables
    B. Making main network routes available to all remote VPN clients
    C. Inserting remote network routes in main network route tables
    D. Exchanging routes both ways between main and branch networks
13. Which Cisco protocol allows wireless users to authenticate over VPN links?
    A. NAT Traversal (NAT-T)
    B. LEAP Bypass
    C. RRI
    D. PPPoE
14. Which of the following is *not* supported by Client Update features?
    A. VPN Software
    B. Firmware on VPN 3002
    C. Push Banner to VPN 3002
    D. VPN configurations
15. Which of the following might create problems for wireless users behind the VPN 3002?
    A. IPSec over NAT-T
    B. Interactive Hardware Client Authentication
    C. Individual User Authentication
    D. AES Support and Diffie-Hellman Group

Answers

1. **B.** Client mode
2. **D.** IPSec over PPTP
3. **D.** None of the above. It is menu-driven, somewhat like the old 1900 switches
4. **B.** Reporting
5. **D.** None of the above. This is a menu-driven process
6. **B.** PPPoE
7. **C.** Set the System Time, Date, and Time Zone
8. **B.** Private interface. Where the LAN connects

9. **B.** Split tunnels, and **C.** Client mode
10. **D.** IPSec backup servers
11. **B.** IPSec Server load balancing
12. **C.** Inserting remote network routes in main network route tables
13. **B.** LEAP Bypass
14. **C.** Push Banner to VPN 3002
15. **B.** Interactive Hardware Client Authentication. The wireless clients would have to wait for a wired user to authenticate the VPN 3002 to the Concentrator.

CHAPTER 16

Cisco VPN 3000 LAN-to-LAN Networks

In this chapter, you will learn to:

- Describe LAN-to-LAN VPNs using VPN Concentrators
- Configure the VPN 3000 Concentrator LAN-to-LAN with preshared keys
- Configure the VPN 3000 Concentrator LAN-to-LAN using digital certificates
- Configure the VPN 3000 Concentrator LAN-to-LAN with NAT features
- Configure the VPN 3000 Concentrator for the IPSec Over UDP and IPSec Over TCP
- Configure the VPN 3000 Concentrator routing

This section discusses configuring VPN 3000 Concentrators to support LAN-to-LAN or site-to-site implementations. This is a rapidly changing technology, so make certain to augment this material with new releases from the Cisco web site.

The VPN Concentrators in LAN-to-LAN VPNs

LAN-to-LAN (site-to-site) VPNs are a quickly expanding alternative or augmentation to leased line or frame relay WAN infrastructures. VPNs are used to create secure tunnels between two networks via an insecure public network, such as the Internet. The Cisco Concentrator supports three types of tunnels: Layer 2 Tunneling Protocol (L2TP), Point-to-Point Tunneling Protocol (PPTP), and IPSec.

Two types of LAN-to-LAN VPN implementations exist.

- *Intranet VPNs* provide secure connections between branch offices to the enterprise network resources.
- *Extranet VPNs* provide secure connections for special third parties, such as business partners, vendors, and customers to the specified enterprise resources.

While this chapter and the certification exam focus mainly on the Cisco VPN 3000 Concentrators for LAN-to-LAN implementations, note that the VPN peer device at the other end of this type of link can be any of the following common technologies:

- Another Cisco VPN Concentrator

- A Cisco VPN 3002 Hardware Client
- A Cisco IOS router
- A Cisco PIX Firewall
- A third-party VPN device

Figure 16-1 shows common intranet and extranet VPNs, as well as the different types of Cisco endpoint devices that might be used.

In a LAN-to-LAN implementation, IPSec creates a secure tunnel between the public interfaces of the two VPN Concentrators or endpoint devices. The endpoint devices forward the secure data received over the VPN to the hosts on their private LANs as unencrypted data. No VPN user authentication or configuration exists in a LAN-to-LAN connection. Hosts configured on the private networks can access hosts on the other side of the connection. Any access is subject to any network authentication, group or user permissions, and router access lists.

To configure a LAN-to-LAN connection fully, you must configure identical basic IKE and IPSec parameters on both endpoint devices.

STUDY TIP Remember, the IPSec VPN related ports on all network devices between the endpoints must be open. The ports are IKE/ISAKMP UDP port 500, ESP IP protocol number 50, and AH IP protocol number 51.

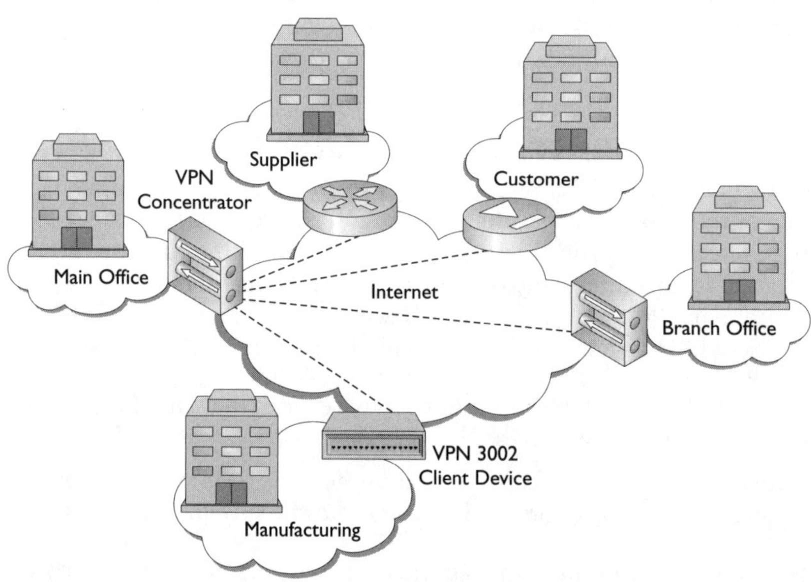

Figure 16-1 Common LAN-to-LAN VPN implementations

Chapter Scenario

The scenario used in the following discussion is quite simple, in case someone wants to follow along with appropriate devices. The configuration is based on Figure 16-2, showing a branch location connecting through a VPN Concentrator to another VPN Concentrator at the main office. The scenario assumes the main office has reserved the 128 class C networks 192.168.0.0 to 192.168.127.0 for its internal use. The other private class C addresses have been assigned as needed to the company's branch locations. The figure shows a branch location assigned the 192.168.144.0 network.

While the diagram assumes a Concentrator at both ends, the central site configuration process won't change much, regardless of the device at the branch. You might need to modify the IKE and IPSec choices based on what the peer device can support.

LAN-to-LAN Networks with Preshared Keys

This section assumes basic Quick Configuration features were set. You must configure a public interface on the VPN Concentrator before you can configure an IPSec LAN-to-LAN connection. Use the Configuration | Interfaces screen to set the interface IP Addresses and default gateway. Figure 16-3 shows the Configuration | Interfaces screen for the Main Office Concentrator.

Device	Private Interface	Subnet Mask	Public Interface	Subnet Mask
Main Office Concentrator	192.168.1.1	255.255.255.0	1.1.1.1	255.255.255.0
Branch Office Concentrator	192.168.144.1	255.255.255.0	1.10.1.1	255.255.255.0

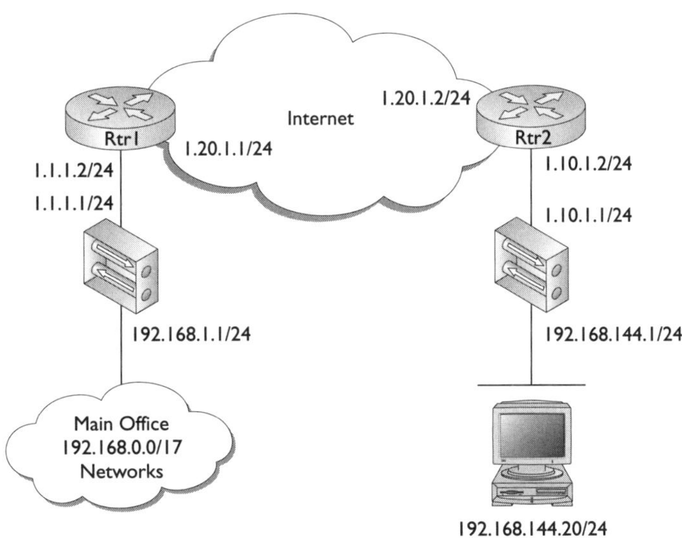

Figure 16-2 VPN 3002 configuration scenario

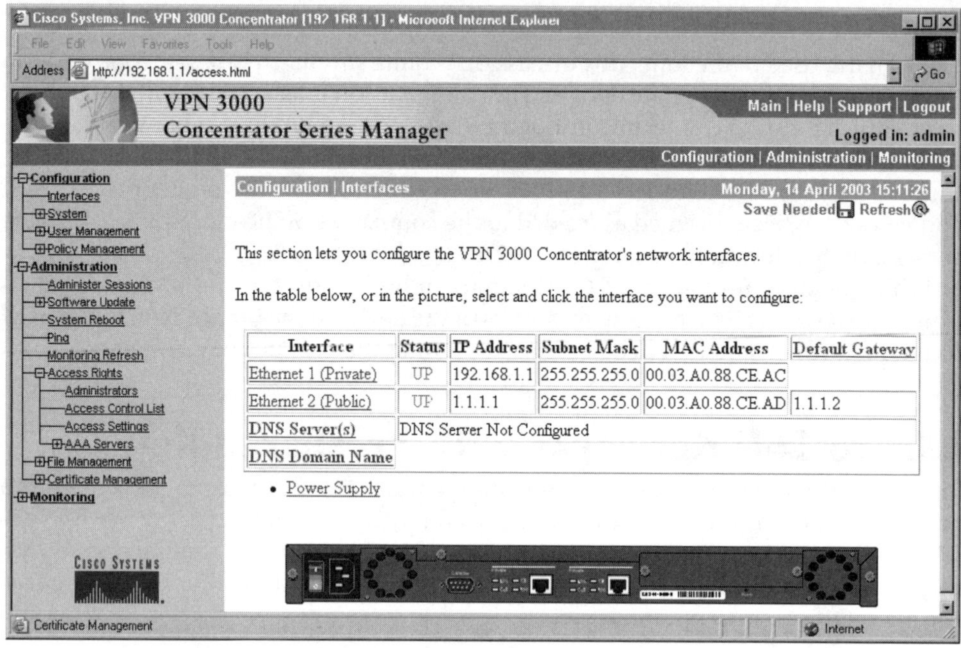

Figure 16-3 Main Office interfaces configuration

Configure Network Lists

The Configuration | Policy Management | Traffic Management screens let you configure network lists, rules, filters, security associations (SA), Network Address Translation (NAT), and bandwidth policies. Together, these features let you control the data traffic through the VPN Concentrator, including what is or isn't protected. The six feature links on this screen include the following:

- **Network lists**—Enable you to create and name lists of network addresses that can be treated as single objects. This can simplify configuring features and filters. Network lists are often a requirement of features like LAN-to-LAN VPNs and IPSec SA filtering.
- **Rules**—Let you filter interface data or limit the data to be protected by IPSec. These named rules enable you to specify protocol, source, and destination addresses (or network lists), port numbers, and what specified action you want to happen to any traffic that meets all criteria. If even one parameter doesn't match, the system ignores the rest of this rule and examines the packet in accordance with the next rule, and so forth. This is similar to each line in router or firewall ACLs.
- **Filters**—Can be used to limit interface traffic, limit groups and user access, and limit application of IPSec security associations.

- **SAs**—Enable you to add, configure, modify, and delete security associations (SAs) to be applied during IPSec tunnel establishment.
- **NAT**—Translates private network addresses into "real world" public network addresses, allowing traffic routing between networks with overlapping private network addresses.
- **Bandwidth**—Defines policies to reserve a minimum amount of bandwidth per session, as well as to limit users within groups to a maximum amount of bandwidth. Once configured, bandwidth policies can be applied to an interface, a group, or both. A policy applied to an interface only applies to each user on the interface. A policy to a group applies only to the users in that group.

Configuring Network Lists

Clicking the Network Lists link brings up the Configuration | Policy Management | Traffic Management | Network Lists screen, as shown in Figure 16-4. In this section, you can define and name lists of networks to be treated as single objects. Network lists can be used for the following common activities:

- Configure IPSec LAN-to-LAN connections (Configuration | System | Tunneling Protocols | IPSec LAN-to-LAN)
- Configure filter rules (Configuration | Policy Management | Traffic Management | Rules)
- Configure split tunneling (Configuration | User Management) for groups and users in remote access network implementations

While a single network list can contain a maximum of 200 network entries, no limit exists to the number of network lists that can be created.

The Network List box displays the names of any existing network lists. If no lists were defined, the field shows "--Empty--". The Add/Modify/Copy/Delete buttons are used to create and manage existing lists. As with everything on the Concentrator, any changes are made live to the active configuration with no Confirmation or Undo options. Click the Save Needed icon in the upper-right corner of the Manager window to save the active configuration to the boot configuration.

LAN-to-LAN Network Lists VPN LAN-to-LAN implementations need a list of the LANs secured behind each endpoint device. In this example, the Main Office would have a list for each LAN-to-LAN connection, plus one for its local LANs. The peer Concentrator would have its own LAN(s) list and Main Office list. These should be reverse images of each other. Any networks not included on the list are invisible to the peer and unable to communicate with the peer network.

Clicking the Add button brings up the Configuration | Policy Management | Traffic Management | Network Lists | Add screen, as shown in Figure 16-5. The screens associated with the other buttons are similar.

1. In the List Name box, type the name for the network list. The name must be unique on this device and is limited to a maximum of 48 case-sensitive

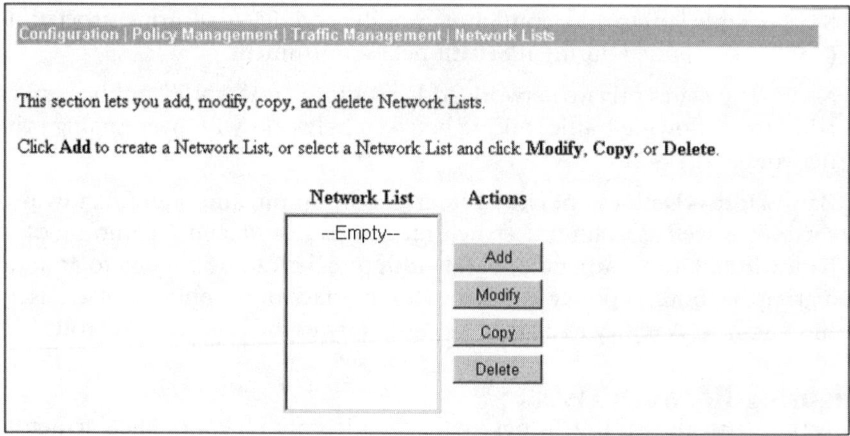

Figure 16-4 Network List creation and management screen

characters. Spaces are allowed. For example, you might use local LANs for the networks attached to this device.

NOTE If the Generate Local List feature (next section) is used, wait to enter this name until after the system generates the network list.

Configuration | Policy Management | Traffic Management | Network Lists | Add

Configure and add a new Network List. Click on **Generate Local List** to generate a network list based on routing entries on the Private interface.

List Name

Network List

Name of the Network List you are adding. The name must be unique.

- Enter the Networks and Wildcard masks using the following format: **n.n.n.n/n.n.n.n** (e.g. 10.10.0.0/0.0.255.255).
- **Note: Enter a *wildcard* mask, which is the reverse of a subnet mask.** A wildcard mask has 1s in bit positions to ignore, 0s in bit positions to match. For example, 10.10.1.0/0.0.0.255 = all 10.10.1.nnn addresses.
- Each Network and Wildcard mask pair must be entered on a single line.
- The Wildcard mask may be omitted if the natural Wildcard mask is to be used.

Add | Cancel | Generate Local List

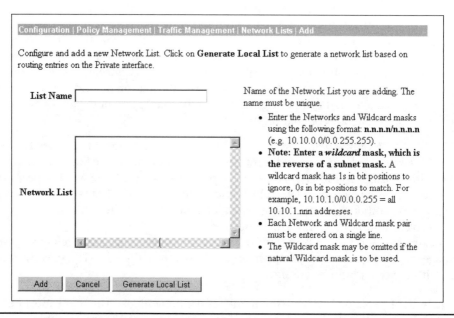

Figure 16-5 Screen to create a new network list

2. In the Network List box, type the networks to be included in this network list. Each entry must be a single line using the format n.n.n.n/w.w.w.w, where w.w.w.w is the wildcard mask (example: 192.168.1.0/0.0.0.255). If the mask is omitted, the Manager will supply the default classful mask. The maximum number of network/wildcard entries in a single network list is 200. The entries for this scenario would be the following:

   Name: *Main Office*
   192.168.0.0 /0.0.127.255 (mask couldn't have been omitted)
   Name: *Tacoma Office*
   192.168.144.1/0.0.0.255 (mask could have been omitted)

Generate Local List The VPN Concentrator has a Generate Local List feature button on the Add or Modify screen, so you needn't explicitly define the entries. Clicking the Generate Local List button causes the Manager to generate a network list automatically, containing the first 200 private networks reachable from the Ethernet 1 (Private) interface. The list is created by reading the routing table (Monitoring | Routing Table). For the feature to work, both devices must be VPN Concentrators and both Concentrators must have inbound RIP routing enabled on the Ethernet 1 (Private) interface (Configuration | Interfaces | Ethernet 1), as shown in Figure 16-6.

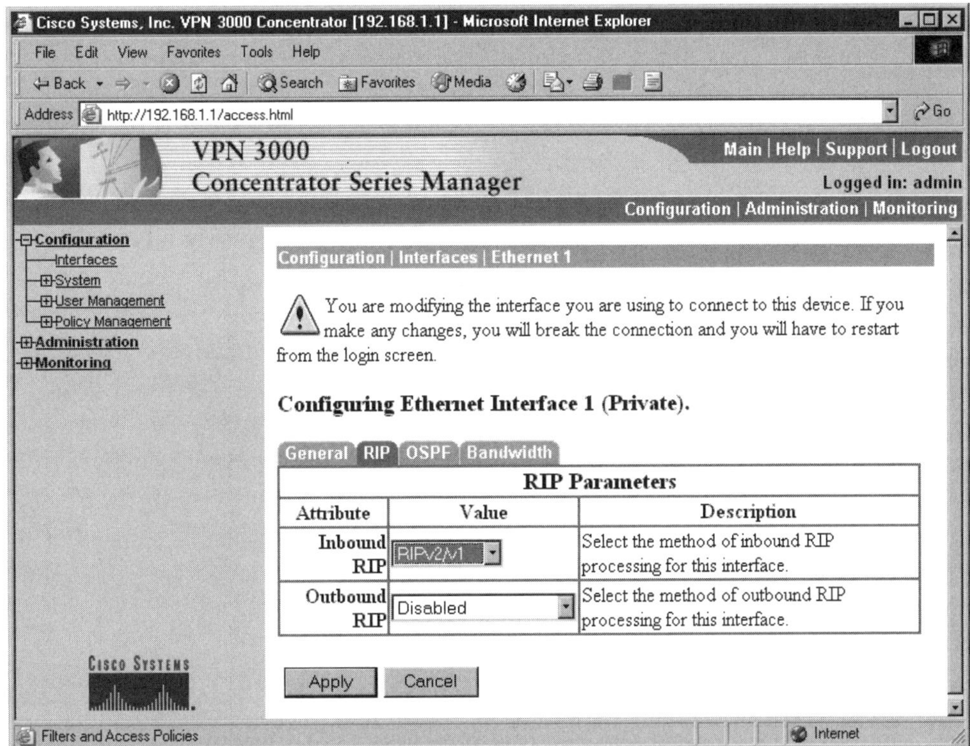

Figure 16-6 Enabling inbound RIP on Ethernet 1

After the Manager refreshes the screen after creating the list, you can edit the Network List entries and enter a name in the List Name box.

Define the IKE Proposals (Optional)

You must also configure any new IKE proposals before you attempt to configure the LAN-to-LAN connections. See the Configuration | System | Tunneling Protocols | IPSec | IKE Proposals screens. If the Cisco defaults are adequate or if any new proposals were defined as part of setting the initial defaults, this process is unnecessary.

If an IKE proposal needs to be added or modified, such as to use digital certificates, you must change settings for IKE negotiation.

IKE Configuration

Use the Manager navigation to locate the Configuration | System | Tunneling Protocols IPSec | IKE Proposals screen, as shown in Figure 16-7. This screen displays both the Active and Inactive IKE options available on the Concentrator.

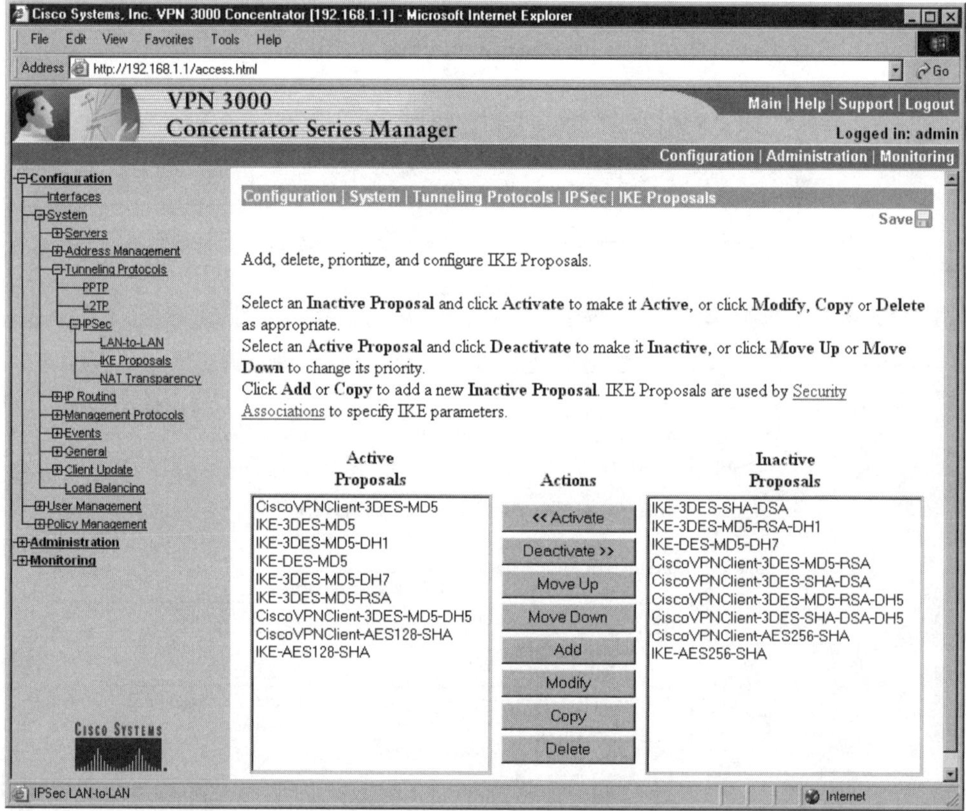

Figure 16-7 IKE Proposal Options

You can change an existing active proposal or create a new one using the Modify or Add buttons, respectively. Either way, a screen similar to the one shown in Figure 16-8 will appear. Make any needed changes, and then click the Apply button.

The resulting IKE proposal will be available in a drop-down list in the next section when it's time to establish the LAN-to-LAN connection.

Create the Tunnel

The Configuration | System | Tunneling Protocols | IPSec | LAN-to-LAN screen lets you configure, add, modify, and delete IPSec LAN-to-LAN connections between two VPN Concentrators. While the VPN Concentrator can establish LAN-to-LAN connections with other protocol-compliant VPN secure gateways, this section assumes VPN Concentrators on both sides.

The following configurations must be done before the tunnel can be implemented.

- Configure the public interfaces.
- Configure identical basic IPSec parameters on both VPN Concentrators.
- Configure mirror-image private network addresses or network lists on both VPN Concentrators.

You can only configure one LAN-to-LAN connection *with each VPN Concentrator (or other secure gateway) peer*. The maximum total number of LAN-to-LAN connections supported is determined by the VPN Concentrator model, as shown in the following table.

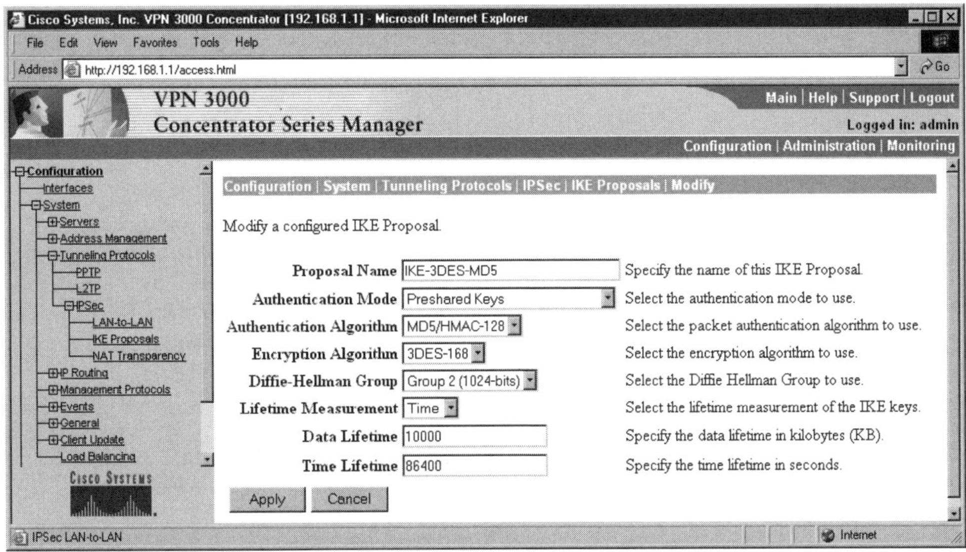

Figure 16-8 IKE Proposal option to be modified

VPN Concentrator Model	Maximum Sessions
3005 & 3015	100
3030	500
3060 & 3080	1,000

Adding a Tunnel

Clicking the Add button brings up the Configuration | System | Tunneling Protocols | IPSec | LAN-to-LAN | Add screen, as shown in Figures 16-9 and 16-10. Any feature or rule with a default setting will be displayed on the Add screen. The Modify screen is similar and is used to make a change to an existing tunnel definition.

NOTE Version 4.0 added an Enable check box above the Name box. Check this box to enable this LAN-to-LAN connection. This debugging feature enables you to disable a LAN-to-LAN configuration without deleting it. To disable this connection, uncheck the check box on either end of the connection. By default, this option is enabled.

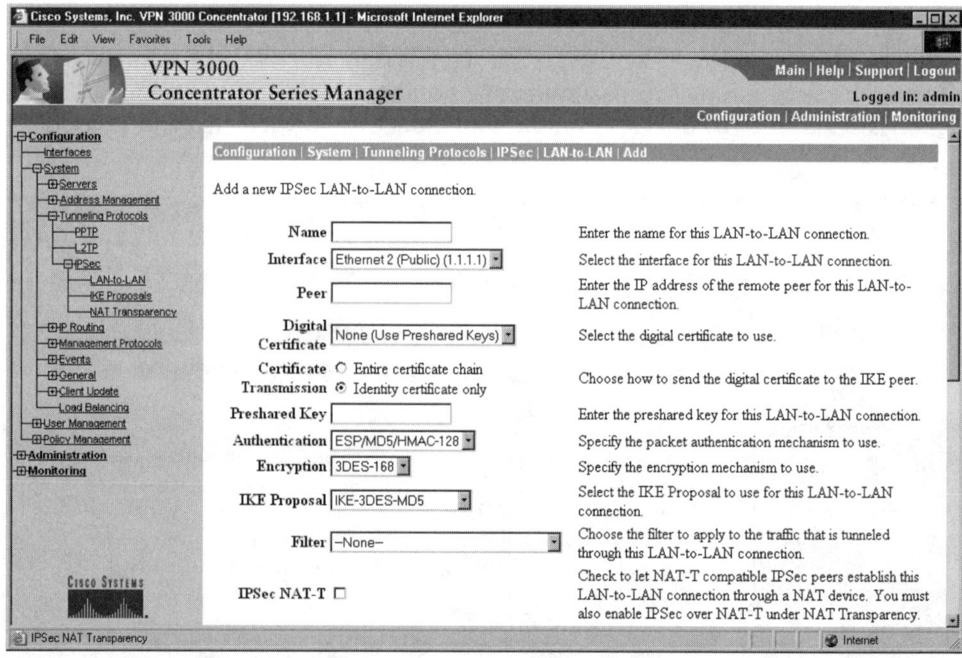

Figure 16-9 Top half of the Tunnel | Add screen

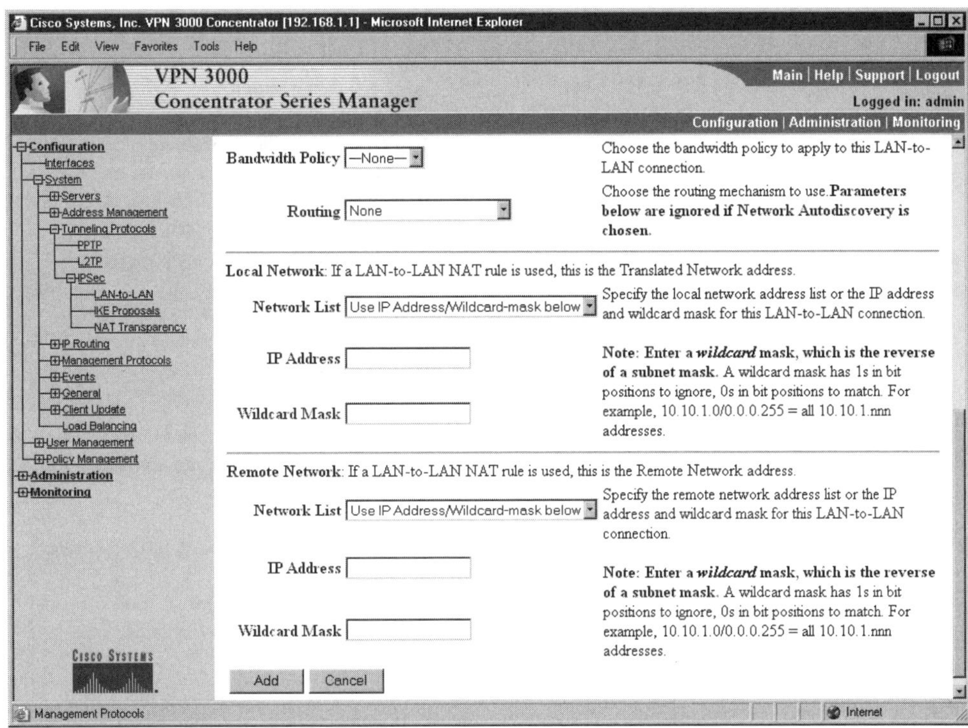

Figure 16-10 Bottom half of the Tunnel | Add screen

The key features and options are as follows:

Name	A unique name up to 32 characters long identifying the tunnel. Because rules and SAs use this name, keep it short and descriptive.
Interface	The drop-down menu to select the public interface from all interfaces with the Public Interface parameter enabled. **Note:** In Modify mode, you can't change the interface. This requires deleting the current connection and adding a new one for the new interface.
Connection Type	Defines the Concentrator role in IKE tunnel establishment: **Bidirectional**—The device can either initiate or accept IKE tunnels. **Answer-only**—The device only accepts IKE tunnels; it can't initiate them. **Originate-only**—The device only initiates IKE tunnels; it can't accept them.
Peers	The IP address of the LAN-to-LAN peer public interface. **Backup Peers:** If this device is the remote-side peer in a backup LAN-to-LAN implementation, you can enter up to ten peers. List the peers from top to bottom, in order of their priority.

Digital Certificate	The drop-down menu to choose preshared keys or a PKI digital certificate to authenticate the peer during Phase 1 IKE negotiations. **None (Use Preshared Keys)**—Use preshared keys (default) or the drop-down list displays any digital certificates that were installed
Certificate Transmission	Digital certificates only, choose the type of certificate transmission. **Entire certificate chain**—Send the identity certificate and all issuing certificates, including the root and any subordinate CA certificates. **Identity certificate only**—Send the peer only the identity certificate.
Preshared Key	Type the preshared key for this connection. (4 to 32 alphanumeric characters) The system displays your entry in Cleartext. This key becomes the password for the IPSec LAN-to-LAN group created. The same key must be entered on the peer VPN Concentrator. This is *not* a manual encryption or authentication key. The system automatically generates those session keys.
Authentication	Specify the data, or packet, authentication algorithm. IPSec Encapsulating Security Payload (ESP) protocol provides both encryption and authentication. Use the Authentication drop-down list to choose the following: **None**—No data authentication **ESP/MD5/HMAC-128**—ESP using HMAC with the MD5 hash function using a 128-bit key. (Default) **ESP/SHA/HMAC-160**—ESP using HMAC with the SHA-1 hash function using a 160-bit key. More secure, but high processing overhead.
Encryption	NULL—Use ESP without packet encryption. **DES-56**—DES encryption with a 56-bit key. **3DES-168**—Triple-DES encryption with a 168-bit key. (Default) **AES-128**—Advanced Encryption Standard (AES) encryption with a 128-bit key. Greater security than DES and more efficient than triple DES. **AES-192**—AES encryption with a 192-bit key. **AES-256**—AES encryption with a 256-bit key.
IKE Proposal	Use the drop-down menu to choose an IKE proposal. The list shows only active IKE proposals in priority order. Default active proposals are **CiscoVPNClient-3DES-MD5**—Preshared keys (XAUTH) and MD5/HMAC-128 authentication. 3DES-168 encryption. D-H Group 2 to generate SA keys. Allows XAUTH user-based authentication. (Default) **IKE-3DES-MD5**—Preshared keys and MD5/HMAC-128 authentication. 3DES-168 encryption. D-H Group 2 to generate SA keys. **IKE-3DES-MD5-DH1**—Preshared keys and MD5/HMAC-128 authentication. 3DES-168 encryption. D-H Group 1 to generate SA keys. Compatible with the Cisco VPN 3000 Client. **IKE-DES-MD5**—Preshared keys and MD5/HMAC-128 authentication. DES-56 encryption. D-H Group 1 to generate SA keys. Compatible with the Cisco VPN 3000 Client. **IKE-3DES-MD5-DH7**—Preshared keys and MD5/HMAC-128 authentication. 3DES-168 encryption. D-H Group 7 (ECC) to generate SA keys. Intended for use with the Movian VPN client. This can also be used with any peer that supports ECC groups for D-H. **IKE-3DES-MD5-RSA**—RSA digital certificate and MD5/HMAC-128 authentication. 3DES-168 encryption. D-H Group 2 to generate SA keys. **IKE-AES128-SHA**—Preshared keys and SHA/HMAC-160 authentication. AES-128 encryption. D-H Group 2 or Group 5 to generate SA keys.

Filter	Use the drop-down menu to select a filter: **--None--**—No filter applied, no restrictions. (Default) **Private (Default)** —Allows all packets, except source-routed IP packets. (Default filter for the private Ethernet interface.) **Public (Default)** —Allow inbound and outbound tunneling protocols, plus ICMP and VRRP. Allow fragmented IP packets. Drop everything else, including source-routed packets. (Default filter for the public Ethernet interface.) **External (Default)** —No rules applied to this filter. Drop all packets. (Default filter for the external Ethernet interface.) Any user-defined filters also appear on the list.
IPSec NAT-T	Check the box to enable NAT-T for this LAN-to-LAN connection. See the LAN-to-LAN Networks with the NAT section for more details.

For the purposes of the scenario, the default settings are okay, but a descriptive connection name must be entered. For the Main Office, this might be as simple as toTacoma, while the branch office might use toMainOffice or TakeMeHome.

Peer addresses must be added to define the peer public interface. On the Main Office, this would be 1.10.1.1, while the branch office would enter 1.1.1.1.

The same Preshared Key must be entered on both sides. The longer and more complex, the less likely it will be compromised. An example might be cZ987hgy943.

The remaining choices: Authentication, Encryption, IKE Proposal, Filter, and IPSec NAT-T must be the same on both peers.

Bandwidth Policy	Use the drop-down list to select a bandwidth policy for this IPSec LAN-to-LAN connection. Select None for no bandwidth policy.
Routing	VPN Concentrator offers two ways to share static LAN-to-LAN routes. **Reverse Route Injection (RRI)** = The local VPN Concentrator adds the addresses of one or more remote networks to its route table and advertises these routes to networks on the local LAN. To use this option, specify the following Local and Remote Network parameters and enable RIP or OSPF routing on the private interface. **Network Autodiscovery** = This feature dynamically discovers and continuously updates the private network addresses on each side of the LAN-to-LAN link. This feature uses RIP by enabling Inbound RIP RIPv2/v1 on the Ethernet 1 (Private) interface of both Concentrators. To use this option, skip the following Local and Remote Network parameters. **None** = Don't advertise static LAN-to-LAN routes.
Local Network	Entries in this section identify the private network(s) on *this* device. The hosts of these LANs can use the LAN-to-LAN connection. The entries must match the Remote Network section on the peer Concentrator. With LAN-to-LAN NAT rule, these are the translated network addresses.
Network List	Use the drop-down list to choose a configured network list that specifies the local network addresses. If you choose a network list, the Manager ignores entries in the IP Address and Wildcard Mask fields.
IP Address	The IP address of the private local network on this VPN Concentrator.

Wildcard Mask	The wildcard mask for the private local network, that is, 0.0.255.255. The system supplies the default wildcard mask for the IP address class.
Remote Network	Entries in this section identify the private network(s) on *this* device. The hosts of these LANs can use the LAN-to-LAN connection. The entries must match the Local Network section on the peer Concentrator. With LAN-to-LAN NAT rule, these are the translated network addresses.
Network List	Use the drop-down list to choose a configured network list that specifies the remote network addresses. If you choose a network list, the Manager ignores entries in the IP Address and Wildcard Mask fields.
IP Address	The IP address of the private remote network on this VPN Concentrator.
Wildcard Mask	The wildcard mask for the private remote network, that is, 0.0.255.255. The system supplies the default wildcard mask for the IP address class.

In the scenario, you would choose the appropriate named lists for the Local (Main Office) and Remote (Tacoma Office) networks.

Once the Apply button is pressed, the Configuration | Policy Management | Traffic Management | Security Associations screen can be used to see a list of the defined IPSec SAs. In the scenario, toTacoma would appear in the list for the Main Office.

No Public Interfaces

The Configuration | System | Tunneling Protocols | IPSec | LAN-to-LAN | No Public Interfaces screen is displayed if a public interface isn't configured on the VPN Concentrator and you try to add an IPSec LAN-to-LAN connection. The public interface needn't be enabled, but it must have an IP address and the Public Interface parameter enabled. Only one VPN Concentrator interface should designate as a public interface.

LAN-to-LAN Networks with Digital Certificates

Ordering, enrolling, and installing digital certificates using SCEP was covered in Chapter 14. Once the certificates are installed, two modifications can be made to use the certificates. These modifications should be done in the following order:

1. Use the Manager navigation to locate the Configuration | System | Tunneling Protocols IPSec | IKE Proposals screen to choose the IKE proposal to be updated to use digital certificates, and then click the Modify button. The Configuration | System | Tunneling Protocols IPSec | IKE Proposals | Modify screen, as shown in Figure 16-11, can be used to update the Authentication Mode to use digital certificates.
2. Use the Configuration | System | Tunneling Protocols | IPSec | LAN-to-LAN screen to modify the existing IPSec LAN-to-LAN connection between the two VPN Concentrators. By selecting the appropriate connection (toTacoma) and clicking the Modify button, the Configuration | System | Tunneling Protocols | IPSec | LAN-to-LAN | Modify screen, previously shown in Figure 16-9, can be used to modify the LAN-to-LAN connection IPSec SA to support the digital certificate.

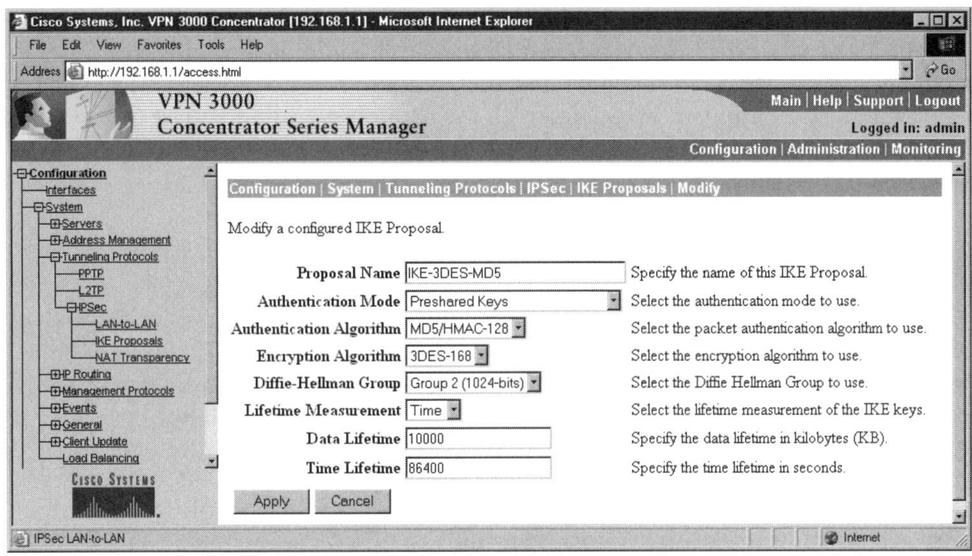

Figure 16-11 Update the Authentication mode to use digital certificates

The digital certificates drop-down list can be used to select the installed certificate. Then choose between Entire certificate chain or Identity certificate only. Choosing Entire certificate chain sends the identity certificate and all issuing certificates, including the root and any subordinate CA certificates. Choosing Identity certificate sends the peer only the identity certificate.

NAT Issues

Chapter 5 covered the various forms of NAT and the implementation for routers. NAT is also used on PIX firewalls, as covered in Chapters 17, 18, and 19. *NAT* is the process of altering the IP header of a packet, so the source local address of the internal host is replaced in the header by real global addresses. In some cases, the destination address might also be modified. This swapping process is performed by a NAT device, usually on the network perimeter. The NAT server then maintains a table of the translations, which allows returning packets to be addressed with the correct internal address.

Static NAT involves permanent, one-to-one address translations. This implementation is typically reserved for devices that must be accessed from the outside, such as shared servers. Dynamic NAT involves temporary address translations to allow inside hosts—often with private IP addresses—to use global addresses, while connecting with the outside world. While NAT works well, it can require a large number of global addresses, often at some monthly cost, to meet the needs of a large number of inside hosts that require global "real" addresses.

Port Address Translation (PAT) involves allowing multiple inside hosts to connect to the outside or to use the Internet as a vehicle to reach a corporate network, while using a single IP address. This one-to-many translation is accomplished by the NAT/PAT device using unique port numbers associated with the IP address to differentiate the sessions. The problem is IPSec won't work with PAT. The next few sections explore Cisco's solutions to this problem.

NAT Transparency

The IPSec NAT Transparency feature deals with the many known incompatibilities among NAT and IPSec. Before IPSec NAT Transparency, a standard IPSec VPN tunnel would fail if one or more devices were implementing NAT or PAT anywhere in the delivery path. The various forms of this feature make NAT IPSec-aware, making it possible for remote access users to use secure IPSec tunnels to home gateways.

The Configuration | System | Tunneling Protocols | IPSec | NAT Transparency screen, shown in Figure 16-12, makes configuring NAT Transparency possible. NAT transparency can take any of the three following forms:

- IPSec over TCP
- IPSec over NAT Traversal (NAT-T)
- IPSec over UDP

The *VPN Concentrator* series of devices can simultaneously support VPN tunnels using standard IPSec, IPSec over TCP, NAT-Traversal, and IPSec over UDP, depending on the requirements of the client with which it's exchanging data. The *VPN 3002 hardware client,* while supporting only one tunnel at a time, can also connect VPN tunnels using

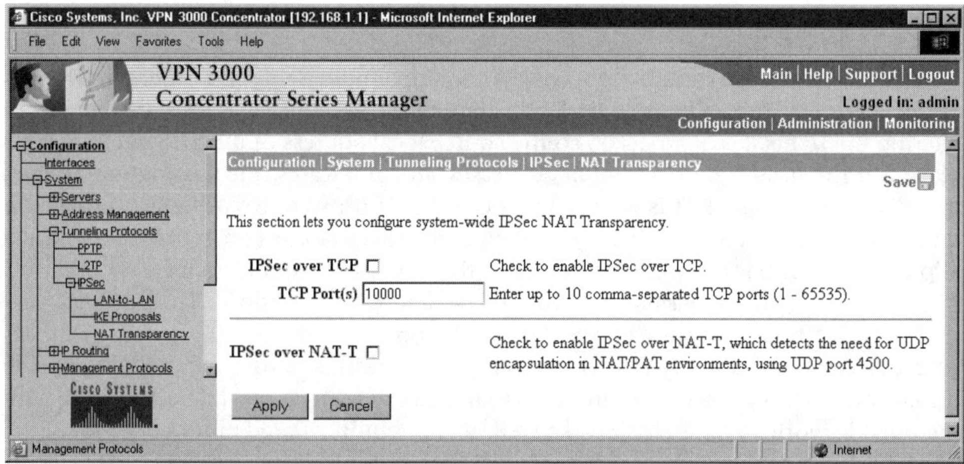

Figure 16-12 Configuring IPSec NAT Transparency

standard IPSec, IPSec over TCP, NAT-Traversal, or IPSec over UDP. The order of precedence is as follows:

- When enabled, IPSec over TCP takes precedence over all other IPSec implementations.
- When both NAT-T and IPSec over UDP are enabled, NAT-T takes precedence.

Figure 16-13 shows the VPN Client software properties screen used to set the features. If TCP is selected, the port number box would be enabled.

IPSec over TCP

IPSec over TCP allows VPN clients to operate in networks where standard ESP (Protocol 50) or IKE (UDP 500) can't operate because the ports are blocked or they can only function by modifying the existing firewall rules. IPSec over TCP enables secure tunneling through both NAT and PAT devices, as well as firewalls by encapsulating both the IKE and IPSec protocols within TCP packets.

IPSec over TCP is a client-to-Concentrator feature, which supports both the VPN software client and the VPN 3002 hardware client. It doesn't work for LAN-to-LAN connections. IPSec over TCP works only on the public interface of the VPN devices. To use IPSec over TCP, both the VPN Concentrator and the client must do the following:

- Run version 3.5 or later of the VPN software.

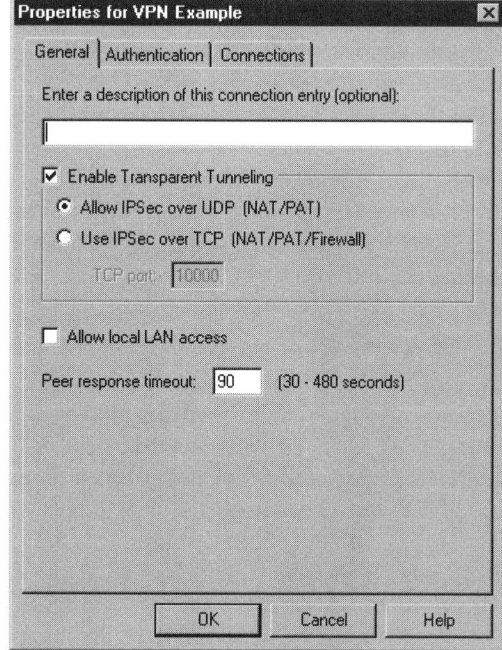

Figure 16-13 Configuring NAT Transparency on the client software

PART III

- Enable IPSec over TCP.
- Configure both the VPN client and the VPN Concentrator to use the same port for IPSec over TCP.

NOTE IPSec over TCP doesn't work with proxy-based firewalls.

Configuring IPSec over TCP on the Concentrator

Use the Configuration | System | Tunneling Protocols | IPSec | NAT Transparency screen shown in the previous Figure 16-12:

1. Check the IPSec over TCP box to enable the feature.
2. Configure up to ten TCP ports, using a comma to separate the ports. Each client configuration must include at least one of the ports you set for the VPN Concentrator. The default port is 10,000. Technically, the range is 1 to 65,635, but ports 0–1,023 were assigned. Other frequently used port numbers exist above that as well. Avoid these numbers to avoid conflicts with the other applications.

The VPN client software or client device must be configured to support the feature (IPSec over TCP (NAT/PAT) Tunnel Encapsulation mode) and selected TCP port number.

NOTE IPSec over TCP is a TCP encapsulation, rather than a true full TCP connection. In VPN software versions prior to 3.6.7.B, the VPN Concentrator didn't implement window size to limit data transmission, resulting in stateful firewalls that sometimes shut down the TCP session. With version 3.6.7.B and later, the VPN Concentrator enforces a 64K window size on the connection to avoid this connection shutdown.

The downside is this: with some large data transfers, packet loss is possible. Because the VPN Concentrator doesn't retransmit dropped packets, the peer application must detect the dropping and recover from it. UDP streaming applications, such as video or voice, might notice choppy transmission.

IPSec over NAT-T

NAT Traversal (NAT-T) allows IPSec peers to establish a connection through a device using NAT. NAT-T accomplishes this by encapsulating IPSec traffic in UDP datagrams, thereby providing NAT devices with needed port information. NAT-T technology autodetects any NAT devices and only encapsulates IPSec traffic when necessary.

The VPN 3002 hardware client uses NAT-T by default and requires no special configuration. The remote-access VPN client first attempts NAT-T, and then, if a NAT device is not autodetected, uses IPSec over UDP. The UDP packets allow IPSec traffic to pass through firewalls that would normally reject and discard it.

To use NAT-T, both the VPN Client and the VPN hardware device must meet the following requirements:

- Run version 3.6 or later software.
- Port 4500 on any firewall and routers between the VPN device and the VPN peer must be open.
- Reconfigure any existing IPSec over UDP using port 4500 to a different port.
- Use the Configuration | Interfaces | Public (3002) or Configuration | Interfaces | Ethernet (Concentrators) screen to select the second or third options for the Fragmentation Policy parameter. These options let traffic travel across NAT devices that don't support IP fragmentation, while not impeding NAT devices that do support IP fragmentation.
- On the Concentrator, use the Configuration | System | Tunneling Protocols | IPSec | NAT Transparency screen, as shown in the previous Figure 16-12, to check the IPSec over NAT-T box to enable the feature.
- In LAN-to-LAN implementations, to enable IPSec over NAT-T on the VPN Concentrator, use the Configuration | System | Tunneling Protocols | IPSec | LAN-to-LAN | Add screen to check the IPSec NAT-T box. The previous Figure 16-9 showed the check box.

VPN Concentrator implementations of NAT-T support IPSec peers behind a single NAT/PAT device, under the following limitations:

- One LAN-to-LAN connection
- Either a single LAN-to-LAN connection or multiple remote access clients, but not a mixture of both
- One Microsoft L2TP/IPSec client, which can support other remote access clients and one L2TP/IPSec client

IPSec over UDP

The VPN client supports UDP NAT/Firewall Transparent IPSec. This technology encapsulates encrypted data traffic within UDP packets to provide secure connections between a VPN client and a VPN Concentrator through a device, such as a firewall performing NAT.

The VPN 3002 uses frequent keepalives to ensure the mappings on the NAT device remain active. The VPN 3002 doesn't require special configuration for this feature, but the following minimum requirements must be met:

- Both the VPN client and the VPN Concentrator must be running Release 3.0.3 or higher.
- IPSec over UDP must be enabled on the VPN Concentrator for the group to which the VPN client belongs. Figure 16-14 shows the Configuration | User Management | Base Group screen used to make the feature a default. If the feature isn't on by default, the Configuration | User Management | Group screen could be used for a specific group.

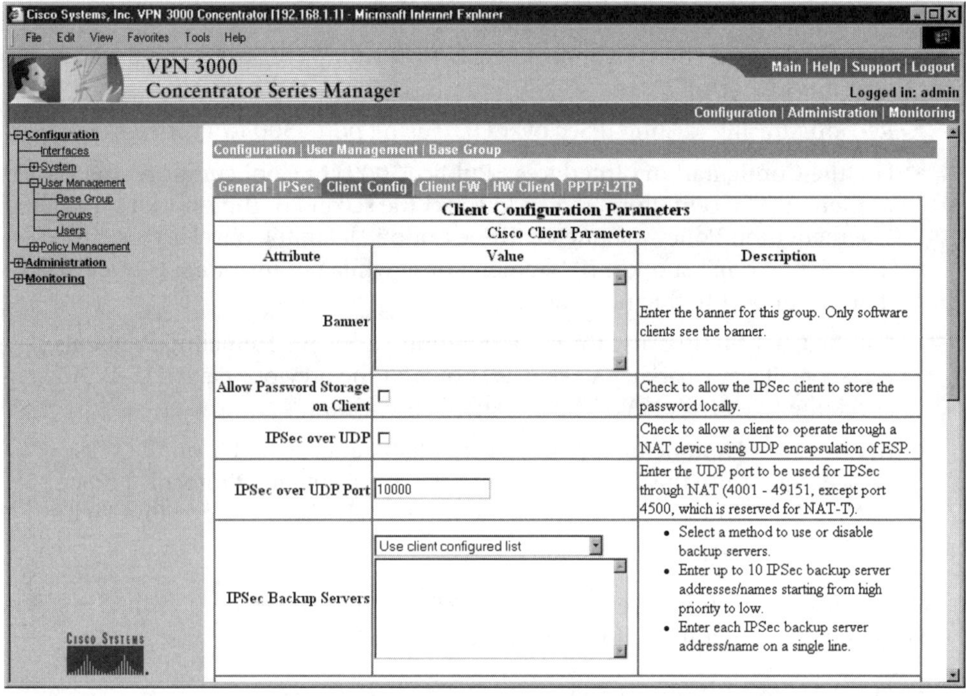

Figure 16-14 Configuring IPSec over UDP on the Concentrator

LAN-to-LAN VPN with Overlapping Network Addresses

One of the problems that can be encountered when two firms merge, business partnerships form, or a business extends its network to a vendor is the possibility of overlapping (duplicated) private IP addresses. This section looks at how to configure a VPN Concentrator in a LAN-to-LAN IPSec VPN with overlapping network addresses. The VPN 3000 Concentrator version 3.6 software introduced the enhanced NAT feature that can translate the overlapping networks on each side of the IPSec VPN tunnel.

Figure 16-15 shows the example scenario. The addresses within the clouds are the local addresses, while the addresses below the clouds represent the new translated addresses. Because Dynamic and PAT implementations are only usable for outgoing connections, the translations will have to be static to allow each network's host to send traffic into the other network.

Use the following steps to configure the VPN 3000 Concentrator for the Main Office:

1. Use the Configuration | System | Tunneling Protocols | IPSec | LAN-to-LAN | Add screen to configure the LAN-to-LAN session parameters for a LAN-to-LAN

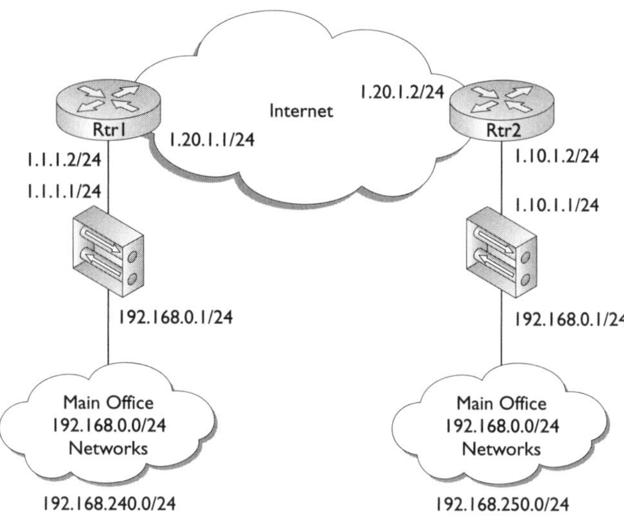

Figure 16-15 Overlapping network address scenario

VPN. Figure 16-16 show the Local and Remote Network fields.

In the Local Network section, enter **192.168.240.0** in the IP Address field

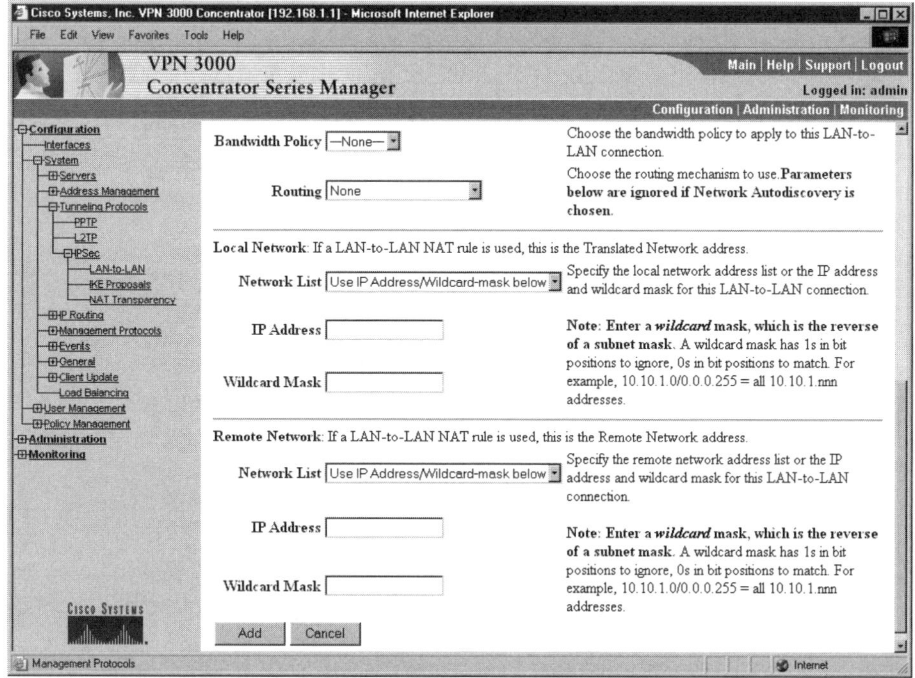

Figure 16-16 Configuring the local and remote networks

and enter **0.0.0.255** in Wildcard Mask field.
In the Remote Network section, enter **192.168.250.0** in the IP Address field and enter **0.0.0.255** in Wildcard Mask field.
Click on Apply when finished.
The Vendor Concentrator would be a mirror image of these entries.

2. Use the Configuration | Policy Management | Traffic Management | NAT | LAN-to-LAN Rules | Modify screen, as shown in Figure 16-17, to define the static NAT translations for the Main Office LAN.
Check the Static option button in the NAT Type section.
Make the following entries in the bottom of the Window, and then click Apply.

	Source Network	Translated Network	Remote Network
IP Address row	192.168.0.0	192.168.240.0	192.168.250.0
Wildcard Mask	0.0.0.255	0.0.0.255	0.0.0.255

The Vendor Concentrator entries would look like this:

	Source Network	Translated Network	Remote Network
IP Address row	192.168.0.0	192.168.250.0	192.168.240.0
Wildcard Mask	0.0.0.255	0.0.0.255	0.0.0.255

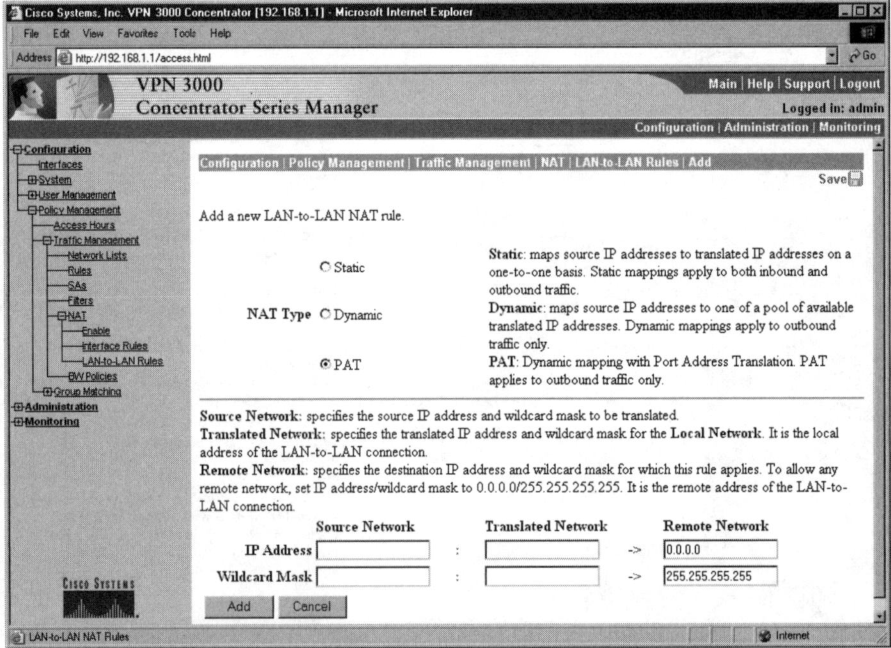

Figure 16-17 Defining the translations

3. Use the Configuration | Policy Management | Traffic Management | NAT | Enable screen, as shown in Figure 16-18, to enable the NAT.
   Check the LAN-to-LAN Tunnel NAT Rule Enabled check box.
   Click Apply.
   The Vendor Concentrator entry would be the same.

LAN-to-LAN Routing

In LAN-to-LAN VPN implementations, VPN Concentrators typically connect to the public network through a perimeter router, which then routes the data traffic through additional routers to the destination Concentrator. Except for small corporate networks, the Concentrator is also connected to the private network through a router.

To share routing information actively with neighbor devices, the VPN Concentrator includes an IP routing subsystem supporting static routing, as well as RIP and OSPF routing protocols. The routing subsystem uses the following order of precedence in selecting routes:

1. Learned routes (RIP and OSPF)
2. Static routes
3. Default gateway (default static route)

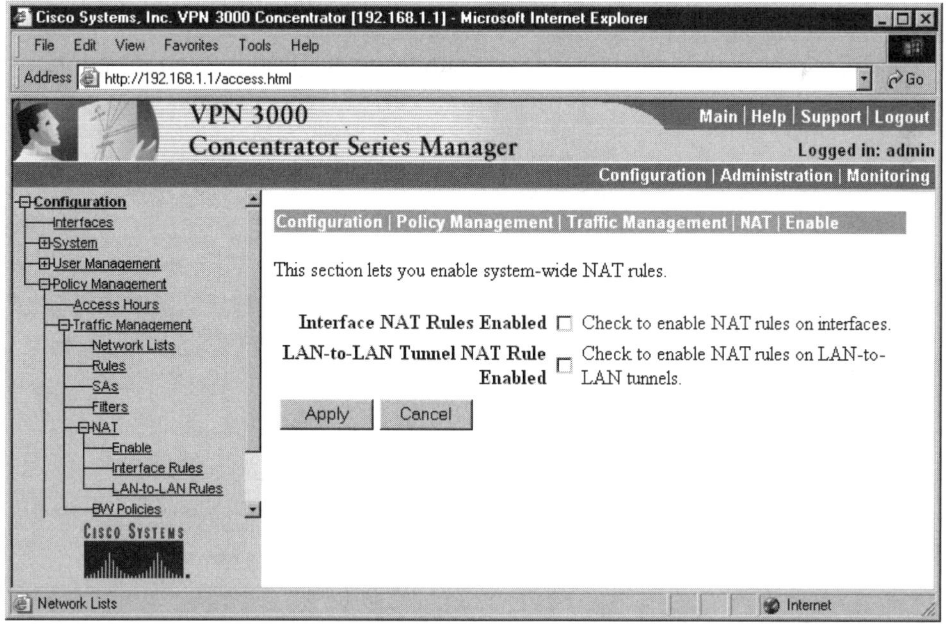

Figure 16-18 LAN-to-LAN Tunnel NAT Rule enabled

PART III

Without a configured default gateway, packets without specific entries in the route table are dropped. The default gateway provides a path of last resort for packets with unrecognized network addresses. The Concentrator has a separate tunnel default gateway for tunneled traffic only.

The Configuration | System | IP Routing screen system is used to configure the following system-wide IP routing options:

- Static Routes—Manually configured routing table entries.
- Default Gateways—Route of last resort for otherwise unroutable traffic.
- OSPF—Open Shortest Path First routing protocol.
- OSPF Areas—Define OSPF areas within the OSPF domain.
- DHCP—Define global parameters for DHCP Proxy and DHCP relay.
- Redundancy—Define Virtual Router Redundancy Protocol (VRRP) parameters.
- Reverse Route Injection—Define reverse route injection (RRI) global parameters.

Adding and modifying static routes were covered in Chapter 14. This section discusses some of the other choices.

Default Gateways

Use the Configuration | System | IP Routing | Default Gateways screen, as shown in Figure 16-19, to define the default gateway for IP routing for non-VPN traffic, as well as to define the tunnel default gateway for VPN traffic.

The *Default Gateway* address box would typically be the IP address on the public network of the near-side interface of the perimeter router. This address can't be the same as any VPN Concentrator interface.

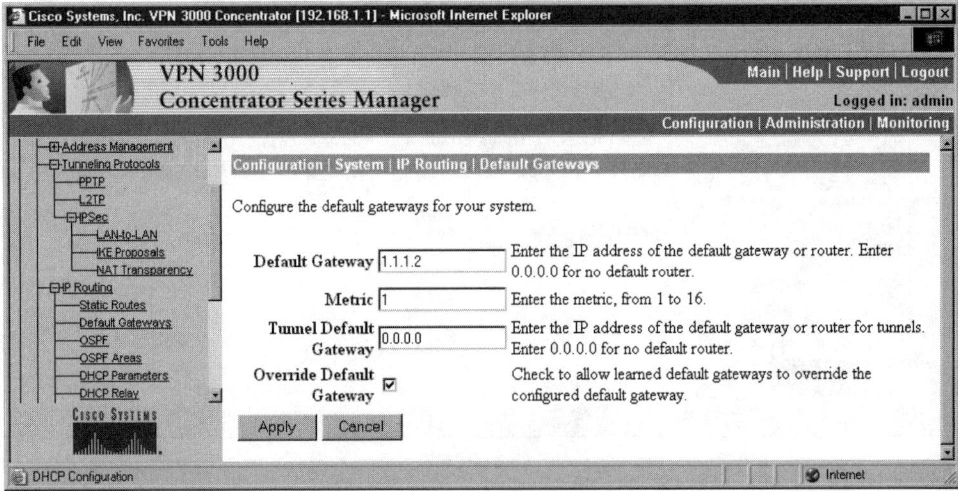

Figure 16-19 Configuring the default gateway

The *Tunnel Default Gateway* address box would typically be a firewall in parallel with the VPN Concentrator, and between the public and private networks. The tunnel default gateway applies to all tunneled traffic, including IPSec LAN-to-LAN traffic. If an external device other than the VPN Concentrator is performing NAT, then the tunnel default gateway must be configured.

Check the Override Default Gateway option box to allow default gateways learned via RIP or OSPF to override the configured default gateway.

Reverse Route Injection

Reverse route injection (RRI) is a feature that allows the VPN Concentrator to add static routes to its routing table, and then to share these routes with routers connected to the private and/or public network using OSPF or RIP. Use the Configuration | System | IP Routing | Reverse Route Injection screen, as shown in Figure 16-20, to configure RRI features. RRI options vary with the type of VPN connection:

- LAN-to-LAN connections—Use the Configuration | System | Tunneling Protocols | IPSec LAN-to-LAN | Add or Modify screen covered earlier in this chapter.
- VPN Software Clients or VPN 3002 Hardware Clients using Client (PAT) mode: *Individual remote access clients*—enable the Client Reverse Route Injection option. *Group remote access clients*—add an entry in the Address Pool Hold Down Routes box.

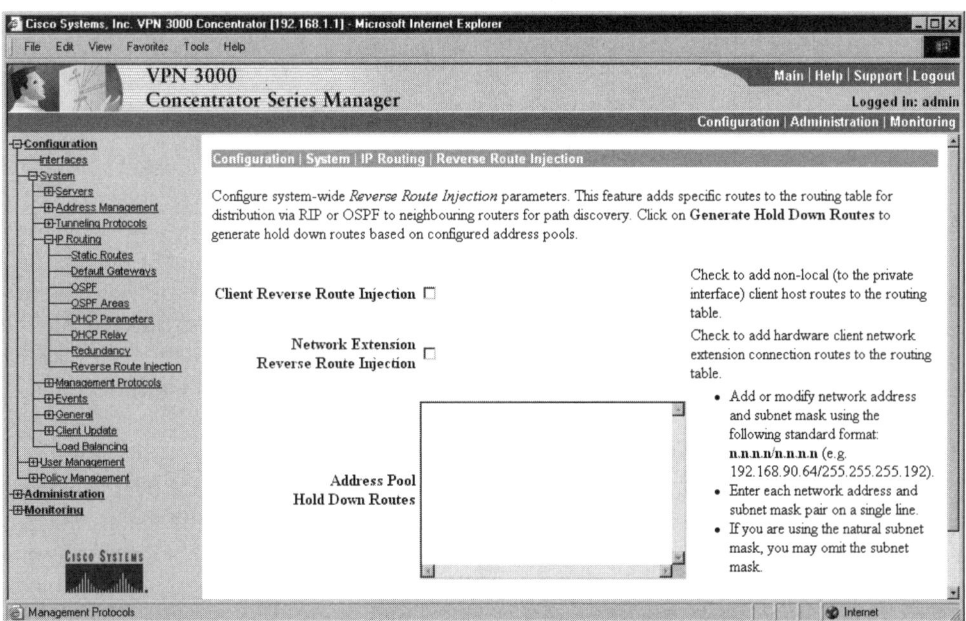

Figure 16-20 RRI configuration screen

- VPN 3002 Hardware Clients using Network Extension mode (NEM) —enable the Network Extension Reverse Route Injection option.

Client Reverse Route Injection	For individual VPN software clients and VPN 3002 hardware clients in Client (PAT) mode. To add host routes for each remote client to the VPN Concentrator routing table. The Concentrator adds the host route when the client connects and deletes it when the client disconnects. Unchecked by default.
Network Extension Reverse Route Injection	For VPN 3002 hardware clients using Network Extension mode only. To add a route for each network behind the VPN 3002 hardware client to the VPN Concentrator routing table. The Concentrator adds the route when the VPN 3002 connects and deletes the route when it disconnects. Unchecked by default.
Address Pool Hold Down Routes	For all VPN software clients and VPN 3002 hardware clients in Client (PAT) mode. This feature ensures that routes remain in the route table, even though the link to the remote client might be inactive—no traffic. Without it, the route would be flushed from all route tables and become unreachable until the client triggered another session. Enter any hold-down routes to be added to the VPN Concentrator routing table. Routes can be entered automatically or manually. To generate a list of hold-down routes automatically, based on currently configured address pools, click the Generate Hold Down Routes button. The list can be edited. To enter routes manually, use the n.n.n.n/m.m.m.m format, for example, 192.168.10.0/255.255.255.0. Put each network address/subnet mask pair on a single line. If Client Reverse Route Injection is also checked, when a remote client connects to the VPN Concentrator, the VPN Concentrator checks first to see if the client address falls in any of the address pool routes listed here. If not, the VPN Concentrator adds the client's route to the routing table.

Advertising the Routes Locally

If you don't want the VPN Concentrator to advertise learned routes to the private network, disable routing on the private interface. To advertise the learned routes to the private network, enable OSPF or RIP on the Concentrator private interface using the Configuration | Interfaces | Ethernet 1 2 3 screen, RIP, or OSPF tabs screen. Figure 16-21 shows the RIP configuration screen. Notice OSPF is another tab on the same screen.

Virtual Router Redundancy Protocol

Virtual Router Redundancy Protocol (VRRP) provides automatic switchover (failover) from one VPN Concentrator to another in a redundant Concentrator installation. This feature ensures users have access to the VPN, even if the primary VPN Concentrator is out of service. VRRP requires two or more VPN Concentrators be in parallel, where one VPN Concentrator is the master system and all others are backup systems. The backup device remains idle unless the active VPN Concentrator fails, so the backup device can't be configured to enable load balancing.

VRRP supports user access via IPSec LAN-to-LAN connections, IPSec client (single-user remote-access) connections, and PPTP client connections.

- **IPSec LAN-to-LAN**—Switchover is fully automatic and typically takes three to ten seconds.
- **Single-User IPSec and PPTP**—Users are disconnected from the failed device, but they can reconnect without changing any settings.

Before configuring or enabling VRRP:

- All Ethernet interfaces that apply to the installation on all redundant VPN Concentrators must be configured. Use the Configuration | Interfaces screens. VRRP can't be used if the VPN Concentrator interfaces are configured as DHCP clients. Use static IP addressing with VRRP.
- Identical IPSec LAN-to-LAN parameters must be configured on the redundant VPN Concentrators. Use the Configuration | System | Tunneling Protocols | IPSec LAN-to-LAN screens.

Interface Failures

If either the public or private interface on the master system goes down in a VRRP implementation, the other interfaces shut down automatically, triggering the backup VPN device to take over. The backup VPN device monitors VRRP messages from the master

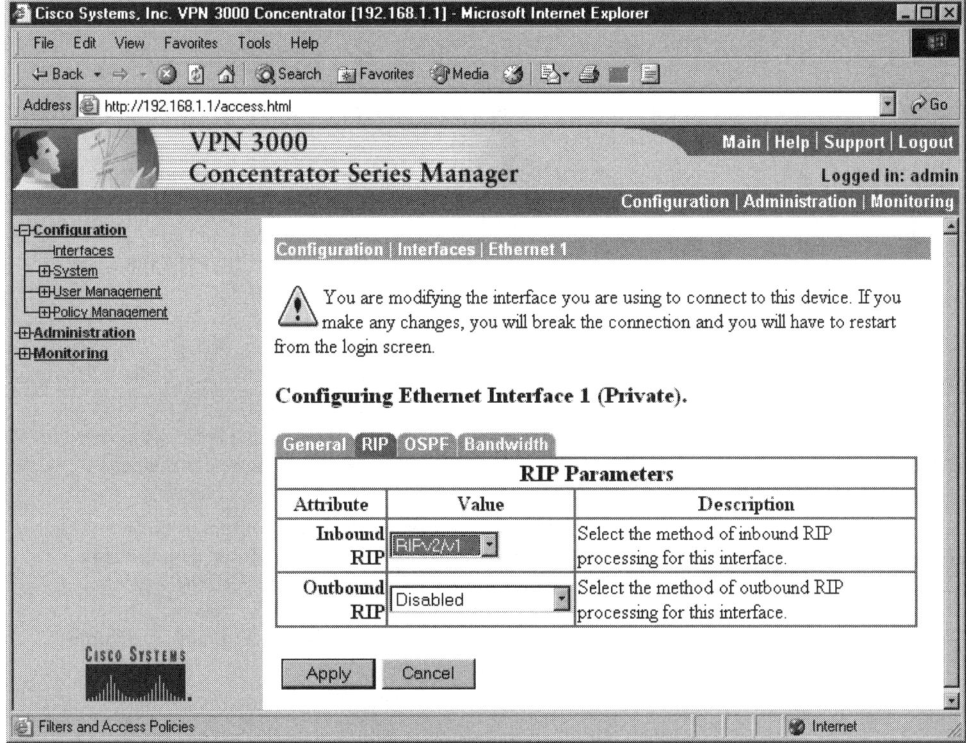

Figure 16-21 Enabling RIP on the private interface

system on both the public and private interfaces. If the backup VPN device stops receiving the messages from the master system, the backup will automatically take over the master system responsibilities.

The VPN Concentrators monitor the interface connections at the link level, so some types of failure might not be detected. If a router or switch fails on a network connecting the master and backup units, the master unit might not detect the failure at the link level. As long as the link layer remains up, the master doesn't detect the interface as "down" and, therefore, doesn't stop sending VRRP messages to the backup device on all its interfaces. Because the backup device still hears VRRP messages on at least one interface, it doesn't take over as the master.

Spanning-Tree Issue

A second issue pertains to the delay (45+ seconds) Spanning-Tree Protocol (STP) introduces when a switch interface changes from down to up status. Enable the Portfast feature on STP-enabled switch ports that are connected to a VRRP implementation. This reduces the delay to 15 seconds.

Configuring VRRP

Use the Configuration | System | IP Routing | Redundancy screen to configure the VRRP parameters, as shown in Figure 16-22.

Enable VRRP	Check to enable VRRP functions. Unchecked by default.
Group ID	A unique number that identifies the group of redundant VPN Concentrators. Must be the same on all systems in the group. Range is 1 to 255. Default is 1.
Group Password	Enter a password for additional security in identifying group devices. Must be the same on all systems in the group. Maximum length is eight characters. Password is displayed and transmitted as Cleartext. Default is no password.
Role	Drop-down menu button to choose the role of this VPN Concentrator. Master—Master system in the group (the default). Configure only one Master in each group (Group ID). Backup 1 through Backup 5—Backup system in the group.
Advertisement Interval	Time interval in seconds between VRRP advertisements to other systems in this group. Range is 1 to 255 seconds. Default is 1. Only the Master system sends advertisements, so this field is ignored on Backup systems while they remain backups. Because a backup can become a Master system, consider the default for all systems.
Group Shared Addresses	Enter the IP addresses to be used by all virtual routers in the group. The Manager displays only the previously configured Ethernet interfaces. *On the Master system*—Entries are the IP addresses configured on its Ethernet interfaces. The Manager supplies them by default. *On a Backup system*—Fields are empty by default and must match the addresses used on the Master system.
1 (Private)	IP address for Ethernet 1 (Private) interface—same on all devices.
2 (Public)	IP address for Ethernet 2 (Public) interface—same on all devices.
3 (External)	IP address for Ethernet 3 (External) interface—same on all devices.

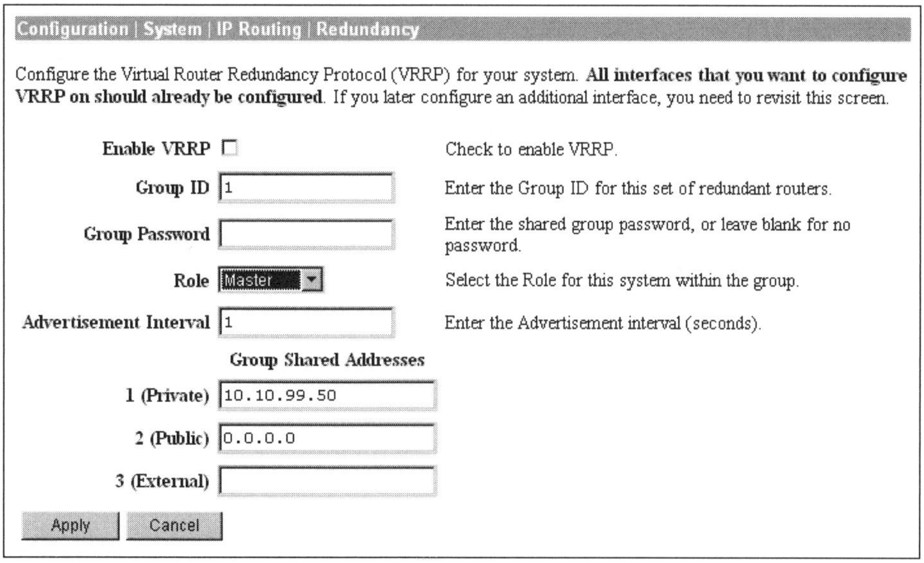

Configuration | System | IP Routing | Redundancy

Configure the Virtual Router Redundancy Protocol (VRRP) for your system. **All interfaces that you want to configure VRRP on should already be configured.** If you later configure an additional interface, you need to revisit this screen.

Enable VRRP	☐	Check to enable VRRP.
Group ID	1	Enter the Group ID for this set of redundant routers.
Group Password		Enter the shared group password, or leave blank for no password.
Role	Master	Select the Role for this system within the group.
Advertisement Interval	1	Enter the Advertisement interval (seconds).
	Group Shared Addresses	
1 (Private)	10.10.99.50	
2 (Public)	0.0.0.0	
3 (External)		

Apply | Cancel

Figure 16-22 Configuring VRRP

Chapter Review

This chapter looked at using Cisco VPN 3000 Series Concentrator devices in LAN-to-LAN VPN implementations. The VPN Concentrator works as an endpoint device in these implementations. While the peer device can be a router, PIX firewall, Cisco VPN 3002 hardware client, or third-party VPN device, this chapter and the features that will be tested on the exam assume Cisco VPN Concentrators will be on both ends of the link.

LAN-to-LAN (site-to-site) VPNs are a rapidly expanding alternative or augmentation to leased line or Frame Relay WAN infrastructures. VPNs are used to create secure tunnels between two networks via an insecure public network, such as the Internet. The Cisco Concentrator supports three types of tunnels: Layer 2 Tunneling Protocol (L2TP), Point-to-Point Tunneling Protocol (PPTP), and IPSec.

Two types of LAN-to-LAN VPN implementations exist.

- Intranet VPNs provide secure connections between branch offices to the enterprise network resources.
- Extranet VPNs provide secure connections for special third parties, such as business partners, vendors, and customers to the specified enterprise resources.

The Concentrator menu-driven system is used to configure basic LAN-to-LAN VPN parameters, as well as to enable and define features like NAT Transparency and VPN routing features, such as reverse route injection (RRI) and Virtual Router Redundancy Protocol (VRRP).

Questions

1. Which one of the following tunnel protocols is *not* supported on Cisco Concentrators?
   A. Layer 2 Tunneling Protocol (L2TP)
   B. Point-to-Point Tunneling Protocol (PPTP)
   C. IP Security (IPSec)
   D. Layer 2 Forwarding (L2F)
2. Which three ports must be open on the entire data path for standard IPSec VPNs?
   A. Protocol 50
   B. Protocol 55
   C. Protocol 51
   D. UDP 500
3. Assuming LAN-to-LAN Network Lists are used, how many lists would a remote branch have in a hub-and-spoke topology?
   A. 1
   B. 2
   C. 1 for each spoke, plus one for the hub
   D. None
4. Which is an example of a valid Network List entry?
   A. 192.168.10.0/255.255.255.0
   B. 192.168.10.0/24
   C. 192.168.10.0/0.0.0.255
   D. 192.168.10.0-192.168.10.255
5. How many LAN-to-LAN connections can be created with each VPN peer?
   A. 1
   B. 100
   C. 500
   D. 1000
6. What is the maximum total number of LAN-to-LAN connections supported on the VPN 3060 Concentrator?
   A. 100
   B. 500
   C. 700
   D. 1000

7. If the Configuration | System | Tunneling Protocols | IPSec | LAN-to-LAN | No Public Interfaces message is displayed, which statement is false?
   A. You can configure the public interface
   B. The LAN-to-LAN connection failed
   C. You need to go to the Configure | Interfaces screen
   D. The LAN-to-LAN connection must be redone
8. Which is *not* an IPSec NAT Transparency feature?
   A. IPSec over TCP
   B. IPSec over PPP
   C. IPSec over UDP
   D. IPSec over NAT Traversal
9. Which statement is *not* true about IPSec over TCP?
   A. It supports both VPN Software Client and VPN 3002 Device
   B. Requires v3.5 or higher of the VPN software
   C. It takes precedence over all other IPSec implementations
   D. Supports LAN-to-LAN connections
10. Which version of the VPN software is required to support NAT Traversal?
   A. 3.2
   B. 3.5
   C. 3.6
   D. 3.7
11. What is the default port for IPSec over TCP?
   A. 520
   B. 4500
   C. 6300
   D. 10000
12. Which of the following could be used to create a LAN-to-LAN VPN connection between two networks with overlapping IP addresses?
   A. NAT one LAN so they are no longer overlapping
   B. Use PAT on the link
   C. NAT both LANs
   D. Renumber one or both LANs

13. Which Concentrator feature allows the VPN Concentrator to add static routes to its routing table, and then to share those routes with connected routers?
    A. Route autodiscovery
    B. VRRP
    C. RRP
    D. RRI
14. Which of the following causes the Concentrator to retain routing table entries that might otherwise be dropped because of link inactivity?
    A. Client Reverse Route Injection
    B. Address Pool Hold Down Routes
    C. Network Extension Reverse Route Injection
    D. Generate Hold Down Routes
15. Which feature provides failover protection for VPN Concentrator users?
    A. Route autodiscovery
    B. VRRP
    C. RRP
    D. RRI

Answers

1. **D.** Layer 2 Forwarding (L2F)
2. **A.** Protocol 50, **C.** Protocol 51, and **D.** UDP 500
3. **B.** 2
4. **C.** 192.168.10.0/0.0.0.255
5. **A.** 1
6. **D.** 1000
7. **C.** You need to go to the Configure | Interfaces screen
8. **B.** IPSec over PPP
9. **D.** Supports LAN-to-LAN connections
10. **C.** 3.6
11. **D.** 10000
12. **C.** NAT both LANs
13. **D.** RRI
14. **B.** Address Pool Hold Down Routes
15. **B.** VRRP

PART IV

PIX Firewalls

CHAPTER 17

CiscoSecure PIX Firewalls

In this chapter, you will learn how to:

- Recognize firewall and firewall security systems
- Discuss the Cisco Secure PIX Firewall products and technology
- Use basic PIX Firewall configuration commands

In this chapter, you will explore the CiscoSecure Private Internet Exchange (PIX) Firewall device or appliance. In the preceding chapter, you learned about the CiscoSecure IOS Firewall feature set that runs on a router. While both perform similar functions in similar ways, they're related in much the same way as a general practitioner and a heart surgeon. Both are doctors, but one has advanced skills developed in a specialty area, and that one works exclusively in that area of specialization.

The CiscoSecure IOS Firewall feature set could well meet the needs in many environments or situations; but when a full-time dedicated security barrier is required, the PIX Firewall device might be the answer.

This chapter looks at the key components of the PIX Firewall device features, and it compares the functionality and limitations to the IOS Firewall feature set.

Firewall and Firewall Security Systems

A *firewall* is, by definition, a system of one or more devices developed to implement the access control policy of the network. Firewalls can be implemented in hardware devices, software features, or a combination of both. In the simplest scenario, a firewall could be the access router running a firewall feature set for a telecommuter, home user, small business network, or smaller branch office when they connect to the Internet. Router and firewall features are often built into the devices used to connect to DSL or cable services.

In larger implementations, the firewall might refer to multiple devices and technologies working together to protect the organization from the outside world, and within the network to provide internal security for specific network segments. As you learned in the preceding two chapters, even protecting a single perimeter connection often includes two or more devices working together to provide multiple layers of defense. This avoids the single point of failure that might expose the organization's digital resources to catastrophic losses.

While a single device might be a firewall, it could also be just a part of a larger system that is the firewall. For clarity, using the terms "firewall device" and "firewall system" might be helpful. A *firewall device* could be a router running a firewall feature set, in addition to its other activities, or it could be a dedicated appliance like a PIX box.

Whether working between Internet users and an organization's internal networks or providing internal security within the company network, firewalls examine all messages passing through and blocks those that don't meet the specified security criteria. For our purposes, we can divide firewall techniques into three categories:

- Packet filter
- Stateful packet filter
- Proxy server

In practice, many firewalls incorporate two or more of these techniques.

Packet Filter

Packet filters are access control lists that look at each packet entering or leaving the network. They accept or reject the packet, based on user-defined rules. As you saw earlier, ACLs can base these decisions on any or all of the following criteria:

- Source IP address
- Destination IP address
- Protocol
- Source port
- Destination port

Packet filtering can be fairly effective and is generally transparent to users. While recognizing the usefulness of ACL Layer 3 and Layer 4 filtering in many cases, it's important to recognize the following limitations in a situation where you might consider relying exclusively on them.

- Because application layer information isn't used or stored, each new packet session must be fully tested.
- Without stateful capabilities, ACLs can't deal with port number changes or multiple session channels required by some applications.
- Fragmented packets will be forwarded, even if the initial packet was denied, thus allowing certain types of DoS attacks.
- Complex ACLs can be difficult to configure and implement.
- ACLs can be susceptible to IP address spoofing.

Proxy Filter

A proxy server stands between the internal network and the outside networks. An internal user wanting to browse a web site creates a session with the proxy server that typically requires authentication. This connection to the proxy might or might not be invisible to the internal user. The proxy can then compare the requested destination URL and/or IP address against a list of blocked sites. Assuming the site isn't on the blocked list, the proxy then establishes a session with the destination. The proxy continues to work as a relay between the user and the outside world. Then, the proxy can apply application layer filtering against any packets. This hides the internal user from the external site and affords a level of content protection. This enhanced screening comes at the cost of reduced end-to-end performance.

Other features some proxies can provide include storing downloaded content, which can then be forwarded to the next interested user. This creates a perception of faster network performance and reduces traffic across WAN links (caching). Many proxies can create detailed access logs, making it possible for network administrators to review and add URLs to the blocked list.

Common problems in using proxy filtering include the following:

- Slower end-to-end performance on true connections to the outside.
- Because proxies are typically servers, any vulnerabilities inherent in that server operating system (OS) could be well known to hackers and easily exploited.
- A proxy can provide a single point of failure, effectively blocking access to the outside world.

Stateful Packet Filter

Stateful packet filtering systems provide a best-of-both-worlds solution that offers greater performance and reduced exposure to attack. By storing complete session state information for each session based on Layer 3, Layer 4, and application layer information, the device can provide more intelligent filtering than packet filters and faster performance than proxy filters.

PIX devices use stateful packet filtering to establish and secure TCP and UDP connections, as well as many common applications. This stateful decision-making allows PIX devices to deal with port number changes or multiple session channels required by some applications.

CiscoSecure PIX Firewall Technology

The *Cisco Secure PIX Firewall series,* formerly *PIX Firewall,* is the top of the firewall product line within the Cisco firewall family, offering high-performance, enterprise-class implementations. The PIX-integrated hardware/software strategy provides high security with minimal impact on network performance. The Cisco Secure PIX Firewall series is both a key component of the Cisco end-to-end security strategy and a leader in the firewall market.

Key features of the Cisco Secure PIX Firewall Series include the following:

- **Non-UNIX, secure, real-time, embedded system** A single-purpose–built firewall appliance that uses a proprietary, hardened OS, which eliminates security risks associated with general purpose OSs. By not having to compromise to support other server services and features, Cisco Secure PIX Firewall series can deliver superior performance of up to 500,000 simultaneous connections and nearly 1.7 Gigabits per second (Gbps) aggregate throughput, dramatically greater than any UNIX-based firewall.
- **Adaptive Security Algorithm (ASA)** *ASA* is a stateful, connection-oriented technology, which is less complex and more robust than ACL-based packet filtering while offering higher performance and better scalability than proxy firewalls. ASA creates and maintains extensive state tables of session flows that include source and destination addresses, randomized TCP sequence numbers, port numbers, and additional TCP flags. To be considered part of an "established" session, traffic must be consistent with these connection table entries.
- **Cut-through proxy** Using CiscoSecure Access Control Server (ACS) this patent- pending method of authentication and authorization offers improved performance advantages over other systems.
- **PIX Firewall Manager** This Java-based, graphical user interface (GUI) configuration tool provides centralized configuration and management of firewall security policies. The tool can provide configuration information common to all system PIX Firewalls, built-in per-user accounting reports showing web sites visited and volume of files transferred, and automatic real-time alerts using e-mail or pager notification for any attempts to breach the firewall.
- **Standards-based VPN support** The PIX Firewall IPSec encryption card is easily installed in the user PC and provides easy-to-use connections for mobile users and remote sites to the corporate network over the Internet or other public IP networks. Triple DES (3DES)–based VPN throughput can be scaled to nearly 100 Mbps using the PIX VPN Accelerator Card (VAC), which offloads CPU-intensive encryption/decryption processes to specialized cryptographic coprocessors.
- **URL filtering** *URL filtering* uses NetPartners WebSENSE software to check outgoing URL requests against the policy defined on a local WebSENSE server (Windows or UNIX). Any connection requests matching web-site characteristics defined as inappropriate are denied. PIX Firewall performance isn't impacted because the filtering is performed on a separate server.
- **Failover/hot standby** Two PIX Firewalls running in parallel provide redundancy both for failure of the primary firewall and during system maintenance or upgrades. Network traffic can be automatically sent to a hot standby unit in case of a failure, while maintaining concurrent connections via automated state synchronization between the primary and standby units.

STUDY TIP Technology changes and improvements come out all the time, so be less concerned with feature details, such as maximum throughput and numbers of interfaces. From a practical standpoint, recognize that in the field, some features might not be implemented on earlier OS versions or device models.

PIX Adaptive Security Algorithm

The key to Cisco Secure Firewall technology is the ASA. Like other stateful technologies, ASA stores key information from outgoing packets, which are then used to screen returning packets. As with others, source and destination addresses and port information are stored, but then randomized TCP sequence numbers are generated and, together, are encrypted into a "signature" used to evaluate new packets. These randomized TCP sequence numbers make hacking considerably more difficult than the often-sequential incrimination used by most systems. These random-sequence numbers and encryption create a secure stateful connection system that's both efficient and fast.

No inbound traffic is allowed unless specifically accepted as part of an existing flow in the state table, or included in a conduit or access list definition. For example, all inbound ICMP packets are blocked unless specifically permitted by the **conduit permit icmp** command.

ASA Security Levels

PIX routers have two or more interfaces, each assigned a security level. Basic PIX ASA operation allows data to travel freely from interfaces with higher security values to interfaces with lower security values. Any two interfaces should have a security level difference that defines the natural flow of data. Data can't flow from a lower security to a higher value, unless a specifically configured static tunnel or conduit is created.

STUDY TIP PIX Firewall releases since 5.1.2 use access lists, instead of static and conduit commands. While this is fine for the Advanced PIX exam, the MCNS exam still includes questions that refer to these earlier commands.

The range of security levels is 0 to 100, with 100 as the most trusted and, therefore, reserved for the inside interface. The lowest trust level is 0, which is reserved for the outside interface. With 0 security level, any hosts accessing the network via the outside interface require explicit permission; otherwise, they'll be rejected. On the simplest two-interface firewall, the inside interface would be assigned a security value of 100 by default, while the outside interface would be assigned 0.

Security levels 1 to 99 are used for protected DMZ interfaces. If the PIX device has a single protected DMZ interface, the security level would be configured between the inside and outside levels, such as 50. Figure 17-1 shows the interfaces just described. With this setting, packets originating from the inside interface could flow to the DMZ. DMZ packets could reply to inside requests, but couldn't originate new traffic to the inside without static tunnels, conduit, or access lists being created. DMZ originating packets can travel to the outside, which is handy for servers, such as e-mail and DNS servers, which must periodically communicate with the outside world. With multiple-protected DMZ interfaces, planning the security-level assignments to make sure security flows properly is important. Two DMZ interfaces with the same security level wouldn't allow

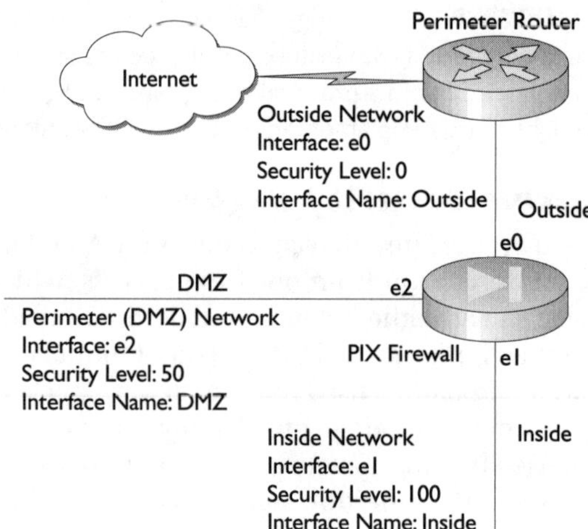

Figure 17-1 PIX security levels with a DMZ interface

flows between them, except with special configuration. Traffic only flows from high- to low-security level without assistance.

The PIX Firewall device using ASA technology and NAT features while working in tandem with a properly configured perimeter router can create an impenetrable barrier to attacks from the outside world.

The PIX Firewall Family

Cisco PIX 500 Series Firewalls security appliances are famous for high levels of security, performance, and reliability. These devices provide a solid package of security services, including stateful firewall inspection, standards-based IPSec VPN, intrusion protection, and much more in several platforms to meet the needs of the smallest office to the largest enterprise.

The following material identifies the target audience for each of the platforms with feature and performance indicators gleaned from current Cisco marketing materials.

NOTE It's important to understand that the actual features and capacities might be dependent on hardware configurations and, more important, the software licensing purchased. Just as with its routers, Cisco offers various software licenses that support certain features and possibly performance enhancements. As with network OSs, the price typically goes up with increased services and the number of users or connections supported. Also like other OSs, router and firewall software licenses are subject to audit and antipiracy enforcement.

Cisco PIX 535 Firewall

The latest and biggest PIX model—the 535—is designed for the largest Enterprise and Service Provider implementations, providing over 1 Gbps of firewall throughput, plus the capability to handle up to 500,000 concurrent connections. Some PIX 535 models include stateful high-availability capabilities, as well as integrated hardware acceleration for VPN, providing up to 95 Mbps of 3DES VPN and support for 2,000 IPSec tunnels. The PIX 535 is a modular chassis with support for up to 10 10/100 Fast Ethernet interfaces or 9 Gigabit Ethernet interfaces.

Cisco PIX 525 Firewall

The 525 was designed for Enterprise and Service Provider environments, providing over 360 Mbps of firewall throughput, plus the capability to handle up to 280,000 concurrent connections. Some PIX 525 models include stateful high-availability capabilities, as well as integrated hardware acceleration for VPN, providing up to 70 Mbps of 3DES VPN and support for 2,000 IPSec tunnels. The PIX 525 is a modular chassis with support for up to eight 10/100 Fast Ethernet interfaces or 3 Gigabit Ethernet interfaces.

Cisco PIX 515E Firewall

The latest version of the 515 platform is the 515E, where the *E* stands for enhanced services. The 515s were designed for small-to-medium business and enterprise environments, providing up to 188 Mbps of firewall throughput with the capability to handle as many as 125,000 simultaneous sessions. Some PIX 515E models include stateful high-availability capabilities, as well as integrated support for 2,000 IPSec tunnels. The PIX 515E is a modular chassis with support for up to six 10/100 Fast Ethernet interfaces.

Cisco PIX 506E Firewall

Another *E* series improvement—the 506E—was designed for branch office implementations, providing up to 20 Mbps of firewall throughput and 16 Mbps of 3DES VPN throughput. The PIX 506E is a fixed interface desktop unit with two autosensing 10 Mbps RJ-45 interfaces. The 506E model has two optional encryption software license options (168-bit 3DES and 56-bit DES), available either at purchase time or as an upgrade.

Cisco PIX 501 Firewall

The 501 was designed for the telecommuter or small office, providing up to 10 Mbps of firewall throughput and 3 Mbps of 3DES VPN throughput. The PIX 501 is a full-fledged member of the PIX family supporting state-of-the-art security with plug-and-play simplicity. The PIX 501 is a fixed interface desktop unit with one 10 Mbps interface for the outside and an integrated 4-port Fast Ethernet (10/100) switch for inside use. The optional software licenses for the 501 include the following:

10-user license	Supports up to ten concurrent source IP addresses from the internal network to pass through the PIX 501, plus DHCP server support for up to 32 internal users.
50-user license	Supports up to 50 concurrent source IP addresses from the internal network to pass through the PIX 501, plus DHCP server support for up to 128 DHCP leases. Additional 10-to-50 user upgrade licenses are also available.
3DES and DES licenses	Two optional encryption licenses (168-bit 3DES and 56-bit DES) are available either at purchase time or as an upgrade.

The following model information is intended to demonstrate this diversity rather than to imply any test objective. As with any rapidly changing technology, going to the Cisco web site is always best—http://www.cisco.com—and either select products or perform a search on PIX Firewalls to see the latest offerings and technical specifications. The current offerings are summarized in the following table:

Models	501	506E	515E	525	535
Processor	133 MHz	300 MHz	433 MHz	600 MHz	1 GHz
RAM	16MB	32MB	32MB or 64MB	128MB or 256MB	512MB or 1GB
Flash	8MB	8MB	16MB	16MB	16MB
PCI slots	None	None	2	3	9
Fixed int.	**	2 10Mb	2 10/100Mb	2 10/100Mb	None
Maximum interfaces	**	2 10Mb	6 10/100Mb	8 10/100Mb or Gb	10 10/100Mb or Gb
VAC*	No	No	Yes	Yes	Yes
Failover	No	No	Yes, UR only	Yes, UR only	Yes, UR only
Connections	3,500	400	125,000	280,000	500,000

*VPN Accelerator Card (VAC) support
**1 10Mb (outside) and a four-port 10/100Mb switch (inside)

In addition, several earlier PIX models still exist, including the Classic, 10000, 510, and 520 protecting networks around the world. Full documentation for each is on the Cisco web site, and, while most can be upgraded to support newer features, the latest features often aren't supported because of hardware limitations.

Interface Modules

The larger PIX models, beginning with the 515, allow additional interface modules for creating additional connections. These modules can include a single RJ-45 or fiberoptic interface, or up to four RJ-45 interfaces. You need to check the current Cisco documentation to verify support for specific modules and to see which slots they can occupy. Slot placement will also impact interface designations. The PIX 535, with nine slots connecting to three different buses at two different speeds, requires special attention.

While PIX 520 and higher devices can support Token Ring and FDDI interfaces, as well as 10/100 Mbps Ethernet, the PIX OS version 5.3 is the last to support these aging technologies. The 525 and 535 devices also support Gbps.

Restricted (R) Software License

The larger PIX models, beginning with the 515, offer a lower cost, reduced-connections model, called a Restricted model, with a product notation like PIX 515E-*R*. Typically the *R* models support fewer connections and interfaces, and contain less memory.

Unrestricted (UR) Software License

The larger PIX models, beginning with the 515, offer Unrestricted models with a product notation like PIX 515E-*UR*. Typically, the *UR* models support more connections and interfaces, contain more memory, and support expanded capabilities, such as stateful failover.

Failover (FO) Software License

The larger PIX models, beginning with the 515, offer Failover models with a product notation like PIX 515E-*FO*. These units are stateful failover units designed for use with a same platform unrestricted (UR) device. With the same hardware configuration as the Cisco PIX UR unit, the FO unit operates in Hot Standby mode, acting as a complete redundant system that maintains current sessions. The discount pricing for the failover units provides a highly cost-effective, high-availability solution.

EXAM TIP The exam covers only the 515 and larger devices; but because the OS and the commands are the same, don't overlook the 501 and 506 units as lower-cost units on which to practice basic commands.

Tested and Certified

PIX Firewalls provide high levels of security. They've been tested and certified to meet certain levels of quality, reliability, and trustworthiness by the leading security organizations, including TruSecure's ICSA Firewall and IPSec certification, and the independent Common Criteria Evaluation Assurance's EAL4 rating. The Common Criteria EAL4 certification requires in-depth analysis of product design and development methodology, backed by extensive testing.

The Common Criteria for Information Technology Security Evaluation (CCITSE) is a set of evaluation criteria agreed to by the United States National Security Agency/National Institute of Standards and Technologies, and equivalent bodies in 13 other countries. The organization's role is to resolve the technical and conceptual differences in existing standards for the evaluation of security systems and products. Common Criteria version 2.1 recently became an international standard—ISO 15408.

PIX Firewalls support a wide range of security and networking services, including Network Address Translation (NAT), Port Address Translation (PAT), DHCP client and server, AAA (both TACACS+ and RADIUS) integration, content filtering (Java/ActiveX), URL filtering, PPP over Ethernet (PPPoE), and Public-Key Infrastructure X.509. PIX Firewall devices support security services for multimedia applications and protocols, including Voice over IP (VoIP), H.323, SIP, Skinny, and Microsoft NetMeeting to allow organizations to securely implement next-generation converged network technologies.

VPN Support

PIX Firewall support enables users to extend their networks safely with secure VPNs to include telecommuters, branch offices, and even trade or industry partners, vendors, and suppliers. PIX Firewalls support a wide range of remote access VPN clients, including

Cisco software VPN clients (available for Windows 95/98/NT/2000/ME/XP, Linux, Solaris UltraSparc-32bit, and Apple Macintosh OS X) and Cisco hardware VPN clients (such as the VPN 3002), as well as PPTP and L2TP clients found within Microsoft Windows OSs.

PIX Management Options

PIX Firewall devices support Cisco's familiar command-line interface (CLI) using access methods including Telnet, Secure Shell (SSH), and an out-of-band console port. While not identical to the router CLI, the differences represent no greater challenge than those encountered when working with Cisco switches.

Administrators can choose from a variety of other solutions for remotely configuring, monitoring, and troubleshooting PIX Firewall devices. These solutions range from an integrated, web-based management interface (PIX Device Manager) to centralized, policy-based management tools. The PIX devices support remote monitoring protocols, such as Simple Network Management Protocol (SNMP) and support Syslog logging features.

Cisco PIX Device Manager (PDM) features an easy-to-use GUI and the capability to provide real-time and historical reports on use trends, performance baselines, and security events. PDM is covered in detail in Chapter 22.

Cisco Mobile Office Support

The PIX Firewall Series supports the Cisco Mobile Office strategy to extend the corporate network by offering high bandwidth and complete access through both wired and wireless solutions. The three components of the Cisco Mobile Office include On The Road, At Home, and At Work. Together, they help to create a network that's secure, flexible, highly manageable, and scalable, and that increases productivity.

For more information, go to http://www.cisco.com/go/mobileoffice.

Cisco Catalyst 6500 Implementation

Cisco has introduced a PIX Firewall implementation—the Firewall Services Module (FWSM)—bringing firewall protection services to the Catalyst 6500 family of IP switches that already support intrusion detection and VPNs, along with multilayer LAN, WAN, and MAN switching capabilities. The FWSM is completely VLAN-aware, offers dynamic routing, and is a fully integrated module within the Cisco Catalyst 6500 Series switches.

FWSM is based on Cisco PIX Firewall technology and, therefore, offers the same security and reliability as the PIX security appliances. In addition, the FWSM capitalizes on the strengths of the Catalyst system to create the industry's highest-performance firewall solution, providing 5GB of throughput per module and scaling to 20GB of bandwidth with multiple modules. The module is based on network processor technology, allowing feature enhancements via software download.

Basic PIX Firewall Configuration

In working with the PIX Firewall device, using the CLI is common because of its similarities to the CLI in Cisco routers and switches. The alternatives include two graphical interface tools: the PIX Firewall Manager (PFM) and the PIX Device Manager (PDM). PFM is the older of the two and is being retired.

The CLI commands are introduced and used in this section.

PIC Command-Line Interface

While similar to the IOS command set, the PIX are somewhat different. You might assume these differences will become less noticeable over time as Cisco moves toward an IOS interface for more and more devices. As with the IOS, it's necessary to be in the correct mode. The four PIX modes are the following:

Unprivileged mode	Like the User mode on the router, this is the first level in accessing a PIX Firewall. This is also called the User EXEC mode and offers a limited set of commands, none of which can change the configuration. The > symbol at the end of the prompt indicates Unprivileged mode. Prompt: **Pixfirewall>**
Privileged mode	Allows the user to change settings and access the Configuration mode. Use the **enable** command to get to this mode, and use **disable**, **exit**, or **quit** to return to the Unprivileged mode. All Unprivileged mode commands have a counterpart in this mode. The # symbol at the end of the prompt indicates Privileged mode. Prompt: **Pixfirewall#**
Configuration mode	Allows configuration changes. All Unprivileged and Privileged mode commands have a counterpart in this mode. Unlike the routers, returning to Privilege mode to see the results of configuration changes is unnecessary. The (config)# at the end of the prompt indicates Configuration mode. Prompt: **Pixfirewall(config)#**
Monitor mode	PIX devices that don't have an internal floppy drive come with a ROM boot monitor program, which is used for upgrading the PIX Firewall's image. Prompt: **Monitor>**

PIX commands can be abbreviated, much like the IOS counterparts; but because of the command differences, the abbreviation might be different. For example, most routers require **config t** to change to Configuration mode, while **co t** will work on the firewall.

The following basic commands are important to know when you start to work with the PIX CLI. While many should be familiar, always be on the lookout for differences.

configure memory	Merges the current configuration with that in Flash memory (startup config). Note, this doesn't replace the copy in Flash, but merges with it.
configure net	Merges a configuration from a TFTP server and the path you specify into the current configuration.

PART IV

enable password	Changes the Privileged (**enablc)** Mode password. This password is encrypted by default. If no Privileged Mode password is set, press ENTER at the Password prompt. To restore the enable password (press ENTER at prompt), type the following: Pixfirewall#**enable password**.
passwd	Sets password for Telnet access to the PIX Firewall console (Privileged mode). The default is **cisco**. Passwords can be up to 16 characters. The **clear passwd** command resets the password back to cisco.
show configure	Displays Flash (startup) configuration on the terminal.
show history	Displays the previously entered commands, same as with routers.
show ip address	Displays the IP addresses that are assigned to interfaces.
show xlate	Displays current translations and connection slot information. Similar in concept to displaying the NAT translations.
write erase	Erases the configuration stored in Flash (startup config).
write floppy	Stores the current configuration on diskette for models with floppy. Not supported by current models. Floppy disk must be in DOS format.
write memory	Stores the current configuration in Flash memory, along with the activation key value and timestamp for when the configuration was last modified. Replaces the existing saved configuration.
write ***server_ip***	Specifies the IP address of the TFTP server. If you specify the full path and filename in the tftp-server command, then use a ":" in the **write** command.
write standby	Writes the current configuration to the failover standby PIX unit from RAM to RAM. This occurs automatically when the Active PIX boots up.
write terminal	Displays current configuration on the terminal.

Commands that are close enough to their IOS counterparts not to present serious problems include the following if you have trouble with abbreviations or optional parameters, the ? help feature works the same as in the IOS.

- host name
- ping
- reload
- show interface
- show version

The next sections look at the basic commands required to configure a PIX Firewall device.

The nameif Command

The **nameif** command can be used to assign a name to an interface if more than two network interfaces are in the PIX Firewall. The first two interfaces are named inside and outside by default. The inside interface has a default security level of 100, while the outside interface has a default security level of 0. The **clear nameif** command restores default interface names and security levels. The syntax is

nameif *hardware_id if_name security_level*
clear nameif

hardware_id	Specifies the interface type and location on the PIX device. Like the interface designations on routers, the names can be spelled out or abbreviated, such as Ethernet 0 or e0.
if_name	Interface names can be up to 48 characters long, but then they must be used for all configuration references. So keep them short and easy to remember. Defaults: e1 is named **inside**, e0 is named **outside**, and any perimeter interface **intf*n*** where *n* is 2 through 5.
security_level	

The following example shows the use of the **nameif** command:

```
Pixfirewall(config)#nameif ethernet2 dmz1 sec50
Pixfirewall(config)#nameif ethernet3 dmz2 sec25
```

The inside interface can't be renamed or given a different security level. You can rename the outside interface, but you can't change the security level. After changing an interface name, use the **clear xlate** command.

The show nameif Command

To displays interface names, use the **show nameif** command. The syntax is

show nameif

The interface Command

Use the **interface** command to define the speed and duplex settings of the network interface boards. After changing an interface command, use the **clear xlate** command. The syntax is

interface *hardware_id* [*hardware_speed*] [shutdown]

PART IV

hardware_id	Specifies the interface type and location on the PIX device. Names can be spelled out or abbreviated, such as Ethernet 0 or e0.
hardware_speed	Network interface speed (optional). Possible Ethernet values include 10baset—10 Mbps Ethernet half-duplex 10full—10 Mbps Ethernet full-duplex 100basetx—100 Mbps Ethernet half-duplex 100full—100 Mbps Ethernet full-duplex 1000sxfull—1000 Mbps Gigabit Ethernet full-duplex 1000basesx—1000 Mbps Gigabit Ethernet half-duplex **1000auto**—1000 Mbps Gigabit Ethernet to autonegotiate full- or half-duplex aui—10 for Mbps Ethernet half-duplex with an AUI cable interface **auto**—Set Ethernet speed automatically bnc—10 Mbps Ethernet half-duplex with a BNC cable interface
shutdown	Disable an interface.

NOTE The previous auto keyword options aren't recommended because of a lack of standards among vendors. Even though the default is the **interface *hardware_id* auto** command, specifying the speed of the network interfaces lets the PIX Firewall operate in network environments, which might include switches or other devices that don't handle autosensing correctly.

The shutdown Option

The *shutdown* option disables the interface. When installing a PIX Firewall, all interfaces are shut down by default. Interfaces must be explicitly enabled by using the command without the shutdown option.

The show interface Command

To display detailed interface information, including the packet-drop count of Unicast RPF for each interface and buffer counters for Ethernet interfaces, use the **show interface** command. The **clear interface** command clears all interface statistics, except the number of input bytes. The command works with all interface types, except Gigabit Ethernet. This command no longer shuts down all system interfaces. The syntax for both commands is

show interface *hardware_id* [*hardware_speed*] [shutdown]
clear interface

```
Pixfirewall#show interface
interface ethernet0 "outside" is up, line protocol is up
 Hardware is i82559 ethernet, address is 00aa.0000.003b
 IP address 209.165.201.7, subnet mask 255.255.255.224
 MTU 1500 bytes, BW 100000 Kbit half duplex
        1184342 packets input, 1222298001 bytes, 0 no buffer
        Received 26 broadcasts, 27 runts, 0 giants
        4 input errors, 0 CRC, 4 frame, 0 overrun, 0 ignored, 0 abort
        1310091 packets output, 547097270 bytes, 0 underruns, 0 unicast rpf drops
        0 output errors, 28075 collisions, 0 interface resets
        0 babbles, 0 late collisions, 117573 deferred
```

```
0 lost carrier, 0 no carrier
input queue (curr/max blocks): hardware (128/128) software (0/1)
output queue (curr/max blocks): hardware (0/2) software (0/1)
```

The ip address Command

The default address for an interface is 127.0.0.1. Use the **ip address** command to assign an IP address to each interface. If you make a mistake, reenter the command with the correct information. After changing an **ip address** command, use the **clear xlate** command. The syntax is

ip address *if_name ip_address* [*netmask*]

if_name	The internal or external interface name designated by the **nameif** command
ip_address	PIX Firewall unit's network interface IP address
netmask	Network mask of *ip_address*

If a *netmask* isn't specified, PIX Firewall assigns one of the following default classful network masks based on the IP address.

- Class A—255.0.0.0
- Class B—255.255.0.0
- Class C—255.255.255.0

NOTE If you're using subnets, the best policy is to specify a network mask with this command. Otherwise, it's possible that PIX using the classful mask could see another address you want to use as being a part of a previously defined network and prevent you from using it.

The show ip Command

To IP addresses on each interface, use the **show ip** command. The following is sample output from the **show ip** command:

```
Pixfirewall#show ip
System IP Addresses:
        ip address outside 209.165.201.2 255.255.255.224
        ip address inside 192.168.2.1 255.255.255.0
        ip address perimeter 192.168.70.3 255.255.255.0
Current IP Addresses:
        ip address outside 209.165.201.2 255.255.255.224
        ip address inside 192.168.2.1 255.255.255.0
        ip address perimeter 192.168.70.3 255.255.255.0
```

The nat Command

NAT allows the network to have any IP addressing scheme, including private addresses, and the PIX Firewall hides these addresses from visibility on the external network. While

PART IV

the implementation is different, the purpose and result are much the same as NAT covered in Chapter 6. With address translation, when a host starts an outbound connection, the IP addresses of the internal network are translated into global addresses, which will be seen by the outside world. The syntax is

nat (*if_name*) *nat_id local_ip* [*netmask*]

if_name	The internal network interface name.
nat_id	The ID number to match with the global address pool.
local_ip	Internal network IP address to be translated. You can use 0.0.0.0 to allow all hosts to start outbound connections. The 0.0.0.0 *local_ip* can be abbreviated as 0.
netmask	Network mask for *local_ip*. You can use 0.0.0.0 to allow all outbound connections to translate with IP addresses from the global pool. The netmask 0.0.0.0 can be abbreviated as 0.

In the following example, the **nat** command statement allows all the hosts on the 192.168.1.0 network to start outbound connections. The default netmask is being used. The nat_id 1 is a pool of global addresses created by the **global** command, in the next section.

```
Pixfirewall(config)#nat (inside) 1 192.168.1.0
```

In the next example, all internal users can use the 1 global address pool to start outbound connections.

```
Pixfirewall(config)#nat (inside) 1 0 0
```

The show nat and show xlate Commands

The **show nat** command displays the **nat** command statements in the current configuration. Use the **show xlate** command to view translation slot information. The **clear xlate** command would clear the translation table.

The following is sample output from the **show xlate** command with three active PATs:

```
Pixfirewall(config)#show xlate
3 in use, 3 most used
PAT Global 192.168.1.97(0) Local 172.16.205.49 ICMP id 340
PAT Global 192.168.1.97(1024) Local 172.16.205.49(1028)
PAT Global 192.168.1.97(1024) Local 172.16.205.49(516)
```

The global Command

Use the **configuration mode global** command to define a pool of global addresses. The global addresses in the pool provide an IP address for each outbound connection and for those inbound connections resulting from outbound connections. To use the global pool of addresses, the **nat** and **global** command statements must use the same **nat_id**. The PIX Firewall assigns the addresses from the beginning of the range (smallest address) to the largest.

The **global** command can't use names with a dash (-) in them because the dash is used by the command to indicate a range of IP addresses. After changing or removing a **global** command statement, use the **clear xlate** command. The syntax is

global (*if_name*) *nat_id* interface | *global_ip* [-*global_ip*] [netmask *global_mask*]

if_name	The external network where you use these global addresses.
nat_id	A positive integer shared with the **nat** command that links the **nat** and **global** command statements together. Valid ID numbers 1 to 2,147,483,647.
interface	Specifies PAT using the IP address of the interface.
global_ip	Single global IP address or the first in a range.
-global_ip	A range ending with *global_ip*.
netmask	(Optional) Reserved word that prefaces the network *global_mask* variable.
global_mask	(Optional) The network mask for *global_ip*.

If subnetting is used, specify a subnet mask; for example, 255.255.255.128 will specify one half of a class C network. If a specified address range in the *global_ip global_ip* overlaps subnets defined by the netmask *global_mask* statement, the global pool won't use any broadcast or network addresses included in the pool of global addresses.

For example, using the 255.255.255.128 and the 192.168.1.0 network would normally be used to define either the first half or the second half of the address pool 192.168.1.0 to 192.168.1.127 or 192.168.1.128 to 192.168.1.255. The following command seems correct.

```
global (outside) 1 192.168.1.0 - 192.168.1.127 netmask 255.255.255.128
```

The pool contains the network address 192.168.1.0 and the broadcast address 192.168.1.127. Both will be ignored by the pool. A better implementation of the command might be the following:

```
global (outside) 1 192.168.1.1 - 192.168.1.126 netmask 255.255.255.128
```

Using nat and global Commands Together

The following example specifies with **nat** command statements, which all the hosts on the 192.168.1.0 and 192.168.100.0 inside networks can use to start outbound connections. The global command statements create a pool of global addresses as follows:

```
nat (inside) 1 192.168.1.0 255.255.255.0
global (outside) 1 1.1.1.1-1.1.1.30 netmask 255.255.255.224
global (outside) 1 215.4.61.0

nat (inside) 3 192.168.100.0 255.255.255.0
global (outside) 3 1.1.11.15-1.1.11.27 netmask 255.255.255.224
```

The show global Command

To display the range of global addresses, use the **show global** command.

The route Command

Use the configuration mode **route** command to define a default or a static route for an interface. To define a default route, set *ip_address* and *netmask* both to 0.0.0.0, or the shortened form of 0. All routes entered using the **route** command are stored in the configuration when it's saved. The **clear route** command removes route command statements that don't contain the **CONNECT** keyword from the configuration. The syntax is

route *if_name ip_address netmask gateway_ip* [*metric*]

if_name	The internal or external network interface name.
ip_address	The internal or external network IP address. Use 0.0.0.0 to specify a default route, which can be abbreviated as 0.
netmask	Specify a network mask to apply to *ip_address*. Use 0.0.0.0 to specify a default route, which can be abbreviated as 0.
gateway_ip	Specify the IP address of the gateway router (the next hop address for this route).
metric	Specify the number of hops to *gateway_ip*. The default is 1.

Static routes are conceptually the same as with the routers. Because PIX devices aren't routers per se, static and default static routes are used to direct packets to their destination. In this example, the PIX Firewall will send all packets destined to the 192.168.12.0 network to the 192.168.0.2 router with this static route statement.

```
Pixfirewall(config)#route dmz1 192.168.12.0 255.255.255.0 192.168.0.2 1
```

To define a default route for the outside interface, use the following command to direct all traffic to the 192.168.44.1 interface on the perimeter router.

```
Pixfirewall(config)#route outside 0 0 192.168.44.1 1
```

The show route Command

Use the **show route** command to confirm static and default route configuration.

Chapter Review

Firewall devices can be broken up into the following three basic types:

- Packet filter
- Stateful packet filter
- Proxy server

Most commercial firewalls incorporate two or more of these techniques. The Cisco PIX Firewall incorporates features from all three to become the heart of the Cisco security strategy.

Because particular models change, and features, such as CPU size, change frequently, using the Cisco web page to confirm or compare features is always best. For the same reason, it's important not simply to assume the features of a unit in the field. Basically, with the 500 series PIX devices, the larger the product number, the more powerful, the larger the throughput, and the higher the cost.

Basic PIX configuration commands are quite similar to those of the IOS-based devices. The PIX has four modes: Unprivileged, Privileged, Configuration, and Monitor. Moving among the first three is much like working with their counterparts on routers.

The six basic configuration commands you saw include the following (each also has a **show** command to confirm the configuration was successful).

- The **nameif** command
- The **interface** command
- The **ip address** command
- The **nat** command
- The **global** command
- The **route** command

Questions

1. True or False. A firewall is always a single device.
   A. True
   B. False
2. True or False. PIX Firewalls rely exclusively on packet filtering to provide security.
   A. True
   B. False
3. Which of the following is *not* one of the basic firewall types?
   A. Intrusion detection
   B. Proxy filter
   C. Packet filter
   D. Stateful packet filter
4. True or False. Packet filtering uses Layers 3 through 5 for filtering decisions.
   A. True
   B. False
5. What does the acronym ASA stand for? ______________

6. True or False. PIX Firewalls are built on reliable UNIX technology.
   A. True
   B. False
7. What is the default security level for the outside interface?
   A. 100
   B. 50
   C. 25
   D. 0
8. What is the default security level for the inside interface?
   A. 0
   B. 50
   C. 100
   D. 200
9. If DMZ1 has a security level of 50 and DMZ2 has a level of 70, which is true?
   A. Data will flow from DMZ1 to DMZ2.
   B. Data will flow from DMZ2 to DMZ1.
   C. Data will flow freely in both directions.
   D. Data never flows between DMZs.
10. Which is the more powerful PIX Firewall?
    A. PIX 501
    B. PIX 525
    C. PIX 535
    D. PIX 610
11. True or False. Data flows in both directions when two interfaces have the same security level.
    A. True
    B. False
12. Which command assigns the security level?
    A. **ip address**
    B. nat
    C. global
    D. nameif

13. True or False. The **interface** command sets both bandwidth and duplex.
    A. True
    B. False
14. What is the default IP address for PIX interfaces?
    A. There is none.
    B. 0.0.0.0
    C. 127.0.0.1
    D. 192.168.0.1
15. Which creates a pool of real IP addresses to be used by NAT?
    A. NAT
    B. Interface
    C. global
    D. route

Answers

1. B. False. A firewall can be an entire system of devices and services.
2. B. False. PIX devices use packet filtering, but they also use stateful filtering to incorporate application layer information.
3. A. Intrusion detection.
4. B. False. Packet filtering can use only Layers 3 and 4.
5. A. Adaptive Security Algorithm
6. B. False. PIX Firewalls use a proprietary OS.
7. D. 0
8. C. 100
9. B. Data will flow from DMZ2 to DMZ1.
10. C. PIX 535
11. B. False. Data won't flow without help.
12. D. nameif
13. A. True
14. C. 127.0.0.1
15. C. global

CHAPTER 18

Getting Started with the Cisco PIX Firewall

In this chapter, you will learn about:

- Basic PIX Firewall configuration
- ICMP traffic to the firewall
- Time setting and NTP support
- Syslog configuration
- DHCP server configuration

This chapter covers a variety of basic PIX Firewall **configuration** commands and processes, which are important for you to know if you want to get the most out of a firewall device. The first section reviews and builds on the basic PIX configuration from the preceding chapter. The fourth section includes an exercise demonstrating how to set up and use a simple Syslog server.

NOTE Some topics covered refer to or use features that have not been covered yet in detail. In this chapter, you will run into Firewall access control lists in several places. I am including them here for complete coverage on the topic. Due to their similarity to ACLs on routers, I am assuming that you will see what the ACLs are doing. If not, they are covered in detail in the next chapter.

Basic PIX Firewall Configuration

In this section, you will implement the commands introduced in Chapter 17, and add those commands that will be useful and/or necessary. The commands from Chapter 17 are used without further explanation because they were covered earlier. These commands make up the six basic commands for initial PIX Firewall configuration.

- The **nameif** command
- The **interface** command
- The **ip address** command
- The **nat** command

- The **global** command
- The **route** command

These commands are approached as if they were a series of steps to be followed each time a firewall needs configuration. This method ensures that you won't overlook a basic step and have trouble implementing an advanced feature because of it.

TIP When I first started with routers, I developed a similar list that has since become a habit. And I have a similar list for switches and servers. The key is to identify those basic commands and to have an efficient order that's required to get up and running (period). Once operating, you can take the time to add additional features. I learned this from my own mistakes, as well as watching the repeated and predictable mistakes of many others.

Step 1: Name the PIX Firewall, assign a privilege-level password, assign a Telnet password, and specify the IP addresses of a host that can Telnet to the PIX.

```
pixfirewall#config t
pixfirewall(config)#hostname Pix
Pix(config)#
Pix(config)#enable password cisco      (privilege mode password)
Pix(config)#passwd letmein            (Telnet password)
Pix(config)#telnet 192.168.1.10
```

Step 2: Name and define the DMZ interface. We'll use the default settings for inside (e1 security100) and outside (e0 security0).

```
Pix(config)#nameif ethernet2 dmz sec50
```

Step 3: Assign IP addresses to the interfaces.

```
Pix(config)#ip address outside 1.1.1.1 255.255.255.0
Pix(config)#ip address inside 192.168.1.1 255.255.255.0
Pix(config)#ip address dmz 192.168.2.1 255.255.255.0
```

Step 4: By default, the interfaces on the PIX are administratively shut down. Use the **interface** command to enable the physical interfaces and set the interface speed and duplex mode. The following example sets the inside and outside to Autodetect mode and the DMZ to 100MB / full-duplex.

```
Pix(config)#interface e0 auto
Pix(config)#interface e1 auto
Pix(config)#interface e2 100full
```

Step 5: Now that you've configured IP addresses for the inside and outside interfaces, you need to specify a default route using the **route** command. The **route outside** command tells the PIX Firewall to send all outbound traffic to the next hop router. The numeral 1 specifies the router is one hop count away. The command could be abbreviated as **route outside 0 0 2.1.1.2 1**.

```
Pix(config)#route outside 0.0.0.0 0.0.0.0 1.1.1.2 1
```

Step 6: To allow all inside hosts to initiate outbound connections using NAT, use the **nat** command, as shown here:

```
Pix(config)#nat (inside) 1 0 0
Pix(config)#nat (dmz) 1 0 0
```

Next, configure a global pool of addresses to be used by inside hosts. You must configure a pool for use when communicating with hosts on the outside and hosts on the DMZ.

```
Pix(config)#global (outside) 1 1.1.1.20-1.1.1.254 netmask 255.255.255.0
```

Step 7: To allow public access to the DMZ web server, create a static mapping between the web server address on the DMZ and the address to be used by outside hosts when they send connection requests to the PIX outside interface. This **static** command specifies the inside interface (dmz) and the outside interface (outside) used for this translation. The first IP specifies the address outside hosts will use, while the second IP address specifies the address to translate to.

```
Pix(config)#static (dmz,outside) 1.1.1.19 192.168.2.2
```

Step 8: Even with the static mapping, the PIX's ASA won't permit outside hosts to connect to the web server on the DMZ. This is because the DMZ's security level (50) is higher than the outside interface's security level (0). Also, ASA won't permit ICMP by default.

IOS versions prior to v5.0.1 used the **conduit** command to get around this. The following **conduit** command permits any outside host to initiate a connection with the web server.

```
Pix(config)#conduit permit tcp host 1.1.1.19 eq www any
```

In PIX software versions 5.0.1 and later, ACLs with access groups can be used instead of conduits. Combining ACLs and conduits on the same configuration isn't good practice. If both are configured, ACLs take preference over the conduits.

The following example shows an ACL entry that permits any outside host to initiate a connection with the web server. The second line applies the ACL to the outside interface.

```
Pix(config)#access-list 101 permit tcp any host 1.1.1.19 eq www
Pix(config)#access-group 101 in interface outside
```

If any time changes are made to the PIX NAT configuration or conduits, a **clear xlate** command must be issued for ASA to apply this change (writing the configuration also applies the new settings).

NOTE Care must be taken when implementing commands that allow outside traffic into the firewall. It's important not to allow more access than intended. The **conduit permit ip any any** or **access-list 101 permit ip any any** command would allow any host on the untrusted outside network to access any host on the trusted network using IP as long as an active translation exists.

Step 9: The final steps are to save the configuration by issuing the **write memory** command, checking the configuration by using the **write terminal** command, and then testing the network connectivity.

Verifying Configuration and Traffic

Pinging the different interfaces of the firewall and getting a response would be a good start in verifying network connectivity. The first four of the following commands check the configuration of the PIX firewall, while the last four confirm activity.

show ip address	Verify the ip address of each interface.
show nat	Verify network address translation.
show route	Verify the default route.
show global	Show the range of global addresses.
show xlate	Shows the current translations built through the PIX.
show interface	Show interface statistics.
show conn	Show the current connections through the PIX.
show traffic	Show how much traffic is passing through the PIX.
debug icmp trace	Show all ICMP echo requests and replies to or through the PIX.

ICMP Traffic to the Firewall

ICMP traffic through the firewall isn't allowed by default and must be specifically allowed by creating **access-list/access-group** commands or **conduit** commands on older IOS versions (4.*x*). These commands are covered in detail in the next chapter. Access lists, including those required to allow ICMP traffic, are also covered in the next chapter.

On the other hand, ICMP traffic originating on or terminating at the firewall is allowed by default. The **configuration mode** command **icmp** controls ICMP traffic that *terminates* anywhere on the PIX Firewall. If no ICMP access control list is configured, then the PIX Firewall *accepts* all ICMP traffic that terminates at the interface. The key word here is "terminates"—the firewall is the destination.

Using the **icmp {permit | deny}** command to allow or block pings to an interface is referred to as *configurable proxy pinging.* Use the no form of the command to remove a specific ICMP statement, or use the **clear icmp** command to remove the entire ICMP control list. The syntax is

```
pix(config)#icmp {permit | deny} [host] src_addr [src_mask] [type] int_name
pix(config)#no icmp {permit | deny} [host] src_addr [src_mask] [type] int_name
pix(config)#clear icmp
```

permit	Allows the PIX Firewall interface to be pinged (default)
deny	Prevents the PIX Firewall interface from being pinged
host *src_addr*	Specifies a host address to be permitted or denied to ping the interface
src_addr src_mask	Defines network address and network mask used with define multiple hosts
type	Describes ICMP message type, as in the following table
int_name	Defines interface name of permitted/denied PIX Firewall interface

The following table lists possible ICMP type values and their literal equivalents. While either form can be used with the command, the literal is much easier to interpret for anyone who has to support the PIX device in the future. The **?** will list the acceptable options while building the command.

Type	Literal	Type	Literal
0	echo-reply	12	parameter-problem
3	unreachable	13	timestamp-reply
4	source-quench	14	timestamp-request
5	redirect	15	information-request
6	alternate-address	16	information-reply
8	echo	17	mask-request
9	router-advertisement	18	mask-reply
10	router-solicitation	31	conversion-error
11	time-exceeded	32	mobile-redirect

It's important to understand that creating an ICMP control list effectively switches the firewall from accepting all ICMP traffic to all interfaces to accepting only that traffic specifically allowed by the ICMP statements. There is, in fact, an implicit **deny any** statement similar to other ACLs. If the new packet is matched first by a permit statement, the ICMP packet continues to be processed normally. But, if the first matched entry is a deny statement or no matching statement exists, then the PIX Firewall discards the ICMP packet and generates the %PIX-3-313001 Syslog message. The Syslog message syntax is

```
%PIX-3-313001: Denied ICMP type=type, code=code from src_addr on
interface int_nam
```

To avoid unintentionally stopping IPSec and PPTP traffic when the ICMP control list is used, create a statement that permits ICMP unreachable (type 3) message traffic to the appropriate interface. Denying the ICMP unreachable messages disables ICMP Path MTU discovery, which is required by IPSec and PPTP. The next examples show the statement.

The following example denies all ping requests directed at the outside interface and permits all unreachable messages at the outside interface. Notice that the ACL keyword **any** can be used as the source address.

```
pix(config)#icmp deny any echo-reply outside
pix(config)#icmp permit any unreachable outside
```

PART IV

This next example will permit host 192.168.1.49 or hosts on the network 192.168.2.0/24 to ping the outside interface. The last line again permits all unreachable messages at the outside interface.

```
pix(config)#icmp permit host 192.168.1.49 echo-reply outside
pix(config)#icmp permit 192.168.2.0 255.255.255.0 echo-reply outside
pix(config)#icmp permit any unreachable outside
```

The show icmp Command

The **show icmp** command displays any **icmp** commands in the configuration.

The debug icmp trace Command

The **debug icmp trace** command shows in real-time all icmp echo requests and replies to or through the PIX.

```
pix#debug icmp trace
1: Outbound ICMP echo request (len 32 id 7 seq 1004) 192.168.1.2 >
172.16.1.78 > 172.16.4.50
2: Inbound ICMP echo reply (Len 32 id 26 seq 1004) 172.16.4.50 >
172.16.1.78 > 192.168.1.2
3: Outbound ICMP echo request (Len 32 id 7 seq 1051) 192.168.1.2 >
172.16.1.78 > 172.16.4.50
4: Inbound ICMP echo reply (Len 32 id 26 seq 1051) 172.16.4.50 >
172.16.1.78 > 192.168.1.2
---- output omitted ----
```

Time Setting and NTP Support

Network Time Protocol (NTP) is an Internet-standard protocol built on top of TCP/IP, which provides a mechanism to synchronize network devices and computers that's accurate to a millisecond. NTP is based on Coordinated Universal Time (UTC), a time scale that couples the highly accurate atomic time with Greenwich Mean Time (GMT), which is based on the rotation rate of the Earth.

NTP ultimately synchronizes distributed time server and client clocks to the United States Naval Observatory Master Clocks in Washington, D.C., and in Colorado Springs, Colorado. This synchronization allows events to be correlated when system logs are created and other time-specific events occur. Some network processes confirm time synchronization and won't accept updates or instructions from a device with an older time. NTP is defined in RFC 1305.

How NTP Works

An NTP server must be accessible to the NTP client device. The NTP network typically gets its time from an authoritative time source, such as a radio clock or an atomic clock attached to a time server. NTP distributes this time across the network.

Running continuously in the background, the NTP client sends periodic time requests to known NTP servers, obtaining server time stamps and using them to adjust the client clock. NTP is extremely efficient, requiring no more than one packet per minute to synchronize two machines to within a millisecond.

NTP uses the term "stratum" to describe the number of NTP hops away a device is from an authoritative time source. A *stratum 1 time server* has a radio or atomic clock directly attached, a *stratum 2 time server* receives its time from a stratum 1 time server, and so on. Any device configured to run NTP client automatically selects the time source device with the lowest stratum number, effectively building a self-organizing tree of NTP speakers.

The NTP devices are organized into associations—devices that will share NTP information—by statically configuring the IP address of all machines with which it should form associations. In a LAN environment, NTP can be configured to use IP broadcast messages with each device configured to send or receive these broadcast messages. The accuracy of timekeeping is only marginally reduced because the information flow is one-way only.

NTP uses the two following techniques to avoid synchronizing to a device whose time might be inaccurate:

- The NTP device never synchronizes to a NTP server that isn't synchronized itself.
- The NTP device first compares the time reported by several NTP servers and won't synchronize to a machine whose time is seriously different than the others, even if its stratum is lower.

NTP and PIX Firewalls

Cisco's NTP implementation devices don't support stratum 1 service because, currently, no way exists to connect to a radio or an atomic clock. Most networks use a host server, such as Windows, UNIX, or Linux, which is running a NTP server service. This server can synchronize with the public NTP servers available on the IP Internet. Also possible is to synchronize directly with one of the Internet-based NTP servers.

Configuring NTP Support

Four **configuration mode** commands are used to synchronize a PIX Firewall with a network time server using the NTP. These **ntp** command variations identify the time server(s) and synchronize the PIX Firewall according to the configured options.

The **ntp authenticate** command enables NTP authentication on the device.

```
pix(config)#ntp authenticate
pix(config)#no ntp authenticate
```

The **ntp authentication-key** command is used if authentication between the firewall and the NTP server is required. Conceptually, this is similar to the **AAA tacacs-server key** command covered in Chapter 3. The key's role is to ensure that only authorized partners are engaging in transactions. If authentication is used, the PIX Firewall and NTP server must share the same key.

pix(config)#ntp authentication-key *number* md5 *value*
pix(config)#no ntp authentication-key *number* md5 *value*

number	The authentication key number (1 to 4294967295).
md5	The encryption algorithm.
value	An arbitrary string of up to 32 characters. This key *value* appears as ********** when the configuration is viewed with the **write terminal** command or the **show tech-support** command.

The **ntp server** command is used to tell the PIX Firewall which interfaces to listen to (port 123) for NTP packets. Any NTP packets arriving on nondefined interfaces or that aren't responses from a NTP request by the PIX Firewall are dropped.

pix(config)#ntp server *ip_address* [key *number*] source *if_name* [prefer]
pix(config)#no ntp server *ip_address*

ip_address	The IP address of the NTP server with which to synchronize
number	The authentication key number (1 to 4294967295)
if_name	The interface to use to send packets to the NTP server
prefer	Designates the network time server specified as the preferred server with which to synchronize time

If authentication is enabled, use the **ntp trusted-key** command to define one or more key numbers the NTP server needs to provide in its NTP packets for the PIX Firewall to accept synchronization with the NTP server.

pix(config)#ntp trusted-key *number*
pix(config)#no ntp trusted-key *number*

trusted-key	Specifies the trusted key against which to authenticate
number	The authentication key number (1 to 4294967295)

Use the **clear ntp** command to remove all NTP configurations, including disabling authentication and removing all authentication keys and NTP server designations.

pix(config)#clear ntp

The following example demonstrates configuring the NTP features:

```
pix(config)#ntp authenticate
pix(config)#ntp authentication-key 9146 md5 HopeThisWorks
pix(config)#ntp trusted-key 9146
pix(config)#ntp server 192.168.4.2 key 9146 source inside prefer
pix(config)#
```

Verifying and Monitoring NTP Support

Use the **show ntp** command to display the current NTP configuration. The following output demonstrates the **show ntp** command:

```
pix(config)#show ntp
ntp authentication-key 9146 md5 ********
ntp authenticate
ntp trusted-key 9146
ntp server 192.168.4.2 key 9146 source inside prefer
pix(config)#
```

Use the **show ntp associations [detail]** command to display the configured NTP server associations. The following is a sample of the possible output from the command without and with the **detail** parameter.

```
pix(config)#show ntp associations
 address       ref clock      st when poll reach  delay offset disp
*~192.168.4.2     172.16.100.5   4  113   128 177   4.5  -0.24  125.2
* master (synced), # master (unsynced), + selected, - candidate, ~ configured

pix(config)#show ntp associations detail
192.168.4.2 configured, our_master, sane, valid, stratum 4
ref ID 172.16.100.5, time c0212639.2ecfc9e0 (10:15:05.101 UTC Wed Nov 13 2002)
our mode client, peer mode server, our poll intvl 128, peer poll intvl 128
root delay 38.04 msec, root disp 9.55, reach 177, sync dist 156.021
delay 3.36 msec, offset -0.2119 msec, dispersion 125.21
precision 2**19, version 3
org time c02128a9.731f127b (10:15:25.313 UTC Wed Nov 13 2002)
rcv time c02128a9.73c1954b (10:15:25.317 UTC Wed Nov 13 2002)
xmt time c02128a9.6b3f729e (10:15:25.309 UTC Wed Nov 13 2002)
filtdelay =   4.47  4.58  4.97  5.63  4.79  5.52  5.87  0.00
filtoffset =  -0.24  -0.36  -0.37  0.30  -0.17  0.57  -0.74  0.00
filterror =   0.02  0.99  1.71  2.69  3.66  4.64  5.62  16000.0
```

Use the **show ntp status** command to display the NTP clock information:

```
pix(config)#show ntp status
Clock is synchronized, stratum 5, reference is 192.168.4.2
nominal freq is 99.9984 Hz, actual freq is 100.0266 Hz, precision is 2**6
reference time is c02128a9.73c1954b (20:29:29.452 UTC Wed Nov 13 2002)
clock offset is -0.2403 msec, root delay is 42.51 msec
root dispersion is 135.01 msec, peer dispersion is 125.21 msec
```

Syslog Configuration

The PIX firewall logging feature can be invaluable in troubleshooting, capacity planning, and dealing with security incidents. For security purposes, the events to log are interface status changes, changes to the system configuration, and access list matches, as well as events detected by the firewall and intrusion-detection features. The PIX Firewall generates Syslog messages for system events, such as security alerts and resource depletion. Syslog messages can be used to create mail alerts and log files, or to display on the console of a designated host using UNIX syslog conventions.

The PIX Firewall Syslog message facility is a useful means to view troubleshooting messages and to watch for network events, such as attacks and service denials. You can view Syslog messages either from the firewall console or from a Syslog server that the PIX Firewall sends Syslog messages to.

NOTE If you don't have access to a Syslog server, go to Kiwi Enterprises at http://www.kiwisyslog.com/index.htm and download its free Kiwi Syslog Daemon. See the exercise at the end of the Logging topic.

When using TCP as the logging transport protocol, the PIX Firewall stops forwarding logging traffic as a security measure if any of the following error conditions occur.

- The PIX Firewall is unable to reach the Syslog server
- The Syslog server is misconfigured
- The disk on the Syslog server is full

UDP-based logging doesn't have a similar mechanism to prevent the PIX Firewall from passing traffic if the Syslog server fails.

The logging Commands

At least a dozen **logging** commands exist and some have various options. This section looks at the main commands, but a search of the Cisco web site for PIX Firewall logging and looking for the latest command reference will include any others.

The logging on Command

The Configuration Mode **logging on** command enables or disables sending informational messages to the console, to a Syslog server, or to a SNMP management station. Use the no form of the command to turn off the feature. The syntax is

```
pix(config)#logging on
pix(config)#no logging on
```

The logging host Command

Use the **logging host** command to specify a Syslog server that will receive the messages sent from the PIX Firewall. Multiple **logging host** commands can be used to specify additional servers that would each receive the Syslog messages. Each server can only be specified to receive either UDP or TCP, but not both. PIX Firewall only sends TCP Syslog messages to the PIX Firewall Syslog Server (PFSS). Use the no form of the command to turn off the feature. The syntax is

```
pix(config)#logging host [in_if_name] ip_address [protocol/port]
pix(config)#no logging host [in_if_name] ip_address
```

For normal Syslog operations to any Syslog server (non-PFSS) on the network, use the default message protocol—UDP—as shown in the following example:

```
pix(config)#logging host dmz1 192.168.1.5
```

The logging trap Command

Set the Syslog message level with the **logging trap** command. The level specified includes all levels up to that level. If Level 3 is specified, Syslog displays 0, 1, 2, and 3 messages. Possible number and string level values are as follows:

Severity Level	Message Type	Description and Examples
0	emergencies	System unusable messages.
1	alerts	Take immediate action. Hardware and failover errors.
2	critical	Critical condition. Connection attempts.
3	errors	Error message. No free IP addresses.
4	warnings	Warning message. PPP errors.
5	notifications	Normal but significant condition. URL/Java blocked.
6	informational	Information message. Authentication denied.
7	debugging	Debug messages and log **FTP** commands and WWW URLs.

Use the no form of the command to turn off the feature. The syntax is

pix(config)#logging trap *level*
pix(config)#no logging trap *level*

An example of setting the logging level with the **logging trap** command is shown in the next line.

```
pix(config)#logging trap debugging
```

The logging history Command

Set the SNMP message level with the **logging history** command. Use the no form of the command to turn off the feature. The syntax is

pix(config)#logging history *level*
pix(config)#no logging history *level*

An example of setting the SNMP message level with the **logging history** command is shown in the next line:

```
pix(config)#logging history notifications
```

PART IV

The logging queue Command

Use the **logging queue** command to define the size of the Syslog message queue for the messages waiting to be processed. When traffic or congestion gets heavy, messages might be discarded.

pix(config)#logging queue *queue_size*

queue *queue_size*	Sets the size of the queue for storing Syslog messages. The queue size defaults to 512 messages. Setting it to 0 (zero) specifies unlimited space (subject to available block memory). The minimum is one message. Use this parameter before the Syslog messages are processed.

The following partial configuration shows some of the **logging** commands used together and demonstrates a few of the commands not addressed earlier.

```
pix(config)#logging on
pix(config)#logging timestamp     Time stamp system messages
pix(config)#no logging standby     Failover device isn't logging
pix(config)#no logging console     Turns off messages to PIX console
pix(config)#no logging monitor     Turns off Telnet session messages
pix(config)#logging buffered errors  Sets message level sent to buffer
pix(config)#logging trap notifications Sets message level sent to syslog
pix(config)#no logging history
pix(config)#logging queue 2048     Sets queue size to 2048 messages
pix(config)#logging host inside 192.168.1.220  syslog server address
```

FTP and URL Logging

Logging FTP commands and WWW URLs with the Syslog feature is possible. FTP and URL messages can be logged at Syslog Level 6. Both inbound and outbound **FTP** commands and URLs are logged, and both can be sent to a Syslog server.

Use the following steps to enable FTP and URL logging:

1. Use the **show fixup** command to make sure the FTP and HTTP **fixup protocol** commands are present in the configuration. They should be on in the default configuration.

   fixup protocol http 80
   fixup protocol ftp 21

2. If all that was required was to enable URL logging, setting the **logging** command(s) to Level 5 would do that. But FTP logging requires setting the **logging** command(s) to Level 6. Because the level includes everything smaller, setting the logging to Level 6 will capture both.

   ```
   pix(config)#logging console 6
   pix(config)#logging trap 6
   ```

The following is an example of a URL logging Syslog message, followed by an FTP logging Syslog message.

```
%PIX-5-304001: user 192.168.1.10 Accessed URL 198.133.219.25: www.cisco.com
%PIX-5-304001: user 192.168.1.10 accessed URL 192.168.4.5/pr_sjones.gif
%PIX-6-303002: 192.168.1.10 Retrieved 172.16.44.34: resume.doc
%PIX-6-303002: 192.168.1.10 Retrieved 172.16.9.21: bigswitch.tar
%PIX-6-303002: 192.168.1.10 Stored 172.30.19.4: budget.zip
```

You can use the **show logging** command to view these messages at the PIX Firewall console.

Verifying and Monitoring Logging

Use the **show logging** command to display which logging options are enabled. If the **logging buffered** command is on, the **show logging** command lists the current message buffer.

This example shows how to set Syslog trap logging and view the results:

```
pix(config)#logging trap debugging
pix(config)#show logging
Syslog logging: enabled
Timestamp logging: disabled
Console logging: disabled
Monitor logging: disabled
Buffer logging: disabled
Trap logging: level debugging, 43 messages logged enabled
```

Use the **show logging queue** command to display the current number of messages in the queue, the highest number recorded, and the number of messages discarded because block memory is unavailable to process them.

The following output shows the results of using the **logging queue** command to set the queue size to Unlimited and **show logging queue** commands:

```
pix(config)#logging queue 0
pix(config)#show logging queue
Logging Queue length limit : Unlimited
Current 9 msg on queue, 2721 msgs most on queue, 3 msg discard.
```

Exercise 18-1

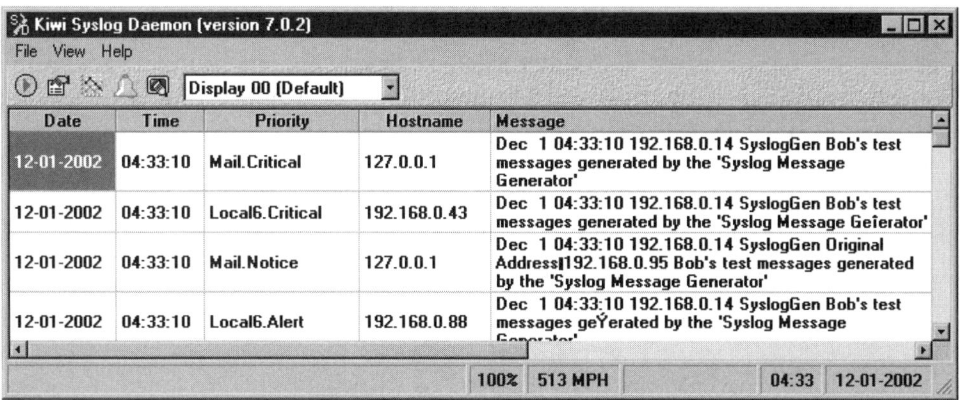

Objective: This lab (which is also available on this book's accompanying CD-ROM) looks at using a Syslog daemon to provide remote storage of system messages. An important part of any project, logging can be used as a debugging tool during development, and a troubleshooting tool once a system has been deployed, and for analyzing and documenting events, such as security breaches. Logging provides a way to see what's happening—good or bad—inside a running system. As such, it should be addressed with care and forethought, rather than used as a last-minute burden.

A Syslog daemon (an open-source logging system) receives, logs, displays, and forwards Syslog system messages from a variety of hosts, such as routers, switches, UNIX hosts/servers, PIX firewall, LinkSys home firewall, SNMP servers, programming projects, and any other Syslog-enabled device. Depending on the Syslog application, customizable options are available, such as the following:

- Display the message in the scrolling window.
- Log the message to a text file.
- Forward the message to another Syslog daemon.
- Log to an ODBC database.
- Log to the Windows Server Application Event Log.
- E-mail an alert message to someone via SMTP.
- Trigger a sound alarm.
- Run an external program, such as a pager notification system.

Actions can be performed on received messages. Messages can be filtered by host name, host IP address, priority, message text, or time of day.

NOTE This lab looks only at using a Syslog daemon and doesn't specifically address using a PIX Firewall with a Syslog server. Once you know how easy it is to set up a Syslog server, it'll be simple enough to add the feature to your next firewall exercise.

Preparation: The purpose of a Syslog daemon (server) is to capture the various log messages that programs like the router's IOS generates. As long as the host with the Syslog software running can be reached from the router or switch, debug, error, and log messages can all be directed to it.

If you don't already have a copy of Kiwi Enterprise's Syslog daemon (or something comparable), consider going to the web site http://www.kiwisyslog.com and downloading it. The software is free to use and runs on Win9X, WinNT, Win2000, and XP. A "for money" version is available from the same site with additional features. The download is 3+MB in size. Several other interesting tools are also on the site to work with the Syslog concepts.

This exercise can be done in any networked environment using TCP/IP. There should be no impact on the network itself.

Download both the Syslog daemon and the SyslogGen tools for this lab. You might want to download the other tools for later self-study.

This lab can be done with the Syslog installed on any number of computers on the same network, or, if necessary, it can be done using one computer. The SyslogGen tool should be on each machine.

1. Use the **winipcfg** or **ipconfig** command to determine the IP address of the machine(s) that will be running the Syslog daemon. If necessary, create a simple map of the room.
2. Start the Syslog daemon using the Start | Programs menu.If you're using the Kiwi daemon, press CTRL-T at the same time to send a test message, which you should be able to read in the Syslog window.The following illustration shows the Syslog with a sample entry.

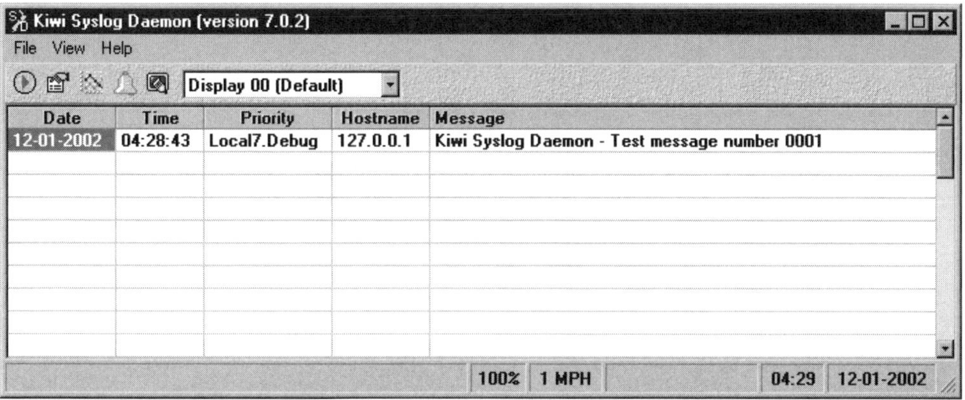

3. The Kiwi Syslog Message Generator can be used to generate Syslog traffic, so you can experiment with different types and volumes of traffic. Start the

SyslogGen tool from the Start menu.The Syslog Message Generator window looks like the following illustration. Look over the options:

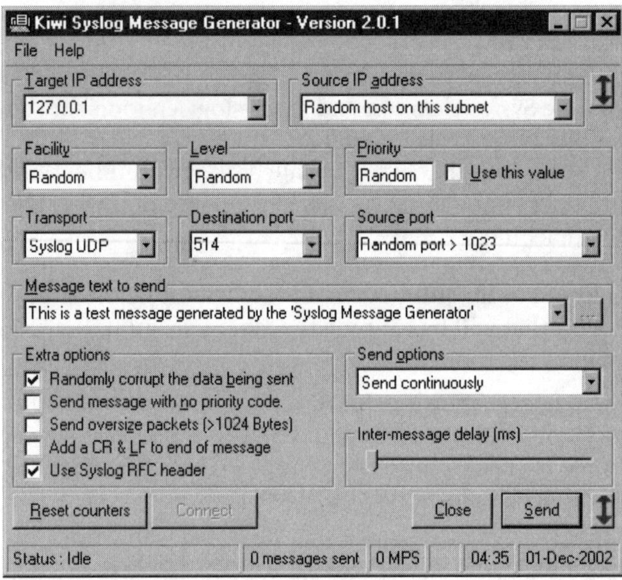

4. The 127.0.0.1 target address means it will send the messages to Syslog running on the local PC. We use this for our first test.
   Confirm the previous settings and, with the Syslog window visible on the screen, click the Send button. Messages should be appearing in the Syslog window. Notice that the status bar at the bottom tells you how many messages have been sent.
   Use the Stop button to halt the traffic.
   Use the scrollbar to look through the messages.

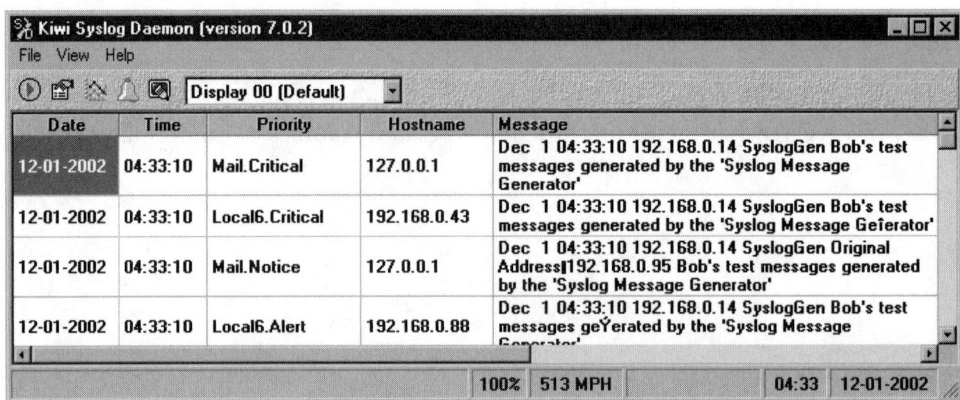

5. On the Syslog machine, choose View | View Syslog Statistics from the menu to bring up the following display and let you view some interesting counters. Use the View | Clear Display to clear the entries.
   Experiment with the features. If possible, change the target to the other host IP address.

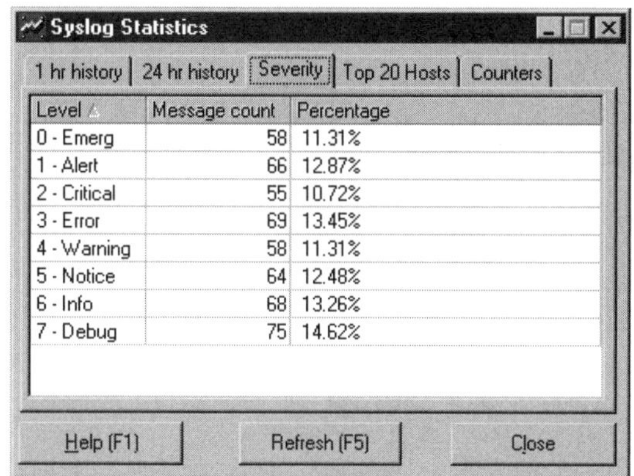

6. Saving the output.
   On the Syslog machine, use the File | Copy Display To Clipboard | Copy Whole Display To Clipboard from the menu or the CTRL-A keys to copy the entire contents of the Syslog window.
   Open a Notepad file and choose Edit | Paste from the menu. The text should appear in the Notepad. This text file can be saved to a disk.
   The saved text file can be opened using MS Excel, MS Access, or the Kiwi LogFile Viewer using the Open | Tab Delimited option to sort and analyze the results.

DHCP Server Configuration

In many small offices and home offices (SOHO) installations, no server exists to provide DHCP services, and, yet, the feature could make adding new users and machines to the LAN much easier. Think about the user who uses their laptop at work in a DHCP environment, and then wants to take the laptop home. Continually configuring and un-configuring static IP addresses would be a pain.

Fortunately, devices like perimeter routers or firewall devices can easily provide DHCP server support in this type of scenario. Cisco's Firewall with DHCP server strategy seems targeted at the PIX 506 and 506e platforms, but the feature is supported throughout the product line. Acting as a DHCP server, the PIX unit provides network configuration information (parameters) to DHCP clients in response to the clients' DHCP polling. These configuration parameters provide the DHCP clients with the networking parameters, such as default gateway, needed to access the network. Once on the network, services such as the DNS and WINS servers can be accessed to facilitate using web browsers or e-mail.

Connecting to a PIX Firewall supporting DHCP server features are PC clients and other network devices configured as DHCP clients. These connections can be nonsecure, not encrypted, for accessing the Internet or corporate resources. A growing market is creating secure, encrypted connections, using IPSec technology, to access corporate resources.

The following table lists the number of concurrent DHCP client connections supported by the PIX Firewall models by versions of the PIX Firewall OS. As with all product details, be sure to check the latest online documentation for maximum clients and the impact on memory requirements.

PIX OS Version	PIX Firewall Platform	Maximum DHCP Clients
v5.2 and earlier	All platforms	10
v5.3 to v6.0	PIX 506/506E	32
	All other platforms	256
v6.1 and higher	PIX 501 (10-user license)	32
	PIX 501 (50-user license)	128
	PIX 506/506E	256
	All other platforms	256

To be considered an active connection for the purpose of comparing to the maximum DHCP clients, a host must have done any one of the following:

- Passed traffic through the PIX device in the last 30 seconds
- Established NAT/PAT through the PIX device
- Established a TCP connection or a UDP session through the PIX device
- Established user authentication through the PIX device

While new versions of the PIX OS might change this, two features aren't supported by the current PIX Firewall DHCP server feature:

- The PIX Firewall DHCP server doesn't support BOOTP requests.
- The PIX Firewall DHCP server doesn't support failover configurations.

NOTE It isn't possible to get 256 clients from a class C network or from a class A or B network subnetted with a 24-bit mask. While the 24-bit mask creates 256 addresses, the first is the network, the last is the broadcast, and one must be configured on the PIX Firewall interface. This leaves 253 DHCP clients.

Configuring the DHCP Server Feature

Since version 5.2 of PIX Firewall OS, the DHCP server daemon can only be enabled on the inside interface and only supports clients directly connected to that interface, in the same network. This means IP Helper and other DHCP request-forwarding techniques won't work with a PIX device working as a DHCP server. Because using any firewall as a DHCP server is a small network solution, this should be a serious limitation.

The PIX Firewall uses variations of the **dhcpd** command to implement the DHCP server features. The following are the most frequently used options. The no form of each command without the variable parameters will remove the command.

The dhcpd address Command

The **dhcpd address** command specifies the DHCP server address pool. This address pool must be within the same subnet as the PIX Firewall DHCP server interface. The size of the pool is limited to the maximum DHCP clients for that platform and license. The *-ipadd2* option is used to define an address range, so interface names can't use names with a "-" (dash). The default interface and only one supported since OS v5.1 is the inside interface. Use the **no dhcpd address** command to remove the DHCP address pool. The syntax is

pix(config)#dhcpd address *ip_add1*[*-ipadd2*] [*if_name*]
pix(config)#no dhcpd address

In the first of the following examples, the address pool is a single address. The second example creates a pool of ten addresses:

```
pix(config)#dhcpd address 192.168.1.2
pix(config)#dhcpd address 192.168.1.2-192.168.1.11
```

The dhcpd dns Command

The **dhcpd dns** command specifies the IP address of one or two DNS servers for DHCP clients. The **no dhcpd dns** command removes the DNS IP address(es) from the configuration. The syntax is

pix(config)#dhcpd dns *dns1* [*dns2*]
pix(config)#no dhcpd dns

The first of the following examples defines one DNS server. The second example defines two DNS servers.

```
pix(config)#dhcpd dns 192.168.100.5
pix(config)#dhcpd dns 192.168.100.5 192.168.101.5
```

The dhcpd wins Command

The **dhcpd wins** command specifies the IP address of one or two WINS servers for DHCP clients. The **no dhcpd wins** command removes the WINS IP address(es) from the configuration. The syntax is

pix(config)#dhcpd wins *wins1* [*wins2*]
pix(config)#no dhcpd wins

The first of the following examples defines one WINS server. The second example defines two WINS servers:

```
pix(config)#dhcpd wins 192.168.100.5
pix(config)#dhcpd wins 192.168.100.5 192.168.101.5
```

The dhcpd lease Command

The **dhcpd lease** command specifies the length of the DHCP lease in seconds. This represents how long the DHCP client can use the IP address assigned by the DHCP granted. The **no dhcpd lease** command restores the lease length with the default value of 3,600 seconds. The syntax is

pix(config)#dhcpd lease *seconds*
pix(config)#no dhcpd lease

This example sets the lease time to 7,200 seconds (two hours).

```
pix(config)#dhcpd lease 7200
```

The dhcpd domain Command

The **dhcpd domain** command defines the DNS domain name for the DHCP clients. The **no dhcpd domain** command removes the DNS domain server from your configuration. The syntax is

pix(config)#dhcpd domain *dom_name*
pix(config)#no dhcpd domain

This example sets the DNS domain name to cisco.com.

```
pix(config)#dhcpd domain cisco.com
```

The dhcpd enable Command

The **dhcpd enable** command turns on DHCP services. This enables the DHCP daemon to begin to listen for the DHCP client requests on the DHCP-enabled interface. While an interface name option exists, since version 5.1, the inside interface is both the default and the only interface supported. The **no dhcpd enable** command disables the DHCP server feature. The syntax is

pix(config)#dhcpd enable
pix(config)#no dhcpd enable

The dhcpd ping_timeout Command

The **dhcpd ping_timeout** command allows a short delay to be configured, in milliseconds, before responding to a DHCP client request. This delay allows the PIX Firewall to work as a backup DHCL server. The **no dhcpd ping_timeout** command removes the delay. The syntax is

pix(config)#dhcpd ping_timeout *timeout*
pix(config)#no dhcpd ping_timeout

This example sets the DHCP ping_timeout to 750 milliseconds.

```
pix(config)#dhcpd ping_timeout 750
```

Using Cisco IP Phones with a DHCP Server

A growing number of organizations with small branch offices are implementing a Cisco IP Telephony VoIP (Voice over IP) solution. A common implementation is to install the Cisco CallManager at the central office and use it to control IP Phones at the small branch offices. The benefits to this implementation include the following:

- Centralizes call processing
- Reduces the equipment required
- Eliminates the administration of additional Cisco CallManager servers
- Eliminates other servers at branch offices

Part of the simplicity of the Cisco IP Telephony solution is that the phones can download their configuration from a TFTP server. To eliminate the need to preconfigure the Cisco IP Phone with the phone IP address and the IP address of the TFTP server, the phone sends out a DHCP request with the **option** parameter set to 150 or 66 to a DHCP server.

PIX Firewall version 6.2 introduced the two new options for the **dhcpd** command specifically to support VoIP installations. Use the no form of the command to remove the configuration entry. The syntax is

pix(config)#dhcpd option 66 ascii {*server_name* | *server_ip_str*}
pix(config)#no dhcpd option 66
pix(config)#dhcpd option 150 ip *server_ip1* [*server_ip2*]
pix(config)#no dhcpd option 150

server_name	TFTP server host name (only one)
server_ip_str	TFTP server host IP address (only one)
server_ip1	IP address of the primary TFTP server
server_ip2	IP address of the secondary TFTP server (maximum of two TFTP servers)

Cisco IP Phones can include both option 150 and 66 requests in a single DHCP request. In this case, the PIX Firewall DHCP server assigns values for both options in the response if they're configured on the PIX Firewall.

The current versions of PIX Firewall DHCP server (v6.2) can only be enabled on the inside interface and, therefore, can only respond to DHCP option 150 and 66 requests from Cisco IP Phones or from other network devices on the internal network. If any outside clients need to connect to the inside TFTP server, then a group of static and access list statements must be created for the TFTP server, instead of using the **dhcpd option** command.

This partial configuration demonstrates configuring the firewall with DHCP support for the dhcpd option 66 and option 150 features. Note, the server IP addresses are on the same network as the inside interface and outside the range of available IP addresses assigned to the DHCP server.

```
pix(config)#ip address inside 192.168.1.1 255.255.255.0
pix(config)#dhcpd address 192.168.1.6-192.168.1.254
pix(config)#dhcpd dns 192.168.100.5 192.168.101.5
pix(config)#dhcpd wins 192.168.100.5
pix(config)#dhcpd domain test.com
pix(config)#dhcpd option 66 ascii 192.168.1.5
pix(config)#dhcpd option 150 192.168.1.4 192.168.1.5
pix(config)#dhcpd enable
```

Verifying and Monitoring DHCP Configuration

In addition to performing a **write terminal** command to see the configuration, the PIX Firewall offers the following commands:

show dhcpd [binding|statistics]	Displays the configured **dhcpd** commands, and binding and statistics information associated with those commands
clear dhcpd [binding|statistics]	Clears all the **dhcpd** commands, binding, and statistics
debug dhcpd event	Displays event information about the DHCP server
debug dhcpd packet	Displays packet information about the DHCP server

This partial configuration demonstrates configuring the DHCP features for a SOHO implementation.

```
pix(config)#ip address inside 192.168.1.1 255.255.255.0
pix(config)#dhcpd address 192.168.1.2-192.168.1.254
pix(config)#dhcpd dns 192.168.100.5 192.168.101.5
pix(config)#dhcpd wins 192.168.100.5
pix(config)#dhcpd lease 7200
pix(config)#dhcpd ping_timeout 750
pix(config)#dhcpd domain test.com
pix(config)#dhcpd enable
```

This next example is sample output from the **show dhcpd** command:

```
pix(config)#show dhcpd
dhcpd address 192.168.1.2-192.168.1.254 inside
dhcpd domain test.com
dhcpd lease 7200
dhcpd ping_timeout 750
dhcpd dhcpd dns 192.168.100.5 192.168.101.5
dhcpd wins 192.168.100.5
dhcpd enable inside
```

This next example is sample output from the **show dhcpd binding** command:

```
pix(config)#show dhcpd binding
IP Address Hardware Address Lease Expiration Type
192.168.1.100 0100.a0c9.868e.43 84985 seconds automatic
```

The following is sample output from the **show dhcpd statistics** command:

```
pix(config)#show dhcpd statistics
Address Pools 1
Automatic Bindings 1
Expired Bindings 1
Malformed messages 0

Message Received
BOOTREQUEST 0
DHCPDISCOVER 1
DHCPREQUEST 2
DHCPDECLINE 0
DHCPRELEASE 0
DHCPINFORM 0

Message Sent
BOOTREPLY 0
DHCPOFFER 1
DHCPACK 1
DHCPNAK 1
```

DHCP Client

Corporate networks tend to use static IP addresses for all key network devices—such as firewalls, routers, switches, and servers—so those IP addresses can be configured as default gateways, used in ACLs, and so forth. But a telecommuter or small office could be using a cable or a DSL service that requires the client to receive their IP address and related information from a DHCP server on the provider's network. In the case of a firewall, this would be the outside interface.

The PIX Firewall **ip address dhcp** command enables the DHCP client feature. Once the DHCP client feature is enabled, the PIX Firewall can accept configuration parameters from a DHCP server. The only configuration parameters the firewall requires are an IP address and a subnet mask for the DHCP client interface, the outside interface. To reset the interface and delete the DHCP lease from the PIX Firewall, configure a static IP address for the interface or use the **clear ip** command to clear all PIX Firewall IP addresses. The syntax is

pix(config)#ip address outside dhcp [setroute] [retry *retry_cnt*]
pix(config)#clear ip

dhcp	Enables the DHCP client features, which then polls for informaton on the defined interface.
Setroute	Tells the PIX to create a default route using the default gateway parameter supplied by the DHCP server.
Retry	Enables PIX to retry a poll for DHCP information.
retry_cnt	The number of times PIX will poll for DHCP information. (4 to16). The default is 4.

If the optional setroute option is configured, the **show route** command output will show that the default route was set by a DHCP server.

The show ip address *if_name* dhcp Command

The **show ip address** *if_name* **dhcp** command displays the DHCP lease details. The following is a sample of what the output might look like:

```
Pix#show ip address outside dhcp
Temp IP Addr:172.16.1.61 for peer on interface:outside
Temp sub net mask:255.255.255.252
DHCP Lease server:172.16.4.5, state:3 Bound
DHCP Transaction id:0x4123
Lease:259200 secs, Renewal:129600 secs, Rebind:226800 secs
Temp default-gateway addr:172.16.1.62
Next timer fires after:91347 secs
Retry count:0, Client-ID:cisco-0000.0000.0000-outside
ip address outside dhcp retry 10
```

NOTE The PIX Firewall DHCP client doesn't support failover configurations.

Using NAT/PAT with DHCP Client

The IP address assigned to the outside interface by the DHCP server can be used as the PAT global address. This means all outbound NAT translations will use the assigned IP address of the outside interface, combined with a unique port number. By using the outside interface, it's unnecessary for the ISP to create a static IP address to the global address pool.

Use the **global** command with the **interface** keyword to enable PAT to use the DHCP-acquired IP address of the outside interface. The syntax is

pix(config)#global (outside) *nat-id* interface

In the following example, the first line enables the DHCP client on the outside interface, uses the acquired gateway address as the default route, and allows ten polling attempts to collect the DHCP information. The second line allows all inside addresses to go out of the network using NAT pool #1. The last line enables PAT using the IP address at the outside interface.

```
pix(config)#ip address outside dhcp setroute retry 10
pix(config)#nat (inside) 1 0 0
pix(config)#global (outside) 1 interface
```

Firewalls as a DHCP Client and Server

In this SOHO scenario, it's likely that the perimeter firewall would be a DHCP client on the outside interface, using PAT to allow internal users to travel out through the router to either the Internet or a corporate network. At the same time, it's entirely possible that the firewall could be providing IP addresses to users on the inside of the network if no resident server exists to provide the feature.

This is, in fact, what happens with virtually all the small perimeter routers manufactured by many vendors, which people are inserting between their home computer systems and their cable or DSL connection. It could be argued that, with a single LAN, the perimeter router is acting only as a firewall and DHCP server/client because no actual routing is occurring. Because most of these small routers rely on another device, such as a cable modem, to prove a LAN (Ethernet) connection to the outside interface, there's every reason to think a true firewall device could be substituted and provide greater protection.

The dhcpd auto_config Command

Use the **dhcpd auto_config** command to enable PIX Firewall to automatically assign DNS, WINS, and domain name values learned by the DHCP client (outside) to the DHCP server (inside). Any of these **auto_config** parameters can be overridden by configuring specific dns, wins, and domain parameters.

pix(config)#dhcpd auto_config [*client_intf_name*]
pix(config)#no dhcpd auto_config

client_intf_name	Currently, this optional argument is irrelevant because the PIX OS only supports the outside interface. If later OS versions support additional interfaces, this argument will specify the interface.

This partial configuration shows an example of how to configure the **auto_config** command to assign the DNS, WINS, and DOMAIN parameters learned from the DHCP client interface (outside). Note that the netmask of the inside interface is 255.255.254.0.

```
pix(config)#ip address outside dhcp setroute retry 10
pix(config)#ip address inside 192.168.1.1 255.255.255.0
pix(config)#dhcpd address 192.168.1.2-192.168.1.254
pix(config)#dhcpd auto_config
pix(config)#dhcpd enable
```

Chapter Review

This chapter looked at the basic commands and techniques for configuring a PIX Firewall device. These commands make up the six basic commands for initial PIX Firewall configuration.

- The **nameif** command
- The **interface** command
- The **ip address** command
- The **nat** command
- The **global** command
- The **route** command

PIX Firewalls don't allow ICMP traffic to pass through by default, but they do allow ICMP traffic directed at the firewall interfaces. You learned how to use the **icmp** command to manage this traffic.

Network Time Protocol (NTP) is an Internet standard protocol to synchronize network devices and computers, which is accurate to a millisecond. You learned about the Cisco NTP implementation that allows PIX Firewalls to synchronize with an established NTP time server, so events and processes can be coordinated and correlated when system logs are created and other time-specific events occur.

The PIX Firewall syslog message facility is a useful means to view and store troubleshooting messages and to watch for network events, such as attacks and service denials. The **logging** commands specify how system messaging will be handled and how to work with a Syslog server to provide reliable logging of PIX activities and processes.

You also learned how having the option to configure a firewall to act as a DHCP client can be useful in working with cable and DSL connections in small offices and SOHO implementations. The capability to act as a DHCP server providing critical network configuration information to host devices is another strong feature of the line, particularly the smaller platforms.

Questions

1. Which one of the following is not one of the six basic commands for initial PIX Firewall configuration?

   A. The **ip address** command

   B. The **nat** command

   C. The **route** command

   D. The **conduit** command

2. Which of the following commands would bring up (enable) a properly configured interface?

   A. **no shutdown**

   B. **nameif ethernet2 dmz sec50**

   C. **interface e0 auto**

   D. **ip address outside 1.1.1.1 255.255.255.0**

3. Which of the following firewall commands would allow a LAN host to successfully ping an Internet site?

   A. **icmp permit any echo-reply outside**

   B. **icmp permit any echo-reply inside**

   C. **both would be required**

   D. None of the above

4. Which command generated the following output?

```
1: Outbound ICMP echo request (len 32 id 7 seq 1004) 192.168.1.2 >
172.16.1.78 > 172.16.4.50
2: Inbound ICMP echo reply (Len 32 id 26 seq 1004) 172.16.4.50 >
172.16.1.78 > 192.168.1.2
```

   A. **show icmp**

   B. **show icmp traffic**

   C. **show icmp trace**

   D. **debug icmp trace**

5. Which one of the following is *not* true about Network Time Protocol (NTP)?

   A. It's an Internet standard protocol.

   B. It's based on Coordinated Universal Time (UTC).

   C. Cisco Firewalls support all NTP service stratum.

   D. NTP devices are organized into associations.

6. Which command enables NTP services on a PIX Firewall?

   A. **ntp authentication-key 9146 md5 HopeThisWorks**

   B. **ntp authenticate**

   C. **ntp trusted-key 9146**

   D. **ntp server 192.168.4.2 key 9146 source inside prefer**

7. Which command shows the NTP configuration?

   A. **show ntp config**

   B. **show ntp status**

   C. **show ntp associations**

   D. **show ntp**

8. Which logging level would need to be set to capture the following output?

```
%PIX-5-304001: user 192.168.1.10 accessed URL 192.168.4.5/pr_sjones.gif
```

   A. 1

   B. 3

   C. 4

   D. 5

9. Which of the following will stop UDP-based logging?

   A. The PIX Firewall is unable to reach the Syslog server.

   B. The Syslog server is misconfigured.

   C. The disk on the Syslog server is full.

   D. None of the above.

PART IV

10. Which PIX Firewall interface does the DHCP client default to?
    A. Inside
    B. Outside
    C. DMZ
    D. No default. It can be enabled anywhere.
11. Which of the following is *not* a PIX Firewall **dhcp** command?
    A. **dhcpd address 192.168.1.6-192.168.1.254**
    B. **dhcpd dns 192.168.100.5 192.168.101.5**
    C. **dhcpd wins 192.168.100.5**
    D. **dhcpd ftp 192.168.100.5**
    E. **dhcpd enable**
12. Which command specifies a Syslog server for logging messages?
    A. **logging trap**
    B. **logging history**
    C. **logging on**
    D. **logging host**
13. For the command **pix(config)#logging trap** 4, what severity levels will be logged?
    A. Level 4
    B. Levels 4 through 7
    C. Levels 1 through 4
    D. Levels 0 through 4
14. What severity level must be trapped to get FTP commands and WWW URLs?
    A. 3
    B. 5
    C. 6
    D. 7
15. Where does the **dhcpd auto_config** command get its source information?
    A. Firewall configuration
    B. CDP packets
    C. DHCP server service
    D. DHCP client service

Answers

1. D. The **conduit** command. This is an old (v4.*x*) command and would come after basic configuration to create exceptions
2. C. **interface e0 auto**
3. D. None of the above. The firewall **icmp** commands only manage ICMP traffic directed at router interfaces, not traffic passing through the device.
4. D. **debug icmp trace**
5. C. Cisco Firewalls support all NTP service stratum. PIX Firewalls do *not* support stratum 1.
6. B. **ntp authenticate**
7. D. **show ntp**
8. D. 5. The number after PIX indicates the level %PIX-5-304001:
9. D. None of the above. Each situation will stop TCP-based logging.
10. B. Outside
11. D. **dhcpd ftp 192.168.100.5**
12. D. **logging host**
13. D. Levels 0 through 4
14. C. 6
15. D. DHCP client service

CHAPTER 19

Access Through the PIX Firewall

In this chapter, you will learn to:

- Use the Adaptive Security Algorithm
- Recognize translations and connections
- Understand Access Control Lists
- Make use of content filtering
- Understand Object Grouping
- Test conduits
- Apply routing configuration

In this chapter, you build on the PIX Firewall basics introduced in the last two chapters. You look at those commands and techniques that make it possible to limit and manage traffic passing through the firewall device. Some of the topics expand on features introduced earlier, such as ASA, access-lists, and routing, but now going into more details and introducing additional options.

Adaptive Security Algorithm

In Chapter 17, Adaptive Security Algorithm (ASA) was introduced as being the heart of the PIX Firewall system. Recognizing that ASA is more than just an algorithm for controlling the direction of traffic flows is important. ASA defines and controls all aspects and features of the PIX devices. While extremely powerful and versatile, ASA is less complex and more robust than packet filtering implementations. ASA provides performance and scalability advantages over application-level proxy firewalls.

ASA concepts introduced in this section, and covered in greater detail throughout this chapter, include the following:

- Security levels
- Stateful system
- Translations
- Connections

Security Levels

Simply stated, every interface on a PIX firewall is assigned a numeric security, or trust, level between 0 and 100. The larger the value, the higher the trust level, with 100 reserved for the inside interface and 0 reserved for the outside interface. Basic PIX ASA operation allows data to travel freely from interfaces with higher security values to interfaces with lower security values. This means, in a two-interface firewall, traffic can always flow without additional assistance from hosts connected to the inside interface out through the outside interface to whatever lies beyond.

Prior to version 5.2 of the PIX OS, Ethernet 1 was reserved for the inside and set to security level 100, and Ethernet 0 was reserved for the outside and set to security level 0. Since 5.2, these are still the defaults, but it's possible to assign any interface as either the inside or the outside. The 100 and 0 security levels must still be assigned to the inside and outside interfaces, respectively.

When you think of security levels, think of data as a liquid and of security levels as elevation. Data would flow freely from the higher elevation to the lower elevation without additional assistance. Unfortunately, the analogy falls apart once you recognize that data, unlike liquids, flows in both directions. This is particularly problematic with data that's in response to a request, returning traffic.

Returning Traffic

While the previous concept is always explained in any discussion of ASA, something that often goes unsaid is this: any resulting return traffic also passes freely through the firewall, unless some configuration prevents it. Simply, if all traffic into the network was the result of outgoing requests from trusted hosts, no need would exist for any additional PIX configuration. Figure 19-1 shows a two-interface firewall and the unassisted traffic flow patterns.

Security Levels 1 to 99

In addition to inside and outside interfaces, a firewall can have one or more protected interfaces connected to shared resources such as web servers. The resulting connections are referred to as *DMZ networks* or *bastion networks*, while the devices are referred to as *DMZ hosts* or *bastion hosts*.

ASA security levels 1 to 99 are used for the DMZ interfaces. If the PIX device has a single, protected DMZ interface, the security level would be configured between the inside and outside levels, such as 50. Figure 19-2 shows the interfaces just described. Packets

Figure 19-1 A two-interface firewall showing data traffic flows

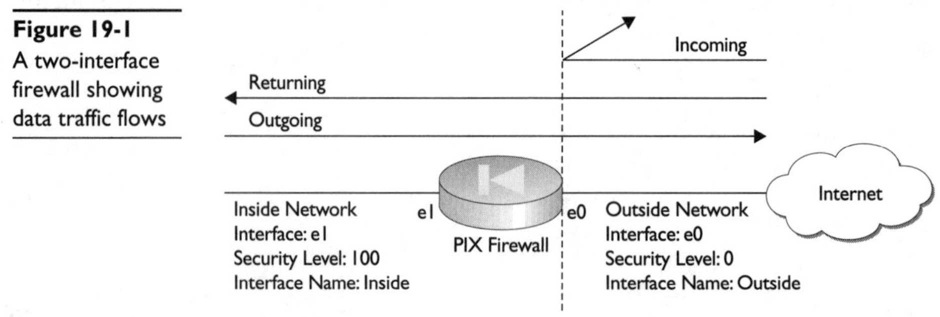

Figure 19-2 PIX security levels with a DMZ interface

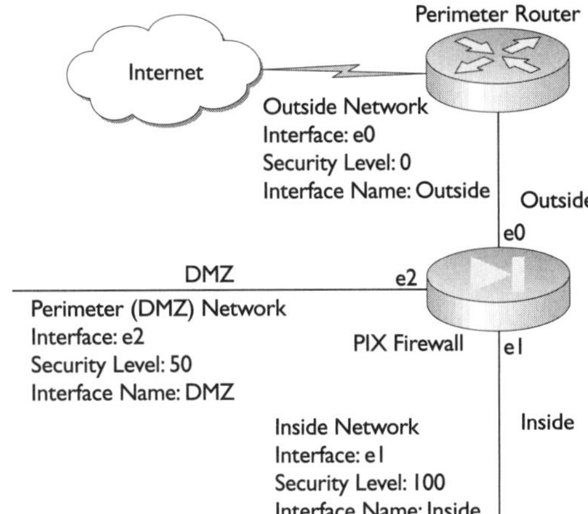

originating from the inside interface could flow freely to the DMZ and reply packets could return to the inside interface. Packets originating in the DMZ that aren't a part of a session originating from the inside interface, couldn't travel to the inside interface without configuration assistance.

DMZ originating packets can travel freely to the outside and can receive reply packets without additional configuration. This is particularly useful for servers, such as e-mail, DNS, and content servers, which must periodically communicate with the outside world.

Multiple protected DMZ interfaces are becoming more common as a way of offering varied levels of security for different types of shared resources. If multiple DMZ interfaces are used, it's important to plan the security level assignments to make sure security flows properly. If two DMZ interfaces have the same security level, no traffic would flow between the interfaces without special configuration in both directions.

The following output shows an example of configuring four DMZ interfaces:

```
Pix(config)# write terminal
   (lines omitted)
nameif ethernet0 outside security0
nameif ethernet1 inside security100
nameif ethernet2 dmz1 security80
nameif ethernet3 dmz2 security60
nameif ethernet4 dmz3 security40
nameif ethernet5 dmz4 security20
hostname Pix
   (lines omitted)
interface ethernet0 auto
interface ethernet1 auto
interface ethernet2 auto
interface ethernet3 auto
interface ethernet4 auto
interface ethernet5 auto
   (lines omitted)
ip address outside 1.1.1.1 255.255.255.0
ip address inside 192.168.1.1 255.255.255.0
ip address dmz1 192.168.2.1 255.255.255.0
ip address dmz2 192.168.3.1 255.255.255.0
ip address dmz3 192.168.4.1 255.255.255.0
ip address dmz4 192.168.5.1 255.255.255.0
```

Inbound Traffic

Because any traffic inbound from a low-security level interface to a higher security level interface is blocked by the ASA, configuring the device to allow for any exceptions is necessary. Combinations of the **static** command and access control lists (ACLs), or *conduits*, are used to allow these specific flows. **Static** commands are discussed in the upcoming section "Static Alone Is Not Enough" and ACLs are discussed in the section "Access Control Lists."

Remember, this discussion is about holes punched through the firewall, each of which represents a vulnerability for the firewall device and protected networks behind them. Therefore, it's only advisable to create these holes if they're specifically allowed by the security policy. An example might be to allow outside users to access the organization's web server on a protected DMZ. In this case, it's important that the resulting hole allows controlled access to the appropriate DMZ, but not to the inside network.

Stateful System

ASA, much like the PIX IOS Firewall CBAC feature covered in Chapter 6, incorporates a stateful approach to evaluating inbound traffic. A *stateful approach* allows the firewall to use knowledge of how certain applications and protocols function to create temporary openings in the firewall to allow effective data exchanges. This effectively creates as-needed application-level filtering capabilities for those supported technologies.

Stateless Firewalls

Firewalls based on the *stateless* packet filtering model can, at most, only create mirror images of outbound traffic, like reflexive ACLs on Cisco routers. By being limited to source and destination address/port combinations, these technologies are effectively limited to Layer 3/Layer 4 filtering. Technologies that change port specifications or port requirements after the initial session exchange, such as multimedia applications, typically can't function within packet filtering-only systems. To accommodate these technologies, the network administrator is often required to create permanent port openings, which could be discovered and exploited by hackers.

Figure 19-3 shows an example of a typical type of filtering that could be created by a stateless, packet filter-based firewall. In this example, an outbound packet to a web server creates a mirror-image inbound filter that would allow the requested information to return. This works well in many situations, particularly with typical TCP traffic. But

Figure 19-3 Stateless firewall with reflexive-type filtering

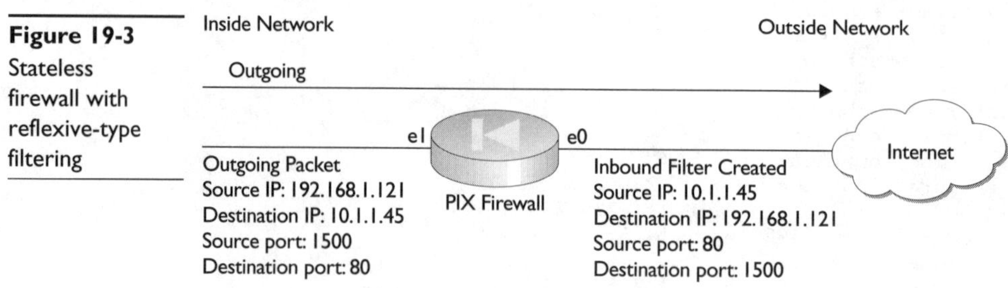

what if the original request was to an FTP server, where the packet was sent to port 20, but port 21 responds? Now the filter isn't right. Remember, firewalls are mindless devices that can only follow rules and can't interpret or be appealed to with logic. The return traffic would probably fail.

Another problem scenario is a client-server type application where the outgoing packet is a request to a SQL server. In meeting the request, the SQL server forwards the packet on to another SQL server. When the reply arrives at the firewall, the source address could be the second server and would, therefore, fail to match the filter. If a permanent ACL entry is created to allow predictable traffic from the SQL data server, it could be detected in a port scan of the firewall and possibly exploited.

That only a stateful firewall that's programmed to support SQL traffic could recognize the returning traffic is a reasonable expectation, based on the stateful table entries created when the original request went out. To maintain security that's as tight as possible, while allowing legitimate inbound traffic, the ASA stateful algorithm looks at other packet fields, such as sequence number, acknowledgment, and code bit fields.

TCP Header Knowledge

ASA's programming allows it to recognize additional TCP fields, such as sequence number, acknowledgement, and code bit fields, as well as the TCP three-step handshake used to establish a session. This programming allows ASA to detect and respond to irregularities, such as too many embryonic (half-open) sessions, sequence number irregularities, or session fragments, all of which could indicate an attack.

Translations

ASA applies to the address translations that are integral to the PIX device in providing security by concealing the internal host addresses from the outside world. These translations can be either *static* (permanent) *translations* for servers and shared devices, which must be reliably accessed from the outside world, or *dynamic translations* to assist internal hosts in venturing out of the network.

As you saw in Chapter 17, and will see again in the next section, static translations use the **static** command, while dynamic translations use the **global** and **nat** commands in either Network Address Translation (NAT) or Port Address Translation (PAT) implementations. Both static and dynamic translations result in translation table entries or translation slots, referred to as *xlates* in the PIX environment.

Connections

You must realize that translations and connections aren't the same thing. A *translation* is literally the substitution of an alias for a local address, but it can't represent an existing connection. For example, a static translation creates an xlate entry to allow outside access to a web server in the DMZ, but there can be no active connection.

Connections, on the other hand, use translations to allow communication from one host to another. In fact, it's possible that a single translation allowing access to a web server might have several active connections underway.

The ASA default rules pertaining to connections include the following:

- No packets can pass through a PIX Firewall without a connection and a state table entry.
- All outbound connections or states are allowed, except those specifically denied by ACLs. Remember, in firewall parlance, "outbound" refers to originating in any higher security-level interface destined to a lower security interface. This means the connection might originate on a DMZ interface destined for the outside interface, as in the case of an e-mail server searching for Internet mail updates.
- All inbound connections or states are denied, except those specifically configured using ACLs or conduits. Inbound connections or states originate on a lower security interface than the destination device.
- All ICMP packets are denied, unless specifically permitted with ACLs or conduits.
- Any packet that can't meet one of the rules, or when no exception has been configured, is dropped and a syslog message is sent.

Translations and Connections

In this section, you see the details of the translation process and the resulting connections. The better these concepts are understood, the easier it is to understand the PIX security algorithms (ASA) and how they work.

To understand how ASA can perform stateful analysis and recognize common attack attempts, it's necessary to review the data encapsulation/deencapsulation process introduced in any basic networking course. Figure 19-4 shows a common depiction of the process, with each layer's encapsulation becoming the next layer's payload. The TCP/IP model combines the top three layers into a single step.

Figure 19-4 OSI model encapsulation process

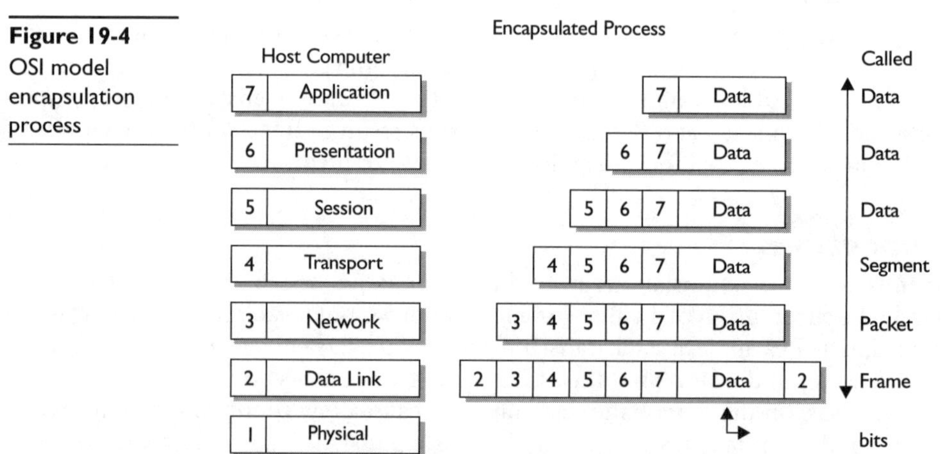

Remember, the little "header" blocks in the diagram are, in fact, multiple binary bits that convey information about the payload. The obvious examples are the bits' designating source and destination IP addresses in the network layer header. But there's additional information that a savvy programmer with a strong algorithm could use to make determinations about what's happening in the communication session. Figure 19-5 shows the IP header information from a packet capture using the Fluke Network Optiview Protocol Expert.

While some of the information, such as the IP addresses, was converted to decimal form, other information, such as the fragmentation bits and Type of Service (TOS) bits, shows the type of detail carried in every IP header. Note that the Protocol ID, converted to decimals, indicates the payload is a TCP segment.

Figure 19-6 shows the TCP header fields from the previous captured packet. Clearly visible are the decimal equivalents of the sequence and acknowledgment numbers used to ensure proper data order and to show no segments are missed. The flag bits are used in the TCP session setup, data exchange, and tear-down processes.

The Source port—139—indicates this is a NetBIOS session service packet. Looking at the session layer information, not shown, reveals the packet is a Session Keepalive Packet. The upper-layer headers, OSI layers 5 to 7, or the TCP/IP application layer can either be quite simple or complex. Figure 19-7 shows only a small portion of an SNMP frame header. The more that ASA programming can interpret these pieces of information, the more granular and powerful it can be in maintaining its "state" table and allowing legitimate traffic flows.

ASA has both the capability to look at these upper-layer fields in the packet and is programmed to recognize appropriate values. This allows ASA to accept packets where an address/port combination might vary from the current state table entry because the upper-layer field entries are consistent with a known possible change.

Figure 19-5 IP header information

```
Internet Protocol (IP)
Version/Header Length   0x45
                           0100 ....    Version 4
                           .... 0101    20 bytes - Header Length
Type of Service         0x00
                           000. ....    Routine
                           ...0 ....    Normal Delay
                           .... 0...    Normal Throughput
                           .... .0..    Normal Reliability
                           .... ..0.    Normal Monetary Cost
                           .... ...0    Not Used
Total Length            44 bytes
Identification          33788
Flags/Fragment Offset   0x4000
                           0... .... .... ....   Not Used
                           .1.. .... .... ....   Don't Fragment
                           ..0. .... .... ....   Last Fragment
                           ...0 0000 0000 0000   Fragment Offset: 0 bytes
Time to Live            128 seconds/hops
Protocol ID             6   (TCP)
CheckSum                0xF564    (Correct)
Source Address          192.168.0.12
Destination Address     192.168.0.14
                        [24 bytes of data]
```

PART IV

Figure 19-6 TCP header information showing flag bits and other fields

Transmission Control Protocol (TCP)	
Source Port	139 (NETBIOS Session Service)
Destination Port	1084
Sequence Number	3291062021
Acknowledgement Number	2222927231
Header Length	0x50
	0101 .... 20 bytes - Header Length
	.... 0000 Not Used
Flags	0x18
	00.. .... Not Used
	..0. .... No URG
	...1 .... Acknowledgement
	.... 1... Push
	.... .0.. No RST
	.... ..0. No SYN
	....0 No FIN
Window Size	65237
CheckSum	0x9092 (Correct)
Urgent Pointer	0
	[4 bytes of data]

Transport Protocols

The PIX Firewall can inspect a variety of protocols at Layer 3 and above. For example, in discovering ICMP packets, ASA automatically blocks them, unless ACLs were created to allow that specific ICMP message type.

Two of the most common protocols are the transport layer protocols TCP and UDP. ASA, such as the PIX IOS CBAC feature, have special processes and techniques for

Figure 19-7 TCP/IP application layer header for SNMP data

Simple Network Management Protocol (SNMP)	
Class	0 (00...... Universal)
Encoding	1 (..1..... Constructed)
Tag Number	16 (Sequence)
Sequence Length	75
Version Class	0 (00...... Universal)
Version Encoding	0 (..0..... Primitive)
Version Tag Number	2 (Integer)
Version Length	1
Version Value	0 (Snmp Version 1)
Community Class	0 (00...... Universal)
Community Encoding	0 (..0..... Primitive)
Community Tag Number	4 (OctetString)
Community Length	6
Community Value	public
PDU Class	2 (10...... Context-Specific)
PDU Encoding	1 (..1..... Constructed)
PDU Tag Number	2 (Get Response)
PDU Length	62
Request ID Class	0 (00...... Universal)
Request ID Encoding	0 (..0..... Primitive)
Request ID Tag Number	2 (Integer)
Request ID Length	1
Request ID Value	15
Error Status Class	0 (00...... Universal)
Error Status Encoding	0 (..0..... Primitive)
Error Status Tag Number	2 (Integer)
Error Status Length	1

managing traffic flows for each. The differences between these two protocols should be familiar from CCNA studies. The implications for firewall filtering are

- **Transmission Control Protocol (TCP),** being connection-oriented with well-defined session setup, data transfer, and tear-down characteristics, this is relatively easy to inspect and monitor.
- **User Datagram Protocol (UDP),** being connectionless and, by definition, somewhat unpredictable in that it simply shows up, this is much more difficult to inspect and monitor.

Transport Control Protocol

TCP traffic, because of its predictable setup, data transfer, and tear-down sequence, allows the PIX firewall to add additional security by substituting a randomized sequence number to make it more difficult for someone eavesdropping on the traffic to insert or replay traffic. In addition, monitoring for an excessive number of half-open, or embryonic, sessions is possible, which could indicate a form of denial of service (DoS) attack is underway.

Figure 19-8 shows an outgoing packet to host 10.2.2.45 before and after the PIX NAT has translated the source IP address and the PIX has created a randomized sequence number. Note that the SYN bit, from Figure 19-6, is the only flag bit set, indicating the first packet of a new session. This information is used by the PIX to create a new xlate table entry, if necessary, and a new state entry in the state table.

Figure 19-9 shows the first returning packet from host 10.2.2.45. The state table is checked for an existing session, and the field details are confirmed as consistent with an expected packet. The PIX retranslates the destination address to the correct local address using the xlate table. The acknowledgment number is the original sequence number incremented, and then is translated before passing into the local network. TCP uses *forward acknowledgment,* meaning the acknowledgement number is the next sequence number expected. The actual acknowledgement number then reflects the "window" increment used for flow control.

Figure 19-8 First step of the TCP setup handshake

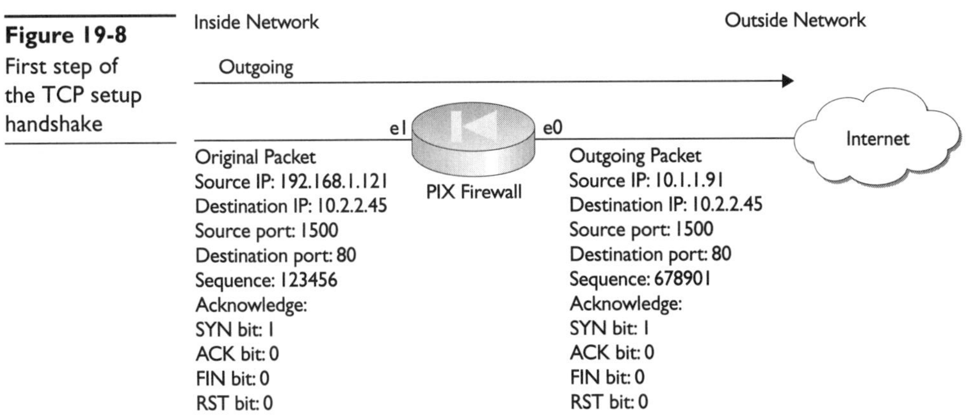

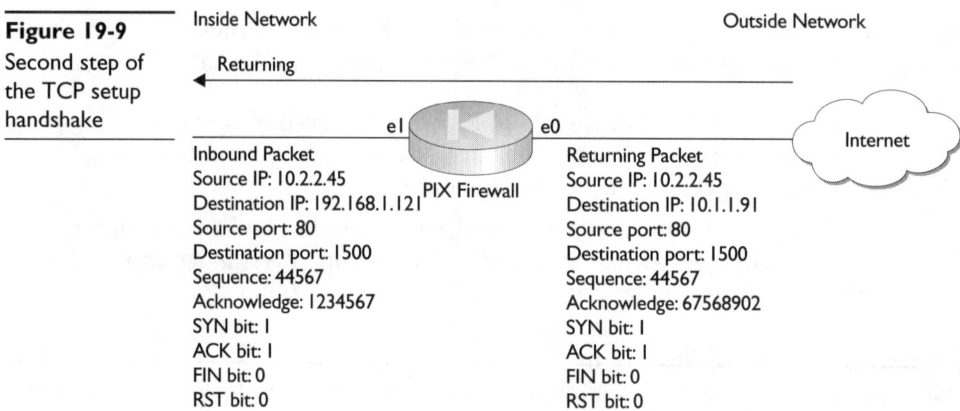

Figure 19-9 Second step of the TCP setup handshake

Note that both the SYN and ACK flag bits are on, which indicates this is the second step in the handshake. If both the SYN and ACK flag bits aren't on, the packet will be dropped for not being the next expected step. The SYN bit is on because host 10.2.2.45 is supplying its synchronization number to the local host.

The next exchange and all exchanges during data transfer would have only the ACK bit set because each exchange acknowledges the last transmission from the other party. The NAT translations would continue as they are. The sequence and acknowledgement fields would be appropriately incremented.

Any packet traffic that doesn't match the key fields of the state table or appears out of order is dropped. Even if the source and destination address/port number combinations are correct, if the packet doesn't fit, the expected step could mean the packet has been manipulated or replayed by someone running a "man-in-the-middle" attack.

FIN and RST Bits If the session is interrupted, a packet with the RST (reset) bit set turned on could be received or, if either host wants to stop the session, the FIN (finish) bit would be turned on. In either case, the PIX device knows the session is ending and removes any related xlate and state table entries, thereby reducing the vulnerability to unauthorized use.

Unauthorized Return Traffic If host 10.2.2.45 were to attempt to send additional packets, even a packet with the SYN bit on and ACK bit off, indicating a new session, the attempt would be blocked because no existing state table entry would be available. Because the original translation was done with NAT (or PAT), there wouldn't be a static entry allowing the unsolicited data.

Authorized Inbound Traffic Assuming the inbound traffic is destined to a shared server, the static address translation is in the xlate table and an enabling access control list allows the unsolicited inbound packet. The SYN bit is on and the ACK bit is off. A state table entry is made, and any necessary translation is performed before the packet passes into the more secure network, typically DMZ, but it could be inside. This state table entry is an "embryonic" TCP session, indicating it's incomplete. The state table entry remains in this state until the three-way handshake is complete and ACK packets are being exchanged.

The inside host then performs Step 2 in the TCP handshake and things progress, as described earlier. Each exchange in both directions is reviewed and the state table is updated as necessary.

SYN Attacks A common form of DoS attack is some variation of a SYN attack where large numbers of SYN packets are received by the inside device and appropriate reply exchanges are prepared and sent. Unfortunately, the sender has no intention of completing these sessions, so the final step of the handshake is never completed. If you recall from Chapter 1, this type of attack can be successful by either overloading the target host or by congesting the link to the target host. Either way, legitimate traffic and activity can't get service.

PIX Firewalls can monitor both the number of embryonic sessions and the time it takes to complete them. This information can be used by the PIX to trigger discarding embryonic sessions to keep the host from being buried. Unfortunately, while the PIX can protect the target device from too many half-open sessions, it might need assistance from an upstream Internet service provider (ISP) to keep the link from becoming clogged.

User Datagram Protocol

Because UDP doesn't establish a connection-oriented session, it's harder to protect. The PIX creates a state table entry any time a UDP packet is sent from a secure interface to a less-secure interface. This entry can only have the basic source, and destination addresses and port numbers. Any UDP traffic arriving from the less-secure interface that matches the state table entries is allowed to pass through.

Common UDP datagrams, such as DNS and NFS, are frequent targets of attacks, so it's important that UDP connections be restricted. PIX units have a feature that only allows one DNS server to respond to a DNS query. Any additional responses are discarded. This reduces the likelihood of an attacker submitting a bogus response and directing output to a bad destination. To reduce exposure further, the state table entries created from the outgoing UDP datagrams have default lives of only two minutes, configurable, to see returning traffic before they're removed.

Static Translations

The PIX **static** command creates a persistent, one-to-one address translation rule to add to the xlate table. This entry is called a *static translation slot* or xlate. In its simplest form, the command maps a local IP address to a global IP address. This is often referred to as a *static NAT translation.*

Static address mappings are created to provide outside access to shared resources, such as web servers. These shared resources must be available to outside users or servers without an originating request from within the more secure interfaces of the firewall. Static mappings shouldn't normally be used with user hosts because their mappings should be added on in an as-needed basis by standard NAT translations. The NAT translations exist only for the time needed and then are removed from the xlate table. Static mappings, on the other hand, stay in the xlate table permanently.

The command syntax includes the interfaces, highest then lowest, followed by the addresses that are reversed to be lowest then highest. Figure 19-10 shows an example of a DMZ server that needs to be accessed from the outside. The next lines show the basic syntax, followed by a simple example translating a protected server—192.168.2.3—to be accessible from the outside as 10.1.1.7. Yes, in real life, this wouldn't be another private address.

```
Pix(config)# static (hi_interface, lo_interface) lo_ip_address hi_ip_address
Pix(config)# static (dmz, outside) 10.1.1.7 192.168.2.3
```

Remember the following about static mappings:

- After changing or removing a **static** command statement, use the **clear xlate** command to make sure the xlate table entries are valid.
- Static mappings always take precedence over mappings created using the NAT command.
- Never use an address in a global address pool for static mapping.

Static Alone Is Not Enough

Note that the xlate table translation created by the **static** command, by itself, won't allow outside traffic to access the server. While the **static** command created a valid global address that could be used, ASA blocks traffic from lower security areas to higher. Enabling the inbound traffic by creating an access-list is still necessary. The **static** command creates the mapping and the access list allows users to use the **static** command mapping. The additional lines required to finish the previous example might look like this:

```
Pix(config)# static (static, outside) 10.1.1.7 192.168.2.3
Pix(config)# access-list acl_server permit tcp any host 10.1.1.7
Pix(config)# access-group acl_server in interface outside
Pix(config)# clear xlate
```

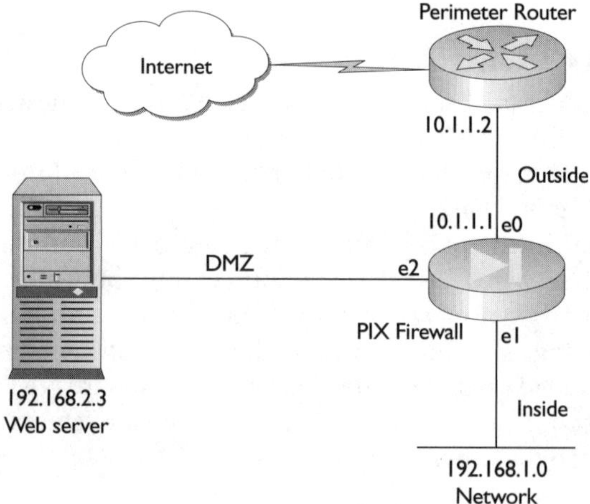

Figure 19-10 Protected DMZ server that must be accessed from the outside

The **access list** command is covered in the section "Access Control Lists," and it won't be included in the remaining **static** command examples, but remember, the **static** command is only part of the solution.

Static Command Options

The **static** command creates a persistent or permanent one-to-one address translation entry in the xlate table. When the translation is between a local IP address and a global IP address, it's called *static NAT*. When the translation is between local and global ports, it is called *static PAT*. The Static Command options might not all be supported on all PIX Firewall OS versions. The following Syntax options are from version 6.2.

Static NAT

Use the following form of the **static** command to perform one-to-one address translation. Use the no form of the command to remove the static translation.

Pix(config)# static [(*hi_interface, lo_interface*)] *global_ip local_ip* [netmask *mask*] [norandomseq] [*max_conn* [*em_limit*]]
Pix(config)# no static [(*hi_interface, lo_interface*)] *global_ip local_ip* [netmask *mask*] [norandomseq] [*max_conn* [*em_limit*]]

hi_interface	The higher security-level interface between the two.
lo_interface	The lower security-level interface between the two.
global_ip	The real global address the *local_ip* is translated to.
local_ip	The internal address to be mapped.
netmask	The key word required before defining a network *mask*.
mask	This network mask applies to both the *global_ip* and *local_ip* addresses. Use 255.255.255.255 for host addresses. For a network or subnet address, use the appropriate mask, for example, 255.255.255.240.
norandomseq	Turns off the randomized TCP/IP packet's sequence number feature for this translation because another firewall is also randomizing sequence numbers and the two together are scrambling the data. Opens a security hole in the firewall.
max_conn	Maximum simultaneous connections permitted through the static. Default is 0, which allows unlimited connections.
em_limit	The embryonic or half-open TCP connection limit. Setting this limit can prevent a common type of DoS attack. Default is 0, which allows unlimited connections.

Mapping a Range of Static Translations While the Netmask Mask option is relatively common to see using 255.255.255.255 for host translations, it might not be obvious that using another mask would define multiple translations. The resulting range of static translations is known as *net statics*. In the following example, the addresses 192.168.2.33 to 192.168.2.46 will be translated to 10.1.1.33 to 10.1.1.46. Figure 19-11 shows a pool of shared servers in the DMZ that need to be mapped to global addresses.

```
Pix(config)# static (inside,outside) 10.1.1.32 192.168.2.32 netmask
255.255.255.240
Pix(config)# clear xlate
```

Figure 19-11 Pool of DMZ servers that need to be mapped to global IP addresses

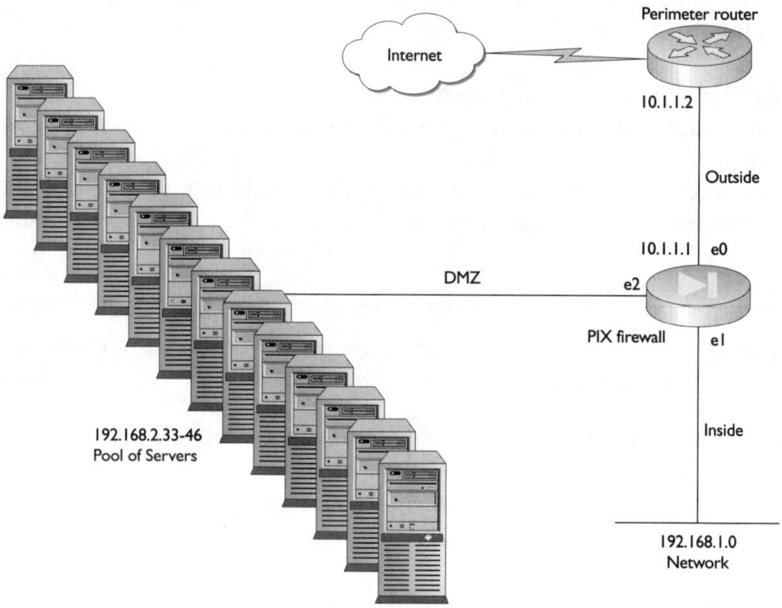

The PIX Firewall won't allow inbound traffic translations that would result in IP addresses identified as either network or broadcast addresses. When the **static** command is used with the Netmask Mask **netmask** ***mask*** option, the PIX Firewall uses the global IP address and mask to determine network and/or broadcast addresses. If a global IP address is a network or broadcast as defined by the mask, the PIX won't allow the xlate table entry. In the previous example, 10.1.1.32 (network) and 10.1.1.47 (broadcast) weren't allowed.

Static PAT

Use the following form of the **static** command to perform one-to-one port translation. Use the no form of the command to remove the static translation.

Pix(config)# static [(*hi_interface, lo_interface*)] {tcp | udp} {*global_ip* | interface} *global_port local_ip local_port* [netmask *mask*][*max_conn*] [*em_limit*] [norandomseq]
Pix(config)# no static [(*hi_interface, lo_interface*)] {tcp | udp} {*global_ip* | interface} *global_port local_ip local_port* [netmask *mask*][*max_conn*] [*em_limit*] [norandomseq]

global_ip	The real global address the *local_ip* is translated to
global_port	The real global port the *local_port* is translated to
interface	Overload the global address from interface
local_ip	The internal address to be mapped
local_port	The internally assigned port to be mapped

In the following example, outside FTP requests to the translated global address 10.1.1.7 are translated to the internal FTP server at 192.168.1.5.

```
Pix(config)# static (inside, outside) tcp 10.1.1.7 ftp 192.168.1.5 ftp
```

No Translation Required

If real global addresses are used in one or more of the DMZs, then translating those addresses isn't necessary. In this case, use the following form of **static** command where the interface IP addresses are the same to literally translate the address to itself. Use the no form of the command to remove the xlate entry.

```
Pix(config)# static (hi_interface, lo_interface) ip_address ip_address
Pix(config)# static (dmz, outside) 10.1.1.7 10.1.1.7
Pix(config)# static (dmz, outside) 10.1.1.32 10.1.1.32 netmask 255.255.255.240
Pix(config)# clear xlate
```

The first example translated a single server to itself, while the second example used a network ID and a subnet mask to define a block of addresses to be mapped to themselves. Figure 19-12 shows the pool of DMZ servers mapped in the previous example.

TCP Intercept Feature

Since version 5.3 of the PIX OS, PIX Firewalls offer a TCP intercept feature. This feature allows the PIX Firewall to step in as a form of proxy for a server being buried by embryonic TCP session requests.

PART IV

Figure 19-12 A pool of DMZ servers that already have global IP addresses

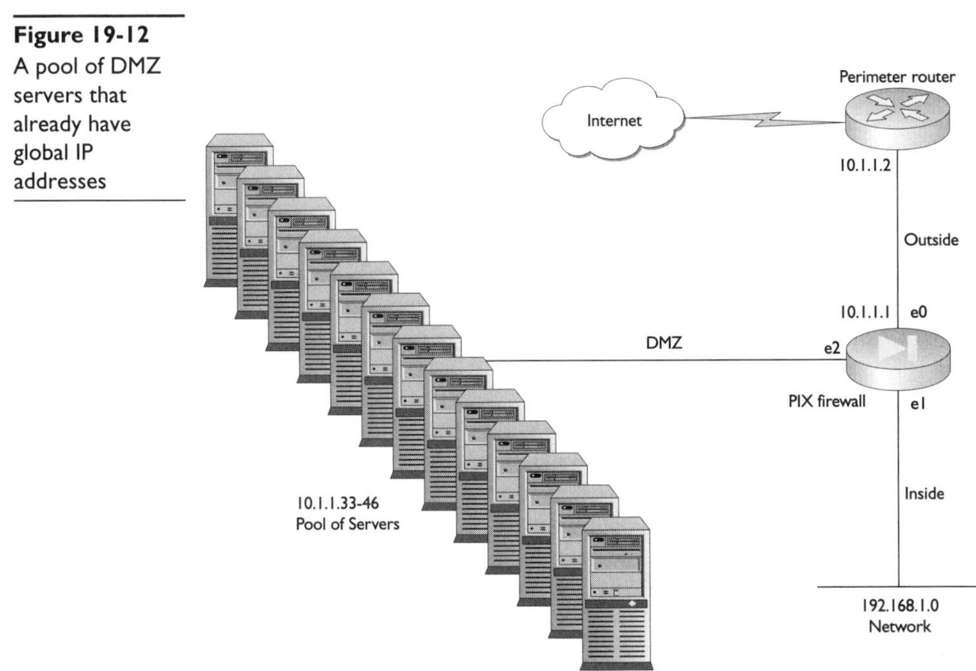

To use the TCP intercept feature, the Embryonic Connection Limit (the previous *em_limit*) option must be configured to something larger than the default 0. Leaving the embryonic connection limit set to 0 directs the PIX Firewall to pass through all new TCP session requests. If the destination server doesn't have TCP SYN attack protection, and most OSs offer only limited protection, then the system's embryonic connection table overloads and all traffic stops. This is a common component of many DoS attacks.

The following example leaves the maximum connection setting unrestricted (0), but sets the embryonic connection limit to 100.

```
Pix(config)# static (inside, outside) 10.1.1.7 192.168.1.3 0 100
```

NOTE The previous example is intended for demonstration purposes only and shouldn't be considered a model for use. Setting either the maximum connections or the maximum embryonic connections can have serious repercussions for the server. Too-high values can provide no protection, while too-low values could unnecessarily restrict access to the device. The actual limits should be set based on the server's performance capabilities. SYN attacks are addressed in the next chapter.

Once the embryonic connection limit is reached, and until the count falls below this limit, every SYN packet (new session request) bound for the mapped server (192.168.1.3) is intercepted by the PIX Firewall. The PIX then responds on behalf of the server with a SYN/ACK (Step 2) packet attempting to complete the connection. The PIX creates a state table entry with the pertinent information from the received packet. The original packet is dropped and the PIX waits for the client's acknowledgment.

If the expected ACK is received (Step 3), completing the three-way handshake, a copy of the client's SYN packet is sent to the local server, and the TCP three-way handshake is performed *between the PIX Firewall and the server.* If this three-way handshake is completed successfully, then the connection between the client and the server resumes as normal.

If, for any reason, the client doesn't respond during the connection phase, then PIX Firewall retransmits the necessary segment using exponential back-offs, just as the server would and, eventually, discards the information.

Prior to version 5.3, if the embryonic connection limit was configured and the level was exceeded, the PIX Firewall simply dropped all new connection attempts. While this might have been better than nothing, the result was that the server was no longer available, which could have been the purpose of the attack.

Network Address Translation

While static address mappings allow permanent outside access to inside resources like servers, users also require address translation to venture into less secure networks, such as the outside. To reduce the window of vulnerability that permanent static mappings introduce, users generally use the **nat/global** command combination to create temporary mappings while they're in the less-secure area. These mappings are removed after the session ends.

NAT syntax and operation were covered in Chapter 17. This section concentrates on those options and implications that might not have been covered earlier. The **nat** and **global** commands are always used together, the **nat** command defining the local host(s) that can be translated to travel to less-secure networks. The **global** command identifies the pool of "real" global IP addresses that can provide access to the less-secure network. The *nat_id* identifies the pool of global addresses that can be accessed by the **nat** command. The two basic command syntaxes are

> Pix(config)# global (*if_name*) ***nat_id*** {*global_ip* [-*global_ip*] [netmask *global_mask*] | interface}
> Pix(config)# nat (*if_name*) ***nat_id*** *local_ip* [*netmask*]

The following example creates a global address\pool, nat_id = 1, that contains all the class C network 215.1.2.0, plus the 31 host addresses included in 1.1.1.1-1.1.1.30. The **nat** command allows all hosts on the 192.168.1.0 inside network to start outbound connections.

```
Pix(config)# global (outside) 1 215.1.2.0
Pix(config)# global (outside) 1 1.1.1.1-1.1.1.30 netmask 255.255.255.224
Pix(config)# nat (inside) 1 192.168.1.0 255.255.255.0
```

Remember the following about global/nat address mappings:

- After changing or removing a **nat** command statement, use the **clear xlate** command.
- You can define up to 256 global pools of addresses.
- Never use an address in a global address pool for static mapping.
- Static mappings always take precedence over mappings created using the **nat** command.

An All Hosts Option

The next examples show a handy shorthand to allow all inside hosts to use NAT to create outbound connections. The **0 0** is a short notation for the *local_ip /netmask* combination 0.0.0.0 0.0.0.0.

```
Pix(config)# nat (inside) 1 0 0
```

Additional NAT Options

The **nat** command lets you enable or disable address translation for one or more internal addresses. Some of the options available, such as norandomseq, *conn_limit*, and *em_limit*, are the same as covered in the **static** command section. To enable NAT for an address or group of addresses, use the following syntax. Use the **no** command to turn off the feature.

> Pix(config)# nat (*if_name*) ***nat_id*** *ip_address* [*netmask*] [outside] [dns] [norandomseq] [timeout *hh:mm:ss*] [*conn_limit*] [*em_limit*]
> Pix(config)# no nat (if_name) ***nat_id*** address [*netmask*] [outside]

PART IV

To disable NAT for an address or group of addresses, use the following syntax. Use the no command to turn off the feature.

```
Pix(config)# nat (if_name) 0 access-list acl_name
Pix(config)# no nat (if_name) 0 [access-list acl_name]
```

nat_id	Values can be **0**, **0 access-list *acl_name***, or a number greater than zero. See the following explanation of the choices.
outside	Enable or disable address translation for the external addresses. Introduced in v6.2 to support access control, IPSec, and AAA that use the real outside address.
dns	Any DNS replies that match the xlate are translated.
timeout *hh:mm:ss*	Sets an idle timer for the translation slot.
access-list *acl_name*	Used with the **nat 0** command to exempt traffic that matches the access list from NAT processing.

NAT_ID Options

The nat_id option in the **nat** command can have serious implications for how the NAT process works. The next paragraphs offer an explanation and examples of each choice.

NAT 0 The **nat 0** turns off NAT translation for the defined address(es). The result is called *identity translation,* which is a translation that maps an address to itself. This command assumes the host address is a valid global address that can be used out in the Internet.

At first glance, this seems like the Static Command option of using the current IP address for both addresses. The difference between this command and the Static option is that this option requires that any resulting traffic must be initiated from an inside host, while the Static Command option allows outside hosts to precipitate access to inside resources. So, if you want the addresses to be visible to the outside, use the **static** command.

In the following example, the first entry shows an identity translation using the **nat 0** command, while the second uses the more public **static** command.

```
Pix(config)# nat (dmz) 0 1.1.1.15
Pix(config)# static (dmz, outside) 1.1.1.15 1.1.1.15
```

The next examples show the same commands using a class C size group of hosts. The first would be used to allow a group of user hosts with valid global IP addresses to travel the Internet without translation. The second would be used to make a large pool of shared servers available to the outside world, assuming appropriate ACLs are created.

```
Pix(config)# nat (dmz) 0 1.1.2.0 255.255.255.0
Pix(config)# static (dmz, outside) 1.1.2.0 1.1.2.0 netmask 255.255.255.0
```

NAT 0 Access-List ACL_Name The NAT 0 Access-List *acl_name* command variation uses an access control list to specify the traffic to exempt from NAT processing. This is particularly useful in VPN configuration where traffic needs to be exempted from

NAT. This command assumes the host address is a valid global address that can be used out in the Internet.

The following example demonstrates using this Command option to permit the internal host 1.1.1.15 to bypass NAT when connecting to outside host 1.1.2.19.

```
Pix(config)# access-list skip-nat permit ip host 1.1.1.15 host 1.1.2.19
Pix(config)# nat (inside) 0 access-list skip-nat
```

NAT_ID Greater Than 0 This is normal NAT with the *nat_id* greater than zero (0), indicating a pool of global IP addresses specified by the **global** command. The same *nat_id* in a **nat** command and **global** command links the two together.

The following example demonstrates using the **global** command to create a global address pool (9) with 508 addresses. The **nat** command allows the hosts on LAN network 192.168.1.0 to access that pool. The *net_id,* which is 9 in all three commands, links them together.

```
Pix(config)# global (outside) 9 1.1.2.1-1.1.2.254
Pix(config)# global (outside) 9 1.1.3.0 netmask 255.255.255.0
Pix(config)# nat (inside) 9 192.168.1.0 255.255.255.0
```

No Network or Broadcast IDs Allowed

ASA won't allow network or broadcast IDs to be included in the xlate table entries. If the Netmask *global_mask* option is used with a network ID to define a pool of addresses, the PIX automatically excludes the host ID and broadcast addresses from the pool available for translations.

ASA specifies a subnet mask, for example, 255.255.255.128 specifies one half of a class C network. If a specified address range in the *global_ip-global_ip* overlaps subnets defined by the netmask global_mask statement, the global pool won't use any broadcast or network addresses included in the pool of global addresses. In the following **global** command, the pool is the first 16 addresses on the 10.1.1.0 network (10.1.1.0-15).

```
Pix(config)# global (outside) 1 10.1.1.0 netmask 255.255.255.240
Pix(config)# nat (inside) 1 192.168.1.0 255.255.255.0
```

Because 10.1.1.0 is the network and 10.1.1.15 is the broadcast address for the network, they'll be excluded from the actual pool, leaving 10.1.1.1 to 10.1.1.14. Another way this could be defined is the following:

```
Pix(config)# global (outside) 1 10.1.1.1-10.1.1.14
Pix(config)# nat (inside) 1 192.168.1.0 255.255.255.0
```

Confirm NAT/Global Configuration

To display the results of the **global** and **nat** commands, use the following commands:

- show global
- show nat
- write terminal
- show xlate

Port Address Translations (PAT)

PAT is a variation of NAT that allows multiple inside hosts to use the same global IP address. Having to maintain a large pool of global addresses can be expensive and puts increased pressure on addresses that are in short supply worldwide. PAT combined with using private addresses within the network can save money and preserve real IP addresses.

The alternative is to have the NAT feature create a unique xlate for each session by using a single global IP address and appending a unique port number, such as 1.1.1.1:1540. While over 64,000 usable port numbers exist (65,536-1,023 reserved), the effective limit is much lower, usually estimated at about 4,000. PAT is often a viable solution when an ISP can't allocate enough unique IP addresses for the organization's outbound connections.

PAT can be enabled by entering a single IP address with the **global** command or by using the Interface option with the same command. The Interface option specifies that the named interface IP address is the one to be used.

Pix(config)# global (*if_name*) **nat_id** {*global_ip* [-*global_ip*] [netmask *global_mask*] | interface}

The first example creates a global address pool with only one "real" address, and then allows all LAN hosts to use the PAT translations.

```
Pix(config)# global (outside) 5 1.1.1.25
Pix(config)# nat (inside) 5 0 0
```

The next example uses the firewall outside interface IP address as the only PAT address, and then allows all LAN hosts to use the PAT translations. This could literally be the DSL or the cable modem connection address for a small network. This is the implementation requiring the smallest number of real IP addresses.

```
Pix(config)# global (outside) 7 interface
Pix(config)# nat (inside) 7 0 0
```

Remember the following about PAT implementations:

- After changing or removing a **nat** command statement, use the **clear xlate** command.
- An IP address used for PAT can't be used in another global or static address pool.
- PAT doesn't work with H.323 applications and caching nameservers.
- Don't use PAT when multimedia applications need to be run through the PIX Firewall. Multimedia applications can conflict with port mappings provided by PAT.
- PAT doesn't work with the TCP ACL "established" option.
- PAT does work with DNS, HTTP, URL filtering, e-mail, FTP, passive FTP, Telnet, outbound traceroute, and the UNIX RPC and rshell protocols.

Using NAT and PAT Together

The pool of available "real" addresses can be made up of multiple global statements. To augment a pool of global addresses with a PAT option, use the same *nat_id* in the global statements. When the pool contains both a global pool and a PAT designation, first the addresses from the global pool are used, and then the next connection uses the PAT address. Whenever a global pool address becomes available, the next connection takes that address.

In this example, a class C-sized global pool is augmented by a PAT argument using the outside interface IP address. All traffic that can't be handled by the 1.1.3.0/24 network will be translated using PAT.

```
Pix(config)# global (outside) 3 1.1.3.0 netmask 255.255.255.0
Pix(config)# global (outside) 3 interface
Pix(config)# nat (inside)3 0 0
```

Names and Name Commands

You can create and use text names for IP addresses in much the same way the **IP Host** command can be used on conventional routers. The **name** command is used to associate a single IP address and a text name. The names created become a host table local to that specific PIX Firewall only. You must first use the **names** command before immediately using the **name** command. Both the **names** command and any name statements created are saved in the configuration. The syntax is

```
Pix(config)# names
Pix(config)# name ip_address name
```

The **clear names** command clears the list of names from the PIX Firewall configuration. The **no names** command disables the use of the text names, but doesn't remove them from the configuration. The **show names** command lists the **name** command statements in the configuration. The following output shows the commands to create three names, the **show names** command, and the result of a **write terminal** command.

```
Pix(config)# names
Pix(config)# name 1.1.1.1 pix_out
Pix(config)# name 192.168.1.1 pix_in
Pix(config)# name 192.168.2.1 pix_dmz
Pix(config)#
Pix(config)# show names
name 1.1.1.1 pix_out
name 192.168.1.1 pix_in
name 192.168.2.1 pix_dmz
Pix(config)#
Pix(config)# write t
Building configuration...
   (output omitted)
names
name 1.1.1.1 pix_out
name 192.168.1.1 pix_in
```

PART IV

```
name 192.168.1.1 pix_in
   (output omitted)
Pix(config)#
```

The next output shows using the name with the **ping** command, instead of the IP address.

```
Pix(config)# ping pix_in
        pix_in response received -- 0ms
        pix_in response received -- 0ms
        pix_in response received -- 0ms
Pix(config)#
```

The next output shows the PIX Firewall assumes you prefer the name and substitutes the name for the address(es) whenever appropriate.

```
Pix(config)# show ip addresses
System IP Addresses:
        ip address outside pix_out 255.255.255.0
        ip address inside pix_in 255.255.255.0
        ip address dmz pix_dmz 255.255.255.0
Current IP Addresses:
        ip address outside pix_out 255.255.255.0
        ip address inside pix_in 255.255.255.0
        ip address dmz pix_dmz 255.255.255.0
Pix(config)#
```

Remember the following about name implementations:

- Only one name can be associated with an IP address.
- Names can use the characters *a* to *z*, *A* to *Z*, 0 to 9, the dash, and the underscore, but no spaces. The name can't be longer than 16 characters or start with a number.
- One reason to create names is to make life easier. Make sure the names you create don't add another level of complexity. The previous names could have been out, in, and dmz. Before you create names, make sure they won't look like keywords or instructions.

Configuring DNS Support

Use the DNS option on the **static** command to create a one-to-one address translation only if the reply is a DNS reply. Use the no form of the command to remove the translation.

> Pix(config)# static (*hi_interface, lo_interface*) *global_ip local_ip* [**dns**] [netmask *mask*] [norandomseq] [*max_conn* [*em_limit*]]
> Pix(config)# no static (*hi_interface, lo_interface*) *global_ip local_ip* [**dns**] [netmask *mask*] [norandomseq] [*max_conn* [*em_limit*]]

The following output is an example of creating the translation for a DNS server in the network depicted in Figure 19-13.

```
Pix(config)# static (dmz, outside) 1.1.1.3 192.168.128.3 dns
```

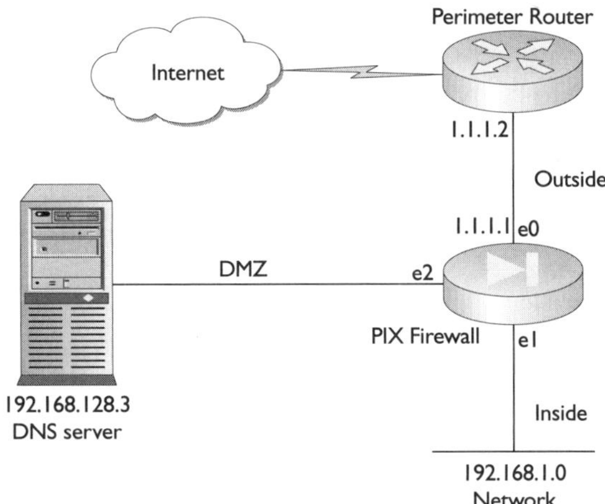

Figure 19-13 Static translation for a DNS server on a DMZ network

Because of the high number of attacks on DNS services, PIX Firewalls now only allow the first DNS reply to pass through, and then they drop all others. This prevents man in the middle attacks, where the attacker sends a second DNS reply, creating a bogus domain name resolution that would direct the browser to the wrong site. Unfortunately, DNS service would accept the later reply and update its table.

The following static PAT translation would direct any DNS traffic directed to the PIX Firewall outside interface to be redirected to the inside DNS server at 192.168.128.3.

```
Pix(config)# static (dns, outside) udp interface domain 192.168.128.3 domain
```

Access Control Lists (ACLs)

Since version 5.3 of the PIX Firewall OS, ACLs similar to the extended ACLs used on all Cisco IOS-based devices are used to control connections between inside and outside networks. Firewall access lists are created using the **access-list** command and applied to an interface with the **access-group** command.

These **ACL** commands replace the **conduit** and **outbound** commands used in earlier PIX Firewall versions. Remember, any **access-list** and **access-group** command statements take precedence over any **conduit/outbound** commands in the configuration.

Conduits are still supported in current OS versions for backward compatibility, but they're discouraged because they offer less-specific control. A brief introduction to conduits is at the end of this section. More detailed information is available online.

Using Access Lists

If internal users could be allowed to venture unrestricted into less-secure areas, bringing back whatever they find, and outside access to the network was absolutely forbidden, it might be possible to get by without using ACLs.

The PIX Firewall is designed around the default of absolute security, but it does allow for exceptions to be specifically configured using access lists. By default, traffic can flow freely from inside to outside, or from higher security to lower, except that specifically denied by an access list. Also, by default, all traffic from the outside toward the inside, lower security to higher, is blocked except that permitted by access lists.

Properly crafted access lists, applied to the proper interfaces, should allow for creating just the right exceptions to maintain acceptable security, while enabling activities that are required to further the organization's mission. All exceptions created with access lists should conform to the security policy. In the next sections, you see a variety of access list implementations.

Access-Group Statement

Use the **configuration mode access-group** command to apply an access list to an interface. The ACL is applied to inbound traffic of the interface. If the matching ACL statement is a Permit option, PIX allows the packet. If the matching ACL statement is a Deny option or no matching statement exists, PIX discards the packet and generates a syslog message. Use the no form of the command to remove the entry. The syntax is

Pix(config)# access-group *acl_id* in interface *int_name*
Pix(config)# no access-group *acl_id* in interface *int_name*

An **access-group** command always overrides the conduit and outbound command statements for the specific interface.

The **show access-group** command displays the current access list applied to interfaces.

In the following example, the **static** command creates a global address of 1.1.1.3 for a DMZ web server at 192.168.2.3. The access-list statement allows any outside host to access the global address for the web server using port 80 (www). The **access-group** command applies the access list to traffic entering the outside interface.

```
Pix(config)# static (dmz,outside) 1.1.1.3 192.168.2.3
Pix(config)# access-list www_ok permit tcp any host 1.1.1.3 eq www
Pix(config)# access-group www_ok in interface outside
```

Basic ACL Statements

PIX ACLs can be used to control connections based on source address, destination address, or protocol information. Because many ACLs are created to allow outside access into the more secure areas of the network, configuring them carefully to allow only the minimum access required is important. Whenever possible, configure ACLs more re strictively by specifying a remote source address, local destination address, and the protocol used, thereby reducing the likelihood of unwanted additional traffic. The **any** and **host** keywords are implemented the same as in IOS ACLs. Use the no form of the command to remove the ACL entry. The basic syntax is

Pix(config)# access-list *acl_id* {deny | permit} *protocol* {*source_addr* | *local_addr*} {*source_mask* | *local_mask*}[*operator* port [*port_id*] {*dest_addr* | *remote_addr*} {*dest_mask* | *remote_mask*} [*operator* port [*port_id*]

acl_id	ACL name. This can be either a name or a number.
permit	Used with the **access-group** command, permit allows the packet to traverse the PIX Firewall. Default is to deny all inbound or outbound traffic. Used with a **crypto map** command, permit selects a packet for IPSec protection using the policy described by the corresponding crypto map command statements.
deny	Used with the **access-group** command, deny doesn't allow a packet to traverse the PIX Firewall. Default is to deny all inbound or outbound traffic. Used with a **crypto map** command statement, deny prevents the traffic from being protected by IPSec in the context of that particular crypto map entry.
protocol	Name or number of an IP protocol. Choices include one of the keywords **ip**, **tcp**, **udp**, **icmp**, or an integer (1 to 254) representing an IP protocol number. Use keyword **ip** to include IP, ICMP, TCP, and UDP.
source_addr	Source network or host address. Use for ACL statement with **access-group**, the **aaa match access-list** command, and the **aaa authorization** command.
local_addr	Network or host address local to the PIX Firewall. Use *local_addr* with ACL statements for a crypto access-list statement, a nat 0 access-list statement, or a vpngroup split-tunnel statement.
source_mask	Netmask mask to be applied to *source_addr*.
local_mask	Netmask mask to be applied to *local_addr*.
operator	Comparison operator: *lt*—less than, *gt*—greater than, *eq*—equal, *neq*—not equal, and *range*—inclusive range. **ACL** command without an operator and port indicates all ports by default.
port *port_id*	Keyword followed by port identifier. Can be a number (0 to 65,535) or a literal, such as www (port 80) or smtp (port 25).
dest_addr	Destination network or host address. Use for ACL statement with **access-group**, the **aaa match access-list,** and **aaa authorization** commands.
remote_addr	Network or host address remote to the PIX Firewall. Use *local_addr* with ACL statements for a crypto access-list statement, a nat 0 access-list statement, or a vpngroup split-tunnel statement.
dest_mask	Netmask mask to be applied to *dest_addr*.
remote_mask	Netmask mask to be applied to *remote_addr*.

In the following example, a static mapping is created for a server, and then outside users are allowed to access that global address for web and FTP activities.

```
Pix(config)# static (dmz,outside) 1.1.1.3 192.168.2.3
Pix(config)# access-list tcp_ok permit tcp any host 1.1.1.3 eq www
Pix(config)# access-list tcp_ok permit tcp any host 1.1.1.3 eq ftp
Pix(config)# access-group tcp_ok in interface outside
```

ICMP ACL Statements

ASA prohibits ICMP traffic through the firewall by default. The last chapter covered managing ICMP traffic and specifically targeting interfaces on the PIX device. In this chapter, you learn about Access-List options used to allow specific ICMP traffic to pass through the PIX Firewall.

Use the following form of the **access-list** command to allow specific ICMP traffic. The **any** and **host** keywords are implemented the same as in IOS ACLs. Use the no form of the command to remove the ACL entry. The basic syntax is

pix(config)# access-list *acl_id* {deny | permit} icmp {*source_addr* | *local_addr*} {*source_mask* | *local_mask*} {*dest_addr* | *remote_addr*} {*dest_mask* | *remote_mask*} *icmp_type*

icmp_type	Non-IPSec implementations only: to permit or deny specific ICMP message types. See the following table for a list of message types. No ICMP types are supported for use with IPSec.

The following table lists possible ICMP type values and their literal equivalents. Either form can be used, but the literal list is easier for the humans to interpret.

Type	Literal	Type	Literal
0	echo-reply	12	parameter-problem
3	unreachable	13	timestamp-reply
4	source-quench	14	timestamp-request
5	redirect	15	information-request
6	alternate-address	16	information-reply
8	echo	17	mask-request
9	router-advertisement	18	mask-reply
10	router-solicitation	31	conversion-error
11	time-exceeded	32	mobile-redirect

The following example creates three static mapping for servers, allows three types of ICMP messages, and then allows outside access to the server global addresses.

```
Pix(config)# static (dmz,outside) 1.1.1.3 192.168.2.3 netmask 255.255.255.255
Pix(config)# static (dmz,outside) 1.1.1.4 192.168.2.4 netmask 255.255.255.255
Pix(config)# static (dmz,outside) 1.1.1.5 192.168.2.5 netmask 255.255.255.255
Pix(config)# access-list 101 permit icmp any any echo-reply
Pix(config)# access-list 101 permit icmp any any time-exceeded
Pix(config)# access-list 101 permit icmp any any unreachable
Pix(config)# access-list 101 permit tcp any host 1.1.1.3 eq www
Pix(config)# access-list 101 permit tcp any host 1.1.1.4 eq ftp
Pix(config)# access-list 101 permit tcp any host 1.1.1.5 eq smtp
Pix(config)# access-group 101 in interface outside
```

TurboACL

Traditional ACLs are composed of a series of permit or deny statements each with one or more test criteria, such as source and destination addresses and possibly protocols.

These statements are processed sequentially from top to bottom, based on the order of creation. Logically, the longer the list of statements and the more elements that must be matched, the longer it can take to process. When an ACL statement is processed by the device, each line must be processed by a command interpreter that converts the text into computer code.

Long ago, programmers learned that text instructions can be compiled by a computer one time to put the same information in a form that can be processed much more quickly. The real benefit to compiling is when the same instructions are used frequently. The PIX Firewall version 6.2 introduced *TurboACL*, which compiles ACLs into a set of binary lookup tables, while maintaining first-match requirements. Because compiling only makes significant improvements on larger ACLs, TurboACL only works on ACLs with 19 or more statements and supports access lists with up to 16,000 statements.

The TurboACL feature requires significant memory resources, including a minimum of 2.1MB, plus approximately 1MB of memory for every 2,000 ACL statements. The feature requiring a minimum of 16MB of Flash combined with the memory requirements is designed for the high-end PIX Firewall models, such as the PIX 525 or the PIX 535.

Global Compiling

TurboACL can either be configured globally, in which case it tags all ACLs with 19 elements or more for compiling, or it can be configured on a per ACL basis. Use the following syntax to configure the feature globally. Use the no form of the command to turn off the feature.

Pix(config)# access-list compiled
Pix(config)# no access-list compiled   the default status

Individual ACL Compiling

Use the following command syntax to enable/disable compiling individual ACLs when TurboACL isn't globally enabled or, if globally configured, to disable compiling individual ACLs.

Pix(config)# access-list [*acl_id*] compiled
Pix(config)# no access-list [*acl_id*] compiled

The following output shows enabling global TurboACL, and then turning the feature off specifically for ACL 105. Any ACLs with less than 19 elements also wouldn't be compiled.

```
Pix(config)# access-list compiled
Pix(config)# no access-list 105 compiled
Pix(config)# access-list 101 permit icmp any any echo-reply
Pix(config)# access-list 101 permit icmp any any time-exceeded
Pix(config)# access-list 101 permit icmp any any unreachable
Pix(config)# access-list 101 permit tcp any host 1.1.1.3 eq www
Pix(config)# access-list 101 permit tcp any host 1.1.1.4 eq ftp
Pix(config)# access-list 101 permit tcp any host 1.1.1.5 eq smtp
Pix(config)# access-group 101 in interface outside
     (additional lines omitted)
```

PART IV

Verifying and Monitoring TurboACL

The standard **show access-list** command displays the memory use of each compiled ACL and the shared memory use for all the turbo-compiled ACLs. The command shows the number of ACEs, the individual ACEs, and activity. The hit count (hitcnt=) is the same information as the "matches" displayed for regular ACLs. The **debug access-list turbo** command allows real-time monitoring.

```
Pix# show access list
TurboACL statistics:
ACL                  State       Memory (KB)
-------------------- ----------- ----------
test1_acl            Operational   5
test2_acl            Operational   2
Shared memory usage: 2046 KB
access-list compiled
access-list test1_acl turbo-configured; 19 elements
access-list test1_acl permit tcp any host 10.1.2.3 (hitcnt=19)
access-list test1_acl permit tcp any host 10.1.2.4 (hitcnt=7)
access-list test1_acl permit tcp any host 10.1.2.5 (hitcnt=0)
access-list test1_acl permit tcp any host 10.1.1.1 eq telnet (hitcnt=8)
access-list test1_acl permit udp any host 10.1.2.3 (hitcnt=4)
     (additional lines omitted)
```

Downloadable ACLs

In Chapter 8, you learned about the CBAC Authentication Proxy feature of the Cisco Secure IOS PIX feature set. This feature allowed ACEs to be downloaded on a per-user or a per-group basis from an AAA server. These ACEs were based on either user or group profile entries added to the Cisco Secure ACS configuration.

The PIX Firewall version 6.2 introduced a similar feature when using a RADIUS server for AAA and Cisco Secure ACS 3.0 or later (Windows). Access lists are configured on the AAA server, and then downloaded to a PIX Firewall during user authentication, eliminating the need to be configured separately on the PIX Firewall. This feature improves scalability when using access lists for individual users. Currently, the feature isn't supported for TACACS+ servers or UNIX ACS.

No additional configuration is needed for the firewall once AAA authorization is configured. The next chapter looks at configuring the Cisco Secure ACS server. Adding downloadable ACLs is covered briefly then.

Cisco Secure ACS Configuration

Remember, as a new feature in the PIX Firewall v6.2 and Cisco Secure ACS v3.0 for Windows, changes and additional options can be expected. Be sure to check the Cisco web site for the latest instructions.

Downloading an ACL

The actual ACL entries can be named or unnamed ACLs, depending on whether the ACL will ultimately be used by multiple users. A *named ACL* should be used when frequent requests occur for downloading a large access list. With a named ACL, after authentication, the ACS server sends the ACL name to the PIX Firewall to see if the ACL already exists. If not, the PIX Firewall requests the ACL to be downloaded. A named ACL isn't down loaded again as long as it exists on the PIX Firewall. *Unnamed ACLs* are always downloaded, so they should be used for unique or short ACLs.

Recognize that not all ACL statements supported by the Cisco IOS software are implemented the same on the PIX Firewall and vice versa. Because no immediate error or typo feedback exists when configuring an ACL on a AAA server, double-checking your work and testing your results is important.

Downloadable Named ACL

The basic Cisco Secure ACS configuration for a named downloadable ACL includes

1. On the Shared Profile Component (SPC) menu, select Downloadable PIX ACLs.
2. Click Add to create an ACL definition with the *acl_name*, description, and the ACL definition. The *ACL definition* consists of one or more valid PIX Firewall ACL statements, each on a separate line. Each command is entered without the keyword **access-list** and the ***acl_name*** (acs_1, as you see in the following). The following is an example:

   ```
   Shared profile Components
   Name: acs_1
   Description:  Basic PIX access example
   ACL Definitions
   permit tcp any host 10.1.2.3
   permit udp any host 10.1.2.3
   permit icmp any host 10.1.2.3
       (balance omitted)
   ```

   Because more than one user or group on the PIX Firewall could have the same ACL lines, the firewall creates a unique *acl_id* by concatenating #ACSACL#-PIX- + *acl_name-* + *unique_num*. *Acl_name* is the ACL name from the SPC and *unique_num* is a unique version ID. The following sample is downloaded from the previous entries:

   ```
   access-list #ACSACL#-PIX-acs_1-4b4119d5 permit tcp any host 10.1.2.3
   access-list #ACSACL#-PIX-acs_1-4b4119d5 permit udp any host 10.1.2.3
   access-list #ACSACL#-PIX-acs_1-4b4119d5 permit icmp any host 10.1.2.3
       (balance omitted)
   ```

3. Use User Setup or Group Setup to include the ACL in the user/group settings.

   Next, enable downloadable ACLs by following these steps:

4. From the ACS main menu, choose Interface Configuration.
5. Choose Advanced Options from the resulting Interface Configuration menu.
6. Depending on how the ACL is to be applied, check either or both of the following:

   User-Level Downloadable ACLs
   Group-Level Downloadable ACLs

PART IV

Downloadable Unnamed ACL

To create a user authentication profile for downloadable unnamed ACLs, perform the following steps on the AAA RADIUS server:

1. On Group Setup or User Setup, choose Cisco IOS/PIX RADIUS Attributes.
2. In the cisco-av-pair field, type the ACL entries, using the following syntax:

   ip:inacl#*nnn*=*acl_command*

ip:inacl#	Keyword string that specifies an input ACL.
nnn	Integer (0 to 999999999) that creates a final sequence order for the ACL statements on the PIX Firewall. Any command with the same *nnn*, including the default 0, will appear in the order created.
acl_command	One or more ACL statements without keyword **access-list** or **acl_name**.

The PIX Firewall assigns a name to a downloaded, unnamed ACL, using the following syntax where *username* is the user name of the authenticated user.

AAA-user-*username*

The following entries demonstrate the syntax and the capability to manage the sequence of statements. This latter feature would be a tremendous improvement to regular ACLs.

```
ip:inacl#5=permit tcp any host 10.1.2.3
ip:inacl#15=permit icmp any host 10.1.2.3
ip:inacl#10=permit udp any host 10.1.2.3
ip:inacl#100=deny tcp any any
ip:inacl#100=deny udp any any
```

The downloaded ACEs on a PIX Firewall would look like the following. Notice that the permit udp statement precedes the permit icmp statement because of the sequence numbers.

```
access-list aaa-user-jkeely permit tcp any host 10.1.2.3
access-list aaa-user-jkeely permit udp any host 10.1.2.3
access-list aaa-user-jkeely permit icmp any host 10.1.2.3
access-list aaa-user-jkeely deny tcp any any
access-list aaa-user-jkeely deny udp any any
```

At a later time, you could add the following line to the configuration. The sequence number 3 would make it the first statement in the downloaded ACL the next time it's called.

```
ip:inacl#3=deny tcp 10.5.5.0 255.255.255.0 host 10.1.2.3
```

Content Filtering

Content filtering features allow administrators to block certain types of web related features or content that may be deemed a threat to the network or inappropriate to the workplace. For example, ActiveX objects and Java applets can represent security vulnerabilities for outside connections because they can contain code intended to attack hosts and servers. You can disable ActiveX objects and remove Java applets with the PIX Firewall **configuration mode filter** command. The **filter** command can work with a Websense server to remove URLs that are inappropriate for the organization. These features are similar to some of the PIX IOS firewall features covered in Chapter 6.

ActiveX Blocking

You can block ActiveX controls from web pages that return to the PIX Firewall from an outbound connection. ActiveX controls, formerly known as OLE or OCX controls, such as custom forms, buttons, calendars, or any of the extensive third-party objects, can be inserted in a web page or other application for gathering or displaying information. These controls can present potential security problems because they can be created to attack network servers or take over a workstation. The user still receives the HTML page, but the web page source for the object can't execute. You might recall that the IOS Firewall can't block ActiveX objects.

Use the **filter activex configuration mode** command to filter out ActiveX. Use 0 for the *local_ip* or *foreign_ip* IP addresses to mean all hosts. No ActiveX blocking occurs if users access an IP address referenced by the **alias** command. The no form of the command turns off the feature. The syntax is the following:

pix(config)# filter activex *port local_ip local_mask foreign_ip foreign_mask*
pix(config)# no filter activex *port local_ip local_mask foreign_ip foreign_mask*

port	Port receiving Internet traffic on the PIX Firewall. Typically, 80, but other values are accepted. The **http** or **url** literal can be used for port 80.
local_ip	The IP address of the highest security-level interface from which access is sought. Set this address to 0.0.0.0 (or in shortened form, 0) to specify all hosts.
local_mask	Network mask of *local_ip*. Use 0.0.0.0 (or 0) to specify all hosts.
foreign_ip	The IP address of the lowest security-level interface to which access is sought. Use 0.0.0.0 (or in shortened form, 0) to specify all hosts.
foreign_mask	Network mask of foreign_ip. Always specify a specific mask value. You can use 0.0.0.0 (or in shortened form, 0) to specify all hosts.

The <object> tag, which is blocked by the **filter activex** command, is also used for Java applets, image files, and multimedia objects.

In the following output, the first example blocks ActiveX for web traffic on port 80 from any local host and for connections to any foreign host. The second example blocks ActiveX for web traffic on port 80 from network 192.168.1.0 to any host.

```
pix(config)#filter activex 80 0 0 0 0
pix(config)#filter activex http 192.168.1.0 255.255.255.0 0 0
```

Java Blocking

The **filter java** command filters out Java applets that return to the PIX Firewall from an outbound connection. The user still receives the HTML page, but the web page source for the applet is commented out, so the applet can't execute. Use 0 for the *local_ip* or *foreign_ip* IP addresses to mean all hosts. If Java applets are known to be in <object> tags, use the **filter activex** command to remove them. The syntax is as follows:

pix(config)#filter java *port*[-*port*] *local_ip local_mask foreign_ip foreign_mask*
pix(config)#no filter java *port*[-*port*] *local_ip local_mask foreign_ip foreign_mask*

-port	Use to define a range of ports.

In the following output, the first example blocks Java for web traffic on port 80 from any local host and for connections to any foreign host. The second example blocks Java for web traffic on port 80 from network 192.168.1.0 to any host.

```
pix(config)#filter java 80 0 0 0 0
pix(config)#filter java http 192.168.1.0 255.255.255.0 0 0
```

Websense Filtering

Websense and *N2H2* are both developers of employee Internet management (EIM) software solution or URL filtering systems. PIX Firewall versions of both companies' products exist. Figure 19-14 shows a typical Websense solution.

The Cisco PIX Firewall Edition of Websense Enterprise allows transparent analysis, management, and reporting of traffic flowing from the internal networks to the Internet. Websense uses pass-through technology to provide accurate, reliable, and scalable Internet filtering. URL filtering allows the PIX Firewall to check outgoing URL requests against the company security policy defined on the Websense server. Websense Enterprise automatically downloads updates to the Master Database daily, including additions, changes, and deletions, so you can be sure you're using the freshest database at all times. Figure 19-15 shows an example of a site-blocked screen.

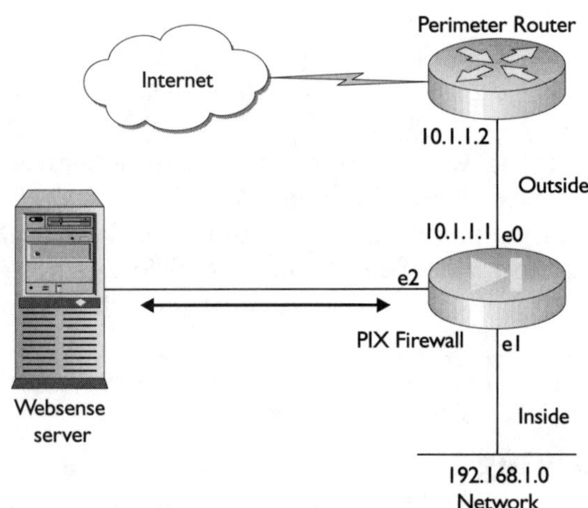

Figure 19-14 A network with a PIX Firewall using a Websense server

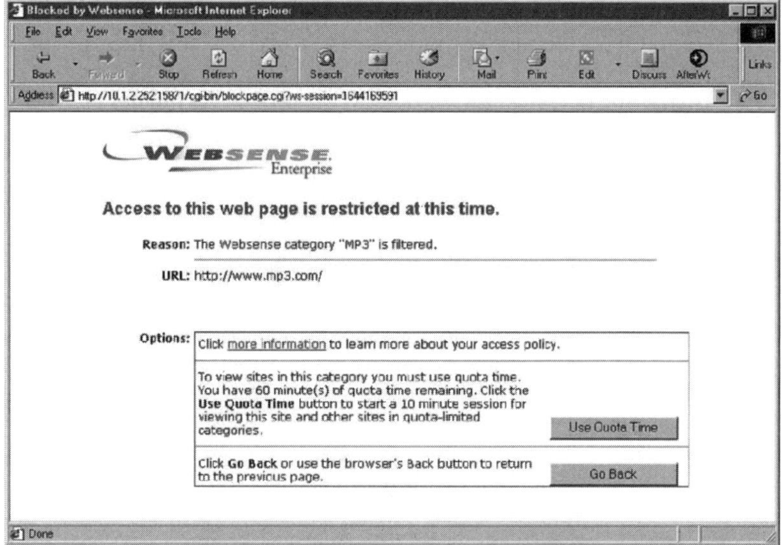

Figure 19-15 Websense screen explaining that the selected site is blocked

Websense protocol enables group and user name authentication between a host and a PIX Firewall. The PIX Firewall performs a user name lookup, and then the Websense server handles URL filtering and user name logging. User name logging tracks the user name, group, and domain name on the Websense server.

Follow these steps to filter URLs:

1. Define a N2H2 or Websense server using the appropriate vendor-specific form of the **url-server** command.
2. Enable filtering with the **filter** command.
3. If needed, improve throughput with the **url-cache** command. This command doesn't update Websense logs, however, which might affect Websense's accounting reports. Accumulate Websense run logs before using the **url-cache** command.
4. Use the **show url-cache stats** and the **show perfmon** commands to view run information.

To perform URL filtering based on N2H2 or Websense server policies, use the **filter url** command. Use the no form of the command to turn the feature off. The syntax is as follows:

pix(config)# filter url [http | *port*[-*port*]] *local_ip local_mask foreign_ip foreign_mask* [allow] [proxy-block] [longurl-*truncate* | longurl-*deny*] [cgi-truncate]
pix(config)#no filter url [http | *port*[-*port*]] *local_ip local_mask foreign_ip foreign_mask* [allow] [proxy-block] [longurl-*truncate* | longurl-*deny*] [cgi-truncate]

To create an exception to a previous filter condition, use the **filter url except** command. Use the no form of the command to turn off the feature. The syntax is

pix(config)# filter url except *local_ip local_mask foreign_ip foreign_mask*
pix(config)# no filter url except *local_ip local_mask foreign_ip foreign_mask*

url	Filters URLs from data passing through the PIX Firewall.
http	Specifies port 80. Can also use http or www to indicate port 80.
except	Creates an exception to a previous filter condition.
allow	Lets outbound connections pass through the PIX Firewall without filtering if the N2H2/Websense server is unavailable. If this option is omitted and the server goes offline, the PIX Firewall stops all outbound port 80 (Web) traffic until the server is back online.
proxy-block	Prevents users from connecting to an HTTP proxy server.
longurl-truncate	Sends only the originating host name or IP address to the Websense server if the URL is over the URL buffer limit.
longurl-deny	Denies the URL request if the URL is over the URL buffer-size limit or the URL buffer is unavailable.
cgi_truncate	Sends a CGI script as a URL.

The **url-server** command defines the server running the N2H2 or Websense URL application. While it's possible to define up to 16 URL servers by repeating the command, you can use only one URL filtering application at a time: either N2H2 or Websense. The syntax is as follows:

Pix(config)#url-server [(*if_name*)] vendor n2h2 host *local_ip* [port *number*] [timeout *seconds*] [protocol {TCP | UDP}]

Pix(config)#url-server [(*if_name*)] vendor websense host *local_ip* [timeout *seconds*] [protocol{TCP | UDP} version]

timeout *seconds*	Maximum idle time permitted before PIX Firewall switches to the next server you specified. The default is five seconds.

This example specifies a Websense server, and then filters all outbound HTTP connections, except those from the host 192.168.1.149.

```
pix(config)#url-server (perimeter) vendor websense host 192.168.100.10
    timeout 15
pix(config)#filter url 80 0 0 0 0
pix(config)#filter url except 192.168.1.149 255.255.255.255 0 0
```

The next example blocks all outbound HTTP connections destined to a proxy server that listens on port 8080:

```
pix(config)#url-server (perimeter) vendor n2h2 host 192.168.100.10
pix(config)#filter url 8080 0 0 0 0 proxy-block
```

The following is an example of the **show url-server stats** command:

```
pix#show url-server stats
URL Server Statistics:
----------------------
URL Server Vendor                  websense
URLs total/allowed/denied          178/135/43

URL Server Status:
------------------
192.168.100.10          UP
192.168.100.12        DOWN
```

More information on Websense, including a good tutorial video on the products tab, is available at the following web site: http://www.websense.com.

N2H2 information is available at http://www.n2h2.com.

Object Grouping

The concept of grouping or forming groups isn't new to network or even human interaction. Groups can be given special privileges or restrictions, and those privileges or restrictions then apply to all members of the group. In the networking world, creating groups—such as employees or marketing employees—is common, and then assigning permission to the group to access certain services, such as department servers and printers. A new employee needs only to be placed in the appropriate group to share the permissions granted that group. By the same token, if a group is denied access to a resource, such as a color printer, then everyone in the group is denied.

Overview of Object Grouping

PIX Firewall version 6.2 introduced grouping to help reduce the complexity of configuration and to improve scalability for large or complex networks. *Object Grouping* allows the definition of groups, and then application of commands or features to a group. This process can reduce the number and the complexity of configuration statements and, thereby, reduce the amount of time spent configuring and troubleshooting large or complex networks.

An example of using Object Grouping would be to group objects of a similar type, so a single access list could apply to all the member objects. Review the following object groups and visualize how they might be used with ACL statements to manage network access.

- **DMZServers** The IP addresses of the shared servers in the DMZ network.
- **Partners** The host and network addresses of trading partners allowed the greatest access to the organization services and servers.
- **DMZServices** Those TCP/UDP port numbers and ICMP message types allowed access to the DMZ network.

Creating a single access rule to allow partner hosts to use the DMZServices with the DMZServers should be possible. If four DMZ servers need to be shared with the current pool of 40 business partner organizations, it's conceivable that, without object groups, hundreds of commands (40 × 4 × the number of ports) might be necessary.

Getting Started with Group Objects

An object group is created with the **command mode** command **object-group**. After the **object-group** command creates the group, the mode changes to a corresponding Subcommand mode. The object group is then defined in the Subcommand mode. The command prompt indicates the Active mode. The object group can neither be created empty nor removed or emptied if it's being used by another command. Use the no form of the command to remove the group. The first line is the basic syntax to create an object group. The last two lines are the actual syntax with options.

Pix(config)# object-group *object-type grp-id*
Pix(config)# no object-group *object-type grp-id*
Pix(config)# object-group {protocol|network|icmp-type} *grp-id*
Pix(config)# object-group service *grp-id* {tcp|udp|tcp-udp}

grp-id	Descriptive name for the group (1 to 64 characters). Can be any combination of letters, digits, dash (-), underscore (_), and period (.) characters.
object-type	Use one of the following object types: **Network**—Group of hosts or subnets **Service**—Group of TCP or UDP port numbers port service literal (www, ftp) **ICMP-type**—Group of ICMP message types **Protocol**—Group of IP protocols. This can be keywords icmp, ip, tcp, or udp, or an IP protocol number (1 to 254). Use IP to include IP, ICMP, TCP, and UDP

Subcommand Mode

The prompt changes to the appropriate Subcommand mode once the **object-group** command is complete. Commands available in the Subcommand mode apply to the object type and group name identified in the **object-group** command. The prompts in each Subcommand mode are as follows:

Pix(config-protocol)#
Pix(config-service)#
Pix(config-icmp-type)#
Pix(config-network)#

Use **exit**, **quit**, or any valid **config-mode** command, such as access list, to close an Object-Group Subcommand mode, and then exit the object-group creation process.

Any **PIX Firewall** command using the keyword **object-group** and followed by the group name applies to every item in that group.

Pix# show object-group *group_name*

Removing Object Groups

Use the **no object-group** ***object-type grp-id*** command to remove a group of previously defined **object-group** commands. The **clear object-group** command form can also be used. Beware, the **clear object-group** command without any parameter removes all defined object groups that aren't being used in a command. Adding the *object_type* parameter removes only the defined object groups that aren't being used in a command.

Verifying Object Groups

Use the **show object-group** command to display a list of the currently configured object groups. The command syntax is

Pix# show object-group [protocol | network | service | icmp-type] | [id *grp_id*]

The **show object-group** command offers the following choices:

- **show object-group id** *grp_id*—Displays all defined object groups by their **grp_id**
- **show object-group** *object_type*—Displays all defined object groups by group type
- **show object-group**—Displays all defined object groups

The following output demonstrates the **show object-group** command.

```
Pix(config)# show object-group
object-group network dmz_servers
  description: The DMZ shared servers
  network-object host 192.168.2.3
  network-object host 192.168.2.4
  network-object host 192.168.2.5
object-group network Partners
  description: The dealer and supplier partners
  network-object host 172.16.21.119
  network-object 192.168.7.0 255.255.255.0
  network-object 192.168.12.0 255.255.253.0
```

Configuring Object Groups with ACLs

The **access-list** command offers an Object Group option for each of the variable choices. The following syntax is the previous basic **ACL** command with an alternative to having to define each element explicitly for what could be many configurations.

Pix(config)# access-list *acl_id* {deny | permit} {protocol | ***object-type protocol-grp-id*** {*source_addr* | *local_addr*} {*source_mask* | *local_mask*} | ***object-type network-grp-id*** [*operator* port [*port*] | ***object-type service-grp-id***] {*dest_addr* | *remote_addr*} {*dest_mask* | *remote_mask*} | ***object-type*** **network-grp-id** [*operator* port [*port*] | ***object-type service-grp-id***]}

The following example creates a service object group to define the DMZ resources you're willing to share. The ACL allows the Partners from the last example to use the services on the DMZ servers defined in the last example.

```
Pix(config)# object-group service dmz_service tcp
Pix(config-service)#port-object eq www
Pix(config-service)#port-object eq ftp
Pix(config-service)#port-object eq smtp
Pix(config-service)#exit
Pix (config)# access-list 101 permit tcp object-group partners dmz_servers eq
dmz_service
```

Nested Object Groups

An *object group* can contain or be contained by other object groups. For example, Partners, from the earlier example, could contain the groups AsiaPartners, EuroPartners, AfricaPartners, and NorthAmericaPartners. Each of those groups could contain other groups, such as NorthAmericaPartners might contain CanadaPartners, MexicoPartners, and USPartners. Each of the smaller subgroups only makes sense if additional resources were limited to each group. The following example demonstrates part of the previous nesting:

```
Pix(config)# object-group network MexicoPartners
Pix (config-network)#network-object 192.168.151.0 255.255.255.0
Pix (config-network)#network-object 192.168.159.0 255.255.255.0
Pix (config-network)#network-object 192.168.210.0 255.255.255.0
Pix(config)# object-group network CanadaPartners
Pix(config-network)# network-object 192.168.251.0 255.255.255.0
Pix(config-network)# network-object 192.168.237.0 255.255.255.0
Pix(config-network)# network-object 192.168.216.0 255.255.255.0
    (additional lines omitted)
Pix(config)# object-group network NorthAmericaPartners
Pix(config-network)# network-object CanadaPartners
Pix(config-network)# network-object MexicoPartners
Pix(config-network)# network-object USPartners
Pix(config-network)# exit
Pix(config)# access-list 101 permit tcp object-group NorthAmericaPartners any
Pix(config)# access-group 101 in interface outside
```

Object Grouping dramatically reduces the number of access list statements required to implement a particular security policy. The last line shows that the NorthAmericaPartners networks are allowed to have TCP access to the network.

Conduit Statements

The **conduit** command can be used to create an exception to the PIX Firewall ASA that prevents traffic originating on a lower-level security traffic interface from passing to higher- level areas. The most obvious example would be allowing outside users to access DMZ or inside shared resources, such as servers.

PIX Firewall version 5.3 introduced ACL features similar to those supported in Cisco IOS-based devices. Although it's strongly recommended that configurations use the more secure **access-list** command approach instead of the conduits, conduits are still supported by the PIX OS for backward compatibility.

STUDY TIP The current PIX Firewall Advanced Exam (CSPFA 9E0-111) assumes PIX OS v6.2, so conduits won't appear on the exam. All CCSP exams after 3/1/2003 also assume ACLS are the preferred approach over the older conduits.

The enhanced security of ACLs over conduits derives from the fact that the scope of ACLs can be easily and explicitly limited because they're applied to specific interfaces with an **access-group** command. The **conduit** command, on the other hand, applies to all but the inside interface, and then relies on proper configuration of **static** and **global** commands to limit access.

Configuring Conduits

The **configuration mode conduit** command, like the newer **access-list** command, supports options for regular traffic filtering, ICMP message filtering, and even object group implementation. Use the no form of each to remove the **conduit** command. The following standard and ICMP message conduit syntax and examples are offered for informational purposes only:

> Pix(config)# conduit {permit | deny} protocol global_ip global_mask [operator port [port]] foreign_ip foreign_mask [operator port [port]]
> Pix(config)# conduit {permit | deny} icmp global_ip global_mask foreign_ip foreign_mask [icmp_type]

The **clear conduit** command removes all **conduit** command statements from your configuration. The **clear conduit counters** command clears the current conduit hit count.

The following examples compare a **conduit** and an **access-list** command used to allow access to a web server on the DMZ. In each case, the static creates the address translation from the DMZ (192.168.2.4) to the global IP address (1.1.1.4).

```
Pix(config)# static (dmz,outside) 1.1.1.4 192.168.2.4 netmask 255.255.255.255
Pix(config)# conduit permit tcp host 1.1.1.4 eq 80 any
```

or

```
Pix(config)# static (dmz,outside) 1.1.1.4 192.168.2.4 netmask 255.255.255.255
Pix(config)# access-list 105 permit tcp any host 1.1.1.4 eq 80
Pix(config)# access-group 105 in interface outside
```

The next example compares a **conduit** and an **access-list** command used to allow ICMP messages though the router. Note that the access list is specifically limited to incoming traffic on the outside interface.

```
pix(config)# conduit permit icmp any any echo-reply
pix(config)# conduit permit icmp any any time-exceeded
```

```
pix(config)# conduit permit icmp any any unreachable

pix(config)# access-list 100 permit icmp any any echo-reply
pix(config)# access-list 100 permit icmp any any time-exceeded
pix(config)# access-list 100 permit icmp any any unreachable
Pix(config)# access-group 100 in interface outside
```

PIX Routing Configuration

Routing represents a multifaceted problem for the PIX Firewall. First, the PIX Firewall is an inline security filter, not a router, and therefore uses static routes to direct traffic out of the interfaces. This nonrouter strategy is reinforced because the PIX interfaces don't support VLAN trunk links and require a "real" router to perform VLAN termination before forwarding traffic on to the firewall.

Second, Cisco security strategy considers sending routing protocols across any firewall to be a serious vulnerability because corrupted or compromised routes received on the unprotected interface would then be transmitted to the protected side of the firewall.

Finally, the PIX Firewall doesn't forward broadcast or multicast packets used by most routing protocols. Not forwarding multicasts also has implications for technologies like IP-TV.

This section looks briefly at the **route** command, and then at possible solutions around the no routing and no multicast restrictions for those exceptional cases. Figure 19-16 shows the router and firewall implementation to use for the examples in this section. The Layer 3 switch connecting the organization's VLANs to the PIX Firewall could also be a router and Layer 2 switch.

The Route Command

Except for organizations using BGP between their networks and their ISPs, most organizations don't share a routing protocol with their ISPs. Instead, they use a static default route to the ISP and the ISP uses one or more static routes back. This reduces router overhead on the organization's routers and limits information about the internal network shared with the outside world, particularly when combined with NAT. The commands for the example in Figure 19-16 might look like the following:

```
Rtr1(config)#ip route 0.0.0.0 0.0.0.0 10.0.2.1
ISP(config)#ip route 10.1.1.0 255.255.255.0 10.0.2.2
```

The **PIX configuration mode route** command performs a similar function for the PIX Firewall. To define a default route, set *ip_address* and *netmask* both to 0.0.0.0, or the shortened form of 0. Use the no form of the command or the **clear route** command to remove the route. The syntax is

Pix(config)# route *int_name ip_address netmask gateway_ip* [*metric*]
Pix(config)# no route [*int_name ip_address* [*netmask gateway_ip*]]
Pix(config)# clear route [*int_name ip_address* [*netmask gateway_ip*]]

gateway_ip	Specify the IP address of the gateway router (the next hop address for this route).
metric	Specify the number of hops to *gateway_ip*. The default is 1.

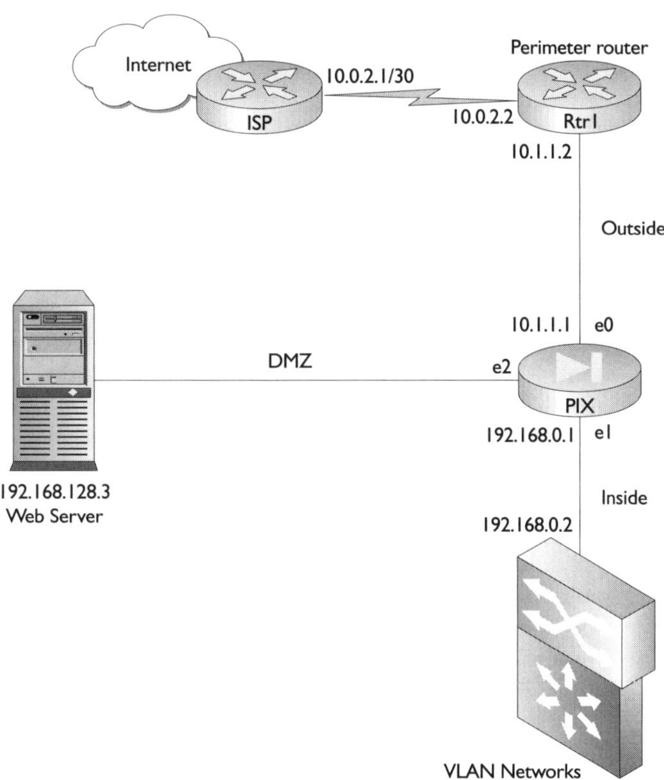

Figure 19-16 Perimeter router, PIX Firewall, and Layer 3 switch implementation

For the sample network in Figure 19-16, use the following command to define a default route for outbound traffic:

```
Pix(config)# route outside 0 0 10.1.1.2 1
```

In the next example, the PIX Firewall directs all traffic for the protected LANs 192.168.0.0 to 192.168.127.0 to the Layer 3 switch.

```
Pix(config)# route inside 192.168.0.0 255.255.128.0 192.168.0.2 1
```

The next example looks at forwarding traffic destined to any shared servers into the DMZ. If the **route** command uses the IP address of a PIX interface as the gateway IP address, the PIX then recognizes the address as local and uses an Address Resolution Protocol (ARP) request for the destination IP address in the packet instead of the gateway IP address.

```
Pix(config)# route dmz 192.168.128.0 255.255.255.0 192.168.128.1 1
```

The show route Command

Use the **show route** command to confirm static and default route configuration. The CONNECT identifier indicates a local network attached directly to a PIX interface. If the target network is labeled with the CONNECT identifier, the PIX will ARP for the destination address.

```
Pix# show route
        outside 0.0.0.0 0.0.0.0 10.1.1.2 1 OTHER static
        inside 192.168.0.0 255.255.128.0 192.168.0.2 1 OTHER static
        dmz 192.168.128.0 255.255.128.0 192.168.128.1 1 CONNECT static
Pix#
```

Routing Options

The PIX Firewall doesn't allow broadcast and multicast traffic to pass between interfaces. Looking at Figure 19-16, it wouldn't be possible to exchange routing between the perimeter router Rtr1 and the Layer 3 switch using an Interior Gateway Protocol (IGP), such as Open Shortest Path First (OSPF), Enhanced Interior Gateway Routing Protocol (EIGRP), or Routing Information Protocol (RIP), all of which use broadcast or multicast packets to exchange routing information.

Possible Workarounds

One possible solution, if it were necessary to send routing updates through the PIX firewall, would be to add neighbor statements to the router configuration on the Layer 3 switch and perimeter router. The *neighbor* statement causes the routing update to be sent to the neighbor router using a unicast, rather than broadcast or multicast. The following output demonstrates what a RIP configuration on the Layer 3 switch might look like. EIGRP and OSPF would support a similar solution.

```
router rip
  version 2
  network 192.168.0.0
  network 192.168.1.0
  network 192.168.2.0
  (other networks omitted)
  neighbor 10.1.1.2
```

The neighbor 10.1.1.2 statement directs routing updates to be sent directly to the perimeter router using a unicast.

Downsides So, if this is so easy, what's the problem? This example intentionally took the easy part of the solution. Little security risk occurs in configuring an outside address on this switch and the firewall naturally allows the packets to flow from the inside to the outside. Things get more complicated coming the other way. What address for the L3 switch would need to be used when the neighbor statement is added to the perimeter router? You don't want to put a "hidden" inside address outside the firewall. Using a translated (static) address and the associated ACL or conduit would involve punching a hole completely through the firewall.

All things considered, this option must be approached carefully, particularly because the Static Route option is within the firewall.

RIP Routing

The PIX Firewall interfaces are configurable for route and RIP information. This means the interfaces can exchange RIP updates with other directly adjacent RIP routers. Unfortunately, those updates still can't be forwarded through the firewall and none of the other routing protocols is supported.

The **configuration mode rip** command enables IP routing table updates from RIP broadcasts received directly on the interface. The PIX Firewall still can't pass RIP updates between interfaces. If RIP version 2 is configured, the RIP updates will be encrypted using MD5 encryption. Use the **no rip** command to disable the PIX Firewall IP routing table updates. The syntax is

Pix(config)# rip *int_name* {default | passive} [version [1 | 2]] [authentication [text | md5 *key* (*key_id*)]]
Pix(config)# no rip *int_name* {default | passive} [version [1 | 2]] [authentication [text | md5 *key* (*key_id*)]]

int_name	The internal or external network interface name
default	Broadcast a default route on the interface
passive	Enable passive RIP on the interface, allowing the PIX to listen for RIP-routing broadcasts and to add that information to its routing table
version	RIP version. (1) Backward compatibility with the older RIP version. (2) RIP update encryption and VLSM and CIDR support
authentication	Enable RIP version 2 authentication
text	Send RIP version 2 updates as clear text (not recommended)
md5	Send RIP version 2 updates using MD5 encryption
key	Key to encrypt RIP version 2 updates (up to 16 characters). Must be the same on any device that provides RIP version 2 updates
key_id	Key identification value (a number from 1 to 255). Must be the same *key_id* on any device that provides RIP version 2 updates

The Passive option enables the PIX Firewall to learn about the network by listening for RIP network updates. This is often called *routing by rumor.* Any networks "discovered" by listening to the interface RIP traffic are added to the PIX Firewall routing tables.

Verifying and Monitoring RIP The **clear rip** command removes all the **rip** commands from the PIX Firewall configuration. The **show rip** command displays the RIP configuration while the **debug rip** command turns on real-time monitoring of the RIP exchanges.

Pix# debug rip [*int_name*]
Pix# show rip [*int_name*]
Pix# clear rip

PART IV

The next example demonstrates version 1 and version 2 **RIP** commands, and the result of the **show rip** command. The first line turns on RIP v1, the second turns on RIP v2 without authentication, and the third enables RIP v2 with authentication using **cisco** as the **key** and **7** as the **key_id**.

```
Pix(config)# rip outside passive
Pix(config)# rip dmz passive version 2
Pix(config)# rip inside passive version 2 authentication md5 cisco 7
Pix(config)# show rip
rip outside passive version 1
rip inside passive version 2 authentication md5 cisco 7
rip dmz passive version 2
```

BGP Routing

Border Gateway Protocol (BGP–RFC 1163) is the routing protocol of the Internet. BGP implementation is complex and well beyond the scope of this text and exams. If an organization needs to pass BGP through a PIX Firewall to achieve redundancy in a multihomed BGP environment, this is made much easier because BGP uses unicast TCP packets on port 179 to communicate with its peers, instead of either broadcast or multicast traffic, which can't pass through the PIX.

Multicast Traffic

IP TV and other streaming media content applications use IP multicast to deliver the content to the end user while preserving bandwidth. Many routing protocols are also using multicast technologies to reduce bandwidth and disruption to unaffected devices. The problem is the PIX Firewall won't pass multicast traffic.

The workaround for this is to encapsulate the multicast packets in a GRE tunnel to pass them through the PIX device.

This isn't an exam requirement and configuring IP multicasting is too complex to go into here. Simply be aware a relatively simple solution exists. Several examples are on the Cisco site: search for PIX Firewall Multicast or PIX Firewall GRE.

Chapter Review

This chapter looked at some of those features and commands required to allow data to pass efficiently through the firewall. The Adaptive Security Algorithm (ASA) was addressed to understand better how the PIX Firewall determines which traffic patterns to allow and which to deny. The basic higher-security to lower-security level flow was expanded to indicate that returning traffic is always approved, unless it's specifically blocked by ACLs.

Static translations create a one-to-one permanent IP address xlate table entry, which can then be enabled with an ACL to create potentially many connections. Static translations are generally used to allow access to shared resources, such as servers. NAT and PAT are used to create temporary, one-to-one xlate table entries, allowing returning traffic from forays into lower security areas. If NAT and PAT are used together, any available NAT address is used before any PAT translations occur.

PIX access lists are created and applied much like those in the Cisco IOS, except they're always implemented inbound on an interface.

Three **filter** commands can be used to block potentially destructive or unpleasant web resources from the network. The **Filter ActiveX** command blocks Active X objects from web pages. The **Filter Java** command does the same thing to Java applets. And, the **Filter URL** command works with either an N2H2 or a Websense server to filter content based on an extensive database. Filter URL also offers web tracking and custom blocking features.

PIX OS v6.2 introduced the concept of object groups that allows a group of similar items to be defined, and then uses ACLs to assign permissions and/or restrictions to the group. An object group can be networks, services, ICMP message types, or protocols. If you understand grouping, you can achieve tremendous savings in configuration time and space on large, complex configurations.

The PIX Firewall doesn't support routing between the interfaces, but it does use a form of static and default routes to direct traffic. It's possible to enable RIP on individual interfaces, allowing the firewall to learn about the attached networks.

Questions

1. Return traffic from an internal user going out on the Internet requires which of the following?

   A. Static address translation

   B. Enabling access control entry

   C. Authenticated access

   D. None of the above

2. In assigning a security level to a DMZ interface, which would be the logical choice?

   A. 0

   B. 1

   C. 50

   D. 100

3. In Cisco terminology, which TCP/IP layer is used in stateful filtering, which is *not* used in stateless?

   A. Data link

   B. Network

   C. Transport

   D. Application

4. What is the relationship between translations and connections?

   A. They're synonymous.

   B. One translation equals one connection.

   C. One connection can support many translations.

   D. One translation can support many connections.

5. Which one of the following is *not* true about connections?
   A. No packets can pass through a PIX Firewall without a connection and a state table entry.
   B. All outbound connections are denied, except those specifically allowed by access control lists.
   C. All ICMP packets are denied unless specifically permitted with ACLs or conduits.
   D. Any packet dropped for failing to meet one of the rules triggers a syslog message to be sent.
6. Which one of the following is easiest for the PIX to monitor the state?
   A. UDP
   B. TCP
   C. ICMP
   D. Java
7. How many address translations result from the following command?

```
Pix(config)# static (inside,outside) 10.1.1.32 192.168.2.32 netmask
255.255.255.240
```

   A. 254
   B. 32
   C. 14
   D. 16
8. Setting the embryonic connection limit triggers what feature?
   A. Static PAT
   B. An All Hosts option
   C. TCP intercept
   D. Static NAT
9. The PIX **filter** command can be used to block which two of the following?
   A. Rogue FTP sessions
   B. ActiveX objects
   C. Bad **e-mail** commands
   D. Java applets
10. Which command filters all outbound HTTP connections?
   A. pix(config)#filter url 80 0 0 0 0
   B. pix#filter url 80 0 0 0 0
   C. pix(config-if)#filter url 80 0 0 0 0
   D. pix(config)#filter url N2H2 80 0 0 0 0

11. In the following syntax, what would be the result of *nat_id* being 0?

```
Pix(config)# nat (if_name) nat_id ip_address
```

    A. The *ip_address* would be reserved for static mapping.
    B. The *ip_address* would be used for PAT translations.
    C. The *ip_address* would *not* be translated.
    D. The *ip_address* would be dropped from the global pool.

12. TurboACL applies to which two of the following?
    A. Compiled access lists
    B. Short, quick ACLs
    C. ACLs with many repeated statements
    D. ACLs with at least 19 statements

13. Which one of the following is *not* true about downloadable ACLs?
    A. Introduced PIX Firewall version 6.2.
    B. Supports TACACS+ servers with Cisco Secure ACS v3.0.
    C. Are based on either user or group profile entries.
    D. Requires no additional configuration for the firewall once AAA authorization is configured.

14. Which one of the following will create an object group?
    A. Pix(config)# object-group service dmz_service tcp
    B. Pix(config)# object group service dmz_service udp
    C. Pix(config)# object-group service dmz_service icmp
    D. Pix# object-group service dmz_service icmp

15. Which statement is *not* true?
    A. The PIX Firewall is *not* a router.
    B. The PIX Firewall does *not* forward broadcast or multicast packets.
    C. Cisco security strategy considers sending routing protocols across any firewall safe, but unnecessary, because of the **route** command.
    D. The PIX interfaces do *not* support VLAN trunk links.

Answers

1. **D.** None of the above. Returning traffic is always allowed, unless it's specifically blocked.
2. **C.** 50 and 100 are reserved (outside/inside) and while 1 would work, it allows no flexibility in security assignment if another DMZ was added

PART IV

3. **D.** Application layer.
4. **D.** One translation can support many connections.
5. **B.** All outbound connections are denied except those specifically allowed by access control lists. Just the opposite, all are allowed unless denied by an ACL.
6. **B.** TCS because it has a session setup and a termination routine.
7. **C.** 14. The mask includes 16 addresses, but one is the network and one is the broadcast.
8. **C.** TCP intercept.
9. **B. and D.** ActiveX objects and Java applets.
10. **A.** **pix(config)#filter url 80 0 0 0 0**.
11. **C.** The *ip_address* would *not* be translated. Nat 0 turns off NAT for that address.
12. **A. and D.** Compiled access lists and ACLs with at least 19 statements.
13. **B.** Supports TACACS+ servers with Cisco Secure ACS v3.0. Actually, it's RADIUS.
14. **A.** Pix(config)# object-group service dmz_service tcp.
15. **C.** Cisco security strategy considers sending routing protocols across any firewall safe, but unnecessary, because of the **route** command. Cisco does *not* consider it safe.

CHAPTER 20

Advanced PIX Firewall Features

In this chapter, you will learn how to:

- Work with remote access using Telnet, HTTP, and SSH features
- Use authentication, authorization, and accounting
- Apply advanced protocol handling
- Understand attack guards
- Recognize Intrusion detection
- Use shunning
- Manage SNMP services

Many of the advanced concepts and configurations in this chapter should be somewhat familiar to you because of their counterparts in the Cisco router environment and from the IOS Firewall chapters 6 through 8. As the PIX Firewall moves to be more fully IOS command compatible with each new release, your existing strengths are leveraged further.

STUDY TIP If you aren't familiar with Cisco's Voice over IP (VoIP) strategy and implementation, give serious thought to looking over a few of the related documents available on the Cisco web site. While this chapter discusses the protocols that facilitate VoIP through the PIX Firewall, a little higher overview might help you gain perspective. Because this is one of the technologies Cisco has identified as its future, having a little broader understanding can't hurt.

Remote Access

The PIX Firewall serial console port allows a single administrator to configure the unit, but it requires close proximity to the device. This close proximity requirement, or limiting access to a single administrator, can severely limit the flexibility on an administrator team. The PIX Firewall allows additional console access via Telnet, HTTP, and Secure Shell (SSH).

Telnet Access

Telnet allows host console access from any internal interface, much like the Telnet access to a Cisco router or switch. If the PIX Firewall is configured for IPSec, it's possible to allow Telnet sessions from the outside interface. PIX Firewall IPSec support, including for Telnet sessions, is covered in Chapter 21.

Up to 16 host or network addresses can be configured to access the PIX Firewall console with Telnet, and up to five hosts can access the unit simultaneously. The **configuration mode telnet** command is used to define which hosts can access the PIX Firewall console with Telnet. While you can enable Telnet on all interfaces, the PIX OS requires that IPSec be configured on the outside interface to allow Telnet traffic. Use the **no telnet** or **clear telnet** command to remove Telnet access assigned to an IP address. The syntax is

Pix(config)# telnet *ip_address* [*netmask*] [*if_name*]
Pix(config)# clear telnet [*ip_address* [*netmask*] [*if_name*]]
Pix(config)# no telnet [*ip_address* [*netmask*] [*if_name*]]

The default *netmask* is 255.255.255.255, or the host address mask. The default *if_name* is all inside interfaces. To allow any host, use 0.0.0.0 0.0.0.0 (or 0 0) for *ip_address* and *netmask*.

In the following, the first example shows a single host (1.1.1.11) allowed to use Telnet to access from the outside, while the entire 192.168.1.0 network can access the inside address. The second example allows all internal hosts to access any inside interface in the PIX using a web browser.

```
Pix(config)# telnet 1.1.1.11 outside
Pix(config)# telnet 192.168.1.0 255.255.255.0 inside

Pix2(config)# telnet 0 0
Pix2(config)# show telnet
0.0.0.0 0.0.0.0 inside
0.0.0.0 0.0.0.0 dmz
Pix2(config)#
```

If the IP address assigned Telnet access is outside of the network or on any lower security interface, then it's necessary to add access list entries and possibly address translations to complete the configuration.

Use the **telnet timeout *minutes*** command to set an idle timer to close any inactive, but open, Telnet console sessions. The acceptable range is 1 to 60 minutes. The default is five minutes. Setting the timer to 15 to 20 minutes until the configuration and testing is completed might be useful.

The **show telnet** command lists the IP addresses configured to Telnet to the PIX Firewall. The **show telnet timeout** command displays the current Telnet idle timer value.

The passwd Command

The **passwd password** command is used to set a Telnet password for access to the PIX console. The default Telnet password is **cisco** and a Telnet user is prompted with the PIX passwd: message. The password doesn't appear when entered. The following output demonstrates the previous commands:

```
Pix(config)# passwd cisCo123
Pix(config)# telnet 192.168.1.10 255.255.255.255 inside
Pix(config)# telnet 192.168.1.47 255.255.255.255
Pix(config)# telnet 192.168.2.0 255.255.255.0 inside
Pix(config)# telnet 1.1.1.10 255.255.255.255 outside
Pix(config)# telnet timeout 10
Pix(config)# show telnet
          192.168.1.10 255.255.255.255 inside
          192.168.1.47 255.255.255.255 inside
          192.168.1.47 255.255.255.255 dmz
          192.168.1.47 255.255.255.255 intf3
          192.168.2.0 255.255.255.0 inside
          1.1.1.10 255.255.255.255 outside
Pix(config)# show telnet timeout
telnet timeout 10 minutes
```

The who and kill Commands

The **who** command is used to see the IP addresses currently accessing the unit. The output includes a session ID followed by the IP address. The **kill** ***session_id*** command is used to end an active Telnet console session. The following output shows the **who** and **kill** commands.

```
pix# who
0: From 192.168.1.10
1: From 192.168.2.210
pix# kill 0
pix# who
1: From 192.168.2.210
```

PART IV

HTTP Access

The PIX Firewall, like many other Cisco devices, provides a graphical user interface that can be used for configuration tasks. Two **configuration mode http** commands are required to use a web browser, such as Internet Explorer, to access the firewall console. The **http server enable** command turns on the feature. The second command defines the host(s) that can use the feature. It's possible to have up to 16 simultaneous HTTP console sessions. Use the no form of each command to remove the configuration. The syntax is

> Pix(config)# http server enable
> Pix(config)# [no] http server enable
> Pix(config)# http *ip_address* [*netmask*] [*if_name*]
> Pix(config)# no http *ip_address* [*netmask*] [*if_name*]

The default *netmask* is 255.255.255.255 or the host address mask. The default *if_name* is the inside interface. To allow any host, use 0.0.0.0 0.0.0.0 (or 0 0) for *ip_address* and *netmask*. In the following, the first example shows a single host (1.1.1.11) allowed to use a web browser to access from the outside, while the entire 192.168.1.0 network can access the inside address. The second example allows all internal hosts to access any inside interface on the PIX unit using a web browser.

```
Pix(config)# http server enable
Pix(config)# http 1.1.1.11 outside
```

```
Pix(config)# http 192.168.1.0 255.255.255.0

Pix2(config)# http server enable
Pix2(config)# http 0 0
Pix2(config)# show http
0.0.0.0 0.0.0.0 inside
Pix2(config)#
```

To access the PIX Firewall using a web browser, use the **http** command followed by the appropriate interface. The web browser prompts for a user name and a password. Always use **admin** for the user name and the Telnet password specified with the **passwd** command.

NOTE Cisco PIX Device Manager (PDM) requires the PIX Firewall to have the HTTP server feature enabled. Chapter 22 covers PDM.

Secure Shell (SSH) Access

The PIX Firewall supports SSH console access for configuration tasks. The **configuration mode ssh *ip_address*** command defines the host(s) or network(s) that can initiate an SSH connection to the PIX Firewall. The no form of the command removes the address(es). The syntax is

Pix(config)# ssh *ip_address* [*netmask*] [*if_name*]
Pix(config)# no ssh *ip_address* [*netmask*] [*if_name*]
Pix(config)# ssh timeout *minutes*

The **no ssh *ip_address*** command removes the specified ssh command statement from the configuration, while the **clear ssh** command removes all ssh command statements.

No default *netmask* exists. The default *if_name* is all inside interfaces. To allow any host, use 0.0.0.0 0.0.0.0 (or 0 0) for *ip_address* and *netmask*.

The **ssh timeout** command defines an idle timer of 1 to 60 minutes (default is five minutes).

The **show ssh** command shows the addresses that are allowed SSH access. The **show ssh sessions** command displays all active SSH sessions to the PIX Firewall. The output includes a session ID for each connection. The **ssh disconnect *session_id*** command will disconnect the specific session. The following output demonstrates the previous commands:

```
Pix# config t
Pix(config)# ssh 1.1.1.47 255.255.255.255 outside
Pix(config)# ssh timeout 15
Pix(config)# show ssh
1.1.1.47 255.255.255.255 outside
0.0.0.0 0.0.0.0 inside
0.0.0.0 0.0.0.0 dmz
Pix(config)#
Pix# show ssh sessions
```

```
Session ID   Client IP       Version Encryption   State    Username
    0        192.168.1.19    1.5     3DES          4        -
    1        192.168.1.116   1.5     DES           6        pix
    2        192.168.1.41    1.5     3DES          4        -
Pix# ssh disconnect 1
```

To use SSH, your PIX Firewall must have a DES or 3DES activation key.

To gain access to the PIX Firewall console via SSH, when prompted for the user name and password, use **pix** and the Telnet password (set with the **passwd** command). SSH permits user names up to 100 characters and passwords up to 50 characters.

AAA Support for Telnet, HTTP, and SSH Sessions

The PIX Firewall supports AAA authentication for Telnet, HTTP, and SSH sessions using the **aaa authentication** command. Use the no form of the command to turn off the authentication. The syntax is

Pix(config)# aaa authentication [serial | enable | telnet | ssh | http] console *group_tag*
Pix(config)# no aaa authentication [serial | enable | telnet | ssh | http] console *group_tag*

The AAA support is covered in the next section.

AAA on the PIX Firewall

The Cisco PIX Firewall supports AAA network security services. This chapter assumes familiarity with Authentication, Authorization, and Accounting (AAA), introduced in Chapter 4, and basic installation of Cisco Secure ACS software, covered in Chapter 5. AAA configuration involves defining the AAA server(s), and then the services that will use AAA authentication. Optionally, AAA authorization and accounting can be configured.

Defining the AAA Server

Use the **configuration mode aaa-server** commands to specify AAA server groups. AAA server groups are defined by a tag name. If the first authentication server defined in the group fails, AAA fails over to the next server in the tag group. There can be up to 14 tag groups, and each group can have up to 14 AAA servers, for a total of up to 196 AAA servers.

Creating a Server Group (Optional)

The following command creates a server group, assigns a name (*server_tag*) to the group, and—most important—specifies which protocol is used by the group. Use the **clear aaa-server** command to remove a named server group. The syntax is

Pix(config)# aaa-server *server_tag* protocol [tacacs+ | radius]
Pix(config)# clear aaa-server *server_tag*

This command is optional because three default server groups are defined on the PIX Firewall in v6.2 that can be used. The **show aaa-server** command shows the default groups.

```
Pix(config)# show aaa-server
aaa-server TACACS+ protocol tacacs+
aaa-server RADIUS protocol radius
aaa-server LOCAL protocol local
Pix(config)#
```

Notice the group name (tag) is nothing more than the protocol name. This provides backward compatibility to older OS versions. Another group should only be created if several AAA servers exist and it would help to keep their functions straight. The LOCAL group was added in version 6.2, and can be used for authentication and command authorization. This new feature is covered in the next section.

The following output shows creating separate TACACS+ server groups for inbound and outbound traffic, plus a RADIUS group for accounting functions. The server tags are up to the administrator, but should be descriptive. The server tags are case sensitive.

```
Pix(config)# aaa-server TacIn protocol tacacs+
Pix(config)# aaa-server TacOut protocol tacacs+
Pix(config)# aaa-server RadAcctg protocol radius
```

The remaining AAA commands use the group tag to identify which group of servers will perform the AAA function.

Defining the Server Group

The next command defines the connecting PIX interface, server IP address, an optional encryption key shared with the AAA server, and an optional retransmit timer. The default interface is (inside). If more than one server is defined in the group, they'll be used in order of entry. This command doesn't verify the existence of the server(s). Use the no form of the command to remove the server from the group. The syntax is

Pix(config)# aaa-server *server_tag* [(*if_name*)] host *server_ip* [*key*] [timeout *seconds*]
Pix(config)# no aaa-server *server_tag* [(*if_name*)] host *server_ip* [*key*] [timeout *seconds*]

host *server_ip*	IP address of the TACACS+ or RADIUS server.
key	Case-sensitive, alphanumeric key up to 127 characters, shared by the PIX and AAA server for encrypting data between them. No spaces, but most special characters are allowed.
timeout *seconds*	Retransmit timer. The time the PIX unit waits for each transmit attempt. After four failed attempts to reach the AAA server, PIX transmits to the next server. Default: five seconds (range 1 to 30 seconds).

NOTE The *server_tag* is case sensitive. The way you type it here determines how it must be addressed in future AAA commands. If you type one of the default groups TACACS+ or RADIUS in any other case, then you create a new server group using the default protocol tacacs+.

This example tries to demonstrate this case importance. The first command, **show aaa-server**, displays the default groups. Lines 5 and 6 show an attempt to assign a server to each of the default server groups (TACACS+ and RADIUS). The next **show aaa-server** command reveals that two new groups were created and they both use the tacacs+ protocol.

```
Pix(config)# show aaa-server
aaa-server TACACS+ protocol tacacs+
aaa-server RADIUS protocol radius
aaa-server LOCAL protocol local
Pix(config)# aaa-server tacacs+ (inside) host 192.168.1.3 3key timeout 20
Pix(config)# aaa-server radius host 192.168.1.4 4key
Pix(config)# show aaa-server
aaa-server TACACS+ protocol tacacs+
aaa-server RADIUS protocol radius
aaa-server LOCAL protocol local
aaa-server tacacs+ protocol tacacs+
aaa-server tacacs+ (inside) host 192.168.1.3 3key timeout 20
aaa-server radius protocol tacacs+
aaa-server radius (inside) host 192.168.1.4 4key timeout 10
Pix(config)#
```

The following example creates the RadIn and TacOut server groups and defines two inside servers to each. From the previous example, you know Line 1 is necessary, but Line 4 could be omitted.

```
Pix(config)# aaa-server RadIn protocol radius
Pix(config)# aaa-server RadIn (inside) host 192.168.1.5 5key timeout 10
Pix(config)# aaa-server RadIn (inside) host 192.168.1.6 6key
Pix(config)# aaa-server TacOut protocol tacacs+
Pix(config)# aaa-server TacOut host 192.168.1.7 7key timeout 20
Pix(config)# aaa-server TacOut host 192.168.1.8 8key
```

PART IV

Local User Database

PIX Firewall software v6.2 introduced the concept of the local user authentication database, common in router configurations to the PIX Firewall family. Like its router relatives, the local PIX Firewall user authentication database consists of the users entered with the **username** command. The PIX Firewall **login** command can use this database for authentication. Use the no form of the command to remove a user from the database. The syntax is

> Pix(config)# username *usr_name* {[{nopassword | password *password*} [encrypted]] [privilege *level*]}
> Pix(config)# no username *usr_name*

The minimum *usr_name* and *password* are four and three alphanumeric characters, respectively. Because the PIX automatically encrypts all passwords, the encrypted option means the entry will already be encrypted.

Use the **show username** [*usr_name*] command to display the users defined in the local PIX Firewall user authentication database.

```
Pix(config)# username admin7 password cisCo7 privilege 7
Pix(config)# username bill password pearson privilege 12
Pix(config)# username mike password chow privilege 15
Pix(config)# show username
username mike password 6NVlMI5JXIWRfMS7 encrypted privilege 15
username admin7 password zs7H.SH1jCsgkxKA encrypted privilege 7
username bill password 7/y5W7TBQ4r2o7OF encrypted privilege 12
Pix(config)#
Pix(config)# no username bill
Pix(config)# no username mike
Pix(config)# no username admin7
Warning:Local user database is empty and there are still 'aaa' commands for
'LOCAL'.
Pix(config)#
```

The preceding example shows how to remove users from the local user database. The warning shows the result of removing the last user if some features, such as AAA, are using the local user database.

The login Command

The login command can be used to log a user into the PIX Firewall, another privilege level, or another Command mode using the local user authentication database. This command is available in Unprivileged mode. The user can use the logout, exit, or quit commands to go back to Unprivileged mode. The following example shows the prompt after a login command.

```
Pix> login
Username:
Username: mike
Password: ****
Pix#
```

Local User Database and AAA

Cisco Secure ACS AAA services support using the local user database (LOCAL) as an alternative to TACACS+ or RADIUS servers for user authentication and command authorization tasks. The following output shows using the local user database with AAA commands. The details of these commands are reviewed in the next pages.

```
Pix(config)# aaa authentication telnet console LOCAL
Pix(config)# aaa authentication enable console LOCAL
Pix(config)# aaa authorization command LOCAL
```

Verifying AAA Services Use the **show aaa** (not **show AAA**) command to list AAA services configured, as shown in the following example:

```
Pix(config)# sho aaa
aaa authentication telnet console LOCAL
aaa authentication enable console LOCAL
aaa authorization command LOCAL
Pix(config)#
```

Configuring AAA Features

After designating at least one authentication server with the **aaa-server** command, it's time to define the AAA services to be used by the PIX Firewall. The **help aaa** command displays the syntax and use for the **aaa authentication**, **aaa authorization**, **aaa accounting**, and **aaa proxy-limit** commands in summary form.

Server Group Case-Sensitivity Issues

Be aware that AAA does some strange things with case sensitivity. The local user database must be referred to as LOCAL or you get the error "bad auth-server groupname local." The **show aaa** command returns an Ambiguous command if the aaa is in uppercase.

The first seven lines of the following output you saw earlier created a new server group called tacacs+ because of the case difference between Line 1 and the default group name.

```
Pix(config)# aaa-server tacacs+ (inside) host 192.168.1.4 4key timeout 20
Pix(config)# sho aaa-server
aaa-server TACACS+ protocol tacacs+
aaa-server RADIUS protocol radius
aaa-server LOCAL protocol local
aaa-server tacacs+ protocol tacacs+
aaa-server tacacs+ (inside) host 192.168.1.4 4key timeout 20
Pix(config)#
Pix(config)# aaa authentication telnet console TACACS+
No authentication servers found!
Pix(config)# aaa authentication telnet console Tacacs+
bad auth-server groupname Tacacs+
Pix(config)# aaa authentication telnet console tacacs+
Pix(config)#
```


Line 9 shows that if you revert back to TACACS+ in the **aaa authentication** command, you're notified that no servers are in that group name. They were assigned to tacacs+.

Line 11 shows a straight case mismatch issue and the resulting "bad auth-server groupname Tacacs+" message.

The last two lines confirm that once the case is correct, the command will be accepted.

Authenticating Console Sessions

AAA can be used to authenticate the four types of console connections, plus allowing for unique enable passwords. The **configuration mode aaa authentication console** command requires authentication verification to access the PIX Firewall unit's console features. Use the no form of the command to remove the authentication. The syntax is

> Pix(config)# aaa authentication [serial | enable | telnet | ssh | http] console *group_tag*
> Pix(config)# no aaa authentication [serial | enable | telnet | ssh | http] console *group_tag*

The *group_tag* can include any *server_tag* or the local user database (LOCAL). Examples of each of these might look like this:

```
Pix(config)# aaa authentication serial console LOCAL
Pix(config)# aaa authentication enable console LOCAL
Pix(config)# aaa authentication telnet console TACACS+
Pix(config)# aaa authentication ssh console TACACS+
Pix(config)# aaa authentication http console MyRadius
```

The Serial Connection and Enable Privilege mode access will be authenticated by the local user database. Telnet and SSH connections are authenticated by the default TACACS+ group, while HTTP connections are authenticated by a named group of RADIUS servers.

Feature Characteristics The Telnet, HTTP, and SSH connections were covered at the beginning of this chapter.

The Serial option refers to console cable connection. If configured with AAA authentication, it requires a user name and a password combination to gain user-level access (unprivileged). The serial console option also logs any configuration changes made from the serial console to a Syslog server.

The Enable option refers to the enable password that allows access to the Privilege mode from any of the other four console connections. The password required is now the same password used to authenticate into the console session. The Enable option prompts only for a password, not a user name/password combination, regardless of what the documentation might say.

The following output shows that exiting from Privilege mode now logs the user out, and requires a user name and password. The first password effort shows the word "chow" was rejected. Even though chow is a valid password in the user database, it isn't the same as the login password (pearson).

```
Pix# exit
Logoff

Username: bill
Password: *******                   (pearson from earlier example)
Type help or '?' for a list of available commands.
Pix> en
Password: ****                      (chow entered)
Password: *******                   (pearson entered)
Pix#
```

The Enable and SSH options allow only three attempts before stopping with an access denied message. The Serial and Telnet options prompt continually until a successful login.

If the specified server or user database is unavailable, try user name *pix* and either the Telnet password (set with the **passwd** command) or **enable password** for the password. The PIX default if AAA authentication is not configured is no user name and the enable password for the password.

Authenticating User Sessions

The PIX Firewall interacts with FTP, HTTP (Web access), and Telnet protocols to display the correct prompts for logging in to the network or logging in to exit the network. For each IP address, one **aaa authentication** command is permitted for inbound connections and one for outbound connections. The no form of the command removes the entry from the configuration. The syntax is

Pix(config)# aaa authentication {include | exclude} *authen_service if_name local_ip local_mask* [*foreign_ip foreign_mask*] *server_tag*

Pix(config)# no aaa authentication {include | exclude} *authen_service if_name local_ip local_mask [foreign_ip foreign_mask] server_tag*

authentication	Enable or disable user authentication, prompts user for user name and password, and verifies information with AAA authentication server.
include	Create a new rule for the specified service.
exclude	Create an exception to a previously defined rule by excluding the specified service from authentication, authorization, or accounting to the specified host.
authen_service	Application used to access the network. Use **any** (tcp/0), **ftp**, **http**, or **telnet**. PIX Firewalls only use FTP, HTTP, and Telnet for authentication. The Any option includes ftp, http, and telnet only.
if_name	Interface name from which users require authentication.
local_ip	IP address of host or network to be authenticated or authorized. 0 combined with 0 *local_mask* includes all hosts.
local_mask	Netmask of *local_ip* to define specific host(s). Use 255.255.255.255 for a host address. Use 0 if *local_ip* is set to 0 to include all hosts.
foreign_ip	IP address of the host(s) to access the *local_ip* address. 0 to include all hosts.
foreign_mask	Netmask of *foreign_ip* to define specific host(s). Use 255.255.255.255 for a host. Use 0 if the *foreign_ip* address is 0 to include all hosts.
server_tag	The AAA server group tag defined by the **aaa-server** command. Note, protocol "local" is available only for console authentication.

Outbound connections will need a NAT translation pass through the PIX Firewall. Inbound connections still need **static** and **access-list** command statements to allow access to inside IP addresses through the PIX Firewall from the outside network.

If both the optional *foreign_ip* and *foreign_mask* are omitted, then the default 0 0 is assumed allowing all other hosts. There are no other defaults.

Inbound vs. Outbound The combination of the *if_name, local_ip,* and *foreign_ip* variables defines the flow of the connection being authenticated. The *local_ip* address is always on the higher security level interface, while the *foreign_ip* is always on the lower security level. This means the *foreign_ip* is asking the interface's (*if_name*) permission to access the *local_ip*.

The following example assigns server, 192.168.1.3, to the tacacs+ server group, located on the inside interface. Lines 2 and 3 create two new authentication rules, while Line 4 creates an exception to the rule created by Line 3. The rest of the lines show the resulting entries. Notice the exclude statement moved to the top of the list.

```
Pix(config)# aaa-server tacacs+ (inside) host 192.168.1.3 3key timeout 20
Pix(config)# aaa authentication include any inside 192.168.1.0 255.255.255.0
 1.10.1.0 255.255.255.0 tacacs+
Pix(config)# aaa authentication include any outside 0 0 tacacs+
Pix(config)# aaa authentication exclude ftp outside 0 0 tacacs+
Pix(config)# show aaa
aaa authentication exclude ftp outside 0.0.0.0 0.0.0.0 0.0.0.0 0.0.0.0 tacacs+
aaa authentication include tcp/0 inside 192.168.1.0 255.255.255.0 1.10.1.0
 255.255.255.0 tacacs+
aaa authentication include tcp/0 outside 0.0.0.0 0.0.0.0 0.0.0.0 0.0.0.0 tacacs+
Pix(config)#
```

Authorizing Access

Except for its use with command authorization, the **aaa authorization** command can't function alone: it requires a previous **aaa authentication** command. Current PIX OS versions support only TACACS+ servers for this command. RADIUS servers and LOCAL aren't supported. For each IP address, only one **aaa authorization** command is permitted. To authorize more than one service, use the **any** parameter for the service type. The no form of the command removes the entry from the configuration. The syntax is

Pix(config)# aaa authorization {include | exclude} *author_service if_name local_ip local_mask [foreign_ip foreign_mask] server_tag*
Pix(config)# no aaa authorization {include | exclude} *author_service if_name local_ip local_mask [foreign_ip foreign_mask] server_tag*

authorization	Enable or disable TACACS+ server to perform user authorization.
author_service	The services that require authorization. Use *any*, *ftp*, *http*, *telnet*, or *protocol/port* combination. Services not specified are authorized implicitly. Services defined in the **aaa authentication** command don't affect the services that require authorization.

To use Protocol/Port option, use a format like udp/53. The details are as follows:

protocol	The protocol TCP (6), UDP (17), or ICMP (1)
port	TCP, UDP, or ICMP destination port number, such as udp/69 or tcp/25. TCP and UDP protocols can use port range, like tcp/1024–49151. Using 0 for the port means to include all ports, like udp/0. Use *any* for all TCP services. Protocols other than TCP, UDP, and ICMP won't work and shouldn't be used.

Outbound connections need a NAT translation to pass through the PIX Firewall. Inbound connections still need **static** and **access-list** command statements to allow access to inside IP addresses through the PIX Firewall from the outside network.

If both the optional *foreign_ip* and *foreign_mask* are omitted, then the default 0 0 is assumed and allows all other hosts. No other defaults exist.

The following example shows a variety of protocol/port specifications and the resulting configuration statements. Notice icmp is replaced by the number 1, while tcp/23 is replaced by telnet. The exclude statements move to the top of the configuration.

```
Pix(config)# aaa authorization include udp/53 inside 0 0 0 0 tacacs+
Pix(config)# aaa authorization include tcp/0 inside 0 0 0 0 tacacs+
Pix(config)# aaa authorization include icmp/0 inside 0 0 0 0 tacacs+
Pix(config)# aaa authorization exclude tcp/23 inside 0 0 0 0 tacacs+
Pix(config)# aaa authorization exclude udp/23 inside 0 0 0 0 tacacs+
Pix(config)# show aaa
aaa authorization exclude udp/23 inside 0.0.0.0 0.0.0.0 0.0.0.0 0.0.0.0 tacacs+
aaa authorization exclude telnet inside 0.0.0.0 0.0.0.0 0.0.0.0 0.0.0.0 tacacs+
aaa authorization include udp/53 inside 0.0.0.0 0.0.0.0 0.0.0.0 0.0.0.0 tacacs+
aaa authorization include tcp/0 inside 0.0.0.0 0.0.0.0 0.0.0.0 0.0.0.0 tacacs+
aaa authorization include 1/0 inside 0.0.0.0 0.0.0.0 0.0.0.0 0.0.0.0 tacacs+
Pix(config)#
```

Accounting for Resource Usage

User accounting services keep a record of which network services a user has accessed, and these records are stored on the designated AAA server. Accounting information is only sent to the active server in a server group. The **aaa accounting** command always follows the **aaa authentication** command. The no form of the command removes the entry from the configuration. The syntax is

Pix(config)#aaa accounting {include | exclude} *acct_service if_name local_ip local_mask* [*foreign_ip foreign_mask*] *server_tag*
Pix(config)#no aaa accounting {include | exclude} *acct_service if_name local_ip local_mask* [*foreign_ip foreign_mask*] *server_tag*

accounting	Enable or disable accounting services with authentication server. Must be a TACACS+ or RADIUS servers. Local user database isn't supported.
acct_service	The accounting service. Accounting is provided for all services or you can limit it to one or more services. Use *any*, *ftp*, *http*, *telnet*, or *protocol/port* combination. Use *any* to provide accounting for all TCP services. The Protocol/Port option is the same as in aaa authorization.

Outbound connections need a NAT translation pass through the PIX Firewall. Inbound connections still need **static** and **access-list** command statements to allow access to inside IP addresses through the PIX Firewall from the outside network.

If both the optional *foreign_ip* and *foreign_mask* are omitted, then the default 0 0 is assumed and allows all other hosts. No other defaults exist.

The following example demonstrates the **aaa accounting** commands.

```
Pix(config)# aaa accounting include any outside 0 0 0 0 tacacs+
Pix(config)# aaa accounting include udp/0 outside 0 0 0 0 tacacs+
Pix(config)# show aaa
aaa accounting include tcp/0 outside 0.0.0.0 0.0.0.0 0.0.0.0 0.0.0.0 tacacs+
aaa accounting include udp/0 outside 0.0.0.0 0.0.0.0 0.0.0.0 0.0.0.0 tacacs+
Pix(config)#
```

Access Lists with AAA

You can use an access list to determine the addresses that will be allowed to authenticate. The access list is then linked to the **aaa** command via the match acl_name feature. The keyword **permit** means "yes" and deny means "no." The syntax for this command is as follows:

Pix(config)# aaa {authentication | authorization | accounting} match *acl_name if_name server_tag*
Pix(config)# no aaa {authentication | authorization | accounting} match *acl_name if_name server_tag*

```
Pix(config)# access-list acl_out permit tcp 192.168.1.0 255.255.255.0 any
Pix(config)# aaa authentication match acl_out outside tacacs+
Pix(config)# show aaa
aaa authentication match acl_out outside tacacs+
Pix(config)#
```

PART IV

Command-Level Authorization

Beginning with PIX Firewall software v6.2, the PIX Firewall devices support command-level authorization. This is user-defined command privilege levels (0 to 15) for PIX Firewall CLI commands, similar to the privilege levels supported on Cisco routers (Chapter 2) and switches. Local command authorization is done by assigning privilege levels to commands and users with the **privilege** and **user name** commands, respectively. Remote command authorization is done through one or more TACACS+ AAA servers.

By using a Cisco Secure ACS server, you can define authorized CLI command sets on a per-user basis without needing to define command sets across all users. This feature is consistent with other downloadable Cisco Secure ACS features covered in several chapters.

Privilege-level command tracing is supported using the PIX Firewall Syslog features. Privilege configuration updates are displayed in the **show version** command output.

Remote Command Authorization

As seen earlier in this chapter, PIX Firewall users can authenticate using an AAA TACACS+ or RADIUS server, or by using the LOCAL user database. Command authorization can be implemented using the LOCAL database or a TACACS+ server. Implementing command authorization assumes the following software and hardware versions:

- PIX Software version 6.2
- CiscoSecure Access Control Server (ACS) for Windows version 3.0 (CSNT)
- CiscoSecure ACS for UNIX (CSUnix) version 2.3.6

NOTE Command-level authorization sets work correctly with Cisco Secure ACS for Windows Version 3.0.2 or higher. Other 3.0 users should look for the patch available on the PIX Software download page.

Use the Configuration mode **aaa authorization command** command to enable command authorization. Only one command authorization method can be defined at a time. Use the no form of the command to remove the entry. The syntax is as follows:

Pix(config)# aaa authorization command {LOCAL | *tacacs_server_tag*}
Pix(config)# no aaa authorization command {LOCAL | *tacacs_server_tag*}

The following example shows defining the LOCAL database to perform command authorization:

```
Pix(config)# aaa authorization command LOCAL
Pix(config)# show aaa
aaa authorization command LOCAL
Pix(config)#
```

The next section looks at the privilege-level features incorporated into the PIX Firewall to facilitate command-level authorization.

Firewall Privilege Levels

Use the **configuration mode privilege** command to set user-defined privilege levels for specified PIX Firewall commands. This command is modeled after the Cisco IOS privilege command feature. The structure of this command makes it easy to set different privilege levels for related **configuration**, **show**, and **clear** commands.

When both commands and users have privilege levels set, the two can be compared to determine if the user can execute a specific command. If the user's privilege level is lower than the command's privilege level, the user is prevented from using the command. Use the no form of the command to remove the privilege declaration. The syntax is

Pix(config)# privilege [show | clear | configure] level *level* [mode {enable | configure}] command *command*
Pix(config)# no privilege [show | clear | configure] level *level* [mode {enable | configure}] command *command*

show	Sets the privilege level for the specified **show** command.
clear	Sets the privilege level for the specified **clear** command.
configure	Sets the privilege level for the specified **configure** command.
level *level*	Privilege level (0 to 15). The lower the numbers, the lower the privilege.
enable	For commands in both Enable and Configuration modes, indicates the **enable mode** command.
configure	For commands in both Enable and Configuration modes, indicates the **configure mode** command.
command *command*	The command to allow. Use the **no command** form to disallow.

Any **aaa authentication** and **aaa authorization** commands must be updated to include any new privilege levels before they can be used with the AAA server configuration.

Use the **show curpriv** command to display the current privilege level for a user and **show privilege [all | command *command* | level *level*]** to display the privileges for a command or set of commands.

The following output shows creating a user admin7 assigned to privilege level 7, and then a series of **show** commands available to privilege level 7.

```
Pix(config)# username admin7 password cisCo7 privilege 7
Pix(config)# show username
username admin7 passowrd zs7H.SH1jCsgkxKA encrypted privelege 7
Pix (config)# privilege show level 7 command ip
Pix (config)# privilege show level 7 command interface
Pix (config)# privilege show level 7 command nat
Pix (config)# privilege show level 7 command xlate
Pix (config)# privilege show level 7 command global
```

PART IV

The following output shows the results of logging in as admin7, the **show curpriv** command showing the privilege level, and an attempt to run two commands not defined for privilege level 7. P_UNPR indicates user (unprivileged) level, P_PRIV indicates that the enable command has been issued.

```
Pix# exit
Logoff

Username: admin7
Password: ******
Type help or '?' for a list of available commands.
Pix> show curpriv
Username : admin7
Current privilege level : 1
Current Mode/s : P_UNPR
Pix> en
Password: ******
Pix# show curpriv
Username : admin7
Current privilege level : 7
Current Mode/s : P_PRIV
Pix# show username
Command authorization failed
Pix# reload
Command authorization failed
Pix#
```

Configuring Cisco Secure ACS for Windows

Understanding the process of configuring Cisco Secure ACS for Windows is an exam objective, and this topic was covered in Chapters 4 and 8. Review that material, and, if possible, get a little hands-on experience configuring an ACS server.

Advanced Protocol Handling

The PIX Firewall offers a number of advanced features to support the many protocols available on the Internet, while maintaining a safe internal environment. Some of these features are configurable using skills already covered or by using the **fixup protocol** commands, covered in the upcoming section "The fixup protocol Command." Others are in place and can't be modified or disabled, such as the attack guards covered in the later section "Attack Guards." All involve some form of higher-layer awareness than would be available from traditional access control lists (ACLs), which, by definition, are limited to Layer 3– and Layer 4–filtering capabilities. The PIX Firewall Adaptive Security Algorithm (ASA) uses application layer (OSI Layers 5–7) inspection to establish and maintain its stateful access control and traffic-monitoring security.

Application Inspection

The PIX Firewall ASA performs stateful application inspection to provide secure use of external applications and services. In some cases, this involves monitoring for and defending against threatening traffic patterns or activity. In other cases, application inspection is used to facilitate outside connections for specific protocols.

Establishing and maintaining outside connections is easy enough with many applications because all address and port information is established by the inside client in its initial transmission to the outside host. But some sessions require special attention from the PIX Firewall application inspection function. Specifically, those applications and protocols that embed IP address information in the data portion of the packet or those that open additional channels on dynamically assigned ports create impossible problems for standard access list filtering.

Because the application inspection feature can look at the upper layer portions of the packet, it can work with NAT to identify embedded address information. NAT can then translate those embedded addresses and, equally important, update any checksum or other fields affected by the translation. Without this attention to detail, the packets could easily be rejected by the destination host or the firewall.

Note, like CBAC in Chapter 6, this application-inspection function is meticulously programmed for a limited number of common programs or protocols. Application inspection uses upper-level field information and a knowledge of the application/protocols processes to make "informed" decisions about what's expected and what returning traffic should be allowed.

This application-aware capability allows application inspection to monitor and permit dynamic port number usage by those supported protocols that open additional TCP or UDP ports to improve performance. These applications use the initial session well-known port numbers to negotiate additional dynamically assigned port numbers, which are then opened by the PIX for only the life of the session. The alternative would be the permanent opening of ranges of port numbers and the inherent vulnerability associated with that.

The fixup protocol Command

Application inspection is frequently referred to as *fixup* because the **fixup protocol** command can be used to configure the application inspection for many of the supported protocols. Note, other protocols are supported that don't support configuration. The **show fixup** command displays the applications/protocols and their default port settings that use the **fixup protocol** command. These defined port numbers are the ones the PIX Firewall listens to for each respective service. The following output is the default **fixup protocol** commands enabled on a PIX Firewall version 6.2.

```
Pix(config)# show fixup
fixup protocol ftp 21
fixup protocol http 80
fixup protocol h323 h225 1720
fixup protocol h323 ras 1718-1719
fixup protocol ils 389
fixup protocol rsh 514
fixup protocol rtsp 554
fixup protocol smtp 25
fixup protocol sqlnet 1521
fixup protocol sip 5060
fixup protocol skinny 2000
Pix(config)#
```

If necessary, the port numbers can be changed for each service, except **rsh** and **sip**. Remember, if a protocol like HTTP is set to use another port number, any connections established to that port number will be interpreted as if they're HTTP data.

Using the fixup protocol Command

Use the **configuration mode fixup protocol** commands to change, enable, or disable the access of supported services or protocols through the PIX Firewall. The command is global and any changes apply to both inbound and outbound connections. The command can't be restricted by any port address changes in **static** command statements. The basic syntax looks like the following, where *protocol* is limited to the 11 supported options in the preceding output.

Pix(config)# fixup protocol *protocol* [*port_options*]

The **clear fixup** command resets the fixup default settings, but it doesn't remove the default **fixup protocol** commands. To disable a fixup for a specific protocol, use the **no fixup protocol** ***protocol*** command without any options. The **no fixup protocol** is stored in the configuration.

Changes made using the **fixup** command only affect future connection sessions. For any change to take effect immediately, you must use the **clear xlate** command to remove all existing application inspection entries.

The next pages look at the applications supported by the PIX Firewall application inspection features and a few examples of working with the **fixup protocol** commands. For more information, a search on fixup on the www.cisco.com site offers a wide selection of documents. Particularly for "hot" technologies such as VoIP, checking the latest documentation for the fixup protocol is always wise.

Supported Applications and Protocols

Some fixup protocols support multiple applications, while other applications benefit from application inspection without having a fixup protocol for Configuration options. Features provided often include extending NAT capabilities to IP addresses embedded within the data payload, including adjusting related checksum values, dynamic implementation of additional port connections, and event logging. The following represents a partial list of supported applications.

Basic Internet Protocols

The PIX Firewall uses application inspection to assist common Internet protocols, such as the following. Those followed by an asterisk have **fixup** command configuration support.

- Domain Name System (DNS)
- File Transfer Protocol (FTP)*
- Hypertext Transfer Protocol (HTTP)*
- NetBIOS over IP
- Simple Mail Transfer Protocol (SMTP)*

Voice over IP (VoIP)

The VoIP application inspection supports the following protocols used by Cisco IP Phones, Cisco CallManager, and other Cisco IP Telephony products. Version 6.2 of the PIX OS adds PAT support for H.323 and SIP. This helps to expand your address space to accommodate the large number of endpoints involved when implementing VoIP networks. Those followed by an asterisk have **fixup** command configuration support.

- H.323*
- Session Initiation Protocol (SIP)*
- Skinny Client Control Protocol (SCCP)*

Multimedia

Multimedia applications represent troublesome challenges to a firewall because multimedia protocols dynamically open additional port connections to improve performance. The PIX Firewall application inspection feature opens and closes UDP ports for secure multimedia connections. Other firewall implementations typically must open a large range of UDP ports, creating security risks, or they must configure one port for inbound multimedia data requiring client reconfiguration.

The PIX-enhanced ASA supports multimedia—with or without NAT—without compromising security. This represents a major advantage over firewall installations that must choose between NAT and multimedia, which either limits multimedia applications to registered users or exposes inside network addresses to the Internet.

NOTE While NAT works well with multimedia applications, don't use PAT while running these applications through the PIX Firewall. Multimedia protocol attempts to dynamically access additional port connections can conflict with port mappings used by PAT.

The multimedia applications supported by the PIX Firewall application inspection include the following. Those followed by an asterisk have **fixup** command configuration support.

- CU-SeeMe
- Intel Internet Phone
- IRC
- RealAudio
- Real Time Streaming Protocol*
- Streamworks
- VDO Live
- Vxtreme
- Windows Media (Netshow)

Database and Directory Support

The database and directory applications supported by the PIX Firewall application inspection include the following. Those followed by an asterisk have **fixup** command configuration support.

- Network File System (NFS) and Sun Remote Procedure Call (RPC)
- Oracle SQL*Net (V1/V2)*
- Internet Locator Service (ILS)*

Management Protocols

The PIX Firewall application inspection-supported management protocols include the following. Those followed by an asterisk have **fixup** command configuration support.

- Internet Control Message Protocol (ICMP)
- Remote Shell (RSH)*
- X Display Manager Control Protocol (XDMCP)

Fixup Protocol Examples

The next three topics—FTP, SMTP, and VoIP—are included as examples of the application-inspection features and **fixup** commands. The Cisco site has more details and examples for any of the other supported protocols or applications.

FTP

The default application inspection for FTP sessions performs the following four tasks:

- NATs any IP addresses embedded within the application payload
- Prepares dynamic secondary data connections for FTP data transfer
- Tracks FTP command-response sequence
- Generates a detailed audit trail

The following output shows the command syntax, plus an example of the Strict option and adding port 3021 for the PIX to listen to for FTP traffic. Our only concern is with the FTP listening ports because the PIX stateful inspection will dynamically prepare the data connection as needed.

Pix(config)# fixup protocol ftp [strict] [*port*]

```
Pix(config)#fixup protocol ftp strict 21
Pix(config)#fixup protocol ftp 3021
```

The Strict option causes each **FTP** command and response sequence to be monitored for various RFC violations, including web browsers embedding commands in FTP requests.

Any connections discovered to contain embedded commands or that have been manipulated are dropped. Each FTP command must be acknowledged before a new command is allowed.

SMTP—Disabling Fixup Protocol Example

The Mail Guard feature provides safe access for Simple Mail Transfer Protocol (SMTP) connections from the outside to an inside e-mail server. *Mail Guard* allows a mail server to be safely deployed on the inside network, without the need for an external mail relay (or bastion host) system.

SMTP servers respond to client requests with numeric reply codes and optional human readable strings. The SMTP servers are vulnerable to mischief because of the simplicity of these messages and because some mail systems, such as Microsoft Exchange, don't fully comply with RFC 821. Mail Guard enforces a safe minimal set of SMTP commands to avoid an SMTP server system from being compromised. Mail Guard performs the following three primary tasks:

- Restricts SMTP requests to seven commands included in RFC 821: HELO, MAIL, RCPT, DATA, RSET, NOOP, and QUIT.
- Monitors the SMTP command and response sequence looking for a series of common anomalous signatures. Unacceptable characters or commands are replaced by Xs, which are then rejected by the internal server.
- Generates a detailed audit trail by logging all SMTP connections.

The **SMTP application inspection** command syntax and an example of disabling the Mail Guard feature are as follows:

Pix(config)# fixup protocol smtp [*port*[-*port*]]

```
Pix(config)# no fixup protocol smtp 25
```

The pervasiveness of Exchange servers in the workplace is reason enough to be aware that Mail Guard could cause Exchange servers and Microsoft Outlook clients to have problems in communicating through a PIX Firewall. It might be necessary to disable the SMTP application inspection and use an access list instead.

The following example demonstrates disabling Mail Guard, while allowing outside access to the DMZ e-mail server. The **static** command assigns a global address to the server. The ACL let_in allows outside users access to the e-mail server global address via SMTP port (25). The DNS server needs to point to the 1.1.1.6 address, so mail can be sent to this address.

```
Pix(config)# static (dmz,outside) 1.1.1.6 192.168.2.6 netmask
 255.255.255.255
Pix(config)# access-list let_in permit tcp any host 1.1.1.6 eq smtp
Pix(config)# access-group let_in in interface outside
Pix(config)# no fixup protocol smtp 25
```

Voice over IP (VoIP)

VoIP involves using H.323 gateways to convert traditional voice analog traffic into IP data packets. The challenges of highly time-sensitive packets in a LAN environment are compounded exponentially when VoIP has to deal with firewalls and NAT. Fortunately, the PIX Firewall application-layer inspection (fixup) features smooth out most of these wrinkles across all the protocols.

- H.323
- Media Gateway Control Protocol (MGCP)
- Session Initiation Protocol (SIP)
- Skinny Client Control Protocol (SCCP)
- Real-Time Transport Protocol (RTP)
- RTP Control Protocol (RTCP)

This section looks at three protocol suites that provide or facilitate call signaling, call control, and media communications. Depending on the VoIP protocols used, the communications between the devices might use either one channel or many different channels. The channels are Transmission Control Protocol (TCP)/User Datagram Protocol (UDP) ports used for the connections between two network devices.

Session Initiation (or Initiated) Protocol (SIP) Session Initiation (or Initiated) Protocol (SIP) is a signaling protocol for Internet conferencing, telephony, events notification, presence, and instant messaging. The protocol initiates call setup, routing, authentication, and other feature messages to end-stations in an IP network. The PIX Firewall application-inspection capabilities support SIP VoIP gateways, VoIP proxy servers, and dynamically allocated UDP ports.

Use the **fixup protocol** command to change the default port assignment for SIP or to add additional ports the PIX will "listen" to. The command syntax is as follows:

```
Pix(config)# fixup protocol sip [port[- port]]
Pix(config)# no fixup protocol sip [port[- port]]
```

H.323 *H.323* is a suite of protocols defined by the International Telecommunication Union (ITU) enabling multimedia conferences over LANs, even though hosts are using different applications. PIX Firewall software versions 6.2 and higher support PAT for H.323. The PIX Firewall supports the secure use of H.323 Version 2 to provide the following features:

- Fast Connect or Fast Start Procedure for faster call setup.
- H.245 tunneling for resource conservation, call synchronization, and reduced setup time.
- Conferencing—the conference is established only after the endpoints agree to participate.
- Call redirection.

Use the **fixup protocol** command to change the default port assignment for H.323 or add additional ports the PIX will "listen" to. The command syntax and default settings are as follows:

Pix(config)# fixup protocol h323 {h225 | ras} [*port*[- *port*]]
Pix(config)# no fixup protocol h323 {h225 | ras} [*port*[- *port*]]

```
Pix(config)# show fixup
fixup protocol h323 h225 1720
fixup protocol h323 ras 1718-1719
```

Skinny `(Simple)` **Client Control Protocol (SCCP)** Secure handling of SCCP in VoIP networks is necessary to use Cisco IP Phones, Cisco CallManager, and other Cisco IP Telephony products. When coupled with an H.323 Proxy, an SCCP client can coexist with H.323-compliant terminals. The PIX application-inspection capabilities ensure proper NAT translation of all SCCP signaling and media packets passing through the firewall.

PIX Firewall version 6.2 introduced support for DHCP options 150 and 166 (discussed in Chapter 18), which allow the PIX Firewall to send the location of a TFTP server to Cisco IP Phones and other DHCP clients.

Use the **fixup protocol** command to change the default port assignment for SCCP or add additional ports the PIX will "listen" to. The command syntax is as follows:

Pix(config)# fixup protocol skinny [*port*[- *port*]]
Pix(config)# no fixup protocol skinny [*port*[- *port*]]

Two problems still exist for SCCP:

- If the Cisco CallManager server address is configured for NAT and outside phones register to it using TFTP, the connection will fail because PIX Firewall currently doesn't support NAT TFTP messages.
- The PIX Firewall currently can't handle fragmented SCCP packets, such as those that occur with a voice-conferencing bridge. The SCCP inspection checks each packet and drops what appear to be bad packets because the internal checksums aren't accurate.

Other Supported Protocols and Applications

This section looks at PIX Firewall support for secure use of the following additional important protocols and applications.

Configurable Proxy Ping (ICMP)

The configurable proxy pinging feature, covered in Chapter 18, allows controlling ICMP access to the PIX Firewall interfaces. While ICMP access through the firewall is denied by ASA, access to the interfaces is unrestricted. The **icmp {permit | deny}** command allows configuring access on a per-interface/per-message–type basis. This feature can shield the PIX Firewall interfaces from detection by users on an external network.

While a temptation exists to deny all ICMP access to the firewall interfaces, permitting ICMP Unreachable (type 3) messages will allow ICMP Path MTU discovery, which is required by IPSec and PPTP traffic.

Internet Group Management Protocol (IGMP)

Internet Group Management Protocol (IGMP) is the protocol that facilitates forwarding router multicast transmissions, which can provide the broad-reach data distributions in an internetwork without the inherent congestion associated with broadcasts and multiple unicasts. IGMP dynamically registers specific LAN hosts in a multicast group with a multicast-enabled router. The enabled routers and supporting Cisco Group Management Protocol (CGMP)–enabled LAN switches efficiently distribute the multicast transmissions to the registered hosts.

PIX Firewall version 6.2 introduced Stub Multicast Routing (SMR) to allow the firewall to function as a *stub router,* an IGMP proxy agent. The firewall, like any stub router, isn't a full multicast router, but simply forwards IGMP messages between hosts and multicast routers.

NetBIOS over IP

The NetBIOS over IP support allows connections from the internal network to the external network. This support is important to Microsoft clients on the internal network that need to access external network servers running older versions of Windows, such as Windows NT. This allows the organization security policies to include Microsoft servers across the Internet and inside an intranet, while still allowing access controls native to the Microsoft environment.

RIP Version 2

As covered in Chapter 19, the PIX Firewall is *not* a router and, as such, won't forward routing information to other interfaces. Instead, the PIX only "listens" in Passive mode and can be configured to broadcast a default route.

The PIX Firewall supports Cisco IOS software standards, including support for RIP v2, which provides optional MD5 authentication of encryption keys. The RIP v2 support includes one key and key ID per interface. While the key has an infinite lifetime, best practices would indicate more frequent changes consistent with the security policy. Don't forget, using Telnet to change the configuration might inadvertently expose the key and the key ID on the network.

Attack Guards

The PIX Firewall offers a family of features to defend the device and protected networks from attack. The PIX application-inspection capabilities and IDS features work together to provide services similar to those covered in Chapters 6 (IDS) and 7 (CBAC). *Attack guards* refer to the PIX Firewall application-layer inspection capabilities that have been programmed to prevent specific kinds of common attacks. This section looks at the following attack guards.

- DNS Control
- Flood Defender
- FragGuard and Virtual Reassembly
- TCP Intercept
- Unicast Reverse Path Forwarding
- ActiveX Blocking, Java Filtering, and URL Filtering

DNS Control

To defend against the growing threat of DNS attacks, Cisco introduced an always-on feature called *DNS Guard*. Because DNS Guard can neither be turned off nor configured, DNS has no **fixup protocol** command.

Generic UDP handling of DNS queries leaves connections open longer than is prudent. Instead, the PIX Firewall identifies each outbound DNS resolve request, and then tears down the connection as soon as a single reply is received. While a host might query several servers for a response in case the first server is down or congested, only the first answer to that request is allowed. Additional responses are dropped. This prevents a hacker from following a legitimate DNS reply with a modified version directing traffic to another site.

PIX Firewall version 6.2 supports NAT and PAT of DNS messages originating from both inside (more secure) and outside (less secure) interfaces. The embedded addresses in both the query and reply message are now translated, and names resolution works as expected.

Flood Defender

The *Flood Defender* feature is used to reclaim PIX Firewall resources if the user authentication subsystem runs out of resources. If an inbound or an outbound authentication connection is being attacked or overused, the PIX Firewall actively reclaims TCP user resources. The feature is enabled by default. The Flood Defender feature is enabled/disabled with the **floodguard** command using the following syntax:

```
Pix(config)# floodguard enable
Pix(config)# floodguard disable
Pix(config)# no floodguard
Pix(config)# clear floodguard
```

The **show floodguard**, **show running-config**, and **write terminal** commands will all display the flood-defender status.

PART IV

As resource depletion gets more serious, the PIX Firewall starts reclaiming TCP user resources in the following order, depending on urgency of the shortage:

1. Timewait
2. FinWait
3. Embryonic
4. Idle

FragGuard and Virtual Reassembly

FragGuard and *Virtual Reassembly* are default features that provide IP fragment protection for traffic passing through the PIX Firewall. FragGuard fully reassembles all ICMP error messages and performs virtual reassembly of all other IP fragments.

Syslog messages are generated by any fragment overlapping and small fragment offset anomalies, common to variations of the teardrop attack. *Teardrop attacks* work by sending deliberately constructed IP fragments, which are reassembled into an invalid UDP datagram. Overlapping offsets work by causing additional fragments to overwrite data in the middle of the UDP header. This is contained in the first fragment in such a way that the datagrams are left incomplete.

The **configuration mode fragment** command provides additional management of packet fragmentation and improves compatibility with NFS. The syntax is as follows:

Pix(config)# fragment {size|chain|timeout} *limit* [*int_name*]
Pix(config)# clear fragment
Pix(config)# show fragment [*int_name*]

size *database-limit*	Maximum number of packets in the fragment database. Default is 200. Maximum is 1,000,000.
chain *chain-limit*	Maximum number of packets a full IP packet can be fragmented to. Default is 24. Maximum is 8,200.
timeout *seconds*	Maximum total seconds after the first fragment is received that fragments can wait to be reassembled, after which the fragments are discarded. Default is five seconds. Maximum is 30 seconds.

The **clear fragment** command clears the fragment databases and resets all defaults. Any fragments waiting for reassembly are discarded.

The **show fragment [*int_name*]** command displays the settings and statistics of the fragment database for the specified interface. If ***int_name*** isn't specified, the command applies to all interfaces. The following output shows a sample with the default settings:

```
Pix(config)# show fragment
Interface: outside
    Size: 200, Chain: 24, Timeout: 5
    Queue: 0, Assemble: 0, Fail: 0, Overflow: 0
Interface: inside
    Size: 200, Chain: 24, Timeout: 5
    Queue: 0, Assemble: 0, Fail: 0, Overflow: 0
Interface: dmz
```

```
    Size: 200, Chain: 24, Timeout: 5
    Queue: 0, Assemble: 0, Fail: 0, Overflow: 0
Pix(config)#
```

The PIX Firewall, by default, accepts up to 24 fragments to reassemble a full IP packet. To increase network security, consistent with the security policy, configure the firewall *not* to accept fragmented packets with the Fragment Size 1 command option. Using a limit of one means only whole packets will be accepted.

The following output shows increasing the fragment size and timeout on all interfaces, plus eliminating fragments on the less-secure interfaces.

```
Pix(config)# fragment size 500
Pix(config)# fragment chain 1 outside
Pix(config)# fragment chain 1 dmz
Pix(config)# fragment timeout 10
Pix(config)# show fragment
Interface: outside
    Size: 500, Chain: 1, Timeout: 10
    Queue: 0, Assemble: 0, Fail: 0, Overflow: 0
Interface: inside
    Size: 500, Chain: 24, Timeout: 10
    Queue: 0, Assemble: 0, Fail: 0, Overflow: 0
Interface: dmz
    Size: 500, Chain: 1, Timeout: 10
    Queue: 0, Assemble: 0, Fail: 0, Overflow: 0
Pix(config)#
```

PART IV

The sysopt security fragguard Command

The **sysopt** commands are used to modify about a dozen PIX Firewall system options. Our interest at this point is specifically the **sysopt security fragguard** command. Although it's disabled by default, once this feature is enabled, it enforces two addition security checks beyond those recommended by RFC 1858 (IP fragment–style attacks, such as teardrop, land, and so forth).

- Each noninitial IP fragment must be associated with a known valid initial IP fragment.
- IP fragments are limited to 100 per second to each internal host.

The feature operates on all PIX Firewall interfaces and can't be selectively enabled or disabled by interface. No Security FragGuard options exist. The syntax is as follows:

```
Pix(config)# sysopt security fragguard
Pix(config)# no sysopt security fragguard
```

The **clear sysopt** command resets *all* **sysopt** commands to default settings.

NOTE While the **sysopt security fragguard** command deviates from the standard for handling IP fragments, it opts on the side of security by greatly reducing the possibility of IP fragmentation attacks.

TCP Intercept

The TCP Intercept feature protects inside systems (servers) from a common type of denial of service (DoS) attack, which is perpetrated by flooding an interface with TCP SYN packets that create half-open TCP (embryonic) connections. The feature is enabled by setting the maximum Embryonic (*em_limit*) Connections option on the **nat** and **static** commands. Both features were covered in Chapter 19. The syntax is the following:

Pix(config)# static [(*hi_interface, lo_interface*)] *global_ip local_ip* [netmask *mask*] [norandomseq] [*max_conn [em_limit]*]
Pix(config)# nat (*if_name*) *nat_id ip_address* [*netmask*] [outside] [dns] [norandomseq] [timeout *hh:mm:ss*] [*conn_limit*] [*em_limit*]

em_limit	The embryonic or half-open TCP connection limit. Default is 0, which allows unlimited connections.

Once the embryonic connection limit is reached, and until the embryonic connection count falls below this threshold, the firewall intercepts additional SYN packets. The PIX Firewall works as a proxy and responds on behalf of the server, with a SYN/ACK reply turning the session over to the server if it's successfully established.

Unicast Reverse Path Forwarding

Spoofing IP source addresses in the IP protocol is a common tool for evil doers to attempt to conceal their identities. Unicast Reverse Path Forwarding (Unicast RPF), or *reverse route lookup,* provides inbound and outbound filtering to help prevent IP address spoofing. The feature verifies that source addresses of inbound packets are verifiable by routes in the local PIX routing table. Realistically, the **ip verify reverse-path interface** command is most useful in reducing the chances of internal hosts becoming parties to an attack and outsiders spoofing a trusted inside address. The syntax is

Pix(config)# ip verify reverse-path interface *int_name*
Pix(config)# no ip verify reverse-path interface *int_name*

Because Unicast RPF is limited to verifying addresses against those in the local route table, the following two conditions are critical:

- A default route statement (0.0.0.0 0.0.0.0) must be configured for the outside interface.
- **Static route** commands must exist for every network on the protected interfaces.

The following example defines IP addresses for three interfaces, creates a default route to the outside, defines the four networks expected on the other side of an inside router, and assumes all DMZ hosts will be connected locally to the 192.168.128.0 network.

```
Pix(config)# ip address outside 1.1.1.1 255.255.255.0
Pix(config)# ip address inside 192.168.1.1 255.255.255.0
Pix(config)# ip address dmz 192.168.128.1 255.255.255.0
```

```
Pix(config)# route outside 0.0.0.0 0.0.0.0 1.1.1.2 1
Pix(config)# route inside 192.168.4.0 255.255.255.0 192.168.1.2 1
Pix(config)# route inside 192.168.5.0 255.255.255.0 192.168.1.2 1
Pix(config)# route inside 192.168.6.0 255.255.255.0 192.168.1.2 1
Pix(config)# route inside 192.168.7.0 255.255.255.0 192.168.1.2 1
Pix(config)# ip verify reverse-path interface outside
Pix(config)# ip verify reverse-path interface inside
Pix(config)# ip verify reverse-path interface dmz
```

The **ip verify reverse-path interface outside** command ensures no packets arrive from the outside with sources addresses defined for the inside or DMZ networks. The **ip verify reverse-path interface inside** command prevents any packets coming from the inside with source addresses that aren't defined to that interface. The final command limits packets coming in from the DMZ to source addresses in the 192.168.128.0 network.

The following output shows using the **show ip verify** command to confirm configuration and the **show ip verify statistics** command to show activity.

```
Pix(config)# show ip verify
ip verify reverse-path interface outside
ip verify reverse-path interface inside
ip verify reverse-path interface dmz
Pix(config)# show ip verify statistics
interface outside: 2 unicast rpf drops
interface inside: 0 unicast rpf drops
interface dmz: 0 unicast rpf drops
Pix(config)#
```


ActiveX Blocking, Java Filtering, and URL Filtering

These three features were covered in Chapter 19 as content filtering using the **filter** command. All three are made possible because of the **fixup protocol http [*port*]** command. They are included here as attack guards.

ActiveX Blocking	ActiveX controls (formerly OLE or OCX controls) are embedded web page components that can introduce potential problems to network clients.
Java Filtering	Java applets are executable programs that can enable certain methods of attacking a protected network.
URL Filtering	Uses products like Websense or N2H2 servers to prevent outbound access to specific configurable web sites deemed inappropriate for the user(s).

Intrusion Detection

The Cisco Secure PIX Firewall, like the Cisco Secure IOS Firewall covered in Chapter 7, added intrusion-detection technology to extend the Cisco Secure IDS technology. IDS sensor incorporation into the firewall is ideal for locations requiring additional security between network segments. It can also provide enhanced visibility at intranet, extranet, and branch-office Internet perimeters.

PIX Firewall IDS v6.2 audits (monitors) 53 attack signatures, representing a broad cross section of severe security breaches and the most common information-gathering scans. The PIX Firewall IDS technology auditing is performed by looking at the IP packets as they arrive at an input interface. If a packet matches an active signature, the IDS can perform any or all of the following actions based on the predefined router configuration:

- **Alarm** Sends an alarm to a Syslog server and/or a Cisco Secure IDS Director
- **Drop** Discards the packet
- **Reset** Resets the questionable TCP connection

Any packet that triggers a *signature* for which the configured action doesn't drop the packet, can then trigger additional signatures.

PIX Firewall IDS supports both inbound and outbound auditing, as well as interface specific auditing.

Define Default Audit Actions

Use the **global configuration mode ip audit** command to specify the default audit action(s). Use the no form of this command to set the default action for info signatures. The syntax is the following:

Pix(config)# ip audit {info | attack} {action [alarm] [drop] [reset]}
Pix(config)# no ip audit {info | attack}

info	For info-type signatures (reconnaissance attacks).
attack	For attack-type signatures.
action	Sets an action for the info signature to take when a match occurs.
alarm	Sends an alarm to all configured Syslog servers. The default option.
drop	Drops the packet.
reset	Drops the packet and closes any related TCP session.0.+.

In the following example, the default action for info and attack signatures is set:

```
Pix(config)# ip audit info action alarm
Pix(config)# ip audit attack action reset
```

Disabling Individual Signatures

Use the **global configuration mode ip audit signature** command to attach a policy to a signature and disable the signature. Use the no form of this command to remove the policy and reenable the signature. The syntax is as follows:

Pix(config)# ip audit signature *signature-id* disable
Pix(config)# no ip audit signature *signature-id*

signature-id	Unique integer specifying a signature in the Director Network Security Database.

In this example, the two signatures are disabled. The **show ip audit signature** command is used to display the disabled signatures, and then one is reenabled.

```
Pix(config)# ip audit signature 1001 disable
Pix(config)# ip audit signature 1004 disable
Pix(config)# show ip audit signature
ip audit signature 1001 disable
ip audit signature 1004 disable
Pix(config)# no ip audit signature 1001 disable
```

The **show ip audit count** command lists the active signatures:

```
Pix(config)# show ip audit count
Signature                               Global
1000 I Bad IP Options List              0
1001 I Record Packet Route              0
1002 I Timestamp                        0
1003 I Provide s,c,h,tcc                0
1005 I SATNET ID                        0
1006 I Strict Source Route              0
```

Create Named Audit Rules

An *audit rule* (audit policy) defines the actions for all active signatures that can be applied to an interface. Each audit rule/policy is identified by a unique user-defined case-sensitive name. Each interface can have two policies: one each for informational and attack signatures. If a policy is defined without actions, then the defined default actions are used. Each policy requires a different name.

Use the **global configuration mode** command **ip audit name** to create audit rules for info and attack signature types. Any signatures disabled with the **ip audit signature** command don't become part of the audit rule created with the **ip audit name** command. Use the no form of this command to delete an audit rule. The syntax is

Pix(config)ip audit name *audit-name* {info | attack} [action [alarm] [drop] [reset]]
Pix(config)no ip audit name *audit-name* {info | attack}

The following example shows creating an audit policy—Audit.99—and then using the **show ip audit name** command to display the named policies.

```
Pix(config)# ip audit name Audit.99 info action alarm drop reset
Pix(config)# show ip audit name
ip audit name Audit.99 info action alarm drop reset
Pix(config)#
```

Apply the Audit Rule to the Interface(s)

The audit rule is applied to an interface on the PIX Firewall using the **ip audit interface** command. The no form of the command removes a policy from the interface. The syntax is

Pix(config)# ip audit interface *int_name audit-name*
Pix(config)# no ip audit interface *int_name*

The following example shows an attempt to assign the policy to the outside interface with a case error on the name. This is followed by a correct entry, and then the **show ip audit interface** command verifying the interface assignments.

```
Pix(config)# ip audit interface outside audit.99
Could not locate an IDS policy with name audit.99
Pix(config)# ip audit interface outside Audit.99
Pix(config)# show ip audit interface
ip audit interface outside Audit.99
Pix(config)#
```

PIX Firewall IDS Syslog Messages

PIX Firewall IDS Syslog messages all start with %PIX-4-4000nn IDS:*signature_id* . . . . The PIX-4 indicates trapping level 4 at least would be needed to capture these messages. The following sample messages include an info (2003) and attack (4051) message:

```
%PIX-4-400013 IDS:2003 ICMP redirect from 192.168.2.1 to 192.168.1.1 on interface dmz
%PIX-4-400032 IDS:4051 UDP Snork attack from 10.1.4.1 to 192.168.1.10 on interface
outside
```

Shunning

The **shun** command enables a dynamic response to an attacking host by dropping any defined connections and preventing new connections. An administrator or a Cisco Secure IDS device can instruct the PIX Firewall to shun the source of traffic when that source is considered malicious. The shun command-blocking function is applied whether or not a connection with the specified host address is currently active. Because the **shun** command is used dynamically to block attacks, it isn't displayed in your configuration. The syntax is as follows:

Pix(config)# shun *src_ip* [*dest_ip src_port dest_port* [*protocol*]]
Pix(config)# no shun *src_ip* [*dest_ip src_port dest_port* [*protocol*]]

The **show shun** command lists any shunning underway, while the **show shun statistics** command shows the interfaces, the number of packets blocked, and how long shunning has been on.

If the **shun** command is used with only the source IP address, no further traffic from the offending host is allowed. The following **show shun** output shows other variables default to 0. Notice the PIX knew that the address to be shunned was on the inside interface.

```
Pix(config)# shun 192.168.1.10
Shun 192.168.1.10 successful
Pix(config)# show shun
Shun 192.168.1.10 0.0.0.0 0 0
```

```
Pix(config)# show shun statistics
outside=OFF, cnt=0
inside=ON, cnt=0
dmz=OFF, cnt=0
intf3=OFF, cnt=0
Shun 192.168.1.10 cnt=42, time=(0:05:52)
Pix(config)#
```

Shunning statistics are also available from PDM. The **clear shun statistics** command clears the counts, while **clear shun** removes all shunning.

Managing SNMP Services

Simple Network Management Protocol (SNMP) is an Internet standard application-layer protocol developed to exchange management data between network devices. SNMP-compliant devices, called *agents*, collect data about themselves and store that data in Management Information Bases (MIBs). These MIBs are sent to SNMP management stations or devices for storage and analysis. MIB data, such as device system messages, packets per second, or network error rates, can be used by network administrators to monitor network performance, find and solve network problems, and facilitate planning for network growth.

SNMP version 1 (SNMPv1) was developed in the early 1980s. Version 2 (SNMPv2) introduced increased security capabilities and improved interoperability by rigorously defining the specifications for SNMP implementation. The SNMPv3 Working Group is preparing recommendations for the next generation of SNMP with increasing network security as an important objective.

PIX Firewall SNMP Support

The PIX Firewall, like its router and switch cousins, is considered an SNMP agent or SNMP server that collects data in MIB form. The management station is often a UNIX or Windows network host running the SNMP program that receives and processes the SNMP MIB data. This program could be a network management program, such as CiscoWorks or HP OpenView, a tool like Fluke Networks OptiView, or one of many network mapping and analysis programs, such as nMAP or Ethereal. Figure 20-1 shows an example of an SNMP management station on the internal network. The security policy and scope of the management station might dictate whether the DMZ servers and the perimeter router would report to the station.

Accessibility to PIX Firewall MIBs is based on configuration, MIB support, and authentication based on the community string. By default, the PIX Firewall is configured to allow polling from all configured SNMP management hosts on the inside interface. Unsuccessful polling attempts, except for failed community string authentication, aren't logged or otherwise reported.

Use the **snmp-server** command to identify location, management station, community string, and contact information for the PIX Firewall.

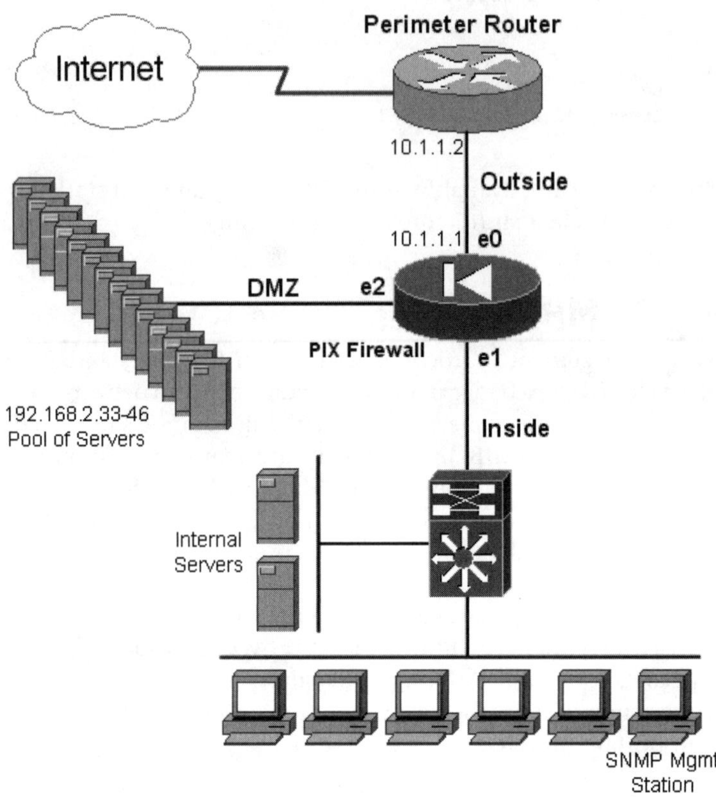

Figure 20-1 SNMP management station in the inside network

SNMP Contact and Location

You can use the **configuration mode snmp-server {contact | location}** command to identify the PIX Firewall system administrator and the unit location. Each item can be up to 127 characters and is case sensitive. Spaces are allowed, but multiple spaces are shortened to a single space. Some security policies might limit what's entered here because the information could be useful to a hacker engaging in reconnaissance. Telephone numbers and contact names might be a useful tool to a person trying to act as if he belongs there or is deserving of assistance. Use the no form of the command to turn off the feature. Typing either command with new information overwrites the old entries. The syntax is

Pix(config)# snmp-server {contact | location} *text*
Pix(config)# no snmp-server {contact | location}

The following example shows a simple configuration:

```
Pix(config)# snmp-server location Building 19-67B
Pix(config)# snmp-server contact Network Security
```

SNMP Management Station

Use the **configuration mode snmp-server host** command to define the interface and the IP address of the SNMP management station(s) to which traps will be sent and/or from which the SNMP polls (requests) will be accepted. By default, both the *traps* and *polls* features are on—adding either keyword to the end of the command limits the command to only that activity. For example, using the Trap option would allow traps, but not polls. Up to 32 SNMP stations can be defined by creating multiple commands. Use the no form of the command to turn the feature off. The syntax is

Pix(config)#snmp-server host [*if_name*] *ip_addr* {trap | poll}
Pix(config)#no snmp-server [if_name] *ip_addr*

The default interface is "inside." If an interface other than inside is used, a security warning like the one shown in the next example appears, but the entry will be accepted.

The following example shows a simple configuration:

```
Pix(config)# snmp-server host 192.168.1.3
Pix(config)# snmp-server host dmz 192.168.2.3 trap
Warning: Sending SNMP traps to a non-inside interface may be insecure
Pix(config)#
```

SNMP Community Key

The SNMP community string is a shared "secret" among the SNMP management station and the SNMP network agents being managed. This is called a *community key* because it can be used to define a data-exchanging group of agent and management stations within a larger network. The default key for the PIX Firewall, like many network devices, is **public**. This is also a routine default entry in most sniffer, mapping, or other reconnaissance tools, so common sense says to change it.

The PIX Firewall uses the community key to determine if the incoming SNMP request is valid. Use the **configuration mode snmp-server community** command to enter the key value used by the SNMP management station(s). The key is case sensitive and can be up to 32 characters long. No spaces are allowed. Typing a new **snmp-server community** command replaces the default public entry or any other existing community key. Use the no form of the command to turn off the feature. The syntax is

Pix(config)# snmp-server community *key*
Pix(config)# no snmp-server community *key*

Enabling SNMP Traps

Use the **configuration mode snmp-server enable traps** command to enable or disable sending log messages as SNMP trap notifications. Use the no form of the command to turn off the feature. The syntax is

Pix(config)# snmp-server enable traps
Pix(config)# no snmp-server enable traps

Verify SNMP Configuration

Use the **show snmp-server** command to display the current SNMP configuration:

```
Pix(config)# show snmp-server
snmp-server host inside 192.168.1.3
snmp-server host dmz 192.168.2.3
snmp-server location Building 19-67B
snmp-server contact Network Security
snmp-server community MySNMP
snmp-server enable traps
Pix(config)#
```

The **clear snmp-server** command clears most of the SNMP entries. It restores the community key "public" and leaves the **snmp-server enable traps** command.

Logging to the SNMP Management Station

You can have PIX Firewall system messages sent to the defined SNMP management unit instead of, or in addition to, a Syslog server. Use the **configuration mode logging history** command to set the message level. This command is the SNMP counterpart to the **logging trap** command used with Syslog messages. Use the no form of the command to turn off the feature. The syntax is

Pix(config)# logging history *level*
Pix(config)# no logging history *level*

The levels are the same eight levels (0–7) covered in the "Syslog Configuration" section in Chapter 18 where the level includes all message levels up to the one used. For example, the following example would send all system messages 0 through 5 to the SNMP host(s).

```
Pix(config)# logging history 5
```

For more information about SNMP, tutorials, SNMP tools, PowerPoint presentations, and so forth, try the following web sites:

http://www.simpleweb.org/
http://www.snmplink.org/
http://www.snmpworld.com/
http://www.cisco.com/warp/public/535/3.html

Chapter Review

This chapter looked at some of the more-advanced features of the PIX Firewall.

You saw the alternatives to establishing a console cable session with the router, including Telnet, HTTP, and SSH. The configuration and case sensitivity are more involved than working with routers.

Configuring AAA on the PIX Firewall is similar to working with AAA on the routers. First, the AAA server must be specified and the host key configured. This key must match the one configured on the AAA server. The key is used to get the AAA server to accept the AAA requests from the PIX device. The next step involves configuring the authentication, authorization, and accounting commands, so target users and resources are identified.

AAA support for all the console session methods and the **enable** command add a higher level of secure authentication to the activity. With PIX v6.2, AAA now supports command authorization, as well as the Local User Database for authentication and command authorization.

Advanced protocol handling involves application-layer inspection to maintain stateful table entries to allow return traffic from those applications and protocols that either embed IP addresses in the data payload or make dynamic port requests after the initial session setup. The **fixup protocol** commands are a portion of the advanced protocol handling that allows the PIX administrator to view, change, enable, or disable the use of a variety of common applications or protocols through the PIX Firewall. The specified ports define the ones the PIX Firewall will listen at for each respective service.

Attack guards are another implementation of application-layer inspection implemented to monitor for common network threats or undesirable traffic and to block them. Features like DNS Control, Flood Defender, TCP Intercept, FragGuard and Reverse Path Forwarding are examples of efforts to block common attack strategies. Three **filter** commands can be used to block potentially destructive or unpleasant web resources from the network: the **Filter activex** command blocks Active X objects from web pages, the **Filter Java** command does the same thing to Java applets, and the **Filter URL** command works with either an N2H2 or a Websense server to filter content based on an extensive database. URL filtering also offers web tracking and custom blocking features.

New IDS sensor capabilities extend the Cisco Secure IDS strategy to include the PIX Firewall, adding visibility to the Internet, intranet, and extranet. Shunning allows the PIX Firewall to receive **dynamic** commands from an IDS unit to block traffic that's determined as a threat.

The SNMP server commands allow the PIX Firewall administrator to configure SNMP to be more secure, while still providing an easy-to-implement method of remote administration and monitoring for a wide variety of network devices.

Questions

1. Looking at the following output, what will be the result of the second statement?

```
Pix(config)# telnet 192.168.1.10 255.255.255.255 inside
Pix(config)# telnet 192.168.1.47 255.255.255.255
Pix(config)# telnet 192.168.2.0 255.255.255.0 inside
Pix(config)# telnet 1.1.1.10 255.255.255.255 outside
```

   A. It will allow Telnetting from the host on the default outside interface.

   B. The command will fail because no interface is specified.

   C. It will enable Telnet from the host on all nonoutside interfaces.

   D. It will enable Telnet from the host only on the interface to that address.

2. The Telnet timeout 10 command does what?

   A. Gives the firewall a ten-minute break

   B. Sets the Telnet idle timer to ten seconds

   C. Sets the Telnet idle timer to ten minutes

   D. Sets the Telnet session limit to ten minutes

3. A group_tag refers to which one of the following?

   A. AAA authentication protocol

   B. Pool of AAA servers

   C. The name of a AAA server

   D. A AAA header field

4. What does the following AAA command do? Pick the best answer.

```
Pix(config)# aaa-server radius host 192.168.1.4 4key
```

   A. It assigns server 192.168.1.4 to the default RADIUS group.

   B. It creates a new group radius—protocol RADIUS—and assigns server 192.168.1.4 to it.

   C. It will fail because no group radius exists.

   D. It creates a new group radius—protocol TACACS+—and assigns server 192.168.1.4 to it.

5. What command displays the syntax and usage for the aaa authentication, aaa authorization, aaa accounting, and aaa proxy-limit commands in summary form?

   A. show aaa

   B. show aaa options

   C. help aaa

   D. show aaa help

6. Which of the following statements is *not* true?
   - A. The local user database requires only a user name and a password.
   - B. PIX Firewall v6.2 introduced the local user database command to firewalls.
   - C. The local user database can be used to authenticate users.
   - D. The local user database can be used for command authorization.
7. What feature does the PIX ASA use to establish and maintain its stateful access control and traffic-monitoring security?
   - A. Application layer inspection
   - B. Access control lists
   - C. ip audit command
   - D. The Filter command
8. With the Fixup Protocol command, what is typically the only variable?
   - A. Source address
   - B. Port number or port range
   - C. Destination address
   - D. Enable/disable
9. The PIX Java and ActiveX filtering is an example of which one of the following?
   - A. Fixup protocol
   - B. Attack guards
   - C. Shunning
   - D. Flood defender
10. Which is *not* a Voice over IP (VoIP) fixup protocol?
    - A. H.323
    - B. Session Initiation Protocol (SIP)
    - C. Skinny Client Control Protocol (SCCP)
    - D. Internet Locator Service (ILS)
11. What does the FragGuard fragment size 1 command do?
    - A. Limits fragments to 1 byte
    - B. Limits fragments to 1 kilobyte
    - C. Blocks fragmenting
    - D. Limits fragmentation time to one minute
12. Which command specifies an SMTP trap level for logging messages?
    - A. logging trap
    - B. logging history

C. logging on

D. logging host

13. What two additional security checks are added by the sysopt security fragguard command?

A. Each noninitial IP fragment must be associated with known valid initial IP fragments.

B. All IP fragments are blocked.

C. IP fragments are limited to 100 per second to each internal host.

D. Only RFC 1858 fragmentation protection is allowed.

14. Which attack guard uses the firewall route table to look for spoofed addresses?

A. Virtual Reassembly

B. TCP Intercept

C. Unicast Reverse Path Forwarding

D. Flood Defender

15. Which command is an example of setting an IDS audit default action?

A. ip audit name Audit.99 info action alarm drop reset

B. ip audit signature 1001 disable

C. ip audit attack action reset

D. ip audit interface outside audit.99

Answers

1. C. It will enable Telnet from the host on all nonoutside interfaces.
2. C. Sets the Telnet idle timer to ten minutes
3. B. Pool of AAA servers
4. D. It creates a new group radius—protocol TACACS+—and assigns server 192.168.1.4 to it. Remember, group names are case sensitive, and if none matches the name used, a new TACACS+ group is formed.
5. C. Help aaa displays the syntax and usage for the aaa authentication, aaa authorization, aaa accounting, and aaa proxy-limit commands in summary form.
6. A. The local user database requires only a user name and a password is false because, on the firewall, the password is optional.
7. A. Application layer inspection
8. B. Port number or port range
9. B. Attack guards

10. **D.** Internet Locator Service (ILS)
11. **C.** Blocks fragmenting
12. **B.** Logging history
13. **A and C.** Each noninitial IP fragment must be associated with known valid initial IP fragments, and IP fragments are limited to 100 per second to each internal host.
14. **C.** Unicast Reverse Path Forwarding
15. **C.** ip audit attack action reset

CHAPTER 21

Firewalls and VPN Features

In this chapter, you learn to:

- See how Pix Firewall enables a secure VPN
- Use IPSec configuration tasks
- Understand Cisco VPN Client
- Scale PIX Firewall VPNs
- Know about PPPoE and the PIX Firewall

In this chapter, you look at configuring IPSec VPNs on PIX Firewalls. Because the fundamentals of IPSec were addressed extensively in Chapters 9 through11, that material won't be repeated. Terminology and concepts like Internet Key Exchange (IKE), Certification Authority (CA), preshared keys, and so forth are identical when connecting to a firewall. The differences are limited to the **implementation** commands.

STUDY TIP As you prepare for the exam, be sure to check the Cisco site for the PIX OS version covered. At press time, the current test version is 6.2. Be careful when verifying commands against the Cisco online resources. Many documents haven't been fully updated to 6.2. Old defaults and syntax have changed, so when in doubt, go to a device and try it out.

Pix Firewall Enables a Secure VPN

Virtual private networks (VPNs) using IPSec provide standards-based authentication and encryption services to protect against modification or unauthorized viewing of the data within a network or as it passes through an unprotected network, such as the public Internet. The correct configuration steps and commands depend on several factors, which include making decisions about the following basic IPSec issues.

1. Choosing between the two IPSec implementations—remote access or site-to-site— is necessary. You look at each in this chapter. Figure 21-1 shows a site-to-site VPN implementation.

Remote access	This implementation allows VPN clients, such as mobile users or telecommuters, to establish secure remote access to centralized network resources, often over the Internet.
Site-to-site	This implementation is used between two IPSec security gateways, such as PIX Firewall. A site-to-site VPN connects geographically separated networks, such as branch locations, to the corporate network.

2. Which of the two security protocols supported by the IPSec standard will be used? The need for encryption may be the deciding factor.

Authentication Header (AH)	Implements authentication and antireplay services.
Encapsulating Security Protocol (ESP)	Implements authentication, antireplay services, plus encryption.

3. Which of the two IPSec modes will be required, based on the previous choices?

Tunnel mode	The typical IPSec implementation between two security gateways, such as PIX Firewall units, using an untrusted network, such as the public Internet, for connectivity. See Figure 21-1.
Transport mode	This method of implementing IPSec for remote access to corporate network resources. This method frequently involves Windows 2000 VPN clients authenticating with L2TP. See Figure 21-2.

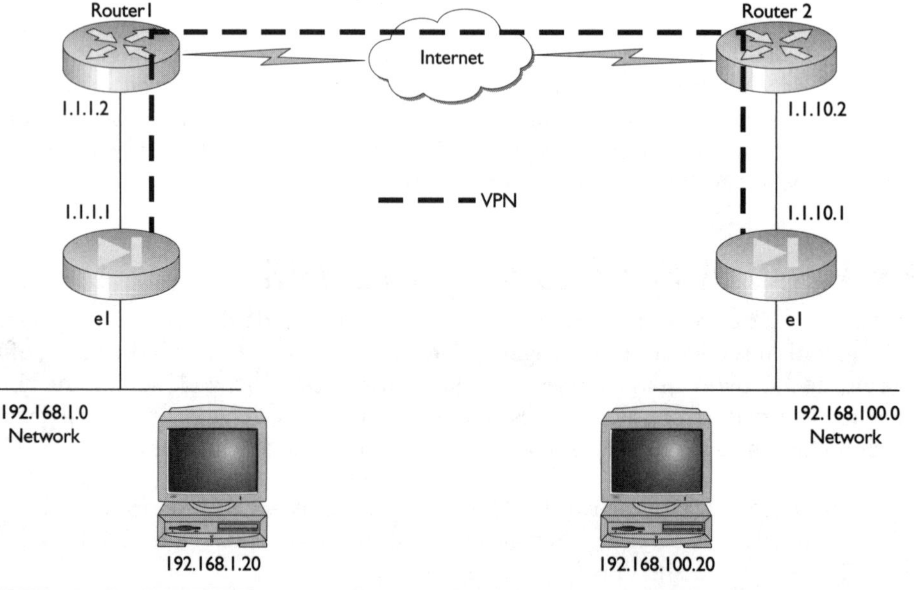

Figure 21-1 IPSec site-to-site VPN implementation (tunnel mode)

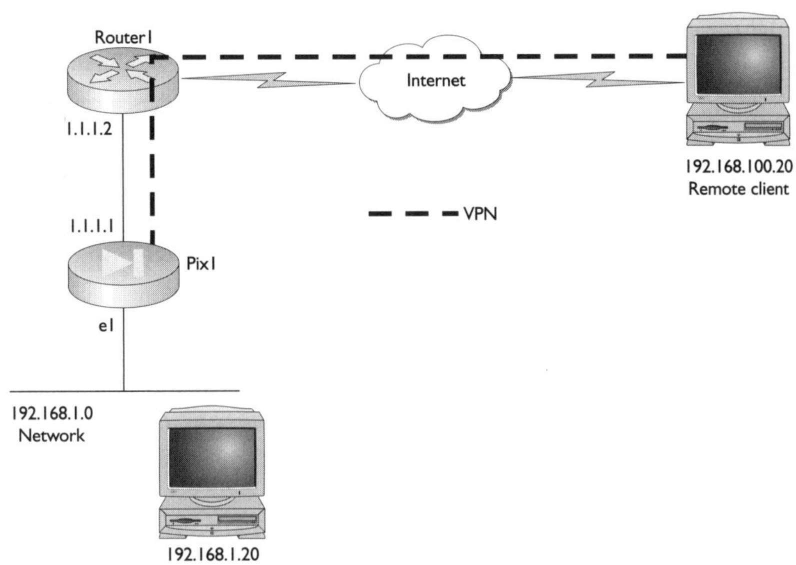

Figure 21-2 IPSec remote access VPN implementation (transport mode)

IPSec VPN Establishment

The role of IPSec is to facilitate the private and secure exchange of information over an inherently insecure link. IPSec uses encryption to secure the information, making it virtually useless to someone who might capture or monitor the exchange. For encryption to work, both the sending and receiving entities need to share a common secret (key) used for encryption and decryption of the data.

IPSec uses a two-phase process to establish the confidential exchange of that shared secret. If Phase 1 can't be established, then Phase 2 isn't attempted and data can't be exchanged.

Phase 1	The negotiation of security parameters required to establish a secure channel between two IPSec peers. Phase 1 can be implemented using IKE protocol or manually configured using preshared keys.
Phase 2	Using the secure connection established in Phase 1, exchange the security parameters necessary to exchange data.

In both phases of IPSec, the agreed-on parameters are called security associations (SAs) that will be used at each IPSec end point.

Five Steps of IPSec

The basic IPSec process can be summarized in the following five steps:

1. Interesting traffic initiates the IPSec process. Traffic is deemed interesting when the IPSec security policy configured in the IPSec peers starts the IKE process.

2. IKE Phase One—IKE authenticates IPSec peers and negotiates IKE SAs during this phase, setting up a secure channel for negotiating IPSec SAs in Phase two.
3. IKE Phase Two—IKE negotiates IPSec SA parameters and sets up matching IPSec SAs in the peers.
4. Data transfer—Data is transferred between IPSec peers, based on the IPSec parameters and keys stored in the SA database.
5. IPSec tunnel termination—IPSec SAs terminate through deletion or by timing out.

NOTE Don't make this any more difficult than it already is. If you strip out the acronyms and encryption, this process isn't all that different than ISDN. While more steps exist, they're basically identifying "interesting" traffic, creating a link, opening a session, transmitting data, and then bringing down the link.

IPSec Configuration Tasks

Configuring IPSec has four major tasks, which are

- Task 1: Prepare to configure VPN support.
- Task 2: Configure IKE parameters.
- Task 3: Configure IPSec parameters.
- Task 4: Test and verify VPN configuration.

Each of these tasks requires several steps. The following sections look at each of these configuration tasks in greater detail.

Task 1: Prepare to Configure VPN Support

This task consists of several steps to determine IKE and IPSec policies, ensure the network works before encryption, and ensure the PIX Firewall can support IPSec. Successful implementation of an IPSec network requires advance preparation before beginning configuration of individual devices.

Configuring IPSec encryption can be complicated and, at times, confusing. To reduce both, it's essential to plan ahead. If you get in a hurry, this can only lead to lost time and frustration. Because this process was defined in detail in Chapter 10, it won't be repeated here. Follow these basic planning steps:

Step 1.1: Determine IKE (IKE Phase one) policy to be used between IPSec peers, including whether to use preshared keys or CAs.

Step 1.2: Determine IPSec (IKE Phase two) policy, including the IPSec peer details, such as IP addresses and IPSec modes to be used when configuring the crypto maps.

Step 1.3: Check the current configuration to see if IPSec is currently being used on the devices. Use the **write terminal**, **show isakmp [policy]**, **show crypto map**, and other **show** commands covered later in this chapter.

Step 1.4: Verify the network works without encryption. Verify basic connectivity among all devices with the **ping** command.

NOTE All Cisco documentation includes this step, but it seems this should be Step 1. Without basic connectivity, the rest is just spinning your wheels. Consider it in "real world" implementations.

Step 1.5: Make sure any access lists are compatible with IPSec. Verify perimeter routers and the PIX Firewall outside interfaces permit IPSec traffic. Implicitly permit IPSec packets to bypass PIX Firewall access lists and conduits. Use the **show access-lists** command.

NOTE As you learned in the VPN chapters, there might only be four or five major tasks, but each task can have a similar number of steps. To make this easier to track, we'll again use a decimal notation to link tasks, steps, and substeps. For example, Step 1.5 indicates Task 1 Step 5. If Step 1.5 had multiple parts, they would be noted by a second decimal (Step 1.5.3).

Task 2: Configure IKE Parameters

The second major task in configuring the PIX Firewall is to configure the IKE parameters developed in Task 1. This task involves several steps to make sure IKE can establish secure channels to the appropriate IPSec peers. Only after this process is successfully completed can IKE set up the IPSec SAs that allow IPSec data exchanges. Configuring the IKE parameters involves the following four steps:

- Step 2.1: Enable or disable IKE.
- Step 2.2: Create IKE policies.
- Step 2.3: Configure preshared keys.
- Step 2.4: Verify IKE configuration.

Step 2.1 Enable or Disable IKE

The **isakmp enable** command is used to enable ISAKMP negotiation on an interface on which the IPSec peer communicates with the PIX Firewall. ISAKMP is enabled by default. Use the no form of the command to disable IKE. The syntax and an example are as follows:

```
Pix(config)# isakmp enable interface-name
Pix(config)# no isakmp enable interface-name
Pix(config)# no isakmp enable inside
```

PIX Firewall version 5.0 software supported IPSec termination on the outside interface only. Since version 5.1, the PIX Firewall supports IPSec termination on any interface. A good practice is to disable IKE on interfaces that don't terminate IKE and IPSec to prevent possible denial-of-service attacks on those interfaces.

Step 2.2 Create IKE Policies

To define an IKE policy to be used instead of the default settings, use a unique priority number. *Priority numbers* are integers between 1 and 65,534, with 1 as the highest priority

PART IV

and 65,534 as the lowest. The priority number is used with up to five **isakmp policy** ***priority*** commands. If one of the **isakmp policy** commands isn't configured, then the default value is assumed. Use the **no isakmp policy** ***priority*** command to remove the entire policy from the configuration. To enable and configure IKE, perform the following steps.

Specify Encryption Algorithm Use the configuration mode **isakmp policy** ***priority*** **encryption** command to specify the encryption algorithm. The **no isakmp policy** ***priority*** **encryption** command resets the encryption algorithm to the default value, DES. The syntax and an example are as follows:

```
Pix(config)# isakmp policy priority encryption {des | 3des}
Pix(config)# isakmp policy 100 encryption des
```

Specify the Hash Algorithm Use the configuration mode **isakmp policy** ***priority*** **hash** command to specify the hash algorithm. The **no isakmp policy** ***priority*** **hash** command resets the hash algorithm to the default value of SHA-1. The syntax and an example are as follows:

```
Pix(config)# isakmp policy priority hash {md5 | sha}
Pix(config)# isakmp policy 100 hash md5
```

Specify Authentication Method Use the configuration mode **isakmp policy** ***priority*** **authentication** command to specify the authentication method. The **no isakmp policy** ***priority*** **authentication** command resets the authentication method to the default value of RSA signatures. The syntax and an example are as follows:

```
Pix(config)# isakmp policy priority authentication {pre-share | rsa-sig}
Pix(config)# isakmp policy 100 authentication rsa-sig
```

With RSA signatures, configuring the PIX Firewall and its peer to obtain certificates from a CA is necessary. With preshared keys, the preshared keys must be configured on both the PIX Firewall and the peer. See Step 2.3, Configuring Authentication Method, in this chapter.

Specify Diffie–Hellman Group Use the configuration mode **isakmp policy** ***priority*** **group** command to specify the Diffie–Hellman group to be used in an IKE policy. The 1,024-bit Diffie–Hellman (Group 2) provides stronger security, but requires greater CPU resources. The **no isakmp policy** ***priority*** **group** command resets the Diffie–Hellman group identifier to the default value of group 1 (768-bit Diffie–Hellman). The syntax and an example are as follows:

```
Pix(config)# isakmp policy priority group {1 | 2}
Pix(config)# isakmp policy 100 group 2
```

The new Cisco VPN Client version 3.*x* for remote access uses Diffie–Hellman group 2.

Specify Security Association's Lifetime Use the configuration mode **isakmp policy** ***priority*** **lifetime** command to specify the security association's lifetime. The seconds is an integer between 120 and 86,400 seconds. The **no isakmp policy** ***priority*** **lifetime**

command resets the security association lifetime to the default value of 86,400 seconds (one day). The syntax and an example are as follows:

```
Pix(config)# isakmp policy priority lifetime seconds
Pix(config)# isakmp policy 100 lifetime 5000
```

The following example shows two defined IKE policies. The highest priority—Policy 100—would be preferred by this device.

```
Pix(config)# isakmp policy 100 encryption 3des
Pix(config)# isakmp policy 100 hash md5
Pix(config)# isakmp policy 100 authentication rsa-sig
Pix(config)# isakmp policy 100 group 2
Pix(config)# isakmp policy 100 lifetime 10000
Pix(config)# isakmp policy 200 encryption des
Pix(config)# isakmp policy 200 authentication pre-share
```

In the previous example, the third and sixth lines wouldn't appear in the PIX configuration because they use the default values for those options.

Step 2.3: Configure Preshared Keys

With preshared keys, the preshared keys must be configured on both the PIX Firewall and the peer. With RSA signatures, you must configure the PIX Firewall and its peer to obtain certificates from a CA.

Configuring Preshared Keys Configure the IKE preshared key by completing the following substeps.

Step 2.3.1: Specify the ISAKMP identity for the PIX using the configuration mode **isakmp identity** command. When two peers use IKE to establish IPSec security associations, each peer sends its ISAKMP identity to the remote peer. The identity can be configured as the PIX hostname (default), the PIX IP address, or a define key-id. Use the no form of the command to reset the ISAKMP identity to the default value of the host name. The syntax and two examples follow.

```
Pix(config)# isakmp identity {address | hostname | key-id} [key-id-string]
Pix(config)# isakmp identity address
Pix(config)# isakmp identity key-id cisco123
```

Reliability will increase if the PIX Firewall and its peer's identities are set using the same method to avoid an IKE negotiation failure caused by either peer not recognizing its peer's identity. If the host name is used as the *key-string* in the **isakmp key** command, using the host name would make sense.

Step 2.3.2: (Optional.) Define a name-to-address mapping similar to the **IP Host** command in the router **IOS** commands using the **name** command. Use the no form of the command to remove a name-to-address mapping. The syntax and an example follow.

```
Pix(config)# name ip_addr name
Pix(config)# name 1.1.40.110 seattle
```

This step isn't necessary if host names are resolved using a DNS server.

Step 2.3.3: Use the **isakmp key** command to specify a preshared authentication key and associate the key with an IPSec peer address or host name. You would configure the preshared key at both peers whenever you specify preshared key in an IKE policy. Otherwise, the policy can't be used because it won't be submitted for matching by the IKE process. Use the no form of the command to delete a preshared authentication key and its associated IPSec peer address. The syntax and two examples follow.

```
Pix(config)# isakmp key key-string address peer_addr [netmask mask] [no-xauth]
[no-config-mode]
Pix(config)# isakmp key cisco123 address 1.1.100.40
Pix(config)# isakmp key cisco456 address 0.0.0.0 netmask 0.0.0.0
```

The following are some things to consider with the **isakmp key** command:

- The *peer-addr* can be a host or a wildcard address.
- If no netmask is defined, the default 255.255.255.255 is used. The wildcard netmask, 0.0.0.0, allows any IPSec peer with the valid preshared key to be a valid peer. Cisco strongly recommends using a unique key for each peer.
- While it's possible for the PIX Firewall or any IPSec peer to use the same authentication key with multiple peers, this isn't as secure as using a unique authentication key for each pair of peers.
- The preshared *keystring* must be configured identically at both peers.
- The *keystring* can be any combination of alphanumeric characters up to 128 bytes.
- You can use the peer's host name for the preshared key. This would seem to make the most sense with remote access implementations.
- Preshared keys are easy to configure, but not very scalable.

Step 2.3.4: (Optional.) To see the IKE entries, use the **show isakmp** command. The following is an example of the output after the policies created earlier:

```
Pix(config)# show isakmp
isakmp enable outside
isakmp key ******** address 1.1.100.40 netmask 255.255.255.255
isakmp key ******** address 0.0.0.0 netmask 0.0.0.0
isakmp identity address
isakmp policy 100 authentication rsa-sig
isakmp policy 100 encryption 3des
isakmp policy 100 hash md5
isakmp policy 100 group 2
isakmp policy 100 lifetime 10000
isakmp policy 200 authentication pre-share
isakmp policy 200 encryption des
isakmp policy 200 hash sha
isakmp policy 200 group 1
isakmp policy 200 lifetime 86400
Pix(config)#
```

Configuring CAs The following steps are used to enable the PIX Firewall to interoperate with a CA and obtain PIX Firewall certificate(s).

NOTE The PIX Firewall clock must be set to Greenwich Mean Time (GMT), month, day, and year before configuring CA. Otherwise, the CA might reject certificates based on a bad timestamp. The PIX Firewall uses the clock to make sure a CRL isn't expired.

Step 2.3.1: Use the **hostname** command to configure the PIX Firewall host name. The syntax and examples follow.

```
pixfirewall(config)# hostname name
pixfirewall(config)# hostname Pix
Pix(config)#
```

Step 2.3.2: Use the **domain-name** command to configure the PIX Firewall domain name. The syntax and an example follow.

```
Pix(config)# domain-name name
Pix(config)# domain-name test.com
```

Step 2.3.3: Use the **ca generate rsa key** command to configure the generation of the RSA key pair(s). The syntax and an example follow.

```
Pix(config)# ca generate rsa key key_modulus_size
Pix(config)# ca generate rsa key 512
```

In the example, one general purpose RSA key pair is to be generated with a key modulus set to 512.

The following is an example of using the **show ca mypubkey rsa** to see the RSA key pair(s).

```
Pix(config)# show ca mypubkey rsa
% Key pair was generated at: 15:46:58 UTC Jan 26 2003
Key name: Pix.test.com
 Usage: General Purpose Key
 Key Data:
  305c300d 06092a86 4886f70d 01010105 00034b00 30480241 00c11fac 224f11ea
  05b81343 6f14e27c 1be96be3 11a5b63b 8ca615c8 39a1844f 89cc48ec 0039423c
  1aeb56b8 c07f3da4 e496c23e d291d458 7aef9c57 cb0ff327 bd020301 0001
Pix(config)#
```

Step 2.3.4: Use the **ca identity** command to declare a CA. The syntax and an example follow.

```
Pix(config)# ca identity ca_nickname ca_ipaddr [:ca_script_location] [ldap_ip
addr]
Pix(config)# ca identity testca.test.com 1.1.100.100
```

In the example, 1.1.100.100 is the IP address of the CA, testca.test.com.

Step 2.3.5: Use the **ca configure** command to configure the parameters of communication between the PIX Firewall and the CA. Use the no form of the command to reset the communication parameters to the default value. The syntax and an example follow.

```
Pix(config)# ca configure ca_nickname {ca | ra} retry_period retry_count
[crloptional]
Pix(config)# ca configure testca.test.com ca 1 15 crloptional
```

PART IV

CA | RA	Whether to contact the CA or the registration authority (RA) with the **ca configure** command.
retry_period	Number of minutes the PIX waits before resending a certificate request to the CA if it doesn't get a response. Range 1 to 60 minutes. Default is one minute.
retry_count	How many attempts the PIX Firewall will make to resend a request if it doesn't get a response. Range 0 to 100. Default is 0, indicating no limit.
crloptional	Allows other peers' certificates to be accepted by the PIX even if the certificate revocation list (CRL) isn't available. Default is without the crloptional.

Use the **show ca configure** command to display the current settings stored in RAM.

Step 2.3.6: Use the **ca authenticate** command to allow the PIX to authenticate its CA by obtaining the CA's self-signed certificate, which contains the CA's public key. When using the RA mode (**ca configure** command) and when issuing the **ca authenticate** command, the RA signing and encryption certificates will be returned from the CA, as well as the CA certificate. The syntax and an example follow.

```
Pix(config)# ca authenticate ca_nickname [fingerprint]
Pix(config)# ca authenticate testca.test.com 0123456789ABCDEF0123
```

The optional fingerprint (0123456789ABCDEF0123), when used, authenticates the CA's public key within its certificate. The PIX will discard the CA certificate if this fingerprint doesn't match the fingerprint in the CA's certificate.

Step 2.3.7: Use the **ca enroll** command to request signed certificates from your CA for *all* PIX RSA key pairs. One command gets all pairs. Contact the CA administrator before running this command because the administrator must authenticate the PIX Firewall manually before granting its certificate(s). The syntax and an example follow.

```
Pix(config)# ca enroll ca_nickname challenge_password [serial] [ipaddress]
Pix(config)# ca enroll testca.test.com mypassword1234567 serial ipaddress
```

challenge_password	Required password the CA administrator uses when a user calls to ask for a certificate to be revoked. Up to 80 characters in length.
serial	Get the PIX unit's serial number from the certificate.
ipaddress	Get the PIX unit's IP address from the certificate.

NOTE This password is most important and is required to revoke a certificate. Note this password and store it in a safe place.

Step 2.3.8: Use the **show ca certificate** to verify the process was successful.

The following is sample output from the **show ca certificate** command including a PIX Firewall general purpose certificate and the RA and CA public-key certificates:

```
Pix(config)# show ca certificate
Subject Name
Name: Pix.test.com
IP Address: 1.1.1.1
Status: Available
Certificate Serial Number: 47d16514
```

```
Key Usage: General Purpose
RA Signature Certificate
Status: Available
Certificate Serial Number: 47d165f7
Key Usage: Signature
CA Certificate
Status: Available
Certificate Serial Number: 47d165e2
Key Usage: Not Set
RA KeyEncipher Certificate
Status: Available
Certificate Serial Number: 47d165f6
Key Usage: Encryption
```

Step 2.3.9: Save the configuration:

Step 2.4: Verify IKE Configuration

To see the IKE entries, use the **show isakmp** command. The following is an example of the output after the policies created earlier. Notice the default parameters are listed for the items not specifically configured.

```
Pix(config)# show isakmp
isakmp enable outside
isakmp policy 100 authentication rsa-sig
isakmp policy 100 encryption 3des
isakmp policy 100 hash md5
isakmp policy 100 group 2
isakmp policy 100 lifetime 10000
isakmp policy 200 authentication pre-share
isakmp policy 200 encryption des
isakmp policy 200 hash sha
isakmp policy 200 group 1
isakmp policy 200 lifetime 86400
Pix(config)#
```

Use the **show isakmp policy** command to view all existing IKE policies. The following is an example of the output after the policies created earlier. Notice the default parameters are listed at the bottom.

```
Pix(config)# show isakmp policy
Protection suite of priority 100
      encryption algorithm:   3DES - Data Encryption TripleDES (168 bit keys)
      hash algorithm:         Message Digest 5
      authentication method: Rivest-Shamir-Adleman Signature
      Diffie-Hellman group:   #2 (1024 bit)
      lifetime:               10000 seconds, no volume limit
Protection suite of priority 200
      encryption algorithm:   DES - Data Encryption Standard (56 bit keys)
      hash algorithm:         Secure Hash Standard
      authentication method: Pre-Shared Key
      Diffie-Hellman group:   #1 (768 bit)
      lifetime:               86400 seconds, no volume limit
Default protection suite
      encryption algorithm:   DES - Data Encryption Standard (56 bit keys)
      hash algorithm:         Secure Hash Standard
      authentication method: Rivest-Shamir-Adleman Signature
      Diffie-Hellman group:   #1 (768 bit)
      lifetime:               86400 seconds, no volume limit
Pix(config)#
```

PART IV

Use the **show isakmp sa** command to view all current IKE security associations between the PIX Firewall and its peer. The following output is an example of the **show isakmp sa** command after IKE negotiations were successfully completed between the PIX Firewall and a peer.

```
Pix(config)# show isakmp sa
        dst              src            state      pending    created
     1.1.10.10        1.1.1.14        QM_IDLE        0           1
```

Task 3: Configure IPSec Parameters

The next major task is to configure the IPSec parameters you determined in Task 1. This task consists of five basic configuration steps that define IPSec SA parameters between peers and the set global IPSec values. The steps are as follows.

- Step 3.1: Configure crypto access lists.
- Step 3.2: Configure transform set suites.
- Step 3.3: Configure global IPSec SA lifetimes (optional).
- Step 3.4: Configure crypto maps.
- Step 3.5: Apply crypto maps to the terminating/originating interface.

Bypassing Interface ACLs

The PIX security model requires that any inbound session must be explicitly permitted by an access list or conduit statement. With IPSec connections, the secondary access list filtering could be redundant. Use the **sysopt connection permit-ipsec** command in IPSec configurations to permit IPSec traffic to pass through the firewall without inspection by the interface access list or conduit command statements.

Without the **sysopt connection permit-ipsec** command, it's necessary to explicitly configure an access-list command statement to permit IPSec traffic to traverse the PIX Firewall. Use the no form of the command to disable the option. The syntax and an example follow.

```
Pix(config)# sysopt connection {permit-pptp | permit-l2tp | permit-ipsec}
Pix(config)# sysopt connection permit-ipsec
```

Step 3.1: Configure Crypto Access Lists

The first major step in configuring PIX Firewall IPSec is to configure crypto access lists to define which IP traffic is interesting and will be protected by IPSec, and which traffic won't be protected by IPSec. Crypto access lists perform the following functions:

- Define the data traffic to be protected by IPSec.
- Filter inbound traffic and discard any traffic that should have been protected by IPSec.
- Determine whether to accept requests for IPSec SAs for the requested dataflows when processing IKE negotiations.

Define a crypto access list with the **access-list global configuration** command. Use the no form of the command to delete an entire access list. The syntax and an example follow.

```
Pix(config)# access-list acl-name {deny | permit} protocol src-addr src-netmask
[operator port [port]] dest dest-netmask [operator port [port]]
Pix(config)# access-list 150 permit ip 1.1.40.0 255.255.255.0 1.1.2.0
 255.255.255.0
```

While the access list syntax is the same as those applied to PIX Firewall interfaces, the meanings are slightly different for crypto access lists. Permit statements specify that any matching packets must be encrypted, while deny statements specify that any matching packets needn't be encrypted.

Some additional details for access lists are as follows.

- Any unprotected inbound traffic matching a permit statement in the crypto access list for a crypto map is dropped because it should have been encrypted.
- Using port ranges can dramatically increase the number of IPSec tunnels the PIX Firewall can originate or terminate. A new tunnel is created for each port.
- Creating two different crypto access lists would be necessary to define two different types of traffic that require different combinations of IPSec protection. One type could define the traffic requiring authentication and encryption, while the second type might define traffic requiring authentication only.

Keyword Any Issues Extreme care should be used with the **any** keyword to define source or destination addresses. Particularly the **permit any any** statement, which would cause all outbound traffic to be protected and sent to the peer defined in the corresponding crypto map statement. It would also require protection for all inbound traffic and, any not protected, would be silently dropped.

Before using the **any** keyword in any permit statement, it's important to preface that statement with a series of deny statements to filter out any traffic that doesn't need to be protected.

PART IV

Step 3.2: Configure Transform Set Suites

The next step in configuring PIX Firewall IPSec is to use the IPSec security policy to define a transform set. A *transform set* is a combination of individual IPSec transforms grouped to define a specific security policy for traffic. During IKE phase two negotiation for IPSec SA, the peers agree to use a particular transform set for protecting a particular dataflow. Transform sets combine the following IPSec factors:

- Payload authentication: AH transform
- Payload encryption: ESP transform
- IPSec mode (transport or tunnel)

Transform sets equal a combination of an AH transform, an ESP transform, and the IPSec mode, Tunnel (default) or Transport mode. Transform sets are limited to up to one AH and up to two ESP transforms. IPSec peers must have at least one matching transform set configured.

If you specify an ESP protocol in a transform set, you can specify only an ESP encryption transform or both an ESP encryption transform and an ESP authentication transform. The PIX Firewall supports the following IPSec transforms.

ah-md5-hmac	AH-HMAC-MD5 transform
ah-sha-hmac	AH-HMAC-SHA transform
esp-des	ESP transform using DES cipher (56 bits)
esp-3des	ESP transform using 3DES(EDE) cipher (168 bits)
esp-md5-hmac	ESP transform with HMAC-MD5 authentication used with an esp-des or esp-3des transform to provide additional integrity of ESP packet
esp-sha-hmac	ESP transform with HMAC-SHA authentication used with an esp-des or esp-3des transform to provide additional integrity of ESP packet

AH's lack of compatibility with NAT and PAT, as well as the fact that ESP is now available with authentication using the esp-sha-hmac and esp-md5-hmac transforms, makes AH an infrequent choice.

Use the configuration mode **crypto ipsec transform-set** command to define a transform set with up to three transoms. Before a transform set can be included in a crypto map entry, it must be defined using the **crypto ipsec transform-set** command. Use the no form of the command to delete a transform set. The syntax and an example follow.

```
Pix(config)# crypto ipsec transform-set trans-name [ah-md5-hmac |
  ah-sha-hmac] [esp-des | esp-null] [esp-md5-hmac|esp-sha-hmac]
Pix(config)# crypto ipsec transform-set seattle esp-des esp-md5-hmac
```

Windows 2000 Issue The Windows 2000 L2TP/IPSec client uses IPSec Transport mode, so Transport mode must be selected on the transform set. The default is Tunnel mode. The **crypto ipsec transform-set** ***trans -name*** **mode transport** command specifies IPSec Transport mode for a transform set.

For PIX Firewall version 6.0 and higher, L2TP is the only protocol that can use the IPSec Transport mode. All other types of packets using IPSec Transport mode will be discarded by the PIX Firewall. Use the no form of the command to reset the mode to the default value of Tunnel mode.

```
Pix(config)# crypto ipsec transform-set trans-name mode transport
Pix(config)# crypto ipsec transform-set tacoma ah-md5-hmac esp-des esp-sha-hmac
Pix(config)# crypto ipsec transform-set tacoma mode transport
```

The following is sample output for the **show crypto ipsec transform-set** command displaying the result of the previous transform definition. The syntax and an example follow:

```
Pix(config)# show crypto ipsec transform-set
Transform set seattle: { esp-des esp-md5-hmac  }
   will negotiate = { Tunnel,  },

Transform set tacoma: { ah-md5-hmac  }
   will negotiate = { Transport,  },
   { esp-des esp-sha-hmac  }
   will negotiate = { Transport,  },
Pix(config)#
```

Step 3.3: Configure Global IPSec SA Lifetimes (Optional)

The IPSec SA lifetime defines how long IPSec SAs remain valid before they're renegotiated. The configuration mode **crypto ipsec security-association lifetime** command defines a global lifetime value that applies to all crypto maps. This global value can be overridden within a crypto map entry. The lifetime can be defined in either seconds or kilobytes. Use the no form of the command to reset a lifetime to the default value. The syntax and two examples follow.

```
Pix(config)# crypto ipsec security-association lifetime {seconds seconds |
 kilobytes kilobytes}
Pix(config)# crypto ipsec security-association lifetime seconds 2700
Pix(config)# crypto ipsec security-association lifetime kilobytes 2304000
```

seconds *seconds*	Seconds a SA lives before expiring. Default: 28,800 (eight hours).
kilobytes *kilobytes*	Traffic volume (in kilobytes) that can pass between IPSec peers using a SA before it expires. Default: 4,608,000 (approximately 10 Mbps of traffic for one hour).

The following output is an example of using the **show crypto ipsec security-association lifetime** command to see the previous entries.

```
Pix(config)# show crypto ipsec security-association lifetime
Security association lifetime: 2304000 kilobytes/2700 seconds
Pix(config)#
```


Step 3.4: Configure Crypto Maps

Crypto map statements must be configured for IPSec to set up SAs for traffic flows that must be encrypted. Crypto map statements set up SA parameters, tying together the various parts required to set up IPSec SAs, including the following:

- The type and granularity of traffic to be protected by IPSec. Uses a crypto access list to define.
- Where outbound IPSec-protected traffic should be sent (the remote IPSec peer).
- The local address to use for the IPSec traffic.
- What type of IPSec security, transform sets, should be applied to the traffic.
- Whether SAs are established via ISAKMP or manually configured.
- The IPSec SA lifetime.

Use the following substeps to configure a crypto map with the following forms of the **crypto map** command.

Step 3.4.1: Use the **crypto map ipsec-manual | ipsec-isakmp** command to create or modify a crypto map entry. Use the *ipsec-manual* option to create or modify an ipsec-manual crypto map entry. Use the *ipsec-isakmp* option to create or modify an ipsec-isakmp crypto map entry. A **crypto map** command without a keyword creates an ipsec-isakmp entry by default. Use the **no crypto map** command to delete a crypto map entry or set. The syntax and two examples follow.

```
Pix(config)# crypto map map-name seq-num [ipsec-isakmp | ipsec-manual]
Pix(config)# crypto map testmap 10 ipsec-isakmp
Pix(config)# crypto map testmap2 10 ipsec-manual
```

Step 3.4.2: Assign a crypto access list, created earlier, to the crypto map entry to be used by IPSec to determine which traffic should be protected by IPSec crypto and which traffic doesn't need protection. Permit traffic will be protected, while deny traffic won't be protected by IPSec.

The defined crypto access list is used to evaluate both inbound and outbound traffic. *Outbound traffic* is evaluated to determine if it should be protected by crypto and, if so (traffic matches a permit entry), which crypto policy to apply. *Inbound traffic* is evaluated to determine if it should have been protected by crypto. If the inbound traffic should have been protected, but wasn't, it's discarded as suspect.

The access list is also used to identify the flow for which the IPSec security associations are established. In the outbound case, the permit entry is used as the dataflow identity (in general). In the inbound case, the data flow identity specified by the peer must be "permitted" by the crypto access list.

Use the following syntax to assign a crypto access list to a crypto map. Use the no form of the command to reverse the command. The syntax and an example follow.

```
Pix(config)# crypto map map-name seq-num match address acl-name
Pix(config)# crypto map testmap 10 match address 150
```

Remember, the crypto access list doesn't determine whether to permit or deny traffic through the interface. An access list applied directly to the interface with the **access- group** command makes that determination.

Step 3.4.3: Use the **crypto map set peer** command to define the IPSec peer in a crypto map entry. The peer is the terminating interface of the IPSec peer. This command is required for all static crypto maps, except for a dynamic crypto map (with the **crypto dynamic-map** command). Use the no form of the command to remove an IPSec peer from a crypto map entry. The syntax and an example follow.

```
Pix(config)# crypto map map-name seq-num set peer {hostname | ip-address}
Pix(config)# crypto map testmap set peer 1.1.40.25
```

You can specify multiple peers for **ipsec-isakmp** crypto entries by repeating the command. The peer that packets are sent to is determined by the last peer the PIX Firewall received either traffic or a negotiation request from for a given data flow. If the attempt fails with the first peer, IKE tries the next peer on the crypto map list.

You can only specify one peer per crypto map with ipsec-manual crypto entries. To change a peer, you must first delete the old peer, and then specify the new peer.

Step 3.4.4: IPSec peers negotiate a matching transform set during IKE phase two. Only one transform set can be defined for an ipsec-manual crypto map, but both ipsec-isakmp and dynamic crypto map entries can have up to six transform sets. When defining multiple transform sets, list them in preference (priority) starting with the highest priority. The most secure transforms should be the highest priority and, therefore, early in the list.

Use the **crypto map set transform-set** command to define which transform set(s) can be used with the crypto map entry. *Before a transform set can be included in a crypto mapset entry, it must be defined using the* ***crypto ipsec transform-set*** *command.* Use the **no crypto map set transform-set** command to remove all transform sets from a crypto map entry. The syntax and an example follow.

```
Pix(config)# crypto map map-name seq-num set transform-set trans-name1
[trans-name2, trans-name6]
Pix(config)# crypto ipsec transform-set seattle esp-des esp-md5-hmac
Pix(config)# crypto map testmap 10 set transform-set seattle
```

Step 3.4.5: (Optional.) Perfect forward secrecy (PFS) requires a new Diffie–Hellman exchange every time a new SA is negotiated for ipsec-isakmp crypto map entries and dynamic crypto map entries. PFS adds an additional level of security because if one key is ever compromised, only the data sent with that key will be affected. This additional security does require additional processing resources and time. PFS isn't on by default.

Use the **crypto map set pfs** command to ask for PFS and the no form of the command to turn off the feature. The default (group1) is used if the set pfs statement doesn't specify a group. The 1024-bit Diffie–Hellman group2 provides more security than group1, but it also consumes more processing time than group1. The syntax and two examples follow.

```
Pix(config)# crypto map map-name seq-num set pfs [group1 | group2]
Pix(config)# crypto map testmap 10 set pfs
Pix(config)# crypto map testmap 10 set pfs group2
```

Step 3.4.6: (Optional.) Use the **crypto map set security-association lifetime** command to override the global lifetime value for a particular crypto map entry. The global lifetime is used when negotiating IPSec security associations. While the command increases security levels, this is at the expense of additional CPU resources. This option is only available for ipsec-isakmp crypto map entries and dynamic crypto map entries. Use the no form of the command to reset a crypto map entry's lifetime value to the global value. The syntax and an example follow.

```
Pix(config)# crypto map map-name seq-num set security-association lifetime
 {seconds seconds | kilobytes kilobytes}
Pix(config)# crypto map testmap 10 set security-association lifetime
 seconds 2700
```

Step 3.4.7: (Optional.) Five **crypto dynamic-map** commands cover many of the IPSec parameters just introduced. These commands can be used to define dynamic crypto map features. A *dynamic crypto map entry* is basically a crypto map entry without all the parameters configured. It acts as a policy template where the missing parameters are later dynamically configured to match a peer's requirements as the result of an IPSec negotiation. This allows peers to exchange IPSec traffic with the PIX Firewall, even if the PIX Firewall doesn't have a crypto map entry specifically configured to meet all the peer's requirements.

The following is the syntax of the commands:

crypto dynamic-map *dyn-map-name dyn-seq-num* match address *acl-name*
crypto dynamic-map *dyn-map-name dyn-seq-num* set peer {*hostname* | *ip-address*}
crypto dynamic-map *dyn-map-name dyn-seq-num* set pfs [group1 | group2]
crypto dynamic-map *dyn-map-name dyn-seq-num* set security-association lifetime seconds
seconds | kilobytes *kilobytes*
crypto dynamic-map *dyn-map-name dyn-seq-num* set transform-set trans-set-name1
[trans-set-name9]

PART IV

The following output shows an example of using each of the commands:

```
Pix(config)# crypto dynamic-map reachus 20 match address 150
Pix(config)# crypto dynamic-map reachus 20 set peer 1.1.70.25
Pix(config)# crypto dynamic-map reachus 20 set pfs group2
Pix(config)# crypto dynamic-map reachus 20 set security-association lifetime
  seconds10000
Pix(config)# crypto dynamic-map reachus 20 set transform-set tacoma
```

The **show crypto dynamic-map** command is used to display the dynamic crypto map information.

The following output shows the minimum commands required for crypto map configuration when IKE is used to establish the security associations.

```
Pix(config)# access-list 150 permit ip 1.1.40.0 255.255.255.0 1.1.2.0
  255.255.255.0
Pix(config)# crypto transform-set testset ah-md5-hmac esp-sha-hmac
Pix(config)# crypto map testmap 10 ipsec-isakmp
Pix(config)# crypto map testmap 10 match address 150
Pix(config)# crypto map testmap 10 set transform-set testset
Pix(config)# crypto map testmap 10 set peer 1.1.40.7
```

The following example shows the minimum required crypto map configuration when the security associations are manually established.

```
Pix(config)# access-list 150 permit ip 1.1.40.0 255.255.255.0 1.1.2.0
  255.255.255.0
Pix(config)# crypto transform-set testset2 ah-md5-hmac esp-des
Pix(config)# crypto map testmap2 10 ipsec-manual
Pix(config)# crypto map testmap2 10 match address 150
Pix(config)# crypto map testmap2 10 set transform-set testset2
Pix(config)# crypto map testmap2 10 set peer 1.1.40.7
Pix(config)# crypto map testmap2 10 set session-key inbound ah 256
  12093487567854903212093487568903
Pix(config)# crypto map testmap2 10 set session-key outbound ah 256
  asdfghjklpoiuytrewqzxcvbnmqazxsw
Pix(config)# crypto map testmap2 10 set session-key inbound esp 256
  cipher 8765432167890543
Pix(config)# crypto map testmap2 10 set session-key outbound esp 256
  cipher plokmnjiuhbvgytf
Pix(config)#
```

Step 3.5: Apply Crypto Maps to the Terminating/Originating Interface

The next step in configuring IPSec is to apply the crypto map set to an interface before that interface can provide IPSec services. Only one crypto map set can be assigned to an interface. If multiple crypto map entries have the same map name, but have a different seq-num, they're considered as part of the same crypto map set and will all be applied to the interface. The crypto map entries with the lowest seq-num are considered the highest priority and will be processed first. A single crypto map set can contain a combination of ipsec-isakmp and ipsec-manual crypto map entries.

While the current PIX software, since 5.1, supports IPSec termination on any active interface, this doesn't mean you terminate traffic coming from the outside on the inside interface. VP traffic terminated on any interface originated on the networks attached to that interface. Traffic terminated on the inside interface originated from the inside network—the same with the outside interface and any DMZs.

Use the **crypto map interface** command to assign a crypto map set to any active PIX Firewall interface. Use the no form of the command to remove the crypto map set from an interface. The syntax and an example follow.

```
Pix(config)# crypto map map-name interface int-name
Pix(config)# crypto map testmap interface outside
```

Task 4: Test and Verify VPN Configuration

The final task is to verify the IPSec configuration and confirm it's working properly. Several commands were introduced throughout the section, but a summary of those commands that would be most useful includes the following.

The **show crypto map** command is used to display the crypto map configuration. The **show crypto map [interface *interface* | tag *map-name*]** command can be used to limit the display to a single interface or a crypto map name.

```
Pix(config)# show crypto map
Crypto Map: "testmap" interfaces: { outside }
Crypto Map "testmap" 10 ipsec-isakmp
        access-list 150; 1 elements
        access-list 150 permit ip 1.1.40.0 255.255.255.0 1.1.2.0 255.255.255.0 (
hitcnt=0)
        Current peer: 0.0.0.0
        Security association lifetime: 2304000 kilobytes/2700 seconds
        PFS (Y/N): Y
        DH group:  group2
        Transform sets={ seattle, }
Pix(config)#
```

To view the configured transform sets, use the **show crypto ipsec transform-set** command.

```
Pix(config)# show crypto ipsec transform-set
Transform set seattle: { esp-des esp-md5-hmac  }
   will negotiate = { Tunnel,  },
Transform set tacoma: { ah-md5-hmac  }
   will negotiate = { Tunnel,  },
   { esp-des esp-sha-hmac  }
   will negotiate = { Tunnel,  },
Pix(config)#
```

The **show crypto ipsec security-association lifetime** command displays the security-association lifetime value configured for a particular crypto map entry.

```
Pix(config)# show crypto ipsec security-association lifetime
Security association lifetime: 2304000 kilobytes/2700 seconds
Pix(config)#
```

The **show access-list** command displays all current ACLs, as well as an activity counter (hitcnt=#), which indicates the number of times the statement was used since the last time a **clear access-list** command was issued or the device was rebooted. If the **acl-id** is added to the command, the output is limited to that access list.

```
Pix(config)# show access-list
access-list 150; 1 elements
access-list 150 permit ip 1.1.40.0 255.255.255.0 1.1.2.0 255.255.255.0
 (hitcnt=7)
Pix(config)#
```

The **show crypto ipsec sa** command displays the settings used by current security associations. If no keyword is used, all security associations are displayed. First, they're sorted by interface, and then they're sorted by traffic flow (for example, source/destination address, mask, protocol, port). Within a flow, the security associations are listed by protocol (ESP/AH) and direction (inbound/outbound).

```
Pix(config)# show crypto ipsec sa
interface: outside
    Crypto map tag: testmap, local addr. 1.1.1.1
Pix(config)#
```

The **debug crypto isakmp** and **debug crypto ipsec** commands can be used to monitor the related activity in real time.

Cisco VPN Client

The PIX Firewall OS version 6.2 introduced the use of the PIX unit as an Easy VPN Remote device (client) when connecting to any Easy VPN Server, such as a Cisco VPN 3000 Concentrator, another PIX Firewall, or in later releases of Cisco IOS Software. The Easy VPN Remote feature for the PIX is also referred to as hardware client/EzVPN client. This "hardware client" feature allows the PIX unit to establish a VPN tunnel to an Easy VPN Server. Host devices on the PIX Firewall–protected LAN can connect through the Easy VPN Server without having to run any VPN client software.

To enable the PIX Firewall as an Easy VPN Remote device, you must select one of the following modes of operation.

Client Mode

In the Client mode, the VPN connections are initiated by traffic, using resources only as needed. In Client mode, the PIX unit performs NAT on all IP addresses of all LAN clients connected through the inside (higher security) interface. This mode also requires the DHCP server to be enabled on the inside interface, as covered in Chapter 18.

Network Extension Mode

In the Network Extension mode, the VPN connections are maintained, even when they aren't transmitting traffic. This option doesn't perform NAT on any client IP addresses connected through the inside (higher security) interface.

In Network Extension mode, the IP addresses of clients on the inside interface are received without change at the Easy VPN Server. If these are legal global, they can be forwarded to the public Internet without further processing. Otherwise, the Easy VPN

Server can provide NAT for them or they can be forwarded to a private network without translation.

Establishing Preliminary Connectivity

Before attempting to create a VPN connection between the PIX Firewall Easy VPN Remote device and an Easy VPN Server, you must establish network connectivity between both devices through their respective ISPs. This connectivity could include using a DSL or cable modem. Verify connectivity before continuing.

Easy VPN Remote Configuration

Because the Easy VPN Server controls the policy enforced on any Easy VPN Remote device, the remote device configuration is simplified considerably. The basic local configuration can be performed using the command-line interface or by using Cisco PIX Device Manager (PDM), covered in Chapter 22. The local configuration steps required include the following.

The **vpnclient** commands used to configure the Easy VPN Remote device stores the configuration information in the flash memory of the PIX Firewall, so it's preserved when the device reboots.

Step 1: Define the VPN group and password by entering the following command:

Pix(config)# vpnclient vpngroup *groupname* password *preshared_key*

group_name	VPN group configured on the Easy VPN server. Up to 63 characters
preshared_key	IKE preshared key used for authentication by the Easy VPN Server

Step 2: (Optional.) If the Easy VPN Server uses extended authentication (Xauth) to authenticate the PIX Firewall client, enter the following command:

Pix(config)# vpnclient username *xauth_username* password *xauth_password*

xauth_username	User name to be used for user authorization. Up to 127 characters
xauth_password	User password to be used for user authorization. Up to 127 characters

Step 3: Identify the remote Easy VPN Server by entering the following command:

Pix(config)# vpnclient server *ip_primary* [*ip_secondary_n*]

ip_primary	Primary IP address for the Easy VPN Remote Server
ip_secondary_1, ip_secondary_2, . . . , ip_secondary_n	Any secondary IP addresses (backup VPN headends), from 1 to *n*, for the Easy VPN Remote Server. The limit will be determined by the device platform

Step 4: Set the Easy VPN Remote mode by entering the following command:

Pix(config)# vpnclient mode {client-mode | network-extension-mode}

PART IV

Step 5: Enable Easy VPN Remote by entering the following command:

Pix(config)# vpnclient enable

The **no vpnclient enable** command closes all established VPN tunnels and prevents new VPN tunnels from initiating until you enter a **vpnclient enable** command. The **clear vpnclient** command removes all **vpnclient** commands from your configuration.

Step 6: (Optional.) Use the **show vpnclient** command to display the current status and configuration of Easy VPN Remote. Enter the following command:

Pix(config)# show vpnclient

The following is an example Easy VPN Remote basic configuration.

```
Pix(config)# vpnclient vpngroup testgrp_a password testkey_a
Pix(config)# vpnclient username testuser_1 password testpass_1
Pix(config)# vpnclient server 1.1.250.1
Pix(config)# vpnclient mode client-mode
Pix(config)# show vpnclient
Local Configuration
vpnclient vpngroup testgrp_a password ********
vpnclient username testuser_1 password ********
vpnclient server 1.1.250.1
vpnclient mode client-mode
Pix(config)#
```

Scale PIX Firewall VPNs

The Cisco Secure PIX Firewall support of the IETF IPSec standard allows an organization to scale its VPNs with much lower administrative costs. The IPSec use of public digital keys administered by a CA, a third-party vendor that registers public keys, allows for tremendous flexibility and scalability in the evolution of the network.

Basic PIX Firewall features that further enhance the scalability of the network security strategy include NAT/PAT, extensive protocol support such as PPPoE and DHCP, the variety of interface NICs to support various connectivity solutions, and PIX Firewall series capability to support from 64,000 to 256,000 simultaneous connections. This strategy protects the organization's investment in security technology.

Network Management Options

PIX Firewalls with VPN support are incorporated into several Cisco network management software solutions. Some of the key examples are introduced in the next paragraphs.

CiscoWorks VPN/Security Management Solution (VMS)

CiscoWorks VPN/Security Management Solution (VMS) is Cisco's flagship integrated security management solution, which provides web-based tools for configuring, monitoring, and troubleshooting enterprise VPNs, PIX, and IOS firewalls, along with network and host-based intrusion detection systems (IDS). CiscoWorks VMS is an integral part of the SAFE strategy for network security.

A key component of CiscoWorks VMS is the CiscoWorks Management Center for PIX Firewalls and Auto Update Server Software that provides unprecedented manageability for the PIX Firewall devices. The Management Center maintains the Web-based "look and feel" of its smaller cousin, the Cisco PIX Device Manager, but provides centralized management scalability for up to 1,000 Cisco PIX Firewalls.

CiscoWorks VMS is composed of a series of tools that reside on a network management server (or servers), such as Windows 2000 Professional or Server.

Cisco Secure Policy Manager (CSPM)

With Cisco Secure Policy Manager (CSPM), it's possible to configure, manage, and monitor end-to-end any Cisco Systems security networks. *CSPM* is a policy-based product that allows abstracting the complexities of security networking to create high-level security policies, which are independent of underlying device platforms and software releases. CSPM is Cisco's strategic security management platform for Cisco Secure PIX Firewalls, Cisco Secure IOS Firewalls, Cisco IOS VPN routers, and Cisco Secure Intrusion Detection System (IDS) sensors.

CSPM provides the following benefits:

- Time savings using a configuration GUI
- Centralized configuration and monitoring of remote security devices
- Enhanced scalability by using policy inheritance
- Easy security device monitoring with e-mail notification and basic reports

Latest versions of CSPM can be installed on systems running Windows 2000 Professional or Windows 2000 Server with at least Service Pack 2. Earlier versions support Windows NT 4.0 with Service Pack 6a. The GUI in client/server installations can be installed on Windows 95, 98, 2000, and NT 4.0 systems. Report viewing is available through Netscape or Microsoft web browsers using Secure Socket Layer (SSL).

Cisco PIX Device Manager

The Cisco PDM is a browser-based configuration tool for configuring and monitoring the PIX Firewall. This is particularly useful for those administrators who lack a solid knowledge of the PIX Firewall command-line interface (CLI). By using a web browser to activate PDM, it can be used to configure and monitor multiple PIX Firewall units from a single workstation. Figure 21-3 shows the System Properties page of the PDM.

PDM facilitates configuring the PIX Firewall unit using a Windows-like interface with drop-down menus and browser features, which are then converted internally to the correct CLI commands for the PIX unit to process. PDM performs the following functions.

Configuration wizards, such as the Startup Wizard and VPN Wizard, provide step-by-step instructions through otherwise complex configuration tasks.

PDM monitoring features include real-time graphs and data, including connection, IDS, and throughput information for the selected PIX Firewall. You can view up to five days of historical data. The tabbed-page graphical interface with Windows Explorer–like controls on the left side makes it easy to check the setting, configuration, or performance.

The PIX Device Manager is covered in greater detail in the next chapter.

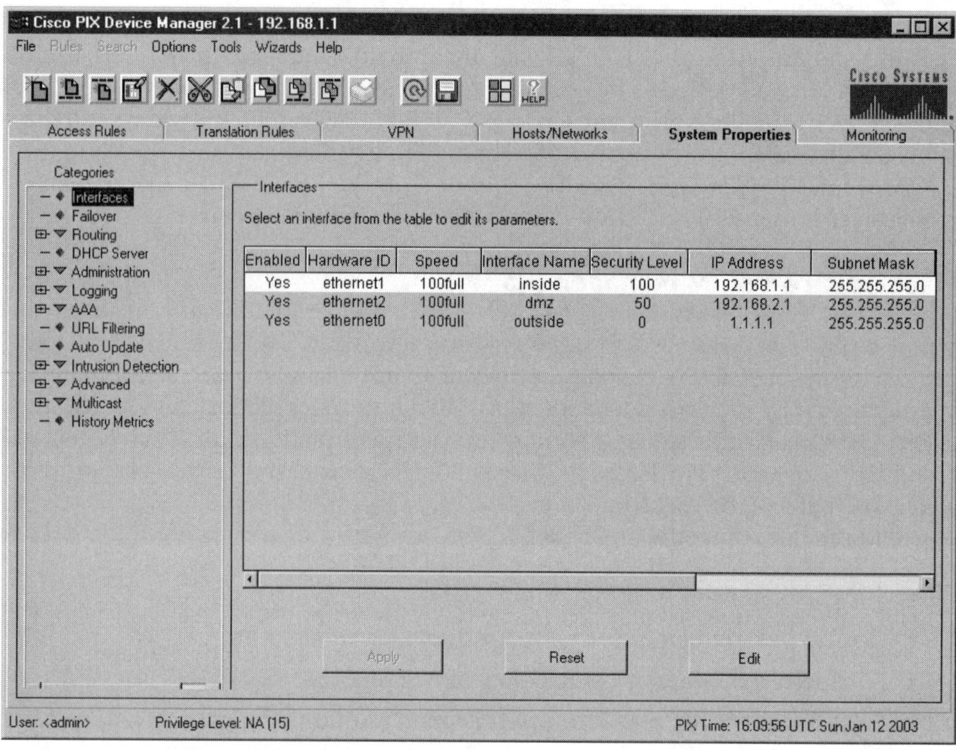

Figure 21-3 Basic PIX Firewall supporting PPPoE

PPPoE and the PIX Firewall

Point-to-Point Protocol over Ethernet (PPPoE) incorporates two widely used and understood standards: PPP and Ethernet. The PPPoE specification connects hosts on an Ethernet to the Internet through a common broadband medium, such as DSL line, cable modem, or wireless device. With PPPoE, the principles of Ethernet supporting multiple users in a LAN are combined with the principles of PPP, which uses serial connections. Figure 21-4 shows a simple PPPoE installation.

PPPoE client was introduced on the PIX Firewall with PIX OS version 6.2. The Cisco PPPoE implementation is specifically targeted for smaller implementations using the low-end PIX (501/506) devices. PPPoE is currently only supported on the outside inter-

Figure 21-3 PDM graphical interface showing the System Properties page

face of the PIX Firewall devices. Layer Two Tunneling Protocol (L2TP) and Point-to-Point Tunneling Protocol (PPTP) aren't currently supported with PPPoE in PIX OS version 6.2.

Once configured, all traffic is encapsulated with PPPoE/PPP headers with Password Authentication Protocol (PAP) as the default authentication mechanism. You can configure Challenge Handshake Authentication Protocol (CHAP) or MS-CHAP manually.

The following are the basic commands required to configure PPPoE features for the inbound connections:

1. Use the **vpdn group** ***group_name*** **request dialout pppoe** command to define a VPDN group to be used for PPPoE. Unless the VPDN group for PPPoE is configured, PPPoE won't be able to establish a connection. The *group_name* is an ASCII string up to 63 characters in length.
2. If the ISP requires authentication, use the **vpdn group** ***group_name*** **ppp authentication {PAP | CHAP | MSCHAP}** command to select the authentication protocol used by the ISP. The Windows dial-up networking client setting allows selecting PAP, CHAP, or MS-CHAP authentication protocol to use. The protocol specified on the client must match the setting on the PIX Firewall. If an authentication protocol isn't specified on the client, the PIX will use PPP as the default. Do *not* specify the ppp authentication option in the configuration.
3. Use the **vpdn group** ***group_name*** **localname** ***username*** command to associate the user name assigned by your ISP with the VPDN group. This is also the user name used in the **vpdn username** command (Step 4).
4. Use the **vpdn username** ***username*** **password** ***password*** command to create a user name and password pair to be used for the PPPoE connection. The user name must be a user name already used in the **vpdn group** command (Step 3).
5. The PPPoE client functionality is turned off by default, so after VPDN configuration, enable PPPoE with the **ip address** ***if_name*** **pppoe [setroute]** command. The Setroute option causes a default route to be created if no default route exists. The **PPPoE vpdn** commands must be configured before enabling PPPoE with the **ip address pppoe** command.

The following is a sample PPPoE configuration:

```
Pix(config)# vpdn group pppoegrp1 request dialout pppoe
Pix(config)# vpdn group pppoegrp1 localname test1
Pix(config)# vpdn group pppoegrp1 ppp authentication pap
Pix(config)# vpdn username test1 password test1pass
Pix(config)# ip address outside pppoe setroute
```

Use the **show vpdn tunnel [pppoe]** command to display tunnel information:

```
Pix# show vpdn tunnel pppoe
PPPoE Tunnel Information (Total tunnels=1 sessions=1)
Tunnel id 1 is up, remote id is 7, 1 active sessions
  Tunnel state is established, time since change 12 secs
  Remote Internet Address 192.168.100.20, port 1701
  Local Internet Address 192.168.65.97, port 1701
  37 packets sent, 63 received, 511 bytes sent, 5719 received
  Control Ns 3, Nr 4
  Local RWS 16, Remote RWS 8
```

PART IV

```
  Retransmission time 1, max 1 seconds
  Unsent queuesize 0, max 0
  Resend queuesize 0, max 1
  Total resends 0, ZLB ACKs 2
  Retransmit time distribution: 0 0 0 0 0 0 0 0 0
pix#
```

Use the **show vpdn username** command to display the user name. The password is always encrypted.

```
Pix# show vpdn username
vpdn username test1 password *********
Pix#
```

Use the **show vpdn session** command to display the session information and the **show vpdn pppinterface** command to display the interface identification value.

Chapter Review

This chapter looked at using the PIX Firewall with various VPN implementations. The basic tasks and steps of configuring VPNs on the firewall aren't significantly different than working with router VPNs, although the command syntax is unique.

Remember, basic VPN terms and technology were covered in Chapters 9 through 11, and they should be reviewed before taking the certification exam.

This chapter looked at the tasks and steps involved in configuring PIX IPSec. The steps and related commands are summarized in the following task list.

Configuring IPSec

Task 1. Prepare for IPSec

- Step 1.1: Determine IKE (IKE phase one) policy
- Step 1.2: Determine IPSec (IKE phase two) policy
- Step 1.3: Check the current configuration

  write terminal

  show isakmp policy

  show isakmp

- Step 1.4: Ensure the network works without encryption

  ping - all devices

- Step 1.5: Ensure access control lists (ACLs) are compatible with IPSec

  show access-lists

  sysopt connection permit-ipsec

Task 2. Configure IKE

- Step 2.1: Enable or disable IKE

  isakmp enable ***interface-name***

- Step 2.2: Create IKE Phase 1 policy

  isakmp policy commands

  encryption

  hash

  authentication

  group

  lifetime

- Step 2.3: Configure pre-shared keys (preshared keys)

  isakmp identity

  name

  isakmp key

- Step 2.3: Configure pre-shared keys (CA Support)

  hostname

  domain-name

  ca generate rsa key

  ca identity

  ca configure

  ca authenticate

  ca enroll

  show ca certificate

- Step 2.4: Verify the IKE configuration

  show isakmp policy

  show isakmp

  show isakmp sa

Task 3. Configure IPSec

- Step 3.1: Configure crypto ACLs to define interesting traffic

  access-list

- Step 3.2: Configure transform set suites
  crypto ipsec transform-set
- Step 3.3: Configure global IPSec security association lifetimes
  crypto ipsec security-association lifetime
- Step 3.4: Configure crypto maps
  crypto map
  ipsec-manual | ipsec-isakmp
  match address acl-name
  set peer
  set transform-set
  set pfs
  set security-association lifetime
  crypto dynamic-map
- Step 3.5: Apply the crypto maps to the terminating/originating interface
  interface
  crypto map interface

Task 4. Test and verify IPSec

- Step 4.1: Display your configured IKE policies
  show isakmp
  show isakmp policy
- Step 4.2: Display your configured transform sets
  show crypto ipsec transform-set
- Step 4.3: Display the current state of your IPSec SAs
  show isakmp sa
  show crypto ipsec security-association lifetime
- Step 4.4: View your configured crypto maps
  show crypto map
- Step 4.5: Debug IKE and IPSec traffic through the Cisco IOS
  debug crypto ipsec
  debug crypto isakmp

Configuring IPSec for RSA Encrypted Nonces

Task 1. Prepare for IPSec to determine a detailed security policy for RSA encryption to include how to distribute the RSA public keys.

Task 2. Configure RSA keys manually.

- Step 2.1: Plan for RSA keys
- Step 2.2: Configure the router's host name and domain name
  hostname *name*

  ip domain-name *name*

- Step 2.3: Generate the RSA keys

  crypto key generate rsa *usage key*

- Step 2.4: Enter peer RSA public keys—Detail is important, any mistake entering the keys will cause them not to work.

  crypto key pubkey-chain

  crypto key pubkey-chain rsa

  addressed-key *key address*

  named-key *key name*

  key-string *string*

- Step 2.5: Verify the key configuration

  show crypto key mypubkey rsa

  show crypto key pubkey-chain rsa

- Step 2.6: Manage RSA keys—Remove old keys to free up space

  crypto key zeroize rsa

Task 3. Configure ISAKMP for IPSec to select RSA encryption as the authentication method in an ISAKMP policy.
Task 4. Configure IPSec—typically done the same as in preshare.
Task 5. Test and verify IPSec and exercise additional commands to view and manage RSA public keys.

Configuring CA Support Tasks

Task 1. Prepare for IPSec

- Step 1.1: Plan for CA support

  A. Determine the type of CA server to use

  B. Identify the CA server's IP address, host name, and URL. Required for Lightweight Directory Protocol (LDAP).

C. Identify the CA server administrator contact information.

- Step 1.2: Determine IKE (IKE phase one) policy
- Step 1.3: Determine IPSec (IKE phase two) policy
- Step 1.4: Check the current configuration
  show running-config
  show crypto isakmp [*policy*]
  show crypto map
- Step 1.5: Ensure the network works without encryption
  ping all devices
- Step 1.6: Ensure access control lists (ACLs) are compatible with IPSec
  show access-lists

Task 2. Configure CA Support

- Step 2.1: Manage the nonvolatile RAM (NVRAM) memory usage (optional)
  crypto ca certificate query
- Step 2.2: Set the router's time and date
  clock timezone *zone hours* [*minutes*]
  clock set *hh:mm:ss day month year*
  clock set *hh:mm:ss month day year*
- Step 2.3: Configure the router's host name and domain name
  hostname *name*
  ip domain-name *name*
  ip host *name address1* [*address2. . . address8*]
- Step 2.4: Generate an RSA key pair—used to identify to the remote VPN peer
  crypto key generate rsa [*usage key*]
- Step 2.5: Declare a CA
  crypto ca identity *name*
- Step 2.6: Authenticate the CA
  crypto ca authenticate *name*
- Step 2.7: Request your own certificate
  crypto ca enroll *name*
- Step 2.8: Save the configuration
  copy run start

- Step 2.9: Monitor and maintain CA interoperability (optional)

  A. Request a CRL

  B. Delete your router's RSA keys

  C. Delete both public and private certificates from the configuration

  D. Delete peer's public keys
  crypto ca identity *name*

- Step 2.10: Verify the CA support configuration

  show crypto ca certificates

  show crypto key {mypubkey | pubkey-chain} rsa

Task 3. Configure IKE

- Step 3.1: Enable or disable IKE

  crypto isakmp enable

- Step 3.2: Create IKE policies

  crypto isakmp policy priority

- Step 3.3: Configure preshared keys

  crypto isakmp key and associated commands

- Step 3.4: Verify the IKE configuration

  show crypto isakmp policy

  show crypto isakmp sa

Task 4. Configure IPSec

- Step 4.1: Configure transform set suites

  crypto ipsec transform-set

- Step 4.2: Configure global IPSec security association lifetimes

  crypto ipsec security-association lifetime

- Step 4.3: Configure crypto ACLs

  access-list

  crypto map
- Step 4.5: Apply the crypto maps to the terminating/originating interface
  interface
- crypto map

Task 5. Test and verify IPSec

- Step 5.1: Display your configured IKE policies
  show crypto isakmp policy
- Step 5.2: Display your configured transform sets
  show crypto ipsec transform set
- Step 5.3: Display the current state of your IPSec SAs
  show crypto ipsec sa
- Step 5.4: View your configured crypto maps
  show crypto map
- Step 5.5: Debug IKE and IPSec traffic through the Cisco IOS
  debug crypto ipsec
  debug crypto isakmp
- Step 5.6: Debug CA events
  debug crypto key-exchange
  debug crypto pki

The PIX Firewall OS version 6.2 introduced the Easy VPN Remote device (client) for connecting to any Easy VPN Server. This implementation greatly reduces configuration on the remote host and relies on the server policies for configuration decisions.

Scaling PIX Firewall VPN solutions includes the basic device features plus a variety of network management software applications to provide Web-based, centralized, configu ration, monitoring, and reporting. Example applications include CiscoWorks VPN/ Security Management Solution (VMS), Cisco Secure Policy Manager (CSPM), and Cisco PIX Device Manager (PDM), which is covered in the next chapter.

PPPoE client was introduced on the PIX Firewall with PIX OS version 6.2. Point-to-Point Protocol over Ethernet (PPPoE) incorporates two widely used and understood standards: PPP and Ethernet. The PPPoE specification connects hosts on an Ethernet to the Internet through a common broadband medium, such as DSL line, cable modem, or wireless device.

Questions

1 Which two of the following are PIX Firewall IPSec implementations?

A. Remote access

B. Host-to-host

C. Site-to-site
D. Lock and key

2. Which IPSec mode runs between two security gateways, such as PIX Firewall units?
   A. Remote access
   B. Transport
   C. Tunnel
   D. VPN Free Client

3. Which command enables IKE on a PIX Firewall?
   A. **IKE enable**
   B. **isakmp enable**
   C. **isakmp policy**
   D. **isakmp identity**

4. Which command defines the Diffie–Hellman configuration?
   A. **Pix(config)# isakmp policy 100 encryption des**
   B. **Pix(config)# isakmp policy 100 hash md5**
   C. **Pix(config)# isakmp policy 100 authentication rsa-sig**
   D. **Pix(config)# isakmp policy 100 group 2**

5. In the **isakmp policy 100 authentication rsa-sig** command, what does **rsa-sig** mean?
   A. Preshared keys will be used for authentication
   B. Hash keys will be used for authentication
   C. CAs will be used for authentication
   D. RSA keys will be used for authentication

6. Of the following IKE policies, which is the highest priority?
   A. 100
   B. 200
   C. 500
   D. 1000

7. Which VPN feature requires device times to be set to GMT?
   A. Preshared keys
   B. Tunnel mode
   C. Transport mode
   D. CAs

8. Which command is *not* required to configure IPSec CAs?
    A. **pixfirewall(config)# hostname Pix**
    B. **Pix(config)# domain-name test.com**
    C. **Pix(config)# ca generate rsa key 512**
    D. **Pix(config)# show ca mypubkey rsa**
9. What does the **sysopt connection permit-ipsec** command do?
    A. Enables IPSec on the PIX unit
    B. Logs IPSec connection info to a Syslog server
    C. Permits IPSec traffic to pass through the firewall without inspection by the interface ACLs
    D. Activates remote IPSec configuration
10. Which is *not* a function performed by crypto access lists?
    A. Filters inbound traffic and discards any traffic that should have been protected by IPSec
    B. Determines whether to accept requests for IPSec SAs for the requested dataflows when processing IKE negotiations
    C. Deny statements that specify any matching packets will be discarded
    D. Defines the data traffic to be protected by IPSec
11. Which is an example of a Cisco VPN Client implementation?
    A. PIX Remote VPN
    B. Easy VPN Remote device
    C. Easy VPN Server
    D. PIX ISAKMP
12. Which command specifies a Syslog server for logging messages?
    A. **logging trap**
    B. **logging history**
    C. **logging on**
    D. **logging host**
13. Which is Cisco's flagship-integrated security-management solution?
    A. CiscoWorks VMS
    B. Cisco Secure Policy Manager (CSPM)
    C. AVVID
    D. Cisco PIX Device Manager (PDM)

14. Point-to-Point Protocol over Ethernet (PPPoE) uses which default authentication protocol?
    A. AAA
    B. CHAP
    C. PAP
    D. MS-CHAP
15. Which statement is true about PPPoE on PIX Firewalls?
    A. It's an industry standard that has been supported since PIX OS 5.1
    B. It encapsulates PPP traffic in Ethernet frames to travel across the LAN
    C. It's only supported on the outside interface of the PIX
    D. PPPoE implementation is specifically targeted for larger links and devices

Answers

1. **A. and C.** Remote access and Site-to-site
2. C. Tunnel
3. B. **isakmp enable**
4. D. **Pix(config)# isakmp policy 100 group 2**
5. C. CAs will be used for authentication
6. A. 100
7. D. CAs
8. D. **Pix(config)# show ca mypubkey rsa**
9. C. Permits IPSec traffic to pass through the firewall without inspection by the interface ACLs
10. C. Denies statements that specify any matching packets will be discarded
11. B. Easy VPN Remote device
12. D. **logging host**
13. A. CiscoWorks VMS
14. C. PAP
15. C. It's only supported on the outside interface of the PIX

CHAPTER 22

Managing and Maintaining the PIX Firewall

In this chapter, you will learn to:

- Understand the PDM overview
- Understand PDM operating requirements
- Prepare for PDM
- Use PDM to configure the PIX Firewall
- Make use of PDM to create a site-to-site VPN
- Use PDM to create a remote access VPN
- Use CiscoWorks Management Center for PIX Firewalls
- Distinguish failover features
- Recognize password recovery
- Upgrade the PIX OS

In this chapter, you look at the PIX Device Management application that adds a graphical interface to configuring and monitoring the PIX Firewall. In addition to the GUI, PDM has included two wizards to help with initial firewall configuration and setting up VPN connections.

This chapter also covers the PIX failover system, which allows implementing PIX Firewalls in pairs for redundancy. System requirements and Configuration options are covered in detail.

Two maintenance issues—password recovery and PIX OS upgrades— are detailed at the end of the chapter.

PDM Overview

The Cisco PIX Device Manager (PDM) is a browser-based configuration tool for configuring and monitoring the PIX Firewall. This is particularly useful for those administrators who lack a solid knowledge of the PIX Firewall command-line interface (CLI). By using a web browser to activate PDM, it can be used to configure and monitor multiple PIX Firewall units from a single workstation. Figure 22-1 shows the System Properties page of the PDM.

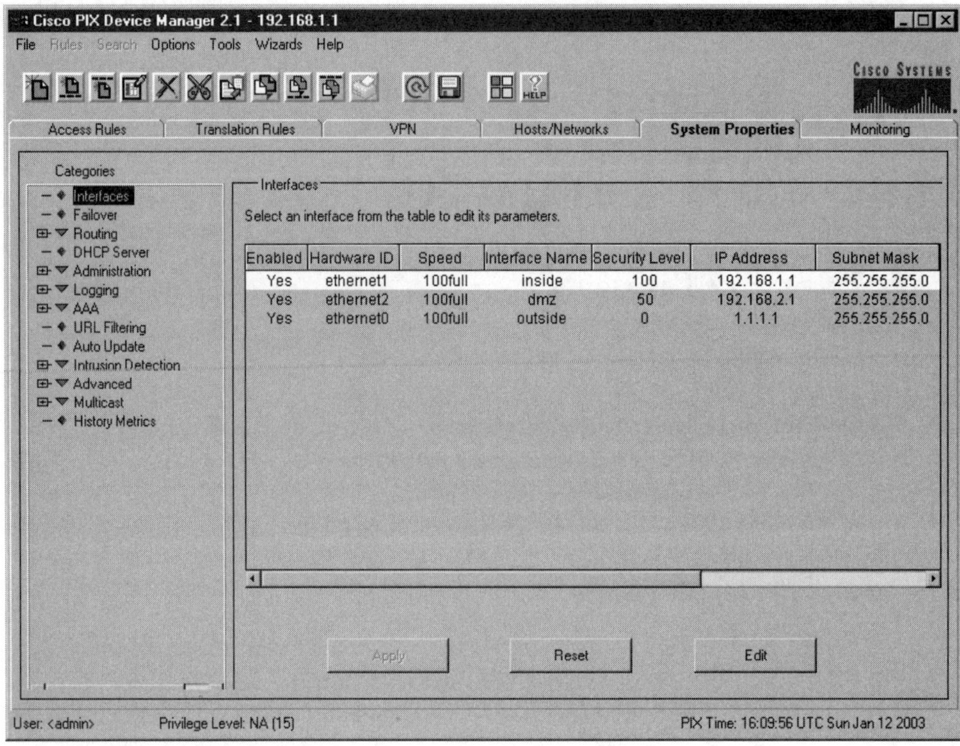

Figure 22-1 PDM graphical interface showing the System Properties page

PDM facilitates configuring the PIX Firewall unit using a Windows-like interface with drop-down menus and browser features, which are then converted internally to the correct **CLI** commands for the PIX unit to process.

Configuration Wizards, such as the Startup Wizard and the VPN Wizard, provide step-by-step instructions through otherwise complex configuration tasks.

PDM monitoring features include real-time graphs and data, including connection, IDS, and throughput information for the selected PIX Firewall. You can view up to five days of historical data. The tabbed-page graphical interface with Windows Explorer-like controls on the left side makes it easy to check setting, configuration, or performance.

You can run more than one PDM session on a single workstation. The practical maximum number of sessions will vary depending on the workstation resources, such as memory, CPU speed, and browser type.

The time required to launch the PDM applet is dependent on the link(s) to the host station because the applet must be transferred from the PIX to the host. LAN bandwidth would obviously be better than serial links. PDM does support serial links of 56 Kbps; but 1.5 Mbps or higher is recommended. Once the PDM applet is running on the host workstation, the link speed has negligible impact.

Versions and Device Support

This book looks exclusively at PDM version 2.1, which works with PIX Firewall version 6.2 and newer. Version 2.1 can be used with the PIX 501, PIX 506/506e, PIX 515/515e, PIX 520, PIX 525, and PIX 535 units running at least version 6.2. PDM Version 2.1 also runs on the Firewall Services Module (FWSM) Version 1.1 for the Catalyst 6500.

PDM version 1.1 works with older versions of the PIX OS, up through version 6.1. Installation and operation instructions for PDM Version 1.1 are available on the Cisco web site.

PDM Operating Requirements

If the PIX firewall was preinstalled with version 6.2 on any of the PIX 501, PIX 506/506e, PIX 515/515e, PIX 520, PIX 525, and PIX 535 platforms, then PDM 2.1 is already installed and supported. Several areas of concern need to be addressed to use PDM successfully. For PDM version 2.1, consider the following:

- PIX Firewall requirements
- Workstation requirements
- Cisco Secure Policy Manager considerations
- Web browser considerations

PIX Firewall Requirements

The PIX Firewall must be running PIX Firewall software version 6.2 for PDM Version 2.1 to run. The PIX installation requirements for PIX OS 6.2 are the same as for PDM v2.1, which means if the PIX Firewall is running PIX Firewall software version 6.2, then the requirements to install PDM v2.1 have already been met.

PIX Firewall unit must meet the following requirements to install and run PDM v2.1 successfully:

- The PIX unit must have an activation key for Data Encryption Standard (DES) or triple DES (3DES) for its Secure Socket Layer (SSL) connection.
- At least 8MB of Flash memory are required.
- The optimal PIX configuration file size for use with PDM is less than 100K, approximately 1,500 lines. Configuration files over 100K might impair the performance of PDM on the workstation. The **show flashfs** command can be used to determine the size of the configuration file. The "file 1" **length** is the size of the configuration file in bytes. The following example shows a config file size of 1.857K.

```
Pix# show flashfs
flash file system:  version:2  magic:0x12345679
  file 0: origin:        0 length:1540152
  file 1: origin: 1572864 length:1857
```

```
  file 2: origin:       0 length:0
  file 3: origin: 2621440 length:4748324
  file 4: origin: 8257536 length:280
Pix#
```

Workstation Requirements

PDM host requirements depend on the platform. PDM isn't supported on Macintosh, Windows 3.1, or Windows 95 devices. PDM currently supports the following host systems:

- Windows
- SUN Solaris
- Linux

This section looks at the requirements for each.

Windows Requirements

The following are minimum requirements to run PDM v2.1 with Windows:

- Windows 2000, Windows NT 4.0, or Windows XP/Me/98 operating system (OS). Windows 3.1 and 95 aren't supported.
- Pentium or Pentium-compatible processor running at 350 MHz or higher.
- 128MB RAM minimum, 192 MB or more recommended.
- 800 × 600 (256 colors) display minimum, 1,024 × 768 with at least High Color (16-bit) colors recommended.
- Cisco recommends Internet Explorer with PDM because it loads faster on this platform. Supported browsers include Internet Explorer 5.0 or higher and Netscape Communicator versions 4.5*x* or 4.7*x* only. PDM doesn't currently support Netscape 6.*x* or 7.

Virus-checking software increases the time required for PDM to start, particularly with Netscape Communicator and Windows 2000 with any browser. Because turning off the virus check has its own downside, just recognize the delay and be patient.

SUN Solaris Requirements

The following are minimum requirements to run PDM v2.1 with Sun SPARC:

- Sun Solaris 2.6 or later running CDE or Sun's OpenWindows interfaces.
- SPARC microprocessor.
- 128MB RAM minimum.
- 800 × 600 (256 colors) display minimum, 1,024 × 768 with at least High Color (16-bit) colors recommended.
- Supported browsers include Netscape Communicator versions 4.5*x* or 4.7*x* only: PDM doesn't currently support Netscape 6.*x* or 7.

PDM doesn't currently support Intel-based Solaris implementations.

Linux Requirements

The following are minimum requirements to run PDM v2.1 with Linux:

- Red Hat Linux 7.0, 7.1, 7.2, or 7.3 running the GNOME or KDE 2.0 desktop environment.
- 64MB RAM minimum.
- 800 × 600 (256 colors) display minimum, 1,024 × 768 with at least High Color (16-bit) colors recommended.
- Supported browsers include Netscape Communicator versions 4.7*x* only. PDM doesn't currently support Netscape 6.*x* or 7.

Cisco Secure Policy Manager Considerations

Cisco Secure Policy Manager (CSPM) is a topology-based GUI application that allows network administrators to define high-level security policies visually for multiple Cisco firewalls, IOS devices, and VPN gateways. These end-to-end policies can then be distributed from the centrally located CSPM host, eliminating time-consuming configuration of security commands on a device-by-device basis. The CSPM application can import existing PIX and IOS device security policies. CSPM provides system-auditing functions, monitoring, event notification, and web-based reporting.

For network using CSPM, PDM can only be used for monitoring. Any PDM configuration changes to the PIX Firewall units would be overwritten the next time CSPM synchronizes with the PIX Firewall. While PDM can monitor any configuration—whether created using the command-line interface or CSPM—these changes to the firewall configuration aren't communicated automatically to the PDM. In this circumstance, clicking Refresh in PDM is necessary to update the current firewall configuration.

Web Browser Considerations

PDM is a signed Java applet that uses certificates and HTTPS (HTTP over SSL) to transmit all information securely between PDM and the PIX Firewall. As a Java applet, PDM can run on a variety of platforms without requiring a plug-in or complex software installation. The PDM applet resides in the PIX unit Flash memory and uploads to the workstation when the PIX is accessed using a web browser. PDM uses the SSL protocol to ensure communication with the PIX Firewall unit is secure.

Note, the Web browser used to access PDM must be Java-enabled and support SSL connection. Both features can be set/confirmed on Internet Explorer 6.*x* using the Tools | Internet Options | Advanced tab, as shown in Figure 22-2.

PDM uses the native Java Virtual Machine (JVM) in the browser, not in the Java browser plug-in. If Java plug-in is present for other applications, it can't be your default JVM.

To use PDM with Microsoft Internet Explorer, it must use JDK Version 1.1.4. To verify the current version, use the Help | About Cisco PDM from the PDM menu. Figure 22-3

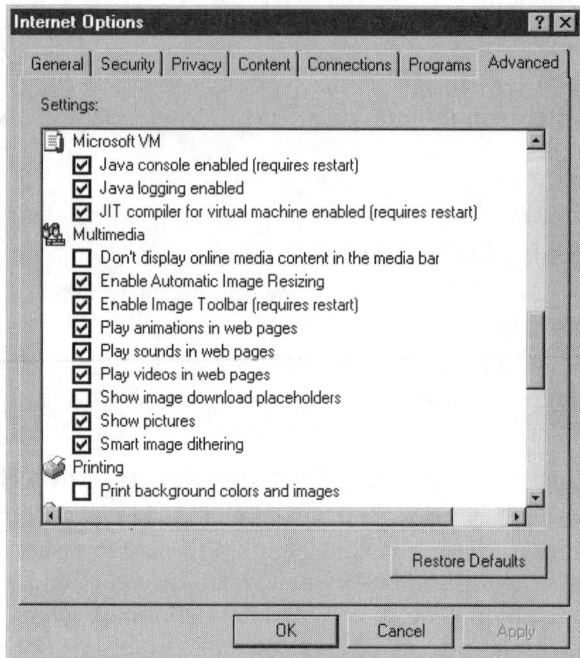

Figure 22-2 Internet Explorer Advanced Options tab

shows the resulting output and the JDK information in the lower-right corner. This same information is available on the PDM opening screen. Notice the screen has a

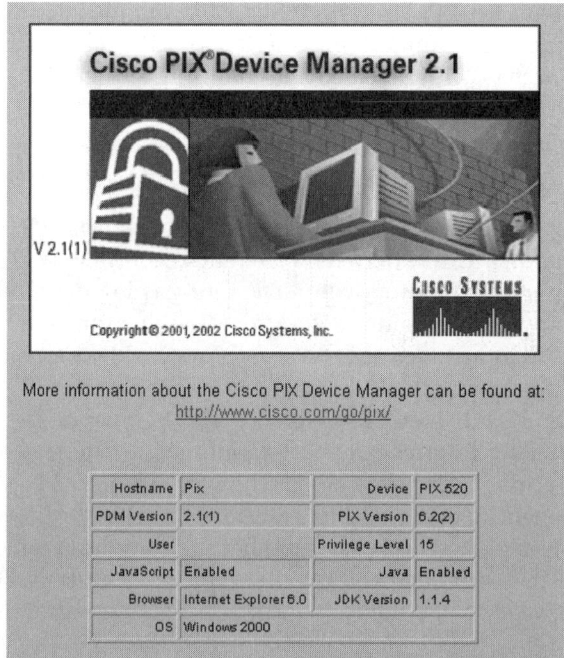

Figure 22-3 The Help | About Cisco PDM screen

model and version information about PDM, the PIX unit, host OS, the browser, and the user privilege level.

The latest version of JVM is available from Microsoft by downloading the product called Virtual Machine.

Prepare for PDM

If the PIX Firewall unit shipped with PIX Firewall software Version 6.2 or higher, PDM v2.1 is already installed in the Flash memory. Otherwise, the following steps should be taken before you install PDM v2.1:

- When performing an upgrade, you must get the PDM software from Cisco using the same methods and, typically, at the same time as securing upgraded PIX Firewall OS software. That process is covered in the last two sections of this chapter.
- Save the PIX Firewall configuration by issuing a **write terminal** command to display the configuration, and then use cut-and-paste to save it to a text file.
- Record the activation key. One method would be to use cut-and-paste with the **show version** command to save it to a text file.

If the network design incorporates a PIX Firewall failover pair, then it's necessary to upgrade both units to be the same PIX OS and PDM version. The failover feature is covered in the next section of this chapter.

Installing PDM on a PIX Firewall

If the process of using TFTP is unfamiliar to you, it's covered in detail in the "Password Recovery" and "Upgrading" sections at the end of this chapter. The following limited commands assume the PIX is configured to function in a network.

Make sure the TFTP server is running, the PDM file (pdm-211.bin) is copied to the TFTP source file folder, and the firewall can ping the TFTP server.

The single step syntax to copy the PDM image file into the PIX Firewall is as follows:

pix# copy tftp://*tftp_server_ip_address*/*pdm_filename* flash:pdm

Or, you can enter the **follow** command to follow the prompts:

pix# copy tftp flash:pdm

The following example shows this latter method. The process prompts for the TFTP server address (address or name of the remote host) and the name of the PDM file. Don't forget the .bin extension. After confirming the request, the process runs unattended:

```
Pix# copy tftp flash:pdm
Address or name of remote host [127.0.0.1]? 192.168.1.10
Source file name [cdisk]? pdm-211.bin
copying tftp://192.168.1.10/pdm-211.bin to flash:pdm
```

```
[yes|no|again]? yes
Erasing current PDM file
Writing new PDM file
!!!!!!!!!!!!!!!!!!!!!!!!!!!!!!!!!!!!!!!!!!!!!!!!!!!!!!!!!!!!!!!!!!!!!!!!!!!!!!!!
   (lines omitted)
!!!!!!!!!!!!!!!!!!!!!!!!!!!!!!!!!!!!!!!!!!!!!!!!
PDM file installed.
Pix#
```

Minimum PIX Configuration

The PDM requires a minimum of the following items configured on the PIX Firewall for the PDM to be accessible. Most of these items should be familiar.

Enable Password	
Clock (UTC)	Universal Coordinated Time (UTC). Enter the year, month, day, and time. Enter time in 24-hour time as hh:mm:ss
Inside IP address	
Inside network mask	
PIX host name	
Domain name	Domain name for the PIX Firewall
IP address of host running PDM	A specific host address

Many of these items would probably already be configured on a working firewall and the others could be configured conventionally. For a new or unconfigured PIX, the **command mode setup** command could also be used, which would then prompt for each item. This is the same autoconfiguration process offered when an unconfigured PIX starts up. Either way, the resulting entries would look something like the following:

```
Enable password: cisco
Clock (UTC): 21:11:47 Jan 12 2003
Inside IP address: 192.168.1.1
Inside network mask: 255.255.255.0
Host name: Pix
Domain name: mypix.com
IP address of host running PIX Device Manager: 192.168.1.20
```

Starting PDM

Once the minimum required PIX configuration is in place and the web browser is set up to be both Java-enabled and support HTTPS (HTTP over SSL), use the following commands to launch PDM:

1. Use a web browser on the workstation designated as **running PIX Device Manager** in the PIX configuration. Enter the following, using the PIX inside interface address to launch PDM:

   https://pix_inside_ address

2. Accept the security certificate. If you don't accept the certificate, the PDM won't launch.

3. A user name/password box will appear. Leave the user name blank and use the enable password as the password. If no enable password is set, click OK to continue.
4. If prompted, accept the second certificate presented. This VeriSign certificate ensures the certificate originated from Cisco Systems and enables PDM to run as a signed applet.

The PDM should launch after the certificates are accepted. Follow the instructions on the screen. If the PDM detects this is the first PDM session, then it launches the Startup Wizard. Figure 22-4 shows the Startup Wizard opening screen (the next section covers this wizard). Or, you can use the Cancel button to close the wizard and work from the menus. If the Startup Wizard gets closed, it can be reactivated at any time from the Wizards menu.

The online help provides information on how to use PDM.

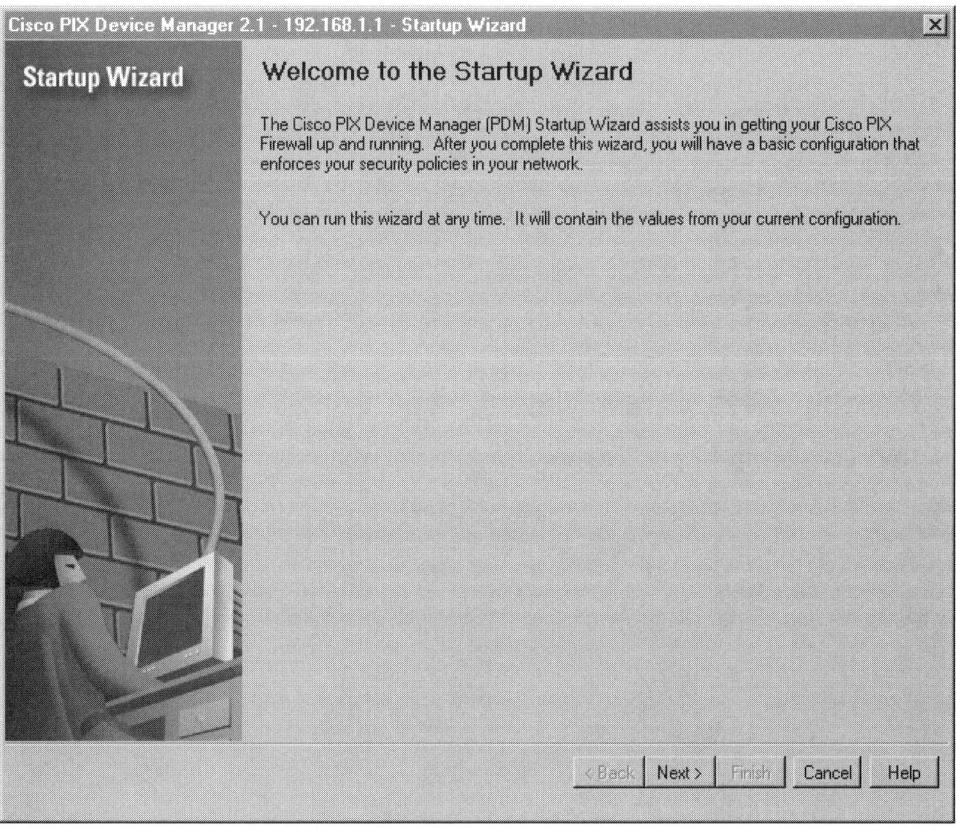

Figure 22-4 The PDM Startup Wizard opening screen

Using the PDM Startup Wizard

The PDM Startup Wizard is a good place to begin configuring a new or erased PIX Firewall. Using the PIX **setup** command, followed by the Startup Wizard, provides the basic requirements needed to implement a network security policy for the PIX Firewall.

If the Start Wizard isn't on the screen after PDM launches, use the following steps from the PDM control panel:

1. Choose Wizards | Startup Wizard from the main menu.
2. After reading the Welcome to the Startup Wizard page, click the Next button. The next screen allows changing the host name, the domain name, and enable password, as shown in Figure 22-5. Each screen has a Help button for assistance. Click the Next button to advance.
3. The next screen allows changing the outside interface configuration, including features like DHCP client and PPPoE. Click the Next button to advance.
4. Other screens allow configuring the other interfaces, NAT/PAT, and DHCP server on the inside interface.

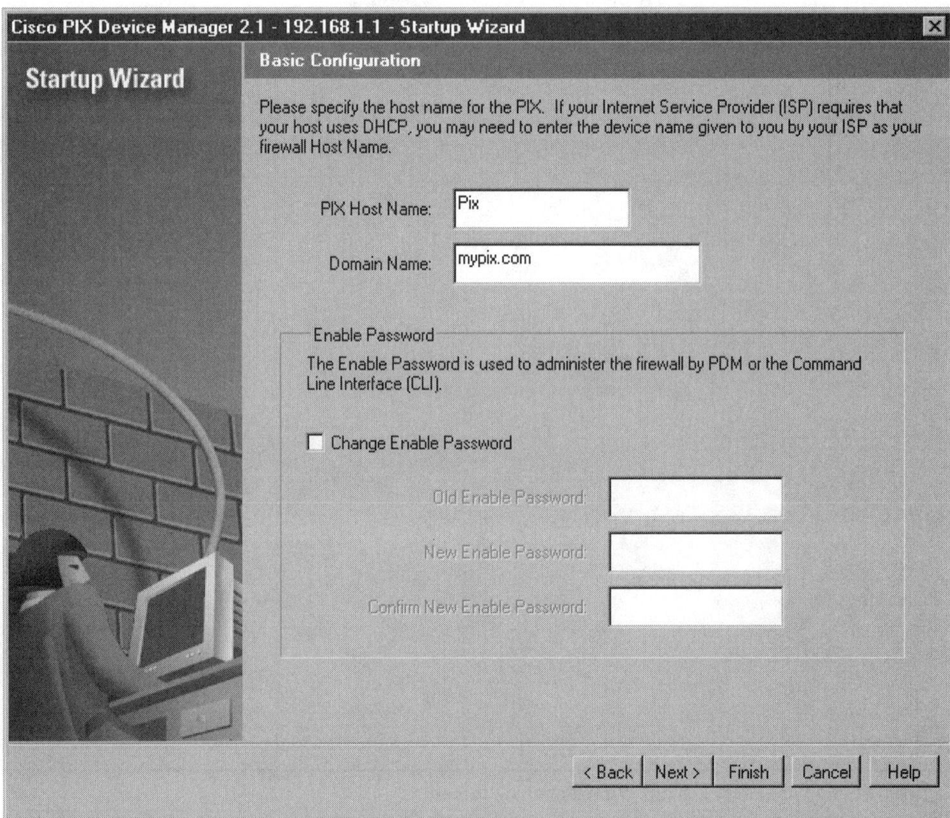

Figure 22-5 Screen 2 of the PDM Start Wizard changes PIX names and password

5. When you finish with the wizard pages, the Startup Wizard Completed page appears. Click the Finish button to send the configuration to the firewall, and then exit the wizard or click Back to edit previous pages.

Using PDM to Configure the PIX Firewall

The Startup Wizard provides basic configuration, but many more advanced features and services can be configured by working on the PDM tabbed pages and using the menus. To a great extent, exploration and experimentation are the best way to learn how to use the tool.

A simple example involves configuring Telnet access to the inside interface. Figure 22-6 shows the System Properties tab with Administration | Telnet selected on the Explorer-like left-side panel. Initially, no entry existed, but the Add button and a pop-up window prompted for the entries you see, and they provided an opportunity to set the idle timer.

Notice the other Administration features that can be configured with similar pages. Features like AAA, IDS, fixup protocols, and URL filtering can all be easily configured using basic graphical interface concepts.

Another example involves configuring Logging and the use of a Syslog Server. Figure 22-7 shows the System Properties tab with Logging | Syslog selected on the Explorer-like left-side panel. Initially, no entry existed, but the Add button and a pop-up window prompted for the entries you see and provided an opportunity to set the packet type (UDP/TCP). A pop-up notice even appears because additional configuration must

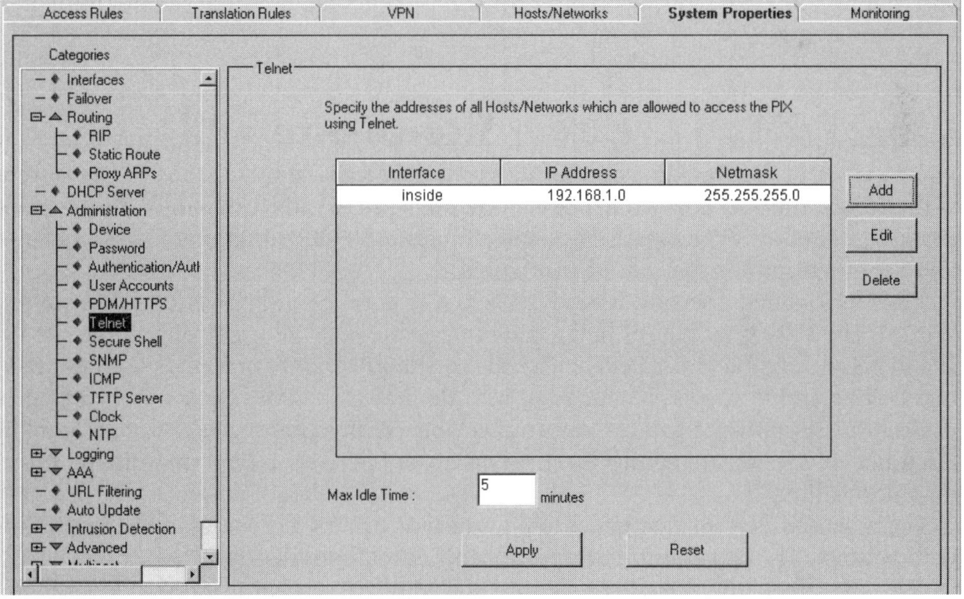

Figure 22-6 Configuring Telnet access using PDM

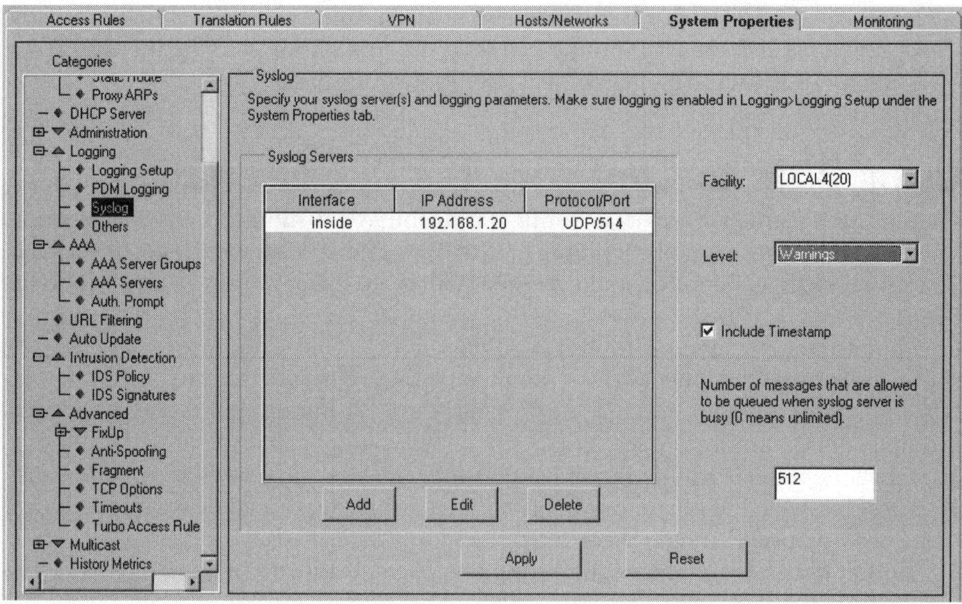

Figure 22-7 Configuring a Syslog Server with PDM

be done (enable logging) to complete this request. PDM will take care of this, but it asks your permission first. Notice you can now see the other features that can be configured with similar pages.

Using PDM to Create a Site-to-Site VPN

The PDM VPN tab allows for configuring the many details of site-to-site VPN consistent with those techniques covered in the VPN chapters (9–16) and in Chapter 21, the chapter on PIX Firewall VPN. Figure 22-8 shows an example of configuring the IKE policies and the other options that can be configured.

PDM v2.1 added a second wizard that's just as friendly and powerful as the Startup Wizard. The VPN Wizard uses half a dozen pages to walk through configuring site-to-site VPNs and remote access VPNs. The site-to-site VPN configuration is used between two IPSec security gateways, which can include firewalls, VPN concentrators, or other devices that support site-to-site IPSec connectivity. With a site-to-site VPN, the local PIX Firewall provides secure connectivity between the LAN and a LAN in a different geographic location.

Figure 22-8 shows the first step is to pick the type of VPN to be created and the PIX interface to use. The Next button accepts the entries and moves on to the next screen.

The next screen, the Remote Site Peer panel, allows the administrator to identify the IP address of the remote IPSec peer that will terminate the VPN tunnel and select whether to use preshared keys or certificates for authentication. Figure 22-10 shows a possible set of choices.

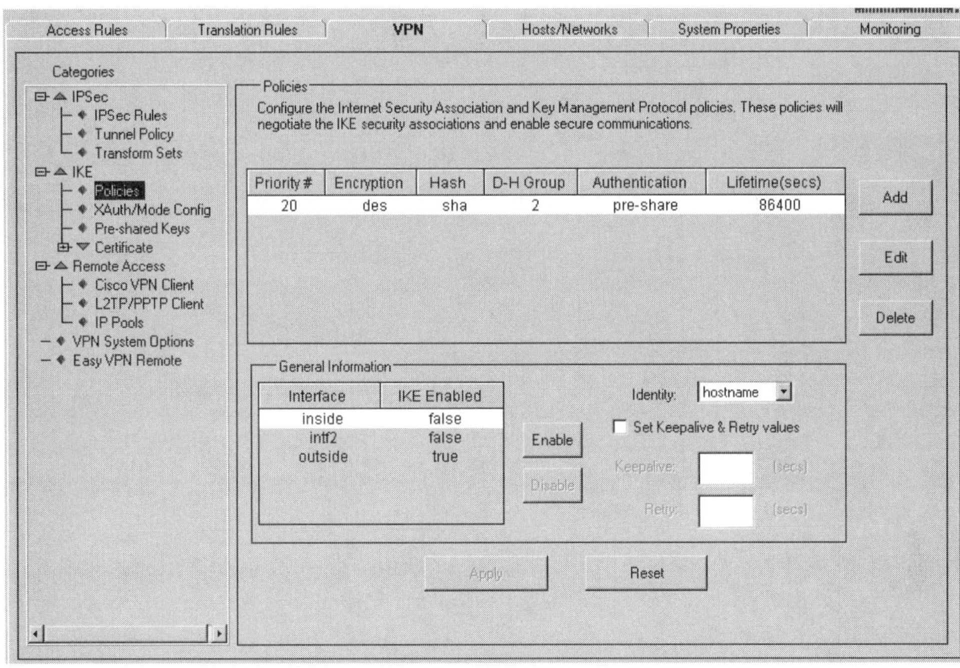

Figure 22-8 VPN IKE policy configuration using PDM

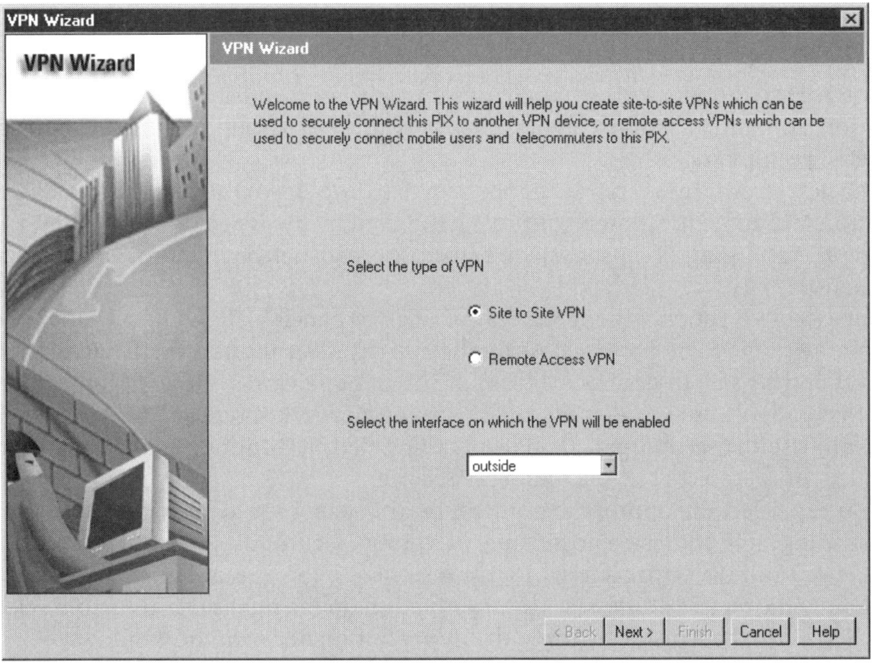

Figure 22-9 VPN Wizard opening screen with VPN type selection

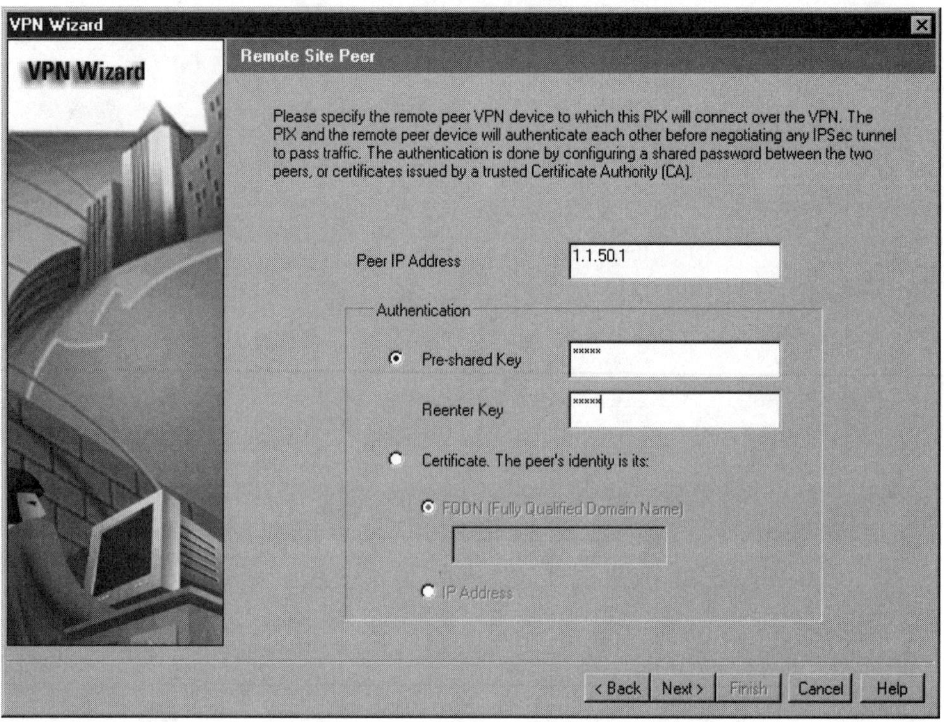

Figure 22-10 VPN remote peer definition and authentication type

The next screen, IKE Policy panel, uses three drop-down list boxes to specify the encryption and authentication algorithms, plus the DH Group to be used by the IKE (Phase 1) setup process.

The next screen, Transform Set panel, uses two drop-down list boxes to specify the encryption and authentication algorithms to be used by the IPSec (Phase 2) VPN Tunnel setup process. Figure 22-11 shows the Transform Set panel, but it's also representational of the IKE Policy.

The next two panels—the IPSec Traffic Selector panels—allow the administrator to define the traffic to be protected using the current IPSec tunnel. The IPSec tunnel will protect packets sent to or received from the hosts or networks selected on these panels. The first panel is used to identify the hosts and networks protected by your local PIX Firewall. Use the second panel—IPSec Traffic Selector (continued)—to identify hosts and networks protected by the remote IPSec peer.

You can select the appropriate button on this panel for identifying hosts and networks using an IP address, a host name, or a group. Figure 22-12 shows a portion of the first IPSec Traffic Selector panels, but this is similar to the one used on the second panel to identify the remote addresses. The *any* notation on the right side came from selecting the choices on the left side by using the upper button between the windows.

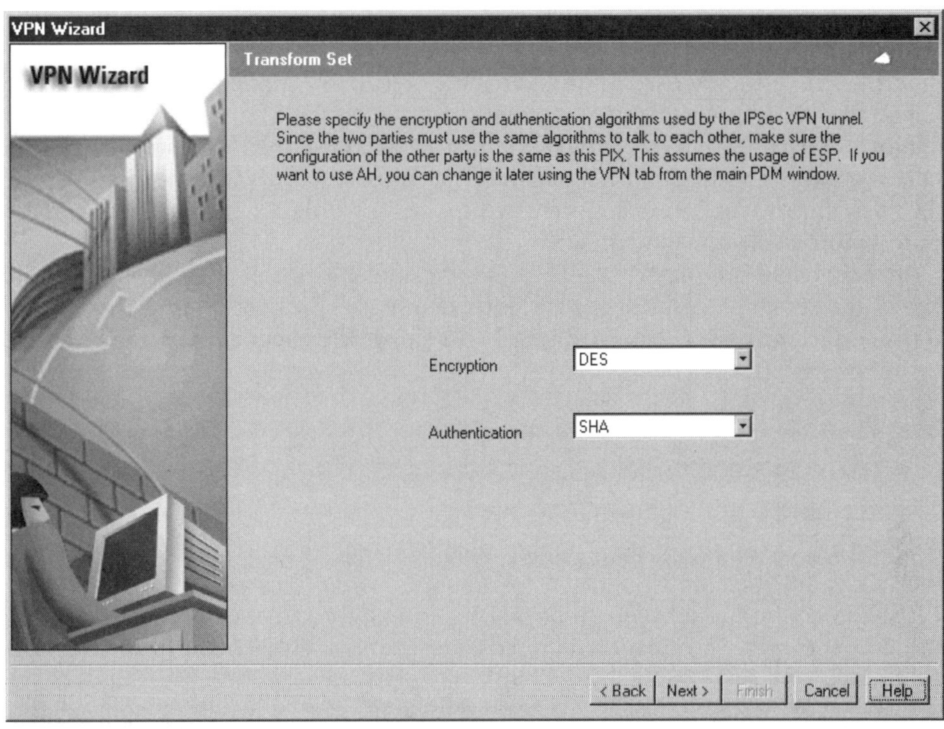

Figure 22-11 Transform Set panel for defining encryption and authentication

At this point the wizard is done. Clicking the Finish button will write the changes to the PIX configuration.

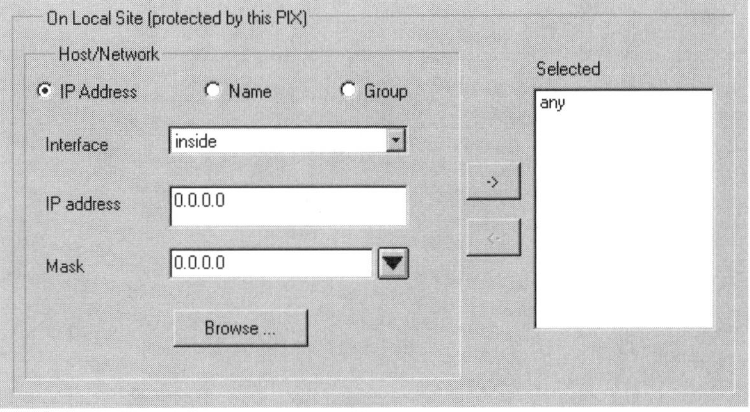

Figure 22-12 IPSec Traffic Selector panels for designating protected addresses

Using PDM to Create a Remote Access VPN

The same VPN Wizard is used to create a remote-access VPN configuration. A *remote access configuration* allows secure remote access for outside VPN clients, such as telecommuters or employees traveling for a company. These remote users will then have secure access centralized network resources much like at their own desks. Using the remote access VPN, the PIX Firewall provides secure connectivity between individual remote users and the resources protected by the local firewall.

After choosing Remote Access VPN and indicating the outside interface on the initial wizard, the Remote Access Client panel is used to specify the type of remote access client to connect to the new VPN link. Figure 22-13 shows the client choices, which include the following:

- Cisco VPN Client, Release 3.*x* or higher
- Cisco VPN 3000 Client, Release 2.5/2.6
- Microsoft Windows client using PPTP
- Microsoft Windows client using L2TP

The choices on the subsequent panels depend on the client choice made here. Figure 22-14 shows the information required when choosing either of the first two options.

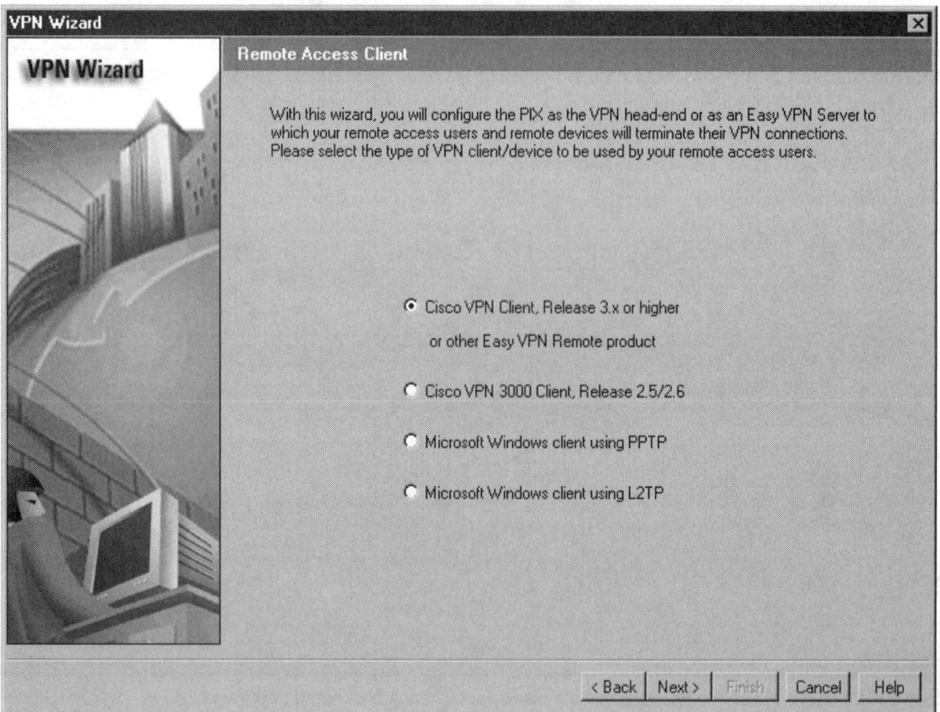

Figure 22-13 Remote Access Client panel for selecting the client type

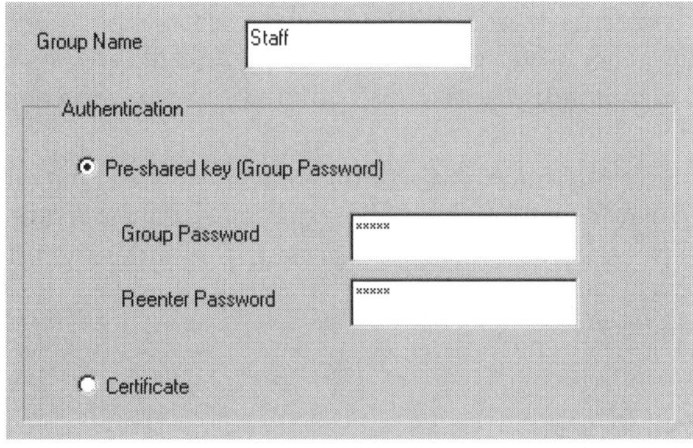

Figure 22-14 VPN Client Group panel for defining the VPN groups

The VPN Client Group panel is used to group remote access users using Cisco VPN Client, so attributes associated with a group will be applied and downloaded to the client(s) that are part of a given group. The group password is a preshared key to be used for IKE authentication.

The group name must also be configured on the remote-access client software to make sure any group attributes are properly downloaded.

The next screen, the Extended Client Authentication panel, is an optional feature that would require remote VPN clients to authenticate using an AAA server before being able to access the private network.

Extended Authentication (Xauth) is a feature within the IKE protocol that allows deploying IPSec VPNs using TACACS+ or RADIUS as the authentication method. The VPN clients would be prompted for a user name and password combination, which would then be verified with the information stored in a TACACS+ or a RADIUS database.

If this feature is selected, an AAA server must be defined using the New button, which opens the AAA Server Group panel. These panel entries define the group name, the protocol used for AAA, and the location of the AAA server. An option also exists to specify a one-time-password OTP. Figure 22-15 shows the Extended Client Authentication panel choices.

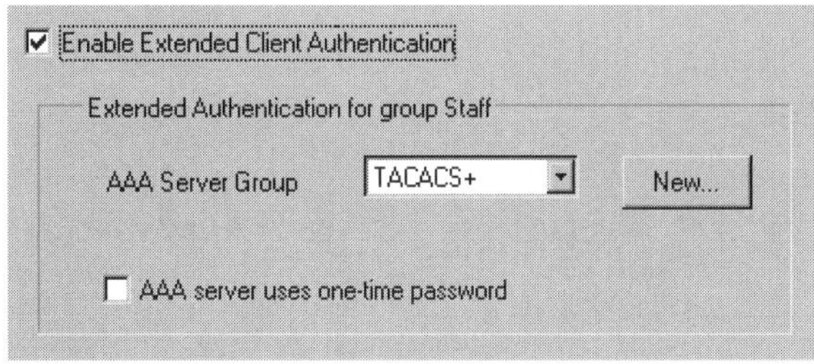

Figure 22-15 Extended Client Authentication panel choices

PART IV

The next wizard screen, the Address Pool panel, creates a pool of local addresses that can be dynamically assigned to remote VPN clients, running Cisco VPN Client v3.*x* or higher. It's necessary to define a pool name, and then a beginning and ending address to define the range.

The next screen, the Attributes Pushed to Client (Optional) panel, is used to provide the other DHCP-type information that will be necessary for the remote client to function within the local network. The information provided includes the following:

- Primary DNS Server
- Secondary DNS Server
- Primary WINS Server
- Secondary WINS Server
- Default Domain Name

The next two screens define the IKE Policy (Phase one) and Transform Set (Phase two), exactly the same as in the previous Site-to Site Wizard.

Figure 22-16 shows the final screen—the Address Translation Exemption (Optional) panel—used to define local hosts/networks that are to be exempted from address translation (NAT). The considerable security provided by NAT might cause problems for

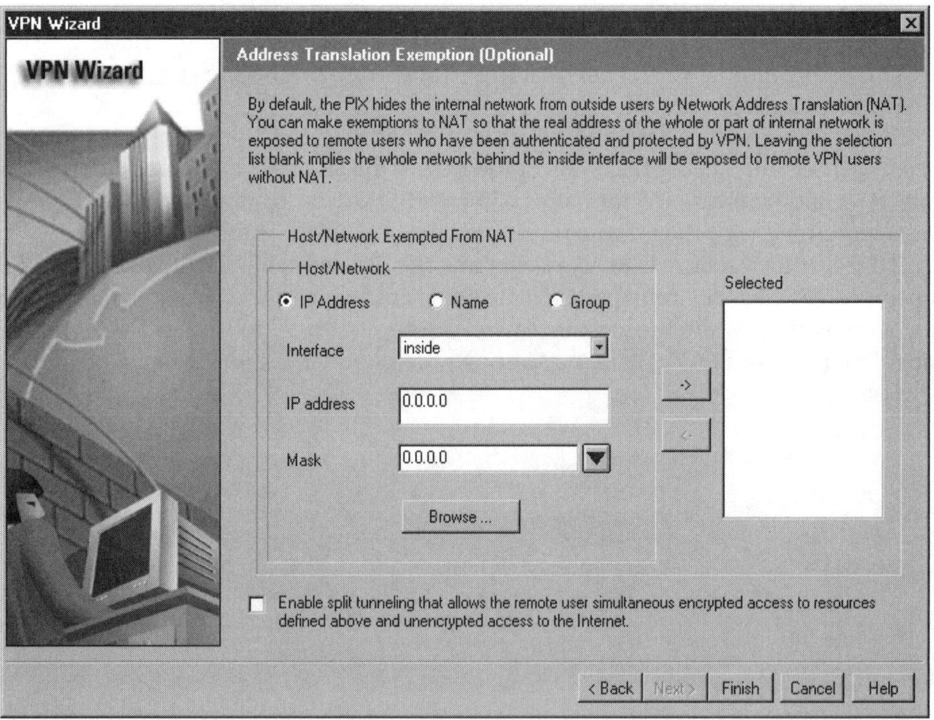

Figure 22-16 Address Translation Exemption panel

those hosts that have been authenticated and protected by VPN. If an inside host is translated to the outside address using a randomly selected public addresses, remote VPN clients would be unable to connect to that host. You can specify which networks will be seen by connecting VPN clients using this exemption rule.

CiscoWorks Management Center for PIX Firewalls (PIX MC)

PIX MC v1.1 for Windows 2000 is a web-based interface with the look-and-feel of the PIX Device Manager (PDM), but it offers centralized management scalability for up to 1,000 PIX firewalls and Firewall Services Modules (FWSM) on Catalyst 6500 switches.

The PIX MC provides the entire Cisco SAFE security strategy and supports centralized management of PIX firewall features such as access rules, NAT, intrusion detection, and EZ-VPN on PIX units. With PIX MC, it is possible to configure new PIX Firewalls or import the configurations from existing firewalls. Once developed, PIX MC can deploy these configurations to the appropriate network devices. At the same time PIX MC provides workflow enhancements for monitoring and controlling changes made to the network, showing any configuration and status changes. The PIX MC can even roll back a device to the previously deployed configuration for those times when things go wrong.

The PIX MC supports centralized management of virtually any PIX firewall security network, including remote access, DMZ, SOHO, voice networks, storage networks, wireless networks, Internet security, and management security provider scenarios. The latest release supports the following PIX Firewall 6.2 features. Later releases of PIX MC will support all of the remaining features in Cisco PIX Firewall Version 6.2.

- LAN-based failover
- DHCP options 66 and 150
- Additional fixup command support
- Turbo ACL
- PPPoE
- Auto-update capability for firewall device configuration files and software images

System Requirements

As with other CiscoWorks implementations, PIX MC uses a centralized management station (server) that contains the PIX MC software and associated databases. The application and features can then be accessed from Web browsers on Windows workstations. This section will look at both of the following system requirements.

- Server Requirements
- Client Requirements

Server Requirements

The minimum hardware requirements to run PIX MC server on Windows 2000 systems are as follows.

- Intel-based computer with 1GHz or faster Pentium processor
- 10 Mbps or faster NIC (obviously faster is better)
- Color monitor with video card capable of 256 colors or more
- CD-ROM drive
- 1 GB RAM minimum
- 9 GB minimum available disk drive space
- NTFS file system recommended
- 2 GB virtual memory

The minimum software requirements to run PIX MC server on Windows 2000 systems are as follows.

- ODBC Driver Manager 3.510 or later
- Either Windows 2000 Professional or Windows 2000 Server with service pack 2 or 3

Client Requirements

The minimum requirements to access all server-based product features from a client workstation are as follows.

- Intel-based computer with 300MHz or faster Pentium processor running one of the following versions of Windows.
- Windows 98
- Windows NT 4.0
- Windows 2000 Server or Professional (Service pack 2)
- 256 MB RAM minimum
- 400 MB virtual memory disk drive space
- Internet Explorer 6.0 or 5.5 (service pack 2) with Java Virtual Machine 5.0.3182 or later

PIX Failover Feature

The firewall's critical role in the network security design makes device failure of any kind a serious consideration. The failover feature allows an identical PIX firewall unit to provide redundancy if the primary unit fails. One unit is considered the "active" or "primary" unit, while the other is considered the "standby" or "secondary" unit. The *active* unit performs its normal network functions, while the *standby* unit only monitors the other unit, ready to take control if the active unit fails.

Since PIX OS v5.1, PIX models support stateful failover, allowing the system to maintain connection state information for the TCP connection during the failover from the primary unit to the standby unit. If failover occurs, the secondary unit assumes the IP and MAC addresses of the primary unit and begins accepting traffic. Because the other network devices don't see any change in these addresses, no ARP entries change or timeouts occur anywhere in the network.

Understanding Failover

Traditionally, the two PIX Firewall units are connected by a special high-speed serial cable when using cable-based failover, although a faster solution involves a dedicated Ethernet connection to a dedicated switch/hub (or VLAN) for LAN-based failover. When using stateful failover, a separate, dedicated 100 Mbps or Gigabit Ethernet connection is required for cable-based failover and is recommended for LAN-based failover.

Once the primary unit is configured and the necessary cabling attached, the primary unit automatically copies the configuration to the standby unit when it's powered up.

If the failover feature is enabled, the ACT indicator light on the front of the PIX 515e, PIX 525, and PIX 535 is lighted when the unit is the active unit and it's off when the device is the standby unit.

Figure 22-17 shows a simple failover system without protected DMZ(s). Each firewall connects to an inside and an outside switch, while the failover serial cable connects the

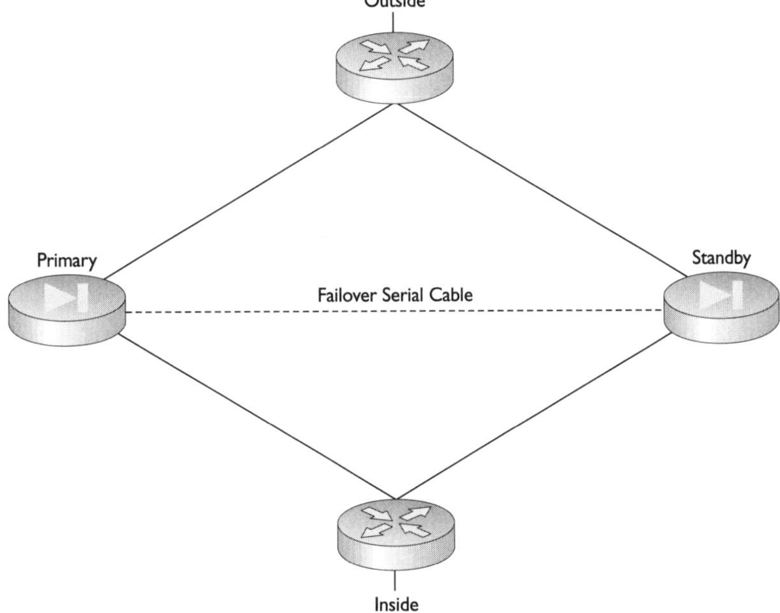

Figure 22-17 Two PIX Firewall units forming a simple serial failover pair

two directly together. If a protected DMZ existed, each firewall's perimeter interface would have to connect to a switch in the DMZ.

Identical Units

The two PIX units hardware must be configured exactly the same to appear as a single unit to the network. Failover requires two units that are identical in the following respects:

- Platform (PIX 515 and PIX 515e won't work together)
- Interfaces
- Software version
- Amount of RAM
- Flash memory
- Activation key type (DES or 3DES)

Software licensing is an issue when choosing units to create a failover pair. At least one of the failover pair must have an Unrestricted (UR) license. The second unit can have either a Failover (FO) or a UR license. Restricted (R) units can't be used as any part of a failover pair and two FO licensed units can't be used to create a failover pair. PIX 501/506/506E units don't support the failover features.

NOTE Cisco's pricing strategy for failover units means a substantial financial savings exists when an unrestricted/failover pair is used compared to two unrestricted units. The failover unit can cost one third as much as an unrestricted unit.

Communicating a Failover

The two PIX failover devices can maintain communication and facilitate rapid failover transitions using either of the following:

- Special modified RS-232 serial failover cable with transfer rates of 115K
- Faster dedicated LAN connection from 10MB half-duplex to Gigabit full-duplex

This connection allows the units to exchange unit identification, and to monitor the power status of the other unit and other failover related communications. Power or cable failure is detected within 15 seconds and triggers a failover switch.

The failover pair uses the failover connection and all network interfaces to exchange special failover "hello" packets every 15 seconds. If two consecutive hello packet cycles are missed, the failover process starts testing the interfaces to determine which unit failed and transfers active control to the secondary unit, if appropriate.

The default 15-second hello cycle can be modified with the **failover poll** ***seconds*** command. The minimum value is 3 seconds and the maximum is 15 seconds. A shorter poll time can allow the PIX Firewall to detect a failure faster and trigger the handoff, but it could be fooled by temporary network congestion.

Failover Serial Cable

The special serial failover cable ends are labeled, and they define the primary and secondary units. If the failover cable connection is presently identifying the unit as primary, the unit becomes the active unit and the configuration is copied to the standby unit. If a PIX unit comes up without a failover cable, then it automatically becomes the active unit.

The serial failover cable allows each unit to detect if the cable is connected at both ends, connected locally but disconnected at the other end, or disconnected locally and the other end is unknown. In addition, the cable can tell if the power is interrupted at the other end. A failure of any of these parameters on the active unit causes the standby unit to trigger a failover.

Because both units will have identical IP and MAC addresses, if both units are powered down, it's critical that the failover cable be in place when power is restored. If not, both units will come up active and create duplicate address problems.

Configuration Replication

The two PIX Firewall units should be exactly the same and running the same software release. Unless stateful failover is configured, only the primary unit is configured by the administrator. That configuration is replicated over the failover cable from the active unit to the standby unit in three ways:

- After the standby unit boots up, the active unit replicates its configuration via the failover cable to the standby unit.
- Commands entered on the active unit are automatically replicated via the failover cable to the standby unit.
- The **write standby** command on the active unit sends the entire configuration in memory via the failover cable to the standby unit.

Configuration replication only occurs from Flash memory to Flash memory so, after making configuration changes, use the **write memory** command to write the configuration into Flash memory. Because the failover cable is a serial link, the replication can take a while with a large configuration.

When the Primary Fails

If a primary unit failure occurs, Syslog messages are sent indicating the cause of the failure, and then the switchover occurs. The standby unit assumes the IP and MAC addresses of its immediate predecessor and starts accepting traffic. After the primary unit is fixed and placed back online, it can't automatically resume as the active unit because of the duplicate addresses, so it comes up as the standby unit.

A switchover can be manually initiated from either unit. The **failover active** command on the primary unit or the **no failover active** command on the secondary unit triggers the change. When a failover occurs and both devices are operational, each will assume the IP address and MAC address of its immediate predecessor. The new active unit will start accepting traffic.

Stateful Failover

Since PIX OS v5.1, stateful failover allows per-connection state table information to be continuously sent to the standby unit. If a failover occurs, both devices have same connection state information allowing end user sessions to be transferred without interruption. With systems not using stateful failover links, the standby unit does not have the state information requiring all active connections to be dropped until they can be reestablished.

Stateful failover can be triggered by any of the following situations:

- The active PIX Firewall loses power or is turned off
- The stateful failover dedicated link goes down for two "hello" cycles as defined by the **failover poll** command (default 30 seconds)
- The **failover active** command is used on the standby unit
- The **no failover active** command is used on the active unit
- The active PIX Firewall is rebooted, including a **reload** command
- Block memory exhaustion for 15 consecutive seconds or more on the active unit

After a stateful failover, the standby unit will assume the active unit configuration, TCP connection table, including the timeout information of each connection, xlate table, and system up time. What won't be assumed by the new active unit are the user authentication (uauth) table, the ISAKMP and IPSec SA table, the ARP table, and the routing information.

Stateful Failover Hardware Requirements Stateful failover requires a dedicated 100 Mbps or Gigabit Ethernet link between the units with a MTU set to 1500 to be used exclusively for passing state information between the two PIX Firewall units. No hosts or routers should be connected to this link. The interface implementations that can be used for this dedicated stateful failover link include the following:

- Cat 5 crossover cable directly connecting the two units
- 100BaseTX half-duplex switch using straight Cat 5 cables
- Full-duplex 100BaseTX using a dedicated switch or a dedicated VLAN on a switch
- Full-duplex 1000BaseTX using a dedicated switch or a dedicated VLAN on a switch

The failover serial cable must be installed and working properly.

Figure 22-18 shows the same simple design as earlier with a stateful failover link installed using crossover cable.

Stateful failover is a new feature, so requirements and configuration commands are in transition. Be sure to check the correct documentation for the Firewall OS version. Early versions didn't support the crossover cable and v6.1 didn't support half-duplex failover links.

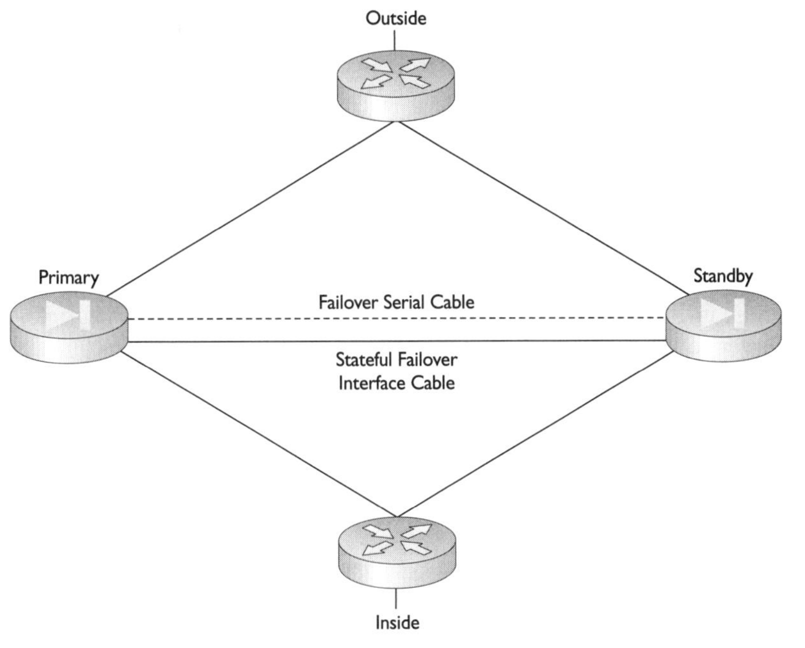

Figure 22-18 Failover system with stateful failover cable installed

Failover Configuration with Failover Cable

Before configuring, make certain the two PIX Firewall units are identical, as discussed earlier, and the standby unit is powered off. The steps to configure failover with a failover cable are as follows:

1. Set the clock on the active PIX Firewall unit using the **clock set *time*** command or using the **Network Time Protocol** (NTP) commands introduced in Chapter 18 for version 6.2 and newer.
2. Connect the failover serial cable to the units. Make sure the end labeled "Primary" attaches to the primary unit and the end labeled "Secondary" connects to the secondary unit. Don't power up the secondary unit.
3. If stateful failover is planned, attach a crossover cable between the primary and secondary units for the network interfaces.
4. Go to Configuration mode with the **configure terminal** command.
5. Always specify the speed for the interface, such as **10baset** for 10 Mbps or **100basetx** for 100 Mbps. Don't use the **auto** or the **1000auto** option on any interface. Verify that the interface speed and duplex settings match any connected devices. Use the **write terminal** command to confirm the settings.

For stateful failover, set the dedicated interface speed, using either the **100full** or the **1000sxfull** command. Set the link maximum transfer unit by using the **mtu** ***interface_name*** **1500** command. For PIX Firewall version 6.2, the MTU size must be at least 1,500 for the stateful failover link and at least 576 for the LAN-based failover link.

6. Use the **clear xlate** command after changing the **interface** command.
7. Use the **ip address** command to assign IP addresses to each interface. The following output shows examples of the commands so far.
8. Use the **failover** command statement to enable the failover feature. The **no failover** command will disable the failover feature.

   The related **failover active** command on the standby unit triggers a failover switch, causing that unit to become the active unit. The **no failover active** command from the active unit triggers a failover switch to make the standby unit become the active unit. This command is used to force an active unit offline for maintenance and to return a updated unit to service.

```
Pix# clock set 14:27:0 jun 1 2004
Pix# config t
Pix(config)# nameif ethernet2 intf2 sec50
Pix(config)# ip address outside 10.1.1.1 255.255.255.0
Pix(config)# ip address inside 192.168.1.1 255.255.255.0
Pix(config)# ip address intf2 192.168.2.1 255.255.255.252
Pix(config)# interface e0 100full
Pix(config)# interface e1 100full
Pix(config)# interface e2 100full
Pix(config)# mtu intf2 1500
Pix(config)# clear xlate
Pix(config)# failover
```

9. Use the **show ip address** command to see the addresses. The **Current IP Addresses** is the same as the **System IP Addresses** on the failover active unit.

```
Pix(config)# show ip address
System IP Addresses:
     ip address outside 10.1.1.1 255.255.255.0
     ip address inside 192.168.1.1 255.255.255.0
     ip address intf2 192.168.2.1 255.255.255.252
Current IP Addresses:
     ip address outside 10.1.1.1 255.255.255.0
     ip address inside 192.168.1.1 255.255.255.0
     ip address intf2 192.168.2.1 255.255.255.252
```

10. Use the **show failover** command to verify the failover feature by looking for the **This host: primary - Active** statement. You can see failover is on and the other unit isn't powered up.

```
Pix(config)# show failover
Failover On
Cable status: Other side powered off
Reconnect timeout 0:00:00
Poll frequency 15 seconds
    This host: primary - Active
                Active time: 330 (sec)
                Interface intf2 (192.168.2.1): Normal (Waiting)
```

```
                Interface outside (10.1.1.1): Normal (Waiting)
                Interface inside (192.168.1.1): Normal (Waiting)
    Other host: secondary - Standby
                Active time: 0 (sec)
                Interface intf2 (0.0.0.0): Unknown (Waiting)
                Interface outside (0.0.0.0): Unknown (Waiting)
                Interface inside (0.0.0.0): Unknown (Waiting)
```

Interface flag	Indicates
Failed	Interface has failed
Link Down	Interface line protocol is down
Normal	Interface is working correctly
Shut Down	Interface has been administratively shut down
Unknown	IP address isn't configured for the interface, so it can't determine the status
Waiting	Monitoring the other unit's network interface hasn't started yet

11. Use the **failover IP address** ***int_name ip_addr*** command to define the standby unit's interface addresses. The IP addresses for the standby unit are different from the active unit's addresses, but in the same subnet for each interface. The standby unit needn't be powered up for this command to work correctly.

    Without setting, the failover IP addresses failover won't work, the **show failover** command will display 0.0.0.0 for the IP address, and monitoring of the interfaces will remain in the "waiting" state.

```
Pix(config)# failover ip address inside 192.168.1.2
Pix(config)# failover ip address outside 10.1.1.2
Pix(config)# failover ip address intf2 192.168.2.2

Pix(config)# show failover
Failover On
Cable status: Other side powered off
Reconnect timeout 0:00:00
Poll frequency 15 seconds
        This host: primary - Active
                Active time: 740 (sec)
                Interface intf2 (192.168.2.1): Normal (Waiting)
                Interface outside (10.1.1.1): Normal (Waiting)
                Interface inside (192.168.1.1): Normal (Waiting)
    Other host: secondary - Standby
                Active time: 0 (sec)
                Interface intf2 (192.168.2.2): Unknown (Waiting)
                Interface outside (10.1.1.2): Unknown (Waiting)
                Interface inside (192.168.1.2): Unknown (Waiting)
```

12. Use the **failover link** [***stateful_if_name***] command to enable stateful failover. Use the **no failover link** command to disable the feature.

```
Pix(config)# failover link intf2
Pix(config)# show failover
Failover On
Cable status: Other side powered off
Reconnect timeout 0:00:00
```

```
Poll frequency 15 seconds
        This host: primary - Active
                Active time: 740 (sec)
                Interface intf2 (192.168.2.1): Normal (Waiting)
                Interface outside (10.1.1.1): Normal (Waiting)
                Interface inside (192.168.1.1): Normal (Waiting)
    Other host: secondary - Standby
                Active time: 0 (sec)
                Interface intf2 (192.168.2.2): Unknown (Waiting)
                Interface outside (10.1.1.2): Unknown (Waiting)
                Interface inside (192.168.1.2): Unknown (Waiting)
```

13. If necessary, use the **failover poll *seconds*** command to set a hello interval shorter than 15 seconds (range 3 to 15).
14. Power up the secondary unit. The primary unit will detect it and start synchronizing the configurations. The messages "Sync Started" and "Sync Completed" will appear.
15. If any other changes are made to the active unit configuration, use the **write memory** command to save the configuration and to synchronize the standby unit.

LAN-Based Failover Configuration

PIX Firewall version 6.2 introduces support for LAN-based failover, eliminating the need for the Failover serial cable to connect the primary and secondary units. LAN-based failover overcomes the six-foot distance limitations of the Failover cable.

A dedicated LAN interface and a dedicated switch/hub (or VLAN) is required to implement LAN-based failover. An Ethernet crossover cable can't be used to connect the two PIX Firewalls.

Because failover messages might be transmitted over Ethernet connections that are relatively less secure than the dedicated Failover serial cable, PIX Firewall version 6.2 provides message encryption and authentication using a manual preshared key.

The four **command mode failover lan** commands include the following syntax. Each uses the no form of the command to remove the feature.

Pix(config)# failover lan unit {primary | secondary}
Pix(config)# failover lan interface *if_name*
Pix(config)# failover lan key *key_secret*
Pix(config)# failover lan enable

enable	Enables LAN-based failover; otherwise, serial cable failover is used
key	Enables encryption and authentication of LAN-based failover messages
key_secret	The shared secret key for encryption
primary | secondary	Specifies the unit to be primary or secondary PIX Firewall to use for LAN-based failover. Equivalent of serial cable labels

The basic configuration of the active firewall doesn't change and won't be restated here. The LAN-based failover does require some configuration on the standby unit and those commands are addressed here. If properly configured, the LAN-based failover configurations for the two units will be different, reflecting which is primary and which is secondary. To configure LAN-based failover, follow these steps:

1. Don't connect the failover LAN interfaces until told to do so.
2. Configure the primary PIX Firewall unit as previously discussed.
3. Still on the primary unit, connect the LAN failover interface to the network and add the following lines to configure the LAN-based failover. *Lanlink* is the interface (Ethernet4) used for the failover connection, while **1234567** is the key used for encrypting traffic over the LAN failover link.

```
Pix(config)# no failover
Pix(config)# failover lan unit primary
Pix(config)# failover lan interface lanlink
Pix(config)# failover lan key 1234567
Pix(config)# failover lan enable
Pix(config)# failover
```

4. Use the **write memory** command to save the primary unit configuration to Flash.
5. Power on the secondary unit without the LAN-based failover interface connected. The following commands are necessary for the secondary unit to connect to the primary unit using the LAN-based failover interface. Once this connection is established, the rest of the primary unit configuration is replicated over the failover connection.

```
Pix2(config)# nameif ethernet4 lanlink security20
Pix2(config)# interface ethernet4 100full
Pix2(config)# ip address lanlink 192.168.3.1 255.255.255.0
Pix2(config)# failover ip address lanlink 192.168.3.2
Pix2(config)# failover lan unit secondary                  (optional)
Pix2(config)# failover lan interface lanlink
Pix2(config)# failover lan key 1234567
Pix2(config)# failover lan enable
Pix2(config)# failover
```

6. Use the **write memory** command to save the secondary unit configuration to Flash.
7. Reboot both units and connect the LAN-based failover interfaces to the designated failover switch, hub, or VLAN.
8. If any of the **failover lan** command needs to be changed, you need to disconnect the LAN-based failover interface and repeat the preceding steps.

Verifying Failover Configuration

Use the following commands to verify that failover configuration is correct.

- **show failover** Use the **show failover** command to verify the status of the connection and to determine which unit is active. You saw sample output earlier in this section.

- **show failover [lan [detail]]** The **show failover lan** command displays the LAN-based failover information useful for debugging purposes.

```
pix(config)# show failover lan
Lan Based Failover is Active
        interface lanlink (192.168.3.1): Normal, peer (192.168.3.2): Normal
```

The **show failover lan detail** command displays the connection details, as well as traffic summary information.

```
pix(config)# show failover lan detail
Lan Failover is Active
This Pix is Primary
Command Interface is lanlink
Peer Command Interface IP is 192.168.3.2
My interface status is 0x1
Peer interface status is 0x1
Peer interface downtime is 0x0
Total msg send: 103093, rcvd: 103031, droped: 0, retrans: 13, send_err: 0
Total/Cur/Max of 51486:0:5 msgs on retransQ
msgs on retransQ if any
LAN FO cmd queue, count: 0, head: 0x0, tail: 0x0
Failover config state is 0x5c
Failover config poll cnt is 0
Failover pending tx msg cnt is 0
Failover Fmsg cnt is 0
```

Password Recovery

Password recovery for a PIX Firewall is quite simple if you can get physical access to the device and know the version of the PIX OS. The actual steps depend on whether the unit has a floppy drive like the 520 model. This section looks at both the floppy disk models and the newer units.

Password recovery on the PIX Firewall units erases only the password, not the configuration. With PIX OS version 6.2, if Telnet or console AAA authentication is configured, the process will also prompt to remove these.

To perform password recovery, you must have a PC that can create a terminal session with the PIX device, such as HyperTerm, and a Cisco configuration cable kit. The router has to be down for about ten minutes. For firewalls with a floppy disk drive, a 3.5″ floppy is required and, for newer firewalls, a PC running TFTP server is needed. If necessary, the TFTP server software can run on the console PC and the software can be downloaded from Cisco.

Before Getting Started

If this is the first time you're performing password recovery on this device, use a web browser to go to http://www.cisco.com and do a search on PIX Firewall password recovery. One of the first documents will have a title like "Cisco PIX 500 Series Firewalls: Password Recovery and AAA Configuration Recovery Procedure." This document contains step-by-step instructions for password recovery, plus links to utilities that are required in the process.

To perform the password recovery procedure, you must have the PIX Password Lockout Utility appropriate for the PIX software release running on the device. The web document found in the last paragraph lists the lockout utility files and should include hyperlinks to download each one. At press time, the list looked like the following. Download the utility that matches the PIX OS of the device. The files are small, under 100K each.

nppix.bin (4.3 and earlier releases)
np44.bin (4.4 release)
np50.bin (5.0 release)
np51.bin (5.1 release)
np52.bin (5.2 release)
np53.bin (5.3 release)
np60.bin (6.0 release)
np61.bin (6.1 release)
np62.bin (6.2 release)

You'll see two other files listed with download links. The rawrite exe file is only needed for PIX units with a floppy drive, and the TFTP Server Download Utility file is needed for all other PIX units. If another TFTP server is already available, it's unnecessary to use this one.

NOTE If you haven't already installed a TFTP server on your laptop, this isn't a bad unit and it's free. If I thought I might face this situation again in the near future, I'd download each of the utilities, the rawrite.exe, the TFTP software, and the PDF of this document, and put them all in a folder for future reference.

PIX Devices with a Floppy Drive

If the PIX unit has a floppy drive, perform the following steps. A 3.5″ floppy disk is required. It will be formatted and unreadable by DOS/Windows when done.

1. Place the 3.5″ disk in the floppy drive. Note: Trying to direct the output to other media or a folder failed when I tried it.
2. Execute the **rawrite.exe** file on your PC and answer the questions on the screen using the correct password recovery filename for the first question. Type **a** or the appropriate drive letter for the floppy for the second question. Pressing ENTER for the third question causes the floppy disk to be formatted and written to. The screen looked like the following:

```
RaWrite 1.2 - Write disk file to raw floppy diskette
Enter source file name: np62.bin
Enter destination drive: a:
Please insert a formatted diskette into drive A: and press -ENTER- :
```

3. Start a console session with the PIX unit console port. Because you're locked out, you should see a password prompt only.

4. Insert the PIX Password Lockout Utility disk into the floppy drive of the PIX.
5. Push the Reset button on the lower-left corner of the PIX front panel. The PIX will reboot from the floppy and print a message to the console. The message for 6.2 looked like this:

```
Rebooting....
Cisco Secure PIX Firewall BIOS (3.6)
Booting Floppy
..................................à
Cisco Secure PIX Firewall floppy loader (3.0) #0: Wed Mar 27 11:02:14 PST 2002
Reading installation media......
Cisco Secure PIX Firewall password tool (3.0) #0: Wed Mar 27 11:02:16 PST 2002
Flash=i28F640J5 @ 0x300
BIOS Flash=AT29C257 @ 0xd8000

Do you wish to erase the passwords? [yn] y
The following lines will be removed from the configuration:
        enable password toXbRG4.WPapU9O3 encrypted
        passwd 2KFQnbNIdI.2KYOU encrypted

Do you want to remove the commands listed above from the configuration? [yn] y
Passwords and aaa commands have been erased.
```

6. You're prompted to answer two questions. Before answering **y** to both, eject the floppy disk because the system will reboot when you press ENTER for the second question.

   There should be no enable password. The Telnet password is cisco.
7. In Configuration mode, use **passwd** ***new_password*** to create a new Telnet password and use **enable password** ***new_enable_password*** to create an enable password, and then save your changes with the **write memory** command.

PIX Devices Without a Floppy Drive

If the PIX device is a newer unit without a floppy drive, perform the following steps. In this process, you type a series of one-word commands, followed by an IP address or a filename. Look at Step four for the information you need.

NOTE I tried this on my 520 (with floppy and v6.2) and it wouldn't respond to Step 3.

1. Start a console session with the PIX unit console port. Because you're locked out, you should only see a password prompt.
2. Make sure the TFTP server is running and the appropriate Password Lockout Utility file was copied to the folder TFTP uses as its source.
3. Power on the PIX Firewall and, as soon as the startup messages appear, send a BREAK character or press the ESC key. For Windows HyperTerminal, use CTRL+BREAK. You might have to do his several times. The **monitor>** prompt will indicate success.

4. Make the following entries, pressing ENTER after each. The command is repeated or responded to on the next line.

```
monitor> interface 1                          (PIX interface to TFTP)
0: i8255X @ PCI(bus:0 dev:14 irq:10)
1: i8255X @ PCI(bus:0 dev:13 irq:11)
Using 1: i82557 @ PCI(bus:0 dev:13 irq:11), MAC: 0002.b945.a23c
monitor> address 192.168.1.1                  (PIX interface address)
address 192.168.1.1
monitor> server 192.168.1.10                  (TFTP server address)
server 192.168.1.10
monitor> file np622.bin                       (PIX Lockout Utility)
file pix622.bin
monitor> ping 192.168.1.10                    (Test connectivity to TFTP)
Sending 5, 100-byte 0xcde2 ICMP Echoes to 192.168.1.10, timeout is 4 seconds:
!!!!!
Success rate is 100 percent (5/5)
monitor> tftp                                 (starts TFTP copy)

Do you wish to erase the passwords? [yn] y    (removes passwords)
Passwords have been erased.
Rebooting....
```

5. With PIX OS v 6.2, if **AAA authentication Telnet** or **console** commands are set, the system will also prompt to remove those.

   There should be no enable password. The telnet password is cisco.

6. In Configuration mode, use **passwd *new_password*** to create a new Telnet password and use **enable password *new_enable_password*** to create an enable password, and then save your changes with the **write memory** command.

PART IV

Upgrading the PIX OS

If the PIX Firewall unit is currently running an OS versions 5.1.1 or later and has a DES or 3DES activation key, use the **copy tftp flash** command to download the latest software image from a TFTP server. The **copy tftp flash** command process is virtually identical to the typical method for upgrading an IOS on a Cisco router. The new image is used by the PIX Firewall on the next reload (reboot).

Regardless of the upgrade method, the latest PIX OS can be downloaded from the PIX Software Download page on the www.cisco.com site. A CCO account is necessary to get to this site. If necessary, Cisco TFTP Server software can be downloaded from this same site. The PIX images have names like **pix622.bin**.

Use the following steps to upgrade the PIX unit using the **copy tftp flash** command.

1. Make sure the TFTP server is running and the appropriate PIX Firewall binary image (pix*nnn*.bin) file was copied to the folder TFTP uses as its source.
2. Confirm connectivity between the PIX unit and the TFTP server by pinging the server from PIX Privilege mode prompt.

3. At the PIX Privilege mode prompt, type the **copy tftp flash** command.
4. Type the TFTP server IP address when prompted for the remote host.
5. Type the PIX binary filename when prompted for the source filename.
6. Type **yes** to confirm the process.

The screen output should look something like this:

```
Pix# copy tftp flash
Address or name of remote host [127.0.0.1]? 192.168.1.10
Source file name [cdisk]? pix622.bin
copying tftp://192.168.1.10/pix622.bin to flash:image
[yes|no|again]?yes
!!!!!!!!!!!!!!!!!!!!!!!!!!!!!!!!!!!!!!!!!!!!!!!!!!!!!!!!!!!!!!!!!!!!!!!!!!!!!!
!!!!!!!!!!!!!!!!!!!!!!!!!!!!!!!!!!!!!!!!!!!!!!!!!!!!!!!!!!!!!!!!!!!!!!!!!!!!!!
!!!!!!!!!!!!!!!!!!!!!!!!!!!!!!!!!!!!!!!!!!!!!!!!!!!!!!!!!!!!!!!!!!!!!!!
!!!!!!!!!!!!!!!!!!!!!!!!!!!!!!!!!!!!!!!!!!!!!!!!!!!!!!!!!!!!!!!!!!!!!!!
!!!!
Received 1658880 bytes.
Erasing current image.
Writing 1540152 bytes of image.
!!!!!!!!!!!!!!!!!!!!!!!!!!!!!!!!!!!!!!!!!!!!!!!!!!!!!!!!!!!!!!!!!!!!!!!
!!!!!!!!!!!!!!!!!!!!!!!!!!!!!!!!!!!!!!!!!!!!!!!!!!!!!!!!!!!!!!!!!!!!!!!
!!!!!!!!!!!!!!!!!!!!!!!!!!!!!!!!!!!!!!!!!!!!!!!!!!!!!!!!!!!!!!!!!!!!!!!
!!!!!!!!!!!!!!!!!!!!!!!!!!!!!!!!!!!!!!!!!!!!!!!!!!!!!!!!!!!!!!
Image installed.
Pix#
```

NOTE While this, undoubtedly, was a temporary problem, I couldn't get these instructions by searching from the www.cisco.co site. Only the older instructions appeared (see the next section). Going to the Cisco TAC site www.cisco.com/tac did locate the latest PIX upgrade document. The point is this: don't forget that site as an additional resource for Cisco technologies.

Older Upgrade Methods

If the PIX Firewall unit is currently running an OS version earlier than 5.1.1 or doesn't have a DES or a 3DES activation key (requiring a new activation key), it will be necessary to use a method virtually identical to the password recovery process.

PIX Units Without a Floppy Drive

Use exactly the same steps as the password recovery, except use the PIX binary image file, such as **pix622.bin**, as the source filename. In this process, you type a series of one-word commands, followed by an IP address or filename.

1. Start a console session with the PIX unit console port.
2. Make sure the TFTP server is running and the appropriate PIX Firewall binary image (pix*nnn*.bin) file was copied to the folder TFTP uses as its source.
3. Power on the PIX Firewall and, as soon as the startup messages appear, send a BREAK character or press the ESC key. For Windows HyperTerminal, use CTRL+BREAK.

You might have to do this several times. The **monitor>** prompt will indicate success.

4. Make the following entries, pressing ENTER after each. The command is repeated or responded to on the next line.

   After the image downloads, when you're prompted to install the new image, type **y** to install the image in Flash. When you're prompted to enter a new activation key, type **y** if you want to enter a new activation key, or type **n** to keep the existing key.

```
monitor> interface 1                          (PIX interface to TFTP)
0: i8255X @ PCI(bus:0 dev:14 irq:10)
1: i8255X @ PCI(bus:0 dev:13 irq:11)
Using 1: i82557 @ PCI(bus:0 dev:13 irq:11), MAC: 0002.b945.a23c
monitor> address 192.168.1.1                  (PIX interface address)
address 192.168.1.1
monitor> server 192.168.1.10                  (TFTP server address)
server 192.168.1.10
monitor> file pix622.bin                      (PIX image name)
file pix622.bin
monitor> ping 192.168.1.10                    (Test connectivity to TFTP)
Sending 5, 100-byte 0xcde2 ICMP Echoes to 192.168.1.10, timeout is 4 seconds:
!!!!!
Success rate is 100 percent (5/5)
monitor> tftp                                 (execute the TFTP copy)
tftp pix622.bin@192.168.1.10.........................................
Received 1658880 bytes
Cisco Secure PIX Firewall admin loader (3.0) #0: Tue Dec 7:35:46 PST 2002
Flash=i28F640J5 @ 0x300
BIOS Flash=AT29C257 @ 0xfffd8000
Flash version 6.2.2, Install version 6.2.2

Do you wish to copy the install image into flash? [n] y
Installing to flash
Serial Number: 480380761 (0x1ca20759)
Activation Key: 760754d0 39f62229 a4a0245f b5b87e80

Do you want to enter a new activation key? [n] n
Writing 1540152 bytes image into flash...
```

PIX Units with a Floppy Drive

For PIX Classic, 10000, 510, and 520, only two reasons exist to upgrade using a bootable floppy disk:

- The current PIX Software OS version is earlier than 5.1.1.
- The current PIX Software OS version is earlier than 6.1 and the activation key doesn't support DES or 3DES.

Use the following steps to create a bootable floppy disk in Windows.

1. Go to the PIX Software Download page on the www.cisco.com site and download the **rawrite.exe** utility, the PIX binary image (pix*nnn*.bin), and the boothelper (bh*nn*.bin) binary file that matches the upgrade version. For an upgrade to 6.1(1), the three files would be rawrite.exe, pix611.bin, and bh61.bin.

PART IV

2. Place a blank 3.5″ floppy disk in the computer floppy drive, and run the **rawrite.exe**. When prompted, type the name of the file you want written to the floppy disk. If upgrading to PIX versions 5.1 or earlier, type the PIX image itself (**pixnnn.bin**); for upgrading to PIX versions 5.2 or later, type the PIX boothelper file (**bhnn.bin**).
   The following output shows the boothelper results:

   ```
   C:\>rawrite
   RaWrite 1.2 - Write disk file to raw floppy diskette
   Enter source file name: bh61.bin
   Enter destination drive: a:
   Please insert a formatted diskette into drive A: and press -ENTER- :
   Number of sectors per track for this disk is 18.
   Writing image to drive A:. Press ^C to abort.
   Track: 11 Head: 1 Sector: 16
   Done.
   C:\>
   ```

3. Insert the 3.5″ floppy disk just created in the PIX Firewall diskette drive and reboot or power up the PIX.
4. If upgrading to PIX 5.1 or earlier, remove the floppy disk from the PIX drive and reboot the PIX. The new image is loaded.
5. If upgrading to PIX 5.2 or later with the boothelper program on the floppy, the PIX will come up in boothelper mode or Monitor mode. To complete the upgrade, follow the steps for PIX without floppy drive in the last section.

Chapter Review

This chapter looked at the Cisco PIX Device Manager (PDM) as a graphical interface tool to facilitate configuration and monitoring one or more PIX Firewalls. While particularly useful for those administrators who lack a solid knowledge of the PIX Firewall command-line interface (CLI), the PDM is an easy tool for any administrator to use to access most of the PIX functionality.

PDM monitoring features include real-time graphs and data, including connection, IDS, and throughput information for the selected PIX Firewall. You can view up to five days of historical data. The tabbed-page graphical interface with Windows Explorer-like controls on the left side makes it easy to check setting, configuration, or performance.

PDM v2.1, which runs on any PIX Firewall supporting the v6.2 operating system, added two wizards to greatly simplify the basic PIX Firewall setup, as well as both site-to-site and remote access VPN connections.

The failover features are available on the larger PIX devices to provide rapid and reliable redundancy. The two units that make up a failover pair must be physically identical. After configuring the primary unit, the standby will receive the configuration, making it identical to the primary right down to the IP and MAC addresses. Each time the primary boots up, the configuration is copied to the standby unit, or a **write standby** command can be used to accomplish the same thing.

Password recovery and OS upgrade procedures were also covered.

Questions

1 Which one of the following statements is false about Cisco PIX Device Manager (PDM)?

A. It's a Java applet that resides in the PIX Flash

B. It supports Windows (except 3.1 and 95), Sun UNIX, and Red Hat Linux

C. It's a wizards-based application used exclusively for feature setup

D. Version 2.1 requires PIX OS 6.2 or higher

2. Which one of the following statements is false about PDM v2.1?

A. The PIX unit must have an activation key for DES or 3DES

B. It will run on any PIX Firewall

C. If the PIX Firewall is running software version 6.2, then the PDM requirements to install v2.1 have already been met

D. At least 8MB of Flash memory is required

3. Which one of the following statements is false about web browsers for PDM v2.1?

A. It must be Java-enabled

B. All versions of Netscape are supported on all three platforms

C. It must support HTTPS (HTTP over SSL)

D. Cisco recommends Internet Explorer on the Windows hosts for PDM

4. Which one of the following commands will upgrade the PDM software?

A. **pixfirwall# copy tftp flash:pdm**

B. **pixfirwall# copy tftp flash**

C. **pixfirwall# copy tftp pdm-211.bin flash**

D. **C:> copy pdm-211.bin \flash**

5. Which command would launch PDM?

A. **http://192.168.1.1**

B. **http://192.168.1.1/pdm**

C. **https://192.168.1.1**

D. **http://192.168.1.1:pdm**

6. If a **write erase** and **reload** command are issued on a PIX, what command will prompt for the minimum configuration required to run PDM?

A. **startup**

B. **Wizards | Startup Wizard**

C. **setup**

D. **autoconfig**

7. Which one is not a PDM Wizard in v2.1?
   A. Site-to-site VPN
   B. AAA setup
   C. Startup
   D. Remote access VPN
8. How many missed failover hellos trigger a PIX failover?
   A. 1
   B. 2
   C. 4
   D. It can be configured to any value
9. Which PIX platform can't be used with the failover feature?
   A. 506/506e
   B. 515/515e
   C. 520s
   D. 535
10. Which two pairs of software licenses can be used for a PIX failover pair?
   A. Unrestricted (UR)/Unrestricted (UR)
   B. Failover (FO)/Failover (FO)
   C. Unrestricted (UR)/Failover (FO)
   D. Unrestricted (UR)/Restricted (R)
11. Which failover method yields the least disruption of dataflows?
   A. Serial failover
   B. LAN failover
   C. Stateful failover
   D. Dynamic failover
12. Which is a PIX 500 Firewall password recovery lockout utility name?
   A. lu62.bin
   B. pix62.bin
   C. pix62.lu
   D. np62.bin
13. Which one statement is true about PIX password recovery?
   A. V6.2 password recovery is the same as for routers
   B. V6.2 password recovery is the same on all PIX platforms

C. Password recovery is dependent on the PIX platform and the current OS version

D. Password recovery requires a floppy disk and the rawrite file

14. To use the **copy tftp flash** command for OS upgrades, what two conditions must be true?

A. PIX Firewall unit is currently running an OS versions 5.1.1 or later

B. PIX Firewall unit has a floppy disk drive

C. PIX Firewall unit has a DES or 3DES activation key

D. PIX Firewall unit doesn't have a floppy disk drive

15. Which is a PIX Firewall OS filename?

A. pix622.bin

B. bh622.bin

C. pix622.exe

D. np622.bin

Answers

1. **C.** It's a wizards-based application used exclusively for feature setup. While it has two wizards, it can also be used for routine admin and monitoring
2. **B.** It will run on any PIX Firewall. It will run only on those supporting OS v6.2
3. **B.** All versions of Netscape are supported on all three platforms. Netscape 6.*x* or 7 aren't supported
4. **A.** **pixfirwall# copy tftp flash:pdm**
5. **C.** **https://192.168.1.1**
6. **C.** **setup**
7. **B.** AAA setup
8. **B.** 2
9. **A.** 506/506e
10. **A.** Unrestricted (UR)/Unrestricted (UR). and C. Unrestricted (UR)/Failover (FO)
11. **C.** Stateful failover
12. **D.** np62.bin
13. **C.** Password recovery is dependent on the PIX platform and the current OS version
14. **D. and C.** PIX Firewall unit is currently running an OS versions 5.1.1 or later, and PIX Firewall unit has a DES or 3DES activation key
15. **A.** pix622.bin

PART V

Intrusion Detection Systems (IDS)

CHAPTER 23

Intrusion Detection System Overview

In this chapter, you will learn to:

- Explain intrusion detection
- Identify the four types of security threats
- Identify the three types of attacks
- Understand the three phases of an attack
- Explain the difference between host-based and network-based intrusion detection
- Understand the difference between anomaly and misuse triggering mechanisms

The purpose of an intrusion detection system (IDS) is to notify the appropriate personnel when an intrusion or attack is discovered. You can detect attacks or intrusion into your computer network or systems in numerous ways and various IDS systems exist to detect these attacks. Just as a burglar alarm can be installed in a business to notify the police of an intrusion, an IDS system can be installed on your computer network to detect intrusions and notify security personnel.

This chapter provides an overview of intrusion detection by describing the four types of security threats, the types of attacks, and the phases of an attack. Additionally, this chapter examines the different types of IDS, and discusses the strengths and weaknesses of each type.

Security Threats

To protect your systems completely, you must first recognize who or what you're protecting them from. What typically comes to mind when discussing network security is protecting the network from mysterious hackers operating from a dark room full of sophisticated computer systems. This is rarely the case. According to the FBI, up to 80 percent (1999) of all security breaches reported are from internal sources. Internal security threats range from a novice server administrator or user who unknowingly installs software or opens an e-mail attachment to a disgruntled employee who attempts to delete source code from a development server.

To prepare for and defend against threats properly, you must first understand the types of threats to your network security. Four basic network security threats exist.

- Internal threats
- External threats
- Unstructured threats
- Structured threats

Internal Threats

The term "internal attack" is used to describe an attack being implemented from a person or organization with some level of authorized access on your network. Internal attacks are performed from within the trusted area of the network. This type of threat can be more difficult to defend against because employees already have access to the network and private company data. To compound the internal threat further, most companies only have firewalls at the edge of their networks, and they rely strictly on access control lists (ACL) and server permission to regulate internal security. Server permissions typically protect resources located on the local servers, but provide little or no protection for the network. Internal threats are typically executed by disgruntled employee(s) who want to "get back" at the company.

Many, if not all, of the security measures are logically connected to the perimeter of the network, protecting the inside networks from the external connections, such as the Internet. While the perimeter of the network is secured, the inside or trusted portion of the network tends to be soft. Once an intruder has made it through the hard outer shell of the network, compromising one system after another is usually simple.

Wireless networks introduce a new area of concern for Security Administrators. Unlike cabled networks, wireless networks create a realm of coverage that can be intercepted and used by anyone with the right software and a wireless network adapter. Not only can all network data be viewed and recorded, but network attacks can also be launched from inside the network where the infrastructure is much more vulnerable. Because of the severe security implications, strong encryption should always be used with wireless networks.

External Threats

External threats are posed by any organization, government, or individual that attempts to gain access from outside the company's network and includes anyone that doesn't have authorized access to the internal network. Typically, external attackers attempt to gain access from dialup servers or Internet connections. External threats are what companies spend the most time and money trying to prevent.

STUDY TIP External threats are from anyone that doesn't have authorized access on the internal network.

Unstructured Threats

Unstructured threats are the most prevalent threats to a company's system infrastructure. Novice hackers, commonly called *script kiddies,* download software developed by more advanced hackers and use this software to gain information, access, or perform a DoS attack against a target system or company. Script kiddies rely on the software and experience of the more advanced hackers.

While script kiddies don't have much experience or knowledge, they can wreak havoc on an unsuspecting and/or unprepared company. What kiddies lack in sophistication, they make up for in shear numbers. While this might seem like a game to the kiddies, the companies that fall prey to these basic attacks stand to lose millions of dollars, as well as the public's trust. If a company's web server is broken into and defaced, the public believes hackers have successfully broken through the companies' security, when hackers have only hacked into one vulnerable server. Web, FTP, SMTP, and any other servers offering services on the Internet are all much more vulnerable to attack, while more important and mission-critical servers reside behind multiple levels of security. The general public doesn't understand that breaking into a company web site is much easier than cracking the company's credit card database. The public has to trust that a company is competent in securing its private information.

Structured Threats

Structured threats are the hardest to prevent and defend against because they come from organizations or individuals that use some sort of methodology to gain unauthorized access. Intelligence organizations, organized crime, and governments are the potential backers of a structured threat. Hackers with advanced knowledge, experience, and equipment make up structured threats.

Experienced hackers understand how packets are formed and can develop code to exploit vulnerabilities within the protocol structure. Organizations or individuals that perform structured attacks are also aware of the countermeasures used to prevent unauthorized access, as well as the IDS systems and how they detect intruders. They know methods of evading those protective measures. These highly motivated and technically competent intruders can create customized code, use existing tools, or even modify existing applications to perform according to their methodology.

STUDY TIP In some cases, a structured attack is performed by or with the assistance of someone on the inside. This is referred to as a *structured internal threat.* Structured and unstructured threats can be either internal threats or external threats.

The Attack Types and Phases

Attacks on network systems can be divided into three types and three phases. The three types of attacks are reconnaissance, access, and denial of service (DoS). The first phase is defining the objective of the attack. The second phase, reconnaissance, is both a type of an attack and a phase of the attack. The third and final phase is the actual intrusion or attack on the network resources. As the phases of an attack progress, the type of attack can also change. The second phase of an attack, reconnaissance, would, by definition, include a reconnaissance attack, while the third phase, attack, would include a DoS or an access attack. DoS attacks are discussed in the section "Denial of Service (DoS) Attacks."

Attack Types

As stated, the three types of attacks are reconnaissance, access, and DoS. Reconnaissance is both a type of attack and a phase of an attack. Intruders typically perform reconnaissance on a target network before attempting to access or disrupt the network resources. The performing of reconnaissance on a target network is considered an attack.

Reconnaissance Attacks

Reconnaissance is the unauthorized data collection of system resources, vulnerabilities, or services. Access and DoS attacks are normally preceded by reconnaissance attacks. Hackers obviously have to know what's available to attack before launching any intrusion. Reconnaissance is analogous to a bank robber casing a bank to find out how many security guards are on duty, how many cameras exist and their placement, and what escape route to use. Reconnaissance is more than a type of attack—it's also a phase of attack. Discussion of the need for, and the tools used for, reconnaissance attacks are discussed in more detail in several upcoming sections on reconnaissance and the section "Reconnaissance Tools."

Access Attacks

Access is a broad term used to describe any attack that requires the intruder to gain unauthorized access to a secure system with the intent to manipulate data, elevate privileges, or simply access the system. The term "access attack" is used to describe any attempt to gain system access, perform data manipulation, or elevate privileges.

System Access Attacks *System access* is the act of gaining unauthorized access to a system for which the attacker doesn't have a user account. Hackers usually gain access to a device by running a script or a hacking tool, or exploiting a known vulnerability of an application or service running on the host.

Data Manipulation Access Attacks Data manipulation occurs when an intruder simply reads, copies, writes, deletes, or changes data that isn't intended to be accessible by the intruder. This could be as simple as finding a share on a Windows 9*x* or NT computer, or as difficult as attempting to gain access to a credit bureau's information, or breaking into the department of motor vehicles to change a driving record.

Elevating Privileges Access Attacks Elevating privileges is a common type of attack. By elevating privileges an intruder can gain access to files, folders or application data that the user account was not initially granted access to. Once the hacker has gained a high-enough level of access, they can install applications, such as *backdoors* and *Trojan horses,* to allow further access and reconnaissance. A common goal of hackers is to gain root or administrator-level access. Once administrator or root-level access is accomplished, the intruder can gain complete control of the server, host, or network system.

Denial of Service (DoS) Attacks

DoS attacks are performed with the intent of disabling, corrupting, or crashing network resources to prevent the use of these systems by the intended users. This electronic vandalism is one of the worst types of attacks faced by e-businesses because the only intent of the hackers is to prevent customers from using the company's electronic storefront. The intent of this type of attack is simply to do damage and prevent the target company from conducting business.

Some script tools attempt to take advantage of a known exploit to damage a host or network, while others generate large amounts of network traffic. A hacker with a home PC would have a difficult time in generating enough traffic to overload an Internet class server. To perform an effective DoS attack, hackers use many different computers in an attempt to overwhelm the target host. Using many computer systems to attack a host or network is called a distributed denial of service attack (DDoS). This type of attack has been successful when used against the web sites of Yahoo!, eBay, and CNN.com. One hacker who performed this type of attack was later caught and prosecuted. See http://www.nipc.gov/investigations/mafiaboy.htm for more details on this attack.

NOTE A known exploit or vulnerability is simply a security flaw in an application, service, or operating system (OS) that can be used by an intruder to violate or bypass system security. Vendors of these software products usually release patches to fix these security flaws. This is why it's important to keep current with all security patches for any software installed on your network.

Hackers could use one or all of these attack types to gain unauthorized access to a target network or system. Most access and DDoS attacks are preceded by a reconnaissance attack, which might have been ongoing for days, weeks, or even months. A hacker could also perform a DoS attack on one portion of the network, while attempting to gain access to other network resources.

Attack Phases

Attacks follow a general structure that takes them from planning through execution and, if they aren't detected and halted, success. The structure consists of three core phases that, though they could vary in detail, are designed toward the same goal. The three phases are objective, reconnaissance, and attack.

Phase One—Objective

The first phase is the objective phase. The first thing to understand in any project, hacking included, is what is the objective or goal. For example, the goal of a DDoS attack is different from that of a system access attack. As a result of identifying the objective of the attack, the determination of appropriate tools and methodology is made. The tools and methodology used to perform a DDoS attack are different than the tools and methodology of attempting to gain system access. The objective is simply the overall goal of the intruder. If the attacker is motivated by revenge, then a DoS attack might suit their needs. If the attacker is a competitor, system access and data manipulation could be the objective.

As the intruder goes through the phases of an attack, the objectives can, and usually do, change. If the overall objective is to manipulate data, then the first objective is to gain system access. Once system access is obtained, the intruder can then attempt to elevate privileges for a compromised user account. Once the privileges have been elevated, the intruder can then use the account to access the objective server and change the data. This is an example of a structured attack.

Another significant factor in determining the objective is the motivation behind the intrusions. Most script kiddies are motivated by revenge, as well as the thrill and excitement, while more advanced hackers are motivated by the intellectual challenge, revenge, or monetary gain.

Phase Two—Reconnaissance

The *reconnaissance phase,* as the name implies, is the stage in which the hacker uses various resources to collect information about the target network or system. The collection of information isn't limited to information about the network or hosts on the network, however. Sophisticated and experience hackers will collect information about the target company, such as company location, phone numbers, employee names, e-mail addresses, and company vendors, all of which can be useful to the experienced intruder.

Reconnaissance—Public Information Employee names and e-mail addresses provide a good start in guessing the user name for an employee's account. Common practice is to use an employee's first initial and last name as the user name for their network computer account. E-mail addresses are also a common user name for computer accounts. Large companies usually have their phone numbers assigned in blocks from the local telephone company and many large corporations have their own dialing prefix. By using this information, the intruder can begin war dialing all the company's phone numbers looking for a dial-up server. Once a dial-up server is found, the intruder can begin guessing account user names, based on an employee's first initial and last name or e-mail addresses. Brute-force password crackers are freely available on the Internet. Once a user name is guessed, it's only a matter of time before a weak password can be cracked.

NOTE A *war dialer* is a program used to dial blocks of phone numbers until it finds a computer on the other end of the line. Once a computer is found, the war dialer application records the number dialed for later use by the intruder.

To use a user account on a server or a network, you must first have the user name and password. Discovering the user names is a fairly straightforward process, as you can see in the preceding paragraph. Attackers use password crackers to crack the passwords to user accounts. Some password crackers find the encrypted password files on the server and decrypt them. When a hacker is unable to retrieve the password files, then brute-force password crackers are used. Brute-force password crackers attempt to log in to a computer account over and over, using multiple password combinations. Some cracking software uses dictionary files, while others attempt every combination of each key on the keyboard, an extremely time-consuming ordeal.

Commonly used password crackers are the following:

Microsoft Windows	UNIX
L0phtCrack 4	Qcrack by the Crypt Keeper
PWLVIEW	CrackerJack by Jackal
Pwlhack 4.10	John the Ripper by Solar Designer
PWL-Key	Crack by Alec Muffet
ntPassword	

Internet Protocol (IP) address information is publicly available via the ARIN and many other Internet-registering authorities. From www.arin.net, anyone can begin a search using a single known IP address. The search will yield the complete block of IP addresses belonging to the company. Domain Naming Systems (DNS) is another publicly available system that can provide a wealth of information regarding the IP addressing and naming strategies of virtually any company connected to the Internet.

For a company to host its own e-mail, web, ftp, or any other service on the Internet, it must first have each of these servers listed within the DNS infrastructure. These DNS servers list the name of the servers, along with the IP addresses that can be used to access these services. To mitigate these risks, security-conscious companies might choose to host these servers and services outside their private networks with a hosting company. Companies can then host these services for their customers and users, without the worry of hackers using these servers or services to attack their private network.

Electronic Reconnaissance The attacker must perform electronic reconnaissance to find what systems and resources are on the network. Unless the attacker has prior knowledge of the target network, he or she must find where the company's resources are logically located. Once the company's IP addresses are known (see the previous Public Information section), the attacker can begin to probe and scan the network. The intruder can scan the network looking for vulnerable hosts, applications, or infrastructure equipment.

Scanning the network is typically done using a ping sweep utility that will ping a range of IP addresses. The purpose of this scanning is to find what hosts are currently live on the network. The ping sweep identifies viable targets on the network. Once the IP address of viable hosts is known, the attacker can then begin to probe those hosts to gather additional information, such as the OS or applications running on those hosts.

Probing is defined as attempting to discover information about the hosts on the network. Probing is accomplished by looking for open ports on the available host computers. *Ports* are like virtual doorways to the computer. For a computer to offer or use services on the network, it must first have an open port. Web servers typically use port 80, while FTP servers use port 21. An attacker can find out what services are running on a computer by discovering what ports that computer has opened.

NOTE TCP/IP uses port addresses to locate services running on host computers. The port numbers used by the application are that application's address on that host. The address for a web application located on host 10.0.0.1 would be 10.0.0.1:80. This address specifies the host address 10.0.0.1 and the application address of 80. Most common applications use well-defined port numbers. A list of well-known port numbers managed by the Internet Assigned Number Authority (IANA) can be viewed at http://www.iana.org/assignments/port-numbers.

The more open ports, the more potential for someone to exploit the services running on the host computer. Once the attacker knows which ports are open, he or she can use this information further to discover the OS and application servicing the port.

The purpose of this scanning and probing is to find weaknesses on the network. Intruders know the vulnerabilities of certain OSs and the applications they run. The intruder increases his or her chance of succeeding by finding the weakest point on the network and, later, attacking that vulnerability. The attacker continues to discover information about the network until he has a complete map of the hosts, servers, and weaknesses to exploit in the future.

Reconnaissance Tools The most common and widely available hacking tools are reconnaissance (recon) tools. The purpose of most recon tools is to assist engineers in troubleshooting, documenting, or maintaining their networks, but hackers use these tools to map network resources illegally. Many of these tools have been developed or modified by hackers to aid them in their illicit activities. Many tools are also developed under the guise of being a legitimate tool for network engineers but, in truth, are built to aid hackers.

As security and intrusion detection have become more sophisticated, so has the software used by hackers. Intrusion-detection software looks for people or software probing or scanning the network. Hackers know scanning and probing a network is likely to create suspicion and could generate alarms. Because of this, hackers have begun to develop new software that attempts to hide the true purpose of its activity. Reconnaissance tools commonly used today include the following:

NMAP	WHOIS
SATAN	Ping
Portscanner	Nslookup
Strobe	Trace

Phase Three—Attack Phase

The final phase is the attack phase. In the *attack phase,* the intruder begins to attempt accessing network and system resources on the network. Using information gathered during the reconnaissance phase, the hacker already knows the host IP addresses, open ports, and OSs in use. Some hackers might go as far as to build a test bed, mimicking the target systems. With this test bed, the hacker can practice attacking the system over and over until a vulnerability is found that can be exploited. Once the hacker has found a vulnerability and is confident in their ability, they will begin to attack the actual target system.

Once a hacker has successfully gained access to a host on the network, that host is described as being compromised. Any systems that have a trust relationship with the compromised host must also be considered compromised.

Attacking IP Trust Relationships Common practice is to establish IP trust relationships between computer and network systems. A trust relationship simply means host A will only accept connections to a particular port from host B with a known and trusted IP address. Any other connection attempts from other IP addresses or hosts are denied. These trust relationships can be configured within the OSs of the hosts or as access lists configured on the routers between the hosts. A common use for these trust relationships is to allow web servers to connect to database servers within the trusted network.

As you can see in Figure 23-1, the firewall has been configured to deny any packets from the Internet with the destination address of the database server. Because the web server needs access to the database server, the firewall has also been configured to permit packets from only the web server to the database server. The database server could also be

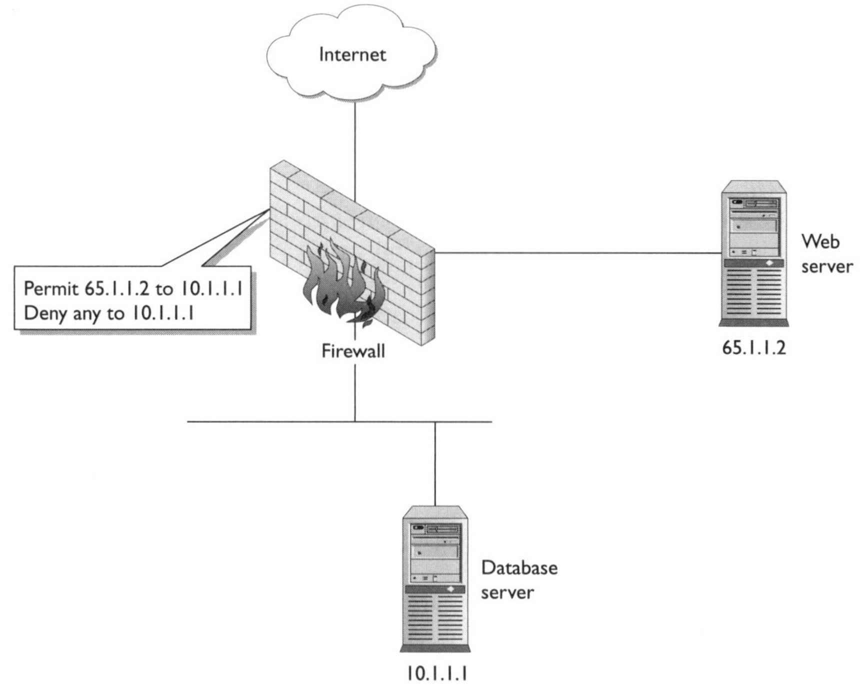

Figure 23-1 Attacking IP trust relationships between compromised hosts

configured to allow access from only the web server, as well. Once a hacker has compromised the web server, the hacker could use this trust relationship to continue the attack on the database server. Once the database server has been compromised, the hacker can continue to use each trust relationship to access each machine on the network.

Trust relationships are easy to attack and use by intruders because they're based on weak or no authentication. IP provides no way to authenticate that a packet came from the source address listed in the IP header. Another weak authentication mechanism used in trust relationships is DNS-based authentication. DNS-based authentication suffers from the same weaknesses as IP-based authentication in that no method exists to insure an address isn't being spoofed.

STUDY TIP *Spoofing* is the act of changing the source IP address listed in the IP header. IP packets include the sending computer's IP address in the IP header, which is called the *source address.* This information is read by the receiving host, allowing it to respond to the sending host. Some hacking software allows the hacker to change the source address to be any address they want, and is typically changed to an address within the internal network or a nonroutable IP address.

Intrusion Detection Systems Overview

Firewalls are the modern-day equivalent to dead bolts and security bars. The purpose of a firewall is to prevent unauthorized access. Just as locks can be manipulated, firewalls can also be compromised. Enterprises long ago learned not to rely on locks alone. Someone or something must be present to protect the company's assets once someone or something has breached the first line of defense. IDSs are the modern-day equivalent to the burglar alarm. IDSs constantly monitor the network to look for suspicious activity and, once discovered, can be configured to notify security personnel of the suspected intrusion. Unlike burglar alarms, which can only send an alert that a breach has been made, an IDS can also be configured to take action to prevent further access, while sending alarms and recording information about the intruder(s).

While the basic function of all IDS systems is to detect intruders, two different types of intrusion-detection systems exist—host-based IDSs and network-based IDSs—and two different methodologies are used to detect intruders. Each can use one of two methods to detect intruders. Host-based IDSs are typically software installed on host computers and are used to analyze all traffic received by the host computer. Network-based intrusion detection uses probes to analyze and monitor all traffic on the target network.

IDS systems can use one of two possible methods to detect intruders. The first method—profile-based IDS—uses profiles created by the security administrator to define normal traffic and activity. Traffic that doesn't match a configured profile is called an *anomaly.* Because profile-based detection will alarm once a set threshold of anomalies is exceeded, profile-based detection is also referred to as *anomaly detection.* The second method of detection is called signature-based detection. *Signature-based detection systems* have a preconfigured set of signatures that are compared with network traffic to detect an attack or intrusion. Just as virus scanners use signatures to recognize viruses, IDSs use signatures to recognize common attacks or exploits used by hackers.

While numerous IDS vendors and methods exist, all IDSs can be described and evaluated by examining the type of IDS, host, or network, plus the methods used to trigger an alarm, profile, or signature. IDS systems that use a combination of host and network, or trigger on both signatures and profiles, are called hybrid systems. *Hybrid systems* attempt to combine the strengths of each type and detection method, while eliminating the weaknesses.

Host- and Network-Based IDSs

IDS systems can be installed on a host, on the network, or on a combination of both. Each monitoring location has its own benefits and drawbacks. *Network monitoring* requires the installation of probes on the network that's to be monitored, while *host-based monitoring* requires that software be installed on all host systems to be monitored. Both types of IDS are configured to send alarms and events to a central location.

Host-based and network-based IDSs send alerts and alarms to a centralized location where security administrators can view them. CIDS sensors can be managed using Cisco Secure Policy Manager (CSPM). Additionally, sensors can be configured using the built in Device Manager application included with the sensor software. Alarms and events can be collected and viewed using Cisco's Event Viewer. These applications are discussed in more detail in Chapter 25.

Host-Based Detection

By installing a software agent on all hosts, host-based IDSs monitor all system activities, log files, and network traffic received. Host-based systems might also monitor the OS, system calls, audit logs, and error messages on the host system. While network probes can detect an attack, only host-based systems can determine whether the attack was successful. Additionally, host-based systems can record what the attacker performed on the compromised host.

Not all attacks are performed over the network. By gaining physical access to a computer system, an intruder can attack a system or data without generating any network traffic. Host-based systems can detect attacks that are out-of-band or performed from the console, but a savvy intruder with knowledge of the IDSs can quickly disable any detection software once physical access is accomplished. Neither host nor network-based IDS is a replacement for proper physical security.

NOTE *Out-of-band* is a term used to describe any traffic or access that doesn't traverse the public or monitored network. Common out-of-band access methods are a private network, a console connection, or an RS232 serial connection between two or more hosts.

Another advantage for host-based monitoring is its capability to detect stealth attacks. Some network-based IDS systems can be fooled by playing with the fragmentation or TTL of the packets. For a host to process traffic, it must be received and reassembled, and, therefore, it's subject to monitoring by the host-based IDS. Packet fragmentation and Time to Live (TTL) manipulation are discussed in the section "Network-Based IDS."

Host-Based Drawbacks Host-based IDSs have four key disadvantages or weaknesses:

- Manageability
- Micro view of network attacks
- Compromised hosts
- Operating systems limitations

Depending on host-based IDSs requires the IDS software be installed on all hosts. This can become an administrative nightmare as version control, software maintenance, and software configuration become a time-consuming and complicated task.

Because host-based systems only analyze traffic received by the host, they can't detect common reconnaissance attacks performed against the host or a range of hosts. Host-based IDSs won't detect ping sweeps or port scans performed across a range of hosts.

When a host-based IDS detects an attack, it sends a notification to the management station or the sensor responsible for collecting and recording alarms. If the host is compromised, it might be possible for the intruder to disable the IDS software or that host's network connection. If the IDS software or the network connection are disabled, the host won't generate an alert.

IDS software must be installed on each system on the network to provide complete coverage of the network. In heterogeneous environments, this can become a problem because the IDS software must support so many different OSs. Before deciding on an IDS system, you should ensure the IDS software will run on each OS present on the network.

Network-Based IDSs

Network-based IDSs uses probes or sensors installed throughout the network. These probes sniff the network looking for traffic that matches a defined profile or signature. Sensors receive and analyze traffic in real time. Once a traffic pattern or signature is recognized, the probe sends an alert to the management platform and can be configured to take action to prevent any additional access.

NOTE *Sniffing the network* is a term used to describe a network interface that receives all network traffic. Typically, a network interface only processes packets that are specifically addressed to the host or the broadcast address. By placing the interface in Promiscuous mode, the interface can receive, process, and analyze all traffic traversing the network, regardless of the Layer 2 or 3 address. Legitimate tools used by network engineers to view all network traffic are commonly called *network sniffers*.

Network-based detection has the advantage of seeing intrusions from a network perspective. While host-based detection can't detect a ping sweep or a port scan across multiple hosts, network-based IDSs can easily detect such reconnaissance attacks. Network-based sensors generate an alert when these reconnaissance attacks are discovered.

Network-based IDSs don't depend on the resources of a host machine and, therefore, won't use valuable network and CPU cycles on mission-critical servers. Additionally, because there's no software to install, there are no issues with OS compatibility. With network-based IDSs, the IDS software runs only on the director and the sensors.

Sensors have an interface used for monitoring the network (monitoring interface) and a second interface used for command and control (command and control interface). Sensors can't send network traffic on the monitoring interface (MI) and are, thereby, invisible to anyone unfamiliar with the security features of the network. The command and control interface (CCI) can send and receive management traffic, and this is the interface used to communicate with the management or director computer(s).

To ensure proper security, the network-based IDS should have a separate and highly secure management network. The director platforms and sensors will communicate with one another via this secured management network. Each probe will use this network to send alarms to the director platform, and the director platform will use this management network to configure and update each network sensor.

Network-Based Drawbacks Network-based intrusion detection has four basic weaknesses:

- Bandwidth
- Packet fragmentation and reassembly
- TTL manipulation
- Encryption

One of the more difficult weaknesses to compensate for is the bandwidth limitation of network-based intrusion detection. Network probes must receive all network traffic, reassemble that traffic, and analyze the traffic. As network speeds increase, so must the capabilities of the intrusion detection probes. The solution is to ensure the network is designed properly to allow the strategic placement of multiple probes. As the network grows, more probes can be added to ensure proper coverage and security.

One way hackers attempt to conceal their activity from network-based IDS is to fragment their packets. Each protocol has a maximum packet size. If data to be sent across the network is larger than the maximum packet size, the packet must be fragmented. *Fragmentation* is simply the process of breaking up data into smaller pieces. These pieces must be put back together in the correct order for proper analyzing. Some OSs reassemble packets first to last, while others reassemble packets last to first. The order of reassembly isn't an issue as long as no overlap occurs. If a fragmentation overlap occurs, the sensor must know the correct reassembly process. Many hackers attempt to prevent detection by sending overlapping fragmented packets. A sensor won't detect intrusion activity if the sensor is unable to reassemble the packets correctly.

NOTE Maximum packet size, also known as maximum transmission unit (MTU), is dependant on the type of network used. Ethernet typically has a MTU of 1,500 bytes, while token ring, for example, can have an MTU of 8,000 bytes or more.

Manipulating the TTL field on multiple packets is another technique used to fool network-based sensors. All TCP/IP packets have a TTL field, which specifies how long a packet should be considered valid on the network. The initial value of the TTL field can range from 1 to 255. Each time a packet passes through a router, the TTL is decremented by 1. When the TTL value reaches zero, the packet is discarded and is no longer forwarded. Figure 23-2 shows how an attacker might use a TTL attack to try and fool a network-based IDS. As you can see in Figure 23-2, the attacker can send packets with a lowered TTL that will reach the sensor, but not the host. Additional packets are sent that reach both the sensor and the host. TTL manipulation is ineffective if the probe and the host are located on the same local area network (LAN).

Using a TTL attack, an intruder can send hundreds of packets to the target network with a lowered TTL. Packets with the lowered TTL reach the sensor, but won't be forwarded to the host. When the packets reach the router, the TTL is decremented and the packet is discarded. At the same time, the intruder could then send actual attack traffic with a normal TTL that will reach both the sensor and the host. In essence, the attacker is

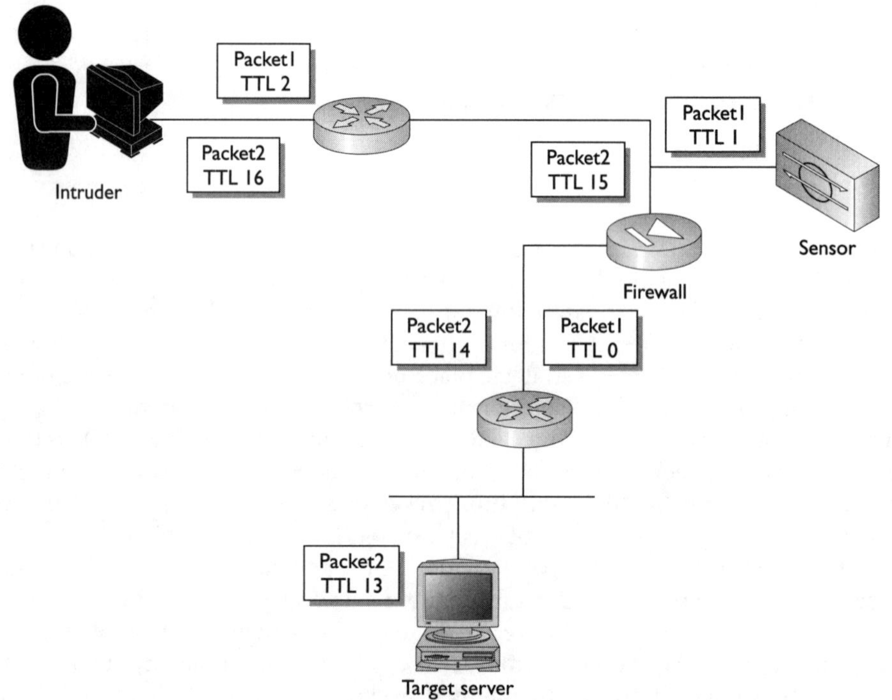

Figure 23-2 Manipulating network-based sensors using TTL

attempting to confuse the sensor by hiding malicious traffic within a stream of valid or nonsuspicious traffic. Because an attacker must have a detailed view of the network beforehand, this isn't a simple attack to use successfully. This type of attack can only be used against network-based IDSs.

The third weakness of network-based IDSs is created through the use of encryption. To work properly, an IDS must read the contents of packets that cross the network. If the data held within the packet is encrypted, the sensor has no way of viewing the contents. If your network uses VPNs, IPSec, or any other form of encryption, then it's important to place sensors outside the encrypted tunnels. Outside the encrypted tunnel, packets are no longer encrypted and, therefore, can be read by the sensor.

Hybrid IDSs

Hybrid IDSs attempt to combine the benefits of each type of IDS, while eliminating the weaknesses. In a hybrid system, both the sensors and the hosts report to a centralized management or director platform.

Presenting information gathered from both network-based sensors and host-based software can be a challenge for hybrid IDS vendors. While more information is usually better, too much information from too many sources can be difficult to manage and understand.

While hybrid systems attempt to combine the benefits of both network and host-based systems, they also can incorporate both signature-based and anomaly-triggering mechanisms. Triggering mechanisms, discussed in the next section, describe how an IDS system detects intruders.

IDS Triggers

The purpose of an IDS system is to alert the appropriate personnel once an intrusion is detected. Burglar alarm systems trigger an alarm based on a motion detector, a broken window, or an opened door. IDS also have two types of triggering mechanisms.

IDSs are merely packet sniffers with the capability to do some basic analyzing. These systems don't inherently know the difference between normal traffic and malicious traffic. For the IDS to recognize malicious traffic or activity, you must first "teach" the IDS what constitutes an attack. The IDS then compares actual network traffic or computer activity with what has been defined as malicious and, if a match is made, an alarm is triggered.

Not all systems use the same method of triggering an alarm and each type of triggering system has its own strengths and weaknesses. To choose the appropriate IDS system for your environment, you must first understand each type of triggering system, as well as the benefits and drawbacks of each. Modern IDSs use two types of triggering mechanisms:

- Anomaly Detection (Profile based)
- Misuse Detection (Signature based)

STUDY TIP The terms "anomaly detection" and "profile based," and the terms "misuse detection" and "signature based" are used interchangeably.

Misuse Detection

Misuse detection is commonly referred to as signature-based detection. *Misuse detection* requires the use of signature files that identify intrusive activity. The signature files used in misuse detection are analogous to signature files commonly used in virus-scanning software to identify viruses on computer systems.

A *signature file* is a set of rules used to identify common intrusive activity. The research of highly skilled engineers discovered attacks, patterns, and methods to write signature files to identify them. As more attack methods and exploits are discovered, the IDS vendor will provide updates to signature files, just as virus-scanning vendors provide updates to their own software. Once the signature files are updated, the IDS system will begin analyzing all activity searching for a match. If activity or traffic is found that matches the signature, an alarm is triggered. IDS systems typically come with a database of signatures for common attacks and exploits.

Signature-Based Benefits

Signature files are created based on known attack methods and activity, so if a match is made, a high probability exists that an attack is underway. Misuse detection, unlike anomaly detection, will have fewer false positive reports because matches are based on a known intrusive activity, not just unusual traffic. Signature-based detection doesn't monitor traffic patterns or look for anomalies. Instead, it monitors activity simply looking for a match to any configured signature.

Because misuse detection relies on signatures—not traffic patterns—the IDS system can be configured and can begin protecting the network immediately. The signatures contained in the signature database contain the known intrusive activity and a description of the signature. Each signature in the database can be viewed, enabled, or disabled. Different levels of alarms, as well as different preventative actions, can be configured for individual signatures, giving security administrators granular control of their IDS systems.

Misuse detection is easier to understand and configure than anomaly-based systems. Signature files can be viewed so administrators can understand what actions must be matched for an alarm to be generated. Security administrators can enable signatures, and then perform a test on the network and view the resulting alarm that's generated. Because misuse detection is easier to understand, implement, and test, administrators have a higher degree of control and more confidence in their IDSs.

Misuse Detection Drawbacks

While there are many benefits to misuse detection triggers, some drawbacks exist to this form of intrusion detection. Misuse detection is simpler to configure and understand, but this simplicity comes at a cost of lost functionality and administrative overhead. Misuse detection has the following drawbacks:

- Inability to detect new or unknown attacks
- Inability to detect variations of known attacks
- Signature database administration
- Sensors must maintain state information

Inability to Detect New Attacks Misuse detection accomplishes its mission by comparing computer network activity to known intrusive activity defined in the signature database. If an attack is instigated that doesn't match a known intrusive activity, the sensors typically won't generate and alert. The IDS system using misuse detection must be aware of the activity of an attack before it can identify that attack. New attacks that haven't previously been used or discovered normally won't be detected by a misuse detection IDS. Signature files are created to be as flexible as possible and, in some cases, a previously unknown attack will be detected by the IDS. Even though an exact match might not occur, the IDS could detect a previously unknown attack that uses a similar method of attack or intrusion activity. IDS systems must be updated with the latest signatures to be effective. Even if an IDS system has been updated with the latest signature database, it's possible that new types of attacks will won't generate an alert.

Inability to Detect Attack Variations Intruders also have access to the signature files and IDS systems used by security administrators. Because this information is available to everyone, hackers can use this information to test and alter their attack. By altering the attack in some minor way, an intruder might be able to perform an intrusion without being detected (false positive). Signature files are static—they don't adapt as some anomaly-based systems do. If an attack doesn't match a signature file, the sensors won't generate an alarm. Because the signature files are included with the IDS systems, intruders are aware of what will and what won't generate an alarm. Armed with this knowledge, an intruder can customize their attacks to defeat the IDS.

Signature File Administration The responsibility of the security administrator is to ensure the database file is current. The security administrator must also configure the probes with the signatures they want the probes to use, as well as the severity level of each matched signature. Keeping the signature database current with constant updates and applying those updates to all sensors can be a difficult and time-consuming task.

State Information Just like firewalls, sensors must maintain state data. Sensors simply match activity or traffic to preconfigured signatures. In some cases, the amount of data to match a signature could be spread across multiple packets and a variable amount of time. Additionally, hackers might fragment their packets before sending them across the network in an attempt to prevent the packets from being analyzed. Sensors must record this information and recompile it to match it against any signatures. The maximum amount of time a probe must record the state—from the first packet until a match is made—is called the *event horizon*.

The event horizon can range from minutes for some signatures to days or weeks for others. For example, a security administrator might want to be alerted if anyone performs a port scan against their network, but might not want to be notified if only one or two ports are scanned. Some patient hackers might only scan two ports every four hours for a month. Within a couple of weeks, this hacker could have found all the services available on the network, which means it's important for the sensor to remember what ports have been scanned and by whom. But how long should the sensor remember this information? The amount of time the sensor is configured to keep state information for a given signature is called the event horizon for that signature. Some signature files, such as those that detect reconnaissance attacks, have an event horizon that spans weeks, while other attacks have an event horizon that spans the time the user is logged into the network. The event horizon is a variable contained in the signature files.

Sensors have a limited amount of storage available. Most sensors keep this state information recorded in memory for fast retrieval, but the storage space is limited. Hackers might attempt to disable your IDS systems by sending them so much information that the sensor(s) run out of resources and can no longer record state data. Once the sensor has reached its memory limits, it no longer analyzes any additional information. This would be an example of a DoS attack against the IDS itself.

Anomaly Detection

Anomaly- or *profile-based triggering* analyzes computer activity and network traffic looking for anomalies. If an anomaly is found, an alarm is triggered. An anomaly is any deviation or departure from the normal or common order, form, or rule. Because this type of detection is looking for any activity or traffic that isn't normal, the security administrator must first define what is normal activity or traffic. Security administrators can define normal activity by creating user group profiles.

A *user group profile* represents a baseline of normal computer activity and network traffic for a given user group. User groups are defined by the security engineer and can be used to represent users or computers with common job functions, or users and computers within the same departments. Typically, user groups should be divided according to the activities and network resources each group uses. A web server farm could have its own profile based on web traffic, while mail servers could have another profile based on SMTP. You wouldn't expect telnet traffic destined for your web servers or SSH traffic destined for your mail servers. For these reasons, you should have different profiles for each type of service offered on your network.

Various techniques are used for building user profiles and some IDS can be configured to build their own profiles. The typical methods used to build user group profiles are statistical sampling, rule-based, and neural networks. Each profile is used as a definition for normal user and network activity. If a user deviates too far from their defined profile, the IDS system will generate an alert.

Building Profiles Using Statistical Sampling With statistical sampling, alarms are generated based on deviations from a normal state. *Normal state* is defined by sampling normal activity and traffic for a given period of time. *Normalcy* is based on the average or median of all activity or traffic. *Deviations* are measured by calculating the standard deviations.

Standard deviations are simply the amount of activity or data that matches, or doesn't match, a sample, and they measure the deviation from a normal state. For example, if 60 percent of all your data falls within one standard deviation and 35 percent of all your traffic falls within two standard deviations, then only 5 percent of your data falls within three or more deviations. Using this method, the IDS system can detect how abnormal specific activity or traffic is.

Building Profiles Using the Rule-Based Approach *Rule-based profile building* is accomplished by defining rules to define normal user behavior. You must create rules that define normal user activity, and these are created by sampling computer and network activity for a given amount of time. Once the data set has been collected, rules can be created to define normal activity. The rules are models representing normal computer and network activity. Any traffic that doesn't match the rules is considered abnormal and generates alarms.

Building Profiles Using Neural Networks Just as a psychologist can use inkblots to discover how you relate information in your mind, neural networks can use matrix(s) to relate normal activity on your network or computer systems. *Neural networks* are built or trained by presenting the IDS system with large amounts of data and rules about data relationships. Neural networks attempt to use artificial intelligence to build matrixes based on the given information. Relationships between these data inputs are used to build a matrix modeled after the biological neurons, such as those found in the human brain. Once the neural network is established, it can be used as a model or definition of normal activity. Any activity that doesn't map correctly to the matrix or neural network is considered abnormal and generates an alarm.

Anomaly Detection Benefits

Using anomaly detection as the triggering mechanism has many benefits. With anomaly-based detection, the intruder never knows what might or might not generate an alarm, because he or she doesn't have access to the profiles used to detect an attack. User group profiles are much like a dynamic signature database that changes as your network changes. With signature-based detection, the intruder can test on their own IDS system what will generate an alert. Signature files are provided with a purchased IDS system, so a hacker could use their own IDS system to perform testing. Once the hacker understands what will generate an alert, the attacker can then customize his or her attack methodology and tools to defeat the IDS. Because anomaly detection doesn't use a preconfigured signature database, intruders can't be sure what activity will generate an alert.

Anomaly detection can quickly detect an internal attack using a compromised user account. If a user account belonging to an administrative assistant is being used to perform system administration, the IDS system using anomaly detection will generate an alarm as long as that account isn't normally used for system administration.

The biggest advantage to anomaly- or profile-based detection is it isn't based on a set of preconfigured signatures or known attacks. Profiles can be dynamic and can use artificial intelligence to determine what normal activity is. Because profile-based detection isn't based on known signatures, it's better suited to detect previously unknown or unpublished attacks as long as the attack deviates from normal activity (profile). Profile-based detection can be used to detect new attack methods, which signature-based detection won't detect.

Anomaly-Based Drawbacks

While many benefits exist to using anomaly- or profile-based detection, many drawbacks also exist with this method of intrusion detection. Many of the drawbacks of anomaly detection have to do with the creation of user group profiles, as well as the quality of these profiles. Drawbacks with anomaly detection include the following:

- High initial prep time
- No protection during initial training time
- Constant update of profiles as users' habits change
- Defining normal behavior can be difficult
- False positives, false negatives
- Hard to understand

Difficulties with User Group Profiles Anomaly-based detection relies on the use of user group profiles. The IDS is only as good as the profiles being used to define what normal activity is. *Profiles* are a baseline of normal activity, created by sampling network traffic and activity over a set period of time. While creating the user profiles, it's vital no intrusive activity occurs on the network and all systems are free of backdoors or Trojan horses. If intrusive activity occurs on the network during the initial training time, the intrusive activity will be included in the profile and, therefore, the activity will seen as normal activity.

The initial training time should consist of enough data to truly represent normal activity and traffic. The training time could range from days to weeks or even months. Defining normal activity can be a daunting task. What normal activity is in one month could or could not be normal the next month. Users aren't compelled to use the same applications and perform the same functions without deviation. Defining normal activity is even more challenging in environments where users' jobs or responsibilities change often. As users' habits change, the profiles describing normal activity for those users must also change. Additionally, while the system is being "trained," the IDS provides no protection, so it's vital no intrusive activity occurs during this training period.

Creating user profiles can be difficult for advanced users or diverse groups of users. If a user group contains a vast amount of users that all perform different functions, then it's difficult to differentiate normal activity from intrusive activity. System administrators, network engineers, and Unix administrators all generate activity that wouldn't be permissible for other types of users. For this reason, segregating different users according to resources and applications each group uses is important.

Some systems can be configured to update the profile constantly, based on traffic and activity as it's being measured. Statistical sampling, discussed in the previous section, constantly monitors the network and uses the data collected to update the profile. The benefit is this: the profile is always kept current with user activity changes, however, a hacker can use this feature to manipulate the IDS. A hacker could slowly begin performing intrusive activity over a long period of time. Starting with small amounts of activity, and slowly increasing the amount of traffic and activity, the hacker can train the IDS to ignore the intrusive activity. The IDS system will slowly begin to consider the intrusive activity as normal, which will result in false negatives.

False Reporting A *false negative* is a situation when intrusive activity is on the network or systems, yet the intrusive activity goes undetected by the IDS system. If the activity is considered normal, then an alert won't be generated. Anomaly detection is only as good as the profile used to detect intrusive activity. Signature-based detection systems tend to have more false negatives than anomaly-based systems because they aren't suited to discovering new methods of attack.

A *false positive* occurs when the IDS system generates an alarm for activity that isn't considered intrusive. Car alarms, for example, commonly report false positives. IDS systems should be continually tuned to strike a balance between false negatives and false positives. Too many false positives and the IDS system will soon be ignored, much like car alarms are today. Even worse, too many false negatives could result in a great deal of damage. Anomaly-based systems tend to have more false positives because they're looking for anything out of the ordinary.

Difficult to Understand The last major drawback to anomaly-based detection is its complexity. Statistical sampling, rule-based, and neural networks are all profile-building strategies that are hard to explain and understand. Signature-based detection is much simpler to understand: if a given activity matches a signature, then an alarm is sent, along with a notification of which signature was matched. Anomaly detection requires a more in-depth understanding and it's harder to discover why the system generated an alert. Because of its complexity, many security administrators have a difficult time understanding the system and are uncomfortable with the IDS. This lack of understanding might also cause lack of confidence in their IDS.

Summary

IDSs are hardware or software systems used to detect intruders on your network. IDS systems differ according to where they're installed: on the host or on the network, as well as how they detect intruders, misuse detection and anomaly detection. While different types of IDS systems exist, each type of IDS has its own benefits and drawbacks.

A host-based IDS consists of software installed on each host. The IDS software monitors the host and its log files looking for intrusive activity. If an attack is performed on the host, alarms are generated and sent to the management platform. The advantage to host-based IDS is its capability to record whether an attack was successful. The disadvantage to a host-based IDS is its inability to detect common reconnaissance attacks against the host or a range of hosts.

Network-based IDS relies on the use of network sensors strategically placed throughout the network. These probes monitor and analyze all network traffic traversing the local network. Network traffic is compared to a signature database or a defined profile to detect intrusive activity. If the monitored traffic matches a profile or signature, an alarm is generated. Additionally, sensors can be configured to take corrective action to stop an attack once it's been detected. The advantage to a network-based IDS is its macro view of the network. A network-based IDS has the advantage of viewing the entire network and, therefore, isn't limited to viewing only the traffic to a single host. The drawback to a network-based

IDS is its cost. A network-based IDS relies on additional hardware in the form of network probes. Additional drawbacks to network-based IDS are the following:

- IDS manipulation with fragmentation and TTL exploits
- Encryption
- Bandwidth

Although different types of IDS systems exist, each type must support at least one triggering mechanism. Triggering mechanisms are simply how an alarm is generated. There are two types of triggering mechanisms:

- Anomaly based
- Misuse based

Anomaly-based systems use profiles created by the IDS or the security administrator. These profiles are then used to detect an attack and generate an alarm. Traffic patterns or computer activity that doesn't match a defined profile generates an alert. The advantage of anomaly detection is it has the capability to detect previously unknown attacks or new types of attacks. The drawback to anomaly detection is an alarm is generated any time traffic or activity deviates from the defined "normal" traffic patterns or activity. This means it's up to the security administrator to discover why an alarm was generated. Anomaly-based systems have a higher rate of false positives because alarms are generated any time a deviation from normal occurs. Defining normal traffic and activity can be a difficult and time-consuming task.

Profile- or misuse-based IDSs rely on the use of a signature database to discover attacks and generate alarms. Signature files contained within the database are used exactly as virus-detection software uses signatures to discover computer viruses. These signature files are created by highly skilled engineers and are based on rules that match exploits and patterns of known intrusive activity. Once a signature is matched, an alarm is generated listing the type and severity of the attack, as well as the specific signature that was matched. Signature-based IDS have a lower occurrence of false positives that are common with anomaly detection. Unlike anomaly detection systems, signature-based systems contain a preconfigured signature database and, therefore, can begin protecting the network immediately. The drawback to signature-based systems is their inability to detect new or previously unknown attacks. If no signature exists to match an attack type, the new attack will go undetected. Therefore, keeping your signature database current is important.

Some vendors attempt to combine both host-based and network-based intrusion detections systems, while also combining anomaly and misuse triggering mechanisms into one overall IDS system. While these types of hybrid IDS provide the most benefits with the least drawbacks, they can be difficult to administer. Combining alarms and data from many different sources and types of sources into one manageable interface is a difficult task.

Questions

1. What is the purpose of an intrusion detection system (IDS)?
   A. To prevent unauthorized access to network resources
   B. To prevent users from accessing network resources
   C. To detect intrusions on the network
   D. To detect security flaws
2. What are the three phases of an attack?
   A. Reconnaissance, Attack, DoS
   B. DoS, Objective, Attack
   C. Attack, Reconnaissance, DoS
   D. Objective, Reconnaissance, Attack
3. What are the three types of attacks?
   A. Attack, Reconnaissance, data manipulation
   B. DoS, Reconnaissance, Access
   C. Objective, Reconnaissance, Access
   D. Objective, Reconnaissance, Attack
4. What is the difference between host-based and network-based intrusion detection?
   A. Host-based systems detect attacks on the hosts and network-based systems don't
   B. Network-based systems detect attacks against the IDS and host-based systems only detect attacks against the host
   C. Host-based IDSs only determine if an attack was successful
   D. Network-based IDSs rely on the use of network probes, while host-based systems rely on software installed on each host
5. What are the four types of security threats?
   A. Internal, external, secured, nonsecured
   B. External, Structured-internal, Unstructured-external, Internal
   C. Internal, Structured, Unstructured, External
   D. Internal-structured, External-structured, Internal-structured, Internal-unstructured
6. What is a false negative?
   A. Results when an attack or an intrusion goes undetected
   B. An alert sent to an incorrect management station

C. Results when the IDS system reports an alarm, although an actual intrusion doesn't occur on the network

D. There is no such thing as a false negative

7. What type of triggering mechanism is most likely to create a false negative?

   A. Anomaly detection

   B. Misuse detection

   C. Profile based

   D. Network based

8. What is a false positive?

   A. A false positive results when an attack or intrusion causes an alarm to be generated

   B. A false positive is an alert sent to an incorrect management station

   C. A false positive results when the IDS system reports an alarm, although no actual intrusion occurs on the network

   D. There is no such thing as a false positive

9. What type of triggering mechanism is most likely to create a false positive?

   A. Anomaly detection

   B. Misuse detection

   C. Network based

   D. Host based

10. Which of the following is a limitation to host-based intrusion detection?

   A. Unable to detect attacks launched from the system console

   B. Unable to detect attacks launched against the host from the network

   C. Unable to detect attacks against the host from multiple locations

   D. Unable to detect reconnaissance attacks

11. Which of the following is a benefit of host-based intrusion detection?

   A. Easier to manage

   B. Can detect if an attack is successful

   C. Detect more intrusions

   D. Administrators have a higher degree of confidence in host-based IDSs

12. Which of the following is a limitation of network-based intrusion detection?

   A. Can only detect attacks performed over the network

   B. Can only detect attacks against the network infrastructure

C. Can't detect new attack methods

D. Easy to manipulate

13. Which of the following is a benefit of network-based intrusion detection?

A. Can determine if an attack was successful

B. Have a lower occurrence of false positives

C. Have a higher occurrence of false negatives

D. Have a complete view of network traffic

14. What are the two types of triggering mechanisms used by an IDS?

A. Network based and host based

B. Misuse and anomaly detection

C. Signature and misuse detection

D. Anomaly and profile-based detection

15. What is the difference between anomaly detection and misuse detection?

A. Anomaly detection uses profiles, while misuse detection uses signatures

B. Misuse detection uses profiles, while anomaly uses signatures

C. Anomaly detection uses network-based, while misuse detection uses host based

D. No difference exists between misuse detection and anomaly detection

16. In the context of an IDS, what is an anomaly?

A. A normal traffic pattern

B. Any computer activity that matches a user profile

C. Any traffic or activity that isn't normal

D. Any traffic pattern or activity that matches a signature in the signature database

17. What is a signature and what is it used for?

A. A definition of intrusive activity and is used to build user profiles

B. A definition of intrusive activity and is used to detect intrusions

C. A definition of normal activity and is used to distinguish normal activity from intrusive activity

D. A set of rules describing intrusive activity and is used to build rule-based profiles

18. What are the three ways to build user profiles?

A. Signatures, neural networks, rule based

B. Rule based, neural networks, statistical sampling

C. Host statistical sampling, network statistical sampling, neural networks

D. Signatures, statistical sampling, neural networks

19. Which of the following is a benefit of misuse detection?

A. Lower occurrence of false negatives

B. Easier to install and understand

C. Can detect new attack methods

D. Can be used for both network based and host based

20. Which of the following is a benefit of anomaly detection?

A. Easier to understand

B. Easier to configure

C. Can be used to prevent intrusions

D. Can be used to detect new attack methods

21. What is a major drawback to misuse detection?

A. Unable to detect new attack methods

B. Hard to understand and configure

C. Results in too many false positives

D. Can only be used with host-based IDSs

22. What is a major drawback to anomaly detection?

A. Results in a high number of false negatives

B. Hackers are aware of what activity will generate an alert

C. Relies on a defined profile defining normal activity

D. Has no major drawbacks

Answers

1. C. To detect intrusions on the network
2. D. Objective, Reconnaissance, Attack
3. B. DoS, Reconnaissance, Access
4. D. Network-based IDSs rely on the use of network probes, while host-based systems rely on software installed on each host
5. C. Internal, Structured, Unstructured, External
6. A. A false negative results when an attack or intrusion goes undetected
7. B. Misuse detection

8. C. A false positive results when the IDS system reports an alarm, although no actual intrusion occurs on the network
9. A. Anomaly detection
10. D. Unable to detect reconnaissance attacks
11. B. Host-based systems can detect if an attack is successful
12. A. Network-based intrusion detection can only detect attacks performed over the network
13. D. A network-based IDS has a complete view of network traffic
14. B. Misuse and anomaly detection
15. A. Anomaly detection uses profiles, while misuse detection uses signatures
16. C. An anomaly is any traffic or activity that isn't normal
17. B. A signature is a definition of intrusive activity and is used to detect intrusions
18. B. Rule-based, neural networks, statistical sampling
19. B. Easier to install and understand
20. D. Anomaly detection can be used to detect new attack methods
21. A. Misuse detection is unable to detect new attack methods
22. C. Anomaly detection relies on a defined profile defining normal activity

CHAPTER 24

Cisco Secure Intrusion Detection System

In this chapter, you will learn to:

- Explain the functions and features of CIDS
- List all CIDS Sensor platforms and their features
- Classify all CIDS Director platforms and their features
- Understand the function and features of the IDS PostOffice protocol
- Apply the addressing scheme used by the PostOffice protocol
- List and understand the common daemons used with CIDS
- Use common commands to configure and view the configurations of CIDS components
- Understand the architecture of both the sensor and director platforms
- Recognize the directory structure of CIDS
- Understand the type of log files generated by the CIDS infrastructure

Cisco's IDS (CIDS) is a network-based intrusion detection system that uses signatures to trigger alarms and detect attacks. The Cisco IDS is composed of network probes that provide constant real-time monitoring of the network and the director platform that's used to display alarms and manage the IDS environment. Communication between the sensors and the director platforms is facilitated by the Cisco proprietary PostOffice protocol. With network probes and the accompanying director platforms, CIDS allows security managers to have real-time views of their network security. As the network grows and changes, probes can be added or moved to provide continual IDS coverage, regardless of network size.

This chapter focuses on the functions and features of the Cisco IDS system. Additionally, this chapter discusses Cisco's two director platforms, Cisco's 4200 series network sensors, and the Intrusion Detection System Module (IDSM) for the Catalyst 6500 series switch.

CIDS Operations and Functionality

CIDS is a network-based IDS system that uses both a director platform and network sensors. The director platform(s) are used to view alarms generated by the sensors, configure the sensors, and maintain the IDS environment. The sensor is the most critical component of Cisco's IDS system because it monitors, analyzes, responds to, and reports intrusions to the director platform.

The basic operations and functionality of the CIDS can be described in the following five steps:

- Step 1 Monitoring
- Step 2 Analyzing
- Step 3 Communications
- Step 4 Centralized Alarm Display and Management
- Step 5 (Optional) Sensor Response

Monitoring

Monitoring is accomplished with network sensors. Sensors have two interfaces: one monitoring interface, and one command and control interface. The monitoring interface is used to capture all network traffic from the network to which it's connected. Sensors capture all packets on the network and, if configured to do so, will reassemble fragmented packets in order to defend against a common IDS defeating technique.

The command and control interface is used to configure the sensor, communicate with the director platform, and perform device management. When an intrusion signature is matched, the sensor is responsible for logging the event, and notifying the director through the command and control interface. *Device management* is the term used to describe the sensor's capability to reconfigure Cisco routers, firewalls, and switches to stop an intrusion. Device management is discussed in more detail in the section "IP Blocking."

Cisco currently has four different network sensors. Three of the sensors are all members of the 4200 series; the fourth sensor is an integrated switch module for the Catalyst 6500 series switch. Each of these four sensors has been engineered and tuned for optimum performance.

Cisco 4200 Series Sensors

The 4200 series network sensors are stand-alone components running their own operating system (OS) and are referred to as *appliances*. To protect the sensors, the host OS on the 4200 series sensors should be secured and patched, and any unneeded services should be removed. The three network sensor appliances belonging to the 4200 series are the following:

- 4210

- 4235 (replaces the 4230)
- 4250

The model 4210 is the entry-level network sensor capable of monitoring up to 45Mbps of network traffic. The back panel of the 2410 is illustrated in Figure 24-1. The 4210 has a console port located on the front panel, much like the 2600 and 3600 series routers, but some Cisco documentation shows the com port on the rear panel labeled as the console port. For an Ethernet network configuration:

- Use the **iprb1** interface for command and control.
- Use the **iprb0** interface for capturing packets.

Some of the features of the 4210 include the following:

- Performance: 45Mbps
- Network Interface: 10/100Base-T
- Chassis: 1U

The model 4235 is a replacement for model 4230 and represents the mid-level network sensor. The 4235 is capable of monitoring up to 200Mbps of data. The back panel of the 4230 is illustrated in Figure 24-2. For an Ethernet network configuration:

- Command and Control interface: **e1000g1**
- Sniffing interface: **e1000g0**

Some of the features of the 4235 include the following:

- Performance: 200Mbps

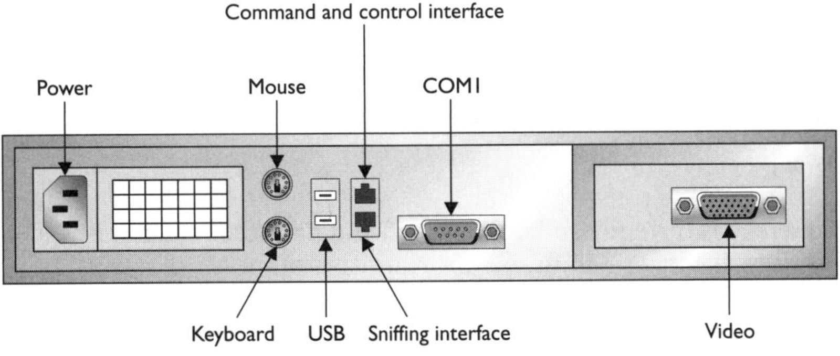

Figure 24-1 Model 4210 rear panel

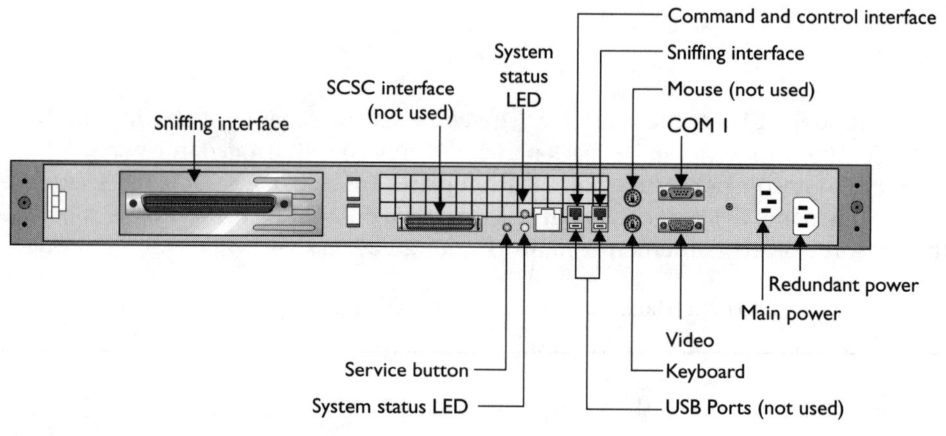

Figure 24-2 Models 4235 and 4250 rear panel

- Network Interface: 10/100/1000Base-TX
- Chassis: 1U

The model 4250 is Cisco's latest addition to the 4200 series and represents the highest level of network performance. The 4250 is capable of monitoring and analyzing up to 500Mbps. The back panels of the 2450 and the 2435 are identical and are illustrated in Figure 24-2. For an Ethernet network configuration:

- Command and Control interface: **e1000g1**
- Sniffing interface (Copper, next to C&C): **e1000g0** (IDS-4250-TX)
- Sniffing interface (Fiber, PCI add on card): **e1000g3** (IDS-4250-SX)

The features of the 4250 include the following:

- : 10/100/1000Base-TX, 1000Base-SX (Fiber)
- **Chassis: Performance:** 500Mbps
- **Network Interface** 1U

The Cisco sensor is currently end of life (EOL) and has been replaced by the 4235. For exam purposes, Figure 24-3 illustrates the rear panel of the 4U chassis.

STUDY TIP You should be familiar with the network interfaces (monitoring, and command and control), as well as the console port locations for each model of the 4200 series network sensors' appliances.

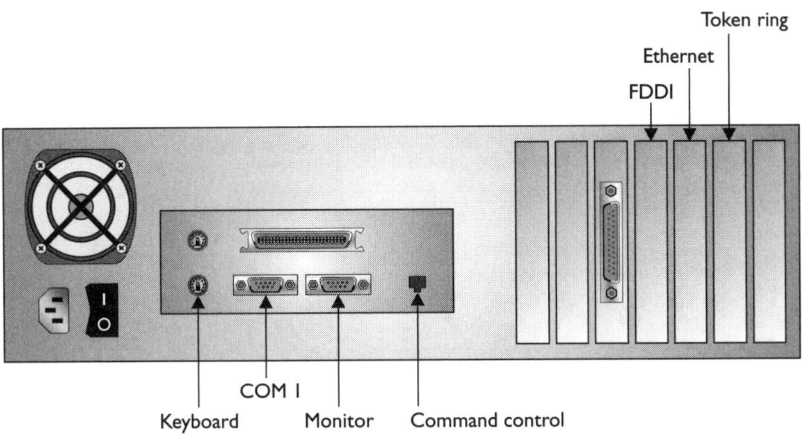

Figure 24-3 Model 4230 rear panel

Table 24-1 compares the features for each member of the 4200 series network sensors.

Catalyst 6000 Intrusion Detection System Module (IDSM)

The Cisco IDSM was designed to allow the inclusion of IDS into enterprise networks by integrating IDS functionality directly into the switching fabric. The IDSM is a passive monitoring module that inspects copies of packets and isn't in the switch-forwarding path. Because the module isn't in the switch-forwarding path, the IDS module doesn't impact switch performance. The IDSM is a blade module that can be inserted into any available slot on any 6000 series Catalyst switch, as shown in Figure 24-4.

The IDSM monitors and analyzes traffic, just as the 4200 series network appliances. If an intrusion is detected, an alarm is generated and sent to the director platform. The IDS module captures packets directly off the catalyst's backplane. Two methods can be used

	Cisco IDS Sensor 4210	Cisco IDS Sensor 4235	Cisco IDS Sensor 4250
Performance	45Mbps	200Mbps	500Mbps
Network Interface	10/100 Base-T	10/100/1000Base-TX	10/100/100Base-TX 1000Base-SX (Fiber)
Performance Upgradeable	No	No	Yes

Table 24-1 Comparison of 4200 Series Network Sensors

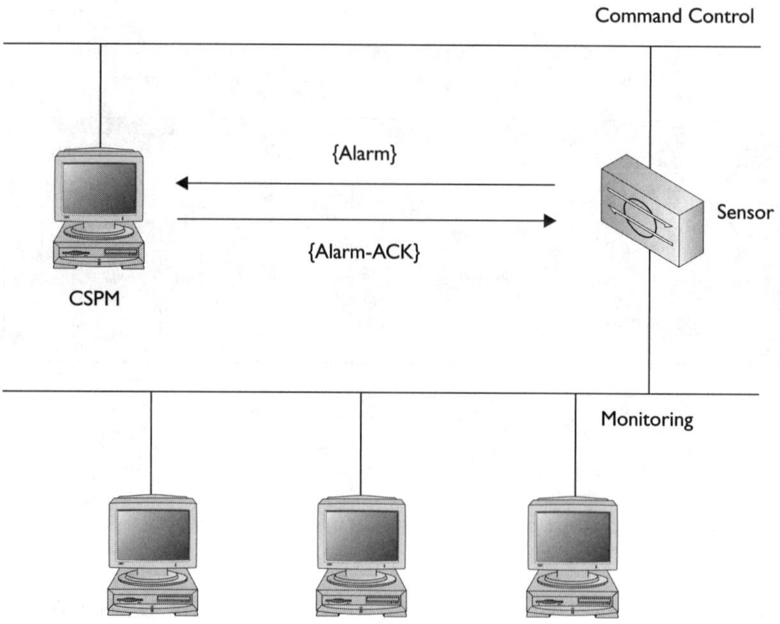

Figure 24-4 Cisco Catalyst 6000 IDS module

to direct copies of packets from the backplane to the IDS module, and the two methods are the following:

- Switch Port Analyzer (SPAN)
- Virtual LAN access control lists (VLAN ACL)

Spanning is a feature that allows the switch administrator to configure a port as a SPAN port. The term "SPAN" isn't associated with the common Spanning Tree protocol. The switch can be configured to copy all packets from a particular port/VLAN or to a particular port/VLAN to the SPAN port.

VLAN ACLs allow the IDSM to monitor traffic based on more granular criteria, such as specific IP addresses or network services. The monitoring is passive and only inspects copies of the packets, not the original packets, allowing real-time monitoring without affecting switch performance. The features of the IDSM include the following:

- 100Mbps performance
- Multi-VLAN visibility
- Fully integrated line card
- Complete signature set
- No performance impact

The IDSM also can use the same director platform as the 4200 series network sensors. One director or management platform can be used to monitor and configure both 4200 series network appliances, and one or more IDSMs.

Analyzing

Packets captured by the sensors are reassembled, if required, and then compared against the signature database. When the sensors analyze network traffic, they're looking for patterns of activity that match known intrusive activity. These patterns are defined in the signature database held on the network sensors. Patterns of activity can be as basic as an attempt to access a specific port on a specific host or as complex as a set of operations directed at a number of different hosts over an extended period of time. If a signature is matched, the sensor logs the information and sends an alarm to the director platform through the command and control interface.

Communications

The sensors and the director platforms must have a communication medium to allow for the sending of alarms, sensor configurations, and messages. Cisco's proprietary PostOffice protocol provides this communication vehicle used by the sensors to communicate with one another and management consoles.

PostOffice Protocol

The *PostOffice* protocol is a proprietary protocol only used between the sensors and directors and shouldn't be confused with common e-mail protocols, such as SMTP, IMAP, or POP. The PostOffice protocol is *not* an e-mail protocol. Through the use of the PostOffice protocol, the director platforms can send configuration files to the sensors, and the sensors can send messages and alarms to a centralized sensor or director. The messages sent between the directors and the sensors are controlled by services running on both devices. These services, called *daemons,* run on both the sensors and directors. Daemons are discussed in the sections "CIDS Software Architecture" and "Daemon Configuration Files."

The PostOffice protocol uses User Datagram Protocol (UDP) as the transport layer protocol on port 45000. The PostOffice protocol also uses a proprietary addressing scheme to address all CIDS infrastructure devices. The following are the message types sent among CIDS service, sensors, and directors:

- Command Messages
- Error Messages
- Command Log Messages
- Alarm Messages
- IP log Messages
- Redirect Messages
- Heartbeat Messages

Communication between services on both the sensors and the directors represents a critical component of Cisco's IDS system. Because of its critical nature, Cisco developed the PostOffice protocol to be reliable, redundant, and fault tolerant.

PostOffice Reliability When a sensor detects an intrusion, it must send an alarm to the centralized director or sensor. Because of its critical nature, the PostOffice protocol supports guaranteed delivery of all messages sent from the sensors to the directors. As seen in Figure 24-5, guaranteed delivery is accomplished through the use of acknowledgments. When a sensor sends a message, it expects to receive an acknowledgment (ack) in a predetermined amount of time. If an acknowledgment isn't received, the sensor will repeatedly repeat the message until the director replies with an ack.

PostOffice Redundancy The PostOffice protocol allows for redundancy by allowing sensors to send messages to redundant director or sensor platforms. By sending alarms and messages to multiple platforms located in diverse locations, the CIDS infrastructure can be engineered for both redundancy and fault tolerance. You can configure the sensors to send alarms and messages to a maximum of 255 different destinations. Figure 24-6 illustrates a redundant director platform design.

PostOffice Fault Tolerance The PostOffice protocol allows the configuration of up to 255 alternate IP addresses for any single platform. These alternate IP addresses

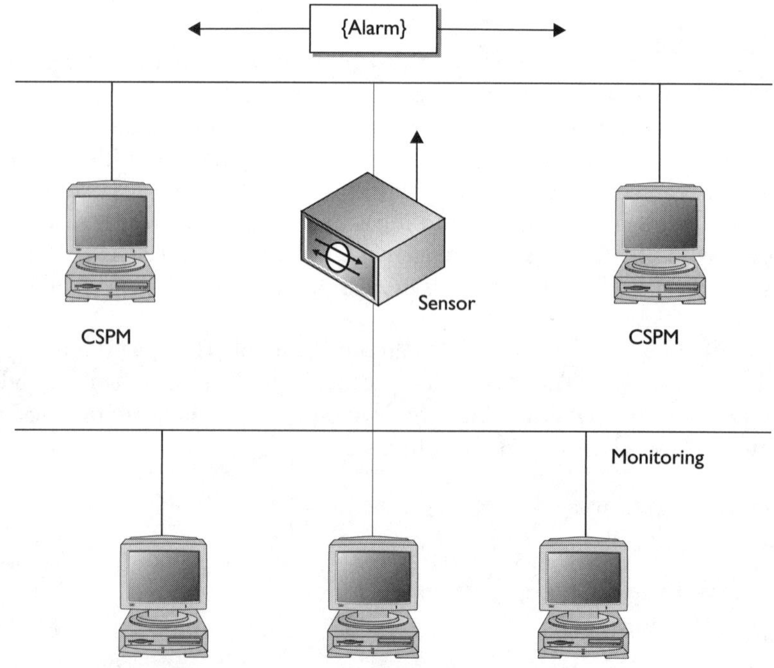

Figure 24-5 Reliable message delivery via the PostOffice protocol

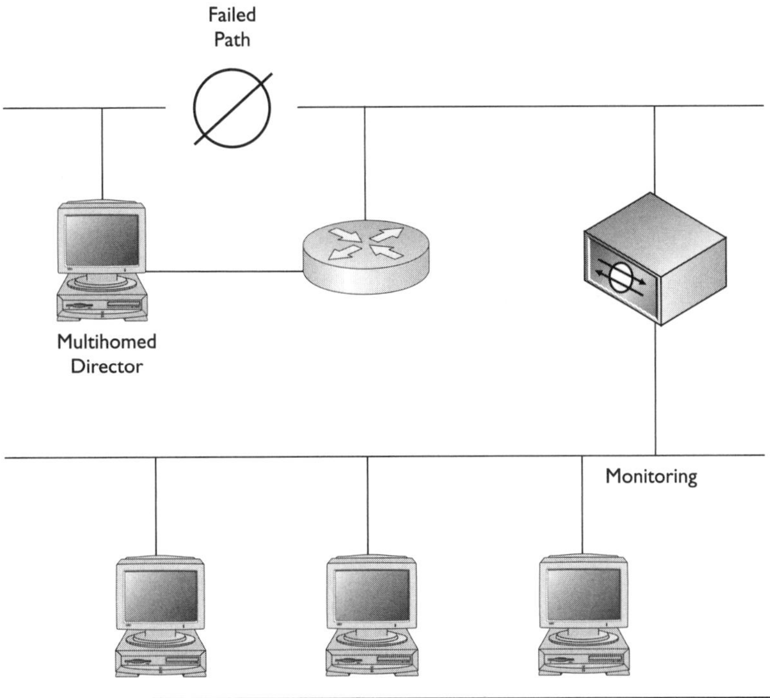

Figure 24-6 Redundant director platforms

can represent separate network interface cards installed on a multihomed director platform, as seen in Figure 24-7. The sensors can be configured to use a primary address to reach a director platform and a secondary address if the primary address is unreachable. Sensors only use the secondary addresses if the primary address is unreachable. The sensors use a watchdog process to detect when the connectivity to the primary IP address is reestablished. Once a connection to the primary address is reestablished, the sensor resumes communications using the primary address.

By placing the director platform on a multihomed system, you allow the director to send and receive traffic on two or more networks. Using multihomed directors provides additional protection from network failures. By multihoming your director platform, you're providing fault tolerance by creating multiple paths between your sensors and your directors. Figure 24-7 illustrates a multihomed director platform design.

NOTE A *multihomed system* is any system that has multiple network interfaces to separate networks. The networks can be logically separated or both physically and logically separated. *Routers*, by definition, are multihomed devices because they receive traffic on one network, and then route that traffic to another network. Multihomed computer systems running Unix or Windows NT/2000/XP can be configured as a router.

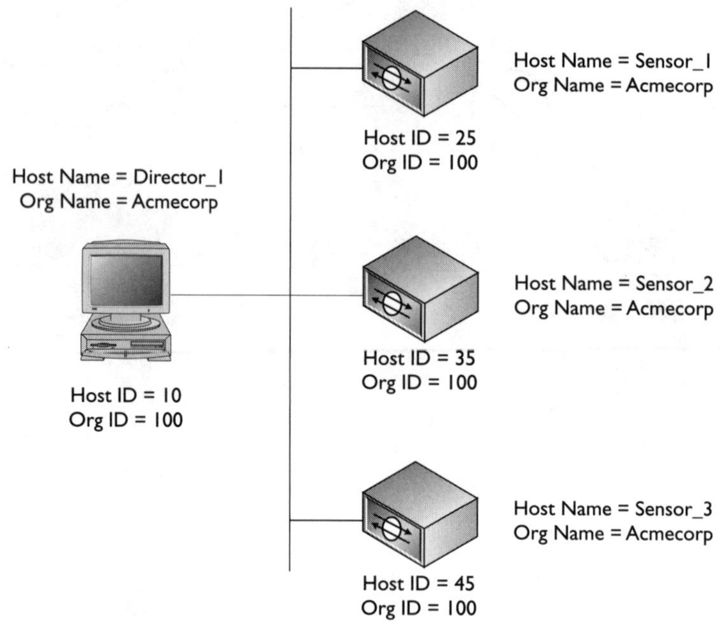

Figure 24-7 CIDS multihomed director platform

PostOffice Protocol Addressing

For devices within the CIDS infrastructure to communicate efficiently, the PostOffice protocol requires a unique protocol specific address for each device. Each device within the CIDS infrastructure has both a numeric identifier and an alphanumeric identifier.

The *numeric identifier* is a combination of the host ID and the organization ID, and is used for network communications. All devices within the same management must have the same organizational ID. Devices contained in the same organizational infrastructure share the same organizational ID, however, each device must have unique host IDs.

The alphanumeric identifier is used as the common name for the devices and is made up of the host name and the organizational name. As seen in Figure 24-8, each sensor and director platform has both a host ID and a host name. Each device also has both an organizational ID and an organizational name.

The host ID and organizational ID are two parts of a three-part addressing scheme used by the PostOffice protocol. The third component that makes up a complete PostOffice protocol address is a unique application ID. All command and control messages are addressed using these three unique identifiers. Application IDs are discussed further in the section "The Services File."

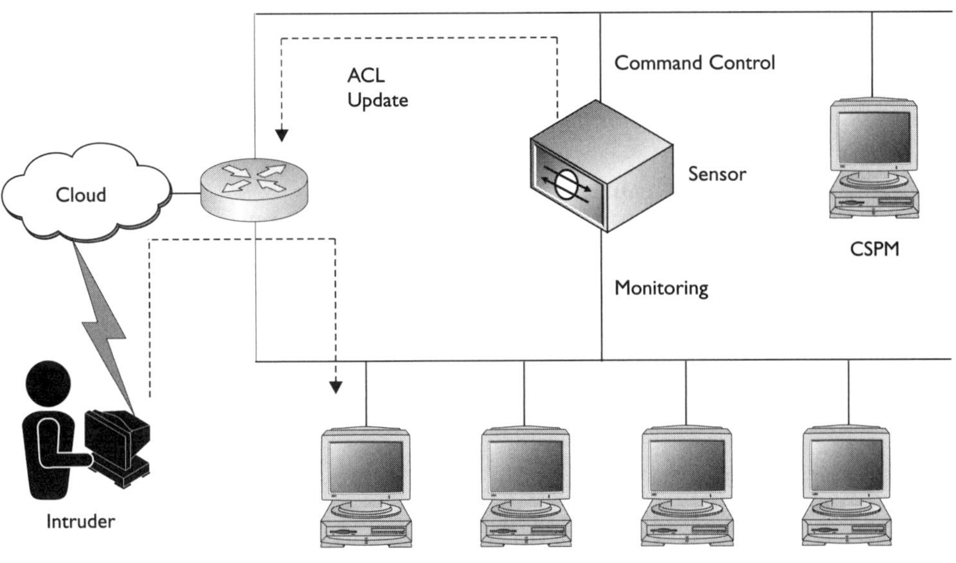

Figure 24-8 PostOffice host and organization addressing

Centralized Alarm Display and Management

The *director platforms* act as centralized management stations for the entire CIDS infrastructure. In addition to displaying alarms, the director platforms are also responsible for manual intrusion response and sensor configuration. Cisco offers two different director platforms that can be used to manage your CIDS environment. Cisco Secure Policy Manager (CSPM) is the director platform of choice for Windows NT, while Cisco Intrusion Detection Director for UNIX (CIDS Director for UNIX) is for use in UNIX environments. Each sensor also has a built-in web interface that can be used to manage and configure the sensor.

Device Manager is an HTTP application installed on each sensor. This web interface can be used to configure and manage the sensor. The *Event Viewer*, a standalone application, can be used to view events and alarms generated by the sensors.

STUDY TIP The CIDS exam focuses on the Device Manager for the configuration and management of network sensors.

Alarm Display

The Event Viewer is a responsible alarm display. Because manually monitoring all the sensors on the network is impractical, the Event Viewer provides a centralized management and alarm notification center. The Event Viewer includes the software necessary to display alarms generated by the sensors within a GUI interface.

PART V

The Event Viewer's GUI interface displays alarms generated by the sensors in a unique color based on the severity of the alarm. Security administrators can quickly view all alarms as they're reported in real time. This detail of alarm displaying allows administrators to examine all security threats quickly across the enterprise.

Manual Intrusion Response

Based on the severity of an alarm, manual and automatic responses can be taken to prevent further activity. The sensors, not the directors, handle this automatic response. In many cases, an automatic response isn't needed or wanted. Manual intrusion response can be accomplished through sensor configuration using the IDS Device Manager. Directly from the sensor platform, the administrator can initiate an IP blocking response, blocking either the offending IP address or the entire network address of the intrusive host.

Sensor Configuration

Configurations can be created on the director platform, and then they can either be pushed to the sensors to update their configuration or individual sensors can be configured using the IDS Device Manager. The UNIX version of the director (CIDS Director for UNIX) allows administrators to create multiple configurations on the Director, and then apply these configurations as needed to any sensor within the infrastructure. The Windows NT version of the director (Cisco Secure Policy Manager) allows administrators to create configuration templates that can be applied to one or more sensors on the network.

Introduced earlier, Cisco offers two different director platforms, which are the following:

- Cisco Secure Policy Manager (CSPM)
- CIDS Director for UNIX

Cisco Secure Policy Manager (CSPM)

Cisco Secure Policy Manager is a Windows NT 4.0 based application that can be used to provide security policy management and enforcement for:

- Cisco PIX firewalls
- Cisco IOS routers with the firewall feature set
- Cisco Secure Integrated virtual private network (VPN)
- Cisco Intrusion Detection System Sensors

CSPM is a vast application, capable of managing an enterprise's entire security infrastructure. Entire books can be written describing all the features and functions of CSPM, but this chapter only details the features and functions of CSPM as they relate to the director platform for CIDS.

Sensor Configuration with CSPM CSPM provides a centralized GUI management platform for the distributed sensor architecture. Sensors can be added to the Network Topology Tree (NTT) using the Add Sensor Wizard within CSPM. Once the sensors are added, CSPM enables security administrators to remotely configure each sensor individually or as a group. Different configurations can be created and saved as a template, and these template configurations can then be applied to one or more sensors within the CIDS infrastructure.

NOTE The *NTT* is a directory containing objects that represent the network and security infrastructure equipment. Much like the active directory in Windows 2000, the NTT provides a graphical view of your network components. The purpose of the NTT is to communicate the locations of objects installed on the network to CSPM. NTT can then be used to locate, view, and configure those objects. Infrastructure equipment that should be defined in the NTT includes networks, gateways, sensors, directors, and hosts.

CSPM Event Viewer The Event Viewer located in CSPM allows security administrators to view, in real time, all suspected intrusive activity on their network. The Event Viewer display has two primary panes: the Connection Status pane and the Grid pane. The Event Viewer can be customized through the use of configurable grids that permit multiple views and instances. The CSPM Event Viewer combines the organization of a spreadsheet and the usability of a browser into a hierarchical collection of audit events called a drillsheet. The *drillsheet* combines data of similar audit event records into the single row of a grid, enabling security administrators to detect patterns in the data.

Cisco Secure Intrusion Detection Director for UNIX

The intrusion detection Director for UNIX is an HP OpenView application that runs on Sun Solaris or HPUX. Like CSPM, the Director provides a GUI interface for centralized management across the distributed sensor architecture.

Sensor Configuration with CIDS Director for UNIX The Director enables security administrators to create and save multiple configuration files. Once a configuration is created, it can be applied to any sensor reporting to the Director platform. The Configuration Management Utility (nrConfigure) component of the director is used to create and save configuration files for later use.

CIDS Director Alarm Display Alarms are recorded and displayed in real time. The Director for UNIX uses an HP OpenView submap to provide a GUI interface for alarm viewing.

Comparing the Two Director Platforms

While the overall objective of both platforms is to provide a centralized management location for all IDS-related activity, CSPM and Director for UNIX offer different features and use different methods to accomplish the same goals. Alarm severities in CSPM are low, medium, and high, while the Director for UNIX has severities of 1 through 5. A severity of 1 represents the lowest severity and 5 represents the highest severity.

CSPM allows security administrators to create configuration templates that can be applied to one or more sensors. When the template is updated, all sensors referencing the template are also updated. The CIDS Director for UNIX allows security administrators to create and save multiple configurations, and then apply those configurations as needed. The CIDS Director for UNIX also has a configuration-versioning mechanism that CSPM doesn't have. When a configuration is changed within the CIDS Director for UNIX, the current configuration is saved as a previous version, allowing security administrators to roll back to a previous version of a configuration. CSPM doesn't offer this versioning feature.

A final feature supported in the CIDS Director for UNIX that isn't supported in CSPM is SNMP. The CIDS director for UNIX can be configured to generate SNMP traps once an alarm is received. CSPM doesn't generate SNMP traps based on alarms. Table 24-2 shows a feature comparison of the two CIDS director platforms.

Sensor Response

When a signature is matched, the Cisco IDS sensors can be configured to take preventative action to stop further intrusive activity. The Cisco Active Response System (CARS) allows the sensor to take control of other systems, such as routers, firewalls, and switches to terminate unauthorized sessions. Sensors can be configured to take different actions based on the configurable severity of the signature matched, so different responses could be configured for different signatures. The configuration of sensor responses is discussed in Chapter 25. The possible actions that can be configured on the sensors are the following:

- Terminate the TCP session
- Block the IP address of the attacking host
- Create an IP session log

Terminating the TCP Session

The transport layer protocol, Transmission Control Protocol (TCP), provides a connection-oriented communication mechanism with a three-way handshake. Both hosts can

Director Features	CSPM	Director for UNIX
Severity Levels	Low, Medium, High	1 through 5
Configuration Templates	Yes	No
Configuration Versioning	No	Yes
Local Logging	Database	Text file
SNMP Traps	No	Yes

Table 24-2 CSPM and Director for UNIX Comparison

terminate this connection-oriented communication by sending and receiving a TCP packet with the FIN bit set to 1 within the TCP header. Additionally, either host can send a TCP reset packet and force the connection between the hosts to be reset immediately.

A TCP reset packet has the RST bit set to 1 in the TCP header. When a reset packet is received by either host, the connection is terminated. Sensors can take advantage of this protocol feature and send a reset packet to the affected hosts, thereby terminating the connection.

NOTE The TCP reset action is only appropriate as an action selection on those signatures associated with a TCP-based service. If selected as an action on non-TCP-based services, no action is taken. Additionally, TCP resets aren't guaranteed to tear down an offending session because of limitations in the TCP protocol.

While resetting the TCP connections is a powerful feature, some drawbacks occur with its use. TCP resets are only effective with communications using the TCP transport layer protocol. Communications using User Datagram Protocol (UDP) aren't affected by TCP resets.

IP Blocking

"Device management" is the term used by Cisco to describe actions taken by the sensors to reconfigure other network infrastructure equipment, such as routers, firewalls, and switches. Sensors can be configured for device management, allowing them to automatically reconfigure ACLs on infrastructure equipment blocking an intruder's IP address or an entire network address range. The blocking of IP addresses through device management is also known as *shunning*. As seen in Figure 24-9, the sensor can reconfigure the ACL on the perimeter router to block the intruders' IP address.

STUDY TIP Perimeter routers are referred to as *Blocking Routers*. Sensors create and maintain a Telnet session to Blocking Routers to reduce the time required to publish the ACL rule sets that block traffic. IP blocking with the use of Device Management is also known as shunning.

IP blocking should be used cautiously. A hacker could take advantage of this response mechanism to perform a DoS attack. This DoS attack could be aimed at the IDS system itself or at other critical network infrastructure equipment. An intruder could spoof the address of an important server or director platform. Using the spoofed address, the intruder could launch an attack, causing the IDS system to block the IP address of the spoofed host. In essence, the hacker is forcing your IDS system to attack your own hosts, by blocking their IP address. Additionally, intruders might have multiple hosts at their disposal and can continue scanning, probing, and attacking your network from hosts that haven't yet been blocked. IP blocking could also be initiated manually from the director platform once an attack is discovered.

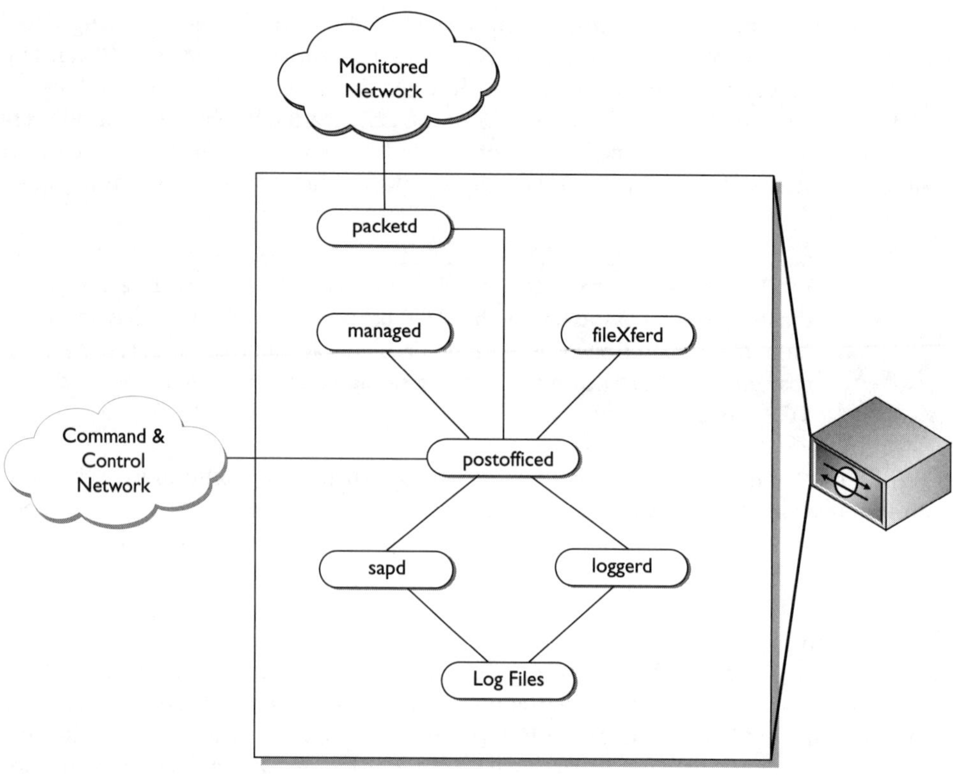

Figure 24-9 Using Device Management to block an IP address

IP Logging

IP session logs can be used to gather information about the suspected intrusive activity. When a signature has been configured for IP logging and that signature is matched, the sensor begins writing every incoming and outgoing packet to a session log. Security administrators can configure how long the sensor should continue to perform IP logging after the signature was matched.

CIDS Architecture

The preceding section described the operations and functionality of CIDS. To understand CIDS completely, you must also understand the architecture that makes up the CIDS. This section discusses the major architecture aspects of the CIDS environment. The following major components of the CIDS architecture are illustrated.

- CIDS Software Architecture
- CIDS Commands

- CIDS Directory Structure
- CIDS Log Files

CIDS Software Architecture

Both the sensors and the director platforms have their own OS and IDS software components. The components that make up the IDS software system are called daemons or services. Each function of CIDS is handled through different daemons or services, running on the sensor, director, or on both platforms. This architecture results in a modular software product that's both fast and scalable.

CIDS is also a highly configurable distributed application. The services operating on a sensor or director platform depend on the configuration of the CIDS system as a whole. Minimally, a sensor must have *packetd, postofficed, fileXferd,* and *loggerd* daemons running, while the director should have *smid, postofficed, fileXferd,* and *loggerd* running.

The daemons each have a corresponding configuration file. This configuration file is used to tune the specific parameters used by the daemons. Parameters, called *tokens,* contained in the configuration files, are read by daemons residing on the sensor and director platforms. Configuration files are used to tune the CIDS system to operate according to your security policy. Another type of file, called *system files,* are used to configure the CIDS operating environment.

System files are used by the sensor and director platforms to describe and configure the environment in which they operate. System files are used to define the security infrastructure in which the host operates, as well as to identify other sensors and directors present on the network. System files provide vital information to the communications infrastructure used between sensors and directors.

The software installed on the director performs a different function than the software installed on the sensors. To describe the architecture of the IDS systems fully, this section first describes the sensor software architecture and then discusses the director software architecture.

Sensor Software Architecture

Sensors are the heart of any IDS system. *Sensors* perform the monitoring, analyzing, and alarm notification. Understanding the architecture of the CIDS sensors can provide a better understanding of the CIDS system as a whole. As seen in Figure 24-10, the architecture of the CIDS sensors is composed of six different services or daemons that work together to form the security system. The architecture of the sensors can be illustrated by defining each of these services and the functions they perform on behalf of the sensor. The services that run on each sensor are the following:

- *packetd*
- *postofficed*
- *loggerd*
- *sapd*

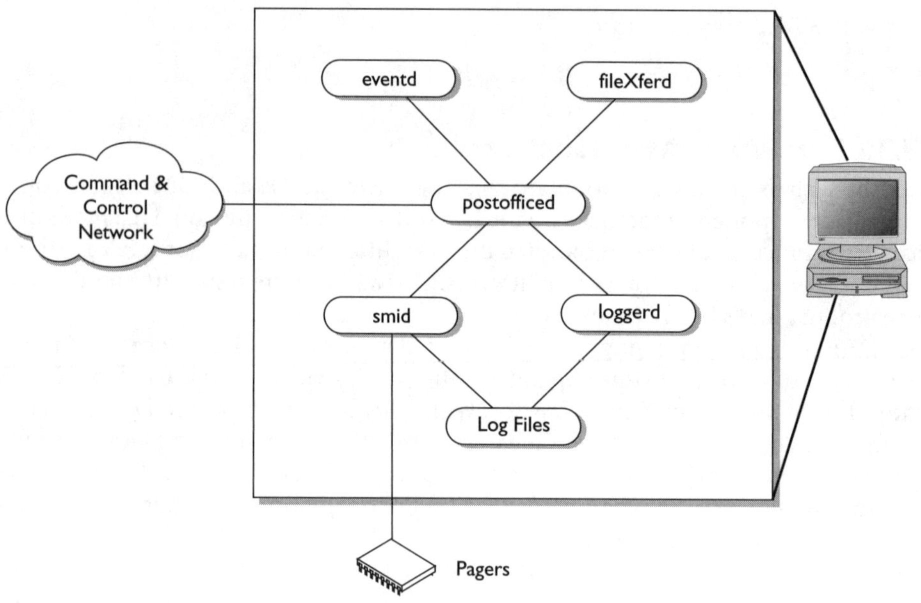

Figure 24-10 CIDS sensor architecture

- *managed*
- *fileXferd*

STUDY TIP You should be familiar with the daemons that make up the IDS system and the functions they perform.

packetd *packetd* is the interface between the network and the sensor. The *packetd* service captures packets on the monitored network and performs an intrusive detection analysis on those packets. If intrusive activity is discovered, *packetd* generates and forwards an alarm to the postofficed service. In addition to generating alarm messages, *packetd* can be configured to automatically instruct managed service to shun an IP address for a specified period of time.

postofficed The *postofficed* service is the communication vehicle for the entire CIDS product. All communication between daemons is routed through this service. Each sensor relies on *postofficed* to maintain communication with the *postofficed* daemon running on other hosts. The *postofficed* daemon service includes the following features:

- A proprietary connection-based protocol that resends a message whenever any of its packets are lost.

- Point-to-point routes that might include intermediate post-office nodes.
- Communication integrity is maintained via alternate routes. When one route fails, communication is switched to an alternate route. Communication is reestablished to the preferred route as soon as it comes back online.

Routing is based on a three-part key that includes the following information:

- Organization ID
- Host ID
- Application ID

loggerd *loggerd* is the logging service used by CIDS; as such, the *loggerd* daemon writes out sensor and error data to flat files received by one or more of the other daemons. This data is passed to *loggerd* via *postofficed*. *loggerd* creates two basic types of flat files: a single sensor event file and one or more IP session logs.

sapd The Security Analysis Package Daemon (sapd) is responsible for file system maintenance, such as file deletion and moving log files to the database staging areas. The *sapd* daemon is a user-configurable scheduler that controls database loading and archival of old event and IP session logs.

managed The *managed* daemon is responsible for the managing and monitoring of all network devices configured for device management. For example, when *packetd* discovers a signature has been matched and the signature is configured for IP blocking, *packetd* sends a **shun** command to *managed* via the *postofficed* service. *managed* is then responsible for reconfiguring the router's ACL. The Director can also send these **shun** commands to the *managed* daemon. *managed* can also be polled for operational statistics, such as:

- The number of network devices being managed
- The type of device being managed

fileXferd The *fileXferd* daemon is responsible for the transfer of configuration files between the director platforms and the sensors. On the sensor, fileXferd is responsible for receiving configuration files from the director platforms.

Cisco Secure Policy Manager Architecture

The architecture of the centralized director platform is illustrated in Figure 24-11. As the sensor monitors the networks and generates alarms, the *postofficed* daemon is responsible for receiving the alarms from *packetd* and forwarding them to the *postofficed* daemon on the director platform. Once an alarm or message is received on the director platform the director's *postofficed* service will route the message or alarm to the appropriate service.

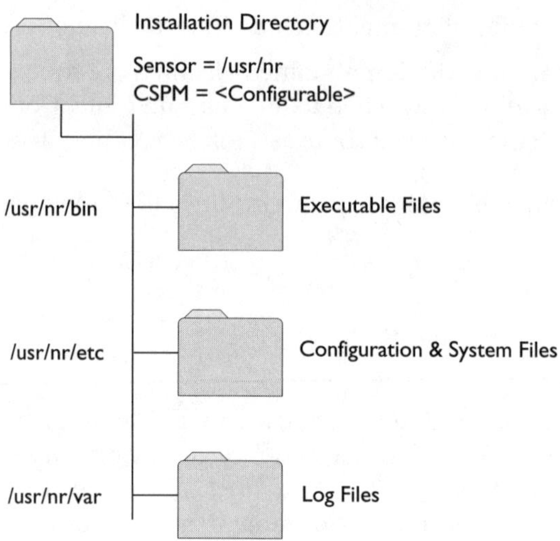

Figure 24-11 Director architecture

The director platform is responsible for alarm management, remote sensor configuration, event processing, and database functions. To accomplish these tasks, the following major daemons are run on the director platform:

- *postofficed*
- *smid*
- *eventd*
- *loggerd*
- *fileXferd*

postofficed The *postofficed* daemon runs on the director as well as sensors and performs the same function on each. The *postofficed* service is responsible for all communications between services residing on the host, as well as all communications between hosts.

smid The *smid* daemon's primary function is to populate the alarm icons on the director's HP OpenView (HPOV) maps, but *smid* can also be used to redirect messages to other daemon services, such as *eventd* and *loggerd.*

eventd The *eventd* daemon can be configured to take specific actions based on messages received from the *smid* service. A common use for this feature is to configure *eventd* to send notification via e-mail to pagers for any alarms of a severity 4 or higher.

loggerd *loggerd* is the logging service used by CIDS. The *loggerd* daemon writes out sensor and error data to flat files received by one or more of the other daemons. This data is passed to *loggerd* via *postofficed.*

fileXferd The *fileXferd* daemon is responsible for the transfer of configuration files between the director platforms and the sensors. The director platform fileXferd is responsible for sending the configuration files.

Daemon Configuration Files

Each daemon, whether on the director or the sensor, has a corresponding configuration file. This configuration file allows security administrators to tune each daemon according to their own security requirements. These configuration files follow a simple naming convention: *<daemon>*.conf, where *<daemon>* is the name of the daemon with which the configuration file is associated. For example, the configuration file for the *packetd* daemon is named *packetd.conf.*

Each configuration file contains tokens. Parameters/tokens include things such as a router's IP address or lists of IP addresses that should never be shunned. When a daemon is started, it reads the values associated with each token in its own configuration file. The values associated with each token are used as the daemon's configuration. For example, the *packetd* daemon's configuration file has a token named *ReassembleFragments.* The value for the *ReassembleFragments* token can be set to 0 or 1. If the value is set to 1, then the *packetd* daemon on the sensor will attempt to reassemble all fragmented packets. If the value is set to 0, the *packetd* daemon on the sensor won't attempt to reassemble fragmented packets.

System Files

System files are used by the CIDS infrastructure to define and configure the environment in which they operate. System files are used to configure the security and network infrastructure of all CIDS components. System files are also used to identify organization, hosts, directors, routes, services, daemons, and signatures. The following list of system files are described in order of their use:

- organization
- hosts
- services
- auths
- destinations
- routes
- daemons
- signatures

The organization File The *organization* file lists all the organization IDs currently registered for a Cisco Secure Intrusion Detection System domain. The entries contained in the organization file must adhere to the following format:

<org_id> <org_name>

The *org_id* is the user-defined organization ID used to identify a group of director and sensor platforms. The *org_name* is the corresponding name associated with the org_id. This file must be exactly the same across all sensor and director platforms within a Cisco Secure IDS domain. A typical organization file might look like the following:

```
125 acmecorp
130 abccorp
135 xyzcorp
```

The hosts File The *hosts* file is much like the \etc\hosts file on UNIX systems or the winnt\system32\etc\hosts file on Windows NT/2000 systems. Just like the associated files, the hosts file is used to identify sensors and directors within the CIDS domain. The hosts file lists the known host IDs, host names, organization IDs, and organization names. Besides listing all known hosts, this file must also have an entry for the local host. The contents of the hosts file should be identical across all sensors and directors, with the exception of the entry for the localhost. The entries contained in the host file must adhere to the following format:

<host_id> . <org_id> <host_name> . <org_name>

A typical hosts file might look like the following:

```
10.120 localhost
10.125 sensor_one.acmecorp
10.130 sensor_two.acemcorp
10.100 director_one.acmecorp
```

NOTE If the hosts files aren't identical across all directors and sensors (with exception to the localhost entry), some systems will generate an "unrecognizable host" error message in /usr/nr/var/errors.postofficed. If you're having communication issues, check for this error message on each sensor and/or director.

The services File The *services* file lists the application IDs of all daemons. When the application_id is combined with the host_id and org_id, these identifiers uniquely identify a specific daemon running on the specified host. CIDS uses these IDs to build a complete Cisco Secure IDS security map. The entries contained in the services file must adhere to the following format:

<application_id> <daemon_name> [<comment>]

The application_id is a Cisco-generated ID number that identifies the CIDS daemon. The <daemon> parameter identifies the name of the daemon the application_id represents. The <comment> parameter is optional and can be set to provide additional information about the service. All sensor platforms should have the same default services file, which contains the following entries:

```
10000    postofficed   #    Provides the IDS communication system
10001    sensord       #    Monitors network traffic when used with STK/Nortel
10002    configd       #    Provides ability to query runtime/configuration info
10003    managed       #    manages IDS components
10004    eventd        #    Configurable shell script support for handling events
10005    loggerd       #    Logs locally generated events and messages
10006    smid          #    Sends data to the director and duplicates messages
10007    sapd          #    File management control and database staging
10008    packetd       #    Monitors network traffic directly or from Cisco router
10009    reserved      #    Reserved for Cisco Systems use
10010    fileXferd     #    File Transfer Service
```

NOTE Changing the application ID for any daemon on any host will cause IDS to fail and should only be done if directed by TAC.

The auths File The *auths* file is used for basic host authentication. This file lists the hosts, as well as which configuration commands these hosts are authorized to perform on the local host. The possible configuration commands that can be issued are **nrget**, **nrgetbulk**, **nrset**, **nrunset**, and **nrexec.** Configuration commands are discussed in the section "Configuration Commands." The entries contained in the *auths* file must adhere to the following format:

<host_name> <configuration_command_1>, [<configuration_command_2....]

The host_name must follow the CIDS naming structure where the host name is <host_name.org_name>. An example *auths* file might contain the following:

```
director_one.acmecorp NRGET, NRGETBULK, NRSET, NRUNSET, NREXEC
director_two.acmecorp NRGET, NRGETBULK
sensor_one.acmecorp GET
```

In the previous example, director_one.acmecorp is allowed full authorization, while director_two.acmecorp is only allowed to read data.

NOTE Each entry in the auths file requires a corresponding host entry in the hosts file.

The destinations File CIDS is a distributed application that allows the exchange, or routing, of information from a given communication service (postofficed) to a daemon service on any host. Using the PostOffice protocol, daemons running on any host

PART V

can communicate with other daemons running on any other host, as long as the following three conditions are met.

1. Both the sending host and the receiving host must be identified in the hosts file (previously mentioned).
2. Any daemons attempting to send or receive messages must be listed in the services file (previously mentioned).
3. An entry in the destinations file permits both the severity and the type of message being sent.

The destinations file defines the type and severity of messages that will get routed to any given daemon on any specific host. The entries contained in the destinations file must adhere to the following format:

```
<destination_id> <host_name> <daemon_name> <message_level> <message_type>
```

An example auths file entry might contain the following:

```
1 director_one.acmecorp smid 2 EVENTS, ERRORS, COMMAND, IPLOG
```

The previous example represents an example configuration on a sensor. In the example, the sensor would send all level 2 and higher events, errors, commands, and IP logs to the host director_one.acmecorp (assuming an entry exists in the hosts file for director_one.acmecorp). You can configure a maximum of 32 different locations in the destinations file.

The *postofficed* daemon can forward messages to the following three services:

- *loggerd*
- *smid*
- *eventd*

The routes File The *routes* file represents the routing table used by the *postofficed* to send messages to remote hosts. The routes file maps the IP address or next hop IP address to the host. The host name used in this file must have a corresponding listing in the hosts file. The entries contained in the routes file must adhere to the following format:

```
<host_name> <connection_num> <ip_address> <udp_port> <type>
```

The host name must match an entry in the hosts file. The <connection_num> represents the priority of this route as compared to other entry's listing routes for the same host. The lower the number, the higher the priority. If two route entries have the same priority, *postofficed* will use the last entry for that priority. The <ip_address> represents the end-point IP address or the next-hop address to reach the specified host name. The <udp_port> represents the UDP port number that should be used when communicating with the host. By default, the UDP port number is 45000. The <type> defines the type of connection that should be used to reach the host, dialup or dedicated. The <type> field currently isn't in use.

An example routes file might contain the following entries:

```
sensor_one.acmecorp 1 192.168.1.1 45000 1
director_one.acmecorp 1 10.10.10.1 45000 1
director_one.acmecorp 3.10.100.100.1 45000 1
```

In the previous example, sensor_one has two different connections that can be used to reach director_one. Sensor_one will prefer to use the IP address 10.10.10.1 to reach director_one because it has a lower *connection_num.*

The daemons File The *daemons* file lists the name of the daemons that should be started when the sensor or director platforms are started. The services file lists all the services that a director or sensor is capable of running, while the daemon file lists which services should be run each time the system is started. The entries contained in the daemons file must adhere to the following format:

<daemon_name>

The following example illustrates a daemons file that would start the *postofficed, loggerd,* and *smid* daemons:

```
nr.postofficed
nr.loggerd
nr.smid
```

The signature File The *signature* file is used primarily by the director platforms to map a common signature name to a signature ID. The signature file shouldn't be modified manually. The entries contained in the routes file must adhere to the following format:

<signature_id> "<signature_name>"

An example signature file would contain the following entries:

```
1000    "Bad Option List"
1001    "Record Packet Rte"
1002    "Timestamp"
1003    "Provide s, c, h, tcc"
1004    "Loose Src Rte"
1005    "SATNET ID"
```

NOTE This file shouldn't be confused with the signature database or the signature files located in the signature database. This is a system file used only to map a common name to a signature ID for use by Cisco Secure IDS applications.

PART V

CIDS Commands

Two different types of commands are available with CIDS: **system** commands and **configuration** commands. *System commands* allow the administrators to view and manage the IDS environment, while ***configuration** commands* are used to view and configure the CIDS sensor and director platforms.

System Commands

Several system commands can be used to view system information, as well as starting and stopping services running on the director or sensor platforms. Some of the more common commands that can be used are

- **idsstart**
- **idsstop**
- **idsconns**
- **idsstatus**
- **idsvers**

STUDY TIP Be aware of the common **system** commands and the functions they perform.

idsstart You can use the ***idsstart*** command to start the CIDS services on your sensor. This command will start all services located in the /usr/nr/etc/daemons configuration file.

idsstop The *idsstop* script can be used to stop the CIDS services running on your sensor.

idsconn The *idsconn* script is provided to assist with troubleshooting communication issues between the sensors and other IDS hosts. The idsconn script can be used to display the status of all connections between the local sensor and other IDS devices, such as a sensor or a director. When this command is issued on the sensor, the script returns a list of open Cisco Secure IDS communication routes.

The script returns the following information for each open connection:

```
<host_name>.<org_name> Connection 1: <ip_address> 45000 1 [Established]
sto:5000
```

If a connection is down, the following is returned:

```
<host_name>.<org_name> Connection 1: <ip_address> 45000 1 [SynSent] sto:5000 syn NOT rcvd!
```

dsstatus To view or confirm that the correct services are running on your sensors, you can use the *idsstatus* script, which returns a list of all IDS daemons currently running on the sensor. The UNIX **ps** command can also be used to list all services running, however, the **ps** command returns a list of all daemons, while the idsstatus script returns a list consisting of only the IDS daemons currently running.

idsvers The *idsvers* script can be used to verify the version of services the sensor is currently running. The idsvers script returns a list of currently running daemons and their version numbers.

Configuration Commands

The sensors can be remotely configured and viewed via the director platforms. The following commands form the bases for remote configuration by the director platforms. Table 24-3 lists the **sensor** commands that allow for remote configuration from the director platform and Table 24-4 lists the syntax parameters used in these commands.

CIDS Directory Structure

The CIDS directory structure follows a hierarchy modeled after the UNIX OS. The organization of the structure allows administrators to locate important system and configuration files quickly. The only variable in the directory structure is the name and location of the installation directory on Windows NT 4.0 servers. As seen in Figure 24-12, below the install directory, each structure is the same on both the director and the sensors. The following are the directories installed on both the sensors and the director platforms:

- Install directory
- bin
- etc
- var

Command	Description	Syntax
nrget	Used to retrieve a single piece of information from a token in a configuration file, such as the IP address of a managed router.	nrget <appid> <hostid> <orgid> <priority> <token> {<identifier>]
nrgetbulk	Used to retrieve multiple pieces of information from a token in a configuration file, such as a list of IP addresses currently being shunned.	nrgetbulk <appid> <hostid> <orgid> <priority> <token> {<identifier>]
nrset	Used to set attributes within a configuration file.	nrset <appid> <hostid> <orgid> <priority> <token> {<identifier>] <value1> [<value2>.....]
nrunset	Used to remove or unset an attribute within a configuration file.	nrunset <appid> <hostid> <orgid> <priority> <token> {<identifier>]
nrexec	Used to execute commands	nrexec <appid> <hostid> <orgid> <priority> <timeout> <token> {<identifier>]

Table 24-3 Configuration Commands with Syntax

Syntax Parameter	Description
<appid>	The application ID. The ID of the service or daemon. A complete list of application IDs can be located in /usr/nr/etc/services.
<hostid>	The PostOffice protocol host identification number, as previously defined.
<identifier> (Optional)	An additional piece of information that can be used to identify a token. This piece of information is optional.
<orgid>	The PostOffice protocol organizational identification number as previously defined.
<priority>	An integer representing the priority of the command.
<timeout>	Used only for **nrexec**, this command specifies the amount of time (in seconds) to wait until the process is considered unreachable.
<token>	The name of the token to set or from which to get information.
<value>	The value to which the specified token should be set.

Table 24-4 Syntax Parameter Description

The Install Directory (/usr/nr)

The *installation* directory on the sensors is the *nr* directory, which is a subdirectory of */usr,* so the installation directory on all sensors is */usr/nr.* Sensor appliances come with the IDS software preinstalled, so the installation directory should always be */usr/nr.*

The bin Directory (usr/nr/bin)

The *bin* directory is used for the storage of all the executable files for CIDS. All CIDS' daemons, services, and functions are stored in the */<install dir>/bin* directory. These files were defined earlier in this chapter. The files stored in the bin directory can be loosely grouped into three categories:

- Daemons
- Configuration Commands
- System Commands

The etc Directory (usr/nr/etc)

The *etc* directory (pronounced *etsee*) is a common UNIX directory used for storing system configuration files. Anyone experienced with the UNIX OS should be familiar with

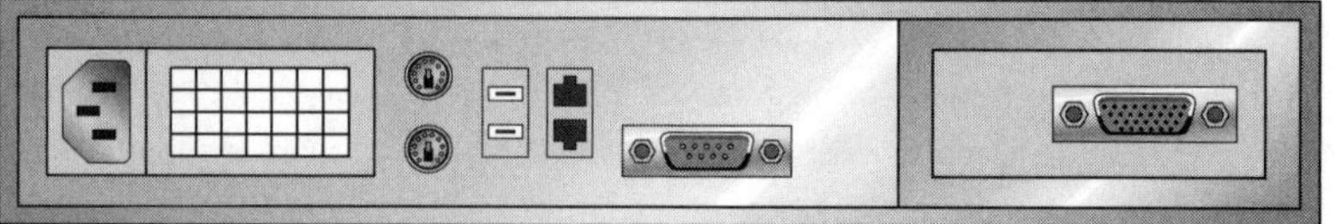

Figure 24-12 IDS Directory structure

the etc directory and the types of files stored there. The etc directory on the sensors and director platforms stores the following two types of files:

- Daemon Configuration files
- System files

The var Directory (usr/nr/var)

The *var* directory is the default directory for all log files. Files created by loggerd and error files for all the daemons are stored in this directory.

CIDS Log Files

During typical operations, the CIDS infrastructure components generate a great deal of information in the form of log files. Log files are created via the *loggerd* daemon. These log files are stored as text files on both the sensor and director platforms. To assist with troubleshooting your system, you should be aware of the types of files, as well as the location of these log files. Additionally, you can create your own custom scripts to pull information from the log files to create custom reports. Cisco Secure IDS provides four types of log files:

- Events
- Service Error
- Commands
- IP Sessions

All event, error, command, and session log data is stored in a common, comma-delimited flat file that can be imported into any database. These four types of logging are written to a text file for performance reasons. Adding text to an open text file is faster than writing the information to a database. Text files are always available and don't rely on a database engine for access to the data, providing greater flexibility to access this important information. For manageability, these text files must periodically be closed, archived, and a new file opened.

Log File Management

For performance and manageability reasons, the log files must be periodically closed and archived. When one log file is closed, another must be opened to take its place. Two factors affect when a log file is closed and a replacement is created: the size of the log file and the time threshold.

Closing Log Files Whenever a log file grows too large or is open too long, a new log file is created to take its place. The name of the new log file depends on the type of log. file and is discussed in the next few sections detailing each type of log file. By default, a log file is closed and another is created when the log file is 60 minutes old or has reached a file size of 1GB, whichever happens first. The 60-minute and 1GB defaults can be changed by modifying tokens in the loggerd.conf daemon configuration file.

The IP session log files have their own set of criteria that determines when a new log file is created. IP session logs are closed every 30 minutes or when the IP session they're recording is terminated.

Storage of Active and Archived Log Files Current event and error log files are stored in the **/usr/nr/var** directory, while archived event and error log files are stored in the **/usr/nr/var/new** directory. Current IP session log files are stored in the **/usr/nr/var/iplog** directory and archived IP session logs are stored in the **/usr/nr/var/iplog/new** directory.

Event Logs

The purpose of any intrusion detection system is to generate alarms when intrusive activity is detected. These alarms, called *events*, are written to log files on the sensors and, in some cases, also on the directors. By default, level 1 and higher events are logged on the sensor, and level 2 to 5 events are forwarded to the director and written to the director's log file. Therefore, level 2 to 5 events are written to the sensor and director log files. Information written to the event logs includes the following:

- Which sensor detected the event
- When the alarm was generated
- The type of alarm
- The source and target of the event

Event logs are written to the /usr/nr/var directory and follow the **log .YYYYMMDDHHMM** naming convention where:

- **Log** Keyword identifying this as an event log
- **YYYY** The four-digit year the file was created
- **MM** The two-digit month the file was created
- **DD** The two-digit day the file was created
- **HH** The two-digit hour the file was created (24-hour clock)
- **MM** The two-digit minute the file was created

An example of a CIDS event log file is

log.200301010001

From the previous example, you can see this log file was created at 12:01 A.M. on 1/1/2003.

Service Error Logs

When any service or daemon generates an error, the error information is written to an error log file. Administrators can then use this error log file to troubleshoot and resolve issues within the CIDS infrastructure. The naming format used for service error log files is **error.service.processID**, where:

- **error**—Keyword identifying this file as a service error log
- **service**—The service or daemon that generated the alert
- **processeID**—Numeric value of the service process identification number

Command Logs

Whenever a service or daemon performs any function that issues a command to the IDS system, the command is logged in a command log file. Information logged includes the name of the daemon that issued the command, the date and time, the host, and the service to which the command was issued.

IP Session Logs

The CIDS system can be configured to log IP session information once a specific event (alarm) is triggered. If a signature is matched, the sensor can respond by recording all IP session activity to a session log. This log provides a permanent record to the intrusion and activity. IP session logs capture all incoming and outgoing TCP packets associated with a specific connection, so they contain binary data.

By default, IP session logs are retained on the sensors until they're needed on the director platforms. This prevents the large amounts of data recorded in IP session logs from impeding CIDS communications during periods of network load.

The naming format used for IP session log files is **iplog.XXX.XXX.XXX.XXX.YYYYMMDDHHMM** where:

- **iplog**—Indicates this is an IP session log file
- **XXX.XXX.XXX.XXX**—Indicates the IP address of the attacking host
- **YYYYMMDDHHMM**—Indicates the year, month, day, hour, and minute the log file was created

An example IP session log might be named as the following:

iplog.192.168.1.1.200212312359

From simply reading the file name, you know a host using the IP address 192.168.1.1 performed some operation that triggered an alarm. The configured response on the sensor, for this alarm, was to create and IP session log. Additionally, you know this attack started on 12/31/2002 at 11:59 P.M. (assuming this is the only IP session log).

Chapter Review

The Cisco Secure Intrusion Detection System (CIDS) is a network-based IDS that uses signatures to detect intrusive activity on your network. The CIDS systems rely on both a sensor platform to capture and analyze network traffic, and an Event Viewer that acts as a centralized alarm and event display platform for the distributed CIDS infrastructure. Communication between these two platforms is handled via the Cisco proprietary PostOffice protocol.

Two types of sensors are available with CIDS:

- 4200 Series Network Sensor Appliance
- 6000 Series Catalyst Intrusion Detection System Module (IDSM)

The 4200 series network sensor appliance consists of three different models. Each model is uniquely tuned for a specific network requirement. These three models and their associated performance features are

- 4210—Capable of monitoring and analyzing 45 Mbps
- 4235—Capable of monitoring and analyzing 200 Mbps
- 4250—Capable of monitoring and analyzing 500 Mbps

The IDSM is a integrated line card that can be inserted into any 6000 series Catalyst switch. The IDSM is capable of copying packets directly off the switch backplane and can monitor up to 100 Mbps. Because the IDSM monitors copies of packets off the switch backplane, it needn't be in the forwarding path of network traffic and won't affect switch throughput performance. Both the 4200 series network appliance and the IDSM can be configured and managed with either director platforms, but the Device Manager can't be installed on an IDSM.

The director platforms allow for centralized configuration and management of the distributed sensor infrastructure. CIDS offers two director platforms, either of which can be used with any type of CIDS sensors. The two director platforms are as follows:

- Cisco Secure Policy Manager (CSPM)
- CIDS Director for UNIX

CSPM is for use on Windows NT 4.0, while CIDS Director for UNIX is an HP OpenView application that runs on Sun Solaris or HPUX. Both offer a GUI interface.

Communication between the sensor and director platforms is facilitated with the Cisco proprietary PostOffice protocol. The PostOffice protocol isn't an e-mail protocol like SMTP, POP, or IMAP. Instead, it's a protocol maintained by Cisco that brings reliability, redundancy, and fault tolerance to the CIDS communication architecture.

Each sensor contains a web application called Device Manager. The Device Manager Application can be used to configure and manage each sensor. The CIDS exam focuses on the use of Device Manager for the configuration of network sensors.

The CIDS application system is made up of services or daemons that each performs a unique function within the CIDS architecture. Daemons run on both the sensors and director platforms, and the most critical daemons, such as *postofficed*, run on both the sensor and director platform. At a minimum, the following daemons must be running on a functioning sensor:

- *packetd*
- *postofficed*
- *fileXferd*
- *loggerd*

The daemons that must be installed and running on a director platform include the following:

- *smid*
- *postofficed*
- *fileXferd*
- *loggerd*

While monitoring the network, the Cisco Secure Intrusion Detection System generates a wealth of information that's stored in log files. These log files include information such as the alarms generated, daemon error conditions, commands issued, and IP session information. Four types of log files are generated by CIDS:

- Event (Alarm) logs
- Command logs
- Service Error logs
- IP Session logs

Questions

1. Which of the following sensor models is capable of delivering 200 Mbps or more of monitoring and analyzing?

   A. The IDSM module for the Catalyst 5500

   B. The IDSM module for the Catalyst 6500

   C. The 4235-network sensor appliance

   D. The 4250-network sensor appliance

2. On which of the following operation systems will CSPM operate properly?

   A. Windows NT 4.0

   B. Windows NT 3.5

C. Windows 2000

D. Sun Solaris or HPUX

3. What is the command that can be used to start the IDS system on a 4200 series network sensor appliance?

A. startids

B. idsstart

C. Idsstart

D. nr.idsstart

4. Which of the following daemons is responsible for the monitoring and analyzing of network traffic?

A. packetd

B. services

C. auth

D. managed

5. Where are archived IP session log files located?

A. /usr/nr/var

B. /usr/nr/var/new

C. /usr/nr/var/iplog

D. /usr/nr/var/iplog/new

6. Which file would you open to see the IP address and UDP port associated with the host name of a CIDS component?

A. auth

B. routes

C. destinations

D. hosts

7. What is the default installation directory on all CIDS sensors?

A. root\usr

B. \usr\var

C. \usr\nr

D. \usr\nr\etc

8. What command would return the current services running and their versions?

A. **idsvers**

B. **showidsver**

C. showver

D. idsshowver

9. What is the protocol used as a communication vehicle between the sensor and director platforms?

A. postofficed

B. SMTP

C. IMAP

D. PostOffice

10. The CIDS Director for UNIX will run on which of the following operating systems?

A. HPUX

B. HPOV

C. Sun Solaris

D. HP OpenView

11. Why should IP blocking be used cautiously?

A. Because it's difficult to configure

B. Because it gives too much control to the sensor

C. Because it's impossible to unblock an address once it's been blocked

D. Because hackers can use this feature to attack your infrastructure

12. What type of files are stored in the /usr/nr/etc directory?

A. Configuration files

B. System files

C. IP session log files

D. Archived log files

13. What is a token?

A. A configuration parameter

B. A configuration file

C. A daemon installed on a sensor

D. A device used in video games

14. What script can assist administrators in troubleshooting communication issues between CIDS devices?

A. auths

B. idscomm

C. idsconn

D. idsstatus

15. Which of the following files should *not* be changed unless directed by Cisco?
    A. signature
    B. hosts
    C. auth
    D. destinations
16. What are the four types of log files?
    A. packetd, postofficed, fileXferd, loggerd
    B. idsstart, idsstop, idsstatus, idsvers
    C. alarm, notification, event, error
    D. event, error, IP session, command
17. The director platform can be configured to respond automatically to an attack by what?
    A. Blocking the offending IP address
    B. Sending a TCP reset packet
    C. Creating an IP Session log
    D. None of the above
18. Which of the following daemons are responsible for file deletion and for moving log files to the database staging area?
    A. loggerd
    B. packetd
    C. fileXferd
    D. sapd
19. Which of the following daemons allow the director platforms to configure sensors remotely?
    A. fileXferd
    B. managed
    C. postofficed
    D. smid
20. Which of the following daemons runs only on the sensor or only on the director, but doesn't run on both?
    A. loggerd
    B. smid
    C. packetd
    D. fileXferd

Answers

1. **C.** and **D.** Both the 4235 and 4250 are capable of 200 Mbps or better
2. **A.** Windows NT 4.0
3. **B.** idsstart
4. **A.** packetd
5. **D.** /usr/nr/var/iplog/new
6. **B.** routes
7. **C.** /usr/nr
8. **A.** idsvers
9. **D.** PostOffice
10. **A.** and **C.** HPUX and Sun Solaris
11. **D.** Because hackers can use this feature to attack your infrastructure
12. **A.** and **B.** Configuration and System files
13. **A.** A configuration parameter
14. **C.** idsconn
15. **A.** signature
16. **D.** event, error, IP session, command
17. **D.** None of the above
18. **D.** sapd
19. **A.** .fileXferd
20. **B. and C.** packetd (sensor), smid (director)

CHAPTER 25

Sensor Installation and Configuration

In this chapter, you will learn to:

- Plan for the proper deployment of CIDS sensors
- Understand the common strategies used to deploy sensors
- Sensor bootstrap configuration
- Use Cisco's IDS Device Manager
- Configure sensors using IDS Device Manager

Sensors form the heart and eyes of the Cisco intrusion detection system (CIDS). For optimum performance, sensors should be deployed at various locations throughout your network. The correct placement of sensors is critical to ensure consistent IDS coverage. This chapter discusses where sensors should be placed, as well as the common strategies used for sensor deployment.

Sensors can be configured using the built-in web application IDS Device Manager. Each sensor can be configure to allow HTTP access to the configuration utility provided in the sensor software. The IDS Device Manager application is preinstalled on each sensor and only must be activated during sensor bootstrap. Once the sensor is bootstrapped, the administrator can connect to the sensor via the IP address configured.

Sensor Deployment Considerations

Extensive planning and preparation are required before deploying sensors on your internetwork. Until some auditing and planning are done, you can't even be sure which sensors are needed. Before you can begin installing your sensors, you must first understand where and how your sensors should be installed. Consider the following factors when you plan the deployment strategy for your network sensors:

- Network entry points
- Network size and complexity
- Amount and type of traffic to be monitored

While each network has its own characteristics and caveats, some common strategies have worked for other Security Engineers across many different and unique network infrastructures. The strategy you choose depends on what you want your intrusion detection system to accomplish. Some IDS systems allow sensors to manage perimeter devices such as routers and firewalls, while other IDS systems are engineered to be passive and only monitor the traffic and actions taking place on the network. Your security policy should dictate the strategy you'll use in engineering your IDS environment and deciding on a sensor deployment strategy.

Network Entry Points

The sensor is designed to monitor all traffic crossing a given network segment. You must consider all external network connections and remote access points you want to protect. The four basic entry points to consider are illustrated in Figure 25-1. Each of the four network entry locations includes the following:

- Internet Connections
- Extranets
- Intranets
- Remote Access

The most common sensor deployment location is between the trusted internal network and the Internet. As seen in Figure 25-1, sensor 1 is located between the trusted network and the Internet. This deployment strategy is referred to as *perimeter protection* and the sensor is commonly paired with one or more firewalls to enforce security policies.

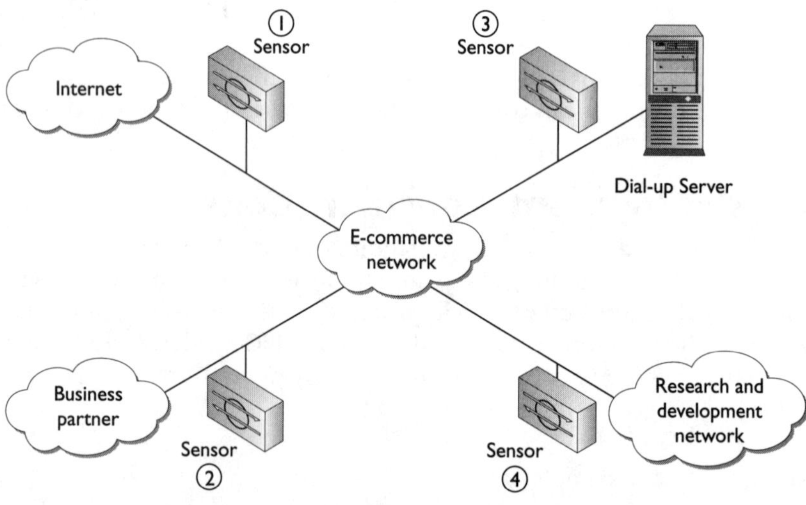

Figure 25-1 Sensor deployment at network entry points

Internet Perimeter Protection Deployment

Different strategies can be used when deploying sensors to monitor perimeter Internet connections. Sensors can be placed in front of a filtering router or a firewall, or they can be placed behind the filtering router or firewall. For the highest level of protection, multiple sensors can be used: one in front of the router/firewall and another behind the router/firewall. As always, advantages and disadvantages exist to each possible physical configuration.

Monitoring Unfiltered Traffic The actual physical placement of the sensor is unimportant. What the sensors are monitoring and where the control interfaces are connected is what's important. As seen in Figure 25-2, the sensor has been logically placed in front of the filtering router by connecting the monitoring interface between the ISP router and the filtering router. In this example, the outermost router is the filtering router/firewall. The sensor monitors all incoming and outgoing traffic, but inbound traffic from the Internet is monitored before it's been filtered by the firewall. If you want (or need) to see all intrusion or denial of service (DoS) attempts before they're filtered, you should consider this deployment strategy.

Because the sensor is placed in front of the filtering device, it will monitor all inbound traffic, including traffic that might be dropped at the filtering device. Another weakness to this deployment strategy is internal network traffic isn't monitored. Hackers could take advantage of this weakness and attack your network resources from an internal host, which would go undetected by the sensor placed in front of the filtering device.

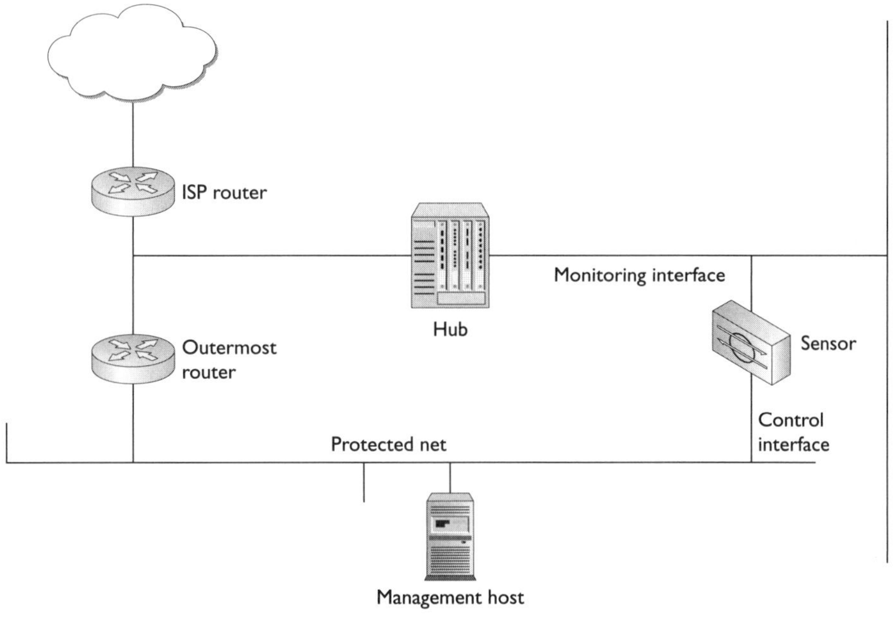

Figure 25-2 Sensor in front of a filtering device

Monitoring Filtered Traffic Sensors can also be placed behind the filtering router or firewall. Figure 25-3 illustrates a common Internet connection where the sensor's monitoring interface is located behind the filtering router. The control interface is connected to the filtering device to allow for device management. This deployment strategy is often called a *firewall sandwich,* because the sensor has an interface connected to the interior network and the control interface is connected to a firewall. Therefore, the firewall or filtering device is sandwiched between the sensors' two interfaces. A firewall sandwich is the Cisco preferred deployment method of using CIDS sensors in conjunction with a firewall.

Placing a sensor's monitoring interface behind a filtering router or firewall prevents the sensor from monitoring traffic the filtering router rejects. One disadvantage to this placement strategy is the sensor is unaware of any policy violations the filtering device stops. To compensate for this, your firewall or filtering router should have some mechanism to notify security personnel when security violations are attempted. To provide the highest level of protection, you can choose to have sensor's located in front of and behind the filtering device.

Monitoring Both Filtered and Unfiltered Traffic To create the highest security posture, you can install a sensor on the inside and the outside of your Internet filtering device. One sensor will monitor all incoming Internet traffic before being filtered and another sensor will monitor internal traffic, as well as all incoming filtered Internet traffic. The only disadvantage to this configuration is the cost associated with purchasing and managing the additional sensors.

Figure 25-3
Sensor behind a filtering device

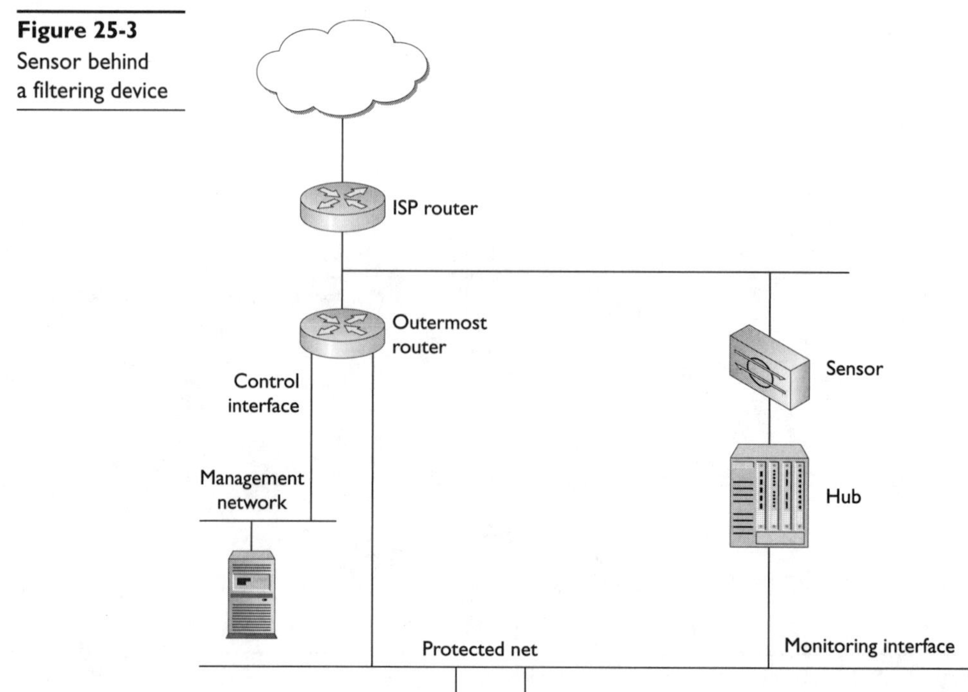

Extranets' Business Partner Networks

Many companies with medium-to-large networks have connections to their business partner networks. These connections include network extensions that connect to vendors, customer companies, and governmental agencies. You might or might not have control over the security policies implemented over these connections. Intruders could manipulate their way into your business partner's networks, and then leverage those connections to compromise your network. In addition, you want to prevent anyone from using your network to attack your business partners. You should deploy sensors to monitor all incoming and outgoing traffic to all business partner networks.

Intranets' Business Divisions

Many large corporations have a hierarchical network design consisting of many different divisional networks, all of which connect to a central corporate backbone. Sensors can be placed at these network boundaries to monitor traffic crossing from one divisional network to another. Different departments commonly have different security policies. For example, company A, an insurance company, could have many different departments with different security policies. The division of the company that processes medical records must adhere to strict governmental security policies, while company A's billing department isn't regulated and can have a less-strict security policy. Sensors can be placed between these two departments to validate that the proper security measures are in place.

Remote Access Networks

Most networks provide a mechanism that allows access to the company network for remote users. This remote access area represents another critical entry point into your network. Hackers will attempt to find and exploit any mechanisms that provide access into your protected network. Remote access networks and servers are a common target of intruders and many intrusions are initiated from these resources. You should monitor all remote access mechanisms, such as servers, VPNs, and dial-up accounts. Placing a sensor between the core network and the remote access network allows security administrators to view and monitor remote incoming traffic.

Network Size and Complexity

The larger and more complex your network, the more likely you'll be forced to deploy multiple sensors throughout the internetwork. Some company departments manage their own Internet and business partner connections, as well as security policies. When the network and security management lacks central control, you're forced to increase the number of sensor and director platforms to monitor your network threats properly. Thankfully, CIDS can be centrally or locally managed, but the more distributed the network, the higher the cost associated with protecting the entire network.

The Amount and Type of Traffic

While some models of the 4200 series network sensor appliance are capable of monitoring up to 500 Mbps, no sensors are capable of monitoring gigabit or multi-gigabit connections.

Some network design changes may be required to allow for the inclusion of your intrusion detection system.

Sensor Installation

Once you decide on the proper placement and deployment strategy, you can then begin to install and configure the sensors. Before you can use Cisco Secure Policy Manager (CSPM) to configure your sensors, though, you must first connect to the sensors and perform basic network connectivity. Once the sensors have a basic configuration, CSPM can be used to configure and manage all sensors in your CIDS infrastructure. This section discusses the management access methods (used to connect initially to the sensor), prepping the sensors for network access (bootstrapping), and configuring the sensors for communication with CSPM.

Once the sensor is properly configured, it can be added as a sensor node in CSPM. After adding the sensor to the NTT tree, you can use CSPM to configure and manage your network sensor appliance.

Connecting to Your Network Sensor Appliance

Once the sensor is installed and powered on, you must gain management access to the sensor. This section describes the methods you can use to connect to your sensor, as well as the default user account you'll use for initial configuration. Three access methods can be used to initially connect to and manage your network sensors. The three access methods include the following:

- Console access using a RS-232 cable
- Telnet to the default initial IP addresses
- Directly with a keyboard and a monitor

NOTE When an IDS 4200 is first plugged into a power source, it powers on momentarily, and then powers off. The Network Interface Controller link lights remain lit as long as a valid link exists. You must press the power switch to boot the system into operation.

When a connection is made, you must then log into the sensor using the preconfigured user account.

Console Access

You can connect to the sensors via their console port. You can use the dual serial communication cable (PN 72-1847-01), included with the sensor, to attach a computer to the console port of the sensor. Once the cable is connected, you can then launch a terminal emulation application, such as Hyperterminal. Table 25-1 lists the terminal settings that must be used for console access.

Table 25-1 Terminal Settings

Terminal Parameters	Terminal Settings
Bits Per Second	9,600
Data Bits	8
Parity	None
Stop Bits	1
Flow Control	Hardware or RTS/CTS

NOTE Cisco recommends using the dual serial communication cable (PN 72-1847-01, included in the accessory kit) rather than a keyboard and monitor because some keyboards and monitors are incompatible with the sensors.

Accessing the Sensor via Telnet

The network sensor appliances come preconfigured with a default IP address of 10.1.9.201. You can use this address to telnet directly to the network sensor, as long as your computer or network has a route-to-host address of 10.1.9.201. If the sensor is installed at a remote location, you probably won't be able to use this option until the default IP address is changed to an address that's routable on your network.

Direct Access with a Keyboard and Monitor

All the 4200 series sensors have both a keyboard and a monitor port located on the back panel. Because the sensor is running the Solaris operating system (OS), you can simply add a keyboard and a monitor, and then begin working on the sensor. Of course, this requires that you also have physical access to the sensor. Some monitors and keyboards are incompatible with the sensors. Cisco provides a list of supported keyboards and monitors in its installation notes. The *Cisco Intrusion Detection System Sensor Installation and Safety Note* has a section devoted to supported monitors and keyboards.

PART V

User Accounts

Two user accounts are created on the sensors. These two user accounts are used to access the OS and the IDS software located on the sensors. The pre-configured default user accounts are root and netrangr. The *root* account is typically used for OS functions and tasks, while the *netrangr* user account is used to administer the CIDS software installed on the host. Table 25-2 shows the common commands used to manage the sensors and the corresponding user account, which must be used to issue the command successfully. Because the sensors run the Solaris OS, these commands are case-sensitive.

The root Account The root account is a Solaris OS user account. This account is used to log in to and perform system-level functions on the sensor. You must be logged in with this account to run the sysconfig-sensor script, which is discussed in more detail in the section "Sensor Bootstrap." The root user must also be used to perform system-level functions on the Solaris OS. Common Solaris commands, such as snoop, can be used when logged in as root. The password used for the root account is attack. The first time you use this account, you're prompted to change the password. Changing the default password for this account is highly recommended.

Command	Description	Log in As
idsstart	Starts the sensor.	netrangr
idsstop	Stops the sensor.	netrangr
idsconns	Displays the state of the current communications' connection.	netrangr
idsvers	Displays software version information.	netrangr
idsstatus	Displays status of Cisco IDS daemons/services.	netrangr
ping	Verifies IP connectivity.	netrangr
snoop -d <sensing interface name>	Displays traffic seen by the monitoring interface.	root
verifySensor	Displays detailed information about the system.	root
shutdown -y -i 0	Shuts down the sensor.	root
traceroute	Traces network traffic to a destination.	root

Table 25-2 Solaris and CIDS User Accounts and Commands

NOTE The snoop command is a common Unix command that configures the OS to display all the network traffic received on a particular network interface. You can use the snoop command to verify the NIC is configured and is receiving network traffic.

The netrangr Account The *netrangr* account is used for administering the IDS system on the sensor. The password for this account is attack. The first time you use this account, you're prompted to change the password. Changing the default password for this account is highly recommended.

Sensor Bootstrap

When a new sensor is installed on the network, it lacks any specific configuration information. In its default state, the sensor has no way of communicating on the network or with any management platform. Before a sensor can be operational, it must first be bootstrapped. *Bootstrapping* a sensor consists of building a basic configuration, which allows the sensor to communicate with remote hosts.

If you're using CSPM to configure and manage your CIDS, you're required to reboot the sensor when PostOffice parameters are changed. For example, if you add a new CSPM platform and you want to manage an existing sensor with the new CSPM server, you rebootstrap the sensor. If you upgrade an existing CSPM with another, yet retain all the settings from the older CSPM platform, you won't have to rebootstrap the sensor.

The IDS Device Manager isn't affected by the PostOffice parameters configured on the sensor. The IDS Device Manager connects to and configures the sensor via an IP address and a web interface, so it isn't affected by changes in the PostOffice protocol.

To bootstrap a server, you must log in to the sensor using the root user account. Stored on each sensor is a configuration script named *sysconfig-sensor,* which provides a menu-driven system that enables you to create a basic configuration on the sensor.

Before running the sysconfig-sensor script, you need to collect and record the relevant information needed to configure the sensor. Table 25-3 is a worksheet that lists the information you should collect and record before running the sysconfig-sensor script.

Performing a Sensor Bootstrap in 12 Easy Steps

The following 12 steps are required to bootstrap a sensor:

- **Step 1** Log in to the sensor using the user name *root* and the password *attack*. You'll be prompted to change the password if this is the first time you've used this account. If you don't know how to log in to the sensor, see the previous section, "Connecting to Your Network Sensor."

Menu Item Number	Information needed for bootstrap
1	What is the IP address of the sensor?
2	What is the netmask to be used by the sensor?
3	What is the sensor's host name?
4	What are the IP address of the sensor's default gateway?
5	What are the IP addresses and/or network range addresses that will be permitted to access the sensor via Telnet, FTP, and TFTP? You must specify the IP addresses of hosts that will be allowed to configure and manage the sensor.
6	What are the values for the following PostOffice communications parameters? **Sensor Host ID**—A unique numeric identifier for the sensor. The expected value is a whole number between 1 and 65,535. **Sensor Organization ID**—A unique numeric identifier for a collection of sensors. The expected value is a whole number between 1 and 65,535. **Sensor Host Name**—A logical name associated with the host ID (not the IP host name). Cisco recommends you use only lowercase letters. **Sensor Organization Name**—A logical name associated with the Sensor Organization ID. Cisco recommends you use only lowercase letters. **CSPM IP Address**—The IP address of your CSPM server. **CSPM Host ID**—A unique numeric identifier for the CSPM host. This value must match the value specified when CSPM was installed. **CSPM Host Name**—A logical name associated with the CSPM Host ID. This value must match the value specified when CSPM was installed.
7	What is the current date, time, and time zone for this sensor?
8	What should the passwords be for both the root and netrangr accounts?
9	For IPSec, you must supply the following values: What is the security parameter index (SPI) for default inbound configuration? If you use custom keys, what are the values for the following inbound and outbound configurations? Cipher key Authentication key

Table 25-3 Bootstrap Information

PART V

- **Step 2** At the command prompt, type **sysconfig-sensor**. When this command is issued, a menu will appear. The following is an example of the menu you'll see on your screen.

```
Cisco IDS Sensor Initial Configuration Utility

Select Options 1 through 6 to initially configure the Sensor.

 1 - IP Address
 2 - IP Netmask
 3 - IP Host Name
 4 - Default Route
 5 - Access Control List
 6 - Communications Infrastructure
 7 - Date/Time and Time Zone
 8 - Passwords
 9 - Secure Communications
10 - Display
11 - IDS Device Manager
 x - Exit

Selection:
```

- **Step 3** Type **1** to enter the **IP Address** screen:

```
IP Address
```

Enter the TCP/IP address the Sensor uses. The new value won't be activated until you restart the Sensor. Write down the new address. You'll need to update the information on the Access Control List menu (Option 5 on the main menu).

```
WARNING: If you do not update the IP address on the Access Control List
menu, you will not be able to log in once the Sensor has rebooted with
the new address:
Current address:10.1.9.201
New address:
```

This screen enables you to configure the new IP address. The existing default IP address is 10.1.9.201. The new IP address won't be activated until the sensor is restarted.

NOTE You must enter this IP address in the list of allowed hosts in the Access Control List screen (Option 5, discussed in a later step).

- **Step 4** Type **2** to enter the **IP Netmask** screen:

```
IP Netmask
Enter the TCP/IP netmask that the Sensor uses. The new value will not
be activated until you restart the Sensor.

Current address:
Current netmask:255.255.255.0

New netmask:
```

The default netmask is 255.255.255.0. Enter the new netmask to be used by this sensor. The new netmask won't be activated until you restart the sensor.

- **Step 5** Type **3** to access the **IP Host Name** screen:

```
IP Host Name

Enter a new host name for the Sensor. The new value will not be
activated until you restart the Sensor.

Current name: sensor
New name:
```

Enter the new hostname to be used by this sensor, such as **sensor1**.

- **Step 6** Type **4** to enter the **Default Route** screen. This is the address of the router that services the local subnet. All nonlocal traffic will be sent to this address.

```
Default Route

Enter the default route for the TCP/IP traffic coming from the Sensor.
The default route is the IP address of the primary router attached to
the same LAN as the Sensor. The new value will not be activated until
you restart the Sensor.

Current default route:
New default route:
```

The current default address is 10.1.9.1. Enter the new default gateway address.

- **Step 7** Type **5** to enter the **Access Control List** screen. Listed here are the IP network and host addresses that should have telnet, TFTP, and FTP access to this sensor. The IP address of the CSPM and the local sensor must be listed here to allow communications between the two hosts.

```
Access Control List

You can modify the list of IP addresses and networks that are allowed
to log into the Sensor. A TCP wrapper application enforces this list.
If a host with an IP address that is not in this list attempts to log
into the Sensor, the TCP connection will automatically be closed.

WARNING: If you have changed the IP address of the Sensor, list the
host addresses from which you log in remotely.

This list must contain only host IP addresses and not host names. The
Sensor by default does not use ANY type of name service (for example,
DNS, NIS, NIS+). List the network addresses with just the network
portion of the address: 192.9.200.

Current list:

   10.

Enter an address to add to the list. If the address entered is already
in the list, it will be deleted from it.

IP address:
```

As you can see, by default, any host with an IP address that starts with 10. is allowed to communicate with this sensor. To delete the 10. entry, simply type **10.** again and it will be removed from the list. To enter an address range, simply type the network portion of the IP address and nothing more, and then press ENTER. For example, to allow all hosts in the 192.168.10.0 /24 network, type **192.168.10.** and press ENTER.

NOTE You should limit the number of hosts that have access to your servers. The more hosts allowed to communicate with your sensor, the greater the potential for an intruder to use the systems to attack your IDS sensors. The IP address of the director platform must be entered.

- **Step 8** Type **6** to enter the Communications Infrastructure screen.

NOTE The communication setting must be configured properly. If a host ID, orgID, or any other ID is inputted incorrectly, the sensor will be unable to communicate with the rest of the CIDS infrastructure.

```
Communications Infrastructure

To create the configuration files necessary to enable communication
between the Sensor and the IDS Manager, enter the following values:

   *Sensor Host ID
   *Sensor Organization ID
   *Sensor Host Name
   *Sensor Organization Name
   *Sensor IP Address

   *IDS Manager Host ID
   *IDS Manager Organization ID
   *IDS Manager Host Name
   *IDS Manager Organization Name
   *IDS Manager IP Address

Do you want to continue (y/n)?
```

Type **y** to enter the PostOffice communications information. Table 25-2 lists these parameters with the acceptable values for each. You must specify this sensor's host and organization information. The Host ID must be unique, however, the organization ID must be the same as the one configured on the other CIDS sensors and infrastructure.

- **Step 9** Type **7** to enter the Date/Time and Time Zone screen.

```
Date/Time and Time Zone

1 - Synchronize Date/Time with Another Host
2 - Set Date/Time
3 - Change Time Zone
x - Exit

Selection:
```

Choose the method you want to use to set the date, time, and time zone information.

- **Step 10** Type **8** to enter the **Password** screen.

```
Select the account whose password you want to change.

1 - netrangr
2 - root
x - Exit

Selection:
```

Change the passwords for both the netrangr and the root user accounts.

- **Step 11** Type **10** to view the **Display** screen.

```
Display

Display Mode: VGA/Terminal

1 - Toggle Display Mode
x - Exit

Selection:
```

Within the Display screen, you can toggle between VGA/Terminal mode and Terminal mode. In *VGA/Terminal mode,* you can connect to the sensor via a console cable or by using a monitor and a keyboard. In this mode, boot messages are only sent to the VGA port.

Terminal mode limits the sensor's display to a terminal connected to the console port, while disabling the VGA port. If you choose Terminal mode, the VGA port won't provide any access to the system. In Terminal mode, boot messages are sent to the terminal, not to the VGA port.

- **Step 12** Type **11** to view the **IDS Device Manager** screen.

```
IDS Device Manager

Current Mode: Enabled

1 - Disable
x - Exit

Selection:
```

Because you're using IDS Device Manager, this option should be enabled. By default, it is enabled.

IDS Device Manager

The *IDS Device Manager* is a web application that comes preinstalled on all sensors version 3.1 or higher. This application can be used to configure and manage your

CIDS sensors. You can access the IDS Device Manager using Netscape or Internet Explorer. Unlike CSPM, this application can't be used to create multiple configurations for multiple sensors.

The IDS Device Manager provides a GUI interface that's used to configure each sensor individually. Figure 25-4 illustrates the IDS Device Manager view displayed during the initial connection using Netscape or Internet Explorer.

Connecting to the IDS Device Manager

Before the IDS Device Manager can be used to configure CIDS sensors, the sensors must first be bootstrapped, as previously discussed. Once the sensors are bootstrapped, you can connect to the sensor using Netscape or Internet Explorer. To connect, simply type **https://<sensor_ip_address>** in the address bar and press ENTER. Notice you must use HTTPS, and not just http.

The sensors contain a web server that's running the Device Manager application. For security reasons, the web server uses an encryption protocol known as Transaction Layer Security (TLS), which is closely related to Secure Socket Layer protocol (SSL). When you enter the URL to the sensor in the address bar, the web browser attempts to connect to the sensor using TLS or SSL. You can disable the security feature by selecting Device | Sensor Setup | Network, where *Device* is the Area, *Sensor Setup* is the Sub-Area, and *Network* is the TOC item.

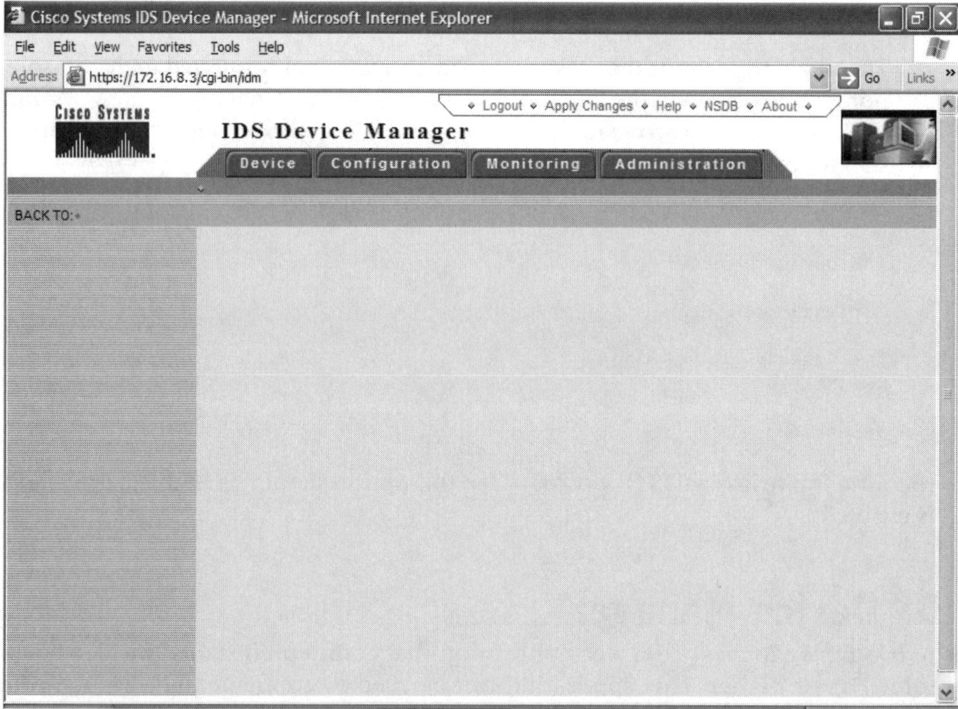

Figure 25-4 IDS Device Manager initial view

When you connect to the Device Manager application, you're presented with a security alert dialog box warning that the certificate being used by the sensor has been issued by an unknown Certificate Authority (CA), as shown in Figure 25-5. The sensor generates its own certificate, so it isn't a trusted CA. To connect to the sensor, you must choose to ignore this warning. To prevent this security alert dialog box from being presented each time you connect to the sensor, you must configure your web browser to trust the sensors as a CA.

NOTE If you change the organization or host name of the sensor, a new certificate is generated. You'll then be required to perform the fingerprint validation again.

The IDS Device Manager application uses cookies for session tracking to provide a consistent view. Device Manager uses only temporary session cookies, not stored cookies. You must enable cookies on your web browser to use the Device Manager application.

When you connect to the Device Manager, you're prompted for a user name and a password. The default user name is netrangr and the password is attack. The user name and the password can be changed once access to the Device Manager is accomplished.

IDS Device Manager GUI Interface

The Device Manager GUI interface consists of the following:

- Area Bar
- Sub-Area Bar
- TOC
- Content Area
- Path Bar
- Tool Bar

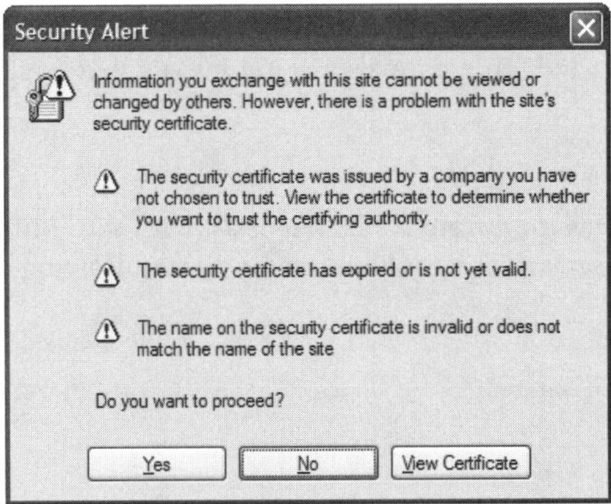

Figure 25-5 Security warning dialog box

Area Bar

The Area Bar contains the four major configuration headings that can be selected to configure specific settings for the IDS sensor. Once an area is selected, a list of corresponding Sub-Areas is listed in the Sub-Area Bar.

The areas include the following:

- Device
- Configuration
- Monitoring
- Administration

Sub-Area Bar

The content of the Sub-Area Bar changes depending on the Area that's selected. The configuration objects that make up the Sub-Area menu are subcategories under the major area. For example, when the Device Area is chosen, the only Sub-Area that can be selected is Sensor Setup, but when the Monitoring area is selected, you can choose from the three Sub-Area categories: Log, Sensing Interfaces Statistics, or IDS Event Viewer. Once a Sub-Area is selected, the Table of Contents (TOC) for that Sub-Area is displayed.

Table of Contents (TOC)

Each Sub-Area selected contains a different Table of Contents (TOC). When an item in the TOC is selected, the content area will display the configuration parameters for the item selected.

Content Area

The *Content Area* is where the configuration parameters for each configurable setting are displayed. From this area, you can add, change, or delete the existing sensor configuration settings from within the Content Area panel. The Content Area is where the configuration parameters are set.

Path Bar

The *Path Bar* displays the current path, including the Area, Sub-Area, and the TOC item currently selected. This path shows the menus that were selected to reach the current destination.

Tool Bar

The *tool bar* has important tools that assist with the configuration and management of the network sensor. The tool bar contains the following tools and links:

- Logout
- Apply Changes
- Help

- NSDB
- About

Logout The *Logout* link can be selected to log out of the current sensor. Only one connection to the sensor is allowed at a time, so logging out of the sensor once you complete the configuration is important.

Apply Changes The *Apply Changes* link must be used to save any configuration changes that were made. The changes made to the sensor aren't applied until the Apply Changes link is selected. If you don't want to apply or save the changes made, you can click reset to remove all the changes made and return the settings to their previous state. As you can see in Figure 25-6, once the changes have been applied, you might be required to reset the sensor.

Help The *Help* link can be selected to provide additional help with the use of Device Manager and the configuration of the CIDS sensor.

NSDB The Network Security Database (NSDB) can be displayed by selecting NSDB from the Tool menu, as seen in Figure 25-7. The NSDB contains specific information regarding the signatures and the types of attacks each signature is used to detect. The NSDB is explained in more detail in the next chapter.

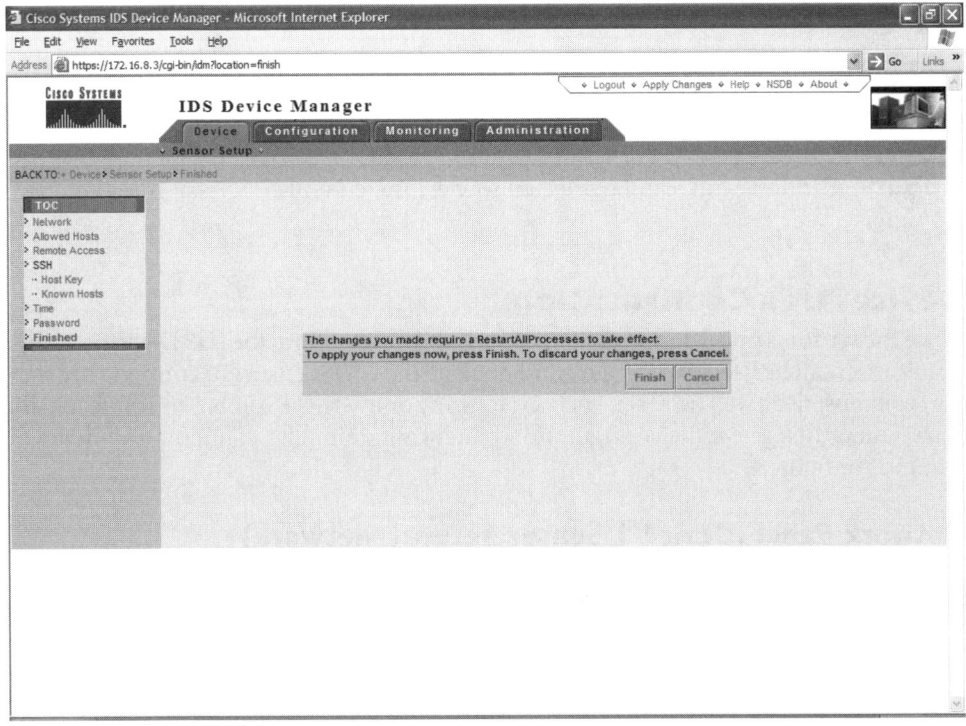

Figure 25-6 Apply changes

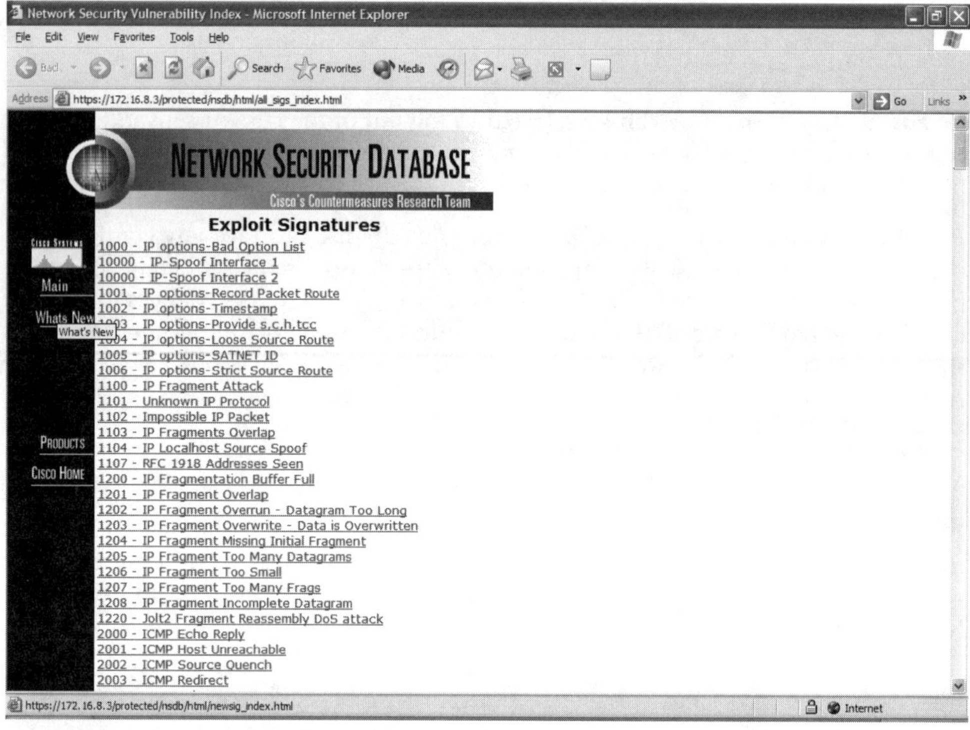

Figure 25-7 Network Security Database

About The *about* link can be selected to view the current IDS version the sensor is running.

Device Area Configuration

Once the sensor is bootstrapped with the correct configuration, the IDS Device Manager application can be used to configure and manage the CIDS sensor. To configure the sensor, you must use a web browser, such as Netscape or Internet Explorer, to connect to the sensor, and then select the configuration panel containing the configuration data you want to configure.

Network Panel (Device | Sensor Setup | Network)

The Network panel can be selected by navigating to Device | Sensor Setup | Network, where *Device* is the Area, *Sensor Setup* is the Sub-Area, and *Network* is the TOC item. Once the Network TOC item is selected, the network panel is displayed in the content area, as seen in Figure 25-8.

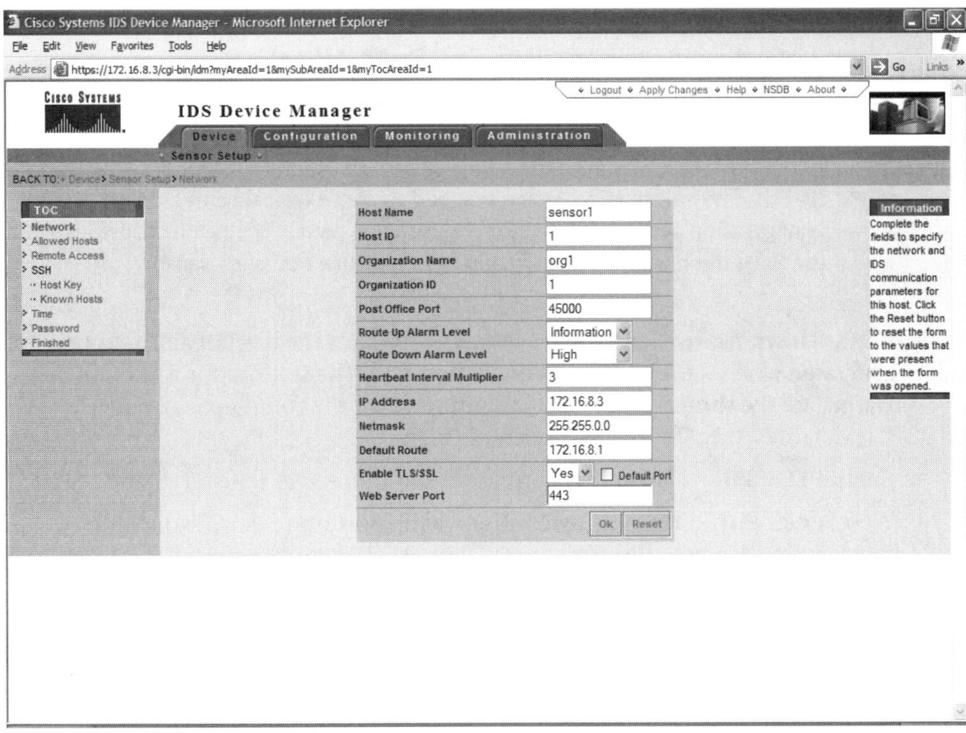

Figure 25-8 IDS Device Manager Network panel

The Network panel lists the configuration parameters that were configured during the sensor bootstrap process. From this panel, the common network and PostOffice setting can be modified. Additional settings that can be configured include the following:

- **Heartbeat Interval** This setting is used to calculate how many attempts the sensor should make to wait for a heartbeat acknowledgement from a remote host before considering the host is down and generating a route-down alarm.
- **Route-Up Alarm Level** This setting configures the level of alarm to be generated when a route-up event is detected. The default setting is Informational. Possible settings include the following:
    - Informational—Categorizes the event as informational in nature and not a risk to security. These events are shown with a blue icon in the IDS Event Viewer.
    - Low—Categorizes the event as mildly severe. These events are displayed with a yellow icon in the IDS Event Viewer.

- Medium—Categorizes the event as a moderate risk. These events are displayed with an orange icon in the IDS Event Viewer.
- Categorizes the event as a high risk. These events are displayed with a red icon in the IDS Event Viewer.

NOTE The values (1 to 5) are mapped to these logical names, based on the configuration settings in the severity mapping panel. The names previously used are the default severity mappings configured on each sensor.

- **Route-Down Alarm Level** This setting configures the level of alarm to be generated when a route-down event is detected. The settings for route-down alarms are the same as previously mentioned for the route-up alarm level. The default setting for this parameter is high.
- **Enable TLS/SSL** This setting configures the web server to use TLS and SSL.
- **Web Server Port** This setting configures the port number on which the sensor's web server will listen for HTTP or HTTPS requests. By default, this parameter is set to 443 for HTTPS communications.

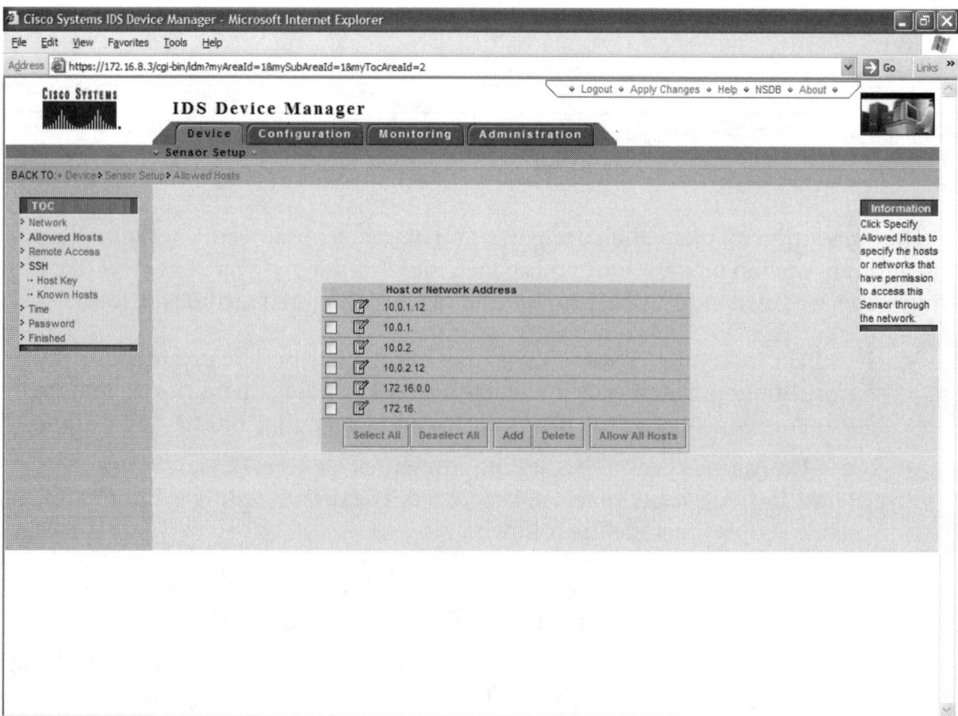

Figure 25-9 Adding allowed hosts

Allowed Hosts (Device | Sensor Setup | Allowed Hosts)

You can configure the allowed hosts during the bootstrapping or from the IDS Device Manager. By default, the sensor only allows access from IP addresses to which the sensor has been configured to allow access. By default, the sensor allows access from any host with an IP address belonging to the 10.0.0.0 /8 network. Before you can connect to the sensor, you must configure the sensor—during bootstrap—to allow the IP address of the host which you'll use to connect to the sensor. Figure 25-9 illustrates the Allowed Hosts panel.

To allow hosts, you can enter the specific host address or the network address. When adding a network address, you only have to enter the octets that make up the network address. For example, if you want to allow all hosts in the 172.30.0.0 /16 network, you could add the first two octets, such as 172.16. In addition, you can allow all hosts to connect to and manage the sensor by clicking Allow All Hosts.

Remote Access (Device | Sensor Setup | Remote Access)

You can allow unsecured access to the sensor via Telnet or FTP. The protocols are considered insecure because they send data in clear text. To enable Telnet or FTP, select the Remote Access item in the TOC and select either protocol by placing a check mark in the corresponding checkbox, as Figure 25-10 shows.

SSH Host Keys (Device | Sensor Setup | SSH)

From the SSH TOC panel, you can generate a new or delete an existing host key. *Host keys* are used by the sensor to connect to PIX firewalls and other hosts. Once the SSH session is open, the sensor can use the connection to perform blocking.

You can configure the sensor to create a new host key by selecting the Generate Host Key link on the Host Key panel. Once the host key is created, apply your configuration settings. With the new key created, you must then update the known host tables on the remote systems with the new key fingerprint. You can delete exiting keys by selecting the Known Hosts TOC item.

NOTE If you're using the sensor to configure blocking on a PIX firewall, you must manually connect to the firewall using SSH, and then accept the SSH key of the PIX firewall.

Setting the Time (Device | Sensor Setup | Time)

You can configure the time, date, and time zone information from the Time panel.

Changing the Password (Device | Sensor Setup | Password)

The password for the netrangr account can be changed from the Password panel. You needn't click Apply Changes on the toolbar for this change to take effect.

PART V

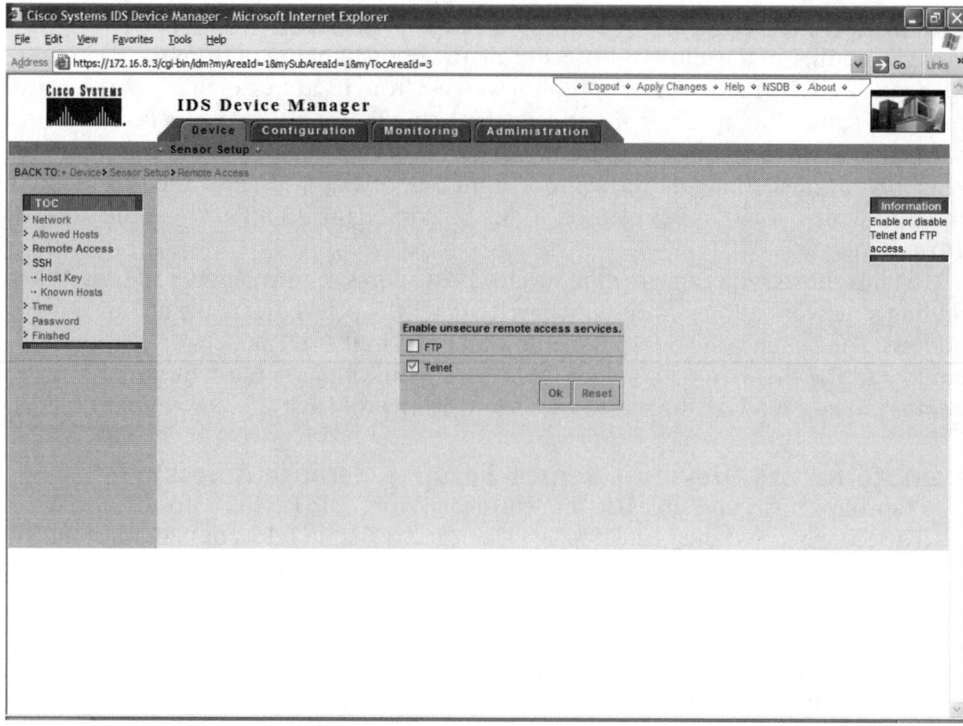

Figure 25-10 Remote Access configuration

Configuration Area

Adding Remote Hosts (Configuration | Communications | Remote Hosts)

By default, the CIDS sensors publish alarm and event data to the host on the host in which you installed IDS Device Manager. You can change or add additional hosts, allowing the sensor to send the event stream to multiple hosts. You must add the IDS Event Viewer as a remote host if alarms are to be sent to the Event Viewer. When adding a remote host, you can specify the level of alarm that should be sent to the remote host. The Remote Hosts panel is illustrated in Figure 25-11.

Event Destinations Event Destinations enables you to configure the level of alarms to be sent to previously configured remote hosts. You can specify the level of alarm to be sent, the service to which the alarm should be sent, and the type of message to be sent.

Signature Configuration (Configuration | Sensing Engine | Signature Configuration)

As discussed in Chapter 23, the sensor uses signatures to detect network intrusions. A signature specifies the types of network attacks for which you want the sensor to detect

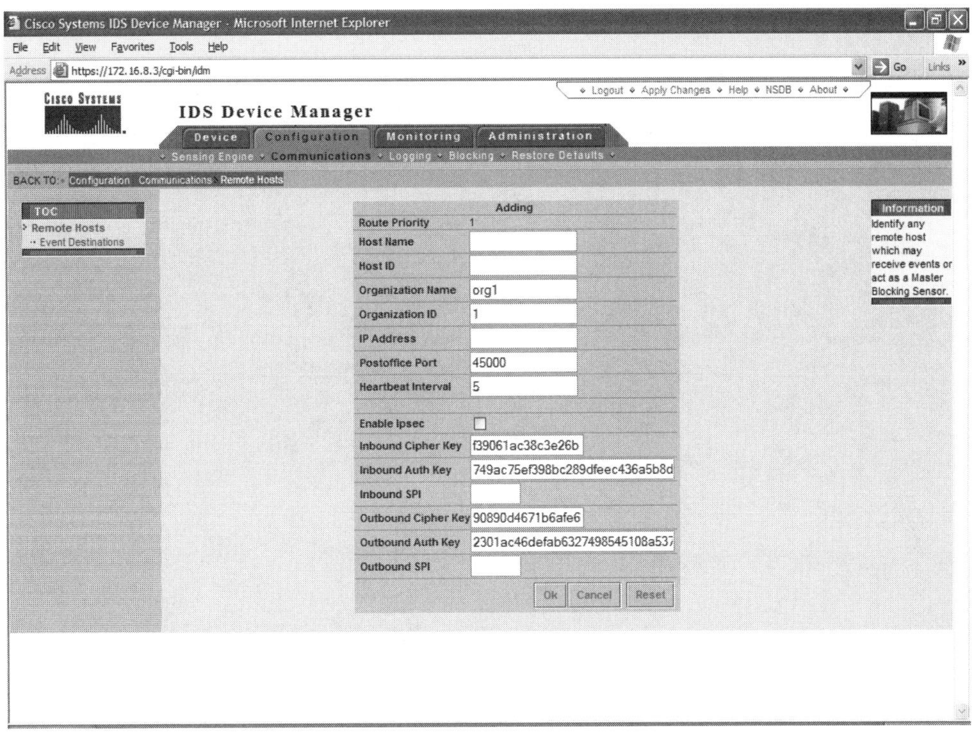

Figure 25-11 Remote Hosts panel

and generate alarms. Signatures are arranged in two different ways. Signatures are arranged in six categories based on the type of traffic that's analyzed. And signatures are also organized into signature groups, based on the signature engine type, as seen in Figure 25-12. Each signature group contains a configuration pane that can be used to configure each specific signature contained in that signature group. From the configuration pane, the signatures can be enable or disabled, the severity can be assigned, and the responsive action can be specified.

The six categories of signatures are as follows:

- Built-in
- Custom
- TCP Connection
- UDP Connection
- String Matching
- ACL

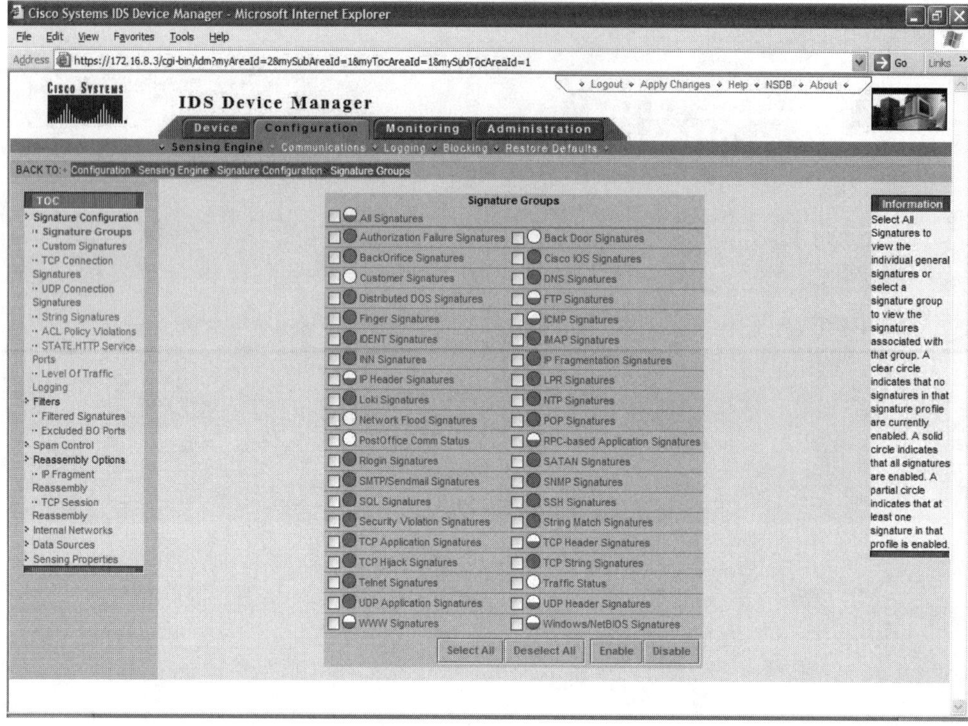

Figure 25-12 Signature groups configuration pane

Built-in signatures are known attack signatures included in the sensor software. The signatures that make up the built-in group can't be added to, removed, or renamed. You can adjust the built-in signatures by adjusting a number of group signature parameters. Figure 25-13 illustrates the configuration pane for built-in and custom signatures.

Custom signatures are user defined. These signatures can be fine-tuned through signature engine parameters.

TCP connection signatures are user-defined signatures based on the TCP port number of the traffic being monitored. As seen in Figure 25-14, you can use the TCP connection signatures configuration pane to enable or disable a TCP connection signature. You can also configure the severity of the signature, as well as the actions to take when the signature is matched.

UDP connection signatures are user-defined signatures based on the UDP port number of the traffic being monitored. As seen in Figure 25-15, the UDP connection configuration pane can be used to configure the UDP connection signatures.

String matching signatures are user-defined signatures that detect malicious activity by analyzing network traffic looking for a specific string match. String-matching signatures

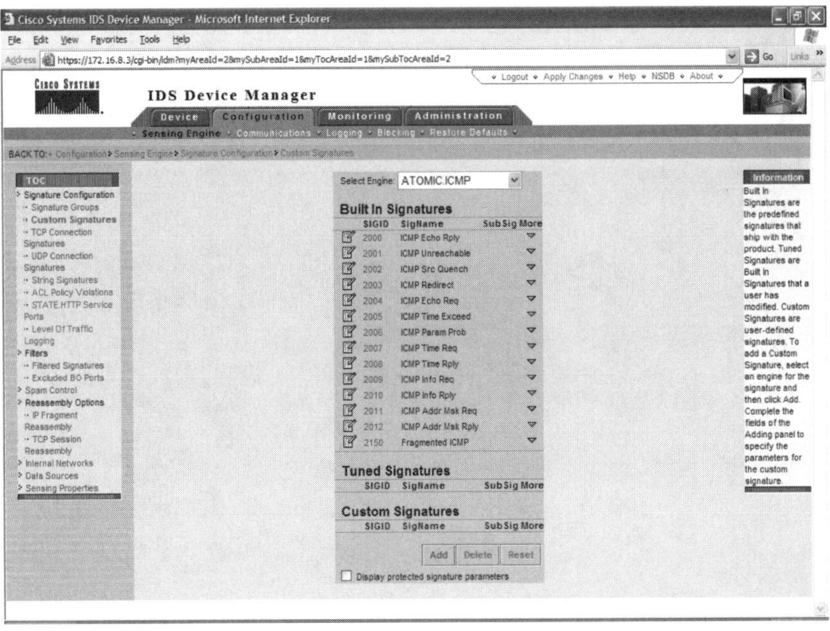

Figure 25-13 Configration panel for built-in and custom signatures

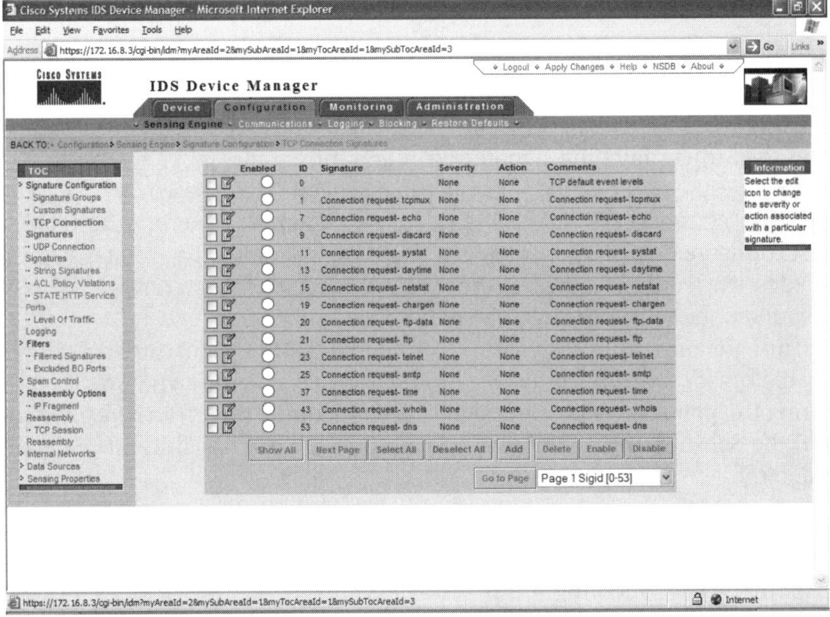

Figure 25-14 TCP connection signatures configuration pane

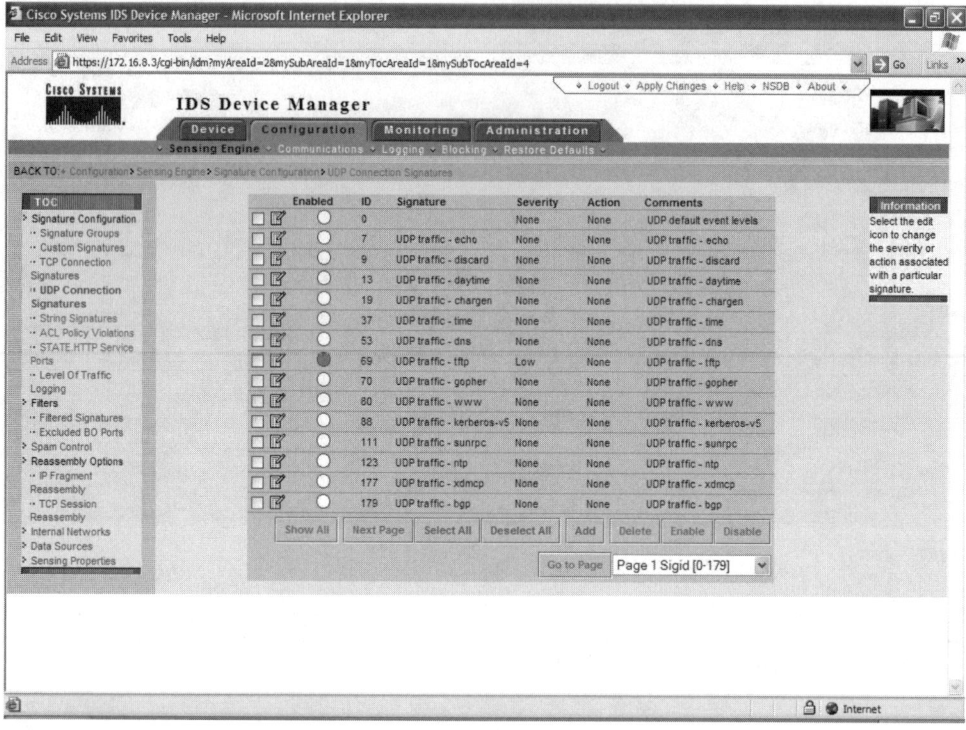

Figure 25-15 UPD connection signatures configuration pane

can be configured to analyze incoming, outgoing, or bidirectional traffic. Figure 25-16 illustrates the String matching signature configuration pane.

ACL signatures are user-defined signatures that generate alerts based on policy violations recorded by access devices. To allow a sensor to send alarms based on ACL violations, you must first configure one or more routers to log ACL violations. The routers must then be configured to send syslog messages to the sensor. When the sensor receives a syslog message from the router, the sensor generates an alarm.

By default, the most critical signatures are enabled. Other signatures must be enabled to allow the sensor to monitor network traffic for that specific signature. Enabling and configuring the parameters for each signature is accomplished from the Configuration Area and the Sensing Engine Sub-Area. Signatures are discussed in more detail in the next chapter.

Level of Traffic Logging From the Configuration Area, you can configure the level of logging the sensor should perform. As seen in Figure 25-17, you can configure the sensor to log the following:

- None
- TCP connection requests and UDP traffic

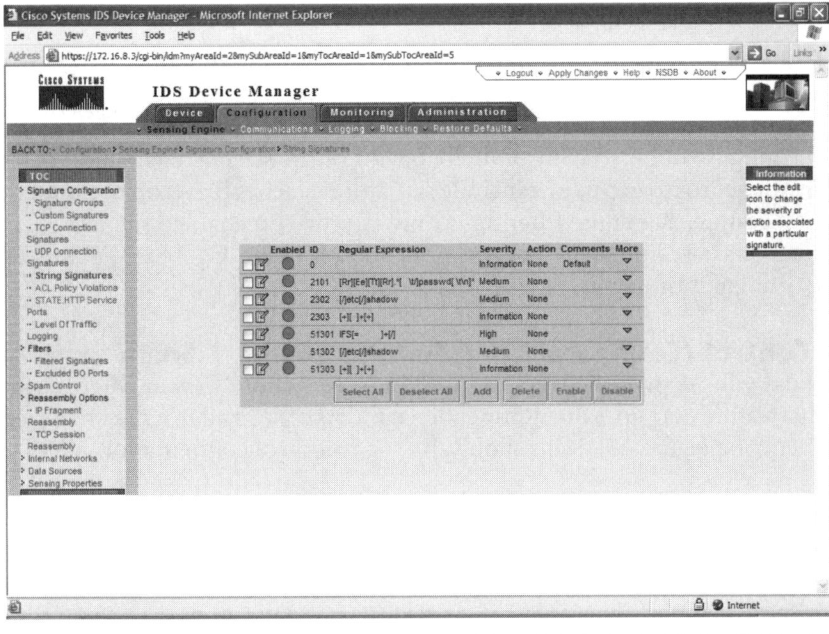

Figure 25-16 String matching signature configuration pane

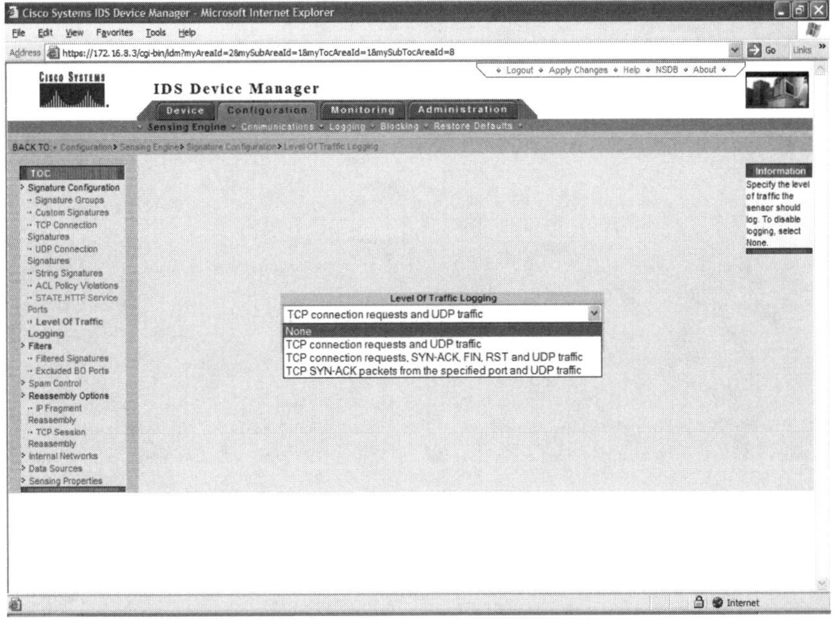

Figure 25-17 Level of logging configuration pane

PART V

- TCP connection requests, SYN-ACK, FIN, RST, and UDP traffic
- TCP SYN-ACK packets from the specified port and UDP traffic

Filter Configuration (Configuration | Sensing Engine | Filters)

You can configure filters to control the behavior of the sensing engine filters. You can configure the sensor to exclude or include signature matches based on the source or destination IP address. Signature filtering is only effective on enabled signatures. You can configure filters based on the IP address or IP address range. Figure 25-18 illustrates the filtering configuration pane.

Spam Control (Configuration | Sensing Engine | Spam Control)

You can use your network sensors to monitor the amount of spam entering your network. This feature examines the number of recipients contained in a mail message crossing the network. Figure 25-19 illustrates the spam control configuration pane.

IP Fragmentation Reassembly (Configuration | Sensing Engine | Reassembly Options)

The reassembly options TOC item contained in the Configuration Area can be used to configure IP fragment reassembly parameters. By configuring this configuration pane,

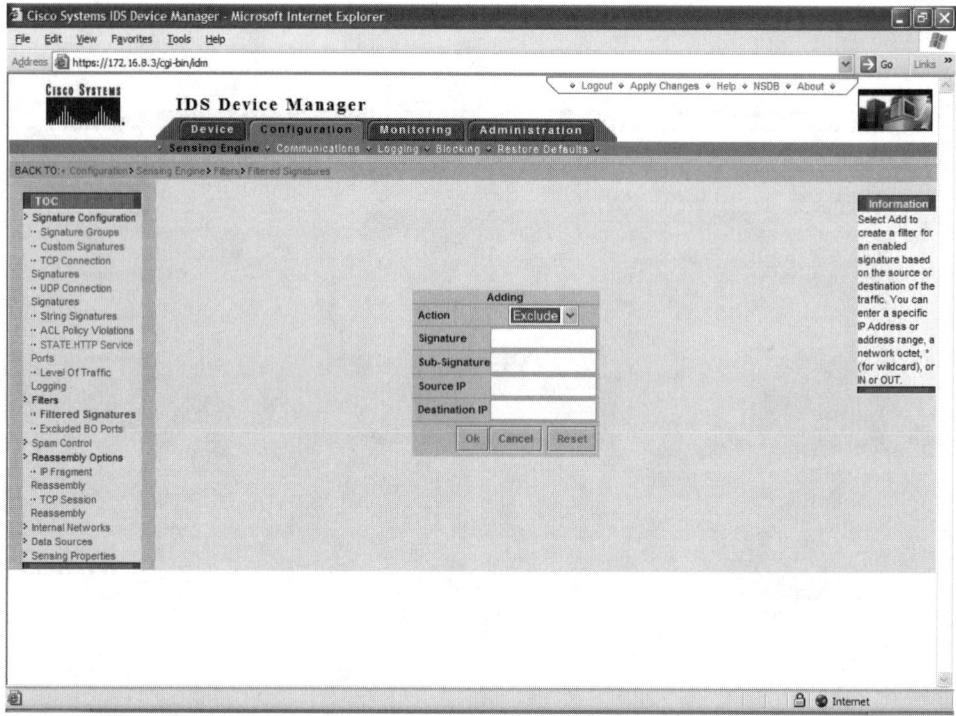

Figure 25-18 Signature filtering configuration pane

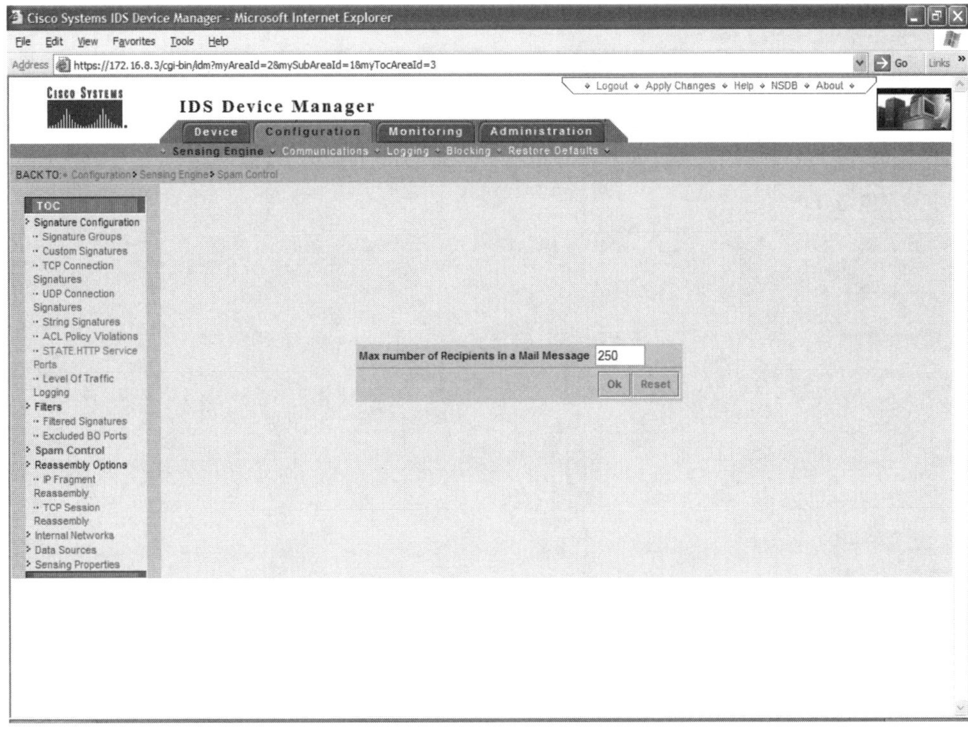

Figure 25-19 Spam control configuration pane

you configure the sensor to reassemble all the fragmented packets before they're compared to the signature database. Figure 25-20 displays the IP fragment reassembly options configuration pane.

Reassembling IP fragments into the complete datagram consumes sensor resources, such as memory and CPU cycles. Without some additional parameters in place, it would be possible for the sensor to run out of resources by attempting to track and reassemble too many datagram fragments. To prevent this from happening you must configure the following parameters:

- Maximum Partial Datagrams
- Maximum Fragments per Datagram
- Fragmented Datagram Timeout

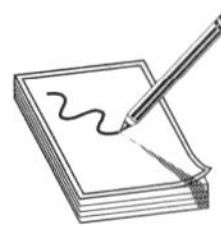

NOTE Cisco recommends you don't modify these settings unless you thoroughly understand your traffic patterns and the likelihood of receiving fragmented packets over a specified amount.

PART V

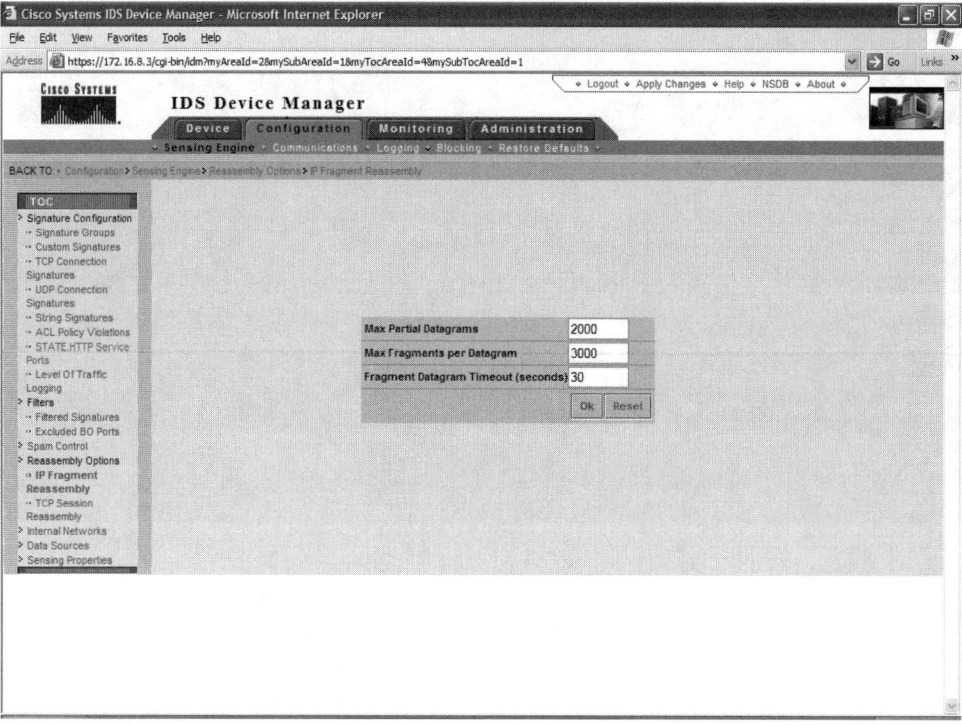

Figure 25-20 IP fragmentation reassembly configuration pane

Maximum Partial Datagrams The *Maximum Partial Datagrams* parameter is used to specify the maximum number of partial datagrams that can be tracked by the sensor. When the sensor receives a fragmented datagram, it must then collect all the associated fragments that make up the entire datagram and reassemble them. This parameter sets the maximum amount of partial datagrams the sensor will attempt to reassemble. The sensor has a limited amount of resources and could be swamped if this limit is set too high.

Maximum Fragments per Datagram The *Maximum Fragments per Datagram* parameter is used to limit the amount of fragments the sensor will track to reassemble a single datagram. This parameter is used to limit the amount of fragments that must be tracked by the sensor.

Fragmented Datagram Timeout The *Fragmented Datagram Timeout* parameter represents the maximum amount of time that can elapse between fragments. The sensor can't wait forever to receive all the fragments that make up a datagram. In addition, hackers could swamp the network with partial datagram fragments in an attempt to overwhelm the sensor's resources. If the sensor doesn't receive any additional fragments for a specific datagram within the timeout period, the existing fragments for that datagram are discarded and the datagram fragments are no longer tracked.

TCP Session Reassembly (Configuration | Sensing Engine > | Reassembly Options)

You can specify which TCP data streams should be analyzed based on the capability of the sensor to rebuild the entire session. Like IP fragment reassembly settings, these settings ensure that system resources, such as memory and CPU cycles, aren't reserved for sessions that are no longer active. The TCP reassembly configuration pane is illustrated in Figure 25-21.

TCP Three-Way Handshake To specify that the sensor track only sessions for which the three-way handshake is completed, select Enabled in the TCP Three Way Handshake list box.

Embryonic Timeout In the TCP Embryonic Timeout field, enter a numerical value between 1 and 180 to specify the number of seconds that can elapse before the sensor frees the resources allocated for an initiated, but not fully established, TCP session. The default number of seconds is five.

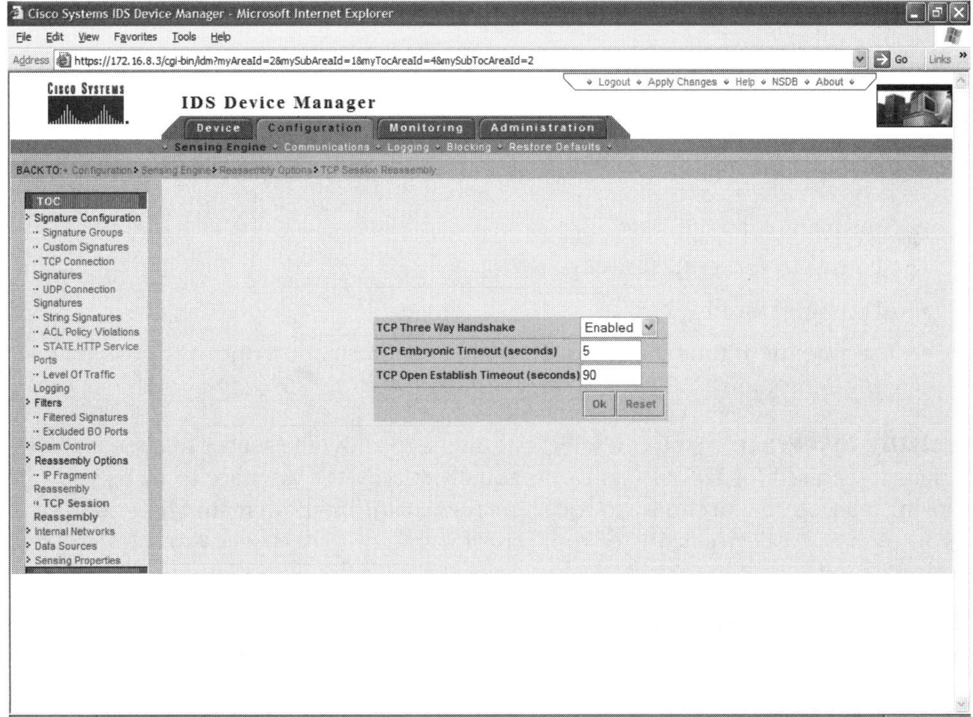

Figure 25-21 TCP reassembly configuration pane

TCP Open Establish Timeout In the TCP Open Establish Timeout field, enter a numerical value between 1 and 3,600 to specify the number of seconds before the sensor frees the resources allocated to a fully established TCP connection when no more packets are being seen for that connection. The default number of seconds is 90.

Internal Networks (Configuration | Sensing Engine | Internal Networks)

You can specify that specific network IP addresses are internal networks for the purpose of logging and reporting. IP addresses that don't match a configured IP internal network are considered external addresses. When the sensor generates an alarm, the IP address of both the source and destination are logged as internal (IN) or external (OUT) to help security administrators to identify the origin and destination of suspected attacks.

Data Sources (Configuration | Sensing Engine | Data Sources)

You must configure data sources when using ACL policy violation signatures. Cisco routers publish syslog messages to the sensors, including attempted ACL policy violations. The Cisco routers represent the data sources for ACL policy violation signatures. In the IP Address field, enter the IP address of the interface of the router that will publish syslog data to the sensor or the IP address of a network, if multiple routers from the same network will be sending syslog data to the sensor.

Sensing Properties (Configuration | Sensing Engine | Sensing Properties)

As shown in Figure 25-22, the Sensing properties configuration panel can be used to configure the following:

- Sensing interface
- Alarm level for traffic flow
- Alarm level for link status
- The amount of time the sensor should store information once a host stops communication

Sensing Interface You can select automatic to allow the sensor to choose the interface to be used for IDS or you can manually specify the interface to be used as the sensing interface. If you choose to configure the sensing interface manually, you need to know the specific device name for your sensor. Table 25-4 lists the sensor interfaces and their names.

Traffic Flow Timeout and Alarm Severity You can configure the sensor to generate an alert when no traffic is seen for a specified amount of time, possibly indicating the sensor is no longer receiving traffic on the network. You can configure the timeout period, the amount of time the sensor will wait to see traffic before generating an alert, and the level of alert that will be generated if the timeout is reached.

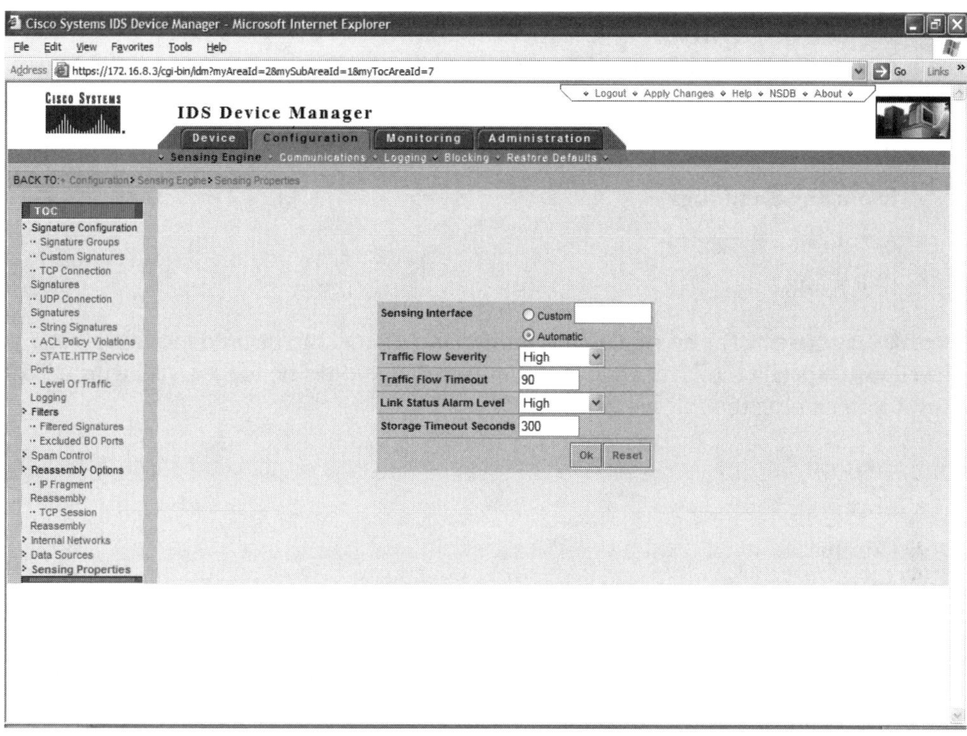

Figure 25-22 Sensing properties configuration panel

Link Status You can configure the sensor to generate an alert if the link fails between the sensing interface and the local access device. If the sensor detects the physical link is non-operational, it generates an alert. You can configure the level of alert to be generated when the link fails.

Storage Timeout Seconds The Storage Timeout Seconds field enables you to configure the amount of time the sensor will store data from a host once that host gone silent.

Packet Capturing Device	Description
/dev/spwr0	All Ethernet sensors except the 4210
/dev/mtok	4200 Series Token ring Sensors where NICs aren't labeled 100/16/4
/dev/mtok36	4200 Series Token ring Sensors where NICs are labeled 100/16/4
/dev/ptpci0	Used with SFDDI and DFDDI interfaces
/dev/iprb0	Monitoring interface on the 4210 series sensor

Table 25-4 Sensor Monitoring Interfaces

Logging (Configuration | Communications | Logging)

The logging Sub-Area can be used to configure specific logging settings on the sensor. The logging Sub-Tab includes four TOC items. TOC items are as follows:

- Event logging
- Exporting event logs
- Automatic IP logging
- IP logging

Event Logging The event logging configuration panel can be used to enable logging, as well as to specify the level and type of events that should be logged. As Figure 25-23 shows, you can log the following:

- Alarms
- Errors
- Commands
- IP logs

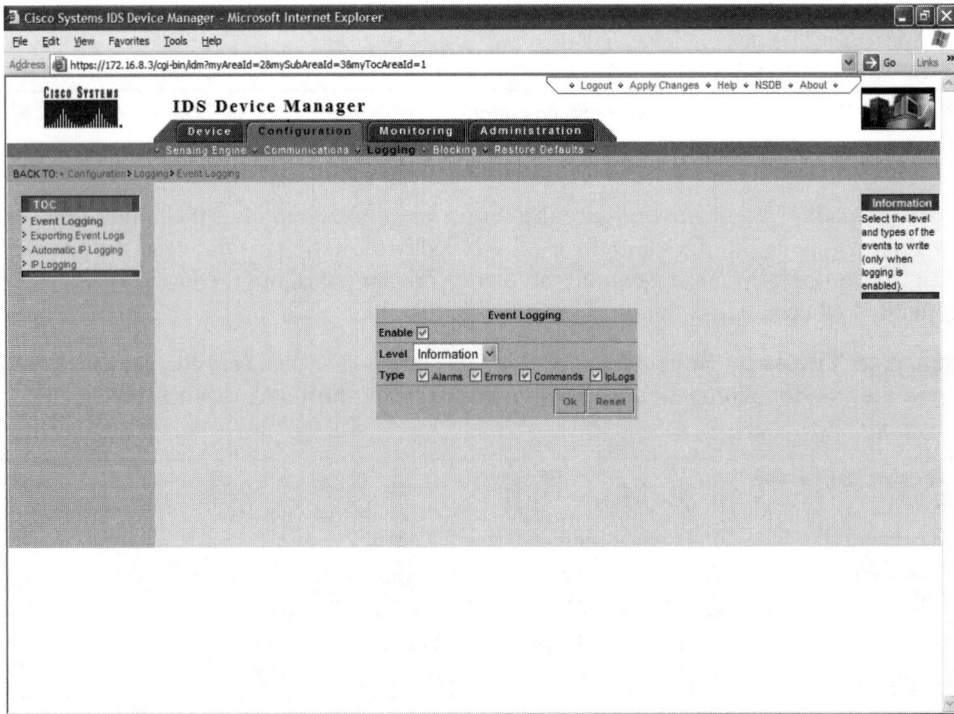

Figure 25-23 Event logging configuration panel

Exporting Event Logs The exporting event logs configuration panel can be used to configure the automatic exporting of event logs to an FTP server. These logs can be stored for future examination, if needed. Figure 25-24 illustrates the exporting event logs configuration panel. You must specify the FTP server, directory, user name, and password to allow the sensor to upload event logs.

Automatic IP Logging *Automatic IP logging* is a responsive action that can be initiated when a signature is matched. When a properly configured signature is matched, the sensor responds by sending an alarm, and then recording all IP packets transmitted by the offending IP address. The automatic IP logging configuration panel enables you to configure the number of minutes the sensor should continue logging once the signature has been matched.

IP Logging Sensors can be configured to log all packets from a specified host or host range. On the IP logging configuration panel, you must specify the host or range of IP addresses that should be logged by the sensor.

Blocking (Configuration > > Blocking)

The 4200 series network appliances are the only sensors that support blocking. The IDSM can't be configured to block IP addresses through device management. The blocking properties configuration panel is illustrated in Figure 25-25.

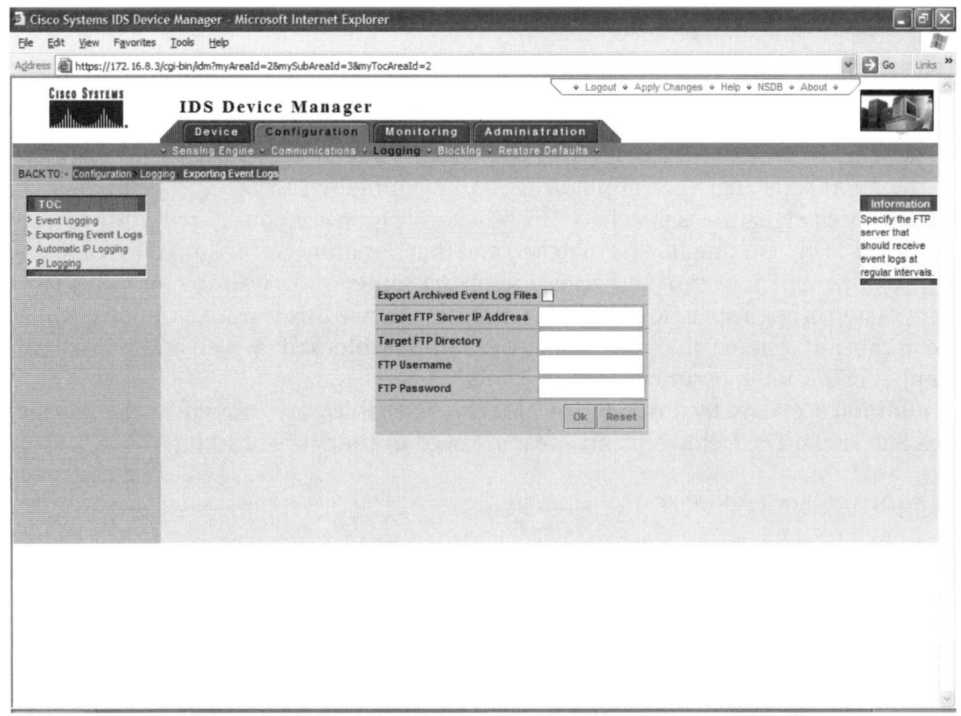

Figure 25-24 Exporting event logs configuration panel

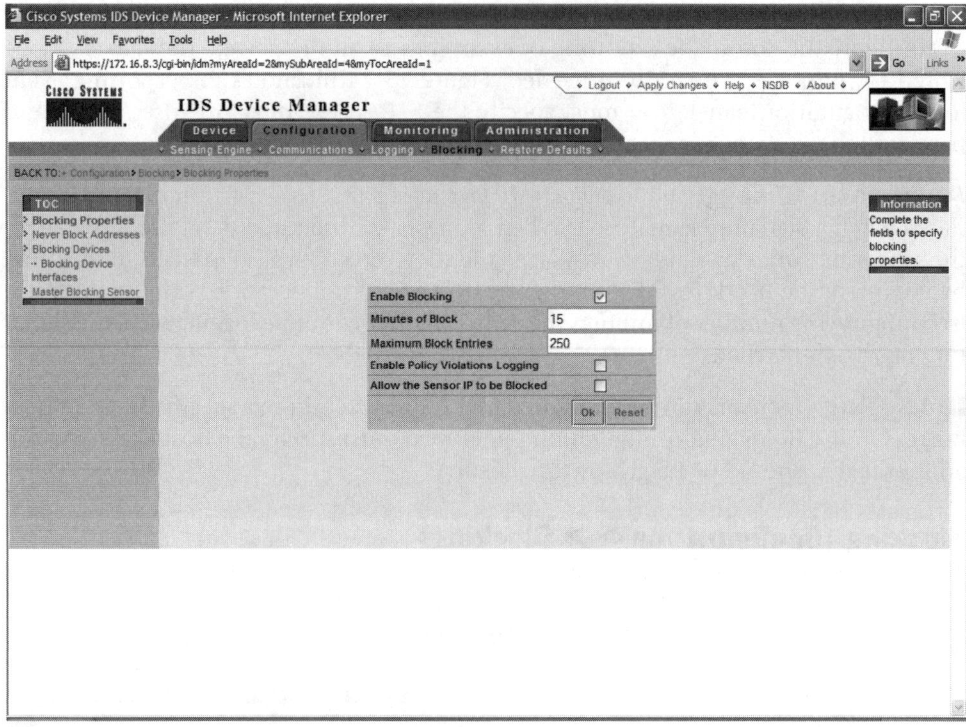

Figure 25-25 The blocking properties configuration panel

The 4200 series network appliances can be configured to block specific host addresses once a signature is matched. The blocking response is configured within the signature file itself. If a signature is matched and that signature is configured for blocking, the network appliance can configure a perimeter router or firewall to block all packets from that host for a specific number of minutes. To use this feature, you must specify the number of minutes the offending host should be blocked, as well as the Cisco ACL number used on the perimeter device.

Additional parameters used when blocking is enabled are located in the Blocking area Sub-Areas. The following Sub-Areas are used to configure blocking:

- Never Block Addresses
- Blocking Devices
- Master Blocking Sensors

STUDY TIP Blocking an IP address is also called shunning a host or IP address.

Never Block Addresses When you enable address blocking, you must specify which addresses should never be blocked. Without this feature, hackers could spoof the address of your event viewer host (for example) and use this address to launch an attack. The sensors, detecting this attack, would then update the ACL on a managed device to block the IP address of your event viewer. If the Event Viewer address is blocked, you could potentially lose communication between your sensors and your Event Viewer host. If communication between the sensors and the Event Viewer host is lost, you won't receive alarm notifications. Figure 25-26 shows the never block addresses configuration panel.

Blocking Devices The *Blocking Devices* area lists the devices managed by the sensor. The router must be configured to allow telnet access from the sensor. Figure 25-27 illustrates the Blocking Device Properties window. You can use a single sensor to manage more than one perimeter device, but a perimeter device can't be managed by more than one sensor. The information that must be configured on this panel to enable the sensors to block IP addresses includes the following:

- The IP address used for telnet access to the router
- The telnet user name and password

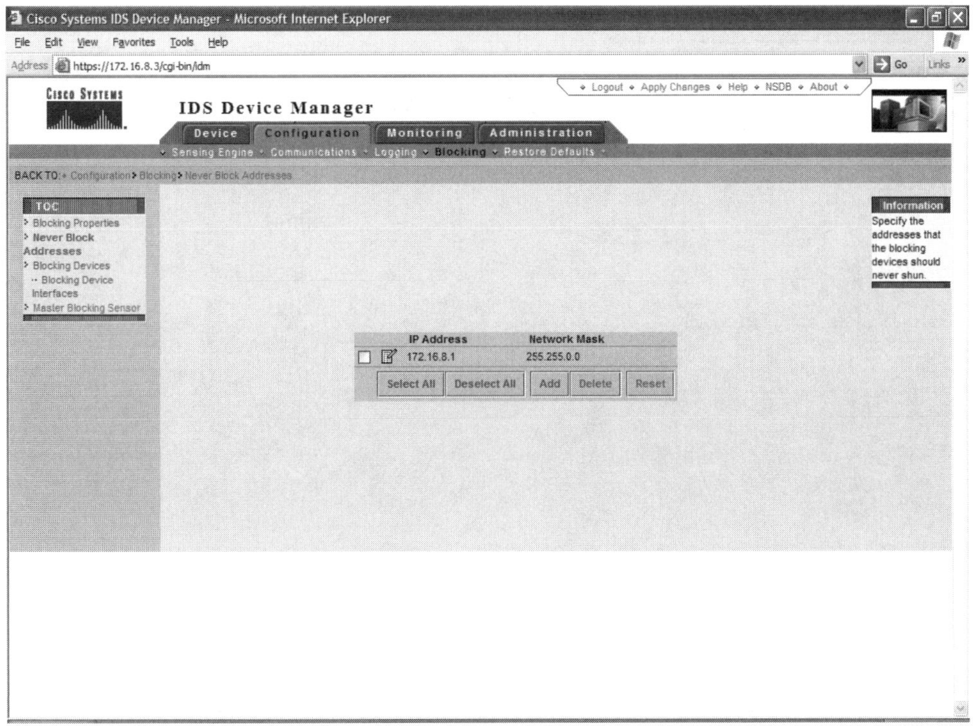

Figure 25-26 Never block addresses configuration panel

- The enable password
- The perimeter device interface address (configured in the Blocking Device interface TOC)

STUDY TIP You should understand how to configure a sensor to manage a perimeter device.

NOTE If the router to be managed doesn't have user names configured, leave the Telnet User field blank.

Master Blocking Sensors Depending on the size and complexity of your network, you could have multiple entry points into your network. Some perimeter routers might be controlled by one sensor, while other perimeter routers are controlled by others. To configure your CIDS environment to allow any managing sensor to block IP addresses on routers controlled by a different sensor, you must enable a master blocking sensor. The

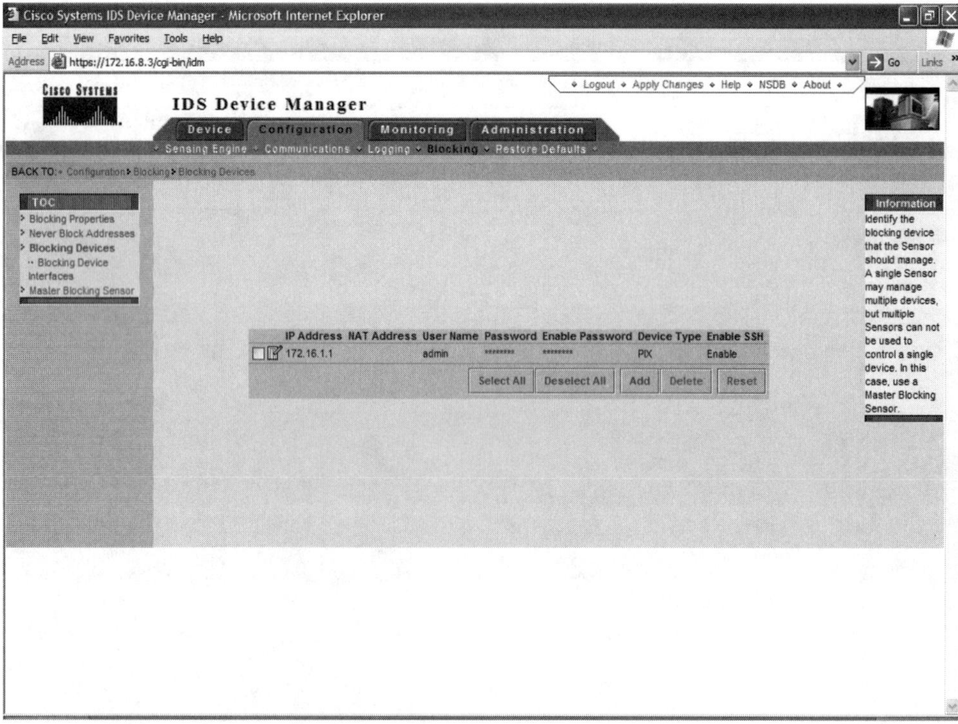

Figure 25-27 Adding a managed device

master blocking sensor sends messages to the managing sensors to update the ACL on the routers that they manage. This master blocking arrangements prevents multiple sensors from attempting to update routers ACLs simultaneously.

Restore Defaults (Configuration | Restore Defaults)

You can restore the factory defaults of the sensor by clicking Reset Configuration on the restore defaults configuration panel. All configuration settings are restored to factory defaults except

- IP address, subnet mask, default gateway
- Allowed hosts
- Password
- Time

Monitoring Area

The *Monitoring Area* contains logs and statistics generated by the sensor. The monitoring area contains the Sub-Areas, Logs, Statistics, and Event Viewer. This Area and the Sub-Area contain information and reports about both the sensor and its operating environment.

Logs (Monitoring | Log)

The Logs Sub-Area contains links to the logs generated by the sensor. These log files provide a record of all events the sensor has detected and can be used by security administrators while investigating an intrusion. The Logs Sub-Area, as seen in Figure 25-28, includes the following TOC items:

- Events
  - Current
  - Archived
- Message
  - sapd
  - idsupdate
- Archived
  - IP Logs
- Errors
  - Current
  - Archived

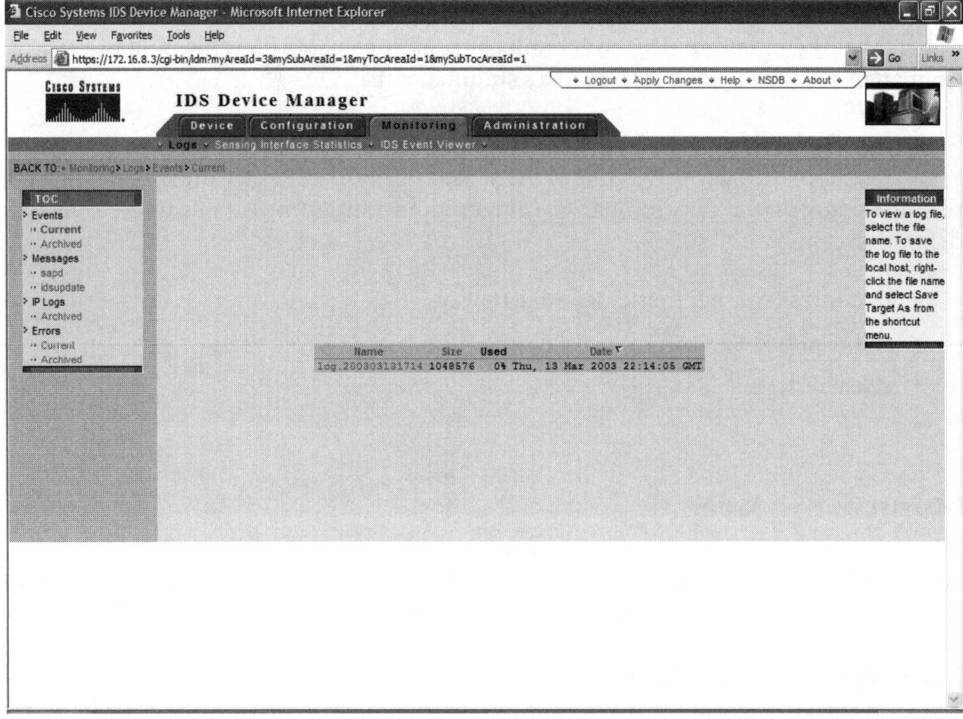

Figure 25-28 The Logs Sub-Area

Sensing Interface Statistics (Monitoring | Sensing Statistics)

The sensing interface statistics panel reports the characteristics of the traffic captured by the sensor's sensing interface, as seen in Figure 25-29.

Event Viewer (Monitoring | Event Viewer)

The event viewer Sub-Area contains links to Cisco's web site detailing technical information and access to the event viewer installation files.

Administration Area

The *Administration Area* is where the administrative functions can be configured and performed. The Administration Area contains the following Sub-Areas:

- System Information
- Update
- Manual Blocking

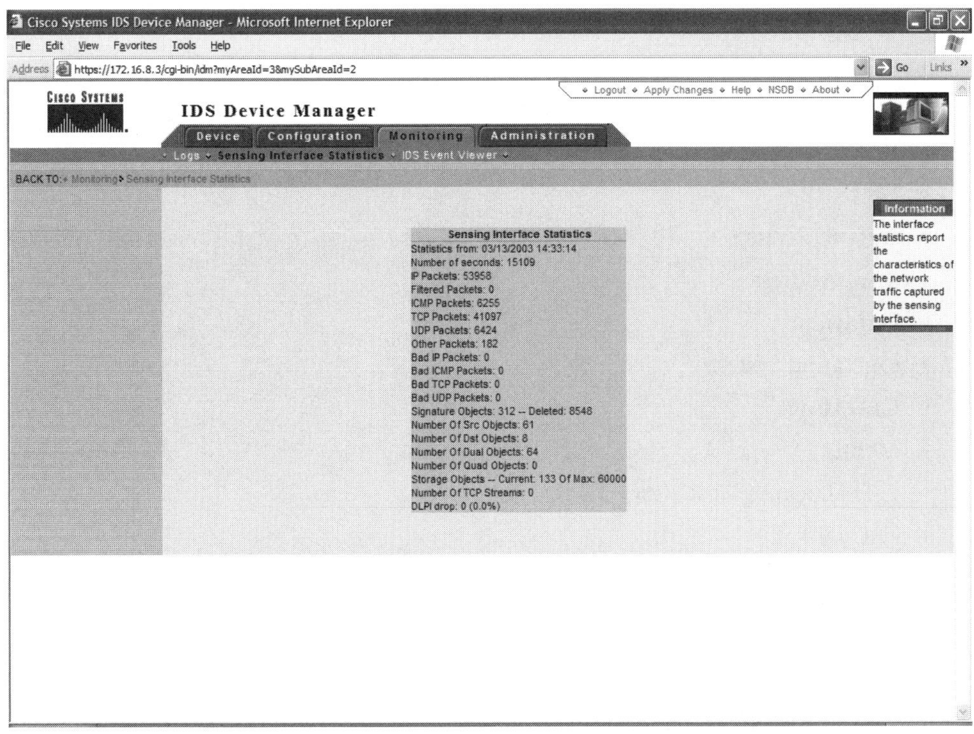

Figure 25-29 Sensor statistics report

- Diagnostics
- System Control
- IDM Properties

System Information (Administration | System Information)

The system information panel lists configuration and system information for the local sensor. As you can see in Figure 25-30, the system information report includes the following information:

- Sensor Version
- Host Name
- Organization Name
- Organization ID
- PostOffice Port
- Web Server Port

- CIDS Daemon Status
- CIDS Connection Status
- CIDS Version
- IP Address
- Netmask
- Default Route
- MAC Address
- Hardware
- Operating System
- CPU Usage
- Memory Usage
- CIDS Logging Disk Usage
- TAC Link

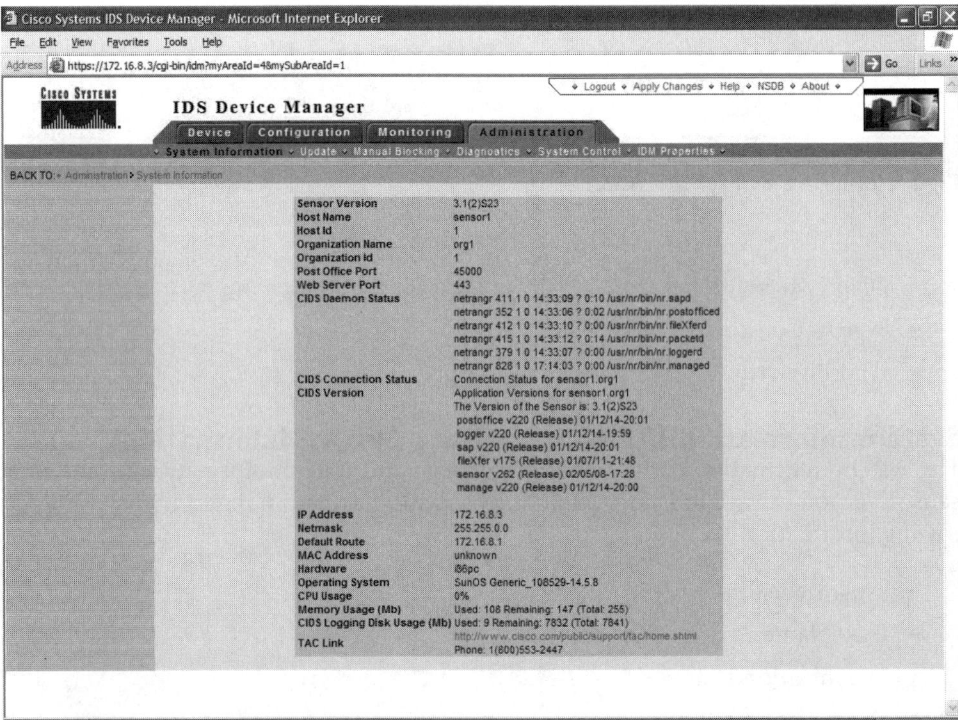

Figure 25-30 System information report

Update (Administration | Update)

The update configuration panel can be used to update the software installed on the sensor. Updates can be initiated manually or they can be scheduled, as shown in Figure 25-31. When performing an update or configuring an automatic update, you must specify the FTP server address, directory, user name, and password.

Manual Blocking (Administration | Manual Blocking)

Manual blocking can be initiated from the Administration Area. You can specify the IP address or the network address you want to block and the amount of time the address(s) should remain blocked, as shown in Figure 25-32.

Diagnostics (Administration | Diagnostics)

The diagnostics Sub-Area can be used to run a new diagnostics test or to view the report generated when the last diagnostics report was generated.

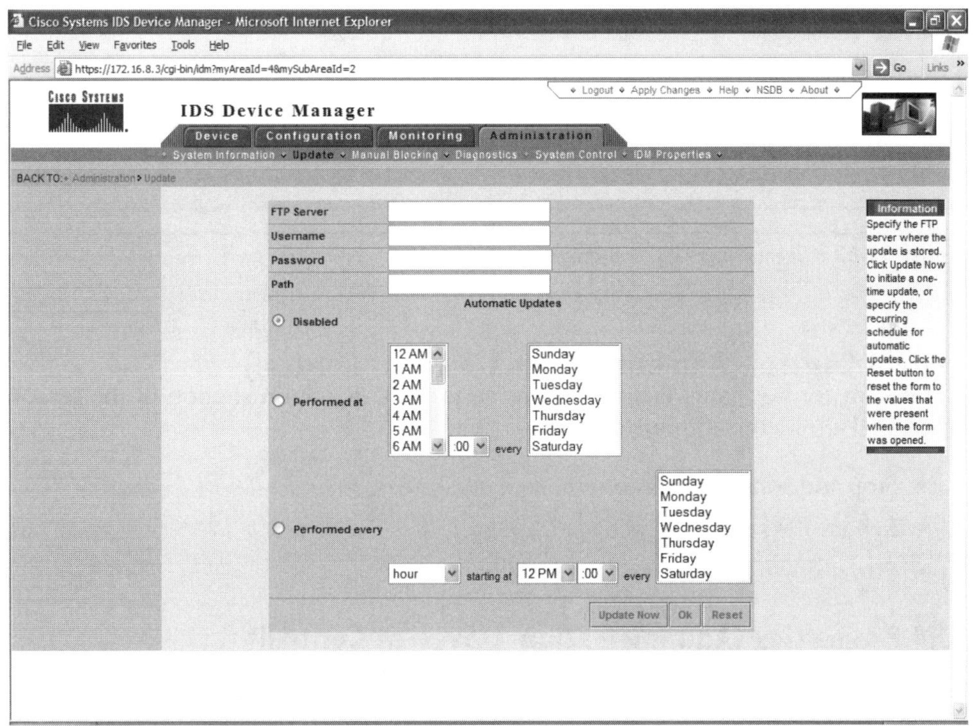

Figure 25-31 Scheduled updates

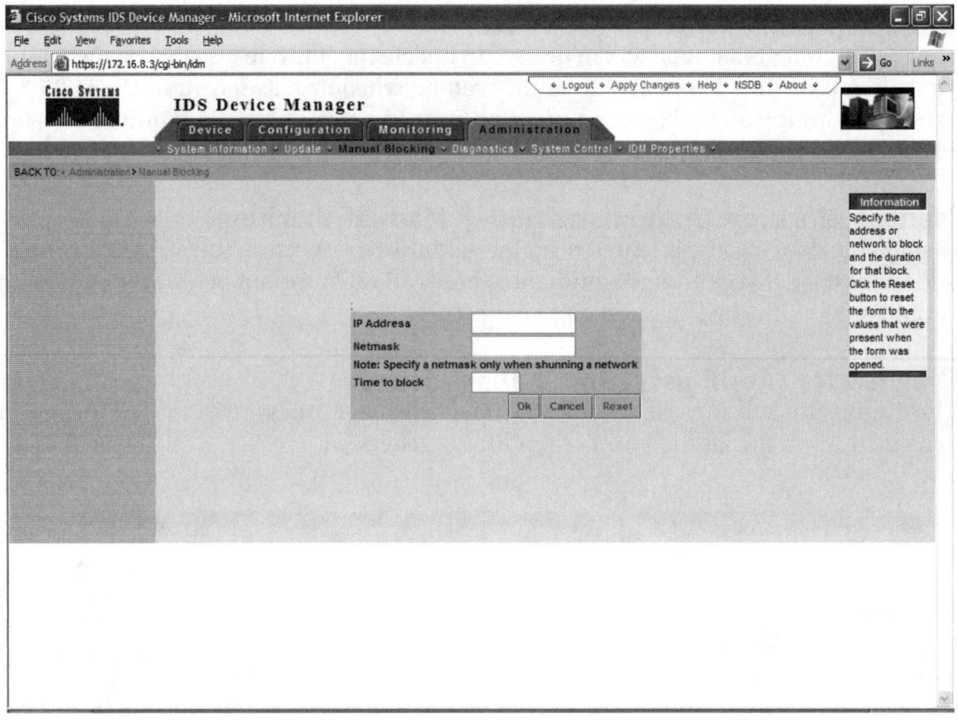

Figure 25-32 Manual blocking configuration panel

System Control (Administration | System Control)

The system control panel enables you to perform basic administration of the sensor. This panel allows the administrator to

- Stop and restart IDS processes
- Reboot the sensor
- Power down the sensor

IDM Properties (Administration | System Control)

The *IDM properties* allow the administrator to customize some configuration settings within the sensor itself. Using the configuration panel in the Sub-Area Severity mapping, you can customize the mapping of severity number (1–5) to the severity names. By default, the mappings are as follows:

- Informational   Categorizes the event as informational in nature and not a risk to security. These events are shown with a blue icon in the IDS Event Viewer.

- Low   Categorized the event as mildly severe. These events are displayed with a yellow icon in the IDS Event Viewer.
- Medium   Categorizes the event as a moderate risk. These events are displayed with an orange icon in the IDS Event Viewer.
- High risk.   High-risk events are displayed with a red icon in the IDS Event Viewer.

The second IDM properties TOC item is signature pagination. This configures the number of signatures listed on a single display page when viewing signature groups.

Chapter Review

Extensive planning and preparation are required before deploying sensors on your Internetwork. Until some auditing and planning are done, you can't even be sure which sensors are needed. This chapter discussed the planning and auditing that can be accomplished to determine where sensors should be deployed throughout the internetwork.

This chapter reviewed the common deployment strategies that have worked in previous IDS deployments and the factors that assist with the deployment strategy, such as

- Network entry points
- Network size and complexity
- The amount and type of traffic to be monitored

This chapter described in detail the methods that can be used to configure the sensors once they've been deployed. The built-in script sysconfig-sensor can be used to configure the sensor for network connectivity. In addition, this application is used to enable the IDS Device Manager.

Once the sensors are bootstrapped, the IDS Device Manager can be used to configure the operations of each sensor, fine-tuning the IDS system. The IDS Device Manager presents the configuration in a common and intuitive web interface to ease the configuration burden. The configuration and management of the sensor through the Device Manager is broken into four configuration and management areas, which are as follows:

- Device
- Configuration
- Monitoring
- Administration

Each area is then broken down into Sub-Areas, which contain Table of Content (TOC) items. Each TOC item has a configuration or report pane that's used to configure the sensor or to display the report.

Questions

1. Which of the following is a disadvantage to placing a single sensor in front of a filtering device?
   A. If the sensor is placed in front of the filtering device, it will be unable to detect interior attacks
   B. If the sensor is placed in front of the filtering device, it will be unable to detect exterior attacks
   C. If the sensor is placed in front of the filtering device, it will be unable to detect any attacks
   D. The sensor will be unable to communicate with the interior CSPM host
2. What is the name of the script used to bootstrap a sensor?
   A. sysconfig.sensor
   B. sysconfig-sensor
   C. sensor.config
   D. sensor-config
3. You must be logged in to the sensor as root to perform which of the following commands?
   A. idsstart
   B. ping
   C. VerifySensor
   D. idsstop
4. IP Blocking response is configured on which of the following?
   A. The sensor
   B. The CSPM host
   C. The router
   D. The firewall
5. To manually configure IP blocking on the sensor, you must define which of the following?
   A. The IP address to blocked
   B. The interface to block
   C. The addresses that shouldn't be blocked
   D. The router's interface
6. What is the default IP address configured on the sensors?
   A. 10.9.201.1
   B. 10.6.202.1

C. 10.1.9.201

D. None of the above

7. Which of the following methods can't be used to connect to a sensor for bootstrapping?

A. Console access

B. CSPM PostOffice connection

C. Telnet

D. Directly, with a keyboard and monitor

Answers

1. A. If the sensor is placed in front of the filtering device, it will be unable to detect interior attacks
2. B. sysconfig-sensor
3. C. VerifySensor
4. A. The sensor
5. D. The router's interface
6. C. 10.1.9.201
7. B. CSPM PostOffice connection

CHAPTER 26

Signature and Alarm Management

In this chapter, you will learn how to:

- Understand the CIDS signature series
- Recognize signature structure and implementation
- Make use of signature types
- Know about signature classes
- Understand signature series
- Use signature categories
- Learn about signature severities
- View and manage alarms
- Use Event Viewer customization
- Configure preference settings
- Understand the Network Security database

Sensors constantly monitor the network, looking for traffic that matches predefined signatures. Once a signature is matched, an alarm is generated, indicating the severity and signature that was matched. Signatures, which allow your sensors to detect intrusive activity, are a vital component of your IDS system. This chapter describes and details the CIDS signatures.

When the sensor matches a signature, an alarm is sent to the director platform. The director platform is then responsible for notifying security personnel. Each alarm has a severity associated with the matched signature. To insure the security of the network, you must be able to view these alarms using Event Viewer. During an actual attack on your network, sensors can generate a large number of alarms in a short period of time. If you're unaware of the functionality of the Event Viewer, you can easily become overwhelmed with the number of alarms generated by your network sensors. To help with the understanding of the Event Viewer and the management of alarms, you should first understand the signatures that generate those alarm events.

CIDS Signatures

CIDS signatures form the intelligence built into your network sensors. A *signature* is a set of rules pertaining to typical intrusion activity that, when matched, generates a unique response.

Signatures can be broken down to be included into a number of different categories to assist with the understanding of how the signature operates and analyzes network traffic. Each of these categories describes the operations of each signature. *Signature implementations* describe what the signature is examining. Signatures can analyze the protocol header information (context) or the data encapsulated in the packet (content). Signature structures categorize signatures based on the number of packets required to match the signature. Some signatures are matched by examining a single packet, while other signatures require multiple packets to make a match. Signature classes detail the type of attack the specific signature is used to detect. As discussed in Chapter 23, different attack types exist and, because there are different attack types, signature classes describe the type of attack the signature was created to detect. Signature types categorize each signature by describing the type of traffic the signature is used to monitor or match. Some signature types monitor protocol connections, while other types monitor SYSLOG output of a router to determine when traffic was denied because of an ACL violation. The last category used to describe a signature is the *signature severity,* which is a configurable parameter that can be used to judge the seriousness of the triggered signature.

To assist you in understanding CIDS signatures, this section discusses the following signature categories in detail:

- Signature Series
- Signature Implementations
- Signature Structures
- Signature Classes
- Signature Types
- Signature Severity

Signature Series

CIDS organizes all the signatures into a series. When an alarm is sent, the signature that generated the alarm is also sent. The Event Viewer displays not only the alarm, but also the signature ID. While recognizing every signature ID that could generate an alarm would be difficult, you can tell from the series of the signature what type of signature was matched. Cisco has organized the signatures to allow for easier identification.

Each of the series is a collection of related signatures. The signature series are 1000, 2000, 3000, 4000, 5000, 6000, 8000, and 10000. The following is a list of all the signature series and the signatures found in each.

STUDY TIP Be aware of each signature series and the type of traffic monitored by each.

1000 Series Signatures—IP Signatures

Includes the following:

- IP Options
- IP fragmentation
- Bad IP Packets

2000 Series Signatures—ICMP Signatures

Includes the following:

- ICMP Traffic Records
- Ping Sweeps
- ICMP Attacks

3000 Series Signatures—TCP Signatures

Includes the following:

- TCP Traffic Records
- TCP Port Scans
- TCP Host Sweeps
- Mail Attacks
- FTP Attacks
- Legacy CIDS Web Attacks (Signature IDs 3200–3233)
- NetBIOS Attacks
- SYN Flood and TCP Hijack Attacks
- TCP Applications

4000 Series Signatures—UDP Signatures

Includes the following:

- UDP Traffic Records
- UDP Port Scans
- UDP Attacks
- UDP Applications

5000 Series Signatures—Web (HTTP) Signatures

Includes the following:

- Web Attacks

6000 Series Signatures—Cross Protocol Signatures

Includes the following:

- DNS Attacks
- RPC Service Attacks
- Authentication Failures
- Loki Attacks
- Distributed DoS Attacks

8000 Series Signatures—String Match Signatures

Includes the following:

- Custom String Matches
- TCP Applications

10000 Series Signatures—ACL Policy Violation Signatures

Includes the following:

- Defined IOS ACL Violations

Signature Implementations

The signature implementations of CIDS signatures come in two types: every signature is either context based or content based. Each of these two types of signature implementations describes which part of the TCP/IP packet is examined.

Context-Based Signatures

Context-based signatures are triggered based on the data contained in the packet header. Information included in the IP headers is used to trigger a context-based signature. The information examined by context-based signatures includes the following:

- IP Options
- IP Fragmentation Parameters
- TCP Flags
- IP Protocol Field
- IP, TCP, and UDP Checksums

- IP Addresses
- Port Numbers

Content-Based Signatures

Content-based signatures search the data portions of the TCP/IP packet, looking for a match. Table 26-1 lists example signatures of the signature definition used to detect these attacks.

Signature Structure

As previously discussed, signature implementations deal with packet headers and packet payloads. The structure of the signatures deals with the number of packets that must be examined to trigger an alarm. Two types of signature structures exist and these are as follows:

- Atomic
- Composite

Atomic Structure

Some attacks can be detected by matching IP header information (context based) or string information contained in a single IP packet (content based). Any signatures that can be matched with a single packet fall into the atomic category. Because atomic signatures examine individual packets, there's no need to collect or store state information.

An example of an atomic signature is the SYN-FIN signature (signature ID 3041). This signature looks for packets that have both the SYN and FIN flags set. The *SYN flag* indicates this is a packet attempting to begin a new connection. The *FIN flag* indicates this packet is attempting to close an existing connection. These two flags shouldn't be used together and, when they are, this is an indication some intrusive activity might exist.

Composite Signatures

Composite signatures require a series of multiple packets to match before an alarm is triggered. Because composite signatures require multiple packets to make a match, the sensor must also keep state information describing the packets that were previously examined. If the sensor analyzes a packet that begins to match a composite signature, the sensor must record this information while it examines additional traffic to complete the signature match.

Table 26-1 Content- and Context-Based Signatures

Signature Name	Signature Implementation
ICMP Echo Request	Content
ICMP Net Sweep w/ Echo	Context
WWW IIS Unicode	Content
TFN Client Request	Content

PART V

An example composite signature is the IP fragments overlap signature (signature ID 1103). The sensor must examine multiple IP fragments to discover an overlap between two or more IP fragments. Because this signature requires the examination of multiple packets to trigger an alarm, this is a composite structure signature.

Signature Classes

CIDS signatures fall into four classes. Signatures belong to one of the four classes, based on the type of attack the signature was designed to detect. As discussed in Chapter 23, there are three types of attacks: Reconnaissance, Access, and Denial of Service (DoS). Signature classes map to these three attack types and add one additional class. The four signature classes are as follows:

- Reconnaissance
- Access
- Denial of Service
- Informational

Reconnaissance Class Signatures

Reconnaissance class signatures are used to detect reconnaissance attacks against your network. Before intruders can launch an attack against your network resources, they must first map your network and network resources. Hackers have many different tools they can use to discover the type, location, and vulnerabilities of your network resources. Reconnaissance class signatures trigger as a result of analyzed activity known to be, or that could lead to, unauthorized discovery of systems, services, or vulnerabilities. Once triggered, these alarms alert security personnel when the sensors detect these tools are being used against your network. Common reconnaissance techniques used by hackers and detected by reconnaissance class signatures are as follows:

- **Ping Sweeps**—Allow intruders to map the active IP addresses on your network.
- **Port Scans**–Scan for open ports on ranges of network resources.
- **DNS Queries**–Allow users and intruders to retrieve information about the topology of your network.

Access Class Signatures

Access class signatures are used to detect access attacks against your network systems. Access class signatures can detect attacks that could lead to unauthorized data retrieval, system access, or privileged escalation. Common access techniques used by hackers and detected by access class signatures are as follows:

- Unix Tooltalk Database server attack
- Internet Information Services (IIS) Unicode attack
- Back Orifice or NetBus

Denial of Service (DoS) Class Signatures

Denial of service class signatures are used to detect DoS attacks against your network. These signatures trigger an activity used for the disablement of a network infrastructure, systems, or services. Common DoS techniques used by hackers and detected by DoS class signatures are as follows:

- Ping of Death
- Tribe Flood Network (TFN) attacks
- Trinoo attacks

Informational Class Signatures

Informational class signatures are used to detect normal network activity, which, in itself, isn't considered malicious, but the information can be used to judge the validity of an attack, as well as for forensic purposes. Common informational events detected by information class signatures are as follows:

- ICMP echo requests
- TCP connection requests
- UDP connections

Signature Types

The *signature types* describe the type of network traffic the signature is used to match. Some signatures detect intrusions by examining the TCP connection requests or UDP connections. Other signature types examine the protocol information in the IP headers or the protocol-dependant application commands located in the packet payload. The four signature types are as follows:

- General
- Connection
- String
- Access control list

General Signature Types

General signatures are used to detect a wide range of intrusive activity. General signatures are used to detect intrusive activity from a number of different protocols included in the TCP/IP protocol suite. Protocols that general signatures monitor include the following:

- IP
- ICMP
- TCP
- UDP

Many of the general signature types are context based because they examine the protocol header data, while attempting to find abnormalities. Other of the general signature types are content based because they examine the application layer protocol information in the payload portion of the packet, such as HTTP web signatures. The following signature series contain general signatures:

- Series 1000 signatures (IP)
- Series 2000 signatures (ICMP)
- Series 5000 signatures (Web/HTTP)
- Series 6000 signatures (cross-protocol)

Connection Signatures

Connection signatures are used to monitor TCP and UDP connection requests between hosts. Connection signatures report the number of connections detected for each transport layer protocol. Connection signatures also have subsignatures, used to identify the port number each connection is using. The following two signature series make up your connection signatures:

- TCP connections, series 3000
- UDP traffic, series 4000

Connection signatures that detect TCP connections are from the 3000 series; UDP traffic is detected and monitored with 4000 series signatures. Each of these connection signatures has subsignatures, used to identify the TCP or UDP port. For example, a Telnet connection request (using TCP) creates an alarm with a 3000 series signature and a subsignature of 23 (Telnet). If the Telnet application is using UDP, a 4000 series signature triggers the alarm. The series identifies the protocol in use—TCP or UDP—while the subsignature identifies the port in use.

String Signatures

String signatures are used to detect text strings within the TCP/IP packets. You can determine and configure the strings that should be detected. String signatures trigger an alarm whenever the configured string is matched using a standard regular expression-matching algorithm. All string-matching signatures fall into the 8000 signature series.

Whenever a string signature is matched, an alarm is generated with a signature ID of 8000. The string subsignature is used to identify which string was matched by the sensor. When you want to configure a string signature, you must also define the subsignature used to specify the string that was matched. For example, you can create a string signature used to search for the string "root," and then configure this signature with a subsignature ID of 11000. When this string is matched, the signature ID will be 8000, with a sub-ID of 11000. Based on this information, you can determine which string your network sensor matched. Some predefined signature series 8000 are configured on your network sensors:

- Telnet-/etc/shadow (ID 8000, SubID 2302)
- Rlogin + + (ID 8000, SubID 51303)

If you receive an alarm on your CSPM host with a signature ID of 8000, you know a string signature was matched. By examining the SubID, you can determine which string was matched.

Access Control Lists

Cisco routers can be configured with access control lists (ACLs) to block traffic that violates defined security policies. If configured to do so, the router can log information anytime an ACL denies traffic into or out of the network. This logged data can then be sent in real time to a SYSLOG server or a sensor. The sensor can monitor this SYSLOG information and generate alarms whenever the ACL is forced to block suspicious traffic. Access control signature types belong to the signature series 10000. All alarms triggered by router ACLs will have a signature ID of 10000. The subsignature ID is used to differentiate the ACL that generated the SYSLOG message.

Signature Severity

The *signature severity* represents the probability that the matched signature represents a real and immediate security threat to your systems and network. Each signature has a default severity assigned to it by Cisco security engineers and these default severities are normally adequate for most network environments.

While each signature already has an assigned severity, this is a configurable parameter and can be changed by security personnel. The three severity levels are low, medium, and high. The severity is based on the alarm level. Alarms can be assigned an alarm level of one to five. Table 26-2 shows how the alarm levels match the alarm severities.

Low Severity

Signatures configured (default) with low-severity alarm levels represent the lowest threat to your network. Many of the signatures configured for a low-severity level are

Severity/ Alarm Level	Description	Probability of an Actual Attack	Immediate Threat
Low, Levels 1–2	Benign activity, but recorded for informational purposes.	Very Low	No
Medium, Levels 3–4	Abnormal activity that could be malicious.	Medium	Low
High, Level 5	Actual attacks are detected that allow access or used for DoS.	Very High	Yes

Table 26-2 Alarm Levels and Severities

PART V

actual informational signatures. Alarms generated by these signatures don't usually indicate intrusive activity. Some signatures configured for a low-severity level are as follows:

- FTP SYST Command (Signature ID 3151)
- Unknown IP protocol (Signature ID 1101)

Medium Severity

Signatures configured with a medium-severity alarm level are used to detect abnormal network traffic that might be perceived as malicious. Some of these signatures are triggered on techniques that were effective in the past, but are usually no longer a threat in modern network environments. Intrusion attempts using these legacy vulnerabilities have a low probability of being successful and, therefore, are assigned a medium- severity level. Examples of signatures that have a medium-severity level include the following:

- TCP SYN Port Sweep (Signature ID 3002)
- ICMP network Sweep with Echo (Signature ID 2100)

High Severity

Signatures configured with a high-severity alarm level represent the most significant threats to your network and system security. Signatures that alarm with a high-severity level detect attacks that intruders use to gain access to network resources. By default, DoS attack signatures are also configured with a high-severity level. The following are examples of signatures configured with a high-severity level:

- WWW IIS Unicode (Signature ID 5114)
- sadmind RPC Buffer Overflow (Signature ID 6194)
- BackOrifice BO2K TCP Non Stealth (Signature ID 3990)

Event Viewer

Network sensors are responsible for generating and sending alarms to the Event Viewer. The Event Viewer host must then receive and display these alarms for security personnel. To insure the integrity of the network, you must understand how to view and manage the alarms, while also understanding the significance of each generated alarm. The Event Viewer provides a GUI interface to assist you with the display and management of your alarm data.

NOTE This section describes and details the Event Viewer included with CSPM.

The *Event Viewer* is a GUI application used to display each alarm and its critical information, as well as provide status information generated by the sensor daemons. A single intrusion on your network can generate a large number of alarms, which can quickly fill the Event Viewer screen. If multiple sensors are installed on the network each sensor can detect the same intrusion, resulting in multiple alarms for a single attack. Your competence and efficiency with the Event Viewer will enable you to disseminate the information received and respond to intrusions in a timely fashion, without being overwhelmed. To assist you in building a thorough understanding of the Event Viewer, this section discusses the following topics:

- Managing Alarms
- Event Viewer Customization
- Preference Settings

Managing Alarms

Alarms are generated by the sensors and sent to the Event Viewer host via the PostOffice protocol. Once received, these alarms are stored in a database. This database can then be viewed with the Event Viewer. This section discusses the following topics that deal with alarm management:

- Opening the Event Viewer
- Alarm Fields
- Resolving Host Names
- Viewing the Context Buffer
- The Network Security Database
- Suspending New Alarms
- Deleting Alarms

Opening the Event Viewer

The Event Viewer can be accessed via CSPM's tool menu. To start the Event Viewer, choose Tools | View Sensor Events | Database. When the View Database Events window appears, you can choose to view all alarms or you can limit the number of displayed alarms by selecting the start time and/or the stop time.

- **Start Time**—The start time is used to view alarms generated after the specified time. Alarms generated before the start time aren't displayed.
- **Stop Time**—The stop time is used to limit the number of alarms received. Alarms generated after the stop time aren't displayed.

- **Event Type**—This is the IDS alarm type. CIDS Alarms is the only option that can be selected.

To open and view alarms using the Event Viewer, use the following steps:

1. Log in to the CSPM host using the administrative account.
2. From within CSPM, select Tools | View Sensor Events | Database.
3. Either select to view all events or specify the start and stop times to limit the scope of alarms displayed.

You can open multiple instances of the Event Viewer. Once an Event Viewer window is open, it can be customized and its display characteristics can be modified independently of all other instances of the Event Viewer. This enables you to open different Event Viewer windows containing the same or different alarms, while adjusting the characteristics of each instance to fulfill a particular need.

Alarm Fields

Each alarm viewed with Event Viewer is displayed as a row in a table. Each row is made up of fields that contain specific data about the alarm. The fields and explanations are provided in Table 26-3.

Resolving Host Names

While viewing alarms in the Event Viewer window, you can easily identify the host names of both the attacking host and the host that was attacked. To resolve the host names, right-click the alarm in question, and then choose Resolve Host Names. A Host Name Resolution window appears, showing the source and destination IP addresses, as well as their associated host name. If the host name can't be resolved, the window displays Cannot be resolved.

Viewing the Context Buffer

For TCP-based, series 3000 signatures, the sensor captures up to 256 characters of the TCP stream. This information is called the *context buffer* and you can use the Event Viewer to display it. By viewing the context buffer, you can determine if this alarm was generated by an actual intrusion attempt or simply an accident.

To view the context buffer, right-click the alarm in question, and then choose Context Buffer from the Shortcut menu. A new window will appear, displaying the information contained in the context buffer. If no context buffer is available, the Shortcut menu won't contain the Context Buffer option.

Network Security Database

Cisco provides a database of network vulnerability information that can be accessed via an HTML browser. If you need additional information for any alarm listed in the Event Viewer, you can search the NSDB for additional information. If the Event Viewer contains

Field	Description
Count	Similar alarms are sometimes consolidated into a single row. The count field specifies the number of alarms consolidated into this row.
Name	The name of the alarm.
Source Address	The source IP address associated with the alarm listed in this row.
Destination Address	The destination IP address associated with the alarm listed in this row.
Destination Port	The destination UDP or TCP port associated with the alarm.
Source Port	The source UDP or TCP port associated with the alarm.
Details	Contains information specific to the signature that generated the alarm. If the signature was a string signature, the string that generated the alarm is listed in this field
Source Location	IN indicates the source IP address is on the local or trusted network. OUT indicates the source IP address is located on a remote or untrusted network.
Destination Location	IN indicates the destination IP address is on the local or trusted network. OUT indicates the destination IP address is located on a remote or untrusted network.
Signature ID	The numeric ID of the signature that generated the alarm.
Subsignature ID	If the signature that generated the alarm has an associated subsignature. the subID is listed in this field. Otherwise, this field is blank.
Severity	The severity of the signature that generated the alarm.
Level	The level, one to five, of the signature that generated the alarm.
Organization Name	The organization name of the sensor that generated the alarm.
Sensor Name	The name of the sensor that generated the alarm.
Application Name	The name of the daemon that generated the alarm. All intrusion alarms are generated by packetd.
Local Date	The date, as recorded by the sensor, when the alarm was generated.
Local Time	The time, as recorded by the sensor, when the alarm was generated.

Table 26-3 Event Viewer Alarm Fields

an alarm you want to examine, you can open the NSDB to view information about that specific alarm. To open the NSDB, you use the following steps:

1. From the Event Viewer, right-click the alarm in question.
2. Choose Network Security Database.

A second method for opening the NSDM is as follows:

1. Select the alarm to examine.
2. Choose Tools | NSDM from the Event Viewer menu bar.

The NSDB Exploit Signature Page contains additional information about the signature that triggered the alarm. Information provided on the NSDB Exploit Signature page includes the following:

- Signature name
- ID
- SubID
- Recommended alarm level
- Signature type
- Signature structure
- Implementation
- Signature description
- Benign triggers
- Related vulnerability
- User notes

STUDY TIP Be aware of how to open and view the NSDB.

Once you gain additional information about the matched signature, you might want or need additional information on the related vulnerability. You can select the link provided on the Exploit Signature page to research additional information about the vulnerability. You can learn the following Information via the Vulnerability page:

- Vulnerability name
- Alias
- ID
- Severity level
- Vulnerability type
- Exploit type
- Affected systems
- Affected programs
- Vulnerability description
- Consequences

- Countermeasures
- Advisory/related information links
- Patch/fix/upgrade links
- Exploit links
- User notes

User Notes Both the Exploit Signatures and Vulnerability page provides a User Notes section. This link allows security administrators to record additional information about the signature or vulnerability. This user-added information is stored permanently in the NSDB database on the CSPM host.

Suspending New Alarms

If desired, you can prevent the Event Viewer from displaying any new or additional alarms. You can use this feature when you're investigating a previous alarm, and you want to prevent any additional alarms from being displayed in the specific Event Viewer window. The alarms are still recorded and stored in the alarm database, and any other instances of the Event Viewer will continue to display additional alarms. To suspend new alarms in a Event Viewer window, do the following:

1. Choose Edit | Suspend New Events on the Event Viewer menu bar.

or

2. Click the Pause Live Feed button on the Event Viewer toolbar.

To resume receiving new alarms:

1. Choose Edit | Resume New Events on the Event Viewer menu bar.

or

2. Click the Resume Live Feed button on the Event Viewer toolbar.

Deleting Alarms

Once you deal with an alarm in the Event Viewer, you might want to remove the alarm record from the view or from the entire alarm database. You can choose to delete an alarm from the current Event Viewer window, from all Event Viewer instances, or from the CSPM database. To delete the alarm from the current Event Viewer window:

1. Right-click the alarm and choose Delete Record.
2. Select From This Grid.

To delete the alarm from all Event Viewer windows:

1. Right-click the alarm and choose Delete Record.
2. Select From All Grids.

To delete the alarm from the entire database:

1. Right-click the alarm and choose Delete Record.
2. Select From Database.

CAUTION If the selected row contains multiple alarms (indicated by a count greater that one) and you choose any of the deletion options, all alarms represented by that row will be deleted. To delete a single alarm represented in a row with multiple alarms, first expand the row, then select the appropriate alarm, and then choose Delete Record.

Event Viewer Customization

Event Viewer combines the functionality of a browser (such as Explorer) with that of a spreadsheet (such as MS Excel) to create a collection of audit event data called a drillsheet. The *drillsheet* allows groups of similar audit-event records to be displayed on a single row, allowing you—quickly and easily—to detect patterns in the data.

Traditional event viewers display events in a single list. Each event fills one row in the list and each data element within an event fills one cell in the row. This display of events is appropriate when the number of events is small. When the number of alarms is large, however, or when events appear quickly, this linear display isn't practical.

The Event Viewer groups alarms together into one row, based on similar information to both alarms. By default, the Event Viewer consolidates or collapses alarms, based on the first two field columns. For example, you might have ten alarms present in the event viewer all triggered by the same signature. Rather than listing ten different rows for each alarm, Event Viewer creates one record (row) listing the name of the alarm with a count field value of 10. Any information common to all ten alarms is listed in the record. Any information different among the ten alarms is listed as a + symbol, indicating additional information exists. You can view the additional information by expanding the record. To expand the record, simply double-click the + sign.

Expanding and Collapsing the Row

As previously mentioned, the Event Viewer is configured by default to collapse alarms into one record, based on identical information contained in the first two field columns. To view additional information about each alarm, you must expand the columns until the information you need is shown. You can expand the additional information by selecting the row you want to expand, and then click the Expand This Branch One Column to the Right button on the tool bar.

If you want to expand the entire row all the way to the right, select the Expand This Branch all the way to the Right button, located on the Event Viewer tool bar. You can collapse a row back to the left by choosing the Collapse This Branch One Column to the Left button or the Collapse This Branch to the Currently Selected Column button on the Event Viewer tool bar.

NOTE Neither of these changes is permanent. If the Event Viewer is closed, all changes to the expanded rows are lost.

By default, all rows are expanded to at least the first two columns. If you want to increase the expansion for all rows beyond the second column, you can configure Event Viewer to do this automatically. To set the default expansion boundary:

1. Select the column which you want to expand.
2. Choose Edit | Set Event Expansion Boundary from the Event Viewer menu bar.

Managing Columns in Event Viewer

Columns can be moved to any position in the Event Viewer. To move a column, click-and-drag the column to the new position. This isn't a permanent change: if one Event Viewer is closed and reopened, the default column placement will be used.

You can delete columns from the Event Viewer Grid. To delete a column, right-click the column you want to delete, and then select Delete Column from the Shortcut menu. Deleting a column isn't a permanent change.

You can also select which columns you want Event Viewer to display, as well as how the information in the columns is sorted. To add or remove a column, use the following steps:

1. Choose Edit | Insert/Modify Column(s) from the Event Viewer menu bar.
2. Select the columns you want to view by placing an *X* in the show field.
3. Click OK.

Preference Settings

This section describes the preference options that can be configured in the Event Viewer. To configure Event Viewer preferences, click the Preferences option from the Edit menu. The following sections make up the Preferences window:

- Actions
- Cells
- Status Events
- Boundaries
- Event Severity Indicator
- Severity Mapping

Actions

The Actions section of the Preference window enables you to set the following parameters:

- **Command Timeout**—This parameter configures how long (in seconds) the Event Viewer should wait for a response from a sensor before it should consider the connection as down. This setting shouldn't be changed unless you've been experiencing excessive timeout errors.
- **Time To Block**—This parameter specifies how long (in minutes) a sensor should block traffic from a specified source when the Block command is issued from the Event Viewer. This block time period applies only to Blocks initiated manually from the Event Viewer, not automatic blocks initiated by the sensor. The default is 1,440 minutes (one day), and can be changed to 1 to 525,600 minutes.
- **Subnet Mask**—The subnet mask is applied to any manually blocked address. If you only want to block the actual attacking host, you should use a netmask of 255.255.255.255. This default subnet mask will be used for all manual blocking.

Cells

The Cells section of the Preference window enables you to configure the following parameters:

- **Blank-Left**—This configures the Event Viewer not to repeat repetitious information in the most left hand column. If ten alarms are all generated by the same signature, Event Viewer lists the name of the alarm in the first row and it won't list anything for that column for the next nine rows below. By default, Blank-left is selected.

- **Blank-Right**—Blank-right affects how the collapsed cells display in the Event Viewer beyond the expansion boundary. By default, Blank-right isn't selected.

Status Events

The Status Events section enables you to decide whether Event Viewer should list status events (route down, route up, PostOffice messages) in the Event Viewer grid. If this option isn't selected, then status events won't be listed in the grid. If you choose Display Popup Window, then all route down messages will generate a pop-up window and other status events won't be displayed.

Boundaries

The Boundaries section in the Preferences window enables you to configure the following:

- **Default Expansion Boundary**—Persistent setting that configures the default expansion boundary. By default, this is set to two.
- **Maximum Events Per Grid**—Configures the maximum amount of rows a single instance of Event Viewer will display. The default is 250,000 alarms and can be changed from 1 to 4,000,000,000.
- **Event Batching Timeout**—Configures how often, in seconds, the Event Viewer is updated during an alarm flood. The default is 0, meaning the Event Viewer is constantly updated with new alarms as they're generated.

Event Severity Indicator

The Event Severity Indicator section of the Preferences window enables you to configure the color and icons used to represent the different signature alarm severities. The colors affect the background of the Count field for each alarm. You can also change the icon used to represent the severity listed for each alarm. The default colors and icons used for each severity are listed in Table 26-4.

Severity Mapping

Alarms are assigned a level of severity from one to five. These alarm levels are mapped to a severity of Low, Medium, or High. Table 26-2 shows the default mapping of alarm levels to severity levels. You can change the default mapping of alarm levels to severity levels using the Severity Mapping section of the Preferences window.

Table 26-4 Alarm Severity Colors and Icons

Severity	Color	Icon
Low	Green	No Icon
Medium	Yellow	Yellow Flag
High	Red	Red Exclamation Point

Chapter Review

Signatures represent the intelligence behind your intrusion detection system. To protect your network infrastructure fully, you must understand both how these signatures are structured and each signature series. A signature is a set of rules used to match activity and traffic present on your network. Once a match is made, the signatures trigger an alarm.

Signatures are broken down into many different categories to facilitate understanding of how they operate and detect intrusions. All signatures are either content based or context based. Content-based signatures analyze the contents of the network packets, while context-based signatures analyze the protocol headers of the network packets. In addition, every CIDS signature is either:

- Atomic
- Composite

Atomic signatures can be matched by analyzing a single network packet. Composite signatures must analyze more than one network packet before a match is made. CIDS signatures also belong to one of four signature classes. The signature classes define the type of attack the signature was designed to detect. The signature classes map closely to the types of attacks discussed in Chapter 23. The four signature classes are as follows:

- Reconnaissance
- Informational
- Access
- Denial of Service

The final signature category all CIDS signatures belong to is the signature series. The signature series defines the protocol the signature is responsible for analyzing. The CIDS signature series includes the following:

- 1000 Series Signatures—IP Signatures
- 2000 Series Signatures—ICMP Signatures
- 3000 Series Signatures—TCP Signatures
- 4000 Series Signatures—UDP Signatures
- 5000 Series Signatures—Web (HTTP) Signatures
- 6000 Series Signatures—Cross Protocol Signatures
- 8000 Series Signatures—String Match Signatures
- 10000 Series Signatures—ACL Policy Violation signatures

The Event Viewer represents your view into your intrusion detection system. Without this powerful application, you would be unaware of the alarms and intrusions on your network. To use the Event Viewer correctly, you should understand the following topics:

- Managing Alarms
- Customizing the Event Viewer
- Preference Settings

You can access the Network Security Database (NSDB) to research information regarding an alarm or a vulnerability. The NSDB is an HTML database containing detailed information on all the CIDS signatures and vulnerabilities. The NSDB also has a User Notes section that allows security administrators to record additional information for later viewing. User Notes are stored within the NSDB.

Review Questions

1. What is a subsignature ID?

   A. The signature ID

   B. The signature ID combined with the host ID

   C. The signature ID combined with the organization ID

   D. The ID of the subsignature associated with the CIDS signature

2. What is the NSDB?

   A. The network security database that contains all CIDS signatures

   B. The network security database that contains all 1000, 2000, 3000, 4000, and 5000 series signatures

   C. The network security database that contains descriptions of all CIDS signatures and vulnerabilities

   D. The network security database located on the sensor and used to define the configured signatures

3. Which of the following accurately lists all the possible alarm levels?

   A. 1, 2, 3, 4, 5

   B. Low, Medium, High

   C. 1, 3, 5

   D. Low, Medium, High, Critical

4. Which of the following accurately lists all the possible severity levels?

   A. 1, 2, 3, 4, 5

   B. Low, Medium, High

C. 1, 3, 5

D. Low, Medium, High, Critical

5. Which of the following categories describes the amount of packets a signature must analyze to make a match? (Choose two.)

   A. Composite

   B. Context

   C. Atomic

   D. Content

6. Which of the following is an example of a signature class?

   A. Denial of service class

   B. General signature class

   C. String signature class

   D. Access control lists

7. Which of the following signatures have an associated subsignature? (Choose two.)

   A. General signatures

   B. String signatures

   C. Access control lists

   D. Reconnaissance class

8. Which of the following is an example of a signature implementation?

   A. Composite

   B. Atomic

   C. Context

   D. Access class

9. Which of the following signature series is responsible for analyzing the IP protocol?

   A. 2000 series

   B. 1000 series

   C. 4000 series

   D. 9000 series

10. Which of the following is *not* a valid CIDS signature series?

   A. 2000 series

   B. 5000 series

C. 7000 series

D. 10000 series

Answers

1. **D.** The ID of the subsignature associated with the CIDS signature
2. **C.** The network security database that contains descriptions of all CIDS signatures and vulnerabilities
3. **A.** 1, 2, 3, 4, 5
4. **B.** Low, Medium, High
5. **A. and C.** Composite and Atomic
6. **A.** Denial of service class
7. **B. and C.** String signatures and access control lists
8. **C.** Context
9. **B.** 1000 series
10. **C.** 7000 series

PART VI

Cisco SAFE Implementation

CHAPTER 27

Cisco SAFE Implementation

In this chapter, you will learn:

- To secure the documents required to prepare for the exam
- The published exam topics
- The skills and knowledge required to assure a successful attempt
- To configure any connections covered in any CCSP exam (simulation)

The Cisco Certified Security Professional (CCSP) certification validates knowledge of how the following devices and technologies can be used to secure a network using Cisco IOS Software, Cisco Secure ACS, Cisco PIX Firewalls, the Cisco VPN 3000 Concentrator Series, IDS technologies, and CiscoWorks VMS. Any concepts and technologies covered in the other four CCSP exams have to be considered fair game for inclusion in this exam.

A CCSP candidate should be able to use the knowledge and skills acquired in preparation for the four main CCSP exams plus the design information from the SAFE document(s) to do the following:

- Design end-to-end network security solutions using the Cisco SAFE Blueprint
- Use Cisco security devices and technologies to implement a defense-in-depth strategy
- Manage network security for maximum productivity

STUDY TIP The following information is as complete and accurate as possible at the time of publication, but Cisco reserves the right to update and modify any of its exams to reflect changes in technology and the industry. It is always prudent to check the Cisco web site for the most recent information.

Preparation Documents

The SAFE Implementation Exam is the capstone exam for the CCSP certification path. The exam tests the knowledge and skills needed to use and implement the principles and technologies contained in the "*SAFE: Extending the Security Blueprint to Small, Midsize, and Remote-User Networks*" (SMR) white paper.

While the exam is based on the SMR, the SMR refers to the original "*SAFE: A Security Blueprint for Enterprise Networks.*" The two documents are a 76 page and 66 page PDFs respectively and are available for free download from www.cisco.com/go/safe. Any SAFE technology document should be considered to be a part of the exam preparation.

In addition to design strategies and security concepts, almost one-half of the SAFE white paper is network diagrams and configuration examples for the various technologies that should make an excellent concise tool for reviewing for the exam.

The white papers reference other Cisco documents that might help if you are feeling weak on a particular topic. Three short papers that can help fill in the gaps include the following. In each case perform a search for the document by name from the www.cisco.com site.

- *Cisco AVVID Network Infrastructure Overview* Good Summary of AVVID. Know this one for sure.
- *Network Security Policy: Best Practices White Paper* Good Summary
- *SAFE Blueprint for Secure E-Business* Q & A Format

Exam Topics

According to the Cisco Web site, the following information provides general guidelines for the content likely to be included on this exam. However, other related topics may also appear on any specific delivery of the exam.

Security Fundamentals

- Need for network security
- Network attack taxonomy
- Network security policy
- Management protocols and functions

Architectural Overview

- Design fundamentals
- Safe axioms
- Security wheel

Cisco Security Portfolio

- Secure connectivity - Virtual Private Network solutions
- Secure connectivity - the 3000 Concentrator series
- Secure connectivity - Cisco VPN optimized routers

- Perimeter security firewalls - Cisco PIX and Cisco IOS Firewall
- Intrusion protection - IDS and Cisco secure scanner
- Identity - Access control solutions
- Security management - VMS and CSPM
- Cisco AVVID

SAFE Small Network Design

- Small network corporate Internet module
- Small network campus module
- Implementation-ISP router
- Implementation-IOS Firewall features and configuration
- Implementation-PIX Firewall

SAFE Medium Network Design

- Medium network corporate Internet module
- Medium network corporate Internet module design guidelines
- Medium network campus module
- Medium network campus module design guidelines
- Medium network WAN module
- Implementation - ISP router
- Implementation - edge router
- Implementation - IOS Firewall
- Implementation - PIX Firewall
- Implementation - NIDS
- Implementation - HIDS
- Implementation - VPN Concentrator
- Implementation - Layer 3 switch

SAFE Remote-User Network Implementation

- Key devices
- Threat mitigation
- Software access option
- Remote site firewall option

- Hardware VPN Client option
- Remote site router option

Skills Required for the Exam

According to Cisco course documentation, as the CCSP candidate studies the SAFE documents and reviews materials from the other four exams in preparation for the *SAFE Implementation Exam* the following specific skills should be used as a readiness measure.

- Describe the four types of security threats.
- Describe common attack methods and techniques used by hackers.
- List the general recommendations for mitigating common attack methods and techniques.
- Identify the components of a complete security policy.
- Identify the security issues implicit in common management protocols.
- Discuss the SAFE design philosophy and how it impacts the decision making process.
- List the devices that are part of the Cisco security portfolio.
- Understand the basic guidelines to use for product selection.
- Identify the functions of the key modules and key devices in a small network.
- Identify the specific threats to a small network.
- Describe the mitigation roles of Cisco devices in a small network.
- Implement specific configurations to apply the mitigation roles in a small network.
- Recommend alternative devices that can fulfill the same mitigation roles in a small network.
- Recommend alternative devices that can fulfill the same mitigation roles in a medium network.

STUDY TIP Early responses from those taking this exam emphasize the importance of knowing all of the technologies covered in the other four exams. Assume that anything covered in the other exams is fair game including simulations evaluating your ability to configure the device or VPN links between any covered technologies.

Chapter Review

The SAFE Implementation Exam is based on the principles and technologies contained in the "*SAFE: Extending the Security Blueprint to Small, Midsize, and Remote-User Networks*"

(SMR) white paper. This document is available as a PDF that can be downloaded from www.cisco.com/go/safe.

The exam topics provide an overview that can be used to guide the study process while the skills required for a successful exam can be used as a checklist to measure progress.

Questions

The following questions are based on the PDFs from the chapter. The actual exam can also include anything from the other four exams.

1. Which one of the following is not one of the Cisco SAFE Axioms?
   A. Switches Are Targets
   B. VPNs Are Targets
   C. Routers Are Targets
   D. Hosts Are Targets
   E. Networks Are Targets
   F. Applications Are Targets
2. Why must IDS be tuned when deployed?
   A. To learn the network devices
   B. To learn the protocols running in the network
   C. To reduce false positives
   D. To ensure compatibility with other security devices
3. To reduce the chances of DoS attacks, filtering should be configured on which two of the following RFCs?
   A. 2827
   B. 1518
   C. 1814
   D. 1918
4. OTP mitigates which of the following common attacks?
   A. Man-in-the-middle attacks
   B. Network reconnaissance attacks
   C. Brute force password attacks
   D. Trojan horse attacks
5. What are the correct first initials for the Cisco Security Wheel?
   A. SMTI
   B. PITR

C. ISPB

D. BPIM

6. The SAFE document considers which of the following architectures to be most secure?

A. In-Band

B. SSL

C. HTTPS

D. Out-of-Band

7. SAFE as a security policy template for company networks provides which one of the following?

A. An all-encompassing design for providing full security for corporate networks

B. A materials list for security purchases

C. A single-vendor approach to end-to-end network security designs

D. The original statement is false; SAFE is not a security policy template

8. According to SAFE, what two reasons account for the increasing threat hackers pose to networks?

A. Computers and networking devices continually becoming less complex

B. Ubiquity of the Internet

C. Pervasiveness of easy-to-use operating systems and development environments

D. Darwin's theory of evolution and natural selection

9. VPN remote users using split tunneling to connect to the Internet outside the VPN tunnel should use which of the following technologies to protect access to the local network?

A. Access lists

B. Layer 2 tunneling

C. PIX failover

D. Personal firewall

10. Which of the following can't mitigate the threat of packet sniffers in the network?

A. Replacing hubs with Layer 2 switches

B. Cryptography

C. Using only static routes in the LAN routers

D. Strong authentication

11. The central theme of Cisco AVVID and Cisco AVVID Network Infrastructure can be split into four general layers of emphasis. Which of the following doesn't belong?
    A. Applications resilience
    B. Business resilience
    C. Hardware resilience
    D. Network resilience
    E. Communications resilience
12. Which is not one of the five primary concerns of network deployment addressed by Cisco AVVID Network Infrastructure?
    A. Quality of service (QoS)
    B. Security
    C. Mobility
    D. Interoperability
    E. High availability
    F. Scalability
13. According to AVVID, Cisco's security suite emphasizes three key areas. Which of the following is not one of them?
    A. External Network Security
    B. Device Security
    C. Internal Network Security
    D. Network Identity
14. What is frequently the only way to thwart a DoS attack?
    A. A strong perimeter router backed up by a firewall
    B. Cooperation with the Internet service provider (ISP)
    C. A strong perimeter firewall backed up by a router
    D. Running TCP Intercept on the perimeter router
15. Which two of the following are advantages of using a VPN hardware client device?
    A. Lower cost than a router
    B. Access and authentication centrally administered
    C. More secure than a firewall device
    D. Individual PCs on the remote-site network do not need VPN client software

Answers

1. **B.** VPNs Are Targets
2. **C.** To reduce false positives
3. **A. and D.** 2827 and 1918
4. **C.** Brute force password attacks
5. **A.** SMTI—Secure, Monitor, Test, Improve
6. **D.** Out-of-Band
7. **D.** The original statement is false, SAFE is not a security policy template
8. **B. and C.** Ubiquity of the Internet, and pervasiveness of easy-to-use operating systems and development environments
9. **D.** Personal firewall
10. **C.** Use only static routes in the LAN routers
11. **C.** Hardware resilience
12. **D.** Interoperability
13. **B.** Device Security
14. **B.** Cooperation with the Internet service provider (ISP)
15. **B. and D.** Access and authentication can be centrally administered, and individual PCs on the remote-site network do not need VPN client software

APPENDIX

Access Control Lists

In this Appendix, you learn to:

- Create and use standard access lists
- Create and use extended access lists
- Create and use named access lists

Access control lists (ACLs) are powerful tools that are often at the heart of many other processes. Activities like traffic filtering, packet manipulation, routing update filtering, using the **debug ip packet** command, and many others use ACLs to make decisions. In each case, the administrator is able to construct a set of test or criteria statements, which are then used to control data flows or limit process scopes. A solid understanding of Cisco ACLs is critical because more devices are using them, including the latest versions of the PIX IOS.

While integral to so many processes, ACLs are often misunderstood by users. In this chapter, you see the two types of ACLS: standard and extended access lists, and, we hope, shed some light on how to build and use them. Undoubtedly, someone is wondering "Isn't there a third type called named access lists?" Well, yes and no. Yes, there are named access lists, but, no, they aren't that different from the other two types. They can be either standard or extended lists, the difference being that named access lists use names instead of numbers as identifiers. After you learn about standard and extended lists, you explore the additional benefits and limitations that named lists bring to the table.

Access List Basics

Access lists are a stack of one-line filters that are processed sequentially to determine whether data packets are allowed to continue on through the router or as a part of a router process. Each statement in the stack tests for one set of criteria and, if the criterion matches, the packet is either permitted or denied, as defined in the same statement.

A simple analogy would be this: while grocery shopping, if the grapes are ripe, I will add them to my basket. The single criterion is whether the grapes are ripe and, based on their being ripe, they're either permitted in my basket or denied. A more complex criterion could be if the grapes need to be ripe *and* from a domestic vineyard.

Two-Step Process

With all access lists, you have two separate and distinct steps in using them: the creation and the implementation. First, the ACL is always created using the access-list statement in Global Configuration mode. Second, the ACL is referenced by a **process** command or applied to an interface with commands unique to the application. If either part isn't done, the ACL typically has no impact, as if it didn't exist at all. The following output is an example of a simple standard access list and applying it to a Fast Ethernet interface.

```
interface Fastethernet 0/0
 ip address 192.168.5.1 255.255.255.0
 ip access-group 50 out
!
access-list 50 deny 192.168.1.10
access-list 50 deny 192.168.2.0 0.0.0.255
access-list 50 permit any
!
```

Access lists, when applied to an interface, called traffic filtering, only filter traffic traveling in the direction specified in the access-group statement. In the previous code output, only the outbound IP traffic is being filtered. While applying two ACLs for the same protocol for traffic going in one direction is impossible, you can have one for each direction for each protocol configured on the interface. The following code shows an example of an interface with multiple ACLs applied:

```
!
interface Fastethernet 0/0
 ip address 192.168.1.1 255.255.255.0
 ip access-group 171 in
 ip access-group 15 out
 appletalk cable-range 10-19 15.11
 appletalk access-group 615 out
 appletalk access-group 601 in
 ipx access-group 805 in
 ipx access-group 809 out
 ipx network 127
!
```

In determining whether to apply the ACL in- or outbound, visualize yourself at the center of the router. Is the data coming at you in the interface or is it traveling out through the interface? The perspective for determining in or out is always the center of the router, never the center of the network segment. A common mistake is to use an inbound filter to block traffic from entering a LAN. While the bad traffic is coming into the LAN, it's passing out of the router. Figure A-1 shows graphically inbound and outbound traffic flows on a basic router.

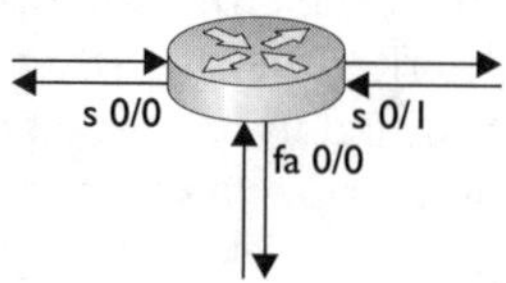

Figure A-1 Inbound and outbound traffic flows on router interfaces

Numbered ACL Common Characteristics

Before looking at the details of standard and extended ACLs, consider the following characteristics of all numbered access lists:

- An ACL is made up of one or more permit or deny statements
- If an ACL doesn't have at least one permit statement, it will deny everything
- All ACL statements with the same number are part of the same ACL
- ACL statements must be entered sequentially in order to be processed
- An ACL can be added to (appended), but not edited. Any attempt to edit an item will delete the entire ACL

TIP By default, router interfaces configured for a protocol "allow" all traffic in both directions without restriction. Once an ACL is applied to an interface, the default flips to "blocking" all traffic for that protocol in the specified direction, except what is explicitly allowed by the ACL.

The Numbers Matter

With numbered ACLs, the number is a list identifier that indicates the protocol used and whether the list is part of a standard or an extended ACL. Each statement in the ACL will have the same number. The following table is a recent listing of the ACL number ranges.

Range	Description
1–99	IP standard access list
1,300–1,999	IP standard access list (expanded range IOS v12.1)
100–199	IP extended access list
2,000–2,699	IP extended access list (expanded range IOS v12.1)
200–299	Protocol type-code access list
300–399	DECnet access list
400–499	XNS standard access list
500–599	XNS extended access list
600–699	Appletalk access list
700–799	48-bit MAC address access list
800–899	IPX standard access list
900–999	IPX extended access list
1,000–1,099	IPX SAP access list
1,200–1,299	IPX summary address access list
1,100–1,199	Extended 48-bit MAC address access list

While this text and the exam focus only on IP ACLs, it's important to remember that similar features exist for IPX, Appletalk, and other even older protocols.

Standard Access Lists

Standard IP access lists filter packets based exclusively on the network layer source address of a data packet. They either block (deny) or allow (permit) traffic, based solely on the origin of the packet. The IP standard access list number ranges are 1 to 99 and, since IOS release 12.1, numbers 1300 to 1399. These lists can be applied to a router interface to manage data traffic, applied to a virtual terminal connection to limit telnet sessions into the router, or used with a process like NAT to identify a pool of acceptable addresses.

A simple analogy for standard ACLs in many American communities would be election polling places. Voters are permitted in the voting area if they live within the election precinct, but denied access if they don't.

Building a Standard ACL

Standard ACLs are created in Global Configuration mode using the **access-list** command. The syntax of a standard ACL statement is simply

access-list *acl#* {permit | deny} {*source* [*source-wildcard*] | any} [log]

acl#	A number (1–99 or 1,300–1,399) that identifies all statements in the list
permit | deny	Choice of whether the packet passes through or not, and whether it lives or dies
source | any	Choice between selected host(s) or keyword ANY includes all hosts
source-wildcard	Used if *source* isn't a single host. The wildcard mask identifies the subnet, network, or supernet (see Wildcard Masks in the following)
log	Turns on the optional logging feature

Unless a packet matches a permit statement before it matches a deny statement or the last statement is processed, the packet will be discarded without recourse or appeal. A simple example would be the following code lines:

```
Rtr1#conf t
Rtr1(config)#access-list 15 deny 192.168.1.14
Rtr1(config)#access-list 15 deny 192.168.1.195
Rtr1(config)#access-list 15 permit 192.168.4.45
Rtr1(config)#access-list 15 permit 192.168.4.211
Rtr1(config)#access-list 15 permit 192.168.1.195
Rtr1(config)#
```

The preceding example shows two host addresses being blocked (denied) and two being permitted. The fifth statement, while valid, serves no purpose because the packet was already discarded in ACL line two and can't be recalled for ACL line five. This often happens when a person decides later to allow an address and adds the line to an existing ACL, where it can only go to the bottom of the stack. To change the order requires deleting the list and re-creating it, although techniques for using Notepad exist that makes this much less work than one might assume.

This clearly becomes tedious if each address must be handled individually. The next section looks at how to handle groups of addresses.

Source Identifier

The source identifier {*source* [*source-wildcard*] | any} is a choice between identified host(s) or any host, which equates to all addresses or all packets. The following example shows a common use of the Any option:

```
Rtr1#conf t
Rtr1(config)#access-list 15 deny 192.168.1.14
Rtr1(config)#access-list 15 deny 192.168.1.195
Rtr1(config)#access-list 15 permit 192.168.4.45
Rtr1(config)#access-list 15 permit 192.168.4.211
Rtr1(config)#access-list 15 permit any
Rtr1(config)#
```

The final statement allows all packets from any source address to be permitted. Looking over the preceding results, what's the impact of ACL Line five on Lines one and two? None, just like last time, it's too late for packets identified by an earlier deny statement.

What is the impact of ACL Line five on Lines three and four? They are now redundant; the result would be the same if they weren't present at all. A small amount of CPU usage could possibly be saved by rewriting the ACL to eliminate them.

What would happen if the line access-list 15 deny 192.168.3.11 was added now? Nothing, because the line would go to the bottom and, even if a packet from that host appeared, it would be permitted by ACL line five before it reached the new line.

Wildcard Masks In identifying ranges of IP addresses, ACLs use a wildcard mask instead of a subnet mask. Initially, they might look quite similar, but closer observation reveals they're basically opposites.

- **Subnet mask**—a 32-bit binary value made up of consecutive 1's indicting the network identifier, which then switches to 0's, indicating the host. The functions and processes using the subnet mask, such as routing or packet forwarding, have no interest in the host bits.
- **Wildcard mask**—a 32-bit binary value made up of consecutive 0's indicating those bits that must match, and then changing to 1's, indicating either bit value (1 or 0) is okay. In most cases, the 0's represent the network identifier and the 1's indicate the hosts to include.

The following example compares the classful subnet mask (netmask) for 192.168.1.0/24 with the wildcard mask. With both types of masks, the actual comparisons in network devices are all being done in binary, not in decimal.

```
Address:   192.168.1.0                11000000.10101000.00000001.00000000
Netmask:   255.255.255.0 == /24       11111111.11111111.11111111.00000000
Wildcard:  0.0.0.255                  00000000.00000000.00000000.11111111
```

In this example, the netmask and wildcard mask are literally opposites. This is true in all cases using classful addresses. The following table shows the default host mask and the three classful netmask/wildcard mask options.

IP Address	Subnet Mask	Wildcard Mask
192.168.1.15	255.255.255.255	0.0.0.0 (default)
192.168.1.0	255.255.255.0	0.0.0.255
112.16.0.0	255.255.0.0	0.0.255.255
15.0.0.0	255.0.0.0	0.255.255.255
45.12.16.0	255.255.255.0	0.0.0.255

The last entry is an example of a class A address subnetted to a series of class C networks. Examples of each are demonstrated in the following code output:

```
Rtr1#conf t
Rtr1(config)#access-list 15 deny 192.168.1.14 0.0.0.0
Rtr1(config)#access-list 15 deny 192.168.1.0 0.0.0.255
Rtr1(config)#access-list 15 permit 112.16.0.0 0.0.255.255
Rtr1(config)#access-list 15 permit 15.0.0.0 0.255.255.255
Rtr1(config)#access-list 15 permit 45.12.16.0.0.0.255
Rtr1(config)#access-list 15 permit any
Rtr1(config)#
```

Classful networks are quite easy because the change occurs on an octet boundary. But what about identifying only a subnet or a supernet? A couple of additional examples in decimal format might help.

IP Address	Subnet Mask	Wildcard Mask
192.168.1.16	255.255.255.240	0.0.0.15
192.168.96.0	255.255.254.0	0.0.1.255

Remember, each octet (8 bits) is interpreted separately when converted to decimal. The following example shows the binary equivalents for the subnet with addresses 192.168.1.16 to 192.168.1.31.

```
Address:   192.168.1.16            11000000.10101000.00000001.00010000
Netmask:   255.255.255.240 = /28   11111111.11111111.11111111.11110000
Wildcard:  0.0.0.15                00000000.00000000.00000000.00001111
```

The remaining rows are for the supernet with address range of 192.168.96.0 to 192.168.97.255.

```
Address:   192.168.96.0            11000000.10101000.01100000.00000000
Netmask:   255.255.254.0 == /23    11111111.11111111.11111110.00000000
Wildcard:  0.0.1.255               00000000.00000000.00000001.11111111
```

To create a wildcard mask for a subnet or supernet requires understanding the previous concepts, but interpreting an existing properly defined one is quite simple. The value 192.168.96.0 /19 (subnet mask: 255.255.224.0) has a wildcard mask of 0.0.31.255. The original value 192.168.96.0 is the starting value. Then add the wildcard mask octet by octet to get the maximum value 192.168.(96+31).(0+255) or 192.168.127.255.

Creating a Wildcard Mask for a Subnet or Supernet Creating a wildcard mask for a subnet or supernet can seem a little overwhelming. After all, there must be an infinite number of possibilities, right? No, like subnets few combinations occur. Figure A-2 shows a simple tool for demonstrating this.

The top table in Figure A-2 shows the eight bit positions in an octet and their corresponding decimal values. The middle table represents carrying the same logic out to 12 bits, which would be handy when working with supernet—networks with more than 8 bits for host addresses. The bottom example shows how the Binary Digits row can be used to calculate the decimal equivalent of binary number. This process works for subnets as well: a 3-bit subnet mask would be ones in the leftmost location equaling 224.

The table is built by counting bit positions, right to left, by ones. The Value row also starts with one, and then doubles with each bit position to the left.

Other information the table reveals is the limited number of subnet increments that can be defined without ambiguity. These are the numbers in the Value row. For example, a subnet mask of 5 bits (248) would have an increment of 8 or values like the following:

Class C	Class B	Class A
192.168.0.0	172.16.0.0	15.0.0.0
192.168.0.8	172.16.8.0	15.8.0.0
192.168.0.16	172.16.16.0	15.16.0.0
192.168.0.24	172.16.24.0	15.24.0.0
to	to	to
192.168.0.240	172.16.240.0	15.240.0.0
192.168.0.248	172.16.248.0	15.248.0.0

Just as each of the previous values is a subnet address, each value would also be the first value used with a wildcard mask. In this case, the wildcard mask would be 0.0.0.7,

Position	8	7	6	5	4	3	2	1
Value	128	64	32	16	8	4	2	1
Binary Digits								
Equals								

Position	12	11	10	9	8	7	6	5	4	3	2	1
Value	2048	1024	512	256	128	64	32	16	8	4	2	1
Binary Digits												
Equals												

Position	8	7	6	5	4	3	2	1	
Value	128	64	32	16	8	4	2	1	
Binary Digits	0	0	1	1	1	1	1	1	
Equals	0	0	32	16	8	4	2	1	= 63

Figure A-2 Binary to decimal conversion tool

as in 192.168.0.24 0.0.0.7, which identifies the range 192.168.0.24–31. In the second octet, this would look like 192.168.24.0 0.0.7.255, which identifies the range 192.168.24.0-192.168.31.255.

Rule of thumb: the starting octet value must be a multiple of a number on the Value line of the table (increment). The wildcard mask for that same octet is the sum of the bits to the right of the Value line entry (always one less than the increment). If the starting value is in the second or third octet, the mask value is unique for that octet, but then all remaining octets must be 255. So, if the increment is 32 and the starting value is 10.96.0.0, then the mask is 0.31.255.255.

Exercise A-1 **Objective:** Practice the skills required to interpret and create wildcard masks.

Required: Use the conversion table covered in the text or any method you choose (except using a subnet calculator). To confirm your results, the correct answers are at the end of the exercise.

1. What would be the starting address (first acceptable) and ending address (last acceptable) for the address/mask combination 192.15.75.0 0.0.0.255?
2. What would be the starting address and ending address for the address/mask combination 172.16.0.0 0.0.255.255?
3. What would be the starting address and ending address for the address/mask combination 210.10.0.0 0.0.1.255?
4. What would be the starting address and ending address for the address/mask combination 209.10.25.128 0.0.0.31?
5. What would be the starting address and wildcard mask for the IP network 210.119.60.0/24?
6. What would be the starting address and wildcard mask for the IP host address 210.119.60.10/24?
7. What would be the starting address and wildcard mask for the third subnet of 192.168.145.0/26?
8. What would be the starting address and wildcard mask for the fifth subnet of 201.110.150.0/30?
9. What would be the starting address and wildcard mask for the second subnet of 145.110.0.0/18?

Answers

1. 192.15.75.0 to 192.15.75.255
2. 172.16.0.0 to 172.16.255.255
3. 210.1.10.0 to 210.1.11.255
4. 209.10.25.128 to 209.10.25.159

5. 210.119.60.0 0.0.0.255
6. 210.119.60.10 0.0.0.0
7. 192.168.145.128 0.0.0.63
8. 201.110.150.16 0.0.0.3
9. 145.110.64.0 0.0.63.255

Removing an Access List

To remove the entire list, type **no access-list** ***acl-num*** in Global Configuration mode or you can unapply the list by typing the **no ip access-group** ***acl-num*** command while in the Interface Configuration mode. The following code demonstrates both techniques:

```
Rtr1#config t
Rtr1(config)#no access-list 50
Rtr1(config)#int e0
Rtr1(config-if)#no ip access-group 50
```

If you remove the list, but leave the **access-group** command on versions of the IOS since v12.0, the result is the same as if there were a single permit any list item. Older versions defaulted to a deny any and would, therefore, block all traffic.

Verifying ACLs

Several basic commands are useful in confirming that ACLs are in place and doing their jobs. Those commands include the following:

- Show run
- Show access lists
- Show IP interfaces

Show Run Command

One way to see your access lists and how they're applied is to use the **show run** command to see the active configuration. The next lines show the output of a **show run** command with some of the unrelated lines removed:

```
Rtr1#show run
hostname Rtr1
!
interface Ethernet0
 ip address 192.168.5.1 255.255.255.0
 ip access-group 50 out
!
interface Serial0
 ip address 192.168.96.2 255.255.255.0
 ip access-group 75 in
!
```

```
access-list 50 deny   192.168.1.10
access-list 50 permit any
access-list 75 deny   192.168.17.123
access-list 75 deny   192.168.1.10
access-list 75 permit any
!
```

This shows that ACL 50 is applied to Ethernet 0 as an inbound access list and ACL 75 is applied to Serial 0 as an outbound list. It also shows the order of the ACL statements.

Show Access-Lists Command

The **show access-lists** command displays all access lists on the router, but doesn't show if or where they're applied. Another command—**show ip access-lists**—would include only IP access lists, which, in this case, would be exactly the same display. Both commands allow specifying an ACL number or name after the command, such as **show ip access-lists 50**, to display only that ACL.

```
Rtr1#show access-lists
Standard IP access list 50
    deny   192.168.1.10 log (23 matches) check=321
    permit any (298 matches)
Standard IP access list 75
    deny   192.168.17.123 (36 matches) check=194
    deny   192.168.1.10 (16 matches) check=158
    permit any (142 matches)
Rtr1#
```

If the ACL has used the results since the last time the counters were cleared, the number of matches will display after each line. The command to clear the results is **clear access-list counters** {*acl-num* | *acl-name*}, like **clear access-list counters 50**.

Show IP Interfaces Command

The **show ip interface** command can be used to tell if an inbound or an outbound access list has been applied to an interface. Rows 9 and 10 of the following output contain the information. The rest of the lines don't pertain to ACLs, so they've been omitted. You should recall that the **show ip interface** command displays all interfaces, but adding the interface ID, such as **show ip interface s0/0**, to the end of the command limits the output to that interface.

```
Rtr1#show ip interface
Ethernet0 is up, line protocol is up
  Internet address is 192.168.5.1/24
  Broadcast address is 255.255.255.255
  Address determined by non-volatile memory
  MTU is 1500 bytes
  Helper address is not set
  Directed broadcast forwarding is disabled
  Multicast reserved groups joined: 224.0.0.9
  Outgoing access list is 50              <-Outbound ACL 50 applied
  Inbound  access list is not set         <-No inbound ACL is applied
  Proxy ARP is enabled.
```

Extended Access Lists

Extended access lists provide a higher level of traffic control by being able to filter packets based on the protocol, source and/or destination IP address, and source and/or destination port number. For example, an extended access list can block an address (or group of addresses) in a particular network from accessing the FTP services on a specific server, while still allowing other services.

Creating an Extended Access List

As with standard lists, the **access-list** command is used to create each condition of the list—one condition per line. The lines are processed sequentially and can't be edited or reordered once in place without the use of a tool like Notepad. The protocol being filtered determines the exact syntax options, but the basic syntax for IOS version 12.*x* includes the following items.

> access-list *acl#* {permit | deny} {*protocol* | *protocol-keyword*} {*source wildcard* | any} [*operator source-port*] {*destination wildcard* | any} [*operator destination-port*] [precedence *precedence*] [tos *tos*] [log | log-input] [options]

acl#	A number (100–199 or 2,000–2,699) that identifies all statements in the list.
permit | deny	The choice between does the packet pass through or not, or does it live or die.
protocol	The name or number of an IP protocol. It can be one of the keywords **eigrp**, **gre, icmp**, **igmp**, **igrp**, **ip**, **ipinip**, **nos**, **ospf**, **pim**, **tcp**, or **udp**, or a number (0 to 255) representing an IP protocol number. Keyword **ip** includes ICMP, TCP, and UDP. Some protocols allow further qualifiers.
source | any	The choice between selected host(s) or keyword ANY includes all hosts.
destination | any	The choice between selected host(s) or keyword ANY includes all hosts.
wildcard	A wildcard mask identifying a host, subnet, network, or supernet. The keyword **host** with the source or destination is the same as **address 0.0.0.0** (example **host 10.0.0.1** is the same as **10.0.0.1 0.0.0.0**).
operator	Compares source or destination ports, include **eq** (equal to), **lt** (less than), **gt** (greater than), **neq** (not equal to), and **range** (inclusive range—requires two port numbers).
source-port *destination-port*	Number (0–65,535) or name of a TCP or UDP port. Used with TCP or UDP filters.
precedence *precedence*	Packets can be filtered by precedence level, as specified by a number from 0 to 7 or by name.
tos *tos*	Packets can be filtered by type of service level, as specified by a number from 0 to 15 or by name.
log | log-input	Logs matches against this entry. Log-input logs match against this entry, including input interface.

Any keywords or components covered in standard access lists are the same, except the Log option now reports relative protocol, source/destination addresses, and source/destination ports. Extended ACLs are applied to interfaces exactly the same as standard ACLs except that, whenever possible, they're placed as close to the source as possible. Placing them close to the source conserves resources by not processing the packet through the network only to kill it off. Some router processes that use ACLs might only use standard, extended, or even named lists.

With extended access lists, every condition listed in the access list statement must match for the statement to match and the permit or deny condition to be applied. As soon as one condition fails, that statement is skipped and the next statement in the access list is compared. If all statements fail to match in their entirety, the packet is then discarded. Remember, once an ACL is applied, the default becomes to deny anything that isn't explicitly permitted. Figure A-3 shows how each line of an extended access list is processed.

Far too many options exist to remember for filtering with extended access lists, but using the question mark (?) help feature displays all the possibilities. The next sections cover the most common ones.

TCP Access Lists

TCP access lists support both source and destination TCP ports, which can be specified using either the port number or mnemonic. Port numbers or name must be preceded with relational operators, such as those shown in the following code output:

```
Rtr1(config)#access-list 101 deny tcp host 10.0.0.97 ?
  eq       Match only packets on a given port number
  gt       Match only packets with a greater port number
  lt       Match only packets with a lower port number
  neq      Match only packets not on a given port number
  range    Match only packets in the range of port numbers
```

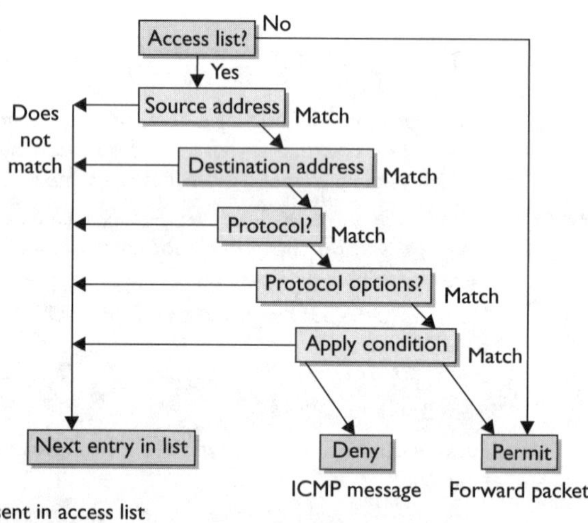

Figure A-3 Extended access list processing steps

After choosing an operator, specify a mnemonic or port number like those shown in the following code output for the TCP port names. The port number appears in parentheses. Because the mnemonics make the access list easier to understand for anyone who might need to support the device later, it's a good idea to use them when they're available.

```
Rtr1(config)#access-list 101 deny tcp host 10.0.0.97 eq ?
  <0-65535>     Port number
  bgp           Border Gateway Protocol (179)
  chargen       Character generator (19)
  cmd           Remote commands (rcmd, 514)
  daytime       Daytime (13)
  discard       Discard (9)
  domain        Domain Name Service (53)
  echo          Echo (7)
  exec          Exec (rsh, 512)
  finger        Finger (79)
  ftp           File Transfer Protocol (21)
  ftp-data      FTP data connections (used infrequently, 20)
  gopher        Gopher (70)
  hostname      NIC hostname server (101)
  ident         Ident Protocol (113)
  irc           Internet Relay Chat (194)
  klogin        Kerberos login (543)
  kshell        Kerberos shell (544)
  login         Login (rlogin, 513)
  lpd           Printer service (515)
  nntp          Network News Transport Protocol (119)
  pim-auto-rp   PIM Auto-RP (496)
  pop2          Post Office Protocol v2 (109)
  pop3          Post Office Protocol v3 (110)
  smtp          Simple Mail Transport Protocol (25)
  sunrpc        Sun Remote Procedure Call (111)
  syslog        Syslog (514)
  tacacs        TAC Access Control System (49)
  talk          Talk (517)
  telnet        Telnet (23)
  time          Time (37)
  uucp          Unix-to-Unix Copy Program (540)
  whois         Nicname (43)
  www           World Wide Web (HTTP, 80)
```

In the following extended ACL example, the first statement blocks network hosts in 192.168.3.0 from accessing the web servers in 192.168.1.0. The second statement blocks the same hosts from accessing any FTP servers. The third statement blocks an address from using the Telnet feature to reach the 192.168.1.0 network:

```
access-list 101 deny tcp 192.168.3.0 0.0.0.255 192.168.1.0 0.0.0.255 eq www
access-list 101 deny tcp 192.168.3.0 0.0.0.255 any eq ftp
access-list 101 deny tcp any 192.168.1.0 0.0.0.255 any eq telnet
access-list 101 permit ip any any
```

The last statement demonstrates an important concept. Recall that any access list changes the default operation from a Permit Anything mode to a Deny Anything mode, except what is explicitly allowed. Implicit in the previous lines is that all protocols are denied, not only TCP. If the final statement were **access-list 101 permit tcp any any**, all remaining TCP ports would, in fact, be permitted, but all UDP and ICMP packets would remain blocked. While this might be the objective, this is a common mistake with people new to ACLs or those in a hurry.

TCP's Established Option The Established option is a TCP-only feature that can use the connection-oriented attributes of the TCP to limit traffic coming into a network or network segment to those sessions that originated from within that network. The established condition is only true if the ACK (acknowledge) or RST (Reset) bits are set to one in the TCP header, indicating an already established connection. A packet with no ACK or RST bit set, but a SYN (synchronize) bit set to one is used to establish a new connection and can then be denied. Figure A-4 demonstrates the three-step "handshake" TCP uses to establish a connection.

The following output demonstrates allowing any host to respond to FTP and Telnet requests that originated within the 192.168.1.0 network, but blocks all other TCP packets.

```
access-list 101 permit tcp any eq www 192.168.1.0 0.0.0.255 eq ftp established
access-list 101 permit tcp any 192.168.1.0 0.0.0.255 any eq telnet established
access-list 101 deny   tcp any any
access-list 101 permit ip  any any
```

The Established option can help reduce the risk of a common type of hacker attack that buries a host in SYN requests, preventing it from handling normal business. Because a sophisticated hacker can manipulate the TCP header bits, this tool needs support from other tools to protect against that threat.

Look over the following ACL statement using the established option. This is a common first effort when trying to limit Web activity to those sessions originating within the network. So what's wrong with the statement?

```
access-list 101 permit tcp any 192.168.1.0 0.0.0.255 eq www established
```

Remember, www is an alias for port 80. A web session originating inside would use port 80 as the destination, but would designate a port above 1024, such as 1065, as the source port. This means the returning packet would have port 80 as the source and port 1065 as the destination. The ACL is looking for port 80 as the destination. The following output might work better:

```
access-list 101 permit tcp any eq www 192.168.1.0 0.0.0.255 established
```

When you work with the established feature, it's important to make sure you understand what the mnemonic stands for and, if you use the port numbers, what any port

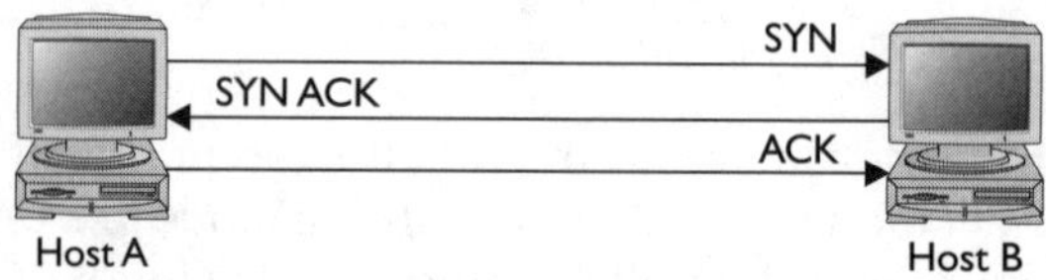

Figure A-4 TCP three-way handshake to establish a session

numbers stand for. Another approach, which allows any established sessions, but blocks all other TCP traffic, is represented in the following code lines:

```
access-list 101 permit tcp any 192.168.1.0 0.0.0.255 established
access-list 101 deny   tcp any any
```

NOTE *Source-port filtering,* the process of filtering data on the source port of a packet, isn't secure because a skilled hacker could easily change a source port on a packet, which could then pass through the filter.

UDP Access Lists

The *UDP access list,* like TCP, supports both source and destination ports, and, like TCP, uses the same relational operators to define the mnemonic or port numbers. The following code output shows some of the most common UDP port names:

```
Rtr1(config)#access-list 101 permit udp any eq ?
  <0-65535>    Port number
  biff         Biff (mail notification, comsat, 512)
  bootpc       Bootstrap Protocol (BOOTP) client (68)
  bootps       Bootstrap Protocol (BOOTP) server (67)
  discard      Discard (9)
  dnsix        DNSIX security protocol auditing (195)
  domain       Domain Name Service (DNS, 53)
  echo         Echo (7)
  isakmp       Internet Security Association and Key Management Protocol (500)
  mobile-ip    Mobile IP registration (434)
  nameserver   IEN116 name service (obsolete, 42)
  netbios-dgm  NetBios datagram service (138)
  netbios-ns   NetBios name service (137)
  netbios-ss   NetBios session service (139)
  ntp          Network Time Protocol (123)
  pim-auto-rp  PIM Auto-RP (496)
  rip          Routing Information Protocol (router, in.routed, 520)
  snmp         Simple Network Management Protocol (161)
  snmptrap     SNMP Traps (162)
  sunrpc       Sun Remote Procedure Call (111)
  syslog       System Logger (514)
  tacacs       TAC Access Control System (49)
  talk         Talk (517)
  tftp         Trivial File Transfer Protocol (69)
  time         Time (37)
  who          Who service (rwho, 513)
  xdmcp        X Display Manager Control Protocol (177)
```

In the following extended ACL example, the first statement blocks network hosts in 192.168.3.0 from sending SNMP packets into the 192.168.1.0 network. The second statement blocks the same hosts from accessing any TFTP servers. The third statement blocks any RIP routing updates from going to the 192.168.1.0 network.

```
access-list 101 deny udp 192.168.3.0 0.0.0.255 192.168.1.0 0.0.0.255 eq snmp
access-list 101 deny udp 192.168.3.0 0.0.0.255 any eq tftp
access-list 101 deny udp any 192.168.1.0 0.0.0.255 any eq rip
access-list 101 permit ip any any
```

The final statement permits the remaining UDP packets, plus all TCP and ICMP packets.

ICMP Access Lists

ICMP (Internet Control Message Protocol—RFC 792) access list syntax doesn't use port numbers, but adds options to allow filtering on ICMP messages. The actual syntax for filtering UDP is as follows:

access-list *acl#* {permit | deny} icmp {*source wildcard* | any} {*destination wildcard* | any} [*icmp-type* | [[*icmp-type icmp-code*] | [*icmp-message*]] [precedence *precedence*] [tos *tos*] [log | log-input] [options]

icmp-type	An ICMP message type is a number between 0 and 255.
icmp-code	An ICMP message code is a number between 0 and 255.
icmp-message	ICMP packets can be filtered by an ICMP message type name or by an ICMP message type and code name.

The following code includes the symbolic names (since IOS v 10.3) that can be used to filter ICMP traffic:

```
Rtr1(config)#access-list 101 permit icmp any any ?
  <0-255>                      ICMP message type
  administratively-prohibited  Administratively prohibited
  alternate-address            Alternate address
  conversion-error             Datagram conversion
  dod-host-prohibited          Host prohibited
  dod-net-prohibited           Net prohibited
  echo                         Echo (ping)
  echo-reply                   Echo reply
  general-parameter-problem    Parameter problem
  host-isolated                Host isolated
  host-precedence-unreachable  Host unreachable for precedence
  host-redirect                Host redirect
  host-tos-redirect            Host redirect for TOS
  host-tos-unreachable         Host unreachable for TOS
  host-unknown                 Host unknown
  host-unreachable             Host unreachable
  information-reply            Information replies
  information-request          Information requests
  log                          Log matches against this entry
  log-input                    Log matches against this entry,
                               including input interface
  mask-reply                   Mask replies
  mask-request                 Mask requests
  mobile-redirect              Mobile host redirect
  net-redirect                 Network redirect
  net-tos-redirect             Net redirect for TOS
  net-tos-unreachable          Network unreachable for TOS
  net-unreachable              Net unreachable
  network-unknown              Network unknown
  no-room-for-option           Parameter required but no room
  option-missing               Parameter required but not present
  packet-too-big               Fragmentation needed and DF set
  parameter-problem            All parameter problems
  port-unreachable             Port unreachable
  precedence                   Match packets with given precedence value
  precedence-unreachable       Precedence cutoff
```

```
protocol-unreachable          Protocol unreachable
reassembly-timeout            Reassembly timeout
redirect                      All redirects
router-advertisement          Router discovery advertisements
router-solicitation           Router discovery solicitations
source-quench                 Source quenches
source-route-failed           Source route failed
time-exceeded                 All time exceededs
timestamp-reply               Timestamp replies
timestamp-request             Timestamp requests
tos                           Match packets with given TOS value
traceroute                    Traceroute
ttl-exceeded                  TTL exceeded
unreachable                   All unreachables
```

RFC 1812 dictates that traffic denied by filtering (ACL) will cause an ICMP Administratively Prohibited message to be sent to the sender, using the sender's address as destination and the filtering router interface address as source. While this might be in formative to the sender, it might not be a good security practice for the network protected by the router. Not sending this message back to external users might be better because of the implication that something is worth protecting or hacking — depending on your point of view. One solution would be to deny ICMP Administratively Prohibited messages outbound at the external interface.

In the following extended ACL example, if the ACL is applied to the outbound traffic on a border router, the first statement blocks any echo replies out of the network. The statement literally prevents ping responses, denying the sender connectivity information about the address. If you ping www.Microsoft.com, you can see this policy in effect. The second statement blocks ICMP Administratively Prohibited messages from notifying the sender that an ACL discarded their packets.

```
access-list 101 deny icmp any any echo-reply
access-list 101 deny icmp any any administratively-prohibited
access-list 101 permit ip any any
```

The final statement permits the remaining ICMP packets, plus all TCP and UDP packets.

Named Access Lists

Since Cisco IOS Release 11.2, you can use a text name for access lists in many cases. Some new features have been added to named ACLs that make them more than just text names. The benefits of using named access lists are the following:

- The name can be meaningful and indicative of the list's purpose. This is particularly important for documentation and maintenance purposes. This can also benefit anyone having to support the ACLs later.
- You can selectively delete specific lines within a named access list, something that can't be done with numbered lists.
- This gets around the limitation on the quantity of numbered ACLs, although this is less of an issue than before the additional numbers added with v12.1.

Some things to consider before you create a named access list for a particular purpose should include the following items:

- Named access lists are incompatible with older IOS releases (pre-11.2).
- A standard access list and an extended access list can't have the same name. This rule means no two access lists can have the same name—not an unusual requirement.
- Names must begin with an alphanumeric character and are case-sensitive. Within the name, almost any character can be included.
- Not all processes that use access lists can use named ACLs.

Named access lists have a different format from numbered access lists. The initial line establishes the type and name of the list. The access-list statement is followed by one or more permit or deny statements. The syntax for a named standard access list is

Router(config)#ip access-list standard *name*
Router(config-std-nacl)# {permit | deny} {*source* [*source-wildcard*] | any} [log]

The following is an example of a named standard access list:

```
Rtr1(config)#ip access-list standard sales_access
Rtr1(config-std-nacl)#permit 192.168.3.0 0.0.0.255
Rtr1(config-std-nacl)#permit 192.168.4.0 0.0.0.255
Rtr1(config-std-nacl)#permit 192.168.5.0 0.0.0.255
Rtr1(config-std-nacl)#permit host 192.168.6.50
Rtr1(config-std-nacl)#interface serial 0
Rtr1(config-if)#ip access-group sales_access out
```

Notice the prompt identifies the ACL as standard (std) and named access list (nacl). This means a new Configuration mode was created for named ACLs because numbered lists are all created at the Global Configuration mode.

The following is what the previous access list looks like in the running configuration. Notice the change in the order and the removal of the wildcards:

```
!
ip access-list standard Sales_access
 permit 192.168.6.50
 permit 192.168.3.0
 permit 192.168.4.0
 permit 192.168.5.0
!
```

The syntax for a named extended access list is

Router(config)#ip access-list extended *name*
Router(config-ext-nacl)# {permit | deny} {*protocol* | *protocol-keyword*} {*source wildcard* | any} [*operator source-port*] {*destination wildcard* | any} [*operator destination-port*] [precedence *precedence*] [tos *tos*] [log | log-input] [options]

The following is an example of a named extended access list to limit TCP and Web access within the network:

```
Rtr1#configure terminal
Rtr1(config)#ip access-list extended server-screen
Rtr1(config-ext-nacl)#permit tcp any host 192.168.2.20 eq 80
Rtr1(config-ext-nacl)#permit tcp host 192.168.1.151 host 192.168.2.20
Rtr1(config-ext-nacl)#int s1
Rtr1(config-if)#ip access-group server-screen out
```

The following is what the previous access list looks like if you show the running configuration. Note, the TCP port 80 was replaced with the mnemonic www:

```
!
ip access-list extended server-screen
 permit tcp any host 192.168.2.20 eq www
 permit tcp host 192.168.1.151 host 192.168.2.20
!
```

APPENDIX B

About the CD

The CD included with this book contains five practice exams—one for each of the following Cisco certification exams:

- **Exam** 642-501 SECUR: SECURING CISCO IOS NETWORKS
- **Exam** 642-521 CSPFA: CISCO SECURE PIX FIREWALLS ADVANCED
- **Exam** 642-511 CSVPN: CISCO SECURE VPN
- **Exam** 642-531 CSIDS: CISCO SECURE INTRUSION DETECTION SYSTEM
- **Exam** 642-541 CSI: CISCO SAFE IMPLEMENTATION

The CD also includes MasterExam, an electronic version of this book, hands-on lab exercises and Session #1 of LearnKey's online training. The software is easy to install on any Windows 98/NT/2000 computer. You must install it to access the MasterExam feature. You can, however, browse the electronic book and the lab exercises directly from the CD without installation. To register for LearnKey's online training and a second bonus MasterExam, click the Online Training link on the Main Page and follow the directions to the free online registration.

System Requirements

The CD software requires Windows 98 or higher, Internet Explorer 5.0 or higher, and 20MB of hard disk space for full installation. The electronic book requires Adobe Acrobat Reader. To access the online training from LearnKey, you must have RealPlayer Basic 8 or the Real1 plug-in, which is installed automatically when you launch the online training.

LearnKey Online Training

The LearnKey Online Training link allows you to access online training from Osborne .Onlineexpert.com. The first session of this course is provided free of charge. You can purchase additional sessions for this course and other courses directly from www .LearnKey.com or by calling (800) 865-0165.

Prior to running the online training, you must add the Real plug-in and the RealCBT plug-in to your system. This is facilitated automatically when you attempt to run the training the first time. You must also register the online product. Follow the instructions for a first-time user. Please be sure to use a valid e-mail address.

Installing and Running MasterExam

If your computer's CD-ROM drive is configured to auto-run, the CD will automatically start up when you insert it. From the opening screen, you can install MasterExam by clicking the MasterExam or MasterSim buttons. This begins the installation process and creates a program group named LearnKey. To run MasterExam, select Start | Programs | LearnKey. If the auto-run feature does not launch your CD, browse to the CD and double-click the RunInstall icon.

MasterExam

MasterExam simulates the actual exam. The number of questions, the type of questions, and the time allowed are intended to represent the exam environment. You have the option to take an open-book exam that includes hints, references, and answers; a closed-book exam; or the timed MasterExam simulation.

When you launch the MasterExam simulation, a digital clock appears in the top center of your screen. The clock counts down to zero unless you end the exam before the time expires.

Electronic Book

The CD includes the entire contents of the Exam Guide in PDF. The Adobe Acrobat Reader is included on the CD to allow you to read the file.

Lab Exercises

Because hands-on experience is key to success with any Cisco exam, we've created exercises for each chapter to provide you with opportunities to put the concepts of the book into practice. These exercises are organized by chapter and are provided in pdf format.

Help

A help file is provided and can be accessed by clicking the Help button on the main page in the lower-left corner. Individual help features are also available through MasterExam, and LearnKey's online training.

Removing Installation(s)

MasterExam is installed on your hard drive. For *best* results for removal of programs, use the Start | Programs | LearnKey | Uninstall options to remove MasterExam.

To remove RealPlayer, use the Add/Remove Programs icon in the Control Panel. You can also remove the LearnKey training program from this location.

Technical Support

For questions regarding the technical content of the electronic book or MasterExam, please visit www.osborne.com or e-mail customer.service@mcgraw-hill.com. For customers outside the United States, please e-mail international_cs@mcgraw-hill.com.

LearnKey Technical Support

For technical problems with the LearnKey software (installation, operation, and removing installations) and for questions regarding LearnKey online training and MasterSim content, please visit www.learnkey.com or e-mail techsupport@learnkey.com.

INDEX

Numeric entries

A

J

K

L

O

P

U

V

W

X

Z

INTERNATIONAL CONTACT INFORMATION

AUSTRALIA
McGraw-Hill Book Company Australia Pty. Ltd.
TEL +61-2-9900-1800
FAX +61-2-9878-8881
http://www.mcgraw-hill.com.au
books-it_sydney@mcgraw-hill.com

CANADA
McGraw-Hill Ryerson Ltd.
TEL +905-430-5000
FAX +905-430-5020
http://www.mcgraw-hill.ca

GREECE, MIDDLE EAST, & AFRICA (Excluding South Africa)
McGraw-Hill Hellas
TEL +30-210-6560-990
TEL +30-210-6560-993
TEL +30-210-6560-994
FAX +30-210-6545-525

MEXICO (Also serving Latin America)
McGraw-Hill Interamericana Editores S.A. de C.V.
TEL +525-117-1583
FAX +525-117-1589
http://www.mcgraw-hill.com.mx
fernando_castellanos@mcgraw-hill.com

SINGAPORE (Serving Asia)
McGraw-Hill Book Company
TEL +65-6863-1580
FAX +65-6862-3354
http://www.mcgraw-hill.com.sg
mghasia@mcgraw-hill.com

SOUTH AFRICA
McGraw-Hill South Africa
TEL +27-11-622-7512
FAX +27-11-622-9045
robyn_swanepoel@mcgraw-hill.com

SPAIN
McGraw-Hill/Interamericana de España, S.A.U.
TEL +34-91-180-3000
FAX +34-91-372-8513
http://www.mcgraw-hill.es
professional@mcgraw-hill.es

UNITED KINGDOM, NORTHERN, EASTERN, & CENTRAL EUROPE
McGraw-Hill Education Europe
TEL +44-1-628-502500
FAX +44-1-628-770224
http://www.mcgraw-hill.co.uk
computing_europe@mcgraw-hill.com

ALL OTHER INQUIRIES Contact:
McGraw-Hill/Osborne
TEL +1-510-420-7700
FAX +1-510-420-7703
http://www.osborne.com
omg_international@mcgraw-hill.com

LICENSE AGREEMENT

THIS PRODUCT (THE "PRODUCT") CONTAINS PROPRIETARY SOFTWARE, DATA AND INFORMATION (INCLUDING DOCUMENTATION) OWNED BY THE McGRAW-HILL COMPANIES, INC. ("McGRAW-HILL") AND ITS LICENSORS. YOUR RIGHT TO USE THE PRODUCT IS GOVERNED BY THE TERMS AND CONDITIONS OF THIS AGREEMENT.

LICENSE: Throughout this License Agreement, "you" shall mean either the individual or the entity whose agent opens this package. You are granted a non-exclusive and non-transferable license to use the Product subject to the following terms:

(i) If you have licensed a single user version of the Product, the Product may only be used on a single computer (i.e., a single CPU). If you licensed and paid the fee applicable to a local area network or wide area network version of the Product, you are subject to the terms of the following subparagraph (ii).

(ii) If you have licensed a local area network version, you may use the Product on unlimited workstations located in one single building selected by you that is served by such local area network. If you have licensed a wide area network version, you may use the Product on unlimited workstations located in multiple buildings on the same site selected by you that is served by such wide area network; provided, however, that any building will not be considered located in the same site if it is more than five (5) miles away from any building included in such site. In addition, you may only use a local area or wide area network version of the Product on one single server. If you wish to use the Product on more than one server, you must obtain written authorization from McGraw-Hill and pay additional fees.

(iii) You may make one copy of the Product for back-up purposes only and you must maintain an accurate record as to the location of the back-up at all times.

COPYRIGHT; RESTRICTIONS ON USE AND TRANSFER: All rights (including copyright) in and to the Product are owned by McGraw-Hill and its licensors. You are the owner of the enclosed disc on which the Product is recorded. You may not use, copy, decompile, disassemble, reverse engineer, modify, reproduce, create derivative works, transmit, distribute, sublicense, store in a database or retrieval system of any kind, rent or transfer the Product, or any portion thereof, in any form or by any means (including electronically or otherwise) except as expressly provided for in this License Agreement. You must reproduce the copyright notices, trademark notices, legends and logos of McGraw-Hill and its licensors that appear on the Product on the back-up copy of the Product which you are permitted to make hereunder. All rights in the Product not expressly granted herein are reserved by McGraw-Hill and its licensors.

TERM: This License Agreement is effective until terminated. It will terminate if you fail to comply with any term or condition of this License Agreement. Upon termination, you are obligated to return to McGraw-Hill the Product together with all copies thereof and to purge all copies of the Product included in any and all servers and computer facilities.

DISCLAIMER OF WARRANTY: THE PRODUCT AND THE BACK-UP COPY ARE LICENSED "AS IS." McGRAW-HILL, ITS LICENSORS AND THE AUTHORS MAKE NO WARRANTIES, EXPRESS OR IMPLIED, AS TO THE RESULTS TO BE OBTAINED BY ANY PERSON OR ENTITY FROM USE OF THE PRODUCT, ANY INFORMATION OR DATA INCLUDED THEREIN AND/OR ANY TECHNICAL SUPPORT SERVICES PROVIDED HEREUNDER, IF ANY ("TECHNICAL SUPPORT SERVICES"). McGRAW-HILL, ITS LICENSORS AND THE AUTHORS MAKE NO EXPRESS OR IMPLIED WARRANTIES OF MERCHANTABILITY OR FITNESS FOR A PARTICULAR PURPOSE OR USE WITH RESPECT TO THE PRODUCT. McGRAW-HILL, ITS LICENSORS, AND THE AUTHORS MAKE NO GUARANTEE THAT YOU WILL PASS ANY CERTIFICATION EXAM WHATSOEVER BY USING THIS PRODUCT. NEITHER McGRAW-HILL, ANY OF ITS LICENSORS NOR THE AUTHORS WARRANT THAT THE FUNCTIONS CONTAINED IN THE PRODUCT WILL MEET YOUR REQUIREMENTS OR THAT THE OPERATION OF THE PRODUCT WILL BE UNINTERRUPTED OR ERROR FREE. YOU ASSUME THE ENTIRE RISK WITH RESPECT TO THE QUALITY AND PERFORMANCE OF THE PRODUCT.

LIMITED WARRANTY FOR DISC: To the original licensee only, McGraw-Hill warrants that the enclosed disc on which the Product is recorded is free from defects in materials and workmanship under normal use and service for a period of ninety (90) days from the date of purchase. In the event of a defect in the disc covered by the foregoing warranty, McGraw-Hill will replace the disc.

LIMITATION OF LIABILITY: NEITHER McGRAW-HILL, ITS LICENSORS NOR THE AUTHORS SHALL BE LIABLE FOR ANY INDIRECT, SPECIAL OR CONSEQUENTIAL DAMAGES, SUCH AS BUT NOT LIMITED TO, LOSS OF ANTICIPATED PROFITS OR BENEFITS, RESULTING FROM THE USE OR INABILITY TO USE THE PRODUCT EVEN IF ANY OF THEM HAS BEEN ADVISED OF THE POSSIBILITY OF SUCH DAMAGES. THIS LIMITATION OF LIABILITY SHALL APPLY TO ANY CLAIM OR CAUSE WHATSOEVER WHETHER SUCH CLAIM OR CAUSE ARISES IN CONTRACT, TORT, OR OTHERWISE. Some states do not allow the exclusion or limitation of indirect, special or consequential damages, so the above limitation may not apply to you.

U.S. GOVERNMENT RESTRICTED RIGHTS: Any software included in the Product is provided with restricted rights subject to subparagraphs (c), (1) and (2) of the Commercial Computer Software-Restricted Rights clause at 48 C.F.R. 52.227-19. The terms of this Agreement applicable to the use of the data in the Product are those under which the data are generally made available to the general public by McGraw-Hill. Except as provided herein, no reproduction, use, or disclosure rights are granted with respect to the data included in the Product and no right to modify or create derivative works from any such data is hereby granted.

GENERAL: This License Agreement constitutes the entire agreement between the parties relating to the Product. The terms of any Purchase Order shall have no effect on the terms of this License Agreement. Failure of McGraw-Hill to insist at any time on strict compliance with this License Agreement shall not constitute a waiver of any rights under this License Agreement. This License Agreement shall be construed and governed in accordance with the laws of the State of New York. If any provision of this License Agreement is held to be contrary to law, that provision will be enforced to the maximum extent permissible and the remaining provisions will remain in full force and effect.